# CHAMBERS

## *School*
## SUPER-MINI
## DICTIONARY

# CHAMBERS

## *SCHOOL* SUPER-MINI DICTIONARY

*edited by*
Imogen Kerr
*and*
Megan Thomson

## CHAMBERS

Chambers Harrap Publishers Ltd
7 Hopetoun Crescent
Edinburgh EH7 4AY

Copyright © Chambers Harrap Publishers Ltd 1997

Previously printed in Integra as Chambers *Super-Mini Dictionary*

A CIP catalogue record for this book is available from the British
Library

ISBN 0550 10020-2

The editors would like to acknowledge with thanks the
help of Serenella Flackett towards the editing of this dictionary.

Typeset by Chambers Harrap Publishers Ltd
Printed in Great Britain by Omnia Books Ltd, Glasgow

# Contents

# How to use your Dictionary

**Guide-words**
The entries in this dictionary are in alphabetical order. At the top of each page, you will see two 'guide-words'.

**abominable**

**absorption**

*The word on the left is the headword for the first entry you will find on this page*

*The word on the right is the headword for the last entry you will find on this page*

---

**Sense numbers**
If a word has more than one meaning, each new definition is marked by a sense (or meaning) number:

**torrent** *noun* **1** a rushing stream **2** a heavy downpour of rain **3** a violent flow of words *etc*: *torrent of abuse* □ **torrential** *adj* like a torrent; rushing violently

---

**Phrasal verbs and idioms**
Phrasal verbs and idioms come at the end of the main entry:

**care** *noun* **1** close attention **2** worry, anxiety **3** protection, keeping: *in my care* □ *verb* to be concerned or worried: *I don't care what happens now* □ **care for 1** to look after **2** to feel affection or liking for □ **careworn** *adj* worn out by anxiety □ **care of** at the house of (often written as **c/o**) □ **take care** to be careful; watch out

---

**Related words**
Most words in this dictionary have a separate entry to themselves. However, some words that are derived from other words can be easily understood from their form, and don't need definitions. In such cases, they may be included at the end of the entry with their part of speech but no separate definition:

**topography** *noun* the description of the features of the land in a certain region □ **topographical** *adj*

---

**Parts of speech**
The part of speech (eg noun, verb, adj) is given in *italic* print after the headword:

If the headword can be used as more that one part of speech, the entry is divided up to show this:

**axiom** *noun* a truth, an accepted principle

**doze** *verb* to sleep lightly □ *noun* a light, short sleep

ix

**Singular nouns/Plural nouns**
Some nouns occur only in a singular form, and always take a singular verb. These nouns are labelled *noun sing*:

Some nouns occur only in a plural form and always take a plural verb. These nouns are labelled *noun pl*:

**civic** *adj* relating to a city or citizens
□ **civics** *noun sing* the study of people's duties as citizens

**catacombs** *noun pl* an underground burial place

---

**Plurals**
The plurals of nouns are occasionally given - sometimes with pronunciation - if there is a possibility that they might be formed incorrectly:

**to-do** *noun* (*pl* **to-dos**) a bustle, commotion

---

**Main forms of verbs**
The main forms of a verb are given if the verb does not follow the normal pattern, look*s*, look*ing*, look*ed* OR search*es*, search*ing*, search*ed*. When the forms are given, they appear in the following order: present tense 3rd person (he/she/it); present participle ('*ing*' form); past tense 3rd person (he/she/it); past participle (if different from past tense):

If the past tense is the same as the past participle, it is not repeated:

**arise** ⇨ aris*es*, aris*ing*, arose, arisen

**catch** *verb* ⇨ catch*es*, catch*ing*, caught

---

**Comparatives and superlatives of adjectives and adverbs**
If the comparative or superlative is formed in an unusual way or if you need to double the final consonant etc; these forms are given in a shaded box:

**far** *adj* ⇨ farth*er*, farth*est*

**hot** ⇨ hot*ter*, hot*test*

---

**Examples**
Examples of the word in use are often given in *italic* print after the definition:

**tomorrow** *adv & noun* **1** (on) the day after today **2** (in) the future: *the children of tomorrow*

| | |
|---|---|
| **Pronunciation**<br>Where pronunciation help is given, it comes in brackets at the start of an entry or section: | **catastrophe** (*say* kat-**as**-tro-fi)<br>*noun* a sudden disaster<br>❑ **catastrophic** (*say* kat-*as*-**trof**-ik)<br>*adj* |
| **Register**<br>Differences in style of language, eg formal language, poetic language or slang, are called differences in register.<br><br>The register labels used in this dictionary are *formal*, *informal* and *slang*. These tell you whether it is appropriate to use the word or phrase in a particular situation. Register, where marked, is given in *italics* at the start of an entry or section: | **ablutions** *noun pl*, *formal* washing of the body<br><br>**ex** *noun*, *informal* a former husband, wife or lover<br><br>**chick** *noun* **1** a chicken **2** *slang* a girl, a young woman |
| **Usage notes**<br>These are to help you use English more effectively, and to warn you against making common mistakes: | **discrete** *adj* separate, distinct<br><br>◆ Do not confuse with: **discreet**. It may help you to think of Crete, which is an island separate from the rest of Greece. |
| **Word origins and language notes**<br>Straightforward word origins are signalled by a clock ⊙ :<br><br>Word histories which tell a story appear in a tinted box: | **ability** *noun* (*pl* **abilities**) **1** power or means to do something **2** talent<br>⊙ From Latin *habilitas* meaning 'skill'<br><br>**Tory** *noun* (*pl* **Tories**) a member of the British Conservative Party<br><br>Originally one of a group of Irish Catholics thrown off their land who waged guerrilla war on British settlers, later applied to any royalist supporter |
| **Alternative words**<br>These are intended to give you ideas for words which you might consider using in place of the headword of this entry. In this way, you can add variety to your writing. Never use a word which is unfamiliar to you without first looking it up at its entry in the dictionary! : | **careful** *adj* attentive, taking care<br>❑ **carefully** *adv*<br><br>▣ cautious, circumspect, chary, vigilant, meticulous, punctilious |
| **Opposites**<br>Direct opposites of words are occasionally included: | **convict** *verb* (*say* kon-**vikt**) to declare or prove that someone is guilty ❑ *noun* (*say* **kon**-vikt) someone found guilty of a crime and sent to prison<br><br>▣ *verb* **acquit** |

# Dictionary Quiz

## Finding what you're looking for

1  Without looking at your dictionary, name three other words which you would expect to find on the pages with guide-words **abstain** to **accessible**, **degrade** to **delphinium** and **quaff** to **quarter-deck**.

2  As well as being a small animal, **mouse** has a special meaning in computing. Find this special meaning in the entry for **mouse**. What is its sense number?

3  What are the adjectives from the nouns (a) **anomaly**, (b) **elephant**, and (c) **climate**?

## Meanings

4  What would (a) a **philologist**, (b) a **numismatist** and (c) an **entomologist** be interested in?

5  What would (a) an **agoraphobic** person and (b) a **hydrophobic** person suffer from?

6  If you were to talk about someone's **emolument**, what would you be referring to? What sort of language would you be using if you used this word? Can you think of some more neutral alternatives?

## Grammar

7  **(a)** Give each of the following words its part of speech: **pint, costly, soon, me, for, although, enjoy, AZT**. Now check in the dictionary to see if you were right.

  **(b)** How many parts of speech do you think the following words have: **master, ship, quick, glimmer, over, contact**? Now check in the dictionary to see if you were right.

8  What is the plural of the following nouns: **criterion, court-martial, bacillus, corpus, calypso**?

9  Insert the correct prepositions in the following phrases:
  *the elegant simplicity peculiar _ Rennie Mackintosh's work*
  *His behaviour is suggestive _ mental illness*
  *She is prone _ tantrums*

## Spelling

**10** Correct the spelling mistakes in this passage:

*I am, of course, refering to the suggestion you made earlier. With plenty of practise, you're playing could be grately improved. Would you consider traveling to Edinburgh for lessons?*

**11** Give the superlative form of the adjective **busy** and make up a sentence using it.

**12** Choose the correct spelling of the word in brackets:

*I enclose two (complementary/complimentary) tickets for the show.*
*My secretary won't ask awkward questions; she's very (discreet/ discrete).*
*It's impossible to get a (straight/ strait) answer from him.*
*Her plan was quite (ingenuous/ ingenious). He was (born/ borne) in India.*

## Pronunciation

**13** Which is the stressed syllable in the words **irrevocable**, **impotent** and **lamentable**?

**14** Which is the silent letter in **alms**?

## Register

**15** Which of the words in the following sentences would you <u>not</u> use in a formal situation? What word might you use instead?

*Do you suppose she's brainy enough to pass the exam?*
*His doctor's advised him to see a shrink.*
*They're too chicken to swim in the river.*
*The steak was served with broccoli, carrots and spuds.*
*She's been chucked out of school.*

## Answers

**1** Check pages 3, 127 and 398 in your dictionary to see if your word is there. **2** sense number 3 **3** (a) anomalous, (b) elephantine, (c) climatic **4** (a) words and their history, (b) coins, (c) insects **5** (a) a fear of open spaces, (b) water **6** their salary; formal language **8** criteria, courts-martial, bacilli, corpora, calypsos **9** to, of, to **10** referring, practice, your, greatly, travelling **11** busiest **12** complimentary, discreet, straight, ingenious, born **13** '-rev-', 'im-', '-lam-', **14** l **15** brainy (intelligent/clever), shrink (psychiatrist), chicken (cowardly), spuds (potatoes), chuck (throw)

# Pronunciation

This dictionary provides help in cases where the pronunciation of a word may not be obvious. Pronunciations are shown in a way which is designed to be immediately understandable. The syllables are separated by hyphens, and the stressed syllable is shown in thick black type. Any vowel or group of vowels which is pronounced as a neutral 'uh' (or *schwa*) sound is shown in italic type. Pronunciations are given in brackets, signalled by the word *say*, for example: **obligatory** (*say* ob-**lig**-*at-o*-ri)

A few sounds are difficult to show in normal English letters. The following list is a guide to the way these sounds are shown in pronunciation sections:

## Consonants

| | |
|---|---|
| 'ng' | shows the sound as in ri**ng** |
| 'ngg' | shows the sound as in fi**ng**er |
| 'th' | shows the sound as in **th**in |
| 'dh' | shows the sound as in **th**is |
| 'sz' | shows the sound as in deci**s**ion, mea**s**ure |
| 'kh' | shows the sound as in lo**ch** |

## Vowels

| | |
|---|---|
| 'uw' | shows the sound as in b**oo**k, p**u**t |
| 'oo' | shows the sound as in m**oo**n, l**o**se |
| 'ah' | shows the sound as in **ar**m, d**a**nce |
| 'aw' | shows the sound as in s**aw**, ign**o**re |
| 'er' | shows the sound as in f**er**n, b**ir**d, h**ear**d |
| 'ei' | shows the sound as in d**ay**, s**a**me |
| 'ai' | shows the sound as in m**y**, p**i**ne |
| 'oi' | shows the sound as in b**oy**, s**oi**l |
| 'oh' | shows the sound as in b**o**ne, n**o**, th**ough** |
| 'ow' | shows the sound as in n**ow**, b**ou**gh |

## Sound-combinations

| | |
|---|---|
| 'eer' | shows the sound as in n**ear**, b**eer**, t**ier** |
| 'eir' | shows the sound as in h**air**, c**are**, th**ere** |
| 'oor' | shows the sound as in p**oor**, s**ure** |
| 'air' | shows the sound as in f**ire**, h**igher** |

# Abbreviations used in the Dictionary

| | | | | |
|---|---|---|---|---|
| *abbrev* | abbreviation | | *N* | North |
| *adj* | adjective | | *orig* | originally |
| *adv* | adverb | | *pl* | plural |
| *Austral* | Australian | | *prep* | preposition |
| *cap* | capital letter | | *pron* | pronoun |
| *comp* | comparative | | *S* | South |
| *conj* | conjunction | | *sing* | singular |
| *E* | East | | *superl* | superlative |
| *eg* | for example | | *TV* | television |
| *etc* | and so on, and other things | | *UK* | United Kingdom |
| *exclam* | exclamation | | *US(A)* | United States (of America) |
| *ie* | that is | | *W* | West |

# Labels used in the Dictionary

All abbreviated labels used in the dictionary are given below; others are used in full (eg *architecture, golf* or *music*):

| | |
|---|---|
| *Austral* | used in Australian English |
| *Brit* | used generally in British English, not in US or Australian English *etc* |
| *euphem* | euphemism |
| *formal* | used mainly in formal English |
| *informal* | common and generally acceptable in spoken or informal English |
| *Irish* | used in Irish English |
| *maths* | mathematics |
| *med* | medicine |
| *offensive* | a word which is offensive to the person addressed or to someone referred to |
| *old* | no longer commonly used in modern English |
| *photog* | photography |
| *S African* | used in South African English |
| *Scot* | used in Scottish English |
| *slang* | less generally acceptable, even in informal English, than informal |
| *taboo* | not generally acceptable, even in informal use |
| *trademark* | a word which is registered as a trademark |
| *US* | used in US (and often Canadian) English |

# Suggestions for language activities

The pen symbol ✐ indicates some suggestions for language activities. If you finish a class activity before the others, look out for the symbol ✐ , and get your thinking cap on! (To start off, you'll find two activities in letter P).

# Aa

**a** or **an** adj **1** one: *a knock at the door* **2** any: *an ant has six legs* **3** in, to or for each: *four times a day*

The form *a* is used before words beginning with a consonant, eg knock; *an* is used before words beginning with a vowel, eg ant

**aback** adverb: **taken aback** surprised

**abacus** (say ab-*a*-kus) noun (pl **abacuses**) a frame with columns of beads for counting

**abandon** verb **1** to leave, without meaning to return to **2** to give up (an idea *etc*) □ noun lack of inhibition: *dancing with gay abandon* □ **abandonment** noun

**abandon** verb ⊷ abandon*s*, abandon*ing*, abandon*ed*

**abase** verb, *formal* to make humble □ **abasement** noun

**abashed** adj embarrassed, confused

**abate** verb to make or grow less □ **abatement** noun

**abattoir** (say ab-*a*-twahr) noun a (public) slaughter-house

**abbess** noun (pl **abbesses**) the female head of an abbey or a convent

**abbey** noun (pl **abbeys**) **1** a monastery or convent ruled by an abbot or an abbess **2** the church now or formerly attached to such a monastery or convent

**abbot** noun the male head of an abbey

**abbreviate** verb to shorten (a word, phrase *etc*) □ **abbreviation** noun a shortened form of a word *etc* used instead of the whole word, eg *maths* for *mathematics*

**abdicate** (say ab-di-kayt) verb to give up (a position, *esp* that of king or queen) □ **abdication** noun

**abdomen** (say ab-*dom*-en) noun the part of the human body between the chest and the hips □ **abdominal** (say ab-**dom**-in-al) adj

**abduct** verb to take away by force or fraud □ **abduction** noun

**abet** verb to help or encourage to do wrong

**abet** ⊷ abet*s*, abet*ting*, abet*ted*

**abeyance** noun: **in abeyance** undecided; not to be dealt with for the time being

**abhor** verb to hate, or look upon with horror □ **abhorrence** noun

**abhor** ⊷ abhor*s*, abhor*ring*, abhor*red*

**abhorrent** adj hateful

**abide** verb to put up with, tolerate □ **abiding** adj lasting □ **abide by** to keep, act according to

**ability** noun (pl **abilities**) **1** power or means to do something **2** talent
Ⓘ From Latin *habilitas* meaning 'skill'

**abject** (say ab-jekt) adj miserable, degraded

**ablaze** adj **1** burning fiercely **2** gleaming like fire

**able** adj **1** having the power or means (to do something) **2** clever □ **ably** adv in an efficient or competent way

**ablutions** noun pl, *formal* washing of the body

**abnormal** adj **1** not normal (in behaviour *etc*) **2** unusual □ **abnormality** noun (pl **abnormalities**) □ **abnormally** adv

**aboard** adv & prep on (to) or in(to) (a ship or aeroplane)

**abode** noun a formal word for a dwelling place

**abolish** verb to put an official end to (eg a custom) □ **abolition** noun □ **abolitionist** noun someone who tries to do away with anything, *esp* slavery

**abominable** *adj* **1** hateful **2** very bad, terrible □ **the Abominable Snowman** (*also called* **Yeti**) a large animal believed to exist in the Himalayas □ **abominably** *adv* (meaning 2): *behave abominably*

**abominate** *verb* to hate very much □ **abomination** *noun* **1** great hatred **2** anything hateful

**Aboriginal** (*say* a-bor-ij-i-nal) or **Aborigine** (*say* a-bor-ij-i-nee) *noun* a member of the original or native people of Australia □ **Aboriginal** *adj* ⓦ From Latin *ab* meaning 'from', and *origo* meaning 'beginning'

**abort** *verb* **1** of a plan *etc*: to come to nothing, stay undeveloped **2** to end a pregnancy deliberately by having an abortion □ **abortion** *noun* an operation to end an unwanted or dangerous pregnancy □ **abortive** *adj* coming to nothing, useless: *an abortive attempt*

**abound** *verb* to be very plentiful □ **abounding in** full of, having many

**about** *prep* **1** around: *look about you* **2** near (in time, size *etc*): *about ten o'clock* **3** here and there in: *scattered about the room* □ *adv* **1** around: *stood about waiting* **2** in motion or in action: *running about* **3** in the opposite direction: *turned about and walked away* □ **about to** on the point of (doing something)

**above** *prep* **1** over, in a higher position than: *above your head* **2** greater than: *above average* **3** too good for: *above jealousy* □ *adv* **1** overhead, on high **2** earlier on (in a letter *etc*): *see above for details* □ **above board** *adj* open □ *adv* openly ⓦ From Old English *bufan* meaning 'above'

**abrasion** *noun* **1** the action of rubbing off **2** a graze on the body

**abrasive** *adj* **1** rough and scratchy **2** having a hurtful manner □ *noun* something used for rubbing or polishing □ **abrasively** *adv* (meaning 2)

**abreast** *adv* side by side □ **abreast of** up to date with: *abreast of current affairs*

**abridge** *verb* to shorten (a book, story *etc*) □ **abridgement** or **abridgment** *noun*

**abroad** *adv* **1** in another country **2** *formal* outside: *witches go abroad after dark*

**abrupt** *adj* **1** sudden, without warning **2** of speech or behaviour: bad-tempered or snappy □ **abruptly** *adv*

**ABS** *abbrev* anti-lock braking system

**abscess** (*say* ab-ses) *noun* (*pl* **abscesses**) a boil or other inflammation filled with pus

**abscond** *verb* to run away secretly: *absconded with the money*

**abseil** (*say* ab-sayl) *verb* to let yourself down a rock face using a double rope ⓦ From German *ab* meaning 'down', and *Seil* meaning 'rope'

**absent** *adj* (*say* ab-sent) away, not present □ *verb* (*say* ab-sent): **absent yourself** to keep away □ **absence** *noun* the state of being away □ **absentee** *noun* someone who is absent □ **absently** *adv* in a dreamy way □ **absent-minded** *adj* forgetful

**absolute** *adj* complete, not limited by anything: *absolute power* □ **absolutely** *adv* **1** completely, certainly **2** (an enthusiastic reply) yes, I agree

**absolve** *verb, formal* to pardon: *absolve me of my sins* □ **absolution** *noun* forgiveness, pardon

**absorb** *verb* **1** to soak up (liquid) **2** to take up the whole attention of

**absorbent** *adj* able to soak up liquid

**absorption** *noun* **1** the act of absorbing **2** complete mental concentration

**abstain** verb **1** to refuse to cast a vote for or against **2** (with **from**) to hold yourself back □ **abstention** noun

**abstemious** (say ab-**steem**-i-us) adj not greedy, sparing in food, drink etc

**abstention** see abstain

**abstinence** (say **ab**-stin-ens) noun abstaining from alcohol etc □ **abstinent** adj

**abstract** adj existing only as an idea, not as a real thing □ noun a summary □ **abstraction** noun **1** a thing existing only as an idea **2** the quality of being based on an idea rather than reality **3** absent-mindedness **4** the industrial process of drawing out some material from a source

**abstruse** (say ab-**stroos**) adj difficult to understand

**absurd** adj clearly wrong; ridiculous □ **absurdity** noun (pl **absurdities**)

**abundance** noun a plentiful supply □ **abundant** adj plentiful □ **abundantly** adv to a great degree, extremely: abundantly obvious

**abuse** verb (say a-**byooz**) **1** to use wrongly **2** to insult or speak unkindly to; treat badly □ noun (say a-**byoos**) **1** wrongful use **2** insulting language or behaviour □ **abusive** adj insulting or rude

**abysmal** (say a-**biz**-mal) adj **1** very bad; terrible **2** bottomless □ **abysmally** adv (meaning 1)

**abyss** (say a-**bis**) noun (pl **abysses**) a bottomless depth

**AC** abbrev alternating current (compare with: **DC**)

**a/c** abbrev account

**acacia** (say a-**kay**-sha) noun a family of thorny shrubs and trees

**academic** adj **1** concerned with theoretical education or complicated ideas: academic qualifications **2** not practical:

purely of academic interest **3** of a university etc □ noun a university or college teacher □ **academically** adv (meaning 1)

**academy** noun (pl **academies**) **1** a college for special study or training **2** a society for encouraging science or art **3** in Scotland, a senior school

Comes from Greek Akademeia, which was Plato's school of philosophy

**acanthus** noun a Mediterranean ornamental shrub

**accede** (say ak-**seed**) verb: **accede** to formal to agree to

**accelerate** verb to increase in speed □ **acceleration** noun
⊕ From Latin celer meaning 'swift'

**accelerator** noun a lever or pedal used to increase the speed of a car etc

**accent** noun **1** (a mark indicating) stress on a syllable or word **2** a mark used in written French to show the quality of a vowel **3** emphasis: the accent must be on hard work **4** the way in which words are pronounced in a particular area etc: a Scottish accent □ **accentuate** (say ak-**sen**-choo-ayt) verb to make more obvious; emphasize

**accept** verb **1** to take something offered **2** to agree or submit to □ **acceptable** adj satisfactory; pleasing □ **acceptably** adv suitably, properly, appropriately for the circumstances □ **acceptance** noun **1** the act of accepting **2** an official statement that someone or something has been accepted: an acceptance from Stirling University

♠ Do not confuse with: **except**

**access** (say **ak**-ses) noun right or means of approach or entry □ **accession** (say ak-**se**-shun) noun a coming to: accession to the throne

**accessible** (say ak-**ses**-i-bl) adj easily approached or reached □ **accessibility** noun

**accessory** (*say* ak-ses-or-i) *noun* (*pl* **accessories**) **1** an item chosen to match or complement a piece of clothing or an outfit, *eg* a piece of jewellery, a handbag *etc* **2** a helper, *esp* in crime

**accident** *noun* **1** an unexpected event causing injury **2** a mishap: *I had a little accident with the cream* **3** chance: *I came upon the book by accident* □ **accidental** *adj* happening by chance □ **accidentally** *adv*

**acclaim** *verb* to welcome enthusiastically □ *noun* enthusiastic reception: *met with critical acclaim* □ **acclamation** *noun* noisy sign of approval

**acclimatize** *verb* to accustom to another climate or situation □ **acclimatization** *noun*

**accommodate** *verb* **1** to find room for **2** to make suitable **3** to be helpful to; supply (with): *accommodate all our customers* □ **accommodating** *adj* making an effort to be helpful □ **accommodation** *noun* a place to live or to stay, lodgings

**accompany** *verb* **1** to go or be with **2** to play an instrument (*eg* a piano) while a singer sings *etc* □ **accompaniment** *noun* **1** something that accompanies **2** the music played while a singer sings *etc* □ **accompanist** *noun* someone who plays an accompaniment

**accompany** ⇌ **accompanies**, **accompanying**, **accompanied**

**accomplice** *noun* someone who helps another person, *esp* to commit a crime

**accomplish** *verb* **1** to complete **2** to manage to do □ **accomplished** *adj* **1** completed **2** skilled, talented □ **accomplishment** *noun* **1** completion **2** a personal talent or skill

**accord** *verb* **1** to agree (with) **2** to give, grant □ *noun* an official

agreement □ **accordance** *noun* agreement: *act in accordance with his wishes* □ **according to 1** as told by **2** in relation to: *paid according to your work* □ **accordingly** *adv* **1** in a way which is in agreement with something already mentioned **2** therefore □ **of your own accord** of your own free will

**accordion** *noun* a musical instrument with bellows, a keyboard and metal reeds □ **accordionist** *noun* an accordion player

**accost** *verb* to approach and speak to in a forceful or threatening way

**account** *verb*: **account for 1** to give a reason (for) **2** to make up: *tax accounts for most of the price* □ *noun* **1** a bill **2** a record of finances **3** a description of events *etc*; an explanation □ **accountable** *adj* answerable, responsible □ **accountant** *noun* a keeper or inspector of accounts □ **on account of** because of

**accoutrements** (*say* a-koo-tre-ments) *noun pl* dress and equipment, *esp* military

**accredited** *adj* having official status, or the official power to act

**accrue** (*say* a-kroo) *verb* to accumulate, collect: *the account accrued no interest* □ **accrue to** to be given or added to: *the benefits that could accrue to the town* □ **accrued** *adj*

**accumulate** *verb* **1** to collect **2** to increase □ **accumulation** *noun* **1** a collection **2** a mass or pile □ **accumulator** *noun* a type of battery used in a car *etc*

**accurate** *adj* correct, exact □ **accuracy** *noun* □ **accurately** *adv*

**accursed** *adj* **1** *formal* under a curse **2** hateful

**accuse** *verb* to bring a (criminal) charge against □ **accusation** *noun* **1** the act of accusing **2** a statement

accusing someone of something
□ **the accused** noun (pl **the accused**)
the person charged with a crime etc
□ **accuser** noun

**accustomed** adj **1** used to **2** usual

**ace** noun **1** the one on playing-cards
**2** an expert: a computer ace **3** tennis
an unreturned first serve □ adj,
informal excellent
   Ⓣ The adjective is a new sense of
'ace', first used in the mid 20th
century

**acetylene** (say a-set-il-een) noun a
gas used for giving light and heat

**ache** noun a continuous pain □ verb
to be in continuous pain

**achieve** verb **1** to get (something)
done, accomplish **2** to win
□ **achievement** noun

**acid** adj **1** of taste: sharp **2** sarcastic
□ noun **1** a substance containing
hydrogen which will dissolve metals
(contrasted with: **alkali**) **2** slang the
drug LSD □ **acidity** noun the state of
being acid □ **acid rain** rain
containing sulphur and nitrogen
compounds and other pollutants

**acidify** verb to make or become acid

**acidify** ← acidifi_es_, acidify_ing_,
acidifi_ed_

**acknowledge** verb **1** to admit the
truth of something **2** to admit that
you know or are aware of
something **3** to (write to) say you
have received something **4** to
express gratitude or thanks
□ **acknowledgement** or
**acknowledgment** noun

**acme** (say ak-mi) noun, formal the
highest point, perfection

**acne** (say ak-ni) noun a common
skin disease with pimples

**acorn** noun the fruit of the oak tree

**acoustic** (say a-koo-stik) adj of
hearing or sound □ **acoustics** (say
a-koo-stiks) noun **1** sing the study of
sound **2** pl the characteristics of a
room etc which affect the hearing of
sound in it

**acquaint** verb to make (someone)
familiar (with) □ **acquaintance** noun
**1** knowledge **2** someone whom you
know slightly

**acquiesce** (say ak-wi-es) verb (often
with **in**) to agree (to): acquiesce to
their demands/ acquiesce in the
terms of the agreement
□ **acquiescence** noun □ **acquiescent**
adj

**acquire** verb to obtain, get □ **acquired**
adj gained; not something you were
born with or have inherited
□ **acquisition** noun **1** the act of
getting **2** something got: our most
recent acquisition

**acquisitive** adj eager to get things,
esp desirable items to add to your
property

**acquit** verb to declare (someone)
innocent of a crime □ **acquittal** noun
a legal judgement of 'not guilty'
□ **acquit yourself well** to do well, be
successful □ **acquit yourself badly** to
do badly, be unsuccessful

**acquit** ← acquit_s_, acquitt_ing_,
acquitt_ed_

**acre** noun a land measure containing
4840 square yards or about 4000
square metres □ **acreage** noun the
number of acres in a piece of land

**acrid** (say ak-rid) adj harsh, bitter

**acrimony** (say ak-rim-on-i) noun
bitterness of feeling or speech
□ **acrimonious** (say ak-rim-oh-ni-us)
adj

**acrobat** noun someone who performs
gymnastic tricks, tightrope-walking
etc □ **acrobatic** adj

**acronym** (say ak-ron-im) noun a
word formed from the initial letters
of other words, eg radar for radio
detecting and ranging

**across** adv & prep to or at the other
side (of): swam across the river/
winked at him across the table
□ **across the board** involving
everyone or everything; sweeping

**acrostic** (say a-kros-tik) noun a poem

*etc* in which the first or last letters of each line, taken in order, spell a word or words

**acrylic** (*say* a-**kril**-ik) *noun* a synthetically produced fibre □ *adj* made with this material

**act** *verb* **1** to do something **2** to behave in a particular way: *act foolishly* **3** to play a dramatic role on stage, film *etc* □ *noun* **1** something done **2** a government law **3** a section of a play □ **act up** *informal* to behave or act wrongly or badly
ⓘ From Latin *actum* meaning 'a thing which has been done'

**action** *noun* **1** a deed, an act **2** a law case **3** dramatic events portrayed in a film, play *etc* □ **actionable** *adj* likely to cause a law case: *actionable statement*

**active** *adj* **1** busy; lively **2** able to perform physical tasks **3** *grammar* describing the form of a verb in which the subject performs the action of the verb, *eg* 'the dog bit the postman' □ **activate** *verb* to start (something) working □ **actively** *adv* in a way which involves doing things: *actively involved in nature conservation* □ **activity** *noun* (*pl* **activities**)

**actor** *noun* someone who acts a part in a play or film

**actress** *noun* (*pl* **actresses**) a female actor

**actual** *adj* real, existing in fact □ **actuality** *noun* fact; reality □ **actually** *adv* really, in fact, as a matter of fact

**actuary** (*say* **ak**-choo-ar-i) *noun* (*pl* **actuaries**) someone who works out the price of insurance □ **actuarial** (*say* ak-choo-**air**-i-al) *adj*

**actuate** *verb* **1** to put into action **2** to drive or urge on

**acumen** (*say* **ak**-yoo-men) *noun* quickness of understanding: *keen business acumen*

**acupressure** (*say* **ak**-yoo-pre-sher) *noun* a method of treating illness by applying pressure to certain key points on the body

**acupuncture** (*say* **ak**-yoo-punk-cher) *noun* a method of treating illness by piercing the skin with needles
ⓘ From Latin *acu* meaning 'needle'

**acute** *adj* **1** quick at understanding **2** severe and causing great discomfort: *acute back pain/ acute difficulties* **3** of an angle: less than a right angle (*contrasted with:* **obtuse**) □ **acute accent** a forward-leaning stroke (´) placed over letters in some languages to show their pronunciation □ **acutely** *adv* extremely, painfully: *an acutely embarrassing situation* □ **acuteness** *noun*

**AD** *abbrev* in the year of our Lord (from Latin *anno Domini*). Used with a date, *eg* AD1900, to show that it refers to the time after the birth of Christ

**▨ BC**

**ad** *noun, informal* an advertisement

**adage** (*say* **a**-dij) *noun* an old saying, a proverb

**adagio** (*say* a-**dah**-jee-oh) *noun* a slow-paced piece of music
ⓘ In Italian *ad agio* means 'at ease'

**adamant** (*say* **ad**-am-ant) *adj* unwilling to give way

**Adam's apple** the natural lump which sticks out from a man's throat

From the story that the lump was part of the forbidden apple stuck in Adam's throat

**adapt** *verb*: **adapt to** to make suitable for; alter so as to fit □ **adaptable** *adj* easily altered to suit new conditions □ **adaptation** *noun*

**adaptor** *noun* a device allowing an electrical plug to be used in a socket for which it was not designed, or several plugs to be used on the same socket

**add** verb **1** to make one thing join another to give a sum total or whole **2** to mix in: *add water to the dough* **3** to say further □ **addition** noun **1** the act of adding **2** something added □ **additional** adj □ **additive** noun a chemical *etc* added to another substance □ **add up 1** to combine, grow to a large quantity: *all these expenses soon add up* **2** to make sense, seem logical: *his story just doesn't add up*

**addendum** (say a-den-dum) noun (pl **addenda**) something added

**adder** noun the common name of the viper, a poisonous snake

**addict** (say a-dikt) noun someone who cannot stop using something, often a drug or alcohol, because they are either physically or mentally dependent on it □ **addicted** (say a-dik-tid) adj: *addicted to* unable to do without □ **addictive** (say a-dik-tiv) adj creating dependence, habit-forming

**address** verb **1** to speak to **2** to write the address on (a letter *etc*) □ noun (pl **addresses**) **1** the name of the house, street, and town where someone lives *etc* **2** a speech

**adenoids** (say a-de-noydz) noun pl tissue at the back of the nose which can swell and make it difficult to breathe

**adept** (say a-dept) adj very skilful

**adequate** adj sufficient, enough □ **adequacy** noun □ **adequately** adv

**adhere** verb **1** to stick (to) **2** to give support (to), be loyal (to): *adhere to a strict dress code* □ **adherence** noun

**adherent** adj sticking (to) □ noun a follower or supporter of a cause *etc*

**adhesion** noun the act of sticking (to)

**adhesive** adj sticky, gummed □ noun something which makes things stick to each other

**ad hoc** adj set up for a particular purpose only

**ad infinitum** (say ad in-fi-nai-tum) adv for ever

**adjacent** (say a-jei-sent) adj (**adjacent to**) lying next to

**adjective** noun a word which tells something about a noun, *eg* 'the *black* cat,' 'times are *hard*' □ **adjectival** adj

**adjoin** verb to be joined to □ **adjoining** adj

**adjourn** verb **1** to stop (a meeting *etc*) with the intention of continuing it at another time or place **2** (with **to**) to go to another place: *adjourn to the lounge* □ **adjournment** noun

**adjudicate** verb **1** to give a judgement on (a dispute *etc*) **2** to act as a judge at a competition □ **adjudication** noun □ **adjudicator** noun

**adjunct** (say aj-unkt) noun something joined or added

**adjust** verb to rearrange or alter to suit the circumstances □ **adjustable** adj □ **adjustment** noun

**ad-lib** verb to speak without plan or preparation □ adj without preparation

**ad-lib** verb ⇔ ad-libs, ad-libbing, ad-libbed

**administer** verb **1** to manage or govern: *South Pacific islands administered by France* **2** to carry out (the law *etc*) **3** to give (help, medicine *etc*)

**administrate** verb to manage or govern □ **administration** noun **1** management **2** (the body that carries on) the government of a country *etc* □ **administrative** adj □ **administrator** noun someone involved in the administration of a country *etc*

**admiral** noun the commander of a navy □ **admiralty** noun the government office which manages naval affairs

**admire** verb 1 to think very highly of 2 to look at with pleasure □ **admirable** adj worthy of being admired □ **admirably** adv □ **admiration** noun □ **admirer** noun

**admit** verb 1 to let in 2 to acknowledge the truth of, confess 3 (with **of**) to leave room for, allow: admits of no other explanation □ **admissible** adj allowable □ **admission** noun 1 (the price of) being let in 2 anything admitted □ **admittance** noun the right or permission to enter

**admit** ↔ admit**s**, admit**ting**, admit**ted**

**admonish** verb 1 to warn 2 to rebuke, scold □ **admonition** noun a warning □ **admonitory** adj

**ad nauseam** (say ad **naw**-zi-am) adv to a tiresome degree

**ado** (say a-**doo**) noun trouble, fuss

**adolescent** noun someone between a child and an adult in age □ adj of this age □ **adolescence** noun

**adopt** verb 1 to take as your own (esp a child of other parents) 2 to take (eg precautions), choose formally □ **adoption** noun □ **adoptive** adj adopted, taken as your own: her adoptive country

**adore** verb 1 to love very much 2 to worship □ **adorable** adj very loveable □ **adoration** noun 1 worship 2 great love

**adorn** verb to decorate (with ornaments etc) □ **adornment** noun ornament

**adrenaline** (say a-**dren**-a-lin) noun a hormone produced in response to fear, anger etc, preparing the body for quick action

**adrift** adv drifting, floating

**adroit** (say a-**droit**) adj skilful

**adulation** (say ad-yoo-**lei**-shun) noun great flattery □ **adulatory** adj

**adult** adj grown up □ noun a grown-up person

**adulterate** verb to make impure by adding something else □ **adulteration** noun

**adultery** noun unfaithfulness to a husband or wife □ **adulterer** or **adulteress** noun

**advance** verb 1 to go forward 2 to put forward (a plan etc): he advanced a number of proposals 3 to help the progress of: research which has advanced our understanding of HIV 4 to pay before the usual or agreed time: Could you advance me £50? □ noun 1 movement forward 2 improvement 3 a loan of money □ **advanced** adj well forward in progress □ **advancement** noun progress □ **in advance** beforehand

**advantage** noun 1 a better position, superiority 2 gain or benefit □ verb to help, benefit □ **advantageous** adj profitable; helpful □ **take advantage of** to make use of (a situation, person etc) in such a way as to benefit yourself

**advent** (say **ad**-vent) noun 1 coming, arrival: before the advent of television 2 (**Advent**) in the Christian church, the four weeks before Christmas

**adventure** noun a bold or exciting undertaking or experience □ **adventurer** noun 1 someone who takes risks, esp in the hope of making a lot of money 2 a mercenary soldier □ **adventurous** adj taking risks, liking adventure

**adverb** noun a word which gives a more definite meaning to a verb, adjective, or other adverb, eg 'eat slowly,' 'extremely hard,' 'very carefully' □ **adverbial** adj of or like an adverb

**adversary** (say **ad**-ve-sar-i) noun (pl **adversaries**) an enemy; an opponent

**adverse** (say **ad**-vers) adj unfavourable: adverse criticism □ **adversity** noun (pl **adversities**) misfortune

**advert** *noun, informal* an advertisement

**advertise** *verb* 1 to make known to the public 2 to stress the good points of (a product for sale)

**advertisement** *noun* a photograph, short film *etc* intended to persuade the public to buy a particular product

**advice** *noun* 1 something said as a help to someone trying to make a decision *etc* 2 a formal notice

🖢 Do not confuse with: **advise**. To help you remember - 'ice' is a noun, 'ise' is not.

**advisable** *adj* wise, sensible □ **advisability** *noun*

**advise** *verb* 1 to give advice to 2 to recommend (an action *etc*) □ **adviser** *noun* □ **advisory** *adj* advice-giving: *advisory body*

🖢 Do not confuse with: **advice**

**advocate** *noun* (*say* **ad**-vo-kat) 1 someone who pleads for another 2 in Scotland, a court lawyer □ *verb* (*say* **ad**-vo-keit) 1 to plead or argue for 2 to recommend

**aegis** (*say* **ee**-jis) *noun* protection; patronage

**aeon** or **eon** (*say* **ee**-on) *noun* a very long period of time, an age

**aerate** (*say* **eir**-reit) *verb* to put air or another gas into (a liquid)

**aerial** *adj* 1 of, in or from the air: *aerial photography* 2 placed high up or overhead: *aerial railway* □ *noun* a wire or rod (or a set of these) by means of which radio or television signals are received or sent

**aero-** *prefix* of air or aircraft ⊕ From Greek *aer* meaning 'air'

**aerobatics** *noun pl* stunts performed by an aircraft

**aerobics** *noun sing* a system of rhythmic physical exercise which aims to strengthen the heart and lungs by increasing the body's oxygen consumption

**aerodrome** *noun* a landing and maintenance station for aircraft

**aeronautics** *noun sing* the science or art of navigation in the air

**aeroplane** or *US* **airplane** *noun* an engine-powered flying machine with fixed wings

**aerosol** *noun* a container of liquid and gas under pressure, from which the liquid is squirted as a mist

**aesthetic** (*say* ees-**thet**-ik) *adj* 1 of beauty or its appreciation 2 artistic, pleasing to the eye □ **aesthetically** *adv*

**affable** *adj* pleasant, easy to speak to □ **affability** *noun*

**affair** *noun* 1 events connected with one person or thing: *the Watergate affair* 2 (**affairs**) personal concerns, transactions *etc*: *his affairs seemed to be in order* 3 business, concern: *that's not your affair* 4 a love affair

**affect** *verb* 1 to act upon 2 to have an effect on; move the feelings of 3 to pretend to feel *etc*: *affect an air of indifference* □ **affectation** *noun* pretence □ **affected** *adj* 1 moved in your feelings 2 not natural, sham □ **affecting** *adj* moving the feelings

🖢 Do not confuse with: **effect**. **Affect** is usually a verb. **Effect** is usually a noun. 'To AFFECT' means 'to have an EFFECT on'.

**affection** *noun* a strong liking □ **affectionate** *adj* loving

**affidavit** (*say* af-i-**dei**-vit) *noun, law* a written statement made on oath

**affiliated** *adj* (with **with** or **to**) connected, attached □ **affiliation** *noun*

**affinity** *noun* (*pl* **affinities**) a close likeness or agreement

**affirm** *verb* to state firmly □ **affirmation** *noun* a firm statement □ **affirmative** *adj* saying 'yes'

**affix** *verb* to attach to

**afflict** *verb* to give continued pain or

distress to □ **afflicted** adj suffering □ **affliction** noun great suffering, misery

**affluent** (say af-loo-ent) adj wealthy □ noun a stream flowing into a river or lake □ **affluence** noun wealth

**afford** verb 1 to be able to pay for 2 formal to give, provide with: I hope the situation will afford me a chance to speak to him

**afforest** verb to cover land with forest □ **afforestation** noun

**affray** noun a fight, a brawl

**affront** verb to insult openly □ noun an insult

**afloat** adv & adj floating

**afoot** adv happening or about to happen: something is afoot

**aforesaid** (say a-faw-sed) adj said or named before: the aforesaid person

**afraid** adj 1 struck with fear 2 informal sorry to have to admit that: I'm afraid there are no tickets left

▣ (meaning 1) frightened, terrified, timorous, fearful, cowardly

**afresh** adv once again, anew

**aft** (say ahft) adv near or towards the stern of a vessel

**after** prep 1 later in time than: after dinner 2 following: arrived one after another 3 in memory or honour of: named after his father 4 in pursuit of: run after the bus 5 about: asked after her health 6 despite: after all my efforts, it still didn't work 7 in the style of: after Rubens □ adv later in time or place: we left soon after □ conj later than the time when: after she arrived, things improved □ **after all 1** all things considered: after all, he's still young 2 despite everything said or done before: I went after all

**after-** prefix later in time or place: aftertaste/ afterthought

**afterbirth** noun the placenta and membranes expelled from the uterus after giving birth

**aftermath** noun the bad results of something: the aftermath of the election

Originally a second crop coming after the main harvest

**afternoon** noun the time between noon and evening □ adj taking place in the afternoon

**aftershave** noun a lotion used on the face after shaving

**afterthought** noun a later thought

**afterwards** adv later

**again** adv 1 once more: say that again 2 in or into the original state, place etc: there and back again 3 on the other hand: again, I might be wrong 4 informal at another later time: see you again

**against** prep 1 in opposition to: against the law/ fight against injustice 2 in the opposite direction to: against the wind 3 on a background of: against the sky 4 close to, touching: lean against the wall 5 as protection from: guard against infection

**age** noun 1 a long period of time 2 the time someone or something has lived or existed □ verb to grow or make visibly older: he has aged ten years in the past six months (= seems to have grown ten years older) □ **aged** adj 1 (say eij-id) old 2 (say eijd) of the age of: aged five □ **of age** legally an adult

**age** verb ⇨ ages, ageing or aging, aged

**ageism** noun discrimination on grounds of age □ **ageist** adj discriminating on grounds of age

**agency** noun (pl agencies) 1 the office or business of an agent 2 action, means by which something is done

**agenda** noun a list of things to be done, esp at a meeting

**agent** noun 1 someone or something that acts 2 someone who acts for another 3 a spy

**aggrandize** *verb* to make greater □ **aggrandizement** (*say* a-gran-diz-ment) *noun*

**aggravate** *verb* 1 to make worse 2 *informal* to annoy □ **aggravating** *adj* □ **aggravation** *noun*

**aggregate** (*say* ag-ri-gat) *noun* a total

**aggressive** *adj* 1 ready to attack first 2 quarrelsome □ **aggression** *noun* □ **aggressor** *noun*

**aggrieved** (*say* a-greevd) *adj* hurt, upset

**aghast** (*say* a-gahst) *adj* struck with horror

**agile** *adj* active, nimble □ **agility** *noun*

**agitate** *verb* 1 to stir up 2 to excite, disturb □ **agitation** *noun* □ **agitator** *noun* someone who stirs up others

**agnostic** (*say* ag-nos-tik) *noun* someone who believes it is impossible to know whether God exists or not □ **agnosticism** *noun*

**ago** *adv* in the past: *that happened five years ago*

**agog** (*say* a-gog) *adj* eager, excited

**agony** *noun* (*pl* **agonies**) great pain □ **agonized** *adj* showing great pain □ **agonizing** *adj* causing great pain □ **agony aunt** someone who gives advice in an agony column □ **agony column** a regular column in a newspaper or magazine in which readers submit and receive advice about personal problems

**agoraphobia** (*say* ag-ra-foh-bi-a) *noun* great fear of open spaces □ **agoraphobic** *noun & adj* (someone) suffering from agoraphobia

**agrarian** *adj* of farmland or farming

**agree** *verb* 1 to be alike in opinions, decisions *etc* 2 to say that you will do something 3 to be the same or consistent, fit together: *their stories don't agree* □ **agreeable** *adj* 1 pleasant 2 ready to agree □ **agreement** *noun* 1 likeness (*esp* of opinions) 2 a written statement making a bargain □ **agree with** 1 to suit 2 to cause no problems in digestion: *the fish didn't agree with me*

**agriculture** *noun* the cultivation of the land, farming □ **agricultural** *adj*

**aground** *adj & adv* stuck on the bottom of the sea or a river: *run aground*

**ahead** *adv* in front; in advance: *finishing ahead of time*

**aid** *verb* to help, assist □ *noun* help

**AIDS** or **Aids** *abbrev* Acquired Immune Deficiency Syndrome

**aikido** (*say* ai-kee-doh) *noun* a Japanese martial art using pressure against the joints

**ail** *verb*, *old* to be or make ill: *What ails thee?*

**ailing** *adj* 1 troubled, in a bad state: *the ailing steel industry* 2 ill

**ailment** *noun* a trouble, disease

**aim** *verb* 1 to point at (*esp* with a gun) 2 to intend to do 3 to have as your purpose □ *noun* 1 the act of, or skill in, aiming 2 the point aimed at, goal, intention □ **aimless** *adj* without aim or purpose □ **aimlessly** *adv*

**air** *noun* 1 the mixture of gases (mainly oxygen and nitrogen) which we breathe, the atmosphere 2 a light breeze 3 fresh air 4 space overhead 5 a tune 6 the look or manner (of a person) □ *verb* 1 to expose to the air 2 to make known (an opinion *etc*) □ **on the air** broadcasting

**airbag** *noun* a bag which automatically inflates inside a car on impact to protect the driver from injury

**airbed** *noun* a mattress which can be inflated

**airborne** *adj* in the air, flying

**air-conditioned** *adj* equipped with a system for filtering and controlling the temperature of the air

**aircraft** *noun* (*pl* **aircraft**) a flying

machine

**air force** the branch of the armed forces using aircraft

**air-gun** *noun* a gun worked by means of compressed air

**airing** *noun* **1** the act of exposing to the air **2** the act of talking about something openly: *give your views an airing*

**airless** *adj* stuffy

**airlock** *noun* **1** a bubble in a pipe obstructing the flow of a liquid **2** a compartment with two doors for entering and leaving an airtight spaceship *etc*

**airplane** *US* for **aeroplane**

**airport** *noun* a place where aircraft land and take off, with buildings for customs, waiting-rooms *etc*

**air-raid** *noun* an attack by aeroplanes

**airship** *noun* a large balloon which can be steered and driven

**airstream** *noun* a flow of air

**airtight** *adj* made so that air cannot pass in or out

**airy** *adj* **1** of or like the air **2** well supplied with fresh air **3** light-hearted □ **airily** *adv* (meaning 3)

**aisle** (*say* ail) *noun* **1** the side part of a church **2** a passage between seats in a theatre *etc*

**ajar** *adv* partly open: *leave the door ajar*

**aka** (*say* ei-kei-ei) *abbrev* also known as: *Stevens, aka The Fly*

**akimbo** *adv* with hand on hip and elbow bent outward

**akin** *adj* similar

**à la carte** *adj & adv* **1** according to the menu **2** each dish chosen and priced separately

**alack!** *exclam, old* alas

**alacrity** *noun* briskness, cheerful readiness

**à la mode** (*say* a la mod) *adj & adv* **1** fashionable **2** *US* served with

ice-cream: *apple pie à la mode*

**alarm** *noun* **1** sudden fear **2** something which rouses to action or gives warning of danger □ *verb* to frighten □ **alarming** *adj* □ **alarmist** *noun* someone who frightens others needlessly

**alas!** *exclamation* a cry showing grief

**albatross** *noun* (*pl* **albatrosses**) a type of large sea-bird

**albino** *noun* (*pl* **albinos**) someone or an animal with no natural colour in their skin, hair and eye irises

**album** *noun* **1** a book with blank pages for holding photographs, stamps *etc* **2** a long-playing record **3** recordings issued under one title

**albumen** (*say* al-byu-men) *noun* the white of eggs

**alchemy** *noun* an early form of chemistry aimed at changing other metals into gold □ **alchemist** *noun* someone who practised alchemy

**alcohol** *noun* **1** the colourless, flammable liquid which you get when you ferment sugar, and which is present in all drinks which can make people drunk **2** any drink which can make people drunk □ **alcoholic** *adj* of or containing alcohol □ *noun* someone addicted to alcohol □ **alcoholism** *noun* addiction to alcohol

**alcove** *noun* a recess in a room's wall

**alder** *noun* a type of tree which grows beside ponds and rivers

**alderman** *noun* **1** *historical* a councillor next in rank to the mayor of a town *etc* **2** *US* a member of the governing body of a city

**ale** *noun* a drink made from malt, hops *etc*

**alert** *noun* signal to be ready for action □ *verb* to make alert, warn □ *adj* **1** watchful **2** quick-thinking □ **on the alert** on the watch (for)

**algae** (*say* al-gi or al-ji) *noun* a group of simple plants which includes seaweed

**algebra** noun a part of mathematics in which letters and signs are used to represent numbers

**alias** adv also known as: Mitchell alias Grassic Gibbon □ noun (pl **aliases**) a false name

**alibi** noun 1 the plea that someone charged with a crime was elsewhere when it was done 2 the state or fact of being elsewhere when a crime was committed

**alien** adj foreign □ noun a foreigner □ **alienate** verb to make someone unfriendly, probably by causing them to feel unwanted or rejected □ **alien to** not in keeping with: alien to her nature

**alight** verb 1 to climb etc down: alight from the train 2 to settle, land □ adj & adv on fire, burning

**alight** verb ▻ alights, alight**ing**, alight**ed**

**align** (say a-**lain**) verb 1 to set in line 2 to take sides in an argument etc □ **alignment** noun arrangement in a line

**alike** adj like one another, similar □ adv in the same way, similarly

**alimentary** adj of food □ **alimentary canal** the passage through the body which begins at the mouth

**alimony** noun an allowance paid by a husband to his wife, or a wife to her husband, to provide support when they are legally separated

**alive** adj 1 living 2 full of activity □ **alive to** aware of

**alkali** noun a substance such as soda or potash (contrasted with: **acid**) □ **alkaline** adj

**all** adj & pronoun 1 every one (of): we are all invited/all letters will be answered 2 the whole of: painted all the house □ adv wholly, completely: dressed all in red □ **all-rounder** noun someone skilled in many kinds of work, sport etc □ **all in** 1 with everything included: all-in

price 2 informal exhausted □ **all over** 1 over the whole of 2 everywhere 3 finished, ended

**Allah** noun in Islam, God

**allay** verb 1 to make less, relieve: allay his fears 2 to calm

**allege** verb to say without proof □ **allegation** noun

**allegiance** noun loyalty

**allegory** noun (pl **allegories**) a story or fable which deals with a subject in a way which is meant to suggest a deeper, more serious subject □ **allegorical** adj

**allergy** noun (pl **allergies**) abnormal sensitiveness of the body to something □ **allergic** adj

**alleviate** verb to make lighter, lessen: try to alleviate their suffering □ **alleviation** noun

**alley** noun (pl **alleys**) 1 a narrow passage or lane 2 an enclosure for bowls or skittles

**alliance** see ally

**alligator** noun a large reptile like a crocodile

**alliteration** noun the repetition of the same sound at the beginning of two or more words close together, eg 'round and round the rugged rock' or 'sing a song of sixpence' □ **alliterative** adj

✎ **Can you think of some short phrases containing alliteration?**

**allocate** verb to allot, share out, reserve for a particular purpose □ **allocation** noun

**allopathic** adj of medicine: conventional, treating disease with drugs which have an effect on the body which is opposite to that of the disease (contrasted with: **homeopathic**)

**allot** verb to give each person a share of, distribute, reserve □ **allotment** noun 1 the act of distributing 2 a small plot of ground for growing vegetables etc

**allot** ⌐ allots, allotting, allotted

**allow** verb **1** to let (someone do something) **2** (with **for**) to take into consideration (in sums, plans etc) **3** to admit, confess **4** to give, esp at regular intervals: she allows him 40 a week ⌐ **allowable** adj

**allowance** noun a fixed sum or amount given regularly ⌐ **make allowances for** to treat differently because of taking into consideration special circumstances etc

**alloy** noun a mixture of two or more metals

**allude** verb: **allude to** to mention in passing

⚠️ Do not confuse with: **elude**

**allure** verb to tempt, draw on by promises etc ⌐ **allurement** noun ⌐ **alluring** adj

**allusion** noun an indirect reference

⚠️ Do not confuse with: **delusion** and **illusion**. An **allusion** is a comment which **alludes to** something.

**allusive** adj referring indirectly, hinting

⚠️ Do not confuse with: **elusive** and **illusive**. **Allusive** is related to the verb **allude** and the noun **allusion**.

**alluvium** noun (pl **alluvia**) earth, sand etc brought down and left by rivers in flood ⌐ **alluvial** adj

**ally** verb to join yourself to by treaty etc ⌐ noun (pl **allies**) someone in alliance with another; a friend ⌐ **alliance** noun a joining together of two people, nations etc, for a common cause ⌐ **allied** adj

**ally** verb ⌐ allies, allying, allied

**almanac** noun a calendar for any year, with information about the phases of the moon etc

**almighty** adj having much power ⌐ **the Almighty** God

**almond** noun the kernel of the fruit of the almond-tree

**almost** adv very nearly but not quite: almost five years old/ almost home

**alms** (say ahmz) noun gifts to the poor

**aloft** adv **1** on high **2** upward

**alone** adj not accompanied by others, solitary: alone in the house ⌐ adv **1** only, without anything else: that alone is bad enough **2** not accompanied by others: do you live alone? ⌐ **leave alone** to let be, leave undisturbed

**along** prep over the length of: walk along the road ⌐ adv onward: come along! ⌐ **alongside** prep beside ⌐ adv near a ship's side ⌐ **along with** together with

**aloof** adj & adv **1** at a distance, apart **2** showing no interest in others

**aloud** adv so as to be heard

**alpha** noun the first letter of the Greek alphabet

**alphabet** noun letters of a language given in a fixed order ⌐ **alphabetic** or **alphabetical** adj in the order of the letters of the alphabet

**alpine** adj of the Alps or other high mountains

**already** adv **1** before this or that time: I've already done that **2** now, before the expected time: you can't have finished already

**alright**

⚠️ It is best to spell this as two words: 'all right'. Some people consider the spelling 'alright' to be incorrect.

**alsatian** noun a German shepherd dog

**also** adv in addition, besides, too: I also need to buy milk ⌐ **also-ran** noun someone or something that competed (as in a race) but was not among the winners

**altar** noun **1** a raised place for offerings to a god **2** in Christian churches, the communion table

**alter** verb to change ⌐ **alteration** noun

**altercation** noun an argument or quarrel

**alter ego 1** a second self **2** a trusted friend, a confidant(e)

**alternate** verb (say **ol**-te-neit) of two things: to do or happen in turn: *meetings alternate between my house and hers* □ adj (say ol-**tern**-ɑt) happening etc in turns: *a grocery van serves the village on alternate days* (= *every other day*) □ **alternation** noun

❧ Do not confuse: **alternate** and **alternative**. 'To ALTERNATE' is to move between two possibilities. **Alternate** is the adjective from this verb.

**alternative** adj offering a second possibility: *an alternative solution* □ noun a second possibility, a different course of action: *I had no alternative but to agree*

**although** conj though, in spite of the fact that

**altimeter** noun an instrument for measuring height above sea level

**altitude** noun height above sea level

**alto** noun (pl **altos**), music **1** the male voice of the highest pitch **2** the female voice of lowest pitch

An alternative term for the female *alto* voice is **contralto**

**altogether** adv **1** considering everything, in all: *there were 20 of us altogether* **2** completely: *not altogether satisfied*

**altruism** noun unselfish concern for the good of others □ **altruistic** adj

**aluminium** (say al-yuw-**min**-i-um) or *US* **aluminum** (say a-**loo**-min-um) noun an element, a very light metal

**always** adv **1** for ever: *he'll always remember this day* **2** every time: *she always gets it wrong*

**Alzheimer's disease** (say alts-hai-mez) an illness affecting the brain and causing dementia in middle-aged and elderly people

**AM** abbrev amplitude modulation

(*compare with:* **FM**)

**am** abbrev before noon (from Latin *ante meridiem*)

**am** see **be**

**amalgam** noun a mixture (*esp* of metals)

**amalgamate** verb **1** to join together, combine □ **amalgamation** noun

**amass** verb to collect in large quantity

**amateur** noun someone who takes part in a thing for the love of it, not for money (*contrasted with:* **professional**) □ **amateurish** adj not done properly; not skilful

**amaze** verb to surprise greatly □ **amazement** noun □ **amazing** adj □ **amazingly** adv

**Amazon** noun **1** one of a nation of mythological warrior women **2** a very strong or manlike woman

**ambassador** noun **1** a government minister sent to look after the interests of one country in another country **2** a representative

**amber** noun a hard yellowish fossil resin used in making jewellery □ adj **1** made of amber **2** of the colour of amber

**ambidextrous** adj able to use both hands with equal skill □ **ambidexterity** noun

**ambience** noun environment, atmosphere □ **ambient** adj surrounding: *ambient temperature*

**ambiguous** adj **1** having two possible meanings **2** not clear □ **ambiguity** noun (pl **ambiguities**) uncertainty in meaning

❧ Do not confuse with: **ambivalent**

**ambition** noun the desire for success, power, fame etc □ **ambitious** adj

**ambivalent** adj having two contrasting attitudes towards something □ **ambivalence** noun

❧ Do not confuse with: **ambiguous**

**amble** verb to walk without hurrying □ noun an unhurried walk

**ambrosia** noun the mythological food of the gods, which gave eternal youth and beauty

**ambulance** noun a vehicle for carrying the sick or injured

**ambush** noun (pl ambushes) **1** the act of lying hidden in order to make a surprise attack **2** the people hidden in this way **3** their place of hiding □ verb to attack suddenly from a position of hiding

**amenable** adj open to advice or suggestion

**amend** verb **1** to correct, improve (a text or statement) by making small additions **2** to alter (a text or statement) slightly by making small additions □ **amendment** noun a change, often in something written □ **make amends** to make up for having done wrong

◣ Do not confuse with: **emend**. **Amending** involves making changes or improvements. **Emending** consists simply of getting rid of errors.

**amenity** noun (pl amenities) a pleasant or convenient feature of a place etc

**amethyst** noun a precious stone of a bluish-violet colour

**amiable** adj likeable; friendly □ **amiability** noun □ **amiably** adv

**amicable** adj friendly

**amid** or **amidst** prep in the middle of, surrounded by: staying calm amidst all the confusion

◣ Use 'amid' or 'amidst' when the thing or things doing the surrounding cannot be counted: amidst the confusion/sitting amidst the wild poppies. Use 'among' or 'amongst' when the thing or things can be counted: celebrate your birthday among friends.

**amiss** adv wrongly; badly

**amity** noun, formal friendship

**ammonia** noun a strong-smelling gas made of hydrogen and nitrogen

**ammunition** noun gunpowder, shot, bullets, bombs etc

**amnesia** noun loss of memory □ **amnesiac** noun & adj (someone) suffering from amnesia

**amnesty** noun (pl amnesties) a general pardon of wrongdoers

**amoeba** (say a-mee-ba) noun (pl amoebas or amoebae - say a-mee-bi or a-mee-bai) a very simple form of animal life found in ponds etc

**amok** or **amuck** adv: run amok to go mad and do a lot of damage, run riot

**among** or **amongst** prep **1** surrounded by or in the middle of: among friends **2** in shares, in parts: divide amongst yourselves **3** in the group of: among all her novels, this is the best

◣ See box at **amid**

**amoral** adj incapable of distinguishing between right and wrong □ **amorality** noun
ⓘ From Greek prefix a- meaning 'the opposite of', and Latin moralis meaning 'moral'

◣ Do not confuse with: **immoral**. An **amoral** person does not understand the difference between right and wrong. An **immoral** person behaves badly in the full knowledge that what they are doing is wrong.

**amorous** adj loving; ready or inclined to love

**amount** noun **1** total, sum **2** a quantity □ **amount to** to add up to

**amp** noun **1** an ampère **2** informal an amplifier

**ampère** noun the standard unit of electric current

**ampersand** noun the character (&) representing and

**amphetamine** (say am-fet-a-meen)

*noun* a type of drug used as a stimulant

**amphibian** *noun* **1** an animal that lives on land and in water **2** a vehicle for use on land and in water □ *adj* living on land and water □ **amphibious** *adj* amphibian

**amphitheatre** *noun* a theatre with seats surrounding a central arena

**ample** *adj* **1** plenty of **2** large enough

**amplify** *verb* **1** to make louder **2** to make more pronounced □ **amplification** *noun* □ **amplifier** *noun* an electrical device for increasing loudness

**amplify** ➣ amplifies, amplifying, amplified

**amplitude** *noun* **1** largeness **2** size

**amputate** *verb* to cut off (*esp* a human limb) □ **amputation** *noun*

**amputee** *noun* someone who has had a limb amputated

**amuck** *another spelling of* **amok**

**amuse** *verb* **1** to make to laugh **2** to give pleasure to □ **amusement** *noun* □ **amusing** *adj* **1** funny **2** giving pleasure

**an** *see* **a**

**anabolic steroids** steroids used to increase the build-up of body tissue, *esp* muscle

**anachronism** (*say* a-**nak**-ro-nizm) *noun* the mention of something which did not exist or was not yet invented at the time spoken about □ **anachronistic** *adj*

**anaconda** *noun* a large South American water snake

**anaemia** or *US* **anemia** (*say both* a-**nee**-mi-a) *noun* a shortage of red cells in the blood

**anaemic** (*say* a-**nee**-mik) *adj* **1** suffering from anaemia **2** pale or ill-looking

**anaerobic** *adj* not requiring oxygen to live

**anaesthesia** or *US* **anesthesia** (*say both* an-es-**thee**-zi-a) *noun* loss of feeling or sensation

**anaesthetic** or *US* **anesthetic** (*say both* an-es-**thet**-ik) *noun* a substance which produces lack of feeling for a time in a part of the body, or which makes someone unconscious □ **anaesthetist** (*say* an-**ees**-the-tist) *noun* a doctor trained to administer anaesthetics

**anagram** *noun* a word or sentence formed by reordering the letters of another word or sentence, *eg* veil is an anagram of *evil*

✎ MAKE THE REAL SHAPES is an anagram of a famous playwright and one of his best-known plays. Can you solve it? Now have a go at inventing some anagrams of your own.

**anal** *adj* of the anus

**analgesic** *adj* causing insensibility to pain

**analogous** *adj* similar, alike in some way

**analogy** *noun* (*pl* **analogies**) a likeness, resemblance in certain ways

**analyse** or *US* **analyze** *verb* **1** to break down, separate into parts **2** to examine in detail

**analysis** *noun* (*pl* **analyses**) **1** a breaking up of a thing into its parts **2** a detailed examination (of something)

**analyst** *noun* **1** someone who analyses **2** a psychiatrist or psychologist

**analyze** *US spelling of* **analyse**

**anarchy** *noun* **1** lack or absence of government **2** disorder or confusion □ **anarchic** or **anarchical** *adj* □ **anarchist** *noun* someone who believes in anarchy

**anathema** (*say* a-**nath**-e-ma) *noun* **1** a curse **2** a hated person or thing: *opera is anathema to him*

**anatomy** *noun* **1** the study of the parts of the body **2** the body

**anatomist** *noun*

**ancestor** *noun* a person from whom someone is descended by birth; a forefather □ **ancestral** *adj* □ **ancestry** *noun* line of ancestors

**anchor** *noun* a heavy piece of iron, with hooked ends, for holding a ship fast to the bed of the sea *etc* □ *verb* **1** to fix by anchor **2** to let down the anchor □ **anchorman, anchorwoman** *noun* the main presenter of a television news programme *etc* □ **cast anchor** to let down the anchor □ **weigh anchor** to pull up the anchor

**anchorage** *noun* a place where a ship can anchor

**anchovy** *noun* (*pl* **anchovies**) a type of small fish of the herring family

**ancient** *adj* **1** very old **2** of times long past

**ancillary** *adj* serving or supporting something more important

**and** *conj* **1** joining two statements, pieces of information *etc*: *black and white film / add milk and stir* **2** in addition to: *2 and 2 make 4*

**android** *noun* a robot in human form

**anecdote** *noun* a short, interesting or amusing story, usually true □ **anecdotal** *adj*

**anemometer** *noun* an instrument for measuring the speed of the wind

**anemone** (*say* a-nem-o-ni) *noun* a type of woodland or garden flower

**aneroid barometer** a barometer which measures air pressure without the use of mercury

**aneurism** (*say* an-yoo-ri-zm) *noun* **1** dilatation of an artery **2** abnormal enlargement

**angel** *noun* **1** a messenger or attendant of God **2** a very good or beautiful person □ **angelic** *adj* □ **angelically** *adv* in a perfectly sweet and virtuous way

**angelica** *noun* a plant whose candied leaf-stalks are used as cake decoration

**anger** *noun* a bitter feeling against someone, annoyance, rage □ *verb* to make angry

**angina** *noun* a form of heart disease causing acute pains

**angle** *noun* **1** the V-shape made by two lines meeting at a point **2** a corner **3** a point of view □ *verb* to try to get by hints *etc*: *angling for a job*

**angler** *noun* someone who fishes with rod and line □ **angling** *noun* the sport of fishing with a rod and line

**Anglican** *adj* of the Church of England □ *noun* a member of the Church of England

**anglicize** *verb* **1** to turn into the English language **2** to make English in character □ **anglicization** *noun*

**Anglo-Saxon** *adj & noun* **1** (of) the people of England before the Norman Conquest **2** (of) their language

**angry** *adj* feeling or showing anger □ **angrily** *adv*

■ cross, irate, incensed, enraged, furious

**anguish** *noun* very great pain or distress

**angular** *adj* **1** having angles **2** thin, bony □ **angularity** *noun*

**animal** *noun* **1** a living being which can feel and move of its own accord **2** an animal other than a human □ *adj* of or like an animal

**animate** *verb* (*say* an-im-eit) **1** to give life to **2** to make lively □ *adj* (*say* an-im-at) living □ **animated** *adj* **1** lively **2** made to move as if alive

■ (adj) inanimate

**animation** *noun* **1** liveliness **2** a film made from a series of drawings that give the illusion of movement when shown in sequence □ **animator** *noun* an artist who works in animation

**animosity** *noun* bitter hatred, enmity

**aniseed** *noun* a seed with a flavour

like that of liquorice

**ankle** *noun* the joint connecting the foot and leg

**annals** *noun pl* yearly historical accounts of events

**annex 1** to take possession of **2** to add, attach □ *noun (also spelled* **annexe)** a building added to another □ **annexation** *noun*

**annihilate** (*say a-nai-i-*leit) *verb* to destroy completely □ **annihilation** *noun*

**anniversary** *noun (pl* **anniversaries)** the day of each year when a particular event is remembered

**annotate** *verb* **1** to make notes upon **2** to add notes or explanation to □ **annotation** *noun*

**announce** *verb* to make publicly known □ **announcement** *noun* □ **announcer** *noun* someone who announces programmes on TV *etc*, or reads the news

**annoy** *verb* to make rather angry; irritate □ **annoyance** *noun*

■ aggravate, irritate, pester, rile, vex, irk

**annual** *adj* yearly □ *noun* **1** a plant that lives only one year **2** a book published yearly □ **annually** *adv* every year

**annuity** *noun (pl* **annuities)** a yearly payment made for a certain time or for life

**annul** *verb* **1** to put an end to **2** to declare no longer valid □ **annulment** *noun*

**annul** ⊷ annuls, annulling, annulled

**anodyne** *adj* **1** soothing, relieving pain **2** bland and harmless: *an anodyne comment* □ *noun* something that soothes pain

**anoint** *verb* to smear with ointment or oil

**anomaly** *noun (pl* **anomalies)** something unusual, not according

to rule □ **anomalous** *adj*

**anon** *abbrev* anonymous

**anonymous** *adj* without the name of the author, giver *etc* being known or given □ **anonymously** *adv*

**anorak** *noun* a hooded waterproof jacket

**anorexia** *noun* **1** *(also called* **anorexia nervosa)** an emotional illness causing the sufferer to refuse food and become sometimes dangerously thin **2** lack of appetite □ **anorexic** *adj* of or suffering from anorexia □ *noun* someone suffering from anorexia

**another** *adj* **1** a different (thing or person): *moving to another job* **2** one more of the same kind: *have another biscuit* □ *pronoun* an additional thing of the same kind: *do you want another?*

**answer** *verb* **1** to speak, write *etc* in return or reply **2** to find the result or solution (of a sum, problem *etc*) **3** (with **for**) to be responsible **4** (with **for**) to suffer, be punished □ *noun* something said, written *etc* in return or reply; a solution □ **answer back** to give a cheeky or aggressive answer to someone in authority □ **answerable** *adj* **1** able to be answered **2** responsible: *answerable for her actions*

**ant** *noun* a very small insect which lives in organized colonies □ **have ants in your pants** to be impatient or restless □ **ant-hill** *noun* an earth mound built by ants as a nest

**antagonist** *noun* **1** an enemy **2** an opponent □ **antagonism** *noun* hostility, opposition, enmity □ **antagonistic** *adj* opposed (to), unfriendly, hostile

**antagonize** *verb* to make an enemy of, cause dislike

**Antarctic** *adj* of the South Pole or regions round it

**ante-** *prefix* before
◉ From Latin *ante* meaning 'before'

**anteater** *noun* an American animal with a long snout which feeds on ants and termites

**ante-bellum** *adj* of the period before a particular war

**antecedent** (*say* ant-i-see-dent) *adj* going before in time □ *noun* **1** someone who lived at an earlier time; an ancestor **2** (**antecedents**) previous conduct, history *etc*

**antedate** *verb* **1** to backdate (= put a date on a document which is earlier than the day you are actually writing it) **2** to be earlier in date than

**antediluvian** *adj* very old or old-fashioned

Literally 'before the flood', in allusion to the Biblical story of Noah

**antelope** *noun* a graceful, swift-running animal like a deer

**antenatal** *adj* **1** before birth **2** relating to pregnancy: *antenatal clinic*

**antenna** *noun* **1** (*pl* **antennae** - *say* an-**ten**-ee) an insect's feeler **2** (*pl* **antennas**) an aerial

**anteroom** *noun* a room leading into a large room

**anthem** *noun* **1** a piece of music for a church choir **2** any song of praise

**anthology** *noun* (*pl* **anthologies**) a collection of specially chosen poems, stories *etc*
  ⊙ From Greek *anthos* meaning 'flower', and *logia* meaning 'collection'

**anthracite** *noun* coal that burns with a hot, smokeless flame

**anthrax** *noun* an infectious disease of cattle, sheep *etc*, sometimes transferred to humans

**anthropoid** *adj* of apes: resembling humans

**anthropology** *noun* the study of mankind □ **anthropological** *adj* □ **anthropologist** *noun*

**anti-** *prefix* against, opposite: *anti-terrorist*
  ⊙ From Greek *anti* meaning 'against'

**antibiotic** *noun* a medicine taken to kill disease-causing bacteria

**antibody** *noun* (*pl* **antibodies**) a substance produced in the human body to fight bacteria *etc*

**anticipate** *verb* **1** to look forward to, expect **2** to see or know in advance **3** to act before (someone or something) □ **anticipation** *noun* **1** expectation **2** excitement □ **anticipatory** *adj*

**anticlimax** *noun* a dull or disappointing ending

**anticlockwise** *adj* & *adv* in the opposite direction to the hands of a clock

**antics** *noun pl* tricks, odd or amusing actions

**anticyclone** *noun* a circling movement of air round an area of high air pressure, causing calm weather

**antidote** *noun* something given to act against the effect of poison

**antifreeze** *noun* a chemical with a low freezing-point, added to a car radiator to prevent freezing

**antihistamine** *noun* a medicine used to treat an allergy

**antipathy** *noun* extreme dislike

**antiperspirant** *noun* a substance applied to the body to reduce sweating

**antipodes** (*say* an-**tip**-od-eez) *noun pl* places on the earth's surface exactly opposite each other, *esp* Australia and New Zealand in relation to Europe □ **antipodean** *adj*

**antique** *noun* an old, interesting or valuable object from earlier times □ *adj* **1** old, from earlier times **2** old-fashioned □ **antiquarian** *noun* a dealer in antiques □ **antiquated** *adj* grown old, or out of fashion

**antiquity** *noun* (*pl* **antiquities**)

**1** ancient times, *esp* those of the Greeks and Romans **2** great age **3** (**antiquities**) objects from earlier times

**antiseptic** *adj* germ-destroying □ *noun* a chemical *etc* which destroys germs

**antisocial** *adj* **1** not fitting in with, harmful to other people **2** disliking the company of other people

**antithesis** *noun* (*pl* **antitheses**) the exact opposite: *the antithesis of good taste* □ **antithetical** *adj*

**antler** *noun* the horn of a deer

**anus** (*say* **ei**-nus) *noun* the lower opening of the bowel through which faeces pass

**anvil** *noun* a metal block on which blacksmiths hammer metal into shape

**anxiety** *noun* (*pl* **anxieties**) worry about what may happen, apprehensiveness

**anxious** *adj* **1** worried, apprehensive **2** eager, keen: *anxious to please*

**any** *adj* **1** some: *is there any milk?* **2** every, no matter which: *any day will suit me* □ *pronoun* some: *there aren't any left* □ *adv* at all: *I can't work any faster* □ **at any rate** in any case, whatever happens

**anybody** *pronoun* any person

**anyhow** *adv* **1** in any case: *I think I'll go anyhow* **2** carelessly: *scattered anyhow over the floor*

**anyone** *pronoun* any person

**anything** *pronoun* something of any kind

**anyway** *adv* at any rate

**anywhere** *adv* in any place

**apart** *adv* **1** aside **2** in or into pieces: *came apart in my hands* **3** in opposite directions □ **apart from 1** separate, or separately, from **2** except for: *who else knows apart from us?*

**apartheid** *noun* the political policy of keeping people of different races apart

**apartment** *noun* **1** a room in a house **2** *US* a flat

**apathy** *noun* lack of feeling or interest □ **apathetic** *adj*

**ape** *noun* a member of a group of animals related to monkeys, but larger, tailless and walking upright □ *verb* to imitate

**aperitif** (*say* a-pe-ri-**teef**) *noun* a drink taken before a meal

**aperture** *noun* an opening, a hole

**apex** *noun* (*pl* **apexes** or **apices** - *say* ei-pi-seez) the highest point of anything

**aphid** (*say* **ei**-fid) *noun* a small insect which feeds on plants

**aphrodisiac** *noun* a drug, food *etc* that increases sexual desire □ *adj* causing increased sexual desire

**apiary** (*say* **ei**-pi-a-ri) *noun* (*pl* **apiaries**) a place where bees are kept □ **apiarist** (*say* **ei**-pi-a-rist) *noun* someone who keeps an apiary or studies bees

**apiece** *adv* to or for each one: *three chocolates apiece*

**aplomb** *noun* self-confidence

**apocalypse** *noun* the destruction of the world □ **apocalyptic** *adj*

**apocryphal** (*say* a-**pok**-rif-al) *adj* unlikely to be true

**apogee** (*say* **ap**-o-jee) *noun* **1** a culmination, a climax **2** the point of an orbit furthest from the earth

**apologize** *verb* to express regret, say you are sorry

**apology** *noun* (*pl* **apologies**) an expression of regret for having done wrong □ **apologetic** *adj* expressing regret

**apoplexy** *noun* sudden loss of ability to feel, move *etc*, a stroke □ **apoplectic** *adj*

**apoptosis** *noun*, *biochemistry* cell death

**apostle** noun 1 a religious preacher, esp one of the disciples of Christ 2 an advocate for a cause

**apostrophe** noun 1 a mark (') indicating possession: the minister's cat 2 a similar mark indicating that a letter etc has been missed out, eg isn't for is not

**apothecary** noun (pl **apothecaries**) old a chemist or druggist

**appal** verb to horrify, shock □ **appalling** adj shocking

**appal** ⇨ appal**s**, appall**ing**, appall**ed**

**apparatus** noun 1 an instrument or machine 2 instruments, tools or material required for a piece of work

**apparel** noun a formal or literary word for clothing

**apparent** adj easily seen, evident □ **apparently** adv

**apparition** noun 1 something remarkable which appears suddenly 2 a ghost

**appeal** verb 1 to ask earnestly (for help etc) 2 law to take a case that has been lost to a higher court 3 to be pleasing (to) □ noun 1 a request for help 2 law the taking of a case to a higher court □ **appealing** adj 1 arousing liking or sympathy 2 asking earnestly

**appear** verb 1 to come into view 2 to arrive 3 to seem □ **appearance** noun

**appease** verb to soothe or satisfy, esp by giving what was asked for

**appendectomy** noun, medical surgical removal of the appendix

**appendicitis** noun, medical inflammation of the appendix

**appendix** noun (pl **appendices** or **appendixes**) 1 a part added at the end of a book 2 a small worm-shaped part of the bowels

**appertain to** verb, formal 1 to belong to 2 to be relevant to

**appetite** noun 1 desire for food 2 taste or enthusiasm (for): no appetite for violence

**appetizer** noun a snack taken before a main meal

**appetizing** adj tempting to the appetite

**applaud** verb 1 to show approval of by clapping the hands 2 to express strong approval of: I applaud the Prime Minister's decision

**applause** noun a show of approval by clapping

**apple** noun a round firm fruit, usually red or green □ **the apple of someone's eye** a person or thing that is greatly loved by someone

**appliance** noun a tool, instrument, machine etc

**applicable** adj 1 able to be applied 2 suitable, relevant

**applicant** noun someone who applies or asks

**application** noun 1 the act of applying 2 something applied, eg an ointment 3 a formal request, usually on paper 4 hard work, close attention

**apply** verb 1 to put on (an ointment etc) 2 to use: apply these rules in each case 3 to ask formally (for) 4 to be suitable or relevant 5 (with to) to affect □ **apply yourself** to work hard

**apply** ⇨ appli**es**, apply**ing**, appli**ed**

**appoint** verb 1 to fix (a date etc) 2 to place in a job: she was appointed manager

**appointment** noun 1 the act of appointing 2 a job, a post 3 an arrangement to meet someone

**apportion** verb to divide in fair shares

**apposite** (say ap-o-zit) adj suitable, appropriate

**appraise** verb to estimate the value or quality of □ **appraisal** noun □ **appraising** adj quickly summing up

**appreciate** verb 1 to see or

understand the good points, beauties *etc* of: *appreciate art* **2** to understand: *I appreciate your point* **3** to rise in value □ **appreciable** *adj* noticeable, considerable □ **appreciation** *noun*

🔄 (meaning 3) depreciate

**apprehend** *verb* **1** to arrest **2** *formal* to understand □ **apprehension** *noun* **1** arrest **2** fear or nervousness **3** *formal* understanding

**apprehensive** *adj* afraid

**apprentice** *noun* someone who is learning a trade □ **apprenticeship** *noun* the time during which someone is an apprentice

**approach** *verb* **1** to come near **2** to be nearly equal to **3** to speak to in order to ask for something □ *noun* (*pl* **approaches**) **1** a coming near to **2** a way leading to a place □ **approachable** *adj* **1** able to be reached **2** easy to speak to, friendly

**approbation** *noun* good opinion, approval

**appropriate** *adj* (*say* a-**proh**-pri-at) suitable, fitting □ *verb* (*say* a-**proh**-pri-eit) **1** to take possession of **2** to set (money *etc*) apart for a purpose □ **appropriately** *adv* □ **appropriation** *noun*

'to appropriate' (meaning 1) is often used as a euphemism for 'to steal'.

**approve** *verb* **1** to agree to, permit **2** to think well (of): *did he approve of the new curtains?* □ **approval** *noun* **1** permission **2** satisfaction, favourable judgement □ **on approval** on trial, for return to a shop if not bought

**approximate** *adj* (*say* ap-**rok**-sim-at) more or less accurate □ *verb* (*say* ap-**rok**-sim-eit): **approximate to** to be or come near to: *the money set aside doesn't approximate to the amount needed* □ **approximately** *adv* □ **approximation** *noun* a rough estimate

**apricot** *noun* an orange-coloured fruit like a small peach

**April** *noun* the fourth month of the year

**a priori** (*say* ei prai-**aw**-ri *or* ah pri-**aw**-ri) *adj* based on accepted principles or arguments

**apron** *noun* **1** a garment worn to protect the front of the clothes **2** a hard surface for aircraft to stand on □ **apron stage** the part of the stage in front of the curtains in a theatre

**apropos** (*say* a-pro-**poh**) *adv*: **apropos of** in connection with, concerning

**apse** *noun* a rounded domed section, *esp* at the east end of a church

**apt** *adj* **1** likely (to): *apt to change his mind* **2** suitable, fitting □ **aptness** *noun* suitability

**aptitude** *noun* talent, ability

**aqua-** *prefix* of or relating to water
ⓘ From Latin *aqua* meaning 'water'

**aqualung** *noun* a breathing apparatus worn by divers

**aquamarine** *noun* **1** a type of bluish-green precious stone **2** a bluish-green colour □ *adj* bluish-green

**aquarium** *noun* (*pl* **aquaria** *or* **aquariums**) a tank or tanks for keeping fish or water animals

**aquatic** *adj* living, growing or taking place in water

**aqueduct** *noun* a bridge for taking a canal *etc* across a valley

**aquiline** *adj* **1** like an eagle **2** of a nose: curved or hooked

**arable** *adj* of land: used for growing crops

**arbiter** *noun* **1** a judge, an umpire, someone chosen by opposing parties to decide between them **2** someone who sets a standard or has influence: *arbiter of good taste* □ **arbitrage** *noun* the practice of buying goods *etc* in one market and selling in another to make a profit

**arbitrary** *adj* **1** fixed according to opinion, not objective rules

**2** occurring haphazardly □ **arbitrarily** adv

**arbitrate** verb to act as a judge between people or their claims etc □ **arbitration** noun **1** the act of judging between claims etc **2** the settlement of a dispute by an arbiter □ **arbitrator** noun someone who arbitrates

**arboreal** (say ah-**baw**-ri-al) adj of trees, living in trees

**arbour** noun a seat in a garden shaded by tree-branches etc

**arc** noun part of the circumference of a circle, a curve □ **arc-lamp** or **arc-light** noun a bright lamp lit by a special kind of electric current

**arcade** noun a covered walk, esp one with shops on both sides

**arch** noun (pl **arches**) the curved part above people's heads in a gateway or the curved support for a bridge, roof etc □ adj mischievous, roguish □ verb to raise or curve in the shape of an arch

**arch-** prefix chief, main: arch-enemy ⊕ From Greek archos meaning 'chief'

**Arch-** is usually pronounced ahch (as in 'March'), but in archangel it is pronounced ahk (like 'ark').

**archaeology** noun the study of the people of earlier times from the remains of their buildings etc □ **archaeological** adj □ **archaeologist** noun

**archaic** (say ahk-**ei**-ik) adj no longer used, old-fashioned □ **archaism** (say **ahk**-ei-i-sm) noun an old-fashioned word etc

**archangel** noun a chief angel

**archbishop** noun a chief bishop

**archdeacon** noun a clergyman next in rank below a bishop

**archduke** noun, historical the title of the ruling princes of Austria

**archer** noun someone who shoots arrows from a bow □ **archery** noun

the sport of shooting with a bow and arrows

**archetype** (say **ahk**-i-taip) noun the original pattern or model from which copies are made □ **archetypal** adj

**archipelago** noun (pl **archipelagoes** or **archipelagos**) a group of small islands

**architect** noun someone who plans and designs buildings

**architecture** noun **1** the study of building **2** the style of a building

**archives** noun pl **1** historical papers, written records etc **2** a building etc in which these are kept

**archway** noun a passage or road beneath an arch

**Arctic** or **arctic** adj **1** (usually **Arctic**) of the district round the North Pole **2** (usually **arctic**) very cold

**ardent** adj eager, passionate □ **ardently** adv □ **ardour** noun

**arduous** adj difficult

**are** see be

**area** noun **1** the extent of a surface measured in square metres etc **2** a region, a piece of land or ground

**arena** noun **1** any place for a public contest, show etc **2** historical the centre of an amphitheatre etc where gladiators fought

**argosy** noun (pl **argosies**) a literary word meaning a large trading-ship with a valuable cargo

**arguable** adj that can be argued as being true □ **arguably** adv in certain people's opinion (although this opinion could be disagreed with): arguably the best film of the year

**argue** verb **1** to quarrel in words **2** to try to prove by giving reasons (that) **3 argue for** or **against something** to give reasons for or against something as a way of persuading people

**argue** ⇢ argues, argu**ing**, argu**ed**

**argument** noun **1** a heated

discussion, quarrel **2** reasoning (for or against something)
□ **argumentative** adj fond of arguing

**aria** noun a song for solo voice in an opera

**arid** adj dry □ **aridity** or **aridness** noun

**arise** verb **1** to rise up **2** to come into being

**arise** ⇌ arises, arising, arose, arisen

**aristocracy** noun those of the nobility and upper class □ **aristocrat** noun a member of the aristocracy □ **aristocratic** adj of the aristocracy

**arithmetic** noun a way of counting and calculating by using numbers □ **arithmetical** adj

**ark** noun the covered boat used by Noah in the Biblical story of the Flood

**arm** noun **1** the part of the body between the shoulder and the hand **2** anything jutting out like this **3** (**arms**) weapons □ verb to equip with weapons □ **armchair** noun a chair with arms at each side □ **armed** adj carrying a weapon, now esp a gun □ **arm-pit** noun the hollow under the arm at the shoulder □ **the long arm of the law** the power or authority of the police force □ **chance your arm** to say or do something which, though a bit risky, could possibly get you what you want

**armada** noun a fleet of armed ships

**armadillo** noun (pl **armadillos**) a small American animal whose body is protected by bony plates

**armageddon** noun a final battle or devastation, an apocalypse

**armaments** noun pl equipment for war, esp the guns of a ship, tank etc

**armistice** noun a halt in fighting during war, a truce

**armour** noun, historical a protective suit of metal worn by knights □ **armoured** adj of a vehicle: protected by metal plates □ **armoury**

noun (pl **armouries**) an arms store

**army** noun (pl **armies**) **1** a large number of soldiers armed for war **2** a great number of anything

**aroma** noun a sweet smell

**aromatherapy** noun a healing therapy involving massage with plant oils

**arose** past form of **arise**

**around** prep **1** in a circle about **2** on all sides of, surrounding **3** all over, at several places in: papers scattered around the room **4** somewhere near in time, place, amount: I left him around here/ come back around three o'clock □ adv all about, in various places: people stood around watching □ **get around 1** of a story: to become known to everyone **2** to be active

**arouse** verb **1** to awaken **2** to stir, move (a feeling or person) □ **arousal** noun

**arpeggio** noun, music a chord with the notes played in rapid succession, not at the same time

**arrange** verb **1** to put in some order **2** to plan, settle □ **arrangement** noun

**array** noun order, arrangement; clothing □ verb **1** to put in order **2** to dress, adorn

**arrears** noun pl: **in arrears** not up to date; behind with payments

**arrest** verb **1** to seize, capture, esp by power of the law **2** to stop **3** to catch (the attention etc) □ noun **1** capture by the police **2** stopping □ **arresting** adj striking, capturing the attention

**arrival** noun **1** the act of arriving **2** someone or something that arrives

**arrive** verb to reach a place □ **arrive at** to reach, come to (a decision etc)

**arrogant** adj proud, haughty, self-important □ **arrogance** noun □ **arrogantly** adv

**arrow** noun **1** a straight, pointed weapon shot from a bow **2** an arrow-shape, eg on a road-sign, showing direction

**arsenal** *noun* a factory or store for weapons, ammunition *etc*

**arsenic** *noun* an element that, combined with oxygen, makes a strong poison

**arson** *noun* the crime of setting fire to a house *etc* on purpose □ **arsonist** *noun*

**art** *noun* **1** drawing, painting, sculpture *etc* **2** cleverness, skill; cunning **3** (**arts**) non-scientific school or university subjects □ **artful** *adj* wily, cunning □ **artless** *adj* simple, frank

**artefact** or **artifact** *noun* a human-made object

**artery** *noun* (*pl* **arteries**) a tube which carries blood from the heart to pass through the body □ **arterial** *adj* of or like arteries □ **arterial road** a main traffic road

**artesian well** a well in which water rises to the surface by natural pressure

**artichoke** *noun* a thistle-like plant with an edible flower-head

**article** *noun* **1** a thing, object **2** a composition in a newspaper, journal *etc* **3** a section of a document **4** (**articles**) an agreement made up of clauses: *articles of apprenticeship* **5** *grammar* the name of the words *the, a, an* □ *verb* to bind (an apprentice *etc*) by articles

**articulate** *adj* (*say* ah-**tik**-yu-lat) expressing thoughts or words clearly □ *verb* (*say* ah-**tik**-yu-leit) to express clearly □ **articulation** *noun* □ **articulated lorry** a lorry with a cab which can turn at an angle to the main part of the lorry, making cornering easier

**artifact** *another spelling of* **artefact**

**artificial** *adj* not natural; human-made □ **artificiality** *noun* □ **artificial insemination** the insertion of sperm into the uterus by means other than sexual intercourse

**artillery** *noun* **1** big guns **2** an army division that uses these

**artisan** *noun* a skilled worker

**artist** *noun* **1** someone who paints pictures **2** someone skilled in anything **3** an artiste □ **artistry** *noun* skill as an artist

**artiste** (*say* ah-**teest**) *noun* a performer in a theatre, circus *etc*

**artistic** *adj* **1** of artists: *the artistic community* **2** having a talent for art

**as** *adv* & *conj* in phrases expressing comparison or similarity: *as good as his brother/ the same as this one* □ *conj* **1** while, when: *happened as I was walking past* **2** because, since: *we stayed at home as it was raining* **3** in the same way that: *he thinks as I do* □ *adv* for instance □ **as for** concerning, regarding □ **as if** or **as though** as it would be if □ **as to** regarding □ **as well** (as) too, in addition (to)

**asbestos** *noun* a thread-like mineral which can be woven and which will not burn □ **asbestosis** *noun* a lung disease caused by inhaling asbestos dust

**ascend** *verb* **1** to climb, go up **2** to rise or slope upwards □ **ascendancy** or **ascendency** *noun* control (over) □ **ascendant** or **ascendent** *adj* rising □ **ascent** *noun* **1** an upward move or climb **2** a slope upwards; a rise □ **ascend the throne** to be crowned king or queen

**ascertain** *verb* **1** to find out **2** to make certain

**ascetic** *noun* someone who keeps away from all kinds of pleasure

**ascribe** *verb*: **ascribe to** to think of as belonging to or due to: *ascribing the blame*

**ash** *noun* (*pl* **ashes**) **1** a type of hard-wood tree with silvery bark **2** (**ashes**) what is left after anything is burnt □ **rise from the ashes** to develop and flourish after experiencing ruin or disaster

This phrase comes from the image of the phoenix, a mythical bird which destroyed itself in fire and was reborn from the ashes.

**ashamed** adj feeling shame

**ashen** adj very pale

**ashore** adv on or on to the shore

**aside** adv on or to one side; apart □ noun words spoken which those nearby are not supposed to hear

**asinine** adj 1 of an ass 2 stupid

**ask** verb 1 to request information about: asked for my address 2 to invite: we've asked over twenty people to come □ **ask after someone** to make enquiries about someone's health and well-being

**askance** adv off the straight □ **look askance at** to look at with suspicion

**askew** adv off the straight, to one side

**asleep** adj 1 sleeping 2 of limbs: numbed

**ASLEF** abbrev Associated Society of Locomotive Engineers and Firemen

**asp** noun a small poisonous snake

**asparagus** noun a plant whose young shoots are eaten as a vegetable

**aspect** noun 1 look, appearance 2 view, point of view 3 side of a building etc or the direction it faces in

**aspen** noun a kind of poplar tree

**asperity** noun 1 harshness, sharpness of temper 2 bitter coldness

**asphalt** noun a tarry mixture used to make pavements, paths etc

**asphyxia** (say as-fik-si-a) noun suffocation by smoke or other fumes □ **asphyxiate** verb to suffocate □ **asphyxiation** noun

**aspidistra** noun a kind of pot-plant with large leaves

**aspire** verb (with to or after) to try to achieve or reach (something difficult, ambitious etc) □ **aspiration** noun a goal which you hope to achieve □ **aspiring** adj trying or wishing to be: an aspiring director

**aspirin** noun a pain-killing drug

**ass** noun (pl asses) 1 a donkey 2 a stupid person

**assail** verb to attack □ **assailant** noun an attacker

**assassin** noun someone who assassinates, a murderer □ **assassinate** verb to murder (esp a politically important person) □ **assassination** noun

Literally 'hashish eater', after an Islamic sect during the Crusades who consumed the drug before assassinating Christians

**assault** noun an attack, esp a sudden one □ verb to attack

**assemblage** noun a collection, a gathering

**assemble** verb 1 to bring (people) together 2 to put together (a machine etc) 3 to meet together

**assembly** noun (pl assemblies) 1 a putting together 2 a gathering of people, esp for a special purpose □ **assembly line** a series of machines and workers necessary for the manufacture of an article

**assent** verb to agree □ noun agreement

**assert** verb 1 to state firmly 2 to insist on (a right etc): women asserting their right to vote □ **assertion** noun □ **assertive** adj not shy, inclined to assert yourself □ **assert yourself** to make yourself noticed, heard etc

**assess** verb 1 to estimate the value, power of etc 2 to fix an amount (to be paid in tax etc) □ **assessment** noun □ **assessor** noun someone who assesses

**asset** noun 1 an advantage, a help 2 (assets) the property of a person, company etc

**assiduous** *adj* persevering; hard-working

**assign** (*say* a-**sain**) *verb* **1** to give to someone as a share or task **2** to fix (a time or place): *assign a date for the meeting* □ **assignation** (*say* as-ig-nei-shun) *noun* an appointment to meet □ **assignment** *noun* **1** an act of assigning **2** a task given

**assimilate** *verb* to take in: *assimilate all the information* □ **assimilation** *noun*

**assist** *verb* to help □ **assistance** *noun* □ **assistant** *noun* **1** a helper, *eg* to a senior worker **2** someone who serves in a shop *etc*

**assizes** *noun pl* the name of certain law courts in England

**associate** *verb* **1** (with **with**) to keep company with **2** (**associate yourself with**) to join (with) in partnership or friendship **3** to connect in thought: *I associate him with hard work* □ *adj* joined or connected (with) □ *noun* a friend, partner, companion

**association** *noun* **1** a club, society, union *etc* **2** a partnership, friendship **3** a connection made in the mind

**assorted** *adj* various, mixed □ **assortment** *noun* a variety, a mixture

**assuage** *verb* to soothe, ease (pain, hunger *etc*)

**assume** *verb* **1** to take upon yourself: *assume responsibility for the errors* **2** to take as true without further proof, take for granted **3** to put on (a disguise *etc*) □ **assumed** *adj* false or pretended: *an assumed air of confidence*

**assumption** *noun* **1** the act of assuming **2** something taken for granted

**assure** *verb* **1** to make (someone) sure **2** to state positively (that) □ **assurance** *noun* **1** a feeling of certainty; confidence **2** a promise **3** insurance □ **assured** *adj* certain; confident

**asterisk** *noun* a star (*) used in printing for various purposes, *esp* to point out a footnote or insertion

**astern** *adv* at or towards the back of a ship

**asthma** (*say* as-ma) *noun* an illness causing wheezing, difficulty in breathing *etc* □ **asthmatic** (*say* as-mat-ik) *adj* suffering from asthma □ *noun* someone with asthma

**astonish** *verb* to surprise greatly □ **astonishing** *adj* □ **astonishment** *noun* amazement, wonder

**astound** *verb* to surprise greatly, amaze □ **astounding** *adj*

**astral** *adj* of the stars

**astray** *adv* out of the right way, straying

**astride** *adv* with legs apart □ *prep* with legs on each side of

**astringent** *noun* a lotion *etc* used for closing up the skin's pores □ *adj* **1** used for closing the pores **2** of manner: sharp, sarcastic

**astro-** or **astr-** *prefix* of or relating to stars or outer space

⊙ From Greek *astron* meaning 'a star'

**astrology** *noun* the study of the stars and their supposed power over the lives of humans □ **astrologer** *noun*

**astronaut** *noun* someone who travels in space

**astronomer** *noun* someone who studies astronomy

**astronomical** *adj* **1** of astronomy **2** of a number: very large

**astronomy** *noun* the study of the stars and their movements

**astute** *adj* cunning, clever □ **astutely** *adv*

**asunder** *adv* a literary word meaning 'apart' or 'into pieces'

**asylum** *noun* **1** a place of refuge or safety **2** *old* a home for the mentally ill

**at** *prep* **1** showing position, time *etc*: *I'll be at home / come at 7 o'clock* **2** costing: *cakes at 25 pence each* □ **at all** in any way: *not worried at all*

**ate** *past form of* **eat**

**atheism** *noun* belief that there is no God □ **atheist** *noun* someone who does not believe in a God □ **atheistic** *adj*

**athlete** *noun* someone good at sport, *esp* running, gymnastics *etc*

**athlete's foot** a fungal condition which affects the feet, making them sore and itchy

**athletic** *adj* **1** of athletics **2** good at sports; strong, powerful □ **athletics** *noun pl* running, jumping *etc* or competitions in these

**atlas** *noun* (*pl* **atlases**) a book of maps

After the mythological *Atlas*, punished by the Greek gods by having to carry the heavens on his shoulders

**atmosphere** *noun* **1** the air round the earth **2** any surrounding feeling: *friendly atmosphere*

**atmospheric** *adj* **1** of the atmosphere **2** with a noticeable atmosphere □ **atmospheric pressure** the pressure exerted by the atmosphere at the earth's surface, due to the weight of the air □ **atmospherics** *noun pl* air disturbances causing crackling noises on the radio *etc*

**atoll** *noun* a coral island or reef

**atom** *noun* **1** the smallest part of an element **2** anything very small

**atom bomb** or **atomic bomb** a bomb in which the explosion is caused by nuclear energy

**atomic** *adj* nuclear □ **atomic energy** nuclear energy

**atomizer** or **atomiser** *noun* an instrument for discharging liquids in a fine spray

**atone** *verb* to make up for wrong-doing: *atone for your sins* □ **atonement** *noun*

**atrocious** *adj* **1** cruel or wicked **2** *informal* very bad

**atrocity** *noun* (*pl* **atrocities**) **1** a terrible crime **2** *informal* something very ugly

**attach** *verb* **1** to fasten or join (to) **2** to think of (something) as having: *don't attach any importance to it* □ **attached** *adj* **1** fastened **2 attached to** fond of □ **attachment** *noun* **1** something attached **2** a joining by love or friendship

**attaché** (*say a-tash-*ei) *noun* a junior member of an embassy staff

**attaché-case** *noun* small case for papers *etc*

**attack** *verb* **1** to fall upon suddenly or violently **2** to speak or write against □ *noun* **1** an act of attacking **2** a fit (of an illness *etc*)

**attain** *verb* to reach; gain □ **attainable** *adj* able to be attained □ **attainment** *noun* act of attaining; the thing attained, an achievement or accomplishment

**attempt** *verb* to try □ *noun* **1** a try or effort: *first attempt* **2** an attack: *an attempt on the president's life*

**attend** *verb* **1** to be present at **2 attend to something** to pay attention to something **3** to wait on, look after **4** to accompany

**attendance** *noun* **1** the fact of being present: *my attendance was expected* **2** the number of people present: *good attendance at the first night*

**attendant** *noun* someone employed to look after a public place, shop *etc*: *cloakroom attendant* □ *adj* accompanying, related: *stress and its attendant health problems*

**attention** *noun* **1** careful notice: *pay attention* **2** concentration **3** care **4** *military* a stiffly straight standing position: *stand to attention*

**attentive** *adj* **1** giving or showing

attention **2** polite □ **attentively** *adv*: *listening attentively*

**attic** *noun* a room just under the roof of a house

From *Attica* in ancient Greece, famous for a type of square architectural column used in upper storeys of classical buildings

**attire** *verb* to dress □ *noun* clothing

**attitude** *noun* **1** a way of thinking or feeling: *positive attitude* **2** a position of the body

**attorney** *noun* (*pl* **attorneys**) **1** someone with legal power to act for another **2** *US* a lawyer

**attract** *verb* **1** to draw to or towards **2** to arouse liking or interest □ **attraction** *noun* **1** the power of attracting **2** something which attracts visitors *etc*: *tourist attraction* □ **attractive** *adj* **1** good-looking, likeable **2** pleasing: *attractive price*

**attribute** *verb* (*say* a-**trib**-yoot) **1** to state or consider as the source or cause of: *attribute the accident to human error* **2** to state as the author or originator of: *attributed to Rembrandt* □ *noun* (*say* **a**-trib-yoot) an attendant characteristic: *attributes of power* □ **attributable** *adj*

**attributive** *adj* **1** expressing an attribute **2** of an adjective: placed immediately before or immediately after the noun it describes, *eg* 'pretty' ('the pretty girl')

Most adjectives can be used in this attributive way. The opposite of 'attributive' (meaning 2) is 'predicative'. An example of an adjective which is only ever used in a predicative way is 'asleep', because you cannot use it to make phrases like 'the asleep girl'.

**aubergine** (*say* oh-*be*-szeen) *noun* an oval dark purple fruit, eaten as a vegetable

**auburn** *adj* of hair: reddish-brown in colour

**auction** *noun* a public sale in which articles are sold to the highest bidder □ *verb* to sell by auction □ **auctioneer** *noun* someone who sells by auction

**audacious** *adj* daring, bold □ **audacity** *noun*

**audible** *adj* able to be heard □ **audibility** *noun*

**audience** *noun* **1** a number of people gathered to watch or hear a performance *etc* **2** a formal interview with someone important: *an audience with the Pope*

**audio** *noun* the reproduction of recorded or radio sound □ *adj* relating to such sound: *an audio tape*

**audio-typist** *noun* a typist able to type from a recording on a tape-recorder

**audio-visual** *adj* concerned with hearing and seeing at the same time □ **audio-visual aids** films, recordings *etc* used in teaching

**audit** *verb* to examine accounts officially □ *noun* an official examination of a company's accounts □ **auditor** *noun* someone who audits accounts

**audition** *noun* a hearing to test an actor, singer *etc*

**auditorium** *noun* (*pl* **auditoria** or **auditoriums**) the part of a theatre *etc* where the audience sits

**auditory** *adj* of hearing

**augment** *verb* to increase in size, number or amount □ **augmentation** *noun* □ **augmentative** *adj* having the quality or power of increasing in size, number or amount

**augur** *verb*: **augur well** to be a good sign for the future □ **augur ill** to be a bad sign for the future

**August** *noun* the eighth month of the year

**august** (*say* aw-**gust**) *adj* full of dignity, stately

**au naturel** (*say* oh nat-yu-**rel**) *adv*

with no additions; plain, natural

**aunt** *noun* a father's or a mother's sister, or an uncle's wife

**au pair** a foreign person, usually a girl, who does domestic duties in return for board, lodging and pocket money

**aural** *adj* relating to the ear
ⓈFrom Latin *auris* meaning 'ear'

✎ Do not confuse with: **oral**. **Oral** means 'relating to the mouth'. It may help to think of the 'O' as looking like an open mouth; and to remember that many words related to listening start with 'AU', like 'audition' and 'auditorium'.

**aurora borealis** the Northern lights

**auspices** *noun pl*: **under the auspices of** under the control or supervision of

**auspicious** *adj* favourable; promising luck

**austere** *adj* **1** severe **2** without luxury; simple, sparse □ **austerity** *noun*

**authentic** *adj* true, real, genuine □ **authenticity** *noun*

**authenticate** *verb* to show to be true or real □ **authentication** *noun*

**author** *noun* the writer of a book, poem, play *etc*

**authoress** *noun, old* a female author

**authoritative** *adj* stated by an expert or someone in authority

**authority** *noun* (*pl* **authorities**)
**1** power or right **2** someone whose opinion is reliable, an expert **3** someone or a body of people having control (over something) **4** (**authorities**) people in power

**authorize** *verb* **1** to give (a person) the power or the right to do something **2** to give permission (for something to be done) □ **authorization** *noun*

**autism** *noun* a disability affecting a person's ability to relate to and communicate with other people □ **autistic** *adj* affected with autism

**auto-** or **aut-** *prefix* **1** self: *autobiography* **2** same **3** self-caused or automatic **4** of or relating to cars
ⓈFrom Greek *autos* meaning 'self' or 'same'

**autobiography** *noun* (*pl* **autobiographies**) the story of someone's life, written or told by themselves □ **autobiographer** *noun* the writer of an autobiography □ **autobiographical** *adj*

**autocrat** *noun* a ruler who has complete power □ **autocracy** *noun* government by an autocrat □ **autocratic** *adj* expecting complete obedience

**autograph** *noun* **1** someone's own signature **2** someone's own handwriting □ *verb* to write your own name on: *autograph the book*

**automate** *verb* to make automatic by introducing machines *etc* □ **automation** *noun* the use of machines for controlling other machines in factories *etc*

**automatic** *adj* **1** of a machine *etc* self-working **2** of an action: unconscious, without thinking □ *noun* **1** something automatic (eg an automatic washing-machine) **2** a kind of self-loading gun □ **automatically** *adv* □ **automatic pilot 1** a device which can be set to control an aircraft on a course **2** the doing of anything unthinkingly or abstractedly

**automaton** *noun* (*pl* **automata**) **1** a mechanical toy or machine made to look and move like a human **2** someone who acts mindlessly, like a machine

**automobile** *noun, US* a car

**autonomy** *noun* the power or right of a country to govern itself □ **autonomous** *adj*

**autopsy** *noun* (*pl* **autopsies**) an examination of a body after death

**auto-reverse** *noun* a feature on a cassette player *etc* allowing it to play the second side of a tape without being changed manually

**autostereogram** *noun* a computer-generated picture which combines two separate images of the same subject, creating a 3-D effect when viewed

**autoteller** *noun* an automatic teller machine

**autumn** *noun* the season of the year following summer, when leaves change colour and fruits are ripe □ **autumnal** *adj* **1** relating to autumn **2** like those of autumn: *autumnal colours*

**auxiliary** *adj* supplementary, additional □ *noun* (*pl* **auxiliaries**) a helper, an assistant

**avail** *verb*: **avail yourself of** to make use of: *avail yourself of an opportunity* □ *noun*: **to no avail** without any effect, of no use

**available** *adj* able or ready to be made use of □ **availability** *noun*

**avalanche** *noun* **1** a mass of snow and ice sliding down from a mountain **2** a great amount: *an avalanche of work*

**avant-garde** *adj* ahead of fashion, very modern: *an avant-garde writer*

**avarice** *noun* greed, *esp* for riches □ **avaricious** *adj* greedy

**avenge** *verb* to take revenge for (a wrong): *avenge his sister's death/determined to avenge herself*

avenge ↔ avenges, aveng*ing*, aveng*ed*

**avenue** *noun* **1** a tree-lined street or approach to a house **2** a means, a way: *avenue of escape*

**average** *noun* the result obtained by adding several amounts and dividing the total by this number, *eg* the average of 3, 7, 9, 13 is 8 (32 ÷ 4) □ *adj* **1** ordinary, usual; of medium size *etc* **2** obtained by working out an average: *the average cost will be*

10 *each* □ *verb* **1** to form an average **2** to find the average of

**averse** *adj* not fond of, opposed (to)

**aversion** *noun* **1** extreme dislike or distaste: *an aversion to sprouts* **2** something that is hated

**avert** *verb*, *formal* **1** to turn away or aside: *avert your eyes* **2** to prevent from happening: *avert the danger*

**aviary** *noun* (*pl* **aviaries**) a place for keeping birds

**aviation** *noun* the practice of flying or piloting aircraft

**aviator** *noun* an aircraft pilot

**avid** *adj* eager, greedy: *an avid reader* □ **avidity** *noun*

**avocado** *noun* **1** a pear-shaped fruit with a rough peel and rich, creamy flesh **2** a light, yellowish-green colour

**avoid** *verb* to escape, keep clear of □ **avoidable** *adj* □ **avoidance** *noun*

**avoirdupois** (*say* av-wah-dyoo-pwah) *noun* the system of measuring weights in pounds and ounces (*compare with*: **metric**)

**avow** *verb*, *formal* to declare openly □ **avowal** *noun* □ **avowed** *adj* openly stated and determinedly sought after

**await** *verb* to wait for

**awake** *verb* **1** to rouse from sleep **2** to stop sleeping □ *adj* not asleep

**awaken** *verb* **1** to awake **2** to arouse (interest *etc*) □ **awakening** *noun* the act or process of waking up or coming into existence

**award** *verb* **1** to give, grant (a prize *etc*) **2** to grant legally □ *noun* something that is awarded, a prize *etc*

**aware** *adj* **1** having knowledge (of), conscious (of): *aware of the dangers* **2** alert

**away** *adv* **1** to a distance from the speaker or person spoken to: *throw that ball away* **2** not here; not at home or work: *she is away all this* *week* **3** in the opposite direction: *he turned away and left* **4** into nothing: *the sound died away* **5** constantly; diligently: *working away* □ **do away with** to abolish, get rid of □ **get away with** to do (something) without being punished □ **make away with** to steal and escape with □ **right away** immediately

**awe** *noun* wonder or admiration mixed with fear □ *verb* to affect with awe: *awed by the occasion* □ **awestruck** *adj* full of awe

**awesome** *adj* **1** causing fear **2** *informal* remarkable, admirable

**awful** *adj* **1** *informal* bad: *an awful headache* **2** *informal* very great: *an awful lot* **3** terrible: *I feel awful about what happened* □ **awfully** *adv, informal* very, extremely: *awfully good of you*

**awkward** *adj* **1** clumsy, not graceful **2** difficult to deal with: *awkward customer*

**awl** *noun* a pointed tool for boring small holes

**awning** *noun* a covering of canvas *etc* providing shelter

**awry** (*say* a-**rai**) *adj & adv* **1** not according to plan, wrong **2** crooked

**axe** *noun* (*pl* **axes**) a tool for chopping □ *verb* **1** to cancel (a plan *etc*) **2** to reduce greatly (costs, services *etc*) □ **have an axe to grind** to have a strong point of view or resentful feelings which you tend to express at any opportunity

**axiom** *noun* a truth, an accepted principle

**axis** *noun* (*pl* **axes**) **1** the line, real or imaginary, on which a thing turns **2** the axis of the earth, from North to South Pole, around which the earth turns **3** a fixed line taken as a reference, as in a graph

**axle** *noun* the rod on which a wheel turns

**ayatollah** *noun* a religious leader of the Shiah sect of Islam

**azalea** *noun* a flowering plant related to the rhododendron

**AZT** *abbrev* azidothymidine, a drug used in the treatment of AIDS

**azure** *adj* sky-coloured, clear blue

---

## Bb

**BA** *abbrev* **1** British Airways **2** Bachelor of Arts

**babble** *verb* to talk indistinctly or foolishly □ *noun* indistinct or foolish talk

**babe** *noun* **1** a baby **2** *informal* a girl or young woman

**baboon** *noun* a large monkey with a dog-like snout

**baby** *noun* (*pl* **babies**) a very young child, an infant □ *verb* to treat like a baby □ **babyhood** *noun* the time when someone is a baby □ **babysitter** *noun* someone who stays in the house with a child while its parents are out

**baby** *verb* -- babies, babying, babied

**bachelor** *noun* an unmarried man □ **Bachelor of Arts, Bachelor of Science** *etc* someone who has passed examinations at a certain level in subjects at a university

**bacillus** (*say* ba-**sil**-*us*) *noun* (*pl* **bacilli** - *say* ba-**sil**-ai) a rod-shaped germ

**back** *noun* **1** the part of the human body from the neck to the base of the spine **2** the upper part of an animal's body **3** the part of anything situated behind: *sitting at the back of the bus* **4** football *etc* a player positioned behind the forwards □ *adj* of or at the back

□ *adv* **1** to or in the place from which someone or something came: *back at the house* / *walked back home* **2** to or in a former time or condition: *thinking back to their youth* □ *verb* **1** to move backwards **2** to bet on (a horse *etc*) **3** (often **back up**) to help or support □ **background** *noun* **1** the space behind the principal figures of a picture **2** details that explain something **3** someone's family and upbringing □ **backhand** *noun, tennis* a stroke played with the back of the hand facing the ball □ **backhanded compliment** a compliment with a double, unflattering meaning □ **backstroke** *noun* a stroke used in swimming on the back □ **back down** to change your opinion *etc* □ **back out 1** to move out backwards **2** to excuse yourself from keeping to an agreement □ **put your back into** to work hard at □ **put someone's back up** to irritate someone □ **with your back to the wall** in desperate difficulties

**backbone** *noun* **1** the spine **2** the main support of something **3** firmness, resolve

**backfire** *verb* **1** of a vehicle: to make an explosive noise in the exhaust pipe **2** of a plan: to go wrong

**backgammon** *noun* a game similar to draughts, played with dice

**backing** *noun* **1** support **2** material used on the back of a picture *etc* **3** a musical accompaniment on a recording

**backlash** *noun* a violent reaction against something

**backward** *adj* **1** to or towards the back **2** slow in learning or development

**backwards** *adv* **1** towards the back: *walked backwards out of the room* **2** in a reverse direction; back to front: *written backwards* **3** towards the past

**backwash** *noun* a backward current,

such as that caused by an outgoing wave

**backwater** *noun* **1** a river pool separate from the main stream **2** a place not affected by what is happening in the outside world

**bacon** *noun* pig's flesh salted and dried, used as food

**bacteria** (*say* bak-tee-ri-a) *noun pl* germs found in air, water, living and dead bodies, and *esp* decaying matter □ **bacterial** *adj*

**bad** *adj* **1** not good; wicked **2** not of a good standard: *bad at maths* **3** (often **bad for**) harmful **4** of food: rotten, decaying **5** severe, serious: *a bad dose of flu* **6** unwell □ **badly** *adv* **1** not well **2** seriously **3** very much

■ (meaning 1) unpleasant, evil, naughty, disobedient; (meaning 2) poor, inferior, deficient, useless; (meaning 3) detrimental, adverse; (meaning 4) putrid, rancid

**badge** *noun* a mark or sign or brooch-like ornament giving some information about the wearer

**badger** *noun* a burrowing animal of the weasel family which comes out at night □ *verb* to pester or annoy

**badminton** *noun* a game resembling tennis, played with shuttlecocks

Although based on a 16th-century game, this was first played in its modern form in *Badminton* House in Avon.

**baffle** *verb* **1** to be too difficult for; puzzle, confound **2** to prevent from being carried out; hinder □ **baffling** *adj* (meaning 1)

**bag** *noun* **1** a holder or container, often of a soft material **2** a quantity of fish or game caught □ *verb* **1** to put in a bag **2** to secure possession of, claim: *bag a seat* **3** to kill (game) in a hunt □ **bag lady** a homeless woman who carries her belongings with her in her shopping bags

**bag** *verb* ⇨ bags, bagging, bagged

**bagatelle** noun a board game, in which balls are struck into numbered holes

**baggage** noun luggage

**baggy** adj of clothes: large and loose □ noun (**baggies**) informal wide, knee-length shorts

**bagpipes** noun pl a wind instrument made up of a bag and several pipes

**bail**[1] noun money given to bail out a prisoner □ **bail out** verb to obtain temporary release of (an untried prisoner) by giving money which will be forfeited if they do not return for trial

  🔺 Do not confuse with: **bale**

**bail**[2] verb: **bail out** to bale out

**bail**[3] noun, cricket one of the crosspieces on the top of the wickets

  🔺 Do not confuse with: **bale**

**bailiff** noun 1 an officer who works for a sheriff 2 a landowner's agent

**bain-marie** (say ban-ma-ree) noun a double-boiler for cooking

Originally an alchemist's pot, named after the Biblical Mary, sister of Moses

**bairn** noun, Scottish a child

**bait** noun 1 food put on a hook to make fish bite, or in a trap to attract animals 2 something tempting or alluring □ verb 1 to put bait on a hook etc 2 to worry, annoy

**baize** (say beiz) noun a coarse woollen cloth

**bake** verb 1 to cook in an oven 2 to dry or harden in the sun or in an oven □ **baker** noun someone who bakes or sells bread etc □ **bakery** or **bakehouse** noun a place used for baking in

**balaklava** noun a knitted covering for the head and neck

**balance** noun 1 steadiness 2 the money needed to make the two sides of an account equal 3 a weighing machine □ verb 1 to be the same in weight 2 to make both sides of an account the same 3 to make or keep

steady: balanced it on her head

**balcony** noun (pl **balconies**) 1 a platform built out from the wall of a building 2 an upper floor or gallery in a theatre etc

**bald** adj 1 without hair 2 plain, frank: a bald statement

**bale**[1] noun a large tight bundle of cotton, hay etc

  🔺 Do not confuse with: **bail**

**bale**[2] verb: **bale out** 1 to escape by parachute from an aircraft in an emergency 2 to scoop water out of a boat (also **bail out**)

**baleful** adj harmful, malevolent

**balk** verb 1 to hinder, baffle 2 (with **at**) to refuse to do something

**ball**[1] noun 1 anything round 2 the round or roundish object used in playing many games □ **ball-bearings** noun pl small steel balls that sit loosely in grooves and ease the revolving of one machinery part over another □ **on the ball** informal in touch with a situation, alert □ **play ball** informal to play along, cooperate

**ball**[2] noun a formal party at which dancing takes place □ **have a ball** informal to have a great time, enjoy yourself

**ballad** noun 1 a narrative poem with a simple rhyme scheme, usually in verses of four lines 2 a simple song

**ballast** noun sand, gravel etc put into a ship to steady it

**ballerina** noun a female ballet dancer

**ballet** noun a form of stylized dancing which tells a story by mime

**ballistic missile** a self-guided missile which falls on to its target

**balloon** noun a bag filled with gas to make it float in the air, esp one made of thin rubber used as a toy etc □ verb to puff or swell out

**ballot** noun a way of voting in secret by marking a paper and putting it into a special box □ verb to collect votes from by ballot

**ballpark** noun, US a sports field for ball-games □ adj rough, estimated

**ballpoint** noun a pen with a tiny ball as the writing point

**ballroom** noun a large room used for public dances etc

**balm** noun 1 something soothing 2 a sweet-smelling healing ointment

**balmy** adj 1 mild, gentle; soothing: balmy air 2 sweet-smelling

**balsam** noun an oily sweet-smelling substance obtained from certain trees

**balsawood** noun a lightweight wood obtained from a tropical American tree

**balustrade** noun a row of pillars on a balcony etc, joined by a rail

**bamboo** noun the woody, jointed stem of a very tall Indian grass

**bamboozle** verb to trick, puzzle □ **bamboozling** adj

**ban** noun an order forbidding something □ verb to forbid officially (the publication of a book etc)

**ban** verb ▷ bans, banning, banned

**banal** adj lacking originality or wit, commonplace □ **banality** noun

**banana** noun the long yellow fruit of a type of tropical tree

**band** noun 1 a group of people 2 a group of musicians playing together 3 a strip of some material to put round something 4 a stripe (of colour etc) 5 a group of wavelengths for radio broadcasts □ verb to join together

**bandage** noun a strip of cloth etc or special dressing for a wound

**bandit** noun an outlaw, robber, esp a member of a gang of robbers

**bandy** adj of legs: bent outward at the knee □ **bandy words** to argue

**bane** noun a cause of ruin or trouble

**bang** noun 1 a sudden, loud noise 2 a heavy blow □ verb 1 to close with a

bang, slam 2 to hit, strike

**bangle** noun a large ring worn on an arm or leg

**banish** verb 1 to order to leave (a country) 2 to drive away (doubts, fear etc) □ **banishment** noun

**banister** noun the posts and handrail of a staircase

**banjo** noun (pl **banjoes** or **banjos**) a stringed musical instrument like a guitar, with a long neck and a round body

**bank** noun 1 a mound or ridge of earth etc 2 the edge of a river 3 a place where money is lent, put for safety etc 4 a place where blood etc is stored till needed 5 a public bin for collecting items for recycling: bottle bank □ **banker** noun someone who manages a bank □ **bank holiday** a day on which all banks and many shops etc are closed □ **banknote** noun a piece of paper money issued by a bank □ **bank on** to depend on, count on

**bankrupt** noun someone who has no money to pay their debts □ adj 1 unable to pay debts 2 utterly lacking in: bankrupt of ideas □ **bankruptcy** noun (pl **bankruptcies**)

**banner** noun 1 a large flag carried in processions etc, often hung between two poles 2 any flag

**banns** noun pl a public announcement of a forthcoming marriage

**banquet** noun a ceremonial dinner

**bantam** noun a small kind of hen

**banter** verb to tease in fun □ noun light teasing

**baptize** verb 1 to dip in, or sprinkle with, water as a sign of admission into the Christian church 2 to christen, give a name to □ **baptism** noun □ **baptismal** adj

**bar** noun 1 a rod of solid material 2 a broad line or band 3 a piece, a cake: bar of soap 4 a hindrance, a block

**5** a bank of sand *etc* at the mouth of a river **6** a room, or counter, where drinks are served in a public house, hotel *etc* **7** a public house **8** the rail at which prisoners stand for trial **9** the lawyers who plead in a court **10** a time division in music □ *prep* except: *all the runners, bar Ian, finished the race* □ *verb* **1** to fasten with a bar **2** to exclude, shut out

bar *verb* ⬦ bars, barring, barred

**barb** *noun* the backward-pointing spike on an arrow, fish-hook *etc* □ **barbed** *adj* having a barb or barbs □ **barbed wire** wire with regular clusters of sharp points, used for fencing *etc*

**barbarian** *noun* an uncivilized person □ *adj* uncivilized □ **barbaric** *adj* **1** uncivilized **2** extremely cruel □ **barbarity** *noun*

**barbecue** *noun* **1** a frame on which to grill food over an open fire **2** an outdoor party providing food from a barbecue □ *verb* to cook (food) on a barbecue

From a Haitian creole term for a wooden grid or frame

**barber** *noun* a men's hairdresser

**barbiturate** *noun* a type of sedative drug

**bard** *noun, formal* a poet

**bare** *adj* **1** uncovered, naked **2** plain, simple **3** empty □ *verb* to uncover, expose □ **barefaced** *adj* impudent, unashamed: *barefaced lie* □ **barely** *adv* hardly, scarcely

**bargain** *noun* **1** an agreement, *esp* about buying or selling **2** something bought cheaply □ *verb* to argue about a price *etc* □ **bargain for** to expect □ **into the bargain** in addition, besides

**barge** *noun* a flat-bottomed boat used on rivers and canals □ *verb* **1** to rush clumsily **2** to push or bump (into) **3** to push your way (into) rudely

**baritone** *noun* **1** a male singing voice

between tenor and bass **2** a singer with this voice

**bark**[1] *noun* the noise made by a dog *etc* □ *verb* **1** to give a bark **2** to speak sharply or angrily

**bark**[2] *noun* the rough outer covering of a tree's trunk and branches

**barley** *noun* a grain used for food and for making malt liquors and spirits □ **barley sugar** sugar candied by melting and cooling to make a sweet

**bar mitzvah** a Jewish ceremony to mark a boy's coming of age

**barn** *noun* a building in which grain, hay *etc* is stored

**barnacle** *noun* a type of shellfish which sticks to rocks, ships' hulls *etc*

**barometer** *noun* an instrument which measures the weight or pressure of the air and shows changes in the weather

**baron** *noun* **1** a nobleman, the lowest in the British peerage **2** a powerful person, *esp* in a business □ **baronial** *adj* (meaning 1)

**baroness** *noun* (*pl* **baronesses**) a baron's wife or a female baron

**baronet** *noun* the lowest title that can be passed on to an heir □ **baronetcy** *noun*

**baroque** *adj* extravagantly ornamented

**barracks** *noun pl* a place for housing soldiers

**barracuda** *noun* a voracious West Indian fish

**barrage** *noun* **1** heavy gunfire against an enemy **2** an overwhelming number **3** a bar across a river to make the water deeper

**barrel** *noun* **1** a wooden cask with curved sides **2** the metal tube of a gun through which the shot is fired

**barren** *adj* not able to reproduce, infertile

**barricade** *noun* a barrier put up to block a street *etc* □ *verb* **1** to block or strengthen against attack **2** to shut behind a barrier

**barrier** noun **1** a strong fence etc used for enclosing or keeping out **2** an obstacle

**barrister** noun a lawyer who pleads cases in English or in Irish courts

**barrow** noun **1** a small hand-cart **2** a mound built over an ancient grave

**barter** verb to give one thing in exchange for another □ noun trading by exchanging goods without using money

**basalt** noun a hard, dark-coloured rock thrown up as lava from volcanoes

**base** noun **1** something on which a thing stands or rests **2** the lowest part **3** a place from where an expedition, military action etc is carried out □ verb to use as a foundation □ adj worthless, cowardly □ **baseless** adj without foundation; untrue □ **basement** noun a storey below ground level in a building

**baseball** noun a North American ball-game in which players make a circuit of four bases on a field

**base jumping** noun the sport of parachuting from low-level objects and structures eg buildings

**bash** verb to hit hard □ noun a heavy blow □ **have a bash** informal to make an attempt

**basic** adj **1** of or forming a base **2** necessary, fundamental □ **basically** adv fundamentally, essentially

**basil** noun an aromatic herb used in cooking

**basilica** noun a church with a large central hall

**basilisk** noun **1** a mythological reptile with a deadly look and poisonous breath **2** a type of American lizard

**basin** noun **1** a wide, open dish **2** a

washhand basin **3** a large hollow holding water **4** the land drained by a river and its tributaries

**basis** noun (pl **bases**) **1** something on which a thing rests, a foundation **2** the main ingredient

**bask** verb **1** to lie in warmth **2** to enjoy, feel great pleasure (in): basking in glory

**basket** noun **1** a container made of strips of wood, rushes etc woven together **2** a related group or collection: basket of currencies

**basketball** noun a team game in which goals are scored by throwing a ball into a raised net

**bass**[1] (say beis) noun (pl **basses**) **1** the low part in music **2** a deep male singing voice **3** a singer with this voice □ adj low or deep in tone □ **bass clef** noun a musical sign (𝄢), placed on a stave to fix the pitch of the notes

**bass**[2] (say bas) noun (pl **bass** or **basses**) a kind of fish of the perch family

**bassoon** noun a musical wind instrument with low notes

**bastard** noun **1** a child born to parents who are not married to each other **2** informal a general term of abuse

**baste**[1] verb to spoon fat over (meat) while roasting to keep (it) from drying out

**baste**[2] verb to sew loosely together with big stitches; tack

**bastion** noun **1** a defensive position, a preserve: the last bastions of male power **2** a tower on a castle etc

**bat**[1] noun a shaped piece of wood etc for striking a ball in some games □ verb to use the bat in cricket etc

**bat** verb ⟳ bats, batting, batted

**bat**[2] noun a mouse-like flying animal

**bat**[3] verb to flutter (eyelids etc)

**bat** verb ⟳ bats, batting, batted

**batch** noun (pl **batches**) a quantity of

things made *etc* at one time

**bated** *adj*: with bated breath anxiously

**bath** *noun* **1** a vessel which holds water in which to wash the body **2** the water in which to wash **3** a washing of the body in water **4** (**baths**) a public building with an artificial pool for swimming □ *verb* to wash (oneself or another person) in a bath □ **bathchair** *noun* an old-fashioned wheelchair

**bathe** *verb* **1** to swim in water **2** to wash gently: *bathe your eyes* **3** to take a bath □ *noun* □ **bathed in** covered with

**baton** *noun* **1** a small wooden stick **2** a light stick used by a conductor of music

**batsman** or **batswoman** *noun* a person who bats in cricket *etc*

**battalion** *noun* a part of a regiment of foot soldiers

**batten** *noun* **1** a piece of sawn timber **2** a strip of wood used to fasten down a ship's hatches during a storm □ *verb*: **batten down** to fasten down firmly

**batter** *verb* to hit repeatedly □ *noun* a beaten mixture of flour, milk and eggs, for cooking □ **battered** *adj* **1** beaten, ill-treated **2** worn out by use **3** dipped in batter and fried □ **battering-ram** *noun, historical* a heavy beam used as a weapon for breaking through walls *etc*

**battery** *noun* (*pl* **batteries**) **1** a number of large guns **2** a device for storing and transmitting electricity **3** a series of cages *etc* in which hens are kept for egg-laying

**battle** *noun* a fight, *esp* between armies □ *verb* to fight □ **battleaxe** *noun* **1** *historical* a kind of axe used in fighting **2** *informal* a fierce, domineering woman □ **battlefield** *noun* the site of a battle □ **battleship** *noun* a heavily armed and armoured warship

**battlement** *noun* a wall on the top of a building, with openings or notches for firing

**bauble** *noun* a brightly-coloured ornament of little value

**bawl** *verb* to shout or cry out loudly □ *noun* a loud cry

**bay** *noun* **1** a wide inlet of the sea in a coastline **2** a space in a room *etc* set back, a recess **3** a compartment in an aircraft *etc* **4** the laurel tree □ *verb* of dogs: to bark □ **bay window** a window that forms a recess □ **hold at bay** to fight off □ **stand at bay** to stand and face attackers *etc*

**bayonet** *noun* a steel stabbing blade that can be fixed to the muzzle of a rifle □ *verb* to stab with this

**bazaar** *noun* **1** a sale of goods for charity *etc* **2** an Eastern market-place **3** a shop

**BBC** *abbrev* British Broadcasting Corporation

**BC** *abbrev* before Christ: *55*BC

■ AD

**be** *verb* **1** to live, exist **2** to have a position, quality *etc*: *he wants to be a dentist*

 ⊕ Present tense: from Anglo-Saxon *beon*, to live or exist; past tense: from Anglo-Saxon *weran*, to be

**be** ⊷ *present form* **am, are, is**, *past form* **was, were**, *past participle* **been** □ **be** is also used to form tenses of other verbs, *eg* I *was* running for the bus/ when *will* you *be* arriving?

**beach** *noun* (*pl* **beaches**) the shore of the sea *etc*, *esp* when sandy or pebbly □ *verb* to drive or haul a boat up on the beach □ **beachcomber** *noun* someone who searches beaches for useful or saleable articles

**beacon** *noun* **1** a flashing light or other warning signal **2** *historical* a fire on a hill used as a signal of danger

**bead** *noun* **1** a small pierced ball of

glass, plastic *etc*, used in needlework or jewellery-making **2** a drop of liquid: *beads of sweat*

**beadle** *noun* an officer of a church or college

**beagle** *noun* a small hound used in hunting hares

**beak** *noun* **1** the hard, horny part of a bird's mouth with which it gathers food **2** a point, a projection

**beaker** *noun* a tall cup or glass, usually without a handle

**beam** *noun* **1** a long straight piece of wood or metal **2** a shaft of light **3** a radio signal **4** the greatest breadth of a ship □ *verb* **1** to shine **2** to smile broadly **3** to divert by radio wave

**bean** *noun* **1** a pod-bearing plant **2** the seed of this used as food

**bear¹** *noun* a heavy animal with shaggy fur and hooked claws

**bear²** *verb* **1** *formal* to carry **2** to endure, put up with **3** to produce (fruit, children *etc*) □ **bearable** *adj* able to be borne or endured □ **bearer** *noun* a carrier or messenger □ **bear in mind** to remember, take into account □ **bear out** to confirm □ **bear with** to be patient with □ **bring to bear** to bring into use

**bear** *verb* ↔ bears, bear*ing*, bore, borne or born □ **born** is used for the past participle when referring to the birth of a child, idea *etc*: *when were you born?*; otherwise the form is borne: *I couldn't have borne it any longer.*

**beard** *noun* the hair that grows on a man's chin and cheeks □ *verb* to face up to, defy

**bearing** *noun* **1** behaviour **2** direction **3** connection **4** part of a machine supporting a moving part

**beast** *noun* **1** a four-footed animal **2** a brutal person □ **beastly** *adj* **1** behaving like an animal **2** horrible **3** unpleasant

**beat** *verb* **1** to hit repeatedly **2** to overcome, defeat **3** of a pulse: to move or throb in the normal way **4** to mark (time) in music **5** to stir (a mixture *etc*) with quick movements **6** to strike bushes *etc* to rouse birds □ *noun* **1** a stroke **2** the regular round of a police officer *etc* □ **beaten** *adj* **1** of metal: shaped **2** of earth: worn smooth by treading **3** defeated □ **beat up** to injure by repeated hitting, kicking *etc*

**beat** *verb* ↔ beats, beat*ing*, beat, beat*en*

**beatific** (*say* bei-*a*-tif-ik) *adj* of, or showing, great happiness

**beautiful** *adj* very attractive or pleasing in appearance, sound *etc* □ **beautifully** *adv* **1** in a way which is pleasing to the eye, *etc* **2** with much skill and sensitivity

**beautify** *verb* to make beautiful

**beautify** ↔ beauti*fies*, beauti*fying*, beauti*fied*

**beauty** *noun* (*pl* beauties) **1** very attractive or pleasing appearance, sound *etc* **2** a very attractive person, *esp* a woman

**beaver** *noun* **1** a gnawing animal that can dam streams **2** a member of the most junior branch of the Scout Association

**becalmed** *adj* of a sailing ship: unable to move for lack of wind

**because** *conj* for the reason that □ *adv* **because of** on account of

**beck** *noun*: **at someone's beck and call** obeying all their orders or requests

**beckon** *verb* to make a sign (with the finger) to summon someone

**become** *verb* **1** to come to be **2** to suit: *that becomes you* □ **becoming** *adj* **1** suiting well **2** of behaviour: appropriate, suitable

**bed** *noun* **1** a place on which to rest or sleep **2** a plot for flowers *etc* in a garden **3** the bottom of a river *etc* □ *verb* **1** to plant in soil *etc* **2** to provide a bed for **3** *informal* to have sexual intercourse with □ **bedclothes** noun pl bedcovers □ **bedding** noun **1** mattress, bedcovers etc **2** straw etc for cattle to lie on □ **bedridden** adj kept in bed by weakness, illness etc □ **bedrock** noun the solid rock under the soil □ **bedroom** noun a room for sleeping □ **bedspread** noun a top cover for a bed □ **bedstead** noun a frame supporting a bed

**bed** verb □ beds, bedding, bedded

**bedlam** noun a place full of uproar and confusion

**bedraggled** adj wet and untidy

**bee** noun **1** a winged insect that makes honey in wax cells **2** a group of people who gather together for some activity □ **beehive** noun a dome or box in which bees are kept □ **make a beeline for** to go directly towards

**beech** noun (pl **beeches**) a forest tree with grey smooth bark

**beef** noun the flesh of an ox or cow, used as food □ **beefy** adj stout, muscular

**beefeater** noun **1** a guardian of the Tower of London **2** a member of the Queen's or King's Guard

**Beelzebub** (say bi-el-zib-ub) noun, old the Devil, Satan

**been** see **be**

**beer** noun an alcoholic drink flavoured with hops

**beet** noun a plant with a carrot-like root, one type (**sugar beet**) used as a source of sugar, the other (**beetroot**) used as a vegetable

**beetle** noun an insect with four wings, the front pair forming hard covers for the back pair

**beetling** adj **1** of cliffs etc: overhanging **2** of eyebrows: heavy, frowning

**befall** verb, formal to happen to, strike

**befall** □ befalls, befalling, befell

**before** prep **1** in front of: before the entrance to the tunnel **2** earlier than: before three o'clock **3** rather than, in preference to: I'd die before telling him □ adv **1** in front **2** earlier □ conj earlier than the time that: before he was born □ **beforehand** adv previously, before the time when something else is done

**befriend** verb to act as a friend to, help

**beg** verb **1** to ask for money etc from others **2** to ask earnestly □ **beg the question** to take as being proved the very point that needs to be proved

**beg** □ begs, begging, begged

**began** past form of **begin**

**beget** verb, formal **1** to be the father of **2** to cause

**beget** □ begets, begetting, begat, begotten

**beggar** noun **1** someone who begs for money **2** a very poor person □ verb to make poor □ **beggarly** adj poor; worthless □ **beggar belief** to be beyond belief, be incredible

**begin** verb to make a start on □ **beginning** noun

**begin** □ begins, beginning, began, begun

**begone** exclamation, formal be off, go away

**begrudge** verb to grudge, envy

**beguile** verb **1** to cheat **2** to pass (time) pleasantly; amuse, entertain

**begun** past participle of **begin**

**behalf** noun: **on behalf of 1** as the representative of: on behalf of my client **2** in aid of: collecting on behalf of the homeless

**behave** verb **1** to act (in a certain way): he always behaves badly at parties **2** to conduct yourself well: can't you behave for just a minute? □ **behaviour** noun

**behead** verb to cut off the head of

**behest** noun, formal command

**behind** prep **1** at or towards the back

of: *behind the door* **2** after **3** in support of, encouraging: *behind him in his struggle* □ *adv* **1** at the back **2** not up to date

**behold** *verb, formal* to look (at), see

**beholden to** *adj* grateful to because of a good turn

**behove** *verb*: **it behoves you to** you ought to

**being** *noun* **1** existence **2** a living person or thing

**belated** *adj* arriving late

**belch** *verb* **1** bring up wind from the stomach through the mouth **2** of a fire *etc*: send up (smoke *etc*) violently

**beleaguer** (*say* be-leeg-er) *verb* to besiege

**belfry** *noun* (*pl* **belfries**) the part of a steeple or tower in which the bells are hung

**belief** *noun* **1** what someone thinks to be true **2** faith

**believe** *verb* **1** to think of as true or as existing **2** to trust (in) **3** to think or suppose □ **make believe** to pretend

**Belisha beacon** *Brit* a pole with an orange globe on top, marking a pedestrian crossing

**belittle** *verb* to make to seem small or unimportant

**bell** *noun* a hollow metal object which gives a ringing sound when struck by the tongue or clapper inside

**bellicose** *adj* inclined to fight, quarrelsome □ **bellicosity** *noun*

**belligerent** *adj* quarrelsome, aggressive □ **belligerence** or **belligerency** *noun*

**bellow** *verb* to roar like a bull □ *noun* a deep roar

**bellows** *noun pl* an instrument for making a blast of air, *eg* to increase a fire

**belly** *noun* (*pl* **bellies**) **1** the abdomen **2** the underpart of an

animal's body **3** the bulging part of anything □ *verb* to swell or bulge out □ **belly-button** *noun, informal* the navel □ **belly-dance** *noun* a sensuous dance performed by women with circling movements of the stomach and hips □ **belly-flop** *noun* an inexpert dive landing face down on the water

**belly** *verb* ⋄ **bellies**, **bellying**, **bellied**

**belong** *verb* **1** to be someone's property **2** to be a member of (a club *etc*) **3** to be born in or live in **4** of an object: to have its place in: *plates belong in the kitchen* □ **belongings** *noun pl* what someone possesses

**beloved** *adj* much loved, very dear □ *noun* someone much loved

**below** *prep* lower in position than: *her skirt reached below her knees* □ *adv* in a lower position: *looking down at the street below*

◼ **above**

**belt** *noun* **1** a strip of leather, cloth *etc* worn around the waist **2** a continuous band on a machine for conveying objects in a factory *etc* **3** a broad strip, *eg* of land □ *verb* **1** to put a belt round **2** to beat with a belt **3** *informal* to beat, hit

**bemoan** *verb* to weep about, mourn

**bench** *noun* (*pl* **benches**) **1** a long seat **2** a work-table **3 the bench** the judges of a court

**bend** *verb* **1** to curve **2** to stoop □ *noun* **1** a curve **2** a turn in a road

**bend** *verb* ⋄ **bends**, **bending**, **bent**

**beneath** *prep* **1** under, in a lower position than **2** covered by: *wearing a black dress beneath her coat* **3** considered too low a task *etc* for: *sweeping floors was beneath him* □ *adv* below

**benediction** *noun* a blessing

**benefactor** *noun* someone who does good to others

**beneficial** *adj* bringing gain or

advantage (to) □ **beneficiary** noun (pl **beneficiaries**) someone who receives a gift, an advantage etc

**benefit** noun **1** something good to receive or have done to you **2** money received from social security or insurance schemes: unemployment benefit □ verb **1** to do good to **2** to gain advantage

**benefit** verb ∾ **benefits, benefiting, benefited**

**benevolence** noun **1** tendency to do good; kindliness **2** a kind act □ **benevolent** adj kindly

**benign** (say bi-nain) adj **1** gentle, kindly **2** of disease: not causing death (contrasted with: **malignant**)

**bent** noun a natural liking or aptitude (for something) □ adj **1** curved, crooked **2** informal dishonest □ **be bent on** to be determined to □ past form of **bend**

**bequeath** verb to leave by will

**bequest** noun money, property etc left in a will

**bereaved** adj suffering from the recent death of a relative or friend □ **bereavement** noun

**bereft** adj lacking, deprived (of)

**beret** (say be-rei) noun a flat, round hat

**berry** noun (pl **berries**) a small juicy fruit enclosing seeds

**berserk** adv in a frenzy, mad

**berth** noun **1** a room for sleeping in a ship etc **2** the place where a ship is tied up in a dock □ verb to moor (a ship) □ **give a wide berth to** to keep well away from

**beryl** noun a type of precious stone such as an emerald or aquamarine

**beseech** verb to ask earnestly

**beset** verb to attack from all sides; surround

**beset** ∾ **besets, besetting, beset**

**beside** prep **1** by the side of, near **2** compared with **3** away from, wide of: beside the point □ **be beside**

**yourself** to lose self-control □ **beside the point** irrelevant

**besides** prep **1** in addition to **2** other than, except □ adv **1** also, moreover: besides, it was your idea **2** in addition: plenty more besides

**besiege** verb **1** to surround (a town etc) with an army **2** to crowd round; overwhelm

**besiege** ∾ **besieges, besieging, besieged**

**besotted** adj: **besotted with** foolishly fond of

**bespoke** adj of clothes: ordered to be made

**best** adj good in the most excellent way □ adv in the most excellent way □ verb to defeat □ **best man** someone who attends a man who is being married □ **best part** the largest or greatest part □ **bestseller** noun a book etc which sells exceedingly well □ **at best** under the most favourable circumstances □ **do your best** to try as hard as you can □ **make the best of** to do as well as possible with

**bestial** adj like a beast, beastly

**bestow** verb to give

**bet** noun money put down to be lost or kept depending on the outcome of a race etc □ verb to place a bet

**bet** verb ∾ **bets, betting, bet or betted**

**bête noire** (say bet **nwahr**) a particular dislike

**betray** verb **1** to give up (secrets, friends etc) to an enemy **2** to show signs of: his face betrayed no emotion □ **betrayal** noun

**betroth** verb, formal to promise in marriage □ **betrothal** noun □ **betrothed to** engaged to be married to

**better** adj **1** good to a greater degree, of a more excellent kind **2** healthier **3** completely recovered from illness □ adv in a more excellent way □ verb to improve □ **better off** in a better position, wealthier □ **get the better of** to defeat, overcome □ **had better** ought to, must □ **think better of** to change your mind about

**between** *prep* **1** in or through the space dividing two people or things **2** in parts, in shares to: *divide the chocolates between you* **3** from one thing to another: *the road between Edinburgh and Glasgow* **4** comparing one to the other

**bevel** *noun* a slanting edge □ *verb* to give a slanting edge to □ **bevelled** *adj*

bevel *verb* ✧ bevels, bevelling, bevelled

**beverage** *noun* a drink

**bevy¹** *noun* (*pl* **bevies**) **1** a group of women or girls **2** a flock of quails

**bevy²** or **bevvy** *noun* (*pl* **bevies** or **bevvies**) *Brit informal* **1** an alcoholic drink **2** a drinking session

**bewail** *verb* to mourn loudly over

**beware** *verb* to watch out for (something dangerous)

**bewilder** *verb* to puzzle, confuse □ **bewildering** *adj* □ **bewilderment** *noun* confusion

**bewitch** *verb* to put under a spell; charm □ **bewitching** *adj* charming; very beautiful

**beyond** *prep* **1** on the far side of **2** later than: *beyond January* **3** more than: *beyond the call of duty* **4** too far gone for: *beyond repair* **5** too difficult or confusing for: *it's beyond me!* □ *adv* on or to the far side, further away

**bi-** *prefix* **1** having two: *biped/ bicycle* **2** occurring twice in a certain period, or once in every two periods: *bi-monthly*
  ⊚ From Latin *bis* meaning 'twice' or 'two'

**biannual** *adj* happening twice a year
  ⊚ From Latin *bi-* meaning 'two' or 'twice', and *annus* meaning 'year'

✧. Do not confuse with: **biennial**

**bias** *noun* **1** the favouring of one person or point of view over any others **2** a tendency to move in a particular direction **3** a weight on or in an object making it move in a particular direction □ *verb* to give a bias to

bias *verb* ✧ biases, biasing, biassing, biased or biassed

**bib** *noun* **1** a piece of cloth put under a child's chin to protect their clothes from food stains *etc* **2** a part of an apron, overalls *etc* above the waist, covering the chest

**Bible** *noun* the holy book of the Christian Church □ **Biblical** *adj*

**bibliography** *noun* (*pl* **bibliographies**) **1** a list of books (about a subject) **2** the art of classifying books □ **bibliographer** *noun* someone who compiles bibliographies, or who studies book classification

**bibliophile** *noun* a lover of books

**bicentenary** *noun* (*pl* **bicentenaries**) the two-hundredth year after an event *eg* someone's birth

**biceps** *noun sing* the muscle in front of the upper part of the arm

**bicker** *verb* to quarrel over small matters

**bicycle** *noun* a vehicle with two wheels, driven by foot-pedals

**bid** *verb* **1** to offer a price (for) **2** to tell, say **3** to command; invite □ *noun* an offer of a price; a bold attempt: *a bid for freedom*

bid *verb* ✧ bids, bidding, bade or bid, bidden or bid

**bidet** (*say* beed-ei) *noun* a low washbasin for washing the genital area and feet

**bier** (*say* beer) *noun* a carriage or frame for carrying a dead body

**big** *adj* **1** large in size, amount, extent *etc* **2** important **3** boastful

big ✧ bigger, biggest

□ (meaning 1) large, great, sizeable,

considerable, immense, substantial, huge, enormous, massive, colossal, gigantic, mammoth, burly, bulky, extensive, spacious, vast, voluminous

**bigamy** noun the crime or fact of having two wives or two husbands at once □ **bigamist** noun □ **bigamous** adj

**bight** noun a small bay

**bigot** noun someone with narrow-minded, prejudiced beliefs □ **bigoted** adj □ **bigotry** noun

**bike** noun, informal a bicycle

**bikini** noun (pl **bikinis**) a woman's two-piece bathing suit

Named after Bikini Atoll atomic test site, because of its supposedly 'explosive' effect on men

**bilateral** adj **1** having two sides **2** affecting two sides, parties etc: bilateral agreement □ **bilaterally** adv

**bilberry** noun a type of plant with an edible dark-blue berry

**bile** noun a fluid coming from the liver

**bilge** noun **1** the broadest part of a ship's bottom **2** bilgewater **3** informal nonsense □ **bilgewater** noun water which lies in the ship's bottom

**bilingual** adj using or fluent in two languages

**bilious** adj **1** ill with too much bile; nauseated **2** greenish-yellow in colour

**bill** noun **1** a bird's beak **2** an account for money **3** an early version of a law before it has been passed by parliament **4** a printed sheet of information

**billet** noun a lodging, esp for soldiers □ verb to lodge (soldiers) in private houses

**billiards** noun a game played with a cue and balls on a table

**billion** noun **1** a million millions (1 000 000 000 000) **2** US (now often in Britain) a thousand millions (1 000 000 000)

**billow** noun **1** a great wave **2** a mass of something such as smoke rising on or being swept along by the wind □ verb to be filled and swelled with, or moved along by, the wind: a billowing sail □ **billowy** adj giving the impression of billowing: billowy clouds

**billy** noun (pl **billies**) or **billycan** a container for cooking, making tea etc outdoors

**billy-goat** noun a male goat

**bin** noun a container for storing goods or rubbish □ verb **1** to put in a bin **2** to throw away

**bin** verb ⇨ bin**s**, binn**ing**, bin**ned**

**binary** adj made up of two □ **binary system** a mathematical system in which numbers are expressed by two digits only, 1 and 0

**bind** verb **1** to tie with a band **2** to fasten together **3** to make to promise □ **binding** noun **1** anything that binds **2** the cover, stitching etc which holds a book together

**bind** ⇨ bind**s**, bind**ing**, bound

**binge** verb eat and drink too much □ noun a spell of over-eating or drinking too much

**bingo** noun a popular gambling game using numbers

**binoculars** noun pl a small double telescope

**biodegradable** adj able to be broken down into parts by bacteria

**biography** noun (pl **biographies**) a written account of someone's life □ **biographer** noun someone who writes a biography □ **biographical** adj

**biology** noun the study of living things □ **biological** adj **1** relating to the way that living organisms grow and behave **2** relating to biology □ **biological warfare** war using as weapons germs which can cause disease ▫ **biologist** noun

**biped** noun an animal with two feet, eg a bird

**birch** noun (pl **birches**) **1** a type of hardwood tree **2** a bundle of birch twigs, used for beating ▫ verb to beat with a birch

**bird** noun a feathered, egg-laying creature ▫ **birdwatching** noun the study of birds in their natural surroundings ▫ **bird of prey** a bird (eg a hawk) which kills and eats small animals or birds ▫ **bird's-eye view** a wide view, as would be seen from above ▫ **get the bird** slang to be booed or hissed at; be dismissed

**birl** verb, Scottish to spin round, whirl

**Biro** noun, trademark a type of ballpoint pen

**birth** noun the very beginning of someone's life ▫ **birthday** noun **1** the day on which someone is born **2** the date of this day each year ▫ **birthmark** noun a mark on the body from birth ▫ **birthright** noun the right which someone may claim because of their parentage

**biscuit** noun dough baked hard in a small cake

**bisect** verb to cut in two equal parts

**bishop** noun a high-ranking member of the clergy (next below an archbishop) in the Roman Catholic Church and the Church of England ▫ **bishopric** noun the district ruled by a bishop

**bison** noun (pl **bison**) a large wild ox with shaggy hair and a fat hump

**bistro** (say **beest**-roh) noun (pl **bistros**) a small bar or restaurant

**bit¹** noun **1** a small piece **2** a small tool for boring **3** the part of the bridle which the horse holds in its mouth **4** computing the smallest unit of information ▫ **do your bit** to do your required share ▫ **bit by bit** gradually ▫ **to bits** apart, in pieces

**bit²** past form of **bite**

**bitch** noun (pl **bitches**) **1** a female dog, wolf etc **2** slang an unpleasant woman ▫ **bitchy** adj catty, malicious

**bite** verb to grip, cut or tear with the teeth ▫ noun **1** a grip with the teeth **2** the part bitten off **3** a nibble at a fishing bait **4** a wound caused by an animal's or insect's bite

**bite** verb ⬦ bite**s**, bit**ing**, bit, bitt**en**

**bitmap** noun, computing a method of screen display where each small element (**pixel**) is assigned on one or more bits of memory ▫ verb to display something using this method ▫ **bitmapped** adj ▫ **bitmapping** noun

**bitmap** verb ⬦ bitmap**s**, bitmap**ping**, bitmap**ped**

**bitten** past participle of **bite**

**bitter** adj **1** unpleasant to the taste; sour **2** harsh: bitter cold **3** resentful, angry through disappointment ▫ **bitterness** noun **1** the quality of being bitter **2** bitter feelings

**bittern** noun a bird resembling a heron

**bitty** (from **bit¹**) adj piecemeal, scrappy

**bivouac** noun an overnight camp outdoors without a tent ▫ verb to sleep outdoors without a tent

**bivouac** verb ⬦ bivouac**s**, bivouac**king**, bivouac**ked**

**bi-weekly** adj happening twice a week or once every two weeks

**bizarre** adj odd, strange

**blab** verb **1** to talk a lot **2** to let out a secret

**blab** ⬦ blab**s**, blab**bing**, blab**bed**

**black** adj dark and colourless ▫ noun black colour ▫ **black-and-blue** adj badly bruised ▫ **black belt** an award for skill in judo or karate ▫ **blackberry** noun (pl **blackberries**) a blackish-purple soft fruit growing on a prickly stem ▫ **blackboard** noun a dark-coloured board for writing on in chalk □ **blacken** *verb* **1** to make black or dark **2** to dishonour, defame: *blackening his name* □ **black eye** a bruised area round the eye as the result of a blow □ **black ice** a thin transparent layer of ice on a road *etc* □ **blacklist** *noun* a list of people to be refused credit, jobs *etc* □ *verb* to put on a blacklist □ **black magic** magic performed for an evil purpose; witchcraft □ **black market** illegal or dishonest buying and selling □ **blackout** *noun* **1** total darkness caused by putting out or covering all lights **2** a temporary loss of consciousness □ **black-pudding** *noun* blood sausage □ **black sheep** someone who is considered a failure or outsider in a group □ **blacksmith** *noun* someone who makes or repairs iron goods, *esp* horseshoes □ **black tie** formal evening dress □ **black widow** a very poisonous American spider, the female of which often eats her mate □ **black out** to become unconscious

**blackball** *verb* to ostracize, exclude from (a club *etc*)

**blackbird** *noun* a type of black, thrush-like bird

**blackguard** *noun, old* a wicked person

**blackleg** *noun* someone who works when other workers are on strike

**blackmail** *noun* the crime of threatening to reveal secrets unless money is paid □ *verb* to threaten by blackmail □ **blackmailer** *noun*

**bladder** *noun* **1** the organ in which urine collects in the body **2** a bag with thin, membrane-like walls

**bladderwrack** *noun* a common seaweed with air bladders on its strands

**blade** *noun* **1** the cutting part of a knife, sword *etc* **2** a leaf of grass or wheat

**blame** *verb* to find fault with; consider responsible for □ *noun* fault; responsibility for something bad □ **blameless** *adj* □ **blameworthy** *adj* deserving blame

**blancmange** (*say* bla-**monsz**) *noun* a jelly-like pudding made with milk

**bland** *adj* **1** mild, not strong or irritating **2** dull, insipid

**blandishments** *noun pl* acts or words meant to flatter

**blank** *adj* **1** clear, unmarked **2** expressionless: *a blank look* □ *noun* **1** an empty space **2** a cartridge without a bullet □ **blank verse** non-rhyming poetry in a metre of 5 feet per line

**blanket** *noun* **1** a bedcovering of wool *etc* **2** a widespread, soft covering: *blanket of snow* □ *adj* covering a group of things: *blanket agreement* □ *verb* to cover widely or thickly □ **blanket bombing** bombing from the air over a widespread area

**blare** *verb* to sound loudly □ *noun* a loud sound, *eg* on a trumpet

**blasé** (*say* blah-zei) *adj* indifferent, unconcerned, *esp* because of being already familiar with something

**blaspheme** *verb* **1** to speak irreverently of a god **2** to swear, curse □ **blasphemer** *noun* □ **blasphemous** *adj* □ **blasphemy** *noun* (*pl* **blasphemies**) **1** the act of speaking irreverently of a god **2** a swear-word

**blast** *noun* **1** a blowing or gust of wind **2** a loud note, *eg* on a trumpet **3** an explosion □ *verb* **1** to break (stones, a bridge *etc*) by explosion **2** to produce a loud noise **3** *formal* to wither, destroy □ *exclamation* damn! □ **blast furnace** a furnace used in iron-smelting into which hot air is blown □ **blast-off** *noun* the moment of the launching of a rocket □ **at full blast** as quickly, strongly *etc* as possible

**blatant** *adj* very obvious; shameless

**blaze** noun a rush of light or flame □ verb 1 to burn with a strong flame 2 to throw out a strong light

**blazer** noun a light jacket often worn as part of a uniform

**bleach** verb to whiten, remove the colour from □ noun (pl bleaches) a substance which bleaches, used for cleaning, whitening clothes etc

**bleak** adj dull and cheerless; cold, unsheltered □ **bleakly** adv sadly, wistfully

**bleary** adj of eyes: tired and inflamed □ **blearily** adv with tired-looking, watery eyes

**bleat** verb 1 to cry like a sheep 2 to complain in an irritating or whining way □ noun 1 a sheep's cry 2 an irritating whine

**bleed** verb 1 to lose blood 2 to draw blood from □ **bleeding** noun a flow of blood

bleed ⋄ bleeds, bleeding, bled

**bleep** noun a high-pitched intermittent sound □ verb to give out such a sound

**blemish** noun (pl blemishes) a stain; a fault or flaw □ verb to stain, spoil

**blend** verb to mix together □ noun a mixture □ **blender** noun an electric machine which mixes thoroughly and liquidizes food

**bless** verb 1 to wish happiness to 2 to make happy 3 to make holy □ **blessed** or (in poetry etc) **blest** adj 1 happy; fortunate 2 made holy, consecrated

**blessing** noun 1 wish or prayer for happiness 2 a source of happiness or relief □ **blessing in disguise** something unexpectedly useful or beneficial

**blether** verb, Scottish to chatter; talk nonsense

**blight** noun 1 a disease which makes plants wither 2 a cause of destruction □ verb to destroy

**blind** adj unable to see □ noun 1 a window screen 2 a deception, a trick □ verb 1 to make blind 2 to dazzle □ **blindness** noun □ **blind alley** a street open only at one end; anything which leads nowhere □ **blindfold** noun a bandage or cover which is put over a person's eyes to prevent them from seeing □ adj with the eyes bandaged or covered, so as not to see □ verb to apply a blindfold to □ **blindman's buff** a game in which a blindfold person tries to catch others

**blink** verb to close the eyes for a moment; shine unsteadily □ noun

**blinkers** noun pl pieces of leather over a horse's eyes to prevent it seeing in any direction except in front

**bliss** noun very great happiness □ **blissful** adj bringing feelings of great happiness, lovely

**blister** noun a thin bubble on the skin full of watery matter □ verb to rise up in a blister

**blithe** adj happy, merry □ **blithely** adv: he blithely imagines he'll pass his exams without studying

**blitz** noun (pl blitzes) 1 an air attack 2 a sudden violent attack

**blizzard** noun a fierce storm of wind and snow

**bloated** adj swollen, puffed out

**bloater** noun a type of smoked herring

**blob** noun 1 a drop of liquid 2 a round spot

**block** noun 1 a lump of wood, stone etc 2 a connected group of buildings 3 an obstruction: road block 4 an engraved piece of wood or metal for printing 5 historical the wood on which people were beheaded □ verb to hinder, prevent from progess □ **block letters** capital letters

**blockade** verb to surround a fort or country so that food etc cannot reach it □ noun the surrounding of a place in this way

**blond** *adj* **1** light-coloured **2** fair-haired

**blonde** *adj* having fair skin and light-coloured hair □ *noun* a woman with this colouring

**blood** *noun* **1** the red liquid which flows in the bodies of human beings and animals **2** someone's descent or parentage: *royal blood* □ **blood donor** someone who gives blood which is stored and given to others in transfusions *etc* □ **blood group** any one of the types into which human blood is divided □ **bloodhound** *noun* a breed of large dog with a good sense of smell □ **bloodless** *adj* without bloodshed □ **bloodshed** *noun* violent loss of life, slaughter □ **bloodshot** *adj* of eyes: inflamed with blood □ **bloodthirsty** *adj* cruel, eager to kill □ **blood-vessel** *noun* a vein or artery in which the blood circulates

**bloody** *adj* **1** covered with blood **2** extremely violent, gory **3** *informal* terrible, awful □ **bloodily** *adv* in a violent way involving lots of blood

**bloom** *verb* **1** of a plant: to flower **2** to be in good health □ *noun* **1** a flower **2** rosy colour **3** freshness, perfection **4** a powder on the skin of fresh fruits

**bloomers** *noun pl* **1** loose underpants with legs gathered above the knee **2** *historical* a woman's outfit of a jacket, skirt and baggy knee-length trousers

After Amelia *Bloomer*, 19th-century US feminist who promoted the use of the outfit for women

**blossom** *noun* **1** a flower **2** the flowers on a fruit-tree □ *verb* **1** to produce flowers **2** to open out, develop, flourish

**blot** *noun* **1** a spot of ink **2** a stain □ *verb* **1** to spot, stain **2** to dry writing with blotting paper □ **blotting paper** thick paper for

absorbing spilled or excess ink □ **blot out** to remove from sight or memory

**blot** *verb* ⊷ blots, blot*ting*, blot*ted*

**blotch** *noun* (*pl* blotch*es*) a spot or patch of colour *etc* □ *verb* to mark with blotches □ **blotched** *adj* □ **blotchy** *adj* with skin or another surface which is temporarily an uneven colour

**blouse** *noun* a loose piece of clothing for the upper body

**blow** *noun* **1** a hard stroke or knock, eg with the fist **2** *informal* a sudden piece of bad luck □ *verb* **1** of wind: to move around **2** to drive air upon or into **3** to sound (a wind instrument) **4** to breathe hard or with difficulty □ **blowlamp** or **blowtorch** *noun* a tool for aiming a very hot flame at a particular spot □ **blowy** *adj* windy □ **blow over** to pass and be forgotten □ **blow up** to destroy by explosion

**blow** *verb* ⊷ blows, blow*ing*, blew, blown

**blubber** *noun* the fat of whales and other sea animals

**bludgeon** *noun* a short stick with a heavy end

**blue** *noun* the colour of a clear sky □ *adj* **1** of this colour **2** *informal* unhappy, depressed **3** containing sexual material: *blue film* □ **the blues** *noun pl* **1** a slow, sad song **2** low spirits, depression □ **bluebell** *noun* **1** the wild hyacinth **2** in Scotland, the harebell □ **blue blood** royal or aristocratic blood □ **bluebottle** *noun* a large fly with a blue abdomen □ **blue-chip** *adj* of a business company: reliable for investment; prestigious □ **Blue Peter** a blue flag with white centre, raised when a ship is about to sail □ **blueprint** *noun* a plan of work to be done □ **out of the blue** unexpectedly

**bluff** *adj* **1** rough and cheerful in

manner **2** frank, outspoken □ *verb* to try to deceive by pretending self-confidence □ *noun* **1** a steep bank overlooking the sea or a river **2** deception, trickery

**blunder** *verb* to make a bad mistake □ *noun* a bad mistake

**blunderbuss** *noun* (*pl* **blunderbusses**) a short hand-gun with a wide mouth

**blunt** *adj* **1** having an edge or point that is not sharp **2** rough in manner □ *verb* to make less sharp or less painful □ **bluntly** *adv* frankly, straightforwardly

**blur** *noun* an indistinct area of something; a smudge, a smear □ *verb* to make indistinct, smudge □ **blurred** *adj*

**blur** *verb* ⇨ blur*s*, blur*ring*, blur*red*

**blurt** *verb*: **blurt out** to speak suddenly and without thinking

**blush** *noun* (*pl* **blushes**) **1** a red glow on the face caused by embarrassment *etc* **2** a reddish glow □ *verb* to go red in the face

**bluster** *verb* **1** to blow strongly **2** to boast loudly □ *noun* **1** a blasting wind **2** empty boasting

**BMA** *abbrev* British Medical Association

**boa** *noun* a long scarf of fur or feathers □ **boa constrictor** a large snake which kills its prey by winding itself round it and crushing it

**boar** *noun* **1** a male pig **2** a wild pig

**board** *noun* **1** a sheet of wood **2** a group of people who run a business: *board of directors* **3** stiff card used to bind books **4** food: *bed and board* □ *verb* **1** to cover with boards **2** to supply with food at fixed terms **3** to enter (a ship, aeroplane *etc*) □ **boarder** *noun* someone who receives food and lodging □ **boarding-house** *noun* a house where paying guests receive meals at a fixed price □ **boarding-school**

*noun* a school in which food and lodging is given

**boat** *noun* **1** a vessel for sailing or rowing; a ship **2** a boat-shaped dish: *sauceboat* □ *verb* to sail about in a boat

**boater** *noun* a straw hat with a brim

**boatswain** or **bosun** (*say both* **boh**-sun) *noun* an officer who looks after a ship's boats, rigging *etc*

**bob**[1] *verb* **1** to move up and down rapidly **2** to cut (hair) to about neck level □ *noun* a bobbed haircut

**bob** *verb* ⇨ bob*s*, bob*bing*, bob*bed*

**bob**[2] *noun* a bobsleigh

**bobbin** *noun* a reel or spool on which thread is wound

**bobby** *noun*, *Brit informal* a police officer

After *Robert* Peel, who introduced the Metropolitan Police Force when Home Secretary in 1828

**bobsleigh** *noun* a long sledge or two short sledges joined together with one long seat

**bode** *verb*: **bode well** or **bode ill** to be a good or bad sign

**bodice** *noun* the close-fitting part of a woman's or a child's dress above the waist

**bodkin** *noun*, *old* a large blunt needle

**body** *noun* (*pl* **bodies**) **1** the whole or main part of a human being or animal **2** a corpse **3** the main part of anything **4** a mass of people **5** *informal* a bodystocking □ **bodily** *adj* of the body □ **bodyguard** *noun* someone or a group of people whose job is to protect another person from harm or attack □ **body language** communication by means of conscious or unconscious gestures, attitudes, facial expressions *etc* □ **bodystocking** *noun* a one-piece woman's undergarment □ **bodywarmer** *noun* a padded sleeveless jacket

**boffin** *noun*, *informal* a research

scientist

Said to come from a scientist who gave his colleagues nicknames from Dickens, Mr Boffin being a character in *Our Mutual Friend*

**bog** *noun* **1** a marsh **2** *slang* a toilet □ **boggy** *adj* marshy □ **bog down** to prevent from making progress

**bogey** *noun* something greatly feared

**boggle** *verb* to be astonished at

**bogus** *adj* false

**bohemian** *noun* someone who lives outside social conventions, *esp* an artist or writer □ *adj* of the lifestyle of a bohemian

**boil** *verb* **1** of a liquid: to reach the temperature at which it turns to vapour **2** to bubble up owing to heat **3** *informal* to be hot **4** *informal* to be angry □ *noun* a kind of inflamed swelling □ **boiling-point** *noun* the temperature at which a liquid turns to vapour (*eg* for water, 100°C)

**boiler** *noun* a container in which water is heated or steam is produced

**boisterous** *adj* **1** wild, noisy **2** of weather: stormy

**bold** *adj* **1** daring, full of courage **2** cheeky **3** striking, well-marked: *bold colours* **4** of printing type: thick and clear □ **boldly** *adj* (meanings 1, 2 and 3)

**bollard** *noun* **1** a post to which ropes are fastened on a ship or quay **2** a short post on a street used for traffic control

**Bolshevik** *noun* **1** *historical* a member of the Extreme Socialist Party in revolutionary Russia **2** *derogatory* a communist

A Russian word based on *bolshe* 'greater', because of the majority held by the Bolsheviks in the Social Democratic Congress of 1903

**bolshy** *adj*, *informal* awkward, uncooperative

Originally a shortening of **Bolshevik**

**bolster** *noun* a long cylindrical pillow or cushion □ **bolster up** to support

**bolt** *noun* **1** a small metal sliding bar used to fasten a door *etc* **2** a large screw or pin **3** a roll of cloth □ *verb* **1** to fasten with a bolt **2** to swallow (food) hurriedly **3** to rush away, escape □ **bolt upright** sitting with a very straight back

**bomb** *noun* **1** a case containing explosive or other harmful material thrown, dropped, timed to go off automatically *etc* **2** the bomb the nuclear bomb □ *verb* to drop bombs on □ **bomber** *noun* **1** an aeroplane built for bombing **2** someone who throws or plants bombs □ **bombshell** *noun* **1** a startling piece of news **2** a stunningly attractive woman

**bombard** *verb* **1** to attack with artillery **2** to overwhelm (with) □ **bombardment** *noun*

**bombast** *noun* pompous language □ **bombastic** *adj* using pompous language

**bona fide** (*say* bohn-*a* fai-dei) *adj* real, genuine: *a bona fide excuse*

In Latin, *bona fide* translates as 'in good faith'

**bond** *noun* **1** something which binds, *eg* a rope **2** something which brings people together **3** a promise to pay or do something □ **in bond** in a bonded warehouse

**bondage** *noun* slavery

**bonded warehouse** a warehouse where goods are kept until taxes have been paid on them

**bone** *noun* **1** a hard material forming the skeleton of animals **2** one of the connected pieces of a skeleton: *the hip bone* □ *verb* to take the bones out of (meat *etc*)

**bony** *adj* **1** full of bones **2** not fleshy, thin **3** made of bone or bone-like substance

**bonfire** *noun* a large fire in the open air

**bonk** *noun* the sound of a blow

**bonnet** *noun* **1** a decorative woman's hat, fastened under the chin **2** the covering over a car engine

**bonny** *adj* good-looking; pretty

**bonsai** (*say* **bon**-sai) *noun* a miniature or dwarf tree created by special pruning

**bonus** *noun* (*pl* **bonuses**) **1** an extra payment in addition to wages **2** something extra

**boo** *verb* to make a sound of disapproval □ *noun* a sound of disapproval

**boob** *noun, informal* a mistake

**booby** *noun* (*pl* **boobies**) an idiot □ **booby prize** a prize for the person who is last in a competition □ **booby trap** a device hidden or disguised as something harmless, intended to injure the first person to come near it

**book** *noun* **1** a number of pages bound together **2** a written work which has appeared, or is intended to appear, in the form of a book □ *verb* to order (places *etc*) beforehand □ **book-keeping** *noun* the keeping of accounts □ **booklet** *noun* a small paperback book □ **bookmaker** *noun* someone who takes bets and pays winnings □ **bookworm** *noun* **1** an avid reader **2** a grub that eats holes in books

**boom** *verb* **1** to make a hollow sound or roar **2** to increase in prosperity, success *etc* □ *noun* **1** a loud, hollow sound **2** a rush or increase of trade, prosperity *etc*: *property boom* **3** a pole along which a sail is stretched

**boomerang** *noun* a curved piece of wood which when thrown returns to the thrower, a traditional hunting weapon of Australian Aboriginals

**boon** *noun* something to be grateful for, a blessing □ **boon companion** a close friend who is good company

**boor** *noun* a rough or rude person □ **boorish** *adj*

**boost** *verb* to push up, raise, increase □ *noun* an increase, a rise

**booster** *noun* **1** a device for increasing the power of a machine *etc* **2** the first of several stages of a rocket

**boot** *noun* **1** a heavy shoe covering the foot and lower part of the leg **2** *Brit* a place for stowing luggage in a car **3** the starting of a computer from its start-up programs **4** a kick □ *verb* to kick □ **boot up** to start (a computer) by running its start-up programs □ **to boot** in addition, as well

**bootee** *noun* a knitted boot for a baby

**booth** *noun* **1** a covered stall, *eg* at a market **2** a small compartment for telephoning, voting *etc*

**booty** *noun* plunder, gains taken in war *etc*

**border** *noun* **1** the edge or side of anything **2** the boundary of a country **3** a flowerbed in a garden □ *verb* **border on** to be near to: *bordering on the absurd*

**bore¹** *verb* **1** to make a hole by piercing **2** to weary, be tiresome to □ *noun* **1** a pierced hole **2** the size across the tube of a gun **3** a tiresome person or thing **4** a wave that rushes up a river mouth at high tide

**bore²** *past form of* **bear**

**boredom** *noun* lack of interest, weariness

**boring** *adj* not at all interesting

**born** *adj* by birth, natural: *a born actor* □ **be born 1** of a baby: to come out of the mother's womb **2** to come into existence

❧ Do not confuse: **born** and **borne**. **Born** is used for the past participle of **bear** when referring to the birth of a child, idea *etc*; otherwise the form is **borne**: *I couldn't have borne it any longer.*

**borne** *past participle of* **bear**

◑. Do not confuse: **borne** and **born**

**borough** noun **1** historical a town with special privileges granted by royal charter **2** a town that elects Members of Parliament

**borrow** verb to get on loan

**bosom** noun the breast; midst, centre: bosom of her family □ adj of a friend: close, intimate

**boss** noun (pl **bosses**) a manager, a chief □ verb to order about in a high-handed way

**bossy** adj tending to boss others, domineering

**bosun** see **boatswain**

**botany** noun the study of plants □ **botanic** or **botanical** adj □ **botanist** noun someone who studies botany □ **botanic garden** a large public garden containing plants and trees from different countries

**botch** verb to mend clumsily; do badly □ noun a badly done piece of work

**both** adj & pronoun the two, the one and the other □ adv equally, together: both willing and able

**bother** verb **1** to be a nuisance to **2** to take time or trouble over something □ noun trouble, inconvenience

**bothy** noun (pl **bothies**) **1** in Scotland, a hut to give shelter to hillwalkers **2** a simply furnished hut for farm workers

**bottle** noun a hollow narrow-necked vessel for holding liquids □ verb to put in a bottle □ **bottle up** to keep in, hold back (feelings)

**bottleneck** noun **1** a narrow part of a road likely to become crowded with traffic **2** a stage in a process where progress is held up

**bottom** noun **1** the lowest part or underside of anything **2** the buttocks □ **bottomless** adj extremely deep

**boudoir** (say **bood-wahr**) noun a lady's private room

**bough** noun a branch of a tree

**bought** past form of **buy**

**boulder** noun a large stone

**bounce** verb **1** to jump up after striking the ground etc **2** to make (a ball etc) do this □ noun a jumping back up □ **bouncing** adj full of life, lively □ **bounce back** to recover after a setback or trouble

**bouncer** noun someone employed to force troublemakers to leave a club etc

**bound¹** noun **1** a leap, a jump **2bounds** borders, limits □ verb **1** to jump, leap **2** to enclose, surround □ **boundless** adj having no limit, vast □ **bound for** ready to go to, on the way to □ **bound to** certain to □ **out of bounds** beyond the permitted limits

**bound²** past form of **bind**

**boundary** noun (pl **boundaries**) **1** an edge, a limit **2** a line etc marking an edge

**bounteous** or **bountiful** adj generous; plentiful

**bounty** noun (pl **bounties**) **1** a gift; generosity **2** money given as a help □ **bounty hunter** someone who tracks down people wanted by the authorities to collect the rewards offered

**bouquet** (say **boo-kei**) noun **1** a bunch of flowers **2** a scent, eg of wine

**bourgeois** (say **boorsz-wah**) adj of the middle class □ **the bourgeoisie** noun a rather insulting name for the kind of middle-class people who have a comfortable but unimaginative lifestyle

**bout** noun **1** a round in a contest **2** a spell, a fit: a bout of flu

**boutique** noun a small shop selling fashionable clothes etc

**bovine** adj **1** of or like cattle **2** stupid

**bow¹** (*say* bow) *verb* **1** to bend **2** to nod the head or bend the body in greeting **3** to give in: *bow to pressure* **4** to weigh down, crush □ *noun* **1** a bending of the head or body **2** the front part of a ship

**bow²** (*say* boh) *noun* **1** anything in the shape of a curve or arch **2** a weapon for shooting arrows, made of a stick of springy wood bent by a string **3** a looped knot **4** a wooden rod with horsehair stretched along it, by which the strings of a violin *etc* are played □ **bow-legged** *adj* having legs curving outwards □ **bow window** a window built in a curve

**bowdlerize** *verb* to censor heavily

After Thomas *Bowdler*, who produced a heavily censored edition of Shakespeare in the 19th century

**bowels** *noun pl* **1** the large and small intestines **2** the innermost or deepest parts of anything: *in the bowels of the earth*

**bower** (*say* bow-er) *noun* a shady spot in a garden

**bowl** *noun* **1** a basin for holding liquids **2** a basin-shaped hollow **3** a heavy wooden ball, used in skittles *etc* **4** (**bowls**) a game played on a green with specially weighted bowls □ *verb* **1** to play at bowls **2** to move speedily like a bowl **3** *cricket* to send the ball at the wicket **4** *cricket* to put out by knocking the wicket with the ball □ **bowl over 1** to knock down **2** to surprise greatly □ **bowler** *noun* **1** someone who plays bowls **2** someone who bowls in cricket **3** a hat with a rounded top

**box** *noun* (*pl* **boxes**) **1** a case for holding anything **2** a hardwood tree **3** an evergreen shrub **4** an enclosure of private seats in a theatre □ *verb* **1** to put in a box **2** to confine in a small space **3** to punch **4** to engage in the sport of boxing □ **box office** an office where theatre tickets *etc* may be bought

**boxer** *noun* **1** someone who boxes as a sport **2** a breed of large smooth-haired dog with a head like a bulldog's □ **boxer shorts** loose-fitting men's underpants

**boxing** *noun* the sport of fighting with the fists wearing padded gloves □ **Boxing Day** the first weekday after Christmas Day

**boy** *noun* **1** a male child **2** a male servant □ **boyish** *adj* **1** of a girl: having an appearance or behaviour which gives an impression of masculinity **2** of a man: having an appearance or behaviour which gives an impression of youthfulness □ **boyhood** *noun* the time of being a boy

**boycott** *verb* to refuse to do business or trade with □ *noun* a refusal to trade or do business

**bra** *noun*, *informal* a brassière

**brace** *noun* **1** an instrument which draws things together and holds them firmly **2** a piece of wire fitted over teeth to straighten them **3** a pair of pheasant, grouse *etc* when shot **4** a carpenter's tool for boring **5** (**braces**) shoulder-straps for holding up trousers □ *verb* to strengthen, give firmness to

**bracelet** *noun* **1** a circular ornament placed around the wrist **2** *slang* a handcuff

**bracing** *adj* giving strength

**bracken** *noun* a coarse kind of fern

**bracket** *noun* **1** a support for something fastened to a wall **2** each of a pair of written or printed marks, *eg* ( ), { }, [ ], used to group together several words **3** a grouping, category: *in the same age bracket* □ *verb* **1** to enclose in brackets **2** to group together

**brackish** *adj* of water: rather salty

**brag** *verb* to boast □ *noun* a boast

**brag** *verb* ▷ brag*s*, brag*ging*, brag*ged*

**braggart** *noun* someone vain and boastful

**braid** verb to plait (the hair) □ noun
1 a plait of hair 2 decorative ribbon
used as trimming

**braille** noun a system of raised marks
on paper which blind people can
read by feeling

Named after its inventor, French
teacher Louis *Braille*

**brain** noun the part of the body inside
the skull, the centre of feeling and
thinking □ verb to knock out the
brains of; hit hard on the head
□ **brainy** adj, informal clever
□ **brainwashing** noun forcing (a
person) to change their views
□ **brainwave** noun a good idea

**braise** verb to stew (meat) in a small
amount of liquid

**brake** noun a part of a vehicle used
for stopping or slowing down □ verb
to slow down by using the brake(s)

**bramble** noun 1 the blackberry bush
2 its fruit

**bran** noun the inner husks of wheat
etc, separated from flour after
grinding

**branch** noun (pl **branches**) 1 an arm-
like limb of a tree 2 a small shop,
bank etc belonging to a bigger one
□ verb to spread out like branches

**brand** noun 1 a make of goods with a
special trademark 2 a burning piece
of wood 3 a permanent mark made
by a red-hot iron □ verb 1 to mark
with a brand 2 to mark
permanently; impress deeply 3 to
mark with disgrace □ **brand-new**
adj absolutely new

**brandish** verb to wave (a weapon etc)
about

**brandy** noun (pl **brandies**) an
alcoholic spirit made from wine

**brass** noun (pl **brasses**) 1 metal
made by mixing copper and zinc
2 music brass wind instruments
□ adj 1 made of brass 2 playing
brass musical instruments: *brass
band* □ **brassy** adj 1 like brass 2 of a
voice: harsh

**brassière** noun an article of women's
underwear for supporting the
breasts

**brat** noun a disapproving name for a
child

**bravado** noun a show of bravery,
bold pretence

**brave** adj ready to meet danger, pain
etc without showing fear;
courageous, noble □ verb to face or
meet boldly and without fear □ noun
a Native American warrior
□ **bravery** noun

**bravo** exclamation well done

**brawl** noun a noisy quarrel; a fight
□ verb to quarrel or fight noisily

**brawn** noun muscle power □ **brawny**
adj big and strong

**bray** noun 1 a cry like that of an ass
2 a pin pressing against a string on a
harp to produce a buzzing effect
□ verb to cry like an ass

**brazen** adj 1 impudent, shameless:
*brazen hussy* 2 of or like brass
□ **brazen it out** to face a difficult
situation with bold impudence

**brazier** noun an iron basket for
holding burning coals

**breach** noun (pl **breaches**) 1 a break,
a gap 2 a breaking of a law, a
promise etc 3 a quarrel □ verb to
make a gap or opening in □ **breach
of the peace** a breaking of the law
by noisy, offensive behaviour

**bread** noun food made of flour or
meal and baked

**breadth** noun 1 distance from side to
side, width 2 extent

**breadwinner** noun someone who
earns a living for a family

**break** verb 1 to (cause to) fall to
pieces or apart 2 to act against (a
law, promise etc) 3 to interrupt (a
silence) 4 to tell (news) 5 to check,
soften the effect of (a fall) 6 to cure
(a habit) 7 of a boy's voice: to drop
to a deep male tone □ noun 1 an
opening 2 a pause 3 informal a

lucky chance ▫ **breakable** *adj* ▫ **breakage** *noun* **1** the act of breaking **2** something broken ▫ **breakdown** *noun* **1** a division into parts **2** a collapse from nervous exhaustion *etc* ▫ **break-in** *noun* illegal forced entry of a house *etc* with intent to steal ▫ **break-through** *noun* a sudden success after some effort ▫ **break down 1** to divide into parts **2** of an engine: to fail **3** to be overcome with weeping or nervous exhaustion ▫ **break in** to tame, train (a wild horse *etc*) ▫ **break into** to enter by force ▫ **break out 1** to appear suddenly **2** to escape **3** **break out in something** to become covered (with a rash *etc*) ▫ **break up 1** to (cause to) fall to pieces or apart **2** to separate, leave one another

**break** *verb* ▫ breaks, breaking, broke, broken

**breaker** *noun* a large wave

**breakfast** *noun* the first meal of the day ▫ *verb* to eat this meal

**breakwater** *noun* a barrier to break the force of waves

**breast** *noun* **1** either of the milk-producing glands on a woman's body **2** the front part of a human or animal body between neck and belly **3** a part of a jacket or coat which covers the breast ▫ **make a clean breast** to make a full confession

**breastbone** *noun* the bone running down the middle of the breast; the sternum

**breastplate** *noun* a piece of armour for the breast

**breath** (*say* breth) *noun* **1** the air drawn into and then sent out from the lungs **2** an instance of breathing **3** a very slight breeze

🔦 Do not confuse: **breath** and **breathe**

**Breathalyser** *noun*, *trademark* a device into which someone breathes to indicate the amount of alcohol in their blood

**breathe** (*say* breedh) *verb* **1** to draw in and send out air from the lungs **2** to whisper

**breathe** ▫ breathes, breathing, breathed

🔦 Do not confuse: **breathe** and **breath**

**breather** *noun* a rest or pause

**breathless** *adj* **1** breathing very fast, panting **2** excited

**bred** *past form* of **breed**

**breech** *noun* the back part, *esp* of a gun

**breeches** (*say* **brich**-iz) *noun pl* trousers reaching to just below the knee

**breed** *verb* **1** to produce (children or a family) **2** to mate and rear (animals) **3** to cause ▫ *noun* **1** a group of animals *etc* descended from the same ancestor **2** type, sort

**breed** *verb* ▫ breeds, breeding, bred

**breeding** *noun* **1** act of producing or rearing **2** good manners; education and training

**breeze** *noun* a gentle wind

**breeze block** a type of large, grey brick used in building

**breezy** *adj* **1** windy, gusty **2** bright, lively ▫ **breezily** *adv* (meaning 2)

**brethren** *noun pl*, *old* brothers

**breve** (*say* breev) *noun* a long musical note (◠) which is 8 beats in length

**brevity** *noun* shortness, conciseness

**brew** *verb* **1** to make beer **2** to make (tea *etc*) **3** to be gathering or forming: *there's trouble brewing* **4** to plot, plan ▫ **brewer** *noun* someone who brews beer *etc*

**brewery** *noun* (*pl* **breweries**) a place where beer is made

**briar** or **brier** *noun* **1** the wild rose **2** a heather plant whose wood is used for making tobacco pipes

**bribe** noun a gift of money etc given to persuade someone to do something □ verb to give a bribe to □ **bribery** noun

**bribe** verb ⊳ bribe*s*, brib*ing*, brib*ed*

**bric-à-brac** noun small odds and ends

**brick** noun **1** a block of baked clay for building **2** a toy building-block of wood etc

**bride** noun a woman about to be married, or newly married □ **bridal** adj of a bride or a wedding □ **bridegroom** noun a man about to be married, or newly married □ **bridesmaid** noun an unmarried woman who attends the bride at a wedding

**bridge**¹ noun **1** a structure built to carry a track or road across a river etc **2** the captain's platform on a ship **3** the bony part of the nose **4** a thin piece of wood holding up the strings of a violin etc □ verb **1** to be a bridge over; span **2** to build a bridge over **3** to get over (a difficulty)

**bridge** verb ⊳ bridge*s*, bridg*ing*, bridg*ed*

**bridge**² noun a card game for two pairs of players

**bridle** noun the harness on a horse's head to which the reins are attached □ verb **1** to put on a bridle **2** to toss the head indignantly □ **bridle path** noun a path for horseriders

**brief** adj short; taking a short time □ noun a set of notes giving information about, esp to a lawyer about a law case □ verb to instruct or inform □ **briefly** adv □ **in brief** in a few words

**briefs** noun pl close-fitting underpants

**brier** another spelling of **briar**

**brigade** noun a body of soldiers, usually two battalions

**brigadier** noun a senior army officer

**brigand** noun, old a robber, a bandit

**bright** adj **1** shining; full of light **2** clever **3** cheerful □ **brighten** verb to make or grow bright

**brilliant** adj **1** very clever **2** sparkling **3** informal very good, excellent □ **brilliance** noun □ **brilliantly** adv

**brim** noun **1** the edge of a cup etc **2** the protruding lower edge of a hat or cap □ verb to be full □ **brimful** adj full to the brim

**brim** verb ⊳ brim*s*, brimm*ing*, brimm*ed*

**brimstone** noun sulphur

**brine** noun salt water □ **briny** adj

**bring** verb **1** to fetch, lead or carry (to a place) **2** to cause to come: the medicine brings him relief □ **bring about** to cause □ **bring home to** to make (someone) realize (something) □ **bring off** to do (something) successfully □ **bring to** to revive □ **bring up 1** to rear, feed and educate **2** to mention **3** informal to vomit

**bring** verb ⊳ bring*s*, bring*ing*, brought

**brink** noun the edge of a cliff etc □ **on the brink of** almost at the point of, on the verge of

**brisk** adj **1** moving quickly **2** lively and efficient: a brisk manner □ **briskly** adv

**bristle** noun a short, stiff hair on an animal, a brush etc □ verb **1** of hair etc: to stand on end **2** to show anger and indignation: he bristled at my remark □ **bristly** adj

**brittle** adj hard but easily broken

**broach** verb **1** to begin to talk about **2** to open, begin using (eg a cask of wine)

**broad** adj **1** wide, extensive **2** of an accent etc: strong, obvious □ **broadly** adv **1** widely **2** generally: broadly speaking, we're all afraid of the same things □ **broaden** verb to make or grow broader

**broadcast** verb to transmit (a

programme *etc*) on radio or television ▫ *noun* a programme transmitted on radio or television

**broad-gauge** *adj* of a railway: having the distance between rails greater than the *standard gauge* (4ft 8in or 1.435 metre)

**broadsheet** *noun* a large-format quality newspaper (*compare with*: **tabloid**)

**broadside** *noun* **1** a strong attack in an argument *etc* **2** a shot by all the guns on one side of a ship

**brocade** *noun* a silk cloth on which fine patterns are sewn

**broccoli** *noun* a hardy variety of cauliflower with small green or purple flower-heads

**brochure** (*say* broh-**shoor** or **broh-**shur) *noun* a booklet, a pamphlet

**brogue**¹ (*say* brohg) *noun* a strong shoe

**brogue**² (*say* brohg) *noun* a broad accent in speaking: *Irish brogue*

**broil** *verb* **1** to make or be very hot **2** *US* to grill

**broke** *past form of* **break** ▫ *adj, informal* having no money

**broken** *past participle of* **break**

**broker** *noun* someone who buys and sells stocks and shares for others ▫ *verb* **1** to act as a broker **2** to negotiate on behalf of others: *broker a deal*

**bromide** *noun* **1** a chemical used as a sedative **2** a dull person **3** a platitude **4** a monochrome photographic print

**bronchitis** (*say* brong-**kait**-is) *noun* an illness affecting the windpipe, causing difficulty in breathing ▫ **bronchial** (*say* **brong**-ki-al) *adj* having to do with the windpipe

**bronco** *noun* (*pl* **broncos**) *US* a half-tamed horse

**brontosaurus** *noun* a large dinosaur

**bronze** *noun* a golden-brown mixture of copper and tin ▫ *adj* of this colour ▫ **bronzed** *adj* suntanned

**brooch** (*say* brohch) *noun* (*pl* **brooches**) an ornament pinned to the clothing

**brood** *verb* **1** of a hen *etc*: to sit on eggs **2** to think anxiously for some time ▫ *noun* **1** a number of young birds hatched at one time **2** young animals or children of the same family

**brook** *noun* a small stream ▫ *verb* to put up with, endure

**broom** *noun* **1** a type of shrub with yellow flowers **2** a brush for sweeping ▫ **broomstick** *noun* the handle of a broom

**brose** *noun, Scottish* a liquid food of boiling water poured on oatmeal *etc*

**broth** *noun* soup, *esp* one made with vegetables

**brothel** *noun* a house where prostitution is practised

Originally *brothel-house, brothel* being a general term of abuse that was later applied specifically to prostitutes

**brother** *noun* **1** a male born of the same parents as yourself **2** a companion, a fellow-worker ▫ **brotherly** *adj* like a brother; affectionate ▫ **brotherhood** *noun* **1** comradeship between men **2** a men's association ▫ **brother-in-law** *noun* **1** the brother of your husband or wife **2** the husband of your sister or sister-in-law

**brought** *past form of* **bring**

**brow** *noun* **1** a forehead **2** an eyebrow **3** the edge of a hill

**browbeat** *verb* to bully

**brown** *noun* a dark colour made by mixing red, yellow, black *etc* ▫ *adj* **1** of this colour **2** *informal* suntanned

**brownie** *noun* **1** a helpful fairy or goblin **2** a Brownie Guide ▫ **Brownie Guide** a junior Guide

**browse** *verb* **1** to glance through a

range of books, shop merchandise *etc* **2** to feed on the shoots or leaves of plants

**bruise** *noun* a discoloured area on the skin, the surface of fruit *etc*, where it has been struck ◻ *verb* to cause bruises (to)

**brunette** *noun* a woman with dark brown hair

**brunt** *noun*: **bear** or **take the brunt** to take the chief strain

**brush** *noun* (*pl* **brushes**) **1** an instrument with tufts of bristles, hair *etc* for smoothing the hair, cleaning, painting *etc* **2** a disagreement, a brief quarrel **3** the tail of a fox ◻ **undergrowth** ◻ *verb* **1** to pass a brush over **2** to remove by sweeping **3** to touch lightly in passing ◻ **brushwood** *noun* **1** broken branches, twigs *etc* **2** undergrowth

**Brussels sprouts** a type of vegetable with sprouts like small cabbages on the stem

**brute** *noun* **1** an animal **2** a cruel person ◻ **brutish** *adj* like a brute, savage, coarse

**BSE** *abbrev* bovine spongiform encephalopathy, a brain disease of cattle

**Bt** *abbrev* baronet

**bubble** *noun* **1** a thin ball of liquid blown out with air **2** a small ball of air in anything ◻ *verb* to rise in bubbles

**bubbly** *adj* **1** full of bubbles **2** lively, vivacious ◻ *noun*, *informal* champagne; sparkling wine

**buccaneer** *noun*, *old* a pirate ◻ **buccaneering** *adj* like a pirate

**buck** *noun* **1** the male of the deer, goat, hare and rabbit **2** *US informal* a dollar ◻ *verb* of a horse *etc*: to attempt to throw a rider by rapid jumps into the air

**bucket** *noun* a container for water *etc*

**buckle** *noun* a clip for fastening

straps or belts ◻ *verb* to fasten with a buckle

**buckler** *noun* a small shield

**bucolic** *adj* of the countryside; pastoral, rural

**bud** *noun* the first shoot of a tree or plant ◻ *verb* to produce buds

**bud** *verb* ⟡ buds, bud*ding*, bud*ded*

**Buddhism** *noun* a religion whose followers worship Buddha ◻ **Buddhist** *noun* & *adj*

**budding** *adj* showing signs of becoming: *budding author*

**budge** *verb* to move slightly, stir

**budge** ⟡ budges, budg*ing*, budg*ed*

**budgerigar** *noun* a kind of small parrot often kept as a pet

**budget** *noun* **1** a government plan for the year's spending **2** any plan of their future spending ◻ *verb* to allow for in a budget

**budgie** *noun*, *informal* a budgerigar

**buff** *noun* **1** a light yellowish brown colour **2** an enthusiast, a fan: *film buff* ◻ *verb* to polish

**buffalo** *noun* (*pl* **buffaloes**) **1** a large Asian ox, used to draw loads **2** the North American bison

**buffer** *noun* something which lessens the force of a blow or collision

**buffet¹** *noun* (*say* **buf**-it) *verb* to strike, knock about ◻ *noun* a slap or a blow

**buffet²** *noun* (*say* **buwf**-ei) **1** a counter or café serving food and drink **2** a range of dishes set out at a party, *etc* for people to serve themselves

**buffoon** *noun* a clown, fool ◻ **buffoonery** *noun* silly behaviour, clowning around

**bug** *noun* **1** a small, *esp* irritating, insect **2** a disease germ **3** a tiny hidden microphone for recording conversations **4** a problem in a computer program causing errors in its execution ◻ *verb* **1** to conceal a microphone in (a room *etc*) **2** to

record with a hidden microphone
**3** *informal* to annoy, harass

**bug** *verb* ⇔ bug**s**, bugg**ing**, bugg**ed**

**bugbear** *noun* something that
frightens or annoys

**buggy** *noun* (*pl* **buggies**) a child's
push-chair

**bugle** *noun* a small military trumpet
□ **bugler** *noun* someone who plays
the bugle

**build** *verb* to put together the parts of
anything □ *noun* physique, physical
character □ **builder** *noun*

**build** *verb* ⇔ build**s**, build**ing**, built

**building** *noun* **1** the act or trade of
building (houses *etc*) **2** a house or
other built dwelling *etc* □ **building
society** an institution like a bank
which accepts investments and
whose main business is to lend
people money to buy a house

**built-up** *adj* of an area: containing
houses and other buildings

**bulb** *noun* **1** the rounded part of the
stem of an onion, tulip *etc*, in which
they store their food **2** a glass globe
surrounding the element of an
electric light □ **bulbous** *adj* bulb-
shaped

**bulge** *noun* **1** a swelling **2** a
noticeable increase □ *verb* to swell
out

**bulge** *verb* ⇔ bulge**s**, bulg**ing**, bulg**ed**

**bulimia** *noun* an eating disorder in
which bingeing is followed by self-
induced vomiting or purging
□ **bulimic** *adj*

**bulk** *noun* **1** large size **2** the greater
part: *the bulk of the population*

**bulkhead** *noun* a wall in the inside of
a ship, meant to keep out water in a
collision

**bulky** *adj* taking up a lot of room
□ **bulkily** *adv*

**bull** *noun* the male of animals of the
ox family, also of the whale,
elephant *etc* □ **bulldog** *noun* a breed
of strong, fierce-looking dog

□ **bullfight** *noun* a public
entertainment in Spain *etc*, in which
a bull is angered and usually killed
□ **bullfinch** *noun* a small pink-
breasted bird □ **bull's-eye** *noun*
**1** the mark in the middle of a target
**2** a striped sweet

**bulldozer** *noun* a machine for
levelling land and clearing away
obstacles □ **bulldoze** *verb* **1** to use a
bulldozer on **2** to force

**bullet** *noun* the piece of metal fired
from a gun □ **bullet-proof** *adj* not
able to be pierced by bullets

**bulletin** *noun* a report of current
news, someone's health *etc*

**bullion** *noun* gold or silver in the
form of bars *etc*

**bullock** *noun* a young bull

**bully** *noun* (*pl* **bullies**) someone who
unfairly uses their size and strength
to hurt or frighten others □ *verb* to
act like a bully

Originally a term of affection that
developed to mean 'pimp' and so to
someone who harasses others

**bulrush** *noun* (*pl* **bulrushes**) a large
strong reed which grows on wet
land or in water

**bulwark** (*say* buwl-wak) *noun* **1** a
strong defensive wall **2** a prop, a
defence

**bum¹** *noun*, *Brit slang* the buttocks
□ **bumbag** *noun* a carrying pouch
strapped round the waist

**bum²** *noun*, *US slang* a tramp □ *adj*
useless, dud □ **give someone the
bum's rush** to get rid of them quickly

**bumble-bee** *noun* a type of large bee

**bumf** *another spelling of* **bumph**

**bump** *verb* **1** to strike heavily **2** to
knock by accident □ *noun* **1** the
sound of a heavy blow **2** an
accidental knock **3** a raised lump

**bumper** *noun* a bar round the front
and back of a car's body to protect it
from damage □ *adj* large: *a bumper
crop*

**bumph** or **bumf** noun, Brit informal miscellaneous, uninteresting papers, leaflets etc

Originally short for 'bum-fodder', ie toilet paper

**bumpkin** noun a clumsy, awkward, country person

**bumptious** adj self-important

**bun** noun 1 a sweet roll made of egg dough 2 hair wound into a rounded mass

**bunch** noun (pl **bunches**) a number of things tied together or growing together □ verb to crowd together

**bundle** noun a number of things loosely bound together □ verb 1 to tie in a bundle 2 to push roughly

**bung** noun the stopper of the hole in a barrel, bottle etc □ verb to stop up with a bung

**bungalow** noun a one-storey detached house

**bungee jumping** the sport of jumping from a height with strong rubber ropes attached to the ankles so that the jumper bounces up before reaching the ground

**bungle** verb 1 to do badly or clumsily 2 to mishandle, mismanage □ noun a clumsy or mishandled action

**bunion** noun a lump or swelling on the joint of the big toe

**bunk** noun a narrow bed, eg in a ship's cabin □ **bunkbed** noun one of a pair of narrow beds one above the other

**bunker** noun 1 a sandpit on a golf course 2 an underground shelter 3 a large box for keeping coal

**bunkum** noun nonsense

From Buncombe county in N Carolina, whose representative once gave a rambling speech in Congress

**bunny** noun (pl **bunnies**) a child's name for a rabbit

**Bunsen burner** a gas-burner used in laboratories

**bunting**¹ noun 1 a thin cloth used for making flags 2 flags

**bunting**² noun a bird of the finch family

**buoy** (say boi) noun 1 a floating mark acting as a guide or warning for ships 2 a float, eg a lifebuoy

**buoyant** adj 1 able to float 2 cheerful, bouncy □ **buoyancy** noun

**bur** another spelling of **burr**

**burden** noun 1 a load 2 something difficult to bear, eg poverty or sorrow 3 old the chorus of a song □ **burdensome** adj

**bureau** (say byoo-roh) noun (pl **bureaux** or **bureaus** - say both byoo-rohz) 1 a writing table 2 an office

A French word which comes from the name of a type of coarse cloth (burel) used as a cover for writing tables

**bureaucracy** (say byoo-**rok**-ra-si) noun government by officials

**bureaucrat** noun an administrative official □ **bureaucratic** adj 1 involving bureaucracy 2 full of complicated and irritating official procedures

**burgh** noun in Scotland, a borough

**burglar** noun someone who breaks into a house to steal □ **burglary** noun (pl **burglaries**) a break-in into a house by a person who wants to steal things □ **burgle** verb to commit burglary

**burial** noun the placing of a body under the ground after death

**burlesque** noun a piece of writing, acting etc, making fun of somebody

**burly** adj broad and strong

**burn**¹ verb 1 to set fire to 2 to be on fire, or scorching 3 to injure by burning □ noun an injury or mark caused by fire □ **burner** noun the part of a lamp or gas-jet from which the flame rises

**burn** verb ➻ burns, burning, burnt or burned

**burn²** noun, Scottish a small stream

**burnish** verb to polish □ noun polish

**burnt** past form of **burn**

**burr** or **bur** noun the prickly seedcase or head of certain plants

**burrow** noun a hole or passage in the ground dug by certain animals for shelter □ verb to make a passage beneath the ground

**burst** verb **1** to break suddenly (after increased pressure) **2** to move, speak etc suddenly or violently

**bury** verb **1** to place (a dead body etc) under the ground **2** to cover, hide

**bury** ⬦ buries, burying, buried

**bus** noun (pl buses) a large road vehicle, often used for public transport □ **bus stop** an official stopping place for buses

**busby** noun (pl busbies) a tall fur hat worn by certain soldiers

**bush** noun (pl bushes) **1** a growing thing between a plant and a tree in size **2** wild, unfarmed country in Africa etc □ **bush telegraph** the quick passing-on of news from person to person

**bushy** adj **1** growing thickly **2** full of bushes □ **bushily** adv in a tangled, dense way

**business** noun (pl businesses) **1** someone's work or job **2** trade, commerce **3** a matter of personal interest or concern □ **businesslike** adj practical, methodical, alert and prompt □ **businessman**, **businesswoman** noun someone who works in commerce

**busk** verb to play or sing in the street for money □ **busker** noun

**bust** noun **1** a woman's breasts **2** a sculpture of someone's head and shoulders

**bustard** noun a large, fast-running bird similar to a turkey

**bustle** verb to busy oneself noisily □ noun **1** noisy activity, fuss **2** historical a stuffed pad worn under a woman's full skirt

**busy** adj having a lot to do □ **busily** adv □ **busybody** noun someone nosey about others □ **busy yourself with** to occupy yourself with

**busy** adj ⬦ busier, busiest

**but** conj **1** showing a contrast between two ideas etc: my brother can swim but I can't **2** except that, without that: it never rains but it pours □ prep except, with the exception of: no one but Tom had any money □ adv only: we can but hope □ **but for** were it not for: but for your car, we would have been late

**butch** adj of a woman: looking or behaving in a masculine way

**butcher** noun someone whose work is to carve up meat and sell it □ verb **1** to kill and carve up (an animal) for food **2** to kill cruelly □ **butchery** noun great or cruel slaughter

**butler** noun the chief manservant in a household who looks after and serves wines etc

**butt** noun **1** a large cask, a barrel **2** someone of whom others make fun **3** the thick heavy end of a rifle etc **4** the end of a cigarette or cigar **5** a push with the head **6** US slang the buttocks □ verb to strike with the head □ **butt in** to interrupt, interfere □ **butt out** slang to stop interfering

**butter** noun a fatty food made by churning cream □ verb to spread over with butter □ **buttermilk** noun the milk that is left after butter has been made □ **butterscotch** noun a hard toffee made with butter □ **butter up** to flatter, soften up

**buttercup** noun a plant with a cup-like yellow flower

**butterfly** noun (pl butterflies) a kind of insect with large, often patterned wings

**buttocks** noun pl the two fleshy parts of the body on which you sit; the rump

**button** *noun* **1** a knob or disc of metal, plastic *etc* used to fasten clothing **2** a knob pressed to work an electrical device □ *verb* to fasten by means of buttons □ **buttonhole** *noun* a hole through which a button is passed □ *verb* to catch the attention of (someone) and force them to listen □ **button up** to be quiet; shut up

**buttress** *noun* (*pl* **buttresses**) a support on the outside of a wall □ *verb* to support, prop up

**buxom** *adj* plump and pretty

**buy** *verb* to get in exchange for money □ *noun* a purchase □ **buyer** *noun*

**buy** *verb* ⊳ buys, buying, bought

**buzz** *verb* **1** to make a humming noise like bees **2** *informal* to call, telephone **3** of aircraft: to fly close to □ *noun* **1** a humming sound **2** *informal* a phonecall

**buzzard** *noun* a large bird of prey

**buzzer** *noun* a signalling device which makes a buzzing noise

**buzzword** *noun* a word well-established in a particular jargon, its use suggesting up-to-date specialized knowledge

**by** *adv* **1** near: *a crowd stood by, watching* **2** past: *people strolled by* **3** aside: *money put by for an emergency* □ *prep* **1** next to, near: *standing by the door* **2** past: *going by*

*the house* **3** through, along, across: *we came by the main road* **4** indicating the person who does something: *written by Burns* **5** of time: not after: *it'll be ready by four o'clock* **6** during the time of: *working by night* **7** by means of: *by train* **8** to the extent of: *taller by a head* **9** used to express measurements, compass directions *etc*: *6 metres by 4 metres* **10** in the quantity of: *sold by the pound* □ **bygone** *adj* past □ **bygones** *noun pl* old grievances or events that have been, or should be, forgotten □ **by-election** *noun* an election for parliament during a parliamentary session □ **by-law** or **bye-law** *noun* a local (not a national) law □ **bypass** *noun* a road built round a town *etc* so that traffic need not pass through it □ **by-product** *noun* something useful obtained during the manufacture of something else □ **byroad** or **byway** *noun* a side road □ **bystander** *noun* someone who stands watching an event or accident □ **byword** *noun* someone or something well-known for a particular quality

**bye** *noun, cricket* **1** a ball bowled past the wicket **2** a run made from this

**byte** (*say* bait) *noun, computing* a unit used to measure data or memory

---

## Cc

**°C** *abbrev* degree(s) Celsius or centigrade

**CAB** *abbrev* Citizens Advice Bureau

**cab** *noun* **1** a taxi **2** *historical* a hired carriage

**cabaret** (*say* **kab**-*a*-rei) *noun* an entertainment consisting of variety acts, *esp* in a club or restaurant

**cabbage** *noun* a type of vegetable

with edible leaves

**caber** (*say* **kei**-ber) *noun* a heavy pole tossed in competition at Highland games

**cabin** *noun* **1** a wooden hut **2** a small room used for living quarters in a ship **3** the part of a commercial aircraft containing passenger seating □ **cabin crew** the flight attendants on a commercial airline

**cabinet** *noun* **1** a cupboard which has shelves and doors **2** a similar container for storage *etc* **3** a wooden case with drawers **4** a selected number of government ministers who decide on policy □ **cabinet-maker** *noun* a maker of fine furniture

**cable** *noun* **1** a strong rope or thick metal line **2** a line of covered telegraph wires laid under the sea or underground **3** a telegram sent by such a line **4** an underground wire **5** *informal* cable television □ *verb* to telegraph by cable □ **cable television** a service transmitting television programmes to individual subscribers by underground cable

**cacao** *noun* a tree from whose seeds cocoa and chocolate are made

**cache** (*say* kash) *noun* **1** a store or hiding place for ammunition, treasure *etc* **2** things hidden ⊕ From French *cacher* meaning 'to hide'

**cackle** *noun* **1** the sound made by a hen or goose **2** a laugh which sounds like this

**cacophony** *noun* (*pl* cacophonies) an unpleasant noise □ **cacophonous** *adj* noisy and unpleasant-sounding

**cactus** *noun* (*pl* cactuses *or* cacti) a type of prickly plant

**CAD** *abbrev* computer-aided design

**cad** *noun, old* a mean, despicable person

**cadaverous** *adj* corpse-like, very pale and thin

**caddie** *noun* an assistant who carries a golfer's clubs

**caddy** *noun* (*pl* caddies) a box for keeping tea fresh

**cadence** *noun* **1** a fall of the voice, *eg* at the end of a sentence **2** a group of chords ending a piece of music

**cadenza** *noun* a musical passage at the end of a movement, concerto *etc*

**cadet** (*say* ka-det) *noun* **1** an officer trainee in the armed forces or police service **2** a school pupil who takes military training

**cadge** *verb* to beg □ **cadger** *noun*

**cadge** ⊷ cadges, cadging, cadged

**Caesarean** (*say* se-zeir-ri-an) *adj* of a birth: delivered by cutting through the walls of the mother's abdomen □ *noun* a Caesarean birth or operation

**café** *noun* a small restaurant serving coffee, tea, snacks *etc*

**cafeteria** *noun* a self-service restaurant

**caffeine** *noun* a stimulating drug found in coffee and tea

**caftan** *noun* a long-sleeved, ankle-length Middle-Eastern garment

**cage** *noun* **1** a barred enclosure for birds or animals **2** a lift used by miners □ *verb* to close up in a cage

**cage** ⊷ cages, caging, caged

**cagey** *or* **cagy** *adj* unwilling to speak freely; wary □ **caginess** *noun*

**cagoule** *noun* a lightweight anorak

**cahoots** *noun pl*: **in cahoots with** in collusion with

**cairn** *noun* **1** a heap of stones marking a grave, or on top of a mountain **2** a breed of small terrier

**cajole** *verb* to coax by flattery □ **cajolery** *noun*

**cake** *noun* **1** a baked piece of dough made from flour, eggs, sugar *etc* **2** something pressed into a lump: *cake of soap* □ *verb* to become dry and hard □ **have your cake and eat it** to enjoy both of two alternative things

**calamine** *noun* a pink powder containing a zinc salt, used to make a skin-soothing lotion

**calamity** *noun* (*pl* calamities) a great disaster, a misfortune □ **calamitous** *adj*

**calcium** *noun* a metal which forms the chief part of lime

**calculate** *verb* **1** to count, work out by mathematics **2** to think out in an exact way □ **calculable** *adj* □ **calculation** *noun* □ **calculator** *noun* a machine which makes mathematical calculations

**calculating** *adj* thinking selfishly

**calculus** *noun* a mathematical system of calculation

**calendar** *noun* a table or list showing the year divided into months, weeks and days

**calf¹** *noun* (*pl* **calves**) **1** the young of a cow or ox **2** the young of certain other mammals, *eg* an elephant or whale **3** calf's skin cured as leather

**calf²** *noun* (*pl* **calves**) the back of the lower part of the leg

**calibrate** *verb* **1** to mark the scale on (a measuring instrument) **2** to check or adjust the scale of (a measuring instrument)

**calibre** or *US* **caliber** *noun* **1** the diameter of a tube or gun **2** of a person: quality of character, ability

**calico** *noun* a patterned kind of cotton cloth

Originally *Calicut cloth*, after the port in SW India from where it was exported

**call** *verb* **1** to cry aloud **2** to name: *what is your cat called?* **3** to summon **4** to make a short visit **5** to telephone □ *noun* **1** a loud cry **2** a short visit **3** a telephone conversation □ **call off** to cancel

**calligraphy** *noun* the art of handwriting

**calling** *noun* a vocation, a job

**callipers** or **calipers** *noun* **1** *pl* an instrument like compasses, used to measure thickness **2** *sing* a splint to support the leg, made of two metal rods

**callous** *adj* cruel, hardhearted □ **callously** *adv*

◈ Do not confuse with: **callus**

**callow** *adj* not mature; inexperienced, naive □ **callowly** *adv*

**callus** *noun* (*pl* **calluses**) an area of thickened or hardened skin

◈ Do not confuse with: **callous**

**calm** *adj* **1** still or quiet **2** not anxious or flustered □ *noun* **1** absence of wind **2** quietness, peacefulness □ *verb* to make peaceful □ **calmly** *adv*

**calorie** *noun* **1** a measure of heat **2** a measure of the energy-giving value of food

**calumny** *noun* (*pl* **calumnies**) a false accusation or lie about a person

**calve** *verb* to give birth to a calf

**calypso** *noun* (*pl* **calypsos**) a West Indian improvised song

**calyx** (*say* **kal**-iks) *noun* (*pl* **calyces** - *say* **kal**-i-seez - or **calyxes**) the outer covering or cup of a flower

**CAM** *abbrev* computer-aided manufacturing

**camaraderie** *noun* comradeship, fellowship

**camber** *noun* a slight curve on a road *etc* making the middle higher than the sides

**camcorder** *noun* a hand-held device combining a video camera and video recorder

**came** *past form of* **come**

**camel** *noun* an animal native to Asia and Africa, with a humped back, used for transport

**cameo** *noun* (*pl* **cameos**) a gem or stone with a figure carved in relief

**camera¹** *noun* an instrument for taking photographs

**camera²** *noun*: **in camera** in private

Literally 'in a room', from the Latin word for 'room' or 'chamber'

**camisole** (*say* **kam**-i-sohl) *noun* a woman's undervest with thin shoulder straps

**camomile** *noun* a plant with pale

yellow flowers, used as a medicinal herb

**camouflage** (say **kam**-ouf-lahsz) noun **1** the disguising of the appearance of something to blend in with its background **2** natural protective colouring in animals □ verb to disguise by camouflage

**camp** noun **1** a group of tents, caravans etc forming a temporary settlement **2** fixed military quarters □ verb **1** to pitch tents **2** to set up a temporary home □ **camp bed** a small portable folding bed □ **campsite** noun an area set aside for pitching tents

**campaign** noun **1** organized action in support of a cause or movement **2** a planned series of battles or movements during a war □ verb **1** to organize support: campaigning against the poll tax **2** to serve in a military campaign

**camphor** noun a pungent solid oil obtained from a cinnamon tree, or a synthetic substitute for it, used to repel insects etc

**campion** noun a plant with pink or white star-shaped flowers

**campus** noun (pl **campuses**) the grounds and buildings of a university or college

**can¹** verb **1** to be able to (do something): can you sing? **2** to have permission to (do something): I asked if I could have the day off □ **can but** can only: we can but hope

**can¹** verb ⇔ present form **can**, past form **could**

Ⓔ From Old English cunnan meaning 'to know how to' or 'to be able'

**can²** noun a sealed tin container for preserving food or liquids □ verb to put into a sealed tin to preserve □ **canned music** pre-recorded bland music

**can²** verb ⇔ **cans**, **canning**, **canned**

**canal** noun an artificial waterway for boats

**canary** noun (pl **canaries**) a songbird with yellow plumage, kept as a pet

**cancan** noun a high-kicking dance performed by women

**cancel** verb **1** to put off permanently, call off: cancel all engagements for the week **2** to mark for deletion by crossing with lines □ **cancel out** to make ineffective by balancing each other

**cancel** ⇔ **cancels**, **cancelling**, **cancelled**

**cancer** noun a serious disease in which cells in the body grow rapidly into lumps which can spread and may cause death □ **cancerous** adj

**candid** adj frank, open, honest □ **candidly** adv

**candida** (say **kan**-did-a) noun an infection caused by a yeastlike fungus

**candidate** noun **1** an entrant for an examination, or competition for a job, prize etc **2** an entrant in a political election □ **candidacy** or **candidature** noun

From a Latin word meaning 'dressed in white', because of the white togas worn by electoral candidates in ancient Rome

**candied** adj cooked or coated in sugar

**candle** noun a stick of wax containing a wick, used for giving light □ **not worth the candle** not worth the effort or expense needed □ **candlestick** noun a holder for a candle

**candour** or US **candor** noun frankness, honesty

**candy** noun **1** sugar crystallized by boiling **2** US (pl **candies**) sweets, chocolate

**cane** noun **1** the woody stem of bamboo, sugar cane etc **2** a walking stick □ verb to beat with a cane □ **cane sugar** sugar extracted from sugar cane

**canine** adj of dogs □ **canine tooth** a

sharp-pointed tooth found on each side of the upper and lower jaw

**canister** *noun* a tin or other container for tea *etc*

**canker** *noun* **1** a spreading sore **2** a disease in trees, plants *etc*

✎ Do not confuse with: **chancre**

**cannabis** *noun* a narcotic drug obtained from the hemp plant

**cannibal** *noun* **1** someone who eats human flesh **2** an animal that eats its own kind □ **cannibalism** *noun* □ **cannibalistic** *adj*

**cannon** *noun* a large gun mounted on a wheel-carriage □ **cannonball** *noun* a solid metal ball shot from a cannon

✎ Do not confuse with: **canon**

**cannot** *verb* **1** used with another verb to express inability to do something: *I cannot understand this* **2** used to refuse permission: *he cannot see me today*

**canny** *adj* wise, shrewd, cautious □ **cannily** *adv*

**canoe** *noun* a light narrow boat driven by paddles

**canon** *noun* **1** a rule used as a standard to judge by **2** a member of the Anglican clergy connected with a cathedral

◉ From Greek *kanon* meaning 'a straight rod'

✎ Do not confuse with: **cannon**

**canon** *noun* another spelling of **canyon**

**canonize** *verb* to put on the list of saints □ **canonization** *noun*

**canopy** *noun* (*pl* **canopies**) a canvas or cloth covering suspended over a bed *etc*

**cant**[1] *noun* **1** the slang or vocabulary of a particular group **2** insincere talk

**cant**[2] *noun* a slope, an incline □ *verb* to tilt from a level position

**can't** *short form* of **cannot**

**cantankerous** *adj* crotchety, bad-tempered, quarrelsome

**cantata** *noun* a short piece of music for a choir

**canteen** *noun* **1** a place serving food and drink in a workplace *etc* **2** a case for storing cutlery **3** a water-flask

**canter** *verb* to move at an easy gallop □ *noun* an easy gallop

Originally *Canterbury gallop*, referring to the pace at which pilgrims rode to the town

**cantilever** *noun* a large projecting bracket used to support a balcony or staircase □ **cantilever bridge** a bridge consisting of upright piers with cantilevers extending to meet one another

**canton** *noun* a federal state in Switzerland

**canvas** *noun* (*pl* **canvases**) **1** coarse, strong cloth used for sails, tents *etc* **2** a piece of this stretched and used for painting on

**canvass** *verb* to go round asking for votes, money *etc* □ **canvasser** *noun*

**canyon** or **canon** *noun* a deep, steep-sided river valley

**cap** *noun* **1** a peaked soft hat **2** a lid, a top **3** a contraceptive diaphragm □ *verb* **1** to put a cap on **2** to set a limit to (a budget *etc*) **3** to do better than, improve on: *no-one can cap this story* **4** to select for a national sports team **5** to confer a university degree on

**cap** *verb* ⇔ **caps**, **capping**, **capped**

**capable** *adj* able to cope with difficulties without help □ **capability** *noun* (*pl* **capabilities**) □ **capable of** able or likely to achieve, produce *etc*: *capable of a better performance* □ **capably** *adv*

**capacious** *adj* roomy, wide □ **capaciously** *adv* □ **capaciousness** *noun*

**capacitor** *noun* a device for

collecting and storing electricity

**capacity** noun (pl **capacities**)
**1** power of understanding **2** ability
to do something: *capacity for
growth* **3** the amount that
something can hold **4** post,
position: *capacity as leader* □ **to
capacity** to the greatest extent
possible: *filled to capacity*

**cape¹** noun a thick shawl or covering
for the shoulders

**cape²** noun a point of land running
into the sea

**caper¹** verb to leap, dance about
□ noun **1** a leap **2** *informal* a prank,
an adventure

**caper²** noun the flower-bud of a
shrub, pickled or salted for eating

**capercaillie** or **capercailzie** (*say*
kap-*e*-**kei**-li or keip-*e*-**kei**-li) noun a
kind of large grouse

**capillary** noun (pl **capillaries**) **1** a
tiny blood vessel **2** a very fine tube
□ adj very fine, like a hair

**capital** adj **1** chief, most important
**2** punishable by death: *capital
offence* **3** *informal* excellent **4** of a
letter: written or printed in upper
case, *eg* A, B or C □ noun **1** the chief
city of a country: *Paris is the capital
of France* **2** an upper-case letter
**3** money for running a business
**4** money invested, accumulated
wealth □ **capital punishment**
punishment by death □ **make
capital out of** to turn to your
advantage

**capitalism** noun a system in which a
country's wealth is owned by
individuals, not by the State
□ **capitalist** noun someone who
supports or practises capitalism
□ **capitalistic** adj

**capitalize** verb **1** to write in capital
letters **2** to turn to your advantage
□ **capitalization** noun

**capitulate** verb to give in to an enemy
□ **capitulation** noun the act of giving
in to an enemy

**caprice** (*say* kap-**rees**) noun a
sudden, impulsive change of mind
or mood

**capricious** adj full of caprice;
impulsive, fickle □ **capriciously** adv
in a way which is characterized by
mood swings or unpredictable
behaviour

**capsize** verb to upset, overturn

**capsule** noun **1** a small gelatine case
containing a dose of medicine *etc*
**2** a dry seed-pod on a plant **3** a self-
contained, detachable part of a
spacecraft

**captain** noun **1** the commander of a
company of soldiers, a ship or an
aircraft **2** the leader of a sports
team, club *etc* □ verb to lead
□ **captaincy** noun (pl **captaincies**)

**caption** noun a heading for a
newspaper article, photograph *etc*

**captious** adj quick to find fault;
judgemental

**captivate** verb to charm, fascinate

**captive** noun a prisoner □ adj **1** taken
or kept prisoner **2** not able to get
away: *captive audience* □ **captivity**
noun **1** the state of being a prisoner
**2** the enclosure of an animal in a zoo
*etc*, not in the wild

**captor** noun someone who takes a
prisoner

**capture** verb **1** to take by force **2** to
get hold of; seize: *capture the
imagination* □ noun **1** the act of
capturing **2** something captured

**car** noun **1** a small enclosed motor
vehicle **2** *US* a train carriage □ **car
park** a place where cars *etc* may be
left for a time □ **car pool 1** a number
of cars owned by a business for use
by employees **2** an arrangement
between car owners to take turns at
driving each other to work *etc*

**carafe** (*say* ka-**raf**) noun a bottle for
serving wine, water *etc*

**caramel** noun **1** sugar melted and
browned **2** a sweet made with sugar
and butter

**carat** *noun* **1** a measure of purity for gold **2** a measure of weight for gemstones

❧ Do not confuse with: **carrot**

**caravan** *noun* **1** a covered vehicle with living accommodation drawn behind a car **2** a number of travellers *etc* crossing the desert together

**caraway** *noun* a plant with spicy seeds used in cooking

**carbohydrate** *noun* a compound of carbon, hydrogen and oxygen, *eg* sugar or starch

**carbon** *noun* an element of which charcoal is one form □ **carbon copy 1** a copy of a document made by using carbon paper **2** an exact copy □ **carbon dioxide** a gas present in the air and breathed out by humans and animals □ **carbon monoxide** a poisonous gas with no smell □ **carbon paper** paper coated with black ink, interleaved between ordinary paper when typing to produce exact copies

**carboniferous** *adj* producing or containing coal or carbon

**carbuncle** *noun* **1** a fiery-red precious stone **2** an inflamed swelling under the skin

**carburettor** or **carburetter** or *US* **carburetor** *noun* the part of a car engine which changes the petrol into vapour

**carcass** or **carcase** *noun* the dead body (of an animal)

**carcinogen** *noun* a substance that encourages the growth of cancer □ **carcinogenic** *adj* causing cancer

**carcinoma** (*say* kah-si-**noh**-ma) *noun* (*pl* **carcinomas** or **carcinomata**) a cancerous growth

**card** *noun* **1** pasteboard or very thick paper **2** an illustrated, folded square of paper sent in greeting *etc* **3** tool for combing wool *etc* **4** (**cards**) any of the many types of games played with a pack of special

cards □ *verb* to comb (wool *etc*)

**cardboard** *noun* stiff pasteboard

**cardiac** *adj* of the heart: *cardiac failure*

ⓘ From Greek *kardia* meaning 'heart'

**cardigan** *noun* a knitted woollen jacket

Named after the 19th-century Earl of *Cardigan* who advocated the use of buttonable woollen jackets

**cardinal** *adj* principal, important □ *noun* the highest rank of priest in the Roman Catholic Church □ **cardinal number** a number which expresses quantity, *eg* 1,2,3 (*contrasted with:* **ordinal number**)

**care** *noun* **1** close attention **2** worry, anxiety **3** protection, keeping: *in my care* □ *verb* to be concerned or worried: *I don't care what happens now* □ **care for 1** to look after **2** to feel affection or liking for □ **careworn** *adj* worn out by anxiety □ **care of** at the house of (often written as **c/o**) □ **take care** to be careful; watch out

**career** *noun* **1** life work; trade, profession **2** course, progress through life **3** headlong rush □ *verb* to run rapidly and wildly: *careering along the road*

**carefree** *adj* having no worries

**careful** *adj* attentive, taking care □ **carefully** *adv*

▣ cautious, circumspect, chary, vigilant, meticulous, punctilious

**careless** *adj* paying little attention; not taking care □ **carelessly** *adv*

**caress** *verb* to touch gently and lovingly □ *noun* (*pl* **caresses**) a gentle touch

**caretaker** *noun* someone who looks after a building □ *adj* in charge temporarily; interim: *caretaker government*

**carfuffle** (*say* ka-**fu**-fl) *noun*

commotion, fuss

**cargo** noun (pl **cargoes**) a ship's load

**caribou** noun the North American reindeer

**caricature** noun a picture of someone which exaggerates certain of their features □ verb to draw a caricature of □ **caricaturist** noun

**caries** (say **kei**-ri-eez) noun decay, esp of the teeth

**carmine** noun a bright red colour □ adj of this colour

**carnage** noun slaughter, killing

**carnation** noun a type of garden flower, often pink, red or white

**carnival** noun a celebration with merriment, feasting etc

**carnivore** noun a flesh-eating animal □ **carnivorous** adj

**carol** noun a hymn or song sung at Christmas □ **caroller** noun □ **carolling** noun

**carouse** verb to take part in a drinking bout □ **carousal** (say ka-**row**-zal) noun

**carousel** (say ka-rou-**sel**) noun **1** US a merry-go-round **2** a rotating conveyor belt for luggage at an airport etc

**carp**[1] noun a freshwater fish found in ponds

**carp**[2] verb to find fault with small errors; complain about nothing

**carpe diem** seize the day; make the most of the present

**carpenter** noun a worker in wood, eg for building □ **carpentry** noun

**carpet** noun the woven covering of floors, stairs etc □ verb to cover with a carpet

**carriage** noun **1** a vehicle for carrying people **2** the act or cost of carrying **3** a way of walking; bearing

**carrier** noun **1** someone who carries goods **2** a machine or container for carrying **3** someone who passes on a

disease □ **carrier pigeon** a pigeon used to carry messages

**carrion** noun rotting animal flesh

**carrot** noun a vegetable with an edible orange-coloured root

**◆◆ Do not confuse with: carat**

**carry** verb **1** to pick up and take to another place **2** to contain and take to a destination: cables carrying electricity **3** to bear, have as a mark: carry a scar **4** of a voice: to be able to be heard at a distance **5** to win, succeed: carry the day **6** to keep for sale: we don't carry cigarettes □ **carried away** overcome by emotion; overexcited □ **carry on** to continue (doing) □ **carry-on** noun a fuss, a to-do □ **carry out** to accomplish; succeed in doing □ **carry-out** noun a take-away meal or alcoholic drink □ **carry the can** to accept responsibility for an error □ **carry weight** to have force or authority

**carry** ◆ carries, carrying, carried

**cart** noun **1** a horse-drawn vehicle used for carrying loads **2** a small wheeled vehicle pushed by hand □ verb **1** to carry by cart **2** to drag, haul: carted off the stage □ **cart-horse** noun a large, heavy work-horse

**cartilage** noun a strong elastic material in the bodies of humans and animals; gristle

**cartography** noun the science of map-making □ **cartographer** noun

**carton** noun a small container made of cardboard, plastic etc

**cartoon** noun **1** a comic drawing, or strip of drawings, often with a caption **2** an animated film **3** a drawing used as the basis for a large painting etc □ **cartoonist** noun

**cartridge** noun **1** a case holding the powder and bullet fired by a gun **2** a spool of film or tape enclosed in a case **3** a tube of ink for loading a pen **4** the part of a record-player which holds the stylus

**cartwheel** noun 1 the wheel of a cart 2 a sideways somersault with hands touching the ground

**carve** verb 1 to make or shape by cutting 2 to cut up (meat) into slices

**cascade** noun 1 a waterfall 2 an abundant hanging display: *cascade of curls* □ verb to fall like or in a waterfall

**case** noun 1 a container or outer covering 2 that which happens, an occurrence 3 a statement of facts, an argument 4 state of affairs, what is true: *if that is the case* 5 a trial in a law-court: *murder case*
◉ meaning 1: from Latin *capsa* meaning 'a holder' or 'a box'; meanings 2,3,4 and 5: from Latin *casus* meaning 'a falling'

**casement** noun 1 a window-frame 2 a window that swings on hinges

**cash** noun money in the form of coins and notes □ verb to turn into, or change for, money □ **cash card** a card issued by a bank *etc* that allows the holder to use a cash dispenser □ **cash dispenser** an automatic teller machine □ **cash register** a machine for holding money that records the amount put in □ **cash in on** to profit from

**cashew** noun a kidney-shaped nut produced by a tropical tree

**cashier** noun someone who looks after the receiving and paying of money □ verb, *military* to dismiss in disgrace

**cashmere** noun fine soft goat's wool

**casino** (say ka-see-noh) noun (pl **casinos**) a building in which gambling takes place

**cask** noun a barrel containing wine *etc*

**casket** noun 1 a small box for holding jewels *etc* 2 *US* a coffin

**cassava** noun a tropical plant with roots from which tapioca is obtained

**casserole** noun 1 a covered ovenproof dish for cooking and serving food 2 food cooked in a casserole

**cassette** noun 1 a small case for film, magnetic recording tape *etc* 2 the magnetic tape itself

**cassock** noun a long robe worn by priests

**cast** verb 1 to throw, fling 2 to throw off; drop, shed 3 to shape in a mould 4 to choose (actors) for a play or film 5 to give a part to (an actor *etc*) □ noun 1 something shaped in a mould 2 plaster encasing a broken limb 3 the actors in a play 4 a small heap of earth thrown up by a worm 5 a type: *cast of mind* 6 an eye squint □ **cast down** adj depressed □ **cast off** adj used by someone else, second-hand

**cast** verb ▷ casts, casting, cast

**castanets** noun pl hollow shells of ivory or hard wood, clicked together to accompany a dance

From a Spanish word for 'chestnuts', because of their shape

**castaway** noun a deserted or shipwrecked person

**caste** noun a class or rank of people, *esp* in the Indian subcontinent

**caster** another spelling of **castor**

**caster oil** a kind of palm oil used medicinally

**castigate** verb to scold, punish □ **castigation** noun

**castle** noun a fortified house or fortress

**castor** or **caster** noun a small wheel, eg on the legs of furniture

**castor sugar** or **caster sugar** very fine granulated sugar

**castrate** verb to remove the testicles of

**casual** adj 1 happening by chance: *casual encounter* 2 not regular, temporary: *casual labour* 3 informal: *casual clothes* 4 not careful, unconcerned: *casual attitude*

**casualty** *noun* (*pl* **casualties**) **1** someone who is killed or wounded **2** a casualty department □ **casualty department** a hospital department for treating accidental injuries *etc*

**cat** *noun* **1** a sharp-clawed furry animal kept as a pet **2** an animal of a family which includes lions, tigers *etc* □ **cat burglar** a burglar who breaks into houses by climbing walls *etc* □ **cat flap** a small door set in a larger door to allow a cat entry and exit □ **cat-o'-nine-tails** *noun* a whip with nine lashes □ **cat's cradle** a children's game of creating patterns by winding string around the fingers □ **cat's-eye** *noun*, *trademark* a small mirror fixed in a road surface to reflect light at night

**cataclysm** *noun* **1** a violent change; an upheaval **2** a great flood of water

**catacombs** *noun pl* an underground burial place

**catalogue** *noun* **1** an ordered list of names, books, objects for sale *etc* □ *verb* **1** to list in order **2** to compile details of (a book) for a library catalogue

**catalyst** *noun* **1** a substance which helps or prevents a chemical reaction without itself changing **2** something that brings about a change

**catamaran** *noun* a boat with two parallel hulls

**catapult** *noun* **1** a small forked stick with a piece of elastic attached, used for firing small stones **2** *historical* a weapon for throwing heavy stones in warfare

**cataract** *noun* **1** a waterfall **2** a disease of the outer eye

**catarrh** *noun* inflammation of the lining of the nose and throat causing a discharge

**catastrophe** (*say* kat-**as**-tro-fi) *noun*

a sudden disaster □ **catastrophic** (*say* kat-as-**trof**-ik) *adj*

**catch** *verb* **1** to take hold of, capture **2** to take (a disease): *catch a cold* **3** to be in time for: *catch the last train* **4** to surprise (in an act): *caught him stealing* □ *noun* **1** a haul of fish *etc* **2** something you are lucky to have got or won **3** a hidden flaw or disadvantage: *where's the catch?* **4** a fastening: *window catch* □ **catching** *adj* infectious □ **catch on** to become popular □ **catch-phrase** or **catchword** *noun* a word or phrase which is popular for a while □ **catch-22** *noun* an absurd situation with no way out □ **catchy** *adj* of a tune: easily remembered □ **catch up on 1** to draw level with, overtake **2** to get up-to-date with (work *etc*)

**catch** *verb* ⋅> **catches**, **catching**, **caught**

**catchment area 1** an area from which a river or reservoir draws its water supply **2** an area from which the pupils in a school are drawn

**catechize** (*say* kat-e-kaiz) *verb* to ask many questions

**categorical** *adj* allowing no doubt or argument: *categorical denial* □ **categorically** *adv*

**categorize** *verb* to divide into categories

**category** *noun* (*pl* **categories**) a class or group of similar people or things

**cater** *verb* **1** to provide food **2** to supply what is required: *cater for all tastes* □ **caterer** *noun*

**caterpillar** *noun* the larva of an insect that feeds on plant leaves □ *adj* moving on rotating metal belts: *caterpillar tractor*

Based on a Latin phrase which translates as 'hairy cat'

**caterwaul** *verb* to howl or yell like a cat

**catgut** *noun* cord made from sheep's stomachs, used to make strings for violins, harps *etc*

**cathedral** *noun* **1** the church of a bishop **2** the chief church in a bishop's district

**Catherine wheel** *noun* a firework which rotates as it burns

**cathode ray tube** a device in a television set *etc*, which causes a narrow beam of electrons to strike against a screen

**Catholic** *adj* of the Roman Catholic Church

**catholic** *adj* wide, comprehensive: *a catholic taste in literature*

**catkin** *noun* a tuft of small flowers on certain trees, *eg* the willow and hazel

**cattle** *noun pl* oxen, bulls and cows, and other grass-eating animals of this family

**caucus** (*say* **kaw-**kus) *noun, US* a meeting of members of a political party to nominate candidates for election *etc*

**caught** *past form of* **catch**

**cauldron** *noun* a large pan

**cauliflower** *noun* a kind of cabbage with an edible white flower-head

**cause** *noun* **1** that which makes something happen **2** a reason for action: *cause for complaint* **3** an aim for which a group or person works □ *verb* to make happen

**causeway** *noun* a raised road over wet ground or shallow water

**caustic** *adj* **1** burning, corroding **2** bitter, severe: *caustic wit* □ **caustically** *adv*

**cauterize** *verb* to burn away flesh with a hot iron *etc* in order to make a wound heal cleanly

**caution** *noun* **1** carefulness because of potential danger: *approach with caution* **2** a warning □ *verb* to warn □ **cautionary** *adj*

**cautious** *adj* careful, showing caution

**cavalcade** *noun* a procession on horseback, in cars *etc*

**cavalier** *noun, historical* a supporter of the king in the English Civil War of the 17th century □ *adj* offhand, careless: *cavalier fashion*

**cavalry** *noun* soldiers mounted on horses

**cave** *noun* a hollow place in the earth or in rock □ **cave in** to fall or collapse inwards □ **caveman, cavewoman** *noun* a prehistoric cave-dweller

**caveat** (*say* kav-i-at) *noun* a warning

**cavern** *noun* a deep hollow place in the earth □ **cavernous** *adj* **1** huge and hollow **2** full of caverns

**caviare** or **caviar** *noun* the pickled eggs of the sturgeon

**cavil** *verb* to make objections over small, unimportant details

**cavil** ➤ cavils, cavilling, cavilled

**cavity** *noun* (*pl* **cavities**) **1** a hollow place, a hole **2** a decayed hollow in a tooth

**cavort** *verb* to dance or leap around

**caw** *verb* to call like a crow □ *noun* a crow's call

**cc** *abbrev* cubic centimetre(s)

**CD** *abbrev* compact disc

**CD-I** *abbrev* compact disc interactive

**CD-R** *abbrev* compact disc recordable

**CD-ROM** *abbrev* compact disc read-only memory

**cease** *verb* to come or bring to an end

**ceasefire** *noun* **1** an order to stop firing weapons **2** an agreed, although maybe temporary, end to active hostilities

**ceaseless** *adj* without stopping

**cedar** *noun* a large evergreen tree with a hard sweet-smelling wood

**cede** *verb* to yield, give up

**ceilidh** (*say* **kei-**li) *noun* an event involving traditional Scottish dancing, sometimes combined with musical performances

**ceiling** noun 1 the inner roof of a room 2 an upper limit

**celandine** noun a small yellow wild-flower

**celebrate** verb to commemorate an event (eg a birthday or marriage) by going out, having a party etc □ **celebrated** adj famous □ **celebration** noun

**celebrity** noun (pl **celebrities**) 1 a famous person, a star 2 fame

**celery** noun a type of vegetable with edible fibrous stalks

**celestial** adj 1 of the sky: celestial bodies (= stars and planets) 2 heavenly

**celibate** adj abstaining from sexual intercourse □ **celibacy** noun

**cell** noun 1 a small room in a prison, monastery etc 2 the smallest, fundamental part of living things 3 the part of an electric battery containing electrodes

**cellar** noun an underground room used for storing coal, wine etc

**cello** (say chel-oh) noun (short for **violoncello**) a large stringed musical instrument, similar in shape to a violin □ **cellist** noun

**cellophane** noun, trademark a thin transparent wrapping material

**cellphone** noun a pocket telephone for use in a cellular radio system based on a network of transmitters

**cellular** adj made of or having cells

**celluloid** noun a very hard elastic substance used for making photographic film etc

**cellulose** noun a substance found in plants and wood used to make paper, textiles etc

**Celsius** (say sel-si-us) adj 1 of a temperature scale: consisting of a hundred degrees, on which water freezes at 0° and boils at 100° 2 of a degree: measured on this scale: 10° Celsius

**cement** noun 1 the mixture of clay and lime used to secure bricks in a wall 2 something used to make two things stick together □ verb 1 to put together with cement 2 to join firmly, fix: cemented their friendship

**cemetery** noun (pl **cemeteries**) a place where the dead are buried

**cenotaph** noun a monument to someone or a group buried elsewhere

**censer** noun a container for burning incense in a church
ⓘ From Latin incens-, a form of incendere meaning 'to burn'

◑ Do not confuse: **censer**, **censor** and **censure**

**censor** noun someone whose job is to examine books, films etc with power to delete any of the contents □ verb to examine (books etc) in this way
ⓘ From Latin censor

◑ Do not confuse: **censor**, **censer** and **censure**

**censorious** adj fault-finding; judgemental

**censure** noun blame, expression of disapproval □ verb to blame, criticize
ⓘ From Latin censura meaning 'censorship'

◑ Do not confuse: **censure**, **censer** and **censor**

**census** noun (pl **censuses**) a periodical official count of the people who live in a country
ⓘ From Latin census meaning 'a register'

◑ Do not confuse with: **consensus**

**cent** noun a coin which is the hundredth part of a larger coin, eg of a US dollar
ⓘ From Latin centum meaning 'a hundred'

**centaur** noun a mythological creature, half man and half horse

**centenary** noun (pl **centenaries**) a hundredth anniversary; the hundredth year since an event took place □ **centenarian** *noun* someone a hundred or more years old □ **centennial** *adj* **1** having lasted a hundred years **2** happening every hundred years □ *noun* a centenary

**centi-** or **cent-** *prefix* hundred; a hundredth part of
ⓖ From Latin *centum* meaning 'a hundred'

**centigrade** *adj* **1** of a temperature scale: consisting of a hundred degrees **2** measured on this scale: *5° centigrade* **3** Celsius

**centilitre** *noun* a hundredth part of a litre

**centimetre** *noun* a hundredth part of a metre

**centipede** *noun* a small crawling insect with many legs

**central** *adj* **1** belonging to the centre **2** chief, main: *central point of the argument* □ **central heating** heating of a building by water, steam or air from a central point □ **central locking** a system whereby all the doors of a vehicle are locked by the locking of the driver's door

**centralize** *verb* to bring (government authority) under one central control □ **centralization** *noun*

**centre** or *US* **center** *noun* **1** the middle point or part **2** a building used for some special activity: *sports centre / shopping centre* □ *verb* to put in the centre

**centre** *verb* ⇔ centres, centr**ing**, centr**ed**

**centrifugal** *adj* moving away from the centre

**centurion** *historical* a commander of 100 Roman soldiers

**century** *noun* (*pl* **centuries**) **1** a hundred years **2** *cricket* a hundred runs

**ceramic** *adj* **1** made of pottery **2** of pottery-making □ *noun* **1** something made of pottery **2** (**ceramics**) the art of pottery

**cereal** *noun* **1** grain used as food **2** a breakfast food prepared from grain

**cerebral** *adj* of the brain

**ceremonial** *adj* with or of ceremony □ **ceremonially** *adv*

**ceremonious** *adj* full of ceremony □ **ceremoniously** *adv*

**ceremony** *noun* (*pl* **ceremonies**) the formal acts that accompany an important event: *marriage ceremony*

**certain** *adj* **1** sure; not to be doubted **2** fixed, settled **3** particular but unnamed: *a certain look* □ **certainly** *adv* definitely, without any doubt **2** of course □ **certainty** *noun* **1** a sure thing **2** the quality of being certain

**certificate** *noun* a written or printed statement giving details of a birth, passed examination *etc*

**certify** *verb* to put down in writing as an official promise or statement *etc*

**certify** *verb* ⇔ certif**ies**, certif**ying**, certif**ied**

**cervical** *adj* of the cervix □ **cervical smear** a collection of a sample of cells from the cervix for examination under a microscope

**cervix** *noun* the neck of the womb

**cessation** *noun* a ceasing or stopping; an ending

**cesspool** *noun* a pool or tank for storing liquid waste or sewage

**cf** *abbrev* compare (from Latin *confer*)

**CFC** *abbrev* chlorofluorocarbon

**chafe** *verb* **1** to make hot or sore by rubbing **2** to wear away by rubbing **3** to become annoyed

**chaff** *noun* **1** husks of corn left after threshing **2** something of little value **3** good-natured teasing □ *verb* to tease jokingly

**chaffinch** *noun* (*pl* **chaffinches**) a small songbird of the finch family

**chagrin** (*say* sha-grin or sha-green) *noun* annoyance, irritation

**chain** *noun* **1** a number of metal links or rings passing through one another **2** (**chains**) these used to tie a prisoner's limbs; fetters **3** a number of connected things: *mountain chain* **4** a group of shops owned by one person or company **5** a number of atoms of an element joined together □ *verb* to fasten or imprison with a chain □ **chain letter** a letter containing promises or threats, requesting the recipient to send a similar letter to several other people □ **chain mail** armour made of iron links □ **chain reaction** a chemical process in which each reaction in turn causes a similar reaction □ **chain saw** a power-driven saw with teeth on a rotating chain □ **chain-smoker** *noun* someone who smokes continuously □ **chain-store** *noun* one of several shops under the same ownership

**chair** *noun* **1** a seat for one person with a back to it **2** a university professorship **3** a chairman or chairwoman □ **chairlift** *noun* a row of chairs on a rotating cable for carrying people up mountains *etc* □ **chairman**, **chairwoman** or **chairperson** *noun* someone who presides at or is in charge of a meeting

It is possible to use chairman when referring to a woman (*eg Madam Chairman*). However, it is more 'politically correct' to use chairman for a man and chairwoman for a woman.

**chalet** (*say* shal-ei) *noun* **1** a small wooden house used by holiday-makers **2** a summer hut used by Swiss herdsmen in the Alps

**chalice** *noun* a cup for wine, used *eg* in church services

**chalk** *noun* **1** a type of limestone **2** a compressed stick of coloured powder used for writing or drawing □ *verb* to mark with chalk □ **chalky** *adj* **1** of chalk **2** white, pale

**challenge** *verb* **1** to question another's right to do something **2** to ask (someone) to take part in a contest, *eg* to settle a quarrel □ *noun* **1** a questioning of another's right **2** a call to a contest □ **challenger** *noun* □ **challenging** *adj* interesting but difficult

**chamber** *noun* **1** a room **2** a place where a parliament meets **3** a room where legal cases are heard by a judge **4** an enclosed space or cavity **5** the part of a gun that holds the cartridges □ **chamber music** music for a small group of players, suitable for performance in a room rather than a large hall

**chamberlain** *noun* an officer appointed by the crown or a local authority to carry out certain duties

**chamberpot** *noun* a receptacle for urine *etc*, used in the bedroom

**chameleon** (*say* ka-meel-yon) *noun* a small lizard able to change its colour to match its surroundings

**chamois** *noun* **1** (*say* sham-wah) a goat-like deer living in mountainous country **2** (*say* sham-i) (*also spelt* **shammy**) a soft kind of leather made from its skin

**champ** *verb* to chew noisily □ **champing at the bit** impatient to act

**champagne** (*say* sham-pein) *noun* a type of white sparkling wine

**champion** *noun* **1** someone who has beaten all others in a competition **2** a strong supporter of a cause: *champion of free speech* □ *verb* to support the cause of □ **championship** *noun* **1** the act of championing **2** a contest to find a champion **3** the title of champion

**chance** *noun* **1** a risk, a possibility **2** something unexpected or unplanned **3** an opportunity □ *verb* **1** to risk **2** to happen by accident □ *adj* happening by accident □ **by chance** not by arrangement, unexpectedly □ **chance upon** to meet or find unexpectedly

**chancel** *noun* the part of a church near the altar

**chancellor** *noun* **1** a high-ranking government minister **2** the head of a university □ **Chancellor of the Exchequer** the minister in the British cabinet in charge of government spending

**chancre** (*say* shang-ker) *noun* a small lump occurring in the early stages of syphilis

◐ Do not confuse with: **canker**

**chancy** *adj* risky

**chandelier** (*say* shan-de-leer) *noun* a fixture hanging from the ceiling with branches for holding lights

**change** *verb* **1** to make or become different **2** to give up or leave (a job, house *etc*) for another **3** to put on different clothes **4** to give (money of one kind) in exchange for (money of another kind) □ *noun* **1** the act of making or becoming different **2** another set of clothing **3** money in the form of coins **4** money returned when a buyer gives more than the price of an article □ **change of life** the menopause

**change** *verb* ⇌ changes, changing, changed

**changeable** *adj* likely to change; often changing

**changeling** *noun* in stories: a fairy child secretly left in place of a human one

**channel** *noun* **1** the bed of a stream **2** a passage for ships **3** a narrow sea **4** a groove; a gutter **5** a band of frequencies for radio or television signals □ *verb* to direct into a particular course

**channel** *verb* ⇌ channels, channelling, channelled

**chant** *verb* to recite in a singing manner □ *noun* a singing recitation

**chaos** (*say* kei-os) *noun* disorder,

confusion □ **chaotic** *adj* □ **chaotically** *adv*

**chap** *noun*, *informal* a man

**chapati** *noun* a round of unleavened Indian bread

**chapel** *noun* **1** a small church **2** a small part of a larger church

**chaperone** *noun* a woman who attends a younger one when she goes out in public □ *verb* to act as a chaperone to

**chaplain** *noun* a member of the clergy accompanying an army, navy *etc*

**chapped** *adj* of skin: cracked by cold or wet weather

**chapter** *noun* **1** a division of a book **2** a branch of a society or organization □ **chapter of accidents** a series of accidents

**char¹** *verb* to burn until black

**char** *verb* ⇌ chars, charring, charred

**char²** *verb* to do odd jobs of housework, cleaning *etc* □ *noun*, *informal* a charwoman

**character** *noun* **1** the nature and qualities of someone **2** the good and bad points which make up a person's nature **3** self-control, firmness **4** someone noted for eccentric behaviour **5** someone in a play, story or film

**characteristic** *noun* a typical and noticeable feature of someone or something □ *adj* typical □ **characteristically** *adv* typically, as always

**characterize** *verb* **1** to be typical of **2** to describe (as) □ **characterization** *noun* the creation and development of the different characters in a book, story or piece of drama

**charade** (*say* sha-rahd *or* sha-reid) *noun* **1** a ridiculous pretence **2** (**charades**) a game in which players have to guess a word from gestures representing its sound or meaning

**charcoal** *noun* wood burnt black, used for fuel or sketching

**charge** *verb* **1** to accuse (someone) of a crime **2** to ask (a price) **3** to ask to do; give responsibility for **4** to load (a gun) **5** to attack in a rush □ *noun* **1** accusation for a crime **2** a price, a fee **3** an attack **4** the gunpowder in a shell or bullet **5** care, responsibility **6** someone looked after by another person □ **in charge** in command or control □ **take charge of** to take command of

**charge** *verb* ⬥ charges, charg*ing*, charged

**charger** *noun* a horse used in battle

**chariot** *noun*, *historical* a wheeled carriage used in battle □ **charioteer** *noun*

**charisma** (*say* ka-**riz**-ma) *noun* a personal quality that impresses others □ **charismatic** *adj*

**charitable** *adj* **1** giving to the poor; kindly **2** of a charity: *charitable status* □ **charitably** *adv*

**charity** *noun* (*pl* **charities**) **1** donation of money to the poor *etc* **2** an organization which collects money and gives it to those in need **3** kindness, humanity

**charlatan** (*say* **shah**-lat-*a*n) *noun* someone who claims to have more knowledge or ability than they really have

**charm** *noun* **1** something thought to have magical powers **2** a magical spell **3** personal power to attract □ *verb* **1** to please greatly, delight **2** to put under a spell □ **charming** *adj* lovely, delightful

**chart** *noun* **1** a table or diagram giving particular information: *temperature chart* **2** a geographical map of the sea **3** a rough map □ *verb* to make into a chart; plot

**charter** *noun* a written paper showing the official granting of rights, lands *etc* □ *verb* to hire (a boat, aeroplane *etc*) □ *adj* hired for a special purpose: *charter flight* □ **chartered** *adj* **1** qualified under the regulations of a professional body: *chartered surveyor* **2** hired for a purpose

**charwoman** *noun* a woman hired to do domestic cleaning *etc*

**chary** *adj* cautious, careful (of)

**chase** *verb* **1** to run after, pursue **2** to hunt □ *noun* **1** a pursuit, a hunt

**chasm** (*say* ka-zm) *noun* **1** a steep drop between high rocks *etc* **2** a wide difference; a gulf

**chassis** (*say* **shas**-i) *noun* (*pl* **chassis** – *say* **shas**-iz) **1** the frame, wheels and machinery of a car **2** an aeroplane's landing carriage

**chaste** *adj* **1** pure, virtuous **2** virgin □ **chastely** *adv* □ **chastity** *noun* virginity

**chasten** *verb* **1** to make humble **2** to scold □ **chastened** *adj* humble or sorry, as a result of receiving a scolding

**chastise** *verb* to punish, *esp* by beating □ **chastisement** *noun*

**chat** *verb* talk in an easy, friendly way □ *noun* a friendly conversation □ **chat-show** *noun* a radio or TV programme in which personalities talk informally with their host

**chat** *verb* ⬥ chats, chat*ting*, chatted

**chateau** (*say* **shat**-oh) *noun* (*pl* **chateaux** – *say* **shat**-ohz) a French castle or country house

**chattels** *noun pl* movable possessions □ **goods and chattels** personal possessions

**chatter** *verb* **1** to talk idly or rapidly; gossip **2** of teeth: to rattle together because of cold □ **chatterbox** *noun* someone who talks a great deal

**chatty** *adj* willing to talk, talkative

**chauffeur** (*say* **shoh**-fer) *noun* someone employed to drive a car

**chauvinist** *noun* **1** a man who practises sexism towards women

□ **chauvinism** *noun* extreme nationalism or patriotism
□ **chauvinistic** *adj*

After Nicholas *Chauvin*, Napoleonic French soldier and keen patriot

**cheap** *adj* **1** low in price, inexpensive **2** of little value, worthless □ **cheapen** *verb* □ **cheaply** *adv*

■ (meaning 1) reasonable, bargain, economical; (meaning 2) tawdry, shoddy, inferior

**cheat** *verb* **1** to deceive **2** to act dishonestly to gain an advantage □ *noun* **1** someone who cheats **2** a dishonest trick

**check** *verb* **1** to bring to a stop **2** to hold back, restrain **3** to see if (a total *etc*) is correct or accurate **4** to see if (a machine *etc*) is in good condition or working properly □ *noun* **1** a sudden stop **2** a restraint **3** a test of correctness or accuracy **4** a square, *eg* on a draughtboard **5** a pattern of squares □ **checked** *adj* patterned with squares □ **check in** or **check out** to record your arrival at or departure from (a hotel *etc*)

◐. Do not confuse with: **cheque**

**checkered** *another spelling of* **chequered**

**checkers** *another spelling of* **chequers**

**checkmate** *noun*, *chess* a position from which the king cannot escape

**checkout** *noun* a place where payment is made in a supermarket

**cheek** *noun* **1** the side of the face below the eye **2** a buttock **3** insolence, disrespectful behaviour

**cheeky** *adj* impudent, insolent □ **cheekily** *adv*

**cheep** *verb* to make a faint sound like a small bird □ *noun* the sound of a small bird

**cheer** *noun* a shout of approval or welcome □ *verb* **1** to shout approval **2** to encourage, urge on **3** to comfort, gladden □ **cheerless** *adj*

sad, gloomy □ **cheer up** to make or become less gloomy

**cheerful** *adj* happy, in good spirits □ **cheerfully** *adv*

**cheerio** *exclamation* goodbye

**cheers** *exclamation* **1** good health! **2** regards, best wishes

**cheery** *adj* lively and merry

**cheese** *noun* a solid food made from milk □ **cheesecloth** *noun* loosely-woven cotton cloth

**cheesy** *adj* **1** tasting of cheese **2** of a smile: broad

**cheetah** *noun* a fast-running animal similar to a leopard

**chef** *noun* a head cook in a restaurant

**chef d'oeuvre** a masterpiece; a life's work

**chemical** *adj* relating to the reactions between elements *etc* □ *noun* a substance formed by or used in a chemical process

**chemist** *noun* **1** someone who studies chemistry **2** someone who makes up and sells medicines; a pharmacist

**chemistry** *noun* the study of the elements and the ways they combine or react with each other

**chemotherapy** (*say* keem-oh-the-rap-i) *noun* treatment of infectious diseases or cancer using chemical compounds

**cheque** or *US* **check** *noun* a written order to a banker to pay money from a bank account to another person □ **cheque book** a book containing cheques

◐. Do not confuse with: **check**

**chequered** or **checkered** *adj* **1** marked like a chessboard **2** partly good, partly bad: *a chequered career*

**chequers** or **checkers** *noun pl* **1** a pattern of squares, *eg* on a chessboard **2** the game of draughts

**cherish** *verb* **1** to protect and treat with fondness or kindness **2** to keep in your mind or heart: *cherish a* *memory*

**cherry** *noun* (*pl* **cherries**) **1** a small bright-red fruit with a stone **2** the tree that produces this fruit

**cherub** *noun* (*pl* **cherubs** or **cherubim**) **1** an angel with a plump, childish face and body **2** a beautiful child

**chess** *noun* a game for two players in which pieces are moved in turn on a board marked in alternate black and white squares □ **chessboard** *noun* □ **chessman** or **chesspiece** *noun*

**chest** *noun* **1** a large strong box **2** the part of the body between the neck and the stomach □ **chest of drawers** a piece of furniture fitted with a set of drawers

**chesterfield** *noun* a kind of sofa

**chestnut** *noun* **1** a reddish-brown edible nut (= **sweet chestnut**), or the tree that produces it **2** a reddish-brown inedible nut (= **horse-chestnut**), or the tree that produces it **3** a reddish-brown horse **4** an old joke

**chevron** *noun* a V-shape, *eg* on a badge or road-sign

**chew** *verb* **1** to break up (food) with the teeth before swallowing **2** to reflect or ponder (on)

**chic** (*say* sheek) *adj* smart and fashionable □ *noun* style, fashionable elegance

**chicanery** (*say* shik-**ein**-*e*-ri) *noun* dishonest cleverness

**chick** *noun* **1** a chicken **2** *slang* a girl, a young woman

**chicken** *noun* **1** the young of birds, *esp* of domestic poultry **2** *informal* a coward □ *adj*, *informal* cowardly □ **chicken-feed** *noun* **1** food for poultry **2** something paltry or worthless □ **chicken-hearted** *adj* cowardly

**chickenpox** *noun* an infectious disease which causes red, itchy spots

**chickpea** *noun* a plant of the pea family with a brown edible seed

**chicory** *noun* **1** a plant with sharp-tasting leaves eaten in salads **2** its root, roasted and ground to mix with coffee

**chide** *verb* to scold with words

**chief** *adj* **1** main, most important **2** largest □ *noun* **1** a leader or ruler **2** the head of a department, organization *etc* □ **chiefly** *adv*

**chieftain** *noun* the head of a clan or tribe

**chiffon** *noun* a thin flimsy material made of silk or nylon

**chihuahua** (*say* chi-**wah**-wah) *noun* a breed of very small dog, originally from Mexico

**chilblain** *noun* a painful swelling on hands and feet, caused by cold weather

**child** *noun* (*pl* **children**) **1** a young human being **2** a son or daughter □ **childhood** *noun* the time of being a child □ **childlike** *adj* innocent ⊚ From Old English *cild*

**childish** *adj* **1** of or like a child **2** silly, immature □ **childishly** *adv*

**chile** *noun* another spelling of **chilli**

**chill** *noun* **1** coldness **2** an illness that causes fever and shivering **3** lack of warmth or enthusiasm □ *adj* cold □ *verb* **1** to make cold **2** to refrigerate □ **chilly** *adj* cold

**chilli** or **chile** *noun* **1** the hot-tasting pod of a kind of pepper, sometimes dried for cooking **2** a dish or sauce made with this

**chime** *noun* **1** the sound of bells ringing **2chimes** a set of bells, *eg* in a clock □ *verb* **1** to ring **2** of a clock: to strike

**chimney** *noun* (*pl* **chimneys**) a passage allowing smoke or heated air to escape from a fire □ **chimneypot** *noun* a metal or earthenware pipe placed at the top of a chimney □ **chimneystack** *noun*

**1** a tall chimney, *eg* in a factory **2** a number of chimneys built up together □ **chimneysweep** *noun* someone employed to clean chimneys

**chimpanzee** *noun* a type of African ape

**chin** *noun* the part of the face below the mouth

**china** *noun* **1** fine kind of earthenware; porcelain **2** articles made of this

**chink** *noun* **1** a narrow opening **2** the sound of coins *etc* striking together

**chintz** *noun* (*pl* **chintzes**) a cotton cloth with brightly coloured patterning

From a Hindi word for painted or multicoloured cotton

**chip** *verb* to break or cut small pieces (from or off) □ *noun* **1** a small piece chipped off **2** a part damaged by chipping **3** a long thin piece of fried potato **4** *US* a potato or corn crisp

**chip** *verb* ⋄ chips, chipp*ing*, chipp*ed*

**chipmunk** *noun* a kind of N American squirrel

**chipolata** *noun* a type of small sausage

**chiropodist** *noun* someone who treats minor disorders and diseases of the feet □ **chiropody** *noun*

**chirp** or **chirrup** *verb* of a bird: make a sharp, shrill sound

**chirpy** *adj* merry, cheerful

**chisel** *noun* a metal tool to cut or hollow out wood, stone *etc* □ *verb* to cut with a chisel

**chisel** *verb* ⋄ chisels, chisel*ling*, chisel*led*

**chit** *noun* **1** a short note **2** a child, a young woman: *chit of a girl*

**chit-chat** *noun* gossip, talk □ *verb* to gossip, talk

**chivalry** (*say* **shiv**-*al*-ri) *noun* **1** kindness, *esp* towards women or the weak **2** *historical* the standard of behaviour expected of knights in medieval times □ **chivalrous** *adj*

**chives** *noun* an onion-like herb used in cooking

**chlamydia** *noun* a sexually transmitted disease that can cause infertility in women

**chlorine** *noun* a yellowish-green gas with a sharp smell, used as a bleach and disinfectant □ **chlorinated** *adj* mixed with chlorine or a substance containing chlorine

**chloroform** *noun* a liquid whose vapour causes unconsciousness if inhaled

**chock-a-block** *adj* completely full or congested

**chockfull** *adj* completely full

**chocolate** *noun* **1** a sweet made from the seeds of the cacao tree **2** a drink made from these seeds (*also called* **cocoa**) □ *adj* dark brown in colour □ **chocolatey** *adj* tasting of chocolate

**choice** *noun* **1** the act or power of choosing **2** something chosen □ *adj* of a high quality: *choice vegetables*

**choir** *noun* **1** a group or society of singers **2** a part of a church where a choir sits

⊚ From Latin *chorus* meaning 'a band of singers and dancers'

❧ Do not confuse with: **quire**

**choke** *verb* **1** to stop or partly stop the breathing of **2** to block or clog (a pipe *etc*) **3** to have your breathing stopped or interrupted, *eg* by smoke □ *noun* a valve in a petrol engine which controls the inflow of air

**cholera** (*say* **kol**-*e*-ra) *noun* an infectious intestinal disease, causing severe vomiting and diarrhoea

**cholesterol** *noun* a substance found in body cells which carries fats through the bloodstream

**chomp** *verb*, *informal* to munch noisily

**choose** *verb* **1** to select and take

from two or several things **2** to decide, prefer to: *we chose to leave before the film began*

**choose** ⇢ **choose**s, **choos**ing, **chose**, **chosen**

▣ (meaning 1) select, designate, adopt; (meaning 2) opt, elect

**chop** *verb* **1** to cut into small pieces **2** to cut with a sudden blow ▫ *noun* **1** a chopping blow **2** a slice of meat containing a bone: *mutton chop* ▫ **chop and change** to keep changing

**chop** *verb* ⇢ **chop**s, **chop**ping, **chop**ped

**chopper** *noun* **1** a knife or axe for chopping **2** *informal* a helicopter

**choppy** *adj* of the sea: not calm, having small waves

**chopsticks** *noun pl* a pair of small sticks of wood, ivory *etc* used instead of a knife and fork for eating Chinese food

**choral** *adj* sung by or written for a choir

**chord¹** *noun* a musical sound made by playing several notes together ⓘ From the word *accord*

**chord²** *noun* a straight line joining any two points on a curve ⓘ From Greek *chorde* meaning 'a string'

◖ Do not confuse with: **cord**

**chore** *noun* **1** a dull, boring job **2** (**chores**) housework

**choreography** *noun* the arrangement of dancing and dance steps ▫ **choreographer** *noun*

**chorister** *noun* a member of a choir

**chortle** *verb* to laugh, chuckle

**chorus** *noun* (*pl* **choruses**) **1** a band of singers and dancers **2** a choir or choral group **3** a part of a song repeated after each verse

**chose** *past form of* **choose**

**chosen** *past participle of* **choose**

**christen** *verb* to baptize and give a

name to ▫ **christening** *noun* the ceremony of baptism

**Christian** *noun* a believer in Christianity ▫ *adj* of Christianity ▫ **Christian name** a first or personal name ▫ **Christianity** *noun* the religion which follows the teachings of Christ

**Christmas** *noun* an annual Christian holiday or festival, in memory of the birth of Christ, held on 25 December ▫ **Christmassy** *adj* typical of, or suitable for Christmas ▫ **Christmas Eve** 24 December ▫ **Christmas tree** an evergreen tree hung with lights, decorations and gifts at Christmas

**chromatic** *adj* **1** of colours **2** coloured **3** *music* of or written in a scale in which each note is separated from the next by a semitone

**chromium** *noun* a metal which does not rust

**chromosome** *noun* a rod-like part of a body cell that determines the characteristics of an individual

**chronic** *adj* **1** of a disease: long-term and progressing slowly **2** *informal* very bad ▫ **chronically** *adv*: *chronically ill*

▣ (meaning 1) acute

**chronicle** *noun* a record of events in order of time ▫ *verb* to write down events in order ▫ **chronicler** *noun*

**chronological** *adj* arranged in the order of the time of happening ▫ **chronologically** *adv*

**chronometer** *noun* an instrument for measuring time

**chrysalis** *noun* an insect (*esp* a butterfly or moth) in its early stage of life, with no wings and encased in a soft cocoon

**chrysanthemum** *noun* a type of garden flower with a large bushy head

**chubby** *adj* plump

**chubby** ⇢ **chubb**ier, **chubb**iest

**chuck** *verb* 1 to throw, toss 2 to pat gently under the chin □ **chuck out** *informal* 1 to throw away, get rid of 2 to expel

**chuckle** *noun* a quiet laugh □ *verb* to laugh quietly

**chuffed** *adj, informal* very pleased

**chum** *informal* a close friend □ **chummy** *adj*

**chump** *noun*: **off your chump** *informal* off your head; mad

**chunk** *noun* a thick piece □ **chunky** *adj*

**church** *noun* (*pl* **churches**) 1 a building for public, *esp* Christian, worship 2 any group of people who meet together for worship □ **churchyard** *noun* a burial ground next to a church

**churlish** *adj* bad-mannered, rude

**churn** *noun* a machine for making butter from milk □ *verb* 1 to make (butter) in a churn 2 to shake or stir about violently

**chute** (*say* shoot) *noun* 1 a sloping trough for sending water, parcels *etc* to a lower level 2 a sloping structure for children to slide down, with steps for climbing back up

**chutney** *noun* (*pl* **chutneys**) a sauce made with vegetables or fruits and vinegar

**CIA** *abbrev* Central Intelligence Agency (in the USA)

**CID** *abbrev* Criminal Investigation Department

**cider** *noun* an alcoholic drink made from fermented apple-juice

**cigar** *noun* a roll of tobacco leaves for smoking

**cigarette** *noun* a tube of fine tobacco enclosed in thin paper

**cinder** *noun* a burnt-out piece of coal

**cinema** *noun* 1 a place where films are shown 2 films as an art form or industry

**cinnamon** *noun* a yellowish-brown spice obtained from tree bark

**cipher** *noun* 1 a secret writing, a code 2 nought, zero 3 someone of no importance

**circa** *prep* about (in dates): *circa 300 BC*

**circle** *noun* 1 a figure formed from an endless curved line 2 something in the form of a circle; a ring 3 a society or group of people 4 a tier of seats in a theatre *etc* □ *verb* 1 to enclose in a circle 2 to move round in a circle

**circuit** *noun* 1 a movement in a circle 2 a connected group of places, events *etc*: *the American tennis circuit* 3 the path of an electric current

**circuitous** *adj* not direct, roundabout

**circular** *adj* round, like a circle □ *noun* a letter sent round to a number of people

**circulate** *verb* 1 to move round 2 to send round: *circulate a memo*

**circulation** *noun* 1 the act of circulating 2 the movement of the blood 3 the total sales of a newspaper or magazine

**circum-** *prefix* round: *circumnavigate*
  ⊚ From Latin *circum* meaning 'all around'

**circumference** *noun* 1 the outside line of a circle 2 the length of this line

**circumlocution** *noun* a roundabout way of saying something

**circumnavigate** *verb* to sail or fly right round something □ **circumnavigator** *noun*

**circumscribe** *verb* 1 to draw a line round 2 to put limits on, restrict □ **circumscription** *noun*

**circumspect** *adj* wary, cautious □ **circumspection** *noun* caution

**circumstance** *noun* 1 a condition of time, place *etc* which affects someone, an action or an event

**2 (circumstances)** the state of someone's financial affairs

**circumstantial** *adj* of evidence: pointing to a conclusion without giving absolute proof

**circumstantiate** *verb* to prove by giving details

**circumvent** *verb* **1** to get round (a difficulty) **2** to outwit □ **circumvention** *noun*

**circus** *noun* (*pl* **circuses**) **1** a travelling company of acrobats, clowns *etc* **2** a large sports arena

**cirrhosis** *noun* a disease of the liver

**cirrus** *noun* a fleecy kind of cloud

**cissy** *noun*, *informal* an effeminate person

**cistern** *noun* a tank for storing water

**citadel** *noun* a fortress within a city

**cite** *verb* **1** to quote as an example or as proof **2** to summon to appear in court □ **citation** *noun*
ⓘ From Latin *citare* meaning 'to call'

◑ Do not confuse with: **sight** and **site**

**citizen** *noun* someone who lives in a city or state □ **citizenry** *noun pl* the inhabitants of a city or state □ **citizenship** *noun* the rights or state of being a citizen

**citric acid** a sharp-tasting acid found in citrus fruits

**citrus fruit** one of a group of fruits including the orange, lemon and lime

**city** *noun* (*pl* **cities**) **1** a large town **2** a town with a cathedral □ **the City** *Brit* the part of London regarded as the centre of business

**civic** *adj* relating to a city or citizens □ **civics** *noun sing* the study of people's duties as citizens

**civil** *adj* **1** relating to a community **2** non-military, civilian **3** polite □ **civil engineer** an engineer who plans bridges, roads *etc* □ **civil law** law concerned with citizens' rights,

not criminal acts □ **civil list** the expenses of the royal household □ **civil marriage** a marriage which does not take place in church □ **civil rights** the rights of a citizen □ **civil service** the paid administrative officials of the country, excluding the armed forces □ **civil war** war between citizens of the same country

**civilian** *noun* someone who is not in the armed forces □ *adj* non-military

**civility** *noun* politeness, good manners

**civilization** *noun* **1** making or becoming civilized **2** life under a civilized system **3** a particular culture: *a prehistoric civilization*

**civilize** *verb* to bring (a people) under a regular system of laws, education *etc* □ **civilized** *adj* living under a system of laws, education *etc*; not savage

**clad** *adj*, *formal* clothed: *clad in leather*

**claim** *verb* **1** to demand as a right **2** to state as a truth; assert (that) □ *noun* an act of claiming

**claimant** *noun* someone who makes a claim

**clairvoyant** *adj* able to see into the future, or to contact the spirit world □ *noun* someone with clairvoyant powers □ **clairvoyance** *noun*

**clam** *noun* a large shellfish with two shells hinged together

**clamber** *verb* to climb awkwardly or with difficulty

**clammy** *adj* moist and sticky

**clamorous** *adj* noisy

**clamour** *noun* a loud, continuous noise or outcry □ *verb* **1** to cry aloud **2** to make a loud demand (for)

**clamp** *noun* a piece of metal, wood *etc* used to fasten things together □ *verb* to bind with a clamp □ **clamp down on** to suppress firmly

**clan** *noun* **1** a number of families with the same surname, traditionally under a single chieftain **2** a sect, a clique

From Scottish Gaelic *clann* meaning 'children'

**clandestine** *adj* hidden, secret, underhand

**clang** *verb* to make a loud, deep ringing sound □ *noun* a loud, deep ring

**clank** *noun* a sound like that made by metal hitting metal □ *verb* to make this sound

**clansman, clanswoman** *noun* a member of a clan

**clap** *noun* **1** the noise made by striking together two things, *esp* the hands **2** a burst of sound, *esp* thunder □ *verb* **1** to strike noisily together **2** to strike the hands together to show approval **3** *informal* to put suddenly, throw: *clap in jail*

**clap** *verb* ⇨ **clap**s, **clap**ping, **clap**ped

**clapper** *noun* the tongue of a bell

**claptrap** *noun* meaningless words, nonsense

**claret** *noun* a type of red wine

**clarify** *verb* to make clear and understandable

**clarify** ⇨ **clarif**ies, **clarif**ying, **clarif**ied

**clarinet** *noun* a musical wind instrument, usually made of wood □ **clarinettist** *noun*

**clarion** *noun*, *old* **1** a kind of trumpet **2** a shrill, rousing noise □ **clarion call** a clear call to action

**clarity** *noun* clearness

**clash** *noun* (*pl* **clashes**) **1** a loud noise made by striking swords *etc* **2** a disagreement, a fight □ *verb* **1** to bang noisily together **2** to disagree **3** of events: to take place at the same time **4** of two colours *etc*: not to look well together

**clasp** *noun* **1** a hook or pin for fastening: *hair clasp* **2** a handshake **3** an embrace □ *verb* **1** to hold closely; grasp **2** to fasten

**class** *noun* (*pl* **classes**) **1** a rank or order of people or things **2** a group of schoolchildren or students taught together **3** a group of plants or animals with something in common □ *verb* **1** to place in a class **2** to arrange in some order

**classify** *verb* **1** arrange in classes **2** put into a class or category □ **classification** *noun*

**classify** ⇨ **classif**ies, **classif**ying, **classif**ied

**classic** *noun* **1** a great book or other work of art **2** something typical and influential of its kind **3** (**classics**) the study of ancient Greek and Latin literature □ *adj* **1** excellent **2** standard, typical of its kind: *a classic example* **3** simple and elegant in style: *a classic black dress*

**classical** *adj* **1** of a classic or the classics **2** of music: serious, not light

**classy** *adj* elegant, stylish

**clatter** *noun* a noise of plates *etc* banged together

**clause** *noun* **1** a part of a sentence containing a finite verb **2** a part of a will, act of parliament *etc*

**claustrophobia** (*say* klos-tro-**foh**-bi-a) *noun* an abnormal fear of enclosed spaces **1** the activity of arranging things into classes or categories **2** the label or name that you give something in order to indicate its class or category □ **claustrophobic** *adj*

**claw** *noun* **1** an animal's or bird's foot with hooked nails **2** a hooked nail on one of these feet □ *verb* to scratch or tear

**clay** *noun* soft, sticky earth, often used to make pottery, bricks *etc* □ **clayey** *adj*

**clean** *adj* **1** free from dirt; pure **2** neat, complete: *a clean break* □ *adv* completely: *got clean away* □ *verb* to make clean; free from dirt □ **cleanliness** (*say* klen-li-nes) *noun* the quality of being free from dirt □ **cleanly** *adv* (meaning 2): *a single blow with the axe split the wood cleanly along its grain* □ **cleaner** *noun* **1** someone employed to clean a building *etc* **2** a substance which cleans

**cleanse** (*say* klenz) *verb* to make clean

**clear** *adj* **1** bright, undimmed **2** free from mist or cloud: *clear sky* **3** transparent **4** free from difficulty or obstructions **5** easy to see, hear or understand **6** after deductions and charges have been made: *clear profit* **7** without a stain **8** without touching: *clear of the rocks* □ *verb* **1** to make clear **2** to empty **3** to free from blame **4** to leap over without touching **5** of the sky: to become bright □ **clearly** *adv* **1** obviously **2** in a clear way □ **clearness** *noun* (adjectives, meanings 1, 2, 3, 4 and 5) □ **clear-cut** *adj* distinct, obvious □ **clear out** or **clear off** to go away

**clearance** *noun* **1** the activity of getting rid of all the things which are in a certain place so that a new start can be made: *a clearance sale* **2** permission to do something: *receive official clearance for the project*

**clearing** *noun* land free of trees

**cleavage** *noun* **1** the hollow between a woman's breasts **2** splitting

**cleave** *verb* **1** to divide, split **2** to crack **3** to stick (to)

**cleave** ⋅- cleaves, cleav*ing*, clove or cleft or cleav*ed*, cloven or cleft or cleav*ed*

**cleaver** *noun* a heavy knife for splitting meat carcases *etc*

**clef** *noun* a musical sign, (𝄞) **treble clef**) or (𝄢) **bass clef**), placed on a stave to fix the pitch of the notes

**cleft** *noun* an opening made by

splitting; a crack □ *past form of* **cleave** □ **cleft palate** a deformity in the roof of the mouth, present in some people at birth

**clement** *adj* mild; merciful □ **clemency** *noun* readiness to forgive; mercy

**clench** *verb* to press firmly together: *clenching his teeth/ clenched his fist*

**clergy** *noun pl* the ministers of the Christian church

**clergyman, clergywoman** *noun* a Christian minister

**clerical** *adj* **1** relating to office work **2** of the clergy

**clerk** *noun* an office worker who writes letters, keeps accounts *etc* □ *verb*

**clever** *adj* **1** quick in learning and understanding **2** intelligent, skilful: *a clever answer* □ **cleverly** *adv*

**cliché** (*say* klee-shei) *noun* an idea, phrase *etc* that has been used too much and has little meaning

From a French word for 'stereotype', in the sense of a fixed printing plate

**click** *noun* a short sharp sound like a clock's tick □ *verb* make this sound

**client** *noun* **1** a customer of a shop *etc* **2** someone who goes to a lawyer *etc* for advice

**clientele** (*say* klee-en-tel or klai-en-tel) *noun* the customers of a lawyer, shopkeeper *etc*

**cliff** *noun* a very steep, rocky slope, *esp* by the sea

**climactic** *adj* most important or intense, of the climax

**climate** *noun* **1** the weather conditions of a particular area **2** general condition or situation: *in the present cultural climate* □ **climatic** *adj* (meaning 1)

**climax** *noun* (*pl* **climaxes**) the point of greatest interest or importance in a situation

**climb** *verb* **1** to go to the top of **2** to go up using hands and feet **3** to

slope upward □ *noun* □ **climber**
*noun* **1** someone who climbs **2** a
plant which climbs up walls *etc*

■ (verb, meaning 1) ascend, mount,
top; (verb, meaning 2) scale,
clamber, shin up; (verb, meaning
3) rise, soar

**clinch** *verb* **1** to grasp tightly **2** to
settle (an argument, bargain *etc*)
□ *noun* (*pl* **clinches**) **1** *boxing* a
position in which the boxers hold
each other with their arms **2** a
passionate embrace

**cling** *verb* to stick or hang on (to)
□ **clingy** *adj*

**cling** ↔ clings, cling**ing**, clung

**clingfilm** *noun* thin transparent
plastic material used to wrap food

**clinic** *noun* a place or part of a
hospital where a particular kind of
treatment is given

**clinical** *adj* **1** of a clinic **2** based on
observation: *clinical medicine*
**3** objective, cool and unemotional:
*clinical approach* □ **clinically** *adv*
according to medical diagnosis:
*clinically depressed*

**clink** *noun* a ringing sound of
knocked glasses *etc* □ *verb*

**clip** *verb* **1** to cut (off) **2** to fasten
with a clip □ *noun* **1** something
clipped off **2** a small fastener
**3** *informal* a smart blow

**clip** ↔ clips, clipp**ing**, clipp**ed**

**clipper** *noun* **1** a fast-sailing ship
**2** (**clippers**) large scissors for
clipping

**clique** (*say* kleek) *noun* a small group
of people who help each other but
keep others at a distance

**clitoris** (*say* klit-or-is) *noun* a small
structure at the front of the external
female sex organs □ **clitoral** *adj*

**cloak** *noun* **1** a loose outer garment
**2** something which hides: *cloak of
darkness* □ *verb* **1** to cover as with a
cloak **2** to hide □ **cloakroom** a place
where coats, hats *etc* may be left for

a time

**cloche** (*say* klosh) *noun* (*pl* **cloches**) a
transparent frame for protecting
plants

**clock** *noun* a machine for measuring
time □ **clock in** or **clock out** to
record your time of arrival at, or
departure from, work

**clockwise** *adj* turning or moving in
the same direction as the hands of a
clock

**clockwork** *adj* worked by machinery
such as that of a clock □ **like
clockwork** smoothly, without
difficulties

**clod** *noun* a thick lump of turf

**clodhopper** *noun* a stupid clumsy
person □ **clodhopping** *adj*

**clog** *noun* a shoe with a wooden sole
□ *verb* to block (pipes *etc*)

**clog** ↔ clogs, clogg**ing**, clogg**ed**

**cloister** *noun* **1** a covered-in walk in
a monastery or convent **2** a
monastery or convent □ **cloistered**
*adj* **1** shut up in a monastery *etc*
**2** sheltered

**close¹** (*say* klohs) *adj* **1** near in time,
place *etc* **2** shut up, with no opening
**3** without fresh air, stuffy **4** narrow,
confined **5** mean **6** secretive
**7** beloved, very dear: *a close friend*
**8** decided by a small amount: *a close
contest* □ *noun* **1** a narrow passage
off a street **2** the gardens, walks *etc*
near a cathedral □ **closely** *adv*
**1** carefully: *listen closely* **2** strongly,
intimately: *he was closely involved in
the action* **3** in a way that brings
things close together: *objects packed
closely together in a box* □ **close-up**
*noun* a film or photograph taken
very near the subject

**close²** (*say* klohz) *verb* **1** to shut **2** to
finish **3** to come closer to and fight
(with) □ *noun* the end

**closed-circuit television** a system of
television cameras and receivers for
use in shops *etc*

**closet** *noun*, *US* a cupboard □ *verb* to

take into a room for a private conference

**closure** *noun* the act of closing

**clot** *noun* **1** a lump that forms in blood, cream *etc* **2** *informal* an idiot □ *verb* to form into clots

**clot** *verb* ⇔ clots, clot**t**ing, clot**t**ed

**cloth** *noun* **1** woven material of cotton, wool, silk *etc* **2** a piece of this **3** a table-cover

**clothe** *verb* **1** to put clothes on **2** to provide with clothes **3** to cover

**clothes** *noun pl* **1** things worn to cover the body and limbs, *eg* shirt, trousers, skirt **2** sheets and coverings for a bed □ **clothing** *noun* clothes

**cloud** *noun* **1** a mass of tiny drops of water or ice floating in the sky **2** a mass of anything: *a cloud of bees* □ *verb* to become dim or blurred □ **clouded** *adj* □ **cloudless** *adj* (noun, meaning 1) □ **cloudburst** *noun* a sudden heavy fall of rain

**cloudy** *adj* **1** darkened with clouds **2** not clear or transparent

**clout** *noun, informal* **1** a blow **2** influence, power □ *verb, informal* to hit

**clove¹** *noun* **1** a flower bud of the clove tree, used as a spice **2** a small section of a bulb of garlic

**clove²** *past form of* **cleave**

**cloven-hoofed** *adj* having a divided hoof like an ox, sheep *etc*

**clover** *noun* a field plant with leaves usually in three parts □ **in clover** in luxury

**clown** *noun* **1** a comedian with a painted face and comical clothes in a circus **2** a fool □ **clowning** *noun* silly or comical behaviour □ **clownish** *adj* like a clown; awkward

**cloy** *verb* of something sweet: to become unpleasant when too much is taken □ **cloying** *adj*

**club** *noun* **1** a heavy stick **2** a stick

used to hit the ball in golf **3** a group of people who meet for social events *etc* **4** the place where these people meet **5** (**clubs**) one of the four suits in playing-cards □ *verb* to beat with a club □ **club together** to put money into a joint fund for some purpose

**club** *verb* ⇔ clubs, club**b**ing, club**b**ed

**cluck** *noun* a sound like that made by a hen □ *verb*

**clue** *noun* a sign or piece of evidence that helps to solve a mystery

**clump** *noun* a cluster of trees or shrubs □ *verb* to walk heavily

**clumsy** *adj* **1** awkward in movement or actions **2** tactless, thoughtless: *clumsy apology* □ **clumsily** *adv*

**clumsy** ⇔ clums**i**er, clums**i**est

**clung** *past form of* **cling**

**cluster** *noun* **1** a bunch of fruit *etc* **2** a crowd □ *verb* to group together in clusters

**clutch** *verb* **1** to hold firmly **2** to seize, grasp □ *noun* (*pl* **clutches**) **1** a grasp **2** part of a car engine used for changing gears **3** a brood of chickens

**clutter** *noun* **1** a muddled or disordered collection of things **2** disorder, confusion, untidiness □ *verb* **1** to crowd together untidily **2 clutter up** to fill or cover in an untidy, disordered way

**Co** *abbrev* **1** Company **2** County

**c/o** *abbrev* care of

**co-** also **col-, con-, com-, cor-** *prefix* joint, working with, together with: *co-author/ coexist/ connect/ compound/ collision/ correspond* ⓔ From Latin *cum* meaning 'with'

**coach** *noun* (*pl* **coaches**) **1** a bus for long-distance travel **2** a closed, four-wheeled horse carriage **3** a railway carriage **4** a private trainer for sportspeople □ *verb* to train or help to prepare for an examination, sports contest *etc*

**coagulate** *verb* to thicken; clot

**coal** *noun* a black substance dug out of the earth and used for burning, making gas *etc* □ **coalfield** *noun* an area where there is coal to be mined □ **coal gas** the mixture of gases obtained from coal, used for lighting and heating □ **coalmine** *noun* a mine from which coal is dug

**coalesce** (*say* koh-*a*-les) *verb* to come together and unite

**coalition** *noun* a joining together of different parts or groups

**coarse** *adj* 1 not fine in texture; rough, harsh 2 vulgar □ **coarsen** *verb* to make coarse

**coast** *noun* the border of land next to the sea □ *verb* 1 to sail along or near a coast 2 to move without the use of power on a bike, in a car *etc* □ **coastal** *adj* of or on the coast □ **coastguard** *noun* someone who acts as a guard along the coast to help those in danger in boats *etc*

**coat** *noun* 1 an outer garment with sleeves 2 an animal's covering of hair or wool 3 a layer of paint □ *verb* to cover with a coat or layer □ **coat of arms** the badge or crest of a family □ **coating** *noun* a covering

**coax** *verb* to persuade to do what is wanted without using force

**cob** *noun* 1 a head of corn, wheat *etc* 2 a male swan

**cobalt** *noun* 1 a silvery metal 2 a blue colouring obtained from this

**cobble** *noun* a rounded stone used in paving roads (*also called* **cobblestone**) □ *verb* 1 to mend (shoes) 2 to repair roughly or hurriedly □ **cobbled** *adj* of streets: paved with cobbles

**cobbler** *noun* someone who mends shoes

**cobra** *noun* a poisonous snake found in India and Africa

**cobweb** *noun* a spider's web

**cocaine** *noun* a narcotic drug

**cock** *noun* 1 the male of most kinds

of bird, *esp* of the farmyard hen 2 a tap or valve for controlling the flow of liquid 3 a hammer-like part of a gun which fires the shot 4 a small heap of hay □ *verb* 1 to draw back the cock of a gun 2 to set (the ears) upright to listen 3 to tilt (the head) to one side

**cockatoo** *noun* a kind of parrot

**cockerel** *noun* a young cock

**cocker spaniel** a breed of small spaniel

**cockle** *noun* a type of shellfish

**cockleshell** *noun* the shell of a cockle

**cockney** *noun* (*pl* **cockneys**) 1 someone born in the East End of London 2 the speech characteristic of this area

**cockpit** *noun* the space for the pilot or driver in an aeroplane or small boat

**cockroach** *noun* (*pl* **cockroaches**) a type of crawling insect

**cocksure** *adj* very confident, often without cause

**cocktail** *noun* a mixed alcoholic drink

**cocky** *adj* conceited, self-confident

**cocoa** *noun* a drink made from the ground seeds of the cacao tree

**coconut** *noun* the large, hard-shelled nut of a type of palm tree

Based on a Portuguese word meaning 'grimace', because of the resemblance of the three holes on the base of the fruit to a human face

**cocoon** *noun* a protective covering of silk spun by the larva of a butterfly, moth *etc*

**cod** *noun* (*pl* **cod**) a fish much used as food, found in the northern seas

**coddle** *verb* to pamper, over-protect

**code** *noun* 1 a way of signalling or sending secret messages, using letters *etc* agreed beforehand 2 a book or collection of laws, rules *etc*

**codger** (*say* koj-er) *noun* an old, eccentric man

**codicil** *noun* a note added to a will or treaty

**codify** *verb* to arrange in an orderly way, classify

**codify ⋄** codifies, codifying, codified

**coed** (*say* koh-**ed**) *adj, informal* coeducational

**coeducation** *noun* the education of boys and girls together
□ **coeducational** *adj*

**coerce** *verb* to make to do; force, compel □ **coercion** *noun*

**coercive** *adj* using force

**coeval** (*say* koh-ee-val) *adj* of the same age or time

**coexist** *verb* to exist at the same time
□ **coexistence** *noun* □ **coexistent** *adj*

**coffee** *noun* **1** a drink made from the roasted, ground beans of the coffee shrub **2** a pale brown colour

**coffer** *noun* a chest for holding money, gold *etc*

**coffin** *noun* a box in which a dead body is buried or cremated

**cog** *noun* a tooth on a wheel
□ **cogwheel** *noun* a toothed wheel

**cogent** *adj* convincing, believable

**cogitate** *verb* to think carefully
□ **cogitation** *noun*

**cognac** *noun* a kind of French brandy

**cohere** *verb* to stick together
□ **cohesion** *noun*

**coherent** *adj* **1** sticking together **2** clear and logical in thought or speech □ **coherence** *noun*

**cohesive** *adj* of a group: consisting of members who are closely linked together or associated with each other

**cohort** *noun, historical* a tenth part of a Roman legion

**coil** *verb* to wind in rings; twist
□ *noun* **1** a wound arrangement of hair, rope *etc* **2** a contraceptive device fitted in the uterus

**coin** *noun* a piece of stamped metal used as money □ *verb* **1** to make metal into money **2** to make up (a new word *etc*)

**coinage** *noun* **1** the system of coins used in a country **2** a newly-made word

**coincide** *verb* (often with **with**) **1** to be the same as: *their interests coincide / his story coincides with mine* **2** to happen at the same time as: *my arrival coincided with his departure*

**coincidence** *noun* the occurrence of two things simultaneously without planning □ **coincidental** *adj* happening by chance, the result of a coincidence □ **coincidentally** *adv*

**coke** *noun* a type of fuel made by heating coal till the gas is driven out

**col-** *see* **co-**

**colander** *noun* a bowl with small holes in it for straining vegetables *etc*

**cold** *adj* **1** low in temperature **2** lower in temperature than is comfortable **3** unfriendly □ *noun* **1** the state of being cold **2** an infectious disease causing shivering, running nose *etc* □ **coldly** *adv* (adjectives, meanings 2 and 3) □ **coldness** *noun* □ **cold-blooded** *adj* **1** of fishes *etc*: having cold blood **2** cruel; lacking in feelings □ **cold feet** lack of courage □ **cold sore** a blister on or near the mouth, caused by a contagious virus similar to that which causes genital herpes □ **cold war** a power struggle between nations without open warfare

■ (adj, meaning 1) unheated, cool, chilled; (adj, meaning 2) raw, biting, wintry, glacial, chill

**coleslaw** *noun* a salad made from raw cabbage

**colic** *noun* a severe stomach pain

**collaborate** *verb* **1** to work together (with) **2** to work with (an enemy) to

betray your country
□ **collaboration** *noun*
□ **collaborator** *noun*
ⓘ From Latin *col-* meaning 'together with', and *laborare* meaning 'to work'

♦ Do not confuse with: **corroborate**

**collage** (*say* ko-**lahsz**) *noun* a design made of scraps of paper pasted on wood, card *etc*

**collapse** *verb* **1** to fall or break down **2** to cave or fall in **3** to become unable to continue □ *noun* a falling down or caving in
□ **collapsible** *adj* of a chair *etc*: able to be folded up

**collar** *noun* **1** a band, strip *etc* worn round the neck **2** part of a garment that fits round the neck □ *verb*, *informal* to seize □ **collarbone** *noun* either of two bones joining the breast bone and shoulderblade

**collate** *verb* **1** to examine and compare **2** to gather together and arrange in order: *collate the pages for the book* □ **collation** *noun* **1** a light, often cold meal **2** a comparison

**collateral** *noun* an additional security for repayment of a debt

**colleague** *noun* someone who works in the same company *etc* as yourself

**collect** *verb* **1** to bring together **2** to gather together □ **collector** *noun* someone who collects a particular group of things: *stamp collector*

**collected** *adj* **1** gathered together **2** calm, composed

**collection** *noun* **1** the act of collecting **2** a number of objects or people **3** money gathered at a meeting, *eg* a church service

**collective** *adj* **1** acting together **2** of several things or people, not of one: *collective decision* □ *noun* a business *etc* owned and managed by the workers

**college** *noun* **1** a building housing students, forming part of a university **2** a higher-education institute □ **collegiate** *adj* of a university: divided into colleges

**collide** *verb* to come together with great force; clash

**collision** *noun* **1** a crash between two moving vehicles *etc* **2** a disagreement, a clash of interests *etc*

**collie** *noun* a breed of long-haired dog with a pointed nose

**collier** *noun* **1** a coal-miner **2** a coal ship □ **colliery** *noun* (*pl* **collieries**) a coalmine

**colloquial** *adj* used in everyday speech but not in formal writing or speaking □ **colloquialism** *noun*
□ **colloquially** *adv*

**collusion** *noun* a secret or clandestine agreement

**cologne** *noun* light perfume made with plant oils and alcohol

**colon**[1] *noun* a punctuation mark (:) used *eg* to introduce a list of examples

**colon**[2] *noun* a part of the bowel

**colonel** (*say* **ker**-nel) *noun* a senior army officer fulfilling a staff appointment

**colonial** *adj* of colonies abroad
□ **colonialism** *noun* the policy of setting up colonies abroad
□ **colonialist** *noun* someone who supports the policy of setting up and maintaining colonies abroad □ *adj*

**colonize** *verb* to set up a colony in

**colonnade** *noun* a row of columns or pillars

**colony** *noun* (*pl* **colonies**) **1** a group of settlers or the settlement they make in another country **2** a group of people, animals *etc* of the same type living together □ **colonist** *noun* a settler

**colossal** *adj* huge, enormous

**colossus** *noun* an enormous statue

**colour** or *US* **color** *noun* **1** a quality that an object shows in the light, *eg* redness, blueness *etc* **2** a shade or tint **3** vividness, brightness **4** (**colours**) a flag or standard □ *verb* **1** to put colour on **2** to blush **3** to influence: *coloured my attitude to life* □ **coloured** *adj* **1** having colour **2** an old-fashioned and possibly offensive adjective meaning 'not white-skinned' □ **colour-blind** *adj* unable to distinguish certain colours, *eg* red and green □ **off colour** unwell

It is generally considered more 'politically correct' to say 'black' for sense 2.

**colourful** *adj* **1** brightly coloured **2** vivid, interesting

**colouring** *noun* **1** shade or combination of colours **2** complexion

**colourless** *adj* **1** without colour **2** dull, bland

**colt** *noun* a young horse

**column** *noun* **1** an upright stone or wooden pillar **2** something of a long or tall, narrow shape **3** a vertical line of print, figures *etc* on a page **4** a regular feature in a newspaper **5** an arrangement of troops *etc* one behind the other □ **columnist** *noun* someone who writes a regular newspaper column

**com-** *see* **co-**

**coma** *noun* unconsciousness lasting a long time

**comatose** *adj* **1** in or of a coma **2** drowsy, sluggish

**comb** *noun* **1** a toothed instrument for separating or smoothing hair, wool *etc* **2** the crest of certain birds **3** a collection of cells for honey □ *verb* **1** to arrange or smooth with a comb **2** to search through thoroughly

**combat** *verb* to fight or struggle against □ *noun* a fight or struggle □ **combatant** *noun* □ *adj*

**combination** *noun* **1** a joining together of things or people **2** a set

of things or people combined **3** a series of letters or figures dialled to open a safe

**combine** *verb* to join together □ *noun* a number of traders *etc* who join together □ **combine harvester** a machine that both cuts and threshes crops

**combustible** *adj* liable to catch fire and burn □ *noun* anything that will catch fire

**combustion** *noun* burning

**come** *verb* **1** to move towards this place (*opposite of* go): *come here!* **2** to draw near **3** to arrive **4** to happen, occur: *the index comes at the end* □ **come about** to happen □ **come across** or **come upon** to meet or find accidentally □ **come by** to obtain □ **come into** to inherit □ **come of age** to reach the age at which you become an adult for legal purposes □ **come round** or **come to** to recover from a faint *etc* □ **come upon** to come across □ **to come in** the future

**come** ⇨ come*s*, com*ing*, *came*, come ① From Old English *cuman*

**comedian** *noun* a performer who tells jokes, acts in comedy *etc*

**comedy** *noun* (*pl* **comedies**) a light-hearted or amusing play (*contrasted with*: **tragedy**)

**comely** *adj* good-looking, pleasing □ **comeliness** *noun*

**comet** *noun* a kind of star which has a tail of light

**comfort** *verb* to help, soothe (someone in pain or distress) □ *noun* **1** ease; quiet enjoyment **2** something that brings ease and happiness

**comfortable** *adj* **1** at ease; free from trouble, pain *etc* **2** giving comfort **3** having enough money for a pleasant lifestyle □ **comfortably** *adv*

**comic** *adj* **1** of comedy **2** amusing, funny □ *noun* **1** a professional comedian **2** a children's magazine with illustrated stories *etc* □ **comic strip** a strip of small pictures outlining a story

**comical** *adj* funny, amusing □ **comically** *adv*

**comma** *noun* a punctuation mark (,) indicating a pause in a sentence

**command** *verb* **1** to give an order **2** to be in charge of **3** to look over or down upon: *commanding a view* □ *noun* **1** an order **2** control: *in command of the situation*

**commandant** *noun* an officer in command of a place or of troops

**commandeer** *verb* to seize (something) *esp* for the use of an army

**commander** *noun* **1** someone who commands **2** a naval officer next in rank below captain

**commandment** *noun* an order or command

**commando** *noun* (*pl* **commandoes**) a soldier in an army unit trained for special tasks

**commemorate** *verb* **1** to bring to memory by some solemn act **2** to serve as a memorial to □ **commemoration** *noun* □ **commemorative** *adj*

**commence** *verb* to begin □ **commencement** *noun*

**commend** *verb* **1** to praise **2** to give into the care of □ **commendation** *noun*

**commendable** *adj* praiseworthy

**comment** *noun* **1** a remark **2** a criticism □ *verb* to remark on; criticize

**commentary** *noun* (*pl* **commentaries**) **1** a description of an event *etc* by someone who is watching it **2** a set of explanatory notes for a book *etc*

**commentator** *noun* someone who gives or writes a commentary

**commerce** *noun* the buying and selling of goods between people or

nations; trade, dealings

**commercial** *adj* **1** of commerce **2** paid for by advertisements: *commercial radio* □ *noun* an advertisement on radio, TV *etc* □ **commercially** *adv*

**commiserate** *verb* to sympathize (with) □ **commiseration** *noun* □ **commiserations** *noun pl* an expression of sympathy when someone has failed to do or achieve something

**commission** *noun* **1** the act of committing **2** a document giving authority to an officer in the armed forces **3** an order for a work of art **4** a fee for doing business on another's behalf **5** a group of people appointed to investigate something □ *verb* to give a commission or power to □ **in** or **out of commission** in or not in use

**commissionaire** *noun* a uniformed doorkeeper

**commissioner** *noun* **1** someone with high authority in a district **2** a member of a commission

**commit** *verb* **1** to give or hand over; entrust **2** to make a promise to do: *committed to finishing this book* **3** to do, bring about: *commit a crime* □ **committal** *noun*

**commit** ← commits, committing, committed

**commitment** *noun* **1** a promise **2** a task that must be done

**committed** *adj* strong in belief or support: *a committed socialist*

**committee** *noun* a number of people chosen from a larger body to attend to special business

**commodious** *adj* roomy, spacious

**commodity** *noun* (*pl* **commodities**) **1** an article to be bought or sold **2** (**commodities**) goods, produce

**commodore** *noun* an officer next above a captain in the navy

**common** *adj* **1** shared by all or many:

*common belief* **2** seen or happening often: *common occurrence* **3** ordinary, normal □ *noun* land belonging to the people of a town, parish *etc*

**commoner** *noun* someone who is not a noble □ **common law** unwritten law based on custom □ **Common Market** the European Community, the EC □ **common noun** a name for any one of a class of things (*contrasted with*: **proper noun**) □ **common room** *noun* a sitting-room for the use of a group in a school *etc* □ **common sense** practical good sense

**commonplace** *adj* ordinary

**Commons** or **House of Commons** the lower House of Parliament

**commonwealth** *noun* an association of self-governing states

**commotion** *noun* a disturbance among several people

**communal** *adj* common, shared **communally** *adv*

**commune** *noun* a group of people living together, sharing work *etc* □ *verb* to talk together

**communicate** *verb* **1** to make known, tell **2** to pass on **3** to get in touch (with) **4** to have a connecting door

**communication** *noun* **1** a means of conveying information **2** a message **3** a way of passing from place to place

**communicative** *adj* willing to give information, talkative

**communion** *noun* **1** the act of sharing thoughts, feelings *etc*; fellowship **2** (**Communion**) in the Christian Church, the celebration of the Lord's supper

**communiqué** (*say* kom-yoon-ik-ei) *noun* an official announcement

**communism** *noun* a form of socialism where industry is controlled by the state □ **communist** *adj* □ *noun*

**community** *noun* (*pl* **communities**) **1** a group of people living in one place **2** the public in general □ **community charge** a local tax in the UK to pay for public services, charged according to property values

**commute** *verb* **1** to travel regularly between two places, *eg* between home and work **2** to change (a punishment) for one less severe

**commuter** *noun* someone who travels regularly some distance to work from their home

**compact** *adj* fitted or packed closely together □ *noun* a bargain or agreement □ **compact disc** a small disc on which digitally recorded sound is registered as a series of pits to be read by a laser beam

**companion** *noun* someone or something that accompanies; a friend □ **companionship** *noun*

**companionable** *adj* friendly

**company** *noun* (*pl* **companies**) **1** a gathering of people **2** a business firm **3** a part of a regiment **4** a ship's crew **5** companionship

**comparable** *adj* roughly similar or equal in some way

**comparative** *adj* **1** judged by comparing with something else; relative: *comparative improvement* **2** near to being: *a comparative stranger* **3** *grammar* the degree of an adjective or adverb between positive and superlative, *eg* blacker, better, more courageous

**compare** *verb* **1** to set things together to see how similar or different they are **2** to liken □ **comparison** *noun* □ **beyond compare** much better than all rivals

**compartment** *noun* a separate part or division, *eg* of a railway carriage

**compass** *noun* (*pl* **compasses**) **1** an instrument with a magnetized needle for showing direction **2** (**compasses**) an instrument with one fixed and one movable leg for drawing circles

**compassion** *noun* pity for another's suffering; mercy □ **compassionate** *adj* □ **compassionately** *adv*

**compatible** *adj* able to live with, agree with, be used with, *etc* □ **compatibility** *noun* □ **compatibly** *adv*

**compatriot** *noun* a fellow-countryman or -countrywoman

**compel** *verb* force to do something

**compel** ↔ compel**s**, compel**ling**, compel**led**

**compensate** *verb* to make up for wrong or damage done, *esp* by giving money □ **compensation** *noun*

**compère** *noun* someone who introduces acts as part of an entertainment □ *verb* to act as compère

**compete** *verb* to try to beat others in a race *etc*

**competent** *adj* 1 capable, efficient 2 skilled; properly trained or qualified □ **competence** *noun* □ **competently** *adv*

**competition** *noun* 1 a contest between rivals 2 rivalry

**competitive** *adj* 1 of sport: based on competitions 2 fond of competing with others

**competitor** *noun* someone who competes; a rival

**compilation** *noun* 1 a collection of several short, related pieces of writing, music or information 2 the activity of compiling something

**compile** *verb* to make (a book *etc*) from information that has been collected □ **compiler** *noun*

**complacence** or **complacency** *noun* a lazy attitude resulting from an exaggerated belief in your own security

**complacent** *adj* self-satisfied and with a tendency to be lazy □ **complacently** *adv*

**complain** *verb* 1 to express dissatisfaction about something 2 to grumble

**complaint** *noun* 1 a statement of dissatisfaction 2 an illness

**complement** *noun* 1 something which completes or fills up 2 the full number or quantity needed to fill something 3 the angle that must be added to a given angle to make up a right angle

❖ Do not confuse with: **compliment**. Remember -COMPLEM**ent** and COMPLE**te** are related in meaning, and the first six letters of both words are the same.

**complementary** *adj* 1 together making up a whole 2 making up a right angle

❖ Do not confuse with: **complimentary**. Complementary is related to the noun **complement**.

**complete** *adj* 1 having nothing missing; whole 2 finished □ *verb* 1 to finish 2 to make whole □ **completely** *adv* totally, absolutely □ **completion** *noun*

**complex** *adj* 1 made up of many parts 2 complicated, difficult □ *noun* (*pl* **complexes**) 1 a set of repressed emotions and ideas which affect someone's behaviour 2 an exaggerated reaction, an obsession: *she has a complex about her height* 3 a group of related buildings: *sports complex*

**complexion** *noun* 1 the colour or look of the skin of the face 2 appearance

**complexity** *noun* (*pl* **complexities**) the quality of being complicated or difficult

**compliance** *noun* the act of complying; agreement with another's wishes □ **compliant** *adj*

**complicate** *verb* to make difficult

**complicated** *adj* difficult to

understand; detailed

**complication** noun **1** a difficulty **2** a development in an illness which makes things worse

**complicity** noun (pl **complicities**) a share in a crime or other misdeed

**compliment** noun **1** an expression of praise or flattery **2 compliments** good wishes □ verb to praise, congratulate

> ♦ Do not confuse with: **complement**. Remember, if you make a **compLIment**, you are being poLIte, and an '**I**' comes after the '**L**' in both words.

**complimentary** adj **1** flattering, praising **2** given free: *complimentary ticket*

> ♦ Do not confuse with: **complementary**. **Complimentary** is related to the noun **compliment**.

**comply** verb to agree to do something that someone else orders or wishes

> **comply** ⤳ complies, complying, complied

**component** adj forming one of the parts of a whole □ noun one of several parts, eg of a machine

**compose** verb **1** to put together or in order; arrange **2** to create (a piece of music, a poem *etc*) □ **composer** noun someone who writes music

**composed** adj quiet, calm

**composite** adj made up of parts

**composition** noun **1** the act of composing **2** a created piece of writing or music **3** a mixture of things

**compos mentis** sane, rational

**compost** noun a mixture of natural manures for spreading on soil

**composure** noun calmness, self-possession

**compound** adj **1** made up of a number of different parts **2** not simple □ noun **1** *chemistry* a

substance formed from two or more elements **2** an enclosure round a building

**comprehend** verb **1** to understand **2** to include □ **comprehension** noun (meaning 1)

**comprehensible** adj able to be understood

**comprehensive** adj taking in or including much or all □ **comprehensive school** a state-funded school providing all types of secondary education

**compress** verb (say kom-**pres**) **1** to press together **2** to force into a narrower or smaller space □ noun (say **kom**-pres) a pad used to create pressure on a part of the body or to reduce inflammation □ **compression** noun

**comprise** verb **1** to include, contain **2** to consist of

> ♦ Do not confuse with: **consist**. Remember, you do not need the word 'of' after **comprise**. You say *the exam comprises three parts*, but *the exam consists of three parts*.

**compromise** noun an agreement reached by both sides giving up something □ verb **1** to make a compromise **2** to put in a difficult or embarrassing position

**compulsion** noun a force driving someone to do something

**compulsive** adj unable to stop yourself, obsessional: *compulsive liar*

> ♦ Do not confuse: **compulsive** and **compulsory**

**compulsory** adj **1** requiring to be done **2** forced upon someone

> ♦ Do not confuse: **compulsory** and **compulsive**

**compunction** noun regret

**computation** noun counting, calculation

**compute** verb to count, calculate

**computer** *noun* an electronic machine that stores and sorts information of various kinds

**comrade** *noun* a companion, a friend

**con** *verb* to trick, play a confidence trick on □ *noun* a trick, a deceit

**con** *verb* ⇔ cons, conning, conned

**con-** *see* co-

**concave** *adj* hollow or curved inwards (*contrasted with*: **convex**) □ **concavity** *noun* (*pl* **concavities**)

**conceal** *verb* to hide, keep secret □ **concealment** *noun*

**concede** *verb* 1 to give up, yield 2 to admit the truth of something

**conceit** *noun* a too high opinion of yourself; vanity □ **conceited** *adj*

**conceivable** *adj* able to be imagined □ **conceivably** *adv*

**conceive** *verb* 1 to form in the mind, imagine 2 to become pregnant

**concentrate** *verb* 1 to direct all your attention or effort towards something 2 to bring together to one place

**concentrated** *adj* made stronger or less dilute □ **concentration** *noun*

**concentric** *adj* of circles: placed one inside the other with the same centre point (*contrasted with*: **eccentric**)

**concept** *noun* a general idea about something

**conception** *noun* 1 the act of conceiving 2 an idea

**concern** *verb* 1 to have to do with 2 to make uneasy 3 to interest, affect □ *noun* 1 anxiety 2 a cause of anxiety, a worry 3 a business □ **concern yourself with** to be worried about

**concerning** *prep* about: *concerning your application*

**concert** *noun* a musical performance

**◆**. Do not confuse with: **consort**

**concerted** *adj* planned or performed together

**concertina** *noun* a type of musical wind instrument, with bellows and keys

**concerto** *noun* (*pl* **concertos**) a long piece of music for a solo instrument with orchestral accompaniment

**concession** *noun* 1 a granting or allowing of something: *a concession for oil exploration* 2 something granted or allowed 3 a reduction in the price of something for children, the unemployed, senior citizens *etc*

**conciliate** *verb* 1 to win over (someone previously unfriendly or angry) 2 to bring peace to two or more people who disagree □ **conciliation** *noun* □ **conciliatory** *adj*

**concise** *adj* brief, using few words

**◆**. Do not confuse with: **precise**

**conclude** *verb* 1 to end 2 to reach a decision or judgement; settle □ **concluding** *adj* last, final

**conclusion** *noun* 1 end 2 decision, judgement

**conclusive** *adj* settling, deciding: *conclusive proof* □ **conclusively** *adv*

**concoct** *verb* 1 to mix together (a dish or drink) 2 to make up, invent □ **concoction** *noun*

**concord** *noun* agreement

**concourse** *noun* 1 a crowd 2 a large open space in a building *etc*

**concrete** *adj* 1 solid, real 2 made of concrete □ *noun* a mixture of gravel, cement *etc* used in building

▣ (adj, meaning 1) abstract

**concur** *verb* to agree □ **concurrence** *noun*

**concur** ⇔ concurs, concurring, concurred

**concurrent** *adj* 1 happening together 2 agreeing □ **concurrently** *adv* (meaning 1)

**concussion** *noun* temporary harm done to the brain from a knock on the head

**condemn** *verb* 1 to blame 2 to

sentence to (a certain punishment) **3** to declare (a building) unfit for use □ **condemnation** noun (meaning 1)

**condensation** noun **1** the act of condensing **2** drops of liquid formed from vapour

**condense** verb **1** to make to go into a smaller space **2** of steam: to turn to liquid

**condescend** verb to act towards someone as if you are better than them □ **condescending** adj □ **condescension** noun

**condiment** noun a seasoning for food, esp salt or pepper

**condition** noun **1** the state in which anything is **2** something that must happen before some other thing happens **3** a point in a bargain, treaty etc

**conditional** adj depending on certain things happening □ **conditionally** adv

**condolence** noun sharing in another's sorrow; sympathy

**condom** noun a contraceptive rubber sheath

**condone** verb to allow (an offence) to pass unchecked

**conducive** adj helping, favourable (to): conducive to peace

**conduct** verb (say kon-dukt) **1** to lead, guide **2** to control, be in charge of **3** to direct (an orchestra) **4** to transmit (electricity etc) **5** to behave: conducted himself correctly □ noun (say **kon**-dukt) behaviour

**conduction** noun transmission of heat, electricity etc

**conductor** noun **1** someone who directs an orchestra **2** someone who collects fares on a bus etc **3** something that transmits heat, electricity etc

**conduit** (say kon-dit) noun a channel or pipe to carry water, electric wires etc

**cone** noun **1** a shape that is round at

the bottom and comes to a point **2** the fruit of a pine or fir-tree etc **3** an ice-cream cornet

**confectioner** noun someone who makes or sells sweets, cakes etc □ **confectionery** noun **1** sweets, cakes etc **2** the shop or business of a confectioner

**confederacy** noun (pl **confederacies**) **1** a league, an alliance **2** (**Confederacy**) US, historical the union of Southern states in the American Civil War

**confederate** adj **1** joined together by treaty **2** US, historical supporting the Confederacy □ noun someone acting in an alliance with others

**confederation** noun a union, a league

**confer** verb **1** to talk together **2** to give, grant: confer a degree

**confer** ⋄ confers, conferring, conferred

**conference** noun a meeting for discussion

**confess** verb to own up, admit to (wrong)

**confession** noun an admission of wrong-doing

**confetti** noun pl small pieces of coloured paper thrown at weddings or other celebrations

**confidant** or **confidante** (say kon-fi-dont) noun a male or female trusted with a secret

⬥ Do not confuse with: **confident**

**confide** verb: **confide in 1** to tell secrets to **2** to hand over to someone's care

**confidence** noun **1** trust, belief **2** self-assurance, boldness **3** something told privately □ **confidence trick** a trick to get money etc from someone by first gaining their trust

**confident** adj **1** very self-assured **2** certain of an outcome □ **confidently** adv

**◑.** Do not confuse with: **confidant** and **confidante**

**confidential** adj **1** to be kept as a secret **2** entrusted with secrets □ **confidentially** adv

**confiding** adj trusting

**confine** verb **1** to shut up, imprison **2** to keep within limits

**confinement** noun **1** the state of being confined **2** imprisonment **3** the time of a woman's labour and childbirth

**confines** (say kon-fainz) noun pl limits

**confirm** verb **1** to make firm, strengthen **2** to make sure **3** to show to be true **4** to admit into full membership of a church

**confirmation** noun **1** a making sure **2** proof **3** the ceremony by which someone is made a full member of a church

**confirmed** adj settled in a habit etc: a confirmed bachelor

**confiscate** verb to take away, as a punishment □ **confiscation** noun

**conflagration** noun a large, widespread fire

**conflict** noun **1** a struggle, a contest **2** a battle **3** disagreement □ verb of statements etc: to contradict each other □ **conflicting** adj

**confluence** noun a place where rivers join

**conform** verb to follow the example of most other people in behaviour, dress etc

**conformity** noun (pl conformities) **1** likeness **2** the act of conforming

**confound** verb to puzzle, confuse

**confront** verb **1** to face, meet: confronted the difficulty **2** to bring face to face (with): confronted with the evidence

**confrontation** noun a situation in which two people or groups are challenging each other openly

**confuse** verb **1** to mix up, disorder

**2** to puzzle, bewilder □ **confusing** adj □ **confusion** noun

**congeal** verb **1** to become solid, esp by cooling **2** to freeze

**congenial** adj agreeable, pleasant □ **congenially** adv

**congenital** adj of a disease: present in someone from birth

**conger** (say kong-ger) noun a kind of large sea-eel

**congested** adj **1** overcrowded, esp with traffic **2** clogged □ **congestion** noun

**conglomeration** noun a heap or collection

**congratulate** verb to express joy to (someone) at their success □ **congratulations** noun pl an expression of joy at someone's success □ **congratulatory** adj

**congregate** verb to come together in a crowd

**congregation** noun a gathering, esp of people in a church

**congress** noun (pl congresses) **1** a large meeting of people from different countries etc for discussion **2** (**Congress**) the parliament of the United States, consisting of the Senate and the House of Representatives

**congruent** adj of triangles: exactly matching

**conical** adj cone-shaped

**conifer** noun a cone-bearing tree □ **coniferous** adj

**conjecture** noun a guess □ verb to guess □ **conjectural** adj

**conjugal** adj of marriage

**conjugate** verb to give the different grammatical parts of (a verb) □ **conjugation** noun

**conjunction** noun **1** grammar a word that joins sentences or phrases, eg and, but **2** a union, a combination □ **in conjunction with** together with, acting with

**conjure** verb to perform tricks that

seem magical □ **conjuror** or **conjurer** noun

**conker** noun **1** a horse-chestnut **2** (**conkers**) a game in which players try to hit and destroy each other's chestnut, held on the end of a string

**con man** noun someone who regularly plays confidence tricks on people in order to cheat them out of money

**connect** verb to join or fasten together

**connection** noun **1** something that connects **2** a state of being connected **3** a train, aeroplane etc which takes you to the next part of a journey **4** an acquaintance, a friend □ **in connection with** concerning

**conning-tower** noun the place on a warship or submarine from which orders for steering are given

**connive** verb: **connive at** to disregard (a misdeed) □ **connivance** noun

**connoisseur** (say kon-o-ser) noun someone with an expert knowledge of a subject: wine connoisseur

**connotation** noun **1** a meaning **2** what is suggested by a word in addition to its simple meaning

**conquer** verb **1** to gain by force **2** to overcome: he conquered his fear of heights □ **conqueror** noun

**conquest** noun **1** something won by force **2** an act of conquering

**conscience** noun an inner sense of what is right and wrong

**conscientious** adj careful and diligent in work etc □ **conscientiously** adv

**conscious** adj **1** aware of yourself and your surroundings; awake **2** aware, knowing **3** deliberate, intentional: a conscious decision □ **consciously** adv □ **consciousness** noun

**conscript** noun (say kon-skript) someone obliged by law to serve in

the armed forces □ verb (say kon-skript) to compel to serve in the armed forces □ **conscription** noun

**consecrate** verb to set apart for sacred use □ **consecration** noun

**consecutive** adj coming in order, one after the other

**consensus** noun an agreement of opinion
ⓘ From Latin consensus meaning 'agreement'
◆◆ Do not confuse with: **census**

**consent** verb to agree (to) □ noun **1** agreement **2** permission □ **age of consent** the age at which someone is legally able to consent to sexual intercourse

**consequence** noun **1** something that follows as a result **2** importance

**consequent** adj following as a result □ **consequently** adv

**consequential** adj **1** following as a result **2** important

**conservation** noun the maintaining of old buildings, the countryside etc in an undamaged state □ **conservationist** noun

**conservative** adj **1** resistant to change **2** moderate, not extreme □ noun **1** someone of conservative views **2** (**Conservative**) a supporter of the Conservative Party

**Conservative Party** a right-wing political party in the UK

**conservatory** (say kon-ser-vat-ri) noun (pl **conservatories**) a glass-house for plants, or a similar room used as a lounge, attached to and entered from, the house

**conserve** verb to keep from being wasted or lost; preserve

**consider** verb **1** to think about carefully **2** to think of as, regard as **3** to pay attention to the wishes of (someone)

**considerable** adj fairly large, substantial □ **considerably** adv

**considerate** adj taking others'

wishes into account; thoughtful

**consideration** noun 1 serious thought 2 thoughtfulness for others 3 a small payment

**considering** prep taking into account: *considering your age*

**consign** (*say* kon-**sain**) verb to give into the care of

**consignment** (*say* kon-**sain**-ment) noun a load, *eg* of goods

**consist** verb to be made up (of)

◆. Do not confuse with: **comprise**. You need the word 'of' after **consist**, but not after **comprise**. You say *the exam consists of three parts*, but *the exam comprises three parts*.

**consistency** noun (*pl* **consistencies**) 1 thickness, firmness 2 the quality of always being the same

**consistent** adj 1 not changing, regular 2 of statements *etc*: not contradicting each other □ **consistently** adv

**consolation** noun something that makes trouble *etc* more easy to bear

**console** verb to comfort, cheer up

**consolidate** verb 1 to make or become strong 2 to unite □ **consolidation** noun

**consonant** noun a letter of the alphabet that is not a vowel, *eg* b, c, d

**consort** noun (*say* **kon**-sawt)1 a husband or wife 2 a companion □ verb (*say* kon-**sawt**): **consort with** to keep company with

◆. Do not confuse with: **concert**

**conspicuous** adj clearly seen, noticeable □ **conspicuously** adv

**conspiracy** noun (*pl* **conspiracies**) a plot by a group of people □ **conspirator** noun

**conspire** verb to plan or plot together

**constable** noun 1 a policeman 2 *historical* a high officer of state

**constabulary** noun the police force

**constant** adj 1 never stopping 2 never changing 3 faithful □ **constancy** noun □ **constantly** adv always

**constellation** noun a group of stars

**consternation** noun dismay, astonishment

**constipation** noun sluggish working of the bowels □ **constipated** adj

**constituency** noun (*pl* **constituencies**) 1 a district which has a member of parliament 2 the voters in such a district

**constituent** adj making or forming □ noun 1 a necessary part 2 a voter in a constituency

**constitute** verb 1 to step up, establish 2 to form, make up 3 to be the equivalent of: *this action constitutes a crime*

**constitution** noun 1 the way in which something is made up 2 the natural condition of a body in terms of health *etc*: *a weak constitution* 3 a set of laws or rules governing a country or organization □ **constitutional** adj of a constitution □ noun a short walk for the sake of your health

**constrain** verb to force to act in a certain way

**constraint** noun 1 compulsion, force 2 restraint, repression

**constrict** verb 1 to press together tightly 2 to surround and squeeze

**construct** verb to build, make

**construction** noun 1 the act of constructing 2 something built 3 the arrangement of words in a sentence 4 meaning

**constructive** adj 1 of construction 2 helping to improve: *constructive criticism* □ **constructively** adv (meaning 2)

**consul** noun 1 someone who looks after their country's affairs in a foreign country 2 *historical* a chief ruler in ancient Rome □ **consular** *adj*

**consulate** *noun* 1 the official residence of a consul 2 the duties and authority of a consul

**consult** *verb* to seek advice or information from

**consultant** *noun* 1 someone who gives professional or expert advice 2 the senior grade of hospital doctor

**consultation** *noun* 1 the activity of looking in *eg* reference books for information 2 a meeting with someone to exchange ideas and opinions 3 discussion

**consume** *verb* 1 to eat up 2 to use (up) 3 to destroy

**consumer** *noun* someone who buys, eats or uses goods

**consummate** *verb* (*say* **kon**-sum-eit or **kon**-syoo-meit) 1 to complete 2 to make (marriage) legally complete by sexual intercourse □ *adj* (*say* **kon**-syoo-mat or kon-sum-at) complete, perfect

**consumption** *noun* 1 the act of consuming 2 an amount consumed 3 *old* tuberculosis

**cont** or **contd** *abbrev* continued

**contact** *noun* 1 touch 2 meeting, communication 3 an acquaintance; someone who can be of help: *business contact* 4 someone who has been with someone suffering from an infectious disease □ *verb* to get into contact with □ **contact lens** a plastic lens worn in contact with the eyeball instead of spectacles

**contagious** *adj* of disease: spreading from person to person, *esp* by touch

**contain** *verb* 1 to hold or have inside 2 to hold back: *she couldn't contain her anger*

**container** *noun* a box, tin, jar *etc* for holding anything

**contaminate** *verb* to make impure or dirty □ **contamination** *noun*

**contd** *another spelling of* cont

**contemplate** (*say* kon-temp-leit) *verb* 1 to look at or think about attentively 2 to consider: *contemplating suicide* □ **contemplation** *noun* □ **contemplative** (*say* kon-**temp**-lat-iv) *adj* quiet and absorbed in thought

**contemporary** *adj* belonging to the same time □ *noun* someone of roughly the same age as yourself

**contempt** *noun* complete lack of respect; scorn □ **contempt of court** deliberate disobedience to and disrespect for the law and those who carry it out

**contemptible** *adj* deserving scorn, worthless

◆ Do not confuse: **contemptible** and **contemptuous**. **Contemptible** is formed from **contempt** + -**ible** ↷ able to be scorned, worthy of scorn. Use it in phrases like *a contemptible little tell-tale*.

**contemptuous** *adj* scornful

**Contemptuous** means 'full of contempt' (for something or someone). Use it in phrases like *a contemptuous laugh* or *he was contemptuous of my achievement*.

**contend** *verb* 1 to struggle against 2 to hold firmly to a belief; maintain (that)

**content** (*say* kon-tent) *adj* happy, satisfied □ *noun* happiness, satisfaction □ *verb* to make happy, satisfy □ *noun* **contents** (*say* **kon**-tents) that which is contained in anything □ **contented** *adj* happy, content □ **contentment** *noun* happiness, content

**contention** *noun* 1 an opinion strongly held 2 a quarrel, a dispute

**contest** *verb* to fight for, argue against □ *noun* a fight, a competition

**contestant** *noun* a participant in a contest

**context** noun **1** the place in a book etc to which a certain part belongs **2** the background of an event, remark etc

**contiguous** adj touching, close □ **contiguity** noun

**continent** noun one of the five large divisions of the earth's land surface (Europe, Asia, Africa, Australia, America) □ **the Continent** Brit the mainland of Europe

**continental** adj **1** of a continent **2** Brit European

**contingency** noun (pl **contingencies**) a chance happening □ **contingency plan** a plan of action in case something does not happen as expected

**contingent** adj depending (on) □ noun a group, esp of soldiers

**continual** adj happening again and again at close intervals □ **continually** adv all the time, repeatedly

❧ Do not confuse with: **continuous**. Something which is **continual** happens often, but there are short breaks when it is not happening. Something which is **continuous** happens all the time without stopping. So you could talk about, for example, continual interruptions, but the continuous lapping of waves on a beach.

**continue** verb to keep on, go on (doing something) □ **continuation** noun **1** the act of continuing **2** a part that continues, an extension

**continuity** noun the state of having no gaps or breaks

**continuous** adj coming one after the other or in a steady stream without any gap or break □ **continuously** adv

❧ Do not confuse with: **continual**

**contort** verb to twist or turn violently □ **contortion** noun a violent twisting □ **contortionist** noun

**contour** noun (often **contours**) outline, shape □ **contour line** a line drawn on a map through points all at the same height above sea-level

**contra-** see **counter-**

**contraband** noun **1** goods legally forbidden to be brought into a country **2** smuggled goods

**contraception** noun the prevention of conceiving children

**contraceptive** adj used to prevent the conceiving of children □ noun a contraceptive device or drug

**contract** verb (say kon-**trakt**) **1** to become or make smaller **2** to bargain for **3** to promise in writing □ noun (say **kon**-trakt) a written agreement □ **contraction** noun **1** a shortening **2** a shortened form of a word **3** a muscle spasm, eg during childbirth

**contractor** noun someone who promises to do work, or supply goods, at an arranged price

**contradict** verb to say the opposite of; deny □ **contradiction** noun □ **contradictory** adj **1** contradicting something **2** of two pieces of information: contradicting each other

**contralto** noun (pl **contraltos**) the lowest singing voice in women

**contraption** noun a machine, a device

**contrary**[1] (say **kon**-tra-ri) adj opposite □ noun the opposite □ **on the contrary** just the opposite

**contrary**[2] (say kon-**treir**-ri) adj always doing or saying the opposite, perverse

**contrast** verb **1** to compare so as to show differences **2** to show a marked difference from □ noun a difference between (two) things

**contravene** verb to break (a law etc) □ **contravention** noun

**contretemps** (say **kon**-tre-tom) noun a mishap at an awkward moment

**contribute** *verb* **1** to give (money, help *etc*) along with others **2** to supply (articles *etc*) for a publication **3** to help to cause □ **contribution** *noun* □ **make a contribution** to give or supply something, play a part □ **contributor** *noun* □ **contributory** *adj*

**con trick** *noun* a confidence trick

**contrite** *adj* very sorry for having done wrong □ **contrition** *noun*

**contrivance** *noun* an act of contriving; an invention

**contrive** *verb* **1** to plan **2** to bring about, manage: *contrived to be out of the office*

**contro-** *see* **counter-**

**control** *noun* **1** authority to rule, manage, restrain *etc* **2** (often **controls**) means by which a driver keeps a machine powered or guided □ *verb* **1** to exercise control over **2** to have power over □ **controlled** *adj* □ **controller** *noun* □ **control tower** an airport building from which landing and take-off instructions are given

**controversial** *adj* likely to cause argument

**controversy** *noun* (*pl* **controversies**) an argument, a disagreement

**conundrum** *noun* a riddle, a question

**conurbation** *noun* a group of towns forming a single built-up area

**convalesce** *verb* to recover health gradually after being ill □ **convalescence** *noun* □ **convalescent** *noun*

**convection** *noun* the spreading of heat by movement of heated air or water

**convector** *noun* a heater which works by convection

**convene** *verb* to call or come together □ **convener** *noun* **1** someone who calls a meeting **2** the chairman or chairwoman of a committee

**convenience** *noun* **1** suitableness, handiness **2** a means of giving ease or comfort **3** *informal* a public lavatory □ **at your convenience** when it suits you best

**convenient** *adj* easy to reach or use, handy □ **conveniently** *adv*

**convent** *noun* a building accommodating an order of nuns

**convention** *noun* **1** a way of behaving that has become usual, a custom **2** a large meeting, an assembly **3** a treaty or agreement □ **conventional** *adj* **1** done by habit or custom **2** having traditional attitudes and behaviour □ **conventionally** *adv*

**converge** *verb* to come together, meet at a point □ **convergence** *noun* □ **convergent** *adj*

**conversation** *noun* talk, exchange of ideas, news *etc* □ **conversational** *adj* **1** of conversation **2** talkative

**converse¹** (*say* kon-**vers**) *verb* to talk □ *noun* conversation

**converse²** (*say* **kon**-vers) *noun* the opposite □ *adj* opposite

**convert** *verb* (*say* kon-**vert**) **1** to change (from one thing into another) **2** to turn from one religion to another □ *noun* (*say* **kon**-vert) someone who has been converted □ **conversion** *noun*

**convertible** *adj* able to be changed from one thing to another □ *noun* a car with a folding roof

**convex** *adj* curved on the outside (*contrasted with:* **concave**) □ **convexity** *noun* (*pl* **convexities**

**convey** *verb* **1** to carry, transport **2** to send **3** *law* to hand over: *convey property*

**conveyance** *noun* **1** the act of conveying **2** a vehicle

**conveyancing** *noun*, *law* the process of handing over from one party to another the legal ownership of property

**conveyor** or **conveyor belt** *noun* an endless moving mechanism for conveying articles, *esp* in a factory

**convict** *verb* (*say* kon-**vikt**) to declare or prove that someone is guilty □ *noun* (*say* **kon**-vikt) someone found guilty of a crime and sent to prison

---

◼ (verb) acquit

---

**conviction** *noun* **1** the passing of a guilty sentence on someone in court **2** a strong belief

**convince** *verb* **1** to make (someone) believe that something is true **2** to persuade (someone) by showing

**convivial** *adj* jolly, festive □ **conviviality** *noun*

**convoy** *verb* to go along with and protect □ *noun* **1** merchant ships protected by warships **2** a line of army lorries with armed guard

**convulsion** *noun* **1** a sudden stiffening or jerking of the muscles **2** a violent disturbance □ **convulse** *verb* to cause to shake violently: *convulsed with laughter* □ **convulsive** *adj*

**coo** *noun* a sound like that of a dove □ *verb* make this sound

**cook** *verb* **1** to prepare (food) by heating **2** *informal* to alter (accounts *etc*) dishonestly □ *noun* someone who cooks and prepares food

**cooker** *noun* **1** a stove for cooking **2** an apple *etc* used in cooking, not for eating raw

**cookery** *noun* the art of cooking

**cool** *adj* **1** slightly cold **2** calm, not excited **3** *informal* acceptable **4** *informal* good, fashionable □ *verb* make or grow cool; calm □ **coolness** *noun* (adjectives, meanings 1 and 2) □ **coolly** *adj* **1** in a calm way **2** in a slightly unfriendly way

**coop** *noun* a box or cage for hens *etc* □ *verb* to shut (up) as in a coop

**co-op** *see* **cooperative society**

**cooper** *noun* someone who makes barrels

**cooperate** *verb* to work or act together □ **cooperation** *noun* □ **cooperative** *noun* a business or farm *etc* owned by the workers

**cooperative society** or **co-op** a trading organization in which the profits are shared among members

**co-opt** *verb* to choose (someone) to join a committee or other body

**co-ordinate** *verb* to make things fit in or work smoothly together □ **co-ordination** *noun* **1** the activity or skill of co-ordinating things **2** the ability to move and use the different parts of your body smoothly together

**coot** *noun* a water-bird with a white spot on the forehead

**cop** *noun, slang* a police officer □ *verb* catch, seize □ **cop it** to land in trouble □ **cop out** to avoid responsibility

---

**cop** *verb* ⇨ cops, copping, copped

---

**cope** *verb* to struggle or deal successfully (with), manage

**coping** *noun* the top layer of stone in a wall

**copious** *adj* plentiful □ **copiously** *adj*

**copper** *noun* **1** a hard reddish-brown metal **2** a reddish-brown colour **3** a coin made from copper **4** a large vessel made of copper, for boiling water

**copperplate** *noun* a style of very fine and regular handwriting

**copra** *noun* the dried kernel of the coconut, yielding coconut oil

**copse** *noun* a wood of low-growing trees

**copy** *noun* (*pl* **copies**) **1** an imitation **2** a print or reproduction of a picture *etc* **3** an individual example of a certain book *etc* □ *verb* **1** to make a copy of **2** to imitate

**copyright** *noun* the right of one

person or body to publish a book, perform a play, print music *etc* ❑ *adj* of or protected by the law of copyright

**coquette** *noun* a flirtatious woman ❑ **coquettish** *adj*

**cor-** *see* **co-**

**coral** *noun* a hard substance made from the skeletons of a tiny animal ❑ **coral reef** a rock-like mass of coral built up gradually from the sea-bed

**cord** *noun* **1** thin rope or strong string **2** a thick strand of anything ⊕ From French *corde* meaning 'a rope'

❧ Do not confuse with: **chord**

**cordial** *adj* cheery, friendly ❑ *noun* a refreshing drink ❑ **cordiality** *noun*

**cordon** *noun* a line of guards, police *etc* to keep people back

**cordon bleu** *adj* of a cook or cooking: first-class, excellent

Literally 'blue ribbon' in French, after the ribbon worn by the Knights of the Holy Ghost

**corduroy** *noun* a ribbed cotton cloth resembling velvet

**core** *noun* the inner part of anything, *esp* fruit ❑ *verb* to take out the core of (fruit)

**corespondent** (*say* koh-res-**pon**-dent) *noun* a man or woman charged with having committed adultery with a wife or husband (the **respondent**)

❧ Do not confuse with: **correspondent**

**corgi** *noun* a breed of short-legged dog

**cork** *noun* **1** the outer bark of a type of oak found in southern Europe *etc* **2** a stopper for a bottle *etc* made of cork ❑ *adj* made of cork ❑ *verb* to plug or stop up with a cork ❑ **corkscrew** *noun* a tool with a screw-like spike for taking out corks ❑ *adj* shaped like a corkscrew

**corm** *noun* the bulb-like underground stem of certain plants

**cormorant** *noun* a type of big sea-bird

**corn** *noun* **1** wheat, oats or maize **2** a small lump of hard skin, *esp* on a toe

**cornea** *noun* the transparent covering of the eyeball

**corned beef** salted tinned beef

**corner** *noun* **1** the point where two walls, roads *etc* meet **2** a small secluded place **3** *informal* a difficult situation ❑ *verb* to force into a position from which there is no escape

**cornerstone** *noun* **1** the stone at the corner of a building's foundations **2** something upon which much depends

**cornet** *noun* **1** a musical instrument like a small trumpet **2** an ice-cream in a cone-shaped wafer

**cornflour** *noun* finely ground maize flour

**cornflower** *noun* a type of plant, with a blue flower

**cornice** *noun* an ornamental border round a ceiling

**coronary** *noun* (*pl* **coronaries**) (*short for* **coronary thrombosis**) a heart disease caused by blockage of one of the arteries supplying the heart

**coronation** *noun* the crowning of a king or queen

**coroner** *noun* a government officer who holds inquiries into the causes of sudden or accidental deaths

**coronet** *noun* **1** a small crown **2** a crown-like head-dress

**corporal**[1] *noun* the rank next below sergeant in the British army

**corporal**[2] *adj* of the body ❑ **corporal punishment** physical punishment by beating

**corporate** *adj* of or forming a whole, united

**corporation** *noun* a body of people acting as one for administrative or business purposes

**corps** (*say* kawr) *noun* (*pl* **corps** - *say* kawz) **1** a division of an army **2** an organized group

◆ Do not confuse: **corps** and **corpse**

**corpse** *noun* a dead body

**corpulent** *adj* fat, obese □ **corpulence** *noun*

**corpus** *noun* (*pl* **corpora**) a collection of writing *etc*

**corpuscle** *noun* **1** a very small particle **2** a blood cell, red or white □ **corpuscular** *adj*

**corral** *noun*, *US* a fenced enclosure for animals □ *verb* enclose, pen

**corral** *verb* ⇔ corrals, corralling, corralled

**correct** *verb* **1** to remove errors from **2** to set right **3** to punish □ *adj* **1** having no errors **2** true **3** suitable and acceptable □ **correction** *noun* **1** the putting right of a mistake **2** punishment □ **corrective** *adj*

**correspond** *verb* **1** to write letters to **2** to be similar (to), match □ **correspondence** *noun* **1** letters **2** likeness, similarity □ **correspondent** *noun* **1** someone who writes letters **2** someone who contributes reports to a newspaper *etc*
℗ From Latin *cor* meaning 'with', and *respondere* meaning 'to answer'

◆ Do not confuse with: **corespondent**

**corridor** *noun* a passageway

**corroborate** *verb* to give evidence which strengthens evidence already given □ **corroboration** *noun*
℗ From Latin *cor-* giving emphasis, and *roborare* meaning 'to make strong'

◆ Do not confuse with: **collaborate**

**corrode** *verb* **1** to rust **2** to eat away at, erode □ **corrosion** *noun*

**corrosive** *adj* **1** able to destroy or wear away materials such as metal by reacting chemically with them: *nitric acid is highly corrosive* **2** having the effect of gradually wearing down or destroying something

**corrugated** *adj* folded or shaped into ridges: *corrugated iron*

**corrupt** *verb* **1** to make evil or rotten **2** to make dishonest, bribe □ *adj* **1** dishonest, taking bribes **2** bad, rotten □ **corruptible** *adj* □ **corruption** *noun*

**corsair** *noun*, *old* **1** a pirate **2** a pirate-ship

**corset** *noun* a tight-fitting undergarment to support the body

**cortège** (*say* kaw-tesz) *noun* a funeral procession

**cosh** *noun* (*pl* **coshes**) a short heavy stick □ *verb* to hit with a cosh

**cosmetic** *noun* something designed to improve the appearance, *esp* of the face □ *adj* **1** applied as a cosmetic **2** superficial, for appearances only

**cosmic** *adj* **1** of the universe or outer space **2** *informal* excellent

**cosmonaut** *noun*, *historical* an astronaut of the former USSR

**cosmopolitan** *adj* **1** including people from many countries **2** familiar with, or comfortable in, many different countries

**cosmos** *noun* the universe

**cosset** *verb* to treat with too much kindness, pamper

**cost** *verb* **1** to be priced at **2** to cause the loss of: *the war cost many lives* □ *noun* what must be paid or suffered in order to get something

**cost** *verb* ⇔ costs, costing, cost

**costly** *adj* high-priced, valuable □ **costliness** *noun*

**costume** *noun* **1** a set of clothes **2** clothes to wear in a play **3** fancy dress **4** a swimsuit □ **costume**

**jewellery** inexpensive, imitation jewellery

**cosy** *adj* warm and comfortable □ *noun* (*pl* **cosies**) a covering to keep a teapot *etc* warm

**cot** *noun* **1** a small high-sided bed for children **2** *US* a small collapsible bed; a camp bed □ **cot death** the sudden unexplained death in sleep of an apparently healthy baby

**cottage** *noun* a small house, *esp* in the countryside or a village □ **cottage cheese** a soft, white cheese made from skimmed milk □ **cottager** *noun*

**cotton** *noun* **1** a soft fluffy substance obtained from the seeds of the cotton plant **2** cloth made of cotton □ *adj* made of cotton □ **cottonwool** *noun* cotton in a fluffy state, used for wiping or absorbing

**couch** *noun* (*pl* **couches**) a sofa □ *verb* to express verbally: *couched in archaic language* □ **couch grass** a kind of grass, a troublesome weed □ **couch potato** someone who spends their free time watching TV *etc*

**cougar** *noun*, *US* a puma

**cough** *noun* a noisy effort of the lungs to throw out air and harmful matter from the throat □ *verb* to make this effort

**could** *verb* **1** the form of the verb **can** used to express a condition: *he could afford it if he tried/ I could understand a small mistake, but this is ridiculous* **2** *past form* of the verb **can**

**council** *noun* a group of people elected to discuss or give advice about policy, government *etc* □ **councillor** *noun* a member of a council
ⓘ From Latin *concilium* meaning 'a calling together'

◥ Do not confuse with: **counsel**

**counsel** *noun* **1** advice **2** *US* someone who gives legal advice; a lawyer □ *verb* to give advice to

□ **counsellor** *noun* someone who gives advice, or who is involved in counselling

**counsel** ⟷ counsel**s**, counsel**ling**, counsel**led**
ⓘ From Latin *consilium* meaning 'advice'

◥ Do not confuse with: **council**

**count¹** *verb* **1** to find the total number of, add up **2** to say numbers in order (1, 2, 3 *etc*) **3** to think, consider: *count yourself lucky!* □ *noun* **1** the act of counting **2** the number counted, *eg* of votes at an election **3** a charge, an accusation **4** a point being considered □ **count on** to rely on, depend on

**count²** *noun* a nobleman in certain countries

**countenance** *noun* **1** the face **2** the expression on someone's face □ *verb* to allow, encourage

**counter¹** *verb* to answer or oppose (a move, act *etc*) by another □ *adv* in the opposite direction □ *adj* opposed; opposite

**counter²** *noun* **1** a token used in counting **2** a small plastic disc used in ludo *etc* **3** a table across which payments are made in a shop

**counter-** also **contra-**, **contro-** *prefix* **1** against, opposing: *counter-argument* **2** opposite
ⓘ From Latin *contra* meaning 'against'

**counteract** *verb* to block or defeat (an action) by doing the opposite

**counterattack** *noun* an attack made by the defenders upon an attacking enemy □ *verb* to launch a counterattack

**counterfeit** *adj* **1** not genuine, not real **2** made in imitation for criminal purposes: *counterfeit money* □ *verb* to make a copy of

**counterfoil** *noun* a part of a cheque, postal order *etc* kept by the payer or sender

**countermand** *verb* to give an order which goes against one already given

**counterpane** *noun* a top cover for a bed

**counterpart** *noun* someone or something which is just like or which corresponds to another person or thing

**counterpoint** *noun* the combining of two or more melodies to make a piece of music

**counterpoise** *noun* a weight which balances another weight

**countersign** *verb* to sign your name after someone else's signature to show that a document is genuine

**countess** *noun* 1 a woman of the same rank as a count or earl 2 the wife or widow of a count or earl

**countless** *adj* too many to be counted, very many

**country** *noun* (*pl* **countries**) 1 a nation 2 a land under one government 3 the land in which someone lives 4 a district which is not in a town or city 5 an area or stretch of land □ *adj* belonging to the country □ **countryside** *noun* the parts of a country other than towns and cities
  ⓗ From Old French *contrée* meaning 'a stretch of land'

**county** *noun* (*pl* **counties**) a division of a country

**coup** (*say* koo) *noun* 1 a sudden outstandingly successful move or act 2 a coup d'état

**coup d'état** (*say* koo dei-**tah**) a sudden and violent change in government

**couple** *noun* 1 a pair, two of a kind together 2 a husband and wife □ *verb* to join together

**couplet** *noun* two lines of rhyming verse

**coupling** *noun* a link for joining railway carriages *etc*

**coupon** *noun* a piece of paper which may be exchanged for goods or money

**courage** *noun* bravery, lack of fear □ **courageous** *adj*

**courgette** *noun* a type of small marrow

**courier** *noun* 1 someone who acts as guide for tourists 2 a messenger

**course** *noun* 1 a path in which anything moves from point to point 3 a track along which athletes *etc* run 4 a direction to be followed 5 line of action 6 a part of a meal 7 a number of things following each other: *a course of twelve lectures* 8 one of the rows of bricks in a wall □ *verb* 1 to move quickly 2 to hunt □ **in due course** after a while, in its proper time □ **in the course of** during

**court** *noun* 1 an open space surrounded by houses 2 an area marked out for playing tennis *etc* 3 the people who attend a monarch *etc* 4 a royal residence 5 a room or building where legal cases are heard or tried □ *verb* 1 to woo as a potential lover 2 to try to gain: *courting her affections* 3 to come near to achieving: *courting disaster* □ **courtship** *noun* the act or time of courting or wooing □ **courtyard** *noun* a court or enclosed space beside a house

**courteous** *adj* polite; obliging □ **courteously** *adv*

**courtesy** *noun* politeness

**courtier** *noun* a member of a royal court

**courtly** *adj* having fine manners

**court-martial** *noun* (*pl* **courts-martial**) an internal court held to try those who break navy or army laws □ *verb* to try in a court-martial

**cousin** *noun* the son or daughter of an uncle or aunt

**cove** *noun* a small inlet on the sea coast; a bay

**covenant** *noun* an important agreement between people to do or not to do something

**cover** *verb* 1 to put or spread something on or over 2 to hide 3 to stretch over: *my diary covers three years* 4 to include, deal with: *covering the news story* 5 to be enough for: *two pounds should cover it* 6 to travel over: *covering 3 kilometres a day* 7 to point a weapon at: *we had the gangster covered* □ *noun* something that covers, hides or protects □ **cover up** 1 to cover completely 2 to conceal deliberately □ **cover-up** *noun* a deliberate concealment, *esp* by people in authority

**coverage** *noun* 1 an area covered 2 the extent of news covered by a newspaper *etc* 3 the amount of protection given by an insurance policy

**coverlet** *noun* a bed cover ⓘ From French *couvrir* meaning 'to cover', and *lit* meaning 'bed'

**covert** *adj* secret, not done openly □ *noun* a hiding place for animals or birds when hunted

**covet** *verb* to desire eagerly, *esp* something belonging to another person □ **covetous** *adj* □ **covetously** *adv*

**covey** *noun* (*pl* **coveys**) a flock of birds, *esp* partridges

**cow** *noun* 1 the female of various types of ox, bred by humans for giving milk 2 the female of an elephant, whale *etc* □ *verb* to frighten, subdue □ **cowboy, cowgirl** *noun* someone who works with cattle on a ranch □ **cowherd** *noun* someone who looks after cows

**coward** *noun* someone who has no courage and shows fear easily □ **cowardice** *noun* lack of courage □ **cowardly** *adj*

**cower** *verb* to crouch down or shrink back through fear

**cowl** *noun* 1 a hood, *esp* that of a monk 2 a cover for a chimney

**cowslip** *noun* a yellow wild flower

**cox** *noun* (*pl* **coxes**) the person who steers a racing crew

**coxswain** *noun* 1 someone who steers a boat 2 an officer in charge of a boat and crew

**coy** *adj* too modest or shy

**coyote** (*say* kai-oh-ti) *noun* (*pl* **coyote** or **coyotes**) a type of small North American wolf

**crab** *noun* 1 a sea creature with a shell and five pairs of legs, the first pair of which have large claws 2 *informal* **crabs** pubic lice □ **crab apple** a type of small, bitter apple □ **crabwise** *adv* sideways like a crab

**crabbed** (*say* **krab**-id) *adj* bad-tempered

**crack** *verb* 1 to (cause to) make a sharp, sudden sound 2 to break partly without falling to pieces 3 to break into (a safe) 4 to decipher (a code) 5 to break open (a nut) 6 to make (a joke) □ *noun* 1 a sharp sound 2 a split, a break 3 a narrow opening 4 *informal* a sharp, witty remark 5 *informal* a pure form of cocaine □ *adj* excellent: *a crack tennis player* □ **cracked** 1 split, damaged 2 mad, crazy □ **crack up** to go to pieces, collapse

**cracker** *noun* 1 a hollow paper tube containing a small gift, which breaks with a bang when the ends are pulled 2 a thin, crisp biscuit 3 *informal* something excellent: *a cracker of a story*

**crackle** *verb* to make a continuous cracking noise

**crackling** *noun* 1 a cracking sound 2 the rind or outer skin of roast pork

**cradle** *noun* 1 a baby's bed, *esp* one which can be rocked 2 a frame under a ship that is being built

**craft** *noun* 1 a trade, a skill 2 a boat, a small ship 3 slyness, cunning □ **craftsman, craftswoman** *noun* someone who works at a trade, *esp* with his or her hands □ **craftworker** *noun*

**crafty** *adj* cunning, sly □ **craftily** *adv*

**crag** *noun* a rough steep rock □ **craggy** *adj* 1 rocky 2 of a face: well-marked, lined

**cram** *verb* 1 to fill full, stuff 2 to learn up facts for an examination in a short time

**cram** ⇨ **cram***s*, **cram***ming*, **cram***med*

**cramp** *noun* 1 a painful stiffening of the muscles 2 (**cramps**) an acute stomach pain □ *verb* 1 to confine in too small a space 2 to hinder, restrict □ **cramped** *adj* 1 without enough room 2 of handwriting: small and closely-written

**cranberry** *noun* (*pl* **cranberries**) a type of red, sour berry

**crane** *noun* 1 a large wading bird with long legs, neck and bill 2 a machine for lifting heavy weights □ *verb* to stretch out (the neck) to see round or over something

**cranium** *noun* (*pl* **crania** or **craniums**) the skull

**crank** *noun* 1 a handle for turning an axle 2 a lever which converts a horizontal movement into a rotating one 3 an eccentric □ *verb* to start (an engine) with a crank □ **cranky** *adj* 1 odd, eccentric 2 cross, irritable

**cranny** *noun* (*pl* **crannies**) a small opening or crack

**crash** *noun* (*pl* **crashes**) 1 a noise of heavy things breaking or banging together 2 a collision causing damage, *eg* between vehicles 3 the failure of a business □ *adj* short but intensive: *crash course in French* □ *verb* 1 to be involved in a crash 2 of a business: to fail 3 of a computer program: to break down, fail 4 *informal* to attend (a party) uninvited (*also called* **gatecrash**) □ **crash-helmet** *noun* a protective covering for the head worn by

motor-cyclists *etc* □ **crash-land** *verb* to land (an aircraft) in an emergency, causing some structural damage □ **crash-landing** *noun*

**crass** *adj* stupid □ **crassly** *adv*

**crate** *noun* a container for carrying goods, often made of wooden slats

**crater** *noun* 1 the bowl-shaped mouth of a volcano 2 a hole made by an explosion

**cravat** (*say* kra-**vat**) *noun* a scarf worn in place of a tie

From a French word for 'Croat', because of the linen neckbands worn by 17th-century Croatian soldiers

**craven** *adj*, *old* cowardly

**crawl** *verb* 1 to move on hands and knees 2 to move slowly 3 to be covered (with): *crawling with wasps* 4 to be obsequious, fawn □ *noun* 1 the act of crawling 2 a swimming stroke of kicking the feet and alternating the arms □ **crawler** *noun*, *informal* an obsequious, fawning person

**crayon** *noun* a coloured pencil or stick for drawing

**craze** *noun* a temporary fashion or enthusiasm

**crazy** *adj* mad, unreasonable □ **crazily** *adv* □ **crazy patchwork** patchwork made with irregular shapes of fabric □ **crazy paving** paving with stones of irregular shape

◼ mad, deranged, crazed, silly, preposterous, impracticable, wild

**creak** *verb* to make a sharp, grating sound like a hinge in need of oiling

**cream** *noun* 1 the fatty substance which forms on milk 2 something like this in texture: *shaving cream* 3 the best part: *the cream of society* □ *verb* to take the cream from 2 to take away (the best part) □ **creamy** *adj*

**crease** *noun* 1 a mark made by folding 2 *cricket* a line showing the position of a batsman and bowler □ **verb 1** to make creases in **2** to become creased

**create** verb **1** to bring into being; make **2** informal to make a fuss □ **creation** noun □ **creative** adj having the ability to create, artistic □ **creativity** noun

**creator** noun the person who has created something □ **the Creator** God

**creature** noun an animal or person

**crèche** noun a nursery for children

**credence** noun belief

**credentials** noun pl documents carried as proof of identity, character etc

**credible** adj able to be believed □ **credibility** noun

● Do not confuse with: **credulous**

**credit** noun **1** recognition of good qualities, achievements etc **2** good qualities **3** a source of honour: a credit to the family **4** trustworthiness in ability to pay for goods **5** the sale of goods to be paid for later **6** the side of an account on which payments received are entered **7** a sum of money in a bank account **8** belief, trust **9** (**credits**) the naming of people who have helped in a film etc □ verb **1** to believe **2** to enter on the credit side of an account **3 credit someone with** to believe them to have: I credited him with more sense □ **credit card** a card allowing the holder to pay for purchased articles at a later date

**creditable** adj bringing honour or good reputation to □ **creditably** adv

**creditor** noun someone to whom money is due

**credulous** adj believing too easily

● Do not confuse with: **credible**

**creed** noun a belief, esp a religious one

**creek** noun **1** a small inlet or bay on the sea coast **2** a short river

**creep** verb **1** to move slowly and silently **2** to move with the body close to the ground **3** to shiver with fear or disgust **4** of a plant: to grow along the ground or up a wall □ noun **1** a move in a creeping way **2** informal an unpleasant person □ **the creeps** informal a feeling of disgust or fear □ **creep up on** to approach silently from behind □ **creepy** adj unsettlingly sinister

**creep** verb ⇔ creeps, creeping, crept

**creeper** noun a plant growing along the ground or up a wall

**cremate** verb to burn (a dead body) □ **cremation** noun

**crematorium** noun a place where dead bodies are burnt

**creosote** noun an oily liquid made from wood tar, used to keep wood from rotting

**crêpe** noun **1** a type of fine, crinkly material **2** a thin pancake □ **crêpe paper** paper with a crinkled appearance

**crept** past form of creep

**crescendo** noun **1** a musical passage of increasing loudness **2** a climax

**crescent** adj shaped like the new or old moon; curved □ noun **1** something in a curved shape **2** a curved road or street

**cress** noun a plant with small, slightly bitter-tasting leaves, used in salads

**crest** noun **1** a tuft on the head of a cock or other bird **2** the top of a hill, wave etc **3** feathers on top of a helmet **4** a badge

**crestfallen** adj down-hearted, discouraged

**cretin** noun, informal an idiot, a fool

**crevasse** (say kre-vas) noun a deep split in snow or ice

● Do not confuse: **crevasse** and **crevice**

**crevice** (*say* krev-is) *noun* a crack, a narrow opening

**crew**[1] *noun* **1** the people who man a ship, aircraft *etc* **2** a gang, a mob □ *verb* to act as a member of a crew □ **crewcut** *noun* an extremely short hairstyle

**crew**[2] *past form of* **crow**

**crib** *noun* **1** a manger **2** a child's bed **3** a ready-made translation of a school text *etc* □ *verb* to copy someone else's work

**crib** *verb* ⇌ cribs, cribbing, cribbed

**cribbage** *noun* a type of card game in which the score is kept with a pegged board

**crick** *noun* a sharp pain, *esp* in the neck □ *verb* to produce a crick in

**cricket** *noun* **1** a game played with bats, ball and wickets, between two sides of 11 each **2** an insect similar to a grasshopper □ **cricketer** *noun* someone who plays cricket

**cried** *past form of* **cry**

**crime** *noun* an act or deed which is against the law

**criminal** *adj* **1** forbidden by law **2** very wrong □ *noun* someone guilty of a crime

**crimson** *noun* a deep red colour □ *adj* of this colour

**cringe** *verb* **1** to crouch or shrink back in fear **2** to behave in too humble a way

**crinkle** *verb* **1** to wrinkle, crease **2** to make a crackling sound □ **crinkly** *adj* wrinkled

**crinoline** *noun* a wide petticoat or skirt shaped by concentric hoops

**cripple** *noun* a disabled person □ *verb* **1** to make lame **2** to make less strong, less efficient *etc*: *their policies crippled the economy*

**crisis** *noun* (pl **crises**) **1** a deciding moment, a turning point **2** a time of great danger or suspense

**crisp** *adj* **1** stiff and dry; brittle **2** cool and fresh **3** firm and fresh

**4** sharp □ *noun* a thin crisp piece of fried potato eaten cold □ **crispy** *adj*

**criss-cross** *adj* having a pattern of crossing lines □ *verb* to move across and back: *railway lines criss-cross the landscape*

Based on the phrase *Christ's cross*

**criterion** *noun* (pl **criteria**) a means or rule by which something can be judged; a standard

**critic** *noun* **1** someone who judges the merits or faults of a book, film *etc* **2** someone who finds faults in a thing or person

**critical** *adj* **1** fault-finding **2** of criticism: *critical commentary* **3** of or at a crisis **4** very ill **5** serious, very important

**criticism** *noun* **1** a judgement or opinion on (something), *esp* one showing up faults **2** the act of criticizing

**criticize** *verb* **1** to find fault with **2** to give an opinion or judgement on

**croak** *verb* to make a low, hoarse sound □ *noun* a low, hoarse sound □ **croaky** *adj* of sounds: low and hoarse

**crochet** (*say* kroh-shei) *noun* a form of knitting done with one hooked needle □ *verb* to work in crochet

**crock** *noun* **1** an earthenware pot or jar **2** a worthless, old and decrepit person or thing

**crockery** *noun* china or earthenware dishes

**crocodile** *noun* **1** a large reptile found in rivers in Asia, Africa *etc* **2** a procession of children walking two by two □ **crocodile tears** pretended tears

**crocus** *noun* (pl **crocuses**) a yellow, purple or white flower which grows from a bulb

**croft** *noun* a small farm with a cottage, *esp* in the Scottish Highlands □ **crofter** *noun* □ **crofting** *noun*

**croissant** noun a curved roll of rich bread dough

**crone** noun an ugly old woman

**crony** noun (pl **cronies**) informal a close friend

**crook** noun **1** a shepherd's or bishop's stick bent at the end **2** a criminal □ verb to bend or form into a hook

**crooked** (say **kruuk**-id) adj **1** bent, hooked **2** dishonest, criminal

**croon** verb to sing or hum in a low voice □ **crooning** noun

**crop** noun **1** natural produce gathered for food from fields, trees or bushes **2** a part of a bird's stomach **3** a riding whip **4** the hair on the head **5** a short haircut □ verb **1** to cut short **2** to gather a crop (of wheat etc) □ **crop up** to happen unexpectedly

**crop** verb ⇔ **crops, cropping, cropped**

**cropper** noun: **come a cropper 1** to fail badly **2** to have a bad fall

**croquet** (say **kroh**-kei) noun a game in which players use long-handled mallets to drive wooden balls through hoops in the ground

**cross** noun **1** a shape (×) or (+) formed of two lines intersecting in the middle **2** a crucifix **3** a street monument marking the site of a market etc **4** the result of breeding an animal or plant with one of another kind **5** a trouble that must be endured □ verb **1** to mark with a cross **2** to go to the other side of (a room, road etc) **3** to lie or pass across **4** to meet and pass **5** to go against the wishes of **6** to draw two lines across to validate (a cheque) **7** to breed (one kind) with (another) □ adj bad-tempered, angry □ **cross-country** adj of a race: across fields etc, not on roads □ **cross-examine** verb question closely in court to test accuracy of a statement etc □ **cross-eyed** adj having a squint □ **crossly**

adv angrily □ **crossness** noun bad temper, sulkiness □ **cross-reference** noun a statement in a reference book directing the reader to further information in another section □ **crossroads** noun sing a place where roads cross each other □ **cross-section** noun **1** a section made by cutting across something **2** a sample taken as representative of the whole: a cross-section of voters

**crossbow** noun a bow fixed crosswise to a wooden stand with a device for pulling back the bowstring

**crossing** noun **1** a place where a street, river etc may be crossed **2** a journey over the sea

**crossword** noun a puzzle in which letters are written into blank squares to form words

**crotch** noun the area between the tops of the legs

**crotchet** noun a musical note (♩) equivalent to a quarter of a whole note or semibreve

**crotchety** adj bad-tempered

**crouch** verb **1** to stand with the knees well bent **2** of an animal: to lie close to the ground

**croup** (say kroop) noun a children's disease causing difficulty in breathing and a harsh cough

**crow** noun **1** a large bird, generally black **2** the cry of a cock **3** the happy sounds made by a baby □ verb **1** to cry like a cock **2** to boast **3** of a baby: to make happy noises □ **as the crow flies** in a straight line □ **crow's-nest** noun a sheltered and enclosed platform near the mast-head of a ship from which a lookout is kept

**crow** verb ⇔ **crows, crowing, crew or crowed** □ **crew** is used as the past form for meaning 1 only; the cock crew; otherwise the form is **crowed**: crowed about his exam results.

**crowbar** *noun* a large iron bar used as a lever

**crowd** *noun* a number of people or things together □ *verb* **1** to gather into a crowd **2** to fill too full **3** to keep too close to, impede

**crown** *noun* **1** a jewelled head-dress worn by monarchs on ceremonial occasions **2** the top of the head **3** the highest part of something **4** *Brit, historical* a coin worth five shillings *verb* **1** to put a crown on **2** to make a monarch **3** *informal* to hit on the head **4** to reward, finish happily: *crowned with success*

**crucial** *adj* extremely important, critical: *crucial question* □ **crucially** *adv*

**crucible** *noun* a small container for melting metals *etc*

**crucifix** *noun* (*pl* **crucifixes**) a figure or picture of Christ fixed to the cross

**crucify** *verb* to put to death by fixing the hands and feet to a cross □ **crucifixion** *noun* **1** the act of crucifying **2** death on the cross, *esp* that of Christ

**crucify** ↔ **crucifies**, **crucifying**, **crucified**

**crude** *adj* **1** not purified or refined: *crude oil* **2** roughly made or done **3** rude, blunt, tactless □ **crudely** *adv* □ **crudity** *noun*

**cruel** *adj* **1** causing pain or distress **2** having no pity for others' sufferings □ **cruelly** *adv* □ **cruelty** *noun* (*pl* **cruelties**)

**cruet** (*say* **kroo**-it) *noun* **1** a small jar for salt, pepper, mustard *etc* **2** two or more such jars on a stand

**cruise** *verb* to travel by car, ship *etc* at a steady speed □ *noun* a journey by ship made for pleasure □ **cruiser** *noun* a middle-sized warship

**crumb** *noun* a small bit of anything, *esp* bread

**crumble** *verb* **1** to break into crumbs or small pieces **2** to fall to pieces □ *noun* a dish of stewed fruit *etc* topped with crumbs □ **crumbly** *adj*

**crumpet** *noun* a soft cake, baked on a griddle and eaten with butter

**crumple** *verb* **1** to crush into creases or wrinkles **2** to become creased **3** to collapse □ **crumple zone** a buffer area in a car *etc* to absorb the impact of a crash

**crunch** *verb* **1** to chew hard so as to make a noise **2** to crush □ *noun* **1** a noise of crunching **2** *informal* a testing moment, a turning-point

**crusade** *noun* **1** a movement undertaken for some good cause **2** *historical* a Christian expedition to regain the Holy Land from the Turks □ **crusader** *noun* someone who goes on a crusade

**crush** *verb* **1** to squeeze together **2** to beat down, overcome **3** to crease, crumple □ *noun* **1** a violent squeezing **2** a pressing crowd of people **3** a drink made by squeezing fruit □ **crushed** *adj* **1** squeezed, squashed **2** completely defeated or miserable

**crust** *noun* a hard outside coating, *eg* on bread, a pie, a planet

**crustacean** (*say* krus-**tei**-shun) *noun* one of a large group of animals with a hard shell, including crabs, lobsters, shrimps *etc*

**crusty** *adj* **1** having a crust **2** cross, irritable

**crutch** *noun* (*pl* **crutches**) **1** a stick held under the armpit or elbow, used for support in walking **2** a support, a prop

**crux** *noun* the most important or difficult part of a problem

**cry** *verb* **1** to make a loud sound in pain or sorrow **2** to weep **3** to call loudly □ *noun* (*pl* **cries**) a loud call □ **crying** *adj* **1** weeping **2** calling loudly **3** requiring notice or attention: *a crying need* □ **cry off** to cancel □ **cry over spilt milk** to be worried about a misfortune that is past

**cry** ⟷ cries, crying, cried

■ (verb, meaning 2) sob, blubber, wail, bawl, whimper, snivel

**crypt** noun an underground cell or chapel, esp one used for burial

**cryptic** adj mysterious, difficult to understand □ **cryptically** adv

**cryptography** noun the art of coding and reading codes

**crystal** noun 1 very clear glass often used for making drinking glasses etc 2 the regular shape taken by each small part of certain substances, eg salt or sugar □ **crystalline** adj

**crystallize** verb 1 to form into the shape of a crystal 2 to take a form or shape, become clear □ **crystallization** noun

**cub** noun 1 the young of certain animals, eg foxes 2 a Cub Scout

**cube** noun 1 a solid body having six equal square sides 2 the answer to a sum in which a number is multiplied by itself twice: 8 is the cube of 2 □ **cubic** adj 1 of cubes 2 in the shape of a cube

**cubicle** noun a small room closed off in some way from a larger one

**Cub Scout** a junior Scout

**cuckoo** noun a bird which visits Britain in summer and lays its eggs in the nests of other birds

**cucumber** noun a creeping plant with a long green fruit used in salads

**cud** noun food regurgitated by certain animals, eg sheep and cows

**cuddle** verb to put your arms round, hug □ noun a hug, an embrace

**cudgel** noun a heavy stick, a club □ verb to beat with a cudgel

**cudgel** ⟷ cudgels, cudgelling, cudgelled

**cue¹** noun 1 a sign to tell an actor when to speak etc 2 a hint, an indication

**cue²** noun the stick used to hit a ball in billiards and snooker

**cuff** noun 1 the end of a sleeve near the wrist 2 the turned-back hem of a trouser leg 3 a blow with the open hand □ verb to hit with the hand □ **off the cuff** without planning or rehearsal □ **cufflinks** noun pl a pair of ornamental buttons etc used to fasten a shirt cuff

**cuisine** (say kwi-zeen) noun 1 the art of cookery 2 a style of cooking: Mexican cuisine

**cul-de-sac** (say kul-de-sak) noun a street closed at one end

**culinary** adj of or used for cookery

**cull** verb 1 to gather 2 to choose from a group 3 to pick out (seals, deer etc) from a herd and kill for the good of the herd □ noun such a killing

**culminate** verb 1 to reach the highest point 2 to reach the most important or greatest point, end (in): culminated in divorce □ **culmination** noun

**culpable** adj guilty, blameworthy

**culprit** noun 1 someone who is to blame for something 2 English and US law a prisoner accused but not yet tried

**cult** noun 1 a religious sect 2 a general strong enthusiasm for something

**cultivate** verb 1 to grow (vegetables etc) 2 to plough, sow 3 to try to develop and improve: cultivated my friendship □ **cultivator** noun 1 a person who cultivates the land 2 a machine or tool that you use for cultivating

**cultivated** adj 1 farmed, ploughed 2 educated, informed □ **cultivation** noun

**culture** noun 1 a type of civilization with its associated customs 2 development of the mind by education 3 educated tastes in art, music etc 4 cultivation of plants

**cultured** *adj* well-educated in literature, art *etc*

**culvert** *noun* an arched drain for carrying water under a road or railway

**cum** *prep* used for both of two stated purposes: *a newsagent-cum-grocer*

**cumbersome** *adj* awkward to handle

**cummerbund** *noun* a sash worn around the waist

**cumulative** *adj* increasing with additions: *cumulative effect*

**cumulus** *noun* a kind of cloud common in summer, made up of rounded heaps

**cunning** *adj* **1** sly, clever in a deceitful way **2** skilful, clever □ *noun* **1** slyness **2** skill, knowledge

**cup** *noun* **1** a hollow container holding liquid for drinking **2** an ornamental vessel given as a prize in sports events □ *verb* to make (hands *etc*) into the shape of a cup □ **cupful** *noun* (*pl* **cupfuls**) as much as fills a cup

**cup** *verb* ⇔ cups, cupping, cupped

**cupboard** *noun* a shelved recess, or a box with drawers, used for storage

**Cupid** (*say* kyoop-id) *noun* the Roman god of sexual love

**cupidity** (*say* kyoo-**pid**-it-i) *noun* greed

**cupola** (*say* kyoop-ol-a) *noun* a curved ceiling or dome on the top of a building

**cur** *noun* **1** a dog of mixed breed **2** a cowardly person

**curable** *adj* able to be treated and cured

**curate** *noun* a member of the Church of England clergy assisting a rector or vicar

**curative** *adj* likely to cure

**curator** *noun* someone who has charge of a museum, art gallery *etc*

**curb** *verb* to hold back, restrain □ *noun* a restraint

**⚫ Do not confuse with: kerb**

**curd** *noun* **1** milk thickened by acid **2** the cheese part of milk, as opposed to the **whey**

**curdle** *verb* to turn into curd □ **curdle someone's blood** to shock or terrify them

**cure** *noun* **1** freeing from disease, healing **2** something which frees from disease □ *verb* **1** to heal **2** to get rid of (a bad habit *etc*) **3** to preserve by drying, salting *etc*

**curfew** *noun* an order forbidding people to be out of their houses after a certain hour

**curio** *noun* (*pl* **curios**) an article valued for its oddness or rarity

**curiosity** *noun* (*pl* **curiosities**) **1** strong desire to find something out **2** something unusual, an oddity

**curious** *adj* **1** anxious to find out **2** unusual, odd □ **curiously** *adv*

**curl** *verb* **1** to twist (hair) into small coils **2** of hair: to grow naturally in small coils **3** of smoke: to move in a spiral **4** to twist, form a curved shape **5** to play at the game of curling □ *noun* a small coil or roll, *eg* of hair

**curler** *noun* **1** something used to make curls **2** someone who plays the game of curling

**curlew** *noun* a wading bird with very long slender bill and legs

**curling** *noun* a game played by throwing round, flat stones along a sheet of ice

**curly** *adj* having curls □ **curliness** *noun* the quality of being curled or of having lots of curls

**currant** *noun* **1** a small black raisin **2** a berry of various kinds of soft fruit

**⚫ Do not confuse: currant and current**

**currency** *noun* (*pl* **currencies**) **1** the money used in a particular country **2** the state of being generally known: *the story gained currency*

**current** *adj* belonging to, talked about and generally known at the present time □ *noun* a stream of water, air or electrical power moving in one direction □ **current account** a bank account from which money may be withdrawn by cheque

**curriculum** *noun* the course of study at a university, school *etc* □ **curriculum vitae** a brief account of the main events of a person's life

**curry¹** *noun* (*pl* **curries**) a dish containing a mixture of spices with a strong, peppery flavour □ *verb* to make into a curry by adding spices □ **curry powder** a selection of ground spices used in making curry

curry *verb* ⊷ curries, currying, curried

**curry²** *verb* to rub down (a horse) □ **curry favour** to try hard to be someone's favourite

**curse** *verb* 1 to use swear words 2 to wish evil towards □ *noun* 1 a wish for evil or a magic spell 2 an evil or a great misfortune or the cause of this □ **cursed** *adj* under a curse; hateful

**cursor** *noun* a flashing device that appears on a VDU screen to show the position for entering data

**cursory** *adj* brief, hurried □ **cursorily** *adv*

**curt** *adj* of someone's way of speaking: clipped and unfriendly □ **curtly** *adv*

**curtail** *verb* to make less, reduce □ **curtailment** *noun*

**curtain** *noun* a piece of material hung to cover a window, stage *etc*

**curtsy** or **curtsey** *noun* (*pl* **curtsies**) a bow made by bending the knees

**curvature** *noun* 1 a curving or bending 2 a curved piece 3 an abnormal curving of the spine

**curve** *noun* a rounded line, a bend □ *verb*

**cushion** *noun* 1 a fabric casing stuffed with feathers, foam *etc*, for resting on 2 a soft pad

**cushy** *adj*, *informal* easy and comfortable: *a cushy job*

**cusp** *noun* a point where two curves join

**custard** *noun* a sweet sauce made from eggs, milk and sugar

**custodian** *noun* 1 a keeper 2 a caretaker, *eg* of a museum

**custody** *noun* 1 care, guardianship 2 imprisonment

**custom** *noun* 1 something done by habit 2 the regular or frequent doing of something; habit 3 the buying of goods at a shop 4 (**customs**) taxes on goods coming into a country 5 (**customs**) the government department that collects these □ **custom-built** *adj* built to suit a particular purpose

**customary** *adj* usual

**customer** *noun* 1 someone who buys from a shop 2 *informal* a person: *an awkward customer*

**cut** *verb* 1 to make a slit in, or divide, with a blade 2 to wound 3 to trim with a blade *etc* 4 to reduce in amount 5 to shorten (a play, book *etc*) by removing parts 6 to refuse to acknowledge (someone you know) 7 to divide (a pack of cards) in two 8 to stop filming 9 *informal* to play truant from (school) □ *noun* 1 a slit made by cutting 2 a wound made with something sharp 3 a stroke, a blow 4 a thrust with a sword 5 the way something is cut 6 the shape and style of clothes 7 a piece of meat □ **cut-and-dried** *adj* arranged carefully and exactly □ **cut glass** glass with ornamental patterns cut on the surface □ **cut-price** *adj* sold at a price lower than usual □ **cut-throat** *noun* a ruffian □ *adj* fiercely competitive: *cut-throat business* □ **cut down** 1 to take down by cutting 2 to reduce □ **cut down on**

to reduce the intake of □ **cut in** to interrupt □ **cut off 1** to separate, isolate **2** to stop: *cut off supplies* □ **cut out 1** to shape (a dress *etc*) by cutting **2** *informal* to stop **3** of an engine: to fail □ **cut-up** *adj* distressed

**cut** *verb* ⇔ **cuts, cutting, cut**

**cute** *adj* **1** smart, clever **2** pretty and pleasing

**cuticle** *noun* the skin at the bottom and edges of finger and toe nails

**cutlass** *noun* (*pl* **cutlasses**) a short broad sword

**cutlery** *noun* knives, forks, spoons *etc*

**cutlet** *noun* a slice of meat with the bone attached

**cutting** *noun* **1** a piece cut from a newspaper **2** a trench cut in the earth or rock for a road *etc* **3** a shoot of a tree or plant □ *adj* wounding, hurtful: *cutting remark*

**cuttlefish** *noun* a type of sea creature like a squid

**cyanide** *noun* a kind of poison

**cycle** *noun* **1** a bicycle **2** a round of events following on from one another repeatedly: *the cycle of the seasons* **3** a series of poems, stories *etc* written about a single person or event □ *verb* **1** to ride a bicycle **2** to move in a cycle; rotate □ **cyclist** *noun*

**cyclone** *noun* **1** a whirling windstorm **2** a system of winds blowing in a spiral □ **cyclonic** *adj*

**cygnet** (*say* sig-net) *noun* a young swan
  ⊚ From Latin *cygnus* meaning 'swan'
  ♠ Do not confuse with: **signet**

**cylinder** *noun* a solid or hollow tube-shaped object; in machines, car engines *etc*, the hollow tube in which a piston works □ **cylindrical** *adj*

**cymbals** (*say* sim-balz) *noun pl* brass, plate-like musical instruments, beaten together in pairs

**cynic** (*say* sin-ik) *noun* someone who believes the worst about people □ **cynicism** *noun* □ **cynical** *adj* sneering; believing the worst of people □ **cynically** *adv*

**cypress** *noun* a type of evergreen tree

**cyst** (*say* sist) *noun* a liquid-filled blister within the body or just under the skin

**cystic fibrosis** a hereditary disease which is present at birth or appears in early childhood

**cystitis** *noun* inflammation of the bladder, often caused by infection

**czar** *another spelling of* **tsar**

**czarina** *another spelling of* **tsarina**

## Dd

**dab** *verb* to touch gently with a pad *etc* to soak up moisture □ *noun* **1** the act of dabbing **2** a small lump of something soft **3** a gentle blow, a pat **4** a small kind of flounder

**dab** *verb* ⇔ **dabs, dabbing, dabbed**

**dabble** *verb* **1** to play in water with hands or feet **2** to do in a half-serious way or as a hobby: *he dabbles in computers*

**dab-hand** *noun, informal* an expert

**dachshund** (*say* daks-huwnt or daks-huwnd) *noun* a breed of dog with short legs and a long body
  ⊚ From German *Dachs* meaning 'badger', and *Hund* meaning 'dog'

**dad** or **daddy** *noun, informal* father

**daffodil** *noun* a type of yellow flower which grows from a bulb

**daft** *adj* silly

**dagger** *noun* a short sword for stabbing

**dahlia** *noun* a type of garden plant with large flowers

Named after Anders *Dahl*, 18th-century Swiss botanist

**daily** *adj & adv* every day □ *noun* (*pl* **dailies**) **1** a paper published every day **2** someone employed to clean a house regularly □ **daily bread** necessary food, means of living

**dainty** *adj* **1** small and neat **2** pleasant-tasting □ *noun* (*pl* **dainties**) a tasty morsel of food □ **daintily** *adv* (adj, meaning 1)

**dairy** *noun* (*pl* **dairies**) **1** a building for storing milk and making butter and cheese **2** a shop which sells milk, butter, cheese *etc* □ **dairy cattle** cows kept for their milk, not their meat □ **dairy farm** a farm concerned with the production of milk, butter *etc* □ **dairy products** food made of milk, butter or cheese

**dais** *noun* (*pl* **daises**) a raised floor at the upper end of a hall

**daisy** *noun* (*pl* **daisies**) a small common flower with white petals □ **daisy-chain** *noun* a string of daisies threaded through each other's stems □ **daisy-wheel** *noun* a flat printing wheel with characters at the end of spokes

Literally 'day's eye', so called because of its opening during the day

**dalai lama** the spiritual leader of Tibetan Buddhism

**dale** *noun* low ground between hills

**dally** *verb* **1** to waste time idling or playing **2** to play (with) □ **dalliance** *noun*

**dally** ⇨ dalli*es*, dally*ing*, dalli*ed*

**Dalmatian** *noun* a breed of large spotted dog

**dam** *noun* **1** a wall of earth, concrete *etc* to keep back water **2** water kept in like this □ *verb* **1** to keep back by a dam **2** to hold back, restrain (tears *etc*)

**dam** ⇨ dam*s*, damm*ing*, damm*ed*

**damage** *noun* **1** hurt, injury **2** (**damages**) money paid by one person to another to make up for injury, insults *etc* □ *verb* to spoil, make less effective or unusable

**damask** *noun* silk, linen or cotton cloth, with figures and designs in the weave

After *Damascus* in Syria, from where it was exported in the Middle Ages

**dame** *noun* **1** a comic woman in a pantomime, played by a man in drag **2** (**Dame**) the title of a woman of the same rank as a knight

**damn** *verb* **1** to sentence to unending punishment in hell **2** to condemn as wrong, bad *etc* □ *exclam* an expression of annoyance

**damnable** *adj* **1** deserving to be condemned **2** hateful □ **damnably** *adv* extremely

**damnation** *noun* **1** unending punishment in hell **2** condemnation

**damning** *adj* leading to conviction or ruin: *damning evidence*

**damp** *noun* **1** moist air **2** wetness, moistness □ *verb* **1** to wet slightly **2** to make less fierce or intense □ *adj* moist, slightly wet

**damp-course** or **damp-proof course** *noun* a layer of damp-proof material inside a wall or under a floor

**dampen** *verb* **1** to make or become damp; moisten **2** to lessen (enthusiasm *etc*)

**damper** *noun*, *music* a pad which touches the strings inside a piano, silencing each note after it has been played □ **put a damper on something** to make it less cheerful

**damsel** *noun*, *old* an unmarried girl

**damson** *noun* a type of small dark-red plum

**dance** *verb* to move in time to music □ *noun* **1** a sequence of steps in time to music **2** a social event with dancing □ **dancer** *noun*

**dandelion** noun a type of common plant with a yellow flower

From the French phrase dent de lion, meaning 'lion's tooth'

**dandruff** noun dead skin which collects under the hair and falls off in flakes

**dandy** noun (pl **dandies**) a man who pays great attention to his dress and looks

**danger** noun **1** something potentially harmful: the canal is a danger to children **2** potential harm: unaware of the danger

**dangerous** adj **1** unsafe, likely to cause harm **2** full of risks ▫ **dangerously** adv

▪ threatening, menacing, reckless, risky, hazardous, perilous, treacherous

**dangle** verb to hang loosely

**dank** adj moist, wet and cold

**dapper** adj small and neat

**dappled** adj marked with spots or splashes of colour

**dare** verb **1** to be brave or bold enough (to): I didn't dare tell him **2** to lay yourself open to, risk **3** to challenge: dared him to cross the railway line ▫ **dare-devil** noun a rash person fond of taking risks ▫ adj rash, risky ▫ **daring** adj bold, fearless ▫ noun boldness ▫ **daringly** adv ▫ **I dare say** I suppose: I dare say you're right

**dark** adj **1** without light **2** black or near to black **3** gloomy **4** evil: dark deeds ▫ noun absence of light, nightfall ▫ **darken** verb to make or grow dark or darker ▫ **darkness** noun ▫ **a dark horse** someone about whom little is known ▫ **in the dark** knowing nothing about something ▫ **keep dark** to keep (something) secret

**darling** noun **1** a word showing affection **2** someone dearly loved

**darn** verb to mend (clothes) with crossing rows of stitches ▫ noun a patch mended in this way

**dart** noun **1** a pointed weapon for throwing or shooting **2** something which pierces ▫ verb to move quickly and suddenly

**dartboard** noun the board used in playing the game of darts

**darts** noun sing a game in which small darts are aimed at a board marked off in circles and numbered sections

**dash** verb **1** to throw or knock violently, esp so as to break **2** to ruin (hopes) **3** to depress, sadden (spirits) **4** to rush with speed or violence ▫ noun (pl **dashes**) **1** a rush **2** a short race **3** a small amount of a drink etc **4** liveliness **5** a short line (-) to show a break in a sentence etc ▫ **dashing** adj **1** hasty **2** smart, elegant

**dastardly** adj, formal cowardly

**data** noun pl (sing **datum**) **1** available facts from which conclusions may be drawn **2** facts stored in a computer

**database** noun, computing a collection of systematically stored files that are often connected with each other

**date¹** noun **1** a statement of time in terms of the day, month and year, eg 23 December 1995 **2** the time at which an event occurs **3** the period of time to which something belongs **4** an appointment ▫ verb **1** to give a date to **2** to belong to a certain time: dates from the 12th century **3** to become old-fashioned: that dress will date quickly

**date²** noun **1** a type of palm tree **2** its blackish, shiny fruit with a hard stone

**datum** sing of **data**

**daub** verb **1** to smear **2** to paint roughly

**daughter** noun a female child ▫ **daughter-in-law** noun a son's wife

**daunt** verb **1** to frighten **2** to be discouraging □ **dauntless** adj unable to be frightened

**Davy-lamp** noun an early kind of safety lamp for coalminers

**dawdle** verb to move slowly □ **dawdler** noun

**dawn** noun **1** daybreak **2** a beginning: dawn of a new era □ verb **1** to become day **2** to begin to appear □ **dawning** noun a rather poetic way of saying 'dawn' □ **dawn chorus** the singing of birds at dawn □ **dawn on** to become suddenly clear to (someone)

**day** noun **1** the time of light, from sunrise to sunset **2** twenty-four hours, from one midnight to the next **3** the time or hours spent at work **4** (often **days**) a particular time or period: in the days of steam □ **daylight** noun **1** the light of day, sunlight **2** a clear space □ **day-release** noun time off from work for training or education □ **day in, day out** on and on, continuously □ **the other day** recently: saw her just the other day

**daydream** noun an imagining of pleasant events while awake □ verb to imagine in this way

**dayglo** noun, trademark a luminously bright colour

**daze** verb **1** to stun with a blow **2** to confuse, bewilder

**dazzle** verb **1** to shine on so as to prevent from seeing clearly **2** to shine brilliantly **3** to fascinate, impress deeply

**DC** abbrev **1** District of Columbia (US) **2** detective constable **3** direct current (compare with: **AC**)

**deacon** noun **1** the lowest rank of clergy in the Church of England **2** a church official in other churches

**deaconess** noun a woman deacon

**dead** adj **1** not living, without life **2** cold and cheerless **3** numb **4** not working; no longer in use

**5** complete, utter: dead silence **6** exact: dead centre **7** certain: a dead shot □ adv **1** completely: dead certain **2** suddenly and completely: stop dead □ noun **1** those who have died: speak well of the dead **2** the time of greatest stillness etc: the dead of night □ **dead-and-alive** adj dull, having little life □ **dead-beat** adj having no strength left □ **dead end 1** a road etc closed at one end **2** a job etc not leading to promotion □ **dead heat** a race in which two or more runners finish equal □ **dead ringer** informal someone looking exactly like someone else

**deaden** verb to lessen (pain etc)

**deadline** noun a date by which something must be done

Originally a line around a military prison, at which any prisoner crossing would be shot on sight

**deadlock** noun a standstill resulting from a complete failure to agree

**deadly** adj **1** likely to cause death, fatal **2** intense, very great: deadly hush □ adv intensely, extremely □ **deadliness** noun

**deadpan** adj without expression on the face

**deaf** adj **1** unable to hear **2** refusing to listen □ **deaf-mute** noun someone who is both deaf and dumb

**deafen** verb **1** to make deaf **2** to be unpleasantly loud **3** to make (walls etc) soundproof □ **deafening** adj extremely loud

**deal** noun **1** an agreement, esp in business **2** an amount or quantity: a good deal of paper **3** the dividing out of playing-cards in a game **4** a kind of softwood □ verb **1** to divide, give out **2** to trade (in) **3** to do business (with) □ **dealer** noun **1** someone who deals out cards at a game **2** a trader **3** a stock-broker □ **deal with** to take action concerning, cope with

**dean** noun **1** the chief religious officer in a cathedral church **2** the head of a faculty in a university

**dear** adj **1** high in price **2** highly valued; much loved □ noun **1** someone who is loved **2** someone who is lovable or charming □ adv at a high price □ **dearly** adv **1** very much, sincerely: love him dearly **2** involving a great cost, either financially or in some other way: His freedom was dearly bought

**dearth** (say derth) noun a scarcity, shortage

**death** noun **1** the state of being dead, the end of life **2** the end of something: the death of steam railways □ **death-blow** noun **1** a blow that causes death **2** an event that causes something to end □ **death-knell** noun **1** a bell announcing a death **2** something indicating the end of a scheme, hope etc □ **death-mask** noun a plastercast taken of a dead person's face □ **death rattle** a rattling in the throat sometimes heard before someone dies □ **death wish** a conscious or unconscious desire to die

**deathly** adj **1** very pale or ill-looking **2** deadly

**debar** verb to keep from, prevent

**debar** ⇔ debars, debarring, debarred

**debase** verb **1** to lessen in value **2** to make bad, wicked etc □ **debased** adj □ **debasement** noun

**debatable** adj arguable, doubtful: a debatable point □ **debatably** adv

**debate** noun **1** a discussion, esp a formal one before an audience **2** an argument □ verb to engage in debate, discuss

**debauched** adj inclined to debauchery

**debauchery** noun excessive indulgence in drunkenness, lewdness etc

**debilitate** verb to make weak

**debility** noun weakness of the body

**debit** noun a debt □ verb to mark down as a debt

**debonair** adj of pleasant and cheerful appearance and behaviour

**debrief** verb to gather information from an astronaut, spy etc after a mission □ **debriefing** noun

**debris** (say deb-ree) noun **1** the remains of something broken, destroyed etc **2** rubbish

**debt** (say det) noun what one person owes to another □ **debtor** (say det-or) noun someone who owes a debt □ **in debt** owing money □ **in someone's debt** under an obligation to them

**début** (say dei-byoo) noun the first public appearance, eg of an actor □ adj first before the public: début concert

**decade** noun **1** a period of ten years **2** a set or series of ten

**decadence** noun a falling from high to low standards in morals, the arts etc □ **decadent** adj

**decaff** adj, informal decaffeinated

**decaffeinated** adj with the caffeine removed

**decamp** verb to run away

**decant** verb to pour (wine etc) from a bottle into a decanter

**decanter** noun an ornamental bottle with a glass stopper for wine, whisky etc

**decapitate** verb to cut the head from □ **decapitation** noun

**decathlon** noun an athletics competition combining contests in ten separate disciplines

**decay** verb to become bad, worse or rotten □ noun the process of rotting or worsening □ **decayed** adj

**decease** noun, formal death

**deceased** adj, formal dead □ noun **(the deceased)** a dead person

**deceit** noun the act of deceiving

**deceitful** adj inclined to deceive;

lying □ **deceitfully** adv

**deceive** verb to tell lies to so as to mislead □ **deceiver** noun

**decelerate** verb to slow down □ **deceleration** noun

**December** noun the twelfth month of the year

**decent** adj 1 respectable 2 good enough, adequate: decent salary 3 kind: decent of you to help □ **decency** noun (meanings 1 and 3) □ **decently** adv

**deception** noun 1 the act of deceiving 2 something that deceives or is intended to deceive

**deceptive** adj misleading: appearances may be deceptive □ **deceptively** adv

**decibel** noun a unit of loudness of sound

**decide** verb 1 to make up your mind to do something: I've decided to take your advice 2 to settle (an argument etc)

**decided** adj 1 clear: decided difference 2 with mind made up: he was decided on the issue □ **decidedly** adv definitely

**deciduous** adj of a tree: having leaves that fall in autumn

**decimal** adj 1 numbered by tens 2 of ten parts or the number 10 □ noun a decimal fraction □ **decimal currency** a system of money in which each coin or note is either a tenth of another or ten times another in value □ **decimal fraction** a fraction expressed in tenths, hundredths, thousandths etc, separated by a decimal point □ **decimal point** a dot used to separate units from decimal fractions, eg $0.1 = \frac{1}{10}$, $2.33 = 2\frac{33}{100}$ □ **decimalize** verb to convert (figures or currency) to decimal form □ **decimalization** noun

**decimate** verb to make much smaller in numbers by destruction

Literally 'reduce by a tenth'

**decipher** verb 1 to translate (a code) into ordinary, understandable language 2 to make out the meaning of: can't decipher his handwriting

**decision** noun 1 the act of deciding 2 clear judgement, firmness: acting with decision

**decisive** adj 1 final, putting an end to a contest etc: a decisive defeat 2 showing decision and firmness: a decisive manner □ **decisively** adv

**deck** noun 1 a platform forming the floor of a ship, bus etc 2 a pack of playing-cards 3 the turntable of a record-player □ verb to decorate, adorn □ **deckchair** noun a collapsible chair of wood and canvas etc □ **clear the decks** to get rid of old papers, work etc before starting something fresh

**declaim** verb 1 to make a speech in impressive dramatic language 2 to speak violently (against) □ **declamation** noun □ **declamatory** adj of a speech or announcement: impressive and dramatic

**declare** verb 1 to make known (goods or income on which tax is payable) 2 to announce formally or publicly: declare war 3 to say firmly 4 cricket to end an innings before ten wickets have fallen □ **declaration** noun

**decline** verb 1 to say 'no' to, refuse: I had to decline his offer 2 to weaken, become worse 3 to slope down □ noun 1 a downward slope 2 a gradual worsening of health etc

**decode** verb to translate (a coded message) into ordinary, understandable language

**decommission** verb to take out of operation (eg a warship, atomic reactor, or weapons used in a war)

**decompose** verb 1 to rot, decay 2 to separate in parts or elements □ **decomposition** noun

**décor** (say dei-kawr) noun the

decoration of, and arrangement of objects in, a room *etc*

**decorate** *verb* **1** to add ornament to **2** to paint or paper the walls of (a room *etc*) **3** to pin a badge or medal on (someone) as a mark of honour □ **decoration** *noun* □ **decorative** *adj* **1** ornamental **2** pretty □ **decorator** *noun* someone who decorates houses, rooms *etc*

**decorous** *adj* behaving in an acceptable or dignified way

**decorum** *noun* good behaviour

**decoy** *verb* to lead into a trap or into evil □ *noun* something or someone intended to lead another into a trap

**decrease** *verb* to make or become less in number □ *noun* a growing less

**decree** *noun* **1** an order, a law **2** a judge's decision □ *verb* to give an order

decree *verb* ⇔ decrees, decreeing, decreed

**decrepit** *adj* **1** weak and infirm because of old age **2** in ruins or disrepair □ **decrepitude** *noun*

**dedicate** *verb* **1** to devote yourself (to): *dedicated to his music* **2** to set apart for a sacred purpose **3** to inscribe or publish (a book *etc*) in tribute to someone or something: *I dedicate this book to my father* □ **dedication** *noun*

**deduce** *verb* to find out something by putting together all that is known

♠. Do not confuse: **deduce** and **deduct**

**deduct** *verb* to subtract, take away (from)

**deduction** *noun* **1** a subtraction **2** finding something out using logic, or a thing which has been found out in this way

**deed** *noun* **1** something done, an act **2** *law* a signed statement or bargain

**deed poll** a document by which someone legally changes their name

From an old meaning of *poll* as 'cut' or

'trimmed', because these were written on paper with cut edges

**deep** *adj* **1** being or going far down **2** hard to understand **3** involved to a great extent: *deep in debt/ deep in thought* **4** intense, strong: *a deep red colour/ deep affection* **5** low in pitch □ *noun* (**the deep**) the sea □ **deepen** *verb* to make or become deep □ **deep freeze** a low-temperature refrigerator that can freeze and preserve food frozen for a long time □ **deep-seated** *adj* firmly fixed, not easily removed □ **in deep water** in serious trouble

**deer** *noun* (*pl* **deer**) an animal with antlers in the male, such as the reindeer

**deface** *verb* to spoil the appearance of, disfigure □ **defacement** *noun*

**defame** *verb* to try to harm the reputation of □ **defamation** *noun* □ **defamatory** *adj* intended to harm, or having the effect of harming, someone's reputation

**default** *verb* to fail to do something you ought to do, *eg* to pay a debt □ **defaulter** *noun* a person who has defaulted □ **by default** because of a failure to do something

**defeat** *verb* to beat, win a victory over □ *noun* a win, a victory

**defect** *noun* (*say* dee-fekt) a lack of something needed for completeness or perfection; a flaw □ *verb* (*say* di-fekt) to desert a country, political party *etc* to join or go to another □ **defection** *noun* **1** failure in duty **2** desertion

**defective** *adj* **1** faulty; incomplete **2** not having normal mental or physical ability

♠. Do not confuse with: **deficient**

**defence** or *US* **defense** *noun* **1** the act of defending against attack **2** a means or method of protection **3** *law* the argument defending the accused person in a case (*contrasted* *with*: **prosecution) 4** *law* the lawyer(s) putting forward this argument □ **defenceless** *adj* without defence

**defend** *verb* **1** to guard or protect against attack **2** *law* to conduct the defence of **3** to support against criticism □ **defendant** *noun* **1** someone who resists attack **2** *law* the accused person in a law case

**defensible** *adj* able to be defended

**defensive** *adj* **1** used for defence **2** expecting criticism, ready to justify actions □ **on the defensive** prepared to defend yourself against attack or criticism

**defer** *verb* **1** to put off to another time **2** to give way (to): *he deferred to my wishes* □ **deference** *noun* **1** willingness to consider the wishes *etc* of others **2** the act of giving way to another □ **deferential** *adj* showing deference, respectful

**defer** ⋄ defers, deferring, deferred

**defiance** *noun* open disobedience or opposition □ **defiant** *adj* □ **defiantly** *adv*

**deficiency** *noun* (*pl* **deficiencies**) **1** lack, want **2** an amount lacking

**deficient** *adj* lacking in what is needed

♠ Do not confuse with: **defective**

**deficit** *noun* an amount by which a sum of money *etc* is too little

**defile** *verb* **1** to make dirty, soil **2** to corrupt, make bad □ **defilement** *noun*

**define** *verb* **1** to fix the bounds or limits of **2** to outline or show clearly **3** to state the exact meaning of

**definite** *adj* **1** having clear limits, fixed **2** exact **3** certain, sure □ **definitely** *adv* certainly, without doubt □ **definite article** the name given to the adjective *the*

**definition** *noun* **1** an explanation of the exact meaning of a word or phrase **2** sharpness or clearness of outline

**definitive** *adj* **1** fixed, final **2** not able to be bettered: *definitive biography* □ **definitively** *adv* (meaning 1)

**deflate** *verb* **1** to let the air out of (a tyre *etc*) **2** to reduce in self-importance or self-confidence □ **deflation** *noun* **1** an economic term describing a reduction in the amount of money available in a country, resulting in a lower level of industrial activity, industrial output and employment, and a lower rate of increase in wages and prices **2** the letting out of air (from *eg* a tyre) **3** the feeling of sadness or disappointment which you get, *eg* when your hopes have been dashed □ **deflationary** *adj* having the purpose of creating economic deflation

**deflect** *verb* to turn aside (from a fixed course) □ **deflection** *noun*

**deform** *verb* **1** to spoil the shape of **2** to make ugly □ **deformed** *adj* badly or abnormally formed □ **deformity** *noun* (*pl* **deformities**) **1** something abnormal in shape **2** the fact of being badly shaped

**defraud** *verb* **1** to cheat **2** (with **of**) to take by cheating or fraud

**defray** *verb* to pay for (expenses)

**defrost** *verb* to remove frost or ice (from); thaw

**deft** *adj* clever with the hands, handy □ **deftly** *adv*

**defunct** *adj* no longer active or in use

**defy** *verb* **1** to dare to do something, challenge **2** to resist openly **3** to make impossible: *its beauty defies description*

**defy** ⋄ defies, defying, defied

**degenerate** *adj* (*say* di-**jen**-*e*-rat) having become immoral or very bad □ *verb* (*say* di-**jen**-*e*-reit) to become or grow bad or worse □ **degeneration** *noun*

**degrade** verb 1 to lower in grade or rank 2 to disgrace □ **degrading** adj humiliating and embarrassing □ **degradation** noun humiliation, loss of dignity

**degree** 1 a step or stage in a process 2 rank or grade 3 amount, extent: *a degree of certainty* 4 a unit of temperature 5 a unit by which angles are measured, one 360th part of the circumference of a circle 6 a certificate given by a university, gained by examination or given as an honour

**dehydrate** verb 1 to remove water from (food *etc*) 2 to lose excessive water from the body □ **dehydrated** adj □ **dehydration** noun

**deign** verb to act as if doing a favour: *she deigned to answer us*

**deity** (say **dei**-i-ti) noun (pl **deities**) a god or goddess

**déjà vu** (say dei-szah **voo**) the feeling of having experienced something before

**dejected** adj gloomy, dispirited □ **dejection** noun

**delay** verb 1 to put off, postpone 2 to keep back, hinder □ noun 1 a postponement 2 a hindrance

**delectable** adj delightful, pleasing □ **delectably** adv

**delectation** noun delight, enjoyment

**delegate** verb (say **del**-ig-eit) to give (a task) to someone else to do □ noun (say **del**-ig-at) someone acting on behalf of another; a representative □ **delegation** noun a group of delegates

**delete** verb to rub or strike out (eg a piece of writing) □ **deletion** noun

**deli** (say **del**-i) noun, *informal* a delicatessen

**deliberate** verb (say di-**lib**-e-reit) to think carefully or seriously (about) □ adj (say di-**lib**-e-rat) 1 intentional, not accidental 2 slow in deciding 3 not hurried □ **deliberately** adv

**deliberation** noun 1 careful thought 2 calmness, coolness 3 (**deliberations**) formal discussions

**delicacy** noun (pl **delicacies**) 1 tact 2 something delicious to eat

**delicate** adj 1 not strong, frail 2 easily damaged 3 fine, dainty: *delicate features* 4 pleasant to taste 5 tactful 6 requiring skill or care: *delicate operation*

**delicatessen** noun a shop selling food cooked or prepared ready for eating

**delicious** adj 1 very pleasant to taste 2 giving pleasure □ **deliciously** adv to just the right degree for maximum pleasure: *The breeze was deliciously cool*

**delight** verb 1 to please greatly 2 to take great pleasure (in) □ noun great pleasure □ **delighted** adj very pleased □ **delightful** adj very pleasing □ **delightfully** adv

**delinquency** noun 1 wrongdoing, misdeeds 2 failure in duty

**delinquent** adj 1 guilty of an offence or misdeed 2 not carrying out your duties □ noun 1 someone guilty of an offence 2 someone who fails in their duty

**delirious** adj 1 raving, wandering in the mind 2 wildly excited □ **deliriously** adv

**delirium** noun 1 a delirious state, *esp* caused by fever 2 wild excitement □ **delirium tremens** a delirious disorder of the brain caused by excessive alcohol

**deliver** verb 1 to hand over 2 to give out (eg a speech, a blow) 3 to set free, rescue 4 to assist at the birth of (a child) □ **deliverance** noun (meaning 3)

**delivery** noun (pl **deliveries**) 1 a handing over, eg of letters 2 the birth of a child 3 a style of speaking

**delphinium** noun a branching garden plant with blue flowers

From a Greek word translating as 'little

dolphin', because of the shape of the flowerheads

**delta** *noun* the triangular stretch of land at the mouth of a river

Originally from a Hebrew word meaning 'tent door'

**delude** *verb* to deceive

**deluge** *noun* **1** a great flood of water **2** an overwhelming amount: *deluge of work* □ *verb* **1** to flood, drench **2** to overwhelm

**delusion** *noun* a false belief, *esp* as a symptom of mental illness

◥. Do not confuse with: **allusion** and **illusion**. **Delusion** comes from the verb **delude**.

**delve** *verb* **1** to dig **2** to rummage, search through: *delved in her bag for her keys*

**demagogue** *noun* a popular leader

**demand** *verb* **1** to ask, or ask for, firmly **2** to insist: *I demand that you listen* **3** to require, call for: *demanding attention* □ *noun* **1** a forceful request **2** an urgent claim: *many demands on his time* **3** a need for certain goods *etc*

**demean** *verb* to lower, degrade

**demeanour** *noun* behaviour, conduct

**demented** *adj* mad, insane

**demise** *noun*, *formal* death

**demobilize** *verb* **1** to break up an army after a war is over **2** to free (a soldier) from army service □ **demobilization** *noun*

**democracy** *noun* government of the people by the people through their elected representatives

**democrat** *noun* **1** someone who believes in democracy **2** (**Democrat**) *US* a member of the American Democratic Party

**democratic** *adj* **1** of or governed by democracy **2** (**Democratic**) *US* belonging to one of the two chief political parties in the USA □ **democratically** *adv* (meaning 1)

**demolish** *verb* **1** to destroy completely **2** to pull down (a building *etc*) □ **demolition** *noun*

**demon** *noun* an evil spirit, a devil □ **demonic** *adj*

**demonstrate** *verb* **1** to show clearly; prove **2** to show (a machine *etc*) in action **3** to express an opinion by marching, showing placards *etc* in public □ **demonstrable** *adj* able to be shown clearly □ **demonstrator** *noun*

**demonstration** *noun* **1** a showing, a display **2** a public expression of opinion by a procession, mass-meeting *etc*

**demonstrative** *adj* **1** pointing out; proving **2** inclined to show feelings openly

**demoralize** *verb* to take away the confidence of □ **demoralization** *noun*

**demote** *verb* to reduce to a lower rank or grade □ **demotion** *noun*

**demur** *verb* to object, say 'no'

**demur** ⇔ demurs, demur**ring**, demur**red**

**demure** *adj* shy and modest □ **demurely** *adv*

**den** *noun* **1** the lair of a wild animal **2** a small private room for working *etc*

**denial** *noun* the act of denying □ **in denial** doggedly refusing to accept something

**denier** (*say* den-i-er) *noun* a unit of weight of nylon, silk *etc*

**denigrate** *verb* to attack the reputation of, defame

**denim** *noun* a hard-wearing cotton cloth used for jeans, overalls *etc*

Denim was first manufactured in the town of Nîmes in the south of France, and this is how it got its name (*de Nîmes* means 'from Nîmes').

**denizen** *noun* a dweller, an inhabitant

**denomination** *noun* **1** name, title **2** a value of a coin, stamp *etc* **3** a religious sect □ **denominational** *adj*

**denominator** *noun* the lower number in a vulgar fraction by which the upper number is divided, *eg* the 3 in $\frac{2}{3}$ (*compare with:* **numerator**)

**denote** *verb* to mean, signify

**dénouement** (*say* dei-**noo**-mon) *noun* the ending of a story where mysteries *etc* are explained

Literally 'untying' or 'unravelling', from French

**denounce** *verb* **1** to accuse publicly of a crime **2** to inform against: *denounced him to the enemy* □ **denunciation** *noun*

**dense** *adj* **1** closely packed together; thick **2** very stupid □ **densely** *adv* (meaning 1)

**density** *noun* (*pl* **densities**) **1** thickness **2** weight (of water) in proportion to volume **3** *computing* the extent to which data can be held on a floppy disk

**dent** *noun* a hollow made by a blow or pressure □ *verb* to make a dent in

**dental** *adj* of or for a tooth or teeth

**dentist** *noun* a doctor who examines teeth and treats dental problems □ **dentistry** *noun* the work of a dentist

**dentures** *noun pl* a set of false teeth

**denude** *verb* to make bare, strip: *denuded of leaves* □ **denudation** *noun*

**denunciation** *see* **denounce**

**deny** *verb* **1** to declare to be untrue: *he denied that he did it* **2** to refuse, forbid: *denied the right to appeal* □ **deny yourself** to do without things you want or need

**deny** ⋅⋅ **denies, denying, denied**

**deodorant** *noun* something that hides unpleasant smells

**depart** *verb* **1** to go away **2** to turn aside from: *departing from the plan* □ **departure** *noun* □ **a new departure** a new course of action

**department** *noun* a self-contained section within a shop, university, government *etc*

**depend** *verb*: **depend on 1** to rely on **2** to receive necessary financial support from **3** to be controlled or decided by: *it all depends on the weather* □ **dependable** *adj* to be trusted

**dependant** *noun* someone who is kept or supported by another

⬥ Do not confuse: **dependant** and **dependent**

**dependent** *adj* relying or depending (on) □ **dependence** *noun* the state of being dependent

**depict** *verb* **1** to draw, paint *etc* **2** to describe

**deplete** *verb* to make smaller in amount or number □ **depletion** *noun*

**deplore** *verb* to disapprove of, regret: *deplored his use of language* □ **deplorable** *adj* regrettable; very bad

**deploy** *verb* to place in position ready for action

**depopulate** *verb* to reduce greatly in population □ **depopulated** *adj*

**deport** *verb* to send (someone) out of a country □ **deportation** *noun*

**deportment** *noun* behaviour, bearing

**depose** *verb* to remove from a high position, *esp* a monarch from a throne □ **deposition** *noun*

**deposit** *verb* **1** to put or set down **2** to put in for safe keeping, *eg* money in a bank □ *noun* **1** money paid in part payment of something **2** money put in a bank account **3** a solid that has settled at the bottom of a liquid **4** a layer of coal, iron *etc* occurring naturally in rock □ **deposit account** a bank account from which money must be withdrawn in person, not by cheque □ **deposition** *noun* a written piece of evidence □ **depository** *noun* (*pl* **depositories**) a place where anything is deposited

**depot** (*say* **dep**-oh) *noun* **1** a storehouse **2** a building where railway engines, buses *etc* are kept and repaired

**deprave** verb to make wicked □ **depraved** adj wicked □ **depravity** (say dip-**rav**-it-i) noun wickedness

**deprecate** (say **dep**-rik-eit) verb to show disapproval of, condemn □ **deprecating** or **deprecatory** adj disapproving, extremely critical □ **deprecation** noun

❧ Do not confuse: **deprecate** and **depreciate**

**depreciate** (say dip-**ree**-shi-eit) verb 1 to lessen the value of 2 to fall in value □ **depreciation** noun

ⓘ From Latin de meaning 'down', and pretium meaning 'price'

❧ Be careful. **Depreciate** is most frequently used to refer to a fall or a bringing down in FINANCIAL value. Don't use it when you really mean **deprecate**.

**depredations** noun pl plundering

**depress** verb 1 to make gloomy or unhappy 2 to press down 3 to make lower in value or intensity □ **depressing** adj

**depression** noun 1 low spirits, gloominess 2 a hollow 3 a lowering in value 4 a low period in a country's economy with unemployment, lack of trade etc 5 a region of low atmospheric pressure

**deprive** verb: **deprive of** to take away from □ **deprivation** noun great hardship □ **deprived** adj suffering from hardship; disadvantaged

**Dept** abbrev department

**depth** noun 1 deepness 2 a deep place 3 the deepest part: from the depth of her soul 4 the middle: depth of winter 5 intensity, strength: depth of colour □ **in depth** thoroughly, carefully □ **out of your depth** concerned in problems too difficult to understand

**deputation** noun a group of people chosen and sent as representatives

**deputy** noun (pl **deputies**) 1 a delegate, a representative 2 a second-in-command □ **deputize** verb to take another's place, act as substitute

**derail** verb to cause to leave the rails □ **derailment** noun

**derange** verb to put out of place, or out of working order □ **deranged** adj mad, insane □ **derangement** noun

**derelict** adj broken-down, abandoned □ **dereliction** noun neglect of what should be attended to: dereliction of duty

**deride** verb to laugh at, mock □ **derision** noun mockery □ **derisive** adj mocking □ **derisory** adj so small or inadequate as to be not worth taking seriously, laughable

**de rigueur** adj required by custom or fashion

**derive** verb 1 to be descended or formed (from) 2 to trace (a word) back to the beginning of its existence 3 to receive, obtain: derive satisfaction □ **derivation** noun □ **derivative** adj not original □ noun 1 a word formed on the base of another word, eg fabulous from fable 2 (**derivatives**) stock market trading in futures and options

**dermatitis** noun inflammation of the skin

**dermatology** noun the study and treatment of skin diseases □ **dermatologist** noun

**derogatory** adj 1 harmful to reputation, dignity etc 2 scornful, belittling, disparaging

**derrick** noun 1 a crane for lifting weights 2 a framework over an oil well that holds the drilling machinery

Named after Derrick, a famous 17th-century hangman in Tyburn, England

**derring-do** noun daring action, boldness

Based on a misprint of a medieval

English phrase *dorring do*, meaning 'daring to do'

**dervish** *noun* a member of an austere Islamic sect

**descant** *noun*, *music* a tune played or sung above the main tune

**descend** *verb* **1** to go or climb down **2** to slope downwards **3** (with **from**) to have as an ancestor: *claims he's descended from Napoleon* **4** to go from a better to a worse state □ **descendant** *noun* someone descended from another

**descent** *noun* **1** an act of descending **2** a downward slope

**describe** *verb* **1** to give an account of in words **2** to draw the outline of, trace

**description** *noun* **1** the act of describing **2** an account in words **3** sort, kind: *people of all descriptions* □ **descriptive** *adj* (meaning 1)

**desecrate** *verb* **1** to spoil (something sacred) **2** to treat without respect □ **desecration** *noun*

**Desecrate** was formed by taking the word 'consecrate' and replacing the 'con-' with the Latin prefix 'de-' (= from).

🔸 Do not confuse with: **desiccate**. Remember that dese**cRate** and sac**Red** related, and they both contain an R.

**desert**[1] *verb* **1** to run away from (the army) **2** to leave, abandon: *deserted his wife/ his courage deserted him* □ **deserter** *noun* (meaning 1) □ **desertion** *noun*

**desert**[2] *noun* a stretch of barren country with very little water □ **desert island** an uninhabited island in a tropical area
 ⊕ From Latin *desertum* meaning 'deserted'

🔸 Do not confuse with: **dessert**

**deserve** *verb* to have earned as a right, be worthy of: *you deserve a*

holiday □ **deservedly** *adv* justly □ **deserving** *adj*

**desiccate** *verb* **1** to dry up **2** to preserve by drying: *desiccated coconut*
 ⊕ From Latin *desiccare* meaning 'to dry up'

🔸 Do not confuse with: **desecrate**

**design** *verb* **1** to make a plan of (*eg* a building) before it is made **2** to intend □ *noun* **1** a plan, a sketch **2** a painted picture, pattern *etc* **3** an intention □ **designing** *adj* crafty, cunning □ **have designs on** to plan to get for yourself

**designate** (*say* dez-ig-neit) *verb* **1** to point out, indicate **2** to name **3** to appoint, select □ *adj* appointed to a post but not yet occupying it: *director designate* □ **designation** (*say* dez-ig-**nei**-shun) *noun* a name, a title

**desirable** *adj* pleasing; worth having □ **desirability** *noun*

**desire** *verb* to wish for greatly □ *noun* **1** a longing for **2** a wish

**desist** *verb*, *formal* to stop (doing something)

**desk** *noun* a table for writing, reading *etc*

**desolate** *adj* **1** deeply unhappy **2** empty of people, deserted **3** barren □ **desolated** *adj* overcome by grief □ **desolation** *noun* **1** deep sorrow **2** barren land **3** ruin

**despair** *verb* to give up hope □ *noun* **1** lack of hope **2** a cause of despair: *she was the despair of her mother* □ **despairing** *adj* in despair

**despatch** *another spelling of* **dispatch**

**desperado** *noun* (*pl* **desperadoes** or **desperados**) a violent criminal

**desperate** *adj* **1** without hope, despairing **2** very bad, awful **3** reckless; violent □ **desperately** *adv* very much, very intensely □ **desperation** *noun*

**despicable** *adj* contemptible, hateful

**despise** verb to look on with contempt

**despite** prep in spite of: we had a picnic despite the weather

**despoil** verb to rob, plunder □ **despoliation** noun

**despondent** adj downhearted, dejected □ **despondency** noun

**despot** (say des-pot) noun a ruler with unlimited power, a tyrant □ **despotic** adj □ **despotism** noun

**dessert** noun fruits, sweets etc served at the end of a meal
  ⊚ From Old French dessert meaning 'the clearing of the table'
**♠** Do not confuse with: **desert**

**destination** noun the place to which someone or something is going

**destine** verb to set apart for a certain use □ **destined** adj 1 bound (for) 2 intended (for) by fate: destined to succeed

**destiny** noun (pl **destinies**) what is destined to happen; fate

**destitute** adj 1 in need of food, shelter etc 2 (with**of**) completely lacking in: destitute of wit □ **destitution** noun

**destroy** verb 1 to pull down, knock to pieces 2 to ruin 3 to kill □ **destroyer** noun 1 someone who destroys 2 a type of fast warship □ **destructible** adj able to be destroyed

**destruction** noun 1 the act of destroying or being destroyed 2 ruin 3 death

**destructive** adj 1 doing great damage 2 of criticism: pointing out faults without suggesting improvements

**desultory** (say dez-ul-tri) adj 1 moving from one thing to another without a fixed plan 2 changing from subject to subject, rambling

**detach** verb to unfasten, remove (from) □ **detachable** adj able to be taken off: detachable lining

**detached** adj 1 standing apart, by itself: detached house 2 not personally involved, showing no emotion □ **detachment** noun 1 the state of being detached 2 a body or group (eg of troops on special service)

**detail** noun a small part, fact, item etc □ verb 1 to describe fully, give particulars of 2 to set to do a special job or task: detailed to keep watch □ **detailed** adj with nothing left out □ **in detail** giving attention to details, item by item

**detain** verb 1 to hold back 2 to keep late 3 to keep under guard

**detect** verb 1 to discover 2 to notice □ **detection** noun

**detective** noun someone who tries to find criminals or watches suspects

**detention** noun 1 imprisonment 2 a forced stay after school as punishment

**deter** verb to discourage or prevent through fear □ **deterrent** noun something, esp a threat of some kind, which deters or discourages people from a particular course of action

**deter** ↔ deters, deterring, deterred

**detergent** noun a soapless substance used with water for washing dishes etc

**deteriorate** verb to grow worse: her health is deteriorating rapidly □ **deterioration** noun

**determine** verb 1 to decide (on) 2 to fix, settle: determined his course of action □ **determination** noun 1 the fact of being determined 2 stubbornness, firmness of purpose □ **determined** adj 1 firmly decided; having a strong intention: determined to succeed 2 fixed, settled

**deterrent** see **deter**

**detest** verb to hate greatly □ **detestable** adj very hateful □ **detestation** noun great hatred

**detonate** *verb* to (cause to) explode □ **detonation** *noun* an explosion □ **detonator** *noun* something which sets off an explosive

**detour** *noun* a circuitous route

**detract** *verb* to take away (from), lessen □ **detraction** *noun*

**detriment** *noun* harm, damage, disadvantage □ **detrimental** *adj* disadvantageous (to), causing harm or damage

**de trop** (*say* de troh) *adj* in the way, unwelcome

**deuce** (*say* dyoos) *noun* **1** a playing-card with two pips **2** *tennis* a score of forty points each

**deus ex machina** (*say* dei-uws eks mak-in-*a*) a contrived solution or way out

Literally a 'god from a machine' referring to the pulley device used in ancient Greek theatres to lower the character of a god on to the stage

**devastate** *verb* **1** to lay in ruins **2** to overwhelm with grief *etc* □ **devastation** *noun*

**develop** *verb* **1** to (make to) grow bigger or more advanced **2** to acquire gradually: *developed a taste for opera* **3** to become active or visible **4** to unfold gradually **5** to use chemicals to make (a photograph) appear □ **developer** *noun* a chemical mixture used to make an image appear from a photograph □ **development** *noun*

**deviate** *verb* to turn aside, *esp* from a standard course □ **deviation** *noun*

**device** *noun* **1** a tool, an instrument **2** a plan **3** a design on a coat of arms

◈. Do not confuse with: **devise**. To help you remember – 'ice' is a noun, '-ise' is the verb!

**devil** *noun* **1** an evil spirit **2** Satan **3** a wicked person □ **devilish** *adj* very wicked □ **devil-may-care** *adj* not caring what happens □ **devilment** or **devilry** *noun* mischief □ **devil's advocate** someone who argues

against a proposal

**devious** *adj* **1** not direct, roundabout **2** not straightforward

**devise** *verb* **1** to make up, put together **2** to plan, plot

◈. Do not confuse with: **device**. To help you remember – 'ice' is a noun...so '-ise' must be the verb!

**devoid** *adj*: **devoid of** empty of, free from: *devoid of curiosity*

**devolution** *noun* the delegation of certain legislative powers to regional or national assemblies □ **devolutionist** *noun* a supporter of devolution

**devolve** *verb* **1** to fall as a duty (on) **2** to delegate (power) to a regional or national assembly

**devote** *verb* to give up wholly (to) □ **devoted** *adj* **1** loving and loyal **2** given up (to): *devoted to her work* □ **devotee** *noun* a keen follower □ **devotion** *noun* great love

**devour** *verb* **1** to eat up greedily **2** to destroy

**devout** *adj* **1** earnest, sincere **2** religious □ **devoutly** *adv*

**dew** *noun* tiny drops of water which form from the air as it cools at night

**dewy** *adj* covered in dew; moist

**dexterity** *noun* skill, quickness □ **dexterous** or **dextrous** *adj*

**diabetes** *noun* a disease in which there is too much sugar in the blood □ **diabetic** *noun* & *adj* (someone) suffering from diabetes

**diabolic** or **diabolical** *adj* devilish, very wicked □ **diabolically** *adv*

**diadem** *noun* a kind of crown

**diagnose** *verb* to identify (a cause of illness) after making an examination □ **diagnosis** *noun* (*pl* **diagnoses**) the identification (of the cause of illness) in a patient □ **diagnostic** *adj*

**diagonal** *adj* going from one corner to the opposite corner □ *noun* a line from one corner to the opposite diagram 134 different

corner □ **diagonally** adv

**diagram** noun a drawing to explain something □ **diagrammatic** or **diagrammatical** adj in the form of a diagram

**dial** noun **1** the face of a clock or watch **2** a rotating disc over the numbers on some telephones □ verb to call (a number) on a telephone using a dial or buttons

**dial** verb ⋄ dials, dialling, dialled

**dialect** noun a way of speaking found only in a certain area or among a certain group of people

**dialogue** noun a talk between two or more people

**dialysis** noun removal of impurities from the blood by a kidney machine

**diameter** noun a line which dissects a circle, passing through its centre

**diamond** noun **1** a very hard, precious stone **2** an elongated, four-cornered shape (♦) **3** a playing-card with red diamond pips

**diaper** noun, US a baby's nappy

Originally a kind of decorated white silk. The current US meaning was used in British English in the 16th century

**diaphragm** noun **1** a layer of muscle separating the lower part of the body from the chest **2** a thin dividing layer **3** a contraceptive device that fits over the cervix

**diarrhoea** noun frequent emptying of the bowels, with too much liquid in the faeces

**diary** noun (pl **diaries**) **1** a record of daily happenings **2** a book detailing these

**diatribe** noun an angry attack in words

**dice** or **die** noun (pl **dice**) a small cube with numbered sides or faces, used in certain games □ verb (**dice**) to cut (food) into small cubes

**dictate** verb **1** to speak the text of (a letter etc) for someone else to write down **2** to give firm commands □

noun an order, a command □ **dictation** noun the act of dictating

**dictator** noun an all-powerful ruler □ **dictatorial** adj like a dictator; domineering

**diction** noun **1** manner of speaking **2** choice of words

**dictionary** noun (pl **dictionaries**) **1** a book giving the words of a language in alphabetical order, together with their meanings **2** any alphabetically ordered reference book

**did** see **do**

**die**[1] verb **1** to lose life **2** to wither □ **diehard** noun an obstinate or determined person □ **die down** to become less intense

**die** verb ⋄ dies, dying, died

**die**[2] noun **1** a stamp or punch for making raised designs on money etc **2** sing form of **dice**

**diesel** noun an internal combustion engine in which heavy oil is ignited by heat generated by compression

**diet**[1] noun **1** food **2** a course of recommended foods, eg to lose weight □ verb to eat certain kinds of food only, esp to lose weight □ **dietetic** adj

**diet**[2] noun **1** a council, an assembly **2** (**Diet**) the national legislature of Japan

**differ** verb **1** **differ from** to be unlike **2** to disagree

**differ** ⋄ differs, differing, differed

**difference** noun **1** a point in which things differ **2** the amount by which one number is greater than another **3** a disagreement

**different** adj: **1** (**different from**) unlike **2** varying, not the same **3** unusual □ **differentiate** verb to make a difference or distinction between

---

▪ (meaning 1) dissimilar; (meaning 2) varied, various, diverse, assorted, disparate, many, several, sundry

**difficult** adj **1** not easy, hard to do, understand or deal with **2** hard to please □ **difficulty** noun (pl **difficulties**) **1** lack of easiness, hardness **2** anything difficult **3** anything which makes something difficult; an obstacle, hindrance etc **4** (**difficulties**) troubles

**diffident** adj shy, not confident □ **diffidence** noun

**diffuse** verb (say di-**fyooz**) to spread in all directions □ adj (say di-**fyoos**) widely spread

**dig** verb **1** to turn up (earth) with a spade etc **2** to make (a hole) by this means **3** to poke or push (something) into □ noun **1** a poke, a thrust **2** an archaeological excavation □ **digger** noun a machine for digging

dig verb ⇨ digs, digging, dug

**digest** verb (say dai-**jest**) **1** to break down (food) in the stomach into a form that the body can make use of **2** to think over □ noun (say **dai**-jest) **1** a summing-up **2** a collection of written material □ **digestible** adj able to be digested □ **digestion** noun the act or power of digesting □ **digestive** adj aiding digestion

**digit** noun **1** a finger or toe **2** any of the numbers 0–9 □ **digital** adj of a clock etc: using the numbers 0–9 □ **digital audio tape** a magnetic audio tape on which sound has been recorded digitally □ **digital recording** the recording of sound by storing electrical pulses representing the audio signal on compact disc, digital audio tape etc

**dignified** adj stately, serious

**dignitary** noun (pl **dignitaries**) someone of high rank or office

**dignity** noun **1** manner showing a sense of your own worth or the seriousness of the occasion **2** high rank

**digress** verb to wander from the point in speaking or writing

□ **digression** noun

**dike** or **dyke** noun **1** a wall; an embankment **2** a ditch

**dilapidated** adj falling to pieces, needing repair

**dilate** verb to make or grow larger, swell out □ **dilatation** or **dilation** noun

**dilatory** (say **dil**-at-o-ri) adj slow to act, inclined to delay

**dilemma** noun a situation offering a difficult choice between two options

**diligent** adj hard-working, industrious □ **diligence** noun □ **diligently** adv

**dilly-dally** verb to loiter, waste time

dilly-dally ⇨ dilly-dallies, dilly-dallying, dilly-dallied

**dilute** verb to lessen the strength of a liquid etc, esp by adding water □ adj: a dilute form of the same substance □ **diluted** adj □ **dilution** noun

**dim** adj **1** not bright or clear **2** not understanding clearly, stupid □ verb to make or become dim □ **dimly** adv □ **dimness** noun

dim verb ⇨ dims, dimming, dimmed

**dime** noun a tenth of a US or Canadian dollar, ten cents

**dimension** noun **1** a measurement of length, width or thickness **2** (**dimensions**) size, measurements

**diminish** verb to make or grow less □ **diminution** noun a lessening □ **diminutive** adj very small

**diminuendo** noun a fading or falling sound

**dimple** noun a small hollow, esp on the cheek or chin

**din** noun a loud, lasting noise □ verb to put (into) someone's mind by constant repetition

din verb ⇨ dins, dinning, dinned

**dine** verb to eat dinner

**dinghy** noun (pl **dinghies**) a small rowing boat

**dingy** adj dull, faded or dirty-looking □ **dinginess** noun

**dinner** noun **1** a main evening meal **2** a midday meal, lunch

**dinosaur** noun any of various types of extinct giant reptile

Coined in the 19th century, from Greek words which translate as 'terrible lizard'

**dint** noun a hollow made by a blow, a dent □ **by dint of** by means of

**diocese** noun a bishop's district

**dip** verb **1** to plunge into a liquid quickly **2** to lower (eg a flag) and raise again **3** to slope down **4** to look briefly into (a book etc) □ noun **1** a liquid in which anything is dipped **2** a creamy sauce into which biscuits etc are dipped **3** a downward slope **4** a hollow **5** a short bathe or swim

**dip** verb ⇨ dips, dipping, dipped

**diphtheria** (say dif-**theer**-i-a) noun an infectious throat disease

**diphthong** noun two vowel-sounds pronounced as one syllable (for example the ow sound in out)

**diploma** noun a written statement conferring a degree, confirming a pass in an examination etc

From a Greek word meaning a letter folded double

**diplomacy** noun **1** the business of making agreements, treaties etc between countries **2** skill in making people agree, tact

**diplomat** noun someone engaged in diplomacy □ **diplomatic** adj **1** of diplomacy **2** tactful

**dire** adj dreadful: in dire need

**direct** adj **1** straight, not roundabout **2** frank, outspoken □ verb **1** to point or aim at **2** to show the way **3** to order, instruct **4** to control, organize **5** to put a name and address on (a letter) □ **directly** adv **1** straight away, immediately **2** straight: I looked directly at him

**3** just, exactly: directly opposite □ **directness** noun frankness □ **direct speech** speech reported in the speaker's exact words

**direction** noun **1** the act of directing **2** the place or point to which someone moves, looks etc **3** an order **4** guidance **5** (**directions**) instructions on how to get somewhere

**director** noun **1** a manager of a business etc **2** the person who controls the shooting of a film etc

**directory** noun (pl **directories**) **1** a book of names and addresses etc **2** a named group of files on a computer disk

**dirge** noun a lament; a funeral hymn

**dirk** noun a kind of dagger

**dirt** noun any unclean substance, such as mud, dust, dung etc □ **dirt track** an earth track for motor-cycle racing

**dirty** adj **1** not clean, soiled **2** obscene, lewd □ verb to soil with dirt □ **dirtily** adv

**dirty** verb ⇨ dirties, dirtying, dirtied

**disable** verb to take away power or strength from, cripple □ **disability** noun (pl **disabilities**) something which disables □ **disabled** adj □ **disablement** noun

**disadvantage** noun an unfavourable circumstance, a drawback □ **disadvantaged** adj suffering a disadvantage, esp poverty or homelessness □ **disadvantageous** adj not advantageous

**disagree** verb **1** (often with **with**) to hold different opinions (from) **2** to quarrel **3** (with **with**) of food: to make feel ill □ **disagreeable** adj unpleasant □ **disagreement** noun a difference of opinion or quarrel

**disallow** verb not to allow

**disappear** verb to go out of sight, vanish □ **disappearance** noun

▣ wane, recede, ebb, evaporate

**disappoint** verb **1** to fail to come up to the hopes or expectations (of) **2** to fail to fulfil □ **disappointed** adj □ **disappointment** noun

**disapprove** verb to have an unfavourable opinion (of) □ **disapproval** noun

**disarm** verb **1** to take (a weapon) away from **2** to get rid of war weapons **3** to make less angry, charm □ **disarmament** noun the removal or disabling of war weapons □ **disarming** adj gaining friendliness, charming: *disarming smile*

**disarray** noun disorder

**disaster** noun an extremely unfortunate happening, often causing great damage or loss □ **disastrous** adj □ **disastrously** adv

**disband** verb to break up, separate: *the gang disbanded* □ **disbandment** noun

**disbelieve** verb not to believe □ **disbelief** noun inability to believe something □ **disbeliever** noun

**disburse** verb to pay out □ **disbursement** noun

**disc** noun **1** a flat, round shape **2** a pad of cartilage between vertebrae **3** a gramophone record □ **disc brakes** vehicle brakes which use pads that are hydraulically forced against discs on the wheels □ **disc jockey** someone who introduces and plays recorded music on radio *etc*

**discard** verb to throw away as useless

**discern** verb to see, realize □ **discernible** adj noticeable: *discernible difference* □ **discerning** adj quick at noticing; discriminating: *a discerning eye* □ **discernment** noun

**discharge** verb **1** to unload (cargo) **2** to set free **3** to dismiss **4** to fire (a gun) **5** to perform (duties) **6** to pay (a debt) **7** to give off (*eg* smoke) **8** to let out (pus) □ noun **1** a discharging **2** dismissal **3** pus *etc* discharged from the body **4** performance (of duties) **5** payment

**disciple** noun **1** someone who believes in another's teaching **2** *historical* one of the followers of Christ

**discipline** noun **1** training in an orderly way of life **2** order kept by means of control **3** punishment **4** a subject of study or training □ verb **1** to bring to order **2** to punish □ **disciplinarian** noun someone who insists on strict discipline □ **disciplinary** adj

**disclaim** verb to refuse to have anything to do with, deny □ **disclaimer** noun a denial

**disclose** verb to uncover, reveal, make known □ **disclosure** noun **1** the act of disclosing **2** something disclosed

**disco** noun (*pl* discos) an event or place where recorded music is played for dancing

**discolour** or *US* **discolor** verb to spoil the colour of; stain □ **discoloration** noun

**discomfit** verb **1** to disconcert **2** to thwart, defeat □ **discomfiture** noun

**discomfort** noun lack of comfort, uneasiness

**disconcert** verb to upset, confuse

**disconnect** verb to separate, break the connection between □ **disconnected** adj **1** separated, no longer connected **2** of thoughts *etc*: not following logically, rambling

**disconsolate** adj sad, disappointed

**discontent** noun dissatisfaction □ **discontented** adj dissatisfied, cross □ **discontentment** noun

**discontinue** verb to stop, cease to continue

**discord** noun **1** disagreement, quarrelling **2** *music* a jarring of notes □ **discordant** adj

**discotheque** noun a disco

**discount** *noun* a small sum taken off the price of something: *10% discount* □ *verb* **1** to leave out, not consider: *completely discounted my ideas* **2** to allow for exaggeration in (*eg* a story)

**discourage** *verb* **1** to take away the confidence, hope *etc* of **2** to try to prevent by showing dislike or disapproval: *discouraged his advances* □ **discouragement** *noun* □ **discouraging** *adj* giving little hope or encouragement

**discourse** *noun* **1** a speech, a lecture **2** an essay **3** a conversation □ *verb* to talk, *esp* at some length

**discourteous** *adj* not polite, rude □ **discourteously** *adv* □ **discourtesy** *noun*

**discover** *verb* **1** to find out **2** to find by chance, *esp* for the first time □ **discoverer** *noun* □ **discovery** *noun* (*pl* **discoveries**) **1** the act of finding or finding out **2** something discovered

**discredit** *verb* **1** to refuse to believe **2** to cause to doubt **3** to disgrace □ *noun* **1** disgrace **2** disbelief □ **discreditable** *adj* disgraceful

**discreet** *adj* wisely cautious, tactful □ **discreetly** *adv* □ **discretion** *noun* wise caution, tact □ **at someone's discretion** according to that person's own judgement

❧ Do not confuse with: **discrete**

**discrepancy** *noun* (*pl* **discrepancies**) a difference or disagreement between two things: *some discrepancy in the figures*

**discrete** *adj* separate, distinct

❧ Do not confuse with: **discreet**. It may help you to think of Crete, which is an island separate from the rest of Greece.

**discretion** *see* **discreet**

**discriminate** *verb* **1** to make differences (between), distinguish **2** to treat (people) differently because of their gender, race *etc*

□ **discriminating** *adj* showing good judgement □ **discrimination** *noun* **1** ability to discriminate **2** adverse treatment on grounds of gender, race *etc*

**discus** *noun* a heavy disc thrown in an athletic competition

**discuss** *verb* to talk about □ **discussion** *noun*

**disdain** *verb* **1** to look down on, scorn **2** to be too proud to do □ *noun* scorn □ **disdainful** *adj*

**disease** *noun* illness □ **diseased** *adj*

**disembark** *verb* to put or go ashore □ **disembarkation** *noun*

**disembodied** *adj* of a soul *etc*: separated from the body

**disengage** *verb* to separate, free □ **disengaged** *adj*

**disentangle** *verb* to free from entanglement, unravel

**disfavour** or *US* **disfavor** *noun* dislike, disapproval

**disfigure** *verb* to spoil the beauty or appearance of □ **disfigurement** *noun*

**disgorge** *verb* **1** to throw out **2** to give up (something previously taken)

**disgrace** *noun* the state of being out of favour; shame □ *verb* to bring shame on □ **disgraceful** *adj* shameful; very bad □ **disgracefully** *adv*

**disgruntled** *adj* sulky, discontented

**disguise** *verb* **1** to change the appearance of **2** to hide (feelings *etc*) □ *noun* **1** a disguised state **2** a costume *etc* which disguises

**disgust** *noun* **1** strong dislike, loathing **2** indignation □ *verb* **1** to cause loathing, revolt **2** to make indignant □ **disgusting** *adj* sickening; causing disgust

**dish** *noun* (*pl* **dishes**) **1** a plate or bowl for food **2** food prepared for eating **3** a saucer-shaped aerial for receiving information from a satellite □ *verb* **1** to serve (food)

**2** to deal (out), distribute

**dishearten** verb to take away courage or hope from □ **disheartened** adj □ **disheartening** adj

**dishevelled** adj untidy, with hair etc disordered

**dishonest** adj not honest, deceitful □ **dishonesty** noun

**dishonour** noun disgrace, shame □ verb to cause shame to □ **dishonourable** adj disgraceful

**disillusion** verb to take away a false belief from □ **disillusioned** adj unhappy and disappointed after your happy impressions of something have been destroyed □ **disillusionment** noun

**disinclined** adj unwilling

**disinfect** verb to destroy disease-causing germs in □ **disinfectant** noun a substance that kills germs

**disinherit** verb to take away the rights of an heir □ **disinheritance** noun □ **disinherited** adj

**disintegrate** verb to fall into pieces; break down □ **disintegration** noun

**disinterested** adj unbiased, not influenced by personal feelings

�😊 Do not confuse with: **uninterested**. It is generally a positive thing to be **disinterested** (= fair), especially if you are trying to make an unbiased decision. It is generally a negative thing to be **uninterested** (= bored).

**disjointed** adj of speech etc: not well connected together

**disk** noun **1** US spelling of **disc 2** computing a flat round magnetic plate used for storing data □ **disk drive** computing part of a computer that records data on to and retrieves data from disks

**dislike** verb not to like, disapprove of □ noun disapproval

**dislocate** verb **1** to put (a bone) out

of joint **2** to upset, disorder □ **dislocation** noun

**dislodge** verb **1** to drive from a place of rest, hiding or defence **2** to knock out of place accidentally

**disloyal** adj not loyal, unfaithful □ **disloyalty** noun

**dismal** adj gloomy; sorrowful, sad

Based on a Latin phrase *diēs malī* 'evil days', referring to two days each month which were believed to be unusually unlucky

**dismantle** verb **1** to remove fittings, furniture etc from **2** to take to pieces

**dismay** verb to make to feel hopeless, upset □ noun: watched in dismay

**dismember** verb **1** to tear to pieces **2** to cut the limbs from

**dismiss** verb **1** to send or put away **2** to remove (someone) from a job, sack **3** to close (a law case) □ **dismissal** noun

**dismount** verb to come down off a horse, bicycle etc

**disobey** verb to fail or refuse to do what is commanded □ **disobedience** noun □ **disobedient** adj refusing or failing to obey

**disorder** noun **1** lack of order, confusion **2** a disease □ verb to throw out of order □ **disorderly** adj **1** out of order **2** behaving in a lawless (noisy) manner □ **disorderliness** noun

**disown** verb to refuse or cease to recognize as your own

**disparage** verb to speak of as being of little worth or importance, belittle □ **disparagement** noun □ **disparaging** adj

**disparity** noun (pl **disparities**) great difference, inequality

**dispassionate** adj **1** favouring no one, unbiased **2** calm, cool □ **dispassionately** adv

**dispatch** or **despatch** verb **1** to send off (a letter etc) **2** to kill, finish off

**3** to do or deal with quickly □ *noun* (*pl* **dispatches** or **despatches**) **1** the act of sending off **2** a report to a newspaper **3** speed in doing something **4** killing **5** (**dispatches**) official papers (*esp* military or diplomatic) □ **dispatch box 1** a case for official papers **2** the box beside which members of parliament stand to make speeches in the House of Commons □ **dispatch rider** a courier who delivers military dispatches by motor-cycle

**dispel** *verb* to drive away, make disappear

> **dispel** ⇨ dispel*s*, dispel*ling*, dispel*led*

**dispense** *verb* **1** to give out **2** to prepare (medicines) for giving out □ **dispensable** *adj* able to be done without □ **dispensary** *noun* (*pl* **dispensaries**) a place where medicines are given out □ **dispensation** *noun* special leave to break a rule *etc* □ **dispenser** *noun* **1** a machine that issues something to you **2** a holder or container from which you can get something one at a time or in measured quantities □ **dispense with** to do without: *dispense with someone's services*

**disperse** *verb* **1** to scatter; spread **2** to (cause to) vanish □ **dispersal** or **dispersion** *noun* a scattering

**dispirited** *adj* sad, discouraged

**displace** *verb* **1** to put out of place **2** to disorder, disarrange **3** to put (someone) out of office □ **displaced person** someone forced to leave his or her own country because of war, political reasons *etc* □ **displacement** *noun*

**display** *verb* to set out for show □ *noun* a show, exhibition

**displease** *verb* not to please; to offend, annoy □ **displeasure** *noun* annoyance, disapproval

**dispose** *verb* **1** to arrange, settle **2** to get rid (of): *they disposed of the body*

**3** to make inclined □ **disposable** *adj* intended to be thrown away □ **disposal** *noun* the act or process of getting rid of something □ **at your disposal** available for your use □ **disposed** *adj* inclined, willing □ **be well disposed towards someone** to favour them and be inclined to treat them well

**disposition** *noun* **1** arrangement **2** nature, personality **3** *law* the handing over of property *etc* to another

**disproportionate** *adj* too big or too little, not in proportion

**disprove** *verb* to prove to be false

**dispute** *verb* to argue about □ *noun* an argument, quarrel □ **disputable** *adj* not certain, able to be argued about □ **disputation** *noun* an argument

**disqualify** *verb* **1** to put out of a competition for breaking rules **2** to take away a qualification or right □ **disqualification** *noun*

> **disqualify** ⇨ disqualif*ies*, disqualif*ying*, disqualif*ied*

**disquiet** *noun* uneasiness, anxiety

**disregard** *verb* to pay no attention to, ignore □ *noun* neglect

**disrepair** *noun* a state of bad repair

**disrepute** *noun* bad reputation □ **disreputable** *adj* having a bad reputation, not respectable

**disrespect** *noun* rudeness, lack of politeness □ **disrespectful** *adj*

**disrupt** *verb* **1** to break up **2** to throw (a meeting *etc*) into disorder □ **disruption** *noun* an obstacle or disturbance □ **disruptive** *adj* causing disorder

**dissatisfy** *verb* to bring no satisfaction, displease □ **dissatisfaction** *noun* displeasure, annoyance □ **dissatisfied** *adj*

> **dissatisfy** ⇨ dissatisf*ies*, dissatisf*ying*, dissatisf*ied*

**dissect** *verb* **1** to cut into parts for

examination **2** to study and criticize □ **dissection** noun

**dissemble** verb to hide, disguise (intentions etc)

**disseminate** verb to scatter, spread □ **dissemination** noun

**dissent** verb **1** to have a different opinion **2** to refuse to agree □ noun disagreement

**dissertation** noun a long piece of writing or talk on a particular (often academic) subject

**disservice** noun harm, a bad turn

**dissident** noun someone who disagrees, esp with a political regime

**dissimilar** adj not the same □ **dissimilarity** noun (pl **dissimilarities**)

**dissipate** verb **1** to (cause to) disappear **2** to waste, squander □ **dissipated** adj worn out by indulging in pleasures; dissolute □ **dissipation** noun

**dissociate** verb to separate □ **dissociate yourself from** to refuse to be associated with

**dissolute** adj having loose morals; debauched

**dissolve** verb **1** to melt **2** to break up **3** to put an end to □ **dissolution** noun (meanings 2 and 3)

**dissonance** noun **1** discord, esp used deliberately for musical effect **2** disagreement □ **dissonant** adj

**dissuade** verb to persuade not to do something □ **dissuasion** noun

**distaff** noun a stick used to hold flax or wool being spun

**distance** noun **1** the space between things **2** a far-off place or point: in the distance **3** coldness of manner

**distant** adj **1** far off or far apart in place or time: distant era/ distant land **2** not close: distant cousin **3** cold in manner □ **distantly** adv **1** with a dreamy or cold manner **2** not closely: distantly related

**distaste** noun dislike □ **distasteful**

adj disagreeable, unpleasant

**distemper** noun **1** a kind of paint used chiefly for walls **2** a viral disease of dogs, foxes etc □ verb to paint with distemper

**distend** verb to swell; stretch outwards □ **distension** noun

**distil** verb **1** to purify (liquid) by heating to a vapour and cooling **2** to extract the spirit or essence from **3** to (cause to) fall in drops □ **distillation** noun □ **distiller** noun □ **distillery** noun (pl **distilleries**) a place where whisky, brandy etc is distilled

**distil** ⬦ distils, distilling, distilled

**distinct** adj **1** clear; easily seen or noticed: a distinct improvement **2** different: the two languages are quite distinct □ **distinction** noun **1** a difference **2** outstanding worth or merit

●\ Do not confuse: **distinct** and **distinctive**

**distinctive** adj different, special, easily recognizable: That singer has a very distinctive voice □ **distinctively** adv

**distinguish** verb **1** to recognize a difference (between) **2** to mark off as different **3** to recognize **4** to give distinction to □ **distinguished** adj **1** outstanding, famous **2** dignified

**distort** verb **1** to twist out of shape **2** to turn or twist (a statement etc) from its true meaning **3** to make (a sound) unclear and harsh □ **distortion** noun

**distract** verb **1** to divert (the attention) **2** to trouble, confuse **3** to make mad □ **distracted** adj mad with pain, grief etc □ **distraction** noun **1** something which diverts your attention **2** anxiety, confusion **3** amusement **4** madness

**distraught** adj extremely agitated or anxious

**distress** noun **1** pain, trouble, sorrow **2** a cause of suffering □ verb to cause pain or sorrow to □ **distressed** adj □ **distressing** adj

**distribute** verb **1** to divide among several **2** to spread out widely □ **distribution** noun

**district** noun a region of a country or town

**distrust** noun lack of trust, suspicion □ verb to have no trust in □ **distrustful** adj

**disturb** verb **1** to confuse, worry, upset **2** to interrupt □ **disturbance** noun **1** an outbreak of violent behaviour, esp in public **2** an act of disturbing, agitating or disorganizing **3** psychological damage or illness □ **disturbed** adj **1** psychology mentally or emotionally ill or damaged **2** full of trouble and anxiety

**disuse** noun the state of being no longer used □ **disused** adj no longer used

**ditch** noun (pl **ditches**) a long narrow hollow trench dug in the ground, esp to carry water

**dither** verb **1** to hesitate, be undecided **2** to act in a nervous, uncertain manner □ noun a state of indecision

**ditto** noun (often written as **do**) the same as already written or said □ **ditto marks** a character (") written below a word in a text, meaning it is to be understood as repeated

**ditty** noun (pl **ditties**) a simple, short song

**divan** noun **1** a long, low couch without a back **2** a bed without a headboard

**dive** verb **1** to plunge headfirst into water **2** to swoop through the air **3** to go down steeply and quickly □ noun an act of diving □ **dive-bomb** verb to bomb from an aircraft in a steep downward dive □ **dive-bomber** noun □ **diver** noun **1** someone who works under water

using special breathing equipment **2** a type of diving bird

**dive** verb ⇔ **dives, diving, dived** or US **dove**

**diverge** verb to separate and go in different directions; differ □ **divergence** noun □ **divergent** adj

**diverse** adj different, various

**diversify** verb to make or become different or varied

**diversify** ⇔ **diversifies, diversifying, diversified**

**diversion** noun **1** turning aside **2** an alteration to a traffic route **3** an amusement

**diversity** noun difference; variety

**divert** verb **1** to turn aside, change the direction of **2** to entertain, amuse □ **diverting** adj entertaining, amusing

**divest** verb to strip or deprive of: divested him of his authority

**divide** verb **1** to separate into parts **2** to share (among) **3** to (cause to) go into separate groups **4** maths to find out how many times one number contains another □ **dividers** noun pl measuring compasses

**dividend** noun **1** an amount to be divided (compare with: **divisor**) **2** a share of profits from a business

**divine** adj **1** of a god; holy **2** informal splendid, wonderful □ verb **1** to guess **2** to foretell, predict □ **diviner** noun someone who claims special powers in finding hidden water or metals

**divinity** noun (pl **divinities**) **1** a god **2** the nature of a god **3** religious studies

**division** noun **1** the act of dividing **2** a barrier, a separator **3** a section, esp of an army **4** separation **5** disagreement □ **divisible** adj able to be divided □ **divisibility** noun □ **divisional** adj of a division □ **divisor** noun the number by which another number (the **dividend**) is divided

**divorce** noun 1 the legal ending of a marriage 2 a complete separation □ verb 1 to end a marriage with 2 to separate (from)

**divulge** verb to let out, make known (a secret etc)

**Diwali** or **Dewali** noun the Hindu and Sikh festival of lamps, celebrated in October or November

**DIY** abbrev do-it-yourself

**dizzy** adj 1 giddy, confused 2 causing giddiness: from a dizzy height □ **dizzily** adv

**DJ** abbrev disc jockey

**djinn** (say jeen or jin) noun pl (sing **djinni** -say jeen-i or jin-ee) a group of spirits in Islamic folklore

**DNA** abbrev deoxyribonucleic acid, a compound carrying genetic instructions for passing on hereditary characteristics

**do** verb 1 to carry out, perform (a job etc) 2 to perform an action on, eg clean (dishes), arrange (hair) etc 3 slang to swindle 4 to act: do as you please 5 to get on: I hear she's doing very well/ how are you doing? 6 to be enough: a pound will do 7 used to avoid repeating a verb: I seldom see him now, and when I do, he ignores me 8 used with a more important verb (1) in questions: do you see what I mean? (2) in sentences with **not**: I don't know; or (3) for emphasis: I do hope she'll be there □ noun (pl dos) informal a social event, a party □ **doer** noun an active person who does a lot of things □ **doings** noun pl actions □ **do away with** to put an end to, destroy □ **do down** informal to get the better of □ **do in** informal 1 to exhaust, wear out 2 to murder □ **done to death** too often repeated □ **do or die** a desperate final attempt at something whatever the consequences □ **do out of** to swindle out of □ **do someone proud** see

proud □ **do up** 1 to fasten 2 to renovate

**do** verb ⊷ does, doing, did, done

**do** abbrev ditto

**docile** adj tame, easy to manage □ **docilely** adv □ **docility** noun

**dock** noun 1 (often **docks**) a deepened part of a harbour where ships go for loading, repair etc 2 the box in a law court where the accused person stands 3 a weed with large leaves □ verb 1 to put in or enter a dock 2 to clip or cut short 3 of a spacecraft: to join on to another craft in space □ **docker** noun someone who works in the docks □ **dockyard** noun a naval harbour with docks, stores etc

**docket** noun a label listing the contents of something

**doctor** noun 1 someone trained in and licensed to practise medicine 2 someone with the highest university degree in any subject □ verb 1 to treat as a patient 2 to tamper with, alter

**doctrine** noun a belief that is taught □ **doctrinal** adj

**document** noun a written statement giving proof, information etc

**documentary** noun (pl **documentaries**) a film giving information about real people or events □ adj 1 of or in documents: documentary evidence 2 of a documentary

**dodder** verb to shake, tremble, esp as a result of old age □ **doddery** adj shaky or slow because of old age

**doddle** noun, informal an easy task

**dodge** verb to avoid by a sudden or clever movement □ noun a trick

**dodo** noun (pl **dodoes** or **dodos**) a type of large extinct bird

**doe** noun the female of certain animals, eg a deer, rabbit or hare

**doff** verb to take off (a hat) in greeting

**dog** noun **1** a four-footed animal often kept as a pet **2** one of the dog family which includes wolves, foxes etc □ adj of certain animals: male □ verb **1** to follow and watch constantly **2** to hamper, plague: dogged by ill health □ **dog-collar** noun **1** a collar for dogs **2** the stiff white collar of a vicar □ **dog-eared** adj of a page: turned down at the corner □ **dog-eat-dog** adj viciously competitive □ **dog-fight** noun a fight between aeroplanes at close quarters □ **dogfish** noun a kind of small shark □ **dog-leg** noun a sharp bend □ **dogsbody** noun, informal someone who is given unpleasant or dreary tasks to do □ **dog-tag** noun **1** a dog's identity disc **2** an identity disc worn by soldiers etc □ **dog-tired** adj completely worn out □ **dog in the manger** someone who stands in the way of a plan or proposal □ **dog's breakfast** or **dog's dinner** a complete mess □ **dog's life** a life of misery □ **go to the dogs** to be ruined

**dog** verb ⊳ dogs, dogging, dogged

**dogged** (say dog-id) adj determined, stubborn: dogged refusal □ **doggedly** adv

**doggerel** noun badly-written poetry

**doggy** adj of or for dogs □ noun, informal a child's name for a dog □ **doggy-bag** noun a bag used to take away left-over food from a restaurant meal □ **doggy-paddle** noun a simple style of swimming

**dogma** noun an opinion, esp religious, accepted or fixed by an authority □ **dogmatic** adj **1** of dogma **2** stubbornly forcing your opinions on others □ **dogmatically** adv

**do-gooder** noun someone who tries to help others in a self-righteous way

**doily** or **doyley** noun (pl **doilies** or **doyleys**) a perforated paper napkin put underneath cakes etc

Originally a light summer fabric, named after Doily's drapery shop in 17th-century London

**Dolby** noun, trademark a system for reducing background noise, used in recording music or soundtracks

**doldrums** noun pl low spirits: in the doldrums

The doldrums take their name from an area of the ocean about the equator famous for calms and variable winds.

**dole** verb to deal (out) in small amounts □ noun, informal unemployment benefit

**doleful** adj sad, unhappy □ **dolefully** adv

**doll** noun a toy in the shape of a small human being

**dollar** noun the main unit of currency in several countries, eg the USA, Canada, Australia and New Zealand

**dolmen** noun an ancient tomb in the shape of a stone table

**dolphin** noun a type of sea animal like a porpoise

**dolt** noun a stupid person □ **doltish** adj

**domain** noun **1** a kingdom **2** a country estate **3** an area of interest or knowledge

**dome** noun **1** the shape of a half sphere or ball **2** the roof of a building etc in this shape □ **domed** adj

**domestic** adj **1** of the home or house **2** of an animal: tame, domesticated **3** not foreign, of your own country: domestic products □ noun a live-in maid etc □ **domesticated** adj **1** of an animal: tame, used for farming etc **2** fond of doing housework, cooking etc □ **domesticity** noun home life □ **domestic science** old cookery, needlework etc, taught as a subject

**domicile** noun the country etc in which someone lives permanently

**dominant** *adj* ruling; most powerful or important □ **dominance** *noun*

**dominate** *verb* 1 to have command or influence over 2 to be most strong, or most noticeable: *the castle dominates the skyline* 3 to tower above, overlook □ **domination** *noun*

**domineering** *adj* overbearing, like a tyrant

**dominion** *noun* 1 rule, authority 2 an area with one ruler or government

**domino** *noun* (*pl* **dominoes**) 1 a piece used in the game of dominoes 2 *historical* a long silk cloak worn at masked balls □ **dominoes** *noun sing* a game played on a table with pieces marked with dots, each side of which must match a piece placed next to it

**don** *noun* a college or university lecturer □ *verb* to put on (a coat *etc*)

**don** *verb* ▷ dons, donning, donned

**donate** *verb* to present a gift □ **donation** *noun* a gift of money or goods

**done** *past participle* of **do** □ *adj* finished

**donkey** *noun* (*pl* **donkeys**) (*also called* **ass**) a type of animal with long ears, related to the horse

**donor** *noun* 1 a giver of a gift 2 someone who agrees to let their body organs be used for transplant operations

**don't** *short for* do not

**doom** *noun* 1 judgement; fate 2 ruin □ **doomed** *adj* 1 destined, condemned 2 bound to fail or be destroyed

**door** *noun* 1 a hinged barrier which closes the entrance to a room or building 2 the entrance itself □ **doorstep** *noun* the step in front of the door of a house □ **doorway** *noun* the space filled by a door, the entrance

**dope** *noun, informal* 1 the drug cannabis 2 an idiot □ *verb* to drug

**dormant** *adj* sleeping, inactive: *a dormant volcano*

▣ active

**dormitory** *noun* (*pl* **dormitories**) a room with beds for several people

**dormouse** *noun* (*pl* **dormice**) a small animal which hibernates
    ⊚ Probably from Latin *dormire* meaning 'to sleep', and English *mouse*

**dorsal** *adj* of the back: *dorsal fin*

**DOS** (*say* dos) *abbrev, computing* disk operating system

**dose** *noun* 1 a quantity of medicine to be taken at one time 2 a bout of something unpleasant: *dose of flu* □ *verb* to give medicine to

**doss** *verb, informal* to lie down to sleep somewhere temporary □ **doss-house** *noun, informal* a cheap lodging-house

**dossier** (*say* dos-i-eh) *noun* a set of papers containing information about a certain person or subject

**dot** *noun* a small, round mark □ *verb* 1 to mark with a dot 2 to scatter □ **on the dot** exactly on time

**dot** *verb* ▷ dots, dotting, dotted

**dotage** *noun* the foolishness and childishness of old age

**dote** *verb*: **dote on** to be foolishly fond of

**double** *verb* 1 to multiply by two 2 to fold □ *noun* 1 twice as much: *he ate double the amount* 2 someone so like another as to be mistaken for them □ *adj* 1 containing twice as much: *a double dose* 2 made up of two of the same sort 3 folded over 4 deceitful □ **doubly** *adv* 1 extra, especially: *check the door to make doubly sure you have locked it* 2 in two ways: *He's doubly responsible for the mess we're in* □ **double agent** a spy paid by each of two rival countries, but loyal to only one of them □ **double bass** a type of large stringed musical instrument □ **double-breasted** adj of a coat: with one half of the front overlapping the other □ **double-cross** verb to cheat □ **double-dealer** noun a deceitful, cheating person □ **double-dealing** noun □ **double-decker** a bus with two floors □ **double-Dutch** noun incomprehensible talk, gibberish □ **double glazing** two sheets of glass in a window to keep in the heat or keep out noise □ **double-take** noun a second look at something surprising or confusing □ **double-think** noun the holding of two contradictory opinions or ideas □ **double-time** noun payment for overtime work etc at twice the usual rate □ **at the double** very quickly □ **double back** to turn sharply and go back the way you have come □ **double up 1** to writhe in pain **2** to share accommodation (with)

**double entendre** (say doob-lon-**ton**-dre) a word or phrase with two meanings, one of them usually sexual

**doublet** noun, historical a man's close-fitting jacket

**doubt** verb **1** to be unsure or undecided about **2** to think unlikely: I doubt that we'll be able to go □ noun a lack of certainty or trust; suspicion □ **doubtful** adj **1** (**doubtful about**) unsure about **2** unlikely, uncertain or unreliable □ **doubtless** adv probably □ **no doubt** probably

**dough** noun **1** a mass of flour, moistened and kneaded **2** informal money

**doughnut** noun a ring-shaped cake fried in fat

**doughty** (say **dowt**-i) adj strong; brave

**dour** (say door) adj dull, humourless

**dove**[1] (say duv) noun a pigeon □ **dovecote** noun a pigeon-house

**dove**[2] (say dohv) US past form of **dive**

**dovetail** verb to fit one thing exactly into another

**dowdy** adj not smart, badly dressed

**down**[1] adv **1** towards or in a lower position: fell down/ sitting down **2** to a smaller size: grind down **3** to a later generation: handed down from mother to daughter **4** on the spot, in cash: 10 down □ prep **1** towards or in the lower part of: rolled back down the hill **2** along: strolling down the road □ adj going downwards: the down escalator □ **down-at-heel** adj worn down, shabby □ **downcast** adj sad □ **downer** noun, slang a tranquillizing or depressant drug □ **downfall** noun ruin, defeat □ **downhearted** adj discouraged □ **downpour** noun a heavy fall of rain □ **downstairs** adj on a lower floor of a building □ adv to a lower floor □ **downstream** adv further down a river, in the direction of its flow □ **downtrodden** adj kept in a lowly, inferior position □ **downwards** adv moving or leading down □ **go down with** or **be down with** to become or be ill with

**down**[2] noun light, soft feathers □ **downy** adj soft, feathery

**downs** noun pl low, grassy hills

**dowry** noun (pl **dowries**) money and property brought by a woman to her husband on their marriage

**doyley** noun another spelling of **doily**

**doze** verb to sleep lightly □ noun a light, short sleep

**dozen** noun twelve

**drab** adj dull, monotonous

**draft** noun **1** a rough outline, a sketch **2** a group of people selected for a special purpose **3** US conscription into the army **4** an order for payment of money **5** US spelling of **draught** □ verb **1** to make a rough plan **2** to select for a purpose **3** US to conscript

♠ Do not confuse with: **draught**

**draftsman, draftswoman** *US*
*spellings of* **draughtsman,
draughtswoman**

**drag** *verb* **1** to pull roughly **2** to
move slowly and heavily **3** to trail
along the ground **4** to search (a
river-bed *etc*) with a net or hook
□ *noun, informal* **1** a dreary task **2** a
tedious person **3** clothes for one sex
worn by the other □ **drag your feet**
or **drag your heels** to be slow to do
something

**dragon** *noun* **1** an imaginary fire-
breathing, winged reptile **2** a fierce,
intimidating person

**dragonfly** *noun* a winged insect with
a long body and double wings

**dragoon** *noun* a heavily-armed horse
soldier □ *verb* to force or bully (into)

**drain** *verb* **1** to clear (land) of water
by trenches or pipes **2** to drink the
contents of (a glass *etc*) **3** to use up
completely □ *noun* a channel or pipe
used to carry off water *etc*
□ **drainage** *noun* the drawing-off of
water by rivers, pipes *etc* □ **drained**
*adj* **1** emptied of liquid **2** sapped of
strength

**drake** *noun* a male duck

**drama** *noun* **1** a play for acting in the
theatre **2** exciting or tense action
□ **dramatist** *noun* a playwright

**dramatic** *adj* **1** relating to plays
**2** exciting, thrilling **3** unexpected,
sudden □ **dramatically** *adv*

**dramatize** *verb* **1** to turn into a play
for the theatre **2** to make vivid or
sensational □ **dramatization** *noun*

**drank** *past form of* **drink**

**drape** *verb* to arrange (cloth) to hang
gracefully □ *noun* (**drapes**) *US*
curtains □ **draper** *noun* a dealer in
cloth □ **drapery** *noun* **1** cloth goods
**2** a draper's shop

**drastic** *adj* severe, extreme
□ **drastically** *adv*

**draught** (*say* drahft) *noun* **1** a

current of air **2** the act of drawing
or pulling **3** something drawn out
**4** a drink taken all at once
**5** (**draughts**) a game for two, played
by moving pieces on a squared
board □ **draughty** *adj* full of air
currents, chilly

♠ Do not confuse with: **draft**

**draughtsman, draughtswoman**
*noun* **1** someone employed to draw
plans **2** someone skilled in drawing

**draw** *verb* **1** to make a picture with
pencil, crayons *etc* **2** to pull after or
along **3** to attract: *draw a large
crowd* **4** to obtain money from a
fund: *drawing a pension* **5** to require
(a depth) for floating: *this ship
draws 20 feet* **6** to approach, come:
*night is drawing near* **7** to score
equal points in a game □ *noun* **1** an
equal score **2** a lottery □ **draw a
blank** to get no result □ **draw a
conclusion** to form an opinion from
evidence heard □ **drawn and
quartered** *historical* disembowelled
and cut in pieces after being hanged
□ **draw on** to approach **2** to use as
a resource: *drawing on experience*
□ **draw out 1** to lengthen **2** to
persuade (someone) to talk and be
at ease □ **draw the line at** to refuse
to allow or accept □ **draw up 1** to
come to a stop **2** to move closer **3** to
plan, write out (a contract *etc*)

**draw** *verb* ⇔ draws, draw*ing*, drew,
drawn

**drawback** *noun* a disadvantage

**drawbridge** *noun* a bridge at the
entrance to a castle which can be
drawn up or let down

**drawer** *noun* **1** someone who draws
**2** (*say* drawr) a sliding box fitting
into a chest, table *etc*

**drawing** *noun* a picture made by
pencil, crayon *etc* □ **drawing-pin**
*noun* a pin with a large flat head for
fastening paper on a board *etc*
□ **drawing-room** *noun* a sitting-
room

**drawl** *verb* to speak in a slow, lazy manner □ *noun* a drawling voice

**drawn** *past participle* of **draw**

**dread** *noun* great fear □ *adj* terrifying □ *verb* to be greatly afraid of □ **dreaded** *adj*

**dreadful** *adj* 1 terrible 2 *informal* very bad □ **dreadfully** *adv*

**dreadlock** *noun* a thick, twisted strand of hair

**dreadnought** *noun*, *historical* a kind of battleship

**dream** *noun* 1 a series of images and sounds in the mind during sleep 2 something imagined, not real 3 something very beautiful 4 a hope, an ambition: *her dream was to go to Mexico* □ *verb* to have a dream □ **dream up** to invent

**dream** *verb* ⇨ dreams, dream*ing*, dream*t* or dream*ed*

**dreamy** *adj* 1 sleepy, half-awake 2 vague, dim 3 *informal* beautiful □ **dreamily** *adv*

**dreary** *adj* gloomy, cheerless □ **drearily** *adv*

**dredge** *verb* 1 to drag a net or bucket along a river- or sea-bed to bring up fish, mud *etc* 2 to sprinkle with (sugar or flour) □ *noun* an instrument for dredging a river *etc* □ **dredger** *noun* 1 a ship which digs a channel by lifting mud from the bottom 2 a perforated jar for sprinkling sugar or flour

**dregs** *noun pl* 1 sediment on the bottom of a liquid: *dregs of wine* 2 last remnants 3 a worthless or useless part

**drench** *verb* to soak

**dress** *verb* 1 to put on clothes or a covering 2 to prepare (food *etc*) for use 3 to arrange (hair) 4 to treat and bandage (wounds) □ *noun* (*pl* dresses) 1 clothes 2 a one-piece woman's garment combining skirt and top 3 a style of clothing: *formal dress* □ *adj* of clothes: for formal use: *a dress shirt* □ **dress rehearsal**

the final rehearsal of a play, in which the actors wear their costumes □ **dressy** *adj* stylish, smart

**dresser** *noun* a kitchen sideboard for dishes

**dressing** *noun* 1 a covering 2 a seasoned sauce poured over salads *etc* 3 a bandage

**dressing-gown** *noun* a loose, light coat worn indoors over pyjamas *etc*

**drew** *past form* of **draw**

**drey** *noun* (*pl* dreys) a squirrel's nest

**dribble** *verb* 1 to (cause to) fall in small drops 2 to let saliva run down the chin 3 *football* to move the ball forward by short kicks

**dried** *see* **dry**

**drift** *noun* 1 snow, sand *etc* driven by the wind 2 the direction in which something is driven 3 the general meaning of someone's words □ *verb* 1 to go with the tide or current 2 to be driven into heaps by the wind 3 to wander about 4 to live aimlessly □ **drifter** *noun* 1 someone who drifts 2 a fishing boat that uses drift-nets □ **drift-net** *noun* a fishing net which stays near the surface of the water □ **driftwood** *noun* wood driven on to the seashore by winds or tides

**drill** *verb* 1 to make a hole in 2 to make with a drill 3 to exercise (soldiers) 4 to sow (seeds) in rows □ *noun* 1 a tool for making holes in wood *etc* 2 military exercise 3 a row of seeds or plants

**drily** *another spelling* of **dryly**

**drink** *verb* 1 to swallow (a liquid) 2 to take alcoholic drink, *esp* excessively □ *noun* 1 liquid to be drunk 2 alcoholic liquids □ **drink in** to listen to eagerly □ **drink to** to drink a toast to □ **drink up** to finish a drink

**drink** *verb* ⇨ drinks, drink*ing*, drank, drunk

**drip** *verb* 1 to fall in drops 2 to let (water *etc*) fall in drops □ *noun* 1 a drop **2** a continual dropping, *eg* of water **3** a device for adding liquid slowly to a vein *etc* □ **drip-dry** *verb* to dry (a garment) by hanging it up to dry without wringing it first □ **dripping** *noun* fat from roasting meat

**drip** *verb* ⇔ drip**s**, drip**ping**, drip**ped**

**drive** *verb* **1** to control or guide (a car *etc*) **2** to go in a vehicle: *driving to work* **3** to force or urge along **4** to hurry on **5** to hit hard (a ball, nail *etc*) **6** to bring about: *drive a bargain* □ *noun* **1** a journey in a car **2** a private road to a house **3** an avenue or road **4** energy, enthusiasm **5** a campaign: *a drive to save the local school* **6** a games tournament: *whist drive* **7** a hard stroke with a club or bat □ **driver** *noun* **1** someone who drives a car *etc* **2** a wooden-headed golf club □ **drive-in** *noun, US* a cinema where the audience watches the screen while staying in their cars □ **what are you driving at?** what are you suggesting or implying?

**drive** ⇔ drive**s**, driv**ing**, drove, driven

**drivel** *noun, informal* nonsense □ *verb* to talk nonsense

**drivel** *verb* ⇔ drivel**s**, drivel**ling**, drivel**led**

**driven** *past participle* of **drive**

**drizzle** *noun* light rain □ *verb* to rain lightly □ **drizzly** *adj*

**droll** *adj* **1** funny, amusing **2** odd

**dromedary** *noun* (*pl* **dromedaries**) an Arabian camel with one hump

**drone** *verb* **1** to make a low humming sound **2** to speak in a dull boring voice □ *noun* **1** a low humming sound **2** a dull boring voice **3** the low-sounding pipe of a bagpipe **4** a male bee **5** a lazy, idle person

**drool** *verb* **1** to produce saliva **2** to anticipate something in an obvious way

**droop** *verb* **1** to hang down: *your hem*

*is drooping* **2** to grow weak or discouraged

**drop** *noun* **1** a small round or pear-shaped blob of liquid **2** a small quantity: *a drop of whisky* **3** a fall from a height: *a drop of six feet* **4** a small flavoured sweet: *pear drop* □ *verb* **1** to fall suddenly **2** to let fall **3** to fall in drops **4** to set down from a car *etc*: *drop me at the corner* **5** to give up, abandon (a friend, habit *etc*) □ **droplet** *noun* a tiny drop □ **droppings** *noun pl* animal or bird dung □ **drop off** to fall asleep □ **drop out** to withdraw from a class, the rat-race *etc*

**drop** ⇔ drop**s**, drop**ping**, drop**ped**

**dross** *noun* **1** scum produced by melting metal **2** waste material, impurities **3** coal dust **4** anything worthless

**drought** *noun* a period of time when no rain falls

**drove** *noun* **1** a number of moving cattle or other animals **2** (**droves**) a great number of people □ *past form* of **drive** □ **drover** *noun* someone who drives cattle

**drown** *verb* **1** to die by suffocating in water **2** to kill (someone) in this way **3** to flood or soak completely **4** to block out (a sound) with a louder one

**drowsy** *adj* sleepy □ **drowsily** *adv*

**drubbing** *noun* a thrashing

**drudge** *verb* to do very humble or boring work □ *noun* someone who does such work □ **drudgery** *noun* hard, uninteresting work

**drug** *noun* **1** a substance used in medicine to treat illness, kill pain *etc* **2** a stimulant or narcotic substance taken habitually for its effects □ *verb* **1** to administer drugs to **2** to make to lose consciousness by drugs □ **druggist** *noun* a chemist □ **drugstore** *noun, US* a shop selling newspapers, soft drinks *etc* as well as medicines

**drug** ↔ drugs, drugging, drugged

**drum** noun **1** a musical instrument of skin etc stretched on a round frame and beaten with sticks **2** a cylindrical container: oil drum/biscuit drum □ verb **1** to beat a drum **2** to tap continuously with the fingers □ **drummer** noun

**drum** ↔ drums, drumming, drummed

**drumstick** noun **1** a stick for beating a drum **2** the lower part of the leg of a cooked chicken etc

**drunk** adj showing the effects (giddiness, unsteadiness etc) of drinking too much alcohol □ noun someone who is drunk, or habitually drunk □ past participle of **drink** □ **drunkard** noun a drunk

**drunken** adj **1** habitually drunk **2** caused by too much alcohol: drunken stupor **3** involving much alcohol: drunken orgy □ **drunkenness** noun

**dry** adj **1** not moist or wet **2** thirsty **3** uninteresting: makes very dry reading **4** reserved, matter-of-fact **5** of wine: not sweet **6** of a sense of humour: funny in a quiet, subtle way □ verb to make or become dry □ **dryly** or **drily** adv □ **dry-clean** verb to clean (clothes etc) with chemicals, not with water □ **dryness** noun □ **dry-rot** noun a disease causing wood to become dry and crumbly

**dry** verb ↔ dries, drying, dried

**dryad** (say drai-ad) noun a mythological wood nymph

**DSS** abbrev Department of Social Services (previously **DHSS** Department of Health and Social Security)

**DTI** abbrev Department of Trade and Industry

**DTP** abbrev desktop publishing

**dual** adj double; made up of two □ **dual carriageway** a road divided by a central barrier or boundary, with each side used by traffic moving in one direction □ **dual-purpose** adj able to be used for two purposes

**♦.** Do not confuse with: **duel**

**dub** verb **1** to declare (a knight) by touching each shoulder with a sword **2** to name or nickname **3** to add sound effects to a film **4** to give (a film) a new sound-track in a different language

**dub** ↔ dubs, dubbing, dubbed

**dubbin** or **dubbing** noun a grease for softening or waterproofing leather

**dubious** adj **1** doubtful, uncertain **2** probably dishonest: dubious dealings □ **dubiety** noun doubt

**ducal** adj of a duke

**ducat** noun, historical an old European gold coin

**duchess** noun (pl duchesses) **1** a woman of the same rank as a duke **2** the wife or widow of a duke

**duchy** noun (pl duchies) the land owned by a duke or duchess

**duck** noun **1** a web-footed bird, with a broad flat beak **2** cricket a score of no runs □ verb **1** to lower the head quickly as if to avoid a blow **2** to push (someone's head) under water □ **duckling** noun a baby duck □ **duck out (of)** to avoid responsibility (for

The meaning in cricket comes from the use of 'duck's egg' to mean a nought on a scoring sheet.

**duck-billed platypus** see platypus

**duct** noun a pipe for carrying liquids, electric cables etc

**ductile** adj easily led, yielding

**dud** adj, informal useless, broken

**dudgeon** noun: in high dudgeon very angry, indignant

**due** adj **1** owed, needing to be paid: the rent is due next week **2** expected to arrive etc: they're due here at six **3** proper, appropriate: due care □ adv directly: due south □ noun **1** something you have a right to: give him his due **2** (**dues**) the amount of money charged for belonging to a club *etc* □ **due to** brought about by, caused by

**duel** *noun, historical* a formalized fight with pistols or swords between two people □ *verb* to fight in a duel □ **duellist** *noun* someone who fights in a duel

⚠ Do not confuse with: **dual**

**duet** (*say* dyoo-et) *noun* a piece of music for two singers or players

**duff** *adj, informal* useless, broken

**duffel bag** a cylindrical canvas bag tied with a drawstring

**duffel coat** a heavy woollen coat, fastened with toggles

After *Duffel*, a town in Belgium where the fabric was first made

**duffer** *noun, informal* a stupid or incompetent person

**dug** *past form of* **dig**

**dugout** *noun* **1** a boat made by hollowing out the trunk of a tree **2** a rough shelter dug out of a slope or bank or in a trench **3** *football* a bench beside the pitch for team managers, trainers, and extra players

**duke** *noun* a nobleman next in rank below a prince □ **dukedom** *noun* the title, rank or lands of a duke

**dulcet** *adj, formal* pleasant-sounding, melodious

**dulcimer** *noun* a musical instrument with stretched wires which are struck with small hammers

**dull** *adj* **1** not lively **2** slow to understand or learn **3** not exciting or interesting **4** of weather: cloudy, not bright or clear **5** not bright in colour **6** of sounds: not clear or ringing **7** blunt, not sharp **8** of pain: present in the background, but not acute □ *verb* to make dull □ **dullness** *noun* □ **dully** *adv* (adj, meanings 1, 5, 6 and 8)

**duly** *adv* at the proper or expected

time; as expected: *he duly arrived*

**dumb** *adj* **1** without the power of speech **2** silent **3** *informal* stupid □ **dumbly** *adv* in silence

**dummy** *noun* (*pl* **dummies**) **1** a mock-up of something used for display **2** a model used for displaying clothes *etc* **3** an artificial teat used to comfort a baby **4** *slang* a stupid person □ **dummy run** a try-out, a practice

**dump** *verb* **1** to throw down heavily **2** to unload and leave (rubbish *etc*) **3** to sell at a low price □ *noun* a place for leaving rubbish □ (**down**) **in the dumps** feeling low or depressed

**dumpling** *noun* a cooked ball of dough

**dumpy** *adj* short and thick or fat

**dun** *adj* greyish-brown, mouse-coloured □ *verb* to demand payment

**dun** *verb* ▷ **duns, dunning, dunned**

**dunce** *noun* a stupid or slow-learning person

Originally a term of abuse applied to followers of the medieval Scottish philosopher, John *Duns Scotus*

**dune** *noun* a low hill of sand

**dung** *noun* animal faeces, manure

**dungarees** *noun pl* trousers with a bib made of coarse, hard-wearing material

**dungeon** *noun* a dark underground prison

**duodenum** *noun* the first part of the small intestine

**dupe** *noun* someone easily cheated □ *verb* to deceive, trick

**duplicate** *adj* exactly the same □ *noun* an exact copy □ *verb* to make a copy or copies of □ **duplication** *noun*

**duplicity** *noun* deceit, double-dealing □ **duplicitous** *adj*

**durable** *adj* lasting, able to last; wearing well □ **durability** *noun*

**duration** *noun* the time a thing lasts

◻ **for the duration** *informal* for a long time, for ages

**duress** (*say* dyoo-**res**) *noun* illegal force used to make someone do something ◻ **under duress** under the influence of force, threats *etc*

**during** *prep* **1** throughout all or part of: *we lived here during the war* **2** at a particular point within: *she died during the night*

**dusk** *noun* twilight, partial dark

**dusky** *adj* dark-coloured ◻ **duskiness** *noun*

**dust** *noun* **1** fine grains or specks of earth, sand *etc* **2** fine powder ◻ *verb* **1** to free from dust: *dusted the table* **2** to sprinkle lightly with powder ◻ **dustbin** *noun* a container for household rubbish ◻ **duster** *noun* a cloth for removing dust ◻ **dust jacket** a paper cover on a book ◻ **dustman** *noun* someone employed to collect household rubbish ◻ **dusty** *adj* covered with dust

**dutiful** *adj* obedient ◻ **dutifully** *adv*

**duty** *noun* (*pl* **duties**) **1** something a person ought to do **2** an action required to be done **3** a tax **4** (**duties**) the various tasks involved in a job ◻ **duty-free** *adj* not taxed

**duvet** (*say* **doo**-vei) *noun* a quilt stuffed with feathers or synthetic material, used instead of blankets

**dwarf** *noun* (*pl* **dwarfs** or **dwarves**) an undersized person, animal or plant ◻ *verb* to make to appear small by comparison ◻ *adj* not

growing to full or usual height: *dwarf cherry-tree*

**dwell** *verb* **1** to live, inhabit, stay **2** (with **on**) to think habitually about something: *dwelling on the past*

**dwindle** *verb* to grow less, waste away

**dye** *verb* to give a colour to (fabric *etc*) ◻ *noun* a powder or liquid for colouring ◻ **dyeing** *noun* the putting of colour into cloth

**dying** *present participle* of **die**

**dyke** *another spelling of* **dike**

**dynamic** *adj* forceful, energetic ◻ **dynamically** *adv*

**dynamics** *noun sing* the scientific study of movement and force

**dynamite** *noun* a type of powerful explosive

**dynamo** *noun* (*pl* **dynamos**) a machine for turning the energy produced by movement into electricity

**dynasty** (*say* **din**-as-ti) *noun* (*pl* **dynasties**) a succession of monarchs, leaders *etc* of the same family ◻ **dynastic** *adj*

**dysentery** *noun* an infectious disease causing fever, pain and diarrhoea

**dyslexia** *noun* difficulty in learning to read and in spelling

**dyslexic** *noun & adj* (someone) suffering from dyslexia

**dyspepsia** *noun* indigestion ◻ **dyspeptic** *adj*

---

# Ee

**E** *abbrev* east; eastern

**each** *adj* of two or more things: every one taken individually: *each person/ each time* ◻ *pronoun* every one individually: *each of them won a prize* ◻ **each other** used when an action takes place between two people: *we don't see each other very*

*often*

**eager** *adj* keen, anxious to do or get (something) ◻ **eagerly** *adv*

◼ anxious

**eagle** *noun* a kind of large bird of prey

**eaglet** *noun* a young eagle

**ear** *noun* **1** the part of the body through which you hear sounds **2** a head (of corn *etc*) □ **eardrum** *noun* the membrane in the middle of the ear □ **ear-lobe** *noun* the soft fleshy part at the bottom of the human ear □ **ear-muffs** *noun pl* two pads of warm material joined by a band across the head, which you use to cover your ears to stop them getting cold □ **earphones** *noun pl* a pair of tiny speakers fitting in or against the ear for listening to a radio *etc* □ **ear-piercing** *adj* very loud or shrill □ **earplugs** *noun pl* a pair of plugs placed in the ears to block off outside noise □ **earshot** *noun* the distance at which a sound can be heard □ **a good ear** the ability to tell one sound from another □ **lend an ear** to listen

**earl** *noun* a member of the British aristocracy between a marquis and a viscount

**early** *adj* **1** in good time **2** at or near the beginning **3** sooner than expected: *you're early!* □ *adv*: *the bus left early* □ **earliness** *noun* □ **early bird 1** an early riser **2** someone who gains an advantage by acting more quickly than rivals

**early** ⇔ **earlier, earliest**

**earmark** *verb* to mark or set aside for a special purpose

**earn** *verb* **1** to receive (money) for work **2** to deserve

**earnest** *adj* serious, serious-minded □ *noun* **1** seriousness **2** money *etc* given to make sure that a bargain will be kept □ **in earnest** meaning what you say or do □ **earnestly** *adv*

**earnings** *noun pl* pay for work done

**earth** *noun* **1** the third planet from the sun; our world **2** its surface **3** soil **4** the hole of a fox, badger *etc* **5** an electrical connection with the ground □ *verb* to connect electrically with the ground □ **earthly** *adj* of the earth as opposed to heaven □ **earthquake** *noun* a shaking of the earth's crust □ **earthshattering** *adj* of great importance □ **earthworm** *noun* the common worm □ **earthy** *adj* **1** like soil **2** covered in soil **3** coarse and natural, not refined

**earthenware** *noun* pottery, dishes made of clay

**earwig** *noun* a type of insect with pincers at its tail

**ease** *noun* **1** freedom from difficulty: *finished the race with ease* **2** freedom from pain, worry or embarrassment **3** rest from work □ *verb* **1** to make or become less painful or difficult **2** to move carefully and gradually: *ease the stone into position* □ **at ease** comfortable, relaxed □ **stand at ease** to stand with your legs apart and arms behind your back

---

■ (verb, meaning 1) alleviate

---

**easel** *noun* a stand for an artist's canvas while painting *etc*

**easily** *adv* **1** without difficulty **2** without pain, worry or discomfort **3** obviously, clearly, beyond doubt or by a long way: *He's easily the best actor in Britain today* **4** more quickly or more readily than most people **5** very possibly: *He could easily be out for a couple of hours* □ **easiness** *noun*

**east** *noun* one of the four chief directions, that in which the sun rises □ *adj* in or from the east: *an east wind* □ **easterly** *adj* □ **eastern** *adj* □ **eastward** or **eastwards** *adj* & *adv* towards the east

**Easter** *noun* **1** the Christian celebration of Christ's rising from the dead **2** the weekend when this is celebrated each year, sometime in spring

**easy** *adj* **1** not hard to do **2** free from pain, worry or discomfort

**easy** ⇔ **easier, easiest**

**eat** verb 1 to chew and swallow (food) 2 to destroy gradually, waste away □ **eatable** adj

eat ⇒ eats, eating, ate, eaten

**eaves** noun pl the edge of a roof overhanging the walls

**eavesdrop** verb to listen secretly to a private conversation □ **eavesdropper** noun

**ebb** noun 1 the flowing away of the tide after high tide 2 a lessening, a worsening □ verb 1 to flow away 2 to grow less or worse

**ebony** noun a type of black, hard wood □ adj 1 made of ebony 2 black

**EC** abbrev European Community

**eccentric** adj 1 odd, acting strangely 2 of circles: not having the same centre (contrasted with: **concentric**) □ **eccentricity** noun (pl **eccentricities**)

**ecclesiastic** or **ecclesiastical** adj of the church or clergy

**echo** noun (pl **echoes**) 1 the repetition of a sound by its striking a surface and coming back 2 something that evokes a memory: echoes of the past □ verb 1 to send back sound 2 to repeat (a thing said) 3 to imitate

**éclair** (say ei-kleir) noun an oblong sweet pastry filled with cream

**eclipse** noun 1 the covering of the whole or part of the sun or moon, eg when the moon comes between the sun and the earth 2 loss of position or prestige □ verb 1 to throw into the shade 2 to blot out (someone's achievement) by doing better

**eco-** prefix relating to the environment: ecofriendly/eco-summit

This prefix has been created by taking the start of 'ecology' and adding different endings.

**ecological** adj 1 having to do with plants, animals etc and their natural surroundings 2 concerned with protecting and preserving plants, animals and the natural environment □ **ecologically** adv

**ecology** noun the study of plants, animals etc in relation to their natural surroundings □ **ecologist** noun

**economic** adj 1 concerning economy 2 making a profit □ **economical** adj thrifty, not wasteful □ **economics** noun sing the study of how money is created and spent □ **economist** noun

**economy** noun (pl **economies**) 1 the management of a country's finances 2 the careful use of something, esp money □ **economize** verb to be careful in spending or using

**ecstasy** noun (pl **ecstasies**) very great joy or pleasure □ **ecstatic** adj □ **ecstatically** adv

**ECT** abbrev electro-convulsive therapy

**eczema** (say ek-sim-a) noun a skin disease causing red swollen patches on the skin □ **eczematous** adj

**eddy** noun (pl **eddies**) a circling current of water or air running against the main stream □ verb to flow in circles

**edge** noun 1 the border of anything, farthest from the middle 2 the cutting side of a blade 3 sharpness: put an edge on my appetite 4 advantage: Brazil had the edge at half-time □ verb 1 to put a border on 2 to move little by little: edge forward □ **edgeways** adv sideways □ **edging** noun a border, a fringe □ **on edge** nervous, edgy □ **set someone's teeth on edge** to grate on their nerves, make them wince

**edgy** adj unable to relax, irritable

**edible** adj fit to be eaten

**edict** noun an order, a command

**edifice** noun a large building

**edify** verb to improve the mind,

enlighten □ **edification** noun
□ **edifying** adj

**edify** ·· edifies, edifying, edified

**edit** verb to prepare (a text, film etc) for publication or broadcasting

**edition** noun **1** the form in which a book etc is published after being edited **2** the copies of a book, newspaper etc printed at one time **3** a special issue of a newspaper, eg for a local area

**editor** noun **1** someone who edits a book, film etc **2** the chief journalist of a newspaper or section of a newspaper: the sports editor □ **editorial** adj of editing □ noun a newspaper column written by the chief editor

**educate** verb to teach (people), esp in a school or college □ **educated** adj knowledgeable and cultured, as a result of receiving a good education □ **educated guess** a guess based on knowledge of the subject involved

**education** noun **1** the process or system of teaching in schools and other establishments **2** the development of a person's knowledge **3** an experience from which you think you have learnt something □ **educational** adj **1** concerned with formal teaching **2** concerned with giving information, rather than simply entertaining or amusing **3** interesting from the point of view of teaching you something which you did not know before

**EEC** abbrev European Economic Community

**eel** noun a long, ribbon-shaped fish

**eerie** adj causing fear of the unknown

Originally a Scots word meaning 'afraid' or 'cowardly'

**efface** verb to rub out □ **efface yourself** to keep from being noticed

**effect** noun **1** the result of an action **2** strength, power **3** an impression

produced: the effect of the sunset **4** general meaning **5** use, operation: that law is not yet in effect **6** (effects) goods, property □ verb to bring about □ **effective** adj **1** producing the desired effect **2** actual □ **effectual** adj able to do what is required □ **effectually** adv

❦ Do not confuse with: affect. Effect is usually a noun. Affect is usually a verb. 'To AFFECT' means 'to have an EFFECT on'.

**effeminate** adj unmanly, womanish

**effervesce** verb **1** to froth up **2** to be very lively, excited etc □ **effervescence** noun □ **effervescent** adj

**effete** adj weak, feeble

**efficacious** adj effective □ **efficacy** noun

**efficient** adj able to do things well; capable □ **efficiency** noun □ **efficiently** adv

**effigy** noun (pl effigies) a likeness of a person carved in stone, wood etc

**effluent** noun **1** a stream flowing from another stream or lake **2** liquid industrial waste; sewage

**effort** noun **1** an attempt using a lot of strength or ability **2** hard work

**effrontery** noun impudence

**effusive** adj speaking freely, gushing □ **effusively** adv

**EFL** abbrev English as a foreign language

**eg** abbrev for example
ⓘ From Latin exempli gratia

**egg** noun **1** an oval shell containing the embryo of a bird, insect or reptile **2** (also called ovum) a human reproductive cell **3** a hen's egg used for eating □ **egg on** to urge, encourage

**eggplant** noun, US an aubergine

**ego** noun **1** the conscious self **2** self-conceit, egotism

**egoism** or **egotism** noun the habit of considering only your own interests, selfishness □ **egoist** or **egotist** noun □ **egoistic** or **egotistic** adj

**eiderdown** noun **1** soft feathers from the eider, a type of northern sea-duck **2** a feather quilt

**eight** noun the number 8 □ adj 8 in number □ **eighth** adj the last of a series of eight □ noun one of eight equal parts

**eighteen** noun the number 18 □ adj 18 in number □ **eighteenth** adj the last of a series of eighteen □ noun one of eighteen equal parts

**eighty** noun the number 80 □ adj 80 in number □ **eightieth** adj the last of a series of eighty □ noun one of eighty equal parts

**either** adj & pronoun **1** one or other of two: either bus will go there **2** each of two, both: there is a crossing on either side of the road □ conj used with **or** to show alternatives: either he goes or I do □ adv any more than another: that won't work either

**ejaculate** verb **1** to emit semen **2** to shout out, exclaim □ **ejaculation** noun

**eject** verb **1** to throw out **2** to force to leave a house, job etc □ **ejection** noun

**eke** verb: **eke out** to make last longer by adding to

**elaborate** verb (say i-**lab**-o-reit) **1** to work out in detail **2** (often **elaborate on**) to explain fully □ adj (say i-**lab**-o-rat) highly detailed and decorated □ **elaboration** noun

**elapse** verb of time: to pass

**elastic** adj able to stretch and spring back again, springy □ noun a piece of cotton etc interwoven with rubber to make it springy □ **elasticity** noun

**elated** adj in high spirits, very pleased □ **elation** noun

**elbow** noun the joint where the arm bends □ verb to push with the elbow, jostle □ **elbow grease** **1** vigorous

rubbing **2** hard work, effort □ **elbow-room** noun plenty of room to move

**elder¹** adj older □ noun **1** someone who is older **2** an office-bearer in the Presbyterian church □ **eldest** adj oldest

**elder²** noun a type of tree with purple-black berries

**elderberry** noun (pl **elderberries**) a berry from the elder tree

**elderly** adj nearing old age

**elect** verb **1** to choose by voting **2** to choose (to): he's elected to stay □ adj **1** chosen **2** chosen for a post but not yet in it: president elect □ **election** noun the choosing by vote of people to sit in parliament etc

**electorate** noun all those who have the right to vote

**electricity** noun a form of energy used to give light, heat and power □ **electric** or **electrical** adj produced or worked by electricity □ **electrician** noun someone skilled in working with electricity □ **electrify** verb **1** to supply with electricity **2** to excite greatly

**electrify** ↔ **electrifies**, **electrifying**, **electrified**

**electro-** prefix electric, of or by electricity

**electrocute** verb to kill by an electric current

**electrode** noun a conductor through which an electric current enters or leaves a battery etc

**electron** noun a very light particle within an atom, having the smallest possible charge of electricity

**electronics** noun sing a branch of physics dealing with electrons and their use in machines etc □ **electronic** adj of or using electrons or electronics

**elegant** adj **1** graceful, well-dressed, fashionable **2** of clothes etc: well-made and tasteful □ **elegance** noun

□ **elegantly** adv

**elegy** noun (pl **elegies**) a poem written on someone's death

**element** noun **1** a part of anything **2** a substance that cannot be split chemically into simpler substances, eg oxygen, iron etc **3** circumstances which suit someone best: she is in her element when singing **4** a heating wire carrying the current in an electric heater **5** (**elements**) first steps in learning **6** (**elements**) the powers of nature, the weather □ **elemental** adj of the elements □ **elementary** adj **1** at the first stage **2** simple

**elephant** noun a very large animal with a thick skin, a trunk and two ivory tusks □ **elephantine** (say el-i-**fan**-tain) adj big and clumsy

**elevate** verb **1** to raise to a higher position **2** to cheer up **3** to improve (the mind) □ **elevation** noun **1** the act of raising up **2** rising ground **3** height **4** a drawing of a building as seen from the side **5** an angle measuring height: the sun's elevation □ **elevator** noun, US a lift in a building

**eleven** noun **1** the number 11 **2** a team of eleven players, eg for cricket □ adj 11 in number □ **eleventh** adj the last of a series of eleven □ noun one of eleven equal parts

**elevenses** noun pl coffee, biscuits etc taken around eleven o'clock in the morning

**elf** noun (pl **elves**) a tiny, mischievous supernatural creature

**elfin**, **elfish** or **elvish** adj like an elf

**elicit** verb to draw out (information etc)
   ⊙ From Latin elicit-, a form of elicere meaning 'to lure out'
   ◈ Do not confuse with: **illicit**

**eligible** adj fit or worthy to be chosen, esp for marriage □ **eligibility** noun

**eliminate** verb **1** to get rid of **2** to exclude, omit □ **elimination** noun

**élite** or **elite** (say ei-**leet**) noun a part of a group selected as, or believed to be, the best

**elixir** (say e-**liks**-eer) noun a liquid believed to give eternal life, or to be able to turn iron etc into gold

**elk** noun a very large deer found in N Europe and Asia, related to the moose

**ellipse** noun (pl **ellipses**) an oval shape

**elliptic** or **elliptical** adj **1** oval **2** having part of the words or meaning left out

**elm** noun a tree with a rough bark and leaves with saw-like edges

**elocution** noun **1** the art of what is thought to be correct speech **2** style of speaking

**elongate** verb to stretch out lengthwise, make longer □ **elongation** noun

**elope** verb to run away from home to get married □ **elopement** noun

**eloquent** adj **1** good at expressing thoughts in words **2** persuasive □ **eloquence** noun

**else** adv otherwise: come inside or else you will catch cold □ adj other than the person or thing mentioned: someone else has taken her place □ **elsewhere** adv in or to another place

**elucidate** verb to make (something) easy to understand

**elude** verb **1** to escape by a trick **2** to be too difficult to remember or understand
   ◈ Do not confuse with: **allude**

**elusive** adj hard to catch
   ◈ Do not confuse with: **allusive** and **illusive**. Elusive comes from the verb elude.

**elves** see elf

**elvish** see elfin

**em-** see in-

**emaciated** adj very thin, like a

skeleton

**E-mail** *noun* electronic mail

**emanate** *verb* to flow, come out from □ **emanation** *noun*

**emancipate** *verb* to set free, *eg* from slavery or repressive social conditions □ **emancipation** *noun*

**embalm** *verb* to preserve (a dead body) from decay by treating it with spices or drugs

**embankment** *noun* a bank of earth or stone to keep back water, or carry a railway over low-lying places

**embargo** *noun* (*pl* **embargoes**) an official order forbidding something, *esp* trade with another country

**embark** *verb* 1 to go on board ship 2 (with **on**) to start (a new career *etc*) □ **embarkation** *noun* (meaning 1)

**embarrass** *verb* to make to feel uncomfortable and self-conscious □ **embarrassing** *adj* □ **embarrassed** *adj* □ **embarrassment** *noun* 1 the state of being embarrassed 2 something which makes you embarrassed

▣ disconcert, mortify, discompose, humiliate

**embassy** *noun* (*pl* **embassies**) the offices and staff of an ambassador in a foreign country

**embellish** *verb* 1 to decorate 2 to add details to (a story *etc*) □ **embellishment** *noun*

**ember** *noun* a piece of wood or coal glowing in a fire

**embezzle** *verb* to use for yourself money entrusted to you □ **embezzlement** *noun*

**emblazon** *verb* 1 to decorate, adorn 2 to show in bright colours or conspicuously

**emblem** *noun* 1 an image which represents something: *the dove is the emblem of peace* 2 a badge

**embody** *verb* 1 to include 2 to express, give form to: *embodying the spirit of the age* □ **embodiment** *noun* a person or thing that perfectly symbolizes some idea or quality

**embody** ⟷ embodi*es*, embodi*ing*, embodi*ed*

**emboss** *verb* to make a pattern in leather, metal *etc*, which stands out from a flat surface □ **embossed** *adj*

**embrace** *verb* 1 to throw your arms round in affection 2 to include 3 to accept, adopt eagerly □ *noun* an affectionate hug

**embrocation** *noun* an ointment for rubbing on the body, *eg* to relieve stiffness

**embroider** *verb* 1 to decorate with designs in needlework 2 to add false details to (a story) □ **embroidery** *noun* 1 the art or practice of sewing designs on to cloth 2 the designs sewn on to cloth

**embroil** *verb* 1 to get (someone) into a quarrel, or into a difficult situation 2 to throw into confusion

**embryo** *noun* (*pl* **embryos**) 1 the young of an animal or plant in its earliest stage 2 the beginning of anything □ **embryonic** *adj*

**emend** *verb* a rather formal word meaning 'to remove faults or errors from' □ **emendation** *noun*

✎ Do not confuse with: **amend**. Emending consists simply of deleting errors. Amending involves making changes or improvements.

**emerald** *noun* a bright green precious stone

**emerge** *verb* 1 to come out 2 to become known or clear □ **emergence** *noun* □ **emergent** *adj* 1 arising 2 newly formed or newly independent: *emergent nation*

**emergency** *noun* (*pl* **emergencies**) an unexpected event requiring very quick action □ **emergency exit** a way out of a building for use in an emergency

**emery** *noun* a very hard mineral, used for smoothing and polishing

**emetic** *adj* causing vomiting □ *noun* an emetic medicine

**emigrant** *noun* someone who emigrates

**emigrate** *verb* to leave your country to settle in another □ **emigration** *noun*

ⓘ From Latin *e* meaning 'from', and *migrare* meaning 'to remove'

❧ Do not confuse with: **immigrate**. You are **Emigrating** when you leave your home country (the E comes from the Latin meaning 'from'). You **IMmigrate** to the country where you plan to start living (the IM comes from the Latin meaning 'into').

**émigré** (*say* ei-mee-grei) *noun* someone who is forced to emigrate for political reasons

**eminence** *noun* **1** distinction, fame **2** a title of honour **3** a hill □ **eminent** *adj* famous, notable □ **eminently** *adv* very, obviously: *eminently suitable*

❧ Do not confuse with: **imminent**

**emit** *verb* to send or give out (light, sound *etc*) □ **emission** *noun*

**emit** ⇢ emits, emit**t**ing, emit**t**ed

**emolument** *noun*, *formal* wages, salary

**emotion** *noun* a feeling that disturbs or excites the mind, *eg* fear, love, hatred □ **emotional** *adj* **1** moving the feelings of a person: having feelings easily excited □ **emotionally** *adv* □ **emotive** *adj* causing emotion rather than thought

**empathy** *noun* the ability to share another person's feelings *etc* □ **empathize** *verb*

**emperor** *noun* the ruler of an empire

**emphasis** *noun* **1** stress placed on a word or words in speaking **2** greater attention or importance □ **emphasize** *verb* □ **emphatic** *adj* spoken strongly: *an emphatic 'no'* □ **emphatically** *adv*

**empire** *noun* **1** a group of nations *etc* under the same ruling power **2** a large business organization including several companies

**empirical** *adj* based on experiment and experience, not on theory alone □ **empiricism** *noun*

**employ** *verb* **1** to give work to **2** to use **3** to occupy the time of □ *noun* employment □ **employee** *noun* someone who works for an employer □ **employer** *noun* someone who gives work to employees □ **employment** *noun* work, occupation

**emporium** *noun* (*pl* emporia or emporiums) a large shop; a market

**empower** *verb* **1** to authorize **2** to give self-confidence to

**empress** *noun* the female ruler of an empire

**empty** *adj* **1** containing nothing or no one **2** unlikely to result in anything: *empty threats* □ *verb* to make or become empty □ *noun* (*pl* empties) an empty bottle *etc* □ **emptiness** *noun* □ **empty-handed** *adj* bringing or gaining nothing □ **empty-headed** *adj* flighty, irresponsible

**empty** ⇢ empties, emptying, emptied

**emu** *noun* a type of Australian bird which cannot fly

**emulate** *verb* to try to do as well as, or better than □ **emulation** *noun*

**emulsion** *noun* a milky liquid, *esp* that made by mixing oil and water

**en-** *see* **in-**

**enable** *verb* to make it possible for, allow

**enact** *verb* **1** to act, perform **2** to make a law

**enamel** noun **1** a glassy coating fired on to metal **2** a paint with a glossy finish **3** the smooth white coating of the teeth □ verb to coat or paint with enamel □ **enamelling** noun

**enamel** verb ⋄ enamels, enamelling, enamelled

**enamoured** adj: **enamoured of** fond of

**encampment** noun a military camp

**encapsulate** verb to capture the essence of; describe briefly and accurately

**enchant** verb **1** to delight, please greatly **2** to put a spell or charm on □ **enchanter, enchantress** noun (meaning 2) □ **enchanting** adj delightful, charming □ **enchantment** noun **1** a feeling of delight and wonder **2** a spell or charm

**enclave** noun an area enclosed within foreign territory

**enclose** verb **1** to put inside an envelope with a letter etc **2** to put (eg a wall) around □ **enclosure** noun **1** the act of enclosing **2** something enclosed eg a small field with a high fence or wall round it

**encompass** verb to surround; to include

**encore** (say ong-kawr) noun **1** an extra performance of a song etc in reply to audience applause **2** a call for an encore

**encounter** verb **1** to meet by chance **2** to come up against (a difficulty, enemy etc) □ noun a meeting, a fight

**encourage** verb **1** to give hope or confidence to **2** to urge (to do) □ **encouragement** noun □ **encouraging** adj (meaning 1)

**encroach** verb to go beyond your rights or land and interfere with someone else's □ **encroachment** noun

**encumber** verb to burden, load down □ **encumbrance** noun

**encyclopedia** or **encyclopaedia** noun a reference book containing information on many subjects, or on a particular subject □ **encyclopedic** or **encyclopaedic** adj

**end** noun **1** the last point or part **2** death **3** the farthest point of the length of something: at the end of the road **4** a result aimed at **5** a small piece left over □ verb to bring or come to an end □ **ending** noun the last part □ **on end 1** standing on one end **2** in a series, without a stop: for days on end

**endanger** verb to put in danger or at risk

**endear** verb to make dear or more dear □ **endearing** adj appealing □ **endearment** noun an expression of love

**endeavour** verb to try hard (to) □ noun a determined attempt

**endemic** adj of a disease: found regularly in a certain area

**endorse** verb **1** to give your support to something said or written **2** to sign the back of a cheque to confirm receiving money for it **3** to indicate on a motor licence that the owner has broken a driving law □ **endorsement** noun

**endow** verb **1** to give money for the buying and upkeep of: he endowed a bed in the hospital **2** to give a talent, quality etc to: nature endowed her with a good brain □ **endowment** noun

**endure** verb to bear without giving way; last □ **endurable** adj □ **endurance** noun

**enema** (say en-im-a) noun the injection of fluid into the bowels

**enemy** noun (pl **enemies**) **1** someone hostile to another; a foe **2** someone armed to fight against another **3** someone who is against something: an enemy of socialism □ **enmity** noun (pl **enmities**) hostility

**energy** noun (pl **energies**) 1 strength to act, vigour 2 a form of power, eg electricity, heat etc □ **energetic** adj active, lively □ **energetically** adv

**enfold** verb to enclose, embrace

**enforce** verb to cause (a law etc) to be carried out

**enfranchise** verb 1 to set free 2 to give the right to vote to

**engage** verb 1 to begin to employ (workers etc) 2 to book in advance 3 to take or keep hold of (someone's attention etc) 4 to be busy with, be occupied (in) 5 of machine parts: to fit together 6 to begin fighting □ **engaged** adj 1 bound by a promise of marriage 2 busy with something 3 of a telephone: in use □ **engagement** noun 1 a promise of marriage 2 an appointment to meet 3 a fight: naval engagement □ **engaging** adj pleasant, charming

**engine** noun 1 a machine which converts heat or other energy into motion 2 the part of a train which pulls the coaches

**engineer** noun 1 someone who works with, or designs, engines or machines 2 someone who designs or makes bridges, roads etc □ verb to bring about by clever planning □ **engineering** noun the science of designing machines, roadmaking etc

**engrave** verb 1 to draw with a special tool on glass, metal etc 2 to make a deep impression on: engraved on his memory □ **engraving** noun a print made from a cut-out drawing in metal or wood

**engross** verb to take up the whole interest or attention

**engulf** verb to swallow up wholly

**enhance** verb to improve, make greater or better

**enigma** noun something or someone difficult to understand, a mystery □ **enigmatic** adj

**enjoy** verb 1 to take pleasure in 2 to experience, have (something beneficial): enjoying good health □ **enjoy yourself** to have a pleasant time □ **enjoyable** adj pleasant and satisfying □ **enjoyment** noun 1 pleasure and satisfaction 2 the experiencing or having (of something beneficial)

**enlarge** verb 1 to make larger 2 **enlarge on** to say much or more about something □ **enlargement** noun 1 an increase in size 2 a larger photograph made from a smaller one

**enlighten** verb 1 to give more knowledge or information to 2 to correct the false beliefs of □ **enlightenment** noun new understanding or awareness □ **The Enlightenment** a French philosophical movement of the 18th century

**enlist** verb 1 to join an army etc 2 to obtain the support and help of

**enliven** verb to make more active or cheerful

**en masse** (say on **mas**) adv all together, in a body

**enmity** see **enemy**

**enormity** noun 1 hugeness 2 extreme badness

**enormous** adj very large □ **enormously** adv 1 very greatly, a great deal 2 extremely: enormously confident

**enough** adj & pronoun (in) the number or amount wanted or needed: do you have enough money? □ adv as much as is wanted or necessary: she's been there often enough to know the way

**enquire** see **inquire**

**enquiring** see **inquiring**

**enquiry** see **inquiry**

**enrage** verb to make angry

**enrol** or **enroll** verb to enter (a name) in a register or list □ **enrolment**

*noun*

**enrol** ⋅⋅ **enrols, enrolling, enrolled**

**en route** (*say* on root) *adv* on the way

**ensconce** *verb*: **ensconce yourself** to settle yourself comfortably

**ensemble** *noun* **1** the parts of a thing taken together **2** an outfit of clothes **3** a group of musicians

**enshrine** *verb* to treat as sacred, cherish

**ensign** *noun* **1** the flag of a nation, regiment *etc* **2** *historical* a young officer who carried the flag

**enslave** *verb* to make a slave of

**ensue** *verb* **1** to follow, come after **2** to result (from)

**ensure** *verb* to make sure

⚫. Do not confuse with: **insure**

**entail** *verb* to bring as a result, involve: *the job entailed extra work*

**entangle** *verb* **1** to make tangled or complicated **2** to involve (in difficulties)

**entente** (*say* on-tont) *noun* a treaty

**enter** *verb* **1** to go or come in or into **2** to put (a name *etc*) on to a list **3** to take part (in) **4** to begin (on)

**enterprise** *noun* **1** an undertaking, *esp* if risky or difficult **2** boldness in trying new things **3** a business concern □ **enterprising** *adj* inventive, clever, original, go-ahead

**entertain** *verb* **1** to amuse **2** to receive as a guest **3** to give a party **4** to consider (*eg* a suggestion) **5** to hold in the mind: *entertain a belief* □ **entertainer** *noun* □ **entertaining** *adj* amusing □ **entertainment** *noun* **1** performances and activities that amuse and interest people **2** a performance or activity organized for the public

**enthral** *verb* to give great delight to

**enthral** ⋅⋅ **enthrals, enthralling, enthralled**

**enthuse** *verb* to be enthusiastic (about)

**enthusiasm** *noun* great interest and keenness □ **enthusiast** *noun* □ **enthusiastic** *adj* □ **enthusiastically** *adv*

**entice** *verb* to attract with promises, rewards *etc* □ **enticement** *noun* □ **enticing** *adj*

**entire** *adj* whole, complete □ **entirely** *adv* □ **entirety** *noun* whole and complete state

**entitle** *verb* **1** to give a name to (a book *etc*) **2** to give (someone) a right to

**entity** *noun* (*pl* **entities**) something which exists; a being

**entomology** *noun* the study of insects □ **entomologist** *noun*

**entrails** *noun pl* the inner parts of an animal's body, the bowels

**entrance**[1] (*say* en-trans) *noun* **1** a place for entering, *eg* a door **2** the act of coming in **3** the right to enter □ **entrant** *noun* someone who goes in for a race, competition *etc*

**entrance**[2] (*say* in-trahns) *verb* **1** to delight, charm **2** to bewitch □ **entrancing** *adj*

**entreat** *verb* to ask earnestly □ **entreaty** *noun* (*pl* **entreaties**) earnest request or plea

**entrenched** *adj* **1** firmly established **2** unmoving, inflexible

**entrepreneur** (*say* on-tre-pre-ner) *noun* someone who undertakes an enterprise, often with financial involvement □ **entrepreneurial** (*say* on-tre-pre-**ner**-ri-al or on-tre-pre-**nyoo**-ri-al) *adj* of an entrepreneur

**entrust** or **intrust** *verb* to place in someone else's care

**entry** *noun* (*pl* **entries**) **1** the act of entering **2** a place for entering, a doorway **3** a name or item in a record book

**E-number** *noun* an identification code for food additives, *eg* E102 for tartrazine

**enumerate** *verb* **1** to count **2** to

mention individually
□ **enumeration** *noun*

**enunciate** *verb* **1** to pronounce distinctly **2** to state formally
□ **enunciation** *noun*

**envelop** (*say* in-**vel**-*op*) *verb* **1** to cover by wrapping **2** to surround entirely: *enveloped in mist*

**envelope** (*say* **en**-vel-*ohp*) *noun* a wrapping or cover, *esp* for a letter

**enviable** *adj* worth envying, worth having

**envious** *adj* feeling envy □ **enviously** *adv*

**environment** *noun* surroundings, circumstances in which someone or an animal lives

**environs** (*say* in-**vai**-*ronz*) *noun pl* surrounding area, neighbourhood

**envisage** *verb* **1** to visualize, picture in the mind **2** to consider, contemplate

**envoy** (*say* **en**-voi) *noun* a messenger, *esp* one sent to deal with a foreign government

**envy** *noun* (*pl* **envies**) greedy desire for someone else's property, qualities *etc* □ *verb* to feel envy for

**envy** *verb* ⇨ envies, envying, envied

**enzyme** *noun* a substance produced in a living body which affects the speed of chemical changes

**eon** *another spelling of* **aeon**

**epaulet** or **epaulette** *noun* a shoulder ornament on a uniform

**ephemeral** *adj* very short-lived, fleeting □ **ephemerality** *noun*

**epi-** or **ep-** *prefix* upon or over: *epidermis*
  ⊚ From Greek *epi* meaning 'on' or 'over'

**epic** *noun* a long poem, story, film *etc* about heroic deeds □ *adj* **1** of an epic; heroic **2** large-scale, impressive

**epicene** *noun* common to both sexes

**epicentre** or *US* **epicenter** *noun* the

centre of an earthquake

**epicure** *noun* a gourmet □ **epicurean** *adj*

**epidemic** *noun* a widespread outbreak of a disease *etc*

**epidermis** *noun* the top covering of the skin □ **epidermal** or **epidermic** *adj*

**epidural** *noun* (short for **epidural anaesthetic**) the injection of anaesthetic into the spine to ease pain in the lower half of the body

**epiglottis** *noun* a piece of skin at the back of the tongue which closes the windpipe during swallowing

**epigram** *noun* a short, witty saying □ **epigrammatic** *adj*

**epilepsy** *noun* an illness causing attacks of unconsciousness and convulsions □ **epileptic** *adj* **1** suffering from epilepsy **2** of epilepsy: *an epileptic fit* □ *noun* someone suffering from epilepsy

**epilogue** or *US* **epilog** *noun* **1** the very end part of a book, programme *etc* **2** a speech at the end of a play

**epiphany** *noun* **1** a Christian festival celebrated on 6 January **2** a sudden revelation or insight

**episcopal** *adj* of or ruled by bishops □ **episcopalian** *adj* belonging to a church ruled by bishops

**episode** *noun* **1** one of several parts of a story *etc* **2** an interesting event □ **episodic** *adj* happening at irregular intervals

**epistle** *noun* a formal letter, *esp* one from an apostle of Christ in the Bible

**epitaph** *noun* words on a gravestone about a dead person

**epithet** *noun* a word used to describe someone; an adjective

**epitome** (*say* i-**pit**-om-i) *noun* **1** a perfect example or representative of something: *the epitome of good taste* **2** a summary of a book *etc*
  □ **epitomize** *verb* to be the epitome

of something

**epoch** (*say* eep-ok) *noun* an extended period of time, often marked by a series of important events □ **epochal** (*say* ep-ok-*al*) *adj* □ **epochmaking** *adj* marking an important point in history

**equable** *adj* **1** of calm temper **2** of climate: neither very hot nor very cold

**equal** *adj* **1** of the same size, value, quantity *etc* **2** evenly balanced **3 equal to** able, fit for: *not equal to the job* □ *noun* someone of the same rank, cleverness *etc* as another □ *verb* **1** to be or make equal to **2** to be the same as □ **equality** *noun* equal treatment for all the people in a group or society □ **equalize** *verb* to make equal □ **equalizer** *noun* a goal *etc* which draws the score in a game □ **equally** *adv*

equal *verb* ⇨ equals, equalling, equalled

**equanimity** *noun* evenness of temper, calmness

**equate** *verb* **1** to regard or treat as the same **2** to state as being equal □ **equation** *noun* a statement, *esp* in mathematics, that two things are equal

**equator** *noun* an imaginary line around the earth, halfway between the North and South Poles □ **equatorial** *adj*

**equerry** *noun* (*pl* **equerries**) *noun* a royal attendant

**equestrian** *adj* **1** of horse-riding **2** on horseback □ *noun* a horse-rider

**equi-** *prefix* equal: *equidistant/ equilateral*
ⓘ From Latin *aequus* meaning 'equal'

**equidistant** *adj* equally distant

**equilateral** *adj* of a triangle: with all sides equal (*compare with*: **isosceles**)

**equilibrium** *noun* **1** equal balance between weights, forces *etc* **2** a balanced state of mind or feelings

**equine** *adj* of or like a horse

**equinox** *noun* either of the times (about 21 March and 23 September) when the sun crosses the equator, making night and day equal in length □ **equinoctial** *adj*

**equip** *verb* to supply with everything needed for a task □ **equipment** *noun* a set of tools *etc* needed for a task; an outfit

equip ⇨ equips, equipping, equipped

**equipoise** *noun* balance

**equitable** *adj* fair, just

**equity** *noun* **1** fairness, just dealing **2** (**Equity**) the trade union for the British acting profession □ **negative equity** *see* **negative**

**equivalent** *adj* equal in value, power, meaning *etc* □ *noun* something that is the equal of another

**equivocal** *adj* having more than one meaning; ambiguous, uncertain □ **equivocally** *adv*

**equivocate** *verb* to use ambiguous words in order to mislead □ **equivocation** *noun*

**era** *noun* a period in history: *the Jacobean era/ the era of steam*

**eradicate** *verb* to get rid of completely □ **eradication** *noun*

**erase** *verb* **1** to rub out **2** to remove □ **eraser** *noun* □ **erasure** *noun* **1** a letter or word that has been rubbed out **2** the complete removal or destruction of something

**ere** *prep* & *conj* before: *ere long*

**erect** *verb* **1** to build **2** to set upright □ *adj* standing straight up □ **erection** *noun* **1** the act of erecting **2** something erected or erect

**ermine** (*say* er-min) *noun* **1** a stoat **2** its white fur

**erode** *verb* to wear away, destroy gradually □ **erosion** *noun*

**erotic** *adj* of or arousing sexual desire □ **erotica** *noun* *pl* erotic art or literature □ **eroticism** noun **1** use of erotic ideas and images **2** sexual excitement □ **eroticize** verb

**err** verb **1** to make a mistake **2** to sin

**errand** noun a short journey to carry a message, buy something etc

**errant** adj **1** doing wrong **2** wandering in search of adventure: knight errant

**erratic** adj **1** irregular, not following a fixed course **2** not steady or reliable in behaviour □ **erratically** adv

**erroneous** adj wrong, mistaken □ **erroneously** adv

**error** noun **1** a mistake **2** wrongdoing

**erudite** adj well-educated or well-read, learned □ **erudition** noun

**erupt** verb to break out or through □ **eruption** noun **1** an outburst from a volcano **2** a rash or spot on the skin

**escalate** verb to increase in amount, intensity etc □ **escalation** noun □ **escalator** noun a moving stairway

**escapade** noun an adventure

**escape** verb **1** to get away safe or free **2** of gas etc: to leak **3** to slip from memory: his name escapes me □ noun the act of escaping □ **escapism** noun the tendency to escape from reality by daydreaming etc □ **escapist** noun & adj

**escarpment** noun a steep side of a hill or rock

**escort** noun someone who accompanies others for protection, courtesy etc □ verb to act as escort to

**Eskimo** noun (pl **Eskimos**) Inuit

**especial** adj **1** special, extraordinary **2** particular □ **especially** adv

**espionage** noun spying, esp by one country to find out the secrets of another

**esplanade** noun a level roadway, esp along a seafront

**espouse** verb to adopt, embrace (a cause)

**espresso** noun strong coffee made by extraction under high pressure

**espy** (say es-**pai**) verb, old to watch, observe

**Esq** abbrev or **Esquire** noun a courtesy title written after a man's name: Robert Brown, Esq

**essay** noun (say es-ei) **1** a written composition **2** an attempt □ verb (say es-ei) to try

**essence** noun **1** the most important part or quality of something **2** a concentrated extract from a plant etc: vanilla essence

**essential** adj absolutely necessary □ noun an absolute requirement □ **essentially** adv **1** basically **2** necessarily

**establish** verb **1** to settle in position **2** to found, set up **3** to show to be true, prove (that) □ **established** adj **1** firmly set up **2** accepted, recognized **3** of a church: officially recognized as national □ **establishment** noun a place of business, residence etc □ **the Establishment** the people holding influential positions in society or a community

**estate** noun **1** a large piece of private land **2** someone's total possessions **3** land built on with houses, factories etc: housing estate/ industrial estate □ **estate agent** someone who sells and leases property for clients □ **estate car** a car with an inside luggage compartment and a rear door

**esteem** verb to think highly of; value □ noun high value or opinion □ **esteemed** adj respected, valued

**estimate** verb (say es-tim-eit) to judge roughly the size, amount or value of something □ noun (say es-tim-at) a rough judgement of size etc □ **estimation** noun opinion, judgement

**estranged** *adj* no longer friendly; separated

**estuary** *noun* (*pl* **estuaries**) the wide lower part of a river, up which the tide travels

**etc** or **&c** *abbrev* and other things of the same sort
ⓘ From Latin *et cetera*

**etch** *verb* to draw on metal or glass by eating out the lines with acid □ **etching** *noun* a picture printed from an etched metal plate

**eternal** *adj* **1** lasting for ever **2** seemingly endless □ **eternally** *adv* for ever □ **eternity** *noun* **1** time without end **2** the time or state after death

**ether** *noun* a colourless liquid used as an anaesthetic, or to dissolve fats

**ethereal** (*say* i-theer-ri-al) *adj* delicate, airy, spirit-like □ **ethereally** *adv* □ **ethereality** *noun*

**ethical** *adj* having to do with right behaviour, justice, duty; right, just, honourable □ **ethically** *adv* □ **ethics** *noun sing* **1** the study of right and wrong **2** (belief in) standards leading to right, ethical behaviour

**ethnic** *adj* **1** of race or culture **2** of the culture of a particular race or group □ **ethnically** *adv* □ **ethnicity** *noun* racial or cultural character □ **ethnic cleansing** the removal of the members of less powerful ethnic groups by the most powerful ethnic group living in an area

**etiquette** *noun* rules governing correct social behaviour

**etymology** *noun* (*pl* **etymologies**) **1** the study of the history of words **2** the history of a word □ **etymological** *adj*

**eucalyptus** *noun* (*pl* **eucalyptuses** or **eucalypti**) a large Australian evergreen tree whose leaves produce a pungent oil

**eucharist** *noun* **1** the Christian sacrament of the Lord's Supper **2** bread and wine *etc* taken as a sacrament

**eulogy** *noun* (*pl* **eulogies**) a speech, poem *etc* in praise of someone □ **eulogize** *verb*

**eunuch** (*say* yoo-nuk) *noun* a castrated man

**euphemism** (*say* yoof-e-mizm) *noun* a vague word or phrase used to refer to an unpleasant subject, *eg* 'passed on' for 'died' □ **euphemistic** *adj*

**euphonium** *noun* a brass musical instrument with a low tone

**euphoria** *noun* a feeling of great happiness, joy □ **euphoric** *adj*

**Euro-** *prefix* of Europe or the European community: *Euro-budget/ Eurocrat*

**Eurosceptic** *noun & adj*, *Brit* (someone) opposed to strengthening the powers of the European community

**euthanasia** *noun* the killing of someone painlessly, *esp* to end suffering

**evacuate** *verb* to (cause to) leave *esp* because of danger; make empty □ **evacuation** *noun* □ **evacuee** *noun* someone who has been evacuated (from danger)

**evade** *verb* to avoid or escape, *esp* by cleverness or trickery □ **evasion** *noun* **1** the act of evading **2** an attempt to avoid the point of an argument or accusation □ **evasive** *adj* with the purpose of evading; not straightforward: *an evasive answer*

**evaluate** *verb* to find or state the value of

**evangelist** *noun* **1** a person who spreads Christian teaching or supports and speaks for some cause **2** (**Evangelist**) an author of a Gospel, *esp* Matthew, Mark, Luke or John □ **evangelistic** *adj* □ **evangelical** *adj*

**evaporate** *verb* **1** to change into vapour **2** to vanish □ **evaporation** *noun*

**eve** noun **1** the evening or day before a festival: New Year's Eve **2** the time just before an event: the eve of the revolution

**even** adj **1** level, smooth **2** equal **3** of a number: able to be divided by 2 without a remainder (contrasted with: odd) **4** calm □ adv **1** used to emphasize another word: even harder than before/ even a child would understand **2** exactly, just □ verb to make even or smooth □ **evenly** adv **1** levelly, smoothly **2** equally **3** calmly □ **evenness** noun □ **even-handed** adv fair, unbiased □ **even out** to become equal □ **get even with** to get revenge on

**evening** noun the last part of the day and early part of the night

**evensong** noun an evening service in the Anglican church

**event** noun **1** an important happening **2** an item in a sports programme etc □ **eventful** adj exciting

**eventual** adj **1** final **2** happening as a result □ **eventuality** noun (pl eventualities) a possible happening □ **eventually** adv

**ever** adv **1** always, for ever **2** at any time, at all: I won't ever see her again **3** that has existed, on record: the best ever □ **evergreen** noun a tree with green leaves all the year round □ **everlasting** adj lasting for ever, eternal □ **evermore** adv, old forever

**every** adj each of several things without exception □ **every other** one out of every two, alternate □ **everybody** or **everyone** pronoun each person without exception □ **everyday** adj **1** daily **2** common, usual □ **everything** pronoun all things □ **everywhere** adv in every place

**evict** verb to force (someone) out of their house, esp by law □ **eviction** noun

**evidence** noun **1** a clear sign; proof

**2** information given in a law case

**evident** adj easily seen or understood □ **evidently** adv seemingly, obviously

**evil** adj wicked, very bad; malicious □ noun wickedness □ **evilly** adv

**evoke** verb to draw out, produce: evoking memories of their childhood □ **evocative** adj evoking memories or atmosphere

**evolution** noun **1** gradual development **2** the belief that the higher forms of life have gradually developed out of the lower □ **evolutionary** adj

**evolve** verb **1** to develop gradually **2** to work out (a plan etc)

**ewe** noun a female sheep

**ewer** noun a large jug with a wide spout

**ex** noun, informal a former husband, wife or lover

**ex-** prefix **1** no longer, former: ex-husband/ ex-president **2** outside, not in: ex-directory number
ⓘ From Latin ex meaning 'out of' or 'from'

**exacerbate** verb to make worse or more severe

🔥 Do not confuse with: **exasperate**

**exact** adj **1** accurate, precise **2** punctual **3** careful □ verb to compel to pay, give etc: exacting revenge □ **exacting** adj **1** asking too much **2** wearying, tiring □ **exactly** adv **1** precisely **2** as a reply to something someone has said: 'that's right' or 'I agree' □ **exactness** noun

**exaggerate** verb to make to seem larger or greater than reality □ **exaggeration** noun

**exalt** verb **1** to raise in rank **2** to praise **3** to make joyful □ **exaltation** noun

**exam** noun an examination

**examine** verb **1** to put questions to (pupils etc) to test knowledge **2** to

**example** 168 **exclamation**

question (a witness) **3** to look at closely, inquire into **4** to look over (someone's body) for signs of illness □ **examination** noun **1** a formal test of knowledge or skill: *driving examination* **2** a close inspection or inquiry **3** formal questioning □ **examiner** noun (verb, meaning 1)

**example** noun **1** something taken as a representative of its kind: *an example of early French glass* **2** a warning: *make an example of someone*

**exasperate** verb to make very angry □ **exasperation** noun
ⓘ From Latin *asperare* meaning 'to make rough'

◐ Do not confuse with: **exacerbate**

**excavate** verb **1** to dig, scoop out **2** to uncover by digging □ **excavation** noun □ **excavator** noun

**exceed** verb to go beyond, be greater than □ **exceedingly** adv very
ⓘ From Latin *ex-* meaning 'beyond', and *cedere* meaning 'to go'

**excel** verb **1** to do very well **2** to be better than

excel ⟶ excels, excelling, excelled

**excellence** noun the fact of being excellent, very high quality □ **excellent** adj

**Excellency** noun (pl **Excellencies**) a title of ambassadors *etc*

**except** prep leaving out, not counting □ conj with the exception (that) □ verb to leave out, not to count □ **except for** with the exception of □ **excepting** prep except

**exception** noun **1** something left out **2** something unlike the rest: *an exception to the rule* □ **take exception to** to object to, be offended by □ **exceptional** adj □ **exceptionally** adv

**excerpt** (say ek-sert) noun a part

chosen from a whole work: *excerpt from a play*

◐ Do not confuse with: **exert**

**excess** noun (say ik-ses) **1** a going beyond what is usual or proper **2** the amount by which one thing is greater than another **3** (**excesses**) very bad behaviour □ adj (say ek-ses) beyond the amount allowed □ **excessive** adj □ **excessively** adv ⓘ (for origin, *see* exceed)

◐ Do not confuse with: **access**

**exchange** verb to give (one thing) and get another in return □ noun **1** the act of exchanging **2** exchanging money of one country for that of another **3** the difference between the value of money in different places: *rate of exchange* **4** a central office or building: *telephone exchange* **5** a place where business shares are bought and sold

**exchequer** noun a government office concerned with a country's finances □ **Chancellor of the Exchequer** see chancellor

From the chequered cloth used to aid calculation in medieval revenue offices

**excise**[1] verb to cut off or out □ **excision** noun

**excise**[2] noun tax on goods *etc* made and sold within a country and on certain licences *etc*

**excite** verb **1** to rouse the feelings of **2** to move to action □ **excitable** adj easily excited □ **excited** adj unable to be calm because of extreme feelings of happiness, impatience or arousal □ **excitement** noun the state of being excited □ **exciting** adj creating feelings of excitement

■ stirred, thrilled, elated, restless, wild

**exclaim** verb to cry or shout out

**exclamation** noun a sudden shout □ **exclamation mark** a punctuation mark (!) used for emphasis, or to indicate surpise *etc*

**exclamatory** (*say* iks-**klam**-at-ri) *adj* exclaiming, emphatic

**exclude** *verb* **1** to shut out **2** to prevent from sharing **3** to leave out of consideration □ **exclusion** *noun*

**exclusive** *adj* **1** only open to certain people, select: *an exclusive club* **2** not obtainable elsewhere: *exclusive offer* □ **exclusive of** not including

**excommunicate** *verb* to expel from membership of a church □ **excommunication** *noun*

**excrement** *noun* the waste matter discharged by humans or animals

**excrescence** *noun* an unwelcome growth, eg a wart

**excrete** *verb* to discharge (waste matter) from the body □ **excreta** *noun pl* discharged waste products

**excruciating** *adj* **1** of pain *etc*: very severe **2** painfully bad: *an excruciating performance*

**exculpate** *verb* to absolve from a crime; vindicate □ **exculpation** *noun* □ **exculpatory** *adj*

**excursion** *noun* an outing for pleasure, eg a picnic

**excuse** *verb* (*say* ek-**skyooz**) **1** to forgive, pardon **2** to set free from a duty or task □ *noun* (*say* ek-**skyoos**) an explanation for having done something wrong □ **excusable** *adj* pardonable

**execrable** *adj* very bad

**execute** *verb* **1** to perform: *execute a dance step* **2** to carry out: *execute commands* **3** to put to death legally □ **execution** *noun* **1** a doing or performing **2** killing by order of the law □ **executioner** *noun* someone with the job of putting condemned prisoners to death

**executive** *adj* having power to act or carry out laws □ *noun* **1** the part of a government with such power **2** a business manager

**executor** *noun* someone who sees that the requests stated in a will are carried out

**exemplary** *adj* **1** worth following as an example: *exemplary conduct* **2** acting as a warning: *exemplary punishment*

**exemplify** *verb* **1** to be an example of **2** to demonstrate by example

**exemplify** ⟿ **exemplifies**, **exemplifying, exemplified**

**exempt** *verb* to grant freedom from an unwelcome task, payment *etc* □ *adj* free (from), not liable for payment *etc* □ **exemption** *noun*

**exercise** *noun* **1** a task for practice **2** a physical routine for training muscles *etc* □ *verb* **1** to give exercise to **2** to use: *exercise great care*

⚠️ Do not confuse with: **exorcize**

**exert** *verb* to bring into action, use: *exerting great influence* □ **exertion** *noun* or **exertions** *noun pl* effort(s); hard work □ **exert yourself** to make a great effort

⊕ From Latin *exsert-*, a form of *exserere* meaning 'to thrust out'

⚠️ Do not confuse with: **excerpt**

**exhale** *verb* to breathe out □ **exhalation** *noun*

**exhaust** *verb* **1** to tire out **2** to use up completely: *we've exhausted our supplies* **3** to say all that can be said about (a subject *etc*) □ *noun* a device for expelling waste fumes from fuel engines □ **exhausted** *adj* **1** tired out **2** emptied; used up □ **exhaustion** *noun* □ **exhaustive** *adj* extremely thorough: *exhaustive research* □ **exhaustively** *adv*

**exhibit** *verb* to show; put on public display □ *noun* something on display in a gallery *etc* □ **exhibitor** *noun*

**exhibition** *noun* a public show, an open display

**exhibitionism** *noun* a tendency to try to attract people's attention □ **exhibitionist** *noun*

**exhilarate** verb to make joyful or lively, refresh □ **exhilarating** adj □ **exhilaration** noun

**exhort** verb to urge (to do) □ **exhortation** noun

**exhume** verb to dig out (a buried body) □ **exhumation** noun

**exile** noun 1 someone who lives outside their own country, by choice or unwillingly 2 a period of living in a foreign country □ verb to drive (someone) away from their own country; banish

**exist** verb 1 to be, have life; live 2 to live in poor circumstances □ **existence** noun □ **existent** adj

**exit** noun 1 a way out 2 the act of going out: a hasty exit

**exodus** noun a going away of many people (esp those leaving a country for ever)

**exonerate** verb to free from blame □ **exoneration** noun

**exorbitant** adj going beyond what is usual or reasonable: exorbitant price □ **exorbitance** noun

**exorcize** verb 1 to drive out (an evil spirit) 2 to free from possession by an evil spirit □ **exorcism** noun □ **exorcist** noun

ⓘ From Greek ex meaning 'out', and horkos meaning 'an oath'

**✎.** Do not confuse with: **exercise**

**exotic** adj 1 coming from a foreign country 2 unusual, colourful

**expand** verb 1 to grow wider or bigger 2 to open out

**expanse** noun a wide stretch of land etc

**expansion** noun a growing, stretching or spreading □ **expansive** adj 1 spreading out 2 talkative, telling much □ **expansively** adv

**expat** noun, informal an expatriate

**expatriate** adj living outside your native country □ noun someone living abroad

**expect** verb 1 to think of as likely to happen or arrive soon: what did you expect her to say? 2 to think, assume: I expect he's too busy □ **expectancy** noun the feeling of excitement that you get when you know something good is about to happen □ **expectant** adj 1 hopeful, expecting 2 waiting to become: expectant mother □ **expectation** noun a firm belief or hope that something will happen □ **expecting** adj, informal pregnant

**expedient** adj done for speed or convenience rather than fairness or truth □ noun something done to get round a difficulty □ **expedience** or **expediency** noun speed or convenience in a particular situation, rather than fairness or truth

**expedite** verb to hasten, hurry on

**expedition** noun 1 a journey with a purpose, often for exploration 2 people making such a journey □ **expeditionary** adj

**expeditious** adj swift, speedy □ **expeditiously** adv

**expel** verb 1 to drive or force out 2 to send away in disgrace, eg from a school

**expel** ⟿ expel**s**, expel**ling**, expel**led**

**expend** verb to spend, use up □ **expenditure** noun an amount spent or used up, esp money

**expense** noun 1 cost 2 a cause of spending: the house was a continual expense 3 (**expenses**) money spent in carrying out a job etc □ **expensive** adj costing a lot of money □ **expensively** adv

**experience** noun 1 an event in which you are involved: a horrific experience 2 knowledge gained from events, practice etc □ verb to go through, undergo □ **experienced** adj skilled, knowledgeable

**experiment** noun a trial, a test (of an idea, machine etc) □ verb to carry out experiments □ **experimental** adj of something new: being done for the first time, to see how successful it will be □ **experimentally** adv

**expert** adj highly skilful or knowledgeable (in a particular subject) □ noun someone who is highly skilled or knowledgeable □ **expertise** (say eks-per-**teez**) noun skill

■ (adj) adroit

**expiate** (say **ek**-spi-eit) verb to make up for (a crime etc) □ **expiation** noun

**expire** verb 1 to die 2 to come to an end, become invalid: your visa has expired □ **expiry** noun

**explain** verb 1 to make clear 2 to give reasons for: please explain your behaviour

■ (meaning 2) justify

**explanation** noun a statement which makes clear something difficult or puzzling; a reason (eg for your behaviour) □ **explanatory** (say ek-**splan**-at-ri) adj intended to make clear

**expletive** noun an exclamation, esp a swear word

**explicable** adj able to be explained

**explicit** adj plainly stated or shown; outspoken, frank □ **explicitly** adv

**explode** verb 1 to blow up like a bomb with loud noise 2 to prove to be wrong or unfounded: that explodes your theory

**exploit** noun (say **ek**-sploit) a daring deed; a feat □ verb (say ik-**sploit**) 1 to make use of selfishly 2 to make good use of (resources etc) □ **exploitation** noun

**explore** verb 1 to make a journey of discovery 2 to think about very carefully, research □ **exploration** noun 1 travel for the sake of discovery 2 the act of searching or searching for something thoroughly □ **exploratory** (say ik-**splo**-rat-ri) adj □ **explorer** noun (meaning 1)

**explosion** noun a sudden violent burst or blow-up

**explosive** adj 1 liable to explode 2 hot-tempered □ noun something that will explode, eg gunpowder

**exponent** noun someone who shows skill in a particular art or craft: an exponent of karate □ **exponential** adj

**export** verb (say ek-**spawt**) to sell goods etc in a foreign country □ noun (say **ek**-spawt) 1 an act of exporting 2 something exported □ **exportation** noun

**expostulate** (say ek-**spos**-chuwl-eit) verb to protest □ **expostulation** noun

**expose** verb 1 to place in full view 2 to show up (a hidden crime etc) 3 to lay open to the sun or wind 4 to allow light to reach and act on (a film) □ **exposure** noun

**expound** verb to explain fully

**express** verb 1 to show by action 2 to put into words 3 to press or squeeze out □ adj 1 clearly stated: express instructions 2 sent in haste: express messenger □ noun a fast train, bus etc □ **expression** noun 1 the look on someone's face 2 showing meaning or emotion through language, art etc 3 a show of emotion in an artistic performance etc 4 a word or phrase: idiomatic expression 5 pressing or squeezing out □ **expressive** adj expressing meaning or feeling clearly

**expulsion** (from expel) noun 1 the act of driving or forcing a person or thing out 2 the sending away of someone in disgrace, eg from a school

**expunge** verb to rub out, remove

**exquisite** (say ek-**skwiz**-it or ik-**skwiz**-it) adj 1 extremely beautiful 2 excellent 3 very great, utter: exquisite pleasure

**extemporize** (say ik-**stem**-po-raiz)

*verb* to make up on the spot, improvise

**extend** *verb* **1** to stretch, make longer **2** to hold out **3** to last, carry over: *my holiday extends into next week* □ **extension** *noun* **1** a part added to a building **2** an additional amount of time on a schedule, holiday *etc* **3** a telephone connected with a main one □ **extensive** *adj* **1** wide; covering a large space **2** happening in many places **3** wide-ranging, sweeping: *extensive changes* □ **extensively** *adv*

**extent** *noun* **1** the space something covers **2** degree: *to a great extent*

**extenuate** *verb* **1** to lessen **2** to make to seem less bad: *extenuating circumstances* □ **extenuation** *noun*

**exterior** *adj* on the outside; outer: *exterior wall* □ *noun* the outside of a building *etc*

**exterminate** *verb* to kill off completely (a race, a type of animal *etc*), wipe out □ **extermination** *noun*

**external** *adj* **1** outside; on the outside **2** not central: *external considerations*

**extinct** *adj* **1** of an old volcano: no longer erupting **2** no longer found alive: *the dodo is now extinct* □ **extinction** *noun*

■ (meaning 1) active

**extinguish** *verb* **1** to put out (fire *etc*) **2** to put an end to □ **extinguisher** *noun* a spray containing chemicals for putting out fires

**extol** *verb* to praise greatly

**extol** ⊷ extols, extol*ling*, extol*led*

**extort** *verb* to take by force or threats □ **extortion** *noun* □ **extortionate** *adj* of a price: much too high

**extra** *adj* more than is usual or necessary; additional □ *adv* unusually; more than is average: *extra large* □ *noun* **1** something extra **2** someone employed to be one of a crowd in a film

**extra-** *prefix* outside, beyond
⊕ From Latin *extra* meaning 'outside'

**extract** *verb* (*say* ek-**strakt**) **1** to draw or pull out, *esp* by force: *extract a tooth* **2** to remove selected parts of a book *etc* **3** to draw out by pressure or chemical action □ *noun* (*say* ek-strakt) **1** an excerpt from a book *etc* **2** a substance obtained by extraction: *vanilla extract* □ **extraction** *noun* **1** the act of extracting **2** someone's descent or lineage: *of Irish extraction*

**extracurricular** *adj* done outside school or college hours

**extradite** *verb* to hand over (someone wanted for trial) to the police of another country □ **extradition** *noun*

**extraneous** *adj* having nothing to do with the subject: *extraneous information*

**extraordinary** *adj* **1** not usual, exceptional **2** very surprising □ **extraordinarily** *adv*

**extrapolate** *verb* to take known facts and use them to infer or predict things which are beyond what is known

**Extrapolate** was created by replacing the 'inter-' beginning of the word 'interpolate' (= to fill in additional details between known facts) with the prefix 'extra-'.

◐. Do not confuse with: **extricate**

**extrasensory** *adj* beyond the range of the ordinary senses: *extrasensory perception*

**extraterrestrial** *adj* from outside the earth □ *noun* a being from another planet

**extravagant** *adj* **1** spending too freely; wasteful **2** too great, overblown: *extravagant praise* □ **extravagantly** *adv* □ **extravagance** *noun*

**extravaganza** *noun* an extravagant

creation or production

**extravert** or **extrovert** noun an outgoing, sociable person

**extreme** adj **1** far from the centre **2** far from the ordinary or usual **3** very great: *extreme sadness* □ noun an extreme point □ **extremely** adv very, exceptionally □ **extremist** noun someone who carries ideas foolishly far □ **extremism** noun □ **extremity** (say ek-**strem**-it-i) noun (pl **extremities**) **1** a part or place furthest from the centre **2** great distress or pain **3** (**extremities**) the hands and feet

**extricate** verb to free from (difficulties etc)
  ⊕ From Latin *extricare* meaning 'to disentangle'
  ◥ Do not confuse with: **extrapolate**

**extrovert** another spelling of **extravert**

**extrude** verb to protrude, stick out

**exuberant** adj in very high spirits □ **exuberantly** adv □ **exuberance** noun

**exude** verb to give off in large amounts: *exuding sweat* / *exuded happiness*

**exult** verb to be very glad, rejoice greatly □ **exultant** adj □ **exultation** noun

**eye** noun **1** the part of the body with which you see **2** the ability to notice: *an eye for detail* **3** sight **4** something the shape of an eye, eg the hole in a needle □ verb to look at with interest □ **eyeball** noun the round part of the eye; the eye itself (the part between the eyelids) □ **eyebrow** noun the hairy ridge above the eye □ **eyeglass** noun a lens to correct faulty eyesight □ **eyelash** noun one of the hairs on the edge of the eyelid □ **eyelet** noun a small hole for a shoelace etc □ **eyelid** noun the skin covering of the eye □ **eye-opener** noun that which shows up something unexpected □ **eyesore** noun anything that is ugly (esp a building) □ **eye-wash** noun a lotion for the eye □ **eyewitness** noun someone who sees a thing done (eg a crime committed)

**eye** verb ⇔ eyes, eyeing, eyed

---

# Ff

**°F** abbrev degree(s) Fahrenheit

**FA** abbrev, Brit Football Association

**fable** noun a story about animals etc, including a lesson or moral

**fabric** noun **1** cloth **2** framework; the external parts of a building etc

**fabricate** verb to make up (lies) □ **fabrication** noun

**fabulous** adj **1** informal very good, excellent **2** imaginary, mythological □ **fabulously** adv extremely, unbelievably: *fabulously rich* □ **fabulousness** noun

**façade** (say fa-**sahd**) noun **1** the front of a building **2** a deceptive appearance or act; a mask

**face** noun **1** the front part of the head **2** the front of anything **3** appearance □ verb **1** to turn or stand in the direction of **2** to stand opposite to **3** to put an additional surface on □ **face up to** to meet or accept boldly: *facing up to responsibilities*

**face-lift** noun **1** a surgical operation to smooth and firm the tissues of the face **2** a renovating process, esp one applied to the outside of a building

**face pack** a cosmetic paste applied to the face and left to dry before being peeled or washed off

**facepowder** noun cosmetic powder

for the face

**facet** noun **1** a side of a many-sided object, eg a cut gem **2** an aspect; a characteristic

**facetious** (say fa-see-shus) adj not meant seriously; joking □ **facetiously** adv

**facial** adj of the face

**facile** (say fas-ail) adj **1** not deep or thorough; superficial, glib **2** fluent □ **facilely** adv

**facilitate** verb to make easy

**facility** noun **1** ease **2** skill, ability **3** (facilities) buildings, equipment etc provided for a purpose: sports facilities

**facsimile** noun an exact copy

**fact** noun **1** something known or held to be true **2** reality **3** law a deed □ **in fact** actually, really
⊙ From Latin factum meaning 'something done or accomplished'

⊠ **in fact** actually, really, indeed

**faction** noun a group that is part of a larger group: rival factions

**factor** noun **1** something affecting the course of events **2** someone who does business for another **3** a number which exactly divides into another (eg 3 is a factor of 6)

**factory** noun (pl **factories**) a workshop producing goods in large quantities

**factotum** noun someone employed to do all kinds of work

**factual** adj consisting of facts; real, not fictional: factual account

**faculty** noun (pl **faculties**) **1** power of the mind, eg reason **2** a natural power of the body, eg hearing **3** ability, aptitude **4** a department of study in a university: Faculty of Arts

**fad** noun **1** an odd like or dislike **2** a temporary fashion □ **faddy** adj having odd likes and dislikes

**fade** verb **1** to (make to) lose colour

or strength **2** to disappear gradually, eg from sight or hearing

**faeces** (say fees-eez) noun pl solid excrement

**faff** verb, informal to dither, fumble: don't faff about

**fag** noun **1** tiring work **2** slang a cigarette **3** informal a young schoolboy forced to do jobs for an older one

**fag end** informal **1** a cigarette butt **2** the very end, the tail end

**fagged out** informal exhausted, tired out

**faggot** or US **fagot** noun **1** a bundle of sticks **2** a meatball

**Fahrenheit** noun a temperature scale on which water freezes at 32° and boils at 212° □ adj measured on this scale: 70° Fahrenheit

**fail** verb **1** to (declare to) be unsuccessful **2** to break down, stop **3** to lose strength **4** to be lacking or insufficient **5** to disappoint □ **failing** noun a fault; a weakness □ **fail-safe** adj made to correct automatically, or be safe, if a fault occurs □ **failure** noun **1** the act of failing **2** someone or something which fails □ **without fail** certainly, for sure

**faint** adj **1** lacking in strength, brightness etc **2** about to lose consciousness: feel faint □ verb **1** to become faint **2** to fall down unconscious □ noun a loss of consciousness □ **faintly** adv dimly, not clearly □ **faintness** noun **1** lack of strength, brightness etc **2** a feeling of weakness, as if you were about to lose consciousness

✦ Do not confuse with: **feint**

**fair**[1] adj **1** of a light colour: fair hair **2** of weather: clear and dry **3** unbiased, just: fair assessment **4** good enough but not excellent **5** beautiful □ **fairly** adv **1** in a just and reasonable way **2** rather, reasonably **3** only moderately, to a limited extent **4** absolutely: *she fairly flung herself at me* □ **fairness** *noun* the quality of being reasonable or just in your treatment of people □ **fair-haired** *adj* having light-coloured hair; blond □ **fair-weather friend** someone who is a friend only when things are going well

■ (meaning 3) just, equitable, dispassionate, impartial, disinterested; (meaning 4) average, moderate, adequate, mediocre

**fair²** *noun* **1** a large market held at fixed times **2** an exhibition of goods from different producers *etc*: *craft fair* **3** a travelling collection of merry-go-rounds, stalls *etc* ⓞ From Late Latin *feria* meaning 'market'

👄 Do not confuse with: **fare**

**fairway** *noun* **1** the mown part on a golf course, between the tee and the green **2** the deep-water part of a river

**fairy** *noun* (*pl* **fairies**) a small imaginary creature, human in shape, with magical powers □ **fairy light** a small coloured light for decorating Christmas trees *etc* □ **fairy story** or **fairy tale 1** a traditional story of fairies, giants *etc* **2** *informal* a lie

**faith** *noun* **1** trust **2** belief in a religion or creed **3** loyalty to a promise: *kept faith with them* □ **faithful** *adj* **1** loyal; keeping your promises **2** true, accurate: *faithful account of events* **3** believing in a particular religion or creed □ **faithfully** *adv* (meanings 1 and 2) □ **faithless** *adj* **1** untrustworthy, inconstant **2** without faith or belief, *esp* in God or Christianity

**fake** *adj* not genuine, forged □ *noun* **1** someone who is not what they pretend to be **2** a forgery □ *verb* to make an imitation or forgery of

**fakir** *noun* an Islamic or Hindu holy man

**falcon** *noun* a kind of bird of prey □ **falconry** *noun* the training of falcons for hunting

**fall** *verb* **1** to drop down **2** to become less **3** of a fortress *etc*: to be captured **4** to die in battle **5** to happen, occur: *Christmas falls on a Monday this year* □ *noun* **1** a dropping down **2** something that falls: *a fall of snow* **3** lowering in value *etc* **4** *US* autumn **5** an accident involving falling **6** ruin, downfall, surrender **7** (**falls**) a waterfall □ **fall flat** to fail to have the intended effect □ **fall guy** a scapegoat □ **fall in love** to begin to be in love □ **fallout** *noun* radioactive dust resulting from the explosion of an atomic bomb *etc* □ **fall out with** to quarrel with □ **fall through** of a plan: to fail, come to nothing

**fall** *verb* ⬦ **falls**, **falling**, **fallen**, **fell**

**fallacy** *noun* (*pl* **fallacies**) a false belief; something believed to be true but really false □ **fallacious** *adj* wrong, because based on false information or on faulty reasoning

**fallible** *adj* liable to make a mistake or to be wrong □ **fallibility** *noun*

**fallopian tubes** two tubes along which egg cells pass from a woman's ovaries to her uterus

**fallow¹** *adj* of land: left unsown for a time after being ploughed

**fallow²** *adj* of a yellowish-brown colour □ **fallow deer** a type of yellowish-brown deer

**false** *adj* **1** untrue **2** not real, fake **3** not natural: *false teeth* □ **falsehood** *noun* a lie, an untruth □ **falseness** or **falsity** *noun*

■ (meaning 2) counterfeit, sham, bogus, assumed; (meaning 3) artificial, synthetic, imitation, mock

**falsetto** *noun* a singing voice forced higher than its natural range

**falsify** verb to make false, alter for a dishonest purpose: falsified his tax forms

**falsify** ⟿ falsifies, falsifying, falsified

**falter** verb to stumble or hesitate

**fame** noun the quality of being well-known, renown

**famed** adj famous

**familiar** adj 1 well-known 2 seen, known etc before 3 well-acquainted (with) 4 over-friendly, cheeky □ **familiarity** noun □ **familiarize** verb to make quite accustomed or acquainted (with)

**family** noun (pl **families**) 1 a couple and their children 2 the children alone 3 a group of people related to one another 4 a group of animals, languages, etc with common characteristics ⓘ From Latin familia meaning 'the slaves in a household'

**famine** noun a great shortage of food

**famished** adj very hungry

**famous** adj well-known, having fame □ **famously** adv, informal very well: get along famously

■ renowned, celebrated, illustrious, eminent, prominent, signal

**fan¹** noun 1 a device or appliance for making a rush of air 2 a small hand-held device for cooling the face □ verb 1 to cause a rush of air with a fan 2 to increase the strength of: fanning her anger □ **fanlight** noun a window above a door, usually semi-circular □ **fan out** to spread out in the shape of a fan

**fan** verb ⟿ fans, fanning, fanned

**fan²** noun an admirer, a devoted follower: a fan of traditional music

**fanatic** noun someone who is over-enthusiastic about something □ adj fanatical □ **fanatical** adj wildly or excessively enthusiastic □ **fanatically** adv

**fancy** noun (pl **fancies**) 1 a sudden liking or desire: he had a fancy for ice-cream 2 imagination 3 something imagined □ adj not plain, elaborate □ verb 1 to picture, imagine 2 to have a liking or a sudden wish for 3 to think without being sure □ **fancier** noun someone whose hobby is to keep prize animals, birds etc: a pigeon fancier □ **fanciful** adj 1 inclined to have fancies 2 imaginary, not real □ **fancy dress** an elaborate costume worn eg for a party, often representing a famous character

**fancy** verb ⟿ fancies, fancying, fancied

**fanfare** noun a loud flourish from a trumpet or bugle

**fang** noun 1 a long tooth of a wild animal 2 the poison-tooth of a snake

**fantastic** adj 1 very unusual, strange 2 informal very great 3 informal excellent

**fantasy** noun (pl **fantasies**) 1 an imaginary scene, story etc 2 an idea not based on reality

**fanzine** noun, informal 1 a magazine for a particular group of fans 2 a small-circulation magazine

**FAO** abbrev for the attention of

**far** adv 1 at or to a long way: far off 2 very much: far better □ adj 1 a long way off, distant: a far country 2 more distant: the far side □ **far-fetched** adj very unlikely: a far-fetched story □ **far-flung** adj extending over a great distance □ **far-sighted** adj foreseeing what is likely to happen and preparing for it □ See also **further**

**far** adj ⟿ farther, farthest

**farce** noun 1 a play with far-fetched characters and plot 2 a ridiculous situation □ **farcical** adj absurd, ridiculous

**fare** verb to get on (either well or badly): they fared well in the competition □ noun 1 the price of a

journey **2** a paying passenger in a taxi *etc* **3** food
ⓘ From Old English *faran*

🔸 Do not confuse with: **fair**

**farewell** *exclam & noun* goodbye

**farm** *noun* **1** an area of land for growing crops, breeding and feeding animals *etc* **2** a place where certain animals, fish *etc* are reared: *a salmon farm* □ *verb* to work on a farm □ **farmer** *noun* the owner or tenant of a farm □ **farmhouse** *noun* the house attached to a farm □ **farmstead** *noun* a farm and farmhouse □ **farmyard** *noun* the yard surrounded by farm buildings □ **farm out** to give (work) to others to do for payment

**farrow** *noun* a litter of baby pigs

**farther** and **farthest** *see* **far**

**farthing** *noun, historical* an old coin, worth $\frac{1}{4}$ of an old penny

**fascinate** *verb* **1** to charm, attract irresistibly **2** to hypnotize □ **fascinating** *adj* extremely interesting □ **fascination** *noun* an intense and deep interest

**fascism** *noun* a form of authoritarian government characterized by extreme nationalism and suppression of individual freedom □ **fascist** *noun* **1** a supporter of fascism **2** a right-wing extremist
ⓘ From Italian word, *fascio* meaning 'bundle' or 'group'

**fashion** *noun* **1** the style in which something is made, *esp* clothes **2** a way of behaving or dressing which is popular for a time **3** a manner, a way: *acting in a strange fashion* □ *verb* to shape, form □ **fashionable** *adj* up-to-date, agreeing with the latest style □ **after a fashion** to some extent, in a way □ **in fashion** fashionable

**fast** *adj* **1** quick-moving **2** of a clock: showing a time in advance of the correct time **3** of dyed colour: fixed, not likely to wash out □ *adv*

**1** quickly **2** firmly: *stand fast* **3** soundly, completely: *fast asleep* □ *verb* to go without food voluntarily, *eg* for religious reasons or as a protest □ *noun* abstinence from food □ **fast-track** *adj* of a career: liable for quick promotion □ **in the fast lane** having an exciting but stressful lifestyle

▪ (adj, meaning 1) quick, swift, accelerated, speedy

**fasten** *verb* to fix; make firm by tying, nailing *etc*

**fastidious** *adj* difficult to please, liking things properly done in every detail □ **fastidiously** *adv* □ **fastidiousness** *noun*

**fat** *noun* an oily substance made by the bodies of animals and by plants □ *adj* **1** having a lot of fat; plump **2** thick, wide □ **fatten** *verb* to make or become fat □ **fatty** *adj* containing a lot of fat

▪ (adj, meaning 1) plump, obese, tubby, stout, corpulent, portly, round, rotund, paunchy, pot-bellied, overweight, heavy, beefy, solid, chubby, podgy, fleshy, flabby, gross

**fatal** *adj* causing death or disaster □ **fatality** *noun* (*pl* **fatalities**) a death, *esp* caused by accident or disaster

**fate** *noun* **1** what the future holds; fortune, luck **2** end, death: *met his fate bravely* □ **fated** *adj* doomed □ **fateful** *adj* with important consequences; crucial, significant

**father** *noun* **1** a male parent **2** a priest **3** the creator or inventor of something: *Poe is the father of crime fiction* □ *verb* to be the father of □ **father-in-law** *noun* the father of someone's husband or wife □ **fatherland** *noun* someone's native country

**fathom** *noun* a measure of depth of water (6 feet, 1.83 metres) □ *verb* to understand, get to the bottom of

**fatigue** (*say* fa-teeg) *noun* **1** great tiredness **2** weakness or strain caused by use: *metal fatigue* □ *verb* to tire out

**fatuous** (*say* fat-yoo-*us*) *adj* very foolish □ **fatuously** *adv*

**fault** *noun* **1** a mistake **2** a flaw, something bad or wrong, *eg* with a machine **3** a long crack in the earth's surface where a section of the rock layer has slipped □ **faultless** *adj* perfect □ **faultlessly** *adv* □ **faulty** *adj* having a fault or faults

**fauna** *noun* the animals of a district or country as a whole

**faux pas** (*say* foh pah) an embarrassing mistake, a blunder

**favour** *noun* **1** a kind action **2** goodwill, approval **3** a gift, a token □ *verb* **1** to show preference for **2** to be an advantage to: *the darkness favoured our escape* □ **in favour of 1** in support of **2** for the benefit of

**favourable** *adj* **1** showing approval **2** advantageous, helpful (to) □ **favourably** *adv* in a positive or advantageous way □ **compare favourably with** to be better than, or at least as good as, the other thing or things mentioned

**favourite** *adj* best liked □ *noun* **1** a liked or best-loved person or thing **2** a competitor, horse, *etc* expected to win a race □ **favouritism** *noun* showing favour towards one person *etc* more than another

**fawn**[1] *noun* **1** a young deer **2** a light yellowish-brown colour □ *adj* of this colour

**fawn**[2] *verb* **1** to show affection as a dog does **2 fawn on** to flatter in a grovelling fashion

**fax** *noun* **1** a machine that scans a document electronically and transfers the information by a telephone line to a receiving machine that produces a corresponding copy **2** a document copied and sent in this way □ *verb* **1** to send by fax **2** to send a fax message to

**FBI** *abbrev, US* Federal Bureau of Investigation

**FE** *abbrev* Further Education

**fear** *noun* an unpleasant feeling caused by danger, evil *etc* □ **fearful** *adj* **1** timid, afraid **2** terrible **3** *informal* very bad: *a fearful headache* □ **fearfully** *adv* **1** timidly, showing fear **2** extremely, dreadfully □ **fearless** *adj* brave, daring □ **fearlessly** *adv*

**feasible** *adj* able to be done, likely □ **feasibility** *noun* □ **feasibly** *adv*

**feast** *noun* **1** a rich and plentiful meal **2** a festival day commemorating some event □ *verb* to eat or hold a feast

**feat** *noun* a deed requiring some effort

**feather** *noun* one of the growths which form the outer covering of a bird □ **feathery** *adj* **1** covered in feathers **2** soft **3** light

**feature** *noun* **1** an identifying mark, a characteristic **2** a special article in a newspaper *etc* **3** the main film in a cinema programme **4** a special attraction **5** (**features**) the various parts of someone's face, *eg* eyes, nose *etc* □ *verb* **1** to have as a feature **2** to take part (in) **3** to be prominent in

**February** *noun* the second month of the year

**fed** *past form* of **feed**

**federal** *adj* joined by treaty or agreement □ **federated** *adj* joined after an agreement is made □ **federation** *noun* a group of states *etc* joined together for a common purpose, a league

**fed up** *adj* tired, bored and disgusted

**fee** *noun* a price paid for work done, or for a special service

**feeble** *adj* weak □ **feebly** *adv*

**feed** *verb* **1** to give food to **2** to eat food **3** to supply with necessary materials □ *noun* food for animals: *cattle feed*

**feed** *verb* ⇔ feed**s**, feed**ing**, **fed**

**feel** *verb* **1** to explore by touch **2** to experience, be aware of: *he felt no pain* **3** to believe, consider **4** to think (yourself) to be: *I feel ill* **5** to be sorry (for): *we felt for her in her grief* □ *noun* an act of touching □ **feelgood** *adj* causing a feeling of comfort or security: *feelgood movie* □ **feel like** to want, have an inclination for: *do you feel like going out tonight?*

**feel** *verb* ⇔ feel**s**, feel**ing**, **felt**

**feeler** *noun* one of two thread-like parts on an insect's head for sensing danger *etc*

**feeling** *noun* **1** sense of touch **2** emotion: *spoken with great feeling* **3** affection **4** an impression, belief □ **feelings** *noun pl* what someone feels inside; emotions

**feet** *pl* of **foot**

**feign** (*say* fein) *verb* to pretend to feel or be: *feigning illness*

**feint** (*say* feint) *noun* **1** a pretence **2** a move to put an enemy off guard □ *adj* of paper: ruled with faint lines: *narrow feint* (= having lines which are close together) □ *verb* to make a feint (noun, meanings 1 and 2)

⚠ Do not confuse with: **faint**

**felicity** *noun* happiness □ **felicitous** *adj* **1** lucky **2** well-chosen, suiting well

**feline** *adj* **1** of or relating to cats **2** like a cat

**fell**[1] *noun* a barren hill

**fell**[2] *verb* to cut down (a tree)

**fell**[3] *adj*, *old* cruel, ruthless

**fell**[4] *past form* of **fall**

**fellow** *noun* **1** an equal **2** one of a pair **3** a member of an academic society, college *etc* **4** a man, a boy

**fellowship** *noun* **1** comradeship, friendship **2** an award to a university graduate

**felon** *noun* a committer of a serious crime

**felony** *noun* (*pl* **felonies**) a serious crime

**felt**[1] *noun* a type of rough cloth made of rolled and pressed wool

**felt**[2] *past form* of **feel**

**female** *adj* of the sex which produces children □ *noun* a human or animal of this sex

**feminine** *adj* **1** of or relating to women **2** characteristic of women □ **femininity** *noun* □ **feminism** *noun* a social and cultural movement aiming to win equal rights for women □ **feminist** *noun* a supporter of feminism □ *adj* relating to this movement: *feminist literature*

**femur** *noun* the thigh bone

**fen** *noun* low marshy land, often covered with water

**fence** *noun* **1** a railing, hedge *etc* for closing in animals or land **2** *slang* a receiver of stolen goods □ *verb* **1** to close in with a fence **2** to fight with swords **3** to give evasive answers when questioned □ **fencing** *noun* **1** material for fences **2** the sport of fighting with swords, using blunted weapons

**fend** *verb*: **fend for yourself** to look after and provide for yourself

**fender** *noun* **1** a low guard round a fireplace to keep in coal *etc* **2** a piece of matting over a ship's side acting as a buffer against the quay **3** *US* the bumper of a car

**ferment** *verb* (*say* fe-ment) **1** to change by fermentation **2** to stir up (trouble *etc*) □ *noun* (*say* ferm-ent) ⊚ From Latin *fermentum* meaning 'yeast'

⚠ Do not confuse with: **foment**

**fermentation** *noun* **1** a reaction caused by bringing certain substances together, *eg* by adding yeast to dough in bread-making **2** great excitement or agitation

**fern** *noun* a plant with no flowers and feather-like leaves

**ferocious** *adj* fierce, savage □ **ferociously** *adv* □ **ferocity** *noun*

**ferret** *noun* a small weasel-like animal used to chase rabbits out of their warrens □ *verb* to search busily and persistently

**ferry** *verb* to carry over water by boat, or overland by aeroplane □ *noun* (*pl* **ferries**) **1** a crossing place for boats **2** a boat which carries passengers and cars *etc* across a channel

‖ **ferry** *verb* ⇔ ferries, ferrying, ferried

**fertile** *adj* **1** able to produce children or young **2** full of ideas, creative, productive □ **fertility** *noun*

**fertilize** *verb* **1** to make (soil *etc*) fertile **2** to start the process of reproduction in an egg or plant by combining them with sperm or pollen □ **fertilization** *noun* □ **fertilizer** *noun* manure or chemicals used to make soil more fertile

**fervent** *adj* very eager; intense □ **fervently** *adv*

**fervour** *noun* ardour, zeal

**fest** *noun* or **-fest** *suffix* a gathering or festival around some subject: *news-fest/ trade fest*
 ⊕ From German *Fest* meaning 'a festival'

**fester** *verb* of a wound: to produce pus because of infection

**festival** *noun* **1** a celebration; a feast **2** a season of musical, theatrical or other performances

**festive** *adj* **1** of a feast **2** in a happy, celebrating mood □ **festivity** *noun* (*pl* **festivities**) a celebration, a feast

**festoon** *verb* to decorate with chains of ribbons, flowers *etc*

**fetch** *verb* **1** to go and get **2** to bring

in (a price): *fetched 100 at auction*

**fete** or **fête** *noun* a public event with stalls, competitions *etc* to raise money □ *verb* to entertain lavishly, make much of

**fetish** *noun* (*pl* **fetishes**) **1** a sacred object believed to carry supernatural power **2** an object of excessive fixation or (*esp* sexual) obsession □ **fetishist** *noun* □ **fetishistic** *adj*

**fetlock** *noun* the part of a horse's leg just above the foot

**fetters** *noun pl, formal* chains for imprisonment

**fettle** *noun*: **in fine fettle** in good health or condition

**feud** (*say* fyood) *noun* a private, drawn-out war between families, clans *etc*

**feudal** (*say* **fyood**-al) *adj, historical* of a social system under which tenants were bound to give certain services to the overlord in return for their tenancies □ **feudalism** *noun* □ **feudalist** *adj*

**fever** *noun* an above-normal body temperature and quickened pulse □ **fevered** *adj* **1** having a fever **2** very excited □ **feverish** *adj* **1** having a slight fever **2** excited **3** too eager, frantic: *feverish pace*

**few** *adj* not many: *only a few tickets left* □ **a good few** or **quite a few** several, a considerable number

‖ **few** ⇔ fewer, fewest

**fez** *noun* (*pl* **fezzes**) a brimless flowerpot-shaped hat, usually with a top tassel

**fiancé** (*say* fi-**on**-sei) *noun* the man a woman is engaged to marry

**fiancée** (*say* fi-**on**-sei) *noun* the woman a man is engaged to marry

**fiasco** *noun* (*pl* **fiascos**) a complete failure

‖ Based on an Italian phrase *far fiasco* 'make a bottle', meaning forget your lines on stage

**fib** verb to lie about something unimportant □ noun an unimportant lie

fib verb ⋄ fibs, fibbing, fibbed

**fibre** noun 1 a thread or string 2 the essence or material of something: *the fibre of her being* 3 roughage in foods □ **fibrous** adj thread-like, stringy □ **fibreglass** noun a lightweight material made of very fine threads of glass, used for building boats *etc* □ **fibre-optic** adj of a cable: made of glass or plastic filaments which transmit light signals

**fickle** adj changeable; not stable or loyal

**fiction** noun 1 stories about imaginary characters and events 2 a lie □ **fictional** adj imagined, created for a story

◈ Do not confuse: **fictional** and **fictitious**

◉ From Latin *fictio* meaning 'a forming'

**fictitious** adj 1 not real, imaginary 2 untrue

◉ From Latin *ficticius* meaning 'counterfeit'

**fiddle** noun, informal 1 a violin 2 a tricky or delicate operation 3 a cheat, a swindle □ verb 1 to play the violin 2 to play aimlessly (with) 3 to interfere, tamper (with) 4 informal to falsify (accounts *etc*) with the intention of cheating

**fiddly** adj needing delicate or careful handling

**fidelity** noun 1 faithfulness 2 truth, accuracy

**fidget** verb to move about restlessly

**field** noun 1 a piece of enclosed ground for pasture, crops, sports *etc* 2 an area of land containing a natural resource: *goldfield/coalfield* 3 a branch of interest or knowledge 4 those taking part in a race □ verb, cricket to catch the ball and return it □ **field-day** noun a day of unusual activity or success □ **fieldglasses** noun pl binoculars □ **field-gun** noun a light, mobile cannon □ **field-marshal** noun the highest ranking army officer

**fiend** noun 1 an evil spirit 2 a wicked person 3 an extreme enthusiast: *a crossword fiend* □ **fiendish** adj 1 evil or wicked 2 extremely bad 3 very complicated or clever

**fierce** adj 1 very angry-looking, hostile, likely to attack 2 intense, strong: *fierce competition* □ **fiercely** adv

**fiery** adj 1 like fire 2 quick-tempered, volatile

**fife** noun a small flute

**fifteen** noun the number 15 □ adj 15 in number □ **fifteenth** adj the last of a series of fifteen □ noun one of fifteen equal parts

**fifth** adj the last of a series of five □ noun one of five equal parts

**fifty** noun the number 50 □ adj 50 in number □ **fiftieth** adj the last of a series of fifty □ noun one of fifty equal parts

**fig** noun 1 a soft roundish fruit with thin, dark skin and red pulp containing many seeds 2 the tree which bears it

**fight** verb 1 to struggle with fists, weapons *etc* 2 to quarrel 3 to go to war with □ noun a struggle; a battle □ **fighter** noun 1 someone who fights 2 a fast military aircraft armed with guns

fight verb ⋄ fights, fighting, fought

**figment** noun an imaginary story or idea

**figurative** adj of a word: used not in its ordinary meaning but to show likenesses, *eg* 'she was a tiger' for 'she was as ferocious as a tiger'; metaphorical (*contrasted with*: **literal**) □ **figuratively** adv

**figure** noun 1 outward form or shape 2 a number 3 a geometrical shape 4 an unidentified person: *a* *shadowy figure approached* **5** a diagram or drawing on a page **6** a set of movements in skating *etc* □ *verb* to appear, take part: *he figures in the story* □ **figured** *adj* marked with a design: *figured silk* □ **figurehead** *noun* **1** a carved wooden figure fixed to the prow of a ship **2** a leader who has little real power □ **figure out** to work out, understand

**filament** *noun* a slender thread, *eg* of wire in a light bulb

**filch** *verb, informal* to steal

**file** *noun* **1** a loose-leaf book *etc* to hold papers **2** an amount of computer data held under a single name **3** a line of soldiers *etc* walking one behind another **4** a steel tool with a roughened surface for smoothing wood, metal *etc* □ *verb* **1** to put (papers *etc*) in a file **2** to rub with a file **3** to walk in a file

**filial** *adj* of or characteristic of a son or daughter

**filibuster** *noun* a long speech given in parliament to delay the passing of a law

**filigree** *noun* very fine gold or silver work in lace or metal

**fill** *verb* **1** to put (something) into until there is no room for more: *fill the bucket with water* **2** to become full: *her eyes filled with tears* **3** to satisfy, fulfil (a requirement *etc*) **4** to occupy: *fill a post* **5** to appoint someone to (a job *etc*): *have you filled the vacancy?* **6** to put something in a hole to stop it up □ *noun* as much as is needed to fill: *we ate our fill* □ **filler** *noun* **1** a funnel for pouring liquids through **2** a substance added to increase bulk **3** a material used to fill up holes in wood, plaster *etc* □ **filling** *noun* something used to fill a hole or gap □ *adj* of food: satisfying □ **filling-station** *noun* a garage which sells petrol □ **fill in 1** to fill (a hole) **2** to complete (a form *etc*) **3** to do

another person's job while they are absent: *I'm filling in for Anne* □ **fill up** to fill completely

**fillet** *noun* a piece of meat or fish with bones removed □ *verb* to remove the bones from

*fillet verb ↔ fillets, filleting, filleted*

**filly** *noun* (*pl* **fillies**) a young female horse

**film** *noun* **1** a thin skin or coating **2** a chemically-coated strip of celluloid on which photographs are taken **3** a narrative photographed on celluloid and shown in a cinema, on television *etc* □ *verb* **1** to photograph on celluloid **2** to develop a thin coating: *his eyes filmed over* □ **filmstar** *noun* a famous actor or actress in films

**Filofax** *noun, trademark* a personal organizer

**filter** *noun* **1** a strainer for removing solid material from liquids **2** a green arrow on a traffic light signalling one lane of traffic to move while the main stream is held up □ *verb* **1** to strain through a filter **2** to move or arrive gradually: *the news filtered through* **3** of cars *etc*: to join gradually a stream of traffic **4** of a lane of traffic: to move in the direction shown by a filter

*filter verb ↔ filters, filtering, filtered*

**filth** *noun* **1** dirt **2** obscene words or pictures □ **filthily** *adv* □ **filthiness** *noun* □ **filthy** *adj*

**fin** *noun* a flexible projecting part of a fish's body used for balance and swimming

**final** *adj* **1** last **2** allowing of no argument: *the judge's decision is final* □ *noun* the last contest in a competition: *World Cup final* □ **finality** *noun* the quality of being final and decisive □ **finalize** *verb* to put (*eg* plans) in a final or finished form □ **finally** *adv* in the end, at last, eventually, lastly

**finale** (*say* fi-**nah**-lei) *noun* the last

part of anything (*eg* a concert)

**finance** *noun* **1** money affairs **2** the study or management of these **3** (**finances**) the money someone has to spend □ *verb* to supply with sums of money □ **financial** *adj* (noun, meaning 1) □ **financially** *adv* (noun, meaning 1) □ **financier** *noun* someone who manages (public) money

**finch** *noun* (*pl* **finches**) a small bird

**find** *verb* **1** to come upon accidentally or after searching: *I found an earring in the street* **2** to discover **3** to judge to be: *she finds it hard to live on her pension* □ *noun* something found, *esp* something of interest or value □ **find out** to discover, detect

> **find** *verb* ⬦ finds, finding, found
> ⓞ From Old English *findan*
>
> ◼ (verb, meaning 1) retrieve, recover, trace; (verb, meaning 2) locate, unearth, expose, detect □ **find out** learn, ascertain

**fine**¹ *adj* **1** made up of very small pieces, drops *etc* **2** not coarse: *fine linen* **3** thin, delicate **4** slight: *a fine distinction* **5** beautiful, handsome **6** of good quality; pure **7** bright, not rainy **8** well, healthy □ **finery** *noun* splendid clothes *etc*

**fine**² *noun* money to be paid as a punishment □ *verb* to compel to pay (money) as punishment

**finesse** (*say* fi-**nes**) *noun* cleverness and subtlety in handling situations *etc*

**finger** *noun* one of the five branching parts of the hand □ *verb* to touch with the fingers □ **fingering** *noun* **1** the positioning of the fingers in playing a musical instrument **2** the showing of this by numbers □ **fingerprint** *noun* the mark made by the tip of a finger, used by the police as a means of identification

**finish** *verb* **1** to end or complete the making of **2** to stop: *when do you*

finish work today?□ *noun* **1** the end (*eg* of a race) **2** the last coating of paint, polish *etc* □ **finished** *adj* **1** ended, complete **2** of a person: ruined, not likely to achieve further success *etc*

**finite** *adj* having an end or limit

**fiord** or **fjord** *noun* a long narrow inlet between steep hills, *esp* in Norway

**fir** *noun* a kind of cone-bearing tree □ **fir-cone** *noun* one of the small, woody cones which grow on a fir tree and hold its seeds

**fire** *noun* **1** the heat and light given off by something burning **2** a mass of burning material, objects *etc* **3** a heating device: *electric fire* **4** eagerness, keenness □ *verb* **1** to set on fire **2** to make eager: *fired by his enthusiasm* **3** to make (a gun) explode, shoot □ **fire alarm** a device to sound a bell *etc* as a warning of fire □ **firearm** *noun* a gun *eg* a pistol □ **fire brigade** a company of firemen □ **fire-damp** *noun* a dangerous gas found in coal mines □ **fire engine** a vehicle carrying firefighters and their equipment □ **fire escape** a means of escape from a building in case of fire □ **firefly** *noun* a type of insect which glows in the dark □ **fire-guard** *noun* a framework of iron placed in front of a fireplace for safety □ **fireman, firewoman** *noun* someone whose job it is to put out fires □ **fireplace** *noun* a recess in a room below a chimney for a fire □ **firewood** *noun* wood for burning on a fire □ **fireworks** *noun pl* **1** squibs, rockets *etc* sent up at night for show **2** *informal* angry behaviour

> **fire** *verb* ⬦ fires, firing, fired

**firm**¹ *adj* **1** not easily moved or shaken **2** with mind made up □ *noun* a business company

**firmament** *noun, formal* the heavens, the sky

**first** *adj & adv* before all others in

place, time or rank □ *adj* before doing anything else □ **first-aid** *noun* treatment of a wounded or sick person before the doctor's arrival □ **first-born** *noun* the eldest child □ **first-class** *adj* of the highest standard, best kind *etc* □ **first-hand** *adj* direct □ **first name** a person's name that is not their surname □ **first-rate** *adj* first-class

**firth** *noun* a narrow arm of the sea, *esp* at a river mouth

**fiscal** *adj* **1** of the public revenue **2** of financial matters

**fish** *noun* (*pl* **fish** or **fishes**) a kind of animal that lives in water, and breathes through gills □ *verb* **1** to try to catch fish with rod, nets *etc* **2** to search (for): *fishing for a handkerchief in her bag* **3** to try to obtain: *fish for compliments* □ **fisherman** *noun* a man who fishes, *esp* for a living □ **fishmonger** *noun* someone who sells fish for eating □ **fishy** *adj* **1** like a fish **2** doubtful, arousing suspicion

**fission** *noun* splitting

**fissure** *noun* a crack

**fist** *noun* a tightly-shut hand □ **fisticuffs** *noun pl, old* a fight with the fists

**fit** *adj* **1** suited to a purpose; proper **2** in good training or health □ *noun* a sudden attack or spasm of laughter, illness *etc* □ *verb* **1** to be of the right size or shape **2** to be suitable □ **fitful** *adj* coming or doing in bursts or spasms □ **fitfully** *adv* □ **fitness** *noun* good physical health and strength □ **fitting** *adj* suitable □ *noun* something fixed or fitted in a room, house *etc*

**fit** *verb* ↪ fits, fitting, fitted

**five** *noun* the number 5 □ *adj* 5 in number □ **fives** *noun pl* a handball game played in a walled court

**fix** *verb* **1** to make firm; fasten **2** to mend, repair □ **fixed** settled; set in position □ **fixedly** *adv* steadily,

intently: *staring fixedly*

**fixture** *noun* **1** a piece of furniture *etc* fixed in position **2** an arranged sports match or race

**fizz** *verb* to make a hissing sound □ *noun* a hissing sound □ **fizzy** *adj* of a drink: forming bubbles on the surface

**fizzle** or **fizzle out** *verb* to fail, coming to nothing

**fjord** *another spelling of* **fiord**

**flabbergasted** *adj* very surprised

**flabby** *adj* not firm, soft, limp; weak, feeble □ **flabbily** *adv*

**flaccid** (*say* fla-sid) *adj* **1** hanging loosely **2** limp, not firm

**flag** *noun* **1** a banner, standard, or ensign **2** a flat paving-stone □ *verb* to become tired or weak

**flag** *verb* ↪ flags, flagging, flagged

**flagon** *noun* a large container for liquid

**flagrant** *adj* **1** conspicuous **2** openly wicked □ **flagrancy** *noun* □ **flagrantly** *adv*

**flail** *verb* to wave or swing in the air □ *noun, old* a tool for threshing corn

**flair** *noun* talent, skill: *a flair for languages*

**flak** *noun* **1** anti-aircraft fire **2** strong criticism

**flake** *noun* **1** a thin slice or chip of anything **2** a very small piece of snow *etc* □ *verb* to form into flakes □ **flaky** *adj* **1** forming flakes, crumbly: *flaky pastry* **2** *US informal* eccentric □ **flake off** to break off in flakes

**flamboyant** *adj* **1** splendidly coloured **2** too showy, gaudy

**flame** *noun* the bright leaping light of a fire □ *verb* **1** to burn brightly **2** *computing slang* to send abusive electronic mail (to) □ **flaming** *adj* **1** burning **2** red **3** violent: *a flaming temper*

**flamingo** *noun* (*pl* **flamingoes**) a type of long-legged bird of pink or bright-red colour

**flammable** *adj* easily set on fire

**flan** *noun* a flat, open tart

**flank** *noun* **1** the side of an animal's body, of an army *etc* **2** to go by the side of **2** to be situated at the side of

**flannel** *noun* **1** loosely woven woollen fabric **2** a small towel or face cloth

**flap** *noun* **1** anything broad and loose-hanging: *tent flap* **2** the sound of a wing *etc* moving through air **3** a panic: *getting into a flap* □ *verb* **1** to hang down loosely **2** to move with a flapping noise **3** to get into a panic

**flap** *verb* ⋄ flaps, flapping, flapped

**flapjack** *noun* **1** *Brit* a biscuit made with rolled oats, butter and sugar **2** *US* a pancake

**flare** *verb* to blaze up □ *noun* a bright light, *esp* one used at night as a signal, to show the position of a boat in distress *etc*

**flare** *verb* ⋄ flares, flaring, flared

**flash** *noun* (*pl* **flashes**) **1** a quick burst of light **2** a moment, an instant **3** a distinctive mark on a uniform □ *verb* **1** to shine out suddenly **2** to pass quickly □ **in a flash** very quickly or suddenly □ **flashlight** *noun* **1** a burst of light in which a photograph is taken **2** an electric torch □ **flashy** *adj* showy, gaudy

**flask** *noun* **1** a narrow-necked bottle **2** a small flat bottle **3** an insulated bottle or vacuum flask

**flat** *adj* **1** level: *a flat surface* **2** of a drink: no longer fizzy **3** leaving no doubt, downright: *a flat denial* **4** below the right musical pitch **5** of a tyre: punctured **6** dull, uninteresting □ *adv* stretched out: *lying flat on her back* □ *noun* **1** an apartment on one storey of a building **2** *music* a sign (♭) which lowers a note by a semitone **3** a punctured tyre □ **flatly** *adv* in a

definite or emphatic way □ **flatness** *noun* the quality of being flat □ **flat race** a race over level ground without hurdles □ **flat rate** a rate which is the same in all cases □ **flatten** *verb* to make or become flat □ **flat out** *adv* as fast as possible, with as much effort as possible

**flatter** *verb* to praise insincerely □ **flattery** *noun*

**flatulence** *noun* wind in the stomach □ **flatulent** *adj*

**flaunt** (*say* flawnt) *verb* to display in an obvious way: *flaunted his wealth*

> ♠ Do not confuse with: **flout**. Remember that the use of **flaunt** is perfectly illustrated in the well-known phrase 'if you've got it, **flaunt** it'. On the other hand, when you **flout** something, you treat it with contempt instead of showing it off, *eg* you might **flout** the rules or **flout** tradition.

**flavour** *noun* **1** taste: *lemon flavour* **2** quality or atmosphere: *an exotic flavour* □ *verb* to give a taste to □ **flavouring** *noun* an ingredient used to give a particular taste: *chocolate flavouring*

**flaw** *noun* a fault, an imperfection □ **flawless** *adj* with no faults or blemishes □ **flawlessly** *adv*

**flax** *noun* a plant whose fibres are woven into linen cloth □ **flaxen** *adj* **1** made of or looking like flax **2** of hair: fair

**flay** *verb* to strip the skin off

**flea** *noun* a small, wingless, blood-sucking insect with great jumping power

**fleck** *noun* a spot, a speck □ **flecked** *adj* marked with spots or patches

**fled** *past form of* **flee**

**fledgling** *noun* a young bird with fully-grown feathers

**flee** *verb* to run away from danger *etc*

**flee** ⋄ flees, fleeing, fled

**fleece** *noun* a sheep's coat of wool

□ *verb* **1** to clip wool from **2** *informal* to rob by cheating □ **fleecy** *adj* soft and fluffy like wool

**fleet** *noun* **1** a number of ships **2** a number of cars or taxis □ *adj* swift; nimble, quick in movement

**fleeting** *adj* passing quickly: *fleeting glimpse* □ **fleetingly** *adv* very briefly

**flesh** *noun* **1** the soft tissue which covers the bones of humans and animals **2** meat **3** the body **4** the soft eatable part of fruit □ **flesh and blood 1** relations, family **2** human, mortal □ **fleshy** *adj* fat, plump

**flew** *past form of* **fly**

**flex** *verb* to bend □ *noun* a length of covered wire attached to electrical devices

**flexible** *adj* **1** easily bent **2** willing to adapt to new or different conditions □ **flexibility** *noun*

**flexitime** *noun* a system in which an agreed number of hours' work is done at times chosen by the worker

**flick** *verb* **1** to strike lightly with a quick movement **2** to remove (dust *etc*) with a movement of this kind □ *noun* a quick, sharp movement: *a flick of the wrist* □ **flick-knife** *noun* a knife with a blade which springs out at the press of a button

**flicker¹** *verb* **1** to flutter **2** to burn unsteadily □ *noun*: *a flicker of hope*

**flicker²** *noun, US* a woodpecker

**flight** *noun* **1** the act of flying **2** a journey by plane **3** the act of fleeing or escaping **4** a flock (of birds) **5** a number (of steps)

**flighty** *adj* changeable, impulsive

**flimsy** *adj* **1** thin; easily torn or broken *etc* **2** weak: *a flimsy excuse*

**flinch** *verb* to move or shrink back in fear, pain *etc*

**fling** *verb* to throw □ *noun* **1** a throw **2** a casual attempt **3** a period of time devoted to pleasure **4** a brief romantic affair

**fling** *verb* ⇨ flings, flinging, flung

**flint** *noun* a kind of hard stone □ *adj* made of flint

**flip** *verb* **1** to toss lightly □ *noun* a light toss or stroke

**flip** *verb* ⇨ flips, flipping, flipped

**flippant** *adj* joking, not serious □ **flippancy** *noun* □ **flippantly** *adv*

**flipper** *noun* **1** a limb of a seal, walrus *etc* **2** a webbed rubber shoe worn by divers

**flirt** *verb* **1** to play at courtship without any serious intentions **2 flirt with** to take an interest in something without committing yourself seriously to it □ *noun* someone who flirts □ **flirt with danger** to take unnecessary risks □ **flirtation** *noun* □ **flirtatious** *adj* fond of flirting

**flit** *verb* **1** to move quickly and lightly from place to place **2** *Scottish* to move house

**flit** ⇨ flits, flitting, flitted

**float** *verb* **1** to keep on the surface of a liquid without sinking **2** to set going: *float a fund* □ *noun* **1** a cork on a fishing line **2** a raft **3** a van delivering milk *etc* **4** a large lorry for transporting cattle **5** a platform on wheels, used in processions **6** a sum of money set aside for giving change

**flock¹** *noun* **1** a number of animals or birds together **2** a large number of people **3** the congregation of a church □ *verb* **1 flock to** to go to in large numbers or in a large crowd **2 flock together** to gather in a crowd

**flock²** *noun* **1** a shred or tuft of wool **2** wool or cotton waste

**floe** (*say* floh) *noun* a sheet of floating ice

**flog** *verb* **1** to beat, lash **2** *slang* to sell □ **flogging** *noun* (meaning 1)

**flog** ⇨ flogs, flogging, flogged

**flood** *noun* **1** a great flow, *esp* of water **2** the rise or flow of the tide

**3** a great quantity: *a flood of letters* ◻ *verb* **1** to (cause to) overflow **2** to cover or fill with water

**floodlight** *verb* to illuminate with floodlighting ◻ *noun* a light used to floodlight ◻ **floodlighting** *noun* strong artificial lighting to illuminate an exterior or stage

**floodlight** ⬦ floodlight*s*, floodlight*ing*, floodl*it*

**floor** *noun* **1** the base level of a room on which people walk **2** a storey of a building: *a third-floor flat* ◻ *verb* **1** to make a floor **2** *informal* to knock flat **3** *informal* to puzzle: *floored by the question*

**flop** *verb* **1** to sway or swing about loosely **2** to fall or sit down suddenly and heavily **3** to move about clumsily **4** to fail badly ◻ *noun* **1** an act of flopping **2** a complete failure ◻ **floppy** *adj* flopping, soft and flexible ◻ **floppy disk** a flexible computer disk, often in a harder case, used to store data

**flop** ⬦ flop*s*, flop*ping*, flop*ped*

**flora** *noun* the plants of a district or country as a whole

**floral** *adj* (made) of flowers

**florist** *noun* a seller or grower of flowers

**floss** *noun* **1** fine silk thread **2** thin, often waxed thread for passing between the teeth to clean them ◻ *verb* to clean (teeth) with dental floss

**flotilla** *noun* a fleet of small ships

**flotsam** *noun* floating objects washed from a ship or wreck

**flounce¹** *verb* to walk away suddenly and impatiently, *eg* in anger

**flounce²** *noun* a gathered decorative strip sewn on to the hem of a dress

**flounder¹** *verb* **1** to struggle to move your legs and arms in water, mud *etc* **2** to have difficulty speaking or thinking clearly, or in acting efficiently

Flounder was probably formed by a gradual blending of 'blunder' and 'founder'.

◈. Do not confuse with: **founder**

**flounder²** *noun* a small flatfish

**flour** *noun* **1** finely-ground wheat **2** any grain crushed to powder: *rice flour* ◻ **floury** *adj* **1** covered with flour **2** powdery

◈. Do not confuse with: **flowery**

**flourish** *verb* **1** to be successful, *esp* financially **2** to grow well, thrive **3** to be healthy **4** to wave or brandish as a show or threat ◻ *noun* (*pl* **flourishes**) **1** fancy strokes in writing **2** a sweeping movement with the hand, sword *etc* **3** showy splendour **4** an ornamental passage in music

**flout** *verb* to treat with contempt, defy openly: *flouted the speed limit* ⓘ Probably from *floute*, a form found in Middle English meaning 'to play the flute'

◈. Do not confuse with: **flaunt**

**flow** *verb* **1** to run, as water **2** to move or come out in an unbroken run **3** of the tide: to rise ◻ *noun* a smooth or unbroken run: *flow of ideas*

**flower** *noun* **1** the part of a plant or tree from which fruit or seeds grow **2** the best of anything ◻ *verb* **1** of plants *etc*: to produce a flower **2** to be at your best, flourish ◻ **flowering** *noun* of plants: producing flowers ◻ **flowery** *adj* **1** full of or decorated with flowers **2** using fine-sounding, fancy language: *flowery prose style*

◈. Do not confuse with: **floury**

**flown** *see* **fly**

**flu** *noun*, *informal* influenza

**fluctuate** *verb* **1** to vary in number, price *etc* **2** to be always changing ◻ **fluctuation** *noun*

**flue** *noun* a passage for air and smoke in a stove or chimney

**fluent** *adj* finding words easily in

speaking or writing without any awkward pauses □ **fluency** *noun*

**fluff** *noun* soft, downy material □ *verb* **1** to spoil something by doing it badly or making a mistake **2 fluff up** or **fluff out** to shake or arrange into a soft mass □ **fluffy** *adj*

**fluid** *noun* a substance whose particles can move about freely, a liquid or gas □ *adj* **1** flowing **2** not settled or fixed: *my plans for the weekend are fluid*

**fluke¹** *noun* a small worm which harms sheep

**fluke²** *noun* the part of an anchor which holds fast in sand

**fluke³** *noun* an accidental or unplanned success

**flume** *noun* a water chute

**flummox** *verb* to bewilder, confuse totally

**flung** *past form of* **fling**

**flunk** *verb, slang* to fail

**fluoride** *noun* a chemical added to water or toothpaste to prevent tooth decay □ **fluoridize** or **fluoridate** *verb* to add fluoride to

**flurry** *noun* (*pl* **flurries**) a sudden rush of wind *etc* □ *verb* to excite

**flurry** *verb* ⋄ **flurries, flurrying, flurried**

**flush** *noun* (*pl* **flushes**) **1** a reddening of the face **2** freshness, glow □ *verb* **1** to become red in the face **2** to clean by a rush of water □ *adj* **1 flush with** having the surface level with the surface around **2** *informal* well supplied with money

**fluster** *noun* excitement caused by hurry □ *verb* to harass, confuse

**flute** *noun* **1** a high-pitched musical wind instrument **2** a tall narrow wine glass □ **fluted** *adj* decorated with grooves

**flutter** *verb* to move (eyelids, wings *etc*) back and forth quickly □ *noun* **1** a quick beating of pulse *etc* **2** nervous excitement: *in a flutter*

**flux** *noun* an ever-changing flow: *in a state of flux*

**fly** *noun* (*pl* **flies**) **1** a small winged insect **2** a fish-hook made to look like a fly to catch fish **3** a flap of material with buttons or a zip, *esp* at the front of trousers □ *verb* **1** to move through the air on wings in an aeroplane **2** to run away □ **flying saucer** a disc-shaped object believed to be an alien spacecraft □ **flying squad** a group of police officers organized for fast action or movement □ **flyover** *noun* a road built on pillars to cross over another □ **flysheet** *noun* the outer covering of a tent □ **flywheel** *noun* a heavy wheel which enables a machine to run at a steady speed

**fly** *verb* ⋄ **flies, flying, flew, flown**

**flyer** *noun* a small poster or advertising sheet

**FM** *abbrev* frequency modulation (*compare with:* **AM**)

**foal** *noun* a young horse □ *verb* to give birth to a foal

**foam** *noun* a mass of small bubbles on liquids □ *verb* to produce foam □ **foam rubber** sponge-like form of rubber for stuffing chairs, mattresses *etc*

**fob¹** *noun* **1** a small watch pocket **2** an ornamental chain hanging from such a pocket

**fob²** *verb* to force to accept (something worthless): *I won't be fobbed off with a silly excuse*

**focal** *adj* central, pivotal: *focal point*

**fo'c'sle** *another spelling of* **forecastle**

**focus** *noun* (*pl* **focuses** or **foci**) **1** the meeting point for rays of light **2** the point to which light, a look, or someone's attention is directed □ *verb* **1** to get the right length of ray of light for a clear picture **2** to direct (one's attention *etc*) to one point

**focus** *verb* ⋄ **focuses, focusing, focused**

**fodder** noun dried food, eg hay or oats, for farm animals

**foe** noun, formal an enemy

**foetal** adj relating to a foetus □ **foetal alcohol syndrome** a range of birth defects caused by an excessive alcohol intake during pregnancy

**foetus** noun a young human being or animal in the womb or egg

**fog** noun thick mist □ verb 1 to cover in fog 2 to bewilder, confuse □ **foggy** adj □ **foghorn** noun a horn used as a warning to or by ships in fog

**fogy** or **fogey** noun someone with old-fashioned views

**foil** verb to defeat, disappoint □ noun 1 metal in the form of paper-thin sheets 2 a dull person against which someone else seems brighter 3 a blunt sword with a button at the end, used in fencing practice

**foist** verb 1 to pass off as genuine 2 to palm off (something undesirable) on someone

**fold** noun 1 a part laid on top of another 2 an enclosure for sheep etc □ verb to lay one part on top of another □ **folder** noun a cover to hold papers

**foliage** noun leaves

**folio** noun (pl **folios**) 1 a leaf (two pages back to back) of a book 2 a page number 3 a sheet of paper folded once

**folk** noun 1 people 2 a nation, race 3 (**folks**) family or relations □ **folklore** noun the study of the customs, beliefs, stories etc of a people □ **folk music** traditional music of a particular culture □ **folksong** noun a traditional song passed on orally

**follicle** noun the pit surrounding a root of hair

**follow** verb 1 to go or come after 2 to happen as a result 3 to act according to: follow your instincts 4 to understand: I don't follow you

5 to work at (a trade) □ **follower** noun 1 someone who follows 2 a supporter, disciple: a follower of Jung □ **following** noun supporters: the team has a large following □ adj next in time: we left the following day □ prep after, as a result of: following the fire, the house collapsed

**folly** noun (pl **follies**) 1 foolishness 2 a purposeless building

**foment** verb to stir up, encourage growth of (a rebellion etc)
ⓔ From Latin fomentum meaning 'a warm lotion' or 'a poultice'

◑ Do not confuse with: **ferment**

**fond** adj 1 loving; tender 2 old foolish □ **fondly** adv □ **fondness** noun □ **fond of** having a liking for

**fondle** verb to caress

**font** noun 1 a basin holding water for baptism 2 a main source: a font of knowledge

**food** noun that which living beings eat □ **food processor** an electrical appliance for chopping, blending etc food □ **foodstuff** noun something used for food

**fool** noun 1 a silly person 2 historical a court jester 3 a dessert made of fruit, sugar and whipped cream □ verb to deceive; play the fool □ **fool about** to behave in a playful or silly manner □ **foolery** noun silliness, foolish behaviour □ **foolhardy** adj rash, taking foolish risks □ **foolish** adj unwise, ill-considered □ **foolishly** adv □ **foolproof** adj unable to go wrong

**foolscap** noun paper for writing or printing, 17 x 13 in (43 x 34 cm)

Referring to the original watermark used on this size of paper, showing a jester's cap and bells

**foot** noun (pl **feet**) 1 the part of the leg below the ankle 2 the lower part of anything 3 12 inches or 30 cm □ verb to pay (a bill etc) □ **football** noun 1 a game played by two teams of 11 on a field with a round ball

**2** *US* a game played with an oval ball which can be handled or kicked **3** a ball used in football □ **foothill** *noun* a smaller hill at the foot of a mountain □ **foothold** *noun* **1** a place to put the foot in climbing **2** a firm position from which to begin something □ **footing** *noun* balance; degree of friendship, seniority *etc* □ **footlight** *noun* a light at the front of a stage, which shines on the actors □ **footloose** *adj* unattached, with no responsibilities □ **footnote** *noun* a note at the bottom of a page □ **footplate** *noun* a driver's platform on a railway engine □ **footprint** *noun* a mark of a foot □ **footsore** *adj* tired out from too much walking □ **footstep** *noun* the sound of someone's foot when walking □ **footwear** *noun* shoes *etc* □ **foot the bill** to pay up □ **my foot!** *exclam* used to express disbelief □ **put a foot wrong** to make a mistake, act inappropriately

**for** *prep* **1** sent to or to be given to: *there is letter for you* **2** towards: *headed for home* **3** during (an amount of time): *waited for three hours* **4** on behalf of: *for me* **5** because of: *for no good reason* **6** as the price of: *£5 for a ticket* **7** in order to obtain: *only doing it for the money*

**for-** *prefix* forms words containing a notion of 'loss' or of 'not having or not doing something': *forbid/ forget* ⊙ From Latin *foris* meaning 'outside'

🔖 Note that **for-** has a different meaning from the prefix **fore-** (which is connected with 'be**fore**', 'in front of' or 'be**fore**hand'). There are a few words which do not fit this general rule of thumb: note the spelling of 'foreclose' and 'forward'. See also the note at 'forgo'.

**forage** *noun* food for horses and cattle □ *verb* to search for food, fuel *etc*

**foray** *noun* **1** a sudden raid **2** a brief journey

**forbade** *past form* of **forbid**

**forbearance** *noun* control of temper

**forbid** *verb* to order not to □ **forbidden** *adj* not allowed □ **forbidding** *adj* rather frightening

**forbid** ↔ forbid*s*, forbid*ding*, forbade, forbid*den*

**force** *noun* **1** strength, violence **2** the police **3** a group of workers, soldiers *etc* **4** (**forces**) those in the army, navy and airforce □ *verb* **1** to make, compel: *they forced him to go* **2** to get by violence: *force an entry* **3** to break open **4** to hurry on **5** to make vegetables *etc* grow more quickly □ **forced** *adj* done unwillingly, with effort: *a forced laugh* □ **forceful** *adj* **1** acting with power **2** persuasive, convincing, powerful □ **forcefully** *adv* □ **forcible** *adj* **1** done by force **2** strong and effective **3** powerful □ **forcibly** *adv*

**forceps** *noun* surgical pincers for holding or lifting

**ford** *noun* a shallow crossing-place in a river □ *verb* to cross (water) on foot

**fore-** *prefix* **1** before **2** beforehand **3** in front

Fore- is a prefix coming from Old English

🔖 Note that **fore-** has a different meaning from the prefix **for-** (which usually indicates some notion of 'loss' or 'not having or not doing something'). There are a few words which do not fit this general rule of thumb: note the spelling of 'foreclose' and 'forward'. See also the note at 'forgo'.

**forearm**¹ (*say* faw-rahm) *noun* the part of the arm between elbow and wrist

**forearm**² (*say* faw-**rahm**) *verb* to prepare beforehand

**foreboding** *noun* a feeling of coming evil

**forecast** *verb* to tell about beforehand, predict □ *noun* a prediction

**forecastle** or **fo'c'sle** (*both say* fohk-sl) **1** a raised deck at the front of a ship **2** the part of a ship under the deck containing the crew's quarters

**foreclose** *verb* **1** to prevent, preclude **2** to bar from redeeming (a mortgage)

**forefather** *noun, formal* an ancestor

**forefinger** *noun* the finger next to the thumb

**forefront** *noun* the very front

**foregoing** *adj* preceding, going before

**foregone** *adj*: **a foregone conclusion** a result that can be guessed rightly in advance □ *see also* **forgo**

**foreground** *noun* the part of a view or picture nearest the person looking at it

**forehead** *noun* the part of the face above the eyebrows

**foreign** *adj* **1** belonging to another country **2** not belonging naturally in a place *etc*: *a foreign body in an eye* **3** not familiar □ **foreigner** *noun* **1** someone from another country **2** somebody unfamiliar

▫ (meaning 1) alien

**foreleg** *noun* an animal's front leg

**forelock** *noun* the lock of hair next to the forehead

**foreman** *noun* (*pl* **foremen**) **1** an overseer of a group of workers **2** the leader of a jury

**foremast** *noun* a ship's mast nearest the bow

**foremost** *adj* the most famous or important

**forensic** *adj* relating to courts of law or criminal investigation: *forensic medicine*

**forerunner** *noun* an earlier example

or sign of what is to follow: *the forerunner of cinema*

**foresee** *verb* to see or know beforehand

**foresee** ⇔ **foresees, foreseeing, foreseen, foresaw**

**foreshore** *noun* the part of the shore between high and low tide-marks

**foresight** *noun* **1** ability to see what will happen later **2** a fitting on the front of the barrel of a gun to help the aim

**forest** *noun* **1** a large piece of land covered with trees **2** a stretch of country kept for game □ **forester** *noun* a worker in a forest □ **forestry** *noun* the science of forest-growing

**forestall** *verb* to upset someone's plan by acting earlier than they expect

**foretaste** *noun* a sample of what is to come

**foretell** *verb* to tell in advance, prophesy

**foretell** ⇔ **foretells, foretelling, foretold**

**forethought** *noun* thought or care for the future

**foretold** *past form of* **foretell**

**forewarn** *verb* to warn beforehand □ **forewarning** *noun*

**forewoman** *noun* a woman overseer

**foreword** (*say* **faw**-werd) *noun* a piece of writing at the beginning of a book

❧ Do not confuse with: **forward**. It is helpful to remember that the foreWORD in a book is made up of WORDs.

**forfeit** *verb* to lose (a right) as a result of doing something: *forfeit the right to appeal* □ *noun* something given in compensation or punishment for an action, *eg* a fine □ **forfeiture** *noun* the loss of something as a punishment

**forge** *noun* **1** a blacksmith's workshop **2** a furnace in which metal is heated □ *verb* **1** to hammer (metal) into shape **2** to imitate for criminal purposes **3** to move steadily on: *forged ahead with the plan* □ **forger** *noun* (verb, meaning 2) □ **forgery** *noun* (*pl* **forgeries**) **1** something imitated for criminal purposes **2** the act of criminal forging

**forge** *verb* ⇔ forge**s**, forg**ing**, forg**ed**

**forget** *verb* to lose or put away from the memory □ **forgetful** *adj* likely to forget, having a tendency to forget things □ **forgetfully** *adv*

**forget** ⇔ forget**s**, forget**ting**, forg**ot**, forg**otten**

**forgive** *verb* **1** to be no longer angry with **2** to overlook (a fault, debt *etc*) □ **forgiveness** *noun* pardon □ **forgiving** *adj* merciful, willing to forgive other people for their faults

**forgive** ⇔ forgive**s**, forgiv**ing**, forgav**e**, forgiv**en**

**forgo** *verb* to give up, do without

**forgo** ⇔ forgo**es**, forgo**ing**, forwent, forgone

🖎 It is possible to spell **forgo** and many of its forms with an 'e' – 'forego', 'forewent' *etc*. However, it is probably less confusing to stick to the basic spellings shown above when you are writing, and to keep the 'e' spelling for **forego** meaning 'to go before' (most commonly used in the expression 'a foregone conclusion'). See also prefix entries **for-** and **fore-**.

**forgot** and **forgotten** *see* **forget**

**fork** *noun* **1** a pronged tool for piercing and lifting things **2** the point where a road, tree *etc* divides into two branches □ *verb* to divide into two branches *etc*

**fork-lift truck** a power-driven truck with steel prongs that can lift and carry heavy packages

**forlorn** *adj* pitiful, unhappy

**forlorn hope** a wish which seems to have no chance of being granted

**form** *noun* **1** shape or appearance **2** kind, type **3** a paper with printed questions and space for answers **4** a long seat **5** a school class **6** the nest of a hare □ *verb* **1** to give shape to **2** to make

**formal** *adj* **1** of manner: cold, business-like **2** done according to custom or convention □ **formally** *adv* □ **formal dress** clothes required to be worn on formal social occasions, *eg* balls and banquets □ **formality** *noun* (*pl* **formalities**) **1** something which must be done but has little meaning: *the nomination was only a formality* **2** cold correctness of manner

**format** *noun* **1** the size, shape *etc* of a printed book **2** the design or arrangement of an event, *eg* a television programme **3** *computing* the description of the way data is arranged on a disk □ *verb* **1** to arrange into a specific format **2** *computing* to arrange data for use on a disk **3** *computing* to prepare (a disk) for use by dividing it into sectors

**format** ⇔ format**s**, format**ting**, format**ted**

**formation** *noun* **1** the act of forming **2** arrangement, *eg* of aeroplanes in flight

**former** *adj* **1** of an earlier time **2** of the first-mentioned of two (*contrasted with*: **latter**) □ **formerly** *adv* in earlier times; previously

**formic** *adj* relating to ants

**formica** *noun*, *trademark* a tough, heat-resistant material used for covering work surfaces

**formidable** *adj* **1** fearsome, frightening **2** difficult to overcome

**formula** *noun* (*pl* **formulae** or **formulas**) **1** a set of rules to be followed **2** an arrangement of signs or letters used in chemistry, arithmetic *etc* to express an idea briefly, *eg* H$_2$O = water □ **formulate** *verb* 1 to set down clearly: *formulate the rules* 2 to make into a formula

**forsake** *verb* to desert □ **forsaken** *adj* deserted; miserable

> **forsake** ⬧ forsake*s*, forsak*ing*, forsook, forsak*en*

**forswear**, *verb*, *formal* to give up

**fort** *noun* a place of defence against an enemy

**forte** (*say* for-tei) *noun* someone's particular talent or specialty

**forth** *adv* forward, onward □ **forthcoming** *adj* 1 happening soon 2 willing to share knowledge; friendly and open □ **forthright** *adj* outspoken, straightforward □ **forthwith** *adv* immediately

**fortieth** *adj* the last of a series of forty □ *noun* one of forty equal parts

**fortify** *verb* to strengthen against attack □ **fortifications** *noun pl* walls *etc* built to strengthen a position

> **fortify** ⬧ fortif*ies*, fortify*ing*, fortif*ied*

**fortitude** *noun* courage in meeting danger or bearing pain

**fortnight** *noun* two weeks □ **fortnightly** *adj or adv* once a fortnight

**FORTRAN** *noun* a computer language

**fortress** *noun* (*pl* **fortresses**) a fortified place

**fortuitous** *adj* happening by chance □ **fortuitously** *adv*

**fortune** *noun* 1 luck (good or bad) 2 large sum of money □ **fortunate** *adj* lucky □ **fortunately** *adv*

**forty** *noun* the number 40 □ *adj* 40 in number

**forum** *noun* 1 a public place where speeches are made 2 a meeting to talk about a particular subject 3 *historical* a market-place in ancient Rome

**forward** *adj* 1 advancing: *a forward*

*movement* 2 near or at the front 3 of fruit: ripe earlier than usual 4 too quick to speak or act, pert □ *verb* 1 to help towards success: *forwarded his plans* 2 to send on (letters) □ *adv* forwards □ **forwards** *adv* onward, towards the front

> ◆ Do not confuse with: **foreword**.
> It is helpful to remember that forWARD is an indication of direction, similar to backWARDs and homeWARDs.

**forwent** *past form of* **forgo**

**fossil** *noun* the hardened remains of the shape of a plant or animal found in rock □ **fossilize** *verb* to change into a fossil

**foster** *verb* 1 to bring up or nurse (a child not your own) 2 to help on, encourage □ **foster-child** *noun* a child fostered by a family □ **foster-parent** *noun* someone who brings up a fostered child

**fought** *past form of* **fight**

**foul** *adj* 1 very dirty 2 smelling or tasting bad 3 stormy: *foul weather/ in a foul temper* □ *verb* 1 to become entangled with 2 to dirty 3 to play unfairly □ *noun* a breaking of the rules of a game □ **foul play** a criminal act

**found**[1] *verb* 1 to establish, set up 2 to shape by pouring melted metal into a mould

**found**[2] *past form of* **find**

**foundation** *noun* 1 that on which anything rests 2 a sum of money left or set aside for a special purpose 3 an organization *etc* supported in this way

**founder**[1] *verb* 1 of a ship: to sink 2 of a horse: to stumble, go lame ⓘ From Old French *fondrer* meaning 'to fall in'

> ◆ Do not confuse with: **flounder**

**founder**[2] (from **found**[1]) *noun* someone who founds

**foundling** noun a child abandoned by its parents

**foundry** noun (pl **foundries**) a workshop where metal founding is done

**fountain** noun 1 a rising jet of water 2 the pipe or structure from which it comes 3 the beginning of anything

**four** noun the number 4 □ adj 4 in number

**fourteen** noun the number 14 □ adj 14 in number □ **fourteenth** adj the last of a series of fourteen □ noun one of fourteen equal parts

**fourth** adj the last of a series of four □ noun 1 one of four equal parts 2 music an interval of four notes

**fowl** noun a bird, esp a domestic cock or hen

**fox** noun (pl **foxes**) a wild animal related to the dog, with reddish-brown fur and a long bushy tail □ verb 1 to trick by cleverness 2 to puzzle, baffle

**foxglove** noun a tall wild flower

**foxy** adj 1 cunning 2 US, informal sexually attractive

**foyer** (say **foi**-ei) noun an entrance hall to a theatre, hotel etc

**fraction** noun 1 a part, not a whole number, eg ½ 2 a small part

**fractious** adj cross, quarrelsome

**fracture** noun a break in something hard, esp in a bone of the body

**fragile** adj easily broken □ **fragility** noun

**fragment** noun (say **frag**-ment) a part broken off; something not complete □ verb (say frag-**ment**) to break into pieces □ **fragmentary** adj consisting of small pieces, not amounting to a connected whole □ **fragmentation** noun breaking up, division into fragments

**fragrance** noun sweet scent □ **fragrant** adj sweet-smelling

**frail** adj weak; easily tempted to do wrong □ **frailty** noun (pl **frailties**)

weakness

**frame** verb 1 to put a frame round 2 to put together, construct 3 slang to make (someone) appear to be guilty of a crime □ noun 1 a case or border round anything 2 build of human body 3 state (of mind) □ **framework** noun the outline or skeleton of something

**frame** verb ⋄ frames, framing, framed

**franc** noun the standard unit of French, Belgian and Swiss money

**franchise** noun 1 the right to vote in a general election 2 a right to sell the goods of a particular company □ verb to give a business franchise to

**frank** adj open, speaking your mind □ verb to mark a letter by machine to show that postage has been paid □ **frankly** adv 1 openly 2 to be honest, I tell you □ **frankness** noun the quality of being frank

**frankincense** noun a sweet-smelling resin used as incense

**frantic** adj wildly excited or anxious □ **frantically** adv

**fraternal** adj brotherly; of a brother □ **fraternally** adv □ **fraternity** noun (pl **fraternities**) 1 a society, a brotherhood 2 a North American male college society (compare with: **sorority**) □ **fraternize** verb to make friends with □ **fratricide** noun 1 the murder of a brother 2 someone who murders their brother

**fraud** noun 1 deceit, dishonesty 2 an impostor; a fake □ **fraudulence** or **fraudulency** noun deceitful or dishonest nature □ **fraudulent** adj deceitful, dishonest □ **fraudulently** adv

**fraught** adj 1 anxious, tense 2 fraught with filled with

**fray** verb to wear away □ noun a fight, a brawl

**freak** noun 1 an unusual event 2 an odd or eccentric person 3 informal a keen fan: film freak

**freckle** *noun* a small brown spot on the skin

**free** *adj* **1** not bound or shut in **2** generous **3** frank, open **4** costing nothing □ *verb* **1** to make or set free **2** (with **from** or **of**) to get rid of □ **freedom** *noun* liberty □ **freehand** *adj* of drawing: done without the help of rulers, tracing *etc* □ **freehold** *adj* of an estate: belonging to the holder or their heirs for all time □ **Freemason** *noun* a member of a certain men's society, sworn to secrecy □ **free-range** *adj* **1** of poultry: allowed to move about freely and feed out of doors **2** of eggs: laid by poultry of this kind □ **freestyle** *adj* of swimming, skating *etc*: in which any style may be used

**freeze** *verb* **1** to turn into ice **2** to make (food) very cold in order to preserve **3** to go stiff with cold, fear *etc* **4** to fix (prices or wages) at a certain level □ **freezer** *noun* a type of cabinet in which food is made, or kept, frozen □ **freezing-point** *noun* the point at which liquid becomes a solid (of water, 0°C)

freeze *verb* ⬦ freezes, freezing, froze, frozen

**freight** *noun* **1** load, cargo **2** a charge for carrying a load □ *verb* to load with goods □ **freighter** *noun* a ship or aircraft that carries cargo □ **freight train** a goods train

**French fries** *US* fried potatoes

**French window** a long window also used as a door

**frenetic** *adj* frantic

**frenzy** *noun* **1** a fit of madness **2** wild excitement □ **frenzied** *adj* mad □ **frenziedly** *adv*

**frequent** *adj* (*say* freek-went) happening often □ *verb* (*say* frik-went) to visit often □ **frequency** *noun* (*pl* **frequencies**) **1** the rate at which something happens **2** the number per second of vibrations, waves *etc*

**fresco** *noun* (*pl* **frescoes** or **frescos**) a picture painted on a wall while the plaster is still damp

**fresh** *adj* **1** new, unused: *fresh sheet of paper* **2** newly made or picked; not preserved: *fresh fruit* **3** cool, refreshing: *fresh breeze* **4** not tired **5** cheeky, impertinent □ *adv* newly: *fresh-laid eggs* □ **freshly** *adv* newly, recently □ **freshen** *verb* to make fresh; to grow strong □ **freshwater** *adj* of inland rivers, lakes *etc*, not of the sea

**fret**[1] *verb* to worry or show discontent □ **fretful** *adj* showing feelings of worry or discontent

fret *verb* ⬦ frets, fretting, fretted

**fret**[2] *noun* one of the ridges on the fingerboard of a guitar

**fretful** *adj* showing feelings of worry or discontent

**fretsaw** *noun* a narrow-bladed, fine-toothed saw for fretwork

**fretwork** *noun* decorated cut-out work in wood

**friar** *noun* a member of one of the Roman Catholic brotherhoods, *esp* someone who has vowed to live in poverty □ **friary** *noun* (*pl* **friaries**) the friars' house

**friction** *noun* **1** rubbing of two things together **2** the wear caused by rubbing **3** quarrelling, bad feeling

**Friday** *noun* the sixth day of the week

**fridge** *noun, informal* refrigerator

**fried** *see* **fry**

**friend** *noun* **1** someone who likes and knows well another person **2** sympathizer, helper
 ⊚ From Old English *freon* meaning 'to love'

 ▪ (meaning 2) ally

**friendly** *adj* **1** kind **2** **friendly with** on good terms with □ *noun* (*pl* **friendlies**) a sports match that is not part of a competition □ **friendliness** *noun*

◨ (meaning 1) amiable, affable, genial; (meaning 2) intimate, close

**friendship** *noun* the state of being friends; mutual affection

**frieze** *noun* **1** a part of a wall below the ceiling, often ornamented with designs **2** a picture on a long strip of paper *etc*, often displayed on a wall

**frigate** *noun* a small warship

**fright** *noun* sudden fear: *gave me a fright/ took fright and ran away* □ **frighten** *verb* to make afraid □ **frightening** *adj*

**frightful** *adj* **1** causing terror **2** *informal* very bad □ **frightfully** *adv* **1** very badly **2** extremely

**frigid** *adj* **1** frozen, cold **2** cold in manner **3** sexually unresponsive □ **frigidity** *noun* □ **frigidly** *adv*

**frill** *noun* **1** an ornamental edging **2** an unnecessary ornament

**fringe** *noun* **1** a border of loose threads **2** hair cut to hang over the forehead **3** a border of soft material, paper *etc* □ *verb* to edge round

**Frisbee** *noun, trademark* a plastic plate-like object skimmed through the air as a game

**frisk** *verb* **1** to skip about playfully **2** *informal* to search someone closely for concealed weapons *etc* □ **frisky** *adj* lively, playful and keen to have fun □ **friskily** *adv*

**fritter** *noun* a piece of fried batter containing fruit *etc*

**fritter away** *verb* to waste, squander

**frivolous** *adj* playful, not serious □ **frivolously** *adv* □ **frivolity** *noun* (*pl* **frivolities**) levity, lack of seriousnes

**frizzy** *adj* of hair: massed in small curls

**fro** *adv*: **to and fro** forwards and backwards

**frock** *noun* **1** a woman's or girl's dress **2** a monk's wide-sleeved

garment □ **frock-coat** *noun* a man's long coat

**frog** *noun* a small greenish jumping animal living on land and in water

**frogman** *noun, informal* an underwater diver with flippers and breathing apparatus

**frolic** *noun* a merry, lighthearted playing □ *verb* to play lightheartedly □ **frolicsome** *adj* in the mood for, or fond of, frolicking

**frolic** *verb* ⬦ frolics, frolicking, frolicked

**from** *prep* **1** used before the place, person *etc* that is the starting point of an action *etc*: *sailing from England to France/ the office is closed from Friday to Monday* **2** used to show separation: *warn them to keep away from there*

**frond** *noun* a leaf-like growth, *esp* a branch of a fern or palm

**front** *noun* **1** the part of anything nearest the person who sees it **2** the part which faces the direction in which something moves **3** the fighting line in a war □ *adj* at or in the front □ **frontage** *noun* the front part of a building □ **frontispiece** *noun* a picture at the very beginning of a book □ **in front of** at the head of, before

**frontier** *noun* a boundary between countries

**frost** *noun* **1** frozen dew **2** the coldness of weather needed to form ice □ *verb* **1** to cover with frost **2** *US* to ice (a cake) □ **frosted** *adj* having an appearance as if covered in frost, *eg* glass with a specially roughened surface □ **frosty** *adj* **1** of weather: cold enough for frost to form **2** cold, unwelcoming: *gave me a frosty look* □ **frosting** *noun, US* icing on a cake *etc*

**froth** *noun* foam on liquids □ *verb* to throw up foam □ **frothy** *adj*

**frown** *verb* to wrinkle the brows in deep thought, disapproval *etc*

□ *noun* **1** a wrinkling of the brows **2** a disapproving look □ **frown on** to look upon with disapproval

**froze** and **frozen** *see* **freeze**

**frugal** *adj* **1** careful in spending, thrifty **2** costing little, small: *a frugal meal* □ **frugality** *noun* □ **frugally** *adv* in a way which reduces spending to a minimum

**fruit** *noun* **1** the part of a plant containing the seed **2** result: *all their hard work bore fruit* □ **fruiterer** *noun* someone who sells fruit □ **fruitful** *adj* **1** producing plenty of fruit **2** producing good results: *a fruitful meeting* □ **fruition** (*say* froo-ish-*u*n) *noun* **1** ripeness **2** a good result □ **fruitless** *adj* useless, done in vain □ **fruit machine** a gambling machine into which coins are put

**frump** *noun* a plain, badly or unfashionably dressed woman □ **frumpish** *adj*

**frustrate** *verb* **1** to make to feel powerless **2** to bring to nothing: *frustrated his wishes* □ **frustration** *noun*

**fry**[1] *verb* to cook in hot fat □ *noun* food cooked in hot fat

**fry** *verb* ⇨ **fries, frying, fried**

**fry**[2] *noun* a young fish □ **small fry** unimportant people or things

**fuchsia** (*say* fyoo-sha) *noun* a plant with long hanging flowers

**fuddle** *verb* to confuse, muddle

**fudge**[1] *noun* a soft, sugary sweet

**fudge**[2] *verb* to cheat □ *noun* a cheat

**fuel** *noun* a substance such as coal, gas or petrol, used to keep a fire or engine going

**fugitive** *adj* running away, on the run □ *noun* someone who is running away from the police *etc*: *a fugitive from justice*

**fugue** (*say* fyoog) *noun* a piece of music with several interwoven tunes

**fulcrum** *noun* (*pl* **fulcrums** or **fulcra**) the point on which a lever turns, or a

balanced object rests

**fulfil** *verb* to carry out (a task, promise *etc*) □ **fulfilment** *noun* **1** successful completion, accomplishment **2** satisfaction with things achieved

**fulfil** ⇨ **fulfils, fulfilling, fulfilled**

**full** *adj* **1** holding as much as can be held **2** plump: *full face* **3** full of having a great deal or plenty of □ *adv* (used with *adjs*) fully: *full-grown* □ **fully** *adv* **1** entirely, completely **2** at least □ **full moon** the moon when it appears at its largest

**fullback** *noun* a defensive player in football *etc*, the nearest to their team's goal-line

**full stop** a punctuation mark (.) placed at the end of a sentence

**fulsome** *adj*, *formal* overdone: *fulsome praise*

**fumble** *verb* **1** to use the hands awkwardly **2** to drop (a thrown ball *etc*)

**fume** *verb* **1** to give off smoke or vapour **2** to be in a silent rage

**fume** *verb* ⇨ **fumes, fuming, fumed**

**fumes** *noun pl* smoke, vapour

**fumigate** *verb* to kill germs by means of strong fumes □ **fumigation** *noun*

**fun** *noun* enjoyment, a good time: *are you having fun?* □ **make fun of** to tease, make others laugh at

■ **make fun of** rag, jeer at, ridicule, laugh at, mock, taunt, tease

**function** *noun* **1** a special job, use or duty of a machine, person, part of the body *etc* **2** an arranged public gathering □ *verb* **1** to work, operate: *the engine isn't functioning properly* **2** to carry out usual duties: *I can't function at this time in the morning*

**fund** *noun* **1** a sum of money for a special purpose: *charity fund* **2** a store or supply

**fundamental** *adj* **1** of great or far-reaching importance **2** basic, essential: *fundamental to her happiness* □ *noun* **1** a necessary part **2** (**fundamentals**) the groundwork, the first stages

**funeral** *noun* the ceremony of burial or cremation

**funereal** *adj* mournful

**funfair** *noun* an amusement park

**fungus** *noun* (*pl* **fungi** - *say* fung-gi) **1** a soft, spongy plant growth, *eg* a mushroom **2** disease-growth on animals and plants

**funk** *noun* **1** funky music **2** *informal* fear, panic □ **funky** *adj*, *informal* **1** of jazz and pop music: unsophisticated, earthy and soulful, like early blues **2** fashionable, trendy **3** odd, eccentric

**funnel** *noun* **1** a cone ending in a tube, for pouring liquids into bottles **2** a tube or passage for escape of smoke, air *etc* □ *verb* to pass through a funnel; channel

**funnel** *verb* ⋄ funnels, funnelling, funnelled

**funny** *adj* **1** amusing **2** odd □ **funnily** *adv* □ **funny bone** part of the elbow which gives a prickly feeling when knocked

---

■ (meaning 1) humorous, entertaining, comical, hilarious, witty, facetious, droll, farcical, laughable, ridiculous, absurd, silly; (meaning 2) strange, curious, puzzling, mysterious

---

**fur** *noun* **1** the short fine hair of certain animals **2** their skins covered with fur **3** a coating on the tongue, on the inside of kettles *etc* □ *verb* to line or cover with fur □ **furry** *adj* covered with fur □ **furrier** (*say* fu-ri-er) *noun* someone who trades in or works with furs

**fur** *verb* ⋄ furs, furring, furred

**furbish** *verb* to rub until bright; burnish

**furious** *adj* **1** extremely angry **2** stormy **3** fast, energetic and rather disorganized □ **furiously** *adv*

**furlong** *noun* one-eighth of a mile (220 yards, 201.17 metres)

**furnace** *noun* a very hot oven for melting iron ore, making steam for heating *etc*

**furnish** *verb* **1** to fit up (a room or house) completely **2** to supply: *furnished with enough food for a week* □ **furnishings** *noun pl* fittings, furniture

**furniture** *noun* movable articles in a house, *eg* tables, chairs

**furore** (*say* fyoo-**raw**-rei) *noun* uproar; excitement

**furrow** *noun* **1** a groove made by a plough **2** a deep groove **3** a deep wrinkle □ *verb* **1** to cut deep grooves in **2** to wrinkle

**further** *adv* & *adj* to a greater distance or degree; in addition □ *verb* to help on or forward □ **furthermore** *adv* in addition to what has been said □ **furthest** *adv* to the greatest distance or degree

**furtive** *adj* stealthy, sly: *furtive glance* □ **furtively** *adv*

**fury** *noun* violent anger

**furze** another name for **gorse**

**fuse** *verb* **1** to melt **2** to join together **3** to put a fuse in (a plug *etc*) **4** of a circuit *etc*: to stop working because of the melting of a fuse □ *noun* **1** easily-melted wire put in an electric circuit for safety **2** any device for causing an explosion to take place automatically

**fuse** *verb* ⋄ fuses, fusing, fused

**fuselage** *noun* the body of an aeroplane

**fusion** *noun* **1** melting **2** a merging: *a fusion of musical traditions*

**fuss** *noun* **1** unnecessary activity, excitement or attention, often about something unimportant: *making a fuss about nothing* **2** strong complaint □ *verb* **1** to be unnecessarily concerned about details **2** to worry too much

**fussy** *adj* **1** over-elaborate **2** choosy, finicky **3** partial, in favour of one thing over another: *either will do; I'm not fussy* □ **fussily** *adv* (meanings 1 and 2) □ **fussiness** *noun* (meanings 1 and 2)

**fusty** *adj* mouldy; stale-smelling

**futile** *adj* useless; having no effect □ **futility** *noun* uselessness

**futon** (*say* **foo**-ton) *noun* a sofa bed with a low frame and detachable mattress

**future** *adj* happening later in time □ *noun* **1** the time to come: *foretell the future* **2** the part of your life still to come: *planning for their future* **3** *grammar* the future tense in verbs

**fuzz** *noun* **1** fine, light hair or feathers **2** *Brit slang* the police

**fuzzy** *adj* **1** covered with fuzz, fluffy **2** tightly curled: *fuzzy hairdo*

## Gg

**g** *abbrev* gramme; gram

**gabble** *verb* to talk fast, chatter □ *noun* fast talk

**gaberdine** *noun* **1** a heavy overcoat **2** a heavy fabric

**gable** *noun* the triangular area of wall at the end of a building with a ridged roof

**gadabout** *noun* someone who loves going out or travelling

**gadget** *noun* a small simple machine or tool

**Gaelic** *noun* **1** the language of the Scottish Highlands **2** the Irish language; Erse □ *adj* written or spoken in Gaelic

**gaff** *noun* **1** a large hook used for landing fish, such as salmon **2** a spar made from a mast, for raising the top of a sail □ **blow the gaff** *informal* to let out a secret

**gag** *verb* to silence by stopping the mouth □ *noun* **1** a piece of cloth *etc* put in or over someone's mouth to silence them **2** *informal* a joke

**gag** *verb* ▸ **gags, gagging, gagged**

**gaggle** *noun* a flock of geese

**gaiety** and **gaily** *see* **gay**

**gain** *verb* **1** to win; earn **2** to reach **3** to get closer, *esp* in a race: *gaining on the leader* **4** of a clock: to go ahead of correct time **5** to take on

(*eg* weight) □ *noun* **1** something gained **2** profit

**gait** *noun* way or manner of walking

◆ Do not confuse with: **gate**

**gaiter** *noun* a cloth ankle-covering, fitting over the shoe, sometimes reaching to the knee

**gala** *noun* **1** a public festival **2** a sports meeting: *swimming gala*

**galaxy** *noun* (*pl* **galaxies**) **1** a system of stars **2** an impressive gathering □ **the Galaxy** the Milky Way

**gale** *noun* a strong wind

**gall** (*say* gawl) *noun* **1** bile, a bitter fluid produced by the liver and stored in the **gallbladder 2** bitterness of feeling **3** a growth caused by insects on trees and plants □ *verb* to annoy

**gallant** *adj* **1** brave; noble **2** polite or attentive towards women □ *noun* a gallant man □ **gallantry** *noun*

**galleon** *noun, historical* a large Spanish sailing ship

**gallery** *noun* (*pl* **galleries**) **1** a long passage **2** the top floor of seats in a theatre **3** a room or building for showing artworks

**galley** *noun* (*pl* **galleys**) **1** *historical* a long, low-built ship driven by oars **2** a ship's kitchen

**galling** *adj* annoying, frustrating

**gallivant** *verb* to travel or go out for pleasure

**gallon** *noun* a measure for liquids (8 pints, 4.546 litres)

**gallop** *verb* **1** to move by leaps **2** to (cause to) move very fast □ *noun* a fast pace

**gallows** *noun sing* a wooden framework on which criminals were hanged

**gallus** (*say* gal-us) *adj, Scottish* spirited, perky; bold

**galore** *adv* in plenty: *whisky galore*

Based on an Irish Gaelic phrase *go leor*, meaning 'sufficient'

**galosh** or **golosh** *noun* (*pl* **galoshes** or **goloshes**) a rubber shoe worn over ordinary shoes in wet weather

**galvanize** *verb* **1** to stir into activity **2** to stimulate by electricity **3** to coat (iron *etc*) with zinc □ **galvanization** *noun*

Named after the Italian physicist, Luigi *Galvani*

**gambit** *noun* **1** *chess* a first move involving sacrificing a piece to make the player's position stronger **2** an opening move in a transaction, or an opening remark in a conversation

**gamble** *verb* **1** to play games for money **2** to risk money on the result of a game, race *etc* **3** to take a wild chance □ *noun* a risk; a bet on a result

**gambol** *verb* to leap playfully

**gambol** ⇨ gambol*s*, gambol*ling*, gambol*led*

**game** *noun* **1** a contest played according to rules **2** (**games**) athletic competition **3** wild animals and birds hunted for sport □ *adj* **1** plucky **2** of a limb: lame □ **gamekeeper** *noun* someone who looks after game birds, animals, fish *etc*

**gaming** *noun* & *adj* gambling

**gammon** *noun* leg of a pig, salted and smoked

**gander** *noun* a male goose

**gang** *noun* **1** a group of people who meet regularly **2** a team of criminals **3** a number of labourers

**gangrene** *noun* the rotting of some part of the body □ **gangrenous** *adj*

**gangster** *noun* a member of a gang of criminals

**gangway** *noun* **1** a passage between rows of seats **2** a movable bridge leading from a quay to a ship

**gannet** *noun* a large white sea bird

**gantry** *noun* (*pl* **gantries**) a platform or structure for supporting a travelling crane *etc*

**gaol** *another spelling of* **jail**

**gaoler** *another spelling of* **jailer**

**gap** *noun* an opening or space between things

**gape** *verb* **1** to open the mouth wide (as in surprise) **2** to be wide open

**garage** *noun* **1** a building for storing a car (or cars) **2** a shop which carries out car repairs and sells petrol, oil *etc*

**garb** *noun, formal* dress □ *verb* to clothe

**garbage** *noun* rubbish

**garble** *verb* to mix up, muddle

**garden** *noun* a piece of ground on which flowers or vegetables are grown □ *verb* to work in a garden □ **gardener** *noun* □ **garden party** a large tea party, held out of doors

**gargantuan** *adj* extremely large, huge

Named after *Gargantua*, a giant with an enormous appetite in a 16th-century French novel by Rabelais

**gargle** *verb* to rinse the throat with a liquid, without swallowing

**gargoyle** *noun* a grotesque carving of a human or animal head, jutting out from a roof

**garish** *adj* tastelessly over-bright: *garish book cover*

**garland** noun flowers or leaves tied or woven into a circle

**garlic** noun an onion-like plant with a strong smell and taste, used in cooking

**garment** noun an article of clothing

**garner** verb, formal to gather; collect and store

**garnet** noun a semi-precious stone, usually red in colour

**garnish** verb to decorate (a dish of food) □ noun (pl **garnishes**) a decoration on food □ **garnishing** noun

**garret** noun an attic room

**garrison** noun a body of troops for guarding a fortress

**garrotte** verb to strangle someone by tightening a noose etc round their neck (originally by tightening an iron collar, also called a **garrotte**)

**garrulous** adj fond of talking □ **garrulity** noun

**garter** noun a broad elastic band to keep a sock or stocking up

**gas** noun (pl **gases**) **1** a substance like air (though you can smell some gases) **2** natural or manufactured form of this which will burn and is used as a fuel **3** US petrol □ verb to poison with gas □ **gas mask** a covering for the face to prevent breathing in poisonous gas □ **gasoline** noun, US petrol □ **gasometer** noun a tank for storing gas □ **gasworks** noun place where gas is made

**gas** verb ⇨ gases, gassing, gassed

**gash** noun (pl **gashes**) a deep, open cut □ verb to cut deeply into

**gasket** noun a layer of padding used to make air-tight or gas-tight joints

**gasp** noun the sound made by a sudden intake of breath □ verb **1** to breathe with difficulty **2** to say breathlessly **3** informal to want badly: gasping for a cup of tea

**gastric** adj relating to the stomach

**gate** noun **1** a door across an opening in a wall, fence etc **2** the number of people at a football match **3** the total entrance money paid by those at a football match □ **gateway** noun **1** an opening containing a gate **2** an entrance

◆. Do not confuse with: **gait**

**gateau** (say gat-oh) noun (pl **gateaus** or **gateaux**) a rich cake, usually layered and filled with cream

**gatecrash** verb to go to a party uninvited □ **gatecrasher** noun

**gather** verb **1** to bring together, or meet, in one place **2** to pick (flowers etc) **3** to increase in: gather speed **4** to learn, come to the conclusion (that): I gather you don't want to go □ **gathering** noun a crowd

**gauche** (say gohsh) adj awkward and clumsy in people's company

Taken from the French word for 'left', because of the supposed awkwardness of using the left hand

**gaudy** adj showy; vulgarly bright in colour □ **gaudily** adv

**gauge** (say geij) verb **1** to measure **2** to make a guess □ noun a measuring device

**gaunt** adj thin, haggard

**gauntlet**[1] noun **1** a long glove (often of leather) with a guard for the wrist, used by motor-cyclists etc **2** historical an iron glove worn with armour □ **take up the gauntlet** to accept a challenge □ **throw down the gauntlet** to offer a challenge

**gauntlet**[2] noun: **run the gauntlet** to expose yourself to criticism, hostility etc

**gauze** noun thin cloth that can be seen through

**gawky** adj awkward

**gay** adj **1** homosexual **2** lively; merry, full of fun **3** brightly coloured □ noun a homosexual □ **gaiety** noun (sense 2) □ **gaily** adv (senses 2 and 3)

**gaze** *verb* to look steadily □ *noun* a fixed look

**gazelle** *noun* a small deer

**gazette** *noun* a newspaper, *esp* one having lists of government notices □ **gazetteer** *noun* a geographical dictionary

**GBH** or **gbh** *abbrev* grievous bodily harm

**GDP** *abbrev* gross domestic product

**gear** *noun* **1** clothing and equipment needed for a particular job, sport *etc* **2** a connection by means of a set of toothed wheels between a car engine and the wheels □ *verb* **gear to** to adapt to, design for what is needed

**geese** *pl* of **goose**

**gelatine** *noun* a jelly-like substance made from hooves, animal bones *etc*, and used in food □ **gelatinous** (*say* jel-**at**-in-*us*) *adj* jelly-like

**geld** *verb* to castrate (an animal) □ **gelding** *noun* a castrated horse

**gem** *noun* **1** a precious stone, *esp* when cut **2** something greatly valued

**gender** *noun* (in grammar, *esp* in languages other than English) any of three types of noun, masculine, feminine or neuter

**gene** *noun* the basic unit of heredity responsible for passing on specific characteristics from parents to offspring

**genealogy** *noun* (*pl* **genealogies**) **1** the history of families from generation to generation **2** a personal family history □ **genealogical** *adj*

**general** *adj* **1** not detailed, broad **2** involving everyone: *a general election* **3** to do with several different things: *general knowledge* **4** of most people: *the general opinion* □ *noun* a high-ranking army officer □ **in general** generally □ **generally** *adv* **1** usually, in most cases **2** by most people: *generally known*

□ **general practitioner** a doctor who treats most ordinary illnesses

**generalize** *verb* to make a broad general statement, meant to cover all individual cases □ **generalization** *noun* a too general view, statement *etc*

**generate** *verb* to produce, bring into being: *generate electricity/ generate good will* □ **generator** *noun* a machine for making electricity *etc*

**generation** *noun* **1** creation, making **2** a step in family descent **3** people born at about the same time: *90s generation*

**generic** *adj* general, applicable to any member of a group or class

**generous** *adj* giving plentifully; kind □ **generosity** *noun* □ **generously** *adv*

**genesis** *noun* beginning, origin

**genetic** *adj* **1** relating to genes **2** inherited through genes: *genetic disease* □ **genetically** *adv*

**genial** *adj* good-natured □ **geniality** *noun* □ **genially** *adv*

**genie** *noun* a guardian spirit

**genitals** *noun pl* the organs of sexual reproduction

**genius** *noun* (*pl* **geniuses**) **1** unusual cleverness **2** someone who is unusually clever

**genocide** *noun* the deliberate extermination of a race of people □ **genocidal** *adj*

**gent** *noun, informal* a man □ **the gents** *informal* a men's public toilet

**genteel** *adj* good-mannered, *esp* excessively

**gentile** (*say* jen-tail) *noun* a non-Jew

**gentility** *noun* **1** aristocracy **2** good manners, refinement, often in excess

**gentle** *adj* **1** mild-mannered, not brutal **2** mild, not extreme: *gentle breeze* **3** having a pleasant light or soft quality, not harsh or forceful □ **gentleness** *noun* □ **gently** *adv*

**gentleman** *noun* (*pl* **gentlemen**) **1** a

man, *esp* one of noble birth **2** a well-mannered man □ **gentlemanly** *adj*

**gentry** *noun* a wealthy, land-owning class of people

**genuine** *adj* **1** real, not fake or pretended **2** honest and straightforward □ **genuinely** *adv* (meaning 1) □ **genuineness** *noun*

**genus** *noun* (*pl* **genera**) a group of living things made up of a number of kinds

**geo-** *prefix* of or relating to the earth: *geography*
ⓖ From Greek *ge* meaning 'earth'

**geography** *noun* the study of the surface of the earth and its inhabitants □ **geographer** *noun* □ **geographic** or **geographical** *adj*

**geology** *noun* the study of the earth's history as shown in its rocks and soils □ **geological** *adj* □ **geologist** *noun*

**geometry** *noun* the branch of mathematics which deals with the study of lines, angles, and figures □ **geometric** or **geometrical** *adj* of a shape or pattern: made up of angles and straight lines

**Geordie** *noun, Brit informal* someone who was born or lives in Newcastle

**geranium** *noun* a plant with thick leaves and bright red or pink flowers

**gerbil** (*say* jerb-il) *noun* a small, rat-like desert animal, often kept as a pet

**germ** *noun* **1** a small living organism which can cause disease **2** the earliest or initial form of something, *eg* a fertilized egg **3** that from which anything grows: *germ of an idea* □ **germicide** *noun* a germ-killing substance

**German shepherd** (*also called* **alsatian**) a breed of large wolf-like dog

**germinate** *verb* to begin to grow; sprout □ **germination** *noun*

**gerrymander** *verb* to rearrange (voting districts *etc*) to suit a political purpose □ **gerrymandering** *noun*

After US governor, Elbridge *Gerry*, who rearranged the map of Massachusetts in 1811 to a shape resembling that of a sala*mander*

**gerund** *noun* an action noun with the ending -*ing*, *eg* watch*ing*, wait*ing*

**gesticulate** *verb* to wave hands and arms about in excitement *etc* □ **gesticulation** *noun*

**gesture** *noun* **1** a meaningful action with the hands, head *etc* **2** an action expressing your feelings or intent: *gesture of good will*

**get** *verb* **1** to go and find, take hold of, obtain: *get a carton of milk on the way home* **2** to go or move **3** to cause to be done: *get your hair cut* **4** to receive: *get a letter* **5** to cause to be in some condition: *get the car started* **6** to arrive: *what time did you get home?* **7** to catch or have (a disease): *I've got flu* **8** to become: *get rich* □ **get at 1** to reach **2** to hint at: *what are you getting at?* **3** to criticize continually: *stop getting at me* **4** *slang* to try to influence by bribes or threats □ **get away with** to escape punishment for □ **get on with** to be on friendly terms with □ **get over** to recover from □ **get to** to affect badly, distress: *the pressure is getting to him* □ **get up 1** to stand up **2** to get out of bed

**get** ⟶ gets, getting, got *US* gets, getting, got, gotten

ⓖ From Old Norse *geta*

✎ Get is one of the most overused words in the English language. Make sure you don't use it too much.

▧ (meaning 1) fetch, catch, seize, acquire, procure, secure, realize; (meaning 6) reach; (meaning 7) develop; (meaning 8) grow

**geyser** (*say* geez-er) *noun* **1** a natural

hot spring **2** a device which heats domestic water when the tap is turned on

**ghastly** adj **1** very ill: feeling ghastly **2** horrible, ugly **3** very pale, death-like **4** very bad □ **ghastliness** noun

**gherkin** noun a small pickled cucumber

**ghetto** noun (pl **ghettos**) a poor residential part of a city in which a certain group (esp of immigrants) lives

**ghost** noun the spirit of a dead person □ **ghostly** adj

**ghoul** (say gool) noun **1** an evil spirit which robs dead bodies **2** someone unnaturally interested in death and disaster □ **ghoulish** adj

**GHQ** abbrev general headquarters

**giant** noun **1** an imaginary being, like a human but enormous **2** a very tall or large person □ adj huge

**gibber** verb **1** to speak nonsense **2** to make meaningless noises; babble □ **gibberish** noun words without meaning; rubbish

**gibbet** noun, historical a gallows where criminals were executed, or hung up after execution

**gibbon** noun a large, tailless ape

**gibe** another spelling of **jibe**

**giblets** noun pl eatable organs from the inside of a chicken etc

**giddy** adj **1** unsteady, dizzy **2** causing dizziness: from a giddy height □ **giddiness** noun (meaning 1)

**gift** noun **1** something freely given, eg a present **2** a natural talent: a gift for music **3** informal something easily done: the exam paper was a gift □ **look a gift horse in the mouth** to find fault with a gift □ **gifted** adj having special natural power or ability

**gigantic** adj huge, of giant size

**giggle** verb to laugh in a nervous or silly manner □ noun a nervous or silly laugh □ **giggly** adj

**gild** (say gild) verb **1** to cover with beaten gold **2** to make bright
&. Do not confuse with: **guild**

**gill** (say gil) noun one of the openings on the side of a fish's head through which it breathes

**gilt** (say gilt) noun beaten gold used for gilding □ adj **1** covered with thin gold **2** gold in colour
&. Do not confuse with: **guilt**. Gilt is a past participle of the verb 'gild'.

**gimlet** (say gim-lit) noun a small tool for boring holes by hand

**gimmick** noun something meant to attract attention

**gin¹** noun an alcoholic drink made from grain, flavoured with juniper berries

**gin²** noun a trap or snare

**ginger** noun a hot-tasting root, used as a seasoning in food □ adj **1** flavoured with ginger **2** reddish-brown in colour □ **gingerbread** noun cake flavoured with ginger

**gingerly** adv very carefully and gently: opened the door gingerly

**gipsy** another spelling of **gypsy**

**giraffe** noun an African animal with very long legs and neck

**gird** verb, formal to bind round

**girder** noun a beam of iron, steel or wood used in building

**girdle** noun **1** a belt for the waist **2** a tight-fitting piece of underwear to slim the waist

**girl** noun a female child or young woman □ **girlhood** noun the state or time of being a girl □ **girlie** adj girlish □ **girlish** adj like a girl

**giro** (say jai-roh) noun (pl **giros**) **1** a system by which payment may be made through banks, post offices etc **2** (also called **girocheque**) a form like a cheque by which such payment is made **3** informal social security paid by girocheque

**girth** noun **1** measurement round the

middle **2** a strap tying a saddle on a horse

**gist** (*say* jist) *noun* the main points or ideas of a story, argument *etc*: *give me the gist of the story*

**give** *verb* **1** to hand over freely or in exchange **2** to utter (a shout or cry) **3** to break, crack: *the bridge gave under the weight of the train* **4** to produce: *this lamp gives a good light* □ **giver** *noun* (meaning I) □ **give-away** *noun* ( *pl* **give-aways**) something that you say or do which reveals a secret to other people □ **give away 1** to hand over (something) to someone without payment **2** to betray □ **give in** to yield □ **give over** *informal* to stop (doing something) □ **give rise to** to cause □ **give up 1** to hand over **2** to yield **3** to stop, abandon (a habit *etc*) □ **give way 1** to yield **2** to collapse **3** to let traffic crossing your path go before you

give ⟷ gives, giving, gave, given

■ (meaning I) present, confer, grant, bestow, endow, furnish, devote; (meaning 4) make, cause, occasion □ **give up** (meaning 2) surrender, capitulate; (meaning 3) abandon, renounce, relinquish

**glacé** *adj* iced or sugared: *glacé cherries*

**glacial** *adj* **1** of ice or glaciers **2** icy, cold: *glacial expression*

**glacier** *noun* a slowly-moving river of ice in valleys between high mountains

**glad** *adj* **1** pleased: *I'm glad you were able to come* **2** giving pleasure: *glad tidings* **3** glad to perfectly willing and happy to □ **gladly** *adv* (meanings 1 and 3) □ **gladness** *noun* (meanings 1 and 2) □ **gladden** *verb* to make glad □ **glad rags** best clothes

**glade** *noun* an open space in a wood

**gladiator** *noun, historical* in ancient Rome, a man trained to fight with other men or with animals for the amusement of spectators □ **gladiatorial** *adj*

**glam** *adj, slang* glamorous

**glamour** *noun* fascination, charm, beauty, *esp* artificial □ **glamorous** *adj*

**glance** *noun* a quick look □ *verb* to take a quick look at □ **glance off** to hit and fly off sideways

**gland** *noun* a part of the body which takes substances from the blood and stores them for later use or elimination by the body

**glandular** *adj* of, or affecting, the glands □ **glandular fever** an infectious disease with symptoms including a slight fever and an enlargement of the glands

**glare** *noun* **1** an unpleasantly bright light **2** an angry or fierce look □ *verb* **1** to shine with an unpleasantly bright light **2** to look angrily

**glaring** *adj* **1** dazzling **2** very clear, obvious: *a glaring mistake* □ **glaringly** *adv* extremely, unmissably: *glaringly obvious*

**glasnost** *noun* a political policy of openness and forthrightness, originally in the Soviet Union in the 1980s

**glass** *noun* (*pl* **glasses**) **1** a hard transparent substance made from metal and other oxides **2** (**glasses**) spectacles **3** a drinking vessel made of glass **4** *old* a mirror □ *adj* made of glass □ **glassy** *adj* **1** of eyes: without expression **2** of surfaces, *esp* water: smooth and shiny with no ripples □ **glass ceiling** a barrier to promotion at work experienced by some women but not officially recognized □ **glasshouse** *noun* a greenhouse

**glaucoma** *noun* an eye disease causing dimness in sight

**glaze** *verb* **1** to cover with a thin coating of glass or other shiny stuff

**2** to ice (a cake *etc*) **3** to put panes of glass in a window **4** of eyes: to become glassy □ *noun* **1** a shiny surface **2** sugar icing □ **glazier** *noun* someone who sets glass in window-frames

**gleam** *verb* **1** to glow **2** to flash □ *noun* **1** a beam of light **2** brightness

**glean** *verb* **1** to collect, gather **2** *old* to gather corn in handfuls after the reapers

**glee** *noun* **1** joy **2** a song in parts □ **gleeful** *adj* merry, usually in a mischievous way □ **gleefully** *adv*

**glen** *noun* in Scotland, a long narrow valley

**glib** *adj* **1** speaking smoothly and fluently (often insincerely and superficially) **2** quick and ready, but showing little thought: *a glib reply* □ **glibly** *adv*

**glide** *verb* **1** to move smoothly and easily **2** to travel by glider □ *noun* the act of gliding □ **glider** *noun* an aeroplane without an engine

**glimmer** *noun* **1** a faint light **2** a faint indication: *a glimmer of hope* □ *verb* to burn or shine faintly

**glimpse** *noun* a brief view □ *verb* to get a brief look at

**glint** *verb* to sparkle, gleam □ *noun* a sparkle, a gleam

**glisten** *verb* to sparkle

**glitter** *verb* to sparkle □ *noun* **1** sparkling **2** shiny granules used for decorating paper *etc* □ **glittery** *adj* shiny, sparkly

**glitz** *noun* showiness, garishness □ **glitzy** *adj*

**gloaming** *noun* twilight, dusk

**gloat** *verb* to look at or think about with malicious joy: *gloating over their rivals' defeat*

**globe** *noun* **1** the earth **2** a ball with a map of the world drawn on it **3** a ball, a sphere **4** a glass covering for a lamp □ **global** *adj* **1** of or affecting

the whole world: *global warming* **2** applying generally

**globule** *noun* **1** a droplet **2** a small ball-shaped piece □ **globular** *adj* ball-shaped

**gloom** *noun* dullness, darkness; sadness □ **gloomy** *adj* **1** sad, depressed **2** miserable, depressing **3** dimly lighted □ **gloomily** *adv*

**glorify** *verb* **1** to make glorious **2** to praise highly

glorify ⇢ glorifies, glorifying, glorified

**glorious** *adj* **1** spendid **2** deserving great praise **3** delightful □ **gloriously** *adv*

**glory** *noun* (*pl* **glories**) **1** fame, honour **2** great show, splendour □ *verb* to rejoice, take great pleasure (in)

**gloss** *noun* brightness on the surface □ *verb* **1** to make bright **2** to explain **3 gloss over** to try to hide (a fault *etc*) by treating it quickly or superficially □ **glossy** *adj* shiny, highly polished

**glossary** *noun* (*pl* **glossaries**) a list of words with their meanings

**glove** *noun* **1** a covering for the hand with a separate covering for each finger **2** a boxing glove

**glow** *verb* **1** to burn without flame **2** to give out a steady light **3** to be flushed from heat, cold *etc* **4** to be radiant with emotion: *glow with pride* □ *noun* **1** a glowing state **2** great heat **3** bright light □ **glowing** *adj* **1** giving out a steady light **2** flushed **3** radiant **4** full of praise: *glowing report* □ **glow-worm** *noun* a kind of beetle which glows in the dark

**glower** *verb* to stare (at) with a frown □ **glowering** *adj* **1** scowling **2** threatening

**glucose** *noun* a sugar found in fruits *etc*

**glue** *noun* a substance for sticking things together □ *verb* to join with glue □ **gluey** adj

**glum** adj sad, gloomy □ **glumly** adv

**glut** verb **1** to feed greedily till full **2** to supply too much to (a market) □ noun an over-supply: a glut of fish on the market

**glut** verb ⋄ gluts, glutting, glutted

**gluten** noun a sticky protein found in wheat and certain other cereals

**glutinous** adj sticky, gluey

**glutton** noun **1** someone who eats too much **2** someone who is eager for anything: a glutton for punishment □ **gluttonous** adj **1** fond of overeating **2** eating greedily □ **gluttony** noun

**glycerine** noun a colourless, sticky, sweet-tasting liquid

**GMT** abbrev Greenwich Mean Time

**gnarled** (say narld) adj knotty, twisted

**gnash** (say nash) verb to grind (the teeth)

**gnat** (say nat) noun a small blood-sucking fly, a midge

**gnaw** (say naw) verb to bite at with a scraping action

**gnome** (say nohm) noun a small, imaginary, human-like creature who lives underground, often guarding treasure

**GNP** abbrev gross national product

**gnu** (say noo or nyoo) noun a type of African antelope

**GNVQ** abbrev General National Vocational Qualification

**go** verb **1** to move: I want to go home/ when are you going to Paris? **2** to leave: time to go **3** to lead: that road goes north **4** to become: go mad **5** to work: the car is going at last **6** to intend (to do): I'm going to have a bath **7** to be removed or taken: the best seats have all gone now **8** to be given, awarded etc: the first prize went to Janet □ noun **1** the act or process of going **2** energy, spirit **3** informal an attempt, a try: have a go

**4** informal fashion, style: all the go □ **go-ahead** adj eager to succeed □ noun permission to act □ **go-between** noun someone who helps two people to communicate with each other □ **go-kart** noun a small low-powered racing car □ **go-slow** noun a slowing of speed at work as a form of protest □ **from the word go** from the start □ **go about** to try, set about □ **go ahead** to proceed (with), begin on □ **go along with** to agree with □ **go back on** to fail to keep (a promise etc) □ **go for 1** to aim to get **2** to attack □ **go off 1** to explode **2** to become rotten **3** to come to dislike □ **go on 1** to continue **2** to talk too much □ **go round** to be enough for everyone: will the trifle go round? □ **go steady with** to court, go out with □ **go the whole hog** to do something thoroughly □ **go under** to be ruined □ **on the go** very active

**go** verb ⋄ goes, going, went, gone

**goad** noun **1** a sharp-pointed stick for driving animals **2** something used to urge action □ verb to urge on by annoying

**goal** noun **1** the upright posts between which the ball is to be driven in football and other games **2** a score in football and other games **3** anything aimed at or wished for: my goal is to pass this exam

**goat** noun an animal of the sheep family with horns and a long-haired coat

**gob** noun, slang the mouth □ **gobsmacked** adj, slang shocked, astonished □ **gobstopper** noun a hard round sweet for sucking

**gobble** verb **1** to eat quickly **2** to make a noise like a turkey

**goblet** noun, historical **1** a large cup without handles **2** a drinking glass with a stem

**goblin** noun a mischievous, ugly spirit in folklore

**god, goddess** *noun* a supernatural being who is worshipped □ **God** *noun* the creator and ruler of the world in the Christian, Jewish *etc* religions □ **godly** *adj* holy, good living □ **godsend** *noun* a very welcome piece of unexpected good fortune

**godfather, godmother** *noun* someone who agrees to see that a child is brought up according to the beliefs of the Christian Church

**goggle-eyed** *adj* with staring eyes

**goggles** *noun pl* spectacles for protecting the eyes from dust, sparks *etc*

**gold** *noun* 1 a precious yellow metal 2 riches □ *adj* made of gold 2 golden in colour □ **goldfish** *noun* a golden-yellow Chinese carp, often kept as a pet □ **gold-leaf** *noun* gold beaten to a thin sheet □ **goldsmith** *noun* a maker of gold articles

**golden** *adj* 1 of or like gold 2 very fine □ **golden handshake** money given by a firm to a retiring employee □ **golden rule** a guiding principle □ **golden wedding** the 50th anniversary of a wedding

**goldfinch** *noun* a small colourful bird

**golf** *noun* a game in which a ball is struck with a club and aimed at a series of holes on a large open course □ **golf club** 1 a club used in golf 2 a society of golf players 3 the place where they meet □ **golfer** *noun*

**golosh** *another spelling of* **galosh**

**gondola** *noun* 1 a canal boat used in Venice 2 a car suspended from an airship, cable railway *etc* 3 a shelved display unit in a supermarket □ **gondolier** *noun* a boatman who rows a gondola

**gone** *past participle of* **go**

**gong** *noun* a metal plate which makes a booming sound when struck, used to summon people to meals *etc*

**good** *adj* 1 having desired or positive qualities: *a good restaurant* 2 having a positive effect: *fruit is good for you* 3 virtuous: *a good person* 4 kind: *she was good to me* 5 pleasant, enjoyable: *a good time* 6 substantial, sufficiently large: *a good income* □ **goodly** *adj* 1 large 2 ample, plentiful □ **good afternoon** a common formal greeting used when meeting or leaving people in the afternoon □ **good-bye** *noun* (*pl* **good-byes**) what you say when leaving people □ **good-day** *noun* an old-fashioned greeting used when meeting or leaving people □ **good evening** a common formal greeting used when meeting or leaving people in the evening □ **good-for-nothing** *adj* useless, lazy □ **good morning** a common formal greeting used when meeting or leaving people in the morning □ **good name** good reputation □ **good-natured** *adj* kind, cheerful □ **goodness** *noun* the quality of being good □ *exclamation* an exclamation of surprise □ **good night** a phrase used when leaving people at night □ **goods** *noun pl* 1 personal belongings 2 things to be bought and sold □ **good taste** good judgement for what is aesthetically pleasing or socially acceptable □ **goodwill** *noun* 1 kind wishes 2 good reputation in business

---

■ (meaning 1) competent, proficient, accomplished, skilful, excellent, commendable; (meaning 2) beneficial, advantageous; (meaning 3) moral, exemplary, righteous; (meaning 5) agreeable; (meaning 6) thorough, considerable, satisfactory

---

**goofy** *adj*, US stupid, silly

**goose** *noun* (*pl* **geese**) a web-footed bird larger than a duck □ **goosebumps** or **goosepimples** *noun pl* small bumps on the skin caused by cold or fear

**gooseberry** *noun* a sour-tasting, pale

green berry

**gore¹** *noun* a mass of blood □ *verb* to run through with horns, tusks *etc*: *gored by an elephant*

**gore²** *noun* a triangular-shaped piece of cloth in a garment *etc*

**Gore-Tex** *noun, trademark* a fabric which is water-repellent, but which has tiny pores to allow air and water vapour to escape from inside

**gorge** *noun* **1** the throat **2** a narrow valley between hills □ *verb* to eat greedily till full

**gorge** *verb* ⟿ gorges, gorging, gorged

**gorgeous** *adj* **1** beautiful, very attractive **2** showy, splendid **3** *informal* excellent, very enjoyable

**gorilla** *noun* the largest kind of ape

♠ Do not confuse with: **guerrilla**

The *Gorillai* were a tribe of hairy women in ancient times.

**gormless** *adj, Brit* stupid, senseless

**gorse** *noun* a prickly bush with yellow flowers

**gory** *adj* full of gore; bloody

**gosling** *noun* a young goose

**gospel** *noun* **1** the teaching of Christ **2** *informal* the absolute truth

**gossamer** *noun* **1** fine spider-threads floating in the air or lying on bushes **2** a very thin material

**gossip** *noun* **1** talk, not necessarily true, about other people's personal affairs *etc* **2** someone who listens to and passes on gossip □ *verb* **1** to engage in gossip **2** to chatter

**gossip** *verb* ⟿ gossips, gossiping, gossiped

Originally *godsibb*, meaning 'godparent'

**got** *past form of* **get**

**gouge** (*say* gowj) *noun* a chisel with a hollow blade for cutting grooves □ *verb* to scoop (out)

**gouge** *verb* ⟿ gouges, gouging, gouged

**goulash** *noun* (*pl* **goulashes**) a stew of meat and vegetables, flavoured with paprika

**gourd** (*say* goord) *noun* **1** a large fleshy fruit **2** the skin of a gourd used to carry water *etc*

**gourmand** (*say* goor-mond) *noun* a glutton

**gourmet** (*say* goor-mei) *noun* someone with a taste for good wines or food

**gout** *noun* a painful swelling of the smaller joints, *esp* of the big toe □ **gouty** *adj* suffering from gout

**govern** *verb* **1** to rule, control **2** to put into action the laws *etc* of a country □ **governess** *noun* a woman who teaches young children at their home □ **government** *noun* **1** rule; control **2** those who rule and administer the laws of a country □ **governor** *noun* someone who rules a state or country *etc*
ⓘ From Latin *gubernare* meaning 'to steer a ship'

**gown** *noun* **1** a woman's formal dress **2** a loose robe worn by members of the clergy, lawyers, teachers *etc*

**GP** *abbrev* general practitioner

**GPO** *abbrev* General Post Office

**grab** *verb* **1** to seize or grasp suddenly **2** to secure possession of quickly: *grab a seat* **3** to get in a hurry: *grab a bite to eat* □ *noun* a sudden grasp or catch

**grab** *verb* ⟿ grabs, grabbing, grabbed

**grace** *noun* **1** beauty of form or movement **2** a short prayer at a meal **3** the title of a duke or archbishop: *Your Grace* **4** favour, mercy: *by God's grace* □ **with bad grace** unwillingly □ **with good grace** willingly □ **graceful** *adj* **1** beautiful in appearance or movement **2** done in a neat way **3** polite □ **gracefully** *adv* □ **grace-note** *noun, music* a short note played before the main note in a melody

**gracious** adj kind, polite □ exclam an exclamation of surprise or shock □ **graciously** adv

**grade** noun a step or placing according to quality or rank; class □ verb to arrange in order, eg from easy to difficult □ **make the grade** to do as well as is necessary □ **gradation** noun arrangement in order of rank, difficulty etc

**gradient** noun a slope on a road, railway etc

**gradual** adj step by step; going slowly but steadily □ **gradually** adv

**graduate** verb (say grad-yoo-eit) 1 to divide into regular spaces 2 to pass university examinations and receive a degree □ noun (say grad-yoo-at) someone who has done so □ **graduation** noun the act of getting a degree from a university, or the ceremony to celebrate this

**graffiti** noun pl words or drawings scratched or painted on a wall etc

**graft** verb 1 to fix a shoot or twig of one plant on to another for growing 2 to fix (skin) from one part of the body on to another part 3 to transfer (a part of the body) from one person to another 4 to get illegal profit □ noun 1 living tissue (eg skin) which is grafted 2 a shoot grafted 3 hard work 4 profit gained by illegal or unfair means

**grain** noun 1 a seed eg of wheat, oats 2 corn in general 3 a very small quantity 4 a very small measure of weight 5 the run of the lines of fibre in wood, leather etc □ **against the grain** against your natural feelings or instincts

**gram** another spelling of **gramme**

**grammar** noun 1 the correct use of words in speaking or writing: his grammar is very bad 2 the rules applying to a particular language: French grammar □ **grammar school**

a kind of secondary school □ **grammatical** adj correct according to rules of grammar □ **grammatically** adv

**gramme** or **gram** noun the basic unit of weight in the metric system

**gramophone** noun, old a record-player

**granary** noun (pl granaries) a storehouse for grain

**grand** adj great; noble; fine □ **grandchild** noun a son's or daughter's child □ **grand-daughter** noun a son's or daughter's daughter □ **grand duke** a duke of specially high rank □ **grandfather** noun a father's or mother's father □ **grand master** a chess-player of the greatest ability □ **grandmother** noun a father's or mother's mother □ **grand piano** a piano with a large flat top □ **grandson** noun a son's or daughter's son □ **grandstand** noun rows of raised seats at a sports ground giving a good view

**grandeur** (say grand-yer) noun greatness

**grandiose** adj planned on a large scale

**granite** noun a hard rock of greyish or reddish colour

**granny** noun (pl grannies) informal a grandmother

**grant** verb 1 to give, allow (something asked for) 2 to admit as true □ noun money awarded for a special purpose □ **granted** or **granting** conj (often with that) even if, assuming: granted that you are right □ **take for granted** 1 to assume that something will happen without checking 2 to treat (someone) casually, without respect or kindness

**granule** noun a tiny grain or part □ **granular** adj made up of grains □ **granulated** adj broken into grains

**grape** noun the green or black smooth-skinned berry from which wine is made

**grapefruit** noun a sharp-tasting fruit like a large yellow orange

**graph** noun lines drawn on squared paper to show changes in quantity, eg in temperature, money spent □ **graphic** adj 1 relating to writing, drawing or painting 2 vivid, well told 3 explicit: graphic violence □ noun a painting, print, illustration or diagram □ **graphically** adv

**graphite** noun a form of carbon used in making pencils

**grapple** verb: grapple with 1 to struggle with 2 to try to deal with (a problem etc)

**grasp** verb 1 to clasp and grip with the fingers or arms 2 to understand □ noun 1 a grip with the hand or arms 2 someone's power of understanding □ **grasping** adj greedy, mean

**grass** noun (pl grasses) 1 the plant covering fields of pasture 2 a kind of plant with long narrow leaves, eg wheat, reeds, bamboo □ **grassy** adj covered with grass □ **grasshopper** noun a type of jumping insect □ **grass-snake** noun a type of harmless snake

**grate** noun a framework of iron bars for holding a fire □ verb 1 to rub down into small pieces 2 to make a harsh, grinding sound 3 to irritate □ **grater** noun an instrument with a rough surface for rubbing cheese etc into small pieces □ **grating** noun a frame of iron bars

**grateful** adj 1 feeling thankful 2 showing or giving thanks □ **gratefully** adv

**gratify** verb to please; satisfy □ **gratification** noun pleasure; satisfaction

**gratify** ← gratifies, gratifying, gratified

**gratis** adv for nothing, without payment

**gratitude** noun thankfulness; desire

to repay kindness

**gratuitous** adj uncalled-for, done without good reason: gratuitous violence □ **gratuitously** adv

**gratuity** noun (pl gratuities) a money gift in return for a service; a tip

**grave** noun a pit in which a dead person is buried □ adj 1 serious, important: grave error 2 not cheerful, solemn □ **gravely** adv □ **graveness** noun □ **gravestone** noun a stone placed to mark a grave □ **graveyard** noun a place where the dead are buried, a cemetery

**grave accent** (say grahv) a backward-leaning stroke (`) placed over letters in some languages to show their pronunciation

**gravel** noun small stones or pebbles

**graven** adj, old carved: graven images

**gravitate** verb to move towards as if strongly attracted (to) □ **gravitation** noun

**gravity** noun 1 seriousness, importance: gravity of the situation 2 lack of levity, solemnity 3 weight 4 the force which attracts things towards earth and causes them to fall to the ground

**gravy** noun (pl gravies) a sauce made from juices of meat that is cooking □ **gravy train** a situation producing large, easy profits

**gray** US spelling of **grey**

**graze** verb 1 to feed on (growing grass) 2 to scrape the skin of 3 to touch lightly in passing □ noun 1 a scraping of the skin 2 a light touch □ **grazing** noun grass land for animals to graze on

**grease** noun 1 thick animal fat 2 an oily substance □ verb to smear with grease, apply grease to □ **greasy** adj 1 full of, or covered in, grease 2 of skin: having a slightly moist appearance because the body releases a lot of natural oils into it 3 wet and slippery

**great** adj **1** very large **2** powerful **3** very important, distinguished **4** very talented: a great singer **5** of high rank, noble **6** informal excellent, very good □ **greatly** adv very much □ **greatness** noun (meanings 1, 2, 3, 4 and 5) □ **great-grandchild** noun the son or daughter of a grandson or grand-daughter □ **great-grandfather**, **great-grandmother** noun the father or mother of a grandfather or grandmother

**grebe** noun a fresh-water diving bird

**greed** noun great and selfish desire for food, money etc □ **greedy** adj □ **greedily** adv

**green** adj **1** of the colour of growing grass etc **2** inexperienced, naive **3** concerned with care of the environment □ noun **1** the colour of growing grass **2** a piece of ground covered with grass **3** (**Green**) a member of the Green Party, an environmentalist **4** (**greens**) green vegetables for food □ **green belt** open land surrounding a city □ **greenery** noun green plants □ **green fingers**: **have green fingers** to be a skilful gardener □ **greenfly** noun (pl **greenfly**) a bright green, small insect which attacks plants □ **greengage** noun a kind of plum, green but sweet □ **greengrocer** noun someone who sells fresh vegetables □ **greenhouse** noun a building with large glass panes in which plants are grown □ **greenhouse effect** the warming-up of the earth's surface due to excess carbon dioxide and certain other gases in the atmosphere □ **the green light** permission to go ahead with a plan □ **Green Party** a political party concerned with conserving natural resources and decentralizing economic and economic power

**greet** verb **1** to meet someone with kind words **2** to say hello etc to **3** to

react to, respond to: greeted the news with relief **4** to become evident to □ **greeting** noun **1** words of welcome or kindness **2** reaction, response

**gregarious** adj **1** sociable, liking the company of others **2** living in flocks and herds

**grenade** noun a small bomb thrown by hand

**grew** past form of **grow**

**grey** or US **gray** adj **1** of a colour between black and white **2** grey-haired, old □ noun **1** grey colour **2** a grey horse □ **greyhound** noun a breed of fast-running dog □ **grey matter** informal brains

**grid** noun **1** a grating of bars **2** a network of lines, eg for helping to find a place on a map **3** a network of wires carrying electricity over a wide area

**grief** noun deep sorrow, esp after bereavement □ **come to grief** to meet with misfortune

**grievance** noun a cause for complaining

**grieve** verb to feel grief or sorrow □ **grievous** adj **1** painful; serious **2** causing grief

**griffin** or **griffon** noun a mythological animal with the body and legs of a lion and the beak and wings of an eagle

**grill** verb **1** to cook directly under heat (provided by an electric or gas cooker) **2** to cook on a grid-iron over a fire **3** to question closely □ noun **1** a frame of bars for grilling food on **2** grilled food **3** the part of a cooker used for grilling **4** a restaurant serving grilled food

**grille** noun a metal grating over a door, window etc

**grim** adj **1** stern, fierce-looking **2** terrible; very unpleasant **3** unyielding, stubborn: grim determination □ **grimly** adv

**grimace** noun a twisting of the face in

fun or pain □ *verb* to make a grimace

**grime** *noun* dirt □ **grimy** *adj*

**grin** *verb* to smile broadly □ *noun* a broad smile □ **grin and bear it** to suffer something without complaining

**grin** *verb* ↔ grins, grinning, grinned

**grind** *verb* **1** to crush to powder **2** to sharpen by rubbing **3** to rub together: *grinding his teeth* □ *noun* hard or unpleasant work □ **grinder** *noun*

**grind** *verb* ↔ grinds, grinding, ground

**grindstone** *noun* a revolving stone for grinding or sharpening tools □ **back to the grindstone** back to work □ **keep your nose to the grindstone** to work hard without stopping

**grip** *noun* **1** a firm hold, a grasp **2** a way of holding or grasping; control: *a loose grip* **3** a handle or part for holding **4** a travelling bag, a holdall □ *verb* to take a firm hold of □ **gripping** *adj* commanding attention, compelling

**grip** *verb* ↔ grips, gripping, gripped

**gripe** *noun* **1** a sharp stomach pain **2** *informal* a complaint □ *verb* to complain

**grisly** *adj* frightful, hideous

**♠. Do not confuse with: grizzly**

**grist** *noun* corn for grinding □ **grist to the mill** something which brings profit or advantage

**gristle** *noun* a tough elastic substance in meat □ **gristly** *adj*

**grit** *noun* **1** a mixture of rough sand and gravel, spread on icy surfaces **2** courage □ *verb* **1** to apply grit to (an icy surface) **2** to clench the teeth □ **gritty** *adj* **1** covered in grit or having a texture like grit **2** courageous **3** honest in the portrayal of harsh realities □ **grittiness** *noun*

**grit** *verb* ↔ grits, gritting, gritted

**grizzled** *adj* grey; mixed with grey

**grizzly** *adj* grey in colour □ **grizzly bear** a type of large bear of North America

ⓞ From French *gris* meaning 'grey'

**♠. Do not confuse with: grisly**

**groan** *verb* **1** to moan in pain, disapproval *etc* **2** to be full or loaded: *a table groaning with food*

**grocer** *noun* a dealer in certain kinds of food and household supplies □ **groceries** *noun pl* food *etc* sold by grocers

**groggy** *adj* weak and light-headed after illness or blows

Originally meaning 'drunk', from *grog*, a mixture of rum and water

**groin** *noun* the part of the body where the inner thigh joins the torso

**groom** *noun* **1** a bridegroom **2** someone in charge of horses □ *verb* **1** to look after (a horse) **2** to make smart and tidy

**groove** *noun* a furrow, a long hollow □ *verb* to cut a groove (in)

**grope** *verb* to search (for) by feeling as if blind: *groping for his socks in the dark*

**gross** *adj* **1** coarse **2** very fat **3** great, obvious: *gross error* **4** of money: total, before any deductions for tax *etc*: *gross profit* **5** *US informal* disgusting, revolting □ *noun* **1** the whole taken together **2** twelve dozen □ **grossly** *adv* extremely □ **grossness** *noun* coarseness

**grotesque** *adj* very odd or unnatural-looking

**grotto** *noun* (*pl* **grottoes** or **grottos**) a cave

**ground**[1] *noun* **1** the surface of the earth **2** (also **grounds**) a good reason: *ground for complaint* **3** (**grounds**) lands surrounding a large house *etc* **4** (**grounds**) dregs: *coffee grounds* □ *verb* **1** of a ship: to strike the sea-bed and become stuck **2** to prevent (aeroplanes) from flying **3** to prevent (someone in your charge) from going out □ **ground floor** the storey of a building at street level □ **grounding** noun the first steps in learning something □ **groundless** adj without reason □ **groundwork** noun the first stages of a task

**ground²** past form of **grind**

**groundnut** same as **peanut**

**group** noun a number of people or things together □ verb **1** to form or gather into a group **2** to classify

**grouse¹** noun (pl grouse) a game bird hunted on moors and hills

**grouse²** noun (pl grouses) a grumble, a complaint □ verb to grumble, complain

**grove** noun a small group of trees

**grovel** verb **1** to crawl or lie on the ground **2** to be overly humble

**grovel** ⇨ grovel*s*, grovel*ling*, grovel*led*

**grow** verb **1** to become bigger or stronger **2** to become: grow old **3** to rear, cause to grow (plants, trees etc): grow from seed

**grow** ⇨ grow*s*, grow*ing*, grew, grown

**growl** verb to utter a deep sound like a dog □ noun an angry dog's deep sound

**grown** past form of **grow**

**growth** noun **1** growing **2** increase: growth in market shares **3** something that grows **4** something abnormal that grows on the body

**grub** noun **1** the form of an insect after being hatched from the egg, eg a caterpillar **2** informal food □ verb to dig

**grub** verb ⇨ grubs, grubbing, grubbed

**grubby** adj dirty □ **grubbily** adv □ **grubbiness** noun

**grudge** verb **1** to be unwilling to grant, accept or allow **2** to give unwillingly or reluctantly □ noun a feeling of resentment: she bears a grudge against me

**gruel** noun a thin mixture of oatmeal boiled in water

**gruelling** adj straining, exhausting

**gruesome** adj horrible

**gruff** adj **1** rough in manner **2** of a voice: deep and harsh

**grumble** verb to complain in a bad-tempered, discontented way □ noun a complaint

**grumpy** adj cross, bad-tempered □ **grumpily** adv

**grunge** noun, informal **1** grime, dirt **2** thrift-shop fashion or its designer equivalent **3** a style of rock music □ **grungy** adj

**grunt** verb to make a sound like that of a pig □ noun a pig-like snort

**guarantee** noun **1** a promise to do something **2** a statement by the maker that something will work well **3** money put down which will be forfeited if a promise is broken □ verb to give a guarantee

**guarantor** noun someone who promises to pay if another person fails to keep an agreement to pay

**guard** verb to keep safe from danger or attack □ noun **1** someone or a group whose duty is to protect **2** a screen etc which protects from danger **3** someone in charge of a railway train or coach **4** sport a position of defence □ **guarded** adj careful, not revealing much: guarded comments

**guardian** noun **1** someone with the legal right to take care of an orphan **2** someone who protects or guards

**guddle** verb, Scottish to fish with the hands by groping under the stones in a river

**guerrilla** noun one of a small band which makes sudden attacks on a larger army but does not fight openly □ adj of fighting: in which many small bands acting independently make sudden raids on an enemy ⓘ From Spanish *guerrilla* meaning 'little war'

🔥 Do not confuse with: **gorilla**

**guess** *verb* 1 to say without sure knowledge 2 *US* to suppose: *I guess I'll go* ◻ *noun* (*pl* **guesses**) an estimate ◻ **guesswork** *noun* guessing

**guest** *noun* a visitor received and entertained in another's house or in a hotel *etc*

**guffaw** *verb* to laugh loudly ◻ *noun* a loud laugh

**guide** *verb* 1 to show the way to, lead, direct 2 to influence ◻ *noun* 1 someone who shows tourists around 2 someone who leads travellers on a route unfamiliar to them 3 a guidebook 4 (**Guide**) a girl belonging to the Guides organization ◻ **guidance** *noun* help or advice towards doing something ◻ **guidebook** *noun* a book with information for tourists about a place ◻ **guided missile** an explosive rocket which after being fired can be guided to its target by radio waves

**guild** *noun* 1 an association for those working in a particular trade or profession 2 a society, a social club

🔥 Do not confuse with: **gild**

**guile** *noun* cunning, deceit

**guillotine** *noun* 1 *historical* an instrument with a falling blade used for executing by beheading 2 a machine with a blade for cutting paper 3 the limiting of discussion time in parliament by prearranging voting times ◻ *verb* 1 to behead with the guillotine 2 to cut (paper) with a guillotine 3 to use a parliamentary guillotine on

Named after Joseph *Guillotin*, a French doctor who recommended its use for executions during the French Revolution

**guilt** *noun* 1 a sense of shame 2 blame for wrongdoing, *eg* breaking the law ◻ **guilty** *adj* 1 ashamed about something bad you have done 2 having done something wrong 3 officially judged to have committed a crime ◻ **guiltily** *adv* (meaning 1)

🔥 Do not confuse with: **gilt**

**guinea** *noun* 1 *historical* a British gold coin 2 a sum of money equal to 1.05, sometimes used in expressing prices, fees *etc*

**guinea-pig** *noun* 1 a rodent about the size of a rabbit 2 someone used as the subject of an experiment

**guise** *noun* appearance, dress, *esp* in disguise: *in the guise of a priest*

**guitar** *noun* a stringed musical instrument with frets and a waisted body

**gulf** *noun* a large inlet of the sea

**gull** *noun* a seagull

**gullet** *noun* a passage by which food goes down into the stomach

**gullible** *adj* easily tricked

**gully** *noun* (*pl* **gullies**) a channel worn by water

**gulp** *verb* to swallow quickly and in large mouthfuls ◻ *noun* a sudden fast swallowing

**gum** *noun* 1 the firm flesh in which the teeth grow 2 sticky juice got from some trees and plants 3 a flavoured gummy sweet, chewing gum ◻ *verb* to stick with gum ◻ **gummy** *adj* sticky ◻ **gum tree** *noun* a tree that gives gum or gum resin, *esp* the eucalyptus

**gum** *verb* ⟷ **gum**s, **gum**m*ing*, **gum**m*ed*

**gumption** *noun* good sense

**gun** *noun* any weapon firing bullets or shells ◻ **gunboat** *noun* a small warship with heavy guns ◻ **gunfire** *noun* the firing of guns ◻ **gunpowder** *noun* an explosive in powder form ◻ **stick to your guns** to keep determinedly to your opinion

**gung-ho** *adj* boisterously enthusiastic

**gunwale** or **gunnel** (*both say* **gun**-el) *noun* the upper edge of a boat's side

**gurgle** *verb* **1** of water: to make a bubbling sound **2** to make such a sound, eg in pleasure □ *noun: the baby's gurgles*

**guru** (*say* **goo**-roo) *noun* **1** a Hindu spiritual teacher **2** a revered instructor, a mentor

**gush** *verb* **1** to flow out in a strong stream **2** to talk at length with exaggerated emotions: *gushing on about the wedding* □ *noun (pl* **gushes**) a strong or sudden flow: *gush of tears*

**gusset** *noun* a piece of material sewn into a seam join to strengthen or widen part of a garment

**gust** *noun* a sudden blast of wind □ **gusty** *adj*

**gusto** *noun* enthusiasm □ **with gusto** enthusiastically

**gut** *noun* **1** a narrow passage in the lower part of the body **2** animal intestines used as strings for musical instruments **3** (**guts**) spirit, courage □ *verb* **1** to take out the inner parts of: *gut a fish* **2** to destroy completely, *esp* by fire: *gutted the building*

**gut** *verb* ▷ **guts, gutting, gutted**

**gutter** *noun* a water channel on a roof, at the edge of a roadside *etc* □ **gutter press** that part of the press that specializes in sensational journalism □ **guttersnipe** *noun, old* a poor child living in the streets

**guttural** *adj* harsh in sound, as if formed in the throat

**guy**[1] *noun* **1** *Brit* a representation of Guy Fawkes, traditionally burned on 5 November **2** *informal* a man

**guy**[2] *noun* a steadying rope for a tent *etc*

**guzzle** *verb* to eat or drink greedily

**gym** *informal* **1** a gymnasium **2** gymnastics

**gymkhana** *noun* a meeting for competitions, *esp* in horse-riding

**gymnasium** *noun (pl* **gymnasiums** or **gymnasia**) a building or room equipped for physical exercises

**gymnastics** *noun pl* exercises to strengthen the body □ **gymnast** *noun* someone who does gymnastics □ **gymnastic** *adj* relating to gymnastics

**gypsy** or **gipsy** *noun (pl* **gypsies** or **gipsies**) a member of a wandering people; a Romany

Based on *Egyptian*, because of the belief that the Romanies came originally from Egypt

**gyrate** *verb* to whirl round □ **gyration** *noun* □ **gyratory** *adj*

# Hh

**haberdashery** *noun* materials for sewing, mending *etc*

**habit** *noun* **1** something you are used to doing: *nasty habits* **2** someone's usual behaviour **3** the dress of a monk or nun □ **make a habit of** to do regularly or frequently

**habitable** *adj* fit to live in

**habitat** *noun* the natural home of an animal or plant

**habitation** *noun* a dwelling place

**habitual** *adj* usual, formed by habit □ **habitually** *adv*

**habituate** *verb* to make accustomed

**hack** *verb* **1** to cut or chop up roughly **2** to ride on horseback, *esp* along ordinary roads □ *noun* **1** a writer who does hard work for low pay **2** a riding horse kept for hire **3** a rough cut, a gash

**hacker** *noun* **1** a skilled computer operator **2** someone who breaks into government or commercial computer systems

**hackles** *noun pl* **1** the feathers on the neck of a farmyard cock **2** the hair on a dog's neck □ **make someone's hackles rise** to make them angry

**hackneyed** *adj* over-used, not fresh or original: *hackneyed phrase*

**hacksaw** *noun* a saw for cutting metal

**haddock** *noun* (*pl* **haddock** or **haddocks**) a small edible N Atlantic fish

**haemoglobin** or *US* **hemoglobin** (*say both* heem-*o*-**globb**-in) *noun* the oxygen-carrying substance in red blood cells

**haemophilia** or *US* **hemophilia** (*say both* heem-*o*-**fil**-i-*a*) *noun* a hereditary disease causing excessive bleeding when cut □ **haemophiliac** (heem-*o*-**fil**-i-ak) *noun* someone suffering from haemophilia

**haemorrhage** or *US* **hemorrhage** (*say both* hem-*o*-rij) *noun* a large amount of bleeding

**haemorrhoids** or *US* **hemorrhoids** (*say both* hem-*o*-roidz) *noun pl* an uncomfortable condition commonly known as 'piles', in which the veins around the anus become dilated

**hag** *noun* **1** an ugly old woman **2** a witch

**haggard** *adj* gaunt and hollow-eyed, from tiredness

Originally a falconer's term for an untamed hawk

**haggis** *noun* (*pl* **haggises**) a Scottish dish made from chopped sheep's offal and oatmeal, traditionally cooked in a sheep's stomach

**haggle** *verb* to argue determinedly over a price

**haiku** *noun* a Japanese form of poem written in three lines of 5, 7 and 5 syllables

**hail¹** *verb* **1** to greet, welcome **2** to call to, attract the attention of □ *noun* **1** a call from a distance **2** greeting, welcome □ **hail-fellow-well-met** *adj* friendly and familiar on first meeting □ **hail from** to come from, belong to

**hail²** *noun* **1** frozen raindrops **2** a falling mass: *a hail of bullets* □ *verb* **1** to shower with hail **2** to descend in a mass □ **hailstone** *noun* a piece of hail

**hair** *noun* a thread-like growth on the skin of an animal; the whole mass of these (as on the head) □ **hair-breadth** or **hair's-breadth** *noun* a very small distance □ **hairdresser** *noun* someone who cuts, washes and sets hair □ **hairdryer** *noun* an electrical device which blows hot air to dry hair □ **hair-raising** *adj* terrifying □ **hairspray** *noun* a fine spray to fix a hairstyle □ **split hairs** to worry about unimportant details; nitpick

**hairy** *adj* **1** covered with hair **2** risky, dangerous

**hake** *noun* an edible sea-fish similar to a cod

**halal** *noun* meat from animals that have been slaughtered according to Islamic law □ *adj* from animals slaughtered in this way

**halcyon** (*say* hal-si-*on*) *adj*: **halcyon days** a time of peace and happiness

From the Greek word for 'kingfisher' in the phrase 'kingfisher days', a period of calm weather in mid-winter

**hale** *adj*: **hale and hearty** healthy

**half** *noun* (*pl* **halves**) one of two equal parts □ *adj* **1** being one of two equal parts: *a half bottle of wine* **2** not full or complete: *a half smile* □ *adv* partly, to some extent □ **half-baked** *adj* not properly thought out, incomplete □ **half-board** noun a hotel charge for bed, breakfast and another meal □ **half-breed** or **half-caste** noun, derogatory, offensive someone with a father and mother of different races □ **half-brother** noun a brother sharing only one parent □ **half-cock** noun: **at half-cock** not completely ready, unprepared □ **half-crown** noun, historical a British coin before decimal currency, worth two shillings and sixpence (12½ pence) □ **half-hearted** adj not eager □ **half-life** noun the time in which the radioactivity of a substance falls to half its original value □ **half-mast** adv of a flag: hoisted half-way up the mast to show that someone important has died □ **halfpenny** (say **heip**-ni) noun, historical a coin worth half of a penny □ **half-sister** noun a sister sharing only one parent □ **half-time** noun an interval half-way through a sports game □ **half-way** adv & adj at or to a point equally far from the beginning and the end □ **half-wit** noun an idiot, a fool □ **half-witted** adj stupid, idiotic

**halibut** noun a large edible flatfish

**hall** noun **1** a passage at the entrance to a house **2** a large public room **3** a large country house

**hallmark** noun **1** a mark put on gold and silver articles to show quality **2** a characteristic sign: the hallmark of a good editor

**hallo** another spelling of **hello**

**hallowed** adj, old holy, sacred

**Hallowe'en** noun the evening of 31 October, traditionally a time when spirits are believed to be around

**hallucination** noun the seeing of something that is not really there □ **hallucinatory** adj causing hallucinations, or like a hallucination

**hallucinogen** noun a substance that causes hallucinations □ **hallucinogenic** adj

**halo** noun (pl **haloes** or **halos**) **1** a circle of light surrounding eg the sun or moon **2** a circle of light depicted around the head of a saint etc as a sign of holiness

**halogen** noun one of a group of elements that includes chlorine and iodine

**halt** verb **1** to come or bring to a stop **2** to be lame, limp **3** to hesitate, be uncertain □ adj, old lame □ noun a stop, a standstill: call a halt **2** stopping place □ **halting** adj hesitant, uncertain

**halter** noun a head-rope for holding and leading a horse

**halve** verb to divide in two

**ham**[1] noun **1** a pig's thigh salted and dried **2** the back of the thigh

**ham**[2] noun, informal **1** an actor who overacts **2** an amateur radio operator

**hamburger** noun a round cake of minced beef, cooked by frying or grilling

**ham-fisted** adj clumsy

**hamlet** noun a small village

**hammer** noun **1** a tool with a heavy metal head for beating metal, driving nails etc **2** a striking piece in a clock, piano, pistol etc □ verb **1** to drive or shape with a hammer **2** to defeat overwhelmingly □ **hammer and tongs** determinedly, violently

**hammock** noun a length of netting, canvas etc hung up by the corners, and used as a bed

**hamper**[1] verb to hinder, impede

**hamper**[2] noun a large basket with a lid

**hamster** noun a small rodent with large cheek pouches, often kept as a pet

**hamstring** noun a tendon at the back of the knee □ verb **1** to make lame by cutting the hamstring **2** to make ineffective or powerless

**hand** noun **1** the part of the human

body at the end of the arm **2** a pointer, *eg* on a clock **3** help, aid: *can you give me a hand?* **4** a measure (four inches, 10.16 centimetres) for the height of horses **5** a worker, a labourer **6** a style of handwriting **7** side, direction: *left-hand side* **8** a group of playing-cards dealt to someone **9** clapping, applause: *a big hand* □ **verb 1** to pass (something) with the hand **2 hand over** to give □ **handbag** *noun* a small bag for personal belongings □ **handbook** *noun* a small book giving information or directions □ **handcuffs** *noun pl* steel bands joined by a short chain, put round the wrists of prisoners □ **hand-in-hand** *adj* **1** holding hands **2** in partnership □ **hand-me-down** *noun* a secondhand piece of clothing, *esp* one that used to belong to another member of the family □ **handout** *noun* a sheet or bundle of information given out at a lecture *etc* □ **hand-picked** *adj* chosen carefully □ **hands-on** *adj* **1** hand-operated **2** involving practical experience □ **hand-to-hand** *adj* of fighting: at close quarters □ **hand-to-mouth** *adj* with barely enough to live on and nothing to spare □ **handwriting** *noun* writing with pen or pencil □ **at hand** near by □ **at first hand** directly from the source □ **change hands** to pass to another owner □ **hand over fist** progressing quickly and steadily □ **in hand 1** in your possession: *cash in hand* **2** in preparation, under control □ **out of hand 1** out of control **2** at once □ **out of someone's hands** no longer their concern □ **take in hand** to take charge of □ **try your hand at** to have a go at, attempt □ **wash your hands of** to give up all responsibility for

**handful** *noun* (*pl* **handfuls**) **1** as much as can be held in one hand **2** a small amount **3** a difficult and demanding child, pet *etc*

**handicap** *noun* **1** something that makes an action more difficult **2** a disadvantage, such as having to run a greater distance, given to the best competitor in a race **3** a race in which handicaps are given **4** a physical or mental disability □ **verb 1** to give a handicap to **2** to burden, impede

**handicapped** *adj* **1** having or given a handicap **2** physically or mentally disabled

**handicraft** *noun* skilled work done by hand, not machine

**handiwork** *noun* **1** thing(s) made by hand **2** something done by a particular person *etc*: *the handiwork of a sick mind*

**handkerchief** *noun* a small cloth for wiping the nose *etc*

**handle** *verb* **1** to touch, hold or use with the hand **2** to manage, cope with □ *noun* **1** the part of anything meant to be held in the hand **2** a way of understanding something

**handlebars** *noun pl* a steering bar at the front of a bicycle with a handle at each end

**handsome** *adj* **1** good-looking **2** generous: *a handsome gift*

**handy** *adj* **1** useful or convenient to use **2** easily reached, near **3** clever with the hands □ **handily** *adv* (meanings 1 and 2) □ **handyman** *noun* a man who does odd jobs

**hang** *verb* **1** to fix or be fixed to a point off the ground **2** to be suspended in the air **3 hang down** to droop or fall downwards **4** to attach (wallpaper) to a wall **5** (*past form* **hanged**) to put a prisoner to death by putting a rope round their neck and letting them fall □ **hangdog** *adj* guilty-looking □ **hang-gliding** *noun* a form of gliding by hanging in a harness under a large kite □ **hanging** *noun* an execution in which the prisoner is hanged □ **hangman** *noun* an executioner who hangs people □ **get the hang of** to understand, learn how to use □ **hang about** or **hang around** to remain near, loiter □ **hang back** to hesitate □ **hang fire** to delay □ **hang on 1** to depend on **2** to wait, linger

**hang** ⇌ hang*s*, hang*ing*, hung or hang*ed*

**hangar** (*say* **hang**-*ar*) *noun* a shed for aeroplanes
ⓘ From French *hangar* meaning 'a shed'

**◑.** Do not confuse: **hangar** and **hanger**

**hanger** *noun* that on which a coat *etc* is hung □ **hanger-on** *noun* (*pl* **hangers-on**) someone who stays near someone in the hope of gaining some advantage

**hangnail** *noun* a torn shred of skin beside a fingernail

**hangover** *noun* **1** uncomfortable after-effects of being drunk **2** something remaining: *a hangover from the 60s*

**hank** *noun* a coil or loop of string, rope, wool *etc*

**hanker** *verb* to long for: *hankering after a chocolate biscuit*

**hankie** or **hanky** *noun* (*pl* **hankies**) *informal* a handkerchief

**Hanukkah** (*say* hah-nuk-*a*) *noun* the Jewish festival of lights held in mid-December

**haphazard** *adj* depending on chance, without planning or system □ **haphazardly** *adv*

**hapless** *adj* unlucky

**happen** *verb* **1** to take place **2** to occur by chance **3** to chance to do: *did you happen to see the news?* □ **happening** *noun* an event

■ (verb, meanings 1 and 2) arise, develop, come about, ensue, transpire

**happy** *adj* **1** joyful **2** contented **3** fortunate, lucky: *a happy coincidence* **4** willing: *happy to help* □ **happily** *adv* □ **happy-go-lucky** *adj* easy-going, taking things as they come

**happy** ⇌ happi*er*, happi*est*

■ (meaning 1) merry, cheerful, glad, pleased, delighted, elated, radiant; (meaning 2) satisfied, content

**harangue** *noun* a loud aggressive speech □ *verb* to deliver a harangue

**harass** *verb* to annoy persistently, pester □ **harassment** *noun*

**harbour** *noun* **1** a place of shelter for ships **2** a shelter, place of safety □ *verb* **1** to give shelter or refuge **2** to store in the mind: *harbouring ill will*

**hard** *adj* **1** solid, firm **2** not easily broken or put out of shape **3** not easy to do, understand *etc* **4** not easy to please **5** not easy to bear **6** having no kind or gentle feelings **7** of water: containing many minerals and so not forming a good lather **8** of drugs: habit-forming □ *adv* strongly, violently □ **hardly** *adv* scarcely; only just; with difficulty □ **hardness** *noun* the state of being hard □ **hardcore** *adj* of pornography *etc*: very explicit, graphic □ **hard disk** *computing* a hard-cased disk able to store large amounts of data, fixed into a base unit □ **harden** *verb* to make hard □ **hard-hearted** *adj* having no kind feelings □ **hard hit** badly affected □ **hard labour** tiring work given to prisoners as part of their punishment □ **hard lines** or **hard luck** bad luck □ **hard-nosed** *adj* tough, unsentimental □ **hardship** *noun* something difficult to bear □ **hard shoulder** the surfaced strip on the outer edges of a motorway, used when stopping in an emergency □ **hard up** *adj* short of

money □ **hardware** *noun*
1 ironmongery 2 the casing,
processor, disk drives *etc* of a
computer, not the programs which
it runs (*contrasted with*: **software**)
□ **hardwood** *noun* the wood of
certain trees including oak, ash, elm
*etc* □ **hard and fast** strict, rigid
□ **hard of hearing** rather deaf

**hardy** *adj* strong, robust, tough
□ **hardiness** *noun*

**hare** *noun* a fast-running animal, like
a large rabbit □ **hare-brained**
*adj* mad, foolish □ **harelip** *noun* a split
in the upper lip at birth, resembling
that of a hare

**harem** (*say* hei-rem or hah-**reem**)
*noun* 1 the women's rooms in an
Islamic house 2 a set of wives and
concubines

**hark** *exclam* listen! □ **hark back to** to
recall or refer to (a previous time,
remark *etc*)

**harlequin** *noun* a comic pantomime
character wearing a multicoloured
costume

**harm** *noun* hurt, damage □ *verb* 1 to
wound, damage 2 to do wrong to
□ **harmful** *adj* having a bad or
damaging effect on people or things
□ **harmless** *adj* 1 safe, *eg* to eat, use
or touch 2 causing no annoyance or
disturbance to anyone

**harmonica** *noun* a mouth organ

**harmony** *noun* (*pl* **harmonies**)
1 agreement of one part, colour or
sound with another 2 agreement
between people: *living in harmony*
3 *music* a part intended to agree in
sound with the melody □ **harmonic**
*adj* relating to harmony □ *noun*,
*music* a ringing sound produced by
lightly touching a string being
played □ **harmonious** *adj*
1 pleasant-sounding 2 peaceful,
without disagreement □ **harmonize**
*verb* 1 to bring into harmony 2 to
agree, go well (with) 3 *music* to add
the different parts to a melody
□ **harmonization** *noun*

**harness** *noun* 1 the leather and other
fittings for a workhorse 2 an
arrangement of straps *etc* attaching
something to the body: *parachute
harness* □ *verb* 1 to put a harness on
a horse 2 to use as a resource:
*harnessing the power of the wind* □ **in
harness** working, not on holiday or
retired

**harp** *noun* a triangular, stringed
musical instrument played upright
by plucking with the fingers □ *verb*
to play the harp □ **harper** or **harpist**
*noun* a harp player □ **harp on about**
to talk too much about

**harpoon** *noun* a spear tied to rope,
used for killing whales □ *verb* to
strike with a harpoon

**harpsichord** *noun* an early musical
instrument with keys, played like a
piano

**harrow** *noun* a frame with iron spikes
for breaking up lumps of earth
□ *verb* 1 to drag a harrow over 2 to
distress greatly

**harrowing** *adj* very distressing

**harry** *verb* 1 to plunder, lay waste
2 to harass, worry

**harry** ⇒ harries, harrying, harried

**harsh** *adj* rough, bitter; cruel
□ **harshly** *adv*

**hart** *noun* the stag or male deer, *esp*
from the age of six years

**harvest** *noun* 1 the time of the year
when ripened crops are gathered in
2 the crops gathered at this time
□ *verb* to gather in (a crop)
□ **harvester** *noun* 1 a farm worker
who helps with the harvest 2 (*also
called* **combine harvester**) a large
machine that cuts and threshes
grain 3 a creature like a spider
□ **harvest home** a feast held after a
harvest is gathered in

**has** *see* **have**

**has-been** *noun* someone no longer
important or popular

**hash** *noun* a dish of chopped meat *etc*
□ **make a hash of** to spoil completely

**hashish** noun the strongest form of the drug made from hemp (*see also* **cannabis**)

**hassle** verb to cause problems for □ noun difficulty, trouble

**hassock** noun a thick cushion used as a footstool or for kneeling on

**haste** noun speed, hurry □ **make haste** to hurry

**hasten** verb 1 to hurry (on) 2 to drive forward

**hasty** adj hurried; done without thinking □ **hastily** adv

**hat** noun a covering for the head □ **hatter** someone who makes or sells hats □ **keep something under your hat** to keep it secret

**hatch** noun (*pl* **hatches**) a door or cover over an opening in a floor, wall *etc* □ verb 1 to produce young from eggs 2 to form and set working: *hatch a plan/ evil* 3 to shade (part of a picture *etc*) with fine lines □ **hatchback** noun a car with a sloping rear door which opens upwards □ **hatchery** noun (*pl* **hatcheries**) a place for hatching eggs (*esp* of fish)

**hatchet** noun a small axe □ **bury the hatchet** to put an end to a quarrel

**hate** verb to dislike very much □ noun great dislike □ **hateful** adj horrible, causing hatred □ **hatred** noun extreme dislike

⬛ (verb) abhor, loathe, detest, abominate

**hat-trick** noun 1 *cricket* the putting out of three batsmen by three balls in a row 2 *football* three goals scored by the same player 3 any action performed three times in a row

**haughty** adj proud, looking on others with scorn □ **haughtily** adv

**haul** verb to drag, pull with force □ noun 1 a strong pull 2 *informal* a difficult or tiring job: *a long haul* 3 an amount gathered at one time: *a*

*haul of fish* 4 a rich find, booty □ **haulage** noun 1 the carrying of goods 2 money charged for this □ **haulier** noun a transporter of goods

**haunch** noun (*pl* **haunches**) 1 the fleshy part of the hip 2 a leg and loin of meat, *esp* venison

**haunt** verb 1 to visit often 2 of a ghost: to inhabit, linger in (a place) □ noun a place often visited □ **haunted** adj inhabited by ghosts

**have** verb 1 used with another verb to show that an action is in the past and completed: *we have decided to move house* 2 to own, possess: *do you have a cat?* 3 to hold, contain: *the hotel has a swimming pool* 4 to give birth to: *have a baby* 5 to suffer from: *have a cold* 6 to cause to be done: *have your hair cut* 7 to put up with: *I won't have him being so rude* □ **have done with** to finish □ **have it out** to settle by argument

**have** ⬠ **has**, **having**, **had**

▨ (meanings 2 and 3) lack

**haven** noun a place of safety

**haver** verb, Scottish 1 to speak nonsense 2 to dawdle, potter

**haversack** noun a bag made of canvas *etc* with shoulder-straps, for carrying on the back

**havoc** noun great destruction

**haw** noun a berry of the hawthorn tree

**hawk** noun a bird of prey like a falcon □ verb 1 to hunt birds with trained hawks 2 to carry goods about for sale □ **hawker** noun a door-to-door salesman

**hawthorn** noun a prickly tree with white flowers and small red berries

**hay** noun cut and dried grass, used as cattle food □ **hay-fever** noun an illness with effects like a bad cold, caused by pollen *etc* □ **hayrick** or **haystack** noun hay built up into a mound

**haywire** *adj* tangled, in a state of disorder

**hazard** *noun* **1** chance **2** risk of harm or danger □ *verb* **1** to risk **2** to put forward (a guess) at the risk of being wrong □ **hazardous** *adj* dangerous, risky

**haze** *noun* a thin mist □ **hazy** *adj* **1** misty **2** not clear, vague □ **hazily** *adv*

**hazel** *noun* a nut-producing tree of the birch family □ *adj* light greenish-brown in colour □ **hazelnut** *noun* a light brown nut produced by the hazel tree

**H-bomb** *noun* a hydrogen bomb

**he** *pronoun* a male person or animal already spoken about (used only as the subject of a verb): *he ate a banana*

**head** *noun* **1** the uppermost part of the body, containing the brain, skull *etc* **2** someone's mind: *can't get that tune out of my head* **3** a person in charge, a chief □ *verb* **1** to lead **2** to go in front of **3** to go in the direction of: *heading for home* **4** to hit (a ball) with the head **5 head off** to turn aside, deflect: *head off an attack* □ **headache** *noun* **1** a pain in the head **2** a worrying problem □ **headband** *noun* a band worn round the head □ **headboard** *noun* a board across the top end of a bed □ **headdress** *noun* a covering for the head □ **header** *noun, football* a shot at goal striking the ball with the head □ **headfirst** *adv* **1** with the head first: *fall headfirst down the stairs* **2** rashly, without thinking □ **heading** *noun* the title of a book or chapter □ **headland** *noun* a point of land running out into the sea, a cape □ **headlight** *noun* a strong light on the front of a car *etc* □ **headline** *noun* a line in large letters at the top of a newspaper page □ **headlong** *adj* & *adv* headfirst □ **headmaster**, **headmistress** or **headteacher** *noun* the principal teacher of a school

□ **head-on** *adj* & *adv* with the head or front first □ **headphones** *noun pl* a listening device that fits over the ears □ **headquarters** *noun sing* and *noun pl* place from which the chief officers of an army *etc* control their operations; the chief office (of a business *etc*) □ **headrest** *noun* a support for the head in a vehicle *etc* □ **headstone** *noun* a gravestone □ **headstrong** *adj* determined, stubborn □ **headway** *noun* forward movement □ **headwind** *noun* a wind blowing straight in your face □ **heady** *adj* exciting □ **head over heels** completely, thoroughly □ **off your head** mad, crazy □ **per head** per person

**heal** *verb* to make or become healthy or sound; cure

**health** *noun* **1** someone's physical condition: *how's your health?* **2** good or natural physical condition □ **healthy** *adj* **1** in good health or condition **2** encouraging good health □ **your** *etc* **health!** (as a toast) a wish that someone may have good health

**heap** *noun* **1** a pile of things thrown one on top of another **2** a great many (of) □ *verb* to throw in a pile

**hear** *verb* **1** to receive (sounds) by the ear **2** to listen to **3** to be told, understand: *I hear you want to speak to me* □ **hearing** *noun* **1** the act or power of listening **2** a court case □ **hearsay** *noun* gossip, rumour □ **hear! hear!** *exclam* a cry to show agreement with a speaker □ **will not hear of** will not allow: *he wouldn't hear of her going there alone*

**hear** ↔ hears, hearing, heard

**hearse** *noun* a car for carrying a dead body to the grave *etc*

**heart** *noun* **1** the part of the body which acts as a blood pump **2** the inner or chief part of anything: *the heart of the problem* **3** courage: *take heart* **4** will, enthusiasm: *his heart isn't in it* **5** love, affection: *with all* *my heart* **6** a sign (♥) representing a heart, or often love **7** this sign used in one of the suits on playing-cards □ **heartache** *noun* sorrow, grief □ **heartbroken** *adj* very upset, very sad □ **heartburn** *noun* a burning feeling in the chest after eating, indigestion □ **hearten** *verb* to cheer on, encourage □ **heart-failure** *noun* the sudden stopping of the heart's beating □ **heartfelt** *adj* felt deeply, sincere □ **heartless** *adj* cruel □ **heart-rending** *adj* very moving, very upsetting □ **heartstrings** *noun pl* inmost feelings of love □ **heart-throb** *noun* a sexually attractive person, with whom others fall in love □ **heart-to-heart** *noun* a frank, intimate discussion

**hearth** *noun* a fireplace

**hearty** *adj* **1** strong, healthy **2** of a meal: large, satisfying **3** eager, over-cheerful □ **heartily** *adv* **1** cheerfully and with great enthusiasm **2** thoroughly, absolutely: *I'm heartily sick of his moaning*

**heat** *noun* **1** high temperature **2** anger **3** a round in a competition, race *etc* □ *verb* to make or become hot □ **heat wave** *noun* a period of hot weather □ **in heat** of a female animal: ready for mating in the breeding season

**heath** *noun* **1** barren, open country **2** heather

**heathen** *noun* someone who does not believe in an established religion, *esp* someone who worships idols □ *adj* of heathens, pagan

**heather** *noun* a plant with small purple or white flowers growing on moorland □ *adj* of the colour of purple heather

**heave** *verb* **1** to lift by force **2** to throw **3** to rise and fall **4** to produce, let out (*esp* a sigh)

**heaven** *noun* **1** the sky (often the **heavens**) **2** the dwelling place of God; paradise **3** any place of great

happiness □ **heavenly** *adj* **1** living in heaven **2** *informal* delightful □ **heavenly bodies** the sun, moon and stars

**heavy** *adj* **1** of great weight **2** great in amount, force *etc*: *heavy rainfall* **3** not easy to bear **4** slow; sleepy **5** loud and deep: *heavy breathing* **6** having a thick, solid appearance: *a heavy oak table* □ **heavily** *adv* **1** with great force, in great amount: *raining heavily* **2** to a serious or great extent, intensely: *heavily in debt* **3** loudly and deeply: *breathing heavily* **4** in a thick, solid-looking way: *He was short, but heavily built* **5** in a slow, sleepy, or sad way □ **heaviness** *noun* □ **heavyhanded** *adj* clumsy, awkward □ **heavy metal** a very loud repetitive form of rock music □ **heavyweight** *noun* **1** a boxer in the highest weight category **2** someone very important or powerful

**heckle** *verb* to shout insults at, or ask awkward questions of, a public speaker □ **heckler** *noun* someone who heckles

**hectare** *noun* 10 000 square metres

**hectic** *adj* rushed; feverish

**hector** *verb* to bully

After *Hector*, the Trojan hero in the *Iliad*

**hedge** *noun* a fence of bushes, shrubs *etc* □ *verb* **1** to make a hedge **2** to shut in with a hedge **3** to avoid giving a straight answer □ **hedgehog** *noun* a small animal with prickly spines on its back □ **hedgerow** *noun* a row of bushes forming a hedge □ **hedge your bets** to keep open two or more possible courses of action

**heed** *verb* to give attention to, listen to □ **heedless** *adj* careless □ **pay heed to** to take notice of

**heel** *noun* the back part of the foot □ *verb* **1** to hit (*esp* a ball) with the heel **2** to put a heel on (a shoe) **3** of a ship: to lean over □ **take to your**

**heels** or **show a clean pair of heels**
to run away

**hefty** *adj* **1** powerful, muscular
**2** heavy

**Hegira** *noun* the Islamic era, dating
from ad 62

**heifer** (*say* hef-er) *noun* a young cow

**height** *noun* **1** the state of being high
**2** distance from bottom to top **3** the
highest point **4** (often **heights**) a
high place □ **heighten** *verb* to make
more intense

**heinous** (*say* heen-us) *adj* extremely
bad, atrocious: *heinous crime*

**heir, heiress** *noun* the legal inheritor
of a title or property on the death of
the owner □ **heir-apparent** *noun*
someone expected to receive a title
or property when the present holder
dies □ **heirloom** *noun* something
that has been handed down in a
family from generation to
generation

**held** *past form of* **hold**

**helicopter** *noun* a flying machine
kept in the air by propellers rotating
on a vertical axis

A coinage based on Greek words
meaning 'spiral wing'

**heliograph** *noun* a means of
signalling, using the sun's rays

**heliotrope** *noun* **1** a plant with small,
sweet-smelling, lilac-blue flowers
**2** a light purple colour

**helium** *noun* a very light gas

**helix** *noun* a screw-shaped coil

**hell** *noun* **1** a place of punishment of
the wicked after death **2** the
dwelling place of the Devil **3** any
place of great misery or pain
□ **hellish** *adj* very bad, unpleasant,
horrible or difficult □ **hellishly** *adv*
extremely, horribly □ **hellbent on**
determined to

**hello** or **hallo** or **hullo** *noun* (*pl* **hellos**
or **helloes** *etc*) a greeting used
between people: *I said hello to him/
Hello! How are you?*

**helm** *noun* the wheel or handle by
which a ship is steered □ **helmsman**
*noun* the person who steers a ship

**helmet** *noun* an armoured or
protective covering for the head

**help** *verb* **1** to aid, do something
useful for **2** to give the means for
doing something to **3** to stop
yourself from (doing): *I can't help
liking him* □ *noun* **1** aid, assistance
**2** someone who assists □ **helpful** *adj*
useful, giving help □ **helpfully** *adv*
□ **helping** *noun* a share, *esp* of food
□ **helpless** *adj* useless; powerless
□ **helplessly** *adv* □ **helpmate** *noun* a
partner □ **help yourself** serve
yourself, take what you wan

**helter-skelter** *adv* in a great hurry, in
confusion □ *noun* a spiral slide in a
fairground *etc*

**hem** *noun* the border of a garment
doubled down and stitched □ *verb* to
put or form a hem on □ **hem in** to
surround

**hem** *verb* ⋄ hems, hemm*ing*,
hemm*ed*

**hemisphere** *noun* **1** a half of a sphere
or ball-shape **2** half of the earth:
*western hemisphere/ southern
hemisphere* □ **hemispherical** *adj* like
half a ball in shape

**hemlock** *noun* a poisonous plant
with spotted leaves

**hemp** *noun* a plant used for making
ropes, bags, sails *etc* and the drug
cannabis

**hen** *noun* **1** a female bird **2** a female
domestic fowl □ **henpecked** *adj* of a
husband: dominated by his wife

**hence** *adv* **1** from this place or time:
*ten years hence* **2** for this reason:
*hence, I am unable to go*
□ **henceforth** or **henceforward** *adv*
from now on

**henchman** *noun* a follower; a servant

**henna** *noun* a reddish plant dye used
for colouring the hair *etc*

**hepatitis** *noun* inflammation of the
liver caused by one of several viruses

**heptagon** noun a seven-sided figure
□ **heptagonal** adj

**her** pronoun a female person already spoken about (used only as the object in a sentence): have you seen her? □ adj belonging to such a person: her house □ **hers** pronoun something belonging to such a person: the idea was hers □ **herself** pronoun 1 used reflexively: she washed herself 2 used for emphasis: she herself won't be there but her brother will

**herald** noun 1 something that is a sign of future things 2 historical someone who carries and reads important notices □ verb 1 to announce loudly 2 to be a sign of □ **heraldic** adj of heraldry □ **heraldry** noun the study of coats of arms, crests etc

**herb** noun a plant used in the making of medicines or in cooking
⊙ From French herbe meaning 'grass'

**herbaceous** adj 1 of a plant: with a stem which dies every year 2 of a flower-bed: filled with such plants

**herbal** adj of or using herbs: herbal remedy □ **herbalism** noun the study and use of plants in medicine

**herbivore** noun an animal which feeds on plants □ **herbivorous** adj

**Herculean** adj requiring tremendous strength or effort: a Herculean task

After the Greek hero, Hercules, who was given twelve seemingly impossible tasks to do by the gods

**herd** noun 1 a group of animals of one kind 2 (**the herd**) most people □ verb to group together like a herd of animals

**here** adv at, in or to this place: he's here already/come here!
□ **hereabouts** adv approximately in this place □ **hereafter** adv after this □ **the hereafter** life after death □ **hereby** adv by this means

**heredity** noun the passing on of physical qualities from parents to children □ **hereditary** adj passed on from parents to children

**heresy** (say he-re-si) noun (pl **heresies**) an opinion which goes against the official (esp religious) view □ **heretic** (say he-re-tik) noun someone who holds or teaches an opinion which goes against the official (esp religious) view □ **heretical** adj

**heritage** noun something passed on by or inherited from an earlier generation

**hermaphrodite** (say her-maf-ro-dait) noun an animal which has the qualities of both male and female sexes

**hermetically** adv: **hermetically sealed** closed completely and airtight

**hermit** noun someone who lives alone, often for religious reasons □ **hermitage** noun the dwelling of a hermit □ **hermit crab** a kind of crab which lives in the abandoned shell of a shellfish

**hernia** noun the bursting out of part of an internal organ through a weak spot in surrounding body tissue

**hero** noun (pl **heroes**), **heroine** 1 someone much admired for their bravery 2 the chief character in a story, film etc □ **heroic** adj 1 brave as a hero 2 of heroes □ **heroically** adv □ **heroism** noun bravery

**heroin** noun a very addictive drug derived from morphine

**heron** noun a large water bird, with long legs and neck

**herpes** noun a name for various types of a skin disease

**herring** noun (pl **herring** or **herrings**) an edible sea fish with silvery colouring, which moves in large shoals

**hers** and **herself** see her

**hertz** noun a unit of frequency for radio waves etc

**hesitate** *verb* **1** to pause because of uncertainty **2** to be unwilling (to do something): *I hesitate to ask* □ **hesitancy** *noun* □ **hesitant** *adj* undecided about whether to do something or not, because of anxiety or worry about the possible results □ **hesitation** *noun*

**hessian** *noun* a type of coarse cloth

**heterodox** *noun* heretical, having an opinion other than the accepted one (*contrasted with*: **orthodox**) □ **heterodoxy** *noun*

**heterogeneous** (*say* het-e-ro-jeen-i-us) *adj* composed of many different kinds (*contrasted with*: **homogeneous**)

**heterosexual** *noun* someone who is sexually attracted to the opposite sex □ *adj* attracted to the opposite sex (*contrasted with*: **homosexual**) □ **heterosexuality** *noun*

**hew** *verb* to cut or shape with an axe *etc*

**hew** ‑> hews, hew*ing*, hew*ed*, hewn or hew*ed*

**hex** *noun* a spell to bring bad luck; a curse

**hexagon** *noun* a six-sided figure □ **hexagonal** *adj*

**heyday** *noun* the time of greatest strength, the prime

From an old English expression *heyda*, meaning 'hurrah'. The *-day* ending and current sense developed much later.

**HGV** *abbrev* heavy goods vehicle

**hi** *exclam*, *informal* **1** hello **2** hey

**hiatus** (*say* hai-**eit**-us) *noun* a gap, a rift

**hibernate** *verb* of an animal: to pass the winter in a sleep-like state □ **hibernation** *noun* □ **hibernator** *noun*

**hiccup** *noun* **1** a sharp gasp, caused by laughing, eating, drinking **2** (**hiccups**) a fit of such gasping **3** a minor setback or difficulty □ *verb* to make a hiccuping sound

**hickory** *noun* (*pl* **hickories**) a N American tree

**hide¹** *verb* to put or keep out of sight □ *noun* a concealed place from which to watch birds *etc* □ **hidden** *adj* **1** concealed, out of sight **2** unknown: *hidden meaning* □ **hidebound** *adj* not open to new ideas

**hide** ‑> hides, hid*ing*, hid, hid*den*

**hide²** *noun* the skin of an animal □ **hiding** *noun* a beating

**hideous** *adj* **1** horrible, ghastly **2** very ugly □ **hideously** *adv* **1** of something horrible, ghastly or very ugly: extremely: *a hideously deformed body* **2** of something unpleasant or unreasonable: extremely: *hideously expensive*

**hierarchy** *noun* a number of people or things arranged in order of rank □ **hierarchical** *adj*

**hieroglyphics** (*say* hai-e-ro-**glif**-iks) *noun pl* ancient Egyptian writing, in which pictures are used as letters

**hi-fi** *adj* short for **high-fidelity** *noun*, *informal* high-quality equipment for reproducing recorded sound

**higgledy-piggledy** *adv & adj* in a complete muddle

**high** *adj* **1** raised far above **2** extending far upwards, tall **3** well up on any scale of measurement, rank *etc* **4** great, large: *high hopes/ high prices* **5** of sound: shrill, acute in pitch **6** of meat: beginning to go bad □ *adv* **1** far above in the air **2** well up on any scale **3** to a high degree □ **highball** *noun*, *US* an alcoholic drink and mixer (*eg* whisky and soda) with ice in a tall glass □ **highbrow** *adj* intellectual, very literary (*contrasted with*: **lowbrow**) □ **High Court** a supreme court □ **Higher** *noun* an examination in Scottish secondary schools, usually taken at the end of the 5th year □ **high-fidelity** *adj* reproducing sound very clearly □ **high-five** *noun* a sign of greeting made by slapping together one another's raised palms □ **high-flier** *noun* a highly ambitious and successful person □ **high-flown** *adj* (of language, style) using words that sound too grand or pompous □ **high-handed** *adj* thoughtless, overbearing □ **high jinks** lively games or play □ **Highlander** *noun* someone who comes from the Highlands □ **highly** *adv* **1** very: *highly delighted* **2** to or at a high level **3** in an approving way: *I've always thought highly of him* □ **highly-strung** *adj* nervous, easily excited □ **high-minded** *adj* having strong principles and high moral standards □ **Highness** *noun* a title of a monarch □ **highroad** *noun* a main road □ **high-spirited** *adj* bold, lively □ **high tea** a cooked meal in the late afternoon □ **high tech** short for **high-technology**, referring to the use of advanced, *esp* electronic, equipment and devices □ *adj* (**high-tech**) modern and sophisticated □ **high tide** or **high water** the time when the tide is farthest up the shore □ **high treason** the crime of acting against the safety of your own country □ **highway** *noun* the public road □ **Highway Code** a set of official rules for road users in Britain □ **highwayman** *noun* a robber who attacked people on the public road □ **the Highlands** a mountainous region, *esp* the north of Scotland □ **the high seas** the open seas □ **for the high jump** expecting trouble or punishment □ **on your high horse** behaving with exaggerated pride or superiority

**highlight** *noun* **1** a bright spot or area in a picture **2** a lighter patch in hair *etc* made obvious by bright light **3** the most memorable part or experience: *the highlight of the week* □ *verb* to emphasize, make the focus of attention □ **highlighter** *noun* a coloured felt-tip pen used to mark but not obscure lines of text

**hijack** *verb* to steal (a car, aeroplane *etc*) while it is moving, forcing the driver or pilot to take a new route □ *noun* the action of hijacking a vehicle *etc* □ **hijacker** *noun*

**hike** *verb* to travel on foot through countryside □ *noun* a country walk □ **hiker** *noun*

**hilarious** *adj* extremely funny □ **hilariously** *adv* of something funny: extremely □ **hilarity** *noun* great amusement and laughter

**hill** *noun* a mound of high land, less high than a mountain □ **hilly** *adj* covered with hills

**hillock** *noun* a small hill

**hilt** *noun* the handle of a sword □ **up to the hilt** thoroughly, completely

**him** *pronoun* a male person already spoken about (used only as the object in a sentence): *I saw him yesterday/ what did you say to him?* □ **himself** *pronoun* **1** used reflexively: *he cut himself shaving* **2** used for emphasis: *he wrote it himself*

**hind** *noun* a female deer □ *adj* placed behind □ **hindmost** *adj* farthest behind □ **hindsight** *noun* wisdom or knowledge got only after something has happened

**hinder** *verb* to keep back, delay, prevent □ **hindrance** *noun* something that hinders

**hinge** *noun* a joint on which a door, lid *etc* turns □ *verb* **1** to move on a hinge **2** to depend (on): *everything hinges on the weather*

**hint** *noun* **1** a remark which suggests a meaning without stating it clearly: *I'll give you a hint* **2** a slight impression, a suggestion: *a hint of panic in her voice* □ *verb* to suggest without stating clearly: *he hinted that he might be there*

**hinterland** *noun* an area lying inland from the coast

**hip¹** *noun* the part of the side of the body just below the waist □ **hip-flask** *noun* a small pocket flask for alcohol

**hip²** *noun* the fruit of the wild rose

**hip³** *adj* very fashionable, trendy

**hip-hop** *noun* a popular culture movement which started in the US in the early 1980's and is associated with rap music, breakdancing, graffiti and baggy sports clothes

**hippie** *noun* a member of a youth movement rebelling against conventional society, dress codes *etc*

**Hippocratic oath** an oath taken by a doctor agreeing to observe a code of medical ethics

**hippodrome** *noun* **1** an arena for horse-racing **2** a large theatre

**hippopotamus** *noun* (*pl* **hippopotami** or **hippopotamuses**) a large African animal living in and near rivers

Based on a Greek word which translates as 'river horse'

**hire** *noun* money paid for work done, or for the use of something belonging to another person □ *verb* to give or get the use of by paying money □ **hire-purchase** *noun* a way of buying an article by paying for it in instalments

**hirsute** *adj* hairy, shaggy

**his** *adj* belonging to him: *his book* □ *pronoun*: *that jacket is his*

**Hispanic** *adj* **1** Spanish **2** Spanish-American

**hiss** *verb* to make a sound like a snake □ *noun* (*pl* **hisses**) such a sound, made to show anger or displeasure

**histamine** *noun* a chemical present in pollen *etc* which can cause an allergic reaction

**history** *noun* (*pl* **histories**) **1** the study of the past **2** a description of past events, society *etc* □ **historian**

*noun* someone who studies or writes history □ **historic** *adj* important, likely to be remembered □ **historical** *adj* **1** of history **2** true of something in the past

**histrionic** *adj* relating to stage-acting or actors □ **histrionics** *noun pl* an exaggerated show of strong feeling

**hit** *verb* **1** to strike with a blow **2** to occur suddenly to: *it finally hit me* □ *noun* **1** a blow, a stroke **2** a shot which hits a target **3** a success **4** a successful song, recording *etc* **5** *slang* a murder by criminals □ **hit-and-miss** *adj* haphazard, sometimes working and sometimes not □ **hit-and-run** *adj* of a driver: driving away after causing injury without reporting the accident □ **hitman** *noun, slang* someone employed to kill or attack others □ **hit the ceiling** or **hit the roof** to explode with anger □ **hit the ground running** to react immediately and efficiently □ **hit the nail on the head** to identify the important point, be exactly right □ **hit upon** to come upon, discover

**hit** *verb* ➠ **hits, hitting, hit**

**hitch** *verb* **1** to fasten with a hook *etc* **2** to lift with a jerk **3** to hitch-hike □ *noun* (*pl* **hitches**) **1** a jerk **2** an unexpected stop or delay **3** a type of knot

**hitchhike** *verb* to travel by getting lifts in other people's vehicles □ **hitchhiker** *noun*

**hi tech** *another spelling of* **high tech**

**hither** *adv* to this place □ **hitherto** *adv* up till now □ **hither and thither** back and forwards

**HIV** *abbrev* human immuno-deficiency virus □ **HIV-positive** *adj* carrying HIV

**hive** *noun* **1** place where bees live **2** a busy place: *hive of industry*

**HM** *abbrev* Her or His Majesty

**HMS** *abbrev* **1** Her or His Majesty's Service **2** Her or His Majesty's Ship

**hoard** *noun* a hidden store of treasure, food *etc* □ *verb* to store up secretly
- ⊕ From Old English *hord* meaning 'treasure' or 'secret place'

♦ Do not confuse with: **horde**

**hoarding** *noun* a fence of boards

**hoar-frost** *noun* white frost

**hoarse** *adj* having a harsh voice, *eg* from a cold or cough

**hoary** *adj* **1** white with age **2** very old

**hoax** *noun* (*pl* **hoaxes**) a trick played to deceive □ *verb* to play a hoax on

**hob** *noun* **1** the top of a cooker, with rings for heating *etc* **2** a small shelf next to a fireplace for keeping pans *etc* hot

**hobble** *verb* **1** to walk with short unsteady steps **2** to tie the legs of (a horse *etc*) loosely **3** to impede, hamper

**hobby** *noun* (*pl* **hobbies**) a favourite way of passing your spare time
- Originally *hobby-horse*, a horse used in morris dances and therefore for amusement or pleasure

**hobby-horse** *noun* **1** a toy wooden horse **2** a favourite subject of discussion

**hobgoblin** *noun* a mischievous fairy

**hobnail** *noun* a large nail used for horseshoes and in the soles of heavy boots

**hobnob** *verb* to be on friendly terms (with); socialize (with)
- **hobnob** ⇨ hobnob*s*, hobnobb*ing*, hobnobb*ed*

**Hobson's choice** the choice of having something as offered, or nothing at all
- Named after *Hobson*, a Cambridge horsekeeper who reputedly gave customers the choice of the horse nearest the door or none at all

**hock**[1] *noun* a joint on the hind leg of an animal, below the knee

**hock**[2] *noun* a white German wine

**hock**[3] *verb, slang* to pawn □ **in hock** pawned

**hockey** *noun* an eleven-a-side ball-game played with clubs curved at one end

**hoe** *noun* a tool used for weeding, loosening earth *etc* □ *verb* to use a hoe

**hog** *noun* a pig □ *verb, informal* to take or use selfishly □ **hogwash** *noun* nonsense, rubbish
- **hog** ⇨ hog*s*, hog*ging*, hog*ged*

**Hogmanay** *noun* the name in Scotland for 31 December and the celebrations held that night
- From an old French word *aguillanneuf*, a gift given at New Year

**hoi polloi** the masses, the rabble
- Taken from a Greek phrase for 'the people'

**hoist** *verb* to lift, raise □ *noun* a lift, an elevator for goods

**hoity-toity** *adj* haughty, superior

**hold** *verb* **1** to keep in your possession or power; have **2** to contain **3** to occupy (a position *etc*) **4** to think, believe **5** to put on, organize: *hold a meeting* **6** to apply: *that rule doesn't hold any longer* **7** to celebrate: *hold Christmas* □ *noun* **1** grip, grasp **2** influence: *a hold over the others* **3** a large space for carrying a ship's cargo □ **holdall** *noun* a large carrying bag with a zip □ **holder** *noun* **1** container **2** someone who holds (a position *etc*) □ **holding** *noun* an amount of land, shares *etc* held □ **hold-up** *noun* **1** an armed attempt at robbery **2** a delay, or something that causes it □ **hold forth** to speak at length □ **hold good** to be true □ **hold out** to refuse to give in □ **hold over** to keep till later □ **hold up 1** to support **2** to hinder **3** to attack and demand money from
- **hold** *verb* ⇨ hold*s*, hold*ing*, held

**hole** *noun* **1** an opening in something

solid **2** a pit, a burrow **3** a miserable place □ **in a hole** in a difficult situation

**holiday** *noun* **1** a day when businesses *etc* are closed **2** a period away from work for rest

**hollow** *adj* **1** having empty space inside, not solid **2** false, unreal: *hollow victory/ hollow smile* □ *noun* **1** a sunken place **2** a dip in the land □ *verb* to scoop (out)

**holly** *noun* (*pl* **hollies**) an evergreen shrub with scarlet berries and prickly leaves

**hollyhock** *noun* a tall garden plant

**holocaust** *noun* a great destruction (by fire)

**hologram** *noun* a 3-D image created by laser beams

**holograph** *noun* a document written entirely by one person

**holster** *noun* a case for a pistol

**holy** *adj* **1** of or like God **2** religious, righteous **3** for religious use; sacred □ **holiness** *noun* **1** the quality of being holy or sacred **2** (**Your Holiness**) the official form of address used for the leader of a religion *eg* the Pope □ **holy of holies** an inner sanctum □ **holier than thou** superior and smug

**holy** ⮕ holi*er*, holi*est*

**homage** *noun* a show of respect; an acknowledgement of debt: *paying homage to the pioneers of cinema*

**home** *noun* **1** the place where someone lives **2** the house of someone's family **3** a centre or place of origin: *Nashville is the home of country music* **4** a place where children, the elderly *etc* live and are looked after □ *adj* **1** of someone's house or family: *home comforts* **2** domestic, not foreign: *home affairs* □ *adv* **1** towards home **2** to the full length: *drive the nail home* □ **home economics** the study of how to run a home □ **homely** *adj* **1** plain but pleasant **2** *US* plain, not

attractive □ **home-made** *adj* made at home □ **home rule** government of a country *etc* by its own parliament □ **Home Secretary** *Brit* the government minister who deals with domestic issues, *eg* law and order, immigration *etc* □ **homesick** *adj* longing for home □ **homestead** *noun* a farmhouse □ **home truth** a frank statement of something true but unpleasant □ **homewards** *adv* towards home □ **homework** *noun* work for school *etc* done at home □ **homing** *adj* of a pigeon: having the habit of making for home □ **bring home to** to make (someone) realize

**homeopathy** or **homoeopathy** *noun* the treatment of illness by small quantities of substances that produce symptoms similar to those of the illness □ **homeopath** *noun* a practitioner of homeopathy □ **homeopathic** *adj* of or using homeopathy (*contrasted with*: **allopathic**)

**homicide** *noun* **1** the killing of a human being **2** someone who kills a person □ **homicidal** *adj* likely to commit murder

**homily** *noun* **1** a plain, practical sermon **2** a talk giving advice

**homoeopathy** *another spelling of* **homeopathy**

**homogeneous** (*say* hom-oh-**jeen**-i-us) *adj* composed of parts of the same kind (*contrasted with*: **heterogeneous**) □ **homogeneity** *noun*

**homogenize** (*say* ho-**moj**-en-aiz) *verb* to treat (milk) so that the cream does not separate and rise to the surface □ **homogenization** *noun*

**homograph** *noun* a word which has the same spelling as, but a different meaning from, another, *eg keen* meaning 'eager' is a homograph of *keen* meaning 'lament'

**homonym** *noun* a word which has the same sound as, but a different meaning from another, *eg pair* is a homonym of *pear*

**homo sapiens** a human being

**homosexual** *noun* someone who is sexually attracted to the same sex □ *adj* sexually attracted to the same sex □ **homosexuality** *noun*

**hone** *verb* to sharpen (a knife *etc*)

**honest** *adj* truthful; not inclined to steal, cheat *etc* □ **honestly** *adv* **1** truthfully **2** without cheating or stealing *etc* **3** when you are trying to convince someone of something: really **4** an expression of annoyance: *Honestly, I don't know why I bother!* □ **honesty** *noun* the quality of being honest, truthful or trustworthy

**honey** *noun* **1** a sweet, thick fluid made by bees from the nectar of flowers **2** *informal* sweetheart, dear

**honeycomb** *noun* a network of wax cells in which bees store honey □ **honeycombed** *adj* patterned with holes like honey cells

**honeymoon** *noun* a holiday spent immediately after marriage □ *verb* to spend a honeymoon

**honeysuckle** *noun* a climbing shrub with sweet-smelling flowers

**honk** *noun* a noise like the cry of the wild goose or the sound of a motor horn □ *verb* to make this sound

**honorary** *adj* **1** done to give honour **2** without payment

**honour** or *US* **honor** *noun* **1** respect for truth, honesty *etc* **2** fame, glory **3** reputation, good name **4** a title of respect, *esp* to a judge: *Your Honour* **5** a privilege **6** (**honours**) recognition given for exceptional achievements □ *verb* **1** to give respect to **2** to give high rank to **3** to pay money when due: *honour a debt* □ **honourable** *adj* worthy of honour □ **honourably** *adv* □ **do the honours** to perform a ceremonial task

**hood** *noun* **1** a covering for the head **2** a protective cover for anything

**3** *US* the bonnet of a car

**hoodwink** *verb* to deceive

**hoof** *noun* (*pl* **hoofs** or **hooves**) the horny part on the feet of certain animals (*eg* horses) □ **on the hoof** *informal* on the move, while moving

**hook** *noun* **1** a bent piece of metal *etc* for hanging things on **2** a piece of metal on the end of a line for catching fish □ *verb* to hang or catch with a hook □ **hooked** *adj* **1** curved, bent **2** caught by a hook **3** *slang* addicted to, fascinated by □ **by hook or by crook** by one means or another, whatever the cost

**hookah** or **hooka** *noun* a tobacco pipe in which the smoke is drawn through water

**hooligan** *noun* a wild, unruly person □ **hooliganism** *noun* unruly behaviour

**hoop** *noun* a thin ring of wood or metal

**hooray** *another spelling of* **hurrah**

**hoot** *verb* **1** to sound (a siren, car horn *etc*) **2** of an owl: to call, cry **3** to laugh loudly □ *noun* **1** the sound made by a car horn, siren or owl **2** a shout of scorn or disgust **3** *informal* someone or something extremely funny □ **hooter** *noun* **1** a siren or horn which makes a hooting sound **2** *slang* a large nose

**Hoover** *noun*, *trademark* a vacuum cleaner □ **hoover** *verb* to vacuum (a floor *etc*)

**hop¹** *verb* to leap on one leg □ *noun* a short jump on one leg

**hop** *verb* ⬦ hops, hopping, hopped

**hop²** *noun* a climbing plant with bitter-tasting fruits which are used in brewing beer

**hope** *noun* **1** the state of expecting or wishing something good to happen **2** something desired □ *verb* to expect or wish good to happen □ **hopeful** *adj* **1** confident or optimistic about something **2** promising, encouraging □ **hopefully** *adv* **1** with

**hope 2** used when expressing hopes: 'I hope that ...' □ **hopeless** adj **1** without hope **2** very bad □ **hopelessly** adv

**hopper** noun a funnel for shaking down corn to a grinding machine

**hopscotch** noun a hopping game over lines drawn on the ground

**horde** noun a large crowd or group ⓖ From Turkish *ordu* meaning 'camp'

**⚠ Do not confuse with: hoard**

**horizon** noun **1** the imaginary line formed where the earth meets the sky **2** the limit of someone's experience or understanding □ **horizontal** adj lying level or flat □ **horizontally** adv

**hormone** noun a substance produced by certain glands of the body, which acts on a particular organ □ **hormonal** adj

**horn** noun **1** a hard growth on the heads of certain animals, *eg* deer, sheep **2** something curved or sticking out like an animal's horn **3** part of a car which gives a warning sound **4** a brass wind instrument (originally made of horn) □ **horned** adj having horns □ **horny** adj hard like horn

**hornet** noun a kind of large wasp □ **stir up a hornet's nest** to cause a commotion or violent reaction

**hornpipe** noun a lively sailor's dance

**horoscope** noun a prediction of someone's future based on the position of the stars at their birth

**horrendous** adj, *informal* awful, terrible

**horrible** adj **1** very unpleasant **2** very bad, awful □ **horribly** adv

**horrid** adj hateful; very unpleasant

**horrific** adj **1** terrifying **2** awful, very bad □ **horrifically** adv

**horrify** verb to frighten greatly, shock: *we were horrified by his behaviour* □ **horrifying** adj

**horrify** ⚬ horrif*ies*, horrify*ing*, horrif*ied*

**horror** noun **1** great fear, terror **2** something which causes fear **3** an unruly or demanding child

**horse** noun **1** a four-footed animal with hooves and a mane **2** a wooden frame for drying clothes on **3** a piece of gymnastic equipment for vaulting □ **horse-chestnut** noun a tree which produces a shiny, inedible nut (a conker) □ **horsefly** noun a large fly which bites □ **horse laugh** a loud, harsh laugh □ **horseplay** noun rough play, fooling around □ **horsepower** noun a unit of mechanical power for car engines (*short form* hp) □ **horseradish** noun a plant with a sharp-tasting root which is used in sauces □ **horseshoe** noun **1** a shoe for horses, made of a curved piece of iron **2** a horseshoe-shaped thing □ **from the horse's mouth** directly from the source, first-hand □ **horses for courses** people will do best in situations that suit them individually

**horticulture** noun the study and art of gardening □ **horticultural** adj

**hosanna** noun an exclamation of praise to God

**hose** noun **1** (*pl* hose) an old-fashioned word meaning 'a covering for the legs or feet', *eg* stockings **2** (*pl* hoses) a rubber tube for carrying water □ **hosiery** noun stockings, tights *etc*

**hospice** noun a home providing special nursing care for incurable invalids

**hospitable** adj showing kindness to guests or strangers □ **hospitably** adv □ **hospitality** noun the quality of being hospitable, or of being friendly and welcoming to guests and strangers, entertaining them with food or drink, or providing them with accommodation

**hospital** noun a building for the

treatment of the sick and injured

**host¹** *noun* **1** someone who welcomes and entertains guests **2** an innkeeper or hotel-keeper **3** the person on a television or radio show who introduces guests and performers to the audience, or interviews them **4** *medicine* or *zoology* the person or animal on which an insect or other organism is living or feeding as a parasite

**host²** *noun* a very large number

**hostage** *noun* someone held prisoner by an enemy to make sure that an agreement will be kept to

**hostel** *noun* a building providing rooms for students *etc*

**hostess** *noun* **1** a woman who welcomes and entertains guests **2** an air hostess

**hostile** *adj* **1** of an enemy **2** not friendly **3** showing dislike or opposition (to) □ **hostility** *noun* **1** unfriendliness, dislike **2** (*pl* **hostilities**) acts of warfare

**hot** *adj* **1** very warm **2** spicy **3** passionate **4** radioactive **5** *slang* stolen **6** *slang* not safe □ **hot air** meaningless talk □ **hotbed** *noun* a centre or breeding ground for anything: *a hotbed of rebellion* □ **hot-blooded** *adj* passionate, easily angered □ **hotdog** *noun* a hot sausage in a long roll □ **hotfoot** *adv* in great haste □ **hot-headed** *adj* inclined to act rashly without thinking □ **hothouse** *noun* a heated glasshouse for plants □ *verb* to give (a child) intensive schooling at an early age □ **hotline** *noun* a direct telephone line between heads of government □ **hot potato** a touchy subject □ **hot seat** a position of responsibility □ **hot on someone's heels** following them closely □ **hot under the collar** indignant, enraged □ **in hot water** in trouble □ **sell like hot cakes** to sell very quickly

**hot** ↔ **hotter, hottest**

**hotel** *noun* a building with several rooms which people can pay to stay in for a number of nights

**hound** *noun* a dog used in hunting □ *verb* to hunt, pursue

**hour** *noun* **1** sixty minutes, the 24th part of a day **2** a time or occasion: *the hour of reckoning* □ **hour-glass** *noun* an instrument which measures the hours by the running of sand from one glass into another □ **hourly** *adj* happening or done every hour □ *adv* every hour

**house** *noun* **1** a building in which people live **2** a household **3** a business firm **4** a building where school boarders stay □ *verb* to provide a house for; accommodate □ **house arrest** confinement under guard in a private house, hospital *etc* □ **houseboat** *noun* a river barge with a cabin for living in □ **housebreaker** *noun* someone who breaks into a house to steal □ **household** *noun* the people who live together in a house □ **a household name** or **a household word** a person or thing that is well known and often mentioned by people □ **householder** *noun* someone who owns or pays the rent of a house □ **housekeeper** *noun* someone employed to look after the running of a house □ **house-proud** *adj* proud of keeping your house clean and tidy □ **house-trained** *adj* of a pet: trained to go outdoors to pass urine and faeces □ **housewarming** *noun* a party held when someone moves into a new house □ **housewife** *noun* a woman who looks after a house and her family □ **housing** *noun* **1** accommodation, *eg* houses, flats *etc* **2** a casing for a machine *etc* □ **like a house on fire** very successfully, extremely well □ **on the house** free, complimentary

**hovel** *noun* a small squalid dwelling

**hover** *verb* **1** to stay in the air in the

same spot **2** to stay near, linger (about) **3** to be undecided or uncertain

**hovercraft** *noun* a craft able to travel over land or sea supported on a cushion of air

**how** *adv* **1** in what manner: *how are they getting there?* **2** to what extent: *how old are you?/ how cold is it outside?* **3** to a great extent: *how young he seems/ how well you play* **4** by what means: *how do you switch this on?* **5** in what condition: *how is she?* □ **however** *adv* **1** no matter how **2** in spite of that

**howl** *verb* **1** to make a long, loud sound like that of a dog or wolf **2** to yell in pain, anger *etc* **3** to laugh loudly □ *noun* a howling sound □ **howler** *noun, informal* a ridiculous mistake

**HP** or **hp** *abbrev* **1** hire-purchase **2** horsepower

**HQ** *abbrev* headquarters

**hub** *noun* **1** the centre part of a wheel through which the axle passes **2** a thriving centre of anything: *the hub of the entertainment industry*

**hubbub** *noun* a confused sound of many voices

Originally meaning 'battle' or 'war cry', based on an Irish Gaelic word

**huddle** *verb* to crowd together □ *noun* a close group

**hue** *noun* colour, shade

**hue and cry** a commotion, a fuss

**huff** *noun* a fit of bad temper and sulking □ **huffy** *adj* inclined to sulk; peevish

**hug** *verb* **1** to hold tightly with the arms **2** to keep close to: *hugging the kerb* □ *noun* a tight embrace

**hug** *verb* ⇔ hug*s*, hug*ging*, hug*ged*

**huge** *adj* extremely big

**hula-hoop** *noun* a light hoop for spinning round the waist

**hulk** *noun* **1** an old ship unfit for use **2** something big and clumsy

**hulking** *adj* big and clumsy

**hull** *noun* the body or framework of a ship

**hullabaloo** *noun* a noisy disturbance

**hullo** *another spelling of* **hello**

**hum** *verb* **1** to make a buzzing sound like that of bees **2** to sing with the lips shut **3** of a place: to be noisily busy □ *noun* **1** the noise of bees **2** any buzzing, droning sound □ **humming-bird** *noun* a small brightly-coloured bird which beats its wings rapidly making a humming noise

**hum** *verb* ⇔ hum*s*, hum*ming*, hum*med*

**human** *adj* **1** relating to people as opposed to animals or gods **2** having natural qualities, feelings *etc* □ *noun* a man, woman or child □ **humanism** *noun* a set of ideas about or interest in ethics and mankind, not including religious belief □ **humanist** *noun* □ **humanitarian** *adj* kind to fellow human beings □ **humanity** *noun* **1** people in general **2** kindness, gentleness

**humane** *adj* kind, showing mercy, gentle □ **humanely** *adv*

**humble** *adj* **1** modest, meek **2** not of high rank, unimportant □ *verb* to make to feel low and unimportant □ **eat humble pie** to admit a mistake openly

**humbug** *noun* **1** nonsense, rubbish **2** a kind of hard minty sweet

**humdrum** *adj* dull, not exciting

**humdudgeon** *noun, Scottish* an unnecessary fuss

**humid** *adj* of air *etc*: moist, damp □ **humidifier** *noun* a device which controls the amount of humidity in the air □ **humidity** *noun* dampness

**humiliate** *noun* make to feel humble or ashamed, hurt someone's pride □ **humiliating** *adj* □ **humiliation** *noun*

**humility** *noun* humble state of mind, meekness

**humongous** or **humungous** *adj*, *informal* enormous, huge

**humorous** *adj* funny, amusing

**humour** or *US* **humor** *noun* **1** the ability to see things as amusing or ridiculous **2** funniness; the amusing side of anything: *failed to see the humour of the situation* **3** state of mind; temper, mood □ *verb* to do as someone else wishes in order to please them □ **humorist** *noun* a comedian, a comic writer

**hump** *noun* **1** a lump, a mound **2** a lump on the back □ **humpback** *noun* **1** a back with a hump **2** someone with a hump on their back □ **humpbacked** *adj* **1** with a hump on the back **2** of a bridge: rising and falling so as to form a hump shape

**humungous** another spelling of **humongous**

**humus** (*say* **hyoom**-*us*) *noun* soil made of rotted leaves *etc*

**hunch** *noun* (*pl* **hunches**) a suspicion that something is untrue or is going to happen *etc* □ *verb* to draw (your shoulders) up towards your ears and forward towards your chest, giving your body a rounded, stooping appearance □ **hunchback** *noun* humpback □ **hunchbacked** *adj* humpbacked

**hundred** *noun* the number 100 □ *adj* 100 in number □ **hundredth** *adj* the last of a hundred (things *etc*) □ *noun* one of a hundred equal parts □ **hundredweight** *noun* 112 lb, 50.8 kilogrammes (often written **cwt**)

**hunger** *noun* **1** a desire for food **2** a strong desire for anything □ *verb* **1** to go without food **2** to long (for) □ **hunger-strike** *noun* a refusal to eat as a protest

**hungover** *adj* suffering from a hangover

**hungry** *adj* wanting or needing food □ **hungrily** *adv*

**hunk** *noun*, *informal* a muscular, sexually attractive man

**hunker** *verb*: **hunker down** to squat

**hunt** *verb* **1** to chase animals or birds for food or sport **2** to search (for) □ *noun* **1** chasing wild animals **2** a search □ **huntsman**, **huntswoman** *noun* someone who hunts

**hurdle** *noun* **1** a light frame to be jumped over in a race **2** a difficulty which must be overcome

**hurdygurdy** *noun* a barrel organ

**hurl** *verb* to throw with force

**hurlyburly** *noun* a great stir, uproar

**hurrah** or **hurray** *exclam* a shout of joy, approval *etc*

**hurricane** *noun* a violent storm of wind blowing at a speed of over 75 miles (120 kilometres) per hour □ **hurricane lamp** a lamp specially made to keep alight in strong wind

**hurry** *verb* **1** to act or move quickly **2** to make (someone) act quickly □ *noun* eagerness to act quickly, haste □ **hurried** *adj* done in a hurry □ **hurriedly** *adv*

**hurry** *verb* ▷ **hurries**, **hurry**ing, **hurried**

**hurt** *verb* **1** to cause pain or distress to **2** to injure physically, wound **3** to damage, spoil □ *noun* **1** pain, distress **2** damage □ **hurtful** *adj* causing pain, distress or damage

**hurtle** *verb* to rush at great speed

**husband** *noun* a married man (the partner of a **wife**) □ *verb* to spend or use (*eg* money, strength) carefully □ **husbandry** *noun* **1** farming **2** management **3** care with money, thrift

**hush** *exclam* be quiet! □ *noun*, *informal* silence, quiet □ *verb* to make quiet □ **hush-hush** *adj*, *informal* top secret □ **hush up** to stop (a scandal *etc*) becoming public

**husk** *noun* the dry thin covering of certain fruits and seeds

**husky¹** *adj* **1** of a voice: deep and

rough **2** big and strong □ **huskily** *adv* (meaning 1)

**husky²** *noun* (*pl* **huskies**) a Canadian sledge-dog

**hussar** (*say* hu-zahr) *noun* a light-armed horse soldier

**hussy** *noun* (*pl* **hussies**) a forward, cheeky girl

**hustings** *noun pl* political campaigning just before an election

**hustle** *verb* **1** to push rudely **2** to hurry

**hut** *noun* a small wooden building

**hutch** *noun* (*pl* **hutches**) a box in which pet rabbits are housed

**hyacinth** *noun* a sweet-smelling flower which grows from a bulb

**hyaena** *another spelling of* **hyena**

**hybrid** *noun* **1** an animal or plant bred from two different kinds, *eg* a mule, which is a hybrid from a horse and an ass **2** a word formed of parts from different languages

**hydra** *noun* **1** a mythological many-headed snake that grew two heads for each one cut off **2** a sea creature that can divide and redivide itself

**hydrant** *noun* a connection to which a hose can be attached to draw water off the main water supply

**hydraulic** *adj* **1** carrying water **2** worked by water or other fluid

**hydro** *noun* (*pl* **hydros**) a hotel with a swimming pool and gymnasium *etc*

**hydro-** or **hydr-** *prefix* water: *hydroelectricity/ hydraulic*
ⓖ From Greek *hydor* meaning 'water'

**hydroelectricity** *noun* electricity obtained from water-power □ **hydroelectric** *adj*

**hydrogen** *noun* the lightest gas, which with oxygen makes up water □ **hydrogen bomb** an extremely powerful bomb using hydrogen

**hydrophobia** *noun* **1** a fear of water, a symptom of rabies **2** rabies □ **hydrophobic** *adj*

**hyena** or **hyaena** *noun* a dog-like wild animal with a howl sounding like laughter

**hygiene** (*say* hai-jeen) *noun* the maintaining of cleanliness as a means to health □ **hygienic** *adj*

**hymn** *noun* a religious song of praise □ **hymnal** or **hymnary** (*pl* **hymnaries**) *noun* a book of hymns

**hype** (*say* haip) *noun*, *informal* extravagant advertisement or publicity □ *verb* to promote extravagantly

**hyper-** *prefix* to a greater extent than usual, excessive: *hypersensitive*
ⓖ From Greek *hyper* meaning 'over'

**hyperbole** (*say* hai-perb-o-li) *noun* exaggeration □ **hyperbolical** *adj*

**hypermarket** *noun* a large self-service store stocking a wide range of goods

**hypernym** *noun* a general word whose meaning contains several specific words, *eg* dance is a hypernym of *waltz* and *reel* (*contrasted with:* **hyponym**)

**hypertension** *noun* high blood pressure

**hypertext** *noun* electronic text containing cross-references which can be accessed by keystrokes *etc*

**hyphen** *noun* a short stroke (-) used to link or separate parts of a word or phrase: *touch-and-go/ re-elect*

**hypnosis** *noun* **1** a sleep-like state in which suggestions are obeyed **2** hypnotism □ **hypnotic** *adj* **1** of hypnosis or hypnotism **2** causing a sleep-like state □ **hypnotism** *noun* the putting of someone into hypnosis □ **hypnotist** *noun* □ **hypnotize** *verb* to put someone into hypnosis

**hypo-** *prefix* below, under: *hypodermic/ hypothermia*
ⓖ From Greek *hypo* meaning 'under'

**hypoallergenic** *adj* specially formulated in order to reduce the risk of allergy

**hypochondria** *noun* over-anxiety about your own health □ **hypochondriac** *noun* someone who is over-anxious about their health, and who is inclined to think they are ill when they are perfectly healthy □ *adj* relating to or affected with hypochondria

**hypocrite** (*say* **hip**-*o*-krit) *noun* someone who pretends to be something they are not, or to believe something they do not □ **hypocrisy** *noun* □ **hypocritical** *adj*

**hypodermic** *adj* used for injecting drugs just below the skin: *a hypodermic needle* □ *noun* a hypodermic syringe

**hyponym** *noun* one of a group of words whose meanings are included in a more general term, *eg guitar* and *piano* are hyponyms of *musical instrument* (*contrasted with:* **hypernym**)

**hypotenuse** (*say* hai-**pot**-*e*-nyooz) *noun* the longest side of a right-angled triangle

**hypothermia** *noun* an abnormally low body temperature caused by exposure to cold

**hypothesis** (*say* hai-**poth**-*e*-sis) *noun* (*pl* **hypotheses**) something taken as true for the sake of argument □ **hypothetical** *adj* supposed, based on an idea or a possibility rather than on facts

**hysterectomy** *noun* (*pl* **hysterectomies**) surgical removal of the womb

**hysteria** *noun* **1** a nervous excitement causing uncontrollable laughter, crying *etc* **2** a nervous illness □ **hysterical** *adj* **1** suffering from a severe emotional disturbance, often as a result of shock **2** wild with panic, excitement or anger **3** very funny □ **hysterically** *adv* □ **hysterics** *noun pl* a fit of hysteria □ **in hysterics** laughing uncontrollably

Based on a Greek word for 'womb', because originally thought to be caused by womb disease or abnormalities

---

# Ii

**I** *pronoun* the word used by a speaker or writer in mentioning themselves (as the subject of a verb): *you and I/I, myself*

**ibex** *noun* (*pl* **ibexes**) a wild mountain goat

**ibid** *adv* in the same book, article *etc*

**ice** *noun* **1** frozen water **2** ice-cream □ *verb* **1** to cover with icing **2** to freeze □ **icy** *adj* **1** covered with ice **2** very cold **3** unfriendly □ **icily** *adv* □ **ice age** an age when the earth was mostly covered with ice □ **iceberg** *noun* a huge mass of floating ice □ **icebox** *noun*, *US* refrigerator □ **ice-cap** *noun* a permanent covering of ice, as at the north and south poles □ **ice-cream** *noun* a

sweet creamy mixture, flavoured and frozen □ **ice hockey** hockey played with a rubber disc (called a **puck**) on an ice rink □ **ice-skate** *noun* a skate for moving on ice □ **ice-skating** *noun*

**icicle** *noun* a hanging, pointed piece of ice formed by the freezing of dropping water

**icing** *noun* powdered sugar, mixed with water or egg-white, spread on cakes or biscuits □ **icing on the cake** an unnecessary extra detail, added to something which is already satisfactory

**icky** *adj*, *informal* disgusting, repulsive

**icon** *noun* **1** a painted or mosaic

image of Christ or a saint (*also* **ikon**) **2** *computing* a small graphic image which is clicked to access a particular program

**ID** *abbrev* identification ▫ *noun*, *US* a means of identification, *eg* a driving licence

**I'd** *short for* I would, I should or I had: *I'd sooner go than stay*

**id** *noun* the unconscious part of the personality, the source of instincts and dreams

**idea** *noun* **1** a thought, a notion **2** a plan

**ideal** *adj* **1** perfect **2** existing in imagination only (*contrasted with*: **real**) ▫ *noun* the highest and best; a standard of perfection ▫ **ideally** *adv* ▫ **idealism** *noun* the belief that perfection can be reached ▫ **idealist** *noun* someone who thinks that perfection can be reached ▫ **idealistic** *adj* ▫ **idealize** *verb* to think of as perfect ▫ **idealization** *noun*

**identical** *adj* the same in all details ▫ **identically** *adv*

**identify** *verb* to claim to recognize, prove to be the same: *he identified the man as his attacker* ▫ **identification** *noun* **1** an official document, such as a passport or driving licence, that proves who you are **2** the process of finding out who someone is or what something is ▫ **identify with 1** to feel close to or involved with **2** to think of as the same, equate: *identifying money with happiness*

**identify** ⇢ **identifies, identifying, identified**

**Identikit (picture)** *trademark* a rough picture of a wanted person which police put together from descriptions

**identity** *noun* (*pl* **identities**) **1** who or what someone or something is **2** the state of being the same

**ideology** *noun* (*pl* **ideologies**) a set of ideas, often political or philosophical ▫ **ideological** *adj* **1** of or relating to an ideology **2** resulting from a clash between different ideologies

**idiocy** (from **idiot**) *noun* feeble-mindedness, foolishness

**idiom** *noun* a common expression whose meaning cannot be guessed from the individual words, *eg* 'I'm feeling *under the weather*' ▫ **idiomatic** *adj* ▫ **idiomatically** *adv*

**idiosyncrasy** *noun* (*pl* **idiosyncrasies**) a personal oddness of behaviour ▫ **idiosyncratic** *adj*

**idiot** *noun* a feeble-minded person; a fool ▫ **idiotic** *adj* extremely foolish, ridiculous ▫ **idiotically** *adv*

**idle** *adj* **1** not working **2** lazy **3** meaningless, without a useful purpose: *idle chatter* ▫ *verb* **1** to spend time in doing nothing **2** of an engine: to run without doing any work ▫ **idler** *noun* ▫ **idly** *adv* (adj, meanings 2 and 3)

**idol** *noun* **1** an image worshipped as a god **2** someone much loved or honoured ▫ **idolize** *verb* to adore, worship

**idolatry** *noun* **1** the worship of an image as if it were a god **2** the excessive loving or honouring of someone or something ▫ **idolatrous** *adj*

**idyll** *noun* **1** a poem on a pastoral theme **2** a time of pleasure and contentment ▫ **idyllic** *adj* very happy and content, blissful

**ie** *abbrev* that is, that means

ⓘ From Latin *id est*

**if** *conj* **1** on condition that, supposing that: *If you go, I'll go* **2** whether: *do you know if she'll be there?*

**iffy** *adj*, *informal* dubious, uncertain

**ig-** *see* **in-**

**igloo** *noun* an Inuit snow hut

**igneous** *adj* **1** relating to fire **2** of rock: formed by the action of great heat within the earth

**ignite** *verb* **1** to set on fire **2** to catch fire □ **ignition** *noun* **1** the act of setting on fire or catching fire **2** the sparking part of a motor engine

**ignoble** *adj* dishonourable; of low birth

**ignominy** (*say* ig-nom-in-i) *noun* disgrace, dishonour □ **ignominious** *adj*

**ignoramus** (*say* ig-no-**rei**-mus) *noun* an ignorant person

**ignorant** *adj* knowing very little □ **ignorance** *noun* □ **ignorant of** unaware of

**ignore** *verb* to take no notice of

**iguana** (*say* ig-**wah**-na) *noun* a type of tree lizard

**ikon** *another spelling of* **icon**

**il-** *see* **in-**

**I'll** *short for* I shall, I will

**ill** *adj* **1** unwell, sick **2** evil, bad **3** unlucky □ *adv* badly □ *noun* **1** evil **2** (ills) misfortunes, troubles □ **illness** *noun* disease, sickness □ **ill-at-ease** *adj* uncomfortable □ **ill-feeling** *noun* dislike, resentment □ **ill-gotten** *adj* got in a dishonest or unethical way □ **ill-humoured** *adj* bad-tempered □ **ill-natured** *adj* bad-tempered □ **ill-treat** *verb* to treat badly □ **ill-use** *verb* to treat badly □ **ill-will** *noun* dislike, resentment

**illegal** *adj* against the law □ **illegality** *noun* (*pl* illegalities)

**illegible** *adj* impossible to read, indistinct □ **illegibility** *noun* □ **illegibly** *adv*

**illegitimate** *adj* born of parents not married to each other

**illicit** *adj* unlawful, forbidden ⓘ From Latin *il-* meaning 'not', and *licitus* meaning 'allowed'

⚠ Do not confuse with: **elicit**

**illiterate** *adj* not able to read or write □ **illiteracy** *noun*

**illogical** *adj* not logical, not showing sound reasoning □ **illogicality** *noun*

□ **illogically** *adv*

**illuminate** *verb* **1** to light up **2** to make more clear □ **illuminated** *adj* of a manuscript: decorated with ornamental lettering □ **illuminations** *noun pl* a decorative display of lights

**illusion** *noun* **1** something which deceives the mind or eye **2** a mistaken belief

⚠ Do not confuse with: **allusion** and **delusion**

**illusive** *adj* misleading, deceptive

⚠ Do not confuse with: **allusive** and **elusive**. Illusive is related to the noun illusion.

**illusory** *adj* mistaken or untrue, despite seeming believable

**illustrate** *verb* **1** to draw pictures for (a book *etc*) **2** to explain, show by example □ **illustration** *noun* **1** a picture in a book *etc* **2** an example which illustrates □ **illustrative** *adj* □ **illustrator** *noun* someone who illustrates books *etc*

**illustrious** *adj* famous, distinguished

**I'm** *short for* I am

**im-** *see* **in-**

**image** *noun* **1** a likeness made of someone or something **2** a striking likeness: *she is the image of her mother* **3** a picture in the mind **4** public reputation □ **imagery** *noun* words that suggest images, used to make a piece of writing more vivid

**imaginary** *adj* existing only in the imagination, not real

⚠ Do not confuse with: **imaginative**

**imagination** *noun* the power of forming pictures in the mind of things not present or experienced

**imaginative** *adj* **1** having a lively imagination **2** done with imagination: *an imaginative piece of writing*

⚠ Do not confuse with: **imaginary**

**imagine** *verb* **1** to form a picture in

the mind, *esp* of something that does not exist **2** to think, suppose

**imam** *noun* **1** the priest who leads the prayers in a mosque **2** (**Imam**) an Islamic leader

**imbecile** *noun* a feeble-minded person; a fool □ **imbecility** *noun*

**imbibe** *verb* to drink (in)

**imbue** *verb* to fill or affect (with): *imbued her staff with enthusiasm*

**imitate** *verb* to try to be the same as, copy □ **imitation** *noun* a copy □ *adj* made to look like: *imitation leather* □ **imitator** *noun* someone who copies, or tries to do the same things as, someone else

**immaculate** *adj* spotless; very clean and neat □ **immaculately** *adv*

**immaterial** *adj* of little importance

**immature** *adj* not mature □ **immaturity** *noun*

**immediate** *adj* **1** happening straight away: *immediate reaction* **2** close: *immediate family* **3** direct: *my immediate successor* □ **immediacy** *noun* of paintings, photographs, writing *etc*: a striking quality, giving the observer a strong sense of involvement □ **immediately** *adv* without delay

**immemorial** *adj* going further back in time than can be remembered

**immense** *adj* very large □ **immensely** *adv* greatly □ **immensity** *noun*

**immerse** *verb* to plunge something into liquid so that it is completely covered □ **immersion** *noun* **1** the plunging of something into liquid so that it is completely covered **2** deep involvement in a certain subject or situation □ **immersion heater** an electric water-heater inside a hot-water tank □ **immerse yourself in** to give your whole attention to

**immigrate** *verb* to come into a country and settle there □ **immigrant** *noun* someone who immigrates □ **immigration** *noun* ⓔ From Latin *in* meaning 'into', and

*migrare* meaning 'to remove'

❧ Do not confuse with: **emigrate**. You IMmigrate to a new country where you plan to start living (the IM comes from the Latin meaning 'into'). You are Emigrating when you leave your original or home country (the E comes from the Latin meaning 'from').

**imminent** *adj* about to happen: *imminent danger*

❧ Do not confuse with: **eminent**

**immobile** *adj* **1** without moving **2** not easily moved □ **immobility** *noun* □ **immobilize** *verb* to put out of action

**immoral** *adj* **1** wrong, unscrupulous **2** sexually improper □ **immorally** *adv* □ **immorality** *noun*

❧ Do not confuse with: **amoral** An **immoral** person behaves badly in the full knowledge that what they are doing is wrong. An **amoral** person behaves badly because they do not understand the difference between right and wrong.

**immortal** *adj* **1** living forever **2** famous forever □ **immortality** *noun* unending life or fame □ **immortalize** *verb* to make immortal or famous forever

**immovable** *adj* not able to be moved or changed □ **immovably** *adv*

**immune** *adj* **1** not likely to catch a particular disease: *immune to measles* **2** not affected by: *she is immune to his charm* □ **immunity** *noun* □ **immunize** *verb* to make someone immune to (a disease), *esp* by inoculation □ **immune system** the natural defensive system of an organism that identifies and neutralizes harmful matter within itself

**imp** *noun* **1** a small malignant spirit **2** a mischievous child □ **impish** *adj*

**impact** *noun* (*say* im-pakt) **1** the

blow of one thing striking another; a collision **2** strong effect: *made an impact on the audience* □ *verb* (say im-**pakt**) to press firmly together □ **impact on** to affect strongly

**impair** *verb* to damage, weaken □ **impairment** *noun*

**impala** *noun* a large African antelope

**impale** *verb* to pierce through with a spear *etc*

**impart** *verb* to tell (information, news *etc*) to others

**impartial** *adj* not favouring one side over another; unbiased □ **impartiality** *noun* □ **impartially** *adv*

**impassable** *adj* of a road: not able to be driven through

**impasse** (say am-**pas**) *noun* a situation from which there seems to be no way out

**impassioned** *adj* moved by strong feeling

**impassive** *adj* not easily moved by strong feeling □ **impassively** *adv*

**impatient** *adj* **1** restlessly eager **2** irritable, short-tempered □ **impatience** *noun* □ **impatiently** *adv*

**impeach** *verb* to accuse publicly of, or charge with, misconduct □ **impeachment** *noun*

**impeccable** *adj* faultless, perfect □ **impeccably** *adv*

**impede** *verb* to hinder, keep back □ **impediment** *noun* **1** a hindrance **2** a speech defect, *eg* a stutter or stammer

**impel** *verb* **1** to urge **2** to drive on □ impel ⟶ impels, impelling, impelled

**impending** *adj* about to happen: *an impending storm*

**impenetrable** *adj* **1** not allowing light *etc* through **2** incomprehensible, inscrutable

**impenitent** *adj* not sorry for wrongdoing, unrepentant

**imperative** *adj* **1** necessary, urgent **2** *grammar* expressing command, *eg read this*

**imperceptible** *adj* so small as not to be noticed

**imperfect** *adj* having a fault or flaw, not perfect □ *noun, grammar* **the imperfect** the tense used to describe continuing or incomplete actions or states in the past: *The sun was shining and the birds were singing* □ **imperfection** *noun* a fault or a flaw □ **imperfectly** *adv* not perfectly or thoroughly

**imperial** *adj* **1** of an emperor or empire **2** commanding, superior □ **imperialism** *noun* the policy of annexing the territory of, and ruling, other nations and people □ **imperialist** *adj* □ **imperious** *adj* having an air of authority, haughty

**impermanence** *noun* lack of permanence, transitoriness □ **impermanent** *adj*

**impermeable** *adj* not able to be passed through: *impermeable by water*

**impersonal** *adj* **1** not influenced by personal feelings **2** not connected with any person □ **impersonally** *adv*

**impersonate** *verb* to dress up as, or act the part of, someone □ **impersonation** *noun* □ **impersonator** *noun*

**impertinent** *adj* **1** cheeky, impudent **2** *old* not pertinent, irrelevant □ **impertinence** *noun* (meaning 1) □ **impertinently** *adv* (meaning 1)

**imperturbable** *adj* not easily worried, calm □ **imperturbably** *adv*

**impervious to** not able to be affected by: *impervious to suggestions*

**impetuous** *adj* rushing into action, rash □ **impetuosity** *noun*

**impetus** (say **im**-pet-*u*s) *noun* **1** moving force, motivation **2** impulse

**impiety** *noun* lack of respect for holy things

**impinge** verb: **impinge on** or **impinge upon** 1 to come in contact with 2 to trespass on, interfere with

**impious** (from impiety, say im-pi-us) adj lacking the proper respect, esp for holy things

**implacable** adj not able to be soothed or calmed □ **implacably** adv

**implant** verb (say im-**plant**) to fix in, plant firmly □ noun (say **im**-plant) an artificial organ, graft etc inserted into the body

**implement** noun a tool □ verb to carry out, fulfil (eg a promise) □ **implementation** noun

**implicate** verb to bring in, involve: the statement implicates you in the crime □ **implication** noun something meant though not actually said

**implicit** adj 1 understood, meant though not actually said 2 unquestioning: implicit obedience □ **implicitly** adv without questioning or doubting

**implode** verb to collapse inwards suddenly □ **implosion** noun

**implore** verb to beg, entreat

**imply** verb to suggest: her silence implies disapproval

○ Do not confuse with: **infer**. **Implying** is an action of expression - you **imply** something by dropping subtle hints about it. **Inferring** is an action of understanding - you **infer** something by drawing conclusions from what you have seen or heard.

**impolite** adj not polite, rude

**imponderable** adj not able to be judged or evaluated

**import** verb (say im-**poht** or **im**-poht) to bring in (goods) from abroad for sale □ noun (say **im**-poht) 1 the act of importing 2 goods imported 3 meaning, significance □ **importation** noun

**important** adj worthy of attention;

special □ **importance** noun □ **importantly** adv

**impose** verb 1 to place (a tax etc) on 2 **impose on** to take advantage of, inconvenience □ **imposing** adj impressive, commanding attention □ **imposition** noun a burden, an inconvenience

**impossible** adj 1 not able to be done or to happen 2 extremely difficult to deal with, intolerable □ **impossibility** noun (meaning 1) □ **impossibly** adv

**impostor** noun someone who pretends to be someone else in order to deceive □ **imposture** noun

**impotent** (say im-pot-ent) adj without power or effectiveness □ **impotence** noun □ **impotently** adv

**impound** verb to seize possession of (something) by law

**impoverish** verb 1 to make financially poor 2 to lessen in quality: an impoverished culture □ **impoverishment** noun

**impracticable** adj not able to be done □ **impracticability** noun

○ Do not confuse: **impracticable** and **impractical**

**impractical** adj lacking common sense □ **impracticality** noun

**imprecise** adj not precise, vague

**impregnable** adj too strong to be taken by attack

**impregnate** verb 1 to make pregnant 2 to saturate: impregnated with perfume

**impresario** noun (pl **impresarios**) the organizer of an entertainment

**impress** verb 1 to arouse the interest or admiration of 2 to mark by pressing upon 3 to fix deeply in the mind □ **impressive** adj having a strong effect on the mind

**impression** noun 1 someone's thoughts or feelings about something: my impression is that it's likely to rain 2 a deep or strong effect: *the film left a lasting impression on me* **3** a mark made by impressing **4** a quantity of copies of a book printed at one time □ **impressionable** *adj* easily influenced or affected □ **impressionism** *noun* an artistic or literary style aiming to reproduce personal impressions of things or events □ **impressionist** *noun* **1** a follower of impressionism **2** an entertainer who impersonates people

**imprint** *verb* (*say* im-**print**) **1** to stamp, press **2** to fix in the mind □ *noun* (*say* **im**-print) **1** the printer's or publisher's name *etc* on a book **2** a common title for a series of related books from one publisher

**imprison** *verb* to shut up as in a prison □ **imprisonment** *noun*

**improbable** *adj* not likely to happen □ **improbability** *noun*

**impromptu** *adj & adv* without preparation or rehearsal

**improper** *adj* **1** not suitable; wrong **2** indecent □ **improper fraction** a fraction greater than 1 (as $\frac{5}{4}\frac{11}{8}$) □ **impropriety** *noun* (*pl* **improprieties**) something improper

**improve** *verb* to make or become better □ **improvement** *noun*

■ ameliorate, enhance, recuperate

**improvident** *adj* giving no thought to future needs □ **improvidence** *noun*

**improvise** *verb* **1** to put together from available materials: *we improvised a stretcher* **2** to create (a tune, script *etc*) spontaneously □ **improvisation** *noun*

**impudent** *adj* cheeky, insolent □ **impudence** *noun* □ **impudently** *adv*

**impulse** *noun* **1** a sudden force or push **2** a sudden urge resulting in sudden action □ **impulsive** *adj* acting on impulse, without taking time to consider □ **impulsively** *adv*

**impunity** *noun* freedom from punishment, injury or loss

**impure** *adj* mixed with other substances; not clean □ **impurity** *noun* (*pl* **impurities**) **1** a small amount of something which is present in, and spoils the quality of, another substance **2** the state of being impure

**impute** *verb* to think of as being caused, done *etc* by someone: *imputing the blame to others* □ **imputation** *noun* suggestion of fault; blame

**in** *prep* **1** showing position in space or time: *sitting in the garden/ born in the 60s* **2** showing state, manner *etc*: *in cold blood* □ *adv* **1** towards the inside, not out **2** in power **3** *informal* in fashion □ *adj* **1** that is in, inside or coming in **2** *informal* fashionable □ **be in for 1** to be trying to get (a prize *etc*) **2** to be about to receive (trouble, punishment)

**in-** *prefix* **1** (also **il-, im-, ir-, em-, en-**) into, on, towards: *inshore/ illusion/ impulse/ embrace* (= to take in the arms)/ *endure* **2** (also **ig-, il-, im-, ir-**) not: *inaccurate/ ignoble* (= not noble)/ *illiterate/ improper/ irregular* (= not regular)

**inability** *noun* (*pl* **inabilities**) lack of power, means *etc* (to do something)

**inaccessible** *adj* not able to be easily reached or obtained

**inaccurate** *adj* **1** not correct **2** not exact □ **inaccuracy** *noun* (*pl* **inaccuracies**)

**inaction** *noun* lack of action □ **inactive** *adj* **1** not active **2** not working, doing nothing □ **inactivity** *noun*

**inadequate** *adj* **1** not enough **2** unable to cope with a situation

**inadvertent** *adj* unintentional

**inadvisable** *adj* not advisable, unwise

**inalienable** *adj* not able to be

removed or transferred: *inalienable rights*

**inane** *adj* silly, foolish, mindless □ **inanity** *noun* (*pl* **inanities**) **1** an empty, meaningless remark **2** silliness, foolishness, mindlessness

**inanimate** *adj* without life

**inappropriate** *adj* not suitable

**inarticulate** *adj* **1** unable to express yourself clearly **2** said indistinctly

**inasmuch as** *conj* because, since

**inattentive** *adj* not paying attention □ **inattention** *noun*

**inaudible** *adj* not loud enough to be heard

**inaugurate** *verb* to mark the beginning of (*eg* a presidency) with a ceremony □ **inaugural** *adj* relating to, or performed at, an inauguration □ **inauguration** *noun* the ceremony to mark the beginning of something (*eg* a presidency)

**inauspicious** *adj* unlucky, unlikely to end in success

**inborn** *adj* innate, natural: *inborn talent*

**inbreeding** *noun* repeated mating and producing of offspring within the same family □ **inbred** *adj* **1** inborn **2** resulting from inbreeding

**inc** *abbrev* **1** incorporated **2** inclusive **3** including

**Inca** *noun* a member of a complex pre-Columbian civilization in Peru □ **Incan** *adj*

**incalculable** *adj* not able to be counted or estimated

**incandescent** *adj* white-hot

**incantation** *noun* a spell

**incapable** *adj* **1** unable (to do what is expected) **2** helpless (through drink *etc*)

**incapacitate** *verb* **1** to take away power, strength or rights **2** to disable □ **incapacity** *noun* **1** inability **2** disability

**incarcerate** *verb* to imprison □ **incarceration** *noun*

**incarnation** *noun* **1** a person whose appearance or behaviour are the perfect example of a particular quality *eg* beauty or honour **2** of a spirit: appearance in a physical form □ **incarnate** *adj* having human form

**incendiary** *adj* meant for setting (buildings *etc*) on fire: *an incendiary bomb*

**incense** *verb* (*say* in-sens) to make angry □ *noun* (*say* **in**-sens) a mixture of resins, gums *etc* burned to give off fumes, *esp* in religious ceremonies

**incentive** *noun* something which encourages someone to do something

**inception** *noun* beginning

**incessant** *adj* going on without pause

**incest** *noun* illegal sexual intercourse between close relatives

**incestuous** *adj* **1** involving incest **2** done within a closely-knit group

**inch** *noun* (*pl* **inches**) one twelfth of a foot (about 2.5 centimetres) □ *verb* to move very gradually

**incidence** *noun* **1** the frequency of something occurring **2** a falling of a ray of light *etc*

**incident** *noun* a happening □ **incidental** *adj* **1** happening in connection with something: *an incidental expense* **2** casual □ **incidentally** *adv* by the way

**incinerate** *verb* to burn to ashes □ **incineration** *noun* □ **incinerator** *noun* an apparatus for burning rubbish *etc*

**incipient** *adj* beginning to exist: *an incipient dislike*

**incise** *verb* to cut into, engrave □ **incision** *noun* **1** cutting into something **2** a cut, a gash □ **incisive** *adj* sharp, clear, firm

**incisor** *noun* a front tooth

**incite** *verb* to move to action; urge on □ **incitement** *noun*

**incivility** *noun* (*pl* **incivilities**) impoliteness

**inclement** *adj* of weather: stormy □ **inclemency** *noun*

**incline** *verb* (*say* in-**klain**) **1** to lean, slope (towards) **2** to bend, bow **3** to have a liking for □ *noun* (*say* in-klain) a slope □ **inclination** *noun* **1** liking, tendency **2** a slope, an angle □ **inclined** *adj* **1** talented or gifted **2 inclined to** having a tendency, or a hesitant desire to

**include** *verb* to count in, along with others □ **inclusion** *noun* □ **inclusive** *adj* including everything mentioned: *from Tuesday to Thursday inclusive is 3 days*

**incognito** (*say* in-cog-**neet**-oh) *adj* & *adv* in disguise, with identity concealed □ *noun* (*pl* **incognitos**) a disguise

**incoherent** *adj* **1** unconnected, rambling **2** speaking in an unconnected, rambling way □ **incoherence** *noun*

**incombustible** *adj* not able to be burned by fire

**income** *noun* **1** personal earnings **2** gain, profit

**incoming** *adj* approaching, next

**incomparable** *adj* without equal

**incompatible** *adj* **1** of statements: contradicting each other **2** of people: not suited, bound to disagree □ **incompatibility** *noun*

**incompetent** *adj* not good enough at doing a job □ **incompetence** *noun*

▨ **able**

**incomplete** *adj* not finished

**incomprehensible** *adj* not able to be understood, puzzling □ **incomprehension** *noun*

**inconceivable** *adj* not able to be imagined or believed

**inconclusive** *adj* not leading to a definite decision or conclusion

**incongruous** *adj* **1** not matching well **2** out of place, unsuitable □ **incongruity** (*pl* **incongruities**)

**inconsequential** *adj* unimportant □ **inconsequence** *noun*

**inconsiderable** *adj* slight, unimportant □ **inconsiderate** *adj* not thinking of others

**inconsistent** *adj* not consistent, contradicting

**inconsolable** *adj* not able to be comforted

**inconspicuous** *adj* not noticeable

**inconstant** *adj* often changing □ **inconstancy** *noun*

**incontinent** *adj* **1** unable to control the bladder or bowels **2** uncontrolled, unrestrained □ **incontinence** *noun*

**incontrovertible** *adj* not to be doubted

**inconvenient** *adj* causing awkwardness or difficulty □ **inconvenience** *noun* minor trouble or difficulty

**incorporate** *verb* **1** to contain as parts of a whole: *the new centre incorporates a theatre and restaurant* **2** to include, take account of: *the new text incorporates the author's changes*

**incorporated** *adj* (*short form* **inc**) formed into a company or society

**incorrect** *adj* wrong

**incorrigible** *adj* too bad to be put right or reformed

**incorruptible** *adj* **1** not able to be bribed **2** not likely to decay

**increase** *verb* (*say* in-**krees**) to grow, make greater or more numerous □ *noun* (*say* in-krees) **1** growth **2** the amount added by growth □ **increasingly** *adv* more and more

**incredible** *adj* impossible to believe □ **incredibility** *noun* □ **incredibly** *adv* extremely, unbelievably ⊚ From Latin *incredibilis* meaning 'beyond belief'

❧ Do not confuse: **incredible** and **incredulous**. IncredIBLE means unbelievABLE. IncredULOUS means unbelievING. You might, for example, be **incredulous** at (= unable to believe) another person's **incredible** (= unbelievable) stupidity.

**incredulous** (*say* in-kred-*yul*-*us*) *adj* not believing what is said □ **incredulity** (*say* in-kred-*yool*-it-i) *noun* disbelief □ **incredulously** *adv* ⊕ From Latin *incredulus* meaning 'unbelieving'

**increment** *noun* an annual increase in a salary

**incriminate** *verb* to show that (someone) has taken part in a crime

**incubate** *verb* to brood, hatch □ **incubator** *noun* **1** a large heated box for hatching eggs **2** a hospital crib for rearing premature babies □ **incubation period** the time that it takes for a disease to develop from infection to the first symptoms

**incumbent** *adj* resting on (someone) as a duty: *it is incumbent upon me to warn you* □ *noun* someone who holds an official position

**incur** *verb* to bring (blame, debt *etc*) upon yourself

**incur** ⊷ incurs, incurring, incurred

**incurable** *adj* unable to be cured

**incurious** *adj* not curious, uninterested

**incursion** *noun* an invasion, a raid

**indebted** *adj* having cause to be grateful: *we are indebted to you for your kindness*

**indecent** *adj* offending against normal or usual standards of (*esp* sexual) behaviour □ **indecency** *noun* □ **indecent assault** an assault involving indecency but not rape

**indecipherable** *adj* **1** illegible **2** incomprehensible

**indecision** *noun* slowness in making

up your mind, hesitation □ **indecisive** *adj* **1** not coming to a definite result **2** unable to make up your mind

**indecorous** *adj* unseemly, inappropriate □ **indecorum** *noun*

**indeed** *adv* **1** in fact **2** (used for emphasis) really: *did he indeed?* □ *exclam* expressing surprise

**indefatigable** *adj* untiring

**indefensible** *adj* **1** unable to be defended **2** inexcusable

**indefinable** *adj* not able to be stated or described clearly

**indefinite** *adj* **1** not fixed, uncertain **2** without definite limits □ **indefinitely** *adv* for an indefinite period of time □ **indefinite article** the name given to the adjs *a* and *an*

**indelible** *adj* unable to be rubbed out or removed

**indelicate** *adj* impolite, rude □ **indelicacy** *noun*

**indemnify** *verb* **1** to compensate for loss **2** to exempt (from)

**indemnify** ⊷ indemnifies, indemnifying, indemnified

**indemnity** *noun* **1** security from damage or loss **2** compensation for loss

**indent** *verb* **1** to begin a new paragraph by going in from the margin **2 indent for** to apply for (stores, equipment *etc*) □ **indentation** *noun* **1** a hollow, a dent **2** an inward curve in an outline, coastline *etc*

**indenture** *noun* a written agreement □ *verb* to bind by a written agreement

**independent** *adj* **1** free to think or act for yourself **2** not relying on someone else for support, guidance *etc* **3** of a country: self-governing □ **independence** *noun*

**indescribable** *adj* not able to be described

**indestructible** *adj* not able to be

destroyed

**indetectable** *adj* not able to be detected

**indeterminate** *adj* not fixed, indefinite

**index** *noun* (*pl* **indexes**) **1** an alphabetical list giving the page number of subjects mentioned in a book **2** an indication **3** (*pl* **indices**) *maths* an upper number which shows how many times a number is multiplied by itself (*eg* $4^3$ means 4 x 4 x 4) **4** a numerical scale showing changes in the cost of living, wages *etc*

**Indian ink** a very black ink used by artists

**Indian summer** a period of summer warmth in autumn

**indiarubber** *noun* a rubber eraser

**indicate** *verb* to point out, show □ **indication** *noun* a sign □ **indicative** *adj* pointing out, being a sign of □ **indicator** *noun* **1** something which indicates; a pointer **2** a flashing light on either side of a vehicle for signalling to other drivers

**indices** *pl* of **index** (meaning 3)

**indict** (*say* in-dait) *verb* to accuse formally of a crime □ **indictment** (*say* in-dait-ment) *noun* something which shows or proves how bad something else is

**indie** (*say* in-di) *noun, informal* an independent record, film or television company □ *adj* of a band: using an independent company to record their music

**indifferent** *adj* **1** neither very good nor very bad **2** **indifferent to** showing no interest in □ **indifference** *noun* (meaning 2)

**indigenous** *adj* native to a country or area

**indigent** *adj* poor, impoverished □ **indigence** *noun*

**indigestion** *noun* discomfort or pain

experienced in digesting food □ **indigestible** *adj* difficult to digest

**indignant** *adj* angry, *esp* because of wrong done to yourself or others □ **indignation** *noun*

**indignity** *noun* (*pl* **indignities**) **1** loss of dignity **2** insult

**indigo** *noun* a purplish-blue colour □ *adj* purplish-blue

**indirect** *adj* **1** not straight or direct **2** not affecting or affected directly □ **indirect speech** speech reported not in the speaker's actual words, *eg they said that they'd leave the next day* (rather than: *they said, 'We'll leave tomorrow.'*) (*contrasted with*: **direct speech**) □ **indirect tax** a tax on particular goods, paid by the customer in the form of a higher price

**indiscreet** *adj* **1** rash, not cautious **2** giving away too much information □ **indiscretion** *noun* a rash or unwise remark or act, rash or unwise behaviour

**indiscriminate** *adj* making no distinction between one person (or thing) and another

**indispensable** *adj* not able to be done without, necessary

**indisposed** *adj* unwell □ **indisposition** *noun*

**indisputable** *adj* not able to be denied

**indistinct** *adj* not clear

**indistinguishable** *adj* **1** difficult to make out **2** too alike to tell apart

**individual** *adj* **1** relating to a single person or thing **2** distinctive, unusual □ *noun* a single person or thing □ **individuality** *noun* **1** separate existence **2** the quality of standing out from others

**indivisible** *adj* not able to be divided

**indoctrinate** *verb* to fill with a certain teaching or set of ideas

**indolent** *adj* lazy □ **indolence** *noun*

**indomitable** *adj* unconquerable,

unyielding

**indoor** adj done etc inside a building □ **indoors** adv in or into a building etc

**indubitable** adj not to be doubted

**induce** verb **1** to persuade **2** to bring on, cause □ **inducement** noun something which encourages or persuades

**induct** verb to introduce, install □ **induction** noun **1** the formal installation of someone in a new post **2** the production of electricity in something by placing it near an electric source **3** the drawing of conclusions from particular cases □ **inductive** adj (meaning 3)

**indulge** verb **1** to be inclined to give into the wishes of; spoil **2** to give way to, not restrain: indulging his sweet tooth □ **indulgence** noun **1** the act of indulging **2** a pardon for a sin □ **indulgent** adj not strict, kind

**industrious** adj hard-working

**industry** noun (pl **industries**) **1** a branch of trade or manufacture: the clothing industry **2** steady attention to work □ **industrial** adj **1** related to or used in trade or manufacture **2** of a country: having highly developed industry □ **industrialist** noun someone involved in organizing an industry

**inebriated** adj drunk

**inedible** adj not eatable

**ineffective** adj useless, having no effect

**ineffectual** adj achieving nothing

**inefficient** adj **1** not efficient, not capable **2** wasting time, energy etc □ **inefficiency** noun (pl **inefficiencies**)

**inelegant** adj not graceful □ **inelegance** noun

**ineligible** adj not qualified, not suitable to be chosen

**inept** adj clumsy, badly done □ **ineptitude** noun

⊚ From Latin ineptus meaning 'useless'

**inequality** noun (pl **inequalities**) **1** lack of equality, unfairness **2** unevenness

**inert** adj **1** not moving or able to move **2** disinclined to move or act **3** not lively **4** chemically inactive □ **inertia** noun

**inescapable** adj unable to be avoided

**inessential** adj not essential, unnecessary

**inestimable** adj too great to be estimated

**inevitable** adj not able to be avoided □ **inevitability** noun

**inexact** adj not exact, approximate

**inexcusable** adj not to be excused

**inexhaustible** adj very plentiful; not likely to be used up

**inexorable** adj not able to be persuaded; relentless

**inexpensive** adj cheap in price

**inexperience** noun lack of (skilled) knowledge or experience □ **inexperienced** adj

**inexpert** adj unskilled, amateurish

**inexplicable** adj not able to be explained

**inexplicit** adj not clear

**inexpressible** adj not able to be described in words

**inextricable** adj not able to be disentangled

**infallible** adj **1** never making an error **2** certain to produce the desired result: infallible cure □ **infallibility** noun

**infamous** adj having a very bad reputation; notorious, disgraceful □ **infamy** noun

**infant** noun a baby □ **infancy** noun **1** early childhood, babyhood **2** the beginning of anything: when psychiatry was in its infancy □ **infantile** adj **1** of babies **2** childish

**infantry** *noun* foot-soldiers

**infatuated** *adj* filled with foolish love □ **infatuation** *noun*

**infect** *verb* **1** to fill with disease-causing germs **2** to pass on disease to **3** to pass on, spread (*eg* enthusiasm) □ **infection** *noun* **1** a disease which can be spread to others **2** something that spreads widely and affects many people □ **infectious** *adj* likely to spread from person to person

**infelicitous** *adj* unfortunate, inappropriate: *an infelicitous remark*

**infer** *verb* to reach a conclusion from facts or reasoning: *Am I to infer from what you say that you wish to resign?* □ **inference** *noun* a conclusion that you reach, based on information which you have been given

**infer** ⟶ infers, inferr*ing*, inferr*ed*

ⓘ From Latin *inferre* meaning 'to bring in'

⚠ Infer is sometimes used to mean 'imply' or 'suggest': *Are you inferring that I'm a liar?*, but this use is considered incorrect by some people.

**inferior** *adj* **1** lower in any way **2** not of best quality □ *noun* someone lower in rank *etc* □ **inferiority** *noun* □ **inferiority complex** a constant feeling that you are less good in some way than other people

**infernal** *adj* **1** of hell **2** *informal* annoying, blasted

**inferno** *noun* **1** hell **2** (*pl* **infernos**) a raging fire

**infertile** *adj* **1** of soil: not producing much **2** not able to bear children or young □ **infertility** *noun*

**infest** *verb* to swarm over: *infested with lice*

**infidel** *adj* someone who does not believe in a particular religion (*esp* Christianity) □ **infidelity** *noun* unfaithfulness, disloyalty

**infiltrate** *verb* to enter (an organization *etc*) secretly to spy or cause damage □ **infiltration** *noun*

**infinite** *adj* without end or limit □ **infinitesimal** *adj* absolutely tiny □ **infinitive** *noun, grammar* the part of a verb which expresses the action but has no subject, *eg* I hate *to lose* □ **infinity** *noun* space or time without end

**infirm** *adj* feeble, weak □ **infirmity** *noun* (*pl* **infirmities**) **1** a physical weakness **2** a character flaw

**infirmary** *noun* (*pl* **infirmaries**) a hospital

**inflame** *verb* **1** to make hot or red **2** to arouse passion in □ **inflamed** *adj* □ **inflammation** *noun* heat in a part of the body, with pain, redness and swelling □ **inflammatory** *adj* arousing passion (*esp* anger)

**inflammable** *adj* **1** easily set on fire **2** easily excited

**inflate** *verb* **1** to blow up (a balloon, tyre *etc*) **2** to puff up (with pride), exaggerate **3** to increase to a great extent □ **inflation** *noun* **1** the act of inflating **2** an economic situation in which prices and wages keep forcing each other to increase

**inflect** *verb* **1** to change the tone of (your voice) **2** to vary the endings of (a verb) to show tense, number *etc* □ **inflection** *noun* **1** change in the tone of your voice **2** a change in the basic form of a word to show tense, number *etc* **3** the new form of a word which has been changed in this way: *The inflections of the verb 'find' are: 'finds', 'finding' and 'found'.* □ **inflectional** *adj*

**inflexible** *adj* not yielding, unbending □ **inflexibility** *noun*

**inflict** *verb* to bring down (blows, punishment *etc*) on □ **infliction** *noun*

**in-flight** *adj* happening or used during an air flight: *in-flight movie*

**inflow** *noun* a flowing in, influx

**influence** *noun* the power to affect

other persons or things □ verb to have power over □ **influential** adj

**influenza** noun an infectious illness with fever, headache, muscle pains etc

**influx** noun 1 a flowing in 2 the arrival of large numbers of people

**info** noun, informal information

**inform** verb 1 to give knowledge to 2 **inform on** to tell on, betray □ **informant** noun □ **information** noun knowledge, news □ **informative** adj giving information □ **informer** noun someone who gives information to the police or authorities

**informal** adj not formal; relaxed, friendly □ **informality** noun

**infra-** prefix below, beneath
ⓘ From Latin infra meaning 'below' or 'underneath'

**infraction** noun a violation, a breach

**infra-red** adj of rays of heat: with wavelengths longer than visible light

**infrastructure** noun inner structure, framework

**infrequent** adj rare, happening seldom

**infringe** verb to break (a rule or law) □ **infringement** noun

**infuriate** verb to drive into a rage □ **infuriating** adj extremely annoying

**infuse** verb 1 to pour on or over 2 to fill the mind (with a desire etc) □ **infusion** noun 1 the act of infusing 2 a tea formed by steeping a herb etc in water

**ingenious** (say in-**jeen**-i-us) adj 1 skilful in inventing 2 cleverly thought out □ **ingenuity** noun cleverness; quickness of ideas

🔥 Do not confuse with: **ingenuous**. It may help you remember which is which if you link the adjective **ingenuous** with the noun **ingénue** (= a

naive young girl).

**ingénue** (say an-szei-noo) noun a naive young girl

**ingenuous** (say in-**jen**-yoo-us) adj frank; without cunning

🔥 Do not confuse with: **ingenious**

**ingot** noun a block of metal (esp gold or silver) cast in a mould

**ingrained** adj deeply fixed: ingrained laziness

**ingratiate** verb to work your way into someone's favour by flattery etc □ **ingratiating** adj

**ingratitude** noun lack of gratitude or thankfulness

**ingredient** noun one of the things of which a mixture is made

**ingrown** adj of a nail: growing into the flesh

**inhabit** verb to live in □ **inhabitant** noun someone who lives permanently in a place

**inhale** verb to breathe in □ **inhalation** noun 1 the act of inhaling 2 a medicine which is inhaled □ **inhaler** noun a device for breathing in medicine, steam etc

**inhere** verb to stick, be fixed (in)

**inherent** adj inborn, belonging naturally

**inherit** verb 1 to receive property etc as an heir 2 to get (a characteristic) from your parents etc □ **inheritance** noun something received by will when someone dies □ **inheritor** noun an heir

**inhibit** verb to hold back, prevent □ **inhibited** adj unable to let yourself go □ **inhibition** noun a holding back of natural impulses etc, restraint

**inhospitable** adj unwelcoming, unfriendly

**inhuman** adj not human; brutal □ **inhumanity** noun

**inhumane** adj cruel

**inimitable** adj impossible to imitate

**iniquity** noun (pl **iniquities**) wickedness; a sin □ **iniquitous** adj unjust; wicked

**initial** adj of or at the beginning: *initial difficulties* □ noun the letter beginning a word, esp someone's name □ verb to sign with the initials of your name

**initial** verb ⇔ initials, initial**ling**, initial**led**

**initiate** verb **1** to begin, start: *initiate the reforms* **2** to give first lessons to **3** to formally make someone a member of a society etc □ **initiation** noun (meanings 1 and 3) □ **initiative** noun **1** the right to take the first step **2** readiness to take a lead

**inject** verb **1** to force (a fluid etc) into the veins or muscles with a syringe **2** to put (eg enthusiasm) into □ **injection** noun

**in-joke** noun a joke only understood by a particular group

**injudicious** adj unwise

**injunction** noun an official order or command

**injure** verb **1** to harm, damage, wrong □ **injured** adj hurt; offended □ **injury** noun (pl **injuries**) **1** hurt, damage, harm **2** a wrong

■ disfigure, mutilate, wound, offend

**injustice** noun **1** unfairness **2** a wrong

**ink** noun a coloured liquid used in writing, printing etc □ verb to mark with ink □ **inky** adj **1** of or covered in ink **2** very dark

**inkling** noun a hint or slight sign

**inlaid** past form of **inlay**

**inland** adj **1** not beside the sea **2** happening inside a country □ adv towards the inner part of a country □ **inland revenue** taxes etc collected within a country

**inlay** noun decoration made by fitting pieces of different shapes and colours into a background □ verb to fit into a background as decoration

□ **inlaid** adj

**inlay** verb ⇔ inlays, inla**ying**, inlaid

**inlet** noun a small bay

**inmate** noun a resident, an occupant (esp of an institution): *the inmates of the prison*

**inmost** adj the most inward, the farthest in

**inn** noun a small country hotel □ **innkeeper** noun someone who keeps an inn

**innate** adj inborn, natural

**inner** adj **1** farther in **2** of feelings etc: hidden □ **innermost** adj farthest in; most secret

**innings** noun sing **1** a team's turn for batting in cricket **2** a turn, a go at something

**innocent** adj **1** not guilty, blameless **2** having no experience of how unpleasant people, and life in general, can be, and therefore tending to trust everyone **3** harmless **4** innocent of lacking, without □ **innocence** noun (meanings 1 and 2)

**innocuous** adj not harmful

**innovation** noun something new

**innuendo** noun (pl **innuendoes**) an indirect reference, a hint

**innumerable** adj too many to be counted

**innumerate** adj not understanding arithmetic or mathematics □ **innumeracy** noun

**inoculate** verb to inject (someone) with a mild form of a disease to prevent them later catching it □ **inoculation** noun

**inoffensive** adj harmless, giving no offence

**inoperative** adj not active, not working

**inopportune** adj at a bad or inconvenient time

**inordinate** adj going beyond the limit, unreasonably great

**inorganic** *adj* not of animal or vegetable origin

**in-patient** *noun* a patient who stays in a hospital during their treatment (*contrasted with:* **out-patient**)

**input** *noun* **1** an amount (of energy, labour *etc*) put into something **2** data fed into a computer (*contrasted with:* **output**)

**inquest** *noun* a legal inquiry into a case of sudden death

**inquire** or **enquire** *verb* to ask □ **inquiring** or **enquiring** *adj* questioning, curious: *an inquiring mind* □ **inquiry** or **enquiry** *noun* (*pl* **inquiries** or **enquiries**) **1** a question; a search for information **2** an official investigation

**inquisition** *noun* a careful questioning or investigation □ **inquisitor** *noun*

**inquisitive** *adj* **1** very curious **2** fond of prying, nosy □ **inquisitively** *adv*

**inroad** *noun* a raid, an advance □ **make inroads into** to use up large amounts of: *the holiday made inroads into their savings*

**insane** *adj* mad, not sane □ **insanity** *noun*

**insanitary** *adj* not sanitary; encouraging the spread of disease

**insatiable** *adj* not able to be satisfied: *insatiable appetite*

**inscribe** *verb* to write or engrave (*eg* a name) on a book, monument *etc* □ **inscription** *noun* the writing on a book, monument *etc*

**inscrutable** *adj* not able to be understood, mysterious

**insect** *noun* a small six-legged creature with wings and a body divided into sections □ **insecticide** *noun* powder or liquid for killing insects □ **insectivorous** *adj* feeding on insects

**insecure** *adj* **1** not safe; not firm **2** lacking confidence, not feeling settled □ **insecurity** *noun*

**inseminate** *verb* **1** to plant, introduce (into) **2** to impregnate, *esp* artificially □ **insemination** *noun*

**insensible** *adj* **1** unconscious, unaware (of) **2** not having feeling

**insensitive** *adj* **1** **insensitive to** not feeling: *insensitive to cold* **2** unsympathetic (to): *insensitive to her grief* **3** unappreciative, crass □ **insensitivity** *noun*

**inseparable** *adj* not able to be separated or kept apart □ **inseparably** *adv*

**insert** *verb* (*say* in-**sert**) to put in or among □ *noun* (*say* in-**sert**) **1** a special feature added to a television programme *etc* **2** a separate leaflet or pullout section in a magazine *etc* □ **insertion** *noun*

**inset** *noun* **1** an insert **2** a small picture, map *etc* in a corner of a larger one

**inshore** *adj & adv* in or on the water but near or towards the shore

**inside** *noun* **1** the side, space or part within **2** indoors □ *adj* **1** being on or in the inside **2** indoor **3** coming from or done by someone within an organization: *inside information* □ *adv* to, in or on the inside □ *prep* to the inside of; within

**insidious** *adj* **1** likely to trap those who are not careful, treacherous **2** of a disease: coming on gradually and unnoticed

**insight** *noun* ability to consider a matter and understand it clearly

**insignia** *noun pl* signs or badges showing that someone holds an office, award *etc*

**insignificant** *adj* of little importance □ **insignificance** *noun*

**insincere** *adj* not sincere □ **insincerity** *noun*

**insinuate** *verb* **1** to hint (at a fault) **2** to put in gradually and secretly **3** to work yourself into (someone's favour *etc*) □ **insinuation** *noun* a sly hint

**insipid** adj 1 dull, without liveliness 2 tasteless, bland

**insist** verb 1 to urge something strongly: *insist on punctuality* 2 to refuse to give way, hold firmly to your intentions: *he insists on walking there* 3 to go on saying (that): *she insists that she saw a UFO* □ **insistence** noun □ **insistent** adj 1 insisting on having or doing something 2 forcing you to pay attention □ **insistently** adv

**insolent** adj rude, impertinent, insulting □ **insolence** noun

**insoluble** adj 1 not able to be dissolved 2 of a problem: not able to be solved

**insolvent** adj not able to pay your debts, impoverished □ **insolvency** noun

**insomnia** noun sleeplessness □ **insomniac** noun

**inspect** verb 1 to look carefully into, examine 2 to look over (troops *etc*) ceremonially □ **inspection** noun careful examination □ **inspector** noun 1 an official who inspects 2 a police officer below a superintendent and above a sergeant in rank

**inspire** verb 1 to encourage, rouse 2 to be the source of creative ideas 3 to breathe in □ **inspiration** noun 1 something or someone that influences or encourages others 2 a brilliant idea 3 breathing in □ **inspirational** adj inspiring, brilliant □ **inspired** adj 1 seeming to be aided by higher powers 2 brilliantly good

**instability** noun lack of steadiness or stability (*esp* in the personality)

**install** or **instal** verb 1 to place in position, ready for use: *instal a telephone* 2 to introduce formally to a new job *etc* □ **installation** noun

**install** ↔ instal**s** or instal**s**, instal**ling**, instal**led**

**instalment** noun 1 a part of a sum of money paid at fixed times until the whole amount is paid 2 one part of a serial story

**instance** noun an example, a particular case □ verb to mention as an example □ **at the instance of** at the request of □ **for instance** for example

**instant** adj 1 immediate, urgent 2 able to be prepared almost immediately: *instant coffee* □ noun 1 a very short time, a moment 2 point or moment of time □ **instantaneous** adj done or happening very quickly □ **instantly** adv immediately

**instead** adv in place of someone or something: *you can go instead* □ **instead of** in place of

**instep** noun the arching, upper part of the foot

**instigate** verb to stir up, encourage □ **instigation** noun: *at someone's instigation* following that person's instructions or wishes

**instil** or **instill** verb to put in little by little (*esp* ideas into the mind)

**instil** ↔ instil**s** or instil**s**, instil**ling**, instil**led**

**instinct** noun a natural feeling or knowledge which someone has without thinking and without being taught □ **instinctive** adj

**institute** verb to set up, establish, start □ noun a society, organization *etc* or the building it uses □ **institution** noun 1 an organization, building *etc* established for a particular purpose (*esp* care or education) 2 an established custom □ **institutional** adj

**instruct** verb 1 to teach 2 to direct, command □ **instruction** noun 1 teaching 2 a command 3 (**instructions**) rules showing how something is to be used □ **instructive** adj containing or giving information or knowledge

□ **instructor** *noun*

**instrument** *noun* **1** something used for a particular purpose, a tool **2** a device for producing musical sounds, *eg* a piano, a harp □ **instrumental** *adj* **1** helpful in bringing (something) about **2** written for or played by musical instruments, without voice accompaniment □ **instrumentalist** *noun*

**insubordinate** *adj* rebellious, disobedient □ **insubordination** *noun*

**insufferable** *adj* not able to be endured

**insufficient** *adj* not enough

**insular** *adj* narrow-minded, prejudiced

**insulate** *verb* **1** to cover with a material that will not let through electrical currents, heat, frost *etc* **2** to cut off, isolate □ **insulation** *noun*

**insulin** *noun* a substance used in the treatment of diabetes

**insult** *verb* to treat with scorn or rudeness □ *noun* a rude or scornful remark □ **insulting** *adj* scornful, rude

**insuperable** *adj* that cannot be overcome

**insure** *verb* to arrange for payment of a sum of money on (something) if it should be lost, damaged, stolen *etc* □ **insurance** *noun*

**♦** Do not confuse with: **ensure**

**insurgent** *adj* rising up in rebellion □ *noun* a rebel □ **insurgency** *noun*

**insurmountable** *adj* not able to be got over

**insurrection** *noun* a rising up in rebellion

**intact** *adj* whole, unbroken

**intake** *noun* an amount of people or things taken in

**intangible** *adj* **1** not able to be felt by touch **2** difficult to define or describe, not clear

**integer** *noun* a whole number, not a fraction

**integral** *adj* **1** of or essential to a whole: *an integral part of the machine* **2** made up of parts forming a whole

**integrate** *verb* **1** to fit parts together to form a whole **2** to enable (racial groups) to mix freely and live on equal terms □ **integration** *noun*

**integrity** *noun* **1** honesty **2** wholeness, completeness

**intellect** *noun* the thinking power of the mind □ **intellectual** *adj* showing or requiring intellect □ *noun* someone of natural ability or with academic interests

**intelligent** *adj* clever, quick at understanding □ **intelligence** *noun* **1** mental ability **2** information sent, news □ **intelligible** *adj* able to be understood

**intelligentsia** *noun* the intellectuals within a particular society

**intend** *verb* to mean or plan to (do something)

**intense** *adj* **1** very great **2** tending to feel strongly, deeply emotional □ **intensely** *adv* □ **intensity** *noun* (*pl* **intensities**) strength, *eg* of feeling, colour *etc*

**intensify** *verb* to increase, make more concentrated

**intensify** ⟷ intensif**ies**, intensif**ying**, intensif**ied**

**intensive** *adj* very thorough, concentrated □ **intensive care** a unit in a hospital where a patient's condition is carefully monitored

**intent** *noun* purpose □ *adj* **1** with all your concentration (on), attentive **2** determined (to) □ **intention** *noun* **1** what someone means to do, an aim **2** meaning □ **intentional** *adj* done on purpose □ **intentionally** *adv*

**inter** (*say* in-ter) *verb* to bury

**inter** ⟷ inter**s**, inter**ring**, inter**red**

⊚ From Latin *in* meaning 'into', and

*terra* meaning 'the earth'

**inter-** *prefix* between, among, together: *intermingle/interplanetary*

⦿ From Latin *inter* meaning 'between', 'among' or 'mutually'

**interact** *verb* to act on one another □ **interactive** *adj* allowing two-way communication, *eg* between a computer and its user

**intercede** *verb* to act as peacemaker between two people, nations *etc* □ **intercession** *noun*

**intercept** *verb* 1 to stop or seize on the way 2 to cut off, interrupt (a view, the light *etc*)

**interchange** *verb* 1 to put each in the place of the other 2 to alternate □ *noun* 1 the act of interchanging 2 a junction of two or more major roads on separate levels □ **interchangeable** *adj* able to be used one for the other

**intercom** *noun* a telephone system within a building, aeroplane *etc*

**intercourse** *noun* 1 communication 2 dealings between people *etc* 3 sexual intercourse

**interdict** *noun* an order forbidding something

**interest** *noun* 1 special attention, curiosity 2 someone's personal concern or field of study 3 advantage, benefit 4 a sum paid for the loan of money □ *verb* to catch or hold the attention of □ **interested** *adj* having or taking an interest □ **interesting** *adj* holding the attention

**interface** *noun, computing* a connection between two parts of the same system

**interfere** *verb* 1 **interfere in** to take part in what is not your business, meddle in 2 **interfere with** to get in the way of, hinder, have a harmful effect on □ **interference** *noun*

**interim** *noun* time between; the meantime □ *adj* temporary

**interior** *adj* 1 inner 2 inside a building 3 inland □ *noun* 1 the inside of anything 2 the inland part of a country

**interject** *verb* 1 to make a sudden remark in a conversation 2 to exclaim □ **interjection** *noun* a word or phrase of exclamation

**interlock** *verb* 1 to lock or clasp together 2 to fit into each other

**interloper** *noun* someone who enters without permission, an intruder

**interlude** *noun* 1 an interval 2 a short piece of music played between the parts of a play, film *etc*

**intermediary** *noun* (*pl* **intermediaries**) someone who acts between two people in trying to settle a quarrel

**intermediate** *adj* in the middle; coming between

**interment** (from inter) *noun* a burial

☙ Do not confuse with: **internment**

**interminable** *adj* never-ending, boringly long

**intermission** *noun* an interval, a pause

**intermittent** *adj* stopping every now and then and starting again

**intern** *verb* to keep (someone from an enemy country) prisoner during a war

**internal** *adj* 1 of the inner part, *esp* the body 2 inside, within a country, organization *etc*: *internal affairs*

**international** *adj* 1 happening between nations 2 concerning more than one nation 3 world-wide □ *noun* a sports match between teams of two countries

**Internet** *noun* an international computer network linking users through telephone lines

**internment** (from intern) *noun* confinement within a country or prison, *esp* during a war

☙ Do not confuse with: **interment**

ⓘ From French *interne* meaning 'internal'

**interplanetary** *adj* between planets

**interplay** *noun* the action of one thing on another

**interpose** *verb* 1 to place or come between 2 to make (a remark *etc*) which interrupts someone

**interpret** *verb* 1 to explain the meaning of something 2 to translate 3 to bring out the meaning of (music, a part in a play *etc*) in performance 4 to take the meaning of something to be □ **interpretation** *noun* □ **interpreter** *noun* someone who translates (on the spot) the words of a speaker into another language

**interregnum** *noun* the time between the end of one reign and the beginning of the next

**interrogate** *verb* to examine by asking questions □ **interrogation** *noun* □ **interrogative** *noun* a word used in asking a question, *eg* who? where? *adj* questioning □ **interrogator** *noun*

**interrupt** *verb* 1 to stop (someone) while they are saying or doing something 2 to stop doing (something) 3 to get in the way of, cut off (a view *etc*) □ **interruption** *noun*

**intersect** *verb* of lines: to meet and cross □ **intersection** *noun* 1 the point where two lines cross 2 a crossroads

**intersperse** *verb* to scatter here and there in □ **interspersion** *noun*

**intertwine** *verb* to twine or twist together

**interval** *noun* 1 a time or space between two things 2 a short pause in a programme *etc*

**intervene** *verb* 1 to come or be between, or in the way 2 to join in (in order to stop) a fight or quarrel between other persons or nations □ **intervention** *noun*

**interview** *noun* a formal meeting of one person with others to apply for a job, give information to the media *etc* □ *verb* 1 to ask questions *etc* of in an interview 2 to conduct an interview

**intestines** *noun pl* the inside parts of the body, *esp* the bowels and passages leading to them □ **intestinal** *adj*

**intimate** *adj* (say **in**-tim-*at*) 1 knowing a lot about, familiar (with) 2 of friends: very close 3 private, personal: *intimate details* 4 having a sexual relationship (with) □ *noun* (say **in**-tim-*at*) a close friend □ *verb* (say **in**-tim-eit) 1 to hint 2 to announce □ **intimacy** *noun* (*pl* **intimacies**) □ **intimately** *adv*

**intimation** *noun* 1 a hint 2 announcement

**intimidate** *verb* to frighten or threaten into submission □ **intimidating** *adj* □ **intimidation** *noun*

**into** *prep* 1 to the inside: *into the room* 2 towards: *into the millennium* 3 to a different state: *a tadpole changes into a frog* 4 maths expressing the idea of division: *2 into 4 goes twice*

**intolerant** *adj* not willing to put up with (people of different ideas, religion *etc*) □ **intolerable** *adj* not able to be endured □ **intolerance** *noun*

**intone** *verb* to speak in a singing manner, chant □ **intonation** *noun* the rise and fall of the voice

**intoxicate** *verb* 1 to make drunk 2 to enthuse, excite □ **intoxication** *noun*
Literally, to affect with arrow-poison

**intra-** *prefix* within
ⓘ From Latin *intra* meaning 'within'

**intractable** *adj* difficult, stubborn □ **intractability** *noun*

**intransigent** *adj* refusing to come to an agreement □ **intransigence** *noun*

**intransitive** *adj, grammar* of a verb: not needing an object, *eg* to *go*, to *fall*

**intrepid** *adj* without fear, brave □ **intrepidity** *noun*

**intricate** *adj* complicated, having many twists and turns □ **intricacy** *noun (pl* **intricacies)**

**intrigue** *noun* **1** a secret plot **2** a secret love affair □ *verb* **1** to plot, scheme **2** to rouse the curiosity of, fascinate □ **intriguing** *adj*

**intrinsic** *adj* belonging to something as part of its nature

**introduce** *verb* **1** to bring in or put in **2** to make (someone) known to another person □ **introduction** *noun* **1** the introducing of someone or something **2** an essay at the beginning of a book *etc* briefly explaining its contents □ **introductory** *adj*

**introspective** *adj* inward-looking, fond of examining your own thoughts and feelings □ **introspection** *noun*

**intrude** *verb* to thrust yourself into somewhere uninvited □ **intruder** *noun* □ **intrusion** *noun* □ **intrusive** *adj*

**intuition** *noun* **1** ability to understand something without thinking it out **2** an instinctive feeling or belief

**Inuit** *noun* **1** the Eskimo people, *esp* those in Greenland, Canada and N Alaska **2** their language

**inundate** *verb* **1** to flood **2** to overwhelm □ **inundation** *noun*

**inure** *verb* to make accustomed (to): *inured to pain*

**invade** *verb* **1** to enter (a country *etc*) as an enemy to take possession **2** to interfere with (someone's rights, privacy *etc*) □ **invader** *noun* □ **invasion** *noun*

**invalid¹** (*say* in-val-id) *adj* not valid, not legally effective □ **invalidity** *noun*

**invalid²** (*say* in-val-id) *noun* someone who is ill or disabled □ *adj* **1** ill or disabled **2** suitable for people who are ill or disabled □ *verb* **1** to make an invalid of **2 invalid out** to discharge from the army as an invalid

**invalidate** *verb* to prove to be wrong, or make legally ineffective

**invaluable** *adj* priceless, essential

**invariable** *adj* unchanging □ **invariably** *adv* always

**invasion** *see* **invade**

**invective** *noun* abusive words; scorn

**inveigle** *verb* to coax, entice □ **inveiglement** *noun*

**invent** *verb* **1** to make or think up for the first time **2** to make up (a story, an excuse) □ **invention** *noun* something invented □ **inventive** *adj* good at inventing, resourceful □ **inventor** *noun*

**inventory** *noun (pl* **inventories)** a detailed list of contents

**invert** *verb* **1** to turn upside down **2** to reverse the order of □ **inverse** *adj* opposite, reverse □ *noun* the opposite □ **inversely** *adv* □ **inversion** *noun* **1** a turning upside-down **2** a reversal □ **inverted commas** *noun pl* commas written or printed upside down (' ' or " ") to show where direct speech begins and ends

**invertebrate** *adj* of an animal: not having a backbone □ *noun* an animal with no backbone, *eg* a worm or insect

**invest** *verb* **1** to put money in a firm, property *etc* to make a profit **2** to give a particular quality to □ **investment** *noun* **1** money invested **2** something in which money is invested **3** *old* a siege □ **investor** *noun*

**investigate** *verb* to search into with care □ **investigator** *noun* □ **investigation** *noun* a careful search

**investiture** noun a ceremony before taking on an important office

**inveterate** adj 1 firmly fixed in a habit: an inveterate gambler 2 deep-rooted □ **inveteracy** noun

**invidious** adj likely to cause ill-will or envy

**invigilate** verb to supervise (an examination etc) □ **invigilator** noun

**invigorate** verb to strengthen, refresh □ **invigorating** adj

**invincible** adj not able to be defeated or overcome □ **invincibility** noun

**invisible** adj not able to be seen □ **invisibility** noun

**invite** verb 1 to ask (someone) to do something, esp to come for a meal etc 2 to seem to ask for: inviting punishment □ **invitation** noun a request to do something □ **inviting** adj tempting, attractive

**invoice** noun a letter sent with goods with details of price and quantity □ verb to make such a list

**invoke** verb 1 to call upon in prayer 2 to ask for (eg help) □ **invocation** noun

**involuntary** adj not done willingly or intentionally □ **involuntarily** adv

**involve** verb 1 to have as a consequence, require 2 to take part (in), be concerned (in): involved in the scandal □ **involved** adj complicated □ **involvement** noun

**invulnerable** adj not vulnerable, not able to be hurt □ **invulnerability** noun

**inward** adj 1 placed within 2 situated in the mind or soul □ adv (also **inwards**) towards the inside □ **inwardly** adv 1 within 2 in your heart, privately

**in-your-face** adj, slang aggressive, demanding attention

**iodine** noun a liquid chemical used to kill germs

**ion** noun an electrically-charged atom or group of atoms

**iota** noun a little bit, a jot

**IOU** short for I owe you, a note given as a receipt for money borrowed

**IQ** abbrev intelligence quotient

**ir-** see **in-**

**IRA** abbrev Irish Republican Army

**irascible** adj easily made angry □ **irascibility** noun

**irate** adj angry

**ire** noun, formal anger

**iridescent** adj 1 coloured like a rainbow 2 shimmering with changing colours □ **iridescence** noun

**iris** noun (pl **irises**) 1 the coloured part of the eye around the pupil 2 a lily-like flower which grows from a bulb

**irk** verb to weary, annoy

**irksome** adj tiresome

**iron** (say ai-on or Scottish ai-ron) noun 1 a common metal, widely used to make tools etc 2 an iron instrument: a branding iron 3 a golf club (originally with an iron head) 4 an appliance for pressing clothes 5 (**irons**) a prisoner's chains □ adj 1 made of iron 2 stern, resolute: iron will 3 of a rule: not to be broken □ verb to press (clothes) with an iron □ **iron out** to smooth out (difficulties) □ **Iron Age** human culture at the stage of using iron for tools etc □ **Iron Curtain** historical the border separating the West from the countries of the former Soviet bloc

**ironmonger** noun a shopkeeper selling household tools, gardening equipment etc

**ironmongery** noun goods sold by an ironmonger

**irony** noun (pl **ironies**) 1 a form of humour in which someone says the opposite of what is obviously true 2 an absurd contradiction or paradox: the irony of it was that she would have given him the money if he *hadn't stolen it* □ **ironic** or **ironical** *adj* □ **ironically** *adv*

**irrational** *adj* against logic or common sense □ **irrationality** *noun*

**irregular** *adj* 1 uneven, variable 2 against the rules □ **irregularity** *noun* (*pl* **irregularities**)

**irrelevant** *adj* not having to do with what is being spoken about □ **irrelevancy** *noun* (*pl* **irrelevancies**)

**irreparable** *adj* not able to be repaired

**irreplaceable** *adj* too good or rare to be replaced

**irrepressible** *adj* not restrainable or controllable

**irreproachable** *adj* not able to be criticized or blamed

**irresistible** *adj* too strong or too charming to be resisted

**irresolute** *adj* not able to make up your mind or keep to a decision

**irrespective** *adj* taking no account of: *irrespective of the weather*

**irresponsible** *adj* having no sense of responsibility, thoughtless

**irreverent** *adj* having no respect, *eg* for holy things □ **irreverence** *noun*

**irrevocable** (*say* i-**rev**-ok-a-bl) *adj* not to be changed

**irrigate** *verb* to supply (land) with water by canals *etc* □ **irrigation** *noun*

**irritate** *verb* 1 to annoy 2 to cause discomfort to (the skin, eyes *etc*) □ **irritable** *adj* cross, easily annoyed □ **irritation** *noun*

■ (meaning 1) aggravate

**Islam** *noun* 1 the Muslim religion, founded by the prophet Mohammed 2 the Muslim world □ **Islamic** *adj*

**island** *noun* 1 an area of land surrounded by water 2 an isolated place, a haven □ **islander** *noun*

**isle** *noun, formal* an island

**ISO** *abbrev* International Standards Organization

**iso-** *prefix* equal: *isobar/ isotherm* ⊙ From Greek *isos* meaning 'equal'

**isobar** *noun* a line on the map connecting places where atmospheric pressure is the same

**isolate** *verb* 1 to place or keep separate from other people or things 2 to consider (something) by itself □ **isolation** *noun*

**isosceles** *adj* of a triangle: having two sides equal (*compare with*: **equilateral**)

**isotope** *noun* an atom with the same atomic number as, but different mass number from, another

**issue** *verb* 1 to go or come out 2 to give out (orders *etc*) 3 to publish □ *noun* 1 a flowing out 2 the copies of a book published at one time 3 one number in a series of magazines *etc* 4 result, consequence 5 the matter which is being discussed □ **take issue with** to disagree with

**it** *pronoun* 1 the thing spoken of: *I meant to bring the book, but I left it at home* 2 used in sentences with no definite subject: *it snowed today* 3 used in phrases as a kind of object: *go it alone*

**italics** *noun pl* a kind of type which slopes to the right □ **italicize** *verb* to print in italics

**itch** *noun* 1 an irritating feeling in the skin, made better by scratching 2 a strong desire □ *verb* 1 to have an itch 2 to be impatient (to do), long (to) □ **itchy** *adj*

**item** *noun* a separate article or detail in a list

**itinerant** *adj* travelling from place to place, *esp* on business □ *noun* someone who travels around, *esp* a tramp, pedlar *etc*

**itinerary** *noun* (*pl* **itineraries**) a route or plan of a journey

**its** *adj* belonging to it: *keep the hat in its box*

**◑.** Do not confuse: **its** and **it's**. Its, meaning 'belonging to it', is spelt with no apostrophe ('). It's means 'it is' or 'it has'.

**it's** *short for* it is *or* it has

**itself** *pronoun* **1** used reflexively: *the cat licked itself* **2** used for emphasis or contrast: *I didn't like the book itself*

**ITV** *abbrev* Independent Television

**IU** or **IUD** *abbrev* intra-uterine (contraceptive) device

**ivory** *noun* (*pl* **ivories**) the hard white substance which forms the tusks of the elephant, walrus *etc*

**ivy** *noun* (*pl* **ivies**) a creeping evergreen plant

## Jj

**jabber** *verb* to talk rapidly and indistinctly

**jack** *noun* **1** a device with a lever for raising heavy weights **2** (*also called* **knave**) the playing-card between ten and queen □ **jack up 1** to raise with a jack **2** to raise (prices *etc*) steeply

**jackal** *noun* a dog-like wild animal

**jackass** *noun* **1** a male ass **2** *informal* an idiot

**jackboots** *noun pl* large boots reaching above the knee

**jackdaw** *noun* a type of small crow

**jacket** *noun* **1** a short coat **2** a loose paper cover for a book

**jacket potato** a baked potato

**jack-in-the-box** *noun* a doll fixed to a spring inside a box that leaps out when the lid is opened

**jack-knife** *noun* **1** a large folding knife **2** a dive forming a sharp angle and then straightening □ *verb* of a vehicle and its trailer: to swing together to form a sharp angle

**jackpot** *noun* a fund of prize money which increases until someone wins it

**Jacobean** *noun*, *historical* relating to the period of James VI of Scotland, I of England (1603–1625)

**Jacobite** *noun*, *historical* a supporter of James VII of Scotland, II of England and his descendants

**Jacuzzi** *noun*, *trademark* a bath fitted with a device that agitates the water

**jade** *noun* a hard green mineral substance used for ornaments

**jaded** *adj* tired

**jagged** *adj* rough-edged, uneven

**jaguar** *noun* a S American animal like a leopard

**jail** *noun* a prison □ **jailbird** *noun* a convict or ex-convict □ **jailer** *noun* someone in charge of a jail or prisoners

**Jain** *noun* a member of an ascetic Indian religion similar to Buddhism

**jam** *noun* **1** fruit boiled with sugar till it is set **2** a crush **3** a blockage caused by crowding **4** *informal* a difficult situation □ *verb* **1** to press or squeeze tight **2** to crowd full **3** to stick and so be unable to move: *the back wheel has jammed* **4** to cause interference with another radio station's broadcast **5** *music* to play with other musicians in an improvised style □ **jam-packed** *adj* packed tightly, congested □ **jam session** an informal gathering to play improvised music

**jam** *verb* ↔ jams, jamm*ing*, jamm*ed*

**▪** (verb, meaning 2) block

**jamb** *noun* the side post of a door

**jamboree** *noun* **1** a large, lively gathering **2** a rally of Scouts

**jangle** *verb* **1** to make a harsh ringing noise **2** to irritate

**janitor** *noun* **1** a caretaker **2** a doorkeeper
ⓘ From Latin *janua* meaning 'a door'

**January** *noun* the first month of the year

**jape** *noun, informal* a trick, a practical joke

**jar** *noun* a glass or earthenware bottle with a wide mouth □ *verb* **1** to have a harsh, startling effect **2** to be discordant, not agree □ **jarring** *adj* harsh, startling

**jar** *verb* ⋯ jars, jarring, jarred

**jargon** *noun* special words used within a particular trade, profession *etc*

**jasmine** *noun* a shrub with white or yellow sweet-smelling flowers

**jaundice** *noun* a disease which causes the skin and eyes to turn yellow □ **jaundiced** *adj* **1** having jaundice **2** discontented, bitter

**jaunt** *noun* a short journey for pleasure

**jaunty** *adj* cheerful □ **jauntily** *adv*

◼ sprightly

**javelin** *noun* a long spear for throwing

**jaw** *noun* **1** the lower part of the face, including the mouth and chin **2** (**jaws**) an animal's mouth

**jay** *noun* a brightly-coloured bird like a crow

**jazz** *noun* a style of music with a strong rhythm, based on African-American folk music □ **jazzy** *adj* **1** resembling or containing certain elements of jazz **2** colourful, flamboyant □ **jazz something up** to make it more lively or colourful

**JCB** *noun* a type of mobile digger used in the construction industry

JCB is an abbreviation of *J C Bamford*, the manufacturer's name.

**jealous** *adj* **1** wanting to have what someone else has; envious **2** guarding closely (possessions *etc*) □ **jealousy** *noun*

**jeans** *noun pl* denim trousers

**Jeep** *noun, trademark* a small army motor vehicle

**jeer** *verb* to make fun of, scoff □ *noun* a scoff

◼ (verb) heckle, taunt

**Jehovah** *noun* the Hebrew God of the Old Testament

**jelly** *noun* (*pl* **jellies**) **1** fruit juice boiled with sugar till it becomes firm **2** a transparent wobbly food, often fruit-flavoured **3** an extremely nervous person **4** (**jellies**) *slang* the drug Temazepam

**jellyfish** *noun* a sea animal with a jelly-like body

**jemmy** *noun* (*pl* **jemmies**) a burglar's iron tool

**jeopardy** *noun* danger □ **jeopardize** *verb* to put in danger or at risk

Originally a gambling term, based on French *jeu parti* meaning 'even chance'

**jerk** *verb* to give a sudden sharp movement □ *noun* a sudden sharp movement □ **jerky** *adj* moving or coming in jerks □ **jerkily** *adv*

**jerkin** *noun* a type of short coat

**jerry-built** *adj* hastily and badly built

**jersey** *noun* (*pl* **jerseys**) a sweater, pullover

**jest** *noun* a joke □ *verb* to joke □ **jester** *noun, historical* a fool employed to amuse a royal court *etc*

**jet** *noun* **1** a hard black mineral, used for ornaments and jewellery **2** a spout of flame, air or liquid **3** a jet plane □ **jet-black** *adj* very black □ **jet lag** tiredness caused by the body's inability to cope with being in a new time zone □ **jet plane** an aeroplane driven by jet propulsion □ **jet propulsion** high-speed forward motion produced by sucking in air or liquid and forcing it out from behind □ **jet set** rich people who enjoy frequent expensive holidays □ **jet stream 1** a band of high-speed winds far above the earth **2** the exhaust of a jet engine

**jetsam** noun goods thrown overboard and washed ashore

**jettison** verb **1** to throw overboard **2** to abandon

**jetty** noun (pl **jetties**) a small pier

**Jew** noun someone who is of the race or religion of the Israelites □ **Jewish** adj of the Jews □ **Jew's harp** a small harp-shaped musical instrument played between the teeth

**jewel** noun **1** a precious stone **2** someone or something highly valued □ **jewelled** or US **jeweled** adj set with jewels □ **jeweller** or US **jeweler** noun someone who makes or sells articles made of precious jewels and metals □ **jewellery** or US **jewelry** noun articles made or sold by a jeweller

**Jezebel** noun a wicked, scheming woman

**jib** noun **1** a three-cornered sail in front of a ship's foremast **2** the jutting-out arm of a crane □ **jib at** to refuse to do, object to

**jib** verb ⇨ jibs, jibbing, jibbed

**jibe** or **gibe** verb to jeer, scoff □ noun a jeer

**Jiffy bag** trademark a padded envelope

**jig** noun a lively dance or tune □ verb to jump about

**jig** verb ⇨ jigs, jigging, jigged

**jigsaw** or **jigsaw puzzle** noun a puzzle consisting of many different-shaped pieces that fit together to form a picture

**jihad** (say jee-had) noun an Islamic holy war

**jilt** verb to cast aside (a lover) after previously encouraging them

**jingle** noun **1** a clinking sound like that of coins **2** a simple rhyme

**jingoism** (say jing-goh-i-zm) noun chauvinism, narrow-minded nationalism □ **jingoistic** adj

**jinx** noun someone or something thought to bring bad luck

Probably from the *Jynx* bird which was once invoked in spells and charms

**jitterbug** noun a dance to rock music

**jitters** noun pl: **have the jitters** to be very nervous

**jittery** adj very nervous, shaking with nerves

▫ edgy

**jive** noun a style of fast dancing to jazz or rock-and-roll music

**job** noun **1** someone's daily work **2** any piece of work □ **job centre** a government office where information about available jobs is shown □ **job-lot** noun a collection of odds and ends □ **job-share** noun the division of one job between two people, each working part-time

**jockey** noun (pl **jockeys**) someone who rides a horse in a race □ verb to push your way into a good position

**jocular** adj joking, merry □ **jocularity** noun □ **jocularly** adv

**jocund** adj merry, cheerful

**jodhpurs** noun pl riding breeches, fitting tightly from knee to ankle

**joey** noun (pl **joeys**) Australian, informal a young kangaroo

**jog** verb **1** to nudge, push slightly **2** to run at a gentle pace □ noun a gentle run □ **jogger** noun someone who runs gently to keep fit □ **jogging** noun (meaning 2)

**jog** verb ⇨ jogs, jogging, jogged

**joggle** verb to shake slightly

**join** verb **1** to put or come together **2** to connect, fasten **3** to become a member of **4** to come and meet □ noun the place where two or more things join □ **join battle** to begin fighting in battle

■ (verb, meanings 1 and 2) attach, connect, link; (verb, meaning 4) meet, converge

**joiner** noun someone who makes wooden fittings, furniture etc

**joint** noun 1 the place where two or more things join 2 the place where two bones are joined, eg an elbow or knee 3 meat containing a bone 4 slang a cannabis cigarette □ adj 1 united 2 shared among more than one □ **jointly** adv together

**joist** noun the beam to which the boards of a floor or the laths of a ceiling are nailed

**joke** noun something said or done to cause laughter □ verb to make a joke, tease

**joker** noun 1 someone who jokes 2 an extra playing-card in a pack

**jolly** adj merry □ **jollification** noun noisy festivity or celebration □ **jolliness** or **jollity** noun merriment

■ jovial

**jolt** verb 1 to shake suddenly 2 to go forward with sudden jerks □ noun a sudden jerk

■ (verb, meaning 1) jog, knock

**jostle** verb to push or knock against

**jot** noun a very small amount □ verb to write down hurriedly or briefly

**jot** verb ▸ jots, jotting, jotted

**jotter** noun a book for taking notes

**joule** noun a unit of energy

**journal** noun 1 a personal account of each day's events; a diary 2 a newspaper, a magazine □ **journalism** noun the business of recording daily events for the media □ **journalist** noun □ **journalistic** adj

**journey** noun (pl **journeys**) a distance travelled □ verb to travel □ **journeyman** noun someone whose apprenticeship is finished

**joust** noun, historical the armed contest between two knights on horseback at a tournament □ verb to fight on horseback at a tournament

**jovial** adj cheerful, good-humoured □ **joviality** noun

**jowl** noun the lower part of the jaw or cheek

**joy** noun gladness □ **joyful** or **joyous** adj full of joy □ **joyless** adj dismal

■ cheerless

**joyride** noun a reckless trip for amusement in a stolen car □ **joyrider** noun

**joy-stick** noun a control-lever for something eg an aeroplane, an invalid car or a video game

**JP** abbrev Justice of the Peace

**Jr** abbrev Junior: John Brown Jr

**jubilant** adj full of rejoicing, triumphant □ **jubilation** noun

**jubilee** noun celebrations arranged for the anniversary of a wedding, coronation etc

From a Hebrew word for 'ram's horn', which was blown to announce the start of a celebratory Jewish year

**Judaism** noun the Jewish religion or way of life □ **Judaic** adj

**judder** noun a strong vibration or jerky movement

**judge** verb 1 to make a decision on (a law case) after hearing all the evidence 2 to form an opinion 3 to decide the winners in a competition etc □ noun 1 an official who hears cases in the law-courts and decides on them according to the country's or state's laws 2 someone skilled in evaluating anything: a good judge of character □ **judgement** or **judgment** noun 1 a decision in a law case 2 an opinion 3 good sense in forming opinions □ **judicial** adj of a judge or court of justice □ **judicially** adv □ **judiciary** noun the judges of a country or state

◾ (verb, meaning 2) ascertain, determine, estimate; (verb, meaning 3) adjudicate, arbitrate

**judicious** *adj* wise □ **judiciously** *adv*

**judo** *noun* a Japanese form of wrestling for self-defence

**jug** *noun* a dish for liquids with a handle and a shaped lip for pouring

**juggernaut** *noun* a large articulated lorry

From a Hindi word for a large wagon used to carry the image of the god Krishna in religious processions

**juggle** *verb* **1** to toss a number of things (balls, clubs *etc*) into the air and catch them in order **2** to handle or present in a deceitful way □ **juggler** *noun* (meaning 1)

◾ (meaning 2) manipulate

**jugular vein** the large vein at the side of the neck

**juice** *noun* the liquid in vegetables, fruits *etc* □ **juicy** *adj* **1** full of juice **2** sensational, scandalous

**jujitsu** *noun* a Japanese martial art similar to judo

**jukebox** *noun* a coin-operated machine which plays selected records automatically

**July** *noun* the seventh month of the year

**jumble** *verb* to throw together without order, muddle □ *noun* **1** a confused mixture **2** second-hand goods to be sold in a jumble sale □ **jumble sale** a sale of odds and ends, cast-off clothing *etc*

**jumbo** *noun* (*pl* **jumbos**) **1** a child's name for an elephant **2** a jumbo jet □ *adj* very large □ **jumbo jet** a large jet aircraft

**jump** *verb* **1** to leap **2** to make a sudden startled movement **3** to pass over without spending time on: *she read the book in an afternoon, jumping all the boring bits* □ *noun* **1** a leap **2** a sudden start □ **jumpy** *adj*

easily startled

◾ (verb, meaning 1) spring, bound, vault, bounce; (verb, meaning 3) omit, skip

**jumper** *noun* a sweater, a jersey

**jump-suit** *noun* a one-piece garment combining trousers and top

**junction** *noun* a place or point of joining, *esp* of roads or railway lines

**juncture** *noun* point: *it's too early to decide at this juncture*

**June** *noun* the sixth month of the year

**jungle** *noun* a dense growth of trees and plants in tropical areas

**junior** *adj* **1** younger **2** in a lower class or rank □ *noun* someone younger: *he is my junior*

**juniper** *noun* an evergreen shrub with berries and prickly leaves

**junk**[1] *noun* worthless articles, rubbish □ **junk food** convenience food with little nutritional value □ **junk mail** unsolicited mail, *esp* advertising material

**junk**[2] *noun* a Chinese flat-bottomed sailing ship, high in the bow and stern

**junkie** or **junky** *noun* (*pl* **junkies**) an insulting name for a drug addict

**jurisdiction** *noun* **1** a legal authority or power **2** the district over which a judge, court *etc* has power

**jurisprudence** *noun* the study or knowledge of law

**jury** *noun* (*pl* **juries**) **1** a group of people selected to reach a decision on whether an accused prisoner is guilty or not **2** a group of judges for a competition *etc* □ **juror**, **juryman**, **jurywoman** *noun* someone who serves on a jury

**just** *adj* **1** fair in judgement; unbiased **2** correct □ *adv* **1** exactly: *just right* **2** not long since: *only just arrived* **3** merely, only **4** really: *just beautiful* □ **justly** *adv* (from *adj*)

**justice** *noun* **1** fairness in making judgements **2** what is right or rightly deserved **3** a judge □ **Justice of the Peace** (*short form* **JP**) a citizen who acts as a judge for certain matters

**justify** *verb* **1** to prove or show to be right or desirable **2** *printing* to make (text) form an even margin down the page □ **justifiable** *adj* able to be justified or defended □ **justifiably** *adv* with good reason □ **justification** *noun* **1** good reason **2** the arrangement of text so that it forms an even margin down the page

**justify** ⬦ justifies, justifying, justified

■ (meaning 1) defend

**jut** *verb* to stand or stick out

**jut** ⬦ juts, jutting, jutted

**jute** *noun* fibre from certain plants for making sacking, canvas *etc*

**juvenile** *adj* **1** young; of young people **2** childish □ *noun* a young person

**juxtapose** *verb* to place side by side □ **juxtaposition** *noun*

# Kk

**kaftan** *another spelling of* **caftan**

**kaiser** (*say* **kaiz**-er) *noun, historical* a German emperor

**kale** *noun* a cabbage with open curled leaves

**kaleidoscope** *noun* a tube held to the eye and turned, so that loose, coloured shapes reflected in two mirrors change patterns □ **kaleidoscopic** *adj* **1** with changing colours **2** changing quickly

**kamikaze** *noun, historical* a Japanese pilot trained to make a suicidal attack □ *adj* suicidal, self-destructive

**kangaroo** *noun* a large Australian animal with long hindlegs and great jumping power, the female carrying its young in a pouch on the front of her body

**kaolin** (*say* **kei**-oh-lin) *noun* China clay

**kaput** (*say* ka-**poot**) *adj, slang* broken, not working

**karaoke** *noun* an entertainment of singing well-known songs against pre-recorded backing music

**karate** *noun* a Japanese form of unarmed fighting using blows and kicks

**karma** *noun* in Buddhist belief, someone's destiny as determined by their actions in a previous life

**kayak** *noun* **1** an Inuit sealskin canoe **2** a lightweight canoe for one person, manoeuvred with a single paddle

**KB** *abbrev, computing* kilobyte

**kebab** *noun* small pieces of meat or vegetables cooked on a skewer

**kedgeree** *noun* a dish made with rice, fish and hard-boiled eggs

**keel** *noun* the piece of a ship's frame that lies lengthways along the bottom □ **keelhaul** *verb, historical* to punish by hauling under the keel of a ship with ropes □ **keelson** *noun* a ship's inner keel □ **keel over** to overturn, fall over

**keen**[1] *adj* **1** eager, enthusiastic **2** very sharp; bitingly cold □ **keenly** *adv* intensely, passionately, alertly □ **keenness** *noun*

■ (meaning 1) anxious

**keen**[2] *verb* to wail in grief; lament □ **keening** *noun*

**keep** *verb* **1** to hold on to, not give or throw away **2** to look after; feed and clothe **3** to have or use **4** to fulfil (a promise) **5** to remain in a position or state **6** (also **keep on**) to continue (doing something): *keep taking the tablets* **7** of food: to stay in good condition **8** to celebrate: *keep Christmas* □ *noun* **1** food, board **2** a castle stronghold □ **in keeping with** suited to □ **keep out 1** to exclude □ **keep out 2** to stay outside □ **keep up** to go on with, continue □ **keep up with** to go as fast *etc* as

**keep** *verb* – keeps, keeping, kept

**keeper** *noun* someone who looks after something: *zookeeper*

**keeping** *noun* care, charge □ **in keeping with** suitable for or fitting in with

**keepsake** *noun* a gift in memory of an occasion *etc*

**keg** *noun* a small cask or barrel

**kelp** *noun* a type of large brown seaweed

**kelvin** *noun* a measure of temperature

**kendo** *noun* a Japanese martial art using bamboo staves

**kennel** *noun* **1** a hut for a dog **2** (**kennels**) a place where dogs can be looked after

**kept** *past form of* **keep**

**kerb** *noun* the edge of something, *esp* a pavement

◗ Do not confuse with: **curb**

**kerchief** *noun* a square of cloth used as a headscarf

**kernel** *noun* **1** a soft substance in the shell of a nut, or inside the stone of a fruit **2** the important part of anything

**kestrel** *noun* a type of small falcon which hovers

**ketchup** *noun* a flavouring sauce made from tomatoes *etc*

Originally spelt *catsup*, as it still is in US English; based on a Chinese word for 'fish brine'

**kettle** *noun* a pot with a spout for heating liquids

**kettledrum** *noun* a drum made of a metal bowl covered with stretched skin *etc*

**key** *noun* **1** a device which is turned in a corresponding hole to lock or unlock, tighten, tune *etc* **2** a lever pressed on a piano *etc* to produce a note **3** a button on a typewriter or computer keyboard which is pressed to type letters **4** the chief note of a piece of music **5** something which explains a mystery or deciphers a code **6** a book containing answers to exercises □ *verb* to type on a typewriter or computer □ *adj* important, essential □ **keyboard** *noun* **1** the keys in a piano or organ arranged along a flat board **2** the keys of a typewriter or computer **3** an electronic musical instrument with keys arranged as on a piano *etc* □ **keyed-up** *adj* excited □ **keyhole** *noun* the hole in which a key of a door is placed □ **keyhole surgery** surgery using miniature instruments, performed through tiny holes instead of large openings in the patient's flesh □ **keynote** *noun* **1** the chief note of a piece of music **2** the chief point about anything □ **keypad** *noun* a device with buttons that can be pushed to operate a television, telephone *etc* □ **keystone** *noun* the stone at the highest point of an arch holding the rest in position

**KGB** *abbrev, historical* Committee of State Security (in Russian, *Komitet Gosudarstvennoi Bezopasnosti*)

**khaki** *adj* greenish-brown in colour □ *noun* **1** greenish-brown **2** cloth of this colour used for military uniforms

From an Urdu word meaning 'dusty'

**kibbutz** *noun* (*pl* **kibbutzim**) a farming settlement in Israel in which all share the work

**kick** *verb* **1** to hit or strike out with

the foot **2** of a gun: to spring back violently when fired □ *noun* **1** a blow with the foot **2** the springing-back of a gun when fired □ **for kicks** *informal* for fun □ **kick-off** *noun* the start (of a football game)

**kid** *noun* **1** *informal* a child **2** a young goat **3** the skin of a young goat □ *adj* made of kid leather □ **with kid gloves** very carefully or tactfully

**kidnap** *verb* to carry (someone) off by force, often demanding money in exchange □ **kidnapper** *noun* □ **kidnapping** *noun*

> **kidnap** ⇨ kidnap**s**, kidnapp**ing**, kidnapp**ed**

> ◪ abduct

**kidney** *noun* (*pl* **kidneys**) either of a pair of organs in the lower back which filter waste from the blood and produce urine □ **kidney bean** a bean with a curved shape like a kidney

**kids' stuff** *informal* something very easy or tame

**kill** *verb* **1** to put to death **2** to put an end to □ *noun* **1** the act of killing **2** the animals killed by a hunter □ **be in at the kill** to be there at the most exciting moment □ **killer** *noun*

> ◪ (verb, meaning 1) slaughter, slay, exterminate, dispatch, annihilate

**killing** *noun*: **make a killing** to make a lot of money quickly

**kiln** *noun* a large oven or furnace for baking pottery, bricks *etc* or for drying grain, hops *etc*

**kilo-** *prefix* a thousand: *kilogramme/ kilometre*
  ⓖ From Greek *chilioi* meaning 'a thousand'

> ◔. In computing terminology **kilo-** does not mean exactly 1000, but 1024 (= 2¹⁰).

**kilobyte** *noun*, *computing* a measure of capacity equal to 1024 bytes

◔. See note at entry for prefix 'kilo-'

**kilocalorie** *noun* a measure of energy equal to 1000 calories

**kilogramme** *noun* a measure of weight equal to 1000 grammes (about 2 lb)

**kilometre** *noun* a measure of length equal to 1000 metres (about ⅝ of a mile)

**kilowatt** *noun* a measure of electrical power equal to 1000 watts

**kilt** *noun* a pleated tartan skirt reaching to the knee, part of traditional Scottish dress

**kimono** *noun* (*pl* **kimonos**) a loose Japanese robe, fastened with a sash

**kin** *noun* members of the same family, relations □ **kinsfolk** *noun pl* relations, relatives □ **kinsman**, **kinswoman** *noun* a close relation □ **kith and kin** *see* **kith** □ **next of kin** your nearest relative

**kind** *noun* **1** a sort, type **2** goods, not money: *paid in kind* □ *adj* having good feelings towards others; generous, gentle □ *adj* kind, warm-hearted □ **kindliness** *noun* □ **kindly** *adv* in a kind way □ **kindhearted** *adj* kind

**kindergarten** *noun* a nursery school

**kindle** *verb* **1** to light a fire **2** to catch fire **3** to stir up (feelings) □ **kindling** *noun* material for starting a fire

**kindred** *noun* relatives, relations □ *adj* of the same sort; related: *a kindred spirit*

**kinetic** *adj* of or expressing motion: *kinetic sculpture* (= sculpture which moves)

**king** *noun* **1** the inherited male ruler of a nation **2** a playing-card with a picture of a king **3** the most important chess piece □ **kingly** *adj* like a king; royal □ **kingdom** *noun* **1** the area ruled by a king **2** any of the three major divisions of natural objects, *ie* animal, vegetable or mineral □ **kingfisher** *noun* a type of fish-eating bird with brightly-coloured feathers

**kink** *noun* **1** a bend or curl in a rope, hair *etc* **2** a peculiarity of the mind □ **kinky** *adj* twisted, contorted

**kiosk** *noun* **1** a small stall for the sale of papers, sweets *etc* **2** a telephone box

**kip** *noun slang* a bed □ *verb* to go to bed, sleep

**kipper** *noun* a smoked and dried herring

**kirk** *noun, Scottish* a church

**kiss** *verb* **1** to touch lovingly with the lips **2** to touch gently □ *noun* (*pl* **kisses**) □ **kiss of life** a mouth-to-mouth method of restoring breathing

**kit** *noun* an outfit of clothes, tools *etc* necessary for a particular job

**kitchen** *noun* a room where food is cooked □ **kitchenette** *noun* a small kitchen □ **kitchen-garden** *noun* a vegetable garden

**kite** *noun* **1** a light frame, covered with paper or other material, for flying in the air **2** a kind of hawk

**kith** *noun*: **kith and kin** friends and relatives

**kitsch** *noun* vulgarly tasteless art *etc*

**kitten** *noun* a young cat □ **kittenish** *adj* behaving like a kitten, playful □ **have kittens** *informal* to make a great fuss

**kitty¹** *noun* (*pl* **kitties**) a sum of money set aside for a purpose

**kitty²** *noun* (*pl* **kitties**) *informal* a cat or kitten

**kiwi** *noun* **1** a fast-running almost wingless bird of New Zealand **2** a kiwi fruit □ **kiwi fruit** an edible fruit with a thin hairy skin and bright green flesh

**kleptomania** *noun* an uncontrollable desire to steal □ **kleptomaniac** *noun* & *adj*

**knack** (*say* nak) *noun* a special talent

**knacker** (*say* nak-er) *noun* a buyer of old horses for slaughter □ *verb,*

*informal* to exhaust, tire out

**knapsack** (*say* **nap**-sak) *noun* a bag for food, clothes *etc* slung on the back

**knave** (*say* neiv) *noun* **1** a cheating rogue **2** in playing-cards, the jack □ **knavery** (*say* neiv-e-ri) *noun* dishonesty □ **knavish** (*say* neiv-ish) *adj* cheating, wicked

**knead** (*say* need) *verb* **1** to work (dough *etc*) by pressing with the fingers **2** to massage

**knee** (*say* nee) *noun* the joint at the bend of the leg □ **kneecap** (*say* nee-kap) *noun* the flat round bone on the front of the knee joint □ *verb* to cause to suffer □ **kneecapping** (*say* nee-kap-ing) *noun* a form of torture or punishment in which the victim is shot or otherwise injured in the kneecap

**kneel** (*say* neel) *verb* to go down on one or both knees

**kneel** ⇨ kneels, kneeling, knelt

**knell** (*say* nel) *noun* **1** the tolling of a bell for a death or funeral **2** a warning of a sad end or failure

**knickerbockers** (*say* nik-e-bok-ez) *noun pl* loose breeches tucked in at the knee

Named after Diedrich *Knickerbocker*, a fictional Dutchman invented by US author Washington Irving in the 19th century

**knickers** (*say* **nik**-ez) *noun pl* women's or girls' underpants

**knick-knack** (*say* **nik**-nak) *noun* a small, ornamental article

**knife** (*say* naif) *noun* (*pl* **knives**) a tool for cutting □ *verb* to stab □ **at knife point** under threat of injury

**knight** (*say* nait) *noun* **1** *historical* an aristocrat trained to use arms **2** a rank, with the title *Sir*, which is not inherited by a son **3** a piece used in chess □ *verb* to raise to the rank of knight □ **knightly** (*say* **nait**-li) *adj* **1** of knights **2** gallant, courageous

▫ **knighthood** (*say* nait-huwd) *noun* the rank of a knight

**knit** (*say* nit) *verb* **1** to form a garment from yarn or thread by making a series of knots using knitting needles **2** to join closely ▫ **knitting** (*say* nit-ing) *noun* work done by knitting ▫ **knitting needles** a pair of thin pointed rods used in knitting

**knit** ▫ knits, knitting, knitted

**knob** (*say* nob) *noun* **1** a small rounded projection **2** a round door-handle

**knock** (*say* nok) *verb* **1** to strike, hit **2** to drive or be driven against **3** to tap on a door to have it opened ▫ *noun* **1** a sudden stroke **2** a tap (on a door) ▫ **knocker** (*say* nok-er) *noun* a hinged weight on a door for knocking with ▫ **knock back** *informal* to eat or drink greedily ▫ **knock down 1** to demolish **2** *informal* to reduce in price ▫ **knock off** *informal* **1** to stop work for the day **2** to plagiarize, copy illegally ▫ **knock out** to hit (someone) hard enough to make them unconscious ▫ **knock up 1** to put together hastily **2** to knock on someone's door to wake them up

▣ (verb, meaning 1) jog, jolt

**knock-kneed** (*say* nok-**need**) *adj* having knees that touch in walking

**knoll** (*say* nohl) *noun* a small rounded hill

**knot** (*say* not) *noun* **1** a hard lump, *eg* one made by tying string, or found in wood at the join between trunk and branch **2** a tangle **3** a small gathering, a cluster of people **4** a measure of speed for ships (about 1.85 kilometre per hour) ▫ *verb* to

tie in a knot ▫ **knotted** (*say* not-id) *adj* full of knots **knotty** (*say* not-i) *adj* **1** having knots **2** difficult, complicated: *knotty problem* ▫ **get knotted!** *exclam*, *informal* expressing anger or defiance towards someone

**knot** *verb* ▫ knots, knotting, knotted

**know** (*say* noh) *verb* **1** to be aware or sure of **2** to recognize ▫ **knowing** (*say* noh-ing) *adj* clever; cunning ▫ **knowingly** (*say* noh-ing-li) *adv* **1** intentionally **2** in a way which shows you understand something which is secret or which has not been directly expressed

**know** ▫ knows, knowing, known, knew

ⓘ From Old English *cnawan*

**knowledge** (*say* nol-ij) *noun* **1** that which is known **2** information **3** ability, skill ▫ **knowledgeable** (*say* nol-ij-*a*-bl) *adj* showing or having knowledge

**knuckle** (*say* nu-kl) *noun* a joint of the fingers ▫ **knuckle under** to give in, yield

**koala** *noun* an Australian tree-climbing animal resembling a small bear

**kohl** *noun* a black powder used as an eyeliner

**Koran** *noun* the sacred book of Islam

**kosher** *adj* **1** pure and clean according to Jewish law **2** *informal* acceptable, all right

**krill** *noun* a small shrimplike creature eaten by whales *etc*

**kudos** (*say* kyood-os) *noun* fame, glory

**kung-fu** *noun* a Chinese form of self-defence

**lab** *noun, informal* a laboratory

**label** *noun* a small written note fixed onto something listing its contents, price *etc* □ *verb* **1** to fix a label to **2** to call something by a certain name

**label** *verb* ⬦ labels, labelling, labelled

**labial** *adj* of the lips

**laboratory** *noun* (*pl* laboratories) a scientist's workroom

**laborious** *adj* requiring hard work; wearisome

**labour** or *US* **labor** *noun* **1** hard work **2** workers on a job **3** the process of childbirth □ *verb* **1** to work hard to move slowly or with difficulty **2** to emphasize (a point) too greatly □ **laboured** *adj* showing signs of effort □ **labourer** *noun* someone who does heavy unskilled work □ **Labour Party** one of the chief political parties of Great Britain, which has the aim of representing the working people and achieving greater social equality

**labrador** *noun* a large black or fawn-coloured dog, often used for retrieving game after it has been shot

**laburnum** *noun* a tree with large clusters of yellow flowers and poisonous seeds

**labyrinth** *noun* a maze

**lace** *noun* **1** a cord for fastening shoes *etc* **2** decorative openwork fabric made with fine thread □ *verb* **1** to fasten with a lace **2** to add alcohol to (a drink)

**lacerate** *verb* **1** to tear, rip **2** to wound □ **laceration** *noun*

**lachrymal** *adj* of tears

**lack** *verb* **1** to be in want **2** to be without □ *noun* want, need

**lackadaisical** *adj* bored, half-hearted

**lackey** *noun* (*pl* lackeys) **1** a manservant **2** someone who acts like a slave

**lacklustre** or *US* **lackluster** *adj* dull, insipid

**laconic** *adj* using few words to express meaning □ **laconically** *adv*

**lacquer** *noun* a varnish □ *verb* to varnish

**lacrosse** *noun* a twelve-a-side ball-game played with sticks having a shallow net at the end

**lad** *noun* a boy, a youth

**ladder** *noun* **1** a set of rungs or steps between two supports, for climbing up or down **2** a run from a broken stitch, in a stocking *etc*

**laden** *adj* loaded, burdened

**lading** *noun* a load; cargo

**ladle** *noun* a large spoon for lifting out liquid □ *verb* to lift with a ladle

**lady** *noun pl* ladies **1** a woman of good manners **2** a title for the wife of a knight, lord or baronet, or a daughter of a member of the aristocracy **3** (ladies) a public lavatory for women □ **ladyship** *noun*: *Her Ladyship* the title used in addressing a titled lady

**ladybird** *noun* a small beetle, usually red with black spots

**lag** *verb* **1** to move slowly and fall behind **2** to cover (a boiler or pipes) with a warm covering □ *noun* a delay □ **laggard** *noun* someone who lags behind □ *adj* lagging behind □ **lagging** *noun* material for covering pipes *etc*

**lag** ⬦ lags, lagging, lagged

**lager** *noun* a light beer

**lagoon** *noun* a shallow stretch of water separated from the sea by low sandbanks, rocks *etc*

**laid** *past form of* **lay**[1]

**laid-back** *adj, informal* relaxed, easy-going

**lain** *past participle of* **lie**[2]

**lair** (*say* leir) *noun* the den of a wild beast
ⓘ From Old English *leger* meaning 'a couch'
⚠ Do not confuse with: **layer**

**laity** (from **lay**[2]) (*say* lei-i-ti) *noun* ordinary people, not clergymen

**lake** *noun* a large stretch of water surrounded by land

**lama** *noun* a Buddhist priest of Tibet

**lamb** *noun* 1 a young sheep 2 the meat of this animal 3 a gentle person

**lambast** *verb* to beat or reprimand severely

**lame** *adj* 1 unable to walk, crippled 2 not good enough, not very convincing or impressive: *a lame excuse* □ *verb* to make lame
□ **lamely** *adv* (*adj*, meaning 2)

**lament** (*say* la-ment) *verb* 1 to mourn, feel or express grief for 2 to regret □ *noun* 1 a show of grief 2 a mournful poem or piece of music
□ **lamentation** *noun*

**lamentable** (*say* lam-en-ta-bl) *adj* 1 pitiful 2 very bad

**laminated** *adj* made by putting layers together: *laminated glass*

**lamp** *noun* a device to give out light, containing an electric bulb, candle *etc*

**lamppost** *noun* a pillar supporting a street lamp

**lamprey** (*say* lamp-ri) *noun* (*pl* **lampreys**) a type of fish like an eel

**LAN** (*say* lan) *abbrev, computing* local area network

**lance** *noun* a long shaft of wood, with a spearhead □ *verb* to cut open (a boil *etc*) with a knife

**lance-corporal** *noun* a soldier with rank just below a corporal

**lancet** *noun* a sharp surgical instrument

**land** *noun* 1 the solid portion of the earth's surface 2 ground 3 soil 4 a part of a country □ *verb* 1 to arrive on land or on shore 2 to set (an aircraft, ship *etc*) on land or on shore □ **landed** *adj* owning lands and estates: *landed gentry* □ **landing** *noun* 1 a coming ashore or to ground 2 a place for getting on shore 3 the level part of a staircase between the flights of steps
□ **landlocked** *adj* almost or completely shut in by land
□ **landlord, landlady** *noun* 1 the owner of land or accommodation for rent 2 the owner or manager of an inn *etc* □ **landlubber** *noun* someone who works on land and knows little about the sea
□ **landmark** *noun* 1 an object on land that serves as a guide 2 an important event □ **land mine** *noun* a bomb laid on or near the surface of the ground which explodes when someone passes over it □ **landslide** *noun* a mass of land that slips down from the side of a hill □ **landslide victory** a win in an election in which a great mass of votes goes to one side

**landscape** *noun* a painting, photograph *etc* of inland scenery
□ **landscape gardening** the art of laying out grounds so as to produce the effect of a picturesque landscape

**lane** *noun* 1 a narrow street or passage 2 a part of the road, sea or air to which cars, ships, aircraft *etc* must keep

**language** *noun* 1 human speech 2 the speech of a particular people or nation

**languid** *adj* lacking liveliness and spirit

**languish** *verb* 1 to grow weak, droop 2 to pine: *the dog was*

*languishing for its master*
□ **languishing** *adj*

**languor** *noun* a languid state, listlessness

**laniard** *another spelling of* **lanyard**

**lank** *adj* **1** tall and thin **2** of hair: straight and limp □ **lanky** *adj* tall and thin

**lanolin** *noun* a fat extracted from sheep's wool

**lantern** *noun* a case for holding or carrying a light

**lanyard** or **laniard** *noun* **1** a short rope used for fastening rigging *etc* on a ship **2** a cord for hanging a whistle *etc* round the neck

**lap** *verb* **1** to lick up with the tongue **2** to wash or flow against **3** **lap up** to accept (praise *etc*) greedily **4** to wrap round, surround **5** to get a lap ahead of other competitors in a race □ *noun* **1** the front part, from waist to knees, of someone seated **2** a fold **3** one round of a racetrack or competition course

**lap** *verb* ⇔ laps, lapping, lapped

**lapdog** *noun* a small pet dog

**lapel** *noun* the part of a coat joined to the collar and folded back on the chest

**lapse** *verb* **1** to fall into bad habits **2** to cease, be no longer valid □ *noun* **1** a mistake, a failure **2** a period of time passing

**laptop** *noun* a compact portable computer combining screen, keyboard and processor in one unit

**lapwing** *noun* (*also called* **peewit**) a type of bird of the plover family

**larceny** *noun* stealing, theft

**larch** *noun* (*pl* **larches**) a cone-bearing deciduous tree

**lard** *noun* the melted fat of a pig □ *verb* **1** to put strips of bacon in meat before cooking **2** to smear, lay on thickly

**larder** *noun* **1** a room or place where food is kept **2** a stock of food

**large** *adj* great in size, amount *etc* □ **largely** *adv* mainly, to a great extent □ **at large 1** at liberty, free **2** in general: *the public at large* ⊚ From French *large* meaning 'broad' or 'wide'

**largesse** (*say* lah-szes) *noun* a generous giving away of money *etc*

**lark** *noun* **1** a general name for several kinds of singing bird **2** a piece of fun or mischief □ *verb* to fool about, behave mischievously

**larva** *noun* (*pl* **larvae**) an insect in its first stage after coming out of the egg, a grub

**laryngitis** *noun* inflammation of the larynx

**larynx** *noun* (*pl* **larynxes** or **larynges**) the upper part of the windpipe containing the cords that produce the voice

**lasagne** *noun pl* flat sheets of pasta □ *noun sing* (or **lasagna**) a baked dish made with this

**lascivious** *adj* lustful; indecent, lewd

**laser** *noun* **1** a very narrow powerful beam of light **2** an instrument that concentrates light into such a beam

An acronym of '*l*ight *a*mplification by *s*timulated *e*mission of *r*adiation'

**lash** *noun* (*pl* **lashes**) **1** a thong or cord of a whip **2** a stroke with a whip **3** an eyelash □ *verb* **1** to strike with a whip **2** to fasten tightly with a rope *etc* **3** to attack with bitter words □ **lash out 1** to kick or swing out without thinking **2** to speak angrily **3** to spend extravagantly

**lass** *noun* (*pl* **lasses**) a girl

**lassitude** *noun* lack of energy, weariness

**lasso** *noun* (*pl* **lassoes** or **lassos**) a long rope with a loop that tightens when the rope is pulled, used for catching wild horses *etc* □ *verb* to catch with a lasso

**lasso** *verb* ⇔ lassoes, lassoing, lassoed

**last** *adj* **1** coming after all the others: *last person to arrive* **2** the final one remaining: *last ticket* **3** most recent: *my last employer* □ *adv* **1** after all others **2** most recently **3** lastly □ *verb* **1** to continue, go on **2** to remain in good condition □ *noun* a foot-shaped tool on which shoes are made or repaired □ **lastly** *adv* finally □ **at last** in the end □ **last rites** religious ceremonies performed for the dying □ **last straw** the last in a series of unpleasant events, which makes a situation unbearable □ **last word** the final comment or decision about something □ **on your last legs** completely worn out, about to collapse □ **to the last** to the end

**latch** *noun* (*pl* **latches**) **1** a wooden or metal catch used to fasten a door **2** a light door-lock □ *verb* to fasten with a latch □ **latchkey** *noun* a key to raise the latch of a door □ **latchkey child** a child who regularly returns home to an empty house

**late** *adj & adv* **1** coming after the expected time: *his train was late* **2** far on in time: *it's getting late* **3** recent: *our late disagreement* **4** recently dead: *the late author* **5** recently, but no longer, holding an office or position: *the late chairman* □ **lately** *adv* recently □ **lateness** *noun* (meanings 1 and 2) □ **of late** recently

**latent** *adj* hidden, undeveloped as yet: *latent ability/ latent hostility*

**lateral** *adj* of, at, to or from the side □ **lateral thinking** thinking which seeks new ways of looking at a problem and does not merely proceed in logical stages

**latex** *noun* the milky juice of plants, *esp* of the rubber tree

**lath** (*say* lahth) *noun* a thin narrow strip of wood

🖐 Do not confuse: **lath** and **lathe**

**lathe** (*say* leidh) *noun* a machine for turning and shaping articles of wood, metal *etc*

🄓 Probably from Old Danish *lad* meaning 'a supporting framework'

**lather** *noun* **1** a foam or froth, *eg* from soap and water **2** *informal* a state of agitation □ *verb* to cover with lather

**Latin** *noun* the language of ancient Rome

**latitude** *noun* **1** the distance, measured in degrees, of a place north or south of the equator (*compare with:* **longitude**) **2** freedom of action or choice: *the new job allows him far more latitude than his previous one*

**latrine** *noun* a toilet in a camp, barracks *etc*

**latter** *adj* **1** the last of two things mentioned (*contrasted with:* **former**): *between working and sleeping, I prefer the latter* **2** recent □ **latterly** *adv* recently □ **latter-day** *adj* of recent times

**lattice** *noun* **1** a network of crossed wooden *etc* strips **2** a window constructed this way

**laud** *verb, formal* to praise □ **laudable** *adj* worthy of being praised □ **laudably** *adv*

**laudanum** (*say* **lawd**-an-um) *noun* an alcoholic solution of opium, taken as a popular medicine in Victorian times

**laudatory** *adj* expressing praise

**laugh** *verb* to make sounds with the voice in showing amusement, scorn *etc* □ *noun* the sound of laughing □ **laughable** *adj* comical, ridiculous □ **laughing stock** an object of scornful laughter □ **laughter** *noun* the act or noise of laughing

▣ (verb) chuckle, giggle, guffaw, snigger, titter, chortle

**launch** *verb* **1** to slide a boat or ship into water, *esp* on its first voyage **2** to fire off (a rocket *etc*) **3** to start off on a course **4** to put (a product) on the market with publicity **5** to throw, hurl □ *noun* (*pl* **launches**) **1** the act of launching **2** a large motor boat

**launder** *verb* to wash and iron clothes *etc* □ **launderette** *noun* a shop where customers may wash clothes *etc* in washing machines □ **laundry** *noun* (*pl* **laundries**) **1** a place where clothes are washed **2** clothes to be washed

**laurel** *noun* **1** the bay tree, from which ceremonial wreaths were made **2** (**laurels**) honours or victories gained □ **rest on your laurels** to be content with past successes and not try for any more

**lava** *noun* molten rock *etc* thrown out by a volcano, becoming solid as it cools

**lavatory** *noun* (*pl* **lavatories**) a toilet

**lavender** *noun* **1** a sweet-smelling plant with small pale purple flowers **2** a pale-purple colour

**lavish** *verb* to spend or give very freely □ *adj* very generous

**law** *noun* **1** the official rules that apply in a country or state **2** one such rule **3** a scientific rule stating the conditions under which certain things always happen □ **law-abiding** *adj* obeying the law □ **law court** a place where people accused of crimes are tried □ **lawful** *adj* allowed by law □ **lawfully** *adv* □ **lawless** *adj* paying no attention to, and not observing, the laws □ **lawsuit** *noun* a quarrel or dispute to be settled by a court of law □ **lawyer** *noun* someone whose work it is to give advice in matters of law

**lawn** *noun* **1** an area of smooth grass, *eg* as part of a garden **2** a kind of fine linen □ **lawnmower** *noun* a machine for cutting grass □ **lawn tennis** tennis played on a hard or grass court

**lax** *adj* **1** not strict **2** careless, negligent □ **laxity** *noun*

**laxative** *noun* a medicine which loosens the bowels

**lay¹** *verb* **1** to place or set down: *lay the book on the table* **2** to put (*eg* a burden, duty) on (someone): *new laws laying more responsibility on teachers/ try to lay the blame on someone else* **3** to beat down: *all the barley in the field had been laid flat by the storm* **4** to settle or subside: *lay a ghost* **5** to set in order, arrange: *lay a trap/ lay the table* **6** of a hen: to produce eggs **7** to bet, wager: *he's sure to be late - I'd lay money on it* □ **lay about someone** to beat them all over □ **lay down 1** to assert: *laying down the law* **2** to store (*eg* wine) □ **lay off 1** to dismiss (workers) temporarily **2** *informal* to stop: *lay off arguing* □ **lay up** to store for future use □ **lay waste** to ruin, destroy

> **lay** *verb* ⊳ **lays, laying, laid**

> ◈. Do not confuse with: **lie**. It may help to remember that the verb **lay** always takes an object, while an object is not used with the verb **lie**.

**lay²** *adj* **1** not of the clergy **2** without special training in a particular subject □ **layman, laywoman** *noun* a person without special training in a subject

**lay³** *noun*, *old* a short poem or song

**layabout** *noun* a lazy idle person

**layby** *noun* a parking area at the side of a road

**layer** *noun* a thickness forming a covering or level □ **layered** *adj* having a number of distinct layers: *layered cake*

> ◈. Do not confuse with: **lair**. Layer comes from the verb 'to lay'.

**laze** *verb* to be lazy; idle

**lazy** *adj* not inclined to work; idle □ **lazily** *adj* □ **lazy-bones** *noun*, *informal* an idler

> **lazy** *adj* ⊳ **lazier, laziest**

■ idle, slothful, lethargic

**lea** *noun*, *old* a meadow

**lead¹** *verb* **1** to show the way by going first **2** to direct, guide **3** to persuade **4** to live (a busy, quiet *etc* life) **5** of a road: to go (to) □ *noun* **1** the first or front place **2** guidance, direction **3** a leash for a dog *etc* □ **leader** *noun* **1** someone who leads or goes first; a chief **2** a column in a newspaper expressing the editor's opinions □ **leadership** *noun* **1** the state of being a leader **2** the ability to lead □ **leading question** one asked in such a way as to suggest the desired answer

**lead** *verb* ↔ leads, leading, led

**lead²** *noun* **1** a soft bluish-grey metal **2** the part of a pencil that writes, really made of graphite **3** a weight used for sounding depths at sea *etc* □ **leaden** *adj* **1** made of lead **2** lead-coloured **3** dull, heavy □ **lead-free** *adj* of petrol: containing no lead

**leaf** *noun* (*pl* **leaves**) **1** a part of a plant growing from the side of a stem **2** a page of a book **3** a hinged flap on a table *etc* □ **leafy** *adj* **1** of a plant or tree: having a lot of leaves **2** of a place: having a lot of trees and plants □ **turn over a new leaf** to begin again and do better

**leaflet** *noun* a small printed sheet

**league** *noun* **1** a union of people, nations *etc* for the benefit of each other **2** an association of clubs for games **3** *old* a measure of distance, approximately 3 miles (about 4.8 kilometres) □ **in league with** allied with

**leak** *noun* **1** a hole through which liquid passes **2** an escape of gas *etc* **3** a release of secret information □ *verb* **1** to escape, pass out **2** to give (secret information) to the media *etc* □ **leakage** *noun* a leaking

**lean** *verb* **1** to slope over to one side **2** to rest (against) **3** to rely (on) □ *adj* **1** thin **2** poor, scanty **3** of

meat: not fat □ **leaning** *noun* a liking for, or interest in, something

**lean** *verb* ↔ leans, leaning, leant

**leap** *verb* **1** to move with jumps **2** to jump (over) □ *noun* a jump □ **leapfrog** *noun* a game in which one player leaps over another's bent back

**leap** *verb* ↔ leaps, leaping, leapt

**leap year** a year which has 366 days (February having 29), occurring every fourth year

**learn** *verb* **1** to get to know (something) **2** to gain skill □ **learned** (*say* ler-nid) *adj* having or showing great knowledge □ **learner** *noun* someone who is learning something □ **learning** *noun* knowledge

**learn** ↔ learns, learning, learnt or learned

**lease** *noun* **1** an agreement giving the use of a house *etc* in return for payment of rent **2** the period of this agreement □ *verb* to let or rent □ **lease-back** *noun* an arrangement in which the buyer of a property leases it back to the seller □ **leasehold** *noun* property or land held by lease

**leash** *noun* (*pl* **leashes**) a lead by which a dog *etc* is held □ *verb* to put (a dog *etc*) on a leash

**least** *adj* the smallest amount of anything: *he had the least money* □ *adv* (often **the least**) the smallest or lowest degree: *I like her least* □ **at least** at any rate, anyway □ **not in the least** not at all

**leather** *noun* the skin of an animal, prepared by tanning for use □ *verb* to beat □ **leathery** *adj* like leather; tough

**leave** *noun* **1** permission to do something (*eg* to be absent) **2** a holiday □ *verb* **1** to allow to remain **2** to abandon, forsake **3** to depart (from) **4** to hand down to someone in a will **5** to give over to someone's responsibility, care *etc*: *leave the choice to her* □ **take your leave of 1** to part from **2** to say goodbye to

**leave** *verb* ⋄ **leaves, leaving, left**

**leaven** *noun* yeast □ **leavened** *adj* raised with yeast

**lecherous** *adj* lustful in a sexual way □ **lechery** *noun*

**lectern** *noun* a stand for a book to be read from

**lecture** *noun* **1** a formal talk on a certain subject given to an audience **2** a scolding □ *verb* **1** to deliver a lecture **2** to scold □ **lecturer** *noun* someone who lectures, *esp* to students

**LED** *abbrev* light-emitting diode

**led** *past form of* **lead**[1]

**ledge** *noun* **1** a shelf or projecting rim: *window-ledge* **2** an underwater ridge

**ledger** *noun* the accounts book of an office or shop

**lee** *noun* the side away from the wind, the sheltered side

**leech** *noun* (*pl* **leeches**) a kind of blood-sucking worm

**leek** *noun* a long green and white vegetable of the onion family

**leer** *noun* a sly, sidelong or lustful look □ *verb* to look sideways or lustfully (at)

**leeward** *adj & adv* in the direction towards which the wind blows

**leeway** *noun* **1** a ship's drift off course **2** lost time, ground *etc*: *a lot of leeway to make up* **3** room to manoeuvre, latitude

**left**[1] *adj* on or of the side of the body that in most people has the less skilful hand (*contrasted with*: **right**) □ *adv* on or towards the left side □ *noun* **1** the left side **2** a political grouping with left-wing ideas *etc* □ **left-handed** *adj* **1** using the left hand rather than the right **2** awkward

**left**[2] *past form of* **leave**

**left-field** *adj, informal* odd, eccentric

**left-wing** *adj* of or holding socialist or radical political views, ideas *etc*

**leg** *noun* **1** one of the limbs by which humans and animals walk **2** a long slender support for a table *etc* **3** one stage in a journey, contest *etc*

**legacy** *noun* (*pl* **legacies**) **1** something which is left by will **2** something left behind by the previous occupant of a house, job *etc*

**legal** *adj* **1** allowed by law, lawful **2** of law □ **legality** *noun* (*pl* **legalities**) the state of being legal □ **legalize** *verb* to make lawful

**legate** *noun* an ambassador, *esp* from the Pope

**legend** *noun* **1** a traditional story handed down, a myth **2** a caption □ **legendary** *adj* **1** of legend; famous **2** not to be believed

**leggings** *noun pl* **1** outer coverings for the lower legs **2** close-fitting trousers for women

**leggy** *adj* having long legs

**legible** *adj* able to be read easily □ **legibility** *noun*

**legion** *noun* **1** *historical* a body of from three to six thousand Roman soldiers **2** a very great number □ **legionary** *noun* (*pl* **legionaries**) a soldier of a legion

**legislate** *verb* to make laws □ **legislation** *noun* □ **legislative** *adj* law-making □ **legislator** *noun* someone who makes laws □ **legislature** *noun* the part of the government which has the powers of making laws

**legitimate** *adj* **1** lawful **2** of a child: born of parents married to each other **3** correct, reasonable □ **legitimacy** *noun*

**leisure** *noun* time free from work, spare time □ **leisured** *adj* not occupied with business □ **leisurely** *adj* unhurried: *leisurely pace*

**lemming** *noun* **1** a small rat-like animal of the arctic regions, reputed to follow others of its kind over sea-cliffs *etc* when migrating **2** someone who follows others unquestioningly

**lemon** *noun* **1** an oval fruit with pale yellow rind and sour juice **2** the tree that bears this fruit □ **lemonade** *noun* a soft drink flavoured with lemons

**lemur** *noun* an animal related to the monkey but with a pointed nose

**lend** *verb* **1** to give use of (something) for a time **2** to give, add (a quality) to someone or something: *his presence lent an air of respectability to the occasion* □ **lend itself to** to be suitable for, adapt easily to

**lend** ⇔ lend*s*, lend*ing*, lent

**length** *noun* **1** extent from end to end in space or time **2** the quality of being long **3** a great extent **4** a piece of cloth *etc* □ **lengthen** *verb* to make or grow longer □ **lengthways** or **lengthwise** *adv* in the direction of the length □ **lengthy** *adj* **1** long **2** tiresomely long □ **at length 1** in detail **2** at last

**lenient** *adj* merciful, punishing only lightly □ **lenience** or **leniency** *noun*

**lens** *noun* (*pl* **lenses**) **1** a piece of glass curved on one or both sides, used in spectacles, cameras *etc* **2** a part of the eye

**Lent** *noun* in the Christian church, a period of fasting before Easter lasting forty days

**lent** *past form of* lend

**lentil** *noun* the seed of a pod-bearing plant, used in soups *etc*

**leopard, leopardess** *noun* an animal of the cat family with a spotted skin

**leotard** *noun* a tight-fitting, stretchy garment worn for dancing, gymnastics *etc*

**lepidopterology** *noun* the study of butterflies and moths

**leprechaun** *noun* a creature in Irish folklore

**leprosy** *noun* a contagious skin disease causing thickening or numbness in the skin □ **leper** *noun* **1** someone with leprosy **2** an outcast

**lesbian** *noun* a female homosexual □ *adj* of a woman: homosexual

**lesion** *noun* a wound

**less** *adj* **1** not as much: *take less* **2** smaller: *think of a number less than 40* □ *adv* not as much, to a smaller extent: *he goes less often than he should* □ *noun* a smaller amount: *he has less than I have* □ *prep* minus: *5 less 2 equals 3* □ **lessen** *verb* to make smaller □ **lesser** *adj* smaller

**lesson** *noun* **1** something which is learned or taught **2** a part of the Bible read in church **3** a period of teaching

**lest** *conj* for fear that, in case

**let** *verb* **1** to allow **2** to grant use of (*eg* a house, shop, farm) in return for payment □ **let down** to fail to act as expected, disappoint □ **let off** to excuse, not punish □ **let up** to become less

**let** *verb* ⇔ let*s*, let*ting*, let

▪ (verb, meaning 1) permit, authorize, give leave □ **let up** subside, abate

**lethal** *adj* causing death

**lethargy** *noun* a lack of energy or interest; sleepiness □ **lethargic** *adj*

**letter** *noun* **1** a mark expressing a sound **2** a written message **3** (**letters**) learning: *a woman of letters* □ **lettering** *noun* letters which have been drawn or painted, usually in a particular style □ **to the letter** according to the exact meaning of the words: *following instructions to the letter*

**lettuce** *noun* a kind of green plant whose leaves are used in a salad

**leukaemia** *noun* a cancerous disease

of the white blood cells in the body

**level** noun **1** a flat, smooth surface **2** a height, position etc in comparison with some standard: water level **3** an instrument for showing whether a surface is level: spirit level **4** personal rank or degree of understanding: a bit above my level □ adj **1** flat, even, smooth **2** horizontal □ verb **1** to make flat, smooth or horizontal **2** to make equal **3** to aim (a gun etc) **4** to pull down (a building etc)

**level** verb ⇔ levels, levelling, levelled

**level crossing** a place where a road crosses a railway track

**lever** noun **1** a bar of metal, wood etc used to raise or shift something heavy **2** a handle for operating a machine **3** a method of gaining advantage □ **leverage** noun **1** the use of a lever **2** power, influence

**leveret** noun a young hare

**levitate** verb to float in the air □ **levitation** noun the illusion of raising a heavy body in the air without support

**levity** noun lack of seriousness, frivolity

**levy** verb to collect by order (eg a tax, army conscripts) □ noun (pl **levies**) money, troops etc collected by order

**levy** ⇔ levies, levying, levied

**lewd** adj taking delight in indecent thoughts or acts

**lexicographer** noun someone who compiles or edits a dictionary □ **lexicography** noun

**liable** adj **1** legally responsible (for) **2** likely or apt (to do something or happen) **3 liable to** likely to have, suffer from: liable to colds □ **liability** noun (pl **liabilities**) **1** legal responsibility **2** a debt **3** a disadvantage

**liaise** (say lee-eiz) verb to make a connection (with), be in touch (with) □ **liaison** (say lee-eiz-on) noun **1** contact, communication **2** a

sexual affair

**liar** (from **lie**[1]) noun someone who tells lies

**lib** noun, informal liberation: women's lib

**Lib Dem** short for Liberal Democrat

**libel** noun something written to hurt another's reputation □ verb to write something libellous about □ **libellous** adj containing a written false statement which hurts a person's reputation

**libel** verb ⇔ libels, libelling, libelled

**liberal** adj generous; broad-minded, tolerant □ noun (**Liberal**) a member of the former Liberal Party, which supported social and political reform □ **liberality** noun □ **Liberal Democrats** one of the chief political parties of Great Britain, formed in 1988 from the Liberal Party and the Social Democratic Party

**liberate** verb to set free □ **liberation** noun

**liberty** noun (pl **liberties**) **1** freedom, esp of speech or action **2** (**liberties**) rights, privileges □ **take liberties** to behave rudely or impertinently

**library** noun (pl **libraries**) **1** a collection of books, records etc **2** a building or room housing these □ **librarian** noun a person employed in or in charge of a library

**libretto** noun (pl **libretti** or **librettos**) the words of an opera, musical show etc

**lice** pl of louse

**licence** noun **1** a form giving permission to do something, eg to keep a television set, drive a car etc **2** too great freedom of action

◆ Do not confuse: **licence** and **license**. Licence / license and practice / practise follow the same pattern: you spell the verbs with an S (licenSe, practiSe), and the nouns with a C (licenCe, practiCe).

**license** verb to permit

**licensee** noun someone to whom a licence is given

**licentious** adj given to behaving immorally or improperly

**lichen** (say laik-en) noun a large group of moss-like plants that grow on rocks etc

**lick** verb 1 to pass the tongue over 2 of flames: to reach up, touch □ noun 1 the act of licking 2 a tiny amount □ **lick into shape** to make vigorous improvements on

**licorice** another spelling of **liquorice**

**lid** noun 1 a cover for a box, pot etc 2 the cover of the eye

**lido** (say lee-doh) noun 1 a bathing beach 2 an open-air swimming pool

**lie¹** noun a false statement meant to deceive □ verb to tell a lie

**lie¹** verb ⇌ lies, lying, lied

■ (verb) fib, fabricate

**lie²** verb 1 to rest in a flat position 2 to be or remain in a state or position: lie dormant □ noun the position or situation in which something lies □ **lie in wait** to keep hidden in order to surprise someone □ **lie low** to keep quiet or hidden □ **the lie of the land** the present state of affairs

**lie²** verb ⇌ lies, lying, lay, lain

◆ Do not confuse with: **lay**. It may help to remember that an object is not used with the verb lie, while the verb lay always takes an object.

**liege** (say leesz) noun 1 a loyal subject 2 a lord or superior

**lieu** (say lyoo or loo) noun: **in lieu of** instead of

**lieutenant** (say lef-ten-ant or US loo-ten-ant) noun 1 an army officer next below captain 2 in the navy, an officer below a lieutenant-commander 3 a rank below a higher officer: lieutenant-colonel

**life** noun (pl **lives**) 1 the period between birth and death 2 the state of being alive 3 liveliness 4 manner of living 5 the story of someone's life 6 living things: animal life □ **lifebelt** noun a ring made of cork or filled with air for keeping someone afloat □ **lifeboat** noun a boat for rescuing people in difficulties at sea □ **life-blood** noun a source of necessary strength or life □ **lifebuoy** noun a float to support someone awaiting rescue at sea □ **life-cycle** noun the various stages through which a living thing passes □ **life drawing** drawing from a live human model □ **life-jacket** noun a buoyant jacket for keeping someone afloat in water □ **lifeless** adj 1 dead 2 not lively, spiritless □ **life-like** adj like a living person □ **lifeline** noun a vital means of communication □ **lifelong** adj lasting the length of a life □ **life-size** adj full size, as in life □ **lifespan** noun the length of someone's life □ **lifestyle** noun the way in which someone lives □ **life-support machine** a device for keeping a human being alive during severe illness, space travel etc □ **lifetime** noun the period during which someone is alive

**lift** verb 1 to raise, take up 2 informal to steal 3 of fog: to disappear, disperse □ noun 1 a moving platform carrying goods or people between floors in a large building 2 a ride in someone's car etc 3 a boost □ **lift-off** noun the take-off of a rocket, spacecraft etc

**ligament** noun a tough substance that connects the bones of the body

**ligature** noun 1 something which binds 2 a printed character formed from two or more letters joined together, eg æ or ffi

**light¹** noun 1 the brightness given by the sun, moon, lamps etc that makes things visible 2 a source of light, eg a lamp 3 a flame on a cigarette

lighter 4 knowledge □ *adj* 1 bright
2 of a colour: pale 3 having light,
not dark □ *verb* 1 to give light to
2 to set fire to □ **lighthouse** *noun* a
tower-like building with a flashing
light to warn or guide ships
□ **lighting** *noun* 1 a means of
providing light 2 the combination
of lights used, *eg* in a theatre or a
disco □ **bring to light** to reveal,
cause to be noticed □ **come to light**
to be revealed or discovered □ **in the
light of** taking into consideration
(information *etc*)

**light** *verb* ↔ light*s*, light*ing*, lit or
light*ed*

**light²** *adj* 1 not heavy 2 easy to bear
or do: *light work* 3 easy to digest
4 nimble 5 lively 6 not grave,
cheerful 7 not serious: *light reading*
8 of rain *etc*: little in quantity
□ **lightly** *adv* 1 gently 2 not
seriously

**light³** *verb, old*: **light on** 1 to land,
settle on 2 to come upon by chance

**light** ↔ light*s*, light*ing*, lit or light*ed*

**lighten** *verb* 1 to make less heavy
2 to make or become brighter 3 of
lightning: to flash

**lighter** *noun* 1 a device with a flame
*etc* for lighting 2 a large open boat
used in unloading and loading ships

**light-fingered** *adj* apt to steal

**light-headed** *adj* dizzy

**light-hearted** *adj* cheerful

**lightning** *noun* an electric flash in the
clouds □ **lightning conductor** a
metal rod on a building *etc* which
conducts electricity down to earth

**lightweight** *noun* a weight category
in boxing □ *adj* not serious enough
to demand much concentration

**light-year** *noun* the distance light
travels in a year (6 billion miles)

**like¹** *adj* the same as or similar to
□ *adv* in the same way as: *he sings
like an angel* □ *noun* something or
someone that is the equal of
another: *you won't see her like again*

□ **liken** *verb* to think of as similar,
compare □ **likeness** *noun*
1 similarity, resemblance 2 a
portrait, photograph *etc* of
someone □ **likewise** *adv* 1 in the
same way 2 also

**like²** *verb* 1 to be pleased with 2 to be
fond of □ **likeable** or **likable** *adj*
attractive, lovable □ **liking** *noun*
1 fondness 2 satisfaction: *to my
liking*

⊕ From Old English *lician* meaning
'to please' or 'to be suitable'

**likely** *adj* 1 probable 2 liable (to do
something) □ *adv* probably
□ **likelihood** *noun* probability

**lilac** *noun* a small tree with hanging
clusters of pale purple or white
flowers □ *adj* of pale purple colour

**lilt** *noun* a striking rhythm or swing
□ *verb* to have this rhythm

**lily** *noun* (*pl* **lilies**) a tall plant grown
from a bulb with large white or
coloured flowers □ **lily-of-the-valley**
*noun* a plant with small white bell-
shaped flowers

**limb** *noun* 1 a leg or arm 2 a branch

**limber** *adj* easily bent, supple
□ **limber up** to exercise so as to
become supple

**limbo¹** *noun* the borderland of Hell,
reserved for those unbaptized
before death □ **in limbo** forgotten,
neglected

**limbo²** *noun* a W Indian dance in
which the dancer passes under a low
bar

**lime** *noun* 1 (*also called* **quicklime**) a
white substance left after heating
limestone, used in making cement
2 a tree related to the lemon 3 the
greenish-yellow fruit of this tree

**limelight** *noun* the glare of publicity
□ **in the limelight** attracting
publicity or attention

**limerick** *noun* a type of humorous
poetry in five-line verses

After *Limerick* in Ireland, the name
of which was repeated in nonsense

songs in an old Victorian parlour game

Limericks are funny poems with five lines and a strict rhyme scheme. Maybe you know this one:
*There was a young lady from Tottenham*
*Whose manners, she quite had forgotten 'em,*
*At tea at the vicar's*
*She took off her knickers*
*Because, she explained, she felt hot in 'em.*

*Can you make up some more?*

**limit** *noun* **1** the farthest point or place **2** a boundary **3** the largest (or smallest) extent, degree *etc* **4** a restriction □ *verb* to set or keep to a limit □ **limitation** *noun* **1** something which limits **2** a weak point, a flaw

**limousine** *noun* a kind of large car, *esp* one with a separate compartment for the driver □ **limo** *noun, informal* a limousine

Named after a type of cloak worn in *Limousin* in France, because the car's roof was supposedly similar in shape

**limp** *adj* **1** not stiff, floppy **2** weak □ *verb* **1** to walk lamely **2** of a damaged ship *etc*: to move with difficulty □ *noun* **1** the act of limping **2** a limping walk

**limpet** *noun* **1** a small cone-shaped shellfish that clings to rocks **2** someone who is difficult to get rid of

**limpid** *adj* clear, transparent

**linchpin** *noun* a pin-shaped rod used to keep a wheel on an axle

**line** *noun* **1** a cord, rope *etc* **2** a long thin stroke or mark **3** a wrinkle **4** a row of people, printed words *etc* **5** a service of ships or aircraft **6** a railway **7** a telephone connection **8** a short letter **9** a family from generation to generation **10** course, direction **11** a subject of interest, activity *etc* **12** (**lines**) army trenches

**13** (**lines**) a written school punishment exercise □ *verb* **1** to mark out with lines **2** (often **line up**) to place in a row or alongside of **3** to form lines along (a street) **4** to cover on the inside: *line a dress* □ **lineage** *noun* descent, traced back to your ancestors □ **lineal** *adj* directly descended through the father, grandfather *etc* □ **linear** *adj* **1** made of lines **2** in one dimension (length, breadth or height) only **3** capable of being represented on a graph by a straight line

**linen** *noun* **1** cloth made of flax **2** articles made of linen: *tablelinen/ bedlinen*

**liner** *noun* a ship or aeroplane working on a regular service

**linesman, lineswoman** *noun* an umpire at a boundary line

**linger** *verb* **1** to stay for a long time or for longer than expected **2** to loiter, delay

**lingerie** *noun pl* women's underwear

**lingo** *noun* (*pl* **lingoes**) a language, a dialect

**linguist** *noun* **1** someone skilled in languages **2** someone who studies language □ **linguistic** *adj* to do with language □ **linguistics** *noun sing* the scientific study of languages and of language in general

**liniment** *noun* an oil or ointment rubbed into the skin to cure stiffness in the muscles, joints *etc*

**lining** *noun* a covering on the inside

**link** *noun* **1** a ring of a chain **2** a single part of a series **3** anything connecting two things □ *verb* **1** to connect with a link **2** to join closely **3** to be connected □ **linkage** *noun*

**links** *noun pl* **1** a stretch of flat or slightly hilly ground near the seashore **2** a golf course

**linnet** *noun* a small songbird of the finch family

**lino-cut** *noun* a design for printing cut into a block of linoleum

**linoleum** *noun* a type of smooth, hard-wearing covering for floors □ **lino** *noun, informal* linoleum

**linseed** *noun* flax seed

**lint** *noun* 1 a soft woolly material for putting over wounds 2 fine pieces of fluff

**lintel** *noun* a timber or stone over a doorway or window

**lion, lioness** *noun* a powerful animal of the cat family □ **the lion's share** the largest share

**lip** *noun* 1 either of the two fleshy flaps in front of the teeth forming the rim of the mouth 2 the edge of a container *etc* □ **lip-reading** *noun* reading what someone says from the movement of their lips □ **lipstick** *noun* a stick of red, pink *etc* colouring for the lips

**liposuction** *noun* a surgical operation to remove unwanted body fat

**lip-service** *noun* saying one thing but believing another: *pay lip-service to the rules*

**liquefy** *verb* to make or become liquid □ **liquefaction** *noun*

**liquefy** ◌ liquefies, liquefying, liquefied

**liqueur** (*say* lik-yoor) *noun* a strong alcoholic drink, strongly flavoured and sweet

◗. Do not confuse with: **liquor**

**liquid** *noun* a flowing, water-like substance □ *adj* 1 flowing 2 looking like water 3 soft and clear □ **liquidize** *verb* 1 to make liquid 2 to make into a purée □ **liquidizer** *noun* a machine for liquidizing

**liquidate** *verb* 1 to close down, wind up the affairs of (a bankrupt business company) 2 *slang* to kill, murder □ **liquidation** *noun* □ **liquidator** *noun*

**liquor** (*say* lik-er) *noun* an alcoholic drink, *esp* a spirit (*eg* whisky)

◗. Do not confuse with: **liqueur**

**liquorice** or **licorice** *noun* 1 a plant with a sweet-tasting root 2 a black, sticky sweet flavoured with this root

**lisp** *verb* 1 to say *th* for *s* or *z* because of being unable to pronounce these letters correctly 2 to speak imperfectly, like a child □ *noun* a speech disorder of this kind

**list**[1] *noun* a series of names, numbers, prices *etc* written down one after the other □ *verb* to write (something) down in this way

**list**[2] *verb* of a ship: to lean over to one side □ *noun* a slope to one side □ **listless** *adj* weary, without energy or interest

**listen** *verb* to hear, pay attention to □ **listener** *noun*

**lit** *past form* of **light**[1] and **light**[3]

**litany** *noun* (*pl* **litanies**) 1 a set form of prayer 2 a long list or catalogue

**liter** *US* spelling of **litre**

**literacy** *noun* ability to read and write

**literal** *adj* following the exact or most obvious meaning (*contrasted with*: **figurative**) □ **literally** *adv* exactly as stated, not just as a figure of speech: *he was literally blinded by the flash*

**literary** *adj* 1 relating to books, authors *etc* 2 knowledgeable about books

**literate** *adj* able to read and write

**literature** *noun* 1 the books *etc* that are written in any language 2 anything in written form on a subject

**lithe** *adj* bending easily, supple, flexible

**lithium** *noun* a metallic element whose salts are used in treating some mental illnesses

**lithograph** *noun* a picture made from a drawing done on stone or metal □ **lithography** *noun* printing done by this method

**litigation** *noun* a law case

**litmus paper** treated paper which changes colour when dipped in an acid or alkaline solution

**litmus test** something which indicates underlying attitudes *etc*

**litre** *noun* a metric measure of liquids (1.76 pint)

**litter** *noun* 1 an untidy mess of paper, rubbish *etc* 2 a heap of straw as bedding for animals 3 a number of animals born at one birth 4 *historical* a bed for carrying the sick and injured □ *verb* 1 to scatter rubbish carelessly about 2 to produce a litter of young

**little** *adj* small in quantity or size □ *adv* 1 a little to a small extent or degree 2 not much 3 not at all: *little does she know* □ *pronoun* a small amount, distance *etc*: *have a little more/ move a little to the right*

**liturgy** (*say* lit-u-ji) *noun* (*pl* **liturgies**) the form of service of a church □ **liturgical** *adj*

**live**[1] (*say* liv) *verb* 1 to have life 2 to dwell 3 to pass your life 4 to continue to be alive 5 to survive 6 to be lifelike or vivid □ **live and let live** to allow others to live as they please □ **live down** to live until (an embarrassment *etc*) is forgotten by others □ **live on** 1 to keep yourself alive 2 to be supported by □ **live up to** to be as good as expected from

**live**[2] (*say* laiv) *adj* 1 having life, not dead 2 full of energy 3 of a television broadcast *etc*: seen as the event takes place, not recorded 4 charged with electricity and apt to give an electric shock □ **liven** *verb* to make lively

**livelihood** (*say* laiv-li-huwd) *noun* someone's means of living, *eg* their daily work

**lively** *adj* full of life, high spirits □ **liveliness** *noun*

**liver** *noun* a large gland in the body that carries out several important functions including purifying the blood

**livery** *noun* (*pl* **liveries**) the uniform of a manservant *etc* □ **at livery** of a horse: being kept at a stable in exchange for payment by its owner

**livestock** *noun* farm animals

**livewire** *noun* a very lively, energetic person

**livid** *adj* 1 of a bluish lead-like colour 2 very angry

**living** *adj* 1 having life 2 active, lively 3 of a likeness: exact □ *noun* means of living

**living-room** *noun* an informal sitting-room

**lizard** *noun* a four-footed reptile

**llama** *noun* a S American animal of the camel family without a hump

**lo** *exclam*, *old* look

**load** *verb* 1 to put on what is to be carried 2 to put the ammunition in (a gun) 3 to put a film in (a camera) 4 to weight for some purpose: *loaded dice* □ *noun* 1 as much as can be carried at once 2 cargo 3 a heavy weight or task 4 the power carried by an electric circuit

**loaf** *noun* (*pl* **loaves**) a shaped mass of bread □ *verb* to pass time idly or lazily □ **loafer** *noun* 1 an idler 2 (**loafers**) casual shoes

**loam** *noun* a rich soil □ **loamy** *adj*

**loan** *noun* something lent, *esp* a sum of money □ *verb* to lend

**loath** or **loth** (*say* lohth) *adj* unwilling (to)

🖤 Do not confuse: **loath** and **loathe**. Remember that loaTHE has an ending common to quite a few other verbs *eg* cloTHE and baTHE.

**loathe** (*say* lohdh) *verb* to dislike greatly □ **loathing** (*say* lohdh-ing) *noun* great hate or disgust □ **loathsome** (*say* lohdh-som) *adj* causing loathing or disgust, horrible

**loaves** *pl* of **loaf**

**lob** *noun* 1 *cricket* a slow, high ball

bowled underhand **2** *tennis* a ball high overhead dropping near the back of the court □ *verb* **1** to send such a ball **2** *informal* to throw

**lob** *verb* ↔ lobs, lob**bing**, lob**bed**

**lobby** *noun* (*pl* lob**bies**) **1** a small entrance hall **2** a passage off which rooms open **3** a group of people who try to influence the government or another authority □ *verb* **1** to try to influence (public officials) **2** to conduct a campaign to influence public officials

**lobby** *verb* ↔ lob**bies**, lob**bying**, lob**bied**

**lobe** *noun* **1** the hanging-down part of an ear **2** a division of the brain, lungs *etc*

**lobotomy** *noun* **1** the surgical operation of cutting into a lobe or gland **2** a surgical operation on the front lobes of the brain which has the effect of changing the patient's character □ **lobotomize** *verb* **1** to perform a lobotomy on **2** to make bland or spiritless

**lobster** *noun* a kind of shellfish with large claws, used for food

**local** *adj* of or confined to a certain place □ *noun*, *informal* **1** the public house nearest someone's home **2** (**locals**) the people living in a particular place or area □ **locale** *noun* scene, location □ **locality** *noun* a particular place and the area round about □ **localize** *verb* to confine to one area, keep from spreading
ⓞ From Latin *locus* meaning 'a place'

**locate** *verb* **1** to find **2** to set in a particular place: *a house located in the Highlands* □ **location** *noun* **1** the act of locating **2** position, situation □ **on location** of filming *etc*: in natural surroundings, not in a studio

**loch** *noun* **1** in Scotland, a lake **2** an arm of the sea

**lock** *noun* **1** a fastening for doors *etc* needing a key to open it **2** a part of a canal for raising or lowering boats **3** the part of a gun which explodes the charge **4** a tight hold **5** a section of hair **6** (**locks**) hair □ *verb* **1** to fasten with a lock **2** to become fastened **3** lock up to shut in with a lock □ **lockjaw** *noun* a form of tetanus which stiffens the jaw muscles □ **locksmith** *noun* a person who makes locks □ **lock-up** *noun* a lockable garage □ **lock, stock and barrel** completely

**locker** *noun* a small cupboard □ **locker-room** *noun* a room for changing clothes and storing personal belongings

**locket** *noun* a little ornamental case hung round the neck

**locomotion** *noun* movement from place to place

**locomotive** *noun* a railway engine □ *adj* of or capable of locomotion

**locum** *noun* (*pl* **locums**) a doctor, dentist *etc* taking another's place for a time

**locus** *noun* (*pl* **loci**) a place, a locality

**locust** *noun* a large insect of the grasshopper family which destroys growing plants

**lodestone** *noun* **1** a form of the mineral magnetite with magnetic properties **2** a magnet

**lodge** *noun* **1** a small house, often at the entrance to a larger building **2** a beaver's dwelling **3** a house occupied during the shooting or hunting season **4** a branch of a society □ *verb* **1** to live in rented rooms **2** to become fixed (in) **3** to put in a safe place **4** to make (a complaint, appeal *etc*) officially □ **lodger** *noun* someone who stays in rented rooms □ **lodging** *noun* **1** a place to stay, sleep *etc* **2** (**lodgings**) a room or rooms rented in someone else's house

**loft** *noun* **1** a room just under a roof

**2** a gallery in a hall, church *etc*

**lofty** *adj* **1** of great height **2** noble, proud □ **loftily** *adv* (meaning 2)

**log** *noun* **1** a thick, rough piece of wood, part of a felled tree **2** a device for measuring a ship's speed **3** a logbook □ *verb* to write down (events) in a logbook □ **logbook** *noun* **1** an official record of a ship's or aeroplane's progress **2** a record of progress, attendance *etc* **3** the registration documents of a motor vehicle

**log** *verb* ↔ logs, logging, logged

**loganberry** *noun* a kind of fruit like a large raspberry

**loggerhead** *noun*: **at loggerheads** quarrelling

**logic** *noun* **1** the study of reasoning correctly **2** correctness of reasoning □ **logical** *adj* according to the rules of logic or sound reasoning □ **logically** *adv*

**logo** *noun* (*pl* **logos**) a symbol of a business firm *etc* consisting of a simple picture or lettering

**loin** *noun* **1** the back of an animal cut for food **2** (**loins**) the lower part of the back □ **loincloth** *noun* a piece of cloth worn round the hips, *esp* in India and south-east Asia

**loiter** *verb* **1** to proceed, move slowly **2** to linger **3** to stand around

**loll** *verb* **1** to lie lazily about **2** of the tongue: to hang down or out

**lollipop** *noun* a large boiled sweet on a stick

**lollipop man, lollipop woman** *Brit* a person employed to stop cars to allow schoolchildren to cross the street, who carries a pole with a disc at the top

**lolly** *noun*, *informal* **1** a lollipop **2** money

**lone** *adj* alone; standing by itself □ **lonely** *adj* **1** lone **2** lacking or needing companionship **3** of a place: having few people

□ **loneliness** *noun* □ **lonesome** *adj* **1** lone **2** feeling lonely

**long** *adj* **1** not short, measuring a lot from end to end **2** measuring a certain amount: *cut a strip 2 cm long/ the film is 3 hours long* **3** far-reaching **4** slow to do something □ *adv* **1** for a great time **2** through the whole time: *all day long* □ *verb* to wish very much (for): *longing to see him again* □ **longevity** *noun* great length of life □ **longhand** *noun* writing in full (*contrasted with*: **shorthand**) □ **longing** *noun* a strong desire □ **longitude** *noun* the distance, measured in degrees, of a place east or west of the Greenwich meridian (*compare with*: **latitude**) □ **long johns** men's under-trousers reaching to the ankles □ **long jump** an athletics contest in which competitors jump as far as possible along the ground from a running start □ **long-range** *adj* **1** able to reach a great distance **2** looking a long way into the future □ **longship** *noun*, *historical* a Viking sailing ship □ **long-sighted** *adj* able to see things at a distance but not those close at hand □ **long-standing** *adj* begun a long time ago, having lasted a long time □ **long-suffering** *adj* putting up with troubles without complaining □ **long-term** *adj* **1** extending over a long time **2** taking the future, not just the present, into account □ **long-wave** *adj* of radio: using wavelengths over 1000 metres (*compare with*: **short wave**) □ **long-winded** *adj* using too many words □ **before long** □ **in the long run** in the end □ **so long** *informal* goodbye

**loo** *noun*, *informal* a toilet

**loofah** *noun* the fibrous fruit of a tropical plant, used as a rough sponge

**look** *verb* **1** to turn the eyes towards so as to see **2** to appear, seem: *you look tired/ it looks as if I can go after* *all* **3** to face: *his room looks south* □ *noun* **1** the act of looking **2** the expression on someone's face **3** appearance **4** (**looks**) personal appearance □ **look-alike** *noun* someone who looks physically like someone else □ **lookout** *noun* **1** (someone who keeps) a careful watch **2** a high place for watching from **3** concern, responsibility □ **look after** to take care of, take responsibility for □ **look alive** *informal* to rouse yourself, get ready for action □ **look down on** to think of as being inferior □ **look for** to search for □ **look forward to** to anticipate with pleasure □ **look into** to investigate □ **look on** **1** to stand by and watch **2** to think of (as): *he looks on her as his mother* □ **look out!** be careful! □ **look over** to examine briefly □ **look sharp** *informal* to be quick, hurry up

■ (verb, meaning 1) observe, view, survey, regard, gaze, study, stare, examine, inspect, scrutinize, glance, contemplate, scan, peep □ **look after** mind, attend to, tend, keep an eye on, supervise, guard

**look-in** *noun* a chance of doing something

**looking-glass** *noun* a mirror

**loom** *noun* a machine for weaving cloth □ *verb* to appear indistinctly, often threateningly

**loony** *noun, informal* a lunatic, an insane person □ *adj* mad, insane

**loop** *noun* **1** a doubled-over part in a piece of string *etc* **2** a U-shaped bend □ **loop the loop** to fly (an aircraft) upwards, back and down as if going round a circle □ **loophole** *noun* **1** a narrow slit in a wall **2** a way of avoiding a difficulty

**loose** (*say* loos) *adj* **1** not tight, slack **2** not tied, free **3** not closely packed **4** vague, not exact **5** careless □ *verb* **1** to make loose, slacken **2** to untie □ **loosen** *verb* to make loose or

looser □ **loose-leaf** *adj* having a cover that allows pages to be inserted or removed □ **break loose** to escape □ **on the loose** free □ **loosely** *adv* (adj, meanings 1, 3, 4 and 5)

◆. Do not confuse with: **lose**

**loot** *noun* goods stolen or plundered □ *verb* to plunder, ransack

**lop** *verb* to cut off the top or ends of □ **lop-eared** *adj* of an animal: having ears hanging down □ **lop-sided** *adj* leaning to one side, not symmetrical

**lop** ⇆ **lops**, **lopping**, **lopped**

**lope** *verb* to run with a long stride

**loquacious** (*say* lok-**wei**-shus) *adj* talkative □ **loquacity** (*pronounced* lok-**was**-it-i) *noun*

**lord** *noun* **1** the owner of an estate **2** a title for a male member of the aristocracy, bishop, judge *etc* **3** *old* a master, a ruler **4** (**the Lord**) God or Christ □ **lordly** *adj* **1** relating to a lord **2** noble, proud □ **lordship** *noun* **1** power, rule **2** used in addressing a lord: *his lordship* □ **drunk as a lord** extremely drunk □ **House of Lords** the upper (non-elected) house of the British parliament □ **lord it over someone** to act in a domineering manner towards them

**lore** *noun* knowledge, beliefs *etc* handed down

**lorgnette** (*pronounced* lawn-**yet**) *noun* eyeglasses with a handle

**lorry** *noun* (*pl* **lorries**) a motor vehicle for carrying heavy loads

**lose** (*pronounced* looz) *verb* **1** to cease to have, have no longer **2** to have (something) taken away from **3** to put (something) where it cannot be found **4** to waste (time) **5** to miss (a train, a chance *etc*) **6** to not win (a game) □ **loser** *noun* **1** someone unlikely to succeed at anything **2** someone who loses a game or contest **3** someone who is put in a disadvantageous situation as the result of a certain event

**lose** ⇌ **loses, losing, lost**

🖐 Do not confuse with: **loose**

**loss** noun (pl **losses**) **1** the act of losing **2** something which is lost **3** waste, harm, destruction □ **at a loss** uncertain what to do or say

**lost** adj **1** not able to be found **2** no longer possessed; thrown away **3** not won **4** ruined □ **lost in** completely taken up by, engrossed in: *lost in thought*

**lot** noun **1** a large number or quantity **2** someone's fortune or fate **3** a separate portion □ **draw lots** to decide who is to do something by drawing names out of a hat *etc*

**loth** *another spelling of* **loath**

**lotion** noun a liquid for treating or cleaning the skin or hair

**lottery** noun (pl **lotteries**) an event in which money or prizes are won through drawing lots

**lotus** noun (pl **lotuses**) **1** a kind of water-lily **2** a mythical tree whose fruit caused forgetfulness

**loud** adj **1** making a great sound; noisy **2** showy, over-bright □ adv in a way that makes a great sound; noisily □ **loudly** adv (adj, meaning 1) □ **loudness** noun (adj, meaning 1) □ **loudhailer** noun a megaphone with microphone and amplifier □ **loudmouth** noun, *informal* someone who talks offensively and too much □ **loudspeaker** noun a device for converting electrical signals into sound

**lounge** verb **1** to lie back in a relaxed way **2** to move about lazily □ noun a sitting-room

**lour** *see* **lower²**

**louse** noun (pl **lice**) a small blood-sucking insect sometimes found on the bodies of animals and people

**lousy** adj **1** swarming with lice **2** *informal* inferior, of poor quality

**lout** noun a clumsy or boorish man

**love** noun **1** a great liking or affection **2** a loved person **3** *tennis* no score, zero □ verb to be very fond of; like very much □ **lovable** adj worthy of love □ **lovely** adj beautiful; delightful □ **loveliness** noun □ **lover** noun **1** someone who loves another **2** an admirer, an enthusiast: *an art lover* **3** someone who is having a love affair □ **lovesick** adj languishing with love □ **loving** adj full of love □ **lovingly** adv □ **love affair** a relationship between people in love but not married □ **in love (with)** **1** feeling love and desire (for) **2** having a great liking (for): *in love with his own voice* □ **make love to** **1** to have sexual intercourse with **2** *old* to make sexual advances to, court

---

🔲 (verb) adore, cherish, idolize, enjoy, delight in

---

**low** adj **1** not high; not lying or reaching far up **2** of a voice: not loud **3** cheap: *low air-fare* **4** feeling sad, depressed **5** humble **6** mean, unworthy □ verb to make the noise of cattle; bellow, moo □ adv **1** in or to a low position **2** not loudly **3** cheaply □ **lowbrow** adj populist, not intellectual (contrasted with: **highbrow**) □ **lowdown** noun damaging information □ **lowkey** adj not elaborate, unpretentious □ **lowland** noun flattish country, without high hills □ **keep a low profile** to not make your feelings or presence known

**lower¹** (pronounced **loh**-er) adj less high □ verb **1** to make less high: *lower the price* **2** to let or come down: *lower the blinds*

**lower²** or **lour** (pronounced **low**-er) verb **1** of the sky: to become dark and cloudy **2** to frown □ **lowering** adj

**lower-case** adj of a letter: not a capital, *eg* a not A (contrasted with: **upper-case**)

**lowly** *adj* low in rank, humble □ **lowliness** *noun*

**loyal** *adj* faithful, true □ **loyally** *adv* □ **loyalist** *noun* someone loyal to their sovereign or country □ **loyalty** *noun* (*pl* **loyalties**) **1** faithful support of *eg* your friends **2** (**loyalties**) feelings of faithful friendship and support, *esp* for a particular person or thing

**lozenge** *noun* **1** a diamond-shaped figure **2** a small sweet for sucking

**Ltd** *abbrev* limited liability

**lubricant** *noun* something which lubricates; an oil

**lubricate** *verb* **1** to apply oil *etc* to (something) to overcome friction and make movement easier **2** *informal* to ply with alcohol □ **lubrication** *noun*

**lucid** *adj* **1** easily understood **2** clear in mind; not confused □ **lucidity** *noun* □ **lucidly** *adv*

**luck** *noun* **1** fortune, either good or bad **2** chance: *as luck would have it* **3** good fortune: *have any luck?* □ **luckless** *adj* unfortunate, unhappy □ **lucky** *adj* **1** fortunate, having good luck **2** bringing good luck: *lucky charm* **3** happening as a result of good luck: *a lucky coincidence* □ **luckily** *adv*

**lucky** ⟷ luck**ier**, luck**iest**

**lucrative** *adj* profitable

**lucre** (*pronounced* **loo**-ker) *noun* gain; money

**Luddite** *noun* an opponent of technological innovation

Originally a group of protesters against the Industrial Revolution in the early 19th century, who based their name on Ned *Ludd*, an earlier opponent of machines for weaving stockings

**ludicrous** *adj* ridiculous □ **ludicrously** *adv*

**ludo** *noun* a game played with counters on a board

**lug¹** *verb* to pull or drag with effort

**lug** ⟷ lug**s**, lug**ging**, lug**ged**

**lug²** *noun*, *informal* the ear

**luge** *noun* a light toboggan □ *verb* to glide on such a sledge as a sport

**luggage** *noun* suitcases and other travelling baggage

**lugger** *noun* a small sailing vessel

**lugubrious** (*pronounced* lu-**goo**-bri-us) *adj* mournful, dismal □ **lugubriously** *adv*

**lukewarm** *adj* **1** neither hot nor cold **2** not very keen, unenthusiastic

**lull** *verb* to soothe or calm □ *noun* a period of calm

**lullaby** *noun* (*pl* **lullabies**) a song to lull children to sleep

**lumbago** *noun* a pain in the lower part of the back

**lumbar** *adj* of or in the lower part of the back

**lumber** *noun* **1** sawn-up timber **2** discarded old furniture *etc* □ *verb* to move about clumsily □ **lumberjack** *noun* someone who fells, saws and shifts trees

**luminescent** *adj* giving out light □ **luminescence** *noun*

**luminous** *adj* **1** giving light **2** shining; clear □ **luminosity** *noun*

**lump** *noun* **1** a small, solid mass of indefinite shape **2** a swelling **3** the whole taken together: *considered in a lump* **4** a heavy, dull person □ *verb* **1** to form into lumps **2** to treat as being alike: *lumped all of us together* □ **lumpish** *adj* heavy, dull □ **lumpy** *adj* full of lumps □ **lump sum** an amount of money given all at once

**lunacy** *noun* madness, insanity

**lunar** *adj* of the moon: *lunar eclipse*

**lunatic** *noun* someone who is insane or crazy □ *adj* insane, mad

**lunch** *noun* (*pl* **lunches**) a midday meal □ *verb* to eat lunch □ **luncheon** *noun* lunch

**lung** *noun* either of the two bag-like

organs which fill with and expel air in the course of breathing

**lunge** *noun* a sudden thrust or push □ *verb* to thrust or plunge forward suddenly

**lupin** *noun* a type of plant with flowers on long spikes

**lurch** *verb* to roll or pitch suddenly to one side; stagger □ *noun* a pitch to one side □ **leave in the lurch** to leave in a difficult position without help

**lure** *noun* something which entices; a bait □ *verb* to attract, entice away

**lurid** *adj* **1** glaring, garish: *lurid shirt* **2** horrifying, sensational: *lurid story* **3** pale, ghostly

**lurk** *verb* **1** to keep out of sight; be hidden **2** to move or act secretly and slyly □ **lurker** *noun* □ **lurking** *adj* vague, hidden

**luscious** *adj* sweet, delicious, juicy

**lush** *adj* of grass *etc*: thick and plentiful

**lust** *noun* **1** a greedy desire for power, riches *etc* **2** a strong sexual desire □ *verb* to have a strong desire (for) □ **lustful** *adj* full of, or showing, strong sexual desire

**luster** *US* spelling of **lustre**

**lustre** or *US* **luster** *noun* brightness, shine, gloss □ **lustrous** *adj* bright, shining

**lusty** *adj* lively, strong □ **lustily** *adv*

**lute** *noun* a stringed musical instrument with a pear-shaped, round-backed body and fretted fingerboard

**luxuriant** *adj* **1** thick with leaves, flowers *etc*: *gardens full of luxuriant*

*plants* **2** richly ornamented

🖊 Do not confuse with: **luxurious**

**luxuriate** *verb* **1** to be luxuriant **2** to enjoy; take delight (in)

🖊 Do not confuse with: **luxuriant**

**luxury** *noun* (*pl* **luxuries**) **1** something very pleasant or expensive but not necessary: *having a car is a luxury* **2** the use or enjoyment of such things □ **luxurious** *adj* full of luxuries; very comfortable: *a luxurious new home* □ **luxuriously** *adv*

**lychgate** (*pronounced* **lich**-geit) *noun* a churchyard gate with a porch

**Lycra** *noun*, *trademark* a lightweight synthetic elastic fabric

**lying** *see* **lie**

**lymph** *noun* a colourless fluid in the body □ **lymph gland** one of the glands carrying lymph

**lynch** *verb* to condemn and put to death without legal trial

Named after William *Lynch*, 19th-century Virginian planter who organized unofficial trials of suspected criminals

**lynx** *noun* (*pl* **lynxes**) a wild animal of the cat family, noted for its keen sight

**lyre** *noun* an ancient stringed musical instrument, played like a harp

**lyric** *noun* **1** a short poem, often expressing the poet's feelings **2** (**lyrics**) the words of a song □ *adj* **1** of a lyric **2** full of joy □ **lyrical** *adj* **1** lyric **2** song-like **3** full of enthusiastic praise □ **lyrically** *adv*

# Mm

**MA** *abbrev* Master of Arts

**macabre** *adj* gruesome, horrible

**macadamize** *verb* to surface (a road) with small broken stones

Named after the 19th-century Scottish engineer John *McAdam* who invented the process

**macaroni** *noun* pasta shaped into

short hollow tubes

**macaroon** *noun* a sweet cake or biscuit made with ground almonds and sugar

**macaw** *noun* a long-tailed brightly-coloured parrot

**mace**¹ *noun* a heavy staff with an ornamental head, carried as a sign of office

**mace**² *noun* a spice made from the covering of a nutmeg

**macerate** *verb* 1 to make into pulp by steeping 2 to emaciate

**machete** (*say* ma-**shet**-i) *noun* a heavy knife used to cut through foliage *etc*

**machinations** *noun pl* a crafty scheme, a plot

**machine** *noun* 1 a working arrangement of wheels, levers *etc* 2 a (motor) bicycle 3 a political party organization □ *verb* to sew *etc* with a machine □ **machinery** *noun* 1 machines in general 2 the working parts of a machine 3 organization: *machinery of local government* □ **machinist** *noun* a machine maker or operator □ **machine code** a system of symbols that can be understood by a computer □ **machinegun** *noun* an automatic rapid-firing gun

**machismo** (*say* ma-**kiz**-moh or ma-**chiz**-moh) *noun* overt or aggressive masculinity

**Mach number** (*say* makh or mahkh) the ratio of the speed of an aircraft to the velocity of sound (*eg* Mach 5 = 5 times the speed of sound)

**macho** (*say* **mach**-oh) *adj* overtly or aggressively masculine

**mackerel** *noun* an edible seafish with wavy markings

**mackintosh** *noun* (*pl* **mackintoshes**) a waterproof overcoat

**macro** *noun, computing* a single instruction that prompts a computer to carry out a series of short instructions embedded in it

**macrobiotic** *adj* of diet: consisting of organic unprocessed food, *esp* vegetables

**mad** *adj* 1 out of your mind, insane 2 wildly foolish 3 furious with anger □ **madly** *adv* 1 insanely 2 extremely: *madly in love* □ **madness** *noun* (meanings 1 and 2) □ **madcap** *noun* a rash, hot-headed person □ *adj* foolishly rash: *madcap scheme* □ **madden** *verb* to make angry or mad □ **maddening** *adj* extremely annoying □ **madhouse** *noun* 1 a place of confusion and noise 2 *historical* an insane asylum □ **madman, madwoman** *noun* someone who is mad □ **like mad** very quickly or energetically

**madam** *noun* a polite form of address to a woman

**made** *past form* of make

**Madonna** *noun* the Virgin Mary as depicted in art

**madrigal** *noun* a part-song for several voices

**maelstrom** (*say* **meil**-strom) *noun* 1 a whirlpool 2 any place of great confusion

**maestro** (*say* **mais**-troh) *noun* (*pl* **maestros**) someone highly skilled in an art, *esp* music

**magazine** *noun* 1 a periodical paper containing articles, stories and pictures 2 a storage place for military equipment 3 a place for extra cartridges in a rifle

The sense of *magazine* as a periodical developed from the military use, being intended as a storehouse or treasury of information.

**magenta** *noun* a reddish-purple colour □ *adj* of this colour

**maggot** *noun* a small worm-like creature, the grub of a bluebottle *etc* □ **maggoty** *adj*

**Magi** *see* **magus**

**magic** *noun* **1** a process which produces results which cannot be explained or which are remarkable **2** conjuring tricks □ *adj* **1** using magic **2** used in magic **3** magical □ **magical** *adj* **1** of or produced by magic **2** very wonderful or mysterious □ **magically** *adv* □ **magician** *noun* someone skilled in magic

▪ (adj) charming, enchanting, bewitching, fascinating, spellbinding

**magistrate** *noun* someone with the power to enforce the law, *eg* a provost or justice of the peace □ **magisterial** *adj* **1** of magistrates **2** having an air of authority

**magma** *noun* molten rock

**magnanimous** (*say* mag-**nan**-im-*us*) *adj* very generous □ **magnanimity** (*say* mag-*n*a-**nim**-it-*i*) *noun* □ **magnanimously** *adv*

**magnate** *noun* someone with great power or wealth

**magnesia** *noun* a white powder formed from magnesium

**magnesium** *noun* a white metal which burns with an intense white light

**magnet** *noun* **1** a piece of iron, steel *etc* which has the power to attract other pieces of metal **2** someone or something that attracts strongly □ **magnetism** *noun* **1** the attractive power of a magnet **2** attraction, great charm □ **magnetize** *verb* **1** to make magnetic **2** to attract, influence

**magnetic** *adj* **1** having the powers of a magnet **2** strongly attractive: *magnetic personality* □ **magnetic north** the direction in which the magnetized needle of a compass points □ **magnetic tape** tape on which sound, pictures, computer material *etc* can be recorded

**magneto** *noun* (*pl* magnetos) a device producing electric sparks, *eg*

for lighting the fuel in a car engine

**magnificent** *adj* **1** splendid in appearance or action **2** excellent, very fine □ **magnificence** *noun* □ **magnificently** *adv*

**magnify** *verb* **1** to make to appear larger by using special lenses **2** to exaggerate □ **magnification** *noun*

**magnify** ⋄ magnif**ies**, magnif**ying**, magnif**ied**

**magnitude** *noun* great size

**magnolia** *noun* a tree which produces large white or purplish sweet-scented flowers

**magnum** *noun* a bottle of wine or champagne equal to two ordinary bottles

**magnum opus** a great work, a masterpiece

**magpie** *noun* a black-and-white bird of the crow family, known for its habit of collecting objects

**magus** *noun* (*pl* magi) an ancient Persian priest or astrologer □ **the Magi** the three wise men who brought gifts to the infant Christ

**Maharajah** *noun* an important Indian prince, *esp* the ruler of a state

**mah-jong** *noun* a Chinese table game played with small painted bricks

**mahogany** *noun* **1** a tropical American hardwood tree **2** its hard reddish-brown wood, often used for furniture

**maid** *noun* **1** a female servant **2** *old* an unmarried woman; a young girl

**maiden** *noun*, *old* an unmarried girl; a virgin □ *adj* **1** of a maiden **2** unmarried: *maiden aunt* **3** first, initial: *maiden speech/ maiden voyage* □ **maiden name** the surname of a married woman before her marriage □ **maiden over** *cricket* an over in which no runs are made

**mail¹** *noun* letters, parcels *etc* carried by post □ *verb* to post □ **mail order** an order for goods to be sent by post □ **mail shot** unsolicited advertising material sent by post

**mail²** *noun* body armour of steel rings or plates

**maim** *verb* to cripple, disable

**main** *adj* chief, most important □ *noun*, *old* **1** the ocean **2** (**the mains**) a chief pipe, wire *etc* supplying gas, water or electricity □ **mainly** *adv* chiefly, mostly □ **mainframe** *noun* the central processing unit and storage unit of a computer □ *adj* of a computer: of the large, powerful type rather than the small-scale kind □ **mainland** *noun* a large piece of land off whose coast smaller islands lie □ **mainstay** *noun* the chief support □ **in the main** for the most part

**maintain** *verb* **1** to keep (something) as it is **2** to continue to keep in good working order **3** to support (a family *etc*) **4** to state (an opinion) firmly □ **maintenance** *noun* **1** the act of maintaining; upkeep, repair **2** means of support, *esp* money for food, clothing *etc*

**maize** *noun* a cereal crop grown in N and S America

**majesty** *noun* (*pl* **majesties**) **1** a title used in addressing a king or queen: *Your Majesty* **2** greatness of rank or manner □ **majestic** *adj* stately, regal

**major** *adj* great in size, importance *etc* (contrasted with: **minor**) □ *noun* a senior army officer □ **majority** *noun* (*pl* **majorities**) **1** the greater number or quantity **2** the difference in amount between the greater and the lesser number **3** the age when someone becomes legally an adult (18 in the UK)

**make** *verb* **1** to form, construct **2** to cause to be: *he makes me mad at times* **3** to bring about: *make trouble* **4** to amount to: *2 and 2 make 4* **5** to earn: *she made £300 last week* **6** to force **7** to undergo (a journey *etc*) **8** to prepare (a meal *etc*) □ *noun* **1** kind, shape, form **2** brand □ **maker** *noun* the person or

organization that has made something □ **meet your maker** to die □ **make-believe** *noun* fantasy □ **makeshift** *adj* used for a time for want of something better □ **make-up** *noun* cosmetics □ **make believe** to pretend □ **make good 1** to do well **2** to carry out (a promise) **3** to make up for (a loss) □ **make light of** to treat as unimportant □ **make much of** to fuss over, treat as important □ **make nothing of 1** to be unable to understand, do *etc* **2** to make light of □ **make off** to run away □ **make out 1** to see in the distance or indistinctly **2** to declare, prove **3** to write out (a bill *etc*) formally □ **make up 1** to form a whole: *eleven players make up the side* **2** to put together, invent (a false story) **3** to put make-up on the face **4** to be friendly again after a quarrel □ **make up for** to give or do something in return for damage done □ **on the make** *informal* **1** looking for personal gain **2** looking for a sexual partner

**make** *verb* ⇨ **makes**, **making**, **made**

ⓘ From Old English *macian*

**maladjusted** *adj* unable to fit in happily in your environment, society *etc*

**maladministration** *noun* bad management, *esp* of public affairs

**malady** *noun* (*pl* **maladies**) illness, disease

**malaise** *noun* a feeling or general air of depression or despondency

**malapropism** *noun* the use of a wrong word which sounds similar to the one intended, *eg* contemptuous for *contemporary*

After Mrs *Malaprop* in Sheridan's play, *The Rivals* (1775), who habitually used the wrong word

**malaria** *noun* a fever caused by the bite of a particular mosquito □ **malarial** *adj*

From an Italian phrase meaning

'bad air', malarial fever being originally thought to be caused by poisonous marsh gases

**male** *adj* of the sex that is able to father children or young; masculine □ *noun* a member of this sex

**malediction** *noun* a curse; cursing □ **maledictory** *adj*

**malefactor** *noun* an evildoer

**malevolent** *adj* wishing ill to others; spiteful □ **malevolence** *noun* □ **malevolently** *adv*

**malformation** *noun* faulty or wrong shape

**malfunction** *verb* to fail to work or operate properly □ *noun* failure to operate

**malice** *noun* ill will; spite □ **malicious** *adj* intending harm; spiteful □ **maliciously** *adv*

**malign** (*say* ma-**lain**) *verb* to speak ill of

**malignant** (*say* ma-**lig**-n*ant*) *adj* 1 wishing harm, spiteful 2 of a disease: likely to cause death (*contrasted with*: **benign**) □ **malignantly** *adv*

**malinger** *verb* to pretend to be ill to avoid work *etc* □ **malingerer** *noun*

**mall** (*say* mol) *noun*, *US* a shopping centre

**malleable** *adj* 1 of metal: able to be beaten out by hammering 2 of people: easy to influence □ **malleability** *noun*

**mallet** *noun* a heavy wooden hammer

**malnutrition** *noun* lack of sufficient or proper food; under-nourishment

**malpractice** *noun* 1 wrongdoing 2 professional misconduct

**malt** *noun* 1 barley or other grain prepared for making beer or whisky 2 a malt whisky

**maltreat** *verb* to treat roughly or unkindly □ **maltreatment** *noun*

**mama** or **mamma** *noun*, *informal* mother

**mammal** *noun* a member of the class of animals of which the female parent feeds the young with her own milk □ **mammalian** *adj*

**mammary** *adj* of a female breast or breasts: *mammary gland*

**mammoth** *noun* a very large elephant, now extinct □ *adj* enormous, huge

**man** *noun* (*pl* **men**) 1 a grown-up human male 2 a human being 3 the human race 4 *informal* a husband 5 a piece in chess or draughts □ *verb* to supply with workers, crew *etc*: *man the boats* □ **manly** *adj* brave, strong □ **manliness** *noun* □ **mannish** *adj* of a woman: behaving, looking like a man □ **manful** *adj* courageous and noble-minded □ **manfully** *adv* □ **manhandle** *verb* to handle roughly □ **manhood** *noun* the state of being a man □ **manhole** *noun* a hole (into a drain, sewer *etc*) large enough to let a man through □ **mankind** *noun* the human race □ **manpower** *noun* the number of people available for work □ **the man in the street** the ordinary person □ **to a man** every single one

**man** *verb* ⇔ mans, man**ning**, man**ned**

ⓘ From Old English *mann*

**manacle** *noun*, *formal* a handcuff □ *verb* to handcuff

**manage** *verb* 1 to have control or charge of 2 to deal with, cope 3 to succeed: *managed to finish on time* □ **manageable** *adj* easily managed or controlled □ **management** *noun* 1 those in charge of a business *etc* 2 the art of managing a business *etc* □ **manager** *noun* someone in charge of a business *etc* □ **manageress** *noun* a woman manager, usually of a shop or restaurant

**mandarin** *noun* a small orange-like citrus fruit

**mandate** *noun* 1 power to act on someone else's behalf 2 a command

**mandatory** *adj* compulsory

**mandible** *noun* the jaw or lower jawbone

**mandolin** or **mandoline** *noun* a round-backed stringed instrument similar to a lute

**mane** *noun* **1** long hair on the head and neck of a horse or male lion **2** a long or thick head of hair

**maneuver** *US spelling of* **manoeuvre**

**manganese** *noun* a hard easily-broken metal of a greyish-white colour

**mange** (*say* meinj) *noun* a skin disease of dogs, cats *etc*

**mangel-wurzel** (*say* mang-gel-wer-zel) *noun* a kind of beetroot used as cattle food

**manger** *noun* a box or trough holding dry food for horses and cattle

**mangle** *noun* a machine for squeezing water out of clothes or for smoothing them ◻ *verb* **1** to squeeze (clothes) through a mangle **2** to crush, tear, damage badly

**mango** *noun* (*pl* **mangoes**) **1** the fruit of a tropical Indian tree, with juicy orange flesh **2** the tree which produces mangoes

**mangrove** *noun* a type of tree which grows in swamps in hot countries

**mangy** *adj* **1** shabby, squalid **2** of an animal: suffering from mange

**mania** *noun* **1** a form of mental illness in which the sufferer is over-active, over-excited and unreasonably happy **2** extreme fondness or enthusiasm ◻ **maniac** *noun* a mad person **2** a very rash or over-enthusiastic person ◻ **manic** *adj* **1** suffering from mania **2** very energetic or excited

**manicure** *noun* **1** the care of hands and nails **2** professional treatment for the hands and nails ◻ *verb* to perform a manicure on ◻ **manicurist** *noun*

**manifest** *adj* easily seen or understood ◻ *verb* to show plainly ◻ **manifestation** *noun* behaviour, actions or events which reveal or display something ◻ **manifestly** *adv*

**manifesto** *noun* (*pl* **manifestoes** or **manifestos**) a public announcement of intentions, *eg* by a political party

**manifold** *adj* many and various

**manioc** *noun* tapioca

**manipulate** *verb* to handle so as to turn to your own advantage

**manna** *noun* an unexpected or delicious treat

The name given in the Bible to the food miraculously provided for the Israelites in the wilderness

**mannequin** *noun* **1** someone who models clothes for prospective buyers **2** a display dummy

**manner** *noun* **1** the way in which something is done **2** the way in which someone behaves **3** (**manners**) polite behaviour towards others ◻ **mannerism** *noun* an odd and obvious habit or characteristic ◻ **mannerly** *adj* polite ◻ **all manner of** all kinds of

**manoeuvre** or *US* **maneuver** *noun* **1** a planned movement of troops, ships or aircraft **2** a trick, a cunning plan ◻ *verb* **1** to perform a manoeuvre **2** to manipulate

**man-of-war** *noun* a warship

**manor** *noun* **1** a large house, usually attached to a country estate **2** *historical* the land belonging to a lord or squire ◻ **manorial** *adj*

**manse** *noun* the house of a minister in certain Christian churches, *eg* the Church of Scotland

**mansion** *noun* a large house

**manslaughter** *noun* killing someone without deliberate intent

**mantelpiece** *noun* a shelf over a fireplace

**mantle** *noun* **1** a cloak or loose outer garment **2** a covering: *mantle of* *snow* **3** a thin, transparent shade around the flame of a gas or paraffin lamp

**mantra** *noun* a word or phrase, chanted or repeated inwardly in meditation

**manual** *adj* **1** of the hand or hands **2** worked by hand **3** working with the hands: *manual worker* □ *noun* a handbook giving instructions on how to use something □ **manually** *adv* (adj, meaning 2)

**manufacture** *verb* to make (articles or materials) in large quantities, usually by machine □ *noun* **1** the process of manufacturing **2** a manufactured article □ **manufacturer** *noun*

**manure** *noun* a substance, *esp* animal dung, spread on soil to make it more fertile □ *verb* to treat with manure

**manuscript** *noun* **1** the prepared material for a book *etc* before it is printed **2** a book or paper written by hand

**Manx cat** a tailless breed of cat

**many** *adj* a large number of □ *pronoun* a large number: *many survived* □ **many a** a large number of: *many a voice was raised*

**map** *noun* a flat drawing of all or part of the earth's surface, showing geographical features □ *verb* **1** to make a map of **2** (**map out**) to plan in detail

**map** *verb* ⇔ map*s*, map*ping*, map*ped*

**maple** *noun* **1** a tree related to the sycamore, one variety of which produces sugar **2** its hard light-coloured wood used for furniture *etc*

**mar** *verb* to spoil, deface

**mar** ⇔ mar*s*, mar*ring*, mar*red*

**maracas** *noun pl* a pair of filled gourds shaken as a percussion instrument

**marathon** *noun* a long-distance foot-race, usually covering 26 miles 385 yards

After the distance run by a Greek soldier from *Marathon* to Athens with news of the victory over the Persians

**maraud** *verb* to plunder, raid □ **marauder** *noun* □ **marauding** *adj*

**marble** *noun* **1** limestone that takes a high polish, used for sculpture, decorating buildings *etc* **2** a small glass ball used in a children's game

**March** *noun* the third month of the year

**march**[1] *verb* **1** to (cause) to walk in time with regular step **2** to go on steadily □ *noun* (*pl* **marches**) **1** a marching movement **2** a piece of music for marching to **3** the distance covered by marching **4** a steady progression of events: *the march of time*

**march**[2] *noun* a boundary or border □ **riding the marches** the traditional ceremony of riding around the boundaries of a town *etc*

**marchioness** *noun* (*pl* **marchionesses**) a woman marquess

**mare** *noun* a female horse

**margarine** *noun* an edible spread similar to butter, made mainly of vegetable fats

**margin** *noun* **1** an edge, a border **2** the blank edge on the page of a book **3** additional space or room; allowance: *margin for error*

**marginal** *adj* **1** of or in a margin **2** borderline, close to a limit **3** of a political constituency: without a clear majority for any one candidate or party **4** of little effect or importance: *marginal improvement* □ *noun* a marginal political constituency □ **marginalize** *verb* to make less important or central □ **marginally** *adv* very slightly, to a very small degree

**marigold** *noun* a kind of plant with a yellow flower

**marijuana** *noun* a drug made from the plant hemp

**marina** noun a place with moorings for yachts, dinghies etc

**marinade** noun a mixture of oil, wine, herbs, spices etc in which food is steeped for flavour □ verb to marinate

**marinate** verb to steep in a marinade

**marine** adj of the sea □ noun a soldier serving on board a ship □ **mariner** (say **ma**-rin-er) noun, old a sailor

**marionette** noun a puppet moved by strings

**marital** adj of marriage

**maritime** adj 1 of the sea or ships 2 lying near the sea

**marjoram** noun a sweet-smelling herb used in cooking

**Mark** noun a Deutschmark, the standard unit of German money

**mark** noun 1 a sign that can be seen 2 a stain, spot etc 3 a target aimed at 4 a trace 5 a point used to assess the merit of a piece of schoolwork etc 6 the starting-line in a race: on your marks! □ verb 1 to make a mark on; stain 2 to observe, watch 3 to stay close to (an opponent in football etc) 4 to award marks to (a piece of schoolwork etc) 5 **mark off** to separate, distinguish □ **marked** adj easily noticed: marked improvement □ **markedly** adv □ **marker** noun 1 someone who marks the score at games 2 a counter etc used to mark a score □ **marksman, markswoman** noun someone who shoots well □ **mark time** 1 to move the feet up and down, as if marching, but without going forward 2 to keep things going without progressing □ **up to the mark** coming up to the required standard

**market** noun 1 a public place for buying and selling 2 (a country, place etc where there is) a need or demand (for certain types of goods) □ verb to put on sale □ **marketing** noun the act or practice of advertising and selling □ **market forces** commerce not restricted by government intervention □ **market garden** a garden in which fruit and vegetables are grown to be sold □ **market leader** a company, or brand of goods, that outsells its competitors □ **on the market** for sale

**marmalade** noun a jam made from citrus fruit, esp oranges

**marmite** noun, trademark a savoury spread made from yeast and vegetable extracts

**marmoset** noun a type of small monkey found in America

**maroon**[1] noun 1 a brownish-red colour 2 a firework used as a distress signal □ adj brownish-red

**maroon**[2] verb 1 to abandon on an island etc without means of escape 2 to leave in a helpless or uncomfortable position

**marquee** (say mah-**kee**) noun a large tent used for large gatherings, eg a wedding reception or circus

**marquess** or **marquis** (both say mah-kwis) noun (pl **marquesses** or **marquises**) a nobleman below a duke in rank

**marriage** noun the ceremony by which two people become husband and wife

**marrow** noun 1 the soft substance in the hollow part of bones 2 a long thick-skinned vegetable

**marry** verb to join, or be joined, together in marriage

**marry** ⟶ marries, marrying, married

**marsh** noun (pl **marshes**) a piece of low-lying wet ground □ **marshy** adj

**marshal** noun 1 a high-ranking officer in the army or air force 2 someone who directs processions etc 3 US a law-court official 4 US the head of a police force □ verb 1 to arrange (troops, facts, arguments etc) in order 2 to show the way, conduct, lead

**marshal** *verb* ⇔ marshal*s*, marshal*ling*, marshal*led*

**marshmallow** *noun* **1** a spongy jellylike sweet made from sugar and egg-whites *etc* **2** a marsh plant with pink flowers, similar to the hollyhock

**marsupial** *noun* an animal which carries its young in a pouch, *eg* the kangaroo

**marten** *noun* an animal related to the weasel

**martial** *adj* **1** of war or battle **2** warlike □ **martial art** a combative sport or method of self-defence □ **martial law** the government of a country by its army

**Martian** *noun* a potential or imaginary being from the planet Mars

**martin** *noun* a bird of the swallow family

**martinet** *noun* someone who keeps strict order; a disciplinarian

Named after Jean *Martinet*, a 17th-century French officer who invented a type of military drill

**Martinmas** *noun* 11 November, the feast of St Martin

**martyr** *noun* someone who suffers death or hardship for their beliefs □ *verb* to execute or cause suffer for beliefs □ **martyrdom** *noun*

**marvel** *noun* something astonishing or wonderful □ *verb* to feel amazement (at)

**marvel** *verb* ⇔ marvel*s*, marvel*ling*, marvel*led*

**marvellous** *adj* **1** astonishing, extraordinary **2** *informal* excellent, very good

**Marxist** *noun* a follower of the theories of Karl Marx; a communist □ **Marxism** *noun*

**marzipan** *noun* a mixture of ground almonds, sugar *etc*, used in cake-making and confectionery

**mascara** *noun* a cosmetic paint used to colour the eyelashes

**mascot** *noun* a person, animal or thing believed to bring good luck

**masculine** *adj* **1** of the male sex **2** manly □ **masculinity** *noun*

**mash** *verb* to beat or crush into a pulp □ *noun* **1** mashed potato **2** a mixture of bran, meal *etc*, used as animal food

**mask** *noun* **1** a cover for the face for disguise or protection **2** a pretence, a disguise □ *verb* **1** to hide, disguise **2** to cover the face with a mask

**masochism** *noun* an unnatural pleasure taken in being dominated, treated cruelly, or made to suffer in any way □ **masochist** *noun* □ **masochistic** *adj*

After Leopold von Sacher-*Masoch*, 19th-century Austrian novelist

**mason** *noun* **1** someone who carves stone **2** a Freemason □ **masonic** *adj* (meaning 2) □ **masonry** *noun* stonework

**masquerade** *noun* **1** a dance at which masks are worn **2** pretence □ *verb* to pretend to be someone else: *masquerading as a journalist*

**mass** *noun* (*pl* **masses**) **1** a lump or quantity gathered together **2** a large quantity **3** the main part or body **4** (**Mass**) a measure of quantity of matter in an object **5** (**Mass**) (in some Christian churches) the celebration of Christ's last supper with his disciples **6** music for a Mass □ *adj* **1** of a mass **2** of or consisting of large numbers or quantities □ *verb* to form into a mass □ **mass media** means of communicating information to a large number of people, *eg* television □ **mass production** production in large quantities of articles all exactly the same □ **the masses** ordinary people

**massacre** *noun* the merciless killing of a large number of people □ *verb* to kill (a large number) in a cruel way

**massage** *noun* the rubbing of parts of the body to remove pain or tension □ *verb* to perform massage on

**masseur, masseuse** *noun* someone who performs massage

**massive** *adj* bulky, heavy, huge □ **massively** *adv*

**mast** *noun* a long upright pole holding up the sails (in a ship, or holding an aerial, flag *etc*

**mastectomy** *noun* the surgical removal of a woman's breast or breasts

**master** *noun* 1 someone who controls or commands 2 an owner of a dog *etc* 3 an employer 4 a male teacher 5 the commander of a merchant ship 6 someone who is very skilled in something, an expert 7 a degree awarded by universities: *Master of Arts* □ *verb* 1 to overcome, defeat 2 to become able to do or use properly □ **mastery** *noun* 1 victory (over) 2 control (of) 3 great skill (in) □ **masterful** *adj* strong-willed and expecting to be obeyed □ **masterly** *adj* showing the skill of an expert or master, clever □ **masterkey** *noun* a key which is so made that it opens a number of different locks □ **mastermind** *verb* to plan, work out the details of (a scheme *etc*) □ *noun: he is the mastermind of the scheme* □ **master of ceremonies** someone who directs the form and order of events at a public occasion; a compère □ **masterpiece** *noun* the best example of someone's work, *esp* a very fine picture, book, piece of music *etc*

**mastic** *noun* a gum resin from Mediterranean trees, used as a varnish or glue

**masticate** *verb, formal* to chew □ **mastication** *noun*

**mastiff** *noun* a breed of large, powerful dog

**masturbate** *verb* to stimulate the sexual organs to a state of orgasm □ **masturbation** *noun*

**mat** *noun* 1 piece of material (coarse plaited plant fibre, carpet *etc*) for wiping shoes on, covering the floor *etc* 2 a piece of material, wood *etc* put below dishes at table □ *adj*, another spelling of **matt**

**matador** *noun* the person who kills the bull in bullfights

**match**[1] *noun* (pl **matches**) a small stick of wood *etc* tipped with a substance which catches fire when rubbed against an abrasive surface

**match**[2] *noun* (pl **matches**) 1 a person or thing similar to or the same as another 2 a person or thing agreeing with or suiting another 3 an equal 4 someone suitable for marriage 5 a contest or game □ *verb* 1 to be of the same make, size, colour *etc* 2 to set (two things, teams *etc*) against each other 3 to hold your own with, be equal to □ **matchless** *adj* having no equal □ **matchbox** *noun* a box for holding matches □ **matchmaker** *noun* someone who tries to arrange marriages or partnerships □ **matchstick** *noun* a single match

**mate** *noun* 1 a friend, a companion 2 an assistant worker: *plumber's mate* 3 a husband or wife 4 the sexual partner of an animal, bird *etc* 5 a merchant ship's officer, next in rank to the captain □ *verb* 1 to marry 2 to bring or come together to breed

**material** *adj* 1 made of matter, able to be seen and felt 2 not spiritual, concerned with physical comfort, money *etc* 3 important, essential: *material difference* □ *noun* 1 something out of which anything is, or may be, made 2 cloth, fabric □ **materially** *adv* 1 to a large extent, greatly 2 relating to objects, possessions or physical comfort, rather than to emotional or spiritual well-being ▫ **materialism** noun **1** a tendency to attach too much importance to material things (eg physical comfort, money) **2** the belief that only things we can see or feel really exist or are important ▫ **materialist** noun ▫ **materialistic** adj ▫ **materialize** verb **1** to appear in bodily form **2** to happen, come about

**maternal** adj **1** of a mother **2** like a mother, motherly **3** related through your mother: maternal grandmother ▫ **maternally** adv

**maternity** noun the state of being a mother, motherhood ▫ adj of or for a woman having or about to have a baby: maternity clothes

**math** noun, US informal mathematics

**mathematics** noun sing the study of measurements, numbers and quantities ▫ **mathematical** adj **1** of or done by mathematics **2** very exact ▫ **mathematician** noun an expert in mathematics

**maths** noun sing, informal mathematics

**matinée** (say mat-in-ei) noun an afternoon performance in a theatre or cinema

**matins** noun pl the morning service in certain churches

**matriarch** (say meit-ri-ahk) noun a woman who controls a family or community ▫ **matriarchal** (say meit-ri-ahk-al) adj

**matrices** pl of matrix

**matriculate** verb to admit, or be admitted, to a university ▫ **matriculation** noun

**matrimony** noun, formal marriage ▫ **matrimonial** adj

**matrix** noun (pl matrices) **1** a mould in which metals etc are shaped **2** a mass of rock in which gems etc are found **3** a rectangular table of data

**matron** (say meit-ron) noun **1** a married woman **2** old a senior nurse in charge of a hospital **3** a woman in charge of housekeeping or nursing in a school, hostel etc ▫ **matronly** (say meit-ron-li) adj **1** of a woman: dignified, staid **2** rather plump

**matt** or **mat** adj having a dull surface; not shiny or glossy

**matted** adj thickly tangled

**matter** noun **1** anything that takes up space, can be seen, felt etc; material, substance **2** a subject written or spoken about (matters) affairs, business **4** trouble, difficulty: what is the matter? **5** importance: of no great matter **6** pus ▫ verb **1** to be of importance: it doesn't matter **2** medical to give out pus ▫ **matter-of-fact** adj keeping to the actual facts; unimaginative, uninteresting ▫ **a matter of course** something that is to be expected ▫ **a matter of opinion** a subject on which different opinions are held ▫ **as a matter of fact** in fact

**matting** noun material from which mats are made

**mattress** noun (pl mattresses) a thick layer of padding covered in cloth, usually as part of a bed

**mature** adj **1** fully grown or developed **2** ripe, ready for use ▫ verb **1** to (cause to) become mature **2** of an insurance policy etc: to be due to be paid out ▫ **maturely** adv ▫ **maturity** noun

**maudlin** adj silly, sentimental

From Mary Magdalene, who was frequently depicted crying in paintings

**maul** verb to hurt badly by rough or savage treatment

**Maundy Thursday** the day before Good Friday in the Christian calendar

**mausoleum** noun a large or elaborate tomb

**mauve** adj of a purple colour

**maverick** *noun* someone who refuses to conform; a determined individualist

*After Samuel Maverick, a Texas rancher who never branded his cattle*

**maw** *noun* **1** an animal's jaws or gullet **2** a wide or gaping cavity

**mawkish** *adj* weak and sentimental

**maxim** *noun* a general truth or rule about behaviour *etc*

**maximum** *adj* greatest, most □ *noun* (*pl* **maxima**) **1** the greatest number or quantity **2** the highest point or degree

**May** *noun* the fifth month of the year

**may** *verb* **1** used with another verb to express permission or possibility: *you may watch the film/ I thought I might find him there* **2** used to express a wish: *may your wishes come true*

**may** ⇨ **may, might**

**maybe** *adv* perhaps

**Mayday** *noun* the first day of May

**mayday** *noun* an international distress signal

**mayfly** *noun* a short-lived insect that appears in May

**mayhem** *noun* widespread chaos or confusion

**mayonnaise** (*say* mei-*o*-**neiz**) *noun* a sauce made of eggs, oil and vinegar or lemon juice

**mayor** *noun* the chief elected public official of a city or town

*Mayor is used for a woman mayor, never mayoress.*

**mayoress** *noun* a mayor's wife

**maypole** *noun* a decorated pole traditionally danced around on Mayday

**maze** *noun* **1** a series of winding paths in a park *etc*, planned to make exit difficult **2** something complicated and confusing: *maze of regulations*

**MBE** *abbrev* Member of the Order of the British Empire

**me** *pronoun* the word used by a speaker or writer in mentioning themselves: *she kissed me*

**mead** *noun* an alcoholic drink made with honey

**meadow** *noun* a field of grass

**meagre** or *US* **meager** *adj* **1** thin **2** poor in quality **3** scanty, not enough

**meal¹** *noun* the food taken at one time, *eg* breakfast or dinner

**meal²** *noun* grain ground to a coarse powder

**mealy-mouthed** *adj* not frank and straightforward in speech

**mean¹** *adj* **1** not generous with money *etc* **2** unkind, selfish **3** lowly, humble □ **meanness** *noun*

**mean²** *adj* **1** midway between two other points, quantities *etc*; middle **2** average □ *noun* **in the meantime** meanwhile

**mean³** *verb* **1** to intend to express; indicate: *what do you mean?* **2** to intend: *how do you mean to do that?* □ **mean well** to have good intentions □ **meaning** *noun* **1** what is intended to be expressed or conveyed **2** purpose, intention □ **meaningful** *adj* full of significance; expressive □ **meaningless** *adj* **1** pointless **2** having no meaning

**mean** ⇨ **means, meaning, meant**

**meander** *verb* **1** of a river: to flow in a winding course **2** to wander about slowly and aimlessly

**means** *noun pl* **1** an action or instrument by which something is brought about **2** money, property *etc*: *a woman of means* □ **by all means** certainly, of course **2** in every way possible □ **by no means** certainly not; not at all

**meanwhile** *adv* in the time between two happenings

**measles** *noun* an infectious disease causing red spots

**measly** *adj, informal* mean, stingy

**measure** *noun* 1 size or amount (found by measuring) 2 an instrument or container for measuring 3 musical time 4 (**measures**) a plan of action 5 a law brought before parliament to be considered □ *verb* 1 to find out the size, quantity *etc* by using some form of measure 2 to be of a certain length, amount *etc* 3 to indicate the measurement of 4 to mark (off) or weigh (out) in portions □ **measured** *adj* steady, unhurried □ **measurement** *noun* 1 the act of measuring 2 the size, amount *etc* found by measuring □ **for good measure** as a bonus

**meat** *noun* animal flesh used as food □ **meaty** *adj* 1 full of meat; tasting of meat 2 of a book *etc*: full of information

**Mecca** *noun* 1 the birthplace of Mohammed 2 a place of pilgrimage

**mechanics** *noun* 1 *sing* the study and art of constructing machinery 2 *pl* the actual details of how something works: *the mechanics of the plan are beyond me* □ **mechanic** *noun* a skilled worker with tools or machines □ **mechanical** *adj* 1 of machinery: *mechanical engineering* 2 worked by machinery 3 done without thinking □ **mechanically** *adv* □ **mechanism** *noun* 1 a piece of machinery 2 the way a piece of machinery works 3 an action by which a result is produced □ **mechanize** *verb* 1 to equip (a factory *etc*) with machinery 2 to supply (troops) with armoured vehicles □ **mechanization** *noun*

**medal** *noun* a metal disc stamped with a design, inscription *etc*, made to commemorate an event or given as a prize □ **medallion** *noun* a large medal or piece of jewellery like one □ **medallist** *noun* someone who has gained a medal

**meddle** *verb* 1 to concern yourself with things that are not your business 2 to interfere or tamper (with) □ **meddler** *noun* □ **meddlesome** *adj*

**media** *noun*: **the media** television, newspapers *etc* as a form of communication

**mediaeval** another spelling of **medieval**

**median** *noun* 1 a straight line from an angle of a triangle to the centre of the opposite side 2 the middle value or point of a series □ *adj* mid, middle

**mediate** *verb* to act as a peacemaker (between) □ **mediation** *noun* □ **mediator** *noun* someone who tries to make peace between people who are quarrelling

**medic** *noun, informal* a medical student

**medical** *adj* of doctors or their work □ *noun* a health check, a physical examination

**medicate** *verb* to give medicine to □ **medicated** *adj* including medicine or disinfectant □ **medication** *noun* 1 medical treatment 2 a medicine

**medicine** *noun* 1 something given to a sick person to make them better 2 the science of the treatment of illness □ **medicine man** a tribal healer or shaman □ **medicinal** *adj* 1 used in medicine 2 used as a medicine □ **medicinally** *adv*

**medieval** *adj* of or in the Middle Ages

**mediocre** *adj* not very good, ordinary □ **mediocrity** *noun*

**meditate** *verb* 1 to think deeply and in quietness 2 to contemplate religious or spiritual matters 3 to consider, think about □ **meditation** *noun* 1 deep, quiet thought 2 contemplation on a religious or spiritual theme □ **meditative** *adj* thinking deeply

**medium** noun (pl **media** or **mediums**) **1** a means or substance through which an effect is produced **2** (pl **mediums**) someone through whom spirits (of dead people) are said to speak □ adj middle or average in size, quality etc □ **the media** see **media**

**medley** noun (pl **medleys**) **1** a mixture **2** a piece of music put together from a number of other pieces

**meek** adj gentle, uncomplaining □ **meekly** adv

**meet** verb **1** to come face to face (with) **2** to come together, join **3** to make the acquaintance of **4** to pay (bills etc) fully **5** to be suitable for, satisfy: meet the demand □ noun a gathering for a sports event □ adj proper, suitable □ **meeting** noun a gathering of people for a particular purpose

**meet** verb ⇨ **meets, meeting, met**

**mega** adj, slang **1** huge **2** excellent, very good

**mega-** prefix **1** great, huge: megaphone **2** a million: megaton ⓘ From Greek megas meaning 'big'

**megalith** noun a huge stone erected in prehistoric times

**megalomania** noun an exaggerated idea of your own importance or abilities

**megaphone** noun a portable cone-shaped device with microphone and amplifier to increase sound

**melancholy** noun lowness of spirits, sadness □ adj sad, depressed □ **melancholic** adj

**mêlée** (say mel-ei) noun a confused fight between two groups of people

**mellow** adj **1** of fruit: ripe, juicy, sweet **2** having become pleasant or agreeable with age **3** of light, colour etc: soft, not harsh □ verb to make or become mellow

**melodious** adj pleasant sounding; tuneful

**melodrama** noun a type of play with a sensational or exaggerated plot □ **melodramatic** adj exaggerated, sensational, over-dramatic

**melody** noun (pl **melodies**) **1** a tune **2** pleasant music □ **melodic** adj

**melon** noun a large round fruit with soft juicy flesh

**melt** verb **1** to make or become liquid, eg by heating **2** to disappear gradually **3** to soften in feeling: his heart melted at the sight

**member** noun **1** someone who belongs to a group or society **2** a limb or organ of the body □ **membership** noun **1** the group of people who are members, or the number of members, in a club etc **2** the state of being a member □ **Member of Parliament** (shortened to **MP**) someone elected to the House of Commons

**membrane** noun a thin skin or covering, esp as part of a human or animal body, plant etc

**memento** noun (pl **mementos**) something by which an event is remembered

**memo** noun (pl **memos**) short for **memorandum**

**memoirs** noun pl a personal account of someone's life; an autobiography

**memorable** adj worthy of being remembered; famous □ **memorably** adv

**memorandum** noun (pl **memoranda**) **1** a note which acts as a reminder **2** a written statement of something under discussion **3** a brief note sent to colleagues in an office etc

**memorial** noun a monument commemorating an historical event or people □ adj commemorating an event or person

**memorize** verb to learn by heart

**memory** noun (pl **memories**) **1** the power to remember **2** the mind's store of remembered things

**3** something remembered **4** *computing* a store of information **5** what is remembered about someone □ **in memory of** in remembrance of, as a memorial of

**menace** *noun* **1** potential harm or danger **2** someone persistently threatening or annoying □ *verb* to be a danger to; threaten □ **menacing** *adj*

**menagerie** (*say* me-**naj**-e-ri) *noun* **1** a collection of wild animals **2** a place where these are kept

**mend** *verb* to repair; make or grow better □ *noun* a repaired part □ **on the mend** getting better, recovering

**mendacious** *adj* not true; lying □ **mendaciously** *adv* □ **mendacity** *noun*

**mendicant** *noun* a beggar □ *adj* begging

**menial** (*say* **meen**-i-al) *adj* of work: unskilled, unchallenging

**meningitis** *noun* an illness caused by inflammation of the covering of the brain

**menopause** *noun* the ending of menstruation in middle age

**menstruation** *noun* the monthly discharge of blood from a woman's womb □ **menstrual** *adj* of menstruation □ **menstruate** *verb* to experience menstruation

**mental** *adj* **1** of the mind **2** done, made, happening *etc* in the mind: *mental arithmetic* **3** of illness: affecting the mind □ **mentally** *adv* □ **mental hospital** a hospital for people suffering from mental illness

**mentality** *noun* (*pl* **mentalities**) **1** mental power **2** type of mind; way of thinking

**menthol** *noun* a sharp-smelling substance obtained from peppermint oil

**mention** *verb* **1** to speak of briefly **2** to remark (that) □ *noun* a mentioning, a remark

**mentor** *noun* someone who gives advice as a tutor or supervisor

After *Mentor*, a friend of Odysseus, who guides Telemachus in his search for his father

**menu** *noun* (*pl* **menus**) **1** (a card with) a list of dishes to be served at a meal **2** *computing* a list of options

**MEP** *abbrev* Member of the European Parliament

**mercantile** *adj* of buying and selling; trading

**mercenary** *adj* **1** working for money **2** influenced by the desire for money □ *noun* (*pl* **mercenaries**) a soldier paid by a foreign country to fight in its army

**merchandise** *noun* goods to be bought and sold

**merchant** *noun* someone who carries on a business in the buying and selling of goods, a trader □ *adj* of trade □ **merchant bank** a bank providing *esp* commercial banking services □ **merchant navy** ships and crews employed in trading

**mercurial** *adj* changeable, volatile

**mercury** *noun* an element, a heavy, silvery liquid metal (also **quicksilver**)

**mercy** *noun* (*pl* **mercies**) lenience or forgiveness towards an enemy *etc*; pity □ **merciful** *adj* **1** willing to forgive or be lenient **2** easing or relieving pain, trouble or difficulty □ **mercifully** *adv* fortunately, to one's great relief □ **merciless** *adj* showing no mercy; cruel □ **mercilessly** *adv* □ **at someone's mercy** in their power

**mere** *adj* nothing more than: *mere nonsense* □ **merely** *adv* only, simply

**merge** *verb* **1** to combine or join together **2** to blend, come together gradually □ **merger** *noun* a joining together, *eg* of business companies

■ (meaning I) amalgamate

**meridian** (*say* me-**rid**-i-an) *noun* **1** an

imaginary line around the globe passing through the north and south poles **2** the highest point of the sun's path **3** in Chinese medicine: a main energy channel in the body

**meringue** (*say* me-rang) *noun* a baked cake or shell made of sugar and egg-white

**merino** *noun* (*pl* **merinos**) **1** a sheep with very fine soft wool **2** its wool, or a soft fabric made from it

**merit** *noun* **1** positive worth or value **2** a commendable quality □ *verb* to deserve

**mermaid** *noun* an imaginary sea creature with a woman's upper body and a fish's tail

**merry** *adj* **1** full of fun; cheerful and lively **2** slightly drunk □ **merrily** *adv* (meaning 1) □ **merry-go-round** *noun*, *Brit* a fairground roundabout with wooden horses *etc* for riding on

**mesh** *noun* (*pl* **meshes**) **1** network, netting **2** the opening between the threads of a net □ *verb* of gears *etc*: to interconnect, engage

**mesmerize** *verb* **1** to hypnotize **2** to hold the attention of completely; fascinate

**mess** (*pl* **messes**) **1** an untidy or disgusting sight **2** disorder, confusion **3** a group of soldiers *etc* who take their meals together, or the place where they eat □ **mess up** to make untidy, dirty or muddled □ **mess with** *US informal* to interfere with, fool with □ **messy** *adj* **1** dirty **2** untidy, disordered □ **messily** *adv*

**message** *noun* **1** a piece of news or information sent from one person to another **2** a lesson, a moral □ **get the message** *informal* to understand, get the point

**messenger** *noun* someone who carries a message

**messiah** *noun* a saviour, a deliverer

**metabolism** *noun* **1** the combined chemical changes in the cells of a living organism that provide energy for living processes and activity **2** the conversion of nourishment into energy □ **metabolic** *adj*

**metal** *noun* any of a group of substances (*eg* gold, silver, iron *etc*) able to conduct heat and electricity □ **metallic** *adj* **1** made of metal **2** shining like metal

Do not confuse with: **mettle**

**metallurgy** *noun* the study of metals □ **metallurgic** or **metallurgical** *adj* □ **metallurgist** *noun*

**metamorphosis** (*say* met-*a*-maw-fos-is) *noun* (*pl* **metamorphoses**) **1** a complete change in appearance or character; a transformation **2** a physical change that occurs during the growth of some creatures, *eg* from a tadpole into a frog □ **metamorphose** (*say* met-*a*-maw-fohz) *verb* to change completely in appearance or character

**metaphor** *noun* a way of describing something by suggesting that it is, or has the qualities of, something else, *eg the camel is the ship of the desert* □ **metaphorical** *adj* □ **metaphorically** *adv*

**meteor** *noun* a small piece of matter moving rapidly through space, becoming bright as it enters the earth's atmosphere □ **meteoric** *adj* **1** of a meteor **2** extremely rapid: *meteoric rise to fame* □ **meteorite** *noun* a meteor which falls to the earth as a piece of rock

**meteorology** *noun* the study of weather and climate □ **meteorological** *adj* □ **meteorologist** *noun*

**mete out** *verb*, *formal* to deal out (punishment *etc*)

**meter**[1] *noun* an instrument for measuring the amount of gas, electricity, *etc* used □ *verb* to measure with a meter

**meter**[2] *US* spelling of **metre**

**methane** *noun* a colourless gas

produced by rotting vegetable matter

**method** noun **1** a planned or regular way of doing something **2** orderly arrangement □ **methodical** adj orderly, done or acting according to some plan □ **methodically** adv

**meths** noun, informal methylated spirits

**methylated spirits** an alcohol with added violet dye, used as a solvent or fuel

**meticulous** adj careful and accurate about small details □ **meticulously** adv

**metre** or US **meter** noun **1** the chief unit of length in the metric system (about 1.1 yards) **2** the arrangement of syllables in poetry, or of musical notes, in a regular rhythm
ⓘ From Greek metron meaning 'measure'

**metric** adj **1** of the metric system **2** metrical □ **metrical** adj **1** of poetry: of or in metre **2** arranged in the form of verse □ **metrication** noun the change-over of a country's units of measurements to the metric system □ **metric system** the system of weights and measures based on tens (1 metre = 10 decimetres = 100 centimetres etc)

**metronome** noun an instrument that keeps a regular beat, used for music practice

**metropolis** noun (pl **metropolises**) a large city, usually the capital city of a country □ **metropolitan** adj

**mettle** formal courage, pluck □ **on your mettle** out to do your best

◆. Do not confuse with: metal

**mew** noun a whining cry made by a cat etc □ verb to cry in this way

**mews** noun buildings (originally stables) built around a yard or in a lane

Originally a cage for hawks, mews took on its present meaning after royal stables were built in the 17th century on a site formerly used to house the King's hawks.

**miaow** noun the sound made by a cat □ verb to make the sound of a cat

**miasma** (say mai-az-ma) noun an unhealthy or depressing atmosphere

**mica** noun a mineral which glitters and divides easily into thin transparent layers

**mice** pl of **mouse**

**Michaelmas** noun the festival of St Michael, 29 September

**mickey** noun: **take the mickey** informal to tease, make fun of someone

**micro** noun, informal (pl **micros**) **1** a microwave oven **2** a microcomputer

**micro-** prefix **1** very small: microchip/ microphone (= an instrument which picks up and can amplify small sounds) **2** using a microscope: microsurgery
ⓘ From Greek mikros meaning 'small'

**microbe** noun a tiny living organism

**microchip** noun a tiny piece of silicon designed to act as a complex electronic circuit

**microcomputer** noun a small desktop computer containing a microprocessor

**microcosm** noun a version on a small scale: a microcosm of society

**microfiche** (say maik-roh-feesh) noun a sheet of microfilm suitable for filing

**microfilm** noun narrow photographic film on which books, newspapers, etc are recorded in miniaturized form □ verb to record on microfilm

**microphone** noun an instrument which picks up sound waves for broadcasting, recording or amplifying

**microprocessor** *noun* a computer processor consisting of one or more microchips

**microscope** *noun* a scientific instrument which magnifies very small objects placed under its lens □ **microscopic** *adj* tiny, minuscule

**microsecond** *noun* a millionth of a second

**microsurgery** *noun* delicate surgery carried out under a microscope □ **microsurgeon** *noun*

**microwave** *noun* **1** a microwave oven **2** a very short radio wave □ **microwave oven** an oven which cooks food by passing microwaves through it

**mid-** *prefix* placed or occurring in the middle: *mid-morning*
ⓖ From Old English *midd*

**midday** *noun* noon

**midden** *noun* a rubbish or dung heap

**middle** *noun* the point or part of anything equally distant from its ends or edges; the centre □ *adj* **1** occurring in the middle or centre **2** coming between extreme positions *etc*: *trying to find a middle way* □ **middling** *adj* **1** of middle size or quality **2** neither good nor bad; mediocre □ **middle-aged** *adj* between youth and old age □ **Middle Ages** the time roughly between AD 500 and AD 1500 □ **middle class** the class of people between the working and upper classes □ **middle-of-the-road** *adj* bland, unadventurous □ **in the middle of** in the midst of doing, busy doing

**midge** *noun* a small biting insect

**midget** *noun* an abnormally small person or thing □ *adj* very small

**midnight** *noun* twelve o'clock at night □ *adj* occurring at midnight

**midriff** *noun* the middle of the body, just below the ribs

**midst** *noun* the middle □ **in our midst**

among us

**midsummer** *noun* the time around 21 June, which is the longest day in the year

**midway** *adv* half-way

**midwife** *noun* (*pl* **midwives**) a nurse trained to assist women during childbirth □ **midwifery** (*say* mid-**wif**-*e*-ri or mid-**waif**-ri) *noun* the practice or occupation of being a midwife

Meaning literally 'with woman'

**midwinter** *noun* the time around 21 December, the winter solstice and shortest day in the year

**mien** (*say* meen) *noun*, *formal* look, appearance, aspect

**might¹** *noun* power, strength

**might²** *past tense* of **may**
ⓖ From Old English *mihte*

**mighty** *adj* very great or powerful □ *adv*, *US informal* very □ **mightily** *adv* **1** extremely, greatly **2** with great strength or force □ **mightiness** *noun*

**mighty** ⬦ mightier, mightiest

**migraine** (*say* mee-grein) *noun* a severe form of headache

**migrant** *noun* **1** someone migrating, or recently migrated, from another country **2** a bird that migrates annually

**migrate** *verb* **1** to change your home or move to another area or country **2** of birds: to fly to a warmer region for the winter □ **migration** *noun* □ **migratory** *adj* **1** migrating **2** wandering

**mike** *noun*, *informal* a microphone

**mild** *adj* **1** not harsh or severe; gentle **2** of taste: not sharp or bitter **3** of weather: not cold **4** of an illness: not serious □ **mildly** *adv* **1** in a mild or calm manner **2** slightly □ **to put it mildly** expressing oneself much less strongly than would be possible in the circumstances

**mildew** *noun* a whitish mark on

plants, fabric *etc* caused by fungus
□ **mildewed** *adj*

**mile** *noun* a measure of length (1.61
kilometre or 1760 yards) □ **mileage**
*noun* **1** distance in miles **2** travel
expenses (counted by the mile) **3** the
amount of use or benefit you can get
out of something □ **milestone** *noun*
**1** a stone beside the road showing
the number of miles to a certain
place **2** something which marks an
important event

**militant** *adj* **1** fighting, warlike
**2** aggressive, favouring or taking
part in forceful action □ *noun*
someone who is militant

**military** *adj* of soldiers or warfare
□ *noun* (**the military**) the army

**militate** *verb* **1** to fight or work
(against) **2** to act to your
disadvantage
  ⓘ From Latin *militare* meaning 'to
  serve as a soldier'

  ◐ Do not confuse with: **mitigate**.
  It may be helpful to remember
  that the idea of fighting is
  contained in the word **MILIT**ate
  (in common with 'military' and
  'militia') but not in **mitigate**.

**militia** *noun* a group of fighters, not
regular soldiers, trained for
emergencies

**milk** *noun* **1** a white liquid produced
by female animals as food for their
young **2** this liquid, *esp* from cows,
used as a drink □ *verb* **1** to draw
milk from **2** to take (money *etc*)
from □ **milk float** a vehicle that
makes deliveries of milk to homes
□ **milkmaid** *noun*, *old* a woman who
milks cows □ **milkman** *noun* a man
who sells or delivers milk □ **milk-
tooth** *noun* a tooth from the first set
of teeth in humans and other
mammals

**milky** *adj* **1** like milk, creamy **2** white
□ **Milky Way** a bright band of stars
seen in the night sky

**mill** *noun* **1** a machine for grinding or

crushing grain, coffee *etc* **2** a
building where grain is ground **3** a
factory □ *verb* **1** to grind **2** to cut
grooves round the edge of (a coin)
**3** to move round and round in a
crowd □ **miller** *noun* someone who
grinds grain □ **millrace** *noun* the
stream of water which turns a
millwheel □ **millstone** *noun* **1** one of
two heavy stones used to grind
grain **2** something felt as a burden
or hindrance □ **millwheel** *noun* a
water-wheel which drives the
machinery of a mill

**millennium** *noun* (*pl* **millennia**) a
period of a thousand years

**millet** *noun* a type of grain used for
food

**milli-** or **mill-** *prefix* thousand; a
thousandth part of: *millimetre/
millennium*
  ⓘ From Latin *mille* meaning
  'thousand'

**milligramme** *noun* a thousandth of a
gramme

**millilitre** *noun* a thousandth of a litre

**millimetre** *noun* a thousandth of a
metre

**milliner** *noun* someone who makes
and sells women's hats □ **millinery**
*noun*

**million** *noun* a thousand thousands
(1 000 000)

**millionaire** *noun* someone who has a
million pounds (or dollars) or more

**millipede** *noun* a small crawling
insect with a long body and many
pairs of legs

**millisecond** *noun* a thousandth of a
second

**mime** *noun* **1** a theatrical art using
body movements and facial
expressions in place of speech **2** a
play performed through mime
□ *verb* **1** to perform a mime **2** to
express through mime

**mimic** *verb* to imitate, *esp* in a
mocking way □ *noun* someone who
mimics □ **mimicry** *noun*

**mimic** *verb* ⬦ mimics, mimicking, mimicked

**mimosa** *noun* a tree producing bunches of yellow, scented flowers

**minaret** *noun* a slender tower on an Islamic mosque

**mince** *verb* **1** to cut or chop into small pieces **2** to walk primly with short steps ▢ *noun* meat chopped finely ▢ **mincer** *noun* a machine for mincing food ▢ **mince-pie** *noun* a pie filled with mincemeat ▢ **not mince matters** to not try to soften an unpleasant fact or statement

**mincemeat** *noun* a chopped-up mixture of dried fruit, suet *etc* ▢ **make mincemeat of** to pulverize, destroy

**mind** *noun* **1** consciousness, intelligence, understanding **2** intention: *I've a good mind to tell him so* ▢ *verb* **1** to see to, look after **2** to watch out for, be careful of **3** to object to: *do you mind if I open the window?* ▢ **minder** *noun* **1** someone who looks after a child *etc* **2** an aide or adviser to a public figure ▢ **mindful** *adj*: mindful of paying attention to ▢ **mindless** *adj* foolish, unthinking; pointless ▢ **change your mind** to change your opinion or intention ▢ **in two minds** undecided ▢ **make up your mind** to decide ▢ **out of your mind** mad, crazy ▢ **presence of mind** ability to act calmly and sensibly ▢ **speak your mind** to speak frankly

**mine**[1] *noun* **1** an underground pit or system of tunnels from which metals, coal *etc* are dug **2** a heavy charge of explosive material ▢ *verb* **1** to dig or work a mine **2** to lay explosive mines in ▢ **miner** *noun* someone who works in a mine ▢ **minefield** *noun* an area covered with explosive mines ▢ **minelayer** *noun* a ship which lays explosive mines ▢ **minesweeper** *noun* a ship which removes explosive mines

**mine**[2] *pronoun* a thing or things belonging to me: *that drink is mine*

**mineral** *noun* a natural substance mined from the earth, *eg* coal, metals, gems *etc* ▢ *adj* of or containing minerals ▢ **mineral water 1** water containing small amounts of minerals **2** *informal* carbonated water

**mineralogy** *noun* the study of minerals ▢ **mineralogist** *noun*

**minestrone** (*say* min-is-troh-ni) *noun* a thick Italian vegetable soup containing rice or pasta

**mingle** *verb* to mix

**mingy** (*say* min-ji) *adj*, *informal* stingy, mean

**Mini** *noun*, *trademark* a small, two-doored British car

**mini-** *prefix* smaller than average; compact: *minibus/ minicab*

The prefix mini- is an abbreviation of 'miniature'.

**miniature** *noun* **1** a small-scale painting **2** a small bottle of spirits ▢ *adj* on a small scale

**minibus** *noun* (*pl* minibuses) a type of small bus

**minim** *music* a note (♩) equal to two crotchets, or half a semibreve, in length

**minimize** *verb* **1** to make to seem small or unimportant **2** to make as small as possible

**minimum** *noun* (*pl* minima) the smallest possible quantity ▢ *adj* the least possible ▢ **minimum wage** the lowest wage per hour which can legally be paid for a particular type of work

**minion** *noun* a slave-like follower

**minister** *noun* **1** the head of a government department: *minister of trade* **2** a member of the clergy **3** an agent, a representative ▢ *verb* **minister to** to help, supply the needs of ▢ **ministerial** *adj*

**ministry** *noun* (*pl* ministries) **1** a government department or its headquarters **2** the work of a member of the clergy

**mink** *noun* a small weasel-like kind of animal or its fur

**minnow** *noun* a type of very small river or pond fish

**minor** *adj* **1** of less importance, size *etc* **2** small, unimportant (*contrasted with*: **major**) □ *noun* someone not yet legally an adult (*ie* in the UK, under 18) □ **minority** *noun* (*pl* **minorities**) **1** the smaller number or part **2** the state of being a minor

**minster** *noun* a large church or cathedral

**minstrel** *noun* **1** *historical* a medieval travelling musician **2** a singer, an entertainer

**mint¹** *noun* a plant with strong-smelling leaves, used as flavouring

**mint²** *noun* **1** a place where coins are made **2** *informal* a large sum of money □ *verb* to make coins □ **in mint condition** in perfect condition

**minuet** *noun* **1** a kind of slow, graceful dance **2** the music for this

**minus** *prep* **1** used to show subtraction, represented by the sign (-): *five minus two equals three or 5-2=3* **2** *informal* without: *I'm minus my car today* □ *adj* of a quantity less than zero

**minuscule** (*say* min-is-kyool) *noun* a small cursive script originally used by monks for manuscripts □ *adj* **1** written in minuscule **2** tiny, minute

**minute¹** (*say* min-it) *noun* **1** a sixtieth part of an hour **2** in measuring an angle, the sixtieth part of a degree **3** a very short time **4** (**minutes**) notes taken of what is said at a meeting

**minute²** (*say* mai-nyoot) *adj* **1** very small **2** very exact

**minx** *noun* (*pl* **minxes**) a cheeky young girl

**miracle** *noun* **1** a wonderful act beyond normal human powers **2** a fortunate happening with no natural cause or explanation □ **miraculous** *adj* □ **miraculously** *adv*

**mirage** *noun* something imagined but not really there, *eg* an oasis seen by travellers in the desert

**mire** *noun* deep mud

**mirror** *noun* a backed piece of glass which shows the image of someone looking into it □ *verb* **1** to reflect like a mirror **2** to copy exactly

**mirth** *noun* merriment, laughter □ **mirthful** *adj* □ **mirthless** *adj*

**mis-** *prefix* wrong(ly), bad(ly): *mispronounce/ misapply*

**misadventure** *noun* an unlucky happening

**misanthropist** *noun* someone who hates humanity □ **misanthropic** *adj* □ **misanthropy** *noun*

**misappropriate** (*say* mis-ap-roh-pri-eit) *verb* to put to a wrong use, *eg* use (someone else's money) for yourself

**misbehave** *verb* to behave badly □ **misbehaviour** *noun*

**miscarriage** *noun* **1** a going wrong, failure: *miscarriage of justice* **2** the accidental loss of a foetus during pregnancy □ **miscarry** *verb* **1** to go wrong or astray **2** to be unsuccessful **3** to have a miscarriage

**miscarry** ⇨ **miscarries**, **miscarrying**, **miscarried**

**miscellaneous** *adj* assorted, made up of several kinds □ **miscellany** *noun* (*pl* **miscellanies**)

**mischance** *noun* an unlucky accident

**mischief** *noun* naughtiness, teasing □ **mischievous** *adj* □ **mischievously** *adv*

**misconceive** *verb* to misunderstand □ **misconception** *noun* a wrong idea, a misunderstanding

**misconduct** *noun* bad or immoral

behaviour

**misconstrue** *verb* to misunderstand □ **misconstruction** *noun*

**miscreant** *noun* a wicked person

**misdeed** *noun* a bad deed; a crime

**misdemeanour** *noun* a minor offence

**miser** *noun* someone who hoards money and spends very little □ **miserly** *adj* stingy; mean

**misery** *noun* (*pl* **miseries**) **1** great unhappiness, pain, poverty *etc* **2** a person who is always sad or bad-tempered □ **miserable** *adj* **1** very unhappy; wretched **2** having a tendency to be bad-tempered and grumpy **3** depressing

**misfire** *verb* **1** of a gun: to fail to go off **2** of a plan: to go wrong

**misfit** *noun* **1** someone who cannot fit in happily in society *etc* **2** something that fits badly

**misfortune** *noun* **1** bad luck **2** an unlucky accident

**misgiving** *noun* fear or doubt, *eg* about the result of an action

**misguided** *adj* led astray, mistaken, unwise

**mishandle** *verb* to treat badly or roughly

**mishap** *noun* an unlucky accident

**misinform** *verb* to inform wrongly

**misinterpret** *verb* to interpret wrongly

**misjudge** *verb* to judge unfairly or wrongly

**mislay** *verb* to put (something) aside and forget where it is; lose

**mislay** ⇔ mislays, mislaying, mislaid

**mislead** *verb* to give a false idea (to); deceive □ **misleading** *adj*

**mislead** ⇔ misleads, misleading, misled

**mismatch** *noun* an unsuitable match

**misnomer** *noun* a wrong or unsuitable name

**misogynist** (*say* mi-so-jin-ist) *noun* a man who hates women

**misplace** *verb* to put in the wrong place; mislay

**misprint** *noun* a mistake in printing

**misquote** *verb* to make a mistake in repeating something written or said

**misrepresent** *verb* to give a wrong idea of (someone's words, actions *etc*)

**Miss** *noun* (*pl* **Misses**) **1** a form of address used before the surname of an unmarried woman **2** (**miss**) a young woman or girl

**miss** *verb* **1** to fail to hit, see, hear, understand *etc* **2** to discover the loss or absence of **3** to feel the lack of □ *noun* (*pl* **misses**) **1** the act of missing **2** a failure to hit a target **3** a loss □ **missing** *adj* lost □ **miss out 1** to leave out **2** to be left out of something worthwhile or advantageous

**missal** *noun* the Mass book of the Roman Catholic Church

**misshapen** *adj* badly or abnormally shaped

**missile** *noun* a weapon or other object that is thrown or fired

**mission** *noun* **1** a task that someone is sent to do **2** a group of representatives sent to another country **3** a group sent to spread a religion **4** the headquarters of such groups **5** someone's chosen task or purpose: *his only mission is to make money*

**missionary** *noun* (*pl* **missionaries**) someone sent abroad *etc* to spread a religion

**missive** *noun* something sent, *eg* a letter

**mist** *noun* a cloud of moisture in the air; thin fog or drizzle □ **mist up** or **mist over** to cover or become covered with mist □ **misty** *adj*

**mistake** *verb* **1** to misunderstand, be wrong or make an error about **2** to take (one thing or person) for another □ *noun* a wrong action or statement; an error □ **mistaken** *adj* making an error, unwise: *mistaken belief*

> **mistake** *verb* ⇨ mistak*es*, mistak*ing*, mistak*en*, mistook

**mistletoe** *noun* a plant with white berries, used as a Christmas decoration

**mistreat** *verb* to treat badly; abuse

**mistress** *noun* (*pl* **mistresses**) 1 a female teacher 2 a female owner of a dog *etc* 3 a woman skilled in an art 4 a woman who is the lover though not the legal wife of a man 5 *full form of* **Mrs**

**mistrust** *noun* a lack of trust or confidence in □ *verb* to have no trust or confidence in

**misunderstand** *verb* to take a wrong meaning from what is said or done □ **misunderstanding** *noun* 1 a mistake about a meaning 2 a slight disagreement

**misuse** *noun* bad or wrong use □ *verb* 1 to use wrongly 2 to treat badly

**mite** *noun* 1 something very small, *eg* a tiny child 2 a very small spider

**mitigate** *verb* to make (punishment, anger *etc*) less great or severe □ **mitigation** *noun*
⊕ From Latin *mitigare* meaning 'to make mild or soft'

> ⬥ Do not confuse with: **militate**. It may be helpful to remember that the idea of fighting is contained in the word **MILIT**ate (in common with 'military' and 'militia') but not in **mitigate**.

**mitre** *noun* 1 the pointed head-dress worn by archbishops and bishops 2 a slanting joint between two pieces of wood

**mitt** or **mitten** *noun* a glove without separate divisions for the four fingers

**mix** *verb* 1 to unite or blend two or more things together 2 (**mix up**) to confuse, muddle 3 to have social contact with other people □ *noun* a mixture, a blending □ **mixed** *adj* 1 jumbled together 2 confused, muddled 3 consisting of different kinds 4 for both sexes □ **mixed-up** *adj* confused, bewildered, emotionally unstable □ **mixer** *noun* 1 a machine that mixes food 2 someone who mixes socially 3 a soft drink added to alcohol □ **mixture** *noun* 1 a number of things mixed together 2 a medicine

> ◪ (verb, meaning 2) jumble; (verb, meaning 3) associate

**mizzen-mast** *noun* the mast nearest the stern of a ship

**mnemonic** (*say* ni-mon-ik) *noun* a rhyme *etc* which helps you to remember something

> ✑ Some people use this mnemonic to help them remember the colours of the rainbow: Richard of York gave battle in vain (red orange yellow green blue indigo violet).
> **Can you think of any more?**

**moan** *noun* a low sound of grief or pain □ *verb* to make this sound

**moat** *noun* a deep trench round a castle *etc*, often filled with water

**mob** *noun* a noisy crowd □ *verb* to crowd round, or attack, in disorder

> **mob** ⇨ mob*s*, mob*bing*, mob*bed*

**mobile** *adj* 1 able to move or be moved easily 2 not fixed, changing quickly 3 portable, not relying on fixed cables *etc*: *mobile phone* □ *noun* 1 a decoration or toy hung so that it moves slightly in the air 2 *informal* a mobile phone □ **mobility** *noun* freedom or ease of movement, either in physical or career terms □ **mobilize** *verb* to gather (troops *etc*) together ready for active service □ **mobilization** *noun*

**moccasin** *noun* a flat soft leather shoe

**mocha** (*say* mok-*a* or mohk-*a*) *noun* 1 a fine coffee 2 coffee and chocolate mixed together 3 a deep brown colour

**mock** *verb* to laugh at, make fun of □ *adj* false, pretended, imitation: *mock battle* □ **mockery** *noun*

**mode** *noun* 1 a manner of doing or acting 2 kind, sort; fashion

**model** *noun* 1 a design or pattern to be copied 2 a small-scale copy of something 3 a living person who poses for an artist 4 someone employed to wear and display new clothes □ *adj* 1 acting as a model 2 fit to be copied, perfect: *model behaviour* □ *verb* 1 to make a model of 2 to shape according to a particular pattern 3 to wear and display (clothes)

**model** *verb* ↔ model*s*, model*ling*, model*led*

**modem** *noun* a device which transmits information from a computer along telephone cables

**moderate** *verb* (*say* mod-*e*-reit) to make or become less great or severe □ *adj* (*say* mod-*e*-rat) 1 keeping within reason, not going to extremes 2 of medium or average quality, ability *etc* □ **moderately** *adv* □ **moderation** *noun* 1 a lessening or calming down 2 the practice of not going to extremes

**modern** *adj* belonging to the present or to recent times; not old □ **modernity** *noun* □ **modernize** *verb* to bring up to date

◼ current, contemporary, advanced, avant-garde, progressive, modernistic, state-of-the-art

**modest** *adj* 1 not exaggerating achievements; not boastful 2 not very large: *modest salary* 3 behaving decently; not shocking □ **modesty** *noun*

**modicum** *noun* (*pl* **modicums**) a small quantity or amount

**modify** *verb* 1 to make a change in: *modified my design* 2 to make less extreme: *modified his demands* □ **modification** *noun*

**modify** ↔ modif*ies*, modify*ing*, modif*ied*

**modish** *adj* fashionable, smart

**modulate** *verb* 1 to vary or soften in tone or pitch 2 *music* to change key □ **modulation** *noun*

**module** *noun* 1 a set course forming a unit in an educational scheme 2 a separate, self-contained section of a spacecraft □ **modular** *adj*

**mogul** *noun* 1 a mound of hard snow forming an obstacle on a ski-slope 2 an influential person; a magnate

**mohair** *noun* 1 the long silky hair of an Angora goat 2 fabric made from this

**Mohammed** *noun* a prophet, the founder of Islam

**moist** *adj* damp, very slightly wet □ **moisten** *verb* to make slightly wet or damp □ **moisture** *noun* slight wetness; water or other liquid in tiny drops in the atmosphere or on a surface □ **moisturize** *verb* □ **moisturizer** *noun* a cosmetic cream that restores moisture to the skin

**molar** *noun* a back tooth used for grinding food

**molasses** *noun sing* a thick dark syrup left when sugar is refined

**mole¹** *noun* 1 a small burrowing animal, with tiny eyes and soft fur 2 a spy who successfully infiltrates a rival organization □ **molehill** *noun* a small heap of earth created by a burrowing mole

**mole²** *noun* a small dark spot on the skin, often raised

**molecule** *noun* the smallest part of a substance that has the same qualities as the substance itself

**molest** *verb* 1 to annoy or torment 2 to injure or abuse sexually

**mollify** verb to calm down; lessen the anger of

> **mollify** ⊸ mollifies, mollifying, mollified

**mollusc** noun one of a group of boneless animals, usually with hard shells, eg shellfish and snails

**mollycoddle** verb to pamper, over-protect

**molten** adj of metal etc: melted

**moment** noun 1 a very short space of time; an instant 2 importance, consequence □ **momentary** adj □ **momentarily** adv □ **momentous** adj of great importance

**momentum** noun (pl momenta) the force of a moving body

**monarch** noun a king, queen, emperor or empress □ **monarchist** noun someone who believes in government by a monarch □ **monarchy** noun (pl **monarchies**) 1 government by a monarch 2 an area governed by a monarch 3 the royal family

**monastery** noun (pl **monasteries**) a building housing a group of monks □ **monastic** adj

**Monday** noun the second day of the week

**monetary** (say mun-it-ri) adj of money or coinage

**money** noun 1 coins and banknotes used for payment 2 wealth □ **moneyed** or **monied** adj

**mongoose** noun (pl **mongooses**) a small weasel-like animal which kills snakes

**mongrel** noun an animal of mixed breed

**monitor** noun 1 an instrument used to check the operation of a system or apparatus 2 a screen in a television studio showing the picture being transmitted 3 a computer screen 4 a school pupil given certain responsibilities □ verb 1 to keep a check on 2 to listen to and report on foreign broadcasts etc

**monk** noun a member of a male religious group living secluded in a monastery

**monkey** noun (pl **monkeys**) 1 a long-tailed mammal which walks on four legs 2 a mischievous child □ **monkey-nut** noun a peanut □ **monkey-puzzle** noun a pine tree with prickly spines along its branches □ **monkey-wrench** noun an adjustable spanner □ **monkey about** to fool about

**monkfish** noun a type of sea-fish, used as food

**mono-** prefix one, single: carbon monoxide (= a gas with only one oxygen atom in its molecule) ⊕ From Greek monos meaning 'single' or 'alone'

**monoboard** noun a wide single ski, controlled with both feet

**monochrome** adj 1 in one colour 2 black and white

**monocle** noun a single eyeglass

**monogamy** noun marriage to one spouse at a time □ **monogamous** adj

**monogram** noun two or more letters, usually initials, made into a single design

**monolith** noun 1 an upright block of stone 2 something unmovable or intractable □ **monolithic** adj

**monologue** noun a long speech by one person

**monoplane** noun an aeroplane with a single pair of wings

**monopoly** noun (pl **monopolies**) 1 an exclusive right to make or sell something 2 complete unshared possession, control etc □ **monopolize** verb 1 to have exclusive rights to 2 to take up the whole of: monopolizing the conversation

**monorail** noun a railway on which the trains run along a single rail

**mono-ski** noun one large ski on

which both feet are placed □ *verb* to ski using a mono-ski

**monosyllable** *noun* a word of one syllable □ **monosyllabic** *adj*

**monotone** *noun* a single, unchanging tone □ **monotonous** *adj* **1** in a single tone **2** unchanging, dull □ **monotonously** *adv* □ **monotony** *noun* lack of variety

**monsoon** *noun* **1** a wind that blows in the Indian Ocean **2** the rainy season caused by the south-west monsoon in summer

**monster** *noun* **1** something of unusual size or appearance **2** a huge terrifying creature **3** an evil person □ *adj* huge

**monstrosity** *noun* (*pl* **monstrosities**) **1** something unnatural **2** something very ugly

**monstrous** *adj* huge, horrible

**montage** (*say* mon-**tahsz**) *noun* **1** a composite picture **2** a film made up of parts of other films

**month** *noun* a twelfth part of a year, approximately four weeks □ **monthly** *adj* & *adv* happening once a month □ *noun* (*pl* **monthlies**) a magazine *etc* published once a month

**monument** *noun* a building, pillar, tomb *etc* built in memory of someone or an event □ **monumental** *adj* **1** of a monument **2** huge, enormous □ **monumentally** *adv* (meaning 2)

**moo** *noun* the sound made by a cow

**mood** *noun* the state of a person's feelings or temper □ **moody** *adj* **1** often changing in mood **2** ill-tempered, cross □ **moodily** *adv* (meaning 2)

**moon** *noun* the heavenly body which travels round the earth once each month and reflects light from the sun □ *verb* **1** to wander (about) **2** to gaze dreamily (at) □ **moonbeam** *noun* a beam of light from the moon □ **moonlight** *noun* the light of the

moon □ *verb* to work secretly at a second job, usually avoiding paying tax on the money earned □ **moonshine** *noun* **1** the shining of the moon **2** rubbish, foolish ideas or talk **3** alcoholic spirits which have been illegally distilled or smuggled

**moor** *noun* a large stretch of open ground, often covered with heather □ *verb* to tie up or anchor (a ship *etc*) □ **moorhen** *noun* a kind of water bird □ **moorings** *noun pl* **1** the place where a ship is moored **2** the anchor, rope *etc* holding it □ **moorland** *noun* a stretch of moor

**moose** *noun* (*pl* **moose**) a large deer-like animal, found in N America

**moot point** a debatable point; a question with no obvious solution

**mop** *noun* **1** a pad of sponge or a bunch of short pieces of coarse yarn *etc* on a handle for washing or cleaning **2** a thick head of hair □ *verb* **1** to clean with a mop **2** to clean or wipe: *mopped his brow* □ **mop up** to clean up

**mop** *verb* ⇔ mop**s**, mop**ping**, mop**ped**

**mope** *verb* to be unhappy and gloomy

**moped** *noun* a pedal bicycle with a motor

**moraine** *noun* a line of rocks and gravel left by a glacier

**moral** *adj* **1** relating to standards of behaviour and character **2** of correct or acceptable behaviour or character □ *noun* **1** the lesson of a story **2** (**morals**) principles and standards of (*esp* sexual) behaviour □ **morality** *noun* moral standards □ **moralize** *verb* to draw a lesson from a story or event □ **moral support** encouragement without active help □ **moral victory** a failure that can really be seen as a success

**morale** (*say* mo-**rahl**) *noun* spirit and confidence

**morass** *noun* (*pl* **morasses**) **1** a

marsh or bog **2** a bewildering mass of something: *a morass of regulations*

**moratorium** *noun (pl* **moratoria)** an official suspension or temporary ban

**morbid** *adj* **1** too concerned with gloomy, unpleasant things, *esp* death **2** diseased, unhealthy □ **morbidity** *noun* □ **morbidly** *adv*

**more** *adj* a greater number or amount of □ *adv* to a greater extent: *more beautiful* □ *noun* **1** a greater proportion or amount **2** a further or additional number □ **moreish** *adj* of food *etc*: enjoyable, making you want more □ **moreover** *adv* besides

**morgue** (*say* mawg) *noun* a place where dead bodies are laid, awaiting identification *etc*

**moribund** *adj* **1** dying **2** stagnant

**morn** *noun, formal* morning

**morning** *noun* the part of the day before noon □ *adj* of or in the morning □ **morning star** Venus when it rises before the sun

**morocco** *noun* a fine goatskin leather first brought from Morocco

**moron** *noun* someone of low mental ability; an idiot □ **moronic** *adj*

**morose** *adj* bad-tempered, gloomy □ **morosely** *adv* □ **morosity** *noun*

**morphia** *noun* morphine

**morphine** *noun* a drug which causes sleep or deadens pain (*also called* **morphia**)

**morris dance** a traditional English country dance in which male dancers carry sticks and wear bells
Originally a *Moorish* dance brought from Spain

**morrow** *noun, old:* **the morrow** tomorrow, the day after

**Morse** or **Morse code** *noun* a signalling code of signals made up of dots and dashes

**morsel** *noun* a small piece, *eg* of food

**mortal** *adj* **1** liable to die **2** causing death; deadly: *mortal injury* □ *noun* a human being □ **mortality** *noun (pl* **mortalities) 1** the state of being mortal **2** death **3** frequency of death; death-rate: *infant mortality* □ **mortally** *adv* **1** fatally: *mortally wounded* **2** very much, dreadfully: *mortally offended*

**mortar** *noun* **1** a heavy bowl for crushing and grinding substances with a pestle **2** a short gun for throwing shells **3** a mixture of lime, sand and water, used for fixing stones *etc*

**mortarboard** *noun* a university or college cap with a square flat top

**mortgage** *noun* a sum of money lent through a legal agreement for buying buildings, land *etc* □ *verb* to offer (buildings *etc*) as security for money borrowed

**mortice** *another spelling of* **mortise**

**mortician** *noun, US* an undertaker

**mortify** *verb* **1** to make to feel ashamed or humble: *I was mortified* **2** of a part of the flesh: to die □ **mortification** *noun* □ **mortifying** *adj*

**mortify** ⇔ mortif*ies*, mortif*ying*, mortif*ied*

**mortise** or **mortice** *noun* a hole in a piece of wood to receive the shaped end (**tenon**) of another piece

**mortise-lock** or **mortice-lock** *noun* a lock whose mechanism is sunk into the edge of a door

**mortuary** *noun (pl* **mortuaries)** a place where dead bodies are kept before burial or cremation

**mosaic** *noun* a picture or design made up of many small pieces of coloured glass, stone *etc*

**Moslem** *another spelling of* **Muslim**

**mosque** *noun* an Islamic place of worship

**mosquito** *noun (pl* **mosquitoes** or **mosquitos)** a biting or blood-sucking insect, often carrying disease

**moss** *noun* (*pl* **mosses**) a very small flowerless plant, found in moist places □ **mossy** *adj*

**most** *adj* the greatest number or amount of □ **1** *adv* very, extremely **2** to the greatest extent: *the most severely injured* □ *noun* the greatest number or amount □ **mostly** *adv* mainly, chiefly □ **at most** not more than □ **for the most part** mostly

**MOT** *noun* a compulsory annual check on behalf of the *Ministry of Transport* on vehicles over a certain age

**motel** *noun* a hotel built to accommodate motorists and their vehicles

**moth** *noun* **1** a flying insect, seen mostly at night **2** the cloth-eating grub of the clothes-moth □ **mothball** *noun* a small ball of chemical used to protect clothes from moths □ *verb* (*also* **put in mothballs**) to put aside for later use *etc* □ **moth-eaten** *adj* **1** full of holes made by moths **2** tatty, shabby

**mother** *noun* **1** a female parent **2** the female head of a convent □ *verb* **1** to be the mother of **2** to care for like a mother □ **motherly** *adj* □ **motherhood** *noun* □ **mother-in-law** *noun* the mother of your husband or wife □ **motherland** *noun* the country of your birth □ **mother-of-pearl** *noun* a hard shiny substance which forms inside certain shells □ **mother tongue** a native language

**motif** (*say* moh-teef) *noun* (*pl* **motifs**) a distinctive feature or idea in a piece of music, a play *etc*

◆. Do not confuse with: **motive**

**motion** *noun* **1** the act or state of moving **2** a single movement **3** a suggestion put before a meeting for discussion □ *verb* **1** to make a signal by a movement or gesture **2** to direct (someone) in this way

□ **motionless** *adj* not moving

**motivate** *verb* to cause (someone) to act in a certain way

**motive** *noun* the cause of someone's actions; a reason

◆. Do not confuse with: **motif**

**motley** *adj* made up of different colours or kinds

**motor** *noun* **1** an engine which causes motion **2** a car □ *verb* to travel by motor vehicle □ **motorist** *noun* someone who drives a car □ **motorize** *verb* to supply with an engine □ **motorbike** *or* **motorcycle** *noun* a bicycle with a petrol-driven engine □ **motorbiker** *noun* □ **motorcyclist** *noun* □ **motorcade** *noun* a procession of cars carrying a head of state *etc* □ **motorway** *noun* a dual carriageway on which traffic is allowed to drive faster than on other roads

**mottled** *adj* marked with spots or blotches

**motto** *noun* (*pl* **mottoes**) a phrase which acts as a guiding principle or rule

**mould**[1] *noun* a shape into which a liquid is poured to take on that shape when it cools or sets □ *verb* **1** to form in a mould **2** to shape

**mould**[2] *noun* **1** a fluffy growth on stale food *etc* **2** soil containing rotted leaves *etc* □ **mouldy** *adj* affected by mould; stale

**moulder** *verb* to crumble away to dust

**moulding** *noun* a decorated border of moulded plaster round a ceiling *etc*

**moult** *verb* of a bird: to shed its feathers

**mound** *noun* **1** a bank of earth or stones **2** a hill; a heap

**mount** *verb* **1** to go up, ascend **2** to climb on to (a horse, bicycle *etc*) **3** to fix (a picture *etc*) on to a backing or support **4** to fix (a gemstone) in a casing **5** to organize (an exhibition) *noun* **1** a support or backing for display **2** a horse, bicycle *etc* to ride on **3** *old* a mountain

**mountain** *noun* **1** a large hill **2** a large quantity □ **mountaineer** *noun* a mountain climber □ **mountain-ash** *noun* the rowan tree □ **mountainous** *adj* **1** having many mountains **2** huge

**mountebank** *noun* a charlatan, a quack

Originally a street pedlar who climbed on a mound or bench to sell his goods

**mourn** *verb* **1** to grieve for **2** to be sorrowful □ **mourner** *noun* □ **mournful** *adj* □ **mourning** *noun* **1** the showing of grief **2** the period during which someone grieves **3** dark-coloured clothes traditionally worn by mourners

**mouse** *noun* (*pl* **mice**) **1** a small gnawing animal, found in houses and fields **2** a shy, timid, uninteresting person **3** *computing* a device moved by hand which causes corresponding cursor movements on a screen □ **mousy** *adj* **1** of a light-brown colour **2** shy, timid, uninteresting

**mousse** *noun* a frothy set dish including eggs, cream *etc*, either sweet or savoury

**moustache** *noun* unshaved hair above a man's upper lip

**mouth** *noun* (*say* mowth) **1** the opening in the head through which an animal or person eats and makes sounds **2** the point of a river where it flows into the sea **3** an opening, an entrance □ *verb* (*say* mowdh) **1** to speak **2** to shape (words) in an exaggerated way □ **mouthful** *noun* (*pl* **mouthfuls**) as much as fills the mouth □ **mouth-organ** *noun* a small wind instrument, moved across the lips □ **mouthpiece** *noun* **1** the part of a musical instrument, tobacco-pipe *etc* held in the mouth

**2** someone who speaks for others

**move** *verb* **1** to (cause to) change place or position **2** to change your house **3** to rouse or affect the feelings of **4** to rouse into action **5** to propose, suggest □ *noun* **1** an act of moving **2** a step, an action **3** a shifting of pieces in a game of chess *etc* □ **movable** *adj* able to be moved, changed *etc* □ **movement** *noun* **1** the act or manner of moving **2** a change of position **3** a division of a piece of music **4** a group of people united in a common aim: *the peace movement* **5** an organized attempt to achieve an aim: *the movement to reform the divorce laws*

**movie** *noun* a cinema film □ **the movies** the cinema

**moving** *adj* **1** in motion **2** causing emotion □ **movingly** *adv* (meaning 2)

**mow** *verb* **1** to cut (grass, hay *etc*) with a scythe or machine **2** (**mow down**) to destroy in great numbers □ **mower** *noun*

**MP** *abbrev* **1** Member of Parliament **2** Military Police

**Mr** *noun* (*short* for **mister**) the form of address used before a man's surname

**Mrs** *noun* (*short* for **mistress**) the form of address used before a married woman's surname

**Ms** *noun* a form of address used before the surname of a married or unmarried woman

**much** *adj* a great amount of □ *adv* to or by a great extent: *much loved/much faster* □ *pronoun* **1** a great amount **2** something important: *made much of it* □ **much the same** nearly the same

**muck** *noun* dung, dirt, filth □ **muck-raking** *noun* looking for scandals to expose

**mucous** *adj* like or covered by mucus

♦ Do not confuse: **mucous** and **mucus**

**mucus** *noun* slimy fluid secreted from the nose *etc*

**mud** *noun* wet, soft earth □ **muddy** *adj* **1** covered with mud **2** unclear, confused □ *verb* to make or become muddy □ **mudguard** *noun* a shield or guard over wheels to catch mud splashes

**muddle** *verb* **1** to confuse, bewilder **2** to mix up **3** to make a mess of □ *noun* **1** a mess **2** a state of confusion

**muesli** *noun* a mixture of grains, nuts and fruit eaten with milk

**muff**¹ *noun* a tube of warm fabric to cover and keep the hands warm

**muff**² *verb* to fail in an opportunity, *eg* to catch a ball

**muffin** *noun* **1** a round, flat spongy cake, toasted and eaten hot with butter **2** *US* a small sweet cake made of flour, cornmeal *etc*

**muffle** *verb* **1** to wrap up for warmth *etc* **2** to deaden (a sound) □ **muffler** *noun* **1** a scarf **2** *US* a silencer for a car

**mufti** *noun* clothes worn by soldiers *etc* when off duty

**mug**¹ *noun* **1** a straight-sided cup **2** *informal* a stupid person **3** *informal* the face

**mug**² *verb* to attack and rob (someone) in the street □ **mugger** *noun*

**mug** ⟿ mug**s**, mug**ging**, mug**ged**

**mug**³ *verb*: **mug up** *informal* to study hard; swot up

**muggy** *adj* of weather: close and damp □ **mugginess** *noun*

**mulberry** *noun* **1** a tree on whose leaves silkworms feed **2** its purple berry

**mule**¹ *noun* an animal bred from a horse and an ass

**mule**² *noun* a backless slipper

**mulish** *adj* stubborn

**mulled** *adj* of wine, *etc*: mixed with spices and served warm

**mullet** *noun* an edible small sea-fish

**mull over** *verb* to think over, ponder over

**multi-** *prefix* many
  ⓘ From Latin *multus* meaning 'many'

**multi-coloured** *adj* many-coloured

**multifarious** *adj* of many kinds

**multimedia** *adj* of a computer: able to run various sound and visual applications

**multimillionaire** *noun* someone who has property worth several million pounds (or dollars)

**multinational** *adj* of a company: having branches in several different countries

**multiple** *adj* **1** affecting many parts: *multiple injuries* **2** involving many things of the same sort, *eg* vehicles in a *multiple crash* □ *noun* a number or quantity which contains another an exact number of times

**multiplex** *adj* of a cinema: including several screens and theatres in one building

**multiplicity** *noun*: **a multiplicity of** a great number of

**multiplier** *noun* the number by which another is to be multiplied

**multiply** *verb* **1** to increase **2** to increase a number by adding it to itself a certain number of times: *2 multiplied by 3 is 6* □ **multiplication** *noun*

**multiply** ⟿ multipl**ies**, multiply**ing**, multipli**ed**

**multitude** *noun* a great number; a crowd □ **multitudinous** *adj*

**mum**¹ *noun, informal* mother

**mum**² *adj* silent

**mumble** *verb* to speak indistinctly

**mummify** ⟿ mummif**ies**, mummify**ing**, mummifi**ed**

**mummy**¹ *noun* (*pl* **mummies**) *informal* mother

**mummy**² *noun* (*pl* **mummies**) a dead

body preserved by wrapping in bandages and treating with wax, spices *etc* ◻ **mummify** *verb*

**mumps** *noun sing* an infectious disease affecting glands at the side of the neck, causing swelling

**munch** *verb* to chew noisily

**munchies**: **the munchies** hunger pangs

**mundane** *adj* dull, ordinary

**municipal** *adj* of or owned by a city or town ◻ **municipality** *noun* a city or town; an area covered by local government

**munificent** *adj* very generous ◻ **munificence** *noun*

**munitions** *noun pl* weapons and ammunition used in war

**Munro** *noun* (*pl* **Munros**) a British or Irish mountain above 3000 feet

Originally applied only to mountains in Scotland, from a list prepared by the Scottish mountaineer, Hugh *Munro*

**mural** *adj* of or on a wall ◻ *noun* a painting or design on a wall

**murder** *verb* to kill someone unlawfully and on purpose ◻ *noun* the act of murdering ◻ **murderer**, *old* **murderess** *noun* someone who commits murder ◻ **murderous** *adj*

**murky** *adj* dark, gloomy ◻ **murkiness** *noun*

**murmur** *noun* **1** a low indistinct continuous sound **2** a hushed speech or tone ◻ *verb* **1** to make a murmur **2** to complain, grumble

**Murphy's Law** the law that if something can go wrong, it will

**muscle** *noun* **1** fleshy tissue which contracts and stretches to cause body movements **2** an area of this in the body **3** physical strength or power ◻ **muscular** *adj* **1** of muscles **2** strong

**muse** *verb* to think (over) in a quiet, leisurely way

**museum** *noun* (*pl* **museums**) a

building for housing and displaying objects of artistic, scientific or historic interest

**mush** *noun* **1** something soft and pulpy **2** an overly sentimental film, song *etc* ◻ **mushy** *adj*

**mushroom** *noun* an edible fungus, usually umbrella-shaped ◻ *verb* to grow very quickly: *buildings mushroomed all over town*

**music** *noun* **1** the art of arranging, combining *etc* certain sounds able to be produced by the voice, or by instruments **2** an arrangement of such sounds or its written form **3** a sweet or pleasant sound ◻ **musical** *adj* **1** of music **2** sounding sweet or pleasant **3** having a talent for music ◻ *noun* a light play or film with a lot of songs and dancing in it ◻ **musically** *adv* ◻ **musician** *noun* **1** a specialist in music **2** someone who plays a musical instrument

**musk** *noun* a strong perfume, obtained from the male musk deer or artificially ◻ **musky** *adj*

**musket** *noun* a kind of gun once used by soldiers

**musketeer** *noun* a soldier armed with a musket

**Muslim** *noun* a follower of the Islamic religion ◻ *adj* Islamic

**muslin** *noun* a fine, soft cotton cloth

**mussel** *noun* an edible shellfish with two separate halves to its shell

**must** *verb* **1** used with another verb to express necessity **2** expressing compulsion: *you must do as you're told* **3** expressing certainty or probability: *that must be right* ◻ *noun* something that must be done; a necessity
ⓔ From Old English *moste*

**mustache** *US spelling of* **moustache**

**mustang** *noun* a North American wild horse

**mustard** *noun* **1** a plant with sharp-tasting seeds **2** a hot yellow paste made from its seeds

**muster** verb to gather up or together (eg troops, courage) □ **pass muster** to be accepted as satisfactory

**musty** adj smelling old and stale □ **mustiness** noun

**mutable** adj changeable

**mute** adj **1** not able to speak; dumb **2** silent **3** of a letter in a word: not pronounced □ noun a mute person □ **muted** adj **1** of a sound: made quieter, hushed **2** of a colour: not bright

**mutilate** verb **1** to inflict great physical damage on; maim **2** to damage greatly □ **mutilation** noun

**mutiny** verb **1** to rise against those in power **2** to refuse to obey the commands of military officers □ noun (pl **mutinies**) refusal to obey commands; rebellion □ **mutineer** noun someone who takes part in a mutiny □ **mutinous** adj rebellious; refusing to obey orders

**mutiny** verb ⊹ mutinies, mutinying, mutinied

**mutt** noun, informal an idiot

**mutter** verb to speak in a low voice; mumble

**mutton** noun meat from a sheep, used as food

**mutual** adj **1** given by each to the other(s): mutual help **2** shared by two or more: mutual friend □ **mutually** adv of a relationship between two people or things: each to the other, in both directions

**muzzle** noun **1** an animal's nose and mouth **2** a fastening placed over an animal's mouth to prevent it biting **3** the open end of a gun □ verb **1** to put a muzzle on (a dog etc) **2** to prevent from speaking freely

**my** adj belonging to me: this is my

book

**myopia** noun short-sightedness □ **myopic** adj

**myriad** noun a very great number □ adj very many, countless

**myrrh** noun a bitter-tasting resin used in medicines, perfumes etc

**myrtle** noun a type of evergreen shrub

**myself** pronoun **1** used reflexively: I can see myself in the mirror **2** used for emphasis: I wrote this myself

**mysterious** adj **1** puzzling, difficult to understand **2** secret, hidden, intriguing □ **mysteriously** adv

**mystery** noun (pl **mysteries**) **1** something that cannot be or has not been explained; something puzzling **2** a deep secret

**mystic** noun someone who seeks knowledge of sacred or mystical things by going into a state of spiritual ecstasy □ **mystical** adj having a secret or sacred meaning beyond ordinary human understanding

**mystify** verb **1** to puzzle greatly **2** to confuse, bewilder

**mystify** ⊹ mystifies, mystifying, mystified

**mystique** (say mis-**teek**) noun an atmosphere of mystery about someone or something

**myth** noun **1** a story about gods, heroes etc of ancient times; a fable **2** something imagined or untrue □ **mythical** adj

**mythology** noun **1** the study of myths **2** a collection of myths □ **mythological** adj

**myxomatosis** noun a contagious disease of rabbits

**N** *abbrev* **1** north **2** northern

**nab** *verb*, *informal* **1** to snatch, seize **2** to arrest

**nab** ➮ nab*s*, nabb*ing*, nabb*ed*

**nadir** *noun* **1** the point of the heavens opposite the zenith **2** the lowest point of anything

**naff** *adj*, *slang* inferior, crass, tasteless

**nag** *verb* to find fault with constantly □ *noun* a horse

**nag** *verb* ➮ nag*s*, nagg*ing*, nagg*ed*

**nail** *noun* **1** a horny covering protecting the tips of the fingers and toes **2** a thin pointed piece of metal for fastening wood *etc* □ *verb* **1** to fasten with nails **2** to enclose in a box *etc* with nails **3** *informal* to catch, trap

**naive** or **naïve** (*say both* nai-**eev**) *adj* **1** simple in thought, manner or speech **2** inexperienced and lacking knowledge of the world □ **naiveté** or **naïveté** (*say both* nai-**eev**-i-tei) *noun*

**naked** *adj* **1** without clothes **2** having no covering **3** bald, blatant: *naked lie* **4** of feelings: bad or unpleasant, and neither hidden nor controlled □ **nakedly** *adv* (meaning 4)

**NALGO** (*say* **nal**-goh) *abbrev* National and Local Government Officers' Association

**namby-pamby** *adj* childish, feeble

Originally a nickname of the 18th-century sentimental English poet, *Ambrose* Philips

**name** *noun* **1** a word by which a person, place or thing is known **2** fame, reputation: *making a name for himself* **3** an offensive description: *don't call people names* **4** authority: *I arrest you in the name*

*of the king* □ *verb* **1** to give a name to **2** to speak of by name, mention **3** to appoint □ **nameless** *adj* without a name, not named □ **namely** *adv* that is to say □ **namesake** *noun* someone with the same name as another

**nanny** *noun* (*pl* **nannies**) a children's nurse

**nanny-goat** *noun* a female goat

**nano-** *prefix* **1** a thousand millionth: *nanosecond* **2** microscopic in size ⊕ From Greek *nanos* meaning 'a dwarf'

**nap** *noun* **1** a short sleep **2** a woolly or fluffy surface on cloth **3** a kind of card game □ *verb* to take a short sleep □ **caught napping** taken unawares

**nap** *verb* ➮ nap*s*, napp*ing*, napp*ed*

**napalm** *noun* petroleum jelly, used to make bombs

**nape** *noun* the back of the neck

**napkin** *noun* a small piece of cloth or paper for wiping the lips at meals

**nappy** *noun* (*pl* **nappies**) a piece of cloth, or thick pad, put between a baby's legs to absorb urine and faeces

**narcissus** *noun* (*pl* **narcissi** or **narcissuses**) a plant like a daffodil with a white, star-shaped flower

**narcotic** *noun* a type of drug that brings on sleep or stops pain

**nark** *noun* a persistent complainer □ *verb* to grumble □ **narky** *adj* irritable, complaining

**narrate** *verb* to tell a story □ **narration** *noun* the telling of a story □ **narrative** *noun* a story □ *adj* telling a story □ **narrator** *noun*

**narrow** *adj* **1** of small extent from side to side, not wide: *a narrow road* **2** with little to spare: *a narrow* *escape* **3** lacking wide interests or experience: *narrow views* □ *verb* to make or become narrow □ **narrowly** *adv* closely; barely □ **narrow-gauge** *adj* of a railway: having the distance between rails less than the **standard gauge** (4ft 8in, or 1.435 metre) □ **narrow-minded** *adj* unwilling to accept or tolerate new ideas □ **narrows** *noun pl* a narrow sea passage, a strait

**NASA** *abbrev*, *US* National Aeronautics and Space Administration

**nasal** *adj* **1** of the nose **2** sounded through the nose

**nascent** *adj* beginning to develop, in an early stage □ **nascency** *noun*

**nasturtium** *noun* a climbing plant with brightly-coloured flowers

**nasty** *adj* **1** very disagreeable or unpleasant **2** of a problem *etc*: difficult to deal with **3** of an injury: serious □ **nastily** *adv* (meaning 1)

**natal** *adj* of birth

**nation** *noun* **1** the people living in the same country, or under the same government **2** a race of people: *the Jewish nation*

**national** *adj* of, relating to or belonging to a nation or race □ *noun* someone belonging to a nation: *a British national* □ **nationally** *adv* □ **national anthem** a nation's official song or hymn □ **national call** a long-distance, but not international, telephone call

**nationalism** *noun* the desire to bring the people of a nation together under their own government □ **nationalist** *noun & adj* □ **nationalistic** *adj* □ **nationality** *noun* membership of a particular nation

**nationalize** *verb* to place (industries *etc*) under the control of the government □ **nationalization** *noun*

**native** *adj* **1** born in a person: *native intelligence* **2** of someone's birth:

*my native land* □ *noun* **1** someone born in a certain place: *a native of Scotland* **2** an inhabitant of a country from earliest times before the discovery by explorers, settlers *etc*

**Nativity**: **the Nativity** the birth of Christ

**NATO** *abbrev* North Atlantic Treaty Organization

**natty** *adj* trim, tidy, smart □ **nattily** *adv*

**natural** *adj* **1** of nature **2** produced by nature, not artificial **3** of a quality *etc*: present at birth, not learned afterwards **4** unpretentious, simple **5** of a result *etc*: expected, normal □ *noun* **1** an idiot **2** someone with a natural ability **3** *music* a note which is neither a sharp nor a flat, shown by the sign (♮) □ **naturally** *adv* **1** by nature **2** simply **3** of course □ **natural gas** gas suitable for burning found in the earth or under the sea □ **natural history** the study of animals and plants □ **naturalist** *noun* someone who studies animal and plant life □ **naturalize** *verb* to give the rights of a citizen to (someone born in another country) □ **natural resources** the natural wealth of a country in its forests, minerals, water *etc* □ **natural selection** evolution by survival of the fittest, who pass their characteristics on to the next generation

**nature** *noun* **1** the things which make up the physical world, *eg* animals, trees, rivers, mountains *etc* **2** the qualities which characterize someone or something: *a kindly nature* □ **-natured** *adj* (added to another word) having a certain temper or personality: *good-natured*

**naturism** *noun* the belief in nudity practised openly □ **naturist** *noun*

**naught** *noun* nothing: *plans came to naught*

🔹 Do not confuse with: **nought**

**naughty** adj bad, misbehaving □ **naughtily** adv

**nausea** noun a feeling of sickness □ **nauseate** verb to make sick, fill with disgust □ **nauseated** adj sickened, disgusted □ **nauseous** adj sickening; disgusting

**nautical** adj of ships or sailors □ **nautical mile** 1.85 kilometre (6080 ft)

**nautilus** noun (pl **nautiluses** or **nautili**) a small sea creature related to the octopus

**naval** see navy

**nave** noun the middle or main part of a church

**navel** noun the small hollow in the centre of the front of the belly

**navigate** verb **1** to steer or pilot a ship, aircraft etc on its course **2** to sail on, over or through □ **navigable** adj able to be used by ships □ **navigation** noun the art of navigating □ **navigator** noun someone who steers or sails a ship etc

**navvy** noun (pl **navvies**) a labourer working on roads etc

**navy** noun (pl **navies**) **1** a nation's fighting ships **2** the men and women serving on these □ **naval** adj of the navy □ **navy blue** dark blue

**nay** adv, old no

**Nazi** (say naht-si) noun, historical a member of the German National Socialist Party, a fascist party ruling Germany in 1933–45 □ **Nazism** noun

**NB** or **nb** abbrev note well
ⓘ From Latin nota bene

**NCO** abbrev non-commissioned officer

**NE** abbrev north-east; north-eastern

**neap** adj of the tide: at its smallest extent between low and high level

**near** adj **1** not far away in place or time **2** close in relationship, friendship etc **3** barely avoiding or almost reaching (something): a near disaster □ adv to or at a short distance; nearby □ prep close to □ verb to approach □ **nearby** adv to or at a short distance: do you live nearby? □ **nearly** adv **1** almost: nearly four o'clock **2** closely: nearly related □ **nearside** adj of the side of a vehicle: furthest from the centre of the road (contrasted with: **offside**) □ **near-sighted** adj short-sighted

**neat** adj **1** trim, tidy **2** skilfully done **3** of an alcoholic drink: not diluted with water etc

**nebula** noun (pl **nebulae**) a shining cloud-like appearance in the night sky, produced by very distant stars or by a mass of gas and dust

**nebulous** adj hazy, vague

**necessary** adj not able to be done without □ noun (pl **necessaries**) something that cannot be done without, such as food, clothing etc □ **necessarily** adv for certain, definitely, inevitably □ **necessitate** verb to make necessary; force □ **necessity** (pl **necessities**) **1** something necessary **2** great need; want, poverty

**neck** noun **1** the part between the head and body **2** a narrow passage or area: neck of a bottle/ neck of land □ **necklace** noun a string of beads or precious stones etc worn round the neck □ **necktie** noun, US a man's tie □ **neck and neck** running side by side, staying exactly equal

**nectar** noun **1** the sweet liquid collected from flowers by bees to make honey **2** the drink of the ancient Greek gods **3** a delicious drink

**nectarine** noun a kind of peach with a smooth skin

**née** (say nei) adj born (in stating a woman's surname before her marriage): Mrs Janet Brown, née Phillips

**need** verb **1** to be without, be in want

of **2** to require □ *noun* **1** necessity, needfulness **2** difficulty, want, poverty □ **needful** *adj* necessary □ **needless** *adj* unnecessary □ **needy** *adj* poor

■ (verb, meaning 1) miss, lack, want; (verb, meaning 2) demand, necessitate, crave

**needle** *noun* **1** a small, sharp piece of steel used in sewing, with a small hole (**eye**) at the top for thread **2** a long thin piece of metal, wood *etc* used *eg* in knitting **3** a thin hollowed-out piece of steel attached to a hypodermic syringe *etc* **4** the moving pointer in a compass **5** the long, sharp-pointed leaf of a pine, fir *etc* **6** a stylus on a record-player □ **needle bank** a place where drug-users can exchange used hypodermic needles for new ones, to help prevent the spread of disease

**ne'er** *adj, formal* never

**nefarious** *adj* very wicked; villainous, shady

**negate** *verb* **1** to prove the opposite **2** to refuse to accept, reject (a proposal *etc*)

**negative** *adj* **1** meaning or saying 'no', as an answer (*contrasted with:* **positive**) **2** of a person, attitude *etc*: timid, lacking spirit or ideas □ *noun* **1** a word or statement by which something is denied **2** the photographic film, from which prints are made, in which light objects appear dark and dark objects appear light □ **negative equity** a situation where the value of a property falls below the value of the mortgage held on it

**neglect** *verb* **1** to treat carelessly **2** to fail to give proper attention to **3** to fail to do □ *noun* lack of care and attention □ **neglectful** *adj* careless, having a habit of not bothering to do things

**negligée** *noun* a women's loose dressing-gown made of thin material

**negligent** *adj* careless □ **negligence** *noun* □ **negligently** *adv*
◉ From Latin *negligens* meaning 'neglecting'
❧ Do not confuse: **negligent** and **negligible**

**negligible** *adj* not worth thinking about, very small: *a negligible amount*
◉ From an old spelling of French *négligeable* meaning 'able to be neglected'

■ appreciable

**negotiate** *verb* **1** to discuss a subject (with) in order to reach agreement **2** to arrange (a treaty, payment *etc*) **3** to get past (an obstacle or difficulty) □ **negotiable** *adj* able to be negotiated □ **negotiation** *noun* (meanings 1 and 2) □ **negotiator** *noun* (meanings 1 and 2)

**Negro** *noun* (*pl* **Negroes**) a Black African, or black person of African descent □ **Negress** *noun* a black woman

**neigh** *verb* to cry like a horse □ *noun* a horse's cry

**neighbour** or *US* **neighbor** *noun* someone who lives near another □ **neighbourhood** *noun* surrounding district or area: *in the neighbourhood of Paris/ a poor neighbourhood* □ **in the neighbourhood of** approximately, nearly □ **neighbouring** *adj* near or next in position □ **neighbourly** *adj* friendly

**neither** *adj & pronoun* not either: *neither bus goes that way/ neither of us can afford it* □ *conj* (sometimes with **nor**) used to show alternatives in the negative: *neither Bill or David knew the answer/ she is neither eating nor sleeping*

**nemesis** *noun* fate, punishment that is bound to follow wrongdoing

**neo-** *prefix* new, recently □ **Neolithic** *adj* relating to the later Stone Age

□ **neologism** *noun* a new word or expression □ **neologistic** *adj*
□ **neonatal** *adj* of newborn babies
□ **neophyte** *noun* **1** a new convert **2** a novice, a beginner
ⓘ From Greek *neos* meaning 'new'

**neon lighting** a form of lighting in which an electric current is passed through a small quantity of gas

**nephew** *noun* the son of a brother or sister, or of a brother-in-law or sister-in-law

**nerd** *noun* a socially inept, irritating person

**nerve** *noun* **1** one of the fibres which carry feeling from all parts of the body to the brain **2** courage, coolness **3** *informal* impudence, cheek □ *verb* to strengthen the nerve or will of □ **nervy** *adj* excitable, jumpy

**nervous** *adj* **1** of the nerves **2** easily excited or frightened; timid **3** worried, frightened or uneasy □ **nervously** *adv* (meaning 3) □ **nervousness** *noun* (meanings 2 and 3) □ **nervous system** the brain, spinal cord and nerves of an animal or human being

**nest** *noun* **1** a structure in which birds (and some animals and insects) live and rear their young **2** a shelter, a den □ *verb* to build a nest and live in it □ **nestling** (*say* nest-ling) *noun* a young newly hatched bird

**nestle** (*say* ne-sl) *verb* **1** to lie close together as in a nest **2** to settle comfortably

**Net** *noun*: **the Net** *informal* the Internet

**net** *noun* **1** a loose arrangement of crossed and knotted cord, string or thread, used for catching fish, wearing over the hair *etc* **2** fine meshed material, used to make curtains, petticoats *etc* □ *adj* (*also* **nett**) **1** of profit *etc*: remaining after expenses and taxes have been paid

**2** of weight: not including packaging □ *verb* **1** to catch or cover with a net **2** to put (a ball) into a net **3** to make by way of profit □ **netball** *noun* a team game in which a ball is thrown into a high net □ **netting** *noun* fabric of netted string, wire *etc* □ **network** *noun* **1** an arrangement of lines crossing one another **2** a widespread organization **3** a system of linked computers, radio stations *etc*

**net** *verb* ▸ **nets, netting, netted**

**nether** *adj* lower □ **nethermost** *adj* lowest

**nett** *see* **net**

**nettle** *noun* a plant covered with hairs which sting sharply □ *verb* to make angry, provoke □ **nettlerash** *noun* a skin rash, like that caused by a sting from a nettle

**neur-** or **neuro-** *prefix* of the nerves: *neuralgia*
ⓘ From Greek *neuron* meaning 'nerve'

**neuralgia** *noun* a pain in the nerves, *esp* in those of the head and face

**neurosis** *noun* a type of mental illness in which the patient suffers from extreme anxiety □ **neurotic** *adj* **1** suffering from neurosis **2** in a bad nervous state □ *noun* someone suffering from neurosis □ **neurotically** *adv*

**neuter** *adj* **1** *grammar* neither masculine nor feminine **2** of an animal: neither male nor female **3** of an animal: infertile, sterile □ *verb* to sterilize (an animal)

**neutral** *adj* **1** taking no side in a quarrel or war **2** of a colour: not strong or definite □ *noun* **1** someone or a nation that takes no side in a war *etc* **2** the gear position used when a vehicle is remaining still □ **neutrality** *noun* (adj, meaning 1) □ **neutralize** *verb* **1** to make neutral **2** to make useless or harmless

**neutron** *noun* one of the uncharged

particles which, together with protons, make up the nucleus of an atom □ **neutron bomb** a nuclear bomb that kills people by intense radiation but leaves buildings intact

**never** adv **1** not ever; at no time **2** under no circumstances □ **nevertheless** adv in spite of that: *I hate opera, but I shall come with you nevertheless*

**new** adj **1** recent; not seen or known before **2** not used or worn; fresh □ **newly** adv (used before past participles) only recently □ **newcomer** noun someone lately arrived □ **newfangled** adj new and not thought very good

**news** noun sing **1** a report of a recent event **2** new information □ **newsagent** noun a shopkeeper who sells newspapers □ **newspaper** noun a paper printed daily or weekly containing news

**newt** noun a small lizard-like animal, living on land and in water

**next** adj nearest, closest in place, time etc: *the next page* □ adv in the nearest place or at the nearest time: *she won and I came next/ do that sum next*
ⓔ From Old English *nehst* meaning 'nearest'

**NHS** abbrev National Health Service

**nib** noun a pen point

**nibble** verb to take little bites (of) □ noun a little bite

**nice** adj **1** agreeable, pleasant **2** careful, precise, exact: *a nice distinction* □ **nicely** adv pleasantly; very well
▣ (meaning I) pleasant, agreeable, delightful, charming, likable, attractive, good, kind, friendly, well-mannered, polite, respectable

**nicety** (say nais-e-ti) noun (pl **niceties**) a small fine detail □ **to a nicety** with great exactness

**niche** (say neesh) noun **1** a hollow in a wall for a statue, vase etc **2** a suitable place in life: *she hasn't yet found her niche* **3** a gap in a market for a type of product

**nick** noun **1** a little cut, a notch **2** slang prison, jail □ verb **1** to cut notches in **2** slang to steal

**nickel** noun a greyish-white metal used for mixing with other metals and for plating **2** US a 5-cent coin

**nickname** noun an informal name used instead of someone's real name, eg for fun or as an insult

**nicotine** noun a poisonous substance contained in tobacco

Named after Jean *Nicot*, 16th-century French ambassador who sent tobacco samples back from Portugal

**niece** noun the daughter of a brother or sister, or of a brother-in-law or sister-in-law

**niff** noun, slang a bad smell

**nifty** adj, slang **1** fine, smart, neat **2** speedy, agile

**niggardly** adj mean, stingy

**niggle** verb to irritate, rankle □ noun **1** an irritation **2** a minor criticism □ **niggling** adj **1** unimportant, trivial, fussy **2** of a worry or fear: small but always present

**nigh** adj, old near

**night** noun **1** the period of darkness between sunset and sunrise **2** darkness □ adj **1** of or for night **2** happening, active etc at night □ **nightly** adj & adv **1** by night **2** every night □ **nightdress** or **nightgown** noun a garment worn in bed □ **nightfall** noun the beginning of night □ **night-watchman** noun someone who looks after a building during the night

**nightingale** noun a small bird, the male of which sings beautifully by night and day

**nightmare** noun a frightening dream

The *-mare* ending comes from an old English word meaning 'evil spirit', nightmares being thought to be caused by an evil spirit pressing on the body.

**nihilism** *noun* belief in nothing, extreme scepticism □ **nihilist** *noun* □ **nihilistic** *adj*

**nil** *noun* nothing

**nimble** *adj* quick and neat, agile □ **nimbly** *adv*

**nimbus** *noun* a rain cloud

**nincompoop** *noun* a weak, foolish person

**nine** *noun* the number 9 □ *adj* 9 in number □ **ninth** *adj* the last of a series of nine □ *noun* one of nine equal parts

**ninepins** *noun* a game in which nine bottle-shaped objects are set up, and knocked down by a ball

**nineteen** *noun* the number 19 □ *adj* 19 in number □ **nineteenth** *adj* the last of a series of nineteen □ *noun* one of nineteen equal parts

**ninety** *noun* the number 90 □ *adj* 90 in number □ **ninetieth** *adj* the last of a series of ninety □ *noun* one of ninety equal parts

**ninja** *noun, historical* an assassin in feudal Japan, trained in martial arts

**ninny** *noun* (*pl* **ninnies**) a foo

**nip** *verb* **1** to pinch, squeeze tightly **2** to be stingingly painful **3** to bite, cut (off) **4** to halt the growth of, damage (plants *etc*) **5** *informal* to go nimbly or quickly □ *noun* **1** a pinch **2** a sharp coldness in the weather: *a nip in the air* **3** a small amount: *nip of whisky*

**nip** *verb* ▷ **nips, nipping, nipp**ed

**nipper** *noun, informal* **1** a child, a youngster **2** (**nippers**) pincers, pliers

**nipple** *noun* the pointed part of the breast from which a baby sucks milk

**nippy** *adj, informal* **1** speedy, nimble

**2** frosty, very cold

**Nirvana** *noun* **1** the state to which a Buddhist or Hindu aspires as the best attainable **2** (**nirvana**) a blissful state

**nit** *noun* **1** the egg of a louse or other small insect **2** *informal* an idiot, a nitwit

**nitrate** *noun* a substance formed from nitric acid, often used as a soil fertilizer

**nitric acid** a strong acid containing nitrogen

**nitrogen** *noun* a gas forming nearly four-fifths of ordinary air

**nitro-glycerine** *noun* a powerful kind of explosive

**nitwit** *noun* a very stupid person

**No** or **no** *abbrev* number

**no** *adj* **1** not any: *they have no money* **2** not a: *she is no beauty* □ *adv* not at all: *the patient is no better* □ *exclam* expressing a negative: *are you feeling better today? No!* □ *noun* (*pl* **noes**) **1** a refusal **2** a vote against □ **no-ball** *noun, cricket* a bowled ball disallowed by the rules □ **nobody** *pronoun* not any person □ *noun* someone of no importance: *just a nobody* □ **no one** or **no-one** *pronoun* not any person, nobody □ **no-show** *noun* someone expected who does not arrive □ **no-win** *adj* of a situation: in which you are bound to lose or fail □ **no dice** no answer, no success □ **no doubt** surely □ **no go** not possible, futile □ **no joke** not something to laugh about or dismiss □ **no way** *informal* under no circumstance

**nobble** *verb, slang* **1** get hold of **2** persuade, coerce **3** seize, arrest

**Nobel prize** an annual international prize awarded for achievements in arts, science, politics *etc*

**noble** *adj* **1** great and good, fine **2** of aristocratic birth □ *noun* an aristocrat □ **nobility** *noun* **1** the aristocracy **2** goodness, greatness of mind or character □ **nobleman, noblewoman** noun □ **nobly** adv

**nocturnal** adj happening or active at night

**nocturne** noun a piece of music intended to have an atmosphere of night-time

**nod** verb **1** to bend the head forward quickly, often as a sign of agreement **2** to let the head drop in weariness □ noun an action of nodding □ **nodding acquaintance with** a slight knowledge of □ **nod off** to fall asleep

**nod** verb ⬦ no**ds**, nod**ding**, nod**ded**

**node** noun **1** the swollen part of a branch or twig where leaf-stalks join it **2** a swelling

**nodule** noun a small rounded lump

**Noël** noun Christmas

**noise** noun a sound, often one which is loud or harsh □ verb, old to spread (a rumour etc) □ **noiseless** adj □ **noisy** adj making a loud sound

**noisy** ⬦ nois**ier**, nois**iest**

**nomad** noun **1** one of a group of people without a fixed home who wander with their animals in search of pasture **2** someone who wanders from place to place □ **nomadic** adj

**no-man's-land** noun land owned by no one, esp that lying between two opposing armies

**nom de plume** noun (pl **noms de plume**) a pen-name

**nomenclature** noun **1** a system of naming **2** names

**nominal** adj **1** in name only **2** very small: a nominal fee

**nominate** verb to propose (someone) for a post or for election; appoint □ **nomination** noun □ **nominee** noun someone whose name is put forward for a post

**non-** prefix not (used with many words to change their meaning to the opposite): non-aggression/ non-event/ non-smoking

⊚ From Latin non meaning 'not'

**nonagenarian** noun someone from ninety to ninety-nine years old

**nonchalant** adj not easily roused or upset, cool □ **nonchalance** noun □ **nonchalantly** adv

**non-commissioned** adj belonging to the lower ranks of army officers, below second-lieutenant

**non-committal** adj unwilling to express, or not expressing, an opinion

**nonconformist** noun someone who does not agree with those in authority, esp in church matters □ adj not agreeing with authority

**nondescript** adj not easily described, lacking anything noticeable or interesting

**none** adv not at all: none the worse □ pronoun not one, not any

**nonentity** noun (pl **nonentities**) someone of no importance

**non-existent** adj not existing, not real

**nonplussed** adj taken aback, confused

**nonsense** noun **1** words that have no sense or meaning **2** foolishness □ **nonsensical** adj

**non sequitur** a remark unconnected with what has gone before

**non-stop** adj going on without a stop

**noodle** noun a long thin strip of pasta, eaten in soup or served with a sauce

**nook** noun **1** a corner **2** a small recess □ **every nook and cranny** informal everywhere

**noon** noun twelve o'clock midday

**no one** see no

**noose** noun a loop in a rope etc that tightens when pulled

**nor** conj used (often with **neither**) to show alternatives in the negative: neither James nor I can speak Japanese

**Nordic** adj **1** relating to Finland or Scandinavia **2** of skiing: involving cross-country and jumping events

**norm** noun a pattern or standard to judge other things by

**normal** adj ordinary, usual according to a standard □ **normality** noun □ **normally** adv

**north** noun **1** one of the four chief directions, that to the left of someone facing the rising sun □ adj & adv in or to the north □ **northerly** adj of, from or towards the north □ **northern** adj of the north □ **north-east** noun the point of the compass midway between north and east □ **north pole** see **pole** □ **northward** or **northwards** adj & adv towards the north □ **north-west** noun the point of the compass midway between north and west

**nose** noun **1** the part of the face by which people and animals smell and breathe **2** a jutting-out part, eg the front of an aeroplane □ verb **1** to track by smelling **2** informal to interfere in other people's affairs, pry (into) **3** to push a way through: the ship nosed through the ice **4** to move forward cautiously □ **nosedive** noun a headfirst dive by an aeroplane □ verb to dive headfirst □ **nosegay** noun, old a bunch of flowers □ **nosey** or **nosy** adj inquisitive, fond of prying

**nostalgia** noun **1** a longing for past times **2** a longing for home □ **nostalgic** adj □ **nostalgically** adv

**nostril** noun either of the two openings of the nose

**not** adv expressing a negative, refusal or denial: I am not going/ give it to me, not to him/ I did not break the window

**notable** adj worth taking notice of; important, remarkable □ noun an important person □ **notability** noun (pl **notabilities**) a well-known person □ **notably** adv **1** in a notable or noticeable way **2** particularly

**notary** noun (pl **notaries**) an official who sees that written documents are drawn up in a way required by law

**notation** noun **1** the showing of numbers, musical sounds etc by signs: sol-fa notation **2** a set of such signs

**notch** noun (pl **notches**) a small V-shaped cut □ verb to make a notch □ **notched** adj

**note** noun **1** a sign or piece of writing to draw someone's attention **2** (**notes**) details for a speech, from a talk etc set down in a short form **3** a short explanation **4** a short letter **5** a piece of paper used as money: £5 note **6** a single sound or the sign standing for it in music **7** a key on the piano etc □ verb **1** to make a note of **2** to notice □ **notebook** noun **1** a small book for taking notes **2** a small laptop computer □ **noted** adj well-known □ **notepaper** noun writing paper □ **noteworthy** adj notable, remarkable □ **of note** well-known, distinguished □ **take note of** to notice particularly

**nothing** noun **1** no thing, not anything **2** nought, zero **3** something of no importance □ adv not at all: he's nothing like his father □ **nothingness** noun **1** non-existence **2** space, emptiness

**notice** noun **1** a public announcement **2** attention: the colour attracted my notice **3** a period of warning given before leaving, or before dismissing someone from, a job □ verb to see, observe, take note of □ **noticeable** adj easily noticed, standing out

**notify** verb **1** to inform **2** to give notice of □ **notifiable** adj that must be reported: a notifiable disease □ **notification** noun

**notify** ⊷ notifies, notifying, notified

**notion** noun **1** an idea **2** a vague belief or opinion

**notorious** *adj* well known because of badness: *a notorious criminal* □ **notoriety** *noun*

**notwithstanding** *prep* in spite of: *notwithstanding his poverty, he refused all help*

**nougat** (*say* noo-gah or nug-et) *noun* a sticky kind of sweet containing nuts *etc*

**nought** *noun* the figure 0, zero

◆. Do not confuse with: **naught**

**noun** *noun, grammar* the word used as the name of someone or something, *eg John* and *tickets* in the sentence *John bought the tickets*

**nourish** *verb* **1** to feed **2** to encourage the growth of □ **nourishing** *adj* giving the body what is necessary for health and growth □ **nourishment** *noun* **1** food **2** an act of nourishing

**nouveau riche** (*say* noo-voh **reesh**) someone who has recently acquired wealth but not good taste

**nova** *noun* (*pl* **novae** - *say* **noh**-vee - or **novas**) a star that suddenly increases in brightness for a period

**novel** (*say* **nov**-el) *adj* new and strange □ *noun* a book telling a long story □ **novelist** (*say* **nov**-el-ist) *noun* a writer of novels

**novelty** (*say* **nov**-el-ti) *noun* (*pl* **novelties**) **1** something new and strange **2** newness **3** a small, cheap souvenir or toy

**November** *noun* the eleventh month of the year

**novice** *noun* a beginner

**now** *adv* **1** at the present time: *I can see him now* **2** immediately before the present time: *I thought of her just now* **3** in the present circumstances: *I can't go now because my mother is ill* □ *conj* (often **now that**) because, since: *you can't go out now that it's raining* □ **nowadays** *adv* in present times, these days □ **now and then** or **now and again** sometimes, from time to time

**nowhere** *adv* not in, or to, any place

**noxious** *adj* harmful: *noxious fumes* ⊕ From Latin *noxius* meaning 'hurtful'

◆. Do not confuse with: **obnoxious**

**nozzle** *noun* a spout fitted to the end of a pipe, tube *etc*

**NSPCC** *abbrev* National Society for the Prevention of Cruelty to Children

**nuance** (*say* **nyoo**-ons) *noun* a slight difference in meaning or colour *etc*

**nub** *noun* a small lump, a knob

**nubile** *adj* of a young woman: attractive, and old enough to be sexually mature □ **nubility** *noun*

**nuclear** *adj* **1** of a nucleus, *esp* that of an atom **2** produced by the splitting of the nuclei of atoms □ **nuclear energy** energy released or absorbed during reactions taking place in atomic nuclei □ **nuclear family** the family unit made up of the mother and father with their children □ **nuclear fission** the splitting of atomic nuclei □ **nuclear fusion** the creation of a new nucleus by merging two lighter ones, with release of energy □ **nuclear missile** a missile whose warhead is an atomic bomb □ **nuclear reactor** apparatus for producing nuclear energy

**nucleus** *noun* (*pl* **nuclei**) **1** the central part of an atom **2** the central part round which something collects or from which it grows: *the nucleus of my book collection* **3** the part of a plant or animal cell that controls its development

**nude** *adj* without clothes, naked □ *noun* **1** an unclothed human figure **2** a painting or statue of such a figure □ **nudism** *noun* □ **nudist** *noun* someone who is in favour of going without clothes in public □ **nudity** *noun* the state of being nude □ **in the nude** naked

**nudge** *noun* a gentle push, *eg* with the elbow or shoulder □ *verb*: *I nudged him*

**nugget** *noun* a lump, *esp* of gold

**nuisance** *noun* someone or something annoying or troublesome

**null** *adj*: **null and void** having no legal force

**nullify** *verb* **1** to make useless or of no effect **2** to declare to be null and void

**nullify** ⟶ nullif*ies*, nullify*ing*, nullif*ied*

**numb** *adj* having lost the power to feel or move □ *verb* to make numb

**number** *noun* **1** a word or figure showing how many, or showing a position in a series **2** a collection of people or things **3** a single issue of a newspaper or magazine **4** a popular song or piece of music □ *verb* **1** to count **2** to give numbers to **3** to amount to in number □ **numberless** *adj* more than can be counted ⓦ From French *nombre* meaning 'number'

**numeral** *noun* a figure (*eg* 1, 2 *etc*) used to express a number

**numerate** (*say* nyoom-*e*-rat) *adj* having some understanding of mathematics and science

**numerator** *noun* the number above the line in vulgar fractions, *eg* 2 in $\frac{2}{3}$ (*compare with*: **denominator**)

**numerical** *adj* of, in, using or consisting of numbers

**numerous** *adj* many

**numismatics** *noun sing* the study of coins □ **numismatist** *noun* someone who collects and studies coins

**numskull** *noun* a stupid person

**nun** *noun* a member of a female religious group living in a convent □ **nunnery** *noun* (*pl* **nunneries**) a house where a group of nuns live, a convent

**nuptial** *adj* of marriage □ **nuptials** *noun pl, formal* a wedding ceremony

**nurse** *noun* someone who looks after sick or injured people, or small children □ *verb* **1** to look after sick people *etc* **2** to give (a baby) milk from the breast **3** to hold or look after with care: *he nurses his tomato plants* **4** to encourage (feelings) in yourself: *nursing her wrath* □ **nursing home** a small private hospital

**nursery** (*pl* **nurseries**) **1** a room for young children **2** a place where young plants are reared **3** a nursery school □ **nursery school** a school for very young children

**nurture** *verb* to bring up, rear; to nourish: *nurture tenderness* □ *noun* care, upbringing; food, nourishment

**NUT** *abbrev* National Union of Teachers

**nut** *noun* **1** a fruit with a hard shell which contains a kernel **2** a small metal block with a hole in it for screwing on the end of a bolt □ **nutcrackers** *noun pl* an instrument for cracking nuts open □ **nutty** *adj* **1** containing, or having the flavour of nuts **2** *informal* mad, insane □ **in a nutshell** expressed very briefly

**nutmeg** *noun* a hard aromatic seed used as a spice in cooking

**nutrient** *noun* a substance which provides nourishment □ **nutriment** *noun* nourishment, food □ **nutrition** *noun* nourishment, food □ **nutritious** or **nutritive** *adj* valuable as food, nourishing

**nuzzle** *verb* **1** to press, rub or caress with the nose **2** to lie close to, snuggle, nestle

**NVQ** *abbrev, Brit* National Vocational Qualification

**NW** *abbrev* north-west; north-western

**nylon** *noun* **1** a synthetic material made from chemicals **2** (**nylons**) stockings made of nylon

**nymph** *noun* **1** a mythological female river or tree spirit **2** a beautiful girl

**3** an insect not yet fully developed

**nymphomania** *noun* excessively strong sexual desire in women

□ **nymphomaniac** *noun* someone suffering from nymphomania

**NZ** *abbrev* New Zealand

## Oo

**O!** or **Oh!** *exclam* expressing surprise, admiration, pain *etc*

**oaf** *noun* (*pl* **oafs**) a stupid or clumsy person

**oak** *noun* **1** a tree which produces acorns as fruit **2** its hard wood □ **oak** or **oaken** *adj* made of oak

**OAP** *abbrev* **1** Old Age Pension **2** Old Age Pensioner

**oar** *noun* a pole for rowing, with a flat blade on the end □ *verb* to row □ **oarsman, oarswoman** *noun* a person who rows □ **put your oar in** to interfere in

**oasis** *noun* (*pl* **oases**) a place in a desert where water is found and trees *etc* grow

**oatcake** *noun* a thin flat cake made of oatmeal

**oath** *noun* (*pl* **oaths**) **1** a solemn promise to speak the truth, keep your word, be loyal *etc* **2** a swear word

**oatmeal** *noun* meal made by grinding down oat grains

**oats** *noun pl* a type of grassy plant or its grain, used as food

**OBE** *abbrev* Officer of the Order of the British Empire

**obedient** *adj* obeying, ready to obey □ **obediently** *adv* □ **obedience** *noun* **1** the act of obeying **2** willingness to obey

**obeisance** *noun* a bow or curtsy showing respect

**obelisk** *noun* a tall four-sided pillar with a pointed top

**obese** *adj* very fat □ **obesity** *noun* the condition of someone who is overweight as a result of the accumulation of excess fat in the body

**obey** *verb* to do what you are told to do: *obey the instructions*

**obituary** *noun* (*pl* **obituaries**) a notice in a newspaper *etc* of someone's death, sometimes with a brief biography

**object** *noun* (*say* ob-jekt) **1** something that can be seen or felt **2** an aim, a purpose: *our main object is not to make money* **3** *grammar* the word in a sentence which stands for the person or thing on which the action of the verb is done, *eg* me in the sentence *he gave me some good advice* □ *verb* (*say* ob-**jekt**) (often **object to something**) to feel or show disapproval of it □ **objection** *noun* **1** the act of objecting **2** a reason for objecting □ **objectionable** *adj* nasty, disagreeable

**objective** *adj* not influenced by personal interests, fair (*contrasted with:* **subjective**) □ *noun* aim, purpose, goal

**oblige** *verb* **1** to force, compel: *we were obliged to go home* **2** to do a favour or service to: *oblige me by shutting the door* □ **obliged** *adj* owing or feeling gratitude □ **obliging** *adj* ready to help others □ **obligation** *noun* **1** a promise or duty by which someone is bound: *under an obligation to help* **2** a debt of gratitude for a favour received □ **obligatory** (*say* ob-**lig**-at-o-ri) *adj* required to be done with no exceptions by law, rule or custom

**oblique** *adj* **1** slanting **2** indirect, not straight or straightforward: *an oblique reference* □ **obliquely** *adv*

**obliterate** *verb* **1** to blot out (writing

*etc*), efface **2** to destroy completely □ **obliteration** *noun* being obliterated, extinction

**oblivion** *noun* **1** forgetfulness **2** the state of being forgotten □ **oblivious** *adj* **1** unaware (of), not paying attention (to) **2** forgetful

**oblong** *noun* a rectangle which is longer than it is wide, *eg* ■ □ *adj* of the shape of an oblong

**obnoxious** *adj* offensive, causing dislike □ **obnoxiously** *adv*
ⓘ From Latin *obnoxious* meaning 'liable to punishment' or 'guilty of'

⚫ Do not confuse with: **noxious**

**oboe** *noun* (*pl* **oboes**) a high-pitched woodwind instrument □ **oboist** *noun* someone who plays the oboe

**obscene** *adj* **1** sexually indecent, lewd **2** disgusting, repellent

**obscenity** *noun* (*pl* **obscenities**) **1** the state or quality of being obscene: *the obscenity of war* **2** an obscene act or word

**obscure** *adj* **1** dark **2** not clear or easily understood **3** unknown, not famous: *an obscure poet* □ *verb* **1** to darken **2** to make less clear □ **obscurity** *noun* **1** the state of being difficult to see or understand **2** the state of being unknown or forgotten

**obsequious** *adj* trying to win favour by flattery, willingness to agree *etc*

**observe** *verb* **1** to notice **2** to watch with attention **3** to remark (that) **4** to obey (a law *etc*) **5** to keep, preserve: *observe a tradition* □ **observe** *verb* **1** to notice **2** to watch with attention **3** to remark (that) **4** to obey (a law *etc*) **5** to keep, preserve: *observe a tradition* □ **observance** *noun* the act of keeping (a law, tradition *etc*) □ **observant** *adj* good at noticing □ **observation** *noun* **1** the act of seeing and noting; attention **2** a remark □ **observatory** *noun* (*pl* **observatories**) a place for making

observations of the stars, weather *etc* □ **observer** *noun* someone sent to listen to, but not take part in, a discussion *etc*

**obsess** *verb* to fill the mind completely □ **obsession** *noun* **1** a feeling or idea which someone cannot stop thinking about **2** the state of being obsessed □ **obsessive** *adj* **1** forming an obsession **2** having or likely to have an obsession
ⓘ From Latin *obsolescere* meaning 'to grow old'

**obsolescent** *adj* going out of date □ **obsolescence** *noun* being obsolescent

**obsolete** *adj* gone out of use
ⓘ From Latin *obsoletus* meaning 'grown old'

⚫ Do not confuse: **obsolete** and **obsolescent**

**obstacle** *noun* something which stands in the way and hinders □ **obstacle race** a race in which obstacles have to be passed, climbed *etc*

**obstetrics** *noun sing* the study of helping women before, during and after childbirth □ **obstetric** or **obstetrical** *adj* of obstetrics □ **obstetrician** *noun* a doctor trained in obstetrics

**obstinate** *adj* **1** of a person: rigidly sticking to decisions or opinions and unwilling to be influenced by persuasion **2** difficult to deal with, defeat or remove □ **obstinacy** *noun* stubbornness

**obstreperous** *adj* noisy, unruly

**obstruct** *verb* **1** to block up, keep from passing **2** to hold back □ **obstruction** *noun* **1** a hindrance **2** something which blocks up

**obtain** *verb* to get, gain □ **obtainable** *adj* able to be got

**obtrude** *verb* **1** to thrust (something unwanted) on someone **2** to thrust (yourself) forward when not wanted

**obtrusion** *noun* an act of obtruding □ **obtrusive** *adj* **1** too noticeable **2** pushy, impudent

**obtuse** *adj* **1** of an angle: greater than a right angle (*contrasted with:* **acute**) **2** blunt, not pointed **3** stupid, not quick to understand

**obverse** *noun* the side of a coin showing the head or main design

**obvious** *adj* easily seen or understood; plain, evident □ **obviously** *adv* in an obvious way; as is obvious, clearly

**occasion** *noun* **1** a particular time: *on that occasion* **2** a special event: *a great occasion* **3** a cause, a reason **4** opportunity □ *verb* to cause □ **occasional** *adj* happening or used now and then □ **occasionally** *adv* on occasions; now and then

**Occident** *noun* the West □ **occidental** *adj* from or relating to the Occident; western

**occult** *adj* **1** secret, mysterious **2** supernatural

**occupy** *verb* **1** to dwell in **2** to keep busy **3** to take up, fill (space, time *etc*) **4** to seize, capture (a town, fort *etc*) □ **occupancy** *noun* (*pl* **occupancies**) the act, fact or period of occupying □ **occupant** *noun* a person who occupies, has, or takes possession of something, not always the owner □ **occupation** *noun* **1** the state of being occupied **2** something which occupies **3** someone's trade or job **4** possession of a house *etc* □ **occupier** *noun* someone who has possession of a house *etc*

**occupy** ⬦ occup*ies*, occupy*ing*, occup*ied*

**occur** *verb* **1** to happen **2** to appear, be found **3 occur to someone** to come into their mind: *that never occurred to me* □ **occurrence** *noun* **1** a happening, an event **2** the act or fact of occurring

**occur** ⬦ occur*s*, occur*ring*, occur*red*

**ocean** *noun* **1** the stretch of salt water surrounding the land of the earth **2** one of five main divisions of this, *ie* the Atlantic, Pacific, Indian, Arctic or Antarctic

**ocelot** *noun* a wild American cat like a small leopard

**ochre** (*say* oh-ker) *noun* a fine pale-yellow or red clay, used for colouring

**octa-** also **octo-, oct-** *prefix* eight: *octave/ octopus/ October* (which was the eighth month in the Roman calendar)
  ⓘ From Latin and Greek *octo* meaning 'eight'

**octagon** *noun* an eight-sided figure □ **octagonal** *adj* having eight sides

**octane** *noun* a colourless liquid found in petroleum and used in petrol

**octave** *noun*, *music* a range of eight notes, *eg* from one C to the C next above or below it

**octet** *noun* a group of eight things which go together *eg* the first eight lines of a sonnet, or a group of eight singers

**octo-** *see* octa-

**October** *noun* the tenth month of the year

**octogenarian** *noun* someone from eighty to eighty-nine years old

**octopus** *noun* (*pl* **octopuses**) a deep-sea creature with eight arms

**ocular** *adj* of the eye

**oculist** *noun* someone who specializes in diseases and defects of the eye

**odd** *adj* **1** of a number: leaving a remainder of one when divided by two, *eg* the numbers 3, 17, 31 (*contrasted with:* **even**) **2** unusual, strange **3** not one of a matching set or group, left over: *an odd glove* □ *noun* **1** (**odds**) chances or probability: *the odds are that they will win* **2** (**odds**) difference: *it makes no odds* □ **oddity** *noun* (*pl*

**oddities**) **1** queerness, strangeness **2** a strange person or thing □ **odd jobs** jobs of different kinds, not part of regular employment □ **oddments** noun pl scraps □ **at odds** quarrelling □ **odds and ends** objects, scraps etc of different kinds

**ode** noun a type of poem, often written to someone or something: ode to autumn

**odious** adj hateful □ **odiously** adv □ **odium** noun dislike, hatred

**odour** noun smell, either pleasant or unpleasant □ **odourless** adj without smell

**oesophagus** (say ee-sof-ag-us) or US **esophagus** (say i-sof-ag-us) noun the gullet

**oestrogen** (say ees-tro-jen) or US **estrogen** (say es-tro-jen) noun a female sex hormone which regulates the menstrual cycle, prepares the body for pregnancy etc

**oeuvre** (say er-vre) noun the complete works of an artist, writer etc

**of** prep **1** belonging to: the house of my parents **2** from (a place, person etc): within two miles of here **3** from among: one of my pupils **4** made from, made up of: a house of bricks **5** indicating an amount, measurement etc: a gallon of petrol **6** about, concerning: talk of old friends **7** with, containing: a class of twenty/ a cup of coffee **8** as a result of: die of hunger **9** indicating removal or taking away: robbed her of her jewels **10** indicating a connection between an action and its object: the joining of the pieces **11** indicating character, qualities etc: a man of good taste/ it was good of you to come **12** US (in telling the time) before, to: ten of eight

**off** adv **1** away from a place, or from a particular state, position etc: he walked off rudely/ switch the light off **2** entirely, completely: finish off your work □ adj **1** cancelled: the

holiday is off **2** rotten, bad: the meat is off **3** not working, not on: the control is in the off position **4** not quite pure in colour: off-white □ prep **1** not on, away from: fell off the table **2** taken away: 10% off the usual price **3** below the normal standard: off his game □ **badly off** poor □ **be off** to go away, leave quickly □ **off and on** occasionally □ **off the cuff** see **cuff** □ **off the wall** see **wall** □ **well off** rich

**offal** noun **1** the parts of an animal unfit for use as food **2** certain internal organs of an animal (heart, liver etc) that are eaten

**off-beam** adj mistaken, misguided

**off-beat** adj not standard, eccentric

**off-chance** noun a slight chance □ **on the off-chance** just in case

**off-colour** adj not feeling well

**offence** or US **offense** noun **1** displeasure, hurt feelings **2** a crime, a sin □ **take offence at** to be angry or feel hurt at

**offend** verb **1** to hurt the feelings of; insult, displease **2** to do wrong □ **offender** noun a person who has committed an offence

**offensive** noun **1** the position of someone who attacks **2** an attack □ adj **1** insulting, disgusting **2** used for attack or assault: an offensive weapon

**offer** verb **1** to put forward (a gift, payment etc) for acceptance or refusal **2** to lay (a choice, chance etc) before **3** to say that you are willing to do something □ noun **1** an act of offering **2** a bid of money **3** something proposed □ **offering** noun **1** a gift **2** a collection of money in church

**offhand** adj **1** said or done without thinking or preparation **2** rude, curt □ adv without preparation; impromptu

**office** noun **1** a place where business is carried on **2** the people working in such a place **3** a duty, a job **4** a position of authority, *esp* in the government acts **5** (**offices**) services, helpful acts

**officer** *noun* **1** someone who carries out a public duty **2** someone holding a commission in the armed forces

**official** *adj* **1** done or given out by those in power: *official announcement/ official action* **2** forming part of the tasks of a job or office: *official duties* **3** having full and proper authority □ *noun* someone who holds an office in the service of the government *etc* □ **officially** *adv* **1** as an official, formally **2** as announced or said in public (though not necessarily truthfully)

◈ Do not confuse with: **officious**. **Official** is a neutral adjective showing neither approval nor disapproval, and it is used most often with reference to position or authority rather than people's characters.

**officiate** *verb* to perform a duty or service, *esp* as a clergyman at a wedding *etc*

**officious** *adj* fond of interfering, *esp* in a pompous way □ **officiously** *adv*

◈ Do not confuse with: **official**. **Officious** is a negative adjective showing disapproval, and it is used to describe people and their characters.

**offing** *noun*: **in the offing** expected to happen soon, forthcoming

**off-licence** *noun* a shop selling alcohol which must not be drunk on the premises

**offload** *verb* **1** to unload **2** to get rid of (something) by passing on to someone else

**offpeak** *adj* not at the time of highest use or demand

**off-putting** *adj* causing aversion

**offset** *verb* to weigh against, make up

for: *the cost of the project was offset by a grant*

**offshoot** *noun* **1** a shoot growing out of the main stem **2** a small business, project *etc* created out of a larger one: *an offshoot of an international firm*

**offshore** *adj & adv* **1** in or on the sea close to the coast **2** at a distance from the shore **3** from the shore: *offshore winds*

**offside** *adj & adv, sport* **1** illegally ahead of the ball, *eg* in football, in a position between the ball and the opponent's goal **2** of the side of a vehicle: nearest to the centre of the road (*contrasted with*: **nearside**)

**offspring** *noun* **1** someone's child or children **2** the young of animals *etc*

**oft** *adv, formal* often

**often** *adv* many times

**ogle** *verb* to eye (someone) impudently in order to show admiration

**ogre** *noun* **1** a mythological man-eating giant **2** someone extremely frightening or threatening

**Oh!** *another spelling of* **O!**

**ohm** *noun* a unit of electrical resistance

**OHMS** *abbrev* On Her (or His) Majesty's Service

**oil** *noun* **1** a greasy liquid obtained from plants (*eg* olive oil), from animals (*eg* whale oil), and from minerals (*eg* petroleum) **2** (**oils**) oil colours for painting □ *verb* to smear with oil, put oil on or in □ **oily** *adj* **1** of or like oil **2** obsequious, too friendly or flattering □ **oil colour** paint made by mixing a colouring substance with oil □ **oilfield** *noun* an area where mineral oil is found □ **oil painting** a picture painted in oil colours □ **oilrig** *noun* a structure set up for drilling an oil-well □ **oilskin** *noun* **1** cloth made waterproof with oil **2** a heavy coat made of this □ **oil-well** *noun* a hole drilled into the earth's surface or into the sea bed to extract petroleum

**oink** noun the noise of a pig ▫ verb to make this noise

**ointment** noun a greasy substance rubbed on the skin to soothe, heal etc

**OK** or **okay** exclam, adj & adv all right ▫ **okay** verb to mark or pass as being all right

**okay** verb ▹ okays, okaying, okayed

**old** adj **1** advanced in age, aged **2** having a certain age: ten years old **3** not new, having existed a long time: an old joke **4** belonging to far-off times **5** worn, worn-out **6** out-of-date, old-fashioned **7** of a person's past, replaced by something different in the present: I preferred my old school to the one I'm at now ▫ **old age** the later part of life ▫ **old-fashioned** adj in a style common in the past, out-of-date ▫ **old guard** the conservative element in an organization etc ▫ **old hand** someone with long experience in a job etc ▫ **old maid 1** derogatory a spinster **2** a game played by passing and matching playing cards ▫ **old timer 1** an old person **2** a veteran, someone with experience ▫ **of old** long ago

**olfactory** adj of or used for smelling: olfactory glands

**oligarchy** (say ol-ig-ahk-i) noun government by a small exclusive group ▫ **oligarch** (say ol-ig-ahk) noun a member of an oligarchy ▫ **oligarchic** (say ol-ig-**ahk**-ik) or **oligarchical** (say ol-ig-**ahk**-ik-al) adj relating to or characteristic of an oligarchy

**olive** noun **1** a small oval fruit with a hard stone, which is pressed to produce a cooking oil **2** the Mediterranean tree that bears this fruit ▫ adj of a yellowish-green colour ▫ **olive branch** a sign of a wish for peace

**ombudsman** noun an official appointed to look into complaints against the government

From a Swedish word meaning 'administration man', introduced into English in the 1960s

**omega** noun the last letter of the Greek alphabet

**omelette** or **omelet** noun beaten eggs fried in a single layer in a pan

**omen** noun a sign of future events

**ominous** adj suggesting future trouble

**omission** noun **1** something omitted **2** the act of omitting

**omit** verb **1** to leave out **2** to fail to do

**omit** ▹ omits, omitting, omitted

**omni-** prefix all: omniscient (= all-knowing)/ omnipotent (= all-powerful) ⓘ From Latin omnis meaning 'all'

**omnibus** noun (pl omnibuses) old a bus ▫ adj **1** widely comprehensive **2** of miscellaneous contents ▫ **omnibus edition** a radio or TV programme made up of material from preceding editions of the series

**omnipotent** adj having absolute, unlimited power: omnipotent ruler ▫ **omnipotence** noun unlimited power

**omnipresent** adj present everywhere at the same time ▫ **omnipresence** noun being present everywhere at the same time

**omniscient** adj knowing everything ▫ **omniscience** noun knowledge of all things

**omnivorous** adj feeding on all kinds of food

**on** prep **1** touching or fixed to the outer or upper side: on the table **2** supported by: standing on one foot **3** receiving, taking etc: suspended on half-pay/ on antibiotics **4** occurring in the course of a specified time: on the next day **5** about: a book on *history* **6** with: *do you have your cheque book on you?* **7** next to, near: *a city on the Rhine* **8** indicating membership of: *on the committee* **9** in the process or state of: *on sale/ on show* **10** by means of: *can you play that on the piano?* **11** followed by: *disaster on disaster* □ *adv* **1** so as to be touching or fixed to the outer or upper side: *put your coat on* **2** onwards, further: *they carried on towards home* **3** at a further point: *later on* □ *adj* **1** working, performing: *the television is on* **2** arranged, planned: *do you have anything on today?* □ **from now on** after this time, henceforth □ **on and off** occasionally, intermittently □ **you're on!** I agree, accept the challenge *etc*

**once** *adv* **1** at an earlier time in the past: *people once lived in caves* **2** for one time only: *I've been to Paris once this year* □ *noun* one time only: *do it just this once* □ *conj* when: *once you've finished, you can go* □ **all at once** suddenly □ **at once** **1** immediately: *come here at once!* **2** (sometimes **all at once**) at the same time, together: *trying to do several things all at once* □ **once and for all** for the last time □ **once upon a time** at some time in the past

**oncoming** *adj* approaching from the front: *oncoming traffic*

**one** *noun* **1** the number 1 **2** a particular member of a group: *she's the one I want to meet* □ *pronoun* **1** a single person or thing: *one of my cats* **2** in formal or pompous English used instead of **you**, meaning anyone: *one must do what one can* □ *adj* **1** 1 in number, a single: *we had only one reply* **2** identical, the same: *we are all of one mind* **3** some, an unnamed (time *etc*): *one day soon* □ **oneself** *pronoun* **1** used reflexively: *wash oneself* **2** used for emphasis: *one usually has to finish the job oneself* □ **one-sided** *adj* with one person,

side *etc* having a great advantage over the other □ **one-way** *adj* meant for traffic moving in one direction only □ **one another** used when an action takes place between two or more people: *they looked at one another*

**onerous** *adj* heavy, hard to bear or do: *onerous task*

**ongoing** *adj* continuing: *ongoing talks*

**onion** *noun* a bulb vegetable with a strong taste and smell □ **oniony** *adj* tasting of onions □ **know your onions** *informal* to know your subject or job well

**onlooker** *noun* someone who watches an event, but does not take part in it

**only** *adv* **1** not more than: *only two weeks left* **2** alone, solely: *you are invited* **3** not longer ago than: *I saw her only yesterday* **4** indicating an unavoidable result: *he'll only be offended if you ask* **5** **only too** extremely: *only too pleased to help* □ *adj* single, solitary: *an only child* □ *conj, informal* but, except that: *I'd like to go, only I have to work*

**ono** *abbrev* or nearest offer

**onomatopoeia** *noun* the forming of a word which sounds like the thing it refers to, *eg* moo, swish □ **onomatopoeic** *adj* relating to or characterized by onomatopoeia

**onrush** *noun* a rush forward

**onset** *noun* **1** beginning **2** a fierce attack

**onslaught** *noun* a fierce attack

**onus** *noun* burden; responsibility

**onward** *adj* going forward in place or time: *the onward march of science* □ **onward** or **onwards** *adv*: *from four o'clock onwards/ we stumbled onward, close to exhaustion*

**onyx** *noun* a precious stone with layers of different colours

**oodles** *noun pl, informal* lots (of), many

**ooze** *verb* to flow gently or slowly □ *noun* **1** soft mud **2** a gentle flow

**opacity** *noun* opaqueness

**opal** *noun* a bluish-white precious stone, with flecks of various colours

**opalescent** *noun* milky and iridescent

**opaque** *adj* not able to be seen through

**OPEC** *abbrev* Organization of Petroleum-Exporting Countries

**open** *adj* **1** not shut, allowing entry or exit **2** not enclosed or fenced **3** showing the inside or inner part; uncovered **4** not blocked **5** free for all to enter **6** honest, frank **7** of land: without many trees □ *verb* **1** to make open; unlock **2** to begin □ **openly** *adv* without trying to hide or conceal anything □ **open-air** any place not indoors or underground □ **open-air** *adj* happening outside □ **open book** something that can be easily seen or understood □ **open-cast** *adj* of a mine: excavating in the open, above ground □ **open-ended** *adj* without definite limits □ **opener** *noun* something that opens: tin opener □ **open-heart** *adj* of surgery: performed on a heart which has been temporarily stopped, with blood being circulated by a heart-lung machine □ **opening** *noun* **1** a hole, a gap **2** an opportunity **3** a vacant job □ **open-minded** *adj* ready to take up new ideas □ **open-plan** *adj* of an office: with desks *etc* in the same room, not divided by walls or partitions □ **in the open** **1** out-of-doors, in the open air **2** widely known, not secret □ **open to** likely or willing to receive: *open to attack/ open to suggestions* □ **with open arms** warmly, enthusiastically

**opera**[1] *noun* a play in which the characters sing accompanied by an orchestra □ **operatic** *adj* of or for opera: *an operatic voice*

**opera**[2] *pl* of **opus**

**operate** *verb* **1** to act, work **2** to bring about an effect **3** to perform an operation □ **operating** *adj* of or for an operation on someone's body □ **operation** *noun* **1** action **2** method or way of working **3** the cutting of a part of the human body to examine or treat disease **4** (**operations**) movements of armies, troops

**operative** *adj* **1** working, in action **2** of a rule *etc*: in force, having effect □ *noun* a workman in a factory *etc*

**operator** *noun* **1** someone who works a machine **2** someone who connects telephone calls

**operetta** *noun* a play with music and singing

**ophthalmic** *adj* relating to the eye: *an ophthalmic surgeon* □ **ophthalmologist** *noun* a doctor who specializes in eye diseases and injuries

**opinion** *noun* **1** what someone thinks or believes **2** professional judgement or point of view: *he wanted another opinion on his son's case* **3** judgement of the value of someone or something: *I have a low opinion of her* □ **opinionated** *adj* having and expressing strong opinions

**opium** *noun* a drug made from the dried juice of a type of poppy

**opossum** *noun* a small American animal that carries its young in a pouch

**opponent** *noun* someone who opposes; an enemy, a rival

**opportune** *adj* coming at the right or convenient time □ **opportunism** *noun* the practice of regulating actions by favourable opportunities rather than by consistent principles □ **opportunist** *noun* someone who takes advantage of a favourable situation □ **opportunistic** *adj*

**opportunity** *noun* (*pl* **opportunities**) a chance (to do something)

**oppose** *verb* **1** to struggle against, resist **2** to stand against, compete against □ **opposition** *noun* **1** resistance **2** those who resist **3** the political party which is against the governing party

**opposite** *adj* **1** facing, across from **2** lying on the other side (of) **3** as different as possible □ *prep* **1** facing, across from: *he lives opposite the post office* **2** acting a role in a play, opera *etc* in relation to another: *she played Ophelia opposite his Hamlet* □ *noun* something as different as possible (from something else): *black is the opposite of white*

**oppress** *verb* **1** to govern harshly like a tyrant **2** to treat cruelly **3** to distress, worry greatly □ **oppression** *noun* **1** the state of suffering cruelty and injustice **2** worry or mental distress □ **oppressive** *adj* **1** oppressing **2** cruel, harsh **3** of weather: close, tiring

**opt** *verb* **1** (with **for**) to choose it **2** to decide (to do) □ **opt out** to decide not to (do something

**optic** or **optical** *adj* relating to the eyes or sight □ **optical illusion** an impression that something seen is different from what it is □ **optician** *noun* someone who makes and sells spectacles □ **optics** *noun sing* the science of light

**optimal** *adj* very best, optimum

**optimism** *noun* the habit of taking a bright, hopeful view of things (*contrasted with:* **pessimism**) □ **optimist** *noun* someone who tends to take a positive view of things □ **optimistic** *adj* relating to or characterized by optimism

**optimum** *adj* best, most favourable: *optimum conditions*

**option** *noun* **1** choice; the right or power to choose **2** something chosen □ **optional** *adj* left to choice, not compulsory

**opulent** *adj* wealthy; luxurious □ **opulence** *noun* riches

**opus** *noun* (*pl* **opera**) an artistic work, *esp* a musical composition

**or** *conj* **1** used (often with **either**) to show alternatives: *would you prefer tea or coffee?* **2** because if not: *you'd better go or you'll miss your bus*

**oracle** *noun* **1** someone thought to be very wise or knowledgeable **2** *historical* a sacred place where a god answered questions **3** someone through whom such answers were made known □ **oracular** *adj* **1** of or like an oracle **2** difficult to interpret; mysterious and ambiguous **3** prophetic

**oral** *adj* **1** spoken, not written: *oral literature* **2** relating to the mouth □ *noun* an oral examination or test □ **orally** *adv* by mouth
Ⓔ From Latin *or-*, a form of *os* meaning 'mouth'

● Do not confuse with: **aural**. **Aural** means 'relating to the ear'. It may help to think of the 'O' as looking like an open mouth.

**orange** *noun* **1** a juicy citrus fruit, with a thick reddish-yellow skin **2** the colour of this fruit

**orang-utan** *noun* a large man-like ape
Based on a Malay phrase which translates as 'wild man'

**oration** *noun* a public speech, *esp* one in fine formal language □ **orator** *noun* a public speaker □ **oratory** *noun* the art of speaking well in public

**oratorio** *noun* (*pl* **oratorios**) a sacred story set to music, performed by soloists, choir and often orchestra

**orb** *noun* anything in the shape of a ball, a sphere

**orbit** *noun* **1** the path of a planet or moon round a sun, or of a space capsule round the earth **2** range or area of influence: *within his orbit* □ *verb* to go round the earth *etc* in space

**orchard** *noun* a large garden of fruit trees

**orchestra** *noun* a group of musicians playing together under a conductor

**orchestrate** *verb* **1** to arrange (a piece of music) for an orchestra **2** to organize so as to produce the best effect

**orchid** *noun* a plant with unusually shaped, often brightly coloured, flowers

**ordain** *verb* **1** to declare something to be law **2** to receive (a member of the clergy) into the Church

**ordeal** *noun* **1** a hard trial or test **2** suffering; a painful experience

**order** *noun* **1** an instruction to act made by someone in authority **2** a request or list of requests: *put an order in with the grocer* **3** an arrangement according to a system **4** an accepted way of doing things **5** a tidy or efficient state **6** peaceful conditions: *law and order* **7** rank, position, class **8** a society or brotherhood, *eg* of monks □ *verb* **1** to give an order to, tell to do **2** to put an order in a request for: *I've ordered another copy of the book* **3** to arrange □ **in order 1** correct according to what is regularly done **2** in a tidy arrangement □ **in order to** for the purpose of: *in order to live you must eat* □ **out of order 1** not working **2** not the correct way of doing things **3** not in a tidy arrangement

**orderly** *adj* **1** in proper order **2** well-behaved, quiet □ *noun* (*pl* **orderlies**) **1** a soldier who carries the orders and messages of an officer **2** a hospital attendant who does routine jobs

**ordinal** *adj* of or in an order □ **ordinal number** a number which shows order in a series, *eg* first, second, third (*compare with*: **cardinal number**)

**ordinance** *noun* a command; a law

**ordinary** *adj* **1** common, usual **2** normal; not exceptional □ **ordinarily** *adv* usually, normally □ **ordinariness** *noun* being ordinary □ **out of the ordinary** unusual

**ordination** *noun* the act or ceremony of ordaining a priest or minister of the church

**Ordnance Survey** a government office which produces official detailed maps

**ore** *noun* a mineral from which a metal is obtained: *iron ore*

**oregano** (*say* o-ri-gah-noh or *US* o-reg-*a*n-oh) *noun* a Mediterranean herb used in cooking

**organ** *noun* **1** an internal part of the body, *eg* the liver **2** a large musical wind instrument with a keyboard **3** a means of spreading information or propaganda, *eg* a newspaper: *an organ of conservatism* □ **organist** *noun* someone who plays the organ

**organdie** (*say* aw-gan-di) *noun* a fine, thin, stiff muslin

**organic** *adj* **1** of or produced by the bodily organs **2** of living things **3** made up of parts each with its separate function **4** of food: grown without the use of artificial fertilizers *etc* □ **organically** *adv*

**organism** *noun* any living thing

**organize** *verb* **1** to arrange, set up (an event *etc*) **2** to form into a whole □ **organization** *noun* **1** the act of organizing **2** a group of people working together for a purpose

**orgasm** *noun* the climax of sexual excitement □ *verb* to experience an orgasm

**orgy** *noun* (*pl* **orgies**) a drunken or other unrestrained celebration

**Orient** *noun, old* the countries of the East □ **oriental** *adj* eastern; from the East

**orientate** *verb* **1** to find your position and sense of direction **2** to set or put facing a particular direction □ **orientation** *noun* **1** the act or an

**orienteering** *noun* the sport of finding your way across country with the help of map and compass

**orifice** *noun, formal* an opening

**origami** *noun* the Japanese art of folding paper

**origin** *noun* 1 the starting point 2 the place from which someone or something comes 3 the cause □ **original** *adj* 1 first in time 2 not copied 3 able to think or do something new □ *noun* 1 the earliest version 2 a model from which other things are made □ **originally** *adv* 1 in or from the beginning: *his family is from Ireland originally* 2 in a new and different way: *she dresses very originally* □ **originate** *verb* 1 to bring or come into being 2 to produce

**Orion** *noun* a constellation containing seven bright stars, forming the shape of a hunter

**ornament** *noun* something added to give or enhance beauty □ *verb* to adorn, decorate □ **ornamental** *adj* used for ornament; decorative □ **ornamentation** *noun* decorating or the state of being decorated

**ornate** *adj* richly decorated □ **ornately** *adv*

**ornithology** *noun* the scientific study of birds and their behaviour □ **ornithological** *adj* relating to or involving ornithology □ **ornithologist** *noun* someone who studies or is an expert on birds

**orphan** *noun* a child who has lost one or both parents □ **orphanage** *noun* a home for orphans

**orthodox** *adj* 1 agreeing with the prevailing or established religious, political *etc* views (*contrasted with:* **heterodox**) 2 normal, generally practised and accepted □ **orthodoxy** *noun* 1 the state of being orthodox or of having orthodox beliefs 2 an orthodox belief or practice

**orthography** *noun* an established system of spelling □ **orthographic** or **orthographical** *adj* relating to spelling

**orthopaedics** or *US* **orthopedics** *noun sing* the branch of medicine which deals with bone diseases and injuries □ **orthopaedic** or *US* **orthopedic** *adj* relating to orthopaedics

**oscillate** *verb* 1 to swing to and fro like the pendulum of a clock 2 to keep changing your mind □ **oscillation** *noun* 1 oscillating 2 a regular movement or change, such as the movement of a pendulum

From Latin *oscillum*, literally 'small face', a mask of the god Bacchus which hung in Roman vineyards and swayed in the wind

**osier** *noun* 1 a type of willow tree whose twigs are used for weaving baskets *etc* 2 a twig from this tree

**osmosis** *noun* 1 diffusion of liquids through a membrane 2 gradual absorption or assimilation

**osprey** *noun* (*pl* **ospreys**) a type of eagle which eats fish

**ostensible** *adj* of a reason *etc*: apparent, but not always real or true

**ostentation** *noun* pretentious display of wealth, knowledge *etc*, *esp* to attract attention or admiration □ **ostentatious** *adj* showy, meant to catch the eye

**osteopathy** *noun* a system of healing or treatment, mainly involving manipulation of the bones and joints and massage of the muscles, that provides relief for many bone and joint disorders □ **osteopath** *noun* someone who practises osteopathy

**osteoporosis** *noun* a disease which makes bones porous and brittle, caused by lack of calcium

**ostracize** verb to banish (someone) from the company of a group of people □ **ostracism** noun social exclusion

Based on *ostrakon*, a piece of pottery used in ancient Greece to cast votes to decide if someone was to be exiled

**ostrich** noun (pl **ostriches**) a large African bird with showy plumage, which cannot fly but runs very fast

**other** adj **1** the second of two: *where is the other sock?* **2** remaining, not previously mentioned: *these are for the other children* **3** different, additional: *there must be some other reason* **4** (**every other**) second: *every other day* **5** recently past: *the other day* □ pronoun **1** the second of two **2** those remaining, those not previously mentioned: *the others arrived later* **3** the previous one: *one after the other* □ **other than** except: *no hope other than to retreat*

□ **someone or other** or **something or other** someone or something not named or specified: *there's always someone or other here*

**OTT** abbrev over-the-top, extravagant

**otter** noun a type of river animal living on fish

**Ottoman** adj, historical relating to the Turkish empire from the 14th to the 19th centuries

**ottoman** noun a low, cushioned seat without a back

**ought** verb **1** used with other verbs to indicate duty or need: *we ought to set an example/ I ought to go* **2** to indicate what can be reasonably expected: *the weather ought to be fine*

**ounce** noun a unit of weight, one-sixteenth of a pound, 28.35 grammes

**our** adj belonging to us: *our house* □ **ours** pronoun something belonging to us: *the green car is ours*

□ **ourselves** pronoun **1** used reflexively: *we exhausted ourselves swimming* **2** used for emphasis: *we ourselves don't like it, but other people may*

**oust** verb **1** to drive out (from) **2** to take the place of: *she ousted him as leader*

**out** adv **1** into or towards the open air: *go out for a walk* **2** from within: *take out a handkerchief* **3** not inside: *out of prison* **4** far from here: *out in the Far East* **5** not at home, not in the office etc: *she's out at the moment* **6** aloud: *shouted out* **7** to or at an end: *hear me out* **8** inaccurate: *the total was five pounds out* **9** informal on strike **10** published: *is the book not out yet?* **11** no longer hidden: *the secret is out* **12** openly admitting to being homosexual **13** dismissed from a game of cricket, baseball etc **14** finished, having won at cards etc **15** no longer in power or office **16** determined: *out to win*

**out-and-out** adj complete, total, thorough

**outback** noun the wild interior parts of Australia

**outbid** verb to offer a higher price than (somebody else)

**outbid** ⇔ outbids, outbidding, outbid

**outboard** adj on the outside of a ship or boat: *an outboard motor*

**outbreak** noun a beginning, a breaking out, eg of war or disease

**outbuilding** noun a building that is separate from the main buildings

**outburst** noun a bursting out, esp of angry feelings

**outcast** noun someone driven away from friends and home

**outcome** noun result

**outcrop** noun the part of a rock formation that can be seen at the surface of the ground

**outcry** *noun* (*pl* **outcries**) a widespread show of anger, disapproval *etc*

**outdo** *verb* to do better than

**outdo** ⊳ outdo**es**, outdo**ing**, outd**id**, outd**one**

**outdoor** *adj* of or in the open air □ **outdoors** *adv* **1** outside the house **2** in or into the open air

**outer** *adj* nearer the edge, surface *etc*; further away □ **outermost** *adj* nearest the edge; furthest away

**outfit** *noun* a set of clothes worn together, often for a special occasion *etc*

**outgoings** *noun pl* money spent or being spent

**outgrow** *verb* to get too big or old for (clothes, toys *etc*)

**outgrow** ⊳ outgrow**s**, outgrow**ing**, outgr**ew**, outgr**own**

**out-house** *noun* a shed

**outing** *noun* a trip, excursion

**outlandish** *adj* looking or sounding very strange

**outlaw** *noun* someone put outside the protection of the law; a robber or bandit □ *verb* **1** to place beyond the protection of the law **2** to ban, forbid

**outlay** *noun* money paid out

**outlet** *noun* **1** a passage to the outside, *eg* for a water-pipe **2** a means of expressing or getting rid of (a feeling, energy *etc*) **3** a market for goods

**outline** *noun* **1** the outer line of a figure in a drawing *etc* **2** a sketch showing only the main lines **3** a rough sketch **4** a brief description □ *verb* to draw or describe an outline of

**outlive** *verb* to live longer than

**outlook** *noun* **1** a view from a window *etc* **2** what is thought likely to happen: *the weather outlook*

**outlying** *adj* far from the centre, distant

**outnumber** *verb* to be greater in number than: *their team outnumbered ours*

**out-of-date** *adj* or **out of date 1** old-fashioned **2** no longer valid: *this voucher is out of date/ an out-of-date ticket*

**out-patient** *noun* a patient who does not stay in a hospital while receiving treatment (*contrasted with*: **in-patient**)

**outpost** *noun* a military station in front of or far from the main army; an outlying settlement

**output** *noun* the goods produced by a machine, factory *etc*; the amount of work done by a person **2** data produced by a computer program (*contrasted with*: **input**)

**outrage** *noun* **1** an act of great violence **2** an act which shocks or causes offence □ *verb* **1** to injure, hurt by violence **2** to insult, shock □ **outrageous** *adj* **1** violent, very wrong **2** not moderate, extravagant

**outright** *adv* completely □ *adj* complete, thorough

**outset** *noun* start, beginning

**outside** *noun* the outer surface or place: *the outside of the box* □ *adj* **1** in, on or of the outer surface or place: *the outside seat* **2** relating to leisure rather than your full-time job: *outside interests* **3** slight: *an outside chance of winning* □ *adv* **1** beyond the limits of: *go outside the building/ locked outside working hours* **2** out-of-doors; in or into the open air: *let's eat outside* □ *prep* beyond the range of, not within □ **at the outside** at the most: *ten miles at the outside*

**outsider** *noun* **1** someone not included in a particular social group **2** a runner *etc* whom no one expects to win

**outsize** *adj* of a very large size

**outskirts** *noun pl* the outer borders of a city *etc*

**outspoken** *adj* bold and frank in speech

**outstanding** *adj* **1** well-known **2** excellent **3** of a debt: unpaid

**outstretched** *adj* reaching out

**outvote** *verb* to defeat by a greater number of votes

**outward** *adj* **1** towards or on the outside **2** of a journey: away from home, not towards it □ **outwardly** or **outwards** *adv* on the outside, externally

**outweigh** *verb* to be more important than: *the advantages outweigh the disadvantages*

**outwit** *verb* to defeat by cunning

**outwit** ⇨ outwits, outwitting, outwitted

**ova** *pl* of **ovum**

**oval** *adj* having the shape of an egg □ *noun* an egg shape

**ovary** *noun* (*pl* **ovaries**) one of two organs in the female body in which eggs are formed

**ovation** *noun* an outburst of cheering, hand-clapping *etc*

**oven** *noun* a covered place for baking; a small furnace

**over** *prep* **1** higher than, above: *the number is over the door/ she won over 200/ we've lived here for over thirty years* **2** across: *going over the bridge* **3** on the other side of: *the house over the road* **4** on top of: *threw his coat over the body* **5** here and there on: *paper scattered over the carpet* **6** about: *they quarrelled over money* **7** by means of: *over the telephone* **8** during, throughout: *over the years* **9** while doing, having *etc*: *fell asleep over his dinner* □ *adv* **1** above, higher up: *two birds flew over our heads* **2** across a distance: *he walked over and spoke* **3** downwards: *did you fall over?* **4** above in number *etc*: *aged four and over* **5** as a remainder: *three left over* **6** through: *read the passage over* □ *adj* finished: *the sale is over* □ *noun*, *cricket* a fixed number of

balls bowled from one end of the wicket □ **over again** once more

**over-** *prefix* too much, to too great an extent: *overcook/ over-excited*

**overall** *noun* **1** a garment worn over ordinary clothes to protect them against dirt **2** hard-wearing trousers with a bib worn as work clothes □ *adj* **1** from one end to the other: *overall length* **2** including everything: *overall cost* □ **over all** altogether

**overawe** *verb* to frighten or astonish into silence

**overbalance** *verb* to lose your balance and fall

**overbearing** *adj* over-confident, domineering

**overboard** *adv* out of a ship into the water: *man overboard*

**overcast** *adj* of the sky: cloudy

**overcoat** *noun* an outdoor coat worn over all other clothes

**overcome** *verb* to get the better of, defeat □ *adj* helpless from exhaustion, emotion *etc*

**overdo** *verb* **1** to do too much **2** to exaggerate: *they rather overdid the sympathy* **3** to cook (food) too long

**overdose** *noun* too great an amount (of medicine, a drug *etc*) □ *verb* to give or take too much medicine *etc*

**overdraft** *noun* the amount of money overdrawn from a bank

**overdraw** *verb* to draw more money from the bank than you have in your account

**overdue** *adj* **1** later than the stated time: *the train is overdue* **2** of a bill *etc*: still unpaid although the time for payment has passed

**overflow** *verb* **1** to flow or spill over: *the river overflowed its banks/ the crowd overflowed into the next room* **2** to be so full as to flow over □ *noun* **1** a running-over of liquid **2** a pipe or channel for getting rid of excess water *etc*

**overgrown** adj **1** covered with wild plant growth **2** grown too large

**overhang** verb to jut out over

**overhaul** verb to examine carefully and carry out repairs □ noun a thorough examination and repair

**overhead** adv directly above: *the aeroplane flew overhead* □ adj placed high above the ground: *overhead cables* □ noun (**overheads**) the general expenses of a business *etc*

**overhear** verb to hear what you were not meant to hear

**overjoyed** adj filled with great joy

**overland** adv & adj on or by land, not sea

**overlap** verb **1** to extend over and partly cover: *the two pieces of cloth overlapped* **2** to cover a part of the same area or subject as another; partly coincide □ noun the amount by which something overlaps

**overleaf** adj on the other side of a leaf of a book

**overload** verb to load or fill too much

**overlook** verb **1** to look down on from a higher point; have or give a view of: *the house overlooked the village* **2** to fail to see, miss **3** to pardon, not punish

**overlord** noun, *historical* a lord with power over other lords

**overly** adv too, excessively

**overmuch** adv too much

**overnight** adv **1** during the night: *staying overnight with a friend* **2** in a very short time: *he changed completely overnight* □ adj **1** for the night: *an overnight bag* **2** got or made in a very short time: *an overnight success*

**overpass** noun a road going over above another road, railway, canal *etc*

**overpower** verb **1** to defeat through greater strength **2** to overwhelm, make helpless □ **overpowering** adj

**1** unable to be resisted **2** overwhelming, very strong: *an overpowering smell*

**overrate** verb to value more highly than is deserved: *his new film is overrated*

**overreach** verb: **overreach yourself** to try to do or get more than you can and so fail

**override** verb to ignore, set aside: *overriding the teacher's authority*

**overrule** verb to go against or cancel an earlier judgement or request

**overrun** verb **1** to grow or spread over: *overrun with weeds* **2** to take possession of (a country)

**overseas** adj & adv abroad; beyond the sea

**oversee** verb to watch over, supervise

**overseer** noun a person who oversees workers, a supervisor

**overshadow** verb to lessen the importance of by doing better than

**oversight** noun **1** something left out or forgotten by mistake **2** failure to notice

**overstep** verb to go further than (a set limit, rules *etc*)

**overt** adj not hidden or secret; openly done

**overtake** verb to catch up with and pass

**overthrow** verb to defeat

**overtime** noun **1** time spent working beyond the agreed normal hours **2** payment for this, usually at a higher rate

**overtone** noun an additional meaning or association, not directly stated

**overture** noun **1** a proposal intended to open discussions: *overtures of peace* **2** a piece of music played as an introduction to an opera

**overwhelm** verb **1** to defeat completely **2** to load with too great an amount: *overwhelmed with work*

**3** to overcome, make helpless: *overwhelmed with grief* □ **overwhelming** *adj* physically or mentally crushing; intensely powerful

**overwork** *verb* to work more than is good for you □ **overworked** *adj* having too much work to do

**overwrought** *adj* excessively nervous or excited, agitated

**ovoid** *adj* egg-shaped □ *noun* an egg-shaped form or object

**ovum** *noun* (*pl* **ova**) the egg from which the young of animals and people develop

**owe** *verb* **1** to be in debt to: *I owe Peter three pounds* **2** to have (a person or thing) to thank for: *he owes his success to his family* □ **owing to** because of

**owl** *noun* a bird of prey which comes out at night □ **owlet** *noun* a young owl

**own** *verb* **1** to have as a possession **2** to admit, confess to be true □ *adj* belonging to the person mentioned:

*is this all your own work?* □ **hold your own** to keep your place or position, not weaken □ **on your own 1** by your own efforts **2** alone

**owner** *noun* someone who possesses anything □ **ownership** *noun* possession

**own goal** a goal scored by mistake against your own side

**ox** *noun* (*pl* **oxen**) a male cow, usually castrated, used for drawing loads *etc*

**oxide** *noun* a compound of oxygen and another element □ **oxidize** *verb* **1** to combine with oxygen **2** to become rusty

**oxygen** *noun* a gas with no taste, colour or smell, forming part of the air and of water □ **oxygenate** *verb* to supply (*eg* the blood) with oxygen

**oyster** *noun* a type of eatable shellfish

**ozone** *noun* a form of oxygen, O₃ □ **ozone layer** a layer of the upper atmosphere which protects the earth from the sun's ultraviolet rays

# Pp

**p** *abbrev* **1** page **2** pence

**pace** *noun* **1** a step **2** rate of walking, running *etc* □ *verb* **1** to measure by steps **2** to walk backwards and forwards □ **pacemaker** *noun* **1** someone who sets the pace in a race **2** a device used to correct weak or irregular heart rhythms

**pacify** *verb* **1** to make peaceful **2** to calm, soothe □ **pacifist** *noun* someone who is against war and works for peace

**pacify** ◁▷ pacif**ies**, pacif**ying**, pacif**ied**

**pack** *noun* **1** a bundle, *esp* one carried on the back **2** a set of playing-cards **3** a group of animals, *esp* dogs or wolves □ *verb* **1** to place (clothes

*etc*) in a case or trunk for a journey **2** to press or crowd together closely □ **pack in** to cram in tightly

**package** *noun* a bundle, a parcel □ *verb* **1** to put into a container **2** to wrap □ **package holiday** or **package tour** a holiday or tour arranged by an organizer with all travel and accommodation included in the price

**packet** *noun* **1** a small parcel **2** a container made of paper, cardboard *etc*

**pack-ice** *noun* a mass of large pieces of floating ice driven together by wind, currents *etc*

**packing** *noun* **1** the act of putting things in cases, parcels *etc*

2 material for wrapping goods to pack 3 something used to fill an empty space □ **send someone packing** to send them away forcefully

**pact** noun 1 an agreement 2 a treaty, a contract

**pad** noun 1 a soft cushion-like object to prevent jarring or rubbing *etc* 2 a bundle of sheets of paper fixed together 3 the paw of certain animals 4 a rocket-launching platform □ verb 1 to stuff or protect with a soft material 2 (often **pad something out**) to fill it up with unnecessary material 3 to walk making a dull, soft noise □ **padding** noun 1 stuffing material 2 words included in a speech, book *etc* just to fill space or time

**pad** verb ▷ pads, pad*ding*, pad*ded*

**paddle** verb 1 to move forward by the use of paddles; row 2 to wade in shallow water □ noun a short, broad, spoon-shaped oar □ **paddle-steamer** noun a steamer driven by two large wheels made up of paddles

**paddock** noun a small closed-in field used for pasture

**paddy-field** noun a muddy field in which rice is grown

**padlock** noun a removable lock with a hinged hook

**paean** (*say* pee-*a*n) noun a song of praise or thanksgiving

**paediatrics** or *US* **pediatrics** noun *sing* the treatment of children's diseases □ **paediatrician** or *US* **pediatrician** noun a doctor specializing in studying and treating children's illnesses

**paedophile** or *US* **pedophile** noun an adult who has sexual desire for children

**pagan** noun someone who does not believe in any religion; a heathen □ adj heathen □ **paganism** noun pagan beliefs and practices

**page** noun 1 one side of a blank, written or printed sheet of paper 2 a boy servant 3 a boy who carries the train of the bride's dress in a marriage service

**pageant** noun 1 a show or procession made up of scenes from history 2 an elaborate parade or display □ **pageantry** noun

**pagoda** noun an Eastern temple, *esp* in China or India

**paid** past form of **pay**

**pail** noun an open vessel of tin, zinc, plastic *etc* for carrying liquids; a bucket

**pain** noun 1 feeling caused by hurt to mind or body 2 threat of punishment: *under pain of death* 3 (**pains**) care: *takes great pains with his work* □ verb to cause suffering to, distress □ **pained** adj showing pain or distress □ **painful** adj 1 causing pain 2 affected by something which causes pain: *a painful finger* 3 causing distress: *a painful duty* 4 laborious: *painful progress* □ **painfully** adv □ **painless** adj without pain □ **painlessly** adv □ **painkiller** noun a medicine taken to lessen pain □ **painstaking** adj very careful □ **painstakingly** adv

**paint** verb 1 to apply colour to in the form of liquid or paste 2 to describe in words □ noun a liquid substance used for colouring and applied with a brush, a spray *etc* □ **painter** noun 1 someone whose trade is painting 2 an artist who works in paint 3 a rope used to fasten a boat □ **painting** noun 1 the act or art of creating pictures with paint 2 a painted picture □ **paintball** noun a type of war game in which the participants fire paint-pellets at one another

**pair** noun 1 two of the same kind 2 a set of two □ verb 1 to join to form a pair 2 to go in twos 3 to mate

**pajamas** another spelling of **pyjamas**

**pal** noun, informal a friend

**palace** noun the house of a king, queen, archbishop or aristocrat

**palaeolithic** or **paleolithic** adj relating to the early Stone Age when people used stone tools

**palatable** adj **1** pleasant to the taste **2** acceptable, pleasing

**palate** (say pal-at) noun **1** the roof of the mouth **2** taste
⊙ From Latin palatum meaning 'the roof of the mouth'

❧ Do not confuse with: **palette** and **pallet**

**palatial** adj like a palace, magnificent

**pale**[1] noun a wooden stake used in making a fence to enclose ground

**pale**[2] adj **1** light or whitish in colour **2** not bright ◻ verb to make or turn pale

**palette** (say pal-et) noun a board or plate on which an artist mixes paints
⊙ From Italian paletta meaning 'a small shovel'

❧ Do not confuse with: **pallet** and **palate**

**palindrome** noun a word or phrase that reads the same backwards as forwards, eg 'level'
⊙ From Greek palindromos, meaning 'running back'

**What is the longest palindrome you can make up?** Remember your palindrome can have several words, so long as it is the same when you read it backwards, like the sentence: 'Able was I ere I saw Elba'.

**paling** noun a row of wooden stakes forming a fence

**palisade** noun a fence of pointed wooden stakes

**pall** (say pawl) noun **1** the cloth over a coffin at a funeral **2** a dark covering or cloud: a pall of smoke ◻ verb to become dull or uninteresting ◻ **pallbearer** noun one of those carrying or walking beside the coffin at a funeral

**pallet** (say pal-et) noun **1** a straw bed or mattress **2** a platform that can be lifted by a fork-lift truck for stacking goods
⊙ Meaning 1: from French paille meaning 'straw'; meaning 2: shares the same origin as 'palette'

❧ Do not confuse with: **palette** and **palate**

**palliative** adj making less severe or harsh ◻ noun something which lessens pain, eg a drug

**pallid** adj pale ◻ **pallor** noun

**palm** noun **1** a tall tree with broad fan-shaped leaves, which grows in hot countries **2** the inner surface of the hand between the wrist and the start of the fingers ◻ **palmist** noun someone who claims to tell fortunes by the lines and markings of the hand ◻ **palmistry** noun the telling of fortunes from the lines and markings of the hand ◻ **palm off** to give with the intention of cheating

**palpable** adj **1** able to be touched or felt **2** easily noticed, obvious

**palpate** verb to examine by touch ◻ **palpation** noun

**palpitate** verb of the heart: to beat rapidly, throb ◻ **palpitations** noun pl

**palsy** noun a loss of power and feeling in the muscles ◻ **palsied** adj

**paltry** adj of little value

**pampas** noun pl the vast treeless plains of South America

**pamper** verb to spoil (a child etc) by giving too much attention to

**pamphlet** noun a small book, stitched or stapled, often with a light paper cover

**pan** noun **1** a broad shallow pot used in cooking, a saucepan **2** a shallow dent in the ground **3** the bowl of a toilet ◻ verb to move a television or film camera so as to follow an object or give a wide view ◻ **pan out 1** to turn out (well or badly) **2** to come to an end

**pan** verb ⇔ pans, pann**ing**, pann**ed**

**pan-** prefix all, whole: pandemonium/ panoply
ⓖ From Greek pan, a form of pas meaning 'all'

**panacea** (say pan-a-see-a) noun a cure for all things

**pancake** noun a thin cake of flour, eggs, sugar and milk, fried in a pan

**panda** noun **1** a large black-and-white bear-like animal found in Tibet etc **2** a raccoon-like animal found in the Himalayas □ **panda car** Brit, informal a police patrol car

**pandemonium** noun a state of confusion and uproar

The name of the capital of Hell in Milton's Paradise Lost (1667)

**pander** noun a pimp □ **pander to** to indulge, easily comply with

After Pandarus, who acts as a go-between in the story of Troilus and Cressida

**Pandora's box** something which causes unexpected havoc

After the story of Pandora, who disobeyed the Greek gods and opened a box containing all the troubles of the world

**pane** noun a sheet of glass

**panegyric** (say pan-i-**ji**-rik) noun a speech praising highly someone, an achievement etc

**panel** noun **1** a flat rectangular piece of wood such as is set into a door or wall **2** a group of people chosen to judge a contest, take part in a television quiz etc

**pang** noun a sudden sharp pain; a twinge

**panic** noun **1** a sudden and great fright **2** fear that spreads from person to person □ verb **1** to throw into panic **2** to act wildly through fear

**panic** verb ⇔ panics, panick**ing**,

panick**ed**

**panoply** noun (pl **panoplies**) the ceremonial dress, equipment etc associated with a particular event: the panoply of a military funeral

**panorama** noun a wide view of a landscape, scene etc

**pansy** noun (pl **pansies**) a flower like the violet but larger

**pant** verb **1** to gasp for breath **2** to say breathlessly **3** to wish eagerly (for)

**pantechnicon** noun a large van for transporting furniture

**panther** noun **1** a large leopard **2** US a puma

**panties** noun pl women's or children's knickers with short legs

**pantomime** noun a Christmas play, with songs, jokes etc, based on a popular fairy tale eg Cinderella

**pantry** noun (pl **pantries**) a room for storing food

**pants** noun pl **1** underpants **2** women's short-legged knickers **3** US trousers

**papa** noun a child's name for **father**

**papacy** noun the position or power of the Pope □ **papal** adj

**paper** noun **1** a material made from rags, wood etc used for writing or wrapping **2** a single sheet of this **3** a newspaper **4** an essay on a learned subject **5** a set of examination questions **6** (**papers**) documents proving someone's identity, nationality etc □ verb to cover up (esp walls) with paper □ **paperback** noun a book bound in a flexible paper cover □ **paper-chase** noun a game in which one runner leaves a trail of paper so that others may track them □ **paperweight** noun a heavy glass, metal etc object used to keep a pile of papers in place

**papier-mâché** (say pap-yei-**mash**-ei) noun a substance consisting of paper pulp and some sticky liquid or glue, shaped into models, bowls *etc*

**paprika** *noun* a type of ground red pepper

**papyrus** *noun* (*pl* **papyri** — *say* pa-**pai**-rai — or **papyruses**) a reed used by the ancient Egyptians *etc* to make paper

**par** *noun* **1** an accepted standard, value *etc* **2** *golf* the number of strokes allowed for each hole if the play is perfect □ **below par 1** not up to standard **2** not feeling very well □ **on a par with** equal to or comparable with

**parable** *noun* a story (*eg* in the Bible) which teaches a moral lesson

**parabola** *noun* **1** a curve **2** the intersection of a cone with a plane parallel to its side

**parachute** *noun* an umbrella-shaped device made of light material and rope which supports someone or something dropping slowly to the ground from an aeroplane □ *verb* to drop by parachute □ **parachutist** *noun*

**parade** *noun* **1** an orderly arrangement of troops for inspection or exercise **2** a procession of people, vehicles *etc* in celebration of some event □ *verb* **1** to arrange (troops) in order **2** to march in a procession **3** to display in an obvious way

**paradise** *noun* **1** heaven **2** a place or state of great happiness

**paradox** *noun* (*pl* **paradoxes**) a saying which seems to contradict itself but which may be true □ **paradoxical** *adj* □ **paradoxically** *adv*

**paraffin** *noun* an oil which burns and is used as a fuel (for heaters, lamps *etc*)

**paragon** *noun* a model of perfection or excellence: *a paragon of good manners*

**paragraph** *noun* **1** a division of a piece of writing shown by beginning the first sentence on a new line **2** a short item in a newspaper

**parakeet** *noun* a type of small parrot

**parallel** *adj* **1** of lines: going in the same direction and never meeting, always remaining the same distance apart **2** similar or alike in some way: *parallel cases* □ *noun* **1** a parallel line **2** something comparable in some way with something else **3** a line to mark latitude, drawn east and west across a map or round a globe at a set distance from the equator

**parallelogram** *noun* a four-sided figure, the opposite sides of which are parallel and equal in length

**paralyse** or *US* **paralyze** *verb* **1** to affect with paralysis **2** to make helpless or ineffective **3** to bring to a halt □ **paralysis** *noun* loss of the power to move and feel in part of the body □ **paralytic** *adj* **1** suffering from paralysis **2** *informal* helplessly drunk □ *noun* a paralysed person

**paramedic** *noun* someone helping doctors and nurses, *eg* a member of an ambulance crew

**parameter** *noun* (often **parameters**) the limiting factors or characteristics which affect the way in which something can be done or made

ⓞ From Greek *para* meaning 'beside' or 'beyond', and *metròn* meaning 'measure'

🖎 Do not confuse with: **perimeter**. Notice that words starting with peri- often relate to the idea of 'going around' - and the **perimeter** of a figure or shape is the line that goes around it.

**paramilitary** *adj* **1** on military lines and intended to supplement the military **2** organized illegally as a military force □ *noun* a member of a paramilitary force

**paramount** *adj* **1** above all others in rank or power **2** very greatest: *of* *paramount importance*

**paranoia** *noun* **1** a form of mental disorder characterized by delusions of grandeur, persecution *etc* **2** intense, irrational fear or suspicion

**parapet** *noun* a low wall on a bridge or balcony to prevent people falling over the side

**paraphernalia** *noun pl* belongings; gear, equipment

Originally a woman's property which was not part of her dowry, and which therefore remained her own after marriage

**paraphrase** *verb* to express (a piece of writing) in other words □ *noun* an expression in different words

**parasite** *noun* an animal, plant or person living on another without being any use in return □ **parasitic** *adj*

**parasol** *noun* a light umbrella used as a sunshade

**paratroops** *noun pl* soldiers carried by air and specially trained to be dropped by parachute into enemy country □ **paratrooper** *noun*

**parboil** *verb* to boil (food) slightly

**parcel** *noun* a wrapped and tied package to be sent by post □ *verb* **1** (**parcel something out**) to divide it into portions **2** (**parcel something up**) to wrap it up as a package □ **part and parcel** an absolutely necessary part

**parcel** *verb* ⇔ parcels, parcel*ling*, parcel*led*

**parch** *verb* **1** to make hot and very dry **2** to make thirsty □ **parched** *adj*

**parchment** *noun* **1** the dried skin of a goat or sheep used for writing on **2** paper resembling this

**pardon** *verb* **1** to forgive **2** to free from punishment **3** to allow to go unpunished □ *noun* **1** forgiveness **2** the act of pardoning □ **pardonable** *adj*

**pare** *verb* **1** to peel or cut off the edge or outer surface of **2** to make smaller gradually □ **parings** *noun pl* small pieces cut away or peeled off

**parent** *noun* a father or mother □ **parentage** *noun* descent from parents or ancestors □ **parental** *adj*

**parenthesis** *noun* (*pl* **parentheses**) **1** a word or group of words in a sentence forming an explanation or comment, often separated by brackets or dashes, *eg* he and his wife (*so he said*) were separated **2** (**parentheses**) brackets □ **parenthetical** *adj*

**pariah** *noun* someone driven out from a community or group; an outcast

Originally a member of a low caste in southern India

**parish** *noun* (*pl* **parishes**) a district with its own church and minister or priest □ **parishioner** (*say* pa-**rish**-on-er) *noun*

**parity** *noun* equality

**park** *noun* **1** a public place for walking, with grass and trees **2** an enclosed piece of land surrounding a country house □ *verb* to stop and leave (a car *etc*) in a place for a time

**parka** *noun* a type of thick jacket with a hood

**parley** *verb* to hold a conference, *esp* with an enemy □ *noun* (*pl* **parleys**) a meeting between enemies to settle terms of peace *etc*

**parley** *verb* ⇔ parleys, parley*ing*, parley*ed*

**parliament** *noun* **1** the chief law-making council of a nation **2** *Brit* the House of Commons and the House of Lords □ **parliamentary** *adj*

**parlour** *noun* a sitting room in a house □ **parlourmaid** *noun* a woman or girl whose job is to wait at table

**parochial** *adj* **1** relating to a parish **2** interested only in local affairs; narrow-minded □ **parochially** *adv*

**parody** noun (pl **parodies**) an amusing imitation of someone's writing style, subject matter etc □ verb to make a parody of

**parody** verb ⋄ parodies, parodying, parodied

**parole** noun the release of a prisoner before the end of a sentence on condition that they will have to return if they break the law □ verb to release on parole

From French parole meaning 'word' because prisoners are released on their word of honour

**paroxysm** noun a fit of pain, rage, laughter etc

**parquet** noun a floor covering of wooden blocks arranged in a pattern

**parrot** noun a bird found in warm countries with a hooked bill and often brightly coloured feathers

**parry** verb to deflect, turn aside (a blow, question etc)

**parry** ⋄ parries, parrying, parried

**parse** verb to name the parts of speech of (words in a sentence) and say how the words are connected with each other

**parsimony** noun great care in spending money, meanness □ **parsimonious** adj

**parsley** noun a bright green leafy herb, used in cookery

**parsnip** noun a plant with an edible yellowish root shaped like a carrot

**parson** noun a member of the clergy, esp one in charge of a parish □ **parsonage** noun a parson's house

**part** noun **1** a portion, a share **2** a piece forming part of a whole **3** a character taken by an actor in a play **4** a role in an action or event: played a vital part in the campaign **5** music the notes to be played or sung by a particular instrument or voice □ verb **1** to divide **2** to separate, send or go in different ways **3** to put or keep apart □ **partly** adv in part, or in some parts; not wholly or completely □ **in good part** without being hurt or taking offence □ **part of speech** one of the grammatical groups into which words are divided, eg noun, verb, adj, prep □ **part with** to let go, be separated from □ **take someone's part** to support them in an argument etc

ⓘ From Latin pars meaning 'a part', 'a section' or 'a share'

**partake** verb: **partake of 1** to eat or drink some of something **2** to take a part in

**partake** ⋄ partakes, partaking, partook, partaken

**partial** adj **1** in part only, not total or complete: partial payment **2** having a liking for (someone or something): partial to cheese □ **partiality** noun **1** the favouring of one thing more than another, bias **2** a particular liking (for something) □ **partially** adv

**participate** verb **1** to take part (in) **2** to have a share in □ **participant** noun □ **participation** noun □ **participatory** adj

**participle** noun **1** a form of a verb which can be used with other verbs to form tenses, eg 'he was eating' or 'she has arrived' **2** used as an adjective, eg 'stolen jewels' **3** used as a noun, eg 'running makes me tired'

**particle** noun a very small piece: a particle of sand

**particular** adj **1** relating to a single definite person, thing etc considered separately from others **2** special: take particular care of the china **3** fussy, difficult to please □ noun (**particulars**) the facts or details about someone or something

**parting** noun **1** the act of separating or dividing **2** a place of separation **3** a going away (from each other), a leave-taking **4** a line dividing hair on the head brushed in opposite directions

**partisan** adj giving strong support or loyalty to a particular cause, theory etc, often without considering other points of view □ noun someone with partisan views

**partition** noun 1 a division 2 something which divides, eg a wall between rooms □ verb 1 to divide into parts 2 to divide by making a wall etc

**partner** noun 1 someone who shares the ownership of a business etc with another or others 2 one of a pair in games, dancing etc 3 a husband, wife or lover □ verb to act as someone's partner □ **partnership** noun

**partridge** noun a type of bird which is shot as game

**party** noun (pl **parties**) 1 a gathering of guests 2 a group of people travelling together 3 a number of people with the same plans or ideas: a political party 4 someone taking part in, or approving, an action

**pass** verb 1 to go, move, travel etc: he passed out of sight over the hill 2 to move on or along: pass the salt 3 to go by 4 to overtake 5 of parliament: to put (a law) into force 6 to be successful in an examination 7 to be declared healthy or in good condition after an inspection 8 to come to an end: the feeling of dizziness soon passed 9 to hand on, give: he passed the story on to his son 10 to spend (time) 11 to make, utter (eg a remark) □ noun 1 a narrow passage over or through a range of mountains 2 a ticket or card allowing someone to go somewhere 3 success in an examination 4 a sexual advance □ **passable** adj 1 fairly good of a river etc: able to be crossed □ **passably** adv (adj meaning 1) □ **pass off** to present (a forgery etc) as genuine □ **pass on** 1 to go forward, proceed 2 to hand on 3 to die □ **pass out** to faint

□ **pass up** to fail to take up (an opportunity)

**pass** verb ⇔ **passes, passing, passed**

**passage** noun 1 the act of passing: passage of time 2 a journey in a ship 3 a corridor 4 a way through 5 a part of the text of a book □ **passageway** noun

**passenger** noun a traveller, not a member of the crew, in a train, ship, aeroplane etc

**passer-by** noun (pl **passers-by**) someone who happens to pass by when something happens

**passing** adj 1 going by: a passing car 2 not lasting long: passing interest 3 casual: a passing remark □ noun 1 the act of someone or something which passes 2 a going away, a coming to an end 3 death

**passion** noun strong feeling, esp anger or love □ **the Passion** the sufferings and death of Christ □ **passionate** adj □ **passionately** adv

**passive** adj 1 making no resistance 2 acted upon, not acting □ **passively** adv □ **passivity** noun □ **passive smoking** the involuntary inhaling of smoke from tobacco smoked by others

**Passover** noun a Jewish festival celebrating the exodus of the Israelites from Egypt

**passport** noun a card or booklet which gives someone's name and description, and which is needed to travel in another country

**password** noun 1 a secret word which allows those who know it to pass 2 a word typed into a computer to allow access to restricted data

**past** noun 1 (**the past**) the time gone by 2 someone's previous life or career 3 grammar the past tense □ adj 1 of an earlier time: past kindnesses 2 just over, recently ended: the past year 3 gone, finished: the time for argument is past □ prep 1 after: it's past midday

**2** up to and beyond, further than □ *adv* by: *she walked past the house*

**pasta** *noun* **1** a dough used in making spaghetti, macaroni *etc* **2** the prepared shapes of this, *eg* spaghetti

**paste** *noun* **1** pastry dough **2** a gluey liquid for sticking paper *etc* together **3** any soft, kneadable mixture: *almond paste* **4** fine glass used to make imitation gems

**pastel** *adj* of a colour: soft, pale □ *noun* **1** a chalk-like crayon used for drawing **2** a drawing made with this

**pasteurize** *verb* to heat food (*esp* milk) in order to kill harmful germs in it

Named after Louis *Pasteur*, the 19th-century French chemist who invented the process

**pastille** *noun* a small sweet, sometimes sucked as a medicine

**pastime** *noun* a hobby, a spare-time interest

**pastor** *noun* a member of the clergy □ **pastoral** *adj* **1** relating to country life **2** of a pastor or the work of the clergy

**pastry** *noun* (*pl* **pastries**) **1** a flour paste used to make the bases and crusts of pies, tarts *etc* **2** a small cake

**pasture** *noun* ground covered with grass on which cattle graze

**pasty**[1] (*say* peis-ti) *adj* **1** like paste **2** pale

**pasty**[2] (*say* pas-ti) *noun* a pie containing meat and vegetables in a covering of pastry

**pat** *noun* **1** a light, quick blow or tap with the hand **2** a small lump of butter *etc* **3** a cake of animal dung □ *verb* to strike gently, tap □ **off pat** memorized thoroughly, to be said when necessary

**pat** *verb* ▷ pats, patt*ing*, patt*ed*

**patch** *verb* **1** to mend (clothes) by putting in a new piece of material to cover a hole **2** (**patch something up**) to mend it, *esp* hastily or clumsily **3** (**patch something up**) to settle (a quarrel) □ *noun* (*pl* **patches**) **1** a piece of material sewn on to mend a hole **2** a small piece of ground □ **patchy** *adj* uneven, mixed in quality □ **patchily** *adv* □ **patchwork** *noun* fabric formed of small patches or pieces of material sewn together

**pate** (*say* peit) *noun, formal* the head

**pâté** *noun* a paste made of finely minced meat, fish or vegetable, flavoured with herbs, spices *etc*

**patent** *noun* an official written statement granting someone the sole right to make or sell something that they have invented □ *adj* **1** protected from copying by a patent **2** open, easily seen □ *verb* to obtain a patent for □ **patently** *adv* openly, clearly: *patently obvious* □ **patent leather** leather with a very glossy surface

**paternal** *adj* **1** of a father **2** like a father, fatherly **3** on the father's side of the family: *my paternal grandfather*

**paternalism** *noun* governmental or managerial benevolence taken to the extreme of over-protectiveness and authoritarianism □ **paternalistic** *adj*

**paternity** *noun* the state or fact of being a father □ **paternity leave** leave of absence from work for a father after the birth of a child

**path** *noun* **1** a way made by people or animals walking on it, a track **2** the route to be taken by a person or vehicle: *in the lorry's path* **3** a course of action, a way of life □ **pathway** *noun*

**pathetic** *adj* **1** causing pity **2** causing contempt; feeble, inadequate: *a pathetic attempt* □ **pathetically** *adv*

**pathology** *noun* the study of diseases □ **pathological** *adj* **1** relating to

disease **2** *informal* compulsive, obsessive: *pathological liar*
□ **pathologist** *noun* **1** a doctor who studies the causes and effects of disease **2** a doctor who makes post-mortem examinations

**pathos** (*say* pei-thos) *noun* a quality that arouses pity

**patience** *noun* **1** the ability or willingness to be patient **2** (*also called:* **solitaire**) a card game played by one person

**patient** *adj* suffering delay, discomfort *etc* without complaint or anger □ *noun* someone under the care of a doctor *etc* □ **patiently** *adv*

**patio** (*say* pat-i-oh) *noun* (*pl* **patios**) a paved open yard attached to a house

**patriarch** (*say* pei-tri-ahk) *noun* **1** the male head of a family or tribe **2** the head of the Greek Orthodox Church □ **patriarchal** (*say* pei-tri-ahk-*al*) *adj* □ **patriarchy** (*say* pei-tri-ahk-i) *noun*

**patrician** *adj* aristocratic

**patriot** *noun* someone who loves and is loyal to their country □ **patriotic** *adj* □ **patriotically** *adv* □ **patriotism** *noun*

**patrol** *verb* to keep guard or watch by moving regularly around an area *etc* □ *noun* **1** the act of keeping guard in this way **2** the people keeping watch **3** a small group of Scouts or Guides □ **patrol car** a police car used to patrol an area

**patrol** *verb* ⇔ patrols, patrolling, patrolled

**patron** (*say* peit-ron) *noun* **1** someone who protects or supports (an artist, a form of art *etc*) **2** a customer of a shop *etc* □ **patronage** *noun* the support given by a patron □ **patronize** *verb* **1** to be a patron towards: *patronize your local shops* **2** to treat (someone) as an inferior, look down on: *don't patronize me* □ **patron saint** a saint chosen as the

protector of a country *etc*

**patter**[1] *verb* of rain, footsteps *etc*: to make a quick tapping sound □ *noun* the sound of falling rain, of footsteps *etc*

**patter**[2] *noun* **1** chatter, rapid talk, *esp* that used by salesmen to encourage people to buy their goods **2** the jargon of a particular group

**pattern** *noun* **1** an example suitable to be copied **2** a model or guide for making something **3** a decorative design **4** a sample: *a book of tweed patterns* □ **patterned** *adj* having a design, not self-coloured

**patty** *noun* (*pl* **patties**) a small flat cake of chopped meat *etc*

**paucity** *noun* smallness of number or quantity

**paunch** *noun* (*pl* **paunches**) a fat stomach

**pauper** *noun* a very poor person

**pause** *noun* **1** a short stop, an interval **2** a break or hesitation in speaking or writing **3** *music* a symbol (⌢) showing the holding of a note or rest □ *verb* to stop for a short time

**pave** *verb* to lay (a street) with stone or concrete to form a level surface for walking on □ **pave the way for** to prepare or make the way easy for □ **pavement** *noun* a paved footway at the side of a road for pedestrians

**pavilion** *noun* **1** a building in a sports ground with facilities for changing clothes **2** a large ornamental building **3** a large tent

**paw** *noun* the foot of an animal □ *verb* **1** of an animal: to scrape with one of the front feet: **2** to handle or touch roughly or rudely **3** to strike out wildly with the hand: *paw the air*

**pawn** *verb* to put (an article of some value) in someone's keeping in exchange for a sum of money which, when repaid, buys back the article

□ *noun* **1** *chess* a small piece of the lowest rank **2** someone who lets themselves be used by another for some purpose □ **in pawn** having been pawned □ **pawnbroker** *noun* someone who lends money in exchange for pawned articles □ **pawnshop** *noun* a pawnbroker's place of business

**pay** *verb* **1** to give (money) in exchange for (goods *etc*): *I paid 30 for it* **2** to suffer the punishment (for) **3** to be advantageous or profitable: *it pays to be prepared* **4** to give (eg attention) □ *noun* money given or received for work; wages □ **payable** *adj* requiring to be paid □ **payee** *noun* someone to whom money is paid □ **pay-as-you-earn** *adj* of income tax: deducted from a salary before it is given to the worker □ **payment** *noun* **1** the act of paying **2** money paid for goods *etc* □ **payphone** *noun* a coin-or card-operated public telephone □ **payroll** *noun* a list of people entitled to receive pay □ **payroll** *noun* the money for paying wages □ **pay off** **1** to pay in full and discharge (workers) owing to lack of work **2** to have good results: *his hard work paid off* □ **pay out** **1** to spend **2** to give out (a length of rope *etc*

> **pay** *verb* ⊷ pays, paying, paid

> ▣ (verb, meaning 1) remit, discharge, remunerate, recompense, reimburse; (verb, meaning 2) atone, compensate, answer

**PAYE** *abbrev* pay as you earn

**PC** *abbrev* **1** police constable **2** privy councillor **3** political correctness

**pc** *abbrev* **1** personal computer **2** postcard **3** percent

**PE** *abbrev* physical education

**pea** *noun* **1** a climbing plant which produces round green seeds in pods **2** the seed itself, eaten as a vegetable

**peace** *noun* **1** quietness, calm

**2** freedom from war or disturbance **3** a treaty bringing this about □ **peaceable** *adj* of a quiet nature, fond of peace □ **peaceful** *adj* □ **peacefully** *adv*

**peach** *noun* (*pl* **peaches**) **1** a juicy, velvet-skinned fruit **2** the tree that bears it **3** an orangey-pink colour

**peacock** *noun* a large bird, the male of which has brightly coloured, patterned tail feathers

**peahen** *noun* a female peacock

**peak** *noun* **1** the pointed top of a mountain or hill **2** the highest point **3** the jutting-out part of the brim of a cap □ *verb* **1** to rise to a peak **2** to reach the highest point: *prices peaked in July and then fell steadily* □ **peaked** *adj* **1** pointed **2** of a cap: having a peak □ **peaky** *adj* looking pale and unhealthy

**peal** *noun* **1** a set of bells tuned to each other **2** the changes rung on such bells **3** a succession of loud sounds: *peals of laughter* □ *verb* to sound loudly

> The noun 'appeal' is said to have gradually lost its inital 'a-' to form the word peal.

> ✹ Do not confuse with: **peel**

**peanut** *noun* a type of nut similar to a pea in shape (*also called* **groundnut, monkey-nut**) □ **peanut butter** a paste of ground roasted peanuts, spread on bread *etc*

**pear** *noun* **1** a fruit which narrows towards the stem and bulges at the end **2** the tree that bears it □ **pear-shaped** *adj*

**pearl** *noun* **1** a gem formed in the shell of the oyster and several other shellfish **2** a valuable remark *etc*: *pearls of wisdom* □ **pearly gates** the entrance to heaven

**peasant** *noun* someone who works and lives on the land, *esp* in an underdeveloped area

**peat** *noun* turf cut out of boggy places, dried and used as fuel

**pebble** *noun* a small, roundish stone

**peccadillo** *noun* (*pl* **peccadilloes** or **peccadillos**) a slight misdemeanour or wrong

**peck** *verb* **1** to strike with the beak **2** to pick up with the beak **3** to eat little, nibble (at) **4** to kiss quickly and briefly □ *noun* **1** a sharp blow with the beak **2** a brief kiss □ **peckish** *adj* slightly hungry

**pectoral** *adj* of the breast or chest: *pectoral muscles*

**peculiar** *adj* **1** belonging to one person or thing only: *a custom peculiar to England* **2** strange, odd □ **peculiarity** *noun* (*pl* **peculiarities**) that which marks someone or something off from others in some way; something odd □ **peculiarly** *adv*

**pecuniary** *adj* of money

**pedagogue** *noun* a teacher □ **pedagogic** or **pedagogical** *adj*

**pedal** *noun* **1** a lever worked by the foot on a bicycle, piano, harp *etc* **2** a key worked by the foot on an organ □ *verb* **1** to work the pedals of **2** to ride on a bicycle

**pedal** *verb* �048 pedal**s**, pedal**ling**, pedal**led**

**pedant** *noun* **1** someone who makes a great show of their knowledge **2** someone overly fussy about minor details □ **pedantic** *adj* over-concerned with correctness □ **pedantry** *noun*

**peddle** *verb* to travel from door to door selling goods

**pedestal** *noun* the foot or support of a pillar, statue *etc*

**pedestrian** *adj* **1** going on foot **2** for those on foot **3** unexciting, dull: *a pedestrian account* □ *noun* someone who goes or travels on foot □ **pedestrian crossing** a place where pedestrians may cross the road when the traffic stops

**pediatrics, pediatrician** *US spelling* of **paediatrics, paediatrician**

**pedicure** *noun* a treatment for the feet including treating corns, cutting nails *etc* □ **pedicurist** *noun*

**pedigree** *noun* **1** a list of someone's ancestors **2** the ancestry of a pure-bred animal **3** a distinguished descent or ancestry □ *adj* of an animal: pure-bred, from a long line of ancestors of the same breed

Literally 'crane's foot', because the forked feet of the bird were thought to resemble the lines of a family tree

**pediment** *noun* a triangular structure over the front of an ancient Greek building

**pedlar** *noun* someone who peddles, a hawker

**peek** *verb* to peep, glance, *esp* secretively □ *noun* a secret look

**peel** *verb* **1** to strip off the outer covering or skin of: *peel an apple* **2** of skin, paint *etc*: to come off in small pieces **3** to lose skin in small flakes, *eg* as a result of sunburn □ *noun* skin, rind
  ⊕ From Latin *pelare* meaning 'to deprive of hair'

🖐 Do not confuse with: **peal**

**peep** *verb* **1** to look through a narrow opening, round a corner *etc* **2** to peep slyly or quickly (at) **3** to begin to appear: *the sun peeped out* **4** to make a high, small sound □ *noun* **1** a quick look, a glimpse, often from hiding **2** a high, small sound

**peer** *verb* to look at with half-closed eyes, as if with difficulty □ *noun* **1** someone's equal in rank, merit or age **2** a nobleman of the rank of baron upwards **3** a member of the House of Lords □ **peerage** *noun* **1** a peer's title **2** the peers as a group □ **peerless** *adj* without any equal, better than all others

**peeved** *adj* annoyed

**peevish** *adj* cross, bad-tempered, irritable

**peewit** *noun* the lapwing

**peg** *noun* **1** a pin or stake of wood, metal *etc* **2** a hook fixed to a wall for hanging clothes *etc* □ *verb* **1** to fasten with a peg **2** to fix (prices *etc*) at a certain level

**peg** *verb* ⋄ pegs, pegging, pegged

**pejorative** *adj* showing disapproval, scorn *etc*

**Pekinese** or **Pekingese** *noun* a breed of small dog with a long coat and flat face

**pelican** *noun* a large waterbird with a pouched bill for storing fish □ **pelican crossing** a street-crossing where the lights are operated by pedestrians

Taken from the phrase '*pe*destrian *li*ght *c*ontrolled cross*ing*'

**pellet** **1** a small ball of shot *etc* **2** a small pill

**pell-mell** *adv* in great confusion; headlong

**pelmet** *noun* a strip or band hiding a curtain rail

**pelt** *noun* the untreated skin of an animal □ *verb* **1** to throw (things) at **2** to run fast **3** of rain: to fall heavily □ **at full pelt** at top speed

**pelvis** *noun* the frame of bone which circles the body below the waist

**pen¹** *noun* an instrument with a nib for writing in ink □ *verb* to write (*eg* a letter) □ **pen-friend** *noun* someone you have never seen (usually living abroad) with whom you exchange letters □ **penknife** *noun* a pocket knife with folding blades □ **pen-name** *noun* a name adopted by a writer instead of their own name

**pen** ⋄ pens, penning, penned

**pen²** *noun* a small enclosure for sheep, cattle *etc* □ *verb* to enclose in a pen

**pen³** *noun* a female swan

**penalize** *verb* **1** to punish **2** to put under a disadvantage □ **penal** *adj* of or as punishment

**penalty** *noun* (*pl* penalties)

**1** punishment **2** a disadvantage put on a player or team for having broken a rule of a game

**penance** *noun* punishment willingly suffered by someone to make up for a wrong

**pence** *pl* of **penny**

**penchant** *noun* an inclination (for), a bias

**pencil** *noun* an instrument containing a length of graphite or other substance for writing, drawing *etc* □ *verb* to draw, mark *etc* with a pencil

**pencil** *verb* ⋄ pencils, pencilling, pencilled

**pendant** *noun* **1** an ornament hung from a necklace *etc* **2** a necklace with such an ornament

**pendent** *adj* hanging

**pending** *adj* awaiting a decision or attention □ *prep* awaiting, until the coming of: *pending confirmation*

**pendulous** *adj* hanging down, drooping

**pendulum** *noun* a swinging weight which drives the mechanism of a clock

**penetrate** *verb* **1** to pierce or pass into or through **2** to enter by force □ **penetrating** *adj* **1** of a sound: piercing **2** keen, probing: *penetrating question* □ **penetration** *noun*

**penguin** *noun* a large sea bird of Antarctic regions, which cannot fly

**penicillin** *noun* a medicine obtained from mould, which kills many bacteria

**peninsula** *noun* a piece of land almost surrounded by water □ **peninsular** *adj*

**penis** *noun* the part of the body which a male human or animal uses in sexual intercourse and for urinating

**penitent** *adj* sorry for your sins □ *noun* a penitent person

□ **penitence** noun □ **penitential** adj □ **penitentiary** noun, US a prison

**pennant** noun a long flag coming to a point at the end

**penny** noun **1** a coin worth $\frac{1}{100}$ of £1 **2** (pl **pence**) used to show an amount in pennies: *the newspaper costs thirty pence* **3** (pl **pennies**) used for a number of coins: *I need five pennies for the coffee machine* □ **penniless** adj having no money □ **penny-farthing** noun a old type of bicycle with a large front wheel and small rear wheel □ **penny-pinching** adj mean, stingy

**pension** noun a sum of money paid regularly to a retired person, a widow, someone wounded in war *etc* □ **pension off** to dismiss or allow to retire with a pension □ **pensioner** noun

**pensive** adj thoughtful □ **pensively** adv

**pent** or **pent-up** adj **1** shut up, not allowed to go free **2** of emotions: not freely expressed

**penta-** prefix five
ⓘ From Greek *pente* meaning 'five'

**pentagon** noun a five-sided figure □ **pentagonal** adj

**pentathlon** noun a five-event contest in the Olympic Games *etc*

**Pentecost** noun **1** a Jewish festival held fifty days after Passover **2** a Christian festival held seven weeks after Easter

**penthouse** noun a luxurious flat at the top of a building

**penultimate** adj last but one

**penumbra** noun a light shadow surrounding the main shadow of an eclipse

**penury** noun poverty, want □ **penurious** adj impoverished, penniless

**peony** noun (pl **peonies**) a type of garden plant with large red, white or pink flowers

**people** noun pl **1** the men, women and children of a country or nation **2** persons generally □ verb **1** to fill with people **2** to inhabit, make up the population of
ⓘ From Latin *populus* meaning 'a people' or 'a nation'

**pep** noun, informal spirit, verve □ **pep up** to invigorate, enliven □ **pep talk** a talk meant to encourage or arouse enthusiasm

**pepper** noun **1** a plant whose berries are dried, powdered and used as seasoning **2** the spicy powder it produces **3** a hot-tasting hollow fruit containing many seeds, eaten raw, cooked or pickled □ verb **1** to sprinkle with pepper **2** (**pepper with**) to throw at or hit: *peppered with bullets* □ **peppery** adj **1** containing much pepper **2** inclined to be hot-tempered □ **peppercorn** noun the dried berry of the pepper plant □ **pepper mill** a small device for grinding peppercorns over food □ **peppermint** noun **1** a type of plant with a powerful taste and smell **2** a flavouring taken from this and used in sweets *etc*

**per** prep **1** in, out of **2** for each: *2 per dozen* **3** in each: *six times per week* □ **per annum** in each year □ **per capita** or **per head** for each person □ **per cent** out of every hundred: *five per cent* (= 5 out of every hundred)

**perambulator** full form of **pram**

**perceive** verb **1** to become aware of through the senses **2** to see **3** to understand

**percentage** noun the rate per hundred

**perception** noun the ability to perceive; understanding □ **perceptible** adj □ **perceptive** adj

**perch¹** noun (pl **perches**) **1** a rod on which birds roost **2** a high seat or position □ verb to roost

**perch²** noun (pl **perches**) a type of

freshwater fish

**percolate** verb **1** of a liquid: to drip or drain through small holes **2** to cause (a liquid) to do this **3** of news etc: to pass slowly down or through □ **percolator** noun: a coffee percolator

**percussion** noun **1** a striking of one object against another **2** musical instruments played by striking, eg drums, cymbals etc □ **percussive** adj

**perdition** noun **1** utter loss or ruin **2** everlasting punishment

**peregrinations** noun pl wanderings

**peregrine** noun a type of falcon used in hawking

**peremptory** adj **1** urgent **2** of a command: to be obeyed at once **3** domineering, dictatorial

**perennial** adj **1** lasting through the year **2** everlasting, perpetual **3** of a plant: growing from year to year without replanting or sowing □ noun a perennial plant

**perestroika** (say pe-ris-**troi**-ka) noun reconstruction, restructuring of the state (originally in the former Soviet Union)

**perfect** adj (say **per**-fikt) **1** complete, finished **2** faultless **3** exact □ verb (say pe-**fekt**) **1** to make perfect **2** to finish □ **perfection** noun □ **perfectly** adv □ **perfectionist** noun

**perfidious** (say pe-**fid**-i-us) adj treacherous, unfaithful □ **perfidy** (say **per**-fi-di) noun

**perforate** verb to make a hole or holes through □ **perforated** adj

**perforce** adv, old of necessity, unavoidably

**perform** verb **1** to do, act **2** to act (a part) on the stage **3** to provide entertainment for an audience **4** to play (a piece of music) □ **performance** noun **1** an entertainment in a theatre etc **2** the act of doing something **3** the level of success of a machine, car etc □ **performer** noun

**perfume** noun **1** smell, fragrance **2** a fragrant liquid put on the skin, scent □ verb **1** to put scent on or in **2** to give a sweet smell to □ **perfumery** noun a shop or factory where perfume is sold or made

**perfunctory** adj done carelessly or half-heartedly: perfunctory inspection □ **perfunctorily** adv

**perhaps** adv it may be (that), possibly

**peri-** prefix around: perimeter ⓘ From Greek peri meaning 'around'

**peril** noun a great danger □ **at your peril** at your own risk □ **perilous** adj □ **perilously** adv

**perimeter** noun **1** the outside line enclosing a figure or shape **2** the outer edge of any area ⓘ From Greek peri meaning 'around', and metron meaning 'measure'

◆ Do not confuse with: **parameter**. Notice that words starting with peri- often relate to the idea of 'going around' - and the perimeter of a figure or shape is the line that goes around it.

**period** noun **1** a stretch of time **2** a stage in the earth's development or in history **3** a full stop after a sentence **4** a time of menstruation □ **periodic** adj **1** of a period **2** happening at regular intervals, eg every month or year **3** happening every now and then □ **periodical** adj issued or done at regular intervals; periodic □ noun a magazine which appears at regular intervals

**peripatetic** adj moving from place to place; travelling

**periphery** noun (pl **peripheries**) **1** the line surrounding something **2** an outer boundary or edge □ **peripheral** adj **1** of or on a periphery; away from the centre **2** not essential, of little importance

**periphrastic** adj of speech:

roundabout, using more words than necessary

**periscope** *noun* a tube with mirrors by which a viewer in a submarine *etc* is able to see objects on the surface

**perish** *verb* **1** to be destroyed, pass away completely; die **2** to decay, rot □ **perishable** *adj* liable to go bad quickly

**periwinkle** *noun* **1** a small shellfish, shaped like a small snail, eaten as food when boiled **2** a creeping evergreen plant with a small blue flower

**perjure** *verb* (**perjure yourself** *etc*) to tell a lie when you have sworn to tell the truth, *esp* in a court of law □ **perjurer** *noun* □ **perjury** *noun*

**perk¹** *noun* something of value allowed in addition to payment for work; a side benefit

**perk²** *verb*: **perk up** to recover energy or spirits □ **perky** *adj* jaunty, in good spirits □ **perkily** *adv*

**perm** *noun* short for **permanent wave** □ *verb* to give a permanent wave to (hair)

**permanent** *adj* lasting, not temporary □ **permanence** or **permanency** *noun* the state of continuing or remaining for a long time or for ever □ **permanently** *adv* □ **permanent wave** a wave or curl put into the hair by a special process and usually lasting for some months

**permeate** *verb* **1** to pass into through small holes, soak into **2** to fill every part of □ **permeable** *adj*

**permit** *verb* (*say* pe-mit) **1** to agree to an action, allow **2** to make possible □ *noun* (*say* **per**-mit) a written order, allowing someone to do something: *a fishing permit* □ **permissible** *adj* □ **permission** *noun* freedom given to do something □ **permissive** *adj* **1** allowing something to be done **2** too tolerant □ **permissiveness** *noun*: *the permissiveness of the 1960s*

**permutation** *noun* **1** the arrangement of numbers, letters *etc* in a certain order **2** the act of changing the order of things

**pernicious** *adj* destructive

**pernickety** *adj* fussy about small details

**peroration** *noun* **1** the closing part of a speech **2** a speech

**peroxide** *noun* a chemical (hydrogen peroxide) used for bleaching hair *etc*

**perpendicular** *adj* **1** standing upright, vertical **2** at right angles (to) □ *noun* a line at right angles to another

**perpetrate** *verb* to commit (a sin, error *etc*) □ **perpetration** *noun* □ **perpetrator** *noun*
ⓔ From Latin *perpetrare* meaning 'to achieve'

🔹 Do not confuse with: **perpetuate**

**perpetuate** *verb* to make to last for ever or for a long time □ **perpetual** *adj* everlasting, unending □ **perpetually** *adv* □ **perpetuity** *noun* □ **in perpetuity 1** for ever **2** for the length of someone's life
ⓔ From Latin *perpetuare* meaning 'to cause to continue uninterruptedly'

🔹 Do not confuse with: **perpetrate**

**perplex** *verb* **1** to puzzle, bewilder **2** to make more complicated □ **perplexity** *noun*

**perquisite** *noun* a perk

**persecute** *verb* **1** to harass over a period of time **2** to cause to suffer, *esp* because of religious beliefs □ **persecution** *noun* □ **persecutor** *noun*
ⓔ From Latin *persequi* meaning 'to follow persistently'

🔹 Do not confuse with: **prosecute**

**persevere** *verb* to keep trying to do a thing (in spite of difficulties) □ **perseverance** *noun*

**persist** *verb* **1** to hold fast to (*eg* an

idea) **2** to continue to do something in spite of difficulties **3** to survive, last □ **persistence** noun □ **persistent** adj □ **persistently** adv

**person** noun **1** a human being **2** someone's body: *jewels hidden on his person* □ **personable** adj good-looking □ **in person** personally, not represented by someone else

**persona** noun the outward part of the personality presented to others; social image

**personage** noun a well-known person

**personal** adj **1** your own; private: *personal belongings* **2** of a remark: insulting, offensive to the person it is aimed at □ **personally** adv **1** speaking from your own point of view **2** by your own action, not using an agent or representative: *he thanked me personally* □ **personal organizer** a small loose-leaf filing system containing a diary and an address book, maps, indexes *etc* □ **personal stereo** a small portable cassette player with earphones ⊙ From Latin *persona* meaning 'an actor's mask'

◕▾ Do not confuse with: **personnel**

**personality** noun (pl **personalities**) **1** all of a person's characteristics as seen by others **2** a well-known person

**personify** verb **1** to talk about things, ideas *etc* as if they were living persons (eg 'Time marches on') **2** to typify, be a perfect example of □ **personification** noun

**personify** ⇨ personifies, personifying, personified

**personnel** (say pers-o-nel) noun the people employed in a firm *etc*

◕▾ Do not confuse with: **personal**. **Personnel** is a noun coming from French company terminology, used to describe the 'person-assets' of a company (= the people who work for it) in contrast to its 'material-assets' (= all its non-human items of value).

**perspective** noun **1** a point of view **2** the giving of a sense of depth, distance *etc* in a painting like that in real life □ **in perspective 1** of an object in a painting *etc*: of a size in relation to other things that it would have in real life **2** of an event: in its true degree of importance when considered in relation to other events: *keep things in perspective*

**perspicacious** adj of clear or sharp understanding □ **perspicacity** noun

**perspire** verb to sweat □ **perspiration** noun

**persuade** verb to bring someone to do or think something, by arguing with them or advising them □ **persuasion** noun **1** the act of persuading **2** a firm belief, *esp* a religious belief □ **persuasive** adj

**pert** adj saucy, cheeky

**pertain to** verb to belong, have to do with: *duties pertaining to the job*

**pertinacious** adj holding strongly to an idea, obstinate □ **pertinacity** noun

**pertinent** adj connected with the subject spoken about, to the point

**perturb** verb to disturb greatly; to make anxious or uneasy □ **perturbation** noun

**peruse** verb to read (with care) □ **perusal** noun

**pervade** verb to spread through: *silence pervaded the room*

**perverse** adj obstinate in holding to the wrong point of view; unreasonable □ **perverseness** or **perversity** noun

**pervert** verb **1** to turn away from what is normal or right: *pervert the course of justice* **2** to turn (someone) to crime or evil; corrupt □ noun someone who commits unnatural or perverted acts □ **perversion** noun

**pessimism** *noun* the habit of thinking that things will always turn out badly (*contrasted with:* optimism) □ **pessimist** *noun* □ **pessimistic** *adj* □ **pessimistically** *adv*

**pest** *noun* **1** a troublesome person or thing **2** a creature that is harmful or destructive, *eg* a mosquito □ **pesticide** *noun* any substance which kills animal pests

**pester** *verb* to annoy continually

**pestilence** *noun* a deadly, spreading disease □ **pestilent** or **pestilential** *adj* **1** very unhealthy **2** troublesome

**pestle** *noun* a tool for pounding things to powder in a mortar

**pet** *noun* **1** a tame animal kept in the home, such as a cat **2** a favourite **3** a fit of sulks □ *adj* **1** kept as a pet **2** favourite **3** chief: *my pet hate* □ *verb* to fondle

**pet** *verb* ⇨ **pets, petting, petted**

**petal** *noun* one of the leaf-like parts of a flower

**petard** *noun*: **hoist with your own petard** caught in a trap of your own making

**peter** *verb*: **peter out** to fade or dwindle away to nothing

**petite** *adj* small and neat in appearance

**petition** *noun* a request or note of protest signed by many people and sent to a government or authority □ *verb* to send a petition to □ **petitioner** *noun* **1** a person who petitions **2** a person who applies for a divorce

**petrel** *noun* a small, long-winged sea-bird

**petrify** *verb* **1** to turn into stone **2** to turn (someone) stiff with fear □ **petrifaction** *noun* the process whereby something is turned into stone

**petrify** ⇨ **petrifies, petrifying, petrified**

**petrol** *noun* petroleum when refined as fuel for use in cars *etc*

**petroleum** *noun* oil in its raw, unrefined form, extracted from natural wells below the earth's surface

**petticoat** *noun* an underskirt worn by women

**pettifogger** *noun* a lawyer who deals in trivial cases

**pettish** *adj* sulky

**petty** *adj* of little importance, trivial □ **pettiness** *noun* □ **petty cash** money paid or received in small sums □ **petty officer** a rank of officer in the navy (equal to a non-commissioned officer in the army)

**petulant** *adj* **1** cross, irritable **2** unreasonably impatient □ **petulance** *noun*

**petunia** *noun* a S American flowering plant related to tobacco

**pew** *noun* a seat or bench in a church

**pewter** *noun* a mixture of tin and lead

**PG** *abbrev* parental guidance (certificate awarded to a film denoting possible unsuitability for young children)

**phalanx** *noun* (*pl* **phalanxes**) **1** a company of foot soldiers in an oblong-shaped formation **2** a group of supporters

**phallus** *noun* a representation of a penis □ **phallic** *adj*

**phantasm** *noun* a vision, an illusion

**phantom** *noun* a ghost

**Pharaoh** *noun*, *historical* a ruler of ancient Egypt

**pharmaceutical** *adj* relating to the making up of medicines and drugs

**pharmacy** *noun* (*pl* **pharmacies**) **1** the art of preparing medicines **2** a chemist's shop □ **pharmacist** *noun*

**pharmacology** *noun* the scientific study of drugs and their effects □ **pharmacological** *adj* □ **pharmacologist** *noun*

**pharynx** *noun* the back part of the throat behind the tonsils

**phase** *noun* **1** one in a series of changes in the shape or appearance of something (*eg* the moon) **2** a stage in the development of something (*eg* a war, a scheme *etc*)

**PhD** *abbrev* Doctor of Philosophy

**pheasant** *noun* a bird with brightly-coloured feathers which is shot as game

**phenomenon** *noun* (*pl* phenomena) **1** an event (*esp* in nature) that is observed by the senses: *the phenomenon of lightning* **2** something remarkable or very unusual, a wonder □ **phenomenal** *adj* very unusual, remarkable □ **phenomenally** *adv* extremely: *phenomenally successful*

**phial** *noun* a small glass bottle

**phil-** *see* philo-

**philander** *verb* to flirt, or have casual love affairs, with women □ **philanderer** *noun*

**philanthropy** *noun* love of mankind, often shown by giving money for the benefit of others □ **philanthropic** *adj* □ **philanthropist** *noun*

**philately** *noun* the study and collecting of stamps □ **philatelist** *noun*

**philharmonic** *adj* (in names of orchestras *etc*) music-loving

**philistine** *noun* someone ignorant of, or hostile to, culture and the arts

After a people of ancient Palestine, enemies of the Israelites

**philo-** or **phil-** *prefix* forms words related to the love of a particular thing: *philharmonic/ philosopher* ⓘ From Greek *philos* meaning 'friend', and *phileein* meaning 'to love'

**philology** *noun* the study of words and their history □ **philologist** *noun*

**philosophy** *noun* (*pl* philosophies)

**1** the study of the nature of the universe, or of human behaviour **2** someone's personal view of life □ **philosopher** *noun* □ **philosophic** or **philosophical** *adj* **1** of philosophy **2** calm, not easily upset

**philtre** *noun* a love potion

**phlegm** (*say* flem) *noun* **1** thick slimy matter brought up from the throat by coughing **2** coolness of temper, calmness □ **phlegmatic** (*say* fleg-mat-ik) *adj* not easily excited

**phobia** *noun* an intense, often irrational, fear or dislike ⓘ From Greek *phobos* meaning 'fear'

**phoenix** (*say* fee-niks) *noun* a mythological bird believed to burn itself and to rise again from its ashes

**phone** *noun short for* telephone □ **phonecard** *noun* a card that can be used instead of cash to operate certain public telephones

**phoneme** *noun* the smallest meaningful unit of sound in a language

**phonetics** *noun sing* **1** the study of the sounds of language **2** a system of writing according to sound □ **phonetic** *adj* **1** relating to the sounds of language **2** of a word: spelt according to sound, *eg flem* for 'phlegm'

**phoney** or **phony** *adj, informal* fake, not genuine

**phosphate** *noun* a soil fertilizer containing phosphorus

**phosphorescence** *noun* faint glow of light in the dark □ **phosphorescent** *adj*

**phosphorus** *noun* a wax-like, poisonous substance that gives out light in the dark

**photo** *noun* (*pl* photos) *informal* a photograph

**photo-** *prefix* **1** of or relating to light: *photosensitive* **2** forms words relating to photography: *photocopy* ⓘ From Greek *photos* meaning 'of light'

**photocopy** *noun* a copy of a document made by a device which photographs and develops images of the document □ *verb* to make a photocopy of

**photofit** *noun, trademark* a method of making identification pictures by combining photographs of individual features

**photogenic** *adj* being a good subject for a photograph; photographing well

**photography** *noun* the art of taking pictures with a camera
□ **photograph** *noun* a picture taken with a camera □ *verb* to take a picture with a camera
□ **photographer** *noun*

**photosynthesis** *noun* the conversion of light into complex compounds by plants

**phrase** *noun* 1 a small group of words expressing a single idea, *eg* 'after dinner', 'on the water' 2 a short saying or expression 3 *music* a short group of bars forming a distinct unit □ *verb* to express in words

**phraseology** (*say* freiz-i-**ol**-oj-i) *noun* someone's personal choice of words and phrases

**physical** *adj* 1 relating to the body 2 relating to things that can be seen or felt □ **physically** *adv*

**physician** *noun* a doctor specializing in medical rather than surgical treatment

**physics** *noun sing* the science which includes the study of heat, light, sound, electricity, magnetism *etc* □ **physicist** *noun*

**physiognomy** *noun* the features or expression of the face

**physiology** *noun* the study of the way in which living bodies work, including blood circulation, food digestion *etc* □ **physiological** *adj* □ **physiologist** *noun*

**physiotherapy** *noun* the treatment of

disease by bodily exercise, massage *etc* rather than by drugs
□ **physiotherapist** *noun*

**physique** *noun* 1 the build of someone's body 2 bodily strength

**piano** *noun* (*pl* **pianos**) a large musical instrument played by striking keys □ **pianist** *noun*

**piccolo** *noun* (*pl* **piccolos**) a small, high-pitched flute

**pick** *verb* 1 to choose 2 to pluck, gather (flowers, fruit *etc*) 3 to peck, bite, nibble (at) 4 to poke, probe (teeth *etc*) 5 to open (a lock) with a tool other than a key □ *noun* 1 choice: *take your pick* 2 the best or best part 3 a pickaxe 4 an instrument for picking, *eg* a toothpick □ **pick a quarrel** to start a quarrel deliberately □ **pick on** 1 to single out for criticism *etc* 2 to nag at □ **pick up** 1 to lift up 2 to learn (a language, habit *etc*) 3 to give (someone) a lift in a car 4 to find or get by chance 5 to improve, gain strength

**pickaxe** *noun* a heavy tool for breaking ground, pointed at one end or both ends

**picket** *noun* 1 a pointed stake 2 a small sentry-post or guard 3 a number of workers on strike who prevent others from going into work □ *verb* 1 to fasten (a horse *etc*) to a stake 2 to place a guard or a group of strikers at (a place)

**pickle** *noun* 1 a liquid in which food is preserved 2 vegetables preserved in vinegar 3 *informal* an awkward, unpleasant situation □ *verb* to preserve with salt, vinegar *etc*

**pickpocket** *noun* someone who robs people's pockets or handbags

**picky** *adj* choosy, fussy

**picnic** *noun* a meal eaten out-of-doors, often during an outing *etc* □ *verb* to have a picnic

**picnic** *verb* ⇔ picnics, picnic*king*, picnic*ked*

**pictorial** *adj* 1 having pictures 2 consisting of pictures 3 calling up pictures in the mind

**picture** *noun* 1 a painting or drawing 2 a portrait 3 a photograph 4 a film 5 (**the pictures**) the cinema 6 a vivid description □ *verb* 1 to make a picture of 2 to see in the mind, imagine □ **picturesque** *adj* such as would make a good or striking picture; pretty, colourful

**pidgin** *noun* a distorted form of a language arising because of its combination with a different language

Pidgin is a distorted form of the word 'business', originally used in Chinese.

🔊 Do not confuse with: **pigeon**

**pie** *noun* meat, fruit or other food baked in a casing or covering of pastry

**piebald** *adj* white and black in patches

**piece** *noun* 1 a part or portion of anything 2 a single article or example 3 an artistic work 4 a coin 5 a man in chess, draughts *etc* □ *verb* to put (together) □ **piecemeal** *adv* by pieces, little by little

**pièce de résistance** (*say* pyes de rei-zis-tons) the best item or work

**pied** *adj* with two or more colours in patches

**pier** *noun* 1 a platform stretching from the shore into the sea as a landing place for ships 2 a pillar supporting an arch, bridge *etc*

**pierce** *verb* to make a hole through; force a way into; move (the feelings) deeply □ **piercing** *adj* shrill, loud; sharp

**piety** *noun* the quality of being pious

**piffle** *noun* nonsense

**pig** *noun* 1 a farm animal, from whose flesh ham and bacon are made 2 an oblong moulded piece of metal (*eg* pig-iron) □ **piggy-back**

*noun* a ride on someone's back with your arms round their neck □ **piggy-bank** *noun* a china pig with a slit along its back to insert coins for saving □ **pig-headed** *adj* stubborn □ **pigsty** *noun* (*pl* **pigsties**) a place where pigs are kept □ **pigtail** *noun* hair formed into a plait

**pigeon** *noun* a bird of the dove family □ **pigeon-hole** *noun* a small division in a case or desk for papers *etc* □ *verb* 1 to lay aside 2 to classify, put into a category

  ⓖ From Latin *pipire* meaning 'to cheep'

🔊 Do not confuse with: **pidgin**

**pigment** *noun* 1 paint or other substance used for colouring 2 a substance in animals and plants that gives colour to the skin *etc* □ **pigmentation** *noun*

**pigmy** *another spelling of* **pygmy**

**pike** *noun* 1 a freshwater fish 2 a weapon like a spear, with a long shaft and a sharp head

**pilchard** *noun* a small sea-fish like a herring, often tinned

**pile** *noun* 1 a number of things lying one on top of another, a heap 2 a great quantity 3 a large building 4 a large stake or pillar driven into the earth as a foundation for a building, bridge *etc* 5 the thick, soft surface on carpets and on cloth such as velvet □ *verb* (often **pile up** or **pile something up**) to make or form a pile or heap

**pilfer** *verb* to steal small things

**pilgrim** *noun* a traveller to a holy place □ **pilgrimage** *noun*

**pill** *noun* 1 a tablet of medicine 2 (often **the pill**) a contraceptive in the form of a small tablet taken by mouth

**pillage** *verb* to seize goods and money, *esp* as loot in war □ *noun* the act of plundering in this way

**pillar** *noun* 1 an upright support for roofs, arches *etc* 2 an upright post

or column as a monument
**3** someone or something that gives support: *a pillar of the community* □ **pillarbox** *noun* a tall box with a slot through which letters *etc* are posted

**pillion** *noun* a seat for a passenger on a motor-cycle

**pillory** *noun* (*pl* **pillories**) *historical* a wooden frame fitted over the head and hands of wrongdoers as a punishment □ *verb* to mock in public

**pillory** *verb* ⊳ **pillories, pillorying, pilloried**

**pillow** *noun* a soft cushion for the head □ *verb* to rest or support on a pillow □ **pillowcase** or **pillowslip** *noun*

**pilot** *noun* **1** someone who steers a ship in or out of a harbour **2** someone who flies an aeroplane **3** a guide, a leader □ *verb* to steer, guide □ **pilot-light** *noun* **1** a small gas-light from which larger jets are lit **2** an electric light showing that a current is switched on

**pimp** *noun* a man who manages prostitutes and takes money from them

**pimpernel** *noun* a plant of the primrose family, with small pink or scarlet flowers

**pimple** *noun* a small round infected swelling on the skin □ **pimpled** or **pimply** *adj*

**pin** *noun* **1** a short pointed piece of metal with a small round head, used for fastening fabric **2** a wooden or metal peg **3** a skittle □ *verb* **1** to fasten with a pin **2** to hold fast, pressed against something: *he was pinned to the ground*

**pin** *verb* ⊳ **pins, pinning, pinned**

**pinafore** *noun* **1** an apron to protect the front of a dress **2** a sleeveless dress worn over a jersey, blouse *etc*

**pinball** *noun* a game played on a slot-machine in which a ball runs down a

sloping board between obstacles

**pincers** *noun pl* **1** a tool like pliers, but with sharp points for gripping, pulling out nails *etc* **2** the claw of a crab or lobster

**pinch** *verb* **1** to squeeze (*esp* flesh) between the thumb and forefinger, nip **2** to grip tightly, hurt by tightness **3** *informal* to steal □ *noun* (*pl* **pinches**) **1** a squeeze, a nip **2** a small amount (*eg* of salt) □ **pinched** *adj* of a face: looking cold, pale or thin □ **at a pinch** if really necessary or urgent □ **feel the pinch** to suffer from lack of mone

**pine** *noun* **1** an evergreen tree with needle-like leaves which produces cones **2** the soft wood of such a tree used for furniture *etc* □ *verb* **1** to waste away, lose strength **2** to long (for something)

**pineapple** *noun* a large tropical fruit shaped like a pine-cone

**ping** *noun* a whistling sound such as that of a bullet □ *verb* to make a brief high-pitched sound

**ping-pong** *noun, trademark* table-tennis

**pinion** *noun* **1** a bird's wing **2** a small toothed wheel □ *verb* **1** to hold (someone) fast by binding or holding their arms **2** to cut or fasten the wings of (a bird)

**pink** *noun* **1** a pale red colour **2** a sweet-scented garden flower like a carnation **3** a healthy or good state: *feeling in the pink* □ *verb* **1** of an engine: to make a faint clinking noise **2** to cut (cloth *etc*) with pinking scissors

**pinkie** *noun, informal* the little finger

**pinking scissors** or **pinking shears** scissors with blades which give cloth a zig-zag edge

**pinnacle** *noun* **1** a slender spire or turret **2** a high pointed rock or mountain **3** the highest point

**pint** *noun* a liquid measure equal to just over $\frac{1}{2}$ litre

**pioneer** noun **1** an explorer **2** an inventor, or an early exponent of somethin □ verb to act as a pioneer

**pious** adj respectful in religious matters

**pip** noun **1** a seed of a fruit **2** a spot or symbol on dice or cards **3** a short bleep as part of a time signal etc on the radio or telephone

**pipe** noun **1** a tube for carrying water, gas etc **2** a tube with a bowl at the end, for smoking tobacco **3** (**pipes**) a musical instrument made of several small pipes joined together **4** (**pipes**) bagpipes □ verb **1** to play (notes, a tune) on a pipe or pipes **2** to whistle, chirp **3** to speak in a shrill high voice **4** to convey (eg water) by pipe □ **piper** noun someone who plays a pipe, esp the bagpipes □ **pipeline** noun a long line of pipes, eg to carry oil from an oil-field □ **in the pipeline** in preparation, soon to become available □ **pipe down** to become silent, stop talking □ **pipe up** to speak up, express an opinion

**pipette** noun a small glass tube used in laboratories

**piping** adj high-pitched, shrill □ noun **1** a length of tubing **2** a system of pipes **3** a narrow ornamental cord for trimming clothes **4** a strip of decorative icing round a cake □ **piping hot** very hot

**pippin** noun a kind of apple

**piquant** (say peek-ant) adj **1** sharp-tasting, spicy **2** arousing interest

**pique** (say peek) noun anger caused by wounded pride, spite, resentment □ verb **1** to wound the pride of **2** to arouse (curiosity)

**piranha** noun a S American river-fish which eats flesh

**pirate** noun **1** someone who robs ships at sea **2** someone who steals or plagiarizes another's work □ **piracy** noun **1** the activity of pirates **2** unauthorized publication or reproduction of copyright material □ **piratical** adj

**pirouette** noun a rapid whirling on the toes in dancing □ verb to twirl in a pirouette

**pistachio** noun (pl **pistachios**) a greenish nut, often used as a flavouring

**pistil** noun the seed-bearing part of a flower

**pistol** noun a small gun held in the hand

**piston** noun a round piece of metal that moves up and down inside a cylinder, eg in an engine

**pit** noun **1** a hole in the ground **2** a place from which coal and other minerals are dug **3** the ground floor of a theatre behind the stalls **4** (often **pits**) a place beside the racecourse for repairing and refuelling racing cars etc □ verb to set one thing or person against another: pitting my wits against his □ **pitted** adj marked with small holes

**pit** verb ⇨ pits, pitting, pitted

**pitch** verb **1** to fix a tent etc in the ground **2** to throw **3** to fall heavily; lurch: pitch forward **4** to set the level or key of a tune □ noun (pl **pitches**) **1** a thick dark substance obtained by boiling down tar **2** a throw **3** an attempt at selling or persuading: sales pitch **4** the height or depth of a note **5** a peak, an extreme point: reach fever pitch **6** the field for certain sports **7** cricket the ground between wickets **8** the slope of a roof etc **9** the spot reserved for a street seller or street-entertainer □ **pitch-dark** adj very dark □ **pitched battle** a battle on chosen ground between sides arranged in position beforehand □ **pitchfork** noun a fork for lifting and throwing hay □ verb to throw suddenly and violently

**pitchblende** noun a black mineral made up of uranium oxides

**pitcher** noun a kind of large jug

**pitfall** noun a trap, a possible danger

**pith** noun 1 the soft substance in the centre of plant stems 2 the white substance under the rind of an orange, lemon etc 3 the important part of anything □ **pithy** adj 1 full of pith 2 full of meaning, to the point: a pithy saying

**pittance** noun a very small wage or allowance

**pity** noun 1 feeling for the sufferings of others, sympathy 2 a cause of grief 3 a regrettable fact □ verb to feel sorry for □ **piteous** or **pitiable** adj □ **pitiful** adj poor, wretched

**pity** verb ⋄ pities, pitying, pitied

**pivot** noun 1 the pin or centre on which anything turns 2 something or someone greatly depended on □ verb 1 to turn on a pivot 2 to depend (on) □ **pivotal** adj 1 acting as a pivot 2 crucially important; critical

**pixie** noun (pl pixies) a kind of fairy

**pizza** noun a flat piece of dough spread with tomato, cheese etc and baked

**pizzicato** adv, music played by plucking the strings rather than bowing

**placard** noun a printed notice (as an advertisement etc) placed on a wall etc

**placate** verb to calm, soothe, make less angry etc

**place** noun 1 a physical location; any area or building 2 a particular spot 3 an open space in a town: market place 4 a seat in a theatre, train, at a table etc 5 a position in football etc 6 a position on a course, in a job etc 7 rank □ verb 1 to put in a particular place 2 to find a place for 3 to give (an order for goods etc) 4 to remember who someone is: I can't place him at all □ **placed** adj 1 having a place 2 among the first three in a competition □ **in place**

1 in the proper position 2 suitable □ **in place of** instead of □ **out of place** 1 not in the proper position 2 unsuitable

**place** verb ⋄ places, placing, placed

ⓘ From Latin platea meaning 'a street'

**placenta** noun a part of the womb that connects an unborn mammal to its mother, shed at birth

**placid** adj calm, not easily disturbed □ **placidity** noun

**plagiarize** verb to steal or borrow from the writings or ideas of someone else without permission □ **plagiarism** noun □ **plagiarist** noun

**plague** noun 1 a fatal infectious disease carried by rat fleas 2 a great and troublesome quantity: a plague of flies □ verb to pester or annoy continually

**plaice** noun a type of edible flatfish

**plaid** noun a long piece of cloth (esp tartan) worn over the shoulder

**plain** adj 1 flat, level 2 simple, ordinary 3 without ornament or decoration 4 clear, easy to see or understand 5 not good-looking, not attractive □ noun a level stretch of land □ **plain-clothes** adj of a police detective: wearing ordinary clothes, not uniform

**plaintiff** noun someone who takes action against another in the law courts

**plaintive** adj sad, sorrowful

**plait** noun 1 a length of hair arranged by intertwining three or more separate pieces 2 threads etc intertwined in this way □ verb to form into a plait

**plan** noun 1 a diagram of a building, town etc as if seen from above 2 a scheme or arrangement to do something □ verb 1 to make a sketch or plan of 2 to decide or arrange to do (something)

**plan** verb ⋄ plans, planning, planned

**plane¹** *short for* **aeroplane**

**plane²** *noun* **1** a level surface **2** a carpentry tool for smoothing wood **3** a standard (of achievement *etc*) □ *adj* flat, level □ *verb* **1** to smooth with a plane **2** to glide over water *etc*

**plane³** *noun* a type of tree with broad leaves

**planet** *noun* any of the bodies (*eg* the earth, Venus) which move round the sun or round another fixed star □ **planetary** *adj*

**plank** *noun* a long, flat piece of timber

**plankton** *noun* tiny living creatures floating in seas, lakes *etc*

**plant** *noun* **1** a living growth from the ground, with a stem, root and leaves **2** a factory or machinery □ *verb* **1** to put (something) into the ground so that it will grow **2** to put (an idea) into the mind **3** to put in position: *plant a bomb* **4** to set down firmly **5** *informal* to place (something) as false evidence

**plantation** *noun* **1** an area planted with trees **2** an estate for growing cotton, sugar, rubber, tobacco *etc*

**planter** *noun* the owner of a plantation

**plaque** *noun* **1** a decorative plate of metal, china *etc* for fixing to a wall **2** a film of saliva and bacteria which forms on the teeth

**plasma** *noun* the liquid part of blood and certain other fluids

**plaster** *noun* **1** a mixture of lime, water and sand which sets hard, for covering walls *etc* **2** (*also called* **plaster of Paris**) a fine mixture containing gypsum used for moulding, making casts for broken limbs *etc* **3** a small dressing which can be stuck over a wound □ *adj* made of plaster □ *verb* **1** to apply plaster to **2** to cover too thickly (with) □ **plasterer** *noun*

**plastic** *adj* **1** easily moulded or

shaped **2** made of plastic □ *noun* a chemically manufactured substance that can be moulded when soft, formed into fibres *etc* □ **plasticity** *noun* □ **plastic surgery** an operation to repair or replace damaged areas of skin, or to improve the appearance of a facial feature

**plate** *noun* **1** a shallow dish for holding food **2** a flat piece of metal, glass, china *etc* **3** gold and silver articles **4** a sheet of metal used in printing **5** a book illustration **6** the part of false teeth that fits to the mouth □ *verb* to cover with a coating of metal

**plateau** *noun* (*pl* **plateaus** or **plateaux**) **1** a broad level stretch of high land **2** a steady, unchanging state: *prices have now reached a plateau*

**platform** *noun* **1** a raised level surface for passengers at a railway station **2** a raised floor for speakers, entertainers *etc*

**platinum** *noun* a heavy and very valuable steel-grey metal

**platitude** *noun* a dull, ordinary remark made as if it were important

**platonic** *adj* of a relationship: not sexual

Although originally an adjective describing anything related to the Greek philosopher Plato, platonic is now most commonly used with the above meaning based on a Renaissance interpretation of his theory.

**platoon** *noun* a section of a company of soldiers

**platter** *noun* a large, flat plate

**platypus** *noun* (*pl* **platypuses**) a small water animal of Australia that has webbed feet and lays eggs (*also called* **duck-billed platypus**)

**plaudits** *noun pl* applause, praise

**plausible** *adj* **1** seeming to be truthful or honest **2** seeming probable or reasonable

□ **plausibility** *noun*

**play** *verb* 1 to amuse yourself 2 to take part in a game 3 to gamble 4 to act (on a stage *etc*) 5 to perform on (a musical instrument) 6 to carry out (a trick) 7 to trifle or fiddle (with) □ *noun* 1 amusement, recreation 2 gambling 3 a story for acting, a drama 4 a way of behaving: *foul play* 5 freedom of movement □ **player** *noun* 1 an actor 2 someone who plays a game, musical instrument *etc*: *a lute player* □ **playful** *adj* 1 wanting to play: *a playful kitten* 2 fond of joking, not serious □ **playfully** *adv* □ **playground** *noun* an open area for playing at school, in a park *etc* □ **playgroup** *noun* a group of young children who play together supervised by adults □ **playing-card** *noun* one of a pack of cards used in playing card games □ **playmate** *noun* a friend with whom you play □ **play-off** *noun* 1 a game to decide a tie 2 a game between the winners of other competitions □ **playschool** *noun* a nursery school or playgroup □ **plaything** *noun* a toy □ **playwright** *noun* a writer of plays □ **play at** to treat in a light-hearted, not serious way: *he only plays at being a businessman* □ **play off** to set off (one person) against another to gain some advantage for yourself □ **play on** to make use of (someone's feelings) to turn to your own advantage □ **a play on words** a pun □ **play the game** to act fairly and honestly
⊚ From Old English verb *plegian*, and noun *plega*

**PLC** *abbrev* public limited company

**plea** *noun* 1 an excuse 2 an accused person's answer to a charge in a law-court 3 an urgent request

**plead** *verb* 1 to state your case in a lawcourt 2 (**plead with someone**) to beg earnestly 3 to give as an excuse □ **plead guilty** or **not guilty**
to admit or deny guilt in a law court

**pleasant** *adj* giving pleasure; agreeable □ **pleasantry** *noun* (*pl* **pleasantries**) a good-humoured joke

**please** *verb* 1 to give pleasure or delight to 2 to satisfy 3 to choose, like (to do): *do as you please* □ *exclamation* added for politeness to a command or request: *please keep off the grass* □ **if you please** please

**pleasure** *noun* 1 enjoyment, joy, delight 2 what you wish: *what is your pleasure?* □ **at your pleasure** when or if you please □ **pleasurable** *adj* delightful, pleasant

**pleat** *noun* a fold in cloth, which has been pressed or stitched down □ *verb* to put pleats in □ **pleated** *adj*

**pleb** *noun, informal* someone of no taste or culture, a boor

**plebeian** *adj* 1 of the ordinary or common people 2 vulgar, lacking culture or taste

**plebiscite** *noun* a vote by everyone in an area on a special issue, for or against

**plectrum** *noun* a small piece of horn, metal *etc* used for plucking the strings of a guitar

**pledge** *noun* 1 something handed over as security for a loan 2 a solemn promise □ *verb* 1 to give as security, pawn 2 to promise solemnly: *pledged himself to carry out the plan* 3 to drink to the health of, toast

**plenary** *adj* full, complete

**plenty** *noun* 1 a full supply, as much as is needed 2 a large number or quantity (of) □ **plenteous** or **plentiful** *adj*

**plethora** *noun* too large a quantity of anything

**pleurisy** *noun* an illness in which the covering of the lungs becomes inflamed

**pliable** *adj* **1** easily bent or folded **2** easily persuaded □ **pliant** *adj*

**pliers** *noun pl* a tool used for gripping, bending and cutting wire *etc*

**plight** *noun* a bad state or situation □ *verb*, *old* to promise solemnly, pledge

**plimsoll** *noun* a light rubber-soled canvas shoe for sports

**Plimsoll line** a ship's loadline

**plinth** *noun* **1** the square slab at the foot of a column **2** the base or pedestal of a statue, vase *etc*

**PLO** *abbrev* Palestine Liberation Organization

**plod** *verb* **1** to travel slowly and steadily **2** to work on steadily □ **plodder** *noun* a dull but hardworking person

**plod** ⬦ plod*s*, plodd*ing*, plodd*ed*

**plop** *noun* the sound made by a small object falling into water □ *verb* to make this sound

**plop** *verb* ⬦ plop*s*, plopp*ing*, plopp*ed*

**plot** *noun* **1** a small piece of ground **2** a plan for an illegal or malicious action **3** the story of a play, novel *etc* □ *verb* **1** to plan secretly **2** to make a chart, graph *etc* of **3** to mark points on one of these

**plot** *verb* ⬦ plot*s*, plott*ing*, plott*ed*

**plough** *noun* a farm tool for turning up the soil **1** to turn up the ground in furrows **2** to work through slowly □ **ploughshare** *noun* the blade of a plough □ **the Plough** a group of seven stars forming a shape like an old plough

**plover** (*say* pluv-er) *noun* any of several kinds of bird that nest on the ground in open country

**ploy** *noun* an activity, an escapade

**pluck** *verb* **1** to pull out or off **2** to pick (flowers, fruit *etc*) **3** to strip off the feathers of (a bird) before cooking □ *noun* courage, spirit □ **plucky** *adj* brave, determined

□ **pluck up courage** to prepare yourself to face a danger or difficult

**plug** *noun* **1** an object fitted into a hole to stop it up **2** a fitting on an appliance put into a socket to connect with an electric current **3** *informal* a brief advertisement □ *verb* **1** to stop up with a plug **2** *informal* to advertise, publicize

**plug** ⬦ plug*s*, plugg*ing*, plugg*ed*

**plum** *noun* **1** a soft fruit, often dark red or purple, with a stone in the centre **2** the tree that produces this fruit □ *adj* very good, very profitable *etc*: *a plum job*

**plumage** (*say* ploo-mij) *noun* the feathers of a bird
   ⊙ From French *plume* meaning 'feather'

**plumb** *noun* a lead weight hung on a string (**plumbline**), used to test if a wall has been built straight up □ *adj* & *adv* standing straight up, vertical □ *verb* to test the depth of (the sea *etc*)

**plumber** *noun* someone who fits and mends water, gas and sewage pipes □ **plumbing** *noun* **1** the work of a plumber **2** the drainage and water systems of a building *etc*

**plume** *noun* **1** a feather, *esp* an ornamental one **2** something looking like a feather: *a plume of smoke*

**plummet** *noun* a weight of lead hung on a line, for taking depths at sea □ *verb* to plunge

**plump** *adj* fat, rounded, well filled out □ *verb* **1** to grow fat, swell **2** to beat or shake (cushions *etc*) back into shape **3** to sit or sink down heavily **4** (**plump for something**) to choose, vote for it

**plunder** *verb* to carry off goods by force, loot, rob □ *noun* goods seized by force

**plunge** *verb* **1** to dive (into water *etc*) **2** to rush or lurch forward **3** to thrust suddenly (into) □ *noun* a thrust; a dive

**plural** *adj* more than one □ *noun, grammar* the form which shows more than one, *eg* mice is the plural of *mouse* □ **plurality** *noun*

**plus** *prep* used to show addition and represented by the sign (+): *five plus two equals seven* □ *adj* of a quantity more than zero □ *adv, informal* and a bit extra: *she earns £20 000 plus*

**plus fours** *noun pl* baggy trousers reaching to just below the knees

So called from the four additional inches of cloth needed for their length

**plush** *noun* cloth with a soft velvety surface on one side □ *adj* luxurious

**plutocrat** *noun* someone who is powerful because of their wealth

**ply** *verb* 1 to work at steadily 2 to make regular journeys: *the ferry plies between Oban and Mull* 3 to use (a tool) energetically 4 to keep supplying with (food, questions to answer *etc*) □ **plywood** *noun* a board made up of thin sheets of wood glued together □ **two-** or **three-** *etc* ply having two or three *etc* layers or strands

ply ⇔ plies, plying, plied

**PM** *abbrev* prime minister

**pm** *abbrev* after noon (from Latin *post meridiem*)

**pneumatic** (*say* nyoo-**mat**-ik) *adj* 1 filled with air 2 worked by air: *pneumatic drill*
ⓘ From Greek *pneuma* meaning 'breath'

**pneumonia** (*say* nyoo-**moh**-ni-*a*) *noun* a disease in which the lungs become inflamed
ⓘ From Greek *pneumon* meaning 'lung'

**PO** *abbrev* 1 post office 2 postal order

**poach** *verb* 1 to cook gently in boiling water or stock 2 to catch fish or hunt game illegally

□ **poacher** *noun*

**pocket** *noun* 1 a small pouch or bag, *esp* as part of a garment 2 a personal supply of money: *well beyond my pocket* 3 a small isolated area: *a pocket of unemployment* □ *verb* 1 to put in a pocket 2 to steal □ **pocket-book** *noun* a wallet □ **pocket money** an allowance of money for personal spending □ **in** or **out of pocket** having gained or lost money on a deal *etc*

**pod** *noun* a long seed-case of the pea, bean *etc* □ *verb* 1 to remove from a pod 2 to form pods

pod *verb* ⇔ pods, podding, podded

**podgy** *adj* short and fat

**podium** *noun* a low pedestal, a platform

**poem** *noun* a piece of imaginative writing set out in lines which often have a regular rhythm or rhyme □ **poet** *noun* □ **poetic** *adj* □ **poetically** *adv* □ **poetry** *noun* 1 the art of writing poems 2 poems

**po-faced** *adj* stupidly solemn, humourless

**pogrom** *noun* an organized killing or massacre of a group of people

**poignant** *adj* 1 sharp, keen 2 very painful or moving; pathetic □ **poignancy** *noun*

**point** *noun* 1 a sharp end of anything 2 a headland 3 a dot: *decimal point* 4 a full stop in punctuation 5 an exact place or spot 6 an exact moment of time 7 the chief matter of an argument 8 the meaning of a joke 9 a mark in a competition 10 a purpose, an advantage: *there is no point in going* 11 a movable rail to direct a railway engine from one line to another 12 an electrical wall socket 13 a mark of character: *he has many good points* □ *verb* 1 to make pointed: *point your toes* 2 to direct, aim 3 to indicate with a gesture 4 to fill (wall joints) with mortar □ **pointed** *adj* 1 having a point, sharp 2 of a remark: obviously aimed at someone □ **pointer** noun 1 a rod for pointing 2 a type of dog used to show where game has fallen after it has been shot □ **pointless** adj having no meaning or purpose □ **point-blank** adj 1 of a shot: fired from very close range 2 of a question: direct ⊙ From French point meaning 'dot' or 'stitch', and pointe meaning 'sharp point'

**poise** verb 1 to balance, keep steady 2 to hover in the air □ noun 1 a state of balance 2 dignity, self-confidence □ **poised** adj 1 balanced, having poise 2 prepared, ready

**poison** noun 1 a substance which, when taken into the body, kills or harms 2 anything harmful □ verb 1 to kill or harm with poison 2 to add poison to 3 to make bitter or bad: poisoned her mind □ **poisonous** adj □ **poison pen** a writer of malicious anonymous letters

**poke** verb 1 to push (eg a finger or stick) into something 2 to prod, thrust at 3 to search about inquisitively □ noun 1 a nudge, a prod 2 a prying search □ **poker** noun 1 a rod for stirring up a fire 2 a card game in which players bet on their chance of winning □ **poky** adj cramped and shabby

**polaroid** noun, trademark 1 a plastic through which light is seen less brightly 2 (**polaroids**) sunglasses 3 a camera that develops individual pictures in a few seconds

**pole** noun 1 a long rounded rod or post 2 the north or south end of the earth's axis (**the north** or **south pole**) 3 either of the opposing points of a magnet or electric battery □ **polar** adj of the regions round the north or south poles □ **polarity** noun the state of having two opposite poles □ **polarize** verb 1 to give polarity to 2 to split into opposing sides □ **pole-star** noun the

star most directly above the north pole □ **pole vault** a sport in which an athlete jumps over a bar with the aid of a flexible pole

**polecat** noun 1 a large kind of weasel 2 US a skunk

**police** noun the body of men and women whose work it is to see that laws are obeyed etc □ verb to keep law and order in (a place) by use of police □ **policeman**, **policewoman** noun a police officer □ **police station** the headquarters of the police in a district

**policy** noun (pl **policies**) 1 an agreed course of action 2 a written agreement with an insurance company

**polio** short for **poliomyelitis**

**poliomyelitis** noun a disease of the spinal cord, causing weakness or paralysis of the muscles

**polish** verb 1 to make smooth and shiny by rubbing 2 to improve (a piece of writing etc) 3 to make more polite □ noun 1 a gloss on a surface 2 a substance used for polishing 3 fine manners, style etc

**polite** adj having good manners, courteous □ **politely** adv

**politic** adj wise, cautious

**politics** noun sing the art or study of government □ **political** adj of government, politicians or politics □ **politician** noun someone involved in politics, esp a member of parliament □ **politicize** verb to make aware of political issues

**polka** noun a lively dance or the music for it

**poll** noun 1 a counting of voters at an election 2 total number of votes 3 (also called **opinion poll**) a test of public opinion by questioning □ verb 1 to cut or clip off (hair, branches etc) 2 to receive (votes) □ **polling station** a place where voting is done □ **poll tax** Brit the community charge

**pollard** *noun* a tree with its top cut off to allow new growth □ *verb* to cut the top off (a tree)

**pollen** *noun* the fertilizing powder of flowers

**pollinate** *verb* to fertilize with pollen □ **pollination** *noun*

**pollute** *verb* **1** to make dirty or impure **2** to make (the environment) harmful to life □ **pollutant** *noun* something that pollutes □ **pollution** *noun*

**polo** *noun* a game like hockey played on horseback □ **polo neck 1** a close-fitting neck with a part turned over at the top **2** a jumper with a neck like this

**poltergeist** *noun* a kind of ghost believed to move furniture and throw objects around a room (literally, 'a ghost which makes a racket')

**poly-** *prefix* **1** many, much: *polygon* **2** *chemistry* a polymer of: *polystyrene* (= a polymer of styrene)
ⓘ From Greek *polys* meaning 'much'

**polyanthus** *noun* a hybrid plant which produces many flowers

**polyester** *noun* a synthetic material often used in clothing

**polygamy** *noun* the fact of having more than one wife or husband at the same time □ **polygamist** *noun* □ **polygamous** *adj*

**polyglot** *adj* speaking, or written in, many languages □ *noun* someone fluent in many languages

**polygon** *noun* a figure with many angles and sides □ **polygonal** *adj*

**polymer** *noun* a chemical compound with large molecules

**polyp** *noun* **1** a small sea-animal with arms or tentacles **2** a kind of tumour

**polystyrene** *noun* a synthetic material which resists moisture, used for packing and disposable cups *etc*

**polytechnic** *noun* a college which teaches technical and vocational subjects

**polythene** *noun* a type of plastic that can be moulded when hot

**polyunsaturated** *adj* of oil: containing no cholesterol

**pomegranate** *noun* a fruit with a thick skin, many seeds and pulpy edible flesh
ⓘ From Old French *pome grenate* meaning 'grainy apple'

**pommel** *noun* **1** the knob on the hilt of a sword **2** the high part of a saddle

**pomp** *noun* solemn and splendid ceremony, magnificence

**pompous** *adj* self-important, excessively dignified □ **pomposity** *noun*

**pond** *noun* a small lake or pool

**ponder** *verb* to think over, consider

**ponderous** *adj* **1** weighty **2** clumsy **3** sounding very important

**pontiff** *noun* **1** a Roman Catholic bishop **2** the Pope □ **pontifical** *adj* **1** of a pontiff **2** pompous in speech □ **pontificate** *verb*

**pontoon**¹ *noun* a flat-bottomed boat used to support a temporary bridge (a **pontoon bridge**)

**pontoon**² *noun* a card-game in which players try to collect 21 points

**pony** *noun* (*pl* **ponies**) a small horse □ **pony-trekking** *noun* riding cross-country in small parties

**poodle** *noun* a breed of dog, with curly hair often clipped in a fancy way

**pool** *noun* **1** a small area of still water **2** a deep part of a river **3** a joint fund or stock (of money, typists *etc*) **4** the money played for in a gambling game □ *verb* to put (money *etc*) into a joint fund □ **football pools** organized betting on football match results

**poop** noun **1** a ship's stern, or back part **2** a high deck in the stern

**poor** adj **1** having little money or property **2** not good **3** lacking (in): *poor in sports facilities* **4** deserving pity: *poor Tom has broken his leg* □ **poorly** adj in bad health, ill □ **the poor** those with little money

■ (meaning 1) impoverished, destitute, straitened, needy; (meaning 4) unfortunate, pitiable

**pop** noun **1** a sharp quick noise, eg that made by a cork coming out of a bottle **2** a fizzy soft drink **3** popular music □ verb **1** to make a pop **2** to move quickly, dash □ adj of music: popular

**pop** verb ⋄ pops, popping, popped

**popadom** or **popadum** noun a thin circle of dough fried in oil until crisp

**popcorn** noun a kind of maize that bursts open when heated

**Pope** or **pope** noun the bishop of Rome, head of the Roman Catholic Church

**poplar** noun a tall, narrow quick-growing tree

**poplin** noun strong cotton cloth

**poppy** noun (pl **poppies**) a plant growing wild in fields etc with large scarlet flowers

**populace** noun the people of a country or area

**popular** adj **1** of the people: *popular vote* **2** liked by most people **3** widely held or believed □ **popularity** noun □ **popularize** verb □ **popularly** adv

**population** noun the number of people living in a place □ **populate** verb □ **populous** adj

**porcelain** noun a kind of fine china

**porch** noun (pl **porches**) a covered entrance to a building

**porcupine** noun a large gnawing animal, covered with sharp quills

**pore** noun **1** a tiny hole **2** the hole of a sweat gland in the skin □ **pore over** study closely or eagerly
ⓘ From Greek *poros* meaning 'a passage'

✎ Do not confuse with: **pour**

**pork** noun the flesh of the pig, prepared for eating

**porn** noun, informal pornography

**pornography** noun literature or art that is sexually explicit and often offensive □ **pornographic** adj

**porous** adj **1** having pores **2** allowing fluid to pass through □ **porosity** noun

**porpoise** noun a blunt-nosed sea animal of the dolphin family

**porridge** noun a food made from oatmeal boiled in water or milk

**porringer** noun a small bowl for soup, porridge etc

**port** noun **1** a harbour **2** a town with a harbour **3** the left side of a ship as you face the front **4** a strong, dark-red sweet wine

**portable** adj able to be lifted and carried □ noun a computer, telephone etc that can be carried around

**portal** noun a grand entrance or doorway

**portcullis** noun (pl **portcullises**) a grating which is let down quickly to close a gateway

**portend** verb to give warning of, foretell

**portent** noun a warning sign □ **portentous** adj

**porter** noun **1** someone employed to carry luggage, push hospital trolleys etc **2** a doorkeeper **3** a kind of dark brown beer

**portfolio** noun (pl **portfolios**) **1** a case for carrying papers, drawings etc **2** the job of a government minister

**port-hole** noun a small round window in a ship's side

**portico** noun (pl **porticoes** or

porticos) a row of columns in front of a building forming a porch or covered walk

**portion** *noun* 1 a part 2 a share, a helping □ *verb* to divide into parts

**portly** *adj* stout and dignified

**portmanteau** *noun* a large leather travelling bag

**portrait** *noun* 1 a drawing, painting, or photograph of a person 2 a description of a person, place *etc*

**portray** *verb* 1 to make a painting or drawing of 2 to describe in words 3 to act the part of □ **portrayal** *noun*

portray ⇔ portrays, portraying, portrayed

**pose** *noun* 1 a position of the body 2 behaviour put on to impress others, a pretence □ *verb* 1 to position yourself for a photograph *etc* 2 (**pose as someone** or **something**) to pretend or claim to be what you are not: *posing as an expert* 3 to put forward (a problem, question *etc*) □ **poser** *noun* 1 someone who poses to impress others 2 a difficult question

**posh** *adj*, *informal* high-class; smart

**position** *noun* 1 place, situation 2 manner of standing, sitting *etc*, posture 3 a rank or job □ *verb* to place

**positive** *adj* 1 meaning or saying 'yes' (*contrasted with*: **negative**) 2 not able to be doubted: *positive proof* 3 certain, convinced 4 definite: *a positive improvement* 5 greater than zero 6 *grammar* of an adj or adv: of the first degree of comparison, *eg big*, not *bigger* or *biggest*

**positron** *noun* a particle with a positive electrical charge

**posse** (*say* pos-i) *noun* a body of police *etc*

**possess** *verb* 1 to own, have 2 to take hold of your mind: *anger possessed her* □ **possessed** *adj* 1 in the power of an evil spirit

2 obsessed 3 self-possessed, calm □ **possession** *noun* □ **possessive** *adj* 1 *grammar* of an adj: showing possession, *eg* the adjectives *my*, *mine*, *your*, *their etc* 2 over-protective and jealous in attitude

**possible** *adj* 1 able to happen or to be done 2 not unlikely □ **possibility** *noun* (*pl* **possibilities**) □ **possibly** *adv* perhaps

ⓔ From Latin *possibilis* meaning 'which may exist' or 'which may be done'

**possum** *noun*: **play possum** to pretend to be asleep or dead

**post** *noun* 1 an upright pole or stake 2 the service which delivers letters and other mail 3 a job 4 a place of duty: *the soldier remained at his post* 5 a settlement, a camp: *military post* □ *verb* 1 to put (a letter) in a postbox for collection 2 to send or station somewhere: *posted abroad* 3 to put up, stick up (a notice *etc*) □ **postal** *adj* □ **postage** *noun* money paid for sending a letter *etc* by post □ **postage stamp** a small printed label to show that postage has been paid □ **postal order** a document bought at a post office which can be exchanged for a stated amount of money □ **postbox** *noun* a box with an opening in which to post letters *etc* □ **postcard** *noun* a card for sending a message by post □ **post code** a short series of letters and numbers, used for sorting mail by machine □ **post-date** *verb* to mark (a cheque) with a date in the future, so that it cannot be cashed immediately □ **post-haste** *adv* with great speed □ **postman**, **postwoman**, *noun* someone who delivers letters □ **postmark** *noun* a date stamp put on a letter at a post office □ **post office** an office for receiving and sending off letters by post *etc*

**post-** *prefix* after: *postgraduate*

ⓔ From Latin *post* meaning 'after'

or 'behind'

**poster** *noun* **1** a large notice or placard **2** a large printed picture

**posterior** *adj* situated behind, coming after □ *noun* the buttocks

**posterity** *noun* **1** all future generations **2** someone's descendants

**postern** *noun* a back door or gate to a castle *etc*

**postgraduate** *adj* of study *etc*: following on from a first university degree □ *noun* someone continuing to study after a first degree

**posthumous** (*say* pos-tyu-mus) *adj* **1** of a book: published after the author's death **2** of a child: born after the father's death

**postilion** or **postillion** *noun*, *old* a carriage driver who rides on one of the horses

**postmortem** *noun* an examination of a dead body to find out the cause of death

**postpone** *verb* to put off to a future time, delay □ **postponement** *noun*

**postscript** *noun* an added remark at the end of a letter, after the sender's name

**postulant** *noun* someone applying to enter a religious order

**postulate** *verb* to assume or take for granted (that)

**posture** *noun* **1** the manner in which someone holds themselves in standing or walking **2** a position, a pose

**postwar** *adj* relating to the time after a war

**posy** *noun* (*pl* **posies**) a small bunch of flowers

**pot** *noun* **1** a deep vessel used in cooking, as a container, or for growing plants **2** *slang* the drug marijuana **3** (**pots**) *informal* a great deal: *pots of money* □ *verb* **1** to plant in a pot **2** to make articles of baked clay □ **take pot-luck** to take

whatever is available or offered □ **potted** *adj* **1** of meat: pressed down and preserved in a jar **2** condensed and simplified: *potted history* □ **pot belly** a protruding stomach □ **pot-boiler** *noun* a book with a sensational plot, written to sell □ **pothole** *noun* **1** a deep cave **2** a hole worn in a road surface □ **potholer** *noun* □ **pot plant** a household plant kept in a pot □ **pot shot** a casual or random shot

**pot** *verb* ⊷ **pots**, **potting**, **potted**

**potash** *noun* potassium carbonate, obtained from the ashes of wood

**potassium** *noun* a type of silvery-white metal

**potato** *noun* (*pl* **potatoes**) **1** a plant with round starchy roots which are eaten as a vegetable **2** the vegetable itself □ **couch potato** *see* **couch**

**potent** *adj* powerful, strong □ **potency** *noun*

**potentate** *noun* a powerful ruler

**potential** *adj* that may develop, possible □ *noun* the possibility of further development □ **potentiality** *noun* (*pl* **potentialities**)

**potion** *noun* a drink, often containing medicine or poison

**potpourri** (*say* poh-poo-ri) *noun* **1** a scented mixture of dried petals *etc* **2** a mixture or medley

**pottery** *noun* **1** articles made of baked clay **2** (*pl* **potteries**) a place where such things are made **3** the art of making them □ **potter** *noun* someone who makes articles of baked clay □ *verb* to do small odd jobs, dawdle

**potty**[1] *adj*, *informal* mad, eccentric

**potty**[2] *noun*, *informal* a child's chamberpot

**pouch** *noun* (*pl* **pouches**) **1** a pocket or small bag **2** a bag-like fold on the front of a kangaroo, for carrying its young

**pouffe** *noun* a low, stuffed seat

without back or arms

**poultice** *noun* a wet dressing spread on a bandage and put on inflamed skin

**poultry** *noun* farmyard fowls, *eg* hens, ducks, geese, turkeys

**pounce** *verb*: **pounce on something** or **someone** to seize, attack them □ *noun* **1** a sudden attack **2** a bird's claw

**pound** *noun* **1** the standard unit of money in Britain, shown by the sign (£), equal to 100 new pence **2** a measure of weight, written 'lb', equal to 16 ounces (about $\frac{1}{2}$ kilogramme) **3** an enclosure for animals □ *verb* **1** to beat into powder **2** to beat heavily **3** to walk or run with heavy steps

**pour** *verb* **1** to flow in a stream **2** to make flow: *pour the tea* **3** to rain heavily
Ⓔ From Middle English *pouren*
🖐 Do not confuse with: **pore**

**pout** *verb* to push out the lips sulkily to show displeasure □ *noun* a sulky look

**poverty** *noun* the state of being poor

**powder** *noun* **1** a substance made up of very fine particles **2** gunpowder **3** cosmetic facepowder □ *verb* **1** to sprinkle or dab with powder **2** to grind down to powder □ **powdered** *adj* □ **powdery** *adj*

**power** *noun* **1** strength, force **2** ability to do things **3** authority or legal right **4** a strong nation **5** someone in authority **6** the force used for driving machines: *electric power* **7** *maths* the product obtained by multiplying a number by itself a given number of times (*eg* $2 \times 2 \times 2$ or $2^3$ is the third power of 2) □ **power-driven** or **powered** *adj* worked by electricity, not by hand □ **powerful** *adj* having great power, strength, vigour, authority, influence, force or effectiveness □ **powerless** *adj* without power or

ability □ **power station** a building where electricity is produced

**pp** *abbrev* pages

**practicable** *adj* able to be used or done
Ⓔ From an old spelling of French *praticable* meaning 'able to be put into practice'

**practical** *adj* **1** preferring action to thought **2** efficient **3** learned by practice, rather than from books: *practical knowledge* □ **practically** *adv* **1** in a practical way **2** in effect, in reality **3** almost: *practically empty* □ **practical joke** a joke consisting of action, not words
Ⓔ From an old spelling of French *pratique* meaning 'handy', + word-ending *-al*

**practice** *noun* **1** habit **2** the actual doing of something: *I always intend to get up early but in practice I stay in bed* **3** repeated performance to improve skill: *piano practice* **4** the business of a doctor, lawyer *etc*
🖐 Do not confuse: **practice** and **practise**. To help you remember - 'ice' is a noun, 'ise' is not.

**practise** or *US* **practice** *verb* **1** to perform or exercise repeatedly to improve a skill **2** to make a habit of: *practise self-control* **3** to follow (a profession)

**practitioner** *noun* someone engaged in a profession: *a medical practitioner*

**pragmatic** or **pragmatical** *adj* practical; matter-of-fact; realistic □ **pragmatism** *noun* a practical, matter-of-fact approach to dealing with problems *etc* □ **pragmatist** *noun*

**prairie** *noun* a stretch of level grassland in N America

**praise** *verb* **1** to speak highly of **2** to glorify (God) by singing hymns *etc* □ *noun* an expression of approval □ **praiseworthy** *adj*

**pram** *noun* a small wheeled carriage

for a baby, pushed by hand (*short for* **perambulator**)

**prance** *verb* **1** to strut or swagger about **2** to dance about **3** of a horse: to spring from the hind legs

**prank** *noun* a trick played for mischief

**prat** *noun, informal* an idiot

**prattle** *verb* to talk or chatter meaninglessly □ *noun* meaningless talk

**prawn** *noun* a type of shellfish like the shrimp

**pray** *verb* **1** to ask earnestly, beg **2** to speak to God in prayer □ **prayer** *noun*
ⓘ From Latin *precarius* meaning 'obtained by prayer'

◈. Do not confuse with: **prey**

**pre-** *prefix* **1** before: *prehistoric* **2** to the highest degree: *pre-eminent*
ⓘ From Latin *prae* meaning 'in front of' or 'before'

**preach** *verb* **1** to give a sermon **2** to teach, speak in favour of: *preach caution* □ **preacher** *noun*

**preamble** *noun* something said as an introduction

**prearrange** *verb* to arrange beforehand

**precarious** *adj* uncertain, risky, dangerous

**precaution** *noun* care taken beforehand to avoid an accident *etc* □ **precautionary** *adj*

**precede** *verb* to go before in time, rank or importance □ **precedence** *noun* the right to go before; priority □ **preceding** *adj*
ⓘ From Latin *praecedere* meaning 'to go before'

◈. Do not confuse with: **proceed**

**precedent** *noun* a past action which serves as an example or rule for the future

**precept** *noun* a guiding rule, a commandment

**precinct** *noun* **1** an area enclosed by the boundary walls of a building **2** (**precincts**) the area closely surrounding any place **3** *US* an administrative district □ **shopping precinct** a shopping centre, often closed to traffic

**precious** *adj* **1** highly valued or valuable **2** over-fussy or precise

**precipice** *noun* a steep cliff

**precipitate** *verb* (*say* pri-**sip**-it-eit) **1** to throw head foremost **2** to force into (hasty action *etc*) **3** to hasten (death, illness *etc*) □ *adj* (*say* pri-**sip**-it-*a*t) **1** headlong **2** hasty, rash □ *noun* (*say* pri-**sip**-it-*a*t) sediment at the bottom of a liquid □ **precipitation** *noun* **1** great hurry **2** rainfall

**precipitous** *adj* very steep

**précis** (*say* **prei**-see) *noun* (*pl* **précis** — *say* **prei**-seez) a summary of a piece of writing

**precise** *adj* **1** definite **2** exact, accurate □ **precisely** *adv* □ **precision** *noun* **1** preciseness **2** exactness, accuracy
ⓘ From Latin *praecisus* meaning 'cut short'

◈. Do not confuse with: **concise**

**preclude** *verb* to prevent, make impossible □ **preclusion** *noun*

**precocious** *adj* of a child: unusually advanced or well-developed □ **precocity** *noun*

**precognitive** *adj* knowing beforehand, foretelling

**preconceive** *verb* to form (ideas *etc*) before having actual knowledge or experience □ **preconception** *noun*

**precursor** *noun* a person or thing which goes before, an early form of something

**predate** *verb* to happen before in time

**predator** *noun* a bird or animal that kills others for food □ **predatory** *adj*

**predecessor** *noun* the previous

holder of a job or office

**predestine** verb to destine beforehand, preordain

**predetermine** verb to settle beforehand

**predicament** noun an unfortunate or difficult situation

**predicate** noun, grammar something said about the subject of a sentence, eg has green eyes in the sentence Anne has green eyes

**predict** verb to foretell, forecast □ **predictable** adj □ **prediction** noun

**predispose** verb 1 to make (someone) in favour of something beforehand: we were predisposed to believe her 2 to make liable (to): predisposed to colds □ **predisposition** noun

**predominant** adj 1 ruling 2 most noticeable or outstanding □ **predominance** noun □ **predominantly** adv mostly, mainly

**predominate** verb 1 to be the strongest or most numerous 2 to have control (over)

**pre-eminent** adj outstanding, excelling all others □ **pre-eminence** noun □ **pre-eminently** adv

**pre-empt** verb to block or stop by making a first move □ **pre-emptive** adj

**preen** verb 1 of a bird: to arrange its feathers 2 to smarten your appearance in a conceited way □ **preen yourself** to show obvious pride in your achievements

**prefabricated** adj made of parts made beforehand, ready to be fitted together

**preface** (say **pref**-is) noun an introduction to a book etc □ verb to precede or introduce (with)

**prefect** noun 1 the head of an administrative district in France etc 2 a senior pupil in some schools with certain powers

**prefer** verb 1 to like better: I prefer tea to coffee 2 to put forward (a claim or request) □ **preferable** (say pref-ra-bl) adj more desirable □ **preference** noun 1 greater liking 2 something preferred: what is your preference? □ **preferential** adj

**prefer** ⇨ prefers, preferring, preferred

**preferment** noun promotion

**prefix** noun (pl prefixes) a syllable or word at the beginning of a word which adds to its meaning, eg dis-, un-, re-, in dislike, unhappy, regain

**pregnant** adj 1 carrying a foetus in the womb 2 full of meaning: pregnant pause □ **pregnancy** noun (pl pregnancies)

**prehensile** adj able to grasp or hold: prehensile tail

**prehistoric** adj relating to the time before history was written down □ **prehistory** noun

**prejudge** verb to decide (something) before hearing the facts of a case

**prejudice** noun 1 an unfair feeling for or against anything 2 an opinion formed without careful thought 3 harm, injury □ verb 1 to fill with prejudice 2 to do harm to, damage: his late arrival prejudiced his chances of success □ **prejudiced** adj □ **prejudicial** adj

**prelate** (say **prel**-it) noun a bishop or archbishop

**preliminary** adj going before, preparatory: preliminary investigation □ noun (pl preliminaries) something that goes before

**prelude** noun 1 a piece of music played as an introduction to the main piece 2 a preceding event: a prelude to a brilliant career

**premature** adj coming, born etc before the right, proper or expected time

**premeditate** verb to think out beforehand, plan: premeditated *murder* □ **premeditation** *noun*

**premier** (*say* prem-i-er) *adj* first, leading, foremost □ *noun* a prime minister

◊. Do not confuse: **premier** and **première**

**première** (*say* prem-i-eir) *noun* a first performance of a play, film *etc*

**premise** or **premiss** *noun* (*pl* **premises** or **premisses**) something assumed from which a conclusion is drawn

**premises** *noun pl* a building and its grounds

**premium** *noun* (*pl* **premiums**) **1** a reward **2** a payment on an insurance policy □ **at a premium** very desirable and therefore difficult to obtain

**premonition** *noun* a feeling that something is going to happen; a forewarning

**prenatal** *adj* before birth, or before giving birth

**preoccupied** *adj* deep in thought □ **preoccupation** *noun* □ **preoccupy** *verb*

**prep** *noun, informal* preparation □ **prep school** a preparatory school

**prepaid** *past form of* **prepay**

**preparatory** *adj* **1** acting as an introduction or first step **2 preparatory to something** before it, in preparation for it □ **preparatory school** a private school educating children of primary-school age

**prepare** *verb* **1** to make or get ready **2** to train, equip □ **preparation** *noun* **1** an act of preparing **2** study for a lesson **3** something prepared for use, *eg* a medicine □ **prepared** *adj* **1** ready **2** willing

**prepay** *verb* to pay beforehand □ **prepayment** *noun*

**prepay** ⟶ **prepays**, **prepay**ing, **prepaid**

**preponderance** *noun* greater

amount or number

**preposition** *noun, grammar* a word placed before a noun or pronoun to show its relation to another word, *eg* '*through* the door', '*in* the town', 'written *by* me'

**prepossessing** *adj* pleasant, making a good impression

**preposterous** *adj* very foolish, absurd

**prerequisite** *noun* something necessary before another thing can happen

**prerogative** *noun* a right enjoyed by someone because of rank or position

**Presbyterian** *adj* **1** of a church: managed by ministers and elders **2** belonging to such a church □ *noun* a member of a Presbyterian church

**presbytery** *noun* (*pl* **presbyteries**) **1** a body of presbyters **2** the house of a Roman Catholic priest

**prescribe** *verb* **1** to lay down as a rule **2** to order the use of (a medicine) □ **prescriptive** *adj* laying down rules
ⓘ From Latin *praescribere* meaning 'to write before'

◊. Do not confuse with: **proscribe**. It may help to remember that the **pre-** in **prescribe** means 'before', and that the whole verb refers to the process by which a doctor has to write down an order for medication before it can be obtained by a patient.

**prescription** *noun* **1** a doctor's written instructions for preparing a medicine **2** something prescribed

◊. Do not confuse with: **proscription**. **Prescription** is related to the verb **prescribe**.

**presence** *noun* **1** the state of being present (*contrasted with*: **absence**) **2** someone's personal appearance, manner *etc* □ **in your presence** while you are present □ **presence of mind** calmness, ability to act

sensibly in an emergency, difficulty
*etc*

**present¹** *adj* **1** here, in this place
**2** happening or existing now □ *noun*
**1** the time now **2** *grammar* the tense
describing events happening now,
*eg* 'we *are* on holiday' □ **presently**
*adv* soon

**present²** *noun* (*say* prez-ent) a gift
□ *verb* (*say* pri-zent) **1** to hand over
(a gift) formally **2** to offer, put
forward **3** to introduce (someone)
to another □ **presentation** *noun*
**1** the giving of a present
**2** something presented **3** a formal
talk or demonstration **4** a showing
of a play *etc* □ **present yourself 1** to
introduce yourself **2** to arrive

**presentiment** *noun* a feeling that
something bad is about to happen, a
foreboding

**preserve** *verb* **1** to keep safe from
harm **2** to keep in existence,
maintain **3** to treat (food) so that it
will not go bad □ *noun* **1** a place
where game animals, birds *etc* are
protected **2** jam □ **preservation**
*noun* preserving or being preserved
□ **preservative** *noun* a substance
added to food to prevent it from
going bad

**preside** *verb* to be in charge at a
meeting *etc*

**president** *noun* **1** the leading
member of a society *etc* **2** the head
of a republic □ **presidency** *noun* (*pl*
**presidencies**)

**press** *verb* **1** to push on, against or
down **2** to urge, force **3** to iron
(clothes *etc*) □ *noun* **1** a crowd **2** a
printing machine **3** the news media,
journalists □ **pressing** *adj* requiring
immediate action, insistent

**pressgang** *noun*, *historical* a group
of men employed to carry off people
by force into the army or navy
□ *verb* **1** *historical* to carry off in a
pressgang **2** to force (someone) to
do something: *pressganged into
joining the committee*

**pressure** *noun* **1** force on or against
a surface **2** strong persuasion,
compulsion **3** stress, strain
**4** urgency □ **pressurize** *verb* **1** to fit
(an aeroplane *etc*) with a device that
maintains normal air pressure **2** to
force (someone) to do something

**prestige** *noun* reputation, influence
due to rank, success *etc*
□ **prestigious** *adj*

**presume** *verb* **1** to take for granted,
assume (that) **2 presume on
something** to take advantage of
(someone's kindness *etc*)
□ **presumably** *adv* I suppose
□ **presumption** *noun* **1** a strong
likelihood **2** impertinent behaviour
□ **presumptuous** *adj*

**presuppose** *verb* to take for granted

**pretend** *verb* **1** to make believe,
fantasize **2** to make a false claim
□ **pretence** *noun* **1** the act of
pretending **2** a false claim
□ **pretender** *noun*

**pretension** *noun* **1** a claim (whether
true or not) **2** self-importance

**pretentious** *adj* self-important;
showy, ostentatious

**pretext** *noun* an excuse

**pretty** *adj* pleasing or attractive to
see, listen to *etc* □ *adv* fairly, quite
□ **prettiness** *noun*

**prevail** *verb* **1 prevail against** or
**over someone** or **something** to
gain control over them **2** to win,
succeed **3** to be most usual or
common □ **prevailing** *adj*

**prevalent** *adj* common, widespread
□ **prevalence** *noun*

**prevaricate** *verb* to avoid telling the
truth □ **prevarication** *noun*
□ **prevaricator** *noun*

**prevent** *verb* to hinder, stop
happening □ *noun* the act of
preventing □ **preventive** *adj* of
medicine: helping to prevent illness

**preview** *noun* a view of a
performance, exhibition *etc* before
its official opening

**previous** *adj* going before in time; former □ **previously** *adv*

**prey** *noun* **1** an animal killed by others for food **2** a victim □ *verb* (**prey on someone** or **something**) **1** to seize and eat them **2** to stalk and harass them
ⓘ From Latin *praeda* meaning 'booty'

✎. Do not confuse with: **pray**

**price** *noun* **1** the money for which something is bought or sold, the cost **2** something that must be given up in order to gain something: *the price of fame* □ **priceless** *adj* **1** very valuable **2** *informal* very funny

**prick** *verb* **1** to pierce slightly **2** to give a sharp pain to **3** to stick up (the ears) □ *noun* a pricking feeling on the skin

**prickle** *noun* a sharp point on a plant or animal □ *verb* **1** to be prickly **2** to feel prickly □ **prickly** *adj*

**pride** *noun* **1** too great an opinion of yourself **2** pleasure in having done something well **3** dignity **4** a group of lions □ **pride yourself on** to feel or show pride in

**priest** *noun* **1** a member of the clergy in the Roman Catholic and Anglican churches **2** an official in a non-Christian religion □ **priestess** *noun* a female, non-Christian priest □ **priesthood** *noun*

**prig** *noun* a smug, self-righteous person □ **priggish** *adj*

**prim** *adj* unnecessarily formal and correct

**prima donna** **1** a leading female opera singer **2** a woman who is over-sensitive and temperamental

**primaeval** *another spelling of* **primeval**

**primary** *adj* **1** first **2** most important, chief □ **primary colours** those from which all others can be made, *eg* red, blue and yellow □ **primary school** a school for the early stages of education

**primate** *noun* **1** a member of the highest order of mammals including humans, monkeys and apes **2** an archbishop

**prime** *adj* **1** first in time or importance **2** best quality, excellent □ *noun* the time of greatest health and strength □ *verb* **1** to prepare the surface of for painting **2** to supply with detailed information: *she was well primed before the meeting* □ **primer** *noun* **1** a simple introductory book on a subject **2** a substance for preparing a surface for painting □ **prime minister** the head of a government

**primeval** or **primaeval** *adj* **1** relating to the beginning of the world **2** primitive, instinctive

**primitive** *adj* **1** belonging to very early times **2** old-fashioned **3** not skilfully made, rough

**primogeniture** *noun* **1** the fact of being born first **2** the rights of a first-born child

**primrose** *noun* a pale-yellow spring flower common in woods and hedges

**prince** *noun* **1** the son of a king or queen **2** a ruler of certain states □ **princely** *adj* splendid, impressive: *a princely reward*

**princess** *noun* (*pl* **princesses**) the daughter of a king or queen

**principal** *adj* most important, chief □ *noun* **1** the head of a school or university **2** a leading part in a play *etc* **3** money in a bank on which interest is paid □ **principality** *noun* (*pl* **principalities**) a state ruled by a prince □ **principally** *adv* chiefly, mostly
ⓘ From Latin *principalis* meaning 'first'

✎. Do not confuse: **principal** and **principle**.
It may help to remember that the adjective **principAL** means 'first or most important', and that it

also contains an A - the first letter of the alphabet.

**principle** *noun* **1** a general truth or law **2** the theory on which the working of a machine is based **3** (**principles**) someone's personal rules of behaviour, sense of right and wrong *etc*
ⓘ From Latin *principium* meaning 'beginning'

**print** *verb* **1** to mark letters on paper with type **2** to write in capital letters **3** to publish in printed form **4** to stamp patterns on (cloth *etc*) **5** to make a finished photograph □ *noun* **1** a mark made by pressure: *footprint* **2** printed lettering **3** a photograph made from a negative **4** a printed reproduction of a painting *etc* **5** cloth printed with a design □ **in print** of a book: published and available to buy □ **printer** *noun* **1** someone who prints books, newspapers *etc* **2** a machine that prints, attached to a computer system □ **printed circuit** a wiring circuit, formed by printing a design on copper foil bonded to a flat base □ **print-out** *noun* the printed information produced by a computer

**prior**[1] *adj* **1** earlier **2** previous (to)

**prior**[2] *noun* the head of a priory

**priority** *noun* (*pl* **priorities**) **1** first position **2** the right to be first **3** something that must be done first: *our priority is to get him into hospital*

**priory** *noun* (*pl* **priories**) a building where a community of monks or nuns live

**prise** *verb* to force open or off with a lever: *prised off the lid*

**prism** *noun* a glass tube with triangular ends that breaks light into different colours

**prison** *noun* **1** a building for holding criminals **2** a place where someone is confined against their will □ **prisoner** *noun* someone held

under arrest or locked up

**pristine** *adj* in the original or unspoilt state

**privacy** *noun* freedom from observation; secrecy

**private** *adj* **1** relating to an individual, not to the general public; personal **2** not open to the public **3** secret, not generally known □ *noun* the lowest rank of ordinary soldier (not an officer) □ **privately** *adv*

**privation** *noun* **1** want, poverty, hardship **2** taking away, loss

**privatize** *verb* to transfer from state to private ownership, denationalize

**privet** *noun* a type of shrub used for hedges

**privilege** *noun* a right available to one person or to only a few people □ **privileged** *adj*

**privy** *adj*: **privy to** knowing about (something secret) □ **privy council** an appointed group of advisers to a king or queen

**prize** *noun* **1** a reward **2** something won in a competition **3** something captured **4** something highly valued □ *adj* very fine, worthy of a prize □ *verb* to value highly

**pro** *short for* **professional**

**pro-** *prefix* **1** before, forward, front **2** in favour of: *pro-devolution* □ **pros and cons** the arguments for and against anything
ⓘ From Latin and Greek *pro* meaning 'before' or 'for'

**probable** *adj* **1** likely to happen **2** likely to be true □ **probability** *noun* (*pl* **probabilities**) □ **probably** *adv* very likely

**probation** *noun* **1** a trial period in a new job *etc* **2** a system of releasing prisoners on condition that they commit no more offences and report regularly to the authorities □ **probationer** *noun* someone who is training to be a member of a profession

**probe** noun **1** a long, thin instrument used to examine a wound **2** a thorough investigation **3** a spacecraft for exploring space □ verb **1** to examine very carefully **2** to investigate thoroughly to find out information

**probity** noun honesty, goodness of character

**problem** noun **1** a question to be solved; a matter which is difficult to deal with □ **problematic** or **problematical** adj doubtful, uncertain

**proboscis** (say pro-boh-sis or pro-bos-kis or pro-bos-kis) noun (pl **proboscises**) **1** an animal's nose, esp an elephant trunk **2** an insect's mouth

**procedure** noun **1** method of doing business **2** a course of action

**proceed** verb **1** to go on with, continue **2** to begin (to do something) **3** to take legal action (against) □ **proceeds** (say proh-seedz) noun pl profit made from a sale etc
ⓘ From Latin procedere meaning 'to go forward'

🔸 Do not confuse with: **precede**

**proceeding** noun **1** a step forward **2** (**proceedings**) a record of the meetings of a society etc **3** a law action

**process** noun (pl **processes**) **1** a series of operations in manufacturing goods **2** a series of events producing change or development **3** a law-court case □ **in the process of** in the course of

**procession** noun a line of people or vehicles moving forward in order

**proclaim** verb to announce publicly, declare openly □ **proclamation** noun an official announcement made to the public

**procrastinate** verb to put things off, delay doing something till a later time □ **procrastination** noun

**procure** verb to obtain; to bring about

**prod** verb to poke; urge on

**prod** ⇔ prod**s**, prod**ding**, prod**ded**

**prodigal** adj spending money recklessly, wasteful □ **prodigality** noun

**prodigy** noun (pl **prodigies**) **1** a wonder **2** someone astonishingly clever: child prodigy □ **prodigious** adj **1** strange, astonishing **2** enormous

**produce** verb (say pro-dyoos) **1** to bring into being **2** to bring about, cause **3** to prepare (a play etc) for the stage **4** to make, manufacture □ noun (say prod-yoos) food grown or produced on a farm or in a garden □ **producer** noun someone who produces a play, film etc

**product** noun **1** something produced **2** a result **3** maths the number that results from the multiplication of two or more numbers □ **production** noun **1** the act of producing; the process of producing or being produced **2** the quantity produced or rate of producing it **3** a particular presentation of a play, opera, ballet etc □ **productive** adj fruitful, producing results □ **productivity** noun the rate of work done

**Prof** abbrev Professor

**profane** adj **1** not sacred **2** treating holy things without respect □ **profanity** (say pro-fan-it-i) noun (pl **profanities**)

**profess** verb **1** to declare (a belief etc) openly **2** to pretend, claim □ **professed** adj

**profession** noun **1** an occupation requiring special training, eg that of a doctor, lawyer, teacher etc **2** an open declaration □ **professional** adj **1** of a profession **2** earning a living from a game or an art (contrasted with: **amateur**) **3** skilful, competent □ noun **1** someone who works in a profession **2** someone who earns

money from a game or art
□ **professionalism** noun **1** a professional status **2** professional expertise or competence
□ **professionally** adv

**professor** noun **1** a teacher of the highest rank in a university **2** US a university teacher

**proffer** verb to offer

**proficient** adj skilled, expert
□ **proficiency** noun

**profile** noun **1** an outline **2** a side view of a face, head etc **3** a short description of someone's life, achievements etc

**profit** noun **1** gain, benefit **2** money got by selling an article for a higher price than was paid for it □ verb to gain (from), benefit □ **profitable** adj □ **profiteer** noun someone who makes large profits unfairly □ verb to make large profits

**profligate** adj **1** living an immoral life **2** very extravagant □ noun a profligate person □ **profligacy** noun

**profound** adj **1** very deep **2** deeply felt **3** showing great knowledge or understanding: a profound comment
□ **profundity** noun

**profuse** adj abundant, lavish, extravagant □ **profusion** noun

**progenitor** noun an ancestor
□ **progeny** noun children

**progesterone** noun a female sex hormone that maintains pregnancy

**prognosis** noun a prediction of the course of a disease

**prognosticate** verb to foretell
□ **prognostication** noun

**program** noun a set of instructions telling a computer to carry out certain actions □ verb **1** to give instructions to **2** to prepare instructions to be carried out by a computer

**program** verb ⋄ programs, programming, programmed

**programme** or US **program** noun

**1** a booklet with details of an entertainment, ceremony etc **2** a scheme, a plan **3** a TV or radio broadcast

**progress** noun **1** advance, forward movement **2** improvement □ verb **1** to go forward **2** to improve
□ **progression** noun □ **progressive** adj

**prohibit** verb **1** to forbid **2** to prevent □ **prohibition** noun the forbidding by law of making and selling alcoholic drinks □ **prohibitive** adj **1** prohibiting **2** of price: too expensive, discouraging

**project** noun (say proj-ekt) **1** a plan, a scheme **2** a task **3** a piece of study or research □ verb (say pro-jekt) **1** to throw out or up **2** to jut out **3** to cast (an image, a light etc) on to a surface **4** to plan, propose

**projectile** noun a missile

**projection** noun an act of projecting; something projected; something which juts out

**projector** noun a machine for projecting cinema pictures on a screen □ **projectionist** noun someone who operates a film projector

**proletariat** noun the ordinary working people □ **proletarian** noun

**proliferate** verb to grow or increase rapidly

**prolific** adj producing a lot, fruitful

**prologue** noun a preface or introduction to a play etc

**prolong** verb to make longer

**prom** informal, short for **1** promenade **2** promenade concert

**promenade** noun **1** a level roadway or walk, esp by the seaside **2** a walk, a stroll □ verb to walk for pleasure
□ **promenade concert** a concert at which a large part of the audience stands instead of being seated

**prominent** adj **1** standing out, easily seen **2** famous, distinguished

◻ **prominence** *noun*

**promiscuous** *adj* **1** having many sexual relationships **2** mixed in kind **3** not making distinctions between people or things
◻ **promiscuity** *noun*

**promise** *verb* **1** to give your word (to do or not do something) **2** to show signs for the future: *the weather promises to improve* ◻ *noun* **1** a statement of something promised **2** a sign of something to come **3** a sign of future success ◻ **promising** *adj* showing signs of being successful

**promontory** *noun* (*pl* **promontories**) a headland jutting out into the sea

**promote** *verb* **1** to raise to a higher rank **2** to help onwards, encourage **3** to advertise, encourage the sales of ◻ **promotion** *noun*
◻ **promotional** *adj*

**prompt** *adj* **1** quick, immediate **2** punctual ◻ *verb* **1** to move to action **2** to supply words to an actor who has forgotten their lines
◻ **prompter** *noun* a person positioned offstage to prompt actors when they forget their lines
◻ **promptly** *adv* ◻ **promptness** *noun*

**promulgate** *verb* to make widely known ◻ **promulgation** *noun*

**prone** *adj* **1** lying face downward **2** inclined (to): *prone to laziness*

**prong** *noun* the spike of a fork
◻ **pronged** *adj*

**pronoun** *noun* a word used instead of a noun, *eg* I, you, who

**pronounce** *verb* **1** to speak (words, sounds) **2** to announce (an opinion), declare ◻ **pronounced** *adj* noticeable, marked
◻ **pronouncement** *noun* a statement, an announcement

**pronunciation** *noun* the way a word is said

**proof** *noun* **1** evidence that makes something clear beyond doubt **2** the standard strength of whisky *etc* **3** a

copy of a printed sheet for correction before publication ◻ *adj* able to keep out or withstand: *waterproof*

**prop** *noun* **1** a support **2** *short for* propeller **3** *short for* stage property (= an item needed on stage for a play) ◻ *verb* to hold up, support
**prop** *verb* ⬦ props, propping, propped

**propaganda** *noun* **1** the spreading of ideas to influence public opinion **2** material used for this, *eg* posters, leaflets

**propagate** *verb* **1** to spread **2** to produce seedlings or young
◻ **propagator** *noun* **1** a person or thing that propagates **2** a heated box with a cover in which plants may be grown from cuttings or seeds

**propel** *verb* to drive forward
◻ **propellant** *noun* **1** an explosive for firing a rocket **2** the gas in an aerosol spray ◻ **propeller** *noun* a shaft with revolving blades which drives forward a ship, aircraft *etc*
**propel** ⬦ propels, propelling, propelled

**propensity** *noun* (*pl* **propensities**) a natural inclination or tendency

**proper** *adj* **1** right, correct **2** full, thorough: *a proper search* **3** prim, well-behaved ◻ **properly** *adv*
◻ **proper noun** or **proper name** *grammar* a name for a particular person, place or thing, *eg* *Shakespeare, York* (*contrasted with:* **common noun**)

**property** *noun* (*pl* **properties**) **1** land or buildings owned **2** a quality **3** (**properties**) the furniture *etc* required by actors in a play

**prophecy** (*say* prof-*es*-i) *noun* (*pl* **prophecies**) **1** foretelling the future **2** something prophesied

🖋 Do not confuse: **prophecy** and **prophesy**.
The spelling with the 'c' is the

noun, the spelling with the 's' the verb. It may help to remember that this is a common pattern, seen also in such pairs as practice/practise, licence/license and advice/advise.

**prophesy** (*say* prof-es-ai) *verb* to foretell the future, predict

**prophesy** ⬦ **prophesi**es, **prophesy**ing, **prophesi**ed

**prophet** *noun* **1** someone who claims to foretell events **2** someone who tells what they believe to be the will of God

**propinquity** *noun* nearness

**propitiate** *verb* to calm the anger of □ **propitious** *adj* favourable

**proponent** *noun* someone in favour of a thing

**proportion** *noun* **1** a part of a total amount **2** relation in size, number *etc* compared with something else □ **in** or **out of proportion** appropriate or inappropriate in size or degree when compared with other things □ **proportional** or **proportionate** *adj* in proportion □ **proportional representation** a voting system in which parties are represented in proportion to their voting strength

**propose** *verb* **1** to put forward for consideration, suggest **2** to intend **3** to make an offer of marriage (to) □ **proposal** *noun* **1** an act of proposing **2** anything proposed **3** an offer of marriage □ **proposition** *noun* **1** a proposal, a suggestion **2** a statement **3** a situation that must be dealt with: *a tough proposition*

**propound** *verb* to state, put forward for consideration

**proprietor, proprietress** *noun* an owner, *esp* of a hotel

**propriety** *noun* (*pl* **proprieties**) **1** fitness, suitability **2** correct behaviour, decency

**propulsion** *noun* an act of driving forward

**prorogue** *verb* to discontinue meetings of (parliament *etc*) for a period □ **prorogation** *noun*

**prosaic** *adj* dull, not interesting □ **prosaically** *adv*

**proscribe** *verb* to ban, prohibit ⓘ From Latin *proscribere* meaning 'to publish in writing'

⬥ Do not confuse with: **prescribe**. It may help to remember that **PRO**scribe and **PRO**hibit share the same three first letters.

**proscription** *noun* proscribing or being proscribed

⬥ Do not confuse with: **prescription**. **Proscription** is related to the verb **proscribe**.

**proscriptive** *adj* tending to proscribe

**prose** *noun* **1** writing which is not in verse **2** ordinary written or spoken language

**prosecute** *verb* **1** to bring a law-court action against **2** to carry on (studies, an investigation *etc*) □ **prosecution** *noun* **1** an act of prosecuting **2** *law* those bringing the case in a trial (*contrasted with*: **defence**) ⓘ From Latin *prosequi* meaning 'to accompany someone on their way forth'

⬥ Do not confuse with: **persecute**

**proselyte** *noun* a convert

**prosody** *noun* study of the rhythms and construction of poetry

**prospect** *noun* (*say* pros-pekt) **1** a view, a scene **2** a future outlook or expectation □ *verb* (*say* pros-pekt) to search for gold or other minerals □ **prospective** *adj* soon to be, likely to be □ **prospector** *noun*

**prospectus** *noun* (*pl* **prospectuses**) a booklet giving information about a school, organization *etc*

**prosper** *verb* to get on well, succeed □ **prosperity** *noun* □ **prosperous** *adj*

**prostitute** *noun* someone who offers sexual intercourse for payment

**prostrate** adj **1** lying flat face downwards **2** worn out, exhausted □ verb **1** to lie on the ground as a sign of respect **2** to exhaust, tire out completely □ **prostration** noun

**protagonist** noun a chief character in a play etc

**protect** verb to shield from danger, keep safe □ **protection** noun □ **protective** adj □ **protector** noun

**protectorate** noun a country which is partly governed and defended by another country

**protégé, protégée** noun a pupil or employee who is taught or helped in their career by someone important or powerful

**protein** noun a substance present in milk, eggs, meat etc which is a necessary part of a human or animal diet

**protest** verb **1** to object strongly **2** to declare solemnly □ noun a strong objection □ **protestation** noun

**Protestant** noun a member of one of the Christian churches that broke away from the Roman Catholic Church at the time of the Reformation

**protocol** noun correct procedure

**proton** noun a particle with a positive electrical charge, forming part of the nucleus of an atom (compare with: **electron**)

**prototype** noun the original model from which something is copied

**protract** verb to lengthen in time

**protractor** noun an instrument for drawing and measuring angles on paper

**protrude** verb to stick out, thrust forward □ **protrusion** noun

**protuberance** noun a swelling, a bulge □ **protuberant** adj

**proud** adj **1** thinking too highly of yourself, conceited **2** feeling pleased at an achievement etc **3** dignified, self-respecting: too

proud to accept the money □ **do someone proud** to treat them grandly

**prove** verb **1** to show to be true or correct **2** to try out, test **3** to turn out (to be)

**provenance** noun source, origin

**provender** noun food, esp for horses and cattle

**proverb** noun a well-known wise saying, eg 'nothing ventured, nothing gained' □ **proverbial** adj well-known, widely spoken of

> In what sort of situation might you say, 'A stitch in time saves nine', or 'Too many cooks spoil the broth'? What would someone mean if they said, 'It's an ill wind that blows nobody any good', or 'Little strokes fell great oaks'?
>
> ✑ **Try writing a short story where the last line takes the form of a proverb.**

**provide** verb to supply □ **providing that** on condition that

**providence** noun **1** foresight; thrift **2** (**Providence**) God □ **provident** adj □ **providential** adj fortunate, coming as if by divine help

**province** noun **1** a division of a country **2** the extent of someone's duties or knowledge **3** (**provinces**) all parts of a country outside the capital □ **provincial** adj **1** of a province or provinces **2** narrow-minded, parochial

**provision** noun **1** an agreed arrangement **2** a rule or condition **3** (**provisions**) a supply of food □ **provisional** adj used for the time being; temporary

**proviso** (say pro-**vai**-zoh) noun (pl **provisos**) a condition laid down beforehand

**provoke** verb **1** to cause, result in **2** to rouse to anger or action: don't let him provoke you □ **provocation** noun (meaning 2) □ **provocative** (say pro-**vok**-at-iv) adj **1** tending to rouse anger **2** likely to arouse sexual interest □ **provoking** adj

**provost** noun the chief magistrate of a burgh in Scotland

**prow** noun the front part of a ship

**prowess** noun skill, ability

**prowl** verb to go about stealthily

**proximity** noun nearness

**proxy** noun (pl **proxies**) someone who acts or votes on behalf of another

**prude** noun an over-modest, priggish person □ **prudery** noun □ **prudish** adj

**prudent** adj wise and cautious □ **prudently** adv □ **prudence** noun

**prune**¹ verb **1** to trim (a tree) by cutting off unneeded twigs **2** to shorten, reduce

**prune**² noun a dried plum

**pry** verb to look closely into things that are not your business □ **prying** adj

**pry** ⇨ pries, prying, pried

**PS** abbrev postscript

**psalm** noun a sacred song □ **psalmist** noun

**p's and q's** correct social manners

**pseud** (say sood) adj, informal pseudo □ noun, informal a fraud

**pseud-** (say sood) or **pseudo-** prefix false: pseudonym
Ⓖ From Greek pseudes meaning 'false'

**pseudo** (say sood-oh) adj, informal false, fake, pretended

**pseudonym** (say sood-o-nim) noun a false name used by an author

**psych-** see psycho-

**psychedelic** adj bright and multi-coloured

**psychiatry** noun the treatment of mental illness □ **psychiatric** (say sai-ki-at-rik) adj □ **psychiatrist** noun

**psychic** (say sai-kik) or **psychical** adj **1** relating to the mind **2** able to read other people's minds, or tell the future

**psycho-** (say sai-koh) or **psych-** prefix relating to the mind: psychology
Ⓖ From Greek psyche meaning 'soul'

**psychoanalysis** noun a method of treating mental illness by discussing with the patient its possible causes in their past □ **psychoanalyse** verb □ **psychoanalyst** noun

**psychology** noun the science which studies the human mind □ **psychologist** noun □ **psychological** adj

**psychosomatic** adj of an illness: having a psychological cause

**psychotherapy** noun treatment of mental illness by psychoanalysis etc □ **psychotherapist** noun

**psychotic** adj, medicine affected by mental illness, mad

**PT** abbrev physical training

**ptarmigan** (say tah-mig-an) noun a mountain-dwelling bird of the grouse family, which turns white in winter

**pterodactyl** (say te-ro-dak-til) noun an extinct flying reptile

**PTO** abbrev please turn over

**pub** short for public house

**puberty** (say pyoob-et-i) noun the time during youth when the body becomes sexually mature

**pubic** (say pyoob-ik) adj of the lowest part of the abdomen: pubic hair

**public** adj **1** relating to or shared by the people of a community or nation in general **2** generally or widely known □ noun people in general □ **publican** noun the keeper of an inn or public house □ **publication** noun **1** the act of making news etc public **2** the act of publishing a book, newspaper etc **3** a published book, magazine etc □ **public house** a building where alcoholic drinks are sold and consumed, a pub

◻ **publicity** noun advertising; bringing to public notice or attention ◻ **publicize** verb to make public, advertise ◻ **public relations 1** the relations between a business etc and the public **2** a department of a business etc dealing with this ◻ **in public** in front of or among other people ◻ **public address system** a system of microphones, amplifiers and loudspeakers used to enable an audience to hear speeches, music etc

**publish** verb **1** to make generally known **2** to prepare and put out (a book etc) for sale ◻ **publisher** noun

**puce** adj of a brownish-purple colour

**pucker** verb to wrinkle ◻ noun a wrinkle, a fold

**pudding** noun **1** the sweet course of a meal **2** a sweet dish made with eggs, flour, milk etc **3** a type of sausage: mealy pudding

**puddle** noun a small, often muddy, pool

**puerile** (say pyoor-rail) adj childish, silly ◻ **puerility** noun
ⓘ From Latin puerilis meaning 'childish'

**puff** verb **1** to blow out in small gusts **2** to breathe heavily, eg after running **3** to blow up, inflate **4** to swell (up or out) ◻ noun **1** a short, sudden gust of wind, breath etc **2** a powder puff **3** a piece of advertising ◻ **puffy** adj **1** swollen, flabby **2** breathing heavily ◻ **puff pastry** a light, flaky kind of pastry

**puffin** noun a type of sea bird, with a short, thick, brightly-coloured beak

**pug** noun a breed of small dog with a snub nose

**pugilist** (say pyoo-jil-ist) noun a boxer

**pugnacious** adj quarrelsome, fond of fighting ◻ **pugnacity** noun
ⓘ From Latin pugnax meaning 'warlike'

**pull** verb **1** to move or try to move (something) towards yourself by force **2** to drag, tug **3** to stretch, strain: pull a muscle **4** to tear: pull to pieces ◻ noun **1** the act of pulling **2** a pulling force, eg of a magnet **3** a handle for pulling **4** informal advantage, influence ◻ **pull yourself together** to regain self-control or self-possession ◻ **pull through** to get safely to the end of a difficult or dangerous experience ◻ **pull up** to stop, halt

**pullet** noun a young hen

**pulley** noun (pl **pulleys**) a grooved wheel fitted with a cord and set in a block, used for lifting weights etc

**pullover** noun a knitted garment for the top half of the body, a jersey

**pulmonary** adj relating to the lungs

**pulp** noun **1** the soft fleshy part of a fruit **2** a soft mass of wood etc which is made into paper **3** any soft mass ◻ verb to reduce to pulp

**pulpit** noun an enclosed platform in a church for the minister or priest

**pulsate** verb to beat, throb

**pulse** noun the beating or throbbing of the heart and blood vessels as blood flows through them ◻ verb to throb, pulsate

**pulses** noun pl beans, peas, lentils and other edible seeds of this family

**pulverize** verb to make or crush into powder

**puma** noun an American wild animal like a large cat

**pumice** noun or **pumice stone** a piece of light solidified lava used for smoothing skin and for rubbing away stains

**pummel** verb to beat with the fists

**pummel** ◦ pummels, pummelling, pummelled

**pump** noun **1** a machine used for making water rise to the surface **2** a machine or device for drawing out or forcing in air, gas etc: bicycle pump **3** a kind of thin-or soft-soled shoe for dancing, gymnastics etc

�‌ *verb* **1** to raise or force with a pump **2** *informal* to draw out information from by clever questioning

**pumpkin** *noun* a large, roundish, thick-skinned, yellow fruit, with stringy edible flesh

**pun** *noun* a play upon words which sound similar but have different meanings, *eg* 'two *pears* make a *pair*' ◌ *verb* to make a pun

**pun** *verb* ⇔ puns, punning, punned

**punch¹** *verb* **1** to hit with the fist **2** to make a hole in with a tool ◌ (*pl* **punches**) **1** a blow with the fist **2** a tool for punching holes ◌ **punchy** *adj* having a powerful effect, striking ◌ **punch line** the words that give the main point to a joke

**punch²** *noun* a drink made of spirits or wine, water, sugar *etc*

**punctilious** *adj* paying attention to details, *esp* in behaviour; fastidious

**punctual** *adj* **1** on time, not late **2** strict in keeping the time of appointments ◌ **punctuality** *noun*

**punctuate** *verb* **1** to divide up sentences by commas, full stops *etc* **2** to interrupt at intervals: *the silence was punctuated by coughs* ◌ **punctuation** *noun* the use of punctuation marks ◌ **punctuation marks** the symbols used in punctuating sentences, *eg* full stop, comma, colon, question mark *etc*

**puncture** *noun* **1** an act of pricking or piercing **2** a small hole made with a sharp point **3** a hole in a tyre

**pundit** *noun* an expert

**pungent** *adj* **1** sharp-tasting or sharp-smelling **2** of a remark: strongly sarcastic

**punish** *verb* **1** to make (someone) suffer for a fault or crime **2** to inflict suffering on **3** to treat roughly or harshly ◌ **punishable** *adj* ◌ **punishment** *noun* pain or constraints inflicted for a fault or crime

**punitive** (*say* pyoo-nit-iv) *adj* inflicting punishment or suffering

**punnet** *noun* a small basket for holding fruit

**punt** *noun* a flat-bottomed boat with square ends ◌ *verb* to move (a punt) by pushing a pole against the bottom of a river

**punter** *noun* **1** a professional gambler **2** a customer, a client **3** an ordinary person

**puny** *adj* little and weak

**pup** *noun* **1** a puppy **2** the young of certain other animals, *eg* a seal

**pupa** (*say* pyoo-pa) *noun* (*pl* **pupae** - *say* pyoo-pee) the stage in the growth of an insect in which it changes from a larva to its mature form, *eg* from a caterpillar into a butterfly ◌ **pupate** (*say* pyoo-peit) *verb*

**pupil** *noun* **1** someone who is being taught by a teacher **2** the round opening in the middle of the eye through which light passes

**puppet** *noun* **1** a doll which is moved by strings or wires **2** a doll that fits over the hand and is moved by the fingers **3** someone who acts exactly as they are told to

**puppy** *noun* a young dog ◌ **puppy fat** temporary fat in childhood or adolescence ◌ **puppy love** immature love when very young

**purchase** *verb* to buy ◌ *noun* **1** the act of buying **2** something which is bought **3** the power to lift by using a lever **4** firm grip or hold ◌ **purchaser** *noun*

**purdah** *noun, historical* the seclusion of Hindu or Islamic women from strangers, behind a screen or under a veil

**pure** *adj* **1** clean, spotless **2** free from dust, dirt *etc* **3** not mixed with other substances **4** free from faults or sin, innocent **5** utter, absolute, nothing but: *pure nonsense* ◌ **purely** *adv*

**purée** *noun* food made into a pulp by

being put through a sieve or liquidizing machine □ *verb* to make into a purée, pulp

**purgative** *noun* a medicine which clears waste matter out of the body □ *adj*

**purgatory** *noun* **1** in the Roman Catholic Church, a place where souls are made pure before entering heaven **2** a state of suffering for a time

**purge** *verb* **1** to make clean, purify **2** to clear (something) of anything unwanted

**purify** *verb* to make pure □ **purification** *noun*

**purify** ⇔ purifies, purifying, purified

**purist** *noun* someone who insists on correctness

**puritan** *noun* **1** someone of strict, often narrow-minded, morals **2** (**Puritan**) *historical* one of a group believing in strict simplicity in worship and daily life □ **puritanical** *adj* □ **puritanism** *noun*

**purity** (*from* pure) *noun* the state of being pure

**purl** *verb* to knit in stitches made with the wool in front of the work

**purloin** *verb* to steal

**purple** *noun* a dark colour formed by the mixture of blue and red

**purport** *noun* meaning □ *verb* **1** to mean **2** to seem, pretend: *he purports to be a film expert*

**purpose** *noun* **1** aim, intention **2** use, function (of a tool *etc*) □ *verb* to intend □ **purposely** *adv* intentionally □ **on purpose** intentionally □ **to the purpose** to the point

**purr** *noun* the low, murmuring sound made by a cat when pleased □ *verb* of a cat: to make this sound

**purse** *noun* **1** a small bag for carrying money **2** *US* a handbag □ *verb* to close (the lips) tightly

**purser** *noun* the officer who looks after a ship's money

**pursue** *verb* **1** to follow after (in order to overtake or capture), chase **2** to be engaged in, carry on (studies, an enquiry *etc*) **3** to follow (a route, path *etc*) □ **pursuer** *noun* □ **pursuit** *noun* **1** the act of pursuing **2** an occupation or hobby

**purvey** *verb* to supply (food *etc*) as a business □ **purveyor** *noun*

**pus** *noun* a thick yellowish liquid produced from infected wounds

**push** *verb* **1** to press hard against **2** to thrust (something) away with force, shove **3** to urge on **4** to make a big effort □ *noun* **1** a thrust **2** effort **3** *informal* energy and determination □ **pushy** *adj* aggressively assertive □ **push-chair** *noun* a folding chair on wheels for a young child

**pusillanimous** (*say* pyoo-si-lan-im-us) *adj* cowardly □ **pusillanimity** *noun*

**pussy** *noun, informal* a cat, a kitten □ **pussy-foot** *verb* to act timidly or non-committally □ **pussy-willow** *noun* an American willow tree with silky catkins

**pustule** *noun* a small pimple containing pus

**put** *verb* **1** to place, lay, set: *put the book on the table* **2** to bring to a certain position or state: *put the light on* **3** to express: *put the question more clearly* □ **put about 1** to change course at sea **2** to spread (news) □ **put by** to set aside, save up □ **put down** to defeat □ **put in for** to make a claim for, apply for □ **put off 1** to delay **2** to turn (someone) away from their plan or intention □ **put out 1** to extinguish (a fire, light *etc*) **2** to annoy, embarrass □ **put up 1** to build **2** to propose, suggest (a plan, candidate *etc*) **3** to let (someone) stay in your house *etc* **4** to stay as a guest in someone's house □ **put up with** to bear patiently, tolerate

**put** ⟷ **puts**, **putting**, **put**

ⓘ From Late Old English *putian*

**putative** *adj* supposed, commonly accepted

ⓘ From Latin *putare* meaning 'to suppose'

**putrefy** *verb* to go bad, rot □ **putrefaction** *noun* □ **putrid** *adj* rotten; stinking

**putrefy** ⟷ **putrefies**, **putrefying**, **putrefied**

**putt** *verb*, *golf* to send a ball gently forward □ **putter** *noun* a golf club used for this

**putty** *noun* a cement made from ground chalk, used in putting glass in windows *etc*

**puzzle** *verb* **1** to present with a difficult problem or situation *etc* **2** to be difficult (for someone) to understand **3 puzzle something out** to consider long and carefully in order to solve (a problem) □ *noun* **1** a difficulty which needs a lot of thought **2** a toy or riddle to test knowledge or skill: *crossword puzzle*

**pygmy** or **pigmy** (*pl* **pygmies** or **pigmies**) *noun* one of a race of very small human beings

**pyjamas** or **pajamas** *noun pl* a sleeping suit consisting of trousers and a jacket

**pylon** *noun* **1** a high, steel tower supporting electric power cables **2** a guiding mark at an airfield

**pyramid** *noun* **1** a solid shape with flat sides which come to a point at the top **2** *historical* a building of this shape used as a tomb in ancient Egypt

**pyre** *noun* a pile of wood on which a dead body is burned

**python** *noun* a large, non-poisonous snake which crushes its victims

# Qq

**QC** *abbreviation* Queen's Counsel

**qed** (*pronounced* kyoo ee **dee**) *abbrev* which was to be demonstrated

ⓘ From Latin *quod erat demonstrandum*

**quack** *noun* **1** the cry of a duck **2** someone who falsely claims to have medical knowledge or training □ *verb* to make the noise of a duck

**quad** *short for* **1** quadruplet **2** quadrangle

**quadrangle** *noun* **1** *maths* a figure with four equal sides and angles **2** a four-sided courtyard surrounded by buildings in a school, college *etc* □ **quadrangular** *adj* having the shape of a quadrangle

**quadrant** *noun* **1** one quarter of the circumference or area of a circle **2** an instrument used in astronomy, navigation *etc* for measuring

heights

**quadri-** or **quadru-** *prefix* four: *quadrilateral/ quadruped*

ⓘ From Latin *quattuor* meaning 'four'

**quadrilateral** *noun* a four-sided figure or area □ *adj* four-sided

**quadrille** *noun* a dance for four couples arranged to form a square

**quadriplegia** *noun* paralysis of both arms and both legs □ **quadriplegic** *noun* someone suffering from quadriplegia

**quadruped** *noun* a four-footed animal

**quadruple** *adj* **1** four times as much or many **2** made up of four parts □ *verb* to make or become four times greater: *quadrupled the price*

**quadruplet** *noun* one of four children

born to the same mother at one
birth

**quaff** (*say* kwahf *or* kwof) *verb* to
drink up eagerly

**quagmire** *noun* wet, boggy ground

**quail** *verb* to shrink back in fear
□ *noun* a type of small bird like a
partridge

**quaint** *adj* pleasantly odd, *esp*
because of being old-fashioned

**quake** *verb* to shake, tremble with
fear □ *noun*, *informal* an earthquake

**quake** *verb* ⇨ quakes, quaking,
quaked

**Quaker** *noun* a member of a religious
group opposed to violence and war,
founded in the 17th century

Originally a nickname given to the
group because their founder, George
Fox, told them to *quake* at the word
of God

**qualify** *verb* **1** to be suitable for a job
or position **2** to pass a test **3** to
lessen the force of (a statement) by
adding or changing words
□ **qualified** *adj* having the necessary
qualifications for a job
□ **qualification** *noun* **1** a qualifying
statement **2** a skill that makes
someone suitable for a job

**quality** *noun* (*pl* **qualities**) **1** an
outstanding feature of someone or
thing: *kindness is a quality admired
by all* **2** degree of worth: *cloth of
poor quality* □ **qualitative** *adj*
relating to quality rather than
quantity

**qualm** *noun* doubt about whether
something is right

**quandary** *noun* (*pl* **quandaries**) **1** a
state of uncertainty **2** a situation in
which it is difficult to decide what to
do

**quango** *noun* (*pl* **quangos**) an official
body, funded and appointed by
government, that supervises some
national activity *etc*

**quantify** *verb* to state the quantity of

□ **quantifiable** *adj* capable of being
quanitified

**quantify** ⇨ quantifies, quantifying,
quantified

**quantity** *noun* (*pl* **quantities**)
**1** amount: *a large quantity of paper*
**2** a symbol which represents an
amount: *x is the unknown quantity*
□ **quantitative** *adj* relating to
quantity, not quality

**quantum leap** a huge, dramatic jump

**quarantine** *noun* the isolation of
people or animals who might be
carrying an infectious disease □ *verb*
to put in quarantine

**quark** *noun*, *physics* a sub-atomic
particle

A word invented by James Joyce in
*Finnegans Wake* (1939)

**quarrel** *noun* an angry disagreement
or argument □ *verb* **1** to disagree
violently or argue angrily (with)
**2** to find fault (with) □ **quarrelsome**
*adj* fond of quarrelling, inclined to
quarrel

**quarrel** *verb* ⇨ quarrels,
quarrelling, quarrelled

**quarry** *noun* (*pl* **quarries**) **1** a pit
from which stone is taken for
building **2** a hunted animal
**3** someone or something eagerly
looked for □ *verb* to dig (stone *etc*)
from a quarry

**quarry** *verb* ⇨ quarries, quarrying,
quarried

**quart** *noun* a measure of liquids,
1.136 litre (2 pints)

**quarter** *noun* **1** one of four equal
parts of something **2** a fourth part
of a year, three months **3** direction:
*no help came from any quarter* **4** a
district **5** mercy shown to an enemy:
*no quarter was given by either side*
**6** (**quarters**) lodgings,
accommodation □ *verb* **1** to divide
into four equal parts **2** to
accommodate

**quarter-deck** *noun* the upper deck of
a ship between the stern and the

mast nearest it

**quarter-final** *noun* a match in a competition immediately before a semi-final

**quarterly** *adj* happening every three months □ *adv* every three months □ *noun* (*pl* **quarterlies**) a magazine *etc* published every three months

**quartet** *noun* 1 a group of four players or singers 2 a piece of music written for such a group

**quartz** *noun* a hard substance often in crystal form, found in rocks

**quash** *verb* 1 to crush, put down (*eg* a rebellion) 2 to wipe out, annul (*eg* a judge's decision)

**quasi-** *prefix* to some extent, but not completely: *quasi-historical* ⓘ From Latin *quasi* meaning 'as if'

**quatrain** *noun* a poetic stanza of four lines

**quaver** *verb* 1 to shake, tremble 2 to speak in a shaking voice □ *noun* 1 a trembling of the voice 2 *music* a note (♪) equal to half a crotchet in length

**quay** (*say* kee) *noun* a solid landing place for loading and unloading boats

**queasy** *adj* 1 feeling nauseous 2 easily shocked or disgusted □ **queasiness** *noun*

**queen** *noun* 1 a female monarch 2 the wife of a king 3 the most powerful piece in chess 4 a high value playing-card with a picture of a queen 5 an egg-laying female bee, ant or wasp □ **queenly** *adj* of or like a queen □ **queen bee** 1 an egg-laying female bee 2 a woman who is the centre of attention □ **queen mother** the mother of the reigning king or queen who was once herself queen

**queer** *adj* 1 odd, strange 2 *informal* (sometimes *derogatory*) homosexual □ *noun*, *informal* (sometimes *derogatory*) a homosexual

**quell** *verb* 1 to crush (a rebellion *etc*) 2 to remove (fears, suspicions *etc*)

**quench** *verb* 1 to drink and so satisfy (thirst) 2 to put out (*eg* a fire

**querulous** *adj* complaining

**query** *noun* (*pl* **queries**) 1 a question 2 a question mark (?) □ *verb* to question (*eg* a statement)

**query** *verb* ⇨ **queries, querying, queried**

**quest** *noun* a search

**question** *noun* 1 something requiring an answer, *eg* 'where do you live?' 2 a subject, matter *etc*: *the energy question/ a question of ability* 3 a matter for dispute or doubt: *there's no question of him leaving* □ *verb* 1 to ask questions of (someone) 2 to express doubt about □ **questionable** *adj* doubtful □ **question mark** a symbol (?) put after a question in writing □ **questionnaire** *noun* a written list of questions to be answered by several people to provide information for a survey □ **out of the question** not even to be considered, unthinkable

**queue** *noun* a line of people waiting, *eg* for a bus □ *verb* to stand in, or form, a queue

**quibble** *verb* to avoid an important part of an argument by quarrelling over details □ *noun* a petty argument or complaint

**quiche** (*say* keesh) *noun* an open pastry case filled with beaten eggs, cheese *etc* and baked

**quick** *adj* 1 done or happening in a short time 2 acting without delay, fast-moving: *a quick brain* □ *noun* a tender area of skin under the nails □ *adv*, *informal* quickly □ **quickly** *adv* without delay, rapidly □ **quicken** *verb* to speed up, become or make faster □ **quickstep** *noun* a ballroom dance like a fast foxtrot □ **quick-tempered** *adj* easily made angry □ **the quick** *old* the living

**quicklime** *noun* lime (= calcium oxide, a white, caustic substance) which has not been mixed with water

**quicksand** *noun* sand that sucks in anyone who stands on it

**quicksilver** *noun* mercury

**quid** *noun, slang* a pound (£1)

**quiddity** *noun* 1 the essence or nature of something 2 a quibble

**quiescent** *adj* not active □ **quiescence** *noun* a quiescent state

**quiet** *adj* 1 making little or no noise 2 calm: *a quiet life* □ *noun* 1 the state of being quiet 2 lack of noise, peace □ *verb* to make or become quiet □ **quieten** *verb* to make or become quiet □ **quietly** *adv* in a quiet way; with little or no sound □ **quietness** *noun* being quiet

◆ Do not confuse with: **quite**

▣ (adj, meaning 1) silent, noiseless, inaudible, hushed, soft, low

**quiff** *noun* a tuft of hair brushed up and back from the forehead

**quill** *noun* 1 a large feather of a goose or other bird made into a pen 2 one of the sharp spines of a porcupine

**quilt** *noun* a bedcover filled with down, feathers *etc*

**quilted** *adj* made of two layers of material with padding between them

**quin** *short for* **quintuplet**

**quince** *noun* a pear-like fruit with a sharp taste, used to make jams *etc*

**quinine** *noun* a bitter drug taken from the bark of a S American tree, used to treat malaria

**quint-** *prefix* fifth
ⓘ From Latin *quintus* meaning 'fifth'

**quintessence** *noun* 1 the most important part of anything 2 the purest part or form of something □ **quintessential** *adj* central, essential

Literally 'fifth essence', sought after by medieval alchemists as the highest essence or ether

**quintet** *noun* 1 a group of five players or singers 2 a piece of music written for such a group

**quintuplet** *noun* one of five children born to a mother at the same time

**quip** *noun* a witty remark or reply □ *verb* to make a witty remark

**quip** *verb* ⋄ quips, quipp*ing*, quipp*ed*

**quire** *noun* a set of 24 sheets of paper
ⓘ Probably from Late Latin *quaternum* meaning 'a set of four sheets'

◆ Do not confuse with: **choir**

**quirk** *noun* 1 an odd feature of someone's behaviour 2 a trick, a sudden turn: *quirk of fate* □ **quirky** *adj* full of sudden twists; unpredictable, inconsistent

**quit** *verb* 1 to give up, stop: *I'm going to quit smoking* 2 *informal* to leave, resign from (a job) □ **be quits** to be even with each other

**quit** ⋄ quits, quitt*ing*, quit or quitt*ed*

**quite** *adv* 1 completely, entirely: *quite empty* 2 fairly, moderately: *quite good*

◆ Do not confuse with: **quiet**

**quiver**¹ *noun* a tremble, a shake □ *verb* to tremble, shake

**quiver**² *noun* a carrying case for arrows

**quixotic** *adj* having noble but foolish and unrealistic aims □ **quixotically** *adv*

After Don *Quixote*, the knight in Cervantes's 16th-century Spanish romance

**quiz** *verb* to question □ *noun* (*pl* **quizzes**) a competition to test knowledge □ **quizzical** *adj* of a look: as if asking a question, *esp* mockingly

**quiz** *verb* ⋄ quizzes, quizzing, quizzed

**quoits** *noun sing* a game in which heavy flat rings (**quoits**) are thrown on to small rods

**quorum** *noun* the least number of people who must be present at a meeting before any business can be done

From Latin phrase *quorum vos .. esse volumus* 'of whom we wish that you be (one, two etc)', used in legal commissions

**quota** *noun* a part or share to be given or received by each member of a group

**quote** *verb* **1** to repeat the words of (someone) exactly as said or written **2** to state (a price for something) □ **quotation** *noun* **1** the act of repeating something said or written **2** the words repeated **3** a price stated □ **quotation marks** marks used in writing to show that someone's words are being repeated exactly, *eg* 'he said, "I'm going out"'

**quoth** *verb*, *old* said

**quotient** *noun*, *maths* the result obtained by dividing one number by another, *eg* 4 is the quotient when 12 is divided by 3

## Rr

**rabbi** *noun* (*pl* **rabbis**) a Jewish priest or teacher of the law

**rabbit** *noun* a small, burrowing, long-eared animal

**rabble** *noun* a disorderly, noisy crowd

**rabid** *adj* **1** of a dog: suffering from rabies **2** violently enthusiastic or extreme: *a rabid nationalist*

**rabies** *noun* (also called: **hydrophobia**) a disease transmitted by the bite of an infected animal, causing fear of water and madness

**raccoon** or **racoon** *noun* a small furry animal of N America

**race¹** *noun* **1** a group of people with the same ancestors and physical characteristics **2** descent: *of noble race* □ **racial** *adj* of or according to race □ **racism** or **racialism** *noun* **1** the belief that some races of people are superior to others **2** prejudice on the grounds of race □ **racist** or **racialist** *noun* someone who believes in, or practises, racism □ *adj* involving racism

**race²** *noun* a competition to find the fastest person, animal, vehicle *etc* □ *verb* **1** to run fast **2** to take part in a race □ **racecourse** or **racetrack** *noun* a course over which races are run □ **racehorse** *noun* a horse bred and used for racing

**rack** *noun* **1** a framework for holding letters, plates, coats *etc* **2** *historical* an instrument for torturing victims by stretching their joints **3** a bar with teeth which fits into and moves a toothed wheel □ **rack and ruin** a state of neglect and decay □ **rack your brains** to think hard about something

**racket¹** or **racquet** *noun* a bat made up of a strong frame strung with gut or nylon for playing tennis, badminton *etc*

**racket²** *noun* **1** a great noise, a din **2** *informal* a dishonest way of making a profit □ **racketeer** *noun* someone who makes money dishonestly

**racoon** another spelling of **raccoon**

**racquet** another spelling of **racket**

**racy** *adj* of a story: full of action, and often involving sexual exploits

**radar** *noun* a method of detecting solid objects using radio waves which bounce back off the object and form a picture of it on a screen

**radiant** *adj* **1** sending out rays of light, heat *etc* **2** showing joy and happiness: *a radiant smile* □ **radiance** *noun* brightness, splendour

**radiate** *verb* **1** to send out rays of light, heat *etc* **2** to spread or send out from a centre □ **radiation** *noun* **1** the giving off of rays of light, heat *etc* or of those from radioactive substances **2** radioactivity □ **radiator** *noun* **1** a device (*esp* a series of connected hot-water pipes) which sends out heat **2** the part of a car which cools the engine

**radical** *adj* **1** thorough: *a radical change* **2** basic, deep-seated: *radical differences* **3** proposing dramatic changes in the method of government □ *noun* someone who has radical political views

**radio** *noun* (*pl* **radios**) a device for sending and receiving signals by means of electromagnetic waves □ *verb* to send a message to (someone) in this way

**radio** *verb* ⋄ **radio**s, **radio**ing, **radio**ed

**radioactive** *adj* giving off rays which are often dangerous but which can be used in medicine □ **radioactivity** *noun* the spontaneous disintegration of the atomic nuclei of some elements, *eg* uranium, resulting in the giving off of radiation

**radiography** *noun* photography of the interior of the body by X-rays □ **radiographer** *noun*

**radiology** *noun* **1** the study of radioactive substances and radiation **2** the branch of medicine involving the use of X-rays and radium □ **radiologist** *noun*

**radiotherapy** *noun* the treatment of certain diseases by X-rays or radioactive substances □ **radiotherapist** *noun*

**radish** *noun* (*pl* **radishes**) a plant with a sharp-tasting root, eaten raw in salads

**radium** *noun* a radioactive metal used in radiotherapy

**radius** *noun* (*pl* **radii**) **1** a straight line from the centre to the circumference of a circle **2** an area within a certain distance from a central point

**RAF** *abbrev* Royal Air Force

**raffia** *noun* strips of fibre from the leaves of a palm tree, used in weaving mats *etc*

**raffish** *adj* flashy, dashing

**raffle** *noun* a way of raising money by selling numbered tickets, one or more of which wins a prize □ *verb* to give as a prize in a raffle

**raft** *noun* a number of logs *etc* fastened together and used as a boat

**rafter** *noun* one of the sloping beams supporting a roof

**rag** *noun* **1** a torn or worn piece of cloth **2** (**rags**) worn-out, shabby clothes □ *adj* made of rags: *a rag doll* □ *verb* to tease, play tricks on □ **ragamuffin** *noun* a ragged, dirty child □ **rag-doll** *noun* a floppy doll made of scrap material □ **ragged** *adj* **1** in torn, shabby clothes **2** torn and tattered

**rag** *verb* ⋄ **rag**s, **rag**ging, **rag**ged

**rage** *noun* great anger, fury □ *verb* **1** to be violently angry **2** of a storm, battle *etc*: to be violent □ **all the rage** very fashionable or popular

**raglan** *noun* a cardigan or coat with the sleeves in one piece with the shoulders

Named after Lord *Raglan*, British commander in the Crimean war

**ragtime** *noun* a style of jazz music with highly syncopated melody

**raid** *noun* **1** a short, sudden attack **2** an unexpected visit by the police to catch a criminal, recover stolen goods *etc* □ *verb* to make a raid on □ **raider** *noun* a person who raids

**rail** noun **1** a bar of metal used in fences **2** (**rails**) strips of steel which form the track on which trains run **3** the railway: *I came here by rail* □ verb (with **against** or **at**) to complain about or criticize them angrily or bitterly □ **railing** noun a fence or barrier of rails □ **railway** or US **railroad** noun a track laid with steel rails on which trains run

**raiment** noun, old clothing

**rain** noun **1** water falling from the clouds in drops **2** a great number of things falling □ verb to pour or fall in drops: *it's raining today* □ **rainy** adj **1** full of rain: *rainy skies* **2** showery, wet: *a rainy day* □ **rainbow** noun the brilliant coloured bow or arch sometimes to be seen in the sky opposite the sun when rain is falling □ **raincheck** noun, US an arrangement to keep an appointment *etc* at a later, postponed date □ **raincoat** noun a waterproof coat to keep out the rain □ **rainfall** noun the amount of rain that falls in a certain time □ **rainforest** noun a tropical forest with very heavy rainfall

**raise** verb **1** to lift up: *raise the flag* **2** to make higher: *raise the price* **3** to bring up (a subject) for consideration **4** to bring up (a child, family *etc*) **5** to breed or grow (*eg* pigs, crops) **6** to collect, get together (a sum of money)

◖ Do not confuse with: **raze**

**raisin** noun a dried grape

**Raj** noun, historical the time of British rule in India, 1858–1947

**rajah** noun, historical an Indian prince

**rake¹** noun a tool, like a large comb with a long handle, for smoothing earth, gathering hay *etc* □ verb **1** to draw a rake over **2** to scrape (together) **3** to aim gunfire at (*eg* a ship) from one end to the other

**rake²** noun, old someone who lives an immoral life

**rakish** adj at a slanting, jaunty angle

**rally** verb **1** to gather again: *rally troops* **2** to come together for a joint action or effort: *the club's supporters rallied to save it* **3** to recover from an illness □ noun (pl **rallies**) **1** a gathering **2** a political mass meeting **3** an improvement in health after an illness **4** tennis a long series of shots before a point is won or lost **5** a competition to test driving skills over an unknown route

**rally** verb ⇔ rallies, rallying, rallied

**RAM** abbrev, computing random access memory

**ram** noun **1** a male sheep **2** something heavy, esp as part of a machine, for ramming □ verb **1** to press or push down hard **2** of a ship, car *etc*: to run into and cause damage to

**ram** verb ⇔ rams, ramming, rammed

**Ramadan** noun **1** the ninth month of the Islamic calendar, a period of fasting by day **2** the fast itself

**ramble** verb **1** to walk about for pleasure, esp in the countryside **2** to speak in an aimless or confused way □ noun a country walk for pleasure □ **rambler** noun **1** someone who goes walking in the country for pleasure **2** a climbing rose or other plant

**ramification** noun **1** a branch or part of a subject, plot *etc* **2** a consequence, usually indirect and one of several

**ramp** noun a sloping surface (*eg* of a road)

**rampage** verb to rush about angrily or violently □ **on the rampage** rampaging

**rampant** adj **1** widespread and uncontrolled **2** heraldry standing on the left hind leg: *lion rampant*

**rampart** noun a mound or wall built

as a defence

**ram-raid** *noun* a raid in which thieves gain access to a shop by smashing into its display window with a stolen car

**ramrod** *noun* **1** a rod for pushing the charge down a gun barrel **2** someone strict or inflexible in their views

**ramshackle** *adj* badly made, falling to pieces

**ran** *past form of* run

**ranch** *noun* (*pl* **ranches**) a large farm in North America for rearing cattle or horses

**rancid** *adj* of butter: smelling or tasting stale

**rancour** *noun* ill-will, hatred □ **rancorous** *adj* resentful, bitter

**random** *adj* done without any aim or plan; chance: *a random sample* □ **at random** without any plan or purpose

**random access memory** a computer memory in which data can be directly located

**range** *noun* **1** a line or row: *a range of mountains* **2** extent, number: *a wide range of goods* **3** a piece of ground with targets for shooting or archery practice **4** the distance which an object can be thrown, or across which a sound can be heard **5** the distance between the top and bottom notes of a singing voice **6** a large kitchen stove with a flat top □ *verb* **1** to set in a row or in order **2** to wander (over) **3** to stretch, extend

**ranger** *noun* a keeper who looks after a forest or park

**rank** *noun* **1** a row or line (*eg* of soldiers) **2** class, order: *the upper ranks of society/ the rank of captain* **3** (**ranks**) ordinary soldiers, not officers □ *verb* **1** to place in order of importance, merit *etc* **2** to have a place in an order: *apes rank above dogs in intelligence* □ *adj* **1** of a

plant: growing too plentifully **2** having a strong, unpleasant taste or smell **3** absolute: *rank nonsense* □ **rank and file 1** soldiers of the rank of private **2** ordinary people, the majority

**rankle** *verb* to cause lasting annoyance, bitterness *etc*

**ransack** *verb* to search thoroughly; plunder

**ransom** *noun* the price paid for the freeing of a captive □ *verb* to pay money to free (a captive)

**rant** *verb* to talk foolishly and angrily for a long time

**rap**[1] *noun* **1** a sharp blow or knock **2** *slang* responsibility for a crime or misdeed □ *verb* **1** (often **rap on something**) to strike it with a quick, sharp blow **2** **rap something out** to say it sharply
**rap** *verb* ▷ raps, rapping, rapped

**rap**[2] *noun* **1** *informal* an informal talk or discussion **2** a style of music accompanied by a rhythmic monologue

**rapacious** *adj* greedy, eager to seize as much as possible

**rape**[1] *verb* to have sexual intercourse with (someone) against their will, usually by force □ *noun* **1** the act of raping **2** the act of seizing and carrying off by force □ **rapist** *noun* someone who commits rape

**rape**[2] *noun* a type of plant like the turnip whose seeds give oil

**rapid** *adj* quick, fast □ **rapidly** *adv* quickly □ **rapidity** *noun* swiftness □ **rapids** *noun pl* a part in a river where the current flows swiftly

**rapier** *noun* a type of light sword with a narrow blade

**rapport** (*say* ra-pawr) *noun* a good relationship, sympathy

**rapt** *adj* having the mind fully occupied, engrossed: *rapt attention*

**rapture** *noun* great delight □ **rapturous** *adj* experiencing or demonstrating rapture

**rare** *adj* **1** seldom found, uncommon **2** of meat: lightly cooked ▫ **rarity** *noun* (*pl* **rarities**) **1** something uncommon **2** uncommonness

▶ Do not confuse with: **unique**. You can talk about something being **rare**, quite **rare**, very **rare** *etc*. It would be incorrect, however, to describe something as very **unique**, since things either are or are not **unique** - there are no levels of this quality.

**rarefy** or **rarify** *verb* to make thin or less dense

**rarefy** or **rarify** ⇔ **rarefies** or **rarifies**, **rarefying** or **rarifying**, **rarefied** or **rarified**

**raring** *adj*: **raring to go** very keen to go, start *etc*

**rascal** *noun* a naughty or wicked person

**rash** *adj* acting, or done, without thought ▫ *noun* redness or outbreak of spots on the skin ▫ **rashness** *noun* the state of being rash

**rasher** *noun* a thin slice (of bacon or ham)

**rasp** *noun* **1** a coarse file **2** a rough, grating sound ▫ *verb* **1** to rub with a file **2** to make a rough, grating noise **3** to say in a rough voice ▫ **rasping** *adj* of a sound: rough and unpleasant

**raspberry** *noun* **1** a type of red berry similar to a blackberry **2** the bush which bears this fruit

**rat** *noun* a gnawing animal, larger than a mouse ▫ *verb* to hunt or kill rats ▫ **rat on** to inform against

**rat** *verb* ⇔ **rats**, **ratting**, **ratted**

**ratchet** *noun* a toothed wheel, *eg* in a watch

**rate** *noun* **1** the frequency with which something happens or is done: *a high rate of road accidents* **2** speed: *speak at a tremendous rate* **3** level of cost, price *etc*: *paid at a higher rate* **4** (**rates**) the sum of money to be paid by the owner of a shop *etc* to pay for local public services ▫ *verb* **1** to work out the value of for taxation *etc* **2** to value: *I don't rate his work very highly*

**rather** *adv* **1** somewhat, fairly: *it's rather cold today* **2** more willingly: *I'd rather do it later* **3** more correctly speaking: *he agreed, or rather he didn't say no*

**ratify** *verb* to approve officially and formally: *ratified the treaty* ▫ **ratification** *noun* ratifying or being ratified

**ratify** ⇔ **ratifies**, **ratifying**, **ratified**

**rating** *noun* a sailor below the rank of an officer

**ratio** *noun* (*pl* **ratios**) the proportion of one thing to another: *a ratio of two parts flour to one of sugar*

**ration** *noun* **1** a measured amount of food given out at intervals **2** an allowance ▫ *verb* **1** to deal out (*eg* food) in measured amounts **2** to allow only a certain amount to (someone)

**rational** *adj* **1** able to reason **2** sensible; based on reason: *rational arguments* ▫ **rationality** *noun* being rational ▫ **rationally** *adv* in a rational way

**rationalize** *verb* **1** to think up a good reason for (an action or feeling) so as not to feel guilty about it **2** to make (an industry or organization) more efficient and profitable by reorganizing it to get rid of unnecessary costs and labour ▫ **rationalization** *noun* rationalizing or being rationalized

**rat-race** *noun* a fierce, unending competition for success or wealth

**rattle** *verb* **1** to give out short, sharp, repeated sounds **2** to fluster or irritate (someone) ▫ *noun* **1** a sharp noise, quickly repeated **2** a toy or instrument which makes such a sound ▫ **rattlesnake** *noun* a poisonous snake with bony rings on

its tail which rattle when shaken
□ **rattle off** to go through (a list of
names *etc*) quickly

**ratty** *adj* irritable

**raucous** *adj* hoarse, harsh: *a raucous
voice*

**raunchy** *adj* sexually suggestive,
lewd

**ravage** *verb* to cause destruction or
damage to; plunder □ *noun pl*
damaging effects: *the ravages of
time*

**rave** *verb* 1 to talk wildly, as if mad
2 *informal* to talk very
enthusiastically (about) □ *noun* a
large party held in a warehouse *etc*
with electronic music

**raven** *noun* a type of large black bird
of the crow family □ *adj* of hair:
black and glossy

**ravenous** *adj* very hungry

**ravine** *noun* a deep, narrow valley
between hills

**raving** *adj* mad, crazy

**ravish** *verb* 1 to plunder 2 to rape
3 to delight □ **ravishing** *adj* filling
with delight

**raw** *adj* 1 not cooked 2 not prepared
or refined, in its natural state: *raw
cotton/ raw text* 3 of weather: cold
4 sore □ **a raw deal** unjust treatment

**ray** *noun* 1 a line of light, heat *etc* 2 a
small degree or amount: *a ray of
hope* 3 one of several lines going
outwards from a centre 4 a kind of
flat-bodied fish

**rayon** *noun* a type of artificial silk

**raze** *verb* to destroy, knock flat (a
town, house *etc*)
ⓔ From French *raser* meaning 'to
shave'

♠. Do not confuse with: **raise**

**razor** *noun* a sharp-edged instrument
for shaving

**razzmatazz** *noun* showiness,
glamorous or extravagant show

**RC** *abbrev* Roman Catholic

**re** *prep* concerning, about

**re-** *prefix* 1 again, once more:
*recreate* 2 back: *reclaim*

re- is a Latin prefix

**reach** *verb* 1 to arrive at: *reach the
summit/ your message never reached
me* 2 to stretch out (the hand) so as
to touch: *I couldn't reach the top
shelf* 3 to extend □ *noun* 1 a distance
that can be travelled easily: *within
reach of home* 2 the distance
someone can stretch their arm 3 a
straight part of a stream or river
between bends

**react** *verb* 1 to act or behave in
response to something done or said
2 to undergo a chemical change:
*metals react with sulphuric acid*

**reaction** *noun* 1 behaviour as a result
of action 2 a chemical change 3 a
movement against a situation or
belief: *a reaction against Victorian
morality*

**reactionary** *adj* favouring a return to
old ways, laws *etc* □ *noun* (*pl*
**reactionaries**) someone who holds
reactionary views

**read** *verb* 1 to look at and
understand, or say aloud written or
printed words 2 to study a subject in
a university or college: *reading law*
□ **readable** *adj* quite interesting to
read □ **reader** *noun* 1 someone who
reads books *etc* 2 someone who
reads manuscripts for a publisher
3 a senior university lecturer 4 a
reading book for children □ **read
only memory** *computing* a memory
device that can only be read, not
written to □ **read-out** *noun* 1 data
from a computer; output 2 data
from a radio transmitter

read ⇔ read*s*, read*ing*, read

**readily** *adv* easily; willingly
□ **readiness** *noun* 1 the state of
being ready and prepared
2 willingness: *the readiness of the
troops to fight*

**ready** *adj* 1 prepared: *packed and*

*ready to go* **2** willing: *always ready to help* **3** quick: *too ready to find fault* **4** available for use: *your coat is ready for collection* □ **readily** *adv* easily; willingly □ **readiness** *noun* **1** the state of being ready and prepared **2** willingness: *the readiness of the troops to fight*

**readymade** *adj* of clothes: made for general sale, not made specially for one person

**real** *adj* **1** actually existing, not imagined **2** not imitation, genuine: *real leather* **3** sincere: *a real love of music* □ **realism** *noun* the showing or viewing of things as they really are □ **realist** *noun* someone who claims to see life as it really is □ **reality** *noun* (*pl* **realities**) that which is real and not imaginary; truth □ **the real Mackay** or **the real McCoy** the genuine article, the real thing

**realistic** *adj* **1** life-like **2** viewing things as they really are □ **realistically** *adv*

**realization** *noun* realizing or being realized

**realize** *verb* **1** to come to understand, know: *I never realized you could sing* **2** to make real, accomplish: *realize an ambition* **3** to get (money) for: *realized £16 000 on the sale of the house* □ **realization** *noun* realizing or being realized

**really** *adv* **1** in fact **2** very: *really dark hair*

---

■ (meaning 1) actually, truly, honestly, sincerely, genuinely, positively, certainly, absolutely, categorically, indeed; (meaning 2) extremely, most

---

**realm** *noun* **1** a kingdom, a country **2** an area of activity or interest

**ream** *noun* **1** a measure for paper, 20 quires **2** (**reams**) a large quantity, *esp* of paper: *she wrote reams in her English exam*

**reap** *verb* **1** to cut and gather (corn *etc*) **2** to gain: *reap the benefits of*

*hard work* □ **reaper** *noun* **1** someone who reaps **2** a machine for reaping

**rear** *noun* **1** the back part of anything **2** the last part of an army or fleet □ *verb* **1** to bring up (children) **2** to breed (animals) **3** of an animal: to stand on its hindlegs □ **rearguard** *noun* troops which protect the rear of an army □ **bring up the rear** to come or be last in a series

**reason** *noun* **1** cause, excuse: *what is the reason for this noise?* **2** purpose: *what is your reason for visiting America?* **3** the power of the mind to form opinions, judge right and truth *etc* **4** common sense □ *verb* **1** to think out (opinions *etc*) **2** (**reason with someone**) to try to persuade them by arguing □ **reasonable** *adj* **1** sensible **2** fair

**reassure** *verb* to take away (someone's) doubts or fears □ **reassurance** *noun* something which reassures, or the feeling of being reassured □ **reassuring** *adj* that reassures

**rebate** *noun* a part of a payment or tax which is given back to the payer

**rebel** *noun* (*say* **reb-**el) someone who opposes or fights against those in power □ *verb* (*say* ri-**bel**) to take up arms against or oppose those in power

**rebel** *verb* ⇨ rebel**s**, rebel**ling**, rebel**led**

**rebellion** *noun* **1** an open or armed fight against those in power **2** a refusal to obey □ **rebellious** *adj* rebelling or likely to rebel □ **rebelliousness** *noun* being rebellious

**reboot** *verb* to restart (a computer) using its start-up programs

**rebound** *verb* (*say* ri-**bownd**) to bounce back: *the ball rebounded off the wall* □ *noun* (*say* **ree-**bownd) **1** the act of rebounding **2** a reaction following an emotional situation or crisis

**rebuff** *noun* a blunt refusal or rejection □ *verb* to reject bluntly

**rebuke** *verb* to scold, blame □ *noun* a scolding

**rebut** *verb* to deny (what has been said) □ **rebuttal** *noun* a rejection or contradiction

**rebut** ⇔ rebuts, rebut*ting*, rebut*ted*

**recalcitrant** *adj* stubborn; disobedient □ **recalcitrance** *noun* stubbornness; disobedience

**recall** *verb* 1 to call back: *recalled to headquarters* 2 to remember □ *noun* 1 a signal or message to return 2 the act of recalling or remembering

**recant** *verb* 1 to take back what you have said 2 to reject publicly your beliefs □ **recantation** *noun* recanting

**recap** *short for* 1 recapitulation 2 recapitulate

**recap** ⇔ recaps, recap*ping*, recap*ped*

**recapitulate** *verb* to go over again quickly the chief points of anything (*eg* a discussion) □ **recapitulation** *noun* an act or instance of recapitulating or summing up

**recapture** *verb* to capture (what has escaped or been lost)

**recast** *verb* to shape in a new form

**recast** ⇔ recasts, recast*ing*, recast

**recede** *verb* 1 to go back 2 to become more distant 3 to slope backwards □ **receding** *adj* 1 going or sloping backwards 2 becoming more distant

**receipt** *noun* 1 the act of receiving (*esp* money or goods) 2 a written note saying that money has been received

**receive** *verb* 1 to have something given or brought to you: *receive a gift/ receive a letter* 2 to meet and welcome: *receiving visitors* 3 to take goods, knowing them to be stolen □ **receiver** *noun* 1 someone who

receives stolen goods 2 the part of a telephone through which words are heard and into which they are spoken 3 an apparatus through which television or radio broadcasts are received

**recent** *adj* happening, done or made only a short time ago □ **recently** *adv* a short time ago

**receptacle** *noun* an object to receive or hold things, a container

**reception** *noun* 1 a welcome: *a warm reception* 2 a large meeting to welcome guests 3 the quality of radio or television signals □ **receptionist** *noun* someone employed in an office or hotel to answer the telephone *etc*

**receptive** *adj* quick to take in or accept ideas *etc*

**recess** *noun* (*pl* **recesses**) 1 part of a room set back from the rest, an alcove 2 the time during which parliament or the law courts do not work 3 remote parts: *in the recesses of my memory*

**recession** *noun* 1 the act of moving back 2 a temporary fall in a country's or world business activities

**recessive** *adj* tending to recede

**recipe** *noun* instructions on how to prepare or cook a certain kind of food

**recipient** *noun* someone who receives

**reciprocate** *verb* to feel or do the same in return: *I reciprocate his dislike of me* □ **reciprocal** *adj* both given and received: *reciprocal affection*

**recite** *verb* to repeat aloud from memory □ **recital** *noun* 1 the act of reciting 2 a musical performance 3 the facts of a story told one after the other □ **recitation** *noun* a poem *etc* recited

**reckless** *adj* rash, careless □ **recklessly** *adv*

**reckon** *verb* 1 to count 2 to consider,

believe □ **reckoning** *noun* **1** the settling of debts, grievances *etc* **2** payment for sins **3** a bill **4** a sum, calculation

**reclaim** *verb* **1** to claim back **2** to win back (land from the sea) by draining, building banks *etc* **3** to make waste land fit for use □ **reclamation** *noun* reclaiming or being reclaimed

**recline** *verb* to lean or lie on your back or side

**recluse** *noun* someone who lives alone and avoids other people □ **reclusive** *adj* solitary

**recognize** *verb* **1** to know from a previous meeting *etc* **2** to admit, acknowledge: *everyone recognized his talent* **3** to show appreciation of: *they recognized his courage by giving him a medal* □ **recognizable** *adj* capable of being recognized □ **recognition** *noun* the act of recognizing someone or something

**recoil** *verb* **1** to shrink back in horror or fear **2** of a gun: to jump back after a shot is fired □ *noun* a shrinking back

**recollect** *verb* to remember □ **recollection** *noun* **1** the act or power of remembering **2** a memory, something remembered

**recommend** *verb* **1** to urge, advise: *I recommend that you take a long holiday* **2** to speak highly of □ **recommendation** *noun* **1** the act of recommending **2** a point in favour of someone or something

**recompense** *verb* to pay money to or reward (a person) to make up for loss, inconvenience *etc* □ *noun* payment in compensation

**reconcile** *verb* **1** to bring together in friendship, after a quarrel **2** to show that two statements, facts *etc* do not contradict each other **3** (with **to**) to agree to accept an unwelcome fact or situation patiently: *I became reconciled to her absence*

□ **reconciliation** *noun* the fact of being friendly with someone again, after an argument, dispute or conflict: *there seems little hope of reconciliation*

**reconnaissance** (*say* ri-kon-is-ens) *noun* a survey to obtain information, *esp* before a battle

**reconnoitre** (*say* rek-o-noi-ter) *verb* to make a reconnaissance of

**reconstitute** *verb* to put back into its original form

**record** *verb* (*say* ri-kawd) **1** to write down for future reference **2** to put (music, speech *etc*) on tape or disc so that it can be listened to later □ *noun* (*say* rek-awd) **1** a written report of facts **2** a round, flat piece of plastic on which sounds are recorded for playing on a record-player **3** the best known performance: *John holds the school record for the mile* □ **recorder** *noun* **1** someone who records **2** a type of simple musical wind instrument **3** a judge in certain courts □ **recording** *noun* **1** the act of recording **2** recorded music, speech *etc* □ **record-player** *noun* a machine for playing records □ **break** or **beat the record** to do better than any previous performance □ **off the record** of a remark *etc*: not to be made public

**recount** *verb* **1** (*say* ree-kownt) to count again **2** (*say* ri-kownt) to tell (the story of) □ *noun* (*say* ree-kownt) a second count, *esp* of votes in an election

**recoup** (*say* ri-koop) *verb* to make good, recover (expenses, losses *etc*) ⊕ From French *recouper* meaning 'to cut back'

⬥ Do not confuse with: **recuperate**

**recourse** *noun*: **have recourse to** to make use of in an emergency

**recover** *verb* **1** to get possession of again **2** to become well again after an illness □ **recoverable** *adj* □ **recovery** *noun* (*pl* **recoveries**) **1** a return to health **2** the regaining of something lost *etc*

**recreation** *noun* a sport, hobby *etc* done in your spare time

**recriminations** *noun pl* accusations made by someone who is themselves accused

**recruit** *noun* a newly-enlisted soldier, member *etc* □ *verb* to enlist (someone) in an army, political party *etc* □ **recruitment** *noun*

**rectangle** *noun* a four-sided figure with all its angles right angles and its opposite sides equal in length, an oblong □ **rectangular** *adj*

**rectify** *verb* to put right □ **rectifiable** *adj*

**rectify** ⟿ rectifies, rectifying, rectified

**rectilineal** or **rectilinear** *adj* in a straight line or lines

**rectitude** *noun* honesty; correctness of behaviour

**rector** *noun* **1** a member of the Anglican clergy in charge of a parish **2** the headmaster of some Scottish secondary schools **3** a Scottish university official elected by the students □ **rectory** *noun* (*plural* **rectories**) the house of an Anglican rector

**rectum** *noun* the lower part of the alimentary canal

**recumbent** *adj* lying down

**recuperate** *verb* to recover strength or health □ **recuperation** *noun*

◖. Do not confuse with: **recoup**

**recur** *verb* to happen again □ **recurrence** *noun* □ **recurrent** *adj*

**recur** ⟿ recurs, recurring, recurred

**recycle** *verb* **1** to remake into something different **2** to treat (material) by some process in order to use it again

**red** *adj* **1** of the colour of blood □ *noun* this colour □ **redden** *verb* to make or grow red □ **red-handed** *adv* in the act of doing wrong □ **red**

**herring** something mentioned to lead a discussion away from the main subject; a false clue □ **Red Indian** *offensive* a Native American □ **red light 1** a danger signal **2** a signal to stop □ **red tape** unnecessary and troublesome rules about how things are to be done □ **see red** to become very angry

**redeem** *verb* **1** to buy back (*eg* articles from a pawnbroker) **2** to save from sin or condemnation **3** to make amends for □ **redeemer** *noun* **1** a person who redeems **2** (**the Redeemer**) Jesus Christ □ **redeeming** *adj* making up for other faults: *a redeeming feature* □ **redemption** *noun* the act of redeeming or state of being redeemed, *esp* the freeing of humanity from sin by Christ

**redolent** *adj* **1** sweet-smelling **2** smelling (of) **3** suggestive, making one think (of): *redolent of earlier times*

**redouble** *verb* to make twice as great: *redouble your efforts*

**redoubtable** *adj* brave, bold

**redress** *verb* to set right, make up for (a wrong *etc*) □ *noun* something done or given to make up for a loss or wrong, compensation

**reduce** *verb* **1** to make smaller **2** to lessen **3** to bring to the point of by force of circumstances: *reduced to begging in the streets* **4** to bring to a lower rank or state **5** to change into other terms: *reduce pounds to pence* □ **reduction** *noun* **1** an act or instance of reducing; the state of being reduced **2** the amount by which something is reduced **3** a reduced copy of a picture, document *etc*

**redundance** or **redundancy** (*pl* **redundancies**) *noun* **1** being redundant, or an instance of this **2** a dismissal or a person dismissed because they are no longer needed □ **redundant** *adj* **1** more than what is needed **2** of a worker: no longer needed because of the lack of a suitable job

**reed** noun **1** a tall stiff grass growing in moist or marshy places **2** a part (originally made of reed) of certain wind instruments which vibrates when the instrument is played □ **reedy** adj **1** full of reeds **2** like a reed **3** sounding like a reed instrument: a reedy voice

**reef** noun a chain of rocks lying at or near the surface of the sea

**reef knot** a square, very secure knot

**reek** noun **1** a strong, unpleasant smell **2** smoke □ verb **1** to send out smoke **2** to smell strongly

**reel** noun **1** a cylinder of plastic, metal or wood on which thread, film, fishing lines etc may be wound **2** a length of cinema film **3** a lively Scottish or Irish dance □ verb **1** to wind on a reel **2** **reel something in** to draw, pull in (a fish on a line) **3** to stagger □ **reel off** to repeat or recite quickly, without pausing

**ref** abbrev **1** referee **2** reference

**refectory** noun (pl **refectories**) a communal dining hall for monks, students etc

**refer** verb: **refer to 1** to mention **2** to turn to for information **3** to relate to, apply to **4** to direct to for information, consideration etc: I refer you to the managing director

**refer** ⟷ refers, referring, referred

**referee** noun **1** someone to whom a matter is taken for settlement **2** a judge in a sports match **3** someone willing to provide a note about someone's character, work record etc

**reference** noun **1** the act of referring **2** a mention **3** a note about a person's character, work etc □ **reference book** a book to be consulted for information, eg an encyclopedia □ **reference library** a library of books to be looked at for

information but not taken away

**referendum** noun (pl **referenda** or **referendums**) a vote given by the people of a country about some important matter

**refine** verb **1** to purify **2** to improve, make more exact etc □ **refined** adj **1** purified **2** polite in manners, free of vulgarity □ **refinement** noun **1** good manners, taste, learning **2** an improvement □ **refinery** noun (pl **refineries**) a place where sugar, oil etc are refined

**refit** verb to repair damages (esp to a ship)

**refit** ⟷ refits, refitting, refitted

**reflect** verb **1** to throw back (light or heat) **2** to give an image of **3** **reflect on someone** to throw blame on them: her behaviour reflects on her mother **4** **reflect on something** to think it over carefully □ **reflection** noun **1** the act of throwing back **2** the image of someone etc reflected in a mirror **3** blame, unfavourable criticism □ **reflective** adj thoughtful □ **reflector** noun something (eg a piece of shiny metal) which throws back light

**reflex** noun (pl **reflexes**) an action which is automatic, not intended, eg jerking the leg when the kneecap is struck □ adj done as an automatic response, unthinking

**reflexive** adj, grammar showing that the object (**reflexive pronoun**) of the verb (**reflexive verb**) is the same as its subject, eg in 'he cut himself', himself is a reflexive pronoun and cut a reflexive verb

**reform** verb **1** to improve, remove faults from **2** to give up bad habits, evil etc □ noun an improvement □ **reformation** noun **1** a change for the better **2** (**the Reformation**) the religious movement in the Christian Church in the 16th century from which the Protestant Church arose □ **reformer** noun someone who wishes to bring about improvements

**refract** *verb* to change the direction of (a wave of light, sound, *etc*) □ **refraction** *noun* a change in the direction of (a wave of light, sound *etc*)

**refractory** *adj* unruly, not easily controlled

**refrain** *noun* a chorus coming at the end of each verse of a song □ *verb* to keep yourself back (from doing something): *please refrain from smoking*

**refresh** *verb* to give new strength, power or life to □ **refreshing** *adj* **1** bringing back strength **2** cooling □ **refresher course** a course of study intended to keep up or increase existing knowledge of a subject □ **refreshments** *noun pl* food and drink □ **refresh your memory** to go over facts again so that they are clear in your mind

**refrigerator** *noun* a storage machine which keeps food cold and so prevents it from going bad □ **refrigerate** *verb* □ **refrigeration** *noun*

**refuel** *verb* to supply with, or take in, fresh fuel

**refuel** ⇨ refuel**s**, refuel**ling**, refuel**led**

**refuge** *noun* a place of safety (from attack, danger *etc*) □ **refugee** *noun* someone who seeks shelter from persecution in another country

**refund** *verb* (*say* ri-**fund**) to pay back □ *noun* (*say* **ree**-fund *or* ri-**fund**) a payment returned, *eg* for unsatisfactory goods

**refuse**[1] (*say* ri-**fyooz**) *verb* **1** to say that you will not do something: *he refused to leave the room* **2** to withhold, not give (*eg* permission) □ **refusal** *noun* **1** an act of refusing **2** the option of accepting or refusing something: *I promised to give him first refusal on my car* (= offer to sell it to him before advertising it generally)

**refuse**[2] (*say* **ref**-yoos) *noun* something which is thrown aside as worthless, rubbish

**refute** *verb* to prove wrong (something that has been said or written) □ **refutation** *noun*

**regain** *verb* **1** to win back again **2** to get back to: *regain the shore*

**regal** *adj* kingly, royal

**regale** (*say* ri-**geil**) *verb* to entertain lavishly

**regalia** *noun pl* symbols of royalty, *eg* a crown and sceptre

**regard** *verb* **1** to look upon, consider **2** to look at carefully **3** to pay attention to □ *noun* **1** concern **2** affection **3** respect **4** (**regards**) good wishes □ **regarding** *prep* concerning, to do with □ **regardless** *adv* not thinking or caring about costs, problems, dangers *etc*; in spite of everything: *carry on regardless* □ **regardless of** paying no care or attention to □ **with regard to** *or* **in regard to** concerning

**regatta** *noun* a meeting for yacht or boat races

From the name of a gondola race held on the Grand Canal in Venice

**regenerate** *verb* to make new and good again

**regeneration** *noun* regenerating or being regenerated

**regent** *noun* someone who governs in place of a king or queen □ **regency** *noun* (*pl* **regencies**) **1** rule by a regent **2** the period of a regent's rule

**reggae** *noun* a strongly rhythmic type of rock music, originally from the West Indies

**régime** *or* **regime** (*say both* rei-**szeem**) *noun* method or system of government or administration

**regiment** *noun* a body of soldiers, commanded by a colonel □ *verb* to organize or control too strictly □ **regimental** *adj*

**region** noun an area, a district □ **in the region of** somewhere near □ **regional** adj

**register** noun **1** a written list (eg of attendances at school, of those eligible to vote etc) **2** the distance between the highest and lowest notes of a voice or instrument □ verb **1** to write down in a register **2** to record, cast (a vote etc) **3** to show, record: a thermometer registers temperature □ **registrar** noun a public official who keeps a register of births, deaths and marriages □ **registry** noun (pl **registries**) an office where a register is kept □ **registry office** one where records of births, marriages and deaths are kept and where marriages may be performed

**regress** verb to go back to an earlier state

**regret** verb **1** to be sorry about **2** to be sorry (to have to say something): we regret to inform you □ noun sorrow for anything □ **regretful** adj □ **regretfully** adv □ **regrettable** adj □ **regrettably** adv

**regret** verb ⊳ regrets, regret**ting**, regret**ted**

**regular** adj **1** done according to rule or habit; usual **2** arranged in order; even: regular teeth **3** happening at certain fixed times **4** having normal bowel movements □ noun a soldier of the regular army □ **regularity** noun □ **regularly** adv

**regulate** verb **1** to control by rules **2** to adjust to a certain order or rate □ **regulation** noun a rule, an order □ **regulator** noun

**regurgitate** verb to bring back into the mouth after swallowing □ **regurgitation** noun

**rehabilitate** verb **1** to give back rights, powers or health to **2** to train or accustom (a disabled person etc) to live a normal life □ **rehabilitation** noun

**rehash** verb to express in different words, do again

**rehearsal** noun **1** a private practice of a play, concert etc before performance in public **2** a practice for a future event or action □ **rehearse** verb **1** to practise beforehand **2** to recount (facts, events etc) in order

**reign** noun **1** rule **2** the time during which a king or queen rules □ verb **1** to rule **2** to prevail: silence reigned at last

**reimburse** verb to pay (someone) an amount to cover expenses □ **reimbursement** noun

**rein** noun **1** one of two straps attached to a bridle for guiding a horse **2** (**reins**) a simple device for controlling a child when walking □ verb to control with reins

**reincarnation** noun the rebirth of the soul in another body after death

**reindeer** noun (pl **reindeer**) a type of deer found in the far North

**reinforce** verb to strengthen (eg an army with men, concrete with iron) □ **reinforcement** noun **1** the act of reinforcing **2** something which strengthens **3** (**reinforcements**) additional troops

**reinstate** verb to put back in a former position □ **reinstatement** noun

**reiterate** verb to repeat several times □ **reiteration** noun

**reject** verb (say ri-jekt) **1** to throw away, cast aside **2** to refuse to take **3** to turn down (eg an application, request) □ noun (say ree-jekt) something discarded or refused □ **rejection** noun

**rejoice** verb to feel or show joy □ **rejoicing** noun

**rejoinder** noun an answer to a reply

**rejuvenate** verb to make young again □ **rejuvenation** noun

**relapse** verb to fall back (eg into ill health, bad habits) □ noun a falling back

**relate** verb **1** to show a connection between (two or more things) **2** to tell (a story) □ **related** adj **1** (often **related to someone**) of the same family (as) **2** connected

**relation** noun **1** someone who is of the same family, either by birth or marriage **2** a connection between two or more things □ **relationship** noun **1** a connection between things or people **2** an emotional or sexual partnership or affair

**relative** noun someone who is of the same family etc □ adj comparative: relative merits □ **relatively** adv more or less: relatively happy

**relax** verb **1** to become or make less tense **2** to slacken (eg your grip or control) **3** to make (laws or rules) less severe □ **relaxation** noun **1** a slackening **2** rest from work, leisure

**relay** verb to receive and pass on (eg a message, a television programme) □ noun **1** the sending out of a radio or television broadcast received from another station **2** a fresh set of people to replace others at a job etc □ **in relays** in groups which take over from one another in series □ **relay race** a race in which members of each team take over from each other, each running a set distance

**relay** verb ⇨ relays, relaying, relayed

**release** verb **1** to set free; let go **2** to allow (news etc) to be made public □ noun a setting free

**relegate** verb **1** to put down (to a lower position, group etc) **2** to leave (a task etc) to someone else □ **relegation** noun

**relent** verb to treat (someone) less severely or strictly □ **relentless** adj **1** without pity **2** refusing to be turned from a purpose □ **relentlessly** adv

**relevant** adj having to do with what is being spoken about □ **relevance**

noun

**reliable** adj able to be trusted or counted on □ **reliability** or **reliance** noun trust

**reliant** adj relying on or having confidence in, trusting

**relic** noun something left over from a past time; an antiquity

**relief** noun **1** a lessening of pain or anxiety **2** release from a post or duty **3** people taking over someone's duty etc **4** help given to those in need: famine relief **5** the act of freeing (a town etc) from a siege **6** a way of carving or moulding in which the design stands out from its background

**relieve** verb **1** to lessen (pain or anxiety) **2** to take over a duty from (someone else) **3** to come to the help of (a town etc under attack)

**religion** noun belief in, or worship of, a god □ **religious** adj

**relinquish** verb to give up, abandon

**relish** verb **1** to enjoy **2** to like the taste of □ noun (pl **relishes**) **1** enjoyment **2** flavour **3** something which adds flavour

**relocate** verb to move to another position, residence etc

**reluctant** adj unwilling □ **reluctance** noun

**rely** verb to have full trust in, depend (on)

**rely** ⇨ relies, relying, relied

**remain** verb **1** to stay, not leave **2** to be left: only two cakes remained **3** to be still the same: the problem remains unsolved □ **remainder** noun **1** something which is left behind after removal of the rest **2** maths the number left after subtraction or division □ **remains** noun pl **1** that which is left **2** a dead body

**remand** verb to put (someone) back in prison until more evidence is found □ **on remand** having been remanded

**remark** verb **1** to say **2** to comment (on) **3** to notice □ noun something said

**remarkable** adj deserving notice, unusual □ **remarkably** adv

**remedial** adj **1** remedying **2** relating to the teaching of slow-learning children

**remedy** noun (pl **remedies**) a cure for an illness, evil etc □ verb **1** to cure **2** to put right

**remember** verb **1** to keep in mind **2** to recall after having forgotten **3** to send your best wishes (to): remember me to your mother

**remembrance** noun **1** the act of remembering **2** memory **3** something given to remind someone of a person or event, a keepsake **4** (**remembrances**) a friendly greeting

**remind** verb **1** to bring (something) back to a person's mind: remind me to post that letter **2** to cause (someone) to think about (someone or something) by resemblance: she reminds me of her sister □ **reminder** noun

**reminisce** verb to think and talk about things remembered from the past □ **reminiscence** noun **1** something remembered from the past **2** (**reminiscences**) memories, esp told or written □ **reminiscent** adj **1** reminding (of): reminiscent of Paris **2** in a mood to remember and think about past events etc

**remiss** adj careless, unthinking

**remission** noun **1** a shortening of a prison sentence **2** a lessening of a disease or illness

**remit** verb **1** to pardon, excuse (a crime etc) **2** to wipe out, cancel (a debt etc) **3** to lessen, become less intense **4** to send (money) **5** to hand over (eg a prisoner to a higher court) □ **remittance** noun **1** the sending of money in payment **2** the money sent

**remit** ⟐ remit*s*, remit*ting*, remit*ted*

**remnant** noun a small piece or number left over

**remonstrate** verb to protest (about)

**remorse** noun regret about something done in the past □ **remorseful** adj □ **remorseless** adj

**remote** adj **1** far away in time or place **2** isolated, far from other people **3** slight: a remote chance

**remove** verb **1** to take (something) from its place **2** to dismiss from a job **3** to take off (clothes etc) **4** to get rid of: remove a stain □ noun a stage away (from): one remove from anarchy □ **removal** noun the act of removing, esp of moving furniture to a new home □ **removed** adj **1** distant (from) **2** of cousins: separated by a generation: first cousin once removed (a cousin's child)

**remunerate** verb to pay (someone) for something done □ **remuneration** noun □ **remunerative** adj

**renaissance** noun **1** a rebirth **2** a period of cultural revival and growth

**renal** adj of the kidneys

**rend** verb to tear (apart), divide

**rend** ⟐ rend*s*, rend*ing*, rent

**render** verb **1** to give (eg thanks) **2** to translate into another language **3** to perform (music etc) **4** to cause to be: his words rendered me speechless □ **rendering** noun **1** a translation **2** a performance

**rendezvous** (say ron-dei-voo) noun (pl **rendezvous** - say ron-dei-vooz) **1** a meeting place fixed beforehand **2** an arranged meeting

**renegade** noun someone who deserts their own side, religion or beliefs

**renew** verb **1** to make as if new again **2** to begin again **3** to make valid for a further period (eg a driving licence) **4** to replace □ **renewal** noun

**rennet** noun a substance used in

curdling milk for making cheeses *etc*

**renounce** *verb* to give up publicly or formally □ **renunciation** *noun*

**renovate** *verb* to make (something) like new again, mend □ **renovation** *noun*

**renown** *noun* fame □ **renowned** *adj* famous

**rent**[1] *noun* payment made for the use of property or land □ *verb* 1 to pay rent for (a house *etc*) 2 (also **rent something out**) to receive rent for (a house *etc*) □ **rental** *noun* money paid as rent

**rent**[2] *noun* a tear, a split □ *verb, past form of* **rend**

**reorganize** *verb* to put in a different order □ **reorganization** *noun*

**rep** *noun, short for* 1 representative: *sales rep* 2 repertory

**repair** *verb* 1 to mend 2 to make up for (a wrong) 3 *old* to go, move: *repair to the drawing room* □ *noun* 1 state, condition: *in bad repair* 2 mending: *in need of repair* 3 a mend, a patch □ **reparation** *noun* compensation for a wrong

**repartee** *noun* 1 an exchange of witty remarks 2 skill in witty conversation

**repast** *noun, old* a meal

**repatriate** *verb* to send (someone) back to their own country □ **repatriation** *noun*

**repay** *verb* 1 to pay back 2 to give or do something in return □ **repayment** *noun*

**repay** ⇔ repays, repaying, repaid

**repeal** *verb* to do away with, cancel (*esp* a law) □ *noun* a cancellation of a law *etc*

**repeat** *verb* 1 to say or do over again 2 to say from memory 3 to pass on (someone's words) □ *noun* a musical passage, television programme *etc* played or shown for a second time □ **repeatedly** *adv* again and again □ **repetition** *noun* □ **repetitive** *adj*

repeating too often, predictable

**repel** *verb* 1 to drive back or away 2 to disgust □ **repellent** *adj* disgusting □ *noun* something that repels: *insect repellent*

**repel** ⇔ repels, repelling, repelled

**repent** *verb* 1 to be sorry for your actions 2 **repent of something** to regret it □ **repentance** *noun* □ **repentant** *adj*

**repercussion** *noun* an indirect or resultant effect of something which has happened

**repertoire** *noun* the range of works performed by a musician, theatre company *etc*

**repertory** *noun* (*pl* **repertories**) repertoire □ **repertory theatre** a theatre with a permanent company which performs a series of plays

**replace** *verb* 1 to put (something) back where it was 2 to put in place of another

**replenish** *verb* to refill (a stock, supply)

**replete** *adj* full

**replica** *noun* an exact copy of a work of art

**reply** *verb* to speak or act in answer to something □ *noun* (*pl* **replies**) an answer

**reply** ⇔ replies, replying, replied

**report** *verb* 1 to pass on news 2 to give a description of (an event) 3 to give information about events for a newspaper 4 to make a formal complaint against □ *noun* 1 a statement of facts 2 an account, a description 3 a news article 4 a rumour 5 a written description of a school pupil's work 6 a loud noise □ **reporter** *noun* a news journalist

**repose** *noun, formal* sleep, rest □ *verb* 1 to rest 2 to place (*eg* trust in a person

**repository** *noun* (*pl* **repositories**) a storage place for safe keeping

**repossess** verb to take back (goods, property), esp because of non-payment

**reprehensible** adj deserving blame

**represent** verb 1 to speak or act on behalf of others 2 to stand for, be a symbol of 3 to claim to be 4 to explain, point out □ **representation** noun 1 an image, a picture 2 a strong claim or appeal □ **representative** adj 1 typical, characteristic 2 standing or acting for others □ noun 1 someone who acts or speaks on behalf of others 2 a travelling salesman for a company

**repress** verb 1 to keep down by force 2 to keep under control □ **repression** noun □ **repressive** adj

**reprieve** verb 1 to pardon (a criminal) 2 to relieve from trouble or difficulty □ noun a pardon, a relief

**reprimand** verb to scold severely, censure □ noun scolding, censure

**reprint** verb to print more copies of (a book etc) □ noun another printing of a book

**reprisal** noun a return of wrong for wrong, a repayment in kind

**reproach** verb to scold, blame □ noun 1 blame, discredit 2 a cause of blame or censure □ **reproachful** adj

**reprobate** noun someone of evil or immoral habits □ adj immoral

**reproduce** verb 1 to produce a copy of 2 to produce (children or young) □ **reproduction** noun

**reproof** noun a scolding, criticism for a fault □ **reprove** verb □ **reproving** adj disapproving

**reptile** noun a creeping, cold-blooded animal, such as a snake, lizard etc

**republic** noun a form of government in which power is in the hands of elected representatives with a president at its head □ **republican** adj

**repudiate** verb to refuse to acknowledge or accept □ **repudiation** noun

**repugnant** adj hateful, distasteful □ **repugnance** noun aversion

**repulse** verb 1 to drive back 2 to reject, snub □ **repulsion** noun □ **repulsive** adj

**reputation** noun 1 opinion held by people in general of a particular person 2 good name □ **reputable** (say **rep**-yut-a-bl) adj having a good reputation, well thought of □ **repute** noun reputation □ **reputed** adj 1 considered, thought (to be something) 2 supposed □ **reputedly** adv in the opinion of most people

**request** verb to ask for □ noun 1 an asking for something 2 something asked for

**requiem** noun a hymn or mass sung for the dead

**require** verb 1 to need 2 to demand, order □ **requirement** noun

**requisite** adj required; necessary □ noun something needed or necessary □ **requisition** noun a formal request for supplies, eg for a school or army □ verb to put in a formal request for

**rerun** verb to run again □ noun a repeated television programme

**rescue** verb 1 to save from danger 2 to free from capture □ noun an act of saving from danger or capture

**research** noun (pl **researches**) close and careful scientific study to try to find out new facts: cancer research □ verb to study carefully □ **researcher** noun

**resemble** verb to look like or be like □ **resemblance** noun

**resent** verb to feel injured, annoyed or insulted by □ **resentful** adj □ **resentment** noun

**reservation** noun 1 the act of reserving, booking 2 an exception or condition: *she agreed to the plan, but with certain reservations* **3** doubt, objection **4** an area of land set aside by treaty for Native American people in the United States

**reserve** *verb* **1** to set aside for future use **2** to book, have kept for you (*eg* a seat, a table) □ *noun* **1** something reserved **2** (**reserves**) troops outside the regular army kept ready to help those already fighting **3** a piece of land set apart for some reason: *nature reserve* **4** shyness, reluctance to speak or act openly □ **reserved** *adj* **1** shy, reluctant to speak openly **2** kept back for a particular person or purpose

**reservoir** *noun* an artificial lake where water is kept in store

**reshuffle** *verb* to rearrange ministerial posts within (a government cabinet) □ *noun* a rearrangement of a cabinet

**reside** *verb* **1** to live, stay (in) **2** of authority *etc*: to be placed (in) □ **residence** *noun* **1** the building where someone lives **2** living, or time of living, in a place □ **resident** *noun* someone who lives in a particular place □ *adj* **1** living in (a place) **2** living in a place of work □ **residential** *adj* of an area: containing houses rather than shops, offices *etc*

**residue** *noun* what is left over □ **residual** *adj*

**resign** *verb* to give up (a job, position *etc*) □ **resign yourself to** to accept (a situation) patiently and calmly □ **resignation** *noun* **1** the act of resigning **2** a letter to say you are resigning **3** patient, calm acceptance of a situation □ **resigned** *adj* patient, not actively complaining

**resilient** *adj* **1** able to recover easily from misfortune, hurt *etc* **2** of an object: readily recovering its original shape after being bent,

twisted *etc* □ **resilience** *noun*

**resin** *noun* a sticky substance produced by certain plants (*eg* firs, pines) □ **resinous** *adj*

**resist** *verb* **1** to struggle against, oppose **2** to stop yourself from (doing something) □ **resistance** *noun* □ **resistant** *adj*

**resit** *verb* to sit (an examination) again □ *noun* a retaking of an examination

**resit** *verb* ↔ resit**s**, resit**ting**, resat

**resolute** *adj* determined, with mind made up □ **resolutely** *adv*

**resolution** *noun* **1** determination of mind or purpose **2** a firm decision (to do something) **3** a proposal put before a meeting **4** a decision expressed by a public meeting

**resolve** *verb* **1** to decide firmly (to do something) **2** to solve (a difficulty) **3** to break up into parts □ *noun* a firm purpose

**resonance** *noun* a deep, echoing tone □ **resonant** *adj*

**resort** *verb* **1** to begin to use **2** to turn (to) in a difficulty: *resort to bribery* □ *noun* a popular holiday destination □ **the last resort** when all else fails

**resound** *verb* **1** to sound loudly **2** to echo □ **resounding** *adj* great: *a resounding victory*

**resourceful** *adj* good at finding ways out of difficulties

**resources** *noun pl* **1** a source of supplying what is required **2** the natural sources of wealth in a country *etc* **3** money or other property **4** an ability to handle situations skilfully and cleverly

**respect** *verb* **1** to feel a high regard for **2** to treat with consideration: *respect his wishes* □ *noun* **1** high regard, esteem **2** consideration **3** a detail, a way: *alike in some respects* **4** (**respects**) good wishes □ **respectability** *noun* □ **respectable** *adj* **1** worthy of respect **2** having a good reputation **3** considerable, fairly good: *a respectable score* □ **respectful** *adj* □ **in respect of** concerning, as regards □ **with respect to** with reference to

**respective** *adj* belonging to each (person or thing mentioned) separately: *my brother and his friends went to their respective homes* (that is, each went to their own home) □ **respectively** *adv*

**respire** *verb* to breathe □ **respiration** *noun* □ **respirator** *noun* **1** a mask worn over the mouth and nose to purify the air taken in **2** a device to help people breathe when they are too ill to do so naturally

**respite** (*say* res-pait *or* res-pit) *noun* a pause, a rest

**resplendent** *adj* very bright or splendid in appearance

**respond** *verb* **1** to answer **2** to react in response to **3** to show a positive reaction to: *responding to treatment*

**respondent** *see* **corespondent**

**response** *noun* **1** a reply **2** an action, feeling *etc* in answer to another **3** an answer made during a church service

**responsible** *adj* **1** (sometimes **responsible for something**) being the cause of **2** liable to be blamed (for): *responsible for the conduct of his staff* **3** involving making important decisions *etc*: *a responsible post* **4** trustworthy □ **responsibility** *noun* (*pl* **responsibilities**)

**responsive** *adj* quick to react, to show sympathy *etc*

**rest** *noun* **1** a break in work **2** a sleep **3** *music* a break in playing or singing for a given number of beats **4** a support, a prop: *book rest* **5** what is left, the remainder **6** the others, those not mentioned: *I went home but the rest went to the cinema* □ *verb* **1** to stop working for a time **2** to be still **3** to sleep **4** to depend (on), be

based on **5** to stop, develop no further: *I can't let the matter rest there* **6** to lean or place on a support □ **restful** *adj* **1** relaxing **2** relaxed □ **restive** *adj* restless, impatient □ **restless** *adj* **1** unable to keep still **2** agitated □ **rest with** to be the responsibility of: *the choice rests with you*

**restaurant** *noun* a place where meals may be bought and eaten □ **restaurateur** *noun* the owner or manager of a restaurant

**restitution** *noun* **1** the return of what has been lost or taken away **2** compensation for harm or injury done

**restore** *verb* **1** to put or give back **2** to repair (a building, a painting *etc*) so that it looks as it used to **3** to cure (a person) □ **restoration** *noun*

**restrain** *verb* **1** to hold back (from) **2** to keep under control □ **restraint** *noun*

**restrict** *verb* **1** to limit, keep within certain bounds **2** to open only to certain people □ **restriction** *noun* □ **restrictive** *adj*

**result** *noun* **1** a consequence of something already done or said **2** the answer to a sum **3** a score in a game □ *verb* **1** (**result from something**) to be the result or effect of it **2** (**result in something**) to have it as a result □ **resultant** *adj*

**resume** *verb* **1** to begin again after an interruption **2** to take again: *he resumed his seat* □ **resumption** *noun*

**résumé** (*say* rez-yoo-mei) *noun* **1** a summary **2** *US* a curriculum vitae

**resurgence** *noun* the act of returning to life, to a state of activity *etc* after a period of decline

**resurrect** *verb* to bring back to life or into use □ **resurrection** *noun* **1** a rising from the dead **2** (**Resurrection**) the rising of Christ from the dead **3** the act of bringing back into use

**resuscitate** verb to bring back to consciousness, revive
□ **resuscitation** noun

**retail** verb 1 to sell goods to someone who is going to use them (not to another seller) 2 to tell (eg a story) fully and in detail □ noun the sale of goods to the actual user □ **retailer** noun

**retain** verb 1 to keep possession of 2 to keep (something) in mind 3 to reserve (someone's services) by paying a fee in advance 4 to hold back, keep in place □ **retainer** noun old a servant (to a family

**retaliate** verb to return like for like, hit back □ **retaliation** noun

**retard** verb 1 to keep back, hinder 2 to make slow or late □ **retardation** noun □ **retarded** adj

**retch** verb to make the actions and sound of vomiting, without actually vomiting

**retention** noun 1 the act of holding in or keeping 2 the act of retaining the services of (eg a lawyer) □ **retentive** adj able to hold or retain well: retentive memory

**reticent** adj unwilling to speak openly and freely, reserved
□ **reticence** noun

**retina** noun (pl **retinas** or **retinae**) the part of the back of the eye that receives the image of what is seen

**retinue** noun the attendants of someone important

**retire** verb 1 to give up work permanently, usually because of age 2 to go to bed 3 to draw back, retreat □ **retired** adj 1 having given up work 2 out-of-the-way, quiet □ **retirement** noun □ **retiring** adj shy, avoiding being noticed

**retort** verb to make a quick and witty reply □ noun 1 a quick, witty reply 2 a bottle of thin glass used for distilling liquids

**retrace** verb to go over again

**retract** verb 1 to take back

(something said or given) 2 to draw back: the cat retracted its claws
□ **retractable** adj □ **retraction** noun

**retreat** verb 1 to draw back, withdraw 2 to go away □ noun 1 a movement backwards corresponding to the advance of an enemy 2 a withdrawal 3 a quiet, peaceful place

**retrenchment** noun economizing in spending

**retribution** noun punishment

**retrieve** verb 1 to get back, recover (something lost) 2 to search for and fetch □ **retriever** noun a breed of dog trained to find and fetch shot birds

**retro-** prefix forms words containing the meaning 'backwards' or 'behind'
ⓞ From Latin retro meaning 'back' or 'behind'

**retroflex** adj bent backwards

**retrograde** adj 1 going backward 2 going from a better to a worse stage

**retrospect** noun: in retrospect considering or looking back on the past □ **retrospective** adj 1 looking back on past events 2 of a law: applying to the past as well as the present and the future

**return** verb 1 to go or come back 2 to give, send, pay etc back 3 to elect to parliament □ noun 1 the act of returning 2 a profit: return on your investment 3 a statement of income for calculating income tax □ **by return** sent by the first post back □ **return match** a second match played between the same team or players □ **return ticket** a ticket which covers a journey both to and from a place

**reunion** noun a meeting of people who have been apart for some time □ **reunite** verb to join after having been separated

**Rev** or **Revd** abbrev Reverend

**rev** noun a revolution of an engine

□ *verb* (often **rev up**) to increase the speed of (an engine

**rev** *verb* ⇨ revs, revving, revved

**revamp** *verb* to renovate, renew the appearance of

**reveal** *verb* **1** to make known **2** to show

**reveille** (*say* ri-**val**-i) *noun* a bugle call at daybreak to waken soldiers

**revel** *verb* **1** to take great delight (in) **2** to celebrate □ *noun* (**revels**) festivities □ **reveller** *noun* □ **revelry** *noun*

**revel** *verb* ⇨ revels, revelling, revelled

**revelation** *noun* **1** the act of revealing **2** something unexpected which is made known

**revenge** *noun* **1** harm done to someone in return for harm they themselves have committed **2** the desire to do such harm □ *verb* **revenge oneself** to take revenge

**revenue** *noun* **1** money received as payment **2** a country's total income

**reverberate** *verb* to echo and re-echo, resound □ **reverberation** *noun*

**revere** *verb* to look upon with great respect □ **reverence** *noun*

**reverend** *adj* **1** worthy of respect **2** (**Reverend**) a title given to a member of the clergy (*short form:* **Rev** or **Revd**)
ⓘ From Latin *reverendus* meaning 'who must be respected'

**✎. Do not confuse: reverend and reverent**

**reverent** or **reverential** *adj* showing respect

**reverie** (*say* **rev**-*e*-ri) *noun* a daydream

**reverse** *verb* **1** to turn upside down or the other way round **2** to move backwards **3** to undo (a decision, policy *etc*) □ *noun* **1** the opposite (of) **2** the other side (of a coin *etc*) **3** a defeat □ **reversal** *noun* □ **reversible** *adj* of clothes: able to

be worn with either side out

**revert** *verb* **1** to go back to an earlier topic **2** to return to a previous owner

**review** *verb* **1** to give an opinion or criticism of (an artistic work) **2** to consider again **3** to inspect (*eg* troops) □ *noun* **1** a critical opinion of a book *etc* **2** a magazine consisting of reviews **3** a second look, a reconsideration **4** an inspection of troops *etc* □ **reviewer** *noun*

**✎. Do not confuse with: revue**

**revile** *verb* to say harsh things about

**revise** *verb* **1** to correct faults in and make improvements **2** to study notes *etc* in preparation for an examination **3** to change (*eg* an opinion) □ **revision** *noun* **1** the act of revising **2** a revised version of a book *etc*

**revive** *verb* to bring or come back to life, use or fame □ **revival** *noun*

**revoke** *verb* **1** to cancel (a decision *etc*) **2** to fail to follow suit in a card-game

**revolt** *verb* **1** to rise up (against), rebel **2** to feel disgust (at) **3** to disgust □ *noun* a rising, a rebellion □ **revolting** *adj* causing disgust

**revolution** *noun* **1** a full turn round a centre **2** the act of turning round a centre **3** a general uprising against those in power **4** a complete change in ideas, way of doing things *etc* □ **revolutionary** *adj* **1** relating to a revolution **2** bringing about great changes **3** turning □ *noun* (*pl* **revolutionaries**) someone who is involved in, or is in favour of, revolution □ **revolutionize** *verb* to bring about a complete change in

**revolve** *verb* to roll or turn round

**revolver** *noun* a kind of hand pistol

**revue** *noun* a light theatre show, with short topical plays or sketches

**✎. Do not confuse with: review**

**revulsion** *noun* **1** disgust **2** a sudden change of feeling

**reward** *noun* **1** something given in return for work done or for good behaviour *etc* **2** a sum of money offered for helping to find a criminal, lost property *etc* □ *verb* **1** to give a reward to **2** to give a reward for (a service) □ **rewarding** *adj* giving pleasure or satisfaction

**rewind** *verb* to wind back (a spool, cassette *etc*) to the beginning

**rewrite** *verb* to write again

**rhapsody** *noun* music or poetry which expresses strong feeling □ **go into rhapsodies over** to show wild enthusiasm for □ **rhapsodize** *verb*

**rhetoric** *noun* **1** the art of good speaking or writing **2** language which is too showy, consisting of unnecessarily long or difficult words *etc* □ **rhetorical** *adj* □ **rhetorical question** one which the asker answers, or which does not need an answer

**rheumatism** *noun* a disease which causes stiffness and pain in the joints □ **rheumatic** *adj*

**rhino** (*pl* **rhinos**) *short for* rhinoceros

**rhinoceros** (*pl* **rhinoceros** or **rhinoceroses**) a large, thick-skinned animal, with a horn (or two) on its nose

**rhododendron** *noun* a flowering shrub with thick evergreen leaves and large flowers

**rhombus** *noun* (*pl* **rhombi** or **rhombuses**) a geometrical figure with four equal straight sides

**rhubarb** *noun* a plant with long red-skinned stalks, edible when cooked

**rhyme** *noun* **1** a similarity in sounds between words or their endings, *eg* humble and crumble **2** a word which sounds like another **3** a short poem □ *verb* (sometimes **rhyme with**) to sound like, be rhymes: *harp rhymes with carp*

**rhythm** *noun* **1** a regular repeated pattern of sounds or beats in music or poetry **2** a regularly repeated pattern of movements □ **rhythm and blues** a type of music combining the styles of rock-and-roll and the blues □ **rhythmic** or **rhythmical** *adj*

**rib** *noun* **1** any of the bones which curve round and forward from the backbone, enclosing the heart and lungs **2** a spar of wood in the framework of a boat, curving up from the keel **3** a ridged knitting pattern □ **ribbed** *adj*

**ribald** *adj* of a joke *etc*: coarse, vulgar

**ribbon** *noun* a narrow strip of silk or other material, used for decoration, tying hair *etc*

**rice** *noun* the seeds of a plant, grown for food in well-watered ground in tropical countries

**rich** *adj* **1** having a lot of money or valuables, wealthy **2** valuable: *a rich reward* **3** (**rich in something**) having a lot of it **4** of food: containing a lot of fat, eggs *etc* **5** of material: heavily decorated or textured, lavish **6** of a colour: deep in tone □ **riches** *noun pl* wealth □ **richly** *adv* □ **richness** *noun*

**rickets** *noun sing* a children's disease caused by lack of calcium, with softening and bending of the bones □ **rickety** *adj* **1** suffering from rickets **2** unsteady: *a rickety table*

**rickshaw** *noun* a two-wheeled carriage pulled by a man, used in Japan *etc*

**ricochet** (*say* rik-osh-ei) *verb* of a bullet: to rebound at an angle from a surface

**ricochet** ⇔ ricochet*s*, ricochet*ing*, ricochet*ed*

**rid** *verb* to free from, clear of: *rid the city of rats* □ **get rid of** to free yourself of

**rid** ⇔ rid*s*, ridd*ing*, rid

**riddance** *noun*: **good riddance to** I am happy to have got rid of

**riddle¹** *noun* **1** a puzzle in the form of a question which describes something in a misleading way **2** something difficult to understand **3** a tray with holes for separating large objects from smaller ones

**riddle²** *verb:* **riddled with** covered with small holes made by: *riddled with woodworm*

**ride** *verb* **1** to travel on a horse or bicycle, or in a vehicle **2** to travel on and control (a horse) **3** of a ship: to float at anchor □ *noun* **1** a journey on horseback, bicycle *etc* **2** a path through a wood, for riding horses □ **rider** *noun* **1** someone who rides **2** something added to what has already been said

ride *verb* ⟷ rides, riding, rode, ridden

**ridge** *noun* **1** a raised part between furrows **2** a long crest on high ground

**ridicule** *verb* to laugh at, mock □ *noun* mockery □ **ridiculous** *adj* deserving to be laughed at, very silly

**rife** *adj* very common: *disease was rife in the country*

**riff-raff** *noun* worthless people

**rifle¹** *verb* **1** to search through and rob **2** to steal

**rifle²** *noun* a gun fired from the shoulder

**rift** *noun* **1** a crack **2** a disagreement between friends □ **rift valley** a long valley formed by the fall of part of the earth's crust

**rig** *verb* **1** (**rig someone out**) to clothe or dress them **2** to fix (an election result) illegally or dishonestly □ **rig up 1** to fit (a ship) with sails and ropes **2** to make or build hastily □ **rigging** *noun* ship's spars, ropes *etc*

rig ⟷ rigs, rigging, rigged

**right** *adj* **1** on or belonging to the side of the body which in most people has the more skilful hand (*contrasted with:* **left**) **2** correct,

true **3** just, good **4** straight □ *adv* **1** to or on the right side **2** correctly **3** straight **4** all the way: *go right to the end* □ *noun* **1** something good which ought to be done **2** something you are entitled to **3** the right-hand side, direction *etc* **4** the conservative side in politics □ *verb* to mend, set in order □ **righteous** *adj* living a good life; just □ **rightful** *adj* by right, proper: *the rightful owner* □ **right angle** an angle like one of those in a square, an angle of 90° □ **right-handed** *adj* using the right hand more easily than the left □ **right-of-way** *noun* a road or path over private land along which people may go as a right □ **right-wing** *adj* of conservative views in politics □ **by right** because you have the right □ **in your own right** not because of anyone else, independently

**rigid** *adj* **1** not easily bent, stiff **2** strict □ **rigidity** *noun*

**rigmarole** *noun* a long, rambling speech

Originally *ragman roll*, a Scots term for a long list or catalogue

**rigour** *noun* strictness; harshness □ **rigorous** *adj*

**rill** *noun* a small stream

**rim** *noun* an edge or border, *eg* the top edge of a cup

**rind** *noun* a thick firm covering, *eg* fruit peel, bacon skin, the outer covering of cheese

**ring** *noun* **1** a small hoop worn on the finger, on the ear *etc* **2** a hollow circle **3** an enclosed space for boxing, circus performances *etc* **4** the sound of a bell being struck **5** a small group of people formed for business or criminal purposes: *a drug ring* □ *verb¹* (*past* ringed) **1** to encircle, go round **2** to mark (a bird *etc*) by putting on a ring □ *verb²* (*past* rang) **1** to make the sound of a bell **2** to strike (a bell *etc*) **3** to telephone □ **ringleader** *noun* someone who takes the lead in mischief etc □ **ringmaster** noun someone who is in charge of the performance in a circus ring □ **ring road** a road that circles a town etc avoiding the centre

**ring** ◇ rings, ringing, rang or ringed, rung or ringed

**ringlet** noun a long curl of hair

**rink** noun a sheet of ice, often artificial, for skating or curling

**rinse** verb 1 to wash lightly to remove soap etc 2 to clean (a cup, your mouth etc) by swilling with water □ noun 1 the act of rinsing 2 liquid colour for the hair

**riot** noun 1 a noisy disturbance by a crowd 2 a hilarious event □ verb to take part in a riot □ **riotous** adj noisy, uncontrolled

**RIP** abbrev may he or she rest in peace

**rip** verb 1 to tear apart or off 2 to come apart □ noun a tear □ **let rip** to express yourself fully, without restraint

**rip** verb ◇ rips, ripping, ripped

**ripe** adj 1 of fruit etc: ready to be picked or eaten 2 fully developed, mature □ **ripen** verb □ **ripeness** noun

**rip-off** noun, slang a cheat, a swindle

**riposte** noun a quick return or reply

**ripple** noun 1 a little wave or movement on the surface of water 2 a soft sound etc that rises and falls quickly and gently: a ripple of laughter

**rise** verb 1 to get up from bed 2 to stand up 3 to move upwards 4 of a river: to have its source (in) 5 to rebel (against) □ noun 1 a slope upwards 2 an increase in wages, prices etc □ **rising** noun 1 an act of rising 2 a rebellion □ **give rise to** to cause

**rise** verb ◇ rises, rising, rose, risen

**risk** noun a chance of loss or injury; a danger □ verb 1 to take the chance

of: risk death 2 to take the chance of losing: risk one's life, health etc □ **risky** adj

**rissole** noun a fried cake or ball of minced meat, fish etc

**rite** noun a solemn ceremony, esp a religious one

**ritual** noun a traditional way of carrying out religious worship etc □ adj relating to a rite or ceremony

**rival** noun someone who tries to equal or beat another □ verb to try to equal □ **rivalry** noun (pl **rivalries**)

**rival** verb ◇ rivals, rivalling, rivalled

**riven** adj, old split

**river** noun a large stream of water flowing across land

**rivet** noun a bolt for fastening plates of metal together □ verb 1 to fasten with a rivet 2 to fix firmly (someone's attention etc)

**rivulet** noun a small stream

**roach** noun (pl **roaches**) a type of freshwater fish

**road** noun 1 a hard, level surface for vehicles and people 2 a way of getting to (somewhere), a route 3 (**roads**) a place where ships may lie at anchor (also called: **roadstead**) □ **road hog** a reckless or selfish driver □ **road movie** a film showing the travels of a character or characters □ **roadway** noun the part of a road used by cars etc □ **roadworthy** adj (of a vehicle) fit to be used on the road

**roam** verb to wander about

**roan** noun a horse with a dark coat spotted with grey or white

**roar** verb 1 to give a loud, deep sound 2 to laugh loudly 3 to say (something) loudly □ noun a loud, deep sound or laugh

**roast** verb to cook or be cooked in an oven or over a fire □ adj roasted: roast beef □ noun 1 meat roasted 2 meat for roasting

**rob** verb to steal from

**rob** ⇔ robs, robbing, robbed

**robber** noun a person who robs; a thief

**robbery** noun (pl **robberies**) the act of stealing

**robe** noun 1 a long loose garment 2 US a dressing-gown 3 (**robes**) the official dress of a judge etc □ verb, formal to dress

**robin** noun a type of small bird, known by its red breast

**robot** noun 1 a mechanical man or woman 2 a machine that can do the work of a person □ **robotic** adj

**robust** adj strong, healthy

**rock** noun 1 a large lump of stone 2 a hard sweet made in sticks 3 music with a heavy beat and simple melody (also called: **rock music**) □ verb to sway backwards and forwards or from side to side □ **rocky** adj 1 full of rocks 2 inclined to rock, unsteady □ **rock-and-roll** or **rock'n'roll** noun a simpler, earlier form of rock music □ **rock cake** a small rough-textured cake □ **rocker** noun a curved support on which a chair, cradle etc rocks □ **rockery** noun (pl **rockeries**) a collection of stones amongst which small plants are grown □ **rocking-chair** noun a chair which rocks backwards and forwards on rockers □ **rocking-horse** noun a toy horse which rocks backwards and forwards on rockers

**rocket** noun 1 a tube containing inflammable materials, used for launching a spacecraft, signalling and as a firework 2 a spacecraft □ verb to move upwards rapidly

**rod** noun 1 a long thin stick 2 a fishing rod 3 historical a measure of distance, about 5 metres

**rode** past form of **ride**

**rodent** noun a gnawing animal, such as a rat, beaver etc

**rodeo** noun (pl **rodeos**) 1 a round-up of cattle for marking 2 a show of riding by cowboys

**roe** noun 1 the eggs of fishes 2 (also **roe deer**) a small kind of deer 3 a female red deer □ **roebuck** noun the male roe deer

**rogue** noun a dishonest or mischievous person, a rascal □ **roguery** noun □ **roguish** adj

**rôle** noun a part played by an actor

**roll** verb 1 to move along by turning over like a wheel 2 of a ship: to rock from side to side 3 of thunder etc: to rumble 4 to wrap round and round 5 to flatten with a roller □ noun 1 a sheet of paper, length of cloth etc rolled into a cylinder 2 a very small loaf of bread 3 a rocking movement 4 a list of names 5 a long, rumbling sound □ **rollcall** noun the calling of names from a list □ **roller** noun 1 a cylindrical tool for flattening 2 a tube over which hair is rolled and styled 3 a small solid wheel 4 a long heavy wave on the sea □ **rollerblades** noun pl rollerskates with the wheels in a single line □ **rollerskates** noun pl skates with wheels at each corner of the shoe □ **rolling pin** a roller for flattening dough □ **rolling stock** the stock of engines, carriages etc that run on a railway

**rollicking** adj noisy and full of fun

**ROM** abbrev, computing read-only memory

**Roman** adj of a number: written in letters, as I, II, III, IV etc for 1, 2, 3, 4 etc □ **Roman Catholic Church** the Church whose head is the Pope, the Bishop of Rome

**romance** noun 1 a story about heroic events not likely to happen in real life 2 a love story 3 a love affair □ verb to write or tell imaginative stories □ **romantic** adj 1 of romance 2 full of feeling and imagination 3 relating to love □ **romanticism** noun (often **Romanticism**) the late 18th-and early 19th-century movement in art, literature and music, characterized by an emphasis on feelings and emotions

**Romany** *noun* **1** a gypsy **2** the gypsy language

**romp** *verb* **1** to play in a lively way **2** to move quickly and easily □ *noun* a lively game

**rompers** or **romper suit** *noun pl* a short suit for a baby

**rondo** *noun* (*pl* **rondos**) a musical composition with a recurring section

**rood** *noun*, *old* **1** a measure of area, equal to a quarter of an acre **2** a cross carrying an image of Christ

**roof** *noun* (*pl* **roofs**) **1** the top covering of a building, car *etc* **2** the upper part of the mouth □ *verb* to cover with a roof

**rook** *noun* **1** a kind of crow **2** *chess* the castle □ **rookery** *noun* (*pl* **rookeries**) **1** a nesting place of rooks **2** a breeding place of penguins or seals

**room** *noun* **1** an inside compartment in a house **2** space **3** (**rooms**) lodgings □ **roomy** *adj*

**roost** *noun* a perch on which a bird rests at night □ *verb* to sit or sleep on a roost □ **rooster** *noun* a farmyard cock

**root** *noun* **1** the underground part of a plant **2** the base of anything, *eg* a tooth **3** a cause, a source **4** a word from which other words have developed □ *verb* **1** to form roots and begin to grow **2** to be fixed **3** of an animal: to turn up ground in a search for food **4** to search (about) □ **root out** or **root up 1** to tear up by the roots **2** to get rid of completely □ **take root 1** to form roots and grow firmly **2** to become firmly fixed □ **rooted** *adj* firmly planted

**rope** *noun* **1** a thick cord, made by twisting strands together **2** anything resembling a thick cord □ *verb* **1** to fasten or catch with a rope **2** to enclose, mark off with a rope □ **ropy** *adj* **1** like ropes, stringy

**2** *informal* bad, not well

**rosary** *noun* (*pl* **rosaries**) **1** a set of prayers **2** a string of beads used in saying prayers **3** a rose garden

**rose¹** *see* **rise**

**rose²** *noun* **1** a type of flower, often scented, usually growing on a prickly bush **2** a deep pink colour □ **rosy** *adj* **1** red, pink **2** (of the future *etc*) bright, hopeful □ **rosehip** *noun* the fruit of the rose □ **rosewood** *noun* a dark Brazilian or Indian wood, which smells of roses when cut

**rosé** *noun* a pink-coloured wine produced by removing red grape-skins during fermentation

**rosemary** *noun* an evergreen sweet-smelling shrub, used as a cooking herb

**rosette** *noun* a badge shaped like a rose, made of ribbons

**roster** *noun* a list showing a repeated order of duties *etc*

**rostrum** *noun* (*pl* **rostrums** or **rostra**) a platform for public speaking

**rot** *verb* to go bad, decay □ *noun* **1** decay **2** *informal* nonsense □ **rotten** *adj* **1** decayed, bad **2** worthless, disgraceful □ **rotter** *noun*, *informal* a very bad, worthless person

**rot** *verb* ⋄ **rots, rotting, rotted**

**rota** *noun* a list of duties *etc* to be repeated in a set order

**rotary** *adj* turning round like a wheel

**rotate** *verb* **1** to turn round like a wheel **2** to go through a repeating series of changes □ **rotation** *noun*

**rote** *noun*: **by rote** off by heart, automatically

**rotor** *noun* a turning part of a motor, dynamo *etc*

**rotund** *adj* round; plump □ **rotundity** *noun*

**rouble** or **ruble** *noun* a standard unit of Russian coinage

**rouge** *noun* a powder or cream used

to add colour to the cheeks

**rough** *adj* **1** not smooth **2** uneven **3** coarse, harsh **4** boisterous, wild **5** not exact: *a rough guess* **6** stormy □ *noun* **1** a hooligan, a bully **2** rough ground □ **roughage** *noun* bran or fibre in food □ **roughen** *verb* □ **rough and ready** not fine or carefully made, but effective □ **rough out** to sketch or shape roughly

**roulette** *noun* a gambling game, played with a ball which is placed on a wheel

**round** *adj* **1** shaped like a circle **2** plump **3** even, exact: *a round dozen* □ *adv & prep* **1** on all sides (of), around: *look round the room* **2** in a circle (about): *the earth moves round the sun* **3** from one (person, place *etc*) to another: *the news went round* □ *noun* **1** a circle, something round in shape **2** a single bullet or shell **3** a burst of firing, cheering *etc* **4** a song in which the singers take up the tune in turn **5** a usual route: *a postman's round* **6** a series of calls or deliveries **7** each stage of a contest □ *verb* **1** to make or become round **2** of a ship: to go round (*eg* a headland) □ **roundly** *adv* boldly, plainly □ **round trip** *US* a journey to a place and back □ **round on** to make a sudden attack on □ **round up** to gather or drive together

**roundabout** *noun* **1** a revolving machine for children to ride on in a park *etc* **2** a meeting place of roads, where traffic must move in a circle □ *adj* not straight or direct: *a roundabout route*

**rounders** *noun sing* a ball game played with a bat in which players run around a series of stations

**Roundhead** *noun* a supporter of Parliament during the English Civil War

**rouse** *verb* **1** to awaken **2** to stir up, excite □ **rousing** *adj*

**rout** *noun* a complete defeat □ *verb* to

defeat utterly

**route** *noun* the course to be followed, a way of getting to somewhere □ *verb* to fix the route of

**routine** *noun* a fixed, unchanging order of doing things □ *adj* regular, usual

**rove** *verb* to wander or roam □ **rover** *noun*

**row¹** *noun* **1** a line of people or things **2** a trip in a rowing boat □ *verb* to drive (a boat) by oars □ **rower** *noun* □ **rowing boat** a boat rowed by oars

**row²** *noun* **1** a noisy quarrel **2** a noise **3** *informal* a scolding

**rowan** *noun* (*also called:* **mountain ash**) a tree with clusters of bright red berries

**rowdy** *adj* noisy, disorderly

**rowlock** *noun* a place to rest an oar on the side of a rowing boat

**royal** *adj* **1** relating to a king or queen **2** splendid, magnificent: *royal welcome* □ **royalty** *noun* (*pl* **royalties**) **1** the state of being royal **2** royal people as a whole **3** a sum paid to the author of a book for each copy sold

**RSVP** *abbrev* please reply (from French *répondez, s'il vous plaît*)

**rub** *verb* **1** to move one thing against the surface of another **2** to clean, polish (something) **3** (**rub something out** or **away**) to remove (a mark) □ *noun* **1** the act of rubbing **2** a wipe □ **rub in 1** to work into (a surface) by rubbing **2** to keep reminding someone of (something unpleasant)

**rub** *verb* ◁ **rubs, rubbing, rubb***ed*

**rubber** *noun* **1** a tough elastic substance made from plant juices **2** a piece of rubber used for erasing pencil marks **3** an odd number (three or five) of games in cards, cricket *etc* □ **rubber stamp** an instrument with rubber figures or letters for stamping dates *etc* on paper

**rubbish** noun 1 waste material, litter 2 nonsense

**rubble** noun small rough stones, bricks etc left from a building

**rubicund** adj red or rosy-faced

**ruble** another spelling of **rouble**

**ruby** noun (pl **rubies**) a type of red, precious stone

**ruck** noun a wrinkle, a crease

**rucksack** noun a bag carried on the back by walkers, climbers etc

**ructions** noun pl a row, a disturbance

**rudder** noun a device fixed to the stern of a boat, or tail of an aeroplane, for steering

**ruddy** adj 1 red 2 of the face: rosy, in good health

**rude** adj 1 showing bad manners, not polite 2 roughly made: a rude shelter 3 rough, not refined 4 startling and sudden: a rude awakening 5 coarse, vulgar, lewd □ **rudely** adv

**rudiments** noun pl the first simple rules or facts of anything □ **rudimentary** adj in an early stage of development

**rue** noun 1 a shrub with bitter-tasting leaves □ verb to be sorry for, regret □ **rueful** adj

**ruff** noun 1 historical a pleated frill worn round the neck 2 a band of feathers round a bird's neck

**ruffian** noun a rough, brutal person □ **ruffianly** adj

**ruffle** verb 1 to make unsmooth, crumple (eg hair, a bird's feathers) 2 to annoy, offend

**rug** noun 1 a floor mat 2 a blanket

**Rugby** or **rugby** noun a form of football using an oval ball which can be handled

Named after *Rugby* School in Warwickshire, where the game was supposedly invented

**rugged** (say rug-id) adj 1 having a rough, uneven appearance 2 strong, robust 3 stern, harsh

**ruin** noun 1 complete loss of money etc 2 a downfall 3 (**ruins**) broken-down remains of buildings □ verb 1 to destroy 2 to spoil completely: ruin your chances 3 to make very poor □ **ruination** noun □ **ruined** adj □ **ruinous** adj

**rule** noun 1 government: military rule 2 a regulation 3 what usually happens 4 a guiding principle 5 a measuring ruler □ verb 1 to govern, be in power 2 to decide (that) 3 to draw (a line) 4 to mark with lines □ **as a rule** usually □ **rule out** to leave out, not consider □ **ruler** noun 1 someone who rules 2 a marked tool for measuring length and drawing straight lines □ **ruling** adj governing; most important □ noun a decision, a rule

**rum¹** noun an alcoholic spirit made from sugar-cane

**rum²** adj, informal strange, odd

**rumble** verb to make a low rolling noise like that of thunder etc □ noun a low rolling noise

**ruminant** noun an animal, such as a cow, that chews the cud □ **ruminate** verb 1 to chew the cud 2 to be deep in thought □ **rumination** noun deep thought

**rummage** verb to turn things over in search □ noun a thorough search

**rummy** noun a card game played with hands of seven cards

**rumour** noun 1 general talk 2 a story passed from person to person which may not be true □ verb 1 to spread a rumour of 2 to tell widely

**rump** noun 1 the hind part of an animal 2 the meat from this part

**rumple** verb 1 to make untidy 2 to crease

**rumpus** noun an uproar, a clamour

**run** verb 1 to move swiftly, hurry 2 to race 3 to travel: the train runs every day 4 of water: to flow 5 to follow a certain route: *the main road running between Glasgow and Edinburgh* **6** of a machine: to work **7** to spread (rapidly): *this colour is running* **8** to continue, extend: *the course runs for two days* **9** to operate (machinery *etc*) **10** to organize, conduct (a business *etc*) **11** to compete with other candidates in an election □ *noun* **1** a trip **2** a distance run **3** a spell of running **4** a continuous period: *a run of good luck* **5** a ladder in a stocking *etc* **6** free use of: *the run of the house* **7** a single score in cricket **8** an enclosure for hens *etc* □ **runaway** *noun* a person that runs away □ *adj* of an animal or vehicle: out of control and moving very fast □ **run-down** *adj* in poor health or condition □ **runner** *noun* **1** someone who runs **2** a messenger **3** a rooting stem of a plant **4** a blade of a skate or sledge □ **do a runner** *slang* to leave without paying a bill □ **runner-up** *noun* (*pl* **runners-up**) someone who comes second in a race or competition □ **running** *noun* **1** the act of moving fast **2** management, control □ *adj* **1** for use in running **2** giving out fluid: *running nose* **3** carried on continuously: *running commentary* □ *adv* one after another: *three days running* □ **in** (or **out of**) **the running** having (or not having) a chance of success □ **run-of-the-mill** *adj* ordinary □ **runway** *noun* a path for aircraft to take off from or land on □ **run a risk** to take a chance of loss, failure *etc* □ **run down 1** to knock (someone) down **2** to speak ill of □ **run into 1** to bump into, collide with **2** to meet accidentally □ **run out of** to become short of □ **run over** to knock down or pass over with a car

**run** *verb* ⇌ **runs, running, ran, run**

**rune** *noun* a letter of an early alphabet used in ancient writings

**rung¹** *noun* a step of a ladder

**rung²** *see* **ring**

**runic** *adj* written in runes

**runrig** *noun, Scottish* a system of dividing land into strips for leasing to tenants

**rupee** *noun* the standard currency of India, Pakistan and Sri Lanka

**rupture** *noun* **1** a breaking, *eg* of a friendship **2** a tear in a part of the body □ *verb* to break, burst

**rural** *adj* of the country (*contrasted with:* **urban**)

**ruse** *noun* a trick, a cunning plan

**rush¹** *verb* **1** to move quickly, hurry **2** to make (someone) hurry **3** to take (a fort *etc*) by a sudden attack □ *noun* (*pl* **rushes**) **1** a quick, forward movement **2** a hurry

**rush²** *noun* (*pl* **rushes**) a tall grasslike plant growing near water

**rusk** *noun* a hard dry biscuit like toast

**russet** *adj* reddish-brown □ *noun* a type of apple of russet colour

**rust** *noun* a reddish-brown coating on metal, caused by air and moisture □ *verb* to form rust □ **rusty** *adj* **1** covered with rust **2** *informal* showing lack of practice: *my French is rusty*

**rustic** *adj* **1** relating to the country **2** roughly made **3** simple, unsophisticated □ *noun* someone who lives in the country

**rusticate** *verb* to live in the country

**rustle** *verb* **1** of silk *etc*: to make a soft, whispering sound **2** to steal (cattle) **3** (**rustle something up**) *informal* to prepare quickly □ *noun* a soft, whispering sound □ **rustler** *noun* someone who steals cattle

**rut** *noun* a deep track made by a wheel *etc* □ **in a rut** having a dull, routine way of life □ **rutted** *adj*

**ruthless** *adj* without pity, cruel

**rye** *noun* a kind of grain

# Ss

**s** *abbrev* **1** south **2** southern

**Sabbath** *noun* the day of the week regularly set aside for religious services and rest (among Muslims, Friday; Jews, Saturday; and Christians, Sunday)

**sabbatical** *noun* a period of paid leave from work

**sable** *noun* a small weasel-like animal with dark brown or blackish fur □ *adj* black or dark brown in colour

**sabotage** (*say* sab-ot-ahsz) *noun* deliberate destruction of machinery, an organization *etc* by enemies or dissatisfied workers □ *verb* to destroy or damage deliberately □ **saboteur** *noun*

**sabre** *noun*, *historical* a curved sword used by cavalry

**sac** *noun* any bag-like part in a plant or animal, *esp* containing liquid

**saccharine** *noun* a very sweet substance used as a sugar substitute

**sachet** (*say* sash-ei) *noun* **1** a small bag to hold handkerchiefs *etc* **2** a small sealed packet containing powder or liquid, eg shampoo

**sack¹** *noun* **1** a large bag of coarse cloth for holding flour *etc* **2 the sack** *informal* dismissal from your job □ *verb*, *informal* to dismiss from a job □ **sacking** *noun* □ **get the sack** *informal* to be dismissed from your job

**sack²** *noun* the plundering of a captured town □ *verb* to plunder

**sacral** (*say* seik-ral) *adj* of the sacrum

ⓘ From Latin *sacrum* meaning 'a sacred object' + word-ending *-al*

 ✦ Do not confuse with: **sacred**

**sacrament** *noun* a religious ceremony, eg baptism or communion

**sacred** *adj* holy

ⓘ From Middle English *sacre* meaning 'make holy', combined with the word-ending *-ed* to give the sense of 'made holy'

 ✦ Do not confuse with: **sacral**

**sacrifice** *noun* **1** the offering of an animal killed for the purpose to a god **2** an animal *etc* offered to a god **3** the giving up of something for the benefit of another person, or to gain something more important **4** something given up for this purpose □ *verb* **1** to offer (an animal *etc*) as a sacrifice to a god **2** to give up (something) for someone or something else □ **sacrificial** *adj*

**sacrilege** *noun* the use of something holy in a blasphemous way □ **sacrilegious** *adj*

**sacrosanct** *adj* **1** very sacred **2** not to be harmed or touched

**sacrum** (*say* sei-krum) *noun* a triangular bone forming part of the human pelvis

**sad** *adj* **1** sorrowful, unhappy **2** showing sorrow **3** causing sorrow: *sad story* **4** *informal* pitiful, feeble □ **sadden** *verb*

■ (meanings 1 and 2) tearful, upset, distressed, miserable, downcast, glum, crestfallen, dejected, downhearted, despondent, melancholy, depressed, low, gloomy, dismal

**saddle** *noun* **1** a seat for a rider on the back of a horse or bicycle **2** a cut or joint of meat from the back of an animal □ *verb* to put a saddle on (an animal) □ **saddle with** to burden with: *saddled with debts*

**sadism** (*say* seid-i-zm) *noun* taking pleasure in cruelty to others □ **sadist**

(*say* **seid**-ist) *noun* □ **sadistic** (*say* sa-dis-tik) *adj*

Sadism is a word which was invented to describe the particular type of sexual cruelty which the 18th-century French author Marquis de *Sade* wrote about in his novels.

**SAE** or **sae** *abbrev* stamped addressed envelope

**safari** *noun* an expedition for observing or hunting wild animals □ **safari park** an enclosed area where wild animals are kept outdoors and on view to visitors

**safe** *adj* 1 unharmed 2 free from harm or danger 3 reliable, trustworthy □ *noun* 1 a lockable box for keeping money and valuables 2 a storage place for meat *etc* □ **safeguard** *noun* anything that gives protection or security □ *verb* to protect □ **safe and sound** unharmed

**safety** *noun* freedom from harm or danger □ *adj* giving protection or safety □ **safety belt** a seat belt □ **safety-pin** *noun* a curved pin in the shape of a clasp, with a guard covering its point

**saffron** *noun* a type of crocus from which is obtained a yellow food dye and flavouring agent

**sag** *verb* to droop or sink in the middle

**sag** ⇨ sags, sagging, sagged

**saga** *noun* 1 an ancient story about heroes *etc* 2 a novel or series of novels about several generations of a family 3 a long detailed story

**sagacious** *adj* very wise, quick at understanding □ **sagaciously** *adv* □ **sagacity** *noun*

**sage** *noun* 1 a type of herb with grey-green leaves which are used for flavouring 2 a wise man □ *adj* wise □ **sagely** *adv*

**sago** *noun* a white starchy substance obtained from a palm-tree, often used in puddings

**said** *adj* mentioned before: *the said shopkeeper* □ *past form of* **say**

**sail** *noun* 1 a sheet of canvas spread out to catch the wind and drive forward a ship or boat 2 a journey in a ship or boat 3 an arm of a windmill □ *verb* 1 to travel in a ship or boat (with or without sails) 2 to navigate or steer a ship or boat 3 to begin a sea voyage 4 to glide along easily □ **sailboard** *noun* a surfboard fitted with a mast and sail □ **sailor** *noun* 1 someone who sails 2 a member of a ship's crew □ **set sail** to set out on a sea voyage

**saint** *noun* 1 a very good or holy person 2 a title conferred after death on a holy person by the Roman Catholic Church (*short form:* **St**) □ **saintly** *adj*

**sake** *noun* 1 cause, purpose: *for the sake of making money* 2 benefit, advantage: *for my sake*

**salaam** *noun* a low bow with the right palm on the forehead, a form of Eastern greeting □ *verb* to perform this greeting

**salad** *noun* a dish of raw vegetables, *eg* lettuce, cucumber *etc*

**salamander** *noun* a kind of small lizard-like animal

**salami** *noun* a type of highly seasoned sausage

**salary** *noun* (*pl* **salaries**) fixed wages regularly paid for work

Based on Latin *salarium*, ration money given to Roman legionaries for buying salt

**sale** *noun* 1 the exchange of anything for money 2 a selling of goods at reduced prices 3 an auction □ **salesman**, **saleswoman** *noun* a person who sells or shows goods to customers

**salient** *adj* 1 pointing outwards: *salient angle* 2 outstanding, chief: *salient points of the speech*

**saline** *adj* containing salt, salty

**saliva** *noun* the liquid that forms in the mouth to help digestion; spittle □ **salivary** *adj* □ **salivate** *verb* 1 to produce saliva 2 to anticipate keenly

**sallow** *adj* of complexion: pale, yellowish

**sally** *noun* (*pl* **sallies**) 1 a sudden rush forward 2 a trip, an excursion 3 a witty remark or retort □ *verb* to rush out suddenly □ **sally forth** to go out, emerge

**sally** *verb* ⋄ sallies, sallying, sallied

**salmon** *noun* a large fish with yellowish-pink flesh

**salmonella** *noun* a bacterium which causes food poisoning

**salon** *noun* 1 a shop in which hairdressing *etc* is done 2 a large room for receiving important guests 3 a gathering of such people

**saloon** *noun* 1 a passengers' dining-room in a ship 2 a covered-in car 3 a public house, a bar

**salt** *noun* 1 a substance used for seasoning, either mined from the earth or obtained from sea water 2 a substance formed from a metal and an acid 3 *informal* a sailor □ *adj* 1 containing salt: *salt water* 2 tasting of salt 3 preserved in salt: *salt herring* □ *verb* 1 to sprinkle with salt 2 to preserve with salt □ **salty** *adj* 1 tasting of salt 2 piquant, racy □ **salt cellar** a small container for salt

**salubrious** *adj* 1 health-giving 2 pleasant, respectable

**salutary** *adj* 1 giving health or safety 2 beneficial, useful: *salutary lesson*

**salute** *verb* 1 to greet with words, an embrace *etc* 2 *military* to raise the hand to the forehead to show respect to 3 to honour someone by a firing of guns *etc* □ *noun* an act or way of saluting □ **salutation** *noun*

**salvage** *noun* 1 goods saved from destruction or waste 2 the act of saving a ship's cargo, goods from a fire *etc* 3 payment made for this act □ *verb* to save from loss or ruin

**salvation** *noun* 1 an act, means or cause of saving 2 the saving of humanity from sin

**salve** *noun* an ointment for healing or soothing □ *verb* to soothe (pride, conscience *etc*

**salver** *noun* a small tray, often of silver

**salvo** *noun* (*pl* **salvos**) a great burst of gunfire, clapping *etc*

**same** *adj* 1 exactly alike, identical 2 not different, unchanged: *he still looks the same* □ *pronoun* the thing just mentioned □ **sameness** *noun* □ **all the same** or **just the same** in spite of that □ **at the same time** still, nevertheless
ⓔ From Old Norse *same*

**samovar** *noun* a Russian tea-urn

**sampan** *noun* a kind of small boat used in Far Eastern countries

**sample** *noun* a small part extracted to show what the whole is like □ *verb* to test a sample of □ **sampler** *noun* 1 someone who samples 2 a piece of needlework *etc* showing skill in different techniques

**sanatorium** *noun* 1 a hospital, *esp* for people suffering from respiratory diseases 2 a sick-room in a school *etc*

**sanctify** *verb* to make holy or sacred □ **sanctification** *noun* □ **sanctity** *noun*

**sanctify** ⋄ sanctifies, sanctifying, sanctified

**sanctimonious** *adj* self-righteous, priggish

**sanction** *noun* 1 permission, approval 2 a penalty for breaking a law or rule 3 (**sanctions**) measures applied to force another country *etc* to stop a course of action

**sanctuary** *noun* (*pl* **sanctuaries**) 1 a sacred place 2 the most sacred part of a temple or church **3** a place of safety from arrest or violence **4** a protected reserve for birds or animals

**sanctum** *noun*: **inner sanctum** a very sacred or private room *etc*

**sand** *noun* **1** a mass of tiny particles of crushed rocks *etc* **2** (**sands**) a stretch of sand on the seashore □ *verb* **1** to sprinkle with sand **2** to add sand to **3** to smooth or polish with sandpaper □ **sandy** *adj* **1** covered with sand **2** like sand **3** of hair: yellowish-red in colour □ **sandbag** *noun* a bag filled with sand, used as a protective barrier □ **sand dune** a ridge of sand blown up by the wind □ **sandpaper** *noun* paper with a layer of sand glued to it for smoothing and polishing □ **sandshoe** *noun* a light shoe with a rubber sole □ **sandstone** *noun* a soft rock made of layers of sand pressed together

**sandal** *noun* a shoe with straps to hold the sole onto the foot

**sandalwood** *noun* a fragrant E Indian wood

**sandwich** *noun* (*pl* **sandwiches**) two slices of bread, or a split roll, stuffed with a filling □ *verb* to fit between two other objects

After the 18th-century Earl of *Sandwich*, said to have invented it to allow him to gamble without interruption for meals

**sane** *adj* **1** of sound mind, not mad **2** sensible □ **sanely** *adv*

**sang** *past form of* **sing**

**sanguinary** *adj* bloodthirsty, bloody
ⓘ From Latin *sanguinarius* meaning 'for blood' or 'blood-thirsty'

❧. Do not confuse: **sanguinary** and **sanguine**

**sanguine** *adj* **1** hopeful, cheerful **2** of a complexion: red, ruddy
ⓘ From Latin *sanguineus* meaning 'blood-stained'

**sanitary** *adj* **1** promoting good

health, *esp* by having good drainage and sewage disposal **2** free from dirt, infection *etc* □ **sanitary towel** a pad of absorbent material worn to soak up menstrual blood

**sanitation** *noun* arrangements for protecting health, *esp* drainage and sewage disposal

**sanity** *noun* **1** soundness of mind **2** mental health **3** good sense or judgement

**sank** *past form of* **sink**

**Sanskrit** *noun* the ancient literary language of India

**sap** *noun* **1** the juice in plants, trees *etc* **2** *informal* a weakling, a fool □ *verb* to weaken (someone's strength *etc*

**sap** *verb* ⬌ **saps, sapping, sapped**

**sapling** *noun* a young tree

**sapphire** *noun* a precious stone of a deep blue colour

**Saracen** *noun, historical* an Islamic opponent of the Crusaders; a Moor

**sarcasm** *noun* **1** scornful humour, characterized by the use of a mocking tone to say the exact opposite of what you really think **2** a hurtful remark made in scorn □ **sarcastic** *adj* **1** of a remark: containing sarcasm **2** often using sarcasm, scornful □ **sarcastically** *adv*

**sarcophagus** *noun* a stone coffin

**sardine** *noun* a young pilchard, often tinned in oil □ **like sardines** crowded closely together

**sardonic** *adj* bitter, mocking, scornful

**sari** *noun* a long cloth wrapped round the waist and brought over the shoulder, traditionally worn by Indian women

**sarong** *noun* a skirt traditionally worn by Malay men and women

**sartorial** *adj* relating to dress or clothes: *sartorial elegance*

**sash¹** *noun* (*pl* **sashes**) a decorative

band worn round the waist or over the shoulder

**sash²** noun (pl **sashes**) a sliding frame for window panes

**Sassenach** noun, Scottish derogatory an English person

**sat** past form of **sit**

**Satan** noun the Devil □ **Satanic** adj

**satchel** noun a small bag for carrying schoolbooks etc

**sate** verb, old to satisfy fully; give more than enough to

**satellite** noun 1 a moon orbiting a larger planet 2 a man-made object launched into space to orbit a planet 3 a state controlled by a more powerful neighbour

**satiate** verb to satisfy fully; to give more than enough to □ **satiety** noun

**satin** noun a closely woven silk with a glossy surface

**satire** noun 1 a piece of writing etc which makes fun of particular people or events 2 ridicule, scorn □ **satirical** adj □ **satirist** noun □ **satirize** verb

**satisfaction** noun 1 the act of satisfying or being satisfied 2 a feeling of pleasure or comfort 3 something that satisfies 4 compensation for damage etc □ **satisfactory** adj 1 satisfying 2 fulfilling the necessary requirements □ **satisfactorily** adv

**satisfy** verb 1 to give enough (of something) to 2 to please, make content 3 to give enough to lessen or quieten: satisfied her curiosity 4 to convince: satisfied that he was innocent 5 to fulfil

satisfy ⋄ satisfies, satisfying, satisfied

**satsuma** noun a small seedless orange

**saturate** verb 1 to soak or immerse in water 2 to cover or fill completely (with): saturated with information □ **saturation** noun

**Saturday** noun the seventh day of the week

**saturnine** adj gloomy, sullen

**satyr** (say sat-er) noun a mythological creature, half man, half goat, living in the woods

**sauce** noun 1 a liquid seasoning added to food to improve flavour 2 informal cheek, impudence □ **saucy** adj impudent, cheeky

**saucepan** noun a deep-sided cooking pan with a long handle

**saucer** noun a small, shallow dish for placing under a cup

**sauna** noun a room filled with dry steam to induce sweating

**saunter** verb to stroll about without hurrying □ noun a leisurely stroll

**sausage** noun minced meat seasoned and stuffed into a tube of animal gut etc

**savage** adj 1 wild, untamed 2 fierce and cruel 3 uncivilized 4 very angry □ noun 1 an uncivilized person 2 someone fierce or cruel □ verb to attack very fiercely □ **savagely** adv □ **savagery** noun

**savanna** or **savannah** noun a grassy, treeless plain

**save** verb 1 to bring out of danger, rescue 2 to protect from harm, damage or loss 3 to keep from spending or using: saves time 4 to put money aside for the future □ prep except (for): all the CDs were damaged save this one □ **savings** noun pl money put aside for the future □ **save up** to put money aside for future use

**saviour** noun 1 someone who saves others from harm or evil 2 (**Saviour**) Christ

**savour** noun 1 characteristic taste or flavour 2 an interesting quality □ verb 1 to taste or smell of 2 to taste with enjoyment 3 to have a trace or suggestion (of): his reaction savours of jealousy 4 to experience

**savoury** adj **1** having a pleasant taste or smell **2** salt or sharp in flavour; not sweet □ noun (pl savouries) a savoury dish or snack

**savoy** noun a type of winter cabbage

**saw**[1] noun a tool with a toothed edge for cutting wood etc □ verb to cut with a saw □ **sawdust** noun a dust of fine fragments of wood, made in sawing □ **sawmill** noun a mill where wood is sawn up

**saw** verb ◇ saws, sawing, sawn, sawed

**saw**[2] past form of **see**

**Saxon** noun, historical one of a Germanic people who invaded Britain in the 5th century

**saxophone** noun a wind instrument with a curved metal tube and keys for the fingers □ **saxophonist** noun

So called because it was invented by a man whose name was Adolphe Sax

**say** verb **1** to speak, utter **2** to express in words, state □ noun **1** the power to speak: no say in the matter **2** the opportunity to speak: I've had my say □ **I say!** interjection **1** expressing surprise or protest **2** used to try to attract attention □ **saying** noun something often said; a proverb □ **that is to say** in other words

**say** verb ◇ says, saying, said
ⓖ From Old English secgan

◻ (verb, meaning 1) pronounce, deliver, exclaim, ejaculate, drawl, mutter, grunt; (verb, meaning 2) tell, declare, assert, affirm, maintain, claim, allege, imply, disclose, divulge

**scab** noun **1** a crust formed over a sore **2** any of several diseases of animals or plants **3** informal a blackleg □ **scabby** adj

**scabbard** noun the sheath in which the blade of a sword is kept

**scabies** noun an itchy skin disease

**scaffold** noun **1** a platform on which people are put to death **2** scaffolding □ **scaffolding** noun a framework of poles and platforms used by people doing repairs on a building etc

**scald** verb **1** to burn with hot liquid or steam **2** to heat (milk etc) just short of boiling point □ noun a burn caused by hot liquid or steam

**scale** noun **1** a set of regularly spaced marks for measurement on a thermometer etc **2** a series or system of increasing values: salary scale **3** music a group of notes going up or down in order **4** the measurements of a map compared with the actual size of the area shown: drawn to the scale 1:50000 **5** the size of a business etc: manufacture on a small scale **6** a small thin flake on the skin of a fish or snake **7** (scales) a weighing machine □ verb **1** to climb up **2** to remove the scales from (eg a fish) **3** to remove in thin layers □ **scaly** adj having scales; flaky

**scallop** noun a shellfish with a pair of hinged fan-shaped shells □ **scalloped** adj of an edge: cut into curves or notches

**scallywag** noun a rogue

**scalp** noun **1** the outer covering of the skull **2** the skin and hair on top of the head □ verb to cut the scalp from

**scalpel** noun a small, thin-bladed knife, used in surgery

**scamp** noun a rascal

**scamper** verb **1** to run about playfully **2** to run off in haste

**scampi** noun pl large prawns

**scan** verb **1** to count the beats in a line of poetry **2** of poetry: to have the correct number of beats **3** to examine carefully **4** informal to read quickly, skim over **5** to pass an X-ray, ultrasonic wave etc over □ noun an act of scanning □ **scanner** noun a machine which scans

□ **scansion** noun scanning of poetry

**scan** verb ⇨ scans, scanning, scanned

**scandal** noun 1 something disgraceful or shocking 2 talk or gossip about people's (supposed) misdeeds □ **scandalize** verb to shock, horrify □ **scandalmonger** noun someone who spreads gossip or scandal □ **scandalous** adj 1 shameful, disgraceful 2 containing scandal □ **scandalously** adv: it is scandalously expensive

**scant** adj not plentiful, hardly enough: pay scant attention □ **scanty** adj little or not enough in amount □ **scantily** adv

**scapegoat** noun someone who bears the blame for the wrongdoing of others

Literally 'escape goat', after an ancient Jewish ritual of transferring the people's sins to a goat which was afterwards let free in the wilderness

**scar** noun 1 the mark left by a wound or sore 2 a mark, a blemish □ verb to mark with a scar

**scar** verb ⇨ scars, scarring, scarred

**scarab** noun a beetle regarded as sacred by the ancient Egyptians

**scarce** adj 1 not plentiful, not enough 2 rare, seldom found □ **make yourself scarce** to go, run away □ **scarcely** adv 1 only just, barely: could scarcely hear 2 surely not: you can scarcely expect me to eat that □ **scarcity** noun (pl **scarcities**) want, shortage

**scare** verb 1 to drive away with fear 2 to startle, frighten □ noun a sudden fright or alarm □ **scary** or **scarey** adj frightening □ **scarecrow** noun a figure set up to scare birds away from crops

**scarf** noun (pl **scarves** or **scarfs**) a strip of material worn round the neck, shoulders or head

**scarlet** noun a bright red colour □ adj

bright red □ **scarlet fever** an infectious illness, causing a rash

**scarper** verb, slang to run away

**scathing** adj cruel, hurtful: scathing remark

**scatter** verb 1 to throw loosely about; sprinkle 2 to spread widely 3 to flee in all directions □ **scattered** adj □ **scattering** noun

**scatterbrain** noun someone who frequently forgets things

**scavenger** noun an animal which feeds on dead flesh

**scenario** (say si-nah-ri-oh) noun 1 a scene-by-scene outline of a play, film etc 2 an outline of a plan or project
ⓘ From Italian scenario meaning 'scenery'

◭ Do not confuse with: **scene**

**scene** noun 1 the place where something happens: scene of the accident 2 a view, a landscape 3 a division of a play or opera 4 an area of activity: the music scene 5 a show of bad temper: don't make a scene □ **scenery** noun 1 the painted background on a theatre stage 2 the general appearance of a stretch of country □ **scenic** adj 1 of scenery 2 picturesque
ⓘ From Latin scaena meaning 'the scene presented' or 'the stage'

◭ Do not confuse with: **scenario**

**scent** verb 1 to discover by the smell 2 to have a suspicion of, sense: scent danger 3 to give a pleasant smell to □ noun 1 perfume 2 an odour, a smell 3 the trail of smell used to track an animal etc

**sceptic** (say skep-tik) noun someone who doubts what they are told □ **sceptical** (say skep-tik-al) adj □ **sceptically** adv □ **scepticism** (say skep-tis-i-zm) noun
ⓘ From Greek skeptikos meaning 'thoughtful'

◭ Do not confuse with: **septic**

**sceptre** (*say* sep-ter) *noun* an ornamental rod carried by a monarch on ceremonial occasions

**schedule** (*say* shed-yool or sked-yool) *noun* **1** the time set for doing something: *I'm a week behind schedule* **2** a written statement of details **3** a form for filling in information □ *verb* **1** to form into a schedule **2** to plan, arrange

**scheme** (*say* skeem) *noun* **1** a plan, a systematic arrangement **2** a dishonest or crafty plan □ *verb* to make schemes, plot □ **schematic** *adj* □ **scheming** *adj*

**scherzo** (*say* sker-tsoh) *noun* (*pl* **scherzos**), *music* a lively movement in triple time

**schism** (*say* si-zm or ski-zm) *noun* a breaking away from the main group

**schizophrenia** (*say* skit-sof-ree-ni-a) *noun* a mental illness involving a distorted perception of reality □ **schizophrenic** (*say* skit-sof-ren-ik) *noun & adj* (someone) suffering from schizophrenia

**scholar** *noun* **1** someone of great learning **2** someone who has been awarded a scholarship **3** a pupil, a student □ **scholarly** *adj* showing or having knowledge, high intelligence and love of accuracy □ **scholarliness** *noun* □ **scholarship** *noun* **1** learning **2** a sum of money given to help a clever student to carry on further studies □ **scholastic** *adj*

**school** *noun* **1** a place for teaching, *esp* children **2** a group of artists *etc* who share the same ideas **3** a large number of fish, whales *etc* □ *verb* **1** to educate in a school **2** to train by practice □ **schooling** *noun* **1** education in a school **2** training □ **schoolmaster**, **schoolmistress** *noun* a teacher at a school

**schooner** *noun* **1** a two-masted sailing ship **2** a large sherry glass **3** *US & Austral* a large beer glass

**sciatica** (*say* sai-at-ik-a) *noun* severe pain in the upper part of the leg

**science** *noun* **1** knowledge obtained by observation and experiment **2** a branch of this knowledge, *eg* chemistry, physics, biology *etc* **3** these sciences considered together □ **scientific** *adj* **1** of science **2** done according to the methods of science □ **scientifically** *adv* □ **scientist** *noun* □ **science fiction** stories dealing with future life on earth, space travel, other planets *etc*

**sci fi** *abbrev* science fiction

**scimitar** *noun* a sword with a short curved blade

**scintillate** *verb* **1** to sparkle **2** to show brilliant wit *etc*

**scion** (*say* sai-on) *noun* **1** a young member of a family **2** a descendant **3** a cutting for grafting on another plant

**scissors** *noun pl* a cutting instrument with two hinged blades

**scoff** *verb* **1** to express scorn **2** (with **at**) to make fun of, mock

**scold** *verb* to tell off; blame or rebuke with angry words □ *noun* a bad-tempered person □ **scolding** *noun* a telling-off

**scone** *noun* a small plain cake made with flour, milk and a little fat

**scoop** *noun* **1** a hollow instrument used for lifting loose material, water *etc* **2** an exclusive news story □ *verb* to lift or dig out with a scoop

**scooter** *noun* **1** a two-wheeled toy vehicle pushed along by foot **2** a low-powered motor-cycle

**scope** *noun* **1** opportunity or room to do something: *scope for improvement* **2** extent, range: *outside the scope of this dictionary*

**scorch** *verb* **1** to burn slightly, singe **2** to dry up with heat □ **scorching** *adj* **1** burning, singeing **2** very hot **3** harsh, severe: *scorching criticism*

**score** *noun* **1** a gash, a notch **2** an account, a debt: *settle old scores*

**3** the total number of points gained in a game **4** a written piece of music showing separate parts for voices and instruments **5** a set of twenty **6** (**scores**) a great many **7** a reason, account: *don't worry on that score* □ *verb* **1** to mark with lines or notches **2** to gain (points) **3** to keep a note of points gained in a game □ **score out** to cross out

**scorn** *verb* **1** to look down on, despise **2** to refuse (help *etc*) because of pride □ *noun* mocking contempt □ **scornful** *adj* □ **scornfully** *adv*

**scorpion** *noun* a spider-like creature with a poisonous sting in its tail

**scotch** *verb* to stamp out, suppress

**scot-free** *adj* unhurt; unpunished

**SCOTVEC** *abbrev* Scottish Vocational Education Council

**scoundrel** *noun* a rascal

**scour** *verb* **1** to clean by hard rubbing; scrub **2** to search thoroughly

**scourge** *noun* **1** a whip **2** a cause of great suffering □ *verb* **1** to whip, lash **2** to afflict, cause to suffer

**scout** *noun* **1** a guide or spy sent ahead to bring back information **2** (**Scout**) a member of the Scout Association

**scowl** *verb* to wrinkle the brows in displeasure or anger □ *noun* a frown

**Scrabble** *noun, trademark* a word-building game

**scrabble** *verb* to scratch or grope about

**scraggy** *adj* **1** long and thin **2** uneven, rugged

**scram** *exclamation* go away

**scramble** *verb* **1** to struggle to seize something before others **2** to wriggle along on hands and knees **3** to mix or toss together: *scrambled eggs* **4** to jumble up (a message) to make it unintelligible without decoding □ *noun* **1** a rush and

struggle to get something **2** a motor-cycle race over rough country

**scrap** *noun* **1** a small piece, a fragment **2** a picture for pasting in a scrapbook **3** *informal* a fight **4** parts of a car *etc* no longer required: *sold as scrap* **5** (**scraps**) small pieces, odds and ends □ *verb* **1** to abandon as useless **2** *informal* to fight, quarrel □ **scrappy** *adj* made up of odd scraps, not well put together □ **scrappily** *adv* □ **scrapbook** *noun* a blank book in which to stick pictures *etc* □ **scrapheap** *noun* a heap of old metal *etc*, a rubbish heap □ **on the scrap-heap** no longer needed □ **scrap metal** metal for melting and re-using

**scrap** *verb* ⋄ scrap**s**, scrap**ping**, scrap**ped**

**scrape** *verb* **1** to rub and mark with something sharp **2** to drag or rub against or across a surface with a harsh grating noise **3** (with **up** or **together**) to collect (money *etc*) with difficulty □ *noun* **1** an act of scraping **2** a mark or sound made by scraping **3** *informal* a difficult situation □ **scrape through** to only just avoid failure

**scratch** *verb* **1** to draw a sharp point across the surface of **2** to mark by doing this **3** to tear or dig with claws, nails *etc* **4** to rub with the nails to relieve or stop itching **5** to withdraw from a competition □ *noun* (*pl* **scratches**) **1** a mark or sound made by scratching **2** a slight wound □ *adj* **1** *golf* too good to be allowed a handicap **2** of a team: made up of players hastily got together □ **come up to scratch** to be satisfactory □ **start from scratch** to start from nothing, right at the beginning

**scrawl** *verb* to write or draw untidily or hastily □ *noun* **1** untidy, hasty or bad writing **2** something scrawled

**scrawny** *adj* thin, skinny

**scream** verb to utter a shrill, piercing cry as in pain, fear etc; shriek □ noun a shrill cry

**scree** noun loose stones covering a steep mountain side

**screech** verb to utter a harsh, shrill and sudden cry □ noun a harsh shrill cry

**screed** noun a long boring speech or letter

**screen** noun 1 a flat covered framework to shelter from view or protect from heat, cold etc 2 something that shelters from wind, danger, difficulties etc 3 the surface on which cinema films are projected 4 the surface on which a television picture, or computer data, appears □ verb 1 to shelter, hide 2 to make a film of 3 to show on a screen 4 to sift, sieve 5 to sort out (the good from the bad) by testing 6 to conduct examinations on someone to test for disease □ **screen off** to hide behind, or separate by, a screen

**screw** noun 1 a nail with a slotted head and a winding groove or ridge (called the **thread**) on its surface 2 a kind of propeller (a **screw-propeller**) with spiral blades, used in ships and aircraft 3 a turn or twist (of a screw etc) □ verb 1 to fasten or tighten with a screw 2 to fix (eg a stopper) in place with a twisting movement 3 to twist, turn round (your head etc) 4 to twist up, crumple, pucker □ **screwdriver** noun a tool for turning screws

**scribble** verb 1 to write carelessly 2 to make untidy or meaningless marks with a pencil etc □ noun 1 careless writing 2 meaningless marks, a doodle

**scribe** noun, historical 1 a clerk who copied out manuscripts 2 a Jewish teacher of law

**scrimp** verb to be sparing or stingy with money: scrimp and save for a holiday

**script** noun 1 the text of a play, talk etc 2 handwriting like print

**scripture** noun 1 sacred writings 2 (**Scripture**) the Christian Bible

**scroll** noun 1 a piece of paper rolled up 2 an ornament shaped like this

**scrotum** noun the bag of skin enclosing the testicles

**scrounge** verb, slang 1 to cadge 2 to get by begging □ noun an attempt to beg or cadge □ **scrounger** noun

**scrub** verb to rub hard in order to clean □ noun countryside covered with low bushes

**scrub** verb ⇔ scrubs, scrubbing, scrubbed

**scruff** noun the back of the neck

**scruffy** adj untidy

**scrum** noun, rugby a struggle for the ball by the forwards of the opposing sides bunched together

**scrumptious** adj, informal delicious

**scrunch** verb to crumple

**scruple** noun doubt over what is right or wrong that keeps someone from doing something □ verb to hesitate because of a scruple

**scrupulous** adj careful over the smallest details

**scrutiny** noun (pl **scrutinies**) careful examination, a close look □ **scrutinize** verb

**scuba** noun breathing apparatus used by skin-divers

**scud** verb to move or sweep along quickly: scudding clouds

**scud** ⇔ scuds, scudding, scudded

**scuffle** noun a confused fight

**scull** noun a short oar □ verb to move (a boat) with a pair of these or with one oar worked at the back of the boat

**scullery** noun (pl **sculleries**) a room for rough kitchen work

**sculpture** noun 1 the art of the sculptor or sculptress 2 a piece of their work □ **sculptor** noun an artist who carves or models figures in wood, stone, clay *etc*

**scum** *noun* **1** foam that rises to the surface of liquids **2** a worthless person or people

**scupper** *noun* a hole in the side of a ship to drain water from the deck □ *verb* to put an end to, ruin

**scurf** *noun* small flakes of dead skin (*esp* on the scalp)

**scurrilous** *adj* insulting, abusive

**scurry** *verb* to hurry along, scamper

**scurry** ⋄ scurries, scurrying, scurried

**scurvy** *noun* a type of disease caused by a lack of fresh fruit and vegetables

**scuttle** *noun* **1** a fireside container for coal **2** an opening with a lid in a ship's deck or side □ *verb* **1** to make a hole in (a ship) in order to sink it **2** to hurry along, scamper

**scythe** (*say* saidh) *noun* a large curved blade, on a long handle, for cutting grass *etc* by hand □ *verb* to cut with a scythe

**SE** *abbrev* south-east; south-eastern

**sea** *noun* **1** the mass of salt water covering most of the earth's surface **2** a great stretch of water of less size than an ocean **3** a great expanse or number: *a sea of faces* □ **sea anemone** a type of small plant-like animal found on rocks at the seashore □ **seaboard** *noun* land along the edge of the sea □ **seafarer** *noun* a traveller by sea, a sailor □ **seafaring** *adj* □ **seafront** *noun* a promenade with its buildings facing the sea □ **seagull** *noun* a type of web-footed sea bird □ **sea-horse** *noun* a type of small fish with a horse-like head and neck □ **sea level** the level of the surface of the sea □ **sea lion** a large kind of seal, the male of which has a mane □ **seaman** *noun* (*pl* **seamen**) a sailor, *esp* a member of a ship's crew who is not an officer □ **seamanship** *noun* the art of steering and looking after ships at sea □ **seaplane** *noun* an aeroplane which can take off from and land on the water □ **seascape** *noun* a picture of a scene at sea □ **seashore** *noun* the land next to the sea □ **seasick** *adj* made ill by the rocking movement of a ship □ **seaside** *noun* the land beside the sea □ **sea urchin** a type of small sea creature with a spiny shell □ **seaward** *adj & adv* towards the sea □ **seaweed** *noun* any of many kinds of plants growing in the sea □ **seaworthy** *adj* in a good enough condition to go to sea □ **at sea 1** on the sea **2** completely puzzled

**seal**¹ *noun* a furry sea animal living partly on land

**seal**² *noun* **1** a piece of wax with a design pressed into it, attached to a document to show that it is legal or official **2** a piece of wax used to keep a parcel closed **3** anything that closes tightly **4** a piece of sticky paper with a picture on it: *a Christmas seal* □ *verb* **1** to mark or fasten with a seal **2** to close up completely **3** to make (legally) binding and definite: *seal a bargain* □ **sealing wax** a hard kind of wax for sealing letters, documents *etc*

**seam** *noun* **1** the line formed by the sewing together of two pieces of cloth **2** a line or layer of metal, coal *etc* in the earth □ **seamstress** *noun* a woman who sews for a living

**seamy** *adj* sordid; disreputable □ **the seamy side** the more unpleasant side (*eg* of life)

**séance** (*say* sei-ons) *noun* a meeting of people to receive messages from the spirits of the dead

**sear** *verb* **1** to scorch, burn **2** to hurt severely

**search** *verb* **1** to look over in order to find something **2** (with **for**) to look for □ *noun* (*pl* **searches**) **1** an act of searching **2** an attempt to find □ **searching** *adj* examining closely and carefully: *searching question*

□ **searchlight** noun a strong beam of light used for picking out objects at night

**season** noun **1** one of the four divisions of the year (spring, summer, autumn, winter) **2** the proper time for anything **3** a time associated with a particular activity: *the football season* □ verb **1** to add (salt *etc*) to improve the flavour of (food) **2** to dry (wood) till it is ready for use □ **seasonable** adj **1** happening at the proper time **2** of weather: suitable for the season □ **seasonal** adj **1** of the seasons or a season **2** of work *etc*: taking place in one particular season only □ **seasoned** adj **1** of food: flavoured **2** of wood: ready to be used **3** trained, experienced: *a seasoned traveller* □ **seasoning** noun something (*eg* salt, pepper) added to food to give it more taste □ **season ticket** a ticket that can be used repeatedly for a certain period of time

**seat** noun **1** a piece of furniture for sitting on **2** the part of a chair on which you sit **3** the buttocks **4** a mansion **5** a place in parliament, on a council *etc* **6** the centre of some activity: *the seat of government* □ verb **1** to make to sit down **2** to have seats for (a certain number): *the room seats forty* □ **seat belt** noun a belt fixed to a seat in a car *etc* to prevent an occupant from being thrown violently forward in the event of a crash

**secateurs** noun pl a tool like scissors, for trimming bushes *etc*

**secede** verb to break away from a group, society *etc* □ **secession** noun **1** seceding **2** a group of seceders

**seclude** verb to keep (yourself) apart from people's notice or company □ **seclusion** noun

**second** adj **1** next after the first in time, place *etc* **2** other, alternate: *every second week* **3** another of the

same kind as: *they thought him a second Mozart* □ noun **1** someone or something that is second **2** an attendant to someone who boxes or fights a duel **3** the 60th part of a minute of time, or of a degree (in measuring angles) **4** an article not quite perfectly made: *these cups are seconds* □ verb **1** to support, back up **2** (*say* se-**kond**) to transfer temporarily to a special job □ **secondly** adv □ **secondary** adj second in position or importance □ **secondary school** a school between primary school and university *etc* □ **second-hand** adj **1** not new; having been used by another **2** of a shop: dealing in second-hand goods □ **second nature** a firmly fixed habit: *organizing people is second nature to her* □ **second-rate** adj not of the best quality, inferior
ⓔ From Latin *secundus* meaning 'following'

**secret** adj **1** hidden from, or not known by, others **2** secretive □ noun a fact, plan *etc* that is not told or known □ **secrecy** noun □ **secretive** adj inclined to hide or conceal your feelings, activities *etc* □ **secret service** a government department dealing with spying

**secretary** noun (pl **secretaries**) **1** someone employed to write letters, keep records *etc* in an office **2** someone elected to deal with the written business of a club *etc* □ **secretarial** adj □ **Secretary of State 1** a government minister in charge of an administrative department **2** *US* the person in charge of foreign affairs

**secrete** verb **1** to hide, conceal in a secret place **2** of a part of the body: to store up and give out (a fluid) □ **secretion** noun

**sect** noun a group of people who hold certain views, *esp* in religious matters □ **sectarian** adj **1** of a sect

2 loyal to a sect 3 narrow-minded
4 of a crime, *esp* a murder:
committed as a result of hatred
between rival religious groups

**section** *noun* 1 a part, a division 2 a
thin slice of a specimen for
examination under a microscope
3 the view of the inside of anything
when it is cut right through or
across: *a section of a plant*

**sector** *noun* 1 a three-sided part of a
circle whose sides are two radii and
a part of the circumference 2 a part,
a section

**secular** *adj* 1 of worldly, not
spiritual or religious things 2 of
music *etc*: not sacred or religious

**secure** *adj* 1 safe, free from danger
or fear 2 confident 3 firmly fixed or
fastened □ *verb* 1 to make safe, firm
or established 2 to seize, get hold of:
*he secured the tickets* 3 to fasten
□ **security** *noun* 1 safety
2 (**securities**) property or goods
which a lender may keep until the
loan is paid back

**sedan** *noun* 1 an enclosed chair for
one person, carried on two poles by
two bearers (*also called:* **sedan
chair**) 2 *US* a saloon car

**sedate** *adj* calm, serious, dignified

**sedative** *adj* calming, soothing
□ *noun* a medicine with this effect
□ **sedation** *noun* the use of sedatives
to calm a patient

**sedentary** *adj* of a job *etc*: requiring
much sitting

**sedge** *noun* a type of coarse grass
growing in swamps and rivers

**sediment** *noun* the grains or solid
parts which settle at the bottom of a
liquid

**sedition** *noun* the stirring up of
rebellion against the government
□ **seditious** *adj*

**seduce** *verb* 1 to tempt (someone)
away from right or moral
behaviour 2 to persuade (someone)
to have sexual intercourse 3 to

attract □ **seducer** *noun* □ **seduction**
*noun* □ **seductive** *adj*

**sedulous** *adj* diligent, painstaking

**see** *verb* 1 to have sight 2 to be
aware of, notice by means of the
eye: *he can see us coming* 3 to form a
picture of in the mind 4 to
understand: *I see what you mean*
5 to find out: *I'll see what is
happening* 6 to make sure: *see that he
finishes his homework* 7 to
accompany: *I'll see you home* 8 to
meet: *I'll see you at the usual time*
□ *noun* the district over which a
bishop or archbishop has authority
□ **seeing that** since, because □ **see
through** 1 to take part in to the end
2 to not be deceived by (a person,
trick *etc*) □ **see to** to take charge of
(the preparation of): *see to a meal*

**see** *verb* ❖ sees, seeing, saw, seen

⊙ From Old English *seon*

■ (verb, meaning 2) perceive,
glimpse, discern, distinguish,
observe, mark, note □ **see to**
attend to, deal with, organize

**seed** *noun* 1 the part of a tree, plant
*etc* from which a new plant may
grow 2 a seed-like part of a grain or
a nut 3 the beginning from which
anything grows: *the seeds of
rebellion* 4 a seeded player in a
tournament 5 *old* children,
descendants □ *verb* 1 of a plant: to
produce seed 2 to sow 3 to remove
the seeds from (*eg* a fruit) 4 to
arrange (good players) in a
tournament so that they do not
compete against each other till the
later rounds □ **go to seed** or **run to
seed** 1 of a plant: to develop seeds
2 of a person, area *etc*: to
deteriorate, become run down
□ **seedling** *noun* a young plant just
sprung from a seed

**seedy** *adj* 1 full of seeds 2 shabby
3 sickly, not very well

**seek** *verb* 1 to look or search for 2 to
try (to do something): *seek to*

*establish proof* **3** to try to get (advice *etc*) □ **sought after** popular, much in demand

**seek** ⇔ **seeks, seeking, sought**

**seem** *verb* **1** to appear to be: *he seems kind* **2** to appear: *she seems to like it* □ **seeming** *adj* apparent but not actual or real: *a seeming success* □ **seemly** *adj* suitable; decent

**seen** *see* **see**

**seep** *verb* to flow slowly through a small opening, leak

**seer** *noun* a prophet

**seersucker** *noun* a lightweight ribbed cotton fabric

**seesaw** *noun* **1** a plank balanced across a stand so that one end of it goes up when the other goes down **2** an up-and-down movement like that of a seesaw □ *verb* **1** to go up and down on a seesaw **2** to move with a seesaw-like movement

**seethe** *verb* **1** to boil **2** to be very angry □ **seething** *adj*

**segment** *noun* **1** a part cut off **2** a part of a circle cut off by a straight line

**segregate** *verb* to separate (someone or a group) from others □ **segregation** *noun* **1** enforced separation into groups **2** the systematic isolation of one group, *esp* a racial or ethnic minority, from the rest of society

**seismic** (*say* **saiz**-mik) *adj* of earthquakes

**seismograph** (*say* **saiz**-mo-grahf) *noun* an instrument that records earthquake shocks and measures their force

**seize** *verb* **1** to take suddenly by force **2** to overcome: *seized with fury* **3** (with **up**) of machinery: to become stuck, break down □ **seizure** *noun* **1** sudden capture **2** a sudden attack of illness, rage *etc*

**seldom** *adv* not often, rarely: *you seldom see an owl during the day*

**select** *verb* to pick out from several according to your preference, choose □ *adj* **1** picked out, chosen **2** very good **3** exclusive, allowing only certain people in □ **selection** *noun* **1** the act of choosing **2** things chosen **3** a number of things from which to choose □ **selective** *adj* selecting carefully

**self** *noun* (*pl* **selves**) **1** someone's own person **2** someone's personality, character □ **selfless** *adj* thinking of others before yourself, unselfish □ **self-assured** *adj* trusting in your own power or ability, confident □ **self-centred** *adj* concerned with your own affairs, selfish □ **self-confident** *adj* believing in your own powers or abilities □ **self-conscious** *adj* too aware of your faults *etc* and therefore embarrassed in the company of others □ **self-contained** *adj* **1** of a house: complete in itself, not sharing any part with other houses **2** of a person: self-reliant □ **self-control** *noun* control over yourself, your feelings *etc* □ **self-defence** *noun* the defence of your own person, property *etc* □ **self-denial** *noun* doing without something, *esp* in order to give to others □ **self-effacing** *adj* keeping yourself from being noticed, modest □ **self-esteem** *noun* respect for yourself; conceit □ **self-evident** *adj* clear enough to need no proof □ **self-expression** *noun* expressing your own personality in your activities □ **self-important** *adj* having a mistakenly high sense of your importance □ **self-indulgent** *adj* too ready to satisfy your own inclinations and desires □ **self-interest** *noun* a selfish desire to consider only your own interests or advantage □ **self-made** *adj* owing success *etc* to your own efforts: *a self-made man* □ **self-portrait** *noun* an artist's portrait of themselves □ **self-possessed** *adj* calm in mind or manner, quietly confident □ **self-raising flour** flour already containing an ingredient to make it rise □ **self-reliant** adj trusting in your own abilities etc □ **self-respect** noun respect for yourself and concern for your own character and reputation □ **self-righteous** adj thinking highly of your own goodness and virtue □ **self-sacrifice** noun the act of giving up your own life, possessions etc in order to do good to others □ **selfsame** adj the very same □ **self-satisfied** adj pleased, smug, satisfied with yourself □ **self-service** adj of a restaurant: where customers help or serve themselves □ **self-sufficient** adj needing no help or support from anyone else □ **self-willed** adj determined to have your own way, obstinate

**selfish** adj caring only for your own pleasure or advantage □ **selfishly** adv

**sell** verb 1 to give or hand over for money 2 to have or keep for sale 3 to be sold for, cost: this book sells for 20 □ **seller** noun

**sell** ⇔ sells, selling, sold

**Sellotape** noun, trademark transparent adhesive tape, esp for use on paper

**selvage** noun the firm edge of a piece of cloth, that does not fray

**semantic** adj relating to the meaning of words etc

**semaphore** noun a form of signalling using the arms to form different positions for each letter

**semblance** noun an outward, often false, appearance: a semblance of listening

**semen** noun the liquid that carries sperm

**semi-** prefix 1 half: semicircle 2 informal partly □ **semibreve** noun, music a whole-note (◯), equal to four crotchets in length □ **semicircle**

noun half of a circle □ **semicolon** noun the punctuation mark (;) □ **semi-detached** adj of a house: joined to another house on one side but not on the other □ **semi-final** noun the stage or match of a contest immediately before the final □ **semi-precious** adj of a stone: having some value, but not considered a gem
◉ From Latin prefix semi- meaning 'half'

**seminar** noun a group of students working on, or meeting to discuss, a particular subject

**seminary** noun (pl **seminaries**) a school or college

**Semitic** adj Jewish

**semolina** noun the hard particles of wheat sifted from flour, used for puddings etc

**senate** noun 1 the upper house of parliament in the USA, Australia etc 2 the governing council of some universities 3 historical the law-making body in ancient Rome □ **senator** noun

**send** verb 1 to make (someone) go 2 to have (something) carried or delivered to a place □ **sender** noun a person who sends something, esp by post □ **send for** to order to be brought

**send** ⇔ sends, sending, sent

**senile** adj 1 of old age 2 showing the mental feebleness of old age □ **senility** noun

**senior** adj older in age or higher in rank □ noun someone older or in a senior position □ **seniority** noun

**senna** noun the dried leaves of certain plants, used as a laxative

**sensation** noun 1 a feeling through any of the five senses 2 a vague effect: a floating sensation 3 a state of excitement □ **sensational** adj

**sense** noun 1 one of the five powers by which humans feel or notice (hearing, taste, sight, smell, touch) 2 a feeling: a sense of loss 3 an

ability to understand or appreciate: *a sense of humour* **4** (**senses**) right mind, common sense: *to take leave of your senses* **5** wisdom, ability to act in a reasonable way **6** ability to be understood: *to make sense* **7** meaning: *to what sense of this word are your referring?* □ *verb* to feel, realize: *sense disapproval*
□ **senseless** *adj* stunned, unconscious; foolish □ **sensory** *adj* of the senses

**sensible** *adj* **1** wise **2** able to be felt or noticed **3 sensible of** aware of □ **sensibility** *noun* (*pl* **sensibilities**) ability to feel, sensitivity

■ (meaning I) prudent, judicious, well-advised, shrewd

**sensitive** *adj* **1** feeling, *esp* strongly or painfully **2** strongly affected by light, movements *etc* □ **sensitivity** *noun* □ **sensitize** *verb* to make sensitive (*esp* to light)

**sensor** *noun* a device that detects and measures physical changes

**sensual** *adj* **1** driven by, or affecting, the senses rather than the mind: *the sensual pleasures of aromatherapy* **2** indulging in bodily pleasures: *a sensual woman* □ **sensuality** *noun*

⚫\ Do not confuse: **sensual and sensuous**

**sensuous** *adj* pleasing to the senses, particularly by being beautiful or luxurious

**sent** *see* **send**

**sentence** *noun* **1** a number of words which together make a complete statement **2** a judgement announced by a judge or court □ *verb* to condemn to a particular punishment

**sentiment** *noun* **1** a thought expressed in words **2** a show of feeling or emotion, often excessive □ **sentimental** *adj* □ **sentimentality** *noun*

**sentinel** *noun* a soldier on guard

**sepal** *noun* one of the green leaves beneath the petals of a flower

**separate** *verb* (*say* sep-a-reit) **1** to set or keep apart **2** to divide into parts **3** to disconnect **4** to go different ways **5** to live apart by choice □ *adj* (*say* sep-a-rat) **1** placed, kept *etc* apart **2** divided **3** not connected **4** different □ **separation** *noun*

**sepia** *noun* a brown colour

**sept-** *prefix* seven: *septet/ September* (which was the seventh month in the Roman calendar)
ⓔ From Latin *septem* meaning 'seven'

**September** *noun* the ninth month of the year

**septet** *noun* a group of seven musicians *etc*

**septic** *adj* of a wound: full of germs that are poisoning the blood
ⓔ From Greek *sepein* meaning 'to putrefy'

⚫\ Do not confuse with: **sceptic**

**septuagenarian** (*say* sep-tyoo-a-ji-neir-ri-an) *noun* someone from seventy to seventy-nine years old

**sepulchre** (*say* sep-ul-ker) *noun* a tomb □ **sepulchral** (*say* sip-**ul**-kral) *adj* **1** of sepulchres **2** dismal, gloomy **3** of a voice: deep, hollow in tone

**sequel** *noun* **1** a result, a consequence **2** a story that is a continuation of an earlier story

**sequence** *noun* **1** the order (of events) in time **2** a number of things following in order, a connected series

**sequestrate** *verb* to keep apart, isolate

**sequin** *noun* a small round sparkling ornament sewn on a dress *etc*

**seraph** *noun* (*pl* **seraphs** or **seraphim**) an angel of the highest rank □ **seraphic** *adj*

**serenade** *noun* music played or sung in the open air at night, *esp* under a woman's window □ *verb* to sing or play a serenade (to)

**serene** *adj* **1** calm **2** not worried, happy, peaceful □ **serenity** *noun*

**serf** *noun, historical* a slave bought and sold with the land on which he worked □ **serfdom** *noun*

**serge** *noun* a strong type of cloth

**sergeant** *noun* **1** an army rank above corporal **2** a rank in the police force above a constable □ **sergeant-major** *noun* an army rank above sergeant

**serial** *noun* a story which is published, broadcast or televised in instalments

**series** *noun* (*pl* **series**) **1** a number of things following each other in order **2** a set of things of the same kind: *a series of books on art*

**serious** *adj* **1** grave, thoughtful: *a serious expression on her face* **2** not joking, in earnest: *a serious remark* **3** important, needing careful thought: *a serious matter* **4** likely to have dangerous results: *a serious accident* □ **seriously** *adv*

**sermon** *noun* a serious talk, *esp* one given in church

**serpent** *noun, old* a snake □ **serpentine** *adj* like a serpent; winding, full of twists

**serrated** *adj* having notches or teeth like a saw

**serried** *adj* crowded together: *serried ranks*

**serum** *noun* **1** a clear watery fluid in blood that helps fight disease **2** a fluid injected into the body to help fight disease

**servant** *noun* **1** someone paid to work for another, *esp* in helping to run a house **2** a government employee: *civil servant*

**serve** *verb* **1** to work for and obey **2** to attend or wait upon at table **3** to give out food, goods *etc* **4** to be able to be used (as): *the cave will serve as a shelter* **5** to be suitable for:

*serve a purpose* **6** to carry out duties as a member of the armed forces **7** to undergo (a sentence in prison *etc*) **8** *tennis* to throw up the ball and hit it with the racket to start play □ **serve someone right** to be deserved by them

**service** *noun* **1** an act of serving **2** the duty required of a servant or other employee **3** a performance of (public) worship **4** use: *bring the new machine into service* **5** time spent in the armed forces **6** (**services**) the armed forces **7** (**services**) help: *services to refugees* **8** a regular supply: *a bus service* **9** (**services**) public supply of water, gas, electricity *etc* **10** a set of dishes: *a dinner service* □ *verb* to keep (a car, machine *etc*) in good working order by regular checks and repairs □ **active service** service in battle □ **at your service** ready to help or be of use □ **serviceable** *adj* useful; lasting a long time: *serviceable clothes*

**serviette** *noun* a table napkin

**servile** *adj* slave-like; showing lack of spirit □ **servility** *noun* □ **servitude** *noun* slavery; the state of being under strict control

**session** *noun* **1** a meeting of a court, council *etc* **2** the period of the year when classes are held in a school *etc* **3** a period of time spent on a particular activity

**set** *verb* **1** to place or put **2** to fix in the proper place (*eg* broken bones) **3** to arrange (a table for a meal, jewels in a necklace *etc*) **4** to fix (a date, a price *etc*) **5** to fix hair (in waves or curls) **6** to adjust (a clock or a machine *etc*) so that it is ready to work or perform some function **7** to give (a task *etc*): *set him three problems* **8** to put in a certain state or condition: *set free* **9** (**set off, out** or **forth**) to start (on a journey *etc*) **10** of a jelly *etc*: to become firm or solid **11** to compose music for: *he* *set the poem to music* **12** of the sun: to go out of sight below the horizon □ *adj* **1** fixed or arranged beforehand; ready: *all set* **2** fixed, stiff: *a set expression on his face* □ *noun* **1** a group of people **2** a number of things of a similar kind, or used together: *set of carving tools* **3** an apparatus: *a television set* **4** scenery made ready for a play *etc* **5** pose, position: *the set of his head* **6** a series of six or more games in tennis **7** a fixing of hair in waves or curls **8** a badger's burrow (*also called:* **sett**) **9** a street paving-block (*also called:* **sett**) □ **setting** *noun* **1** the act of someone who or something that sets **2** an arrangement **3** a background: *against a setting of hills* □ **setback** *noun* a movement in the wrong direction, a failure □ **set-square** *noun* a triangular drawing instrument, with one right angle □ **set about** to begin (doing something) **2** to attack □ **set in** to begin: *winter has set in* □ **set on** to attack

**set** *verb* ⬦ **sets, setting, set**

ⓘ From Old English verb *settan* and noun *set* meaning 'a seat'

**sett** *another spelling of* **set** (senses 8 and 9)

**settee** *noun* a sofa

**setter** *noun* a dog trained to point out game in hunting

**settle** *verb* **1** to place in a position or at rest **2** to come to rest **3** to agree over (a matter): *settle the price* **4** (sometimes with **down**) to become calm or quiet **5** (sometimes with **down**) to make your home in a place **6** to pay (a bill) **7** to fix, decide (on) **8** to bring (a quarrel *etc*) to an end **9** to sink to the bottom □ *noun* a long high-backed bench □ **settlement** *noun* **1** the act of settling **2** a decision, an agreement **3** payment of a bill **4** money given to a woman on her marriage **5** a

number of people who have come to live in a country □ **settler** *noun* someone who goes to live in a new country

**seven** *noun* the number 7 □ *adj* **7** in number □ **seventh** *adj* the last of a series of seven □ *noun* one of seven equal parts

**seventeen** *noun* the number 17 □ *adj* **17** in number □ **seventeenth** *adj* the last of a series of seventeen □ *noun* one of seventeen equal parts

**seventy** *noun* the number 70 □ *adj* **70** in number □ **seventieth** *adj* the last of a series of seventy □ *noun* one of seventy equal parts

**sever** *verb* **1** to cut apart or away, break off **2** to separate, part □ **severance** *noun*

**several** *adj* **1** more than one or two, but not many **2** various **3** different: *going their several ways* □ *pronoun* more than one or two people, things *etc*, but not a great many

**severe** *adj* **1** serious **2** harsh, strict **3** very plain and simple, not fancy □ **severity** *noun*

**sew** *verb* **1** to join together with a needle and thread **2** to make or mend in this way

**sew** ⬦ **sews, sewing, sewed, sewn**

**sewage** *noun* water and waste matter

**sewer** *noun* an underground drain for carrying off water and waste matter

**sex** *noun* **1** either of the two classes (male or female) into which animals are divided according to the part they play in producing children or young **2** sexual intercourse □ **sexy** *adj* sexually attractive or sexually exciting

**sexagenarian** *noun* someone from sixty to sixty-nine years old

**sexist** *noun* someone who treats the opposite sex unfairly or thinks that they are inferior □ *adj* relating to or characteristic of sexism: *a sexist* *attitude* □ **sexism** *noun*

**sextant** *noun* an instrument used for calculating distances by means of measuring angles, *eg* the distance between two stars

**sextet** *noun* a group of six musicians *etc*

**sexton** *noun* someone who has various responsibilities in a church, *eg* bellringing, gravedigging *etc*

**sexual** *adj* 1 of sex or gender 2 relating to sexual intercourse □ **sexuality** *noun* the way in which a person expresses, or their ability to experience, sexual feelings □ **sexually** *adv* □ **sexual intercourse** physical union between a man and a woman involving the insertion of the penis into the vagina

**SF** *abbrev* science fiction

**shabby** *adj* 1 worn-looking 2 poorly dressed 3 of behaviour: mean, unfair □ **shabbily** *adv*

**shack** *noun* a roughly-built hut

**shackle** *verb* 1 to fasten with a chain 2 to hold back, prevent, hinder □ **shackles** *noun pl* chains fastening a prisoner's legs or arms

**shade** *noun* 1 slight darkness caused by cutting off some light 2 a place not in full sunlight 3 a screen from the heat or light 4 (**shades**) *informal* sunglasses 5 the deepness or a variation of a colour 6 the dark parts in a picture 7 a very small amount or difference: *a shade larger* 8 a ghost □ *verb* 1 to shelter from the sun or light 2 to make parts of a picture darker 3 to change gradually, *eg* from one colour into another □ **shading** *noun* the marking of the darker places in a picture □ **shady** *adj* 1 sheltered from light or heat 2 *informal* dishonest, underhand: *a shady character*

**shadow** *noun* 1 shade caused by some object coming in the way of a light 2 the dark shape of that object

on the ground 3 a dark part in a picture 4 a very small amount: *a shadow of doubt* □ *verb* 1 to shade, darken 2 to follow someone about secretly and watch them closely □ **shadow cabinet** leading members of the opposition in parliament

**shaft** *noun* 1 anything long and straight 2 the rod on which the head of an axe, arrow *etc* is fixed 3 an arrow 4 a revolving rod which turns a machine or engine 5 the pole of a cart to which the horses are tied 6 the deep, narrow passageway leading to a mine 7 a deep vertical hole for a lift 8 a ray (of light)

**shaggy** *adj* rough, hairy, or woolly

**shake** *verb* 1 to move backwards and forwards or up and down with quick, jerky movements 2 to make or be made unsteady 3 to shock, disturb: *his parting words shook me* □ *noun* 1 the act of shaking or trembling 2 a shock 3 a drink mixed by shaking or stirring quickly: *milk shake* □ **shaky** *adj* unsteady; trembling □ **shakily** *adv*

**shake** *verb* ⊷ shake*s*, shak*ing*, shak*en*, shook

**shale** *noun* a kind of rock from which oil can be obtained

**shall** *verb* 1 used to form future tenses of other verbs when the subject is *I* or *we*: *I shall tell you later* 2 used for emphasis, or to express a promise, when the subject is *you, he, she, it* or *they*: *you shall go if I say you must* □ *see also* **should**

**shallot** *noun* a kind of onion

**shallow** *adj* 1 not deep 2 not capable of thinking or feeling deeply □ *noun* (often **shallows**) a place where the water is not deep

**sham** *noun* something which is not what it appears to be, a pretence □ *adj* false, imitation, pretended □ *verb* to pretend, feign

**sham** *verb* ⊷ sham*s*, shamm*ing*, shamm*ed*

**shamble** *verb* to walk in a shuffling or awkward manner

**shambles** *noun sing, informal* a mess, confused disorder

**shame** *noun* 1 an uncomfortable feeling caused by realization of guilt or failure 2 disgrace, dishonour 3 *informal* bad luck, a pity: *it's a shame that you can't go* □ *verb* 1 to make to feel shame or ashamed 2 (with *into*) to cause (someone to do something) by making them ashamed: *they shamed him into paying his share* □ **shameful** *adj* disgraceful □ **shameless** *adj* □ **shamefaced** *adj* □ **put to shame** to cause to feel ashamed

**shammy** *another spelling of* **chamois**

**shampoo** *verb* to wash (the hair and scalp) □ *noun* 1 an act of shampooing 2 a soapy liquid used for cleaning the hair 3 a similar liquid used for cleaning carpets or upholstery

**shamrock** *noun* a plant like clover with leaves divided in three

**shank** *noun* 1 the part of the leg between the knee and the foot 2 a long straight part (of a tool *etc*)

**shan't** *short for* shall not

**shanty** *noun* (*pl* **shanties**) 1 a roughly-made hut 2 a sailors' song □ **shantytown** *noun* an area of makeshift, squalid housing

**shape** *noun* 1 the form or outline of anything 2 a mould for a jelly *etc* 3 a jelly *etc* turned out of a mould 4 condition: *in good shape* □ *verb* 1 to make into a certain form 2 to model, mould 3 to develop (in a particular way) □ **shapeless** *adj* □ **shapely** *adj* having an attractive shape

**share** *noun* 1 one part of something that is divided among several people 2 one of the parts into which the money of a business firm is divided □ *verb* 1 to divide out among a number of people 2 to

allow others to use (your possessions *etc*) 3 to have or use in common with someone else □ **shareholder** *noun* someone who owns shares in a business company

**shark** *noun* 1 a large, very fierce, flesh-eating fish 2 *informal* a swindler

**sharp** *adj* 1 cutting, piercing 2 having a thin edge or fine point 3 hurting, stinging, biting: *sharp wind/ sharp words* 4 alert, quick-witted 5 sensitive, perceptive, able to pick up faint signals 6 severe, inclined to scold 7 *music* of a note: raised half a tone in pitch 8 of a voice: shrill 9 of an outline: clear □ *adv* punctually □ *noun, music* a sign (♯) showing that a note is to be raised half a tone □ **sharpen** *verb* to make or grow sharp □ **sharpener** *noun* an instrument for sharpening: *pencil sharpener* □ **sharper** *noun* a cheat, *esp* at cards □ **sharp practice** cheating □ **look sharp** to hurry

**shatter** *verb* to break in pieces; to upset, ruin (hopes, health *etc*)

**shave** *verb* 1 to cut away hair with a razor 2 to scrape away the surface of (wood *etc*) 3 to touch lightly, or just avoid touching, in passing □ *noun* 1 the act of shaving 2 a narrow escape: *a close shave* □ **shaven** *adj* shaved □ **shavings** *noun pl* very thin slices of wood *etc*

**shawl** *noun* a loose covering for the shoulders

**she** *pronoun* a woman, girl or female animal *etc* already spoken about (used only as the subject of a verb): *when the girl saw us, she waved*

**sheaf** *noun* (*pl* **sheaves**) a bundle (*eg* of corn, papers) tied together

**shear** *verb* 1 to clip, cut (*esp* wool from a sheep) 2 to cut through, cut off □ **shears** *noun pl* large scissors

**shear** ↔ shears, shearing, shorn, sheared

◎ From Old English *sceran*, from a

Germanic base meaning 'cut', 'divide', 'shave' or 'shave'

◈. Do not confuse with: **sheer**

**sheath** noun 1 a case for a sword or dagger 2 a long close-fitting covering 3 a condom □ **sheathe** verb to put into a sheath

**shed** noun 1 a building for storage or shelter: bicycle shed 2 an out-house □ verb 1 to throw or cast off (leaves, a skin, clothing) 2 to pour out (tears, blood) 3 to give out (light etc

**sheen** noun brightness, gloss

**sheep** noun 1 an animal whose flesh is used as food and whose fleece is used for wool 2 a very meek person who lacks confidence □ **sheepish** adj shy; embarrassed, shamefaced □ **sheep-dip** noun a liquid for disinfecting sheep □ **sheepdog** noun a dog trained to look after sheep □ **sheepskin** noun 1 the skin of a sheep 2 a kind of leather made from this

**sheepshank** noun a kind of knot, used for shortening a rope

**sheer** adj 1 very steep: sheer drop from the cliff 2 pure, not mixed: sheer nonsense 3 of cloth: very thin or fine □ adv straight up and down, very steeply □ verb to turn aside from a straight line, swerve

ⓘ Adj and adv: come perhaps from the Old English equivalent of Old Norse skærr meaning 'bright'; verb: formed from a combination of Late German or Dutch scheren meaning 'to cut', and an alternative spelling of English shear

◈. Do not confuse with: **shear**

**sheet** noun 1 a large piece of linen, cotton, nylon etc for a bed 2 a large thin piece of metal, glass, ice etc 3 a piece of paper 4 a sail 5 the rope fastened to the lower corner of a sail

**sheikh** noun an Arab chief

**shelf** noun (pl **shelves**) 1 a board fixed on a wall, for laying things on

2 a flat layer of rock, a ledge 3 a sandbank

**shell** noun 1 a hard outer covering (of a shellfish, egg, nut etc) 2 a husk or pod (eg of peas) 3 a metal case filled with explosive fired from a gun 4 a framework, eg of a building not yet completed or burnt out □ verb 1 to take the shell from (a nut, egg etc) 2 to fire shells at □ **shellfish** noun a water creature covered with a shell, eg an oyster, limpet or mussel

**shelter** noun 1 a building which acts as a protection from harm, rain, wind etc 2 the state of being protected from any of these □ verb 1 to give protection to 2 to put in a place of safety or protection 3 to go to, or stay in, a place of safety □ **take shelter** to go to a place of safety

**shelve** verb 1 to put up shelves in 2 to put aside (a problem etc) for later consideration 3 of land: to slope gently

**shepherd, shepherdess** noun someone who looks after sheep □ verb to watch over carefully, guide □ **shepherd's pie** a dish of minced meat covered with mashed potatoes

**sherbet** noun 1 a fizzy drink 2 powder for making this

**sheriff** noun 1 the chief representative of a monarch in a county, whose duties include keeping the peace 2 in Scotland, the chief judge of a county 3 US the chief law-enforcement officer of a county

**sherry** noun a strong kind of wine, often drunk before a meal

**shibboleth** noun a word or attribute which identifies members of a group

Originally a word giving membership to a group, after a Biblical story in which its correct pronunciation was used as a password

**shied** *past form of* **shy**

**shield** *noun* **1** anything that protects from harm **2** a broad piece of metal carried by a soldier *etc* as a defence against weapons **3** a shield-shaped trophy won in a competition **4** a shield-shaped plaque bearing a coat-of-arms ◻ *verb* to protect, defend, shelter

**shift** *verb* **1** to move, change the position of: *shift the furniture* **2** to change position or direction **3** to get rid of ◻ *noun* **1** a change **2** a change of position, transfer **3** a group of workers on duty at the same time: *night shift* **4** a specified period of work or duty **5** a loose-fitting lightweight dress ◻ **shifty** *adj* not to be trusted, looking dishonest ◻ **shift for yourself** to manage to get on by your own efforts

**shilling** *noun, Brit historical* a silver-coloured coin in use before decimalization, worth $\frac{1}{20}$ of £1 (now the 5 pence piece)

**shillyshally** *verb* to hesitate in making up your mind, waver

**shillyshally** ⇔ shillyshall*ies*, shillyshally*ing*, shillyshall*ied*

**shimmer** *verb* to shine with a quivering or unsteady light ◻ *noun* a quivering light

**shin** *noun* the front part of the leg below the knee ◻ **shin up** to climb

**shindy** *noun (pl* **shindies)** *informal* a noise, uproar

**shine** *verb* **1** to give out or reflect light **2** to be bright **3** to polish (shoes *etc*) **4** to be very good at: *he shines at arithmetic* ◻ *noun* **1** brightness **2** an act of polishing ◻ **shining** *adj* **1** very bright and clear **2** admired, distinguished: *a shining example* ◻ **shiny** *adj* glossy, polished

**shine** *verb* ⇔ shin*es*, shin*ing*, shone

**shingle** *noun* coarse gravel of rounded stones on the shores of rivers or of the sea

**ship** *noun* a large vessel for journeys across water ◻ *verb* **1** to take onto a ship **2** to send by ship **3** to go by ship ◻ **shipment** *noun* **1** an act of putting on board ship **2** a load of goods sent by ship ◻ **shipping** *noun* **1** ships as traffic: *a gale warning to shipping* **2** the business of transporting goods and freight, *esp* by ship ◻ **shipshape** *adj* in good order, neat, trim ◻ **shipwreck** *noun* **1** the sinking or destruction of a ship (*esp* by accident) **2** a wrecked ship **3** ruin ◻ **shipwrecked** *adj* ◻ **shipyard** *noun* the yard in which ships are built or repaired

**ship** *verb* ⇔ ship*s*, ship*ping*, ship*ped*

**shire** *noun* a county

**shirk** *verb* to avoid or evade (doing your duty *etc*) ◻ **shirker** *noun*

**shirt** *noun* **1** a garment worn by men on the upper part of the body, having a collar, sleeves and buttons down the front **2** a similar garment for a woman

**shiver** *verb* **1** to tremble with cold or fear **2** to break into small pieces, shatter ◻ *noun* **1** the act of shivering **2** a small broken piece: *shivers of glass*

**shoal** *noun* **1** a group of fishes, moving and feeding together **2** a shallow place, a sandbank

**shock** *noun* **1** a sudden forceful blow **2** a feeling of fright, horror, dismay *etc* **3** a state of weakness or illness following such feelings **4** the effect on the body of an electric current passing through it **5** an earthquake **6** a bushy mass (of hair) ◻ *verb* **1** to give a shock to **2** to upset or horrify ◻ **shocking** *adj* causing horror or dismay; disgusting ◻ **shock-absorber** *noun* a device in an aircraft, car *etc* for lessening the impact or force of bumps

**shod** *adj* wearing shoes ◻ *verb, past form of* **shoe**

**shoddy** *adj* of poor material or

quality

**shoe** *noun* **1** a stiff outer covering for the foot, not reaching above the ankle **2** a rim of iron nailed to the hoof of a horse □ *verb* to put shoes on (a horse) □ **shoehorn** *noun* a curved piece of horn, metal *etc* for making a shoe slip easily over your heel □ **shoelace** *noun* a cord or string used for fastening a shoe □ **shoemaker** *noun* □ **shoestring** *noun, US* a shoelace □ **on a shoestring** with very little money

**shoe** *verb* ⋄ shoes, shoeing, shod

**shone** *past form of* **shine**

**shoo** *exclamation* used to scare away birds, animals *etc* □ *verb* to drive or scare away

**shoo** *verb* ⋄ shoos, shooing, shooed

**shook** *see* **shake**

**shoot** *verb* **1** to send a bullet from a gun, or an arrow from a bow **2** to hit or kill with an arrow, bullet *etc* **3** to let fly swiftly and with force **4** to kick for a goal **5** to score (a goal) **6** of a plant: to grow new buds **7** to photograph, film **8** to move very swiftly or suddenly **9** to slide (a bolt) □ *noun* **1** a new sprout on a plant **2** an expedition to shoot game **3** land where game is shot □ **shooting star** a meteor

**shoot** *verb* ⋄ shoots, shot

**shop** *noun* **1** a place where goods are sold **2** a workshop □ *verb* **1** to visit shops and buy goods **2** *slang* to betray (someone) to the police □ **shopkeeper** *noun* someone who owns and keeps a shop □ **shoplifter** *noun* someone who steals goods from a shop □ **shopper** *noun* someone who shops, a customer □ **shop steward** a worker elected by the other workers as their representative □ **talk shop** *informal* to talk about work when off duty

**shop** *verb* ⋄ shops, shopping, shopped

**shore** *noun* the land bordering on a

sea or lake □ *verb* to prop (up), support

**shorn** *see* **shear**

**short** *adj* **1** not long **2** not tall **3** brief, not lasting long: *short talk* **4** not enough, less than it should be **5** rude, sharp, abrupt **6** of pastry: crisp and crumbling easily □ *adv* **1** suddenly, abruptly: *stop short* **2** not as far as intended: *the shot fell short* □ *noun* **1** a short film **2** a short-circuit **3** a drink of an alcoholic spirit **4** (**shorts**) short trousers □ *verb* to short-circuit □ **shortly** *adv* **1** soon **2** curtly, abruptly **3** briefly □ **shortage** *noun* a lack □ **shortcoming** *noun* a fault, a defect □ **short cut** a short way of going somewhere or doing something □ **shorten** *verb* to make less in length □ **shorthand** *noun* a method of swift writing using strokes and dots to show sounds (*contrasted with:* **longhand**) □ **short list** a list of candidates selected from the total number of applicants or contestants □ **shortlived** *adj* living or lasting only a short time □ **short-sighted** *adj* **1** seeing clearly only things which are near **2** taking no account of what may happen in the future □ **short-tempered** *adj* easily made angry □ **short-term** *adj* intended to last only a short time □ **give short shrift to** to waste little time or consideration on □ **short** in a few words □ **short of 1** not having enough: *short of money* **2** less than, not as much or as far as: *£5 short of the price* **3** without going as far as: *he didn't know how to get the money, short of stealing it*

**shortbread** *noun* a thick biscuit made of butter and flour *etc*

**short-circuit** *noun* the missing out of a major part of an intended electric circuit, sometimes causing blowing of fuses □ *verb* **1** of an electrical appliance: to have a short-circuit **2** to bypass (a difficulty *etc*)

**shot** noun **1** something which is shot or fired **2** small lead bullets, used in cartridges **3** a single act of shooting **4** the sound of a gun being fired **5** the distance covered by a bullet, arrow etc **6** a marksman **7** a throw or turn in a game **8** an attempt at doing something, guessing etc **9** a photograph **10** a scene in a motion picture □ adj **1** of silk: showing changing colours **2** streaked or mixed with (a colour etc) □ verb, past form of **shoot** □ **shotgun** noun a light type of gun which fires shot □ **a shot in the dark** a guess

**should** verb **1** the form of the verb **shall** used to express a condition: I should go if I had time **2** used to mean 'ought to': you should know that already

**shoulder** noun **1** the part of the body between the neck and upper arm **2** the upper part of an animal's foreleg **3** a hump, a ridge: the shoulder of the hill □ verb **1** to carry on the shoulders **2** to bear the full weight of (a burden etc) **3** to push with the shoulder □ **shoulderblade** noun the broad flat bone of the shoulder

**shout** noun **1** a loud cry or call **2** a loud burst (of laughter etc) □ verb to make a loud cry

━━━━━━━━━━━━━━━━━━━━━━
■ call, cry, scream, shriek, yell, roar, bellow, bawl, howl, bay, cheer
━━━━━━━━━━━━━━━━━━━━━━

**shove** verb to push roughly, thrust, push aside □ noun a rough push

**shovel** noun a spade-like tool used for lifting coal, gravel etc □ verb to lift or move with a shovel

**show** verb **1** to allow, or cause, to be seen **2** to be able to be seen: your underskirt is showing **3** to exhibit, display (an art collection etc) **4** to point out (the way etc) **5** to direct, guide: show her to a seat **6** to make clear, demonstrate: that shows that I was right □ noun **1** the act of showing **2** a display, an exhibition

**3** a performance, an entertainment □ **show business** the branch of the theatre concerned with variety entertainments □ **showroom** noun a room where goods are laid out for people to see □ **showy** adj bright, gaudy; (too) obvious, striking □ **show off 1** to show or display (something) **2** to try to impress others with your talents etc □ **show up 1** to make to stand out clearly **2** to expose, make obvious (esp someone's faults

**show** verb ⇔ shows, showing, shown, showed

**shower** noun **1** a short fall of rain **2** a large quantity: a shower of questions **3** a bath in which water is sprayed from above **4** the apparatus which sprays water for this **5** US a party at which gifts are given to someone about to be married □ verb **1** to pour (something) down on **2** to bathe under a shower □ **showerproof** adj of material, a coat etc: able to withstand light rain □ **showery** adj raining from time to time

**shown** see show

**shrank** see shrink

**shrapnel** noun **1** a shell containing bullets etc which scatter on explosion **2** splinters of metal, a bomb etc

After Henry Shrapnel, 18th-century British general who invented the shell

**shred** noun **1** a long, narrow piece, cut or torn off **2** a scrap, a very small amount: not a shred of evidence □ verb to cut or tear into shreds

**shred** verb ⇔ shreds, shredding, shredded

**shrew** noun **1** a small mouse-like type of animal with a long nose **2** a quarrelsome or scolding woman □ **shrewish** adj

**shrewd** adj clever, cunning

**shriek** verb to make a shrill scream or laugh □ noun a shrill scream or laugh

**shrift** noun: **give someone short shrift** to dismiss them quickly

**shrill** adj of a sound or voice: high in tone, piercing □ **shrilly** adv

**shrimp** noun **1** a small, long-tailed edible shellfish **2** informal a small person

**shrine** noun a holy or sacred place

**shrink** verb **1** to make or become smaller **2** to draw back in fear and disgust (from) □ noun, informal a psychiatrist □ **shrinkage** noun

**shrink** ⟡ shrink**s**, shrink**ing**, shrank, shrunk

**shrive** verb, old **1** to hear a confession **2** to confess

**shrive** ⟡ shrive**s**, shriv**ing**, shrove, shriv**en**

**shrivel** verb to dry up, wrinkle, wither

**shrivel** ⟡ shrivel**s**, shrivell**ing**, shrivell**ed**

**shroud** noun **1** a cloth covering a dead body **2** something which covers: a shroud of mist **3** (**shrouds**) the ropes from the mast-head to a ship's sides □ verb to wrap up, cover

**Shrove Tuesday** sometimes called Pancake Day: the day before Ash Wednesday

**shrub** noun a small bush or plant □ **shrubbery** noun (pl **shrubberies**) a place where shrubs grow

**shrug** verb to show doubt, lack of interest etc by drawing up the shoulders □ noun a movement of the shoulders to show doubt, lack of interest etc □ **shrug off** to dismiss, treat as being unimportant

**shrug** ⟡ shrug**s**, shrugg**ing**, shrugg**ed**

**shrunk** see **shrink**

**shrunken** adj shrunk

**shudder** verb to tremble from fear, cold, disgust □ noun a trembling

**shuffle** verb **1** to mix, rearrange (eg playing-cards) **2** to move by dragging or sliding the feet along the ground without lifting them **3** to move (the feet) in this way □ noun **1** a rearranging **2** a dragging movement of the feet

**shun** verb to avoid, keep clear of

**shun** ⟡ shun**s**, shunn**ing**, shunn**ed**

**shunt** verb to move (railway trains, engines etc) onto a side track

**shut** verb **1** to move (a door, window, lid etc) so that it covers an opening **2** to close, lock (a building etc) **3** to become closed: the door shut with a bang **4** to confine, restrain in a building etc □ **shut down** to close (a factory etc) □ **shut up 1** to close completely **2** informal to stop speaking or making other noise

**shut** ⟡ shut**s**, shutt**ing**, shut

**shutter** noun **1** a cover for a window **2** a cover which closes over a camera lens as it takes a picture

**shuttle** noun the part of a weaving loom which carries the cross thread from side to side □ adj of a transport service: going to and fro between two places

**shuttlecock** noun a rounded cork stuck with feathers, used in the game of badminton

**shy** adj **1** of a wild animal: easily frightened, timid **2** lacking confidence in the presence of others **3** not wanting to attract attention □ verb **1** to jump or turn suddenly aside in fear **2** to throw, toss □ noun a try, an attempt □ **shyly** adv □ **fight shy of** to avoid, keep away from

**shy** ⟡ shi**es**, shy**ing**, shi**ed**

**Siamese** adj: **Siamese cat** a fawn-coloured domestic cat □ **Siamese twins** twins joined by their flesh at birth

**sibilant** adj of a sound: hissing

**sibling** noun a brother or sister

**sibyl** noun a prophetess

**sick** adj **1** wanting to vomit **2** vomiting **3** not well, ill **4** (with of) tired of □ **sick bed** or **sick room** a bed or room for people to rest in when ill □ **sicken** verb to make or become sick □ **sickening** adj **1** causing sickness **2** disgusting, revolting □ **sick leave** time off work for illness □ **sickly** adj **1** unhealthy **2** feeble □ **sickness** noun **1** an illness **2** vomiting or nausea □ **be sick** to vomit

**sickle** noun a hooked knife for cutting or reaping grain, hay etc

**side** noun **1** an edge, border or boundary line **2** a surface that is not the top, bottom, front or back **3** either surface of a piece of paper, cloth etc **4** the right or left part of the body **5** a division, a part: the north side of the town **6** an aspect, point of view: all sides of the problem **7** a slope (of a hill) **8** a team or party which is opposing another □ adj **1** on or towards the side: side door **2** indirect, additional but less important: side issue □ verb (with **with**) to support (one person, group etc against another) □ **sideboard** noun a piece of furniture in a dining-room for holding dishes etc □ **sidecar** noun a small car for a passenger, attached to a motor-cycle □ **side effect** an additional (often bad) effect of a drug □ **sideline** noun an extra bit of business outside regular work □ **sidelong** adj & adv from or to the side: sidelong glance □ **sideshow** noun a less important show that is part of a larger one □ **sidestep** verb to avoid by stepping to one side □ **sidetrack** verb to turn (someone) away from what they were going to do or say □ **sidewalk** noun, US a pavement □ **sideways** adv **1** with the side foremost **2** towards the side □ **take sides** to choose to support (a party, person) against another

**sidereal** adj relating to the stars

**siding** noun a short line of rails on which trucks are shunted off the main line

**sidle** verb **1** to go or move sideways **2** to move stealthily, sneak

**siege** (say seej) noun **1** an attempt to capture a town etc by keeping it surrounded by an armed force **2** a constant attempt to gain control □ **lay siege to** to besiege

**sienna** noun a reddish-brown, or yellowish-brown, pigment used in paints

**sierra** noun a range of mountains with jagged peaks

**siesta** noun a short sleep or rest taken in the afternoon

**sieve** (say siv) noun a container with a mesh used to separate liquids from solids, or fine pieces from coarse pieces etc □ verb to put through a sieve

**sift** verb **1** to separate by passing through a sieve **2** to consider and examine closely: sifting all the evidence

**sigh** noun a long, deep-sounding breath, showing tiredness, longing etc □ verb to give out a sigh

**sight** noun **1** the act or power of seeing **2** a view, a glimpse **3** (often **sights**) something worth seeing: the sights of London **4** something or someone unusual, ridiculous, shocking etc: she's quite a sight in that hat **5** a guide on a gun for taking aim □ verb **1** to get a view of, see suddenly **2** to look at through the sight of a gun □ **sight-reading** noun playing or singing from music that has not been seen previously □ **sightseeing** noun visiting the chief buildings, monuments etc of a place ⊛ From Old English sihth meaning 'vision' or 'appearance'

**◈.** Do not confuse with: **site** and **cite**

**sign** noun **1** a mark with a special

meaning, a symbol **2** a gesture (*eg* a nod, wave of the hand) to show your meaning **3** an advertisement or notice giving information **4** something which shows what is happening or is going to happen: *a sign of good weather* □ *verb* **1** to write your name on (a document, cheque *etc*) **2** to make a sign or gesture to **3** to show (your meaning) by a sign or gesture □ **signpost** *noun* a post with a sign, *esp* one showing direction and distances to certain places □ **sign on** to enter your name on a list for work, the army *etc*

**signal** *noun* **1** a gesture, light or sound giving a command, warning *etc*: *air-raid signal* **2** something used for this purpose: *railway signals* **3** the wave of sound received or sent out by a radio *etc* set □ *verb* **1** to make signals (to) **2** to send (information) by signal □ *adj* remarkable: *a signal success* □ **signalman** *noun* someone who works railway signals, or who sends signals

**signal** *verb* ⋅∴⋅ signals, signalling, signalled

**signatory** *noun* (*pl* **signatories**) someone who has signed an agreement *etc*

**signature** *noun* **1** a signed name **2** an act of signing **3** *music* the flats or sharps at the beginning of a piece which show its key, or figures showing its timing □ **signature tune** a tune used to identify a particular radio or television series *etc* played at the beginning or end of the programme

**signet** *noun* a small seal, usually bearing someone's initials □ **signet ring** a ring imprinted with a signet ⊕ From Medieval Latin *signetum* meaning 'a small seal'

⬧ Do not confuse with: **cygnet**

**significant** *adj* meaning much; important: *no significant change* □ **significance** *noun* □ **significantly**

*adv*

**signify** *verb* **1** to mean, be a sign of **2** to show, make known by a gesture: *signifying disapproval* **3** to have meaning or importance

**signify** ⋅∴⋅ signifies, signifying, signified

**silage** *noun* green fodder preserved in a silo

**silence** *noun* **1** absence of sound or speech **2** a time of quietness □ *verb* to cause to be silent □ **silencer** *noun* a device (on a car engine, gun *etc*) for making noise less □ **silent** *adj* □ **silently** *adv*

**silhouette** *noun* **1** an outline drawing of someone, often in profile, filled in with black **2** a dark outline seen against the light

After the 18th-century French finance minister, Etienne de *Silhouette*, possibly because of his notorious stinginess

**silk** *noun* **1** very fine, soft fibres spun by silkworms **2** thread or cloth made from this □ *adj* **1** made of silk **2** soft, smooth □ **silky** *adj* □ **silken** *adj* **1** made of silk **2** smooth like silk □ **silkworm** *noun* the caterpillar of certain moths which spins silk

**sill** *noun* a ledge of wood, stone *etc* below a window or a door

**silly** *adj* foolish, not sensible

**silo** *noun* (*pl* **silos**) **1** a tower for storing grain *etc* **2** a pit or airtight chamber for holding silage **3** an underground chamber built to contain a guided missile

**silt** *noun* sand or mud left behind by flowing water □ **silt up** to become blocked by mud

**silver** *noun* **1** a white precious metal, able to take on a high polish **2** money made of silver or of a metal alloy resembling it **3** objects (*esp* cutlery) made of, or plated with, silver □ *adj* made of, or looking like, silver □ *verb* **1** to cover with silver **2** to become like silver □ **silvery** *adj*

**1** like silver **2** of sound: ringing and musical □ **silversmith** *noun* someone who makes or sells articles of silver □ **silver wedding** the 25th anniversary of a wedding

**simian** *adj* ape-like

**similar** *adj* alike, almost the same □ **similarity** *noun* (*pl* **similarities**) □ **similarly** *adv*

**simile** *noun* an expression using 'like' or 'as', in which one thing is likened to another that is well-known for a particular quality (*eg* 'as black as night', 'to swim like a fish')

**simmer** *verb* to cook gently just below or at boiling-point

**simper** *verb* **1** to smile in a silly manner **2** to say with a simper □ *noun* a silly smile

**simple** *adj* **1** easy, not difficult or complicated **2** plain, not fancy: *a simple house* **3** ordinary **4** of humble rank **5** mere, nothing but: *the simple truth* **6** too trusting, easily cheated **7** foolish, half-witted □ **simplicity** *noun* □ **simply** *adv* **1** in a simple manner **2** merely: *I do it simply for the money* **3** absolutely: *simply beautiful* □ **simpleton** *noun* a foolish person

**simplify** *verb* to make simpler □ **simplification** *noun* **1** an act of making simpler **2** a simple form of anything

**simplify** ⟷ simplifies, simplifying, simplified

**simulate** *verb* **1** to pretend, feign: *she simulated illness* **2** to have the appearance of, look like □ **simulated** *adj* □ **simulation** *noun*

**simultaneous** *adj* happening, or done, at the same time □ **simultaneously** *adv*

**sin** *noun* **1** a wicked act, *esp* one which breaks religious laws **2** wrongdoing **3** *informal* a shame, pity □ *verb* to commit a sin, do wrong □ **sinful** *adj* wicked □ **sinner** *noun* □ **original sin** the supposed sinful nature of all human beings since the time of Adam's sin

**sin** *verb* ⟷ sins, sinning, sinned

**since** *adv* **1** (often **ever since**) from that time onwards: *I have avoided him ever since* **2** at a later time: *we have since become friends* **3** ago: *long since* **4** from the time of: *since his arrival* □ *conj* **1** after the time when: *I have been at home since graduating* **2** because: *since you are going, I will go too*

**sincere** *adj* **1** honest in word and deed, meaning what you say or do, true **2** truly felt □ **sincerely** *adv* □ **sincerity** *noun*

**sinecure** (*say* sin-ik-yoor) *noun* a job for which someone receives money but has little or no work to do ⓘ From Latin *sine* meaning 'without', and *cura* meaning 'care'

**sinew** *noun* **1** a tough cord that joins a muscle to a bone **2** (**sinews**) equipment and resources necessary for something: *sinews of war* □ **sinewy** *adj*

**sing** *verb* **1** to make musical sounds with your voice **2** to utter (words, a song *etc*) by doing this □ **singer** *noun* □ **sing-song** *noun* a gathering of people singing informally together □ *adj* of a speaking voice *etc*: having a fluctuating rhythm

**sing** ⟷ sings, singing, sang, sung

**singe** *verb* to burn slightly on the surface, scorch □ *noun* a surface burn

**single** *adj* **1** one only **2** not double **3** not married **4** for one person **5** between two people: *single combat* **6** for one direction of a journey: *a single ticket* □ **singly** *adv* one by one, separately □ **single-handed** *adj* working *etc* by yourself □ **single-minded** *adj* having one aim only □ **single out** to pick out, treat differently in some way

**singlet** *noun* a vest, an undershirt

**singular** adj **1** grammar the opposite of **plural**, showing one person, thing etc **2** exceptional **3** unusual, strange: a singular sight □ **singularly** adv

**sinister** adj suggesting evil, evil-looking

**sink** verb **1** to go down below the surface of the water etc **2** to go down or become less: my hopes sank **3** of a very ill person: to become weaker **4** to lower yourself (into) **5** to make by digging (a well etc) **6** to push (your teeth etc) deep into (something) **7** to invest (money etc) in a business □ noun a basin in a kitchen, bathroom etc, with a water supply connected to it and a drain for carrying off dirty water etc

**sink** verb ⋄ sinks, sinking, sank, sunk

**sinuous** adj bending in and out, winding

**sinus** noun (pl **sinuses**) an air cavity in the head connected with the nose

**sip** verb to drink in very small quantities □ noun a taste of a drink, a swallow

**sip** verb ⋄ sips, sipping, sipped

**siphon** or **syphon** noun **1** a bent tube for drawing off liquids from one container into another **2** a glass bottle, for soda water etc, containing such a tube □ verb **1** to draw (off) through a siphon **2** (with **off**) to take (part of something) away gradually

**sir** noun **1** a polite form of address used to a man **2** (**Sir**) the title of a knight or baronet

**sire** noun **1** a male parent, esp of a horse **2** historical a title used in speaking to a king □ verb of an animal: to be the male parent of

**siren** noun **1** an instrument that gives out a loud hooting noise as a warning **2** a mythical sea nymph whose singing enchanted sailors and tempted them into danger **3** an

attractive but dangerous woman

**sirloin** noun the upper part of the loin of beef

**sirocco** noun a hot dry wind blowing from N Africa to the Mediterranean coast

**sirrah** noun, old sir

**sisal** noun a fibre from a W Indian plant, used for making ropes

**sister** noun **1** a female born of the same parents as yourself **2** a senior nurse, often in charge of a hospital ward **3** a nun □ adj **1** closely related **2** of similar design or structure: a sister ship □ **sisterly** adj □ **sisterhood** noun **1** the state of being a sister **2** a religious community of women □ **sister-in-law** noun **1** the sister of your husband or wife **2** the wife of your brother or of your brother-in-law

**sit** verb **1** to rest on the buttocks, be seated **2** of a bird: to perch **3** to rest on eggs in order to hatch them **4** to be an official member: sit on a committee **5** of a court etc: to meet officially **6** to pose (for) a photographer, painter etc **7** to take (an examination etc) □ **sitter** noun **1** someone who poses for a portrait etc **2** a babysitter **3** a bird sitting on eggs □ **sit tight** to be unwilling to move □ **sit up 1** to sit with your back straight **2** to stay up instead of going to bed

**sit** verb ⋄ sits, sitting, sat

**sitcom** noun a television comedy series with a running theme

**site** noun a place where a building, town etc is or is to be placed □ verb to select a place for (a building etc)
ⓘ From Latin situs meaning 'situation'

◭ Do not confuse with: **sight** and **cite**

**sitting** noun the state or time of sitting □ adj **1** seated **2** for sitting in or on **3** in office: sitting member of parliament **4** in possession: sitting *tenant* □ **sitting-room** *noun* a room chiefly for sitting in

**situated** *adj* placed

**situation** *noun* **1** the place where anything stands **2** a job, employment **3** a state of affairs, circumstances

**six** *noun* the number 6 □ *adj* 6 in number □ **sixth** *adj* the last of a series of six □ *noun* one of six equal parts □ **at sixes and sevens** in confusion

**sixpence** *noun, old* a silver-coloured coin worth $\frac{1}{40}$ of £1

**sixteen** *noun* the number 16 □ *adj* 16 in number □ **sixteenth** *adj* the last of a series of sixteen □ *noun* one of sixteen equal parts

**sixty** *noun* the number 60 □ *adj* 60 in number □ **sixtieth** *adj* the last of a series of sixty □ *noun* one of sixty equal parts

**size** *noun* **1** space taken up by anything **2** measurements, dimensions **3** largeness **4** a class into which shoes and clothes are grouped according to size **5** a weak kind of glue □ **sizeable** or **sizable** *adj* fairly large □ **size up** to form an opinion of a person, situation *etc*

**sizzle** *verb* **1** to make a hissing sound **2** to fry, scorch

**skate** *noun* **1** a steel blade attached to a boot for gliding on ice **2** a rollerskate **3** a type of large flatfish □ *verb* to move on skates □ **skateboard** *noun* a narrow board on four rollerskate wheels □ **skateboarding** *noun*

**skein** (*say* skein) *noun* a coil of thread or yarn, loosely tied in a knot

**skeleton** *noun* **1** the bony framework of an animal or person, without the flesh **2** any framework or outline □ *adj* of staff *etc*: reduced to a very small or minimum number □ **skeletal** *adj* □ **skeleton key** a key from which the inner part has been cut away so that it can open many different locks

**skerry** *noun* a reef of rock

**sketch** *noun* (*pl* **sketches**) **1** a rough plan or drawing **2** a short or rough account **3** a short play, dramatic scene *etc* □ *verb* **1** to draw roughly **2** to give the chief points of **3** to draw in pencil or ink □ **sketchy** *adj* **1** roughly done **2** not thorough, incomplete: *my music knowledge is rather sketchy*

**skew** *adj & adv* off the straight, slanting □ *verb* to set at a slant □ **skewer** *noun* a long pin of wood or metal for holding meat together while roasting *etc* □ *verb* to fix with a skewer or with something sharp

**ski** *noun* (*pl* **skis**) one of a pair of long narrow strips of wood or metal that are attached to boots for gliding over snow □ *verb* to move or travel on skis □ **ski-jump** *noun* **1** a steep, snow-covered track ending in a platform from which a skier jumps **2** a jump made by a skier from such a platform □ **ski-jumping** *noun*

**ski** *verb* ⇔ ski**s**, ski**ing**, ski**ed**

**skid** *noun* **1** a slide sideways: *the car went into a skid* **2** a wedge put under a wheel to check it on a steep place **3** (**skids**) logs *etc* on which things can be moved by sliding □ *verb* **1** of a wheel: to slide along without turning **2** to slip sideways □ **on the skids** on the way down □ **put the skids under** to hurry along

**skill** *noun* cleverness at doing a thing, either from practice or as a natural gift □ **skilful** *adj* □ **skilfully** *adv* □ **skilled** *adj* **1** having skill, *esp* through training **2** of a job: requiring skill

**skim** *verb* **1** to remove cream, scum *etc* from the surface of (something) **2** to move lightly and quickly over (a surface) **3** to read quickly, missing parts

**skim** ⇔ skim**s**, skim**ming**, skim**med**

**skimp** *verb* **1** to give (someone)

hardly enough **2** to do (a job) imperfectly **3** to spend too little money (on) □ **skimpy** *adj* **1** too small **2** of clothes: too short or tight

**skin** *noun* **1** the natural outer covering of an animal or person **2** a thin outer layer on a fruit **3** a thin film that forms on a liquid □ *verb* to strip the skin from □ **skinny** *adj* very thin □ **skin-deep** *adj* as deep as the skin only, on the surface □ **skin-diver** *noun* a diver who wears simple equipment (originally someone who dived naked for pearls) □ **by the skin of your teeth** very narrowly

**skin** *verb* ⇨ skin**s**, skinn**ing**, skinn**ed**

**skinflint** *noun* a very mean person

**skint** *adj, Brit informal* broke, without much money

**skip** *verb* **1** to go along with a rhythmic step and hop **2** to jump over a turning rope **3** to leap, *esp* lightly or joyfully **4** to leave out (parts of a book, a meal *etc*) □ *noun* **1** an act of skipping **2** the captain of a side at bowls *etc* **3** a large metal container for transporting refuse □ **skipping rope** a rope used in skipping

**skip** *verb* ⇨ skip**s**, skipp**ing**, skipp**ed**

▣ (verb, meaning 4) jump

**skipper** *noun* the captain of a ship, aeroplane or team □ *verb* to act as captain for (a ship, team *etc*)

**skirmish** *noun* (*pl* **skirmishes**) **1** a fight between small parties of soldiers **2** a short sharp contest or disagreement □ *verb* to fight briefly or informally

**skirt** *noun* **1** a garment, worn by women, that hangs from the waist **2** the lower part of a dress **3** (**skirts**) the outer edge or border □ *verb* to pass along, or lie along, the edge of

**skirting** or **skirting-board** *noun* the narrow board next to the floor round the walls of a room (*also called*: **wainscot**)

**skit** *noun* a piece of writing, a short play *etc* that makes fun of a person, event *etc*

**skittish** *adj* frivolous, light-headed

**skittle** *noun* **1** a bottle-shaped object used as a target in bowling, a ninepin **2** (**skittles**) a game in which skittles are knocked over by a ball

**skive** *verb, informal* (often with **off**) to avoid doing a duty □ **skiver** *noun*

**skivvy** *noun, informal* a domestic servant, a cleaner

**skulduggery** or *US* **skullduggery** *noun* trickery, underhand practices

**skulk** *verb* **1** to wait about, stay hidden **2** to move stealthily away, sneak

**skull** *noun* **1** the bony case which encloses the brain **2** the head □ **skull and crossbones** the sign on a pirate's flag □ **skullcap** *noun* a cap which fits closely to the head

**skunk** *noun* **1** a small American animal which defends itself by giving off a bad smell **2** a contemptible person

**sky** *noun* (*pl* **skies**) **1** the upper atmosphere, the heavens **2** the weather, the climate □ **sky-diving** *noun* jumping with a parachute as a sport □ **skylark** *noun* the common lark which sings while hovering far overhead □ **skylight** *noun* a window in a roof or ceiling □ **skyline** *noun* the horizon □ **skyscraper** *noun* a high building of very many storeys

**slab** *noun* a thick flat slice or piece of anything

**slack** *adj* **1** not firmly stretched **2** not firmly in position **3** not strict **4** lazy and careless **5** not busy: *slack holiday season* □ *noun* **1** the loose part of a rope **2** small coal and coal-dust **3** (**slacks**) loose, casual trousers □ *verb* **1** to do less work than you should, be lazy **2** to slacken □ **slacken** *verb* **1** to make or become looser **2** to make or become less active, less busy or less fast *etc*

**slag** noun waste left from metal-smelting □ verb, slang to criticize, make fun of cruelly

**slag** verb ⋄ slags, slagging, slagged

**slain** see **slay**

**slake** verb to quench, satisfy (thirst, longing etc)

**slalom** noun 1 a downhill, zigzag ski run among posts or trees 2 an obstacle race in canoes

**slam** verb 1 to shut (a door, lid etc) with a loud noise 2 to put down with a loud noise □ noun 1 the act of slamming 2 (also **grand slam**) a winning of every trick in cards or every contest in a competition etc

**slam** verb ⋄ slams, slamming, slammed

**slander** noun an untrue statement (in England, a spoken one) aimed at harming someone's reputation □ verb to speak slander against (someone) □ **slanderous** adj

**slang** noun 1 popular words and phrases that are used in informal, everyday speech or writing 2 the special language of a particular group: Cockney slang □ verb to scold, abuse

**slant** verb 1 to slope 2 to lie or move diagonally or in a sloping position 3 to give or present (facts or information) in a distorted way that suits your own purpose □ noun 1 a slope 2 a diagonal direction 3 a point of view

**slap** noun a blow with the palm of the hand or anything flat □ verb to give a slap to

**slap** verb ⋄ slaps, slapping, slapped

**slapdash** adj hasty, careless

**slapstick** adj of comedy: boisterous, funny in a very obvious way □ noun comedy in this style

**slash** verb 1 to make long cuts in 2 to strike at violently □ noun (pl slashes) 1 a long cut 2 a sweeping blow

**slat** noun a thin strip of wood, metal or other material □ **slatted** adj

**slate** noun an easily split blue-grey rock, used for roofing, or at one time for writing upon □ adj 1 made of slate 2 slate-coloured □ verb 1 to cover with slate 2 to say or write harsh things to or about: the play was slated

**slattern** noun a woman of untidy appearance or habits

**slaughter** noun 1 the killing of animals, esp for food 2 cruel killing of great numbers of people □ verb 1 to kill (an animal) for food 2 to kill brutally □ **slaughterhouse** noun a place where animals are killed in order to be sold for food

**slave** noun, historical 1 someone forced to work for a master and owner 2 someone who serves another devotedly 3 someone who works very hard 4 someone who is addicted to something: a slave to fashion □ verb to work like a slave □ **slavery** noun □ **slavish** adj thinking or acting exactly according to rules or instructions

**slaver** noun saliva running from the mouth □ verb to let saliva run out of the mouth

**Slavic** adj relating to a group of E European people or their languages, including Russian, Polish etc

**slay** verb, formal to kill

**slay** ⋄ slays, slaying, slew, slain

**sleaze** noun, informal corrupt or illicit practices, esp in public life □ **sleaziness** noun □ **sleazy** adj

**sled** or **sledge** noun a vehicle with runners, made for sliding upon snow □ verb to ride on a sledge

**sledgehammer** noun a large, heavy hammer

**sleek** adj 1 smooth, glossy 2 of an animal: well-fed and well-cared for 3 elegant, well-groomed

**sleep** verb to rest with your eyes

closed in a state of natural unconsciousness □ **sleepily** *adv* □ **sleepless** *adj* unable to sleep, without sleep □ **sleepy** *adj* **1** drowsy, wanting to sleep **2** looking as if needing sleep **3** quiet, not bustling: *sleepy town* □ **sleeper** *noun* **1** someone who sleeps **2** a beam of wood or metal supporting railway lines **3** a sleeping car or sleeping berth on a railway train □ **sleeping bag** a large warm bag for sleeping in, used by campers *etc* □ **sleepwalker** *noun* someone who walks *etc* while asleep □ **go to sleep 1** to pass into the state of being asleep **2** of a limb: to become numb, tingle □ **put to sleep 1** to make to go to sleep, make unconscious **2** to put (an animal) to death painlessly, *eg* by an injection of a drug □ **sleep with** *informal* to have sexual intercourse with

**sleep** *verb* ⟼ sleep*s*, sleep*ing*, slept

**sleet** *noun* rain mixed with snow or hail

**sleeve** *noun* **1** the part of a garment which covers the arm **2** a cover for a gramophone record **3** a cover for an arm-like piece of machinery □ **sleeveless** *adj*

**sleigh** *noun* a large horse-drawn sledge

**sleight-of-hand** *noun* skill and quickness of hand movement in performing card tricks *etc*

**slender** *adj* **1** thin, narrow **2** slim **3** small in amount: *by a slender margin*

**sleuth** *noun* someone who tracks down criminals, a detective

**slew** *past form of* slay

**slice** *noun* **1** a thin, broad piece of something **2** a broad-bladed utensil for serving fish *etc* □ *verb* **1** to cut into slices **2** to cut through **3** to cut (off from *etc*) **4** *golf* to hit (a ball) in such a way that it curves away to the right

**slick** *adj* **1** smart, clever, often too much so **2** smooth □ *noun* a thin layer of spilt oil

**slide** *verb* **1** to move smoothly over a surface **2** to slip **3** to pass quietly or secretly □ *noun* **1** an act of sliding **2** a smooth, slippery slope or track **3** a chute **4** a groove or rail on which a thing slides **5** a fastening for the hair **6** a picture for showing on a screen **7** a piece of glass on which to place objects to be examined under a microscope

**slide** *verb* ⟼ slide*s*, slid*ing*, slid

**slight** *adj* **1** of little amount or importance **2** small, slender □ *verb* to treat as unimportant, insult by ignoring □ *noun* an insult, an offence

**slim** *adj* **1** slender, thin **2** small, slight: *slim chance* □ *verb* **1** to make slender **2** to use means (such as eating less) to become slender

**slim** *verb* ⟼ slim*s*, slimm*ing*, slimm*ed*

**slime** *noun* sticky, half-liquid material, *esp* thin, slippery mud □ **slimy** *adj*

**sling** *noun* **1** a bandage hanging from the neck or shoulders to support an injured arm **2** a strap with a string attached to each end, for flinging stones **3** a net of ropes *etc* for hoisting and carrying heavy objects □ *verb* **1** to throw with a sling **2** to move or swing by means of a sling **3** *informal* to throw

**sling** *verb* ⟼ sling*s*, sling*ing*, slung

**slink** *verb* to sneak away, move stealthily

**slink** ⟼ slink*s*, slink*ing*, slunk

**slip** *verb* **1** to slide accidentally and lose footing or balance **2** to fall out of place, or out of your control: *the plate slipped from my grasp* **3** to move quickly and easily **4** to move quietly, quickly and secretly **5** to escape from: *slip your mind* □ *noun* **1** the act of slipping **2** an error, a slight mistake **3** a cutting from a plant **4** a strip or narrow piece of anything (*eg* paper) **5** a slim, slight person: *a slip of a girl* **6** a slipway **7** a thin undergarment worn under a dress, an underskirt **8** a cover for a pillow **9** *cricket* a fielding position □ **slippery** *adj* **1** causing skidding or slipping **2** not trustworthy □ **slipknot** *noun* a knot made with a loop so that it can slip □ **slip road** a road by which vehicles join or leave a motorway □ **slipstream** *noun* the stream of air driven back by an aircraft propeller *etc* □ **slip-up** *noun* a mistake □ **slipway** *noun* a smooth slope on which a ship is built □ **slip up** to make a mistake

**slip** *verb* ⟿ slips, slipp*ing*, slipp*ed*

**slipper** *noun* a loose indoor shoe

**slipshod** *adj* untidy, careless

**slit** *verb* **1** to make a long narrow cut in **2** to cut into strips □ *noun* a long narrow cut or opening

**slit** *verb* ⟿ slits, slitt*ing*, slit

**slither** *verb* **1** to slide or slip about (*eg* on mud) **2** to move with a gliding motion □ **slithery** *adj*

**sliver** *noun* a thin strip or slice

**slobber** *verb* to let saliva dribble from the mouth, slaver

**sloe** *noun* the small black fruit of a blackthorn shrub, often used to flavour gin

**slog** *verb* to work or plod on steadily, *esp* against difficulty □ *noun* a difficult spell of work

**slog** *verb* ⟿ slogs, slogg*ing*, slogg*ed*

**slogan** *noun* an easily remembered and frequently repeated phrase, used in advertising *etc*

**sloop** *noun* a one-masted sailing ship

**slop** *verb* **1** to flow over, spill **2** to splash *noun* **1** spilt liquid **2** (**slops**) dirty water **3** (**slops**) thin, tasteless food □ **sloppy** *adj* **1** wet, muddy **2** careless, untidy **3** silly, sentimental

**slop** *verb* ⟿ slops, slopp*ing*, slopp*ed*

**slope** *noun* **1** a position or direction that is neither level nor upright, a slant **2** a surface with one end higher than the other, *eg* a hillside □ *verb* to be in a slanting, sloping position

**slosh** *verb* **1** to splash **2** *informal* to hit

**slot** *noun* **1** a small, narrow opening, *eg* to insert coins □ *verb* **1** to make a slot in **2** (sometimes with **into**) to find a position or place for □ **slot machine** a vending machine worked by putting a coin in a slot

**slot** *verb* ⟿ slots, slott*ing*, slott*ed*

**sloth** *noun* **1** laziness **2** a slow-moving S American animal that lives in trees □ **slothful** *adj* lazy

**slouch** *noun* a hunched-up body position □ *verb* to walk with shoulders rounded and head hanging

**slough**¹ (*say* slow) *noun* a bog, a marsh

**slough**² (*say* sluf) *noun* the cast-off skin of a snake □ *verb* **1** to cast off (*eg* a skin) **2** of skin: to come (off

**slovenly** *adj noun* untidy, careless, dirty

**slow** *adj* **1** not fast **2** not hasty or hurrying **3** of a clock: behind in time **4** not quick in learning, dull □ *verb* (often with **down**) to make or become slower □ **slowly** *adv* □ **slowcoach** *noun* someone who moves, works *etc* slowly □ **slow-motion** *adj* **1** slower than normal movement **2** of a film: slower than actual motion

**sludge** *noun* soft, slimy mud

**slug** *noun* **1** a snail-like animal with no shell **2** a small piece of metal used as a bullet **3** a heavy blow □ **sluggish** *adj* moving slowly

**sluggard** *noun* someone who has slow and lazy habits

**sluice** noun **1** a sliding gate for controlling a flow of water in an artificial channel (also called: **sluicegate**) **2** the stream which flows through this □ verb to clean out with a strong flow of water

**slum** noun **1** an overcrowded part of a town where the houses are dirty and unhealthy **2** a house in a slum

**slumber** verb to sleep □ noun sleep

**slump** verb **1** to fall or sink suddenly and heavily **2** to lose value suddenly □ noun a sudden fall in values, prices etc

**slung** past form of **sling**

**slunk** past form of **slink**

**slur** verb **1** to pronounce indistinctly **2** to damage (a reputation etc), speak evil of □ noun **1** a blot or stain (on someone's reputation) **2** a criticism, an insult

**slur** verb ⬦ slurs, slurring, slurred

**slurp** verb to drink or gulp noisily □ noun a noisy gulp

**slurry** noun **1** thin, liquid cement **2** liquid waste

**slush** noun **1** watery mud **2** melting snow **3** something very sentimental **4** sentimentality □ **slushy** adj

**slut** noun **1** a woman who regularly engages in casual sex **2** a prostitute **3** a dirty, untidy woman

**sly** adj cunning; wily; deceitful □ **slyly** adv □ **on the sly** secretly, surreptitiously

**smack** verb **1** to strike smartly, slap **2** to have a trace or suggestion (of): this smacks of treason etc □ noun **1** an act of smacking **2** the sound made by smacking **3** a boisterous kiss **4** a taste, a flavour **5** a trace, a suggestion **6** a small fishing vessel □ adv with sudden violence: run smack into the door

**small** adj **1** little, not big or much **2** not important **3** not having a large or successful business: a small businessman **4** of a voice: soft

□ noun the most slender or narrow part: the small of the back □ adv into small pieces: cut up small □ **small hours** noun pl the hours just after midnight □ **small-minded** adj having narrow opinions, ungenerous □ **small talk** polite conversation about nothing very important

■ (adj, meaning 1) little, tiny, minute, minuscule, short, slight, puny, petite, diminutive, miniature, mini, young, inadequate, insufficient, scanty, meagre, paltry, mean, limited

**smallpox** noun a serious infectious illness, causing a rash of large pimples (**pocks**)

**smarmy** adj smooth in manner, unctuous, ingratiating

**smart** adj **1** clever and quick in thought or action **2** well-dressed **3** brisk **4** sharp, stinging □ noun a sharp, stinging pain □ verb **1** to feel a sharp, stinging pain **2** to feel annoyed, resentful etc after being insulted

**smash** verb **1** to break in pieces, shatter **2** to strike with force **3** to crash (into etc) □ noun (pl **smashes**) **1** an act of smashing **2** a crash, a collision (of vehicles) **3** the ruin of a business etc

**smattering** noun a very slight knowledge of a subject

**smear** verb **1** to spread (something sticky or oily) **2** to spread, smudge with (something sticky etc) **3** to become smeared **4** to slander, insult □ noun a smudge of something sticky

**smell** noun **1** the sense or power of being aware of things through your nose **2** an act of using this sense **3** something sensed through the nose, a scent □ verb **1** to notice by the sense of smell: I smell gas **2** to use your sense of smell on: smell this fish **3** to give off a smell: this room *smells* □ **smelly** *adj* having a bad smell □ **smelling-salts** *noun pl* strong-smelling chemicals in a bottle, used to revive fainting people □ **smell out** to find out by prying or inquiring closely

**smell** *verb* ⋄ smells, smelling, smelt or smelled

**smelt** *verb* **1** to melt (ore) in order to separate the metal from other material **2** *past form of* smell

**smile** *verb* **1** to show pleasure by drawing up the corners of the lips **2** (sometimes with **on**) to be favourable to: *fortune smiled on him* □ *noun* an act of smiling

**smirch** *verb* to stain, soil □ *noun* a stain

**smirk** *verb* to smile in a self-satisfied or foolish manner □ *noun* a self-satisfied smile

**smite** *verb* to strike, hit hard

**smite** *verb* ⋄ smites, smiting, smitten, smote

**smith** *noun* a worker in metals; a blacksmith □ **smithy** *noun* (*pl* **smithies**) the workshop of a smith

**smithereens** *noun pl* fragments

**smitten** *past participle of* smite: **smitten with** affected by; strongly attracted by

**smock** *noun* a loose shirt-like garment, sometimes worn over other clothes as a protection

**smog** *noun* thick, smoky fog

**smoke** *noun* **1** the cloud-like gases and particles of soot given off by anything burning **2** an act of smoking (a cigarette *etc*) □ *verb* **1** to give off smoke **2** to inhale and exhale tobacco smoke from a cigarette, pipe *etc* **3** to cure or preserve (ham, fish *etc*) by applying smoke **4** to darken (eg glass) by applying smoke □ **smokeless** *adj* □ **smoker** *noun* **1** someone who smokes **2** a railway compartment in which smoking is allowed □ **smoky** *adj* □ **smokescreen** *noun* anything

(originally smoke) meant to confuse or mislead

**smooch** *verb, informal* to kiss, pet

**smooth** *adj* **1** not rough **2** having an even surface **3** without lumps **4** hairless **5** without breaks, stops or jolts: *smooth journey* **6** too agreeable in manner □ *verb* **1** to make smooth **2** to calm, soothe **3** to free from difficulty

**smote** *past form of* smite

**smother** *verb* **1** to kill by keeping air from, *eg* by covering over the nose and mouth **2** to die by this means **3** to cover up, conceal (feelings *etc*) **4** to put down, suppress (a rebellion *etc*)

**smoulder** *verb* **1** to burn slowly without bursting into flame **2** to exist in a hidden state **3** to show otherwise hidden emotion, *eg* anger, hate

**smudge** *noun* a smear □ *verb* to make dirty with spots or smears

**smug** *adj* well-satisfied, too obviously pleased with yourself

**smuggle** *verb* **1** to take (goods) into, or out of, a country without paying the required taxes **2** to send or take secretly □ **smuggler** *noun*

**smut** *noun* **1** a spot of dirt or soot **2** vulgar or indecent talk *etc* □ **smutty** *adj*

**snack** *noun* a light, hasty meal

**snaffle** *verb, slang* to steal

**snag** *noun* a difficulty, an obstacle □ *verb* to catch or tear on something sharp

**snag** *verb* ⋄ snags, snagging, snagged

**snail** *noun* **1** a soft-bodied, small, crawling animal with a shell **2** someone who is very slow

**snake** *noun* **1** a legless reptile with a long body, which moves along the ground with a winding movement **2** anything snake-like in form or movement **3** a cunning, deceitful person

**snap** verb **1** to make a sudden bite **2** (with **up**) to eat up, or grab, eagerly **3** to break or shut suddenly with a sharp noise **4** to cause (the fingers) to make a sharp noise **5** to speak sharply **6** to take a photograph of □ noun **1** the noise made by snapping **2** a sudden spell (eg of cold weather) **3** a card-game in which players try to match cards **4** a photograph □ **snappy** adj irritable, inclined to speak sharply □ **snappily** adv □ **snapshot** noun a quickly taken photograph

**snap** verb ⇔ snaps, snapping, snapped

**snapdragon** noun a garden plant whose flower, when pinched, opens and shuts like a mouth

**snare** noun **1** a noose or loop that draws tight when pulled, for catching an animal **2** a trap **3** a hidden danger or temptation □ verb to catch in or with a snare

**snarl** verb **1** to growl, showing the teeth **2** to speak in a furious, spiteful tone **3** to become tangled □ noun **1** a growl, a furious noise **2** a tangle, a knot **3** a muddled or confused state

**snatch** verb **1** to seize or grab suddenly **2** to take quickly when you have time: snatch an hour's sleep

**sneak** verb **1** to creep or move in a stealthy, secretive way **2** to tell tales, tell on others □ noun **1** someone who tells tales **2** a deceitful, underhand person □ **sneaky** adj underhand, deceitful □ **sneakily** adv

**sneer** verb to show contempt by a scornful expression, words etc □ noun a scornful expression or remark

**sneeze** verb to make a sudden, unintentional and violent blowing noise through the nose and mouth □ noun an involuntary blow through

the nose

**snicker** verb **1** to snigger **2** of a horse: to neigh

**snide** adj mean, malicious: snide remark

**sniff** verb **1** to draw in air through the nose with a slight noise, eg when having a cold, or showing disapproval **2** to smell (a scent etc) **3** (with **at**) to treat with scorn or suspicion □ noun a quick drawing in of air through the nose

**sniffle** noun a light sniff, a snuffle □ verb to sniff lightly

**snigger** verb to laugh in a quiet, sly manner □ noun a quiet, sly laugh

**snip** verb to cut off sharply, esp with a single cut □ noun **1** a cut with scissors **2** a small piece snipped off **3** informal a bargain

**snip** verb ⇔ snips, snipping, snipped

**snipe** noun a bird with a long straight beak, found in marshy places □ verb **1** (with **at**) to shoot at from a place of hiding **2** (with **at**) to attack with critical remarks

**sniper** noun someone who shoots at a single person from cover

**snippet** noun a little piece, esp a piece of information or gossip

**snivel** verb **1** to have a running nose, eg because of a cold **2** to whine or complain tearfully □ noun **1** a running nose **2** a whine

**snivel** verb ⇔ snivels, snivelling, snivelled

**snob** noun someone who looks down on those in a lower social class □ **snobbish** adj □ **snobbery** noun

**snooker** noun a game like billiards, using twenty-two coloured balls

**snoop** verb to spy or pry in a sneaking secretive way □ noun someone who pries

**snooty** adj haughty, snobbish

**snooze** verb to sleep lightly, doze □ noun a light sleep

**snore** verb to make a snorting noise

in your sleep while breathing □ *noun* a snorting sound made in sleep

**snorkel** *noun* **1** a tube with one end above the water, to enable an underwater swimmer to breathe **2** a similar device for bringing air into a submarine

**snort** *verb* **1** to force air noisily through the nostrils **2** to make such a noise to express disapproval, anger, laughter *etc* □ *noun* a loud noise made through the nostrils

**snot** *noun* mucus of the nose □ **snotty** *adj* supercilious

**snout** *noun* the projecting nose and mouth of an animal, *eg* of a pig

**snow** *noun* frozen water vapour which falls in light white flakes □ *verb* to fall down in, or like, flakes of snow □ **snowy** *adj* **1** covered with snow **2** white, pure □ **snowball** *noun* a ball made of snow pressed hard together □ *verb* **1** to throw snowballs **2** to grow increasingly quickly: *unemployment has snowballed recently* □ **snowboard** *noun* a single board used as a ski on snow □ **snowdrift** *noun* a bank of snow blown together by the wind □ **snowdrop** *noun* a small white flower growing from a bulb in early spring □ **snowflake** *noun* a flake of snow □ **snowman** *noun* a figure shaped like a human being, made of snow □ **snowplough** *noun* a large vehicle for clearing snow from roads *etc* □ **snowshoe** *noun* a long broad frame with a mesh, one of a pair for walking on top of snow □ **snowed under** overwhelmed

**snub** *verb* to treat or speak to in an abrupt, scornful way, insult □ *noun* an act of snubbing □ *adj* of a nose: short and turned up at the end

**snub** *verb* ⊷ snubs, snubb*ing*, snubb*ed*

**snuff** *verb* to put out or trim the wick of (a candle) □ *noun* powdered tobacco for drawing up into the nose □ **snuffbox** *noun* a box for holding snuff

**snuffle** *verb* to make a sniffing noise through the nose, *eg* because of a cold □ *noun* a sniffling through the nose

**snug** *adj* **1** lying close and warm **2** cosy, comfortable **3** closely fitting; neat and trim

**snuggle** *verb* **1** to curl up comfortably **2** to draw close to for warmth, affection *etc*

**so** *adv* **1** as shown, *eg* by a hand gesture: *so high* **2** to such an extent, to a great extent: *you look so happy* **3** in this or that way: *point your toes so* **4** correct: *is that so?* **5** (used in contradicting) indeed: *It's not true. It is so* □ *conj* therefore: *you don't need it, so don't buy it* □ **so-and-so** *noun, informal* **1** this or that person or thing **2** *euphemistic* used instead of a stronger insult: *she's a real so-and-so, saying that to you!* □ **so-called** *adj* called by such a name, often mistakenly: *a so-called expert* □ **so-so** *adj* not particularly good □ **so as to** ir. order to □ **so far** up to this or that point □ **so forth** more of the same sort of thing: *pots, pans and so forth* □ **so much for** that is the end of: *so much for that idea!* □ **so that** with the purpose or result that □ **so what?** what difference does it make? does it matter?

**soak** *verb* **1** to let stand in a liquid until wet through **2** to drench (with) **3** (with **up**) to suck up, absorb □ **soaking** *adj* wet through □ *noun* a wetting, drenching □ **soaking wet** thoroughly wet, drenched

**soap** *noun* **1** a mixture containing oils or fats and other substances, used in washing **2** *informal* a soap opera □ *verb* to use soap on □ **soapy** *adj* □ **soap-box** *noun* **1** a small box for holding soap **2** a makeshift platform for standing on when speaking to a crowd out of doors □ **soap opera** a television series about a group of characters and their daily lives □ **soapsuds** *noun pl* soapy water worked into a froth

**soar** *verb* **1** to fly high into the air **2** of prices: to rise high and quickly

**sob** *verb* to weep noisily □ *noun* a noisy weeping □ **sob story** a story told to arouse sympathy

**sob** *verb* ⇔ sobs, sobbing, sobbed

**sober** *adj* **1** not drunk **2** serious, staid **3** not florid, unelaborate □ *verb* (sometimes with **up**) to make or become sober □ **soberly** *adv* □ **sobriety** *noun*

**soccer** *noun* football

**sociable** *adj* fond of the company of others, friendly □ **sociability** *noun*

**social** *adj* **1** relating to society, or to a community: *social history* **2** living in communities: *social insects* **3** of companionship: *social gathering* **4** of rank or level in society: *social class* □ **social security** the system, paid for by taxes, of providing insurance against old age, illness, unemployment *etc* □ **social work** work which deals with the care of the people in a community, *esp* of the poor or underprivileged □ **social worker**

**socialism** *noun* the belief that a country's wealth should belong to the people as a whole, not to private owners □ **socialist** *noun* someone who believes in socialism □ *adj* relating to or characteristic of socialism

**society** *noun* **1** humanity considered as a whole **2** a community of people **3** a social club, an association **4** the class of people who are wealthy, fashionable *etc* **5** company, companionship: *I enjoy his society*

**sociology** *noun* the study of human society □ **sociological** *adj* □ **sociologist** *noun*

**sociopath** *noun* someone who hates the company of others

**sock** *noun* a short stocking

**socket** *noun* a hollow into which something is fitted: *an electric socket*

**sod** *noun* a piece of earth with grass growing on it, a turf

**soda** *noun* **1** the name of several substances formed from sodium **2** soda-water □ **baking soda** sodium bicarbonate, a powder used as a raising agent in baking □ **soda-water** *noun* water through which gas has been passed, making it fizzy

**sodden** *adj* soaked through and through

**sodium** *noun* a metallic element from which many substances are formed, including common salt

**sofa** *noun* a kind of long, stuffed seat with back and arms □ **sofa bed** a sofa incorporating a fold-away bed

**soft** *adj* **1** easily put out of shape when pressed **2** not hard or firm **3** not loud **4** of a colour: not bright or glaring **5** not strict enough **6** lacking strength or courage **7** lacking common sense, weak in the mind **8** of a drink: not alcoholic **9** of water: containing little calcium *etc* □ *adv* gently, quietly □ **soften** *verb* to make or grow soft □ **soft-hearted** *adj* kind and generous

**software** *noun*, *computing* programs *etc* as opposed to the machines (*contrasted with*: **hardware**)

**soggy** *adj* **1** soaked **2** soft and wet

**soil** *noun* **1** the upper layer of the earth in which plants grow **2** loose earth; dirt □ *verb* to make dirty

**sojourn** *verb* to stay for a time □ *noun* a short stay

**solace** *noun* something which makes pain or sorrow easier to bear, comfort □ *verb* to comfort

**solar** *adj* **1** relating to the sun **2** influenced by the sun **3** powered by energy from the sun's rays □ **solar system** the sun with the planets (including the earth) going round it

**sold** *past form of* **sell**

**solder** *noun* melted metal used for joining metal surfaces □ *verb* to join (with solder) □ **soldering-iron** *noun* an electric tool for soldering joints

**soldier** *noun* someone in military service, *esp* someone who is not an officer

**sole¹** *noun* **1** the underside of the foot **2** the underside of a shoe *etc* □ *verb* to put a sole on (a shoe etc)

**sole²** *adj* only □ **solely** *adv*

**sole³** *noun* a small type of flatfish

**solemn** *adj* **1** serious, earnest **2** of an occasion: celebrated with special ceremonies □ **solemnize** *verb* to carry out (a wedding *etc*) with religious ceremonies □ **solemnity** *noun*

**sol-fa** *noun, music* a system of syllables (do, ray, me *etc*) to be sung to the notes of a scale

**solicit** *verb* **1** to ask earnestly for: *solicit advice* **2** to ask (someone for something) **3** to offer yourself as a prostitute

**solicitor** *noun* a lawyer who advises people about legal matters

**solicitous** *adj* **1** anxious **2** considerate, careful □ **solicitously** *adv*

**solicitude** *noun* care or anxiety about someone or something

**solid** *adj* **1** fixed in shape, not in the form of gas or liquid **2** in three dimensions, with length, breadth and height **3** not hollow **4** firm, strongly made **5** made or formed completely of one substance: *solid silver* **6** reliable, sound: *solid business* **7** *informal* without a break: *three solid hours' work* □ *noun* **1** a substance that is solid **2** a figure that has three dimensions □ **solidity** *noun*

**solidarity** *noun* unity of interests *etc*

**solidify** *verb* to make or become firm or solid

**solidify** ⬅ **solidifies**, **solidifying**, **solidified**

**soliloquy** *noun* (*pl* **soliloquies**) a speech made by an actor *etc* to themselves □ **soliloquize** *verb*

**solitaire** *noun* a card-game for one player (*also called:* **patience**)

**solitary** *adj* **1** lone, alone **2** single: *not a solitary crumb remained*

**solitude** *noun* the state of being alone; lack of company

**solo** *noun* (*pl* **solos**) a musical piece for one singer or player □ *adj* performed by one person alone □ **soloist** *noun*

**solstice** *noun* the time of longest daylight (**summer solstice** about 21 June) or longest dark (**winter solstice** about 21 December)

**soluble** *adj* **1** able to be dissolved or made liquid **2** of a problem *etc*: able to be solved □ **solubility** *noun*

**solution** *noun* **1** a liquid with something dissolved in it **2** the act of solving a problem *etc* **3** an answer to a problem, puzzle *etc*

**solve** *verb* **1** to clear up or explain (a mystery) **2** to discover the answer or solution to

**solvency** *noun* the state of being able to pay all debts

**solvent** *adj* able to pay all debts □ *noun* anything that dissolves another substance

**sombre** *adj* gloomy, dark, dismal

**sombrero** *noun* (*pl* **sombreros**) a broad-brimmed Mexican hat

**some** *adj* **1** several **2** a few: *some oranges, but not many* **3** a little: *some bread, but not much* **4** certain: *some people are rich* □ *pronoun* **1** a number or part out of a quantity: *please try some* **2** certain people: *some won't be happy*

**somebody** or **someone** *noun* **1** an unknown or unnamed person: *somebody I'd never seen before* **2** an important person: *he really is* *somebody now*

**somehow** *adv* in some way or other

**somersault** *noun* a forward or backward roll in which the heels go over the head □ *verb* to perform a somersault

**something** *pronoun* **1** a thing not known or not stated **2** a thing of importance **3** a slight amount, a degree: *he has something of his father's looks*

**sometime** *adv* at a time not known or stated definitely

**sometimes** *adv* at times, now and then

**somewhat** *adv* rather: *somewhat boring*

**somewhere** *adv* in some place

**somnambulist** *noun* a sleepwalker

**somnolent** *adj* sleepy; causing sleepiness □ **somnolence** *noun*

**son** *noun* a male child □ **son-in-law** *noun* a daughter's husband

**sonata** *noun* a piece of music with three or more movements, usually for one instrument

**song** *noun* **1** singing **2** a piece of music to be sung □ **for a song** (bought, sold *etc*) very cheaply □ **songbird** *noun* a bird that sings □ **songster** *noun*, *old* a talented (*esp* male) singer

**sonic** *adj* of sound waves

**sonnet** *noun* a type of poem in fourteen lines

**sonorous** *adj* giving a clear, loud sound

**soon** *adv* **1** in a short time from now or from the time mentioned **2** early: *too soon to tell* **3** (**as soon**) as readily, as willingly: *I would as soon stand as sit* □ **sooner** *adv* more willingly, rather: *I would sooner stand than sit* □ **sooner or later** at some time in the future

**soot** *noun* the black powder left by smoke □ **sooty** *adj*

**soothe** *verb* **1** to calm or comfort (a person, feelings *etc*) **2** to help or ease (a pain *etc*) □ **soothing** *adj*

**soothsayer** *noun* someone who predicts the future

**sop** *noun* **1** bread dipped in soup *etc* **2** a bribe given to keep someone quiet □ *verb* to soak (up) □ **sopping** *adj* wet through

**sophist** *noun* a person who uses clever arguments that are fundamentally unsound □ **sophistic** *adj*

**sophisticated** *adj* **1** of a person: full of experience, accustomed to an elegant, cultured way of life **2** of ways of thought, or machinery *etc*: highly developed, complicated, elaborate

**soporific** *adj* causing sleep □ *noun* something which causes sleep

**soppy** *adj* overly sentimental

**soprano** *noun* (*pl* **sopranos**) **1** a singing voice of high pitch **2** a singer with this voice

**sorcery** *noun* magic, witchcraft □ **sorcerer**, **sorceress** *noun* someone who works magic spells; a witch or wizard

**sordid** *adj* **1** dirty, filthy **2** mean, selfish **3** contemptible

**sore** *adj* painful □ *noun* a painful, inflamed spot on the skin □ **sorely** *adv* very greatly: *sorely in need*

**sorority** *noun* (*pl* **sororities**) a society of female students (*compare with:* **fraternity**)

**sorrel** *noun* a type of plant with sour-tasting leaves

**sorrow** *noun* sadness caused by a loss, disappointment *etc* □ *verb* to be sad □ **sorrowful** *adj*

**sorry** *adj* **1** feeling regret for something you have done **2** feeling sympathy or pity (for) **3** miserable: *in a sorry state*

**sort** *noun* a kind of (person or thing) □ *verb* to separate things, putting each in its place: *sort letters* □ **a sort**

**of** used of something which is like something else, but not exactly □ **of a sort** or **of sorts** of a kind, usually inadequate: *a party of sorts* □ **out of sorts** not feeling very well

**sortie** *noun* a sudden attack made by the defenders of a place on those who are trying to capture it

**SOS** *noun* **1** a code signal calling for help **2** any call for help

**sought** *past form of* **seek**

**soul** *noun* **1** the spirit, the part of someone which is not the body **2** a person: *a dear old soul* **3** a perfect example (of): *the soul of kindness* □ **soulful** *adj*

**sound** *noun* **1** anything that can be heard, a noise **2** an impression: *I don't like the sound of him* □ *verb* **1** to strike you as being: *that sounds awful* **2** (with *like*) to resemble in sound: *that sounds like Henry's voice* **3** to make a noise with: *sound a horn* **4** to examine by listening carefully to: *sound a patient's chest* **5** to measure (the depths of water) **6** to try to find out someone's opinions: *I'll sound him out tomorrow* □ *adj* **1** healthy, strong **2** of sleep: deep **3** thorough: *a sound beating* **4** reliable: *sound opinions* □ **soundproof** *adj* built or made so that sound cannot pass in or out □ *verb* to make soundproof □ **soundtrack** *noun* the strip on a film where the speech and music are recorded

**soup** *noun* a liquid food made from meat, vegetables *etc*

**sour** *adj* **1** having an acid or bitter taste, often as a stage in going bad: *sour milk* **2** bad-tempered □ *verb* to make sour

**source** *noun* **1** the place where something has its beginning or is found **2** a spring, *esp* one from which a river flows

**souse** *verb* to soak (*eg* herrings) in salted water

**south** *noun* one of the four chief directions, that to one's left as one faces the setting sun □ *adj & adv* to or in the south □ **south-east** *noun* the point of the compass midway between south and east □ *adj* in the south-east □ **southerly** *adj* **1** towards the south **2** of wind: from the south □ **southern** *adj* of, from or in the south □ **southerner** *noun* someone living in a southern region or country □ **south pole** the southern end of the imaginary axis on which the earth turns □ **southward** or **southwards** *adv* towards the south □ **south-west** *noun* the point of the compass midway between south and west □ *adj* in the south-west

**souvenir** *noun* something bought or given as a reminder of a person, place or occasion

**sou'wester** *noun* a kind of waterproof hat

**sovereign** *noun* **1** a king or queen **2** *historical* a British gold coin worth £1 □ *adj* **1** supreme, highest: *sovereign lord* **2** having its own government: *sovereign state* □ **sovereignty** *noun* highest power

**sow¹** (*say* sow) *noun* a female pig

**sow²** (*say* soh) *verb* **1** to scatter (seeds) so that they may grow **2** to cover (an area) with seeds □ **sower** *noun*

**sow** ⇨ sows, sowing, sown or sowed, sowed

**soya bean** or **soy bean** a kind of bean, rich in protein, used as a substitute for meat

**soya sauce** or **soy sauce** a sauce made from soya beans used in Chinese cooking

**spa** *noun* a place where people go to drink or bathe in the water from a natural spring

**space** *noun* **1** a gap, an empty place **2** the distance between objects **3** an uncovered part on a sheet of paper

**4** length of time: *in the space of a day*
**5** the empty region in which all stars, planets *etc* are situated □ *verb* to put things apart from each other, leaving room between them □ **spacecraft** *noun* a machine for travelling in space □ **spaceman**, **spacewoman** *noun* a traveller in space □ **spaceship** *noun* a manned spacecraft

**spacious** *adj* having plenty of room

**spade** *noun* **1** a tool with a broad blade for digging in the earth **2** one of the four suits of playing-cards □ **call a spade a spade** to say plainly and clearly what you mean

**spaghetti** *noun* a type of pasta made into long sticks

**spake** *verb, old* spoke

**span** *noun* **1** the distance between the tips of the little finger and the thumb when the hand is spread out (about 23 centimetres, 9 inches) **2** the full time anything lasts **3** an arch of a bridge **4** *verb* to stretch across: *the bridge spans the river*

**span** *verb* ◇ spans, spanning, spanned

**spangle** *noun* a thin sparkling piece of metal used as an ornament □ *verb* to sprinkle with spangles *etc*

**spaniel** *noun* a breed of dog with large, hanging ears

**spank** *verb* to strike with the flat of the hand □ *noun* a slap with the hand, *esp* on the buttocks □ **spanking** *noun* a beating with the hand □ *adj* fast: *a spanking pace*

**spanner** *noun* a tool used to tighten or loosen nuts, screws *etc*

**spar** *noun* a long piece of wood or metal used as a ship's mast or its crosspiece □ *verb* **1** to fight with the fists **2** to engage in an argument

**spar** *verb* ◇ spars, sparring, sparred

**spare** *verb* **1** to do without: *I can't spare you today* **2** to afford, set aside: *I can't spare the time* **3** to treat with mercy, hold back from

injuring **4** to avoid causing (trouble *etc*) to □ *adj* **1** extra, not yet in use: *spare tyre* **2** thin, small: *spare but strong* □ *noun* another of the same kind (*eg* a tyre, part of a machine) kept for emergencies □ **sparing** *adj* careful, economical □ **to spare** over and above what is needed

**spark** *noun* **1** a small red-hot part thrown off from something burning **2** a trace: *a spark of humanity* **3** a lively person □ *verb* to make sparks □ **sparking-plug** or **spark-plug** *noun* a device in a car engine that produces a spark to set on fire explosive gases

**sparkle** *noun* **1** a little spark **2** brightness, liveliness **3** bubbles, as in wine □ *verb* **1** to shine in a glittering way **2** to be lively or witty **3** to bubble □ **sparkling** *adj* **1** glittering **2** witty **3** of a drink: bubbling, fizzy

**sparrow** *noun* a type of small dull-coloured bird

**sparse** *adj* **1** thinly scattered **2** not much, not enough

**spartan** *adj* of conditions *etc*: hard, without luxury

**spasm** *noun* **1** a sudden involuntary jerk of the muscles **2** a strong, short burst (*eg* of anger, work) □ **spasmodic** *adj* **1** occurring in spasms **2** coming now and again, not regularly □ **spasmodically** *adv*

**spastic** *adj* suffering from brain damage which has resulted in extreme muscle spasm and paralysis

**spat** *past form of* spit

**spate** *noun* a sudden rush: *a spate of new books*

**spatial** *adj* of or relating to space

**spatter** *verb* to splash (*eg* with mud)

**spatula** *noun* a tool with a broad, blunt blade

**spawn** *noun* a mass of eggs of fish, frogs *etc* □ *verb* **1** of fish *etc*: to lay eggs **2** to cause, produce

**spay** *verb* to remove the ovaries of (a female animal)

**speak** *verb* **1** to say words, talk **2** to hold a conversation (with) **3** to make a speech **4** to be able to talk (a certain language) □ **speak your mind** to give your opinion openly □ **speak up 1** to speak more loudly or clearly **2** to give your opinion openly

**speak** ⇔ speak*s*, speak*ing*, spoke, spoken

**spear** *noun* **1** a long weapon, with an iron or steel point **2** a long, pointed shoot or leaf (*esp* of grass) □ *verb* to pierce with a spear

**special** *adj* **1** not ordinary, exceptional **2** put on for a particular purpose: *special train* **3** belonging to one person or thing and not to others: *special skills* □ **specialist** *noun* someone who studies one branch of a subject or field: *heart specialist* □ **speciality** *noun* (*pl* **specialities**) something for which a person is well-known □ **specialization** *noun* specializing □ **specialize** *verb* to work in, or study, a particular job, subject *etc* □ **specialized** *adj* of knowledge: obtained by specializing

**species** *noun* (*pl* **species**) **1** a group of plants or animals which are alike in most ways **2** a kind (of anything)

**specific** *adj* giving all the details clearly; particular, exactly stated: *a specific purpose* □ **specifically** *adv* **1** particularly or for the purpose stated and no other **2** exactly and clearly

**specify** *verb* **1** to set down or say clearly (what is wanted) **2** to make particular mention of □ **specification** *noun* **1** the act of specifying **2** a full description of details (*eg* in a plan or contract)

**specify** ⇔ specif*ies*, specify*ing*, specif*ied*

**specimen** *noun* something used as a sample of a group or kind of anything, *esp* for study or for putting in a collection

**specious** *adj* looking or seeming good but really not so good

**speck** *noun* **1** a small spot **2** a tiny piece (*eg* of dust)

**speckle** *noun* a spot on a different-coloured background □ **speckled** *adj*

**spectacle** *noun* **1** a striking or wonderful sight **2** (**spectacles**) glasses which someone wears to improve eyesight

**spectacular** *adj* **1** very impressive to see or watch **2** remarkable or dramatic: *a spectacular success* □ **spectacularly** *adv* (meaning 2)

**spectator** *noun* someone who watches (an event *eg* a football match)

**spectre** *noun* a ghost □ **spectral** *adj*

**spectrum** *noun* (*pl* **spectra** or **spectrums**) **1** the band of colours as seen in a rainbow, sometimes formed when light passes through water or glass **2** the range or extent of anything

**speculate** *verb* **1** to guess **2** to wonder (about) **3** to buy goods, shares *etc* in order to sell them again at a profit □ **speculation** *noun* □ **speculative** *adj* □ **speculator** *noun*

**sped** *past form of* **speed**

**speech** *noun* **1** the power of making sounds which have meaning for other people **2** a way of speaking **3** (*pl* **speeches**) a (formal) talk given to an audience □ **speechless** *adj* so surprised *etc* that you cannot speak

**speed** *noun* quickness of, or rate of, movement or action □ *verb* **1** (*past* **sped**) to (cause to) move along quickly, hurry **2** (*past* **speeded**) to drive very fast in a car *etc* (*esp* faster than is allowed by law) □ **speeding** *noun* driving at (an illegally) high speed □ **speedy** *adj* going quickly □ **speed limit** the greatest speed

permitted on a particular road
□ **speedometer** *noun* an instrument that shows how fast you are travelling □ **speedway** *noun* a motor-cycle racing track

**speed** *verb* ○ speeds, speed*ing*, sped or speed*ed*

**speedwell** *noun* a type of small plant with blue flowers

**speleology** *noun* the study or exploration of caves

**spell** *noun* 1 words which, when spoken, are supposed to have magic power 2 magic or other powerful influence 3 a (short) space of time 4 a turn (at work, rest, play) □ *verb* 1 to give or write correctly the letters which make up a word 2 to mean, imply: *this spells disaster for us all* □ **spelling** *noun* 1 the ability to spell words 2 the study of spelling words correctly □ **spellbound** *adj* charmed, held by a spell □ **spell out** to say (something) very frankly or clearly

**spell** *verb* ○ spells, spell*ing*, spelt or spell*ed*

**spelt** *see* spell

**spend** *verb* 1 to use (money) for buying 2 to use (energy *etc*) 3 to pass (time) □ **spendthrift** *noun* someone who spends money freely and carelessly

**spend** ○ spends, spend*ing*, spent

**spent** *adj* exhausted; having lost force or power: *a spent bullet*

**sperm** *noun* (the fluid in a male carrying) the male sex-cell that fertilizes the female egg

**spew** *verb* to vomit

**sphere** *noun* 1 a ball or similar perfectly round object 2 a position or level in society: *he moves in the highest spheres* 3 range (of influence or action) □ **spherical** *adj*

**Sphinx** *noun* 1 a mythological monster with the head of a woman and the body of a lioness 2 the large stone model of the Sphinx in Egypt

3 (**sphinx**) someone whose real thoughts you cannot guess

**spice** *noun* 1 any substance used for flavouring, *eg* pepper, nutmeg 2 anything that adds liveliness, interest □ *verb* to flavour with spice □ **spicy** *adj* 1 full of spices 2 lively and sometimes slightly indecent: *a spicy tale* □ **spiciness** *noun*

**spick-and-span** *adj* neat, clean and tidy

**spider** *noun* a kind of small, insect-like creature with eight legs, that spins a web □ **spidery** *adj* 1 like a spider 2 of handwriting: having fine, sprawling strokes

**spiel** (*say* speel *or* shpeel) *noun*, *informal* a (long or often repeated) story or speech
⊚ From German *spielen* meaning 'to play'

**spike** *noun* 1 a pointed piece of rod (of wood, metal *etc*) 2 a type of large nail 3 an ear of corn 4 a head of flowers □ *verb* 1 to pierce with a spike 2 to make useless 3 *informal* to add an alcoholic drink, *esp* to a soft drink □ **spiky** *adj*

**spill** *verb* to (allow liquid to) run out or overflow □ *noun* 1 a fall 2 a thin strip of wood or twisted paper for lighting a candle, a pipe *etc* □ **spillage** *noun* □ **spill the beans** *informal* to give away a secret, *esp* unintentionally

**spill** *verb* ○ spills, spill*ing*, spilt or spill*ed*

**spin** *verb* 1 to draw out (cotton, wood, silk *etc*) and twist into threads 2 to (cause to) whirl round quickly 3 to travel quickly, *esp* on wheels 4 to produce a fine thread as a spider does □ *noun* 1 a whirling motion 2 a ride (*esp* on wheels) □ **spindrier** *noun* a machine for taking water out of clothes by whirling them round □ **spinning wheel** a machine for spinning thread, consisting of a wheel which drives spindles □ **spin a yarn** to tell a long story □ **spin out** to make to last a long or longer time

**spin** verb ↔ spin**s**, spin**ning**, spun

**spinach** noun a type of plant whose leaves are eaten as vegetables

**spindle** noun **1** the pin from which the thread is twisted in spinning wool or cotton **2** a pin on which anything turns round (eg that in the centre of the turntable of a record-player) □ **spindly** adj long and thin

**spindrift** noun the spray blown from the tops of waves

**spine** noun **1** the line of linked bones running down the back in animals and humans, the backbone **2** a ridge **3** a stiff, pointed spike which is part of an animal's body (eg a porcupine) **4** a thorn □ **spinal** adj □ **spineless** adj

**spinet** noun a kind of small harpsichord

**spinney** noun (pl **spinneys**) a small clump of trees

**spinster** noun a woman who is not married

**spiral** adj **1** coiled round like a spring **2** winding round and round, getting further and further away from the centre □ noun **1** anything with a spiral shape **2** a spiral movement **3** an increase which gets ever more rapid □ verb **1** to move in a spiral **2** to increase ever more rapidly

**spiral** verb ↔ spiral**s**, spiral**ling**, spiral**led**

**spire** noun a tall, sharp-pointed tower (esp on the roof of a church

**spirit** noun **1** the soul **2** a being without a body, a ghost **3** liveliness, boldness **4** a feeling or attitude: a spirit of kindness **5** the intended meaning: the spirit of the laws **6** a distilled liquid, esp alcohol **7** (**spirits**) strong alcoholic drinks in general (eg whisky) **8** (**spirits**) state of mind, mood: in high spirits □ verb (esp **spirit away**) to remove, as if by

magic □ **spirited** adj lively □ **spiritual** adj having to do with the soul or with ghosts □ noun an emotional, religious song of a kind originally developed by the African American slaves □ **spiritualism** noun the belief that living people can communicate with the souls of dead people □ **spiritualist** noun

**spit** noun **1** the liquid which forms in a person's mouth **2** a metal bar on which meat is roasted **3** a long piece of land running into the sea □ verb (past form **spat**) **1** to throw liquid out from the mouth **2** to rain slightly **3** (past form **spitted**) to pierce with something sharp

**spit** verb ↔ spit**s**, spit**ting**, spat or spit**ted**

**spite** noun the wish to hurt (esp feelings) □ verb to annoy out of spite □ **spiteful** adj motivated by spit; malicious □ **in spite of 1** taking no notice of **2** although something has happened or is a fact: the ground was dry in spite of the rain

**spitting image** an exact likeness

**spittle** noun spit

**spittoon** noun a kind of dish into which you may spit

**splash** verb **1** to spatter with water, mud etc **2** to move or fall with a splash or splashes □ noun (pl **splashes**) **1** the sound made by, or the scattering of liquid caused by, something hitting water etc **2** a mark made by splashing (eg on your clothes) **3** a bright patch: a splash of colour □ **make a splash** to attract a lot of attention

**splay** verb to turn out at an angle

**spleen** noun **1** a spongy, blood-filled organ inside the body, near the stomach **2** bad temper

**splendid** adj **1** magnificent, brilliant **2** informal excellent □ **splendidly** adv

**splendour** noun the state or quality of being very grand and beautiful in appearance or style

**splice** *verb* to join (two ends of a rope) by twining the threads together □ *noun* a joint so made

**splint** *noun* a piece of wood *etc* tied to a broken limb to keep it in a fixed position

**splinter** *noun* a sharp, thin, broken piece of wood, glass *etc* □ *verb* to split into splinters

**split** *verb* 1 to cut or break lengthways 2 to crack, break 3 to divide into pieces or groups *etc* □ *noun* a crack, a break □ **splitting** *adj* of a headache: severe, intense □ **the splits** the feat of going down on the floor with one leg stretched forward and the other back □ **a split second** a fraction of a second □ **split your sides** to laugh heartily

**splutter** *verb* 1 to make spitting noises 2 to speak hastily and unclearly

**spoil** *verb* 1 to make useless; damage, ruin 2 to give in to the wishes of (a child *etc*) and so ruin its character 3 of food: to become bad or useless 4 (*past form* **spoiled**) to rob, plunder □ *noun* (often **spoils**) plunder □ **spoil-sport** *noun* someone who won't join in other people's fun □ **spoiling for** eager for (*esp* a fight)

**spoil** *verb* ↔ spoils, spoiling, spoiled

**spoke** *noun* one of the ribs or bars from the centre to the rim of a wheel □ *verb, past form of* **speak**

**spoken** *see* **speak**

**spokesman, spokeswoman** *noun* someone who speaks on behalf of others

**spoliation** *noun* plundering

**sponge** *noun* 1 a sea animal 2 its soft, elastic skeleton which can soak up water and is used for washing 3 an artificial object like this used for washing 4 a light cake or pudding □ *verb* 1 to wipe with a sponge 2 *informal* to live off money *etc* given by others □ **sponger** *noun*,

*informal* someone who lives at others' expense □ **spongy** *adj* soft like a sponge □ **throw in the sponge** to give up a fight or struggle

**sponsor** *noun* 1 someone who takes responsibility for introducing something, a promoter 2 someone who promises to pay a sum of money if another person completes a set task (*eg* a walk, swim *etc*) 3 a business firm which pays for a radio or television programme and advertises its products during it □ *verb* to act as a sponsor to □ **sponsorship** *noun*

**spontaneous** *adj* 1 not planned beforehand 2 natural, not forced □ **spontaneity** *noun*

**spoof** *noun* a trick played as a joke, a hoax

**spook** *noun* a ghost □ **spooky** *adj* frightening

**spool** *noun* a reel for thread, film *etc*

**spoon** *noun* a piece of metal *etc* with a hollow bowl at one end, used for lifting food to the mouth □ *verb* to lift with a spoon □ **spoonfeed** *verb* to teach without encouraging independent thought

**spoonerism** *noun* a mistake in speaking in which the first sounds of words change position, as in *every crook and nanny* for *every nook and cranny*

**spoor** *noun* the footmarks or trail left by an animal

**sporadic** *adj* happening here and there, or now and again □ **sporadically** *adv*

**spore** *noun* the seed of certain plants (*eg* ferns, fungi)

**sporran** *noun* a small pouch worn hanging in front of a kilt

**sport** *noun* 1 games such as football, tennis, skiing *etc* in general 2 any one game of this type 3 a good-natured, obliging person □ *verb* 1 to have fun, play 2 to wear: *sporting a pink tie* □ **sporting** *adj* 1 fond of sport **2** believing in fair play, good-natured □ **sporting chance** a reasonably good chance □ **sports car** a small, fast car with only two seats □ **sportsman, sportswoman** *noun* **1** someone who plays sports **2** someone who shows fair play in sports □ **sportsmanlike** *adj* fair, sporting

**spot** *noun* **1** a small mark or stain (of mud, paint *etc*) **2** a round mark as part of a pattern on material *etc* **3** a pimple **4** a place □ *verb* **1** to mark with spots **2** to catch sight of □ **spotted** or **spotty** *adj* □ **spotless** *adj* very clean □ **spotlight** *noun* a bright light that is shone on an actor on the stage □ *verb* **1** to show up clearly **2** to draw attention to □ **in a spot** in trouble □ **on the spot 1** in the place where someone is most needed **2** right away, immediately **3** in an embarrassing or difficult position

**spot** *verb* ⊷ spot*s*, spot*ting*, spot*ted*

**spouse** *noun* a husband or wife

**spout** *noun* **1** the part of a kettle, teapot *etc* through which liquid is poured out **2** a strong jet of liquid □ *verb* to pour or spurt out

**sprain** *noun* a painful twisting (*eg* of an ankle) □ *verb* to twist painfully

**sprang** *past form of* spring

**sprat** *noun* a small fish similar to a herring

**sprawl** *verb* **1** to sit, lie or fall with the limbs spread out widely **2** of a town *etc*: to spread out in an untidy, irregular way

**spray** *noun* **1** a fine mist of liquid like that made by a waterfall **2** a device with many small holes (*eg* on a watering-can or shower) for producing spray **3** a liquid for spraying **4** a shoot spreading out in flowers □ *verb* to cover with a mist or fine jets of liquid

**spread** *verb* **1** to put more widely or thinly over an area: *spread the butter* on the bread **2** to cover: *spread the bread with jam* **3** to open out (*eg* your arms, a map) **4** to scatter or distribute over a wide area, length of time *etc* □ *noun* **1** the act of spreading **2** the extent or range (of something) **3** a food which is spread on bread: *sandwich spread* **4** *informal* a large meal laid out on a table □ **spread-eagled** *adj* with limbs spread out

**spread** *verb* ⊷ spread*s*, spread*ing*, spread

**spree** *noun* a careless spell of some activity: *a spending spree*

**sprig** *noun* a small twig or shoot

**sprightly** *adj* lively, brisk

**spring** *verb* **1** to jump, leap **2** to move swiftly **3** (with **back**) to return suddenly to an earlier position when released **4** to set off (a trap *etc*) **5** to give, reveal unexpectedly: *he sprang the news on me* **6** to come from: *his bravery springs from his love of adventure* □ *noun* **1** a leap **2** a coil of wire used in a mattress **3** the ability to stretch and spring back **4** bounce, energy **5** a small stream flowing out from the ground **6** the season which follows winter, when plants begin to grow again □ **springy** *adj* able to spring back into its former position *etc*, elastic □ **springboard** *noun* a springy board from which swimmers may dive □ **springbok** *noun* a type of deer found in S Africa □ **spring-cleaning** *noun* a thorough cleaning of a house, *esp* in the spring □ **spring a leak** to begin to leak □ **spring up** to appear suddenly

**spring** *verb* ⊷ spring*s*, spring*ing*, sprang, sprung

**sprinkle** *verb* to scatter or cover in small drops or pieces □ **sprinkler** *noun* something which sprinkles water □ **sprinkling** *noun* a few, a small amount

**sprint** *verb* to run at full speed □ *noun* a short running race □ **sprinter** *noun*

**sprite** *noun* a supernatural spirit

**sprocket** *noun* one of a set of teeth on the rim of a wheel

**sprout** *verb* **1** to begin to grow **2** to put out new shoots □ *noun* **1** a young bud **2** (**sprouts**) Brussels sprouts

**spruce** *adj* neat, smart □ *noun* a kind of fir-tree

**sprung** *see* **spring**

**spry** *adj* lively, active

**spud** *noun, informal* a potato

**spume** *noun* froth, foam

**spun** *past form of* **spin**

**spur** *noun* **1** a sharp point worn by a horse-rider on the heel and used to urge on a horse **2** a claw-like point at the back of a bird's leg **3** anything that urges someone on **4** a small line of mountains running off from a larger range □ *verb* **1** to use spurs on (a horse) **2** to urge on □ **on the spur of the moment** without thinking beforehand

**spur** *verb* ⋄ spurs, spurring, spurred

**spurious** *adj* not genuine, false

**spurn** *verb* to cast aside, reject with scorn

**spurt** *verb* to pour out in a sudden stream □ *noun* **1** a sudden stream pouring or squirting out **2** a sudden increase of effort

**sputter** *verb* to make a noise as of spitting and throw out moisture in drops

**spy** *noun* (*pl* **spies**) someone who secretly collects (and reports) information about another person, country, firm *etc* □ *verb* **1** to catch sight of **2** (with **on**) to watch secretly

**spy** *verb* ⋄ spies, spying, spied

**squabble** *verb* to quarrel noisily □ *noun* a noisy quarrel

**squad** *noun* **1** a group of soldiers, workmen *etc* doing a particular job **2** a group of people

**squadron** *noun* a division of a regiment, section of a fleet or group of aeroplanes

**squalid** *adj* **1** very dirty, filthy **2** contemptible

**squall** *noun* **1** a sudden violent storm **2** a squeal, a scream □ **squally** *adj* stormy

**squalor** *noun* dirty or squalid living conditions

**squander** *verb* to waste (money, goods, strength *etc*)

**square** *noun* **1** a figure with four equal sides and four right angles, of this shape □ **2** an open space enclosed by buildings in a town **3** the answer when a number is multiplied by itself (*eg* the square of 3 is 9) □ *adj* **1** shaped like a square **2** equal in scores in a game **3** of two or more people: not owing one another anything **4** straight, level □ *verb* **1** to make like a square **2** to straighten (the shoulders) **3** to multiply a number by itself **4** to fit, agree: *that doesn't square with what you said earlier* **5** (with **up**) to settle a debt □ *adv* **1** in a straight or level position **2** directly; exactly: *hit square on the nose* □ **square deal** fair treatment □ **square foot** or **square metre** *etc* an area equal to that of a square each side of which is one foot or one metre *etc* long □ **square meal** a large, satisfying meal □ **square root** the number which, multiplied by itself, gives a certain other number (*eg* 3 is the square root of 9)

**squash** *verb* **1** to crush flat or to a pulp **2** to put down, defeat (rebellion *etc*) □ *noun* **1** a crushing or crowding **2** a mass of people crowded together **3** a drink made from the juice of crushed fruit **4** a game with rackets and a rubber ball played in a walled court

**squat** *verb* **1** to sit down on the heels **2** to settle without permission in property which you do not pay rent for □ *adj* short and thick □ **squatter**

*noun* someone who squats in a building, on land *etc*

**squat** *verb* ⟷ squats, squatting, squatted

**squaw** *noun, derogatory* **1** a Native American woman or wife **2** a woman

**squawk** *verb* to give a harsh cry □ *noun* a harsh cry

**squeak** *verb* to give a short, high-pitched sound □ *noun* a high-pitched noise □ **squeaky** *adj* **1** high-pitched **2** tending to squeak: *a squeaky floorboard*

**squeal** *verb* **1** to give a loud, shrill cry **2** *informal* to inform on

**squeamish** *adj* **1** easily sickened or shocked **2** feeling sick

**squeeze** *verb* **1** to press together **2** to grasp tightly **3** to force out (liquid or juice from) by pressing **4** to force a way: *squeeze through the hole in the wall* □ *noun* **1** a squeezing or pressing **2** a few drops got by squeezing: *a squeeze of lemon juice* **3** a crowd of people crushed together

**squelch** *noun* a sound made, *eg* by walking through marshy ground □ *verb* to make this sound

**squib** *noun* a type of small firework

**squid** *noun* a sea animal with tentacles, related to the cuttlefish

**squiggle** *noun* a curly or wavy mark

**squint** *verb* **1** to screw up the eyes in looking at something **2** to have the eyes looking in different directions □ *noun* **1** a fault in eyesight which causes squinting **2** *informal* a quick, close glance

**squire** *noun, historical* **1** a country landowner **2** a knight's servant

**squirm** *verb* to wriggle or twist the body, *esp* in pain or embarrassment

**squirrel** *noun* a small gnawing animal, either reddish-brown or grey, with a bushy tail

**squirt** *verb* to shoot out a narrow jet

of liquid □ *noun* a narrow jet of liquid

**St** *abbrev* **1** saint **2** street **3** strait

**stab** *verb* **1** to wound or pierce with a pointed weapon **2** to poke (at) □ *noun* **1** the act of stabbing **2** a wound made by stabbing **3** a sharp pain □ **have a stab at** to make an attempt at

**stab** *verb* ⟷ stabs, stabbing, stabbed

**stable** *noun* a building for keeping horses □ *verb* to put or keep (horses) in a stable □ *adj* firm, steady □ **stability** *noun* □ **stabilize** *verb*

**staccato** *adj* **1** of sounds: sharp and separate, like the sound of tapping **2** *also adv, music* (with each note) sounded separately and clearly

**stack** *noun* a large pile (of straw, hay, wood *etc*) □ *verb* to pile in a stack

**stadium** *noun* (*pl* **stadiums** or **stadia**) a large sports-ground or race-course with seats for spectators

**staff** *noun* **1** a stick or pole carried in the hand **2** *music* a stave **3** workers employed in a business, school *etc* **4** a group of army officers who assist a commanding officer □ *verb* to supply (a school *etc*) with staff

**stag** *noun* a male deer

**stage** *noun* **1** a platform for performing or acting on **2** (**the stage**) the theatre; the job of working as an actor **3** a step in development: *the first stage of the plan* **4** a landing place (*eg* for boats) **5** a part of a journey **6** a stopping place on a journey □ *verb* **1** to prepare and put on a performance of (a play *etc*) **2** to arrange (an event, *eg* an exhibition) □ **on the stage** in the theatre-world

**stagecoach** *noun, historical* a coach running every day with passengers

**stagger** *verb* **1** to walk unsteadily, totter **2** to astonish **3** to arrange (people's hours of work *etc*) so that they do not begin or end together □ **staggered** *adj* of two or more things: arranged to begin and end at different times □ **staggering** adj astonishing

**stagnant** adj of water: standing still, not flowing and therefore not pure □ **stagnate** verb **1** of water: to remain still and so become impure **2** to remain for a long time in the same situation and so become bored, inactive etc □ **stagnation** noun

**staid** adj set in your ways, sedate

**stain** verb **1** to give a different colour to (wood etc) **2** to mark or make dirty by accident □ noun **1** a liquid which dyes or colours something **2** a mark which is not easily removed **3** something shameful in someone's character or reputation □ **stained glass** coloured glass cut in shapes and leaded together □ **stainless steel** a mixture of steel and chromium which does not rust

**stair** noun **1** one or all of a number of steps one after the other **2** (stairs) a series or flight of steps □ **staircase** noun a stretch of stairs with rails on one or both sides

**stake** noun **1** a strong stick pointed at one end **2** money put down as a bet **3** historical a post to which people were tied to be burned □ verb **1** to mark the limits or boundaries (of a field etc) with stakes **2** to bet (money) **3** to risk □ **at stake 1** be won or lost **2** in great danger □ **have a stake in** to be concerned in (because you have something to gain or lose) □ **stake a claim** to establish ownership or right (to something)

**stalactite** noun a spike of limestone hanging from the roof of a cave, formed by the dripping of water containing lime

**stalagmite** noun a spike of limestone, like a stalactite, rising from the floor of a cave

**stale** adj **1** of food: no longer fresh **2** no longer interesting because

heard, done etc too often before **3** not able to do your best (because of overworking, boredom etc)

**stalemate** noun **1** chess a position in which a player cannot move without putting their king in danger **2** a position in an argument in which neither side can win

**stalk** noun the stem of a plant or of a leaf or flower □ verb **1** to walk stiffly or proudly **2** to go quietly up to animals being hunted to shoot at close range

**stall** noun **1** a division for one animal in a cowshed etc **2** a table on which things are laid out for sale **3** an open-fronted shop **4** a seat in a church (esp for choir or clergy) **5** stalls theatre seats on the ground floor □ verb **1** of a car engine: to come to a halt without the driver intending it to do so **2** of an aircraft: to lose flying speed and so fall out of control **3** informal to avoid action or decision for the time being

**stallion** noun a male horse, esp one kept for breeding purposes

**stalwart** adj brave, stout-hearted □ noun

**stamen** noun one of the thread-like spikes in the middle of a flower which bear the pollen

**stamina** noun strength, power to keep going

**stammer** verb **1** to have difficulty in saying the first letter of words in speaking **2** to stumble over words □ noun a speech difficulty of this kind

**stamp** verb **1** to bring the foot down firmly on the ground **2** to stick a (postage stamp) on **3** to mark with a design cut into a mould and inked **4** to fix or mark deeply: stamped in my memory □ noun **1** the act of stamping **2** a design etc made by stamping **3** a cut or moulded design for stamping **4** kind, sort: he's of a different stamp **5** a postage stamp

◻ **stamp out 1** to put out (a fire) by stamping **2** to suppress, crush

**stampede** *noun* **1** a wild rush of frightened animals **2** a sudden, wild rush of people ◻ *verb* to rush wildly

**stance** *noun* someone's manner of standing

**stanchion** *noun* an upright iron bar used as a support (*eg* in windows, ships)

**stand** *verb* **1** to be on your feet (not lying or sitting down) **2** to rise to your feet **3** of an object: to (cause to) be in a particular place: *it stood by the door* **4** to bear: *I cannot stand this heat* **5** to treat (someone) to: *stand you tea* **6** to remain: *the law still stands* **7** to be a candidate (for): *he stood for parliament* **8** to be short (for): *PO stands for Post Office* ◻ *noun* **1** something on which anything is placed **2** an object made to hold, or for hanging, things: *a hat-stand* **3** lines of raised seats from which people may watch games *etc* **4** an effort made to support, defend, resist *etc*: *a stand against violence* **5** (*US*) a witness box in a law court ◻ **standpoint** *noun* the position from which you look at something (*eg* a question, problem), point of view ◻ **standstill** *noun* a complete stop ◻ **stand by** to be ready or available to be used or help in an emergency *etc* (**standby** *noun*) ◻ **stand down** to withdraw (from a contest) or resign (from a job) ◻ **stand fast** to refuse to give in ◻ **stand in (for)** to take another's place, job *etc* for a time (**stand-in** *noun*) ◻ **stand out** to stick out, be noticeable ◻ **stand to reason** to be likely or reasonable ◻ **stand up for** to defend strongly ◻ **stand up to** to face or oppose bravely

**stand** *verb* ⋄ stand*s*, stand*ing*, stood

**standard** *noun* **1** a level against which things may be judged **2** a level of excellence aimed at: *artistic standards* **3** a large flag *etc* on a pole

◻ *adj* **1** normal, usual: *standard charge* **2** ordinary, without extras: *standard model* ◻ **standard lamp** a kind of tall lamp which stands on the floor of a room *etc* ◻ **standard of living** a level of material comfort considered necessary by a particular group of society *etc*

**standardize** *verb* to make all of one kind or size ◻ **standardization** *noun* standardizing or being standardized

**standby** *noun* **1** something that is kept ready for use, *esp* in an emergency **2** (*usually* **standby ticket**) a ticket for a journey by air that is offered at a reduced price because you must wait until just before the flight takes off to see if there is a seat available

**standing** *noun* social position or reputation ◻ *adj* **1** on your feet **2** placed on end **3** not moving **4** lasting, permanent: *a standing joke*

**stank** *past form of* **stink**

**stanza** *noun* a group of lines making up a part of a poem, a verse

**staple** *noun* **1** a U-shaped iron nail **2** a piece of wire driven through sheets of paper to fasten them together **3** the main item in a country's production, a person's diet *etc* **4** a fibre of wool, cotton *etc* ◻ *verb* to fasten with a staple ◻ *adj* chief, main

**star** *noun* **1** any of the bodies in the sky appearing as points of light **2** the fixed bodies which are really distant suns, not the planets **3** an object, shape or figure with a number of pointed rays (often five) **4** a leading actor or actress or other well-known performer ◻ *adj* for or of a star (in a film *etc*) ◻ *verb* **1** to act the chief part (in a play *etc*) ◻ **2** of a play *etc*: to have as its star ◻ **stardom** *noun* the state of being a leading performer ◻ **starfish** *noun* a type of small sea creature with five points or arms □ **Stars and Stripes** the flag of the United States of America

**star** *verb* ⋄ **stars, starring, starred**

**starboard** *noun* the right side of a ship, as you look towards the bow (or front)

**starch** *noun* (*pl* **starches**) **1** a white carbohydrate (found in flour, potatoes, bread, biscuits *etc*) **2** a form of this used for stiffening clothes □ **starchy** *adj* **1** of food: containing starch **2** stiff and unfriendly

**stare** *verb* to look with a fixed gaze □ *noun* a fixed gaze

**stark** *adj* **1** barren, bare **2** harsh, severe **3** sheer: *stark idiocy* □ *adv* completely: *stark naked*

**starling** *noun* a common bird with dark, glossy feathers

**starry** *adj* full of stars; shining like stars

**start** *verb* **1** to begin (an action) **2** to get (a machine *etc*) working: *he started the car* **3** to jump or jerk (*eg* in surprise) □ *noun* **1** the act of starting (*eg* on a task, journey) **2** a sudden movement of the body **3** a sudden shock: *you gave me a start* **4** in a race *etc* the advantage of beginning before, or farther forward than, others, or the amount of this: *a start of five metres*

**startle** *verb* to give a shock or fright to □ **startling** *adj*

**starve** *verb* **1** to die for want of food **2** to suffer greatly from hunger **3** to deprive (of something needed or wanted badly): *starved of company here* □ **starvation** *noun*

**state** *noun* **1** the condition (of something) **2** the people of a country under a government **3** (*US*) an area and its people with its own laws forming part of the whole country **4** a government and its officials **5** great show, pomp: *the king drove by in state* □ *adj* **1** of the

government **2** national and ceremonial: *state occasions* **3** (*US*) of a certain state of America: *the state capital of Texas is Austin* □ *verb* to tell, say or write (*esp* clearly and fully) □ **stately** *adj* noble-looking; dignified □ **stateliness** *noun*

**statement** *noun* that which is said or written

**statesman** *noun* someone skilled in government

**static** *adj* not moving □ *noun* **1** atmospheric disturbances causing poor reception of radio or television programmes **2** electricity on the surface of objects which will not conduct it *eg* hair, nylons *etc* (*also called*: **static electricity**)

**station** *noun* **1** a building with a ticket office, waiting rooms *etc* where trains, buses or coaches stop to pick up or set down passengers **2** a place which is the centre for work or duty of any kind: *police station* **3** rank, position: *lowly station* □ *verb* **1** to assign to a position or place **2** to take up a position: *stationed himself by the door*

**stationary** *adj* standing still, not moving

ⓕ From Latin *stationarius* meaning 'belonging to a military station'

♦ Do not confuse: **stationary** and **stationery**. Remember that a stationER's shop sells stationERy.

**stationery** *noun* writing paper, envelopes, pens *etc* □ **stationer** *noun*

**statistics 1** *noun pl* figures and facts set out in order: *statistics of road accidents for last year* **2** *noun sing* the study of these □ **statistical** *adj* □ **statistically** *adv* □ **statistician** *noun* someone who produces or studies statistics

**statue** *noun* a likeness of someone or

an animal carved in stone, metal *etc* □ **statuesque** *adj* like a statue in dignity *etc* □ **statuette** *noun* a small statue

**stature** *noun* **1** height **2** importance, reputation

**status** *noun* position, rank (of a person) in the eyes of others □ **status quo** the state of affairs now existing, or existing before a certain time or event □ **status symbol** a possession which is thought to show the high status of the owner (*eg* a powerful car)

**statute** *noun* a written law of a country □ **statutory** *adj* according to law

**staunch** *adj* firm, loyal; trustworthy

**stave** *noun* **1** a set of spaced lines on which music is written **2** one of the strips making the side of a barrel □ *verb* **1** (with **in**) to crush in **2** (with **off**) to keep away, delay

**stave** *verb* ⬦ staves, staving, stove or staved

**stay** *verb* **1** to continue to be: *stayed calm* **2** to live (for a time): *staying in a hotel* **3** *old* to stop □ *noun* **1** time spent in a place **2** a rope running from the side of a ship to the mast-head **3** (**stays**) *old* corsets □ **stay put** to remain in the same place

**stead** *noun* place: *she went in my stead* □ **stand you in good stead** to turn out to be helpful to you

**steadfast** *adj* **1** steady, fixed **2** faithful, loyal

**steading** *noun* farm buildings

**steady** *adj* **1** firm, not moving or changing **2** not easily upset or put off **3** even, regular, unchanging: *moving at a steady pace* □ *verb* to make or become steady □ **steadily** *adj*

**steady** *verb* ⬦ steadies, steadying, steadied

**steak** *noun* a thick slice of meat *etc* for cooking

**steal** *verb* **1** to take (something not belonging to you) without permission **2** to move quietly **3** to take quickly or secretly: *stole a look at him*

**steal** ⬦ steals, stealing, stole, stolen

**stealth** *noun* a secret way of doing, acting *etc* □ **stealthy** *adj* □ **stealthily** *adv*

**steam** *noun* **1** vapour from hot liquid, *esp* from boiling water **2** power produced by steam: *in the days of steam* □ *verb* **1** to give off steam **2** to cook by steam **3** to open or loosen by putting into steam: *steam open the envelope* **4** to move or travel by steam □ **steamy** *adj* **1** full of steam: *steamy atmosphere* **2** *informal* passionate, erotic □ **steam-engine** *noun* an engine (*esp* a railway engine) worked by steam □ **steamer** *noun* a ship driven by steam □ **steamroller** *noun* a steam-driven engine with large and very heavy wheels, used for flattening the surfaces of roads □ **steamship** *noun* a steamer □ **steam up** of glass: to become covered with condensed steam in the form of small drops of water

**steed** *noun*, *old* a horse

**steel** *noun* **1** a very hard mixture of iron and carbon **2** a bar of steel for sharpening knife blades □ **steely** *adj* hard, cold, strong *etc* like steel: *a steely gaze* □ **of steel** hard, strong: *a grip of steel* □ **steel yourself** to get up courage (to)

**steep** *adj* **1** of a slope: rising almost straight up **2** *informal* of a price: too great □ *verb* to soak in a liquid □ **be steeped in something** to be very familiar with something (*eg* a subject of knowledge): *steeped in French literature*

**steeple** *noun* a tower of a church *etc* rising to a point, a spire □ **steeplejack** *noun* someone who climbs steeples or other high buildings to make repairs

**steeplechase** noun 1 a race run across open country, over hedges etc 2 a race over a course on which obstacles (eg walls) have been made

**steer** noun a young ox raised for its beef □ verb 1 to control the course of (a car, ship, discussion etc) 2 to follow (a course) □ **steer clear of** to keep away from

**steering** noun the parts of a ship, car etc which have to do with controlling its course □ **steering-wheel** noun the wheel in a car used by the driver to steer it

**stellar** adj of the stars

**stem** noun 1 the part of a plant from which the leaves and flowers grow 2 the thin support of a wine-glass □ verb 1 to stop, halt: stem the bleeding 2 to start, spring (from): hate stems from envy

**stem** verb ⇔ stems, stemming, stemmed

**stench** noun a strong unpleasant smell

**stencil** noun 1 a sheet of metal, cardboard etc with a pattern cut out 2 the drawing or design made by rubbing ink or brushing paint etc over a cut-out pattern 3 a piece of waxed paper on which words are cut with a typewriter, and which is then used to make copies □ verb to make a design or copy in one of these ways

**stencil** verb ⇔ stencils, stencilling, stencilled

**stentorian** adj 1 of the voice: loud 2 loud-voiced

Named after Stentor, a loud-voiced Greek herald in the Iliad

**step** noun 1 a movement of the leg in walking, running etc 2 the distance covered by this 3 a particular movement of the feet, as in dancing: 4 the sound made by the foot in walking etc: heard a step outside 5 a riser on a stair, or rung on a ladder 6 one of a series of moves in a plan, career etc: take the first step 7 a way

of walking: springy step 8 (steps) a flight of stairs 9 (steps) a step-ladder □ verb 1 to take a step 2 to walk, move: step this way, please □ **step-ladder** noun a ladder with a support on which it rests □ **stepping-stone** noun 1 a stone rising above water or mud, used to cross on 2 anything that helps you to advance □ **in step** 1 of two or more people walking: with the same foot going forward at the same time 2 acting etc in agreement (with) □ **out of step** not in step (with) □ **step up** to increase (eg production) □ **take steps** to begin to do something for a certain purpose

**step** verb ⇔ steps, stepping, stepped

**step-** prefix related as the result of a second marriage: stepfather
ⓘ From Old English prefix steop-meaning 'orphan'

**steppe** noun a dry, grassy treeless plain in SE Europe and Asia

**stereo** adj, short for **stereophonic** □ noun (pl **stereos**) stereophonic equipment, esp a record-player and/or tape recorder, with amplifier and loudspeakers

**stereophonic** adj of sound: giving a life-like effect, with different instruments, voices etc coming from different directions

**stereotype** noun 1 a fixed metal plate for printing, with letters etc moulded onto its surface 2 something fixed and unchanging 3 a characteristic type of person □ **stereotyped** or **stereotypical** adj fixed, not changing: stereotyped ideas

Originally a printing term for a fixed block of type

**sterile** adj 1 unable to have children or reproduce 2 producing no ideas etc: sterile imagination 3 free from germs □ **sterility** noun

**sterilize** verb 1 to make sterile 2 to free from germs by boiling etc

◻ **sterilization** *noun* **1** a surgical operation that is performed on humans or animals so that offspring can no longer be produced **2** the treatment of food *etc* in order to destroy germs

**sterling** *noun* British money, when used in international trading: *one pound sterling* ◻ *adj* **1** of silver: of a certain standard of purity **2** worthy, good: *sterling qualities*

**stern¹** *adj* **1** looking or sounding angry or displeased **2** severe, strict, harsh: *stern prison sentence*
◻ **sternly** *adv* ◻ **sternness** *noun*

**stern²** *noun* the back part of a ship

**steroid** *noun* any of a number of substances, including certain hormones (*see also* **anabolic steroids**)

**stethoscope** *noun* an instrument by means of which a doctor listens to someone's heartbeats, breathing *etc*

**stevedore** *noun* someone employed to load and unload ships

**stew** *verb* to cook by boiling slowly ◻ *noun* **1** a dish of stewed food, often containing meat and vegetables **2** *informal* a state of worry; a flap

**steward** *noun* **1** a flight attendant on an aircraft **2** someone who shows people to their seats at a meeting *etc* **3** an official at a race meeting *etc* **4** someone who manages an estate or farm for someone else
◻ **stewardess** *noun* a female flight attendant (*also called:* **air hostess**)

**stick** *noun* **1** a long thin piece of wood; a branch or twig from a tree **2** a piece of wood shaped for a special purpose: *hockey-stick* **3** a long piece (*eg* of rhubarb) ◻ *verb* **1** to push or thrust (something): *stick the knife in your belt* **2** to fix with glue *etc* **3** to be or become caught, fixed or held back: *stuck in the ditch* **4** to hold fast to, keep to (*eg* a decision) ◻ **sticky** *adj*

**1** clinging closely (like glue, treacle *etc*) **2** covered with something sticky **3** difficult: *a sticky problem* ◻ **stickiness** *noun* ◻ **sticking-plaster** *noun* a kind of tape with a sticky surface, used to protect slight cuts *etc* ◻ **stick-in-the-mud** *noun* someone who is against new ideas, change *etc* ◻ **stick up for** to speak in defence of

**stick** *verb* ⇒ sticks, sticking, stuck

■ (verb, meanings 1 and 3) jam; (verb, meanings 2 and 4) adhere

**stickleback** *noun* a type of small river-fish with prickles on its back

**stickler** *noun* someone who attaches great importance to a particular (often small) matter: *stickler for punctuality*

**stiff** *adj* **1** not easily bent or moved **2** of a mixture, dough *etc*: thick, not easily stirred **3** cold and distant in manner **4** hard, difficult: *stiff examination* **5** severe: *stiff penalty* **6** strong: *stiff drink* ◻ **stiffen** *verb* to make or become stiff

**stifle** *verb* **1** to suffocate **2** to put out (flames) **3** to keep back (tears, a yawn *etc*) ◻ **stifling** *adj* very hot and stuffy

**stigma** *noun* **1** (*pl* **stigmata**) a mark of disgrace **2** (*pl* **stigmas**) in a flower, the top of the pistil
◻ **stigmatize** *verb* to mark, describe as something bad: *stigmatized for life*

**stile** *noun* a step or set of steps for climbing over a wall or fence

**stiletto** *noun* (*pl* **stilettos**) **1** a dagger, or a type of instrument, with a narrow blade **2** (a shoe with) a stiletto heel ◻ **stiletto heel** a high, thin heel on a shoe

**still** *adj* **1** not moving **2** calm, without wind; quiet **3** of drinks: not fizzy ◻ *verb* to make calm or quiet ◻ *adv* **1** up to the present time or the time spoken of: *it was still there* **2** even so, nevertheless: *it's difficult* *but we must still try* **3** even: *still more people* ◻ *noun* an apparatus for distilling spirits (*eg* whisky) ◻ **stillness** *noun* ◻ **stillborn** *adj* of a child: dead at birth ◻ **still life** a picture of something that is not living (as a bowl of fruit *etc*)

**stilted** *adj* stiff, not natural

**stilts** *noun pl* **1** long poles with footrests on which someone may walk clear of the ground **2** tall poles (*eg* to support a house built above water)

**stimulant** *noun* something which makes a part of the body more active or which makes you feel livelier

**stimulate** *verb* **1** to make more active **2** to encourage **3** to excite

**stimulus** *noun* (*pl* **stimuli**) **1** something that brings on a reaction in a living thing **2** something that rouses (someone *etc*) to action or greater effort

**sting** *noun* **1** the part of some animals and plants (*eg* the wasp, the nettle) which can prick the skin and cause pain or irritation **2** the act of piercing with a sting **3** the wound, swelling or pain caused by a sting ◻ *verb* **1** to pierce with a sting or cause pain like that of a sting **2** to be painful, smart **3** to hurt the feelings of: *stung by his words*

**sting** *verb* ⟷ stings, stinging, stung

**stingy** (*say* stin-ji) *adj* mean, not generous ◻ **stinginess** *noun*

**stink** *noun* a bad smell ◻ *verb* to give out a bad smell

**stink** *verb* ⟷ stinks, stinking, stank or stunk, stunk

**stint** *verb* to allow (someone) very little: *don't stint on ...* ◻ *noun* **1** limit: *praise without stint* **2** a fixed amount of work: *my daily stint*

**stipend** *noun* pay, salary, *esp* of a parish minister

**stipple** *verb* to paint or mark with tiny dots from a brush

**stipulate** *verb* to state as a condition (of doing something) ◻ **stipulation** *noun*

**stir** *verb* **1** to set (liquid) in motion, *esp* with a spoon *etc* moved circularly **2** to move slightly: *he stirred in his sleep* **3** to arouse (a person, a feeling *etc*) ◻ *noun* disturbance, fuss ◻ **stirring** *adj* exciting ◻ **stir up** to rouse, cause (*eg* trouble)

**stir** *verb* ⟷ stirs, stirring, stirred

**stirrup** *noun* a metal loop hung from a horse's saddle as a support for the rider's foot

**stitch** *noun* (*pl* **stitches**) **1** the loop made in a thread, wool *etc* by a needle in sewing or knitting **2** a sharp, sudden pain in your side ◻ *verb* to put stitches in, sew

**stoat** *noun* a type of small fierce animal similar to a weasel, sometimes called an ermine when in its white winter fur

**stock** *noun* **1** family, race: *of ancient stock* **2** goods in a shop, warehouse *etc* **3** the capital of a business company divided into shares **4** the animals of a farm (*also called:* **livestock**) **5** liquid (used for soup) obtained by boiling meat, bones *etc* **6** a type of scented garden flower **7** the handle of a whip, rifle *etc* **8** (**stocks**) *historical* a wooden frame, with holes for the ankles and wrists, in which criminals *etc* were fastened as a punishment **9** (**stocks**) the wooden framework upon which a ship is supported when being built ◻ *verb* **1** to keep a supply of (for sale) **2** to supply (a farm with animals *etc*) ◻ *adj* **1** usual, known by everyone: *a stock joke* **2** usually stocked (by a shop *etc*) ◻ **stockbroker** *noun* someone who buys and sells shares in business companies on behalf of others ◻ **stock exchange 1** a place where stocks and shares are bought and sold **2** an association of people who do this □ **stock market** the stock exchange; dealings in stocks and shares □ **stockpile** *noun* a store, a reserve supply □ *verb* to build up a store □ **stocktaking** *noun* a regular check of the goods in a shop or warehouse □ **take stock of** to form an opinion or estimation about (a situation *etc*)

**stockade** *noun* a fence of strong posts set up round an area or building for defence

**stocking** *noun* a close-fitting covering in a knitted fabric (wool, nylon *etc*) for the leg and foot

**stock-still** *adj* perfectly still

**stocky** *adj* short and stout □ **stockiness** *noun*

**stodgy** *adj* 1 of food: heavy, not easily digested 2 of a person, book *etc*: dull □ **stodginess** *noun*

**stoic** *noun* someone who bears pain, hardship *etc* without showing any sign of feeling it □ **stoical** *adj* □ **stoicism** *noun*

**stoke** *verb* to put coal, wood, or other fuel on (a fire)

**stole**[1] *noun* a length of silk, linen or fur worn over the shoulders

**stole**[2] *and* **stolen** *see* **steal**

**stolid** *adj* of someone *etc*: dull; not easily excited □ **stolidity** *noun* □ **stolidly** *adv*

**stomach** *noun* 1 the bag-like part of the body into which the food passes when swallowed 2 desire or courage (for something): *no stomach for a fight* □ *verb* to put up with, bear: *can't stomach her rudeness*

**stomp** *verb* to stamp the feet, *esp* noisily

**stone** *noun* 1 the material of which rocks are composed 2 a (small) loose piece of this 3 a piece of this shaped for a certain purpose: *tombstone* 4 a precious stone (*eg* a diamond) 5 the hard shell around the seed of some fruits (*eg* peach, cherry) 6 a measure of weight (14lb,

6.35 kilogrammes) 7 a piece of hard material that forms in the kidney, bladder *etc*, causing pain □ *verb* 1 to throw stones at 2 to take the stones out of fruit □ *adj* made of stone □ **stony** *adj* 1 like stone 2 covered with stones 3 hard, cold in manner: *stony look* □ **Stone Age** human culture before the use of metal □ **a stone's throw** a very short distance □ **leave no stone unturned** to do everything possible

**stood** *past form of* **stand**

**stooge** *noun* someone who is used by another to do a (usually humble or unpleasant) job

**stool** *noun* a seat without a back

**stoop** *verb* 1 to bend the body forward and downward 2 to be low or wicked enough to do a certain thing: *I wouldn't stoop to stealing* □ *noun* 1 the act of stooping 2 a forward bend of the body

**stop** *verb* 1 to bring to a halt 2 to prevent from doing 3 to put an end to 4 to come to an end: *the rain has stopped* 5 (with **up**) to block (a hole *etc*) □ *noun* 1 the state of being stopped 2 a place where something stops 3 a full stop 4 a knob on an organ which brings certain pipes into use □ **stopcock** *noun* a tap for controlling the flow of liquid through a pipe □ **stopgap** *noun* something which is used in an emergency until something better is found □ **stoppage** *noun* 1 something which blocks up (*eg* a tube or a passage in the body) 2 a halt (*eg* in work in a factory) □ **stopper** *noun* something that stops up an opening (*esp* in the neck of a bottle, jar *etc*) □ **stop press** a space in a newspaper for news put in at the last minute □ **stopwatch** *noun* a watch that can be stopped and started, used in timing races

**stop** *verb* ▷ stops, stopping, stopped

**store** *noun* 1 a supply (*eg* of goods) from which things are taken when needed **2** a place where goods are kept **3** a shop **4** a collected amount or number □ *verb* to put aside for future use □ **storage** *noun* **1** the act of storing **2** the state of being stored: *our furniture is in storage* □ **in store for** awaiting: *trouble in store* □ **set (great) store by** to value highly

**storey** *noun* (*pl* **storeys**) all that part of a building on the same floor

✎. Do not confuse with: **story**

**stork** *noun* a wading bird with a long bill, neck and legs

**storm** *noun* **1** a sudden burst of bad weather (*esp* with heavy rain, lightning, thunder, high wind) **2** a violent outbreak (*eg* of anger) □ *verb* **1** to be in a fury **2** to rain, blow *etc* violently **3** to attack (a stronghold *etc*) violently □ **go down a storm** to be popular or well received □ **storm in a teacup** a great fuss over nothing

**story** *noun* (*pl* **stories**) an account of an event or events, real or imaginary

✎. Do not confuse with: **storey**

**stout** *adj* **1** fat, stocky **2** brave: *stout resistance* **3** strong: *stout walking-stick* □ *noun* a strong, dark-coloured beer □ **stoutness** *noun*

**stove** *noun* an apparatus using coal, gas or electricity *etc*, used for heating, cooking *etc* □ *verb, past form of* **stave**

**stow** *verb* **1** to pack or put away **2** to fill, pack □ **stowaway** *noun* someone who hides in a ship in order to travel without paying a fare

**straddle** *verb* **1** to stand or walk with legs apart **2** to sit with one leg on each side of (*eg* a chair or horse)

**straggle** *verb* **1** to lag behind **2** to grow or spread beyond the intended limits □ **straggler** *noun* □ **straggly** *adj* spread out untidily

**straight** *adj* **1** not bent or curved **2** direct, frank, honest: *a straight*

*answer* **3** in the proper position or order: *your tie isn't straight* **4** of a hanging picture *etc*: placed level with ceiling or floor **5** without anything added: *a straight vodka* **6** expressionless: *he kept a straight face* □ *adv* **1** by the shortest way, directly: *straight across the desert* **2** at once, without delay: *I came straight home* **3** fairly, frankly: *he's not playing straight with you* □ *noun* (**the straight**) the straight part of a racecourse *etc* □ **straighten** *verb* to make straight □ **straightforward** *adj* **1** without any difficulties **2** honest, frank □ **straight away** immediately

⊙ From Old English *streht*

✎. Do not confuse with: **strait**

**strain** *verb* **1** to hurt (a muscle or other part of the body) by overworking or misusing it **2** to work or use to the fullest: *he strained his ears to hear the whisper* **3** to make a great effort: *he strained to reach the rope* **4** to stretch too far, to the point of breaking (a person's patience *etc*) **5** to separate liquid from a mixture of liquids and solids by passing it through a sieve □ *noun* **1** the act of straining **2** a hurt to a muscle *etc* caused by straining it **3** (the effect of) too much work, worry *etc* **4** too great a demand: *a strain on my patience* **5** manner: *they grumbled on in the same strain for hours* **6** a streak: *a strain of selfishness* **7** a tune **8** a kind, breed: *a strain of fowls* □ **strained** *adj* **1** not natural, done with effort: *a strained conversation* **2** unfriendly: *strained relations* □ **strainer** *noun* a sieve

**strait** *noun* **1** a narrow strip of sea between two pieces of land **2** (**straits**) difficulties, hardships: *dire straits*

✎. Do not confuse with: **straight**

**straitened** *adj* poor and needy

**straitjacket** *noun* a jacket with long sleeves tied behind to prevent a violent or insane person from using their arms

**straitlaced** *adj* strict in attitude and behaviour

**strand** *noun* **1** a length of something soft and fine (*eg* hair, thread) **2** *old* the shore of a sea or lake

**stranded** *adj* **1** of a ship: run aground on the shore **2** left helpless without money or friends

**strange** *adj* **1** unusual, odd **2** not known, seen, heard *etc* before, unfamiliar, **3** not accustomed (to) **4** foreign: *a strange country* □ **strangely** *adv* □ **stranger** *noun* **1** someone who is unknown to you **2** a visitor □ **a stranger to** someone who is quite unfamiliar with: *a stranger to hard work*

■ (meaning 1) peculiar, curious, bizarre, funny, perplexing, unexplained; (meaning 2) new, unknown, alien

**strangle** *verb* **1** to kill by gripping or squeezing the throat tightly **2** to keep in, prevent oneself from giving (*eg* a scream, a sigh) **3** to stop the growth of

**strangulate** *verb* to strangle, constrict □ **strangulation** *noun*

**strap** *noun* a narrow strip of leather, cloth *etc* used to hold things in place or together *etc* □ *verb* **1** to bind or fasten with a strap *etc* **2** to beat with a strap □ **strapping** *adj* tall and strong: *strapping young man*

**strap** *verb* ⇔ strap**s**, strap**p**ing, strap**p**ed

**stratagem** *noun* a cunning act, meant to deceive and outwit an enemy

**strategy** *noun* (*pl* **strategies**) the art of guiding, forming or carrying out a plan □ **strategic** *adj* **1** of strategy **2** done according to a strategy: *a strategic retreat* **3** giving an advantage: *a strategic position* □ **strategist** *noun* someone who plans military operations

**stratification** *noun* **1** the formation of strata **2** a stratified condition

**stratosphere** *noun* the layer of the earth's atmosphere between 10 and 60 kilometres above the earth

**stratum** *noun* (*pl* **strata**) **1** a layer of rock or soil **2** a level of society

**straw** *noun* **1** the stalk on which corn grows **2** a paper or plastic tube for sucking up a drink

**strawberry** *noun* a type of small, juicy, red fruit or the low creeping plant which bears it

**stray** *verb* **1** to wander **2** to lose your way, become separated (from companions *etc*) □ *adj* **1** wandering, lost **2** happening *etc* here and there: *a stray example* □ *noun* a wandering animal which has been abandoned or lost

**streak** *noun* **1** a line or strip different in colour from that which surrounds it **2** a smear of dirt, polish *etc* **3** a flash (*eg* of lightning) **4** a trace of some quality in one's character: *a streak of selfishness* □ *verb* **1** to mark with streaks **2** *informal* to move very fast □ **streaked** *adj* having streaks □ **streaky** *adj* marked with streaks □ **streakiness** *noun*

**stream** *noun* **1** a flow (of water, air, light *etc*) **2** a small river, a brook **3** any steady flow of people or thing □ *verb* to flow or pour out

**streamer** *noun* **1** a long strip, usually of paper, used for decorating rooms *etc* (*esp* at Christmas) **2** a narrow flag blowing in the wind

**streamline** *verb* **1** to shape (a vehicle *etc*) so that it may cut through the air or water as easily as possible **2** to make more efficient

**street** *noun* a road lined with houses *etc* □ **streets ahead of** much better *etc* than □ **up someone's street** relating to one's interests or abilities

**strength** *noun* **1** the state of being strong **2** an area of high performance or particular ability: *her greatest strength is her ability to listen to people* □ **on the strength of** encouraged by or counting on □ **strengthen** *verb* to make, or become, strong or stronger

**strenuous** *adj* performed with or needing great effort: *squash is a strenuous game*

**stress** *noun* (*pl* **stresses**) **1** force, pressure, pull *etc* of one thing on another **2** physical or nervous pressure or strain **3** emphasis, importance **4** extra weight laid on a part of a word (as in butter) □ *verb* to put stress, pressure, emphasis or strain on

**stretch** *verb* **1** to draw out to greater length, or too far, or from one point to another **2** to be able to be drawn out to a greater length or width: *this fabric stretches* **3** to (cause to) exert (yourself): *the work stretched him to the full* **4** to hold (out) **5** to make (something, *eg* words, the law) appear to mean more than it does □ *noun* (*pl* **stretches**) **1** the act of stretching **2** the state of being stretched **3** a length in distance or time: *a stretch of bad luck* □ **stretcher** *noun* a light folding bed with handles for carrying the sick or wounded □ **at a stretch** continuously: *working three hours at a stretch* □ **at full stretch** at the limit, using all resources

**strew** *verb* to scatter: *papers strewn over the floor*

**strew** ⋯ strews, strewing, strewed, strewn or strewed

**striated** *adj* streaked

**stricken** *adj* **1** wounded **2** deeply affected (*eg* by illness) **3** struck

**strict** *adj* **1** insisting on exact obedience to rules **2** exact: *the strict meaning of a word* **3** allowing no exception: *strict orders* **4** severe □ **strictly** *adv*

**stricture** *noun* criticism, blame

**stride** *verb* **1** to walk with long steps **2** to take a long step **3** to walk over, along *etc* □ *noun* **1** a long step **2** the distance covered by a step **3** a step forward □ **take in your stride** to manage to do it easily

**stride** ⋯ strides, striding, strode, stridden

**strident** *adj* **1** of a sound: harsh, grating **2** forceful; assertive □ **stridency** *noun*

**strife** *noun* quarrelling; fighting

**strike** *verb* **1** to hit with force **2** to give, deliver (a blow) **3** to knock: *I struck my head on the beam* **4** to attack: *the enemy struck at dawn* **5** to light (a match) **6** to make (a musical note) sound **7** of a clock: to sound (*eg* at ten o'clock with ten chimes) **8** (often with **off** or **out**) to cross out, cancel **9** to hit or discover suddenly: *strike oil* **10** to take a course: *he struck out across the fields* **11** to stop working (in support of a claim for more pay *etc*) **12** to give (someone) the impression of being: *did he strike you as odd?* **13** to affect, impress: *I am struck by her beauty* **14** to make (an agreement *etc*) □ **striking** *adj* **1** noticeable: *a striking resemblance* **2** impressive □ **strike camp** to take down tents □ **strike home 1** of a blow: to hit the point aimed at **2** of a remark: to have the intended effect □ **strike up 1** to begin to play or sing (a tune) **2** to begin (a friendship, conversation *etc*)

**strike** ⋯ strikes, striking, struck

**string** *noun* **1** a long narrow cord for binding, tying *etc* made of threads twisted together **2** a piece of wire or gut producing a note on a musical instrument **3** (**strings**) the stringed instruments in an orchestra **4** a line of objects threaded together: *string of pearls* **5** a number of things coming one after another: *string of abuse* □ *verb* **1** to put on a string **2** to stretch out in a line □ **stringed** *adj*

having strings □ **stringy** adj **1** like
string **2** of meat: tough and fibrous
□ **string along** to give false
expectations to, deceive □ **string up**
to hang

**string** ⇨ string**s**, string**ing**, strung

**stringent** adj strictly enforced:
stringent rules □ **stringency** noun
strictness

**strip** noun a long narrow piece (eg of
paper) □ verb **1** to pull (off) in strips
**2** to remove (eg leaves, fruit) from
**3** to remove the clothes from **4** to
deprive: stripped of his disguise **5** to
make bare or empty: strip the bed
□ **strip-cartoon** noun a line of
drawings which tell a story
□ **striptease** noun an act in which a
performer strips naked

**strip** ⇨ strip**s**, strip**ping**,
strip**ped**

**stripe** noun **1** a band of colour
different from the background on
which it lies **2** a blow with a whip or
rod □ verb to make stripes on
□ **stripy** adj patterned with stripes

**stripling** noun a growing youth

**strive** verb **1** to try hard **2** old to
fight

**strive** ⇨ strive**s**, striv**ing**, strove,
striven

**strobe** noun a light which produces a
flickering beam

**strode** past form of **stride**

**stroke** noun **1** the act of striking **2** a
blow (eg with a sword, whip)
**3** something unexpected: a stroke of
good luck **4** one movement (of a
pen, an oar) **5** one chime of a clock
**6** one complete movement of the
arms and legs in swimming **7** a
particular style of swimming: breast
stroke **8** a way of striking the ball
(eg in tennis, cricket) **9** an
achievement **10** a sudden attack of
illness causing paralysis □ verb to
rub gently, esp as a sign of affection
□ **at a stroke** in a single action or
effort

**stroll** verb to walk slowly in a
leisurely way □ noun a leisurely
walk; an amble

**strong** adj **1** not easily worn away
**2** not easily defeated etc **3** forceful,
not easily resisted: strong wind
**4** very healthy and robust, with
great muscular strength **5** forceful,
commanding respect or obedience
**6** of a smell, colour etc: striking,
very noticeable **7** of a feeling:
intense **8** in number: a workforce
500 strong □ **strongly** adv **1** in a
strong way **2** to a strong degree:
strongly flavoured □ **stronghold**
noun a place built to withstand
attack, a fortress □ **strong point**
something in which a person excels

■ (meaning 1) tough, resilient,
durable, robust, sturdy, stout;
(meaning 4) muscular, lusty,
strapping, burly, beefy, brawny,
sinewy; (meaning 6) intense,
deep, vivid, pungent; (meaning 7)
intense, keen, ardent, vehement

**strop** noun a strip of leather on which
a razor is sharpened □ verb to
sharpen a razor

**strop** ⇨ strop**s**, strop**ping**,
strop**ped**

**stroppy** adj, informal quarrelsome,
disobedient, rowdy

**strove** past form of **strive**

**struck** past form of **strike**

**structure** noun **1** a building; a
framework **2** the way the parts of
anything are arranged: the structure
of the story □ **structural** adj
□ **structurally** adv

**struggle** verb **1** to try hard (to do
something) **2** to twist and fight to
escape **3** to fight (with or against
someone) **4** to move with difficulty:
struggling through the mud □ noun
**1** a great effort **2** a fight

**strum** verb to play (a guitar etc) in a
relaxed way

**strum** ⇨ strum**s**, strum**ming**,

strummed

**strung** *past form of* **string** □ **highly strung** easily excited or agitated

**strut** *verb* to walk in a proud manner □ *noun* **1** a proud way of walking **2** a bar *etc* which supports something

**strut** *verb* ⋄ struts, strutting, strutted

**strychnine** *noun* a bitter, poisonous drug

**stub** *noun* a small stump (*eg* of a pencil, cigarette) □ *verb* **1** to put out, (*eg* a cigarette) by pressure against something **2** to knock (your toe) painfully against something

**stub** *verb* ⋄ stubs, stubbing, stubbed

**stubble** *noun* **1** the short ends of the stalks of corn left after it is cut **2** a short growth of beard

**stubborn** *adj* **1** unwilling to give way, obstinate **2** of resistance *etc*: strong, determined **3** difficult to manage or deal with □ **stubbornly** *adv* □ **stubbornness** *noun*

**stubby** *adj* short, thick and strong: *stubby fingers*

**stucco** *noun* (*pl* **stuccos**) **1** a kind of plaster used for covering walls, moulding ornaments *etc* **2** work done in stucco

**stuck** *past form of* **stick**

**stud** *noun* **1** a nail with a large head **2** a decorative knob on a surface **3** a button with two heads for fastening a collar **4** a collection of horses kept for breeding □ *verb* **1** to cover or fit with studs **2** to sprinkle thickly (with): *the crown is studded with jewels*

**student** *noun* someone who studies, *esp* at college, university *etc*

**studied** *adj* **1** done on purpose, intentional: *a studied insult* **2** too careful, not natural: *a studied smile*

**studio** *noun* (*pl* **studios**) **1** the workshop of an artist or photographer **2** a building or place in which cinema films are made **3** a

room from which television or radio programmes are broadcast

**studious** *adj* **1** studying carefully and much **2** careful: *his studious avoidance of quarrels* □ **studiously** *adv*

**study** *verb* **1** to gain knowledge of (a subject) by reading, experiment *etc* **2** to look carefully at **3** to consider carefully (*eg* a problem) □ *noun* (*pl* **studies**) **1** the gaining of knowledge of a subject **2** a room where someone reads and writes **3** a piece of music which is meant to develop the skill of the player **4** a work of art done as an exercise, or to try out ideas for a later work

**study** *verb* ⋄ studies, studying, studied

**stuff** *noun* **1** the material of which anything is made **2** cloth, fabric **3** substance or material of any kind □ *verb* **1** to pack full **2** to fill the skin of (a dead animal) to preserve it **3** to fill (a prepared bird) with stuffing before cooking □ **stuffing** *noun* **1** feathers, scraps of material *etc* used to stuff a cushion, chair *etc* **2** breadcrumbs, onions *etc* packed inside a fowl or other meat and cooked with it □ **stuffy** *adj* **1** full of stale air, badly ventilated **2** *informal* dull, having old-fashioned ideas □ **stuffily** *adv* □ **stuffed shirt** an inflexible, old-fashioned person □ **get stuffed** *slang* get lost, go away

**stultify** *verb* to dull the mind, make stupid

**stultify** ⋄ stultifies, stultifying, stultified

**stumble** *verb* **1** to trip in walking **2** to walk unsteadily, as if blind **3** to make mistakes or hesitate in speaking **4** (with **on**) to find by chance □ *noun* the act of stumbling □ **stumbling block** a difficulty in the way of a plan or of progress

**stump** *noun* **1** the part of a tree, leg, tooth *etc* left after the main part has been cut away **2** *cricket* one of the three wooden stakes which make up a wicket □ *verb*, *cricket* **1** to put out (a batsman) by touching the stumps with the ball **2** to puzzle completely **3** to walk stiffly or heavily □ **stump up** *informal* to pay up □ **stumpy** *adj* short and thick

**stun** *verb* **1** to knock senseless (by a blow *etc*) **2** to surprise or shock very greatly

**stun** *verb* ⇔ stun*s*, stun*ning*, stun*ned*

**stung** *past form* of **sting**

**stunk** *past form* & *past participle* of **stink**

**stunt** *noun* **1** a daring trick **2** something done to attract attention □ *verb* to stop the growth of □ **stunted** *adj* small and badly shaped

**stupefy** *verb* **1** to make stupid, deaden the feelings of **2** to astonish □ **stupefaction** *noun*

**stupefy** ⇔ stupefie*s*, stupefy*ing*, stupefie*d*

**stupendous** *adj* wonderful, amazing (*eg* because of size and power)

**stupid** *adj* **1** foolish **2** dull, slow at learning **3** stupefied (*eg* from lack of sleep) □ **stupidity** *noun*

◼ (meaning 1) silly, ill-advised, foolhardy, inane, puerile, mindless

**stupor** *noun* the state of being only partly conscious

**sturdy** *adj* strong, well built; healthy □ **sturdily** *adv*

**sturgeon** *noun* a type of large fish from which caviare is taken

**stutter** *verb* to speak in a halting, jerky way; stammer □ *noun* a stammer

**sty**¹ *noun* (*pl* **sties**) a pen in which pigs are kept

**sty**² *or* **stye** *noun* (*pl* **sties** *or* **styes**) an inflamed swelling on the eyelid

**style** *noun* **1** manner of acting, writing, speaking *etc* **2** fashion **3** an air of elegance **4** the middle part of the pistil of a flower □ *verb* to design or arrange something in a certain way □ **stylish** *adj* smart, elegant, fashionable □ **stylized** *adj* elaborate, *esp* creating an impression of unnaturalness □ **in style** with no expense or effort spared

**stylus** *noun* (*pl* **styluses**) a needle for a record-player

**suave** (*say* swahv) *adj* of a person: superficially polite and sophisticated, smooth

**sub-** *prefix* **1** under, below **2** less than **3** lower in rank or importance ⊚ From Latin *sub* meaning 'under' or 'near'

**subaltern** (*say* sub-al-ten) *noun* an officer in the army under the rank of captain

**subconscious** *noun* the contents of the mind of which someone is not themselves aware □ *adj* of the subconscious, not conscious or aware

**subdivide** *verb* to divide into smaller parts □ **subdivision** *noun*

**subdue** *verb* **1** to conquer (an enemy *etc*) **2** to keep under control (*eg* a desire) **3** to make less bright (*eg* a colour, a light) **4** to make quieter

**subject** *adj* (*say* sub-jekt) **1** under the power of another: *a subject nation* **2** (with **to**) liable to suffer from (*eg* colds) **3** (with **to**) depending on: *subject to your approval* □ *noun* (*say* sub-jekt) **1** someone under the power of another: *the king's subjects* **2** a member of a nation with a monarchy: *a British subject* **3** something or someone spoken about, studied *etc* **4** *grammar* the word in a sentence or clause which stands for the person or thing doing the action of the verb (*eg cat* is the subject in 'the *cat* drank the milk') □ *verb* (*say* sub-**jekt**) (often with **to**) to force them to submit (to) □ **subjection** *noun* the act of subjecting or the state of being subjected

**subjective** *adj* based on personal feelings, thoughts *etc*, not impartial (*contrasted with:* **objective**) ▫ **subjectivity** *noun*

**subjugate** *verb* to bring under your power; make obedient

**subjunctive** *adj, grammar* of a verb: in a form which indicates possibility *etc*, *eg* 'were' in: *If I were you* ▫ *noun* a subjunctive form of a verb

**sublet** *verb* to let out (rented property) to another person, *eg* while the original tenant is away

**sublime** *adj* very noble, great or grand ▫ **subliminal** *adj* working below the level of consciousness: *subliminal messages*

**submarine** *noun* a type of ship which can travel under water ▫ *adj* under the surface of the sea

**submerge** *verb* to cover with water; sink ▫ **submergence** or **submersion** *noun*

**submit** *verb* 1 to give in, yield 2 to place (a matter) before someone for making a judgement ▫ **submission** *noun* 1 the act of submitting 2 readiness to yield, meekness 3 an idea, statement *etc* offered for consideration ▫ **submissive** *adj*

**submit** ⟳ submit*s*, submit*ting*, submit*ted*

**subordinate** *adj* (*say* su-baw-din-*a*t) (often *with* **to**) lower in rank or importance (than) ▫ *noun* (*say* su-baw-din-*a*t) someone who is subordinate ▫ *verb* (*say* su-baw-din-eit) (*with* **to**) to consider as being of less importance ▫ **subordination** *noun*

**suborn** *verb* to persuade (someone) to do something illegal, *esp* by bribery

**subpoena** (*say* su-pee-na) *noun* an order for someone to appear in court ▫ *verb* to order to appear in court

**subscribe** *verb* 1 to make a contribution (*esp* of money) towards a charity 2 to promise to take and pay for a number of issues of a magazine *etc* 3 (*with* **to**) to agree with (an idea, statement *etc*) ▫ **subscription** *noun* a payment for *eg* a club membership fee or a number of issues of a magazine for a given period

**subsequent** *adj* following, coming after

**subservient** *adj* weak-willed, ready to do as you are told ▫ **subservience** *noun*

**subside** *verb* 1 to settle down, sink lower 2 of noise *etc*: to get less and less ▫ **subsidence** *noun* a sinking down, *esp* into the ground

**subsidiary** *adj* 1 acting as a help 2 of less importance 3 of a company: controlled by another company

**subsidy** *noun* (*pl* **subsidies**) money paid by a government *etc* to help an industry ▫ **subsidize** *verb*

**subsist** *verb* 1 to exist 2 (*with* **on**) to live on (a kind of food *etc*) ▫ **subsistence** *noun* 1 existence 2 means or necessities for survival

**subsoil** *noun* the layer of the earth just below the surface soil

**substance** *noun* 1 a material that can be seen and felt 2 general meaning (of a talk, essay *etc*) 3 thickness, solidity 4 wealth, property: *a woman of substance*

**substantial** *adj* 1 solid, strong 2 large: *a substantial building* 3 able to be seen and felt 4 in the main, but not in detail: *substantial agreement* ▫ **substantially** *adv* for the most part; *substantially the same*

**substantiate** *verb* to give proof of, or evidence for

**substitute** *verb*: (*with* **for**) to put in place of or instead of ▫ *noun* someone or thing used instead of another ▫ **substitution** *noun* 1 the process of substituting or being substituted

**2** something that is substituted

**subterfuge** *noun* a cunning trick to get out of a difficulty *etc*

**subterranean** *adj* found under the ground

**subtitle** *noun* **1** a second additional title of a book *etc* **2** a translation of a foreign-language film, appearing at the bottom of the screen

**subtle** (*say* su-tl) *adj* **1** difficult to describe or explain: *a subtle difference* **2** cunning: *by a subtle means* □ **subtlety** (*say* su-tl-ti) *noun* (*pl* **subtleties**) □ **subtly** *adv*

**subtotal** *noun* a total of one set of figures within a larger group

**subtract** *verb* **1** to take away (a part from) **2** to take away (one number from another) □ **subtraction** *noun*

**suburb** *noun* a residential area on the outskirts of a town □ **suburban** *adj* □ **suburbia** *noun* the suburbs

**subversive** *adj* likely to overthrow (government, discipline *etc*)

**subway** *noun* **1** an underground crossing for pedestrians *etc* **2** an underground railway

**succeed** *verb* **1** (with **in**) to manage to do what you have been trying to do **2** to get on well **3** to take the place of, follow **4** (often with **to**) to follow in order (to the throne *etc*)

**success** *noun* (*pl* **successes**) **1** the achievement of something you have been trying to do **2** someone who succeeds **3** something that turns out well □ **successful** *adj* **1** having achieved what was aimed at **2** having achieved wealth, importance *etc* **3** turning out as planned

**succession** *noun* **1** the act of following after **2** the right of becoming the next holder (of a throne *etc*) **3** a number of things coming one after the other: *a succession of failures* □ **in succession** one after another □ **successive** *adj* following one after

the other □ **successor** *noun* who comes after, follows in a post *etc*

**succinct** *adj* in a few words, brief, concise: *a succinct reply*

**succour** *verb* to help in time of distress □ *noun* help

**succulent** *adj* **1** juicy **2** of a plant: having thick, juicy leaves or stems

**succumb** *verb* to yield (to)

**such** *adj* **1** of a kind previously mentioned: *such things are difficult to find* **2** similar: *doctors, nurses and such people* **3** so great: *his excitement was such that he gave a yell* **4** used for emphasis: *it's such a disappointment!* □ *pronoun* thing, people *etc* of a kind already mentioned: *such as these are not to be trusted* □ **such-and-such** *adj* & *pronoun* any given (person or thing): *such-and-such a book* □ **as such** by itself □ **such as** of the same kind as

**suck** *verb* **1** to draw into the mouth **2** to draw milk from with the mouth **3** to hold in the mouth and lick hard (*eg* a sweet) **4** (often with **up** or **in**) to draw in, absorb □ *noun* **1** a sucking action **2** the act of sucking

**sucker** *noun* **1** a side shoot rising from the root of a plant **2** a part of an animal's body by which it sticks to objects **3** a pad (of rubber *etc*) which can stick to a surface **4** *informal* someone easily fooled

**suckle** *verb* of a woman or female animal: to give milk from the breast or teat □ **suckling** *noun* a baby or young animal which still sucks its mother's milk

**suction** *noun* **1** the act of sucking **2** the process of reducing the air pressure, and so producing a vacuum, on the surface or between surfaces

**sudden** *adj* happening all at once without being expected □ **suddenly** *adv* □ **suddenness** *noun*

**suds** *noun pl* frothy, soapy water

**sue** verb to start a law case against

**suede** (say sweid) noun a kind of leather with a soft, dull surface

**suet** noun a kind of hard animal fat

**suffer** verb 1 to feel pain or punishment 2 to bear, endure 3 old to allow 4 to go through, undergo (a change etc) □ **suffering** noun pain or distress □ **on sufferance** allowed or tolerated but not really wanted

**suffice** verb to be enough, or good enough

**sufficient** adj enough □ **sufficiently** adv

**suffix** noun (pl **suffixes**) a small part added to the end of a word to make another word, such as -ness to good to make goodness, -ly to quick to make quickly etc

**suffocate** verb 1 to kill by preventing the breathing of 2 to die from lack of air 3 to feel unable to breathe freely: suffocating in this heat □ **suffocation** noun

**suffrage** noun 1 a vote 2 the right to vote

**suffuse** verb to spread over

**sugar** noun a sweet substance obtained mostly from sugar-cane and sugar-beet □ verb to mix or sprinkle with sugar □ **sugary** adj

**suggest** verb 1 to put forward, propose (an idea etc) 2 to put into the mind, hint □ **suggestible** adj easily influenced by suggestions □ **suggestion** noun 1 an act of suggesting 2 an idea put forward 3 a slight trace: a suggestion of anger in her voice □ **suggestive** adj 1 that suggests something particular, esp sexually improper 2 (with of) giving the idea of: suggestive of mental illness

**suicide** noun 1 the taking of your own life 2 someone who kills themselves □ **suicidal** adj 1 of or considering suicide 2 likely to cause your death or ruin: suicidal action

**suit** noun 1 a set of clothes to be worn together 2 a case in a law court 3 old a request for permission to court a woman 4 one of the four divisions (spades, hearts, diamonds, clubs) of playing-cards □ verb 1 to be convenient or suitable for: the climate suits me 2 to look well on: that dress suits you 3 (with **to**) to make fitting or suitable for: suited his words to the occasion □ **suitability** noun □ **suitable** adj □ **suitcase** noun a travelling case for carrying clothes etc □ **follow suit** to do just as someone else has done

**suite** (say sweet) noun 1 a number of things in a set, eg rooms, furniture, pieces of music 2 a group of attendants for an important person

**suitor** noun a man who tries to gain the love of a woman

**sulk** verb to keep silent because of being displeased □ **the sulks** a fit of sulking □ **sulky** adj

**sullen** adj angry and silent, sulky □ **sullenness** noun

**sully** verb to make less pure, dirty □ **sully ⋅** sullies, sullying, sullied

**sulphur** noun a yellow substance found in the ground which gives off a choking smell when burnt, used in matches, gunpowder etc □ **sulphuric acid** a powerful acid much used in industry

**sultan** noun 1 historical the head of the Turkish Ottoman empire 2 an Islamic ruler

**sultana** noun 1 a sultan's wife 2 a light-coloured raisin

**sultry** adj 1 of weather: very hot and close 2 passionate, steamy

**sum** noun 1 the amount made by two or more things added together 2 a quantity of money 3 a problem in arithmetic 4 the general meaning (of something said or written) □ **sum up** to give the main points of (a discussion, evidence in a trial etc)

**summary** noun (pl **summaries**) a shortened form (of a story, statement *etc*) giving only the main points □ *adj* **1** short, brief **2** done without wasting time or words □ **summarily** *adv: he was summarily dismissed* □ **summarize** *verb* to state briefly, make a summary of

**summer** *noun* the warmest season of the year □ *adj* of or in summer □ **summerhouse** *noun* a small house in a garden for sitting in

**summit** *noun* the highest point of a hill *etc*

**summon** *verb* **1** to order (someone) to come to you, appear in a court of law *etc* **2** (with **up**) to gather up (courage, strength *etc*)

**summons** *noun* (*pl* **summonses**) an order to appear in court

**sumo** *noun* a Japanese form of wrestling

**sump** *noun* **1** part of a motor-engine which contains the oil **2** a small drainage pit

**sumptuous** *adj* costly, splendid

**sun** *noun* **1** the round body in the sky which gives light and heat to the earth **2** sunshine □ *verb* (with **yourself**) to lie in the sunshine, sunbathe □ **sunny** *adj* **1** full of sunshine **2** cheerful □ **sunbathe** *verb* to lie or sit in the sun to acquire a suntan □ **sunbeam** *noun* a ray of light from the sun □ **sunburn** *noun* a burning or redness caused by over-exposure to the sun □ **sunburned** or **sunburnt** *adj* affected by sunburn □ **sundial** *noun* an instrument for telling the time from the shadow of a rod on its surface cast by the sun □ **sunflower** *noun* a large yellow flower with petals like rays of the sun □ **sunglasses** *noun pl* spectacles with tinted lenses that shield the eyes from sunlight □ **sunlight** *noun* the light from the sun □ **sunlit** *adj* lighted up by the sun □ **sunrise** *noun* the rising of the sun in the morning □ **sunset** *noun* the setting of the sun in the evening □ **sunshine** *noun* **1** bright sunlight **2** cheerfulness

□ **sunstroke** *noun* a serious illness caused by over-exposure to very hot sunshine □ **suntan** *noun* a browning of the skin caused by exposure to the sun

**sun** *verb* ⇔ **suns, sunning, sunned**

**sundae** *noun* a sweet dish of ice-cream served with fruit, syrup *etc*

**Sunday** *noun* the first day of the week, the Christian Sabbath

**sunder** *verb, old* to separate, part

**sundries** *noun pl* odds and ends

**sundry** *adj* several, various: *sundry articles for sale*

**sung** *past participle* of **sing**

**sunk** *adj* **1** on a lower level than the surroundings; sunken **2** *informal* defeated, done for □ **sunken** *adj* **1** that has been sunk **2** of cheeks *etc*: hollow

**sup** *verb* to eat or drink in small mouthfuls

**sup** ⇔ **sups, supping, supped**

**super** *adj, informal* extremely good

**super-** *prefix* above, beyond, very, too □ **superannuate** *verb* to make (someone) retire from their job because of old age □ **superannuation** *noun* □ **supercilious** *adj* looking down on others, haughty □ **superficial** *adj* **1** of a wound: affecting the surface of the skin only, not deep **2** not thorough or detailed **3** apparent at first glance, not actual: *superficial likeness* **4** of a person: not capable of deep thoughts or feelings □ **superficially** *adv* □ **superficiality** *noun* □ **superfluous** (*say* soo-per-floo-us) *adj* beyond what is enough or necessary □ **superfluity** (*say* soo-pe-**floo**-it-i) *noun* □ **superhuman** *adj* **1** divine, godly **2** greater than would be expected of an ordinary person: *superhuman effort* □ **superimpose** *verb* to lay or place (one thing on another) □ **superintend** *verb* to be in charge or control, manage

□ **superintendent** *noun* **1** someone who is in charge of an institution, building *etc* **2** a police officer above a chief inspector □ **superlative** *adj* **1** better than, or going beyond, all others: *superlative skill* **2** *grammar* an adj or adv of the highest degree of comparison, *eg* kindest, worst, most quickly □ **supersonic** *adj* faster than the speed of sound □ **supervene** *verb* to come after or in addition □ **supervise** *verb* to be in charge of work and see that it is properly done □ **supervision** *noun* □ **supervisor** *noun*

**superb** *adj* magnificent, very fine, excellent: *a superb view*

**superior** *adj* **1** higher in place or rank **2** better or greater than others: *superior goods* **3** having an air of being better than others □ *noun* someone better than, or higher in rank than, others □ **superiority** *noun*

**supermarket** *noun* a large self-service store selling food *etc*

**supernatural** *adj* not happening in the ordinary course of nature, miraculous

**supernova** *noun* an exploding star surrounded by a bright cloud of gas

**supersede** *verb* **1** to take the place of **2** to replace (something with something else)

**superstition** *noun* **1** belief in magic and in things which cannot be explained by reason **2** an example of such belief (*eg* not walking under ladders) □ **superstitious** *adj*

**supine** *adj* **1** lying on the back **2** not showing any interest or energy

**supper** *noun* a meal taken in the evening

**supplant** *verb* to take the place of somebody or of something

**supple** *adj* **1** bending easily, flexible **2** of an object: bending easily without breaking □ **supply** (*say* sup-li) *adv*

**supplement** *noun* **1** something added to supply a need or lack **2** a special section added to the main part of a newspaper or magazine □ *verb* to make or be an addition to □ **supplementary** *adj*

**suppliant** *adj* asking earnestly and humbly □ *noun* someone who asks in this way

**supplicate** *verb* to ask earnestly, beg □ **supplication** *noun*

**supply** *verb* **1** to provide (what is wanted or needed) **2** to provide (someone with something) □ *noun* (*pl* **supplies**) **1** an act of supplying **2** something supplied **3** a stock or store **4** (**supplies**) a stock of essentials, *eg* food, equipment, money *etc* □ *adj* of a teacher: filling another's place or position for a time

**supply** *verb* ⇔ supplies, supplying, supplied

**support** *verb* **1** to hold up, take part of the weight of **2** to help, encourage **3** to supply with a means of living: *support a family* □ *noun* **1** an act of supporting **2** something that supports □ **supporter** *noun* someone who supports (*esp* a football club)

**suppose** *verb* **1** to take as true, assume for the sake of argument: *suppose that we have £100 to spend* **2** to believe, think probable: *I suppose you know* **3** used to give a polite order: *suppose you leave now* □ **supposed** *adj* believed (often mistakenly) to be so: *her supposed generosity* □ **supposedly** *adv* □ **supposition** *noun* □ **be supposed to** to be required or expected to (do) □ **supposing** in the event that: *supposing it rains*

**suppress** *verb* **1** to crush, put down (a rebellion *etc*) **2** to keep back (a yawn, a piece of news *etc*) □ **suppression** *noun*

**supreme** *adj* **1** highest, most powerful **2** greatest: *supreme* *courage* □ **supremacy** *noun* highest power or authority

──────────────

■ (meaning I) absolute

──────────────

**surcharge** *noun* an extra charge or tax

**sure** *adj* 1 having no doubt: *I'm sure that I can come* 2 certain (to do, happen *etc*): *he is sure to be there* 3 reliable, dependable: *a sure method* □ **sure-footed** *adj* unlikely to slip or stumble □ **be sure** to see to it that: *be sure that he does it* □ **make sure** to act so that, or check that, something is sure □ **sure of yourself** confident □ **to be sure** 1 certainly! 2 undoubtedly: *to be sure, you are correct*

**surely** *adv* 1 certainly, without doubt 2 sometimes expressing a little doubt: *surely you won't tell him?* 3 without hesitation, mistake *etc*

**surety** *noun* (*pl* **sureties**) 1 someone who promises that another person will do something (*esp* appear in court) 2 a pledge, a guarantee

**surf** *noun* the foam made by the breaking of waves □ **surfer** *noun* someone who surfs □ **surfing** *noun* the sport of riding on a surfboard □ **surfboard** *noun* a long, narrow board on which someone can ride over the surf

**surface** *noun* the outside or top part of anything (*eg* of the earth, of a road *etc*) □ *verb* 1 to come up to the surface of (water *etc*) 2 to put a (smooth) surface on □ *adj* 1 on the surface 2 travelling on the surface of land or water: *surface mail*

**surfeit** *noun* too much of anything

**surge** *verb* 1 to move (forward) like waves 2 to rise suddenly or excessively □ *noun* 1 the swelling of a large wave 2 a swelling or rising movement like this 3 a sudden rise or increase (of pain *etc*)

**surgeon** *noun* a doctor who performs operations, often cutting

the body open to examine or remove a diseased part

**surgery** *noun* (*pl* **surgeries**) 1 treatment of diseases *etc* by operation 2 a doctor's or dentist's consulting room □ **surgical** *adj* □ **surgically** *adv*

**surly** *adj* gruff, rude, ill-mannered □ **surliness** *noun*

**surmise** *verb* to suppose, guess □ *noun* a supposition

**surmount** *verb* 1 to overcome (a difficulty *etc*) 2 to climb over, get over □ **surmountable** *adj*

**surname** *noun* a person's last name or family name

**surpass** *verb* to go beyond, be more or better than

**surplice** (*say* ser-plis) *noun* a loose white gown worn by members of the clergy
 ⓘ From Late Latin *superpellicium* meaning 'an overgarment'

❧ Do not confuse: **surplice** and **surplus**

**surplus** (*say* ser-plus) *noun* the amount left over after what is needed has been used up □ *adj* left over, extra
 ⓘ From French word-beginning *sur-* meaning 'over', and *plus* meaning 'more'

**surprise** *noun* 1 the feeling caused by an unexpected happening 2 an unexpected happening □ *verb* 1 to cause someone to feel surprise 2 to come upon (someone) suddenly and without warning □ **take by surprise** to come upon, or capture, without warning □ **surprised** *adj*

**surreal** *adj* dreamlike, using images from the subconscious □ **surrealism** *noun* □ **surrealist** *noun* □ *adj*

**surrender** *verb* 1 to give up, give in, yield 2 to hand over: *she surrendered the note to the teacher* □ *noun* an act of surrender, *esp* in a war

**surreptitious** *adj* done in a secret, underhand way

**surrogate** *adj* used or acting as a substitute for another person or thing: *a surrogate mother* □ *noun* a substitute

**surround** *verb* **1** to be all round (someone or something) **2** to enclose, put round □ *noun* a border □ **surroundings** *noun pl* **1** the country lying round a place **2** the people and places with which you have to deal in daily life

**surveillance** *noun* a close watch or constant guard

**survey** *verb* **1** to look over **2** to inspect, examine **3** to make careful measurements of (a piece of land *etc*) □ *noun* (*pl* **surveys**) **1** a general view **2** a detailed examination or inspection **3** a piece of writing giving results of this **4** a careful measuring of land *etc* **5** a map made with the measurements obtained □ **surveyor** *noun* someone who makes surveys of land, buildings *etc*

**survey** *verb* ↔ surveys, survey*ing*, survey*ed*

**survive** *verb* **1** to remain alive, continue to exist (after an event *etc*) **2** to live longer than: *he survived his wife* □ **survival** *noun* **1** the state of surviving **2** a custom, relic *etc* that remains from earlier times □ **survivor** *noun*

**susceptible** *adj* **1** (with **to**) liable to be affected by: *susceptible to colds* **2** easily affected or moved □ **susceptibility** *noun* (*pl* **susceptibilities**) **1** the state or degree of being susceptible to something **2** (**susceptibilities**) strong feelings or sensibilities

**suspect** *verb* (*say* **sus**-pekt) **1** to be inclined to think (someone) guilty **2** to distrust, have doubts about: *I suspected his air of frankness* **3** to guess: *I suspect that we're wrong* □ *noun* (*say* **sus**-pekt) someone thought to be guilty of a crime *etc*

□ *adj* (*say* **sus**-pekt) arousing doubt, suspected

**suspend** *verb* **1** to hang **2** to keep from falling or sinking: *particles suspended in a liquid* **3** to stop for a time: *suspend business* **4** to take away a job, privilege *etc* from for a time: *they suspended the student from classes*

**suspender** *noun* **1** an elastic strap to keep up socks or stockings **2** (**suspenders**) *US* braces

**suspense** *noun* **1** a state of being undecided **2** a state of uncertainty or worry

**suspension** *noun* **1** the act of suspending **2** the state of being suspended **3** the state of a solid which is mixed with a liquid or gas and does not sink or dissolve in it □ **suspension bridge** a bridge which is suspended from cables hanging from towers

**suspicion** *noun* **1** a feeling of doubt or mistrust **2** an opinion, a guess □ **suspicious** *adj* **1** inclined to suspect or distrust **2** arousing suspicion □ **suspiciously** *adv*

**sustain** *verb* **1** to hold up, support **2** to bear (an attack *etc*) without giving way **3** to suffer (an injury *etc*) **4** to give strength to: *the food will sustain you* **5** to keep up, keep going

**sustenance** *noun* food, nourishment

**suzerain** *noun* **1** a feudal lord **2** a supreme ruler

**svelte** *adj* slender, trim

**SW** *abbrev* south-west; south-western

**swab** *noun* **1** a mop for cleaning a ship's deck **2** a piece of cottonwool used for cleaning, absorbing blood *etc* □ *verb* to clean with a swab

**swab** *verb* ↔ swabs, swab*bing*, swab*bed*

**swaddle** *verb* to wrap up (a young baby) tightly □ **swaddling clothes** *old* strips of cloth used to wrap up a young baby

**swag** noun, Austral informal a bundle of possessions

**swagger** verb 1 to walk proudly, swinging the arms and body 2 to boast □ noun a proud walk or attitude

**swain** noun, old a young man

**swallow**[1] verb 1 to pass (food or drink) down the throat into the stomach 2 (with **up**) to make disappear 3 to receive (an insult etc) without objection 4 to keep back (tears, a laugh etc) □ noun an act of swallowing

**swallow**[2] noun a bird with pointed wings and a forked tail

**swamp** noun wet, marshy ground □ verb 1 to fill (a boat) with water 2 to overwhelm: swamped with work

**swan** noun a large, stately water bird, with white feathers and a long neck

**swank** verb, informal to show off

**swan song** the last work of a musician, writer etc

**swap** or **swop** verb to give one thing in exchange for another: swap addresses

**swap** or **swop** verb ⇨ swaps or swops, swapping or swopping, swapped or swopped

**swarm** noun 1 a large number of insects flying or moving together 2 a dense moving crowd □ verb 1 of insects: to gather together in great numbers 2 to move in crowds 3 to be crowded with: swarming with tourists 4 (with **up**) to climb up (a wall etc)

**swarthy** adj dark-skinned

**swashbuckling** adj bold, swaggering

**swastika** noun an ancient design of a cross with bent arms, taken up as a symbol of Nazism

**swat** verb to squash (a fly etc) □ noun an instrument for squashing insects

**swat** verb ⇨ swats, swatting, swatted

**swath** or **swathe** noun 1 a line of

corn or grass cut by a scythe 2 a strip

**swathe**[1] verb to wrap round with clothes or bandages

**swathe**[2] another spelling of **swath**

**sway** verb 1 to swing or rock to and fro 2 to bend in one direction or to one side 3 to influence □ noun 1 a swaying movement 2 rule, power: hold sway over

**swear** verb 1 to promise or declare solemnly 2 to vow 3 to curse, using the name of God or other sacred things without respect 4 to make (someone) take an oath: to swear someone to secrecy □ **swear word** a word used in swearing or cursing □ **swear by** to rely on, have complete faith in

**swear** ⇨ swears, swearing, swore, sworn

**sweat** noun moisture secreted by the skin, perspiration □ verb 1 to give out sweat 2 informal to work hard □ **sweaty** adj wet, or stained with, sweat

**sweater** noun a jersey, a pullover

**swede** noun a kind of large yellow turnip

**sweep** verb 1 to clean (a floor etc) with a brush or broom 2 (often with **up**) to gather up (dust etc) by sweeping 3 to carry (away, along, off) with a long brushing movement 4 to travel over quickly, move with speed: a new fad which is sweeping the country 5 to move quickly in a proud manner (eg from a room) 6 (with **of**) to clear of: sweep the sea of enemy mines 7 to curve widely or stretch far □ noun 1 a sweeping movement 2 a curve, a stretch 3 a chimney sweeper 4 a sweepstake □ **sweeping** adj 1 that sweeps 2 of a victory etc: great, overwhelming 3 of a statement etc: too general, allowing no exceptions, rash

**sweep** verb ⇨ sweeps, sweeping, swept

**sweepstake** *noun* a gambling system in which those who take part stake money which goes to the holder of the winning ticket

**sweet** *adj* 1 having the taste of sugar, not salty, sour or bitter 2 pleasing to the taste 3 pleasant to hear or smell 4 kindly, agreeable, charming □ *noun* 1 a small piece of sweet substance, *eg* chocolate, toffee *etc* 2 something sweet served towards the end of a meal, a pudding □ **sweetly** *adv* in a sweet way □ **sweetness** *noun* a sweet quality □ **sweetbreads** *noun pl* an animal's pancreas used for food □ **sweetcorn** *noun* maize □ **sweeten** *verb* to make or become sweet □ **sweetener** *noun* 1 an artificial substance used to sweeten food or drinks 2 *informal* a bribe □ **sweetheart** *noun* a lover □ **sweetmeat** *noun, old* a sweet, a confection □ **sweet pea** a sweet-smelling climbing flower grown in gardens □ **sweet talk** flattery, persuasion □ **sweet tooth** a liking for sweet-tasting things

**swell** *verb* 1 to grow in size or volume 2 of the sea: to rise into waves □ *noun* 1 an increase in size or volume 2 large, heaving waves 3 a gradual rise in the height of the ground 4 a dandy □ *adj, US informal* fine, splendid □ **swelling** *noun* a swollen part of the body, a lump

**swell** *verb* ↪ swells, swelling, swelled, swollen

**swelter** *verb* to be too hot □ **sweltering** *adj*

**swept** *past form* of **sweep**

**swerve** *verb* to turn quickly to one side □ *noun* a quick turn aside

**swift** *adj* moving quickly; rapid □ *noun* a bird rather like the swallow □ **swiftly** *adv*

**swig** *noun, informal* a mouthful of liquid, a large drink □ *verb, informal* to gulp down

**swig** *verb* ↪ swigs, swigging, swigged

**swill** *verb* 1 to wash out 2 *informal* to drink a great deal □ *noun* 1 partly liquid food given to pigs 2 *informal* a big drink

**swim** *verb* 1 to move on or in water, using arms, legs, fins *etc* 2 to cross by swimming: *swim the Channel* 3 to float, not sink 4 to move with a gliding motion 5 to be dizzy 6 to be covered (with liquid): *meat swimming in grease* □ *noun* an act of swimming □ **swimmer** *noun* someone or something that swims □ **swimming bath** or **swimming pool** a large water-filled tank designed for swimming, diving in *etc* □ **swimming costume** or **swimsuit** *noun* a brief close-fitting garment for swimming in □ **swimmingly** *adv* smoothly, easily, successfully

**swim** *verb* ↪ swims, swimming, swam, swum

**swindle** *verb* 1 to cheat, defraud 2 to get (money *etc* from someone) by cheating □ *noun* a fraud, a deception □ **swindler** *noun* a person who swindles others

**swine** *noun* (*pl* **swine**) 1 *old* a pig 2 *informal* a contemptible person □ **swineherd** *noun, old* someone who looks after pigs

**swing** *verb* 1 to move to and fro, sway 2 to move backwards and forwards on a swinging seat 3 to turn or whirl round 4 to walk quickly, moving the arms to and fro □ *noun* 1 a swinging movement 2 a seat for swinging, hung on ropes *etc* from a support □ **in full swing** going on busily

**swing** *verb* ↪ swings, swinging, swung

⊙ From Old English *swingan*

**swingeing** (*say* swin-jing) *adj* very great: *swingeing cuts in taxation* ⊙ From Old English *swengan* meaning 'to shake'

👆 Do not confuse with: **swinging**

**swipe** verb to strike with a sweeping blow □ noun a sweeping blow

**swirl** verb to sweep along with a whirling motion □ noun a whirling movement

**swish** verb 1 to strike or brush against with a rustling sound 2 to move making such a noise: swishing out of the room in her long dress □ noun a rustling sound or movement

**switch** noun (pl **switches**) 1 a small lever or handle, eg for turning an electric current on and off 2 an act of switching 3 a change: a switch of loyalty 4 a thin stick □ verb 1 to strike with a switch 2 to turn (off or on) by means of a switch 3 to change, turn: switch jobs □ **switchback** noun a road or railway with steep ups and downs or sharp turns □ **switchboard** noun a board with equipment for making telephone connections

**swivel** noun a joint that turns on a pin or pivot □ verb to turn on a swivel, pivot

**swivel** verb ⇔ swivels, swivel**ling**, swivel**led**

**swollen** adj increased in size by swelling □ verb, past form of **swell**

**swoon** verb, old to faint □ noun a fainting fit

**swoop** verb to come down with a sweep, like a bird of prey □ noun a sudden downward rush □ **at one fell swoop** all at one time, at a stroke

**swop** another spelling of **swap**

**sword** noun a type of weapon with a long blade for cutting or piercing □ **swordfish** noun a large type of fish with a long pointed upper jaw like a sword

**swore** past form of **swear**

**sworn** past participle of **swear** □ adj holding steadily to an attitude etc:

they had been sworn friends since childhood

**swot** verb, informal to study hard □ noun someone who studies hard

**sycamore** noun a name given to several different types of tree, the maple, plane, and a kind of fig tree

**sycophant** noun someone who flatters others in order to gain favour or personal advantage □ **sycophantic** adj

**syl-** see **syn-**

**syllable** noun a word or part of a word spoken with one breath (cheese has one syllable, but-ter two, mar-gar-ine three) □ **syllabic** adj

**syllabus** noun (pl **syllabuses** or **syllabi**) a programme or list of lectures, classes etc

**sylph** noun 1 a type of fairy supposed to inhabit the air 2 a slender, graceful woman

**sym-** see **syn-**

**symbol** noun 1 something that stands for or represents another thing, eg the red cross, which stands for first aid 2 a character used as a short form of something, eg the signs + meaning plus, and O meaning oxygen □ **symbolic** or **symbolical** adj □ **symbolism** noun the use of symbols to express ideas esp in art and literature □ **symbolize** verb

**symmetry** noun the equality in size, shape and position of two halves on either side of a dividing line □ **symmetrical** adj □ **symmetrically** adv

**sympathetic** adj feeling or showing sympathy □ **sympathetic to** or **towards** inclined to be in favour of: sympathetic to the scheme □ **sympathetically** adv

**sympathy** noun (pl **sympathies**) 1 a feeling of pity or sorrow for someone in trouble 2 agreement with, or understanding of, the feelings, attitudes etc of others

□ **sympathize** *verb*: **sympathize with** to express or feel sympathy (for)

**symphony** *noun* (*pl* **symphonies**) a long piece of music written for an orchestra of many different instruments

**symptom** *noun* an outward sign indicating the presence of a disease *etc* □ **symptomatic** *adj*

**syn-** also **sym-**, **syl-** *prefix* with, together: *sympathize* (= have so much pity for someone that you feel sorrow with them)/ *syllable* (= sounds which are pronounced together in one breath)
ⓘ From Greek *syn* meaning 'with'

**synagogue** *noun* a Jewish place of worship

**synchronize** *verb* **1** to cause to happen at the same time **2** to set to the same time: *synchronize watches*

**syncopate** *verb*, *music* to change the beat by accenting beats not usually accented □ **syncopation** *noun*

**syndicate** *noun* a number of persons who join together to manage some piece of business

**syndrome** *noun* a pattern of behaviour, events *etc* characteristic of some problem or condition

**synod** *noun* a meeting of members of the clergy

**synonym** *noun* a word which has the same, or nearly the same, meaning as another, *eg* 'ass' and 'donkey', or 'brave' and 'courageous' □ **synonymous (with)** *adj* having the same meaning (as)

**synopsis** *noun* (*pl* **synopses**) a short summary of the main points of a book, speech *etc*

**syntax** *noun* rules for the correct combination of words to form sentences □ **syntactic** or **syntactical** *adj*

**synthesis** *noun* **1** the act of making a whole by putting together its separate parts **2** the making of a substance by combining chemical elements □ **synthesize** *verb* to make (*eg* a drug) by synthesis □ **synthesizer** *noun* a computerized instrument which creates electronic musical sounds □ **synthetic** *adj* **1** made artificially to look like a natural product: *synthetic leather* **2** not natural, pretended: *synthetic charm* □ **synthetically** *adv*

**syphon** *another spelling of* **siphon**

**syringe** *noun* a tubular instrument with a needle and plunger, used to extract blood, inject drugs *etc* □ *verb* to clean out with a syringe

**syrup** *noun* **1** a thick sticky liquid made by boiling water or fruit juice with sugar **2** a purified form of treacle

**system** *noun* **1** an arrangement of several parts which work together: *solar system* **2** a way of organizing: *democratic system of government* **3** a regular method of doing something **4** the body, or its parts, considered as a whole: *my system is run down* □ **systematic** *adj* following a system; methodical □ **systematically** *adv*
ⓘ From Greek *sy-* meaning 'together', and the root of *histanai* meaning 'to set'

---

# Tt

**tab** *noun* **1** a small tag or flap attached to something **2** a running total, a tally

**tabard** *noun* a short sleeveless tunic

**tabby** *noun* (*pl* **tabbies**) or **tabby-cat** a striped (usually female) cat

**tabernacle** *noun* a place of worship

**table** *noun* **1** a flat-topped piece of

**tableau** 505 **tag**

furniture, supported by legs **2** a flat surface, a plateau **3** facts or figures set out in columns: *multiplication tables* □ *verb* **1** to make into a list or table **2** to put forward for discussion: *table a motion* □ **tablecloth** *noun* a cloth for covering a table □ **tablespoon** *noun* a large type of spoon □ **tablespoonful** *noun* (*pl* **tablespoonfuls**) the amount held in a tablespoon □ **table tennis** a form of tennis played across a table with small bats and a light ball

**tableau** *noun* (*pl* **tableaux**) a striking group or scene

**tablet** *noun* **1** a small flat plate on which to write, paint *etc* **2** a small flat piece, *eg* of soap or chocolate **3** a pill **4** a brittle sweet made with sugar and condensed milk

**tabloid** *noun* a small-sized newspaper giving news in shortened and often simplified form

Originally a trademark for a medicine in tablet form, and then, by association, the name for a small-sized newspaper giving information in concentrated form

**taboo** *adj* forbidden by common consent; not approved by social custom □ *noun* a taboo subject or behaviour

**tabular** *adj* set in the form of a table

**tabulate** *verb* to set out (information *etc*) in columns or rows

**tachograph** *noun* an instrument showing a vehicle's mileage, number of stops *etc*

**tacit** (*say* **tas**-it) *adj* understood but not spoken aloud, silent: *tacit agreement*

**taciturn** (*say* **tas**-it-ern) *adj* not inclined to talk □ **taciturnity** (*say* tas-it-**ern**-*i*-t-i) *noun* an unwillingness to talk

**tack** *noun* **1** a short sharp nail with a broad head **2** a sideways movement allowing a yacht *etc* to sail against

the wind **3** a direction, a course **4** a rough stitch to keep material in place while sewing □ *verb* **1** to fasten with tacks **2** to sew with tacks **3** of a yacht *etc*: to move from side to side across the face of the wind □ **change tack** to change course or direction □ **on the wrong tack** following the wrong train of thought

**tackle** *verb* **1** to come to grips with, deal with **2** *football etc* to try to stop, or take the ball from, another player □ *noun* **1** the ropes and rigging of a ship **2** equipment, gear: *fishing tackle* **3** ropes and pulleys for raising heavy weights **4** an act of tackling

**tacky**[1] *adj* sticky, gluey

**tacky**[2] *adj, informal* shabby; vulgar, in bad taste

**tact** *noun* skill in dealing with people so as to avoid giving offence

**tactful** *adj* using tact; avoiding giving offence □ **tactfully** *adv*

**tactical** *adj* **1** involving clever and successful planning **2** diplomatic, politic: *tactical withdrawal*

**tactics** *noun pl* **1** a way of acting in order to gain advantage **2** the art of coordinating military forces in action

**tactile** *adj* of or perceived through touch

**tactless** *adj* giving offence through lack of thought □ **tactlessly** *adv*

**tadpole** *noun* a young frog or toad in its first stage of life

**tae kwon do** (*say* tei kwon **doh**) a Korean martial art similar to karate

**taffeta** *noun* a thin, glossy fabric made mainly of silk

**tag** *noun* **1** a label: *price tag* **2** a familiar saying or quotation **3** a chasing game played by children (*also called* **tig**) □ *verb* **1** to put a tag or tags on □ **tag on to** or **tag after** to follow closely and continually

**t'ai chi** (*say* tai **chee**) a Chinese system of exercise and self-defence stressing the importance of balance and co-ordination

**tail** *noun* **1** an appendage sticking out from the end of the spine on an animal, bird or fish **2** an appendage on a machine *etc*: *tail of an aeroplane* **3** the stalk on a piece of fruit **4** (**tails**) the side of a coin opposite to the head **5** (**tails**) a tail-coat □ *verb* **1** *informal* to follow closely **2** to remove the tails from (fruit *etc*) □ **tailcoat** *noun* a coat with a divided tail, part of a man's evening dress **tail-end** *noun* the very end of a procession *etc* □ **tail off** to become less, fewer or worse □ **turn tail** to run away

**tailor** *noun* someone who cuts out and makes clothes □ *verb* **1** to make and fit (clothes) **2** to make to fit the circumstances, adapt: *tailored to your needs* □ **tailor-made** *adj* exactly suited to requirements

**taint** *verb* **1** to spoil by contact with something bad or rotten **2** to corrupt □ *noun* a trace of decay or evil

**take** *verb* **1** to lay hold of, grasp **2** to choose: *take a card!* **3** to accept, agree to have: *do you take credit cards?/ please take a biscuit* **4** to have room for: *my car only takes four people* **5** to eat, swallow **6** to get or have regularly: *doesn't take sugar* **7** to capture (a fort *etc*) **8** to subtract: *take two from eight* **9** to lead, carry, drive: *take the children to school* **10** to use, make use of: *take care!* **11** to require: *it'll take too much time* **12** to travel by: *took the afternoon train* **13** to experience, feel: *takes great pride in his work* **14** to photograph: *take some shots inside the house* **15** to understand: *took what I said the wrong way* **16** of a plant: to root successfully **17** to become popular, please □ **take-away** *noun* **1** a meal prepared and

bought in a restaurant or shop but taken away and eaten somewhere else **2** a restaurant or shop providing such meals □ **taking** *adj* pleasing, attractive □ *noun* **1** an act of taking **2** (**takings**) money received from things sold □ **take account of** to consider, remember □ **take advantage of 1** to make use of (an opportunity) **2** to treat or use unfairly □ **take after** to be like in appearance or behaviour □ **take care of** to look after □ **take down** to write, note down □ **take for** to believe (mistakenly) to be: *I took him for his brother* □ **take heed** to pay careful attention □ **take ill** to become ill □ **take in 1** to include **2** to receive **3** to understand: *didn't take in what you said* **4** to make smaller: *take in a dress* **5** to cheat, deceive □ **take leave of** to say goodbye to □ **take someone's life** to kill them □ **taken with** attracted to □ **take off 1** to remove (clothes *etc*) **2** to imitate unkindly **3** of an aircraft: to leave the ground □ **take-off** *noun* **1** the act of an aircraft leaving the ground **2** an act of imitating or mimicking □ **take on 1** to undertake (work *etc*) **2** to accept (as an opponent): *take you on at tennis* □ **take over** to take control of □ **takeover** *noun* the act of taking control of something, *esp* a company by buying the majority of its shares □ **take part in** to share or help in □ **take pity on** to show pity for □ **take place** to happen □ **take to 1** to be attracted by **2** to begin to do or use regularly: *took to rising early* □ **take to heart** to be deeply affected or upset by □ **take to your heels** to run away, flee □ **take up 1** to lift, raise **2** to occupy (space, time *etc*) **3** to begin to learn, show interest in: *take up playing the harp*

**take** ·· takes, tak**i**ng, tak**e**n, took

■ (verb, meaning 1) seize, grab, snatch, steal; (verb, meaning 2)

pick, select; (verb, meaning 4)
accommodate; (verb, meaning 7)
seize, capture; (verb, meaning 8)
subtract, deduct; (verb, meaning
9) transport, escort, bring; (verb,
meaning 11) need, necessitate,
demand □ **take in** (meaning 3)
absorb, assimilate □ **take off**
(meaning 1) remove, doff, shed

**talc** *noun* **1** a soft mineral, soapy to
the touch **2** *informal* talcum
powder □ **talcum powder** a fine
powder made from talc, used for
rubbing on the body

**tale** *noun* **1** a story **2** an untrue story,
a lie

**talent** *noun* **1** a special ability or skill:
*a talent for music* **2** *historical* a
measure of weight for gold or silver
□ **talented** *adj* skilled, gifted

**talisman** *noun* (*pl* **talismans**) an
object believed to have magic
powers; a charm

**talk** *verb* **1** to speak **2** to gossip **3** to
give information □ *noun*
**1** conversation **2** gossip **3** the
subject of conversation: *the talk is of
revolution* **4** a discussion or lecture:
*gave a talk on stained glass* □ **talk
over 1** to discuss **2** to persuade
□ **talk round 1** to discuss without
coming to the main point **2** to
persuade □ **talk shop** *see* **shop**

□ (verb, meaning 1) speak, utter;
(verb, meaning 2) chat, chatter,
natter; (verb, meaning 3)
communicate, converse, confer

**talkative** *adj* inclined to chatter

**tall** *adj* **1** high or higher than average
**2** hard to believe: *tall story* □ **tall
order** a request to do something
awkward or unreasonable

**tallow** *noun* animal fat melted down
to make soap, candles *etc*

**tally** *noun* (*pl* **tallies**) **1** an account
**2** a ticket, a label **3** *old* a notched
stick for keeping a score □ *verb* to
agree (with): *his story doesn't tally
with yours*

**tally** *verb* ⟵ **tallies, tallying, tallied**

**tambourine** *noun* a small one-sided
drum with tinkling metal discs set
into the sides

**tame** *adj* **1** of an animal: not wild,
used to living with humans **2** dull,
not exciting □ *verb* to make tame,
subdue

**tamper** *verb*: **tamper with** to meddle
with so as to damage or alter

**tampon** *noun* a plug of cotton-wool
inserted into the vagina to absorb
blood during menstruation

**tan** *verb* **1** to make (animal skin) into
leather by treating with tannin **2** to
make or become brown, *eg* by
exposure to the sun □ *noun* **1** a
yellowish-brown colour **2** a suntan

**tan** *verb* ⟵ **tans, tanning, tanned**

**tandem** *noun* a long bicycle with two
seats and two sets of pedals one
behind the other □ *adv* one behind
the other □ **in tandem** together, in
conjunction

**tandoori** *noun* a style of Indian
cookery in which food is baked over
charcoal in a clay oven

**tang** *noun* a strong taste, flavour or
smell: *the tang of lemons*

**tangent** *noun* a straight line which
touches a circle or curve without
crossing it □ **go off at a tangent** to
go off suddenly in another direction
or line of thought

**tangerine** *noun* a small type of
orange

Originally meaning 'from Tangiers',
from where the fruit was exported in
the 19th century

**tangible** *adj* **1** able to be felt by
touching **2** real, definite: *tangible
profits* □ **tangibly** *adv*

**tangle** *verb* **1** to twist together in
knots **2** to make or become difficult
or confusing □ *noun* **1** a twisted
mass of knots **2** a confused
situation

**tango** *noun* (*pl* **tangos**) a ballroom dance with long steps and pauses, originally from South America

**tank** *noun* **1** a large container for water, petrol *etc* **2** a heavy armoured vehicle which moves on caterpillar wheels

**tankard** *noun* a large drinking mug

**tanker** *noun* **1** a ship or large lorry for carrying liquids, *eg* oil **2** an aircraft carrying fuel

**tanner** *noun* someone who works at tanning leather □ **tannery** *noun* (*pl* **tanneries**) a place where leather is made

**tannin** *noun* a bitter-tasting substance found in tea, red wine *etc*, also used in tanning and dyeing

**tantalize** *verb* to torment by offering something and keeping it out of reach □ **tantalizing** *adj*

**tantamount** *adj*: **tantamount to** coming to the same thing as, equivalent to: *tantamount to stealing*

**tantrum** *noun* a fit of rage or bad temper

**tap** *noun* **1** a light touch or knock **2** a device with a valve for controlling the flow of liquid, gas *etc* □ *verb* **1** to knock or strike lightly **2** to draw on, start using **3** to attach a listening device secretly to (a telephone) □ **on tap** ready, available for use

**tap** *verb* ⇆ taps, tapping, tapped

**tapdance** *noun* a dance done with special shoes that make a tapping sound □ *verb* to perform a tapdance

**tape** *noun* **1** a narrow band or strip used for tying **2** a piece of string over the finishing line on a racetrack **3** a tape-measure **4** a strip of magnetic material for recording sound or pictures □ *verb* **1** to fasten with tape **2** to record on tape □ **tape-measure** *noun* a narrow strip of paper, plastic *etc* used for measuring distance □ **tape-recorder** *noun* a kind of instrument for recording sound *etc* on magnetic tape □ **tapeworm** *noun* a type of long worm sometimes found in the intestines of humans and animals □ **have someone taped** to have a good understanding of their character or worth

**taper** *noun* **1** a long, thin kind of candle **2** a long waxed wick used for lighting oil lamps *etc* □ *verb* to make or become thinner at one end □ **tapering** *adj* becoming gradually thinner at one end

**tapestry** *noun* (*pl* **tapestries**) a cloth with designs or figures woven into it, used to decorate walls or cover furniture

**tapioca** *noun* a starchy food obtained from the root of the cassava plant

**tapir** *noun* a kind of wild animal something like a large pig

**tar** *noun* **1** a thick, black, sticky liquid derived from wood or coal, used in roadmaking *etc* **2** *informal* a sailor □ *verb* to smear with tar □ **tarred with the same brush (as)** having the same faults (as)

**tar** *verb* ⇆ tars, tarring, tarred

**tarantula** *noun* a type of large, poisonous spider

**tardy** *adj* slow; late □ **tardiness** *noun* being late or delayed

**target** *noun* **1** a mark to aim at in shooting, darts *etc* **2** a result or sum that is aimed at: *a target of 3000* **3** someone at whom unfriendly remarks are aimed: *the target of her criticism*

**tariff** *noun* **1** a list of prices **2** a list of taxes payable on goods brought into a country

**tarmac** *noun* the surface of a road or airport runway, made of tarmacadam □ *verb* to surface with tarmacadam

**tarmacadam** *noun* a mixture of small stones and tar used to make road surfaces *etc*

**tarnish** *verb* **1** of metal: to (cause to)

become dull or discoloured **2** to spoil (a reputation *etc*)

**tarot** (*say* ta-roh) *noun* a system of fortune-telling using special cards divided into suits

**tarpaulin** *noun* **1** strong waterproof cloth **2** a sheet of this material

**tarragon** *noun* a herb used in cooking

**tarry**[1] (*say* ta-ri) *verb* **1** to stay behind, linger **2** to be slow or late

**tarry**[2] (*say* tah-ri) *adj* like or covered with tar; sticky

**tart** *noun* a small pie containing fruit, vegetables *etc* □ *adj* sharp, sour

**tartan** *noun* **1** fabric patterned with squares of different colours, traditionally used by Scottish Highland clans **2** one of these patterns: *Macdonald tartan* □ *adj* with a pattern of tartan

**tartar** *noun* **1** a substance that gathers on the teeth **2** a difficult or demanding person **3** a substance that forms inside wine casks □ **cream of tartar** a white powder obtained from the tartar from wine casks, used in baking

**task** *noun* a set piece of work to be done □ **task force** a group of people gathered together with the purpose of performing a special or specific task □ **taskmaster** *noun* someone who sets and supervises tasks □ **take to task** to scold, find fault with

**tassel** *noun* a hanging bunch of threads, used to decorate a hat *etc*

**taste** *verb* **1** to try by eating or drinking a sample **2** to eat or drink some of: *taste this soup* **3** to recognize (a flavour): *can you taste the chilli in it?* **4** to have a particular flavour: *tasting of garlic* **5** to experience: *taste success* □ *noun* **1** the act or sense of tasting **2** a flavour **3** a small quantity of something **4** a liking: *taste for literature* **5** ability to judge what is suitable in behaviour, dress *etc*, or what is fine or beautiful

**tasteful** *adj* showing good taste and judgement □ **tastefully** *adv*

**tasteless** *adj* **1** without flavour **2** not tasteful; vulgar □ **tastelessly** *adv*

**tasty** *adj* having a good flavour

**tattered** *adj* ragged

**tatters** *noun pl* torn, ragged pieces

**tattle** *noun* gossip

**tattoo** *noun* **1** a coloured design on the skin, made by pricking with needles **2** a drumbeat **3** an outdoor military display with music *etc* □ *verb* to prick coloured designs into the skin □ **tattooed** *adj* marked with tattoos

From a Dutch term meaning to shut off beer taps at closing time, later applied to a military drumbeat at the end of the day

**tatty** *adj* shabby, tawdry

**taught** *past form of* **teach**

**taunt** *verb* to tease or jeer at unkindly □ *noun* a jeer

Originally a phrase *taunt for taunt*, based on the French *tant pour tant* meaning 'tit for tat'

**taut** *adj* **1** pulled tight **2** tense, strained

**tauten** *verb* to make or become tight

**tautology** *noun* a form of repetition in which the same thing is said in different ways, *eg* 'he looked *anxious* and *worried*'

**tavern** *noun*, *old* a public house, an inn

**tawdry** *adj* cheap-looking and gaudy

From *St Audrey's lace*, once used to make cheap lace neckties

**tawny** *adj* yellowish-brown

**tax** *noun* (*pl* **taxes**) **1** a charge made by the government on income, certain types of goods *etc* **2** a strain, a burden: *severe tax on my patience* □ *verb* **1** to make to pay a tax **2** to put a strain on: *taxing her strength* □ **taxation 1** the act or system of taxing **2** taxes □ **taxpayer** *noun* someone who pays taxes □ **tax with** to accuse of

**taxi** *noun* (*pl* **taxis**) a vehicle which may be hired, with a driver (*also called:* **taxi-cab**) □ *verb* **1** to travel in a taxi **2** of an aeroplane: to travel on the runway before or after take-off

> **taxi** *verb* ⇔ taxi*es*, taxi*ing*, taxi*ed*

**taxidermy** *noun* the art of preparing and stuffing the skins of animals to make them lifelike □ **taxidermist** *noun* someone who prepares and stuffs the skins of dead animals

**TB** *abbrev* tuberculosis

**tea** *noun* **1** a plant grown in India, China *etc*, or its dried and prepared leaves **2** a drink made by infusing its dried leaves **3** a hot drink, an infusion: *beef tea/ camomile tea* **4** an afternoon or early evening meal □ **teacake** *noun* a light, flat bun □ **tea chest** a tall box of thin wood used to pack tea for export, often used as a packing case when empty □ **teapot** *noun* a pot with a spout, for making and pouring tea □ **teaspoon** *noun* a small spoon □ **tea-towel** *noun* a cloth for drying dishes

**teach** *verb* **1** to give (someone) skill or knowledge **2** to give knowledge of, or training in (a subject): *she teaches French* **3** to be a teacher: *decide to teach*

> **teach** ⇔ teach*es*, teach*ing*, taught

**teacher** *noun* someone employed to teach others in a school, or in a particular subject: *guitar teacher*

**teaching** *noun* **1** the work of a teacher **2** guidance, instruction **3** (**teachings**) beliefs or rules of conduct that are preached or taught

**teacup** *noun* a medium-sized cup for drinking tea □ **storm in a teacup** *see* storm

**teak** *noun* **1** a hardwood tree from the East Indies **2** its very hard wood **3** a type of African tree

**teal** *noun* a small water-bird like a duck

**team** **1** a group of people working together **2** a side in a game: *a football team* **3** two or more animals working together: *team of oxen* □ **team up with** to join together with, join forces with

> ♠ Do not confuse with: **teem**

**tear**[1] (*say* teer) *noun* **1** a drop of liquid from the eye **2** (**tears**) grief □ **tear gas** gas which causes the eyes to stream with tears □ **in tears** weeping

**tear**[2] (*say* teir) *verb* **1** to pull with force: *tear apart/ tear down* **2** to make a hole or split in (material *etc*) **3** to hurt deeply **4** *informal* to rush: *tearing off down the road* □ *noun* a hole or split made by tearing

> **tear** *verb* ⇔ tear*s*, tear*ing*, torn, tor

**tearful** *adj* **1** inclined to weep **2** in tears, crying □ **tearfully** *adv*

**tease** *verb* **1** to annoy, irritate on purpose **2** to pretend to upset or annoy for fun: *I'm only teasing* **3** to untangle (wool *etc*) with a comb **4** to sort out (a problem or puzzle) □ *noun* someone who teases

**teasel** *noun* a type of prickly plant

**teaser** *noun* a problem, a puzzle

**teat** *noun* **1** the part of an animal through which milk passes to its young **2** a rubber object shaped like this attached to a baby's feeding bottle

**technical** *adj* **1** relating to a particular art or skill, *esp* a mechanical or industrial one: *what is the technical term for this?/ a technical expert* **2** according to strict laws or rules: *technical defeat* □ **technically** *adv* according to the rules, strictly speaking

**technicality** *noun* (*pl* **technicalities**) a technical detail or point

**technician** *noun* someone trained in the practical side of an art

**technique** *noun* the way in which a process is carried out; a method

**techno** *noun, short for* **technomusic**

**technological** *adj* relating to or involving technology □ **technologically** *adv: a technologically advanced country* □ **technologist** *noun* a person skilled in technology and its applications

**technology** *noun* **1** science applied to practical (*esp* industrial) purposes **2** the practical skills of a particular civilization, period *etc*

**technomusic** *noun* a style of popular music which uses electronic effects

**teddy** or **teddybear** *noun* (*pl* **teddies** or **teddybears**) **1** a stuffed toy bear **2** (**teddy**) a one-piece woman's undergarment

**tedious** *adj* long and tiresome □ **tediously** *adv* □ **tedium** *noun* boredom

**tee** *noun* **1** the square of level ground from which a golfball is driven **2** the peg or sand heap on which the ball is placed for driving □ **tee up** to place (a ball) on a tee

**teem** *verb* **1** to be full: *teeming with people* **2** to rain heavily

◐ Do not confuse with: **team**

**teenage** *adj* suitable for, or typical of, those in their teens

**teenager** *noun* someone in their teens

**teens** *noun pl* the years of age from thir*teen* to nine*teen*

**teeny** *adj, informal* tiny, minute

**tee-shirt** or **T-shirt** *noun* a short-sleeved shirt pulled on over the head

**teeth** *pl* of **tooth**

**teethe** *verb* of a baby: to grow its first teeth

**teetotal** *adj* never drinking alcohol □ **teetotaller** *noun* a person who never drinks alcohol

**tele-** *prefix* at a distance: *television/telegram*

⊚ From Greek *tele* meaning 'far'

**telecommunications** *noun pl* the sending of information by telephone, radio, television *etc*

**telegram** *noun* a message sent by telegraph

**telegraph** *noun* an instrument for sending messages to a distance using electrical impulses □ *verb* to send (a message) by telegraph □ **telegraphic** *adj* **1** of a telegraph **2** short, brief, concise

**telepathy** *noun* communication between people without using sight, hearing *etc* □ **telepathic** *adj* relating to or involving telepathy

**telephone** *noun* an instrument for speaking over distances, which uses an electric current travelling along a wire, or radio waves □ *verb* to send (a message) by telephone □ **telephonist** *noun* an operator on a telephone switchboard

**telephoto** *adj* of a lens: used to photograph enlarged images of distant objects

**teleprinter** *noun* a typewriter which receives and prints out messages sent by telegraph

**telescope** *noun* a tubular instrument fitted with lenses which magnify distant objects □ *verb* **1** to push or fit together so that one thing slides inside another **2** to force together, compress

**teletex** *noun* a high-speed means of transmitting data, similar to telex

**teletext** *noun* news and general information transmitted by television companies, viewable only on special television sets

**televise** *verb* to broadcast on television: *are they televising the football match?*

**television** *noun* **1** the reproduction on a small screen of pictures sent from a distance **2** an apparatus for receiving these pictures

**teleworker** *noun* someone who works from home and

communicates with their employer by computer, fax *etc*

**telex** *noun* **1** the sending of messages by means of teleprinters **2** a message sent in this way

**tell** *verb* **1** to say or express in words: *she's telling the truth* **2** to give the facts of (a story) **3** to inform, give information: *can you tell me when it's 9 o'clock* **4** to order, command: *tell him to go away!* **5** to make out, distinguish: *I can't tell one wine from the other* **6** to give away a secret: *promise not to tell* **7** to be effective, produce results: *training will tell in the end* □ **teller** *noun* **1** a bank clerk who receives and pays out money **2** someone who counts votes at an election □ **telling** *adj* having a marked effect: *telling remark* □ **all told** altogether, counting all □ **tell off** *informal* to scold □ **tell on 1** to have an effect on **2** to give information about □ **tell tales** to give away information about the misdeeds of others

**tell** ⊷ tells, telling, told

**temerity** *noun* rashness, boldness

**temp** *abbrev* **1** temperature **2** temporary □ *noun, informal* a temporarily employed secretarial worker □ *verb, informal* to work as a temp

**temper** *noun* **1** habitual state of mind: *of an even temper* **2** a passing mood: *in a good temper* **3** a tendency to get angry easily **4** a fit of anger **5** the amount of hardness in metal, glass *etc* □ *verb* **1** to bring (metal) to the right degree of hardness by heating and cooling **2** to make less severe □ **lose your temper** to show anger

**temperament** *noun* someone's nature as it affects the way they feel and act; disposition □ **temperamental** *adj* **1** of temperament **2** excitable, emotional

**temperance** *noun* the habit of not drinking much (or any) alcohol

**temperate** *adj* **1** moderate in temper, eating or drinking *etc* **2** of climate: neither very hot nor very cold

**temperature** *noun* **1** degree of heat or cold: *today's temperature* **2** a body heat higher than normal

**tempest** *noun* a storm, with great wind

**tempestuous** *adj* **1** very stormy and windy **2** passionate, violently emotional

**template** *noun* a thin plate cut in a design for drawing round

**temple¹** *noun* a building used for public worship; a church

**temple²** *noun* a small flat area on each side of the forehead

**tempo** *noun* (*pl* **tempos** or **tempi**) **1** the speed at which music is played **2** the speed or rate of an activity

**temporary** *adj* lasting only for a time, not permanent

**temporize** *verb* to avoid or delay taking action in order to gain time

**tempt** *verb* **1** to try to persuade or entice **2** to attract **3** to make inclined (to): *tempted to phone him up* □ **temptation** *noun* **1** the act of tempting **2** the feeling of being tempted **3** something which tempts □ **tempting** *adj* attractive

**ten** *noun* the number 10 □ *adj* 10 in number □ **tenpin bowling** a game like skittles played by bowling a ball at ten pins standing at the end of a bowling lane

**tenable** *adj* able to be defended; justifiable

**tenacious** *adj* **1** keeping a firm hold or grip **2** obstinate, persistent, determined □ **tenaciously** *adv* □ **tenacity** *noun* persistence, determination

**tenant** *noun* someone who pays rent for the use of a house, land *etc* □ **tenancy** *noun* (*pl* **tenancies**) **1** the holding of a house, farm *etc* by a tenant **2** the period of this holding

**tend** verb **1** to be likely or inclined to do something: *these flowers tend to wilt* **2** to move or slope in a certain direction **3** to take care of, look after

**tendency** noun (pl **tendencies**) a leaning or inclination (towards): *tendency to daydream*

**tender** adj **1** soft, not hard or tough **2** easily hurt or damaged **3** hurting when touched **4** loving, gentle □ verb **1** to offer (a resignation *etc*) formally **2** to make a formal offer for a job □ noun **1** an offer to take on work, supply goods *etc* for a fixed price **2** small boat that carries stores for a large one **3** a truck for coal and water attached to a steam engine □ **legal tender** coins or notes which must be accepted when offered □ **of tender years** very young

**tendon** noun a tough cord joining a muscle to a bone

**tendril** noun **1** a thin curling stem of a climbing plant which attaches itself to a support **2** a curling strand of hair *etc*

**tenement** noun a block of flats

**tenet** noun a belief, opinion

**tenner** noun, *informal* a ten-pound note; ten pounds

**tennis** noun a game for two or four players using rackets to hit a ball to each other over a net □ **tennis court** a place made level and prepared for tennis

**tenon** noun a projecting part at the end of a piece of wood made to fit a **mortise**

**tenor** noun **1** a singing voice of the highest normal pitch for an adult male **2** a singer with this voice **3** the general course: *the even tenor of country life* **4** general meaning: *the tenor of the speech*

**tense**[1] noun the form of a verb that shows time of action, eg *'I was'* (**past**

tense), *'I am'* (**present tense**), *'I shall be'* (**future tense**)

**tense**[2] adj **1** tightly stretched **2** nervous, strained: *feeling tense / tense with excitement* □ **tensile** adj relating to stretching □ **tension** noun **1** the state of being stretched **2** strain, anxiety

**tent** noun a movable shelter of canvas or other material, supported by poles and pegged to the ground

**tentacle** noun a long thin flexible part of an animal used to feel or grasp, eg the arm of an octopus

**tentative** adj **1** experimental, initial: *a tentative offer* **2** uncertain, hesitating: *tentative smile* □ **tentatively** adv

**tenterhooks** noun pl: **on tenterhooks** uncertain and very anxious about what will happen

**tenth** adj the last of ten items □ noun one of ten equal parts

**tenuous** adj slight, weak: *tenuous connection*

**tenure** noun **1** the holding of property or a position of employment **2** the period, or terms or conditions, of this

**tepee** noun a traditional Native American tent made of animal skins

**tepid** adj lukewarm

**term** noun **1** a length of time: *term of imprisonment* **2** a division of an academic or school year: *autumn term* **3** a word, an expression: *dictionary of computing terms* **4 terms** the rules or conditions of an agreement: *what are their terms?* **5** (**terms**) fixed charges **6** (**terms**) footing, relationship: *on good terms with his neighbours* □ verb to name, call □ **come to terms** to reach an agreement or understanding □ **come to terms with** to accept, be able to live with □ **in terms of** from the point of view of

**termagant** noun a bad-tempered, noisy woman

**terminal** adj **1** of or growing at the end: terminal bud **2** of an illness: fatal, incurable □ noun **1** an end **2** a point of connection in an electric circuit **3** a computer monitor connected to a network **4** a terminus **5** an airport building containing arrival and departure areas **6** a bus station in a town centre running a service to a nearby airport

**terminate** verb to bring or come to an end □ **termination** noun

**terminology** noun the special words or expressions used in a particular art, science etc

**terminus** noun (pl **termini** or **terminuses**) **1** the end **2** an end point on a railway, bus route etc

**termite** noun a pale-coloured wood-eating insect, like an ant

**tern** noun a type of sea bird like a small gull

**terrace** noun **1** a raised level bank of earth **2** a raised flat place **3** a connected row of houses □ verb to form into a terrace or terraces

**terracotta** noun a brownish-red mixture of clay and sand used for tiles, pottery etc

**terrain** noun an area of land considered in terms of its physical features: the terrain is a bit rocky

**terrapin** noun a small turtle living in ponds or rivers

**terrestrial** adj of or living on the earth

**terrible** adj **1** causing great fear: terrible sight **2** causing great hardship or distress: terrible disaster **3** informal very bad: a terrible writer □ **terribly** adv, informal **1** badly: sang terribly **2** extremely: terribly tired

**terrier** noun a breed of small dog

**terrific** adj **1** powerful, dreadful **2** huge, amazing **3** informal attractive, enjoyable etc: a terrific party

**terrify** verb to frighten greatly

**terrify** ↔ terrifies, terrifying, terrified

**territorial** adj of, belonging to a territory

**territory** noun (pl **territories**) **1** an area of land, a region **2** land under the control of a ruler or state **3** an area allocated to a salesman etc **4** a field of activity or interest

**terror** noun **1** very great fear **2** something which causes great fear **3** informal an uncontrollable child □ **terrorize** verb to frighten very greatly

**terrorism** noun the organized use of violence or intimidation for political or other ends □ **terrorist** noun someone who practises terrorism

**terse** adj using few words; curt, brusque □ **tersely** adv

**tertiary** adj third in position or order □ **tertiary education** education at university or college level

**test** noun **1** a short examination **2** something done to check soundness, reliability etc: ran tests on the new model **3** a means of finding the presence of: test for radioactivity **4** an event that shows up a good or bad quality: a test of courage □ verb to carry out tests on □ **test match** cricket one of a series of matches between two countries □ **test pilot** a pilot who tests new aircraft □ **test tube** a glass tube closed at one end, used in chemical tests

**testament** noun **1** a written statement **2** a will □ **Old Testament** and **New Testament** the two main divisions of the Christian Bible

**testator** noun the writer of a will

**testicle** noun one of two sperm-producing glands enclosed in the male scrotum

**testify** verb **1** to give evidence in a law court **2** to make a solemn declaration of **3 (testify to)** to show, give evidence of it: *testifies to his ignorance*

**testify** ⊷ testifies, testifying, testified

**testimonial** *noun* **1** a personal statement about someone's character, abilities *etc* **2** a gift given in thanks for services given

**testimony** *noun* (*pl* testimonies) **1** the statement made by someone who testifies **2** evidence

**testosterone** *noun* the chief male sex hormone, secreted by the testicles

**testy** *adj* easily angered, irritable □ **testily** *adv* □ **testiness** *noun*

**tetanus** *noun* a disease, caused *esp* by an infected wound, causing stiffening and spasms in the jaw muscles (*also called*: **lockjaw**)

**tetchy** *adj* irritable, testy □ **tetchily** *adv*

**tether** *noun* a rope or chain for tying an animal to restrict its movement □ *verb* **1** to tie with a tether **2** to limit the freedom of

**text** *noun* **1** the written or printed part of a book, not the pictures, notes *etc* **2** a printed or written version of a speech, play *etc* **3** a Biblical passage used as the basis for a sermon **4** the subject matter of a speech, essay *etc* □ **textbook** *noun* a book used for teaching, giving the main facts about a subject

**textile** *adj* of weaving; woven □ *noun* a woven cloth or fabric

**textual** *adj* of or in a text

**texture** *noun* **1** the quality of cloth resulting from weaving: *loose texture* **2** the quality of a substance in terms of how it looks or feels: *rough texture/ lumpy texture*

**than** *conj* & *prep* used in comparisons: *easier than I expected/ better than usual*

**thank** *verb* to express gratitude to (someone) for a favour, gift *etc*

□ **thank you** or **thanks** a polite expression used to thank someone (*see also* **thanks**) □ **thankless** *adj* neither worthwhile nor appreciated: *thankless task* □ **thanks** *noun pl* gratitude; appreciation: *you'll get no thanks for it* □ **thanks to 1** with the help of: *we arrived on time, thanks to our friends* **2** owing to: *we were late, thanks to our car breaking down*

**thankful** *adj* grateful; relieved and glad □ **thankfully** *adv*: *thankfully, no-one was badly injured in the crash*

**thanksgiving** *noun* **1** a church service giving thanks to God **2 (Thanksgiving)** *US* the fourth Thursday of November, a national holiday commemorating the first harvest of the Puritan settlers

**that** *adj* & *pron* (*pl* those) used to point out a thing or person (*contrasted with*: **this**): *that woman over there/ don't say that* □ *relative pron*: *those are the colours he chose/ that's the man I spoke to* □ *adv* to such an extent or degree: *why were you that late?* □ *conj* **1** used in reporting speech: *she said that she was there* **2** used to connect clauses: *I heard that you were ill*

**thatch** *noun* straw *etc* used to make the roof of a house □ *verb* to cover with thatch

**thaw** *verb* **1** to melt **2** of frozen food: to defrost, become unfrozen **3** to become friendly □ *noun* **1** the melting of ice and snow by heat **2** a change in the weather that causes this

**the** *adj* **1** referring to a particular person or thing: *the boy in the park/ I like the jacket I'm wearing* **2** referring to all or any of a general group: *the horse is of great use to man*

**theatre** or *US* **theater** *noun* **1** a place for the public performance of plays *etc* **2** a room in a hospital for surgical operations **3** the acting profession

**theatrical** adj **1** of theatres or acting **2** over-dramatic, overdone
▫ **theatricality** noun

**thee** pron, old you (sing) as the object of a sentence

**theft** noun stealing

**their** adj belonging to them: their car
▫ **theirs** pron belonging to them: the red car is theirs

🖝 Do not confuse with: **there**. Remember that the 'y' in the pronoun 'they' turns into an 'i' in **their** - and that **there** is spelt the same as 'here' except for the first letter.

**them** pron pl **1** people or things already spoken about (as the object of a verb): we've seen them **2** those: one of them over in the corner ▫ pron sing used to avoid giving the gender of the person being referred to: if anyone phones, ask them to leave their number

**theme** noun **1** the subject of a discussion, essay etc **2** music a main melody which is often repeated
▫ **theme park** a public display in an open area, related to a single theme
▫ **theme song** or **theme tune** a tune that is repeated often in a film, television series etc

**themselves** pron pl **1** used reflexively: they tired themselves out walking **2** used for emphasis: they'll have to do it by themselves

**then** adv **1** at that time: I didn't know you then **2** after that: and then where did you go? ▫ conj in that case, therefore: if you're busy, then don't come

**thence** adv, old from that time or place

**theocracy** noun government of a state according to religious laws
▫ **theocratic** adj

**theology** noun the study of God and religion ▫ **theologian** noun someone who studies theology ▫ **theological** adj

**theorem** noun a proposition to be proved in mathematics etc

**theory** noun (pl **theories**) **1** an explanation that has not been proved or tested **2** the underlying ideas in an art, science etc, compared to practice or performance ▫ **theoretical** adj of theory, not experience or practice
▫ **theoretically** adv: it is theoretically possible to travel from Glasgow to Edinburgh in one hour ▫ **theorize** verb to form theories

**therapeutic** adj **1** of therapy **2** healing, curing

**therapist** noun someone who gives therapeutic treatment: speech therapist

**therapy** noun (pl **therapies**) treatment of disease or disorders

**there** adv at, in or to that place: what did you do there? ▫ pron used (with be) as a subject of a sentence or clause when the real subject follows the verb: there is nobody at home
▫ **thereabouts** adv approximately ▫ **thereafter** adv after that ▫ **thereby** adv by that means ▫ **therefore** adv for this or that reason ▫ **thereof** adv of that ▫ **thereupon** adv **1** because of this or that **2** immediately

🖝 Do not confuse with: **their**. Remember that **there** is spelt the same as 'here' except for the first letter - and that the 'y' in the pronoun 'they' turns into an 'i' in **their**.

**therm** noun a unit of heat used in measuring gas

**thermal** adj **1** of heat **2** of hot springs

**thermodynamics** noun sing the science of the relation between heat and mechanical energy

**thermometer** noun an instrument for measuring temperature

**thermonuclear** adj relating to the fusion of nuclei at high temperatures

**Thermos** *noun, trademark* a kind of vacuum flask

**thermostat** *noun* a device for automatically controlling temperature in a room

**thesaurus** *noun* (*pl* **thesauri** or **thesauruses**) **1** a reference book listing words and their synonyms **2** a dictionary or encyclopedia

**these** *see* **this**

**thesis** *noun* (*pl* **theses**) **1** a long piece of written work on a topic, often part of a university degree **2** a statement of a point of view

**thespian** *noun, formal* an actor

Named after *Thespis*, founder of ancient Greek tragedy

**they** *pron pl* some people or things already mentioned (used only as the subject of a verb): *they followed the others* □ *pron sing* used to avoid giving the gender of the person being referred to: *anyone can come if they like*

**thick** *adj* **1** not thin, of reasonable width: *a thick slice/ two metres thick* **2** of a mixture: containing solid matter, stiff: *a thick soup* **3** dense, difficult to see or pass through: *thick fog/ thick woods* **4** of speech: not clear **5** *informal* stupid **6** *informal* very friendly □ *noun* the thickest, most crowded or active part: *in the thick of the fight* □ **thicken** *verb* to make or become thick □ **thicket** *noun* a group of close-set trees and bushes □ **thickness** *noun* **1** the quality of being thick **2** the distance between opposite sides **3** a layer □ **thickset** *adj* **1** closely set or planted **2** having a thick sturdy body □ **thick-skinned** *adj* not sensitive or easily hurt

**thief** *noun* (*pl* **thieves**) someone who steals

**thieve** *verb* to steal □ **thieving** *noun* stealing □ *adj* that thieves □ **thievish** *adj* inclined to stealing

**thigh** *noun* the thick, fleshy part of the leg between the knee and the hip

**thimble** *noun* a small cap worn over a fingertip, used to push a needle while sewing

**thin** *adj* **1** not very wide between its two sides: *thin paper/ thin slice* **2** slim, not fat **3** not dense or crowded: *thin population* **4** poor in quality: *thin wine* **5** of a voice: weak, not resonating **6** of a mixture: not stiff, watery: *a thin soup* □ *verb* to make or become thin or thinner □ **thinness** *noun*

**thin** *verb* ⋯ thin*s*, thin*ning*, thin*ned*

**thine** *adj, old* belonging to you (used before words beginning with a vowel or a vowel sound): *thine enemies* □ *pron, old* something belonging to you: *my heart is thine*

**thing** *noun* **1** an object that is not living **2** *informal* a person: *a nice old thing* **3** (**things**) belongings **4** an individual object, quality, idea *etc* that may be referred to: *several things must be taken into consideration*

**think** *verb* **1** to work things out, reason **2** to form ideas in the mind **3** to believe, judge or consider: *I think that we should go* **4** (with **of**) to intend: *she is thinking of resigning* □ **think tank** a group of people who give expert advice and come up with ideas □ **think better of** to change your mind about □ **think highly of** or **think much of** to have a good opinion of □ **think nothing of 1** to have a poor opinion of **2** to consider as easy □ **think out** to work out in the mind

**think** *verb* ⋯ think*s*, think*ing*, thought

**third** *adj* the last of a series of three □ *noun* one of three equal parts

**thirst** *noun* **1** a dry feeling in the mouth caused by lack of fluid **2** an eager desire (for): *thirst for knowledge* □ *verb* **1** to feel thirsty

**2** (with *for*) to desire eagerly
□ **thirsty** *adj* **1** having thirst **2** of
earth: parched, dry **3** eager (for)

**thirteen** *noun* the number 13 □ *adj*
thirteen in number □ **thirteenth** *adj*
the last of a series of thirteen □ *noun*
one of thirteen equal parts

**thirty** *noun* the number 30 □ *adj* thirty
in number □ **thirtieth** *adj* the last of
a series of thirty □ *noun* one of thirty
equal parts

**this** *adj & pron* (*pl* **these**) **1** used to
point out someone or something,
*esp* one nearby (*contrasted with*:
**that**): *look at this letter/ take this
instead* **2** to such an extent or
degree: *this early*

**thistle** *noun* a prickly plant with
purple flowers □ **thistledown** *noun*
the feathery bristles of the seeds of
the thistle

**thither** *adv* to that place

**thong** *noun* **1** a thin strap of leather
to fasten anything **2** the lash of a
whip

**thorax** *noun* (*pl* **thoraxes** or
**thoraces**) **1** the chest in the human
or animal body **2** the middle section
of an insect's body

**thorn** *noun* **1** a sharp prickle sticking
out from the stem of a plant **2** a
bush with thorns, *esp* the hawthorn
□ **thorny** *adj* full of thorns;
prickly **2** difficult, causing
arguments: *a thorny problem*
□ **thorn in the flesh** a cause of
constant irritation

**thorough** *adj* **1** complete, absolute: *a
thorough muddle* **2** very careful,
attending to every detail
□ **thoroughly** *adv* **1** completely,
absolutely: *I thoroughly agree*
**2** very carefully: *the product has been
tested thoroughly* □ **thoroughbred**
*noun* an animal of pure breed
□ **thoroughfare** *noun* **1** a public
street **2** a passage or way through:
*no thoroughfare*

**those** *see* **that**

**thou** *pron*, *old* you (as the subject of a
sentence)

**though** *conj* although: *though he
disliked it, he ate it all* □ *adv*,
*informal* however: *I wish I'd never
said it, though*

**thought** *noun* **1** the act of thinking
**2** something which you think, an
idea **3** an opinion **4** consideration:
*after much thought* □ *verb*, *past form*
of **think** □ **thoughtful** *adj* **1** full of
thought **2** thinking of others,
considerate □ **thoughtless** *adj*
showing lack of thought;
inconsiderate

**thousand** *noun* the number 1000
□ *adj* a thousand in number
□ **thousandth** *adj* the last of a series
of a thousand □ *noun* one of a
thousand equal parts

**thrash** *verb* **1** to beat severely **2** to
move or toss violently (about)
**3** (with *out*) to discuss a problem *etc*
thoroughly **4** to thresh (grain)
□ *noun* thrash metal music
□ **thrashing** *noun* a flogging, a
beating □ **thrash metal** very fast,
loud rock music resembling punk
rock, often with violent themes

**thread** *noun* **1** a very thin line of
cotton, wool, silk *etc*, often twisted
and drawn out **2** the ridge which
goes in a spiral round a screw **3** a
connected series of details in correct
order in a story □ *verb* **1** to put a
thread through a needle *etc* **2** to
make (your way) in a narrow space
□ **threadbare** *adj* of clothes: worn
thin

**threat** *noun* **1** a warning that you
intend to hurt or punish someone
**2** a warning of something bad that
may come: *a threat of war*
**3** something likely to cause harm: *a
threat to our plans* □ **threaten** *verb*
**1** to make a threat: *threatened to kill
himself* **2** to suggest the approach of
something unpleasant **3** to be a
danger to

**three** *noun* the number 3 □ *adj* **3** in

number

**3-D** *short for* three-dimensional

**thresh** *verb* to beat out (grain) from straw

**threshold** *noun* **1** a piece of wood or stone under the door of a building **2** a doorway **3** an entry or beginning: *on the threshold of a new era*

**threw** *past form of* **throw**

**thrice** *adv* three times

**thrift** *noun* careful management of money in order to save □ **thrifty** *adj* careful about spending

**thrill** *noun* **1** an excited feeling **2** quivering, vibration □ *verb* **1** to feel excitement **2** to make excited □ **thriller** *noun* an exciting story, often about crime and detection □ **thrilling** *adj* very exciting

**thrive** *verb* **1** to grow strong and healthy **2** to get on well, be successful

**throat** *noun* **1** the back part of the mouth **2** the front part of the neck

**throb** *verb* **1** of a pulse *etc*: to beat, *esp* more strongly than normal **2** to beat or vibrate rhythmically and regularly

> **throb** *verb* ⊹ throb*s*, throb*bing*, throb*bed*

**throes** *noun pl* great suffering or struggle □ **in the throes of** in the middle of (a struggle, doing a task *etc*)

**thrombosis** *noun* the forming of a clot in a blood vessel

**throne** *noun* **1** the seat of a monarch or bishop **2** a monarch or their power

**throng** *noun* a crowd □ *verb* **1** to move in a crowd **2** to crowd, fill (a place)

**throttle** *noun* the part of an engine through which steam or petrol can be turned on or off □ *verb* to choke by gripping the throat

**through** *prep* **1** entering from one direction and out in the other: *through the tunnel* **2** from end to end, or side to side, of: *all through the performance* **3** by way of: *related through his grandmother* **4** as a result of: *through his expertise* **5** *US* from (one date) to (another) inclusive: *Monday through Friday is five days* □ into and out of, from beginning to end: *all the way through the tunnel* □ *adj* **1** without break or change: *through train* **2** *informal* finished: *are you through with the newspaper?* **3** of a telephone call: connected: *I couldn't get through this morning* □ **through-and-through** *adv* completely, entirely: *a gentleman through-and-through* □ **throughout** *prep* **1** in all parts of: *throughout Europe* **2** from start to finish of: *throughout the journey*

**throw** *verb* **1** to send through the air with force **2** of a horse: to make (a rider) fall to the ground **3** to shape (pottery) on a wheel **4** to give (a party) □ *noun* **1** the act of throwing **2** the distance a thing is thrown: *within a stone's throw of the house* □ **throwback** *noun* a reversion to an earlier form □ **throw away** to get rid of

> **throw** *verb* ⊹ throw*s*, throw*ing*, threw, thrown

**thrush** (*pl* thrushes) **1** a type of singing bird with a speckled breast **2** an infection which can affect the mouth, throat or vagina

**thrust** *verb* **1** to push with force **2** to make a sudden push forward with a pointed weapon **3** (with **on**, **upon**) to force (something, yourself) upon □ *noun* **1** a stab **2** a pushing force

> **thrust** *verb* ⊹ thrust*s*, thrust*ing*, thrust

**thud** *noun* a dull, hollow sound like that made by a heavy body falling □ *verb* to move or fall with such a sound

> **thud** *verb* ⊹ thud*s*, thud*ding*,

thudd*ed*

**thug** *noun* a violent, brutal person

**thumb** *noun* the short, thick finger of the hand □ *verb* to turn over (the pages of a book) with the thumb or fingers □ **thumbscrew** *noun, historical* an instrument of torture which worked by squashing the thumbs □ **rule of thumb** a rough-and-ready practical method □ **thumbs down** or **thumbs up** showing disapproval, or approval, of something □ **under someone's thumb** under their control

**thump** *noun* a heavy blow □ *verb* **1** to beat heavily **2** to move or fall with a dull, heavy noise

**thunder** *noun* **1** the deep rumbling sound heard after a flash of lightning **2** any loud, rumbling noise □ *verb* **1** to produce the sound of, or a sound like, thunder **2** to shout out angrily □ **thunderbolt** *noun* **1** a flash of lightning followed by thunder **2** a very great and sudden surprise □ **thunderclap** *noun* a sudden roar of thunder □ **thunderous** *adj* like thunder; very angry □ **thunderstruck** *adj* overcome by surprise □ **thundery** *adj* of weather: sultry, bringing thunder

**Thursday** *noun* the fifth day of the week

**thus** *adv* **1** in this or that manner: *he always talks thus* **2** to this degree or extent: *thus far* **3** because of this, therefore: *thus, we must go on*

**thwart** *verb* **1** to hinder (someone) from carrying out a plan, intention *etc* **2** to prevent (an attempt *etc*) □ *noun* a cross seat for rowers in a boat

**thy** *adj, old* belonging to you: *thy wife and children*

**thyme** *noun* a small sweet-smelling herb used for seasoning food

**thyroid gland** a large gland in the neck which influences the rate at which energy is used by the body

Based on a Greek word meaning 'door-shaped', because of the shape of the cartilage in the front of the throat

**tiara** *noun* a jewelled ornament for the head like a crown

**tic** *noun* a twitching motion of certain muscles, *esp* of the face

**tick**[1] *noun* **1** a light mark (✔) used to mark as correct, or mark off in a list **2** a small quick noise, made regularly by a clock or watch **3** *informal* a moment: *I'll just be a tick* □ *verb* **1** to mark with a tick **2** of a clock *etc*: to produce regular ticks □ **ticking** *noun* the noise made by a clock *etc*

**tick**[2] *noun* a tiny blood-sucking animal

**tickle** *verb* **1** to excite the surface nerves of a part of the body by touching lightly **2** to please or amuse □ **ticklish** *adj* **1** sensitive to tickling **2** not easy to deal with: *ticklish problem* □ **tickly** *adj* ticklish

**tiddlywinks** *noun sing* a game in which small plastic discs (**tiddlywinks**) are flipped into a cup

**tide** *noun* **1** the rise and fall of the sea which happens regularly twice each day **2** *old* season: *Christmastide* □ **tidal** *adj* of the tide □ **tidal wave** an enormous wave in the sea often caused by an earthquake *etc* □ **tide over** to help to get over a difficulty for a time

**tidings** *noun pl* news

**tidy** *adj* **1** in good order, neat **2** *informal* fairly big: *a tidy sum of money* □ *verb* to make neat □ **tidily** *adv*

**tidy** *verb* → tidies, tidying, tidied

**tie** *verb* **1** to fasten with a cord, string *etc* **2** to knot or put a bow in (string, shoelaces *etc*) **3** to join, unite **4** to limit, restrict: *tied to a tight schedule* **5** to score the same number of points (in a game *etc*), draw □ *noun*

**1** a band of fabric worn round the neck, tied with a knot or bow **2** something that connects: *ties of friendship* **3** something that restricts or limits **4** an equal score in a competition **5** a game or match to be played □ **tie-breaker** noun an extra question or part of a tied contest to decide a winner

**tie** verb ⇔ **ties, tying, tied**

**tier** (*say* teer) noun a row of seats in a theatre *etc*, with others above or below it

**tiff** noun a slight quarrel

**tig** another name for **tag**

**tiger** noun a large animal of the cat family with a tawny coat striped with black

**tight** adj **1** packed closely **2** firmly stretched, not loose **3** fitting too closely: *these jeans are a bit tight* **4** *informal* short of money **5** *informal* drunk □ **tighten** verb to make or become tight or tighter □ **tight-fisted** adj stingy □ **tight-lipped** adj uncommunicative □ **tightrope** noun a tightly stretched rope on which acrobats perform

**tights** noun pl a close-fitting garment covering the feet, legs and body as far as the waist

**tigress** noun a female tiger

**tile** noun a piece of baked clay *etc* used in covering floors or roofs □ verb to cover with tiles

**till¹** noun a container or drawer for money in a shop □ verb to cultivate (land); plough

**till²** see **until**

**tiller** noun the handle of a boat's rudder

**tilt** verb **1** to fall into, or place in, a sloping position **2** *historical* to joust **3** *historical* (with **at**) to attack on horseback, using a lance □ noun **1** a slant **2** a thrust, a jab □ **at full tilt** with full speed and force

**timber** noun **1** wood for building *etc*

**2** trees suitable for this **3** a wooden beam in a house or ship

**timbre** noun the quality of a musical sound or voice

**time** noun **1** the hour of the day **2** the period at which something happens **3** (often **times**) a particular period: *in modern times* **4** opportunity: *no time to listen* **5** a suitable or right moment: *now is the time to ask* **6** one of a number of occasions: *he won four times* **7** (**times**) multiplied by: *two times four* **8** the rhythm or rate of performance of a piece of music □ adj **1** of time **2** arranged to go off at a particular time: *a time bomb* □ verb **1** to measure the minutes, seconds *etc* taken to do anything **2** to choose the time for (well, badly *etc*): *time your entrance well* □ **time-honoured** adj respected because it has lasted a long time □ **timeless** adj **1** not belonging to any particular time **2** never ending: *timeless beauty* □ **timely** adj coming at the right moment: *a timely reminder* □ **time-sharing** noun **1** a system of using a computer so that it can deal with several programs at the same time **2** a scheme by which someone buys the right to use a holiday home for a specified period each year □ **timetable** noun a list showing times of classes, arrivals or departures of trains *etc* □ **at times** occasionally □ **do time** *slang* to serve a prison sentence □ **in time** early enough □ **on time** or **up to time** punctual □ **the time being** the present time

**timid** adj easily frightened; shy □ **timidly** adv shyly □ **timidity** noun nervousness, shyness

**timorous** adj very timid

**timpani** or **tympani** noun pl kettledrums

**tin** noun **1** a silvery-white kind of metal **2** a box or can made of **tinplate**, thin iron covered with tin or other metal □ verb **1** to cover with tin **2** to pack (food *etc*) in tins □ **tinfoil** *noun* a very thin sheet of tin, aluminium *etc* used for wrapping □ **tinny** *adj* **1** like tin **2** of sound: thin, high-pitched

**tin** *verb* ▷ **tins**, **tinning**, **tinned**

**tincture** *noun* **1** a slight tinge of colour **2** a characteristic quality **3** a medicine mixed in alcohol

**tinder** *noun* dry material easily set alight by a spark

**tine** *noun* a spike of a fork or of a deer's antler

**tinge** *verb* **1** to tint, colour slightly **2** (with **with**) to add a slight amount of it to □ *noun* a slight amount; a hint: *tinge of pink* / *tinge of sadness*

**tingle** *verb* **1** to feel a sharp prickling sensation **2** to feel a thrill of excitement □ *noun* a sharp prickle

**tinker** *noun* a mender of kettles, pans *etc* □ *verb* **1** to work clumsily or unskilfully **2** to meddle (with)

**tinkle** *verb* to (cause to) make a light, ringing sound; clink, jingle, □ *noun* a light, ringing sound

**tinsel** *noun* a sparkling, glittering material used for decoration

**tint** *noun* a variety or shade of a colour □ *verb* to give slight colour to

**tiny** *adj* very small

**tip** *noun* **1** the top or point of something thin or tapering **2** a piece of useful information **3** a small gift of money to a waiter *etc* **4** a rubbish dump **5** a light stroke, a tap □ *verb* **1** to slant **2** (with **over**) to overturn **3** (with **out** or **into**) to empty out or into **4** (also with **off**) to give a hint to **5** to give a small gift of money **6** to strike lightly

**tip** *verb* ▷ **tips**, **tipping**, **tipped**

**Tipp-Ex** *noun, trademark* correcting fluid for covering over mistakes in typing or writing

**tipple** *verb, informal* to drink small amounts of alcohol regularly □ *noun* an alcoholic drink □ **tippler** *noun*

**tipsy** *adj* rather drunk □ **tipsiness** *noun*

**tiptoe** *verb* **1** to walk on your toes in order to go very quietly □ **on tiptoe** standing or walking on your toes

**tirade** *noun* a long, bitter, scolding speech

**tire**[1] *verb* **1** to make or become weary **2** (with **of**) to lose patience with or interest in □ **tireless** *adj* **1** never becoming weary **2** never resting □ **tiresome** *adj* **1** making weary **2** long and dull **3** annoying: *a tiresome child* □ **tiring** *adj* causing tiredness or weariness: *a tiring journey*

**tire**[2] *US* spelling of tyre

**tired** *adj* **1** weary **2** (with **of**) bored with

> ▬ (meaning I) drowsy, sleepy, flagging, fatigued, exhausted, drained, jaded

**tiro** or **tyro** *noun* (*pl* **tiros** or **tyros**) a beginner

**tissue** *noun* **1** the substance of which body organs are made: *muscle tissue* **2** a mass, a network (of lies, nonsense *etc*) **3** a paper handkerchief **4** finely woven cloth □ **tissue paper** thin, soft paper used for wrapping

**tit** *noun* **1** a type of small bird: *blue tit* / *great tit* **2** a teat □ **tit for tat** blow for blow, repayment of injury with injury

**titanic** *adj* huge, enormous

**titbit** *noun* a tasty piece of food *etc*

**tithe** (*say* taidh) *noun, historical* a tax paid to the church, a tenth part of someone's income or produce

**titillate** *verb* to gently stimulate or arouse (often sexually)
  ⓘ From Latin *titillare* meaning 'to tickle'

  ✎ Do not confuse: **titillate** and **titivate**

**titivate** *verb* to make smarter; improve in appearance

523

It is thought that **titivate** was created by taking 'tidy' and reforming it on the model of the verb 'cultivate'.

**title** noun 1 the name of a book, poem etc 2 a word in front of a name to show rank or office (eg Sir, Lady, Major), or in addressing anyone formally (eg Mr, Mrs, Ms) 3 right or claim to money, an estate etc □ **titled** adj having a title which shows noble rank □ **title deed** a document that proves a right to ownership (of a house etc) □ **title role** the part in a play which is the same as the title eg Hamlet

**titter** verb to giggle □ noun a giggle

**tizzy** noun a state of confusion, a flap

**TNT** abbrev trinitrotoluene, a high explosive

**to** prep 1 showing the place or direction aimed for: going to the cinema/ emigrating to New Zealand 2 showing the indirect object in a phrase, sentence etc: show it to me 3 used before a verb to indicate the infinitive: to err is human 4 showing that one thing belongs with another in some way: key to the door 5 compared with: nothing to what happened before 6 about, concerning: what did he say to that? 7 showing a ratio, proportion etc: odds are six to one against 8 showing the purpose or result of an action: tear it to pieces □ adv almost closed: pull the door to □ **to and fro** backwards and forwards

**toad** noun a type of amphibian like a frog

**toadstool** noun a mushroom-like fungus, often poisonous

**toady** verb to give way to someone's wishes, or flatter them, to gain favour □ noun someone who acts in this way

**toast** verb 1 to brown (bread) by heating at a fire or grill 2 to drink to the success or health of (someone) 3 to warm (your feet etc) at a fire □ noun 1 bread toasted 2 the person to whom a toast is drunk 3 the drinking of a toast □ **toaster** noun an electric machine for toasting bread □ **toast-rack** noun a stand with partitions for slices of toast

**tobacco** noun a type of plant whose dried leaves are used for smoking □ **tobacconist** noun someone who sells tobacco, cigarettes etc

**toboggan** a long, light sledge □ verb to go in a toboggan

**today** adv & noun 1 (on) this day 2 (at) the present time

**toddle** verb to walk unsteadily, with short steps □ **toddler** noun a young child just able to walk

**toddy** noun (pl **toddies**) a hot drink of whisky and honey

**to-do** noun (pl **to-dos**) a bustle, commotion

**toe** noun 1 one of the five finger-like parts of the foot 2 the front part of an animal's foot 3 the front part of a shoe, golf club etc □ **on your toes** alert, ready for action □ **toe the line** to do as you are told

**toffee** noun a kind of sweet made of sugar and butter □ **toffee-nosed** adj, informal snobbish, conceited

**toga** noun, historical the loose outer garment worn by a citizen of ancient Rome

**together** adv 1 with each other, in place or time: we must stay together/ three buses arrived together 2 in or into union or connection: glue the pages together 3 by joint action: together we can afford it

**toggle** noun a cylindrical fastening for a coat □ verb to switch quickly between two positions, states etc (esp between being on and off)

**toil** verb 1 to work hard and long 2 to walk, move etc with effort □ noun hard work

**toilet** noun 1 the act of washing yourself, doing your hair 2 a receptacle for waste matter from the body, with a water-supply for flushing this away **3** a room containing this □ **toilet water** a lightly perfumed, spirit-based liquid for the skin

**toiletries** *noun pl* soaps, cosmetics *etc*

**token** *noun* **1** a mark, a sign: *a token of my friendship* **2** a stamped piece of plastic *etc*, or a voucher, for use in place of money: *bus token/ book token* □ *adj* done for show only, insincere: *token gesture*

**told** *past form of* **tell**

**tolerable** *adj* **1** bearable, endurable **2** fairly good: *tolerable player* □ **tolerably** *adv*

**tolerance** *noun* **1** putting up with and being fair to people with different beliefs, manners *etc* from your own **2** ability to resist the effects of a drug *etc* □ **tolerant** *adj*

**tolerate** *verb* **1** to bear, endure; put up with **2** to allow □ **toleration** *noun* **1** the act of tolerating **2** the practice of allowing people to practise religions which are different to the established religion of the country

**toll¹** *noun* **1** a tax charged for crossing a bridge *etc* **2** loss, damage □ **take toll** to cause damage or loss

**toll²** *verb* **1** to sound (a large bell) slowly, as for a funeral **2** of a bell: to be sounded slowly

**tomahawk** *noun, historical* a Native American light axe used as a weapon and tool

**tomato** *noun* (*pl* **tomatoes**) a juicy red-skinned fruit, used in salads, sauces *etc*

**tomb** *noun* **1** a grave **2** a burial vault or chamber

**tombola** *noun* a kind of lottery

**tomboy** *noun* a high-spirited active girl who enjoys the rough, boisterous activities which people tend to associate with boys

**tombstone** *noun* a stone placed over a grave in memory of the dead person

**tomcat** *noun* a male cat

**tome** *noun* a large heavy book

**tomorrow** *adv & noun* **1** (on) the day after today **2** (in) the future: *the children of tomorrow*

**tomtom** *noun* a type of drum beaten with the hands

**ton** *noun* **1** a measure of weight equal to 2240 pounds, about 1016 kilogrammes **2** a unit (100 cubic feet) of space in a ship □ **metric ton** or **metric tonne** 1000 kilogrammes

**tone** *noun* **1** sound **2** quality of sound: *harsh tone* **3** *music* one of the larger intervals in a scale, *eg* between C and D **4** the quality of a voice expressing the mood of the speaker: *a gentle tone* **5** a shade of colour **6** muscle firmness or strength □ *verb* **1** (sometimes with **in**) to blend, fit in well **2** (with **down**) to make or become softer **3** (with **up**) to give strength to (muscles *etc*)

**tongs** *noun pl* an instrument for lifting and grasping coals, sugar lumps *etc*

**tongue** *noun* **1** the fleshy organ inside the mouth, used in tasting, speaking, and swallowing **2** a flap in a shoe **3** a long, thin strip of land **4** the tongue of an animal served as food **5** a language: *his mother tongue* □ **tongue-tied** *adj* not able to speak freely □ **tongue-twister** *noun* a phrase, sentence *etc* not easy to say quickly, *eg* 'she sells sea shells'

**tonic** *noun* **1** a medicine which gives strength and energy **2** *music* the keynote of a scale **3** tonic water □ *adj* **1** of tones or sounds **2** of a tonic □ **tonic water** aerated water with quinine

**tonight** *adv & noun* (on) the night of the present day

**tonnage** *noun* the space available in a

ship, measured in tons

**tonne** *another spelling of* **ton**

**tonsil** *noun* one of a pair of soft, fleshy lumps at the back of the throat □ **tonsillitis** *noun* reddening and painfulness of the tonsils

**too** *adv* **1** to a greater extent, in a greater quantity *etc* than is wanted: *too hot to go outside/ too many people in the room* **2** (with a negative) very, particularly: *not feeling too well* (ie not feeling very well) **3** also, as well: *I'm feeling quite cold, too*

**took** *past form of* **take**

**tool** *noun* an instrument for doing work, *esp* by hand

**toot** *noun* the sound of a car horn *etc*

**tooth** *noun* (*pl* **teeth**) *noun* **1** any of the hard, bony objects projecting from the gums, arranged in two rows in the mouth **2** any of the points on a saw, cogwheel, comb *etc* □ **toothache** *noun* pain in a tooth □ **toothpaste** or **tooth-powder** *noun* paste or powder for cleaning the teeth □ **toothpick** *noun* a small sharp instrument for picking out food from between the teeth □ **tooth and nail** fiercely, determinedly

**top** *noun* **1** the highest part of anything **2** the upper surface **3** the highest place or rank **4** a lid **5** a circus tent **6** a kind of spinning toy □ *adj* highest, chief □ *verb* **1** to cover on the top **2** to rise above **3** to do better than **4** to reach the top of **5** to take off the top of □ **top dog** *informal* a winner or leader □ **top hat** a man's tall silk hat □ **top-heavy** *adj* having the upper part too heavy for the lower □ **topmost** *adj* highest, uppermost □ **top-secret** *adj* (of information *etc*) very secret

**top** *verb* ⇨ **tops, topping, topped**

**topaz** *noun* a type of precious stone, of various colours

**topiary** *noun* the art of trimming

bushes, hedges *etc* into decorative shapes

**topic** *noun* a subject spoken or written about

**topical** *adj* of current interest, concerned with present events

**topography** *noun* the description of the features of the land in a certain region □ **topographical** *adj*

**topple** *verb* to become unsteady and fall

**topsyturvy** *adj & adv* turned upside down

**torch** *noun* (*pl* **torches**) **1** a small hand-held light with a switch and electric battery **2** a flaming piece of wood or coarse rope carried as a light in processions □ *verb, slang* to set fire to deliberately

**tore** *past form of* **tear**

**toreador** *noun* a bullfighter mounted on horseback

**torment** *verb* **1** to treat cruelly and make suffer **2** to worry greatly **3** to tease □ *noun* **1** great pain, suffering **2** a cause of these □ **tormentor** *noun*

**torn** *past participle of* **tear**

**tornado** *noun* (*pl* **tornadoes**) a violent whirling wind that causes great damage

**torpedo** *noun* (*pl* **torpedoes**) a large cigar-shaped type of missile fired by ships, planes *etc* □ *verb* to hit or sink (a ship) with a torpedo

**torpedo** *verb* ⇨ **torpedoes, torpedoing, torpedoed**

**torpid** *adj* slow, dull, stupid □ **torpidity** or **torpor** *noun* dullness

**torrent** *noun* **1** a rushing stream **2** a heavy downpour of rain **3** a violent flow of words *etc*: *torrent of abuse* □ **torrential** *adj* like a torrent; rushing violently

**torrid** *adj* **1** parched by heat; very hot **2** very passionate: *torrid love affair*

**torsion** *noun* twisting; a twist

**torso** *noun* (*pl* **torsos**) the body,

excluding the head and limbs

**tortoise** *noun* a four-footed, slow-moving kind of reptile, covered with a hard shell □ **tortoiseshell** *noun* the shell of a kind of sea turtle, used in making ornamental articles □ *adj* **1** made of this shell **2** mottled brown, yellow and black: *a tortoiseshell cat*

**tortuous** *adj* winding, roundabout, not straightforward

**torture** *verb* **1** to treat someone cruelly as a punishment or to force them to confess something **2** to cause to suffer □ *noun* **1** the act of torturing **2** great suffering

**Tory** *noun* (*pl* **Tories**) a member of the British Conservative Party

Originally one of a group of Irish Catholics thrown off their land who waged guerrilla war on British settlers, later applied to any royalist supporter

**toss** *verb* **1** to throw up in the air **2** to throw up (a coin) to see which side falls uppermost **3** to turn restlessly from side to side **4** of a ship: to be thrown about by rough water □ **toss-up** *noun* an equal choice or chance □ **toss off** to produce quickly □ **toss up** to toss a coin

**tot¹** *noun* **1** a little child **2** a small amount of alcoholic spirits

**tot²** *verb*: **tot up** to add up

**total** *adj* **1** whole: *total number* **2** complete: *total wreck* □ *noun* **1** the entire amount **2** the sum of amounts added together □ *verb* **1** to add up **2** to amount to **3** *informal* to damage irreparably; wreck □ **totally** *adv* completely

**total** *verb* ⬦ **totals, totalling, totalled**

**totalitarian** *adj* governed by a single party that allows no rivals

**totem** *noun* an image of an animal or plant used as the badge or sign of a Native American tribe □ **totem pole** a pole on which totems are carved and painted

**totter** *verb* **1** to shake as if about to fall **2** to stagger

**toucan** *noun* a type of S American bird with a very big beak

**touch** *verb* **1** to feel (with the hand) **2** to come or be in contact (with): *a leaf touched his cheek* **3** to move, affect the feelings of: *the story touched those who heard it* **4** to mark slightly with colour: *touched with gold* **5** to reach the standard of: *I can't touch him at chess* **6** to have anything to do with: *I wouldn't touch a job like that* **7** to eat or drink: *he won't touch meat* **8** to concern (someone) **9** *informal* to persuade (someone) to lend you money: *I touched him for 10* □ *noun* **1** the act of touching **2** the physical sense of touch **3** a small quantity or degree: *a touch of salt* **4** of an artist, pianist *etc*: skill or style **5** *football* the ground beyond the edges of the pitch marked off by **touchlines** □ **touch-and-go** *adj* very uncertain: *it's touch-and-go whether we'll get it done on time* □ **touching** *prep* about, concerning □ *adj* causing emotion, moving □ **touchstone** *noun* a test or standard of measurement of quality *etc* □ **in** (or **out of**) **touch with 1** in (or not in) communication or contact with **2** aware (or unaware) of □ **touch down** of an aircraft: to land □ **touch off** to cause to happen □ **touch on** to mention briefly □ **touch up** to improve (a drawing or photograph *etc*) by making details clearer *etc*

**touché** (*say* too-**shei**) *exclam* acknowledging a point scored in a game or argument

**touchy** *adj* **1** easily offended **2** needing to be handled with care and tact: *a touchy subject* □ **touchily** *adv* (meaning 1)

**tough** *adj* **1** strong, not easily broken **2** of meat *etc*: hard to chew **3** of strong character, able to stand hardship or strain **4** difficult to cope

with or overcome: *tough opposition*
□ **toughen** *verb* to (cause to)
become tough

**tour** *noun* a journey in which you visit
various places; a pleasure trip □ *verb*
to make a tour (of) □ **tourism** *noun*
the activities of tourists and of those
who cater for their needs □ **tourist**
*noun* someone who travels for
pleasure, and visits places of
interest

**tournament** *noun* **1** a competition
involving many contests and
players **2** *historical* a meeting at
which knights fought together on
horseback

**tourniquet** (*say* toorn-ik-ei) *noun* a
bandage tied tightly round a limb to
prevent loss of blood from a wound

**tousled** *adj* of hair: untidy, tangled

**tout** *verb* to go about looking for
support, votes, buyers *etc* □ *noun*
**1** someone who does this **2** someone
who gives tips to people who bet on
horse races

**tow** *verb* to pull (a car *etc*) with a rope
attached to another vehicle □ *noun*
**1** the act of towing **2** the rope used
for towing □ **towpath** *noun* a path
alongside a canal used by horses
which tow barges □ **in tow** under
protection or guidance □ **on tow**
being towed

**towards** or **toward** *prep* **1** moving in
the direction of (a place, person *etc*):
*walking towards the house* **2** to (a
person, thing *etc*): *his attitude
towards his son* **3** as a help or
contribution to: *I gave 5 towards the
cost* **4** near, about (a time *etc*):
*towards four o'clock*

**towel** *noun* a cloth for drying or
wiping (*eg* the skin after washing)
□ *verb* to rub dry with a towel
□ **towelling** *noun* a cotton cloth
often used for making towels

towel *verb* ↔ towels, towelling,
towelled

**tower** *noun* **1** a high narrow building

**2** a high narrow part of a castle *etc*
□ *verb* to rise high (over, above)
□ **towering** *adj* **1** rising high
**2** violent: *a towering rage*

**town** *noun* a place, larger than a
village, which includes many
buildings, houses, shops *etc* □ **town
crier** *historical* someone who made
public announcements in a town
□ **town hall** the building where the
official business of a town is done

**toxaemia** *noun* poisoning

**toxic** *adj* **1** poisonous **2** caused by
poison □ **toxicology** *noun* the
scientific study of poisons □ **toxic
shock syndrome** a condition which
can be fatal, characterized by high
fever, vomiting and diarrhoea,
sometimes occurring in women
using tampons

**toxin** *noun* a naturally-occurring
poison

**toy** *noun* **1** an object for a child to
play with **2** an object for
amusement only □ **toy with** to play
or trifle with

**trace** *noun* **1** a mark or sign left
behind **2** a footprint **3** a small
amount **4** a line drawn by an
instrument recording a change (*eg*
in temperature) **5** (**traces**) the straps
by which a horse pulls a cart *etc*
along □ *verb* **1** to follow the tracks
or course of **2** to copy (a drawing
*etc*) on transparent paper placed
over it □ **traceable** *adj* able to be
traced (to) □ **tracery** *noun* decorated
stonework holding the glass in some
church windows □ **tracing** *noun* a
traced copy

**track** *noun* **1** a mark left **2** tracks
footprints **3** a path or rough road
**4** a racecourse for runners, cyclists
*etc* **5** a railway line **6** an endless
band on which wheels of a tank *etc*
travel □ *verb* to follow (an animal)
by its footprints and other marks
left □ **tracksuit** *noun* a warm suit
worn while jogging, before and after
an athletic performance *etc* □ **keep**

or **lose track of** to keep or fail to keep aware of the whereabouts or progress of □ **make tracks for** to set off towards □ **track down** to search for (someone or something) until caught or found

**tract** *noun* **1** a stretch of land **2** a short pamphlet, *esp* on a religious subject **3** a system made up of connected parts of the body: *the digestive tract*

**tractable** *adj* easily made to do what is wanted

**traction** *noun* **1** the act of pulling or dragging **2** the state of being pulled □ **traction engine** a road steam-engine

**tractor** *noun* a motor vehicle for pulling loads, ploughs *etc*

**trade** *noun* **1** the buying and selling of goods **2** someone's occupation, craft, job: *a carpenter by trade* □ *verb* **1** to buy and sell **2** to have business dealings (with) **3** to deal (in) **4** to exchange, swap □ **trademark** *noun* a registered mark or name put on goods to show that they are made by a certain company □ **trader** *noun* someone who buys and sells □ **tradesman** *noun* **1** a shopkeeper **2** a workman in a skilled trade □ **trade union** a group of workers of the same trade who join together to bargain with employers for fair wages *etc* □ **trade unionist** a member of a trade union □ **trade-wind** *noun* a wind which blows towards the equator (from the north-east and south-east) □ **trade in** to give as part-payment for something else (*eg* an old car for a new one) □ **trade on** to take advantage of, often unfairly

**tradition** *noun* **1** the handing-down of customs, beliefs, stories *etc* from generation to generation **2** a custom, belief handed down in this way □ **traditional** *adj* of customs: having existed for a long time without changing: *the*

*traditional English breakfast* □ **traditionalist** *noun* someone who believes in maintaining traditions

**traffic** *noun* **1** the cars, buses, boats *etc* which use roads or waterways **2** trade **3** dishonest dealings (*eg* in drugs) □ *verb* **1** to trade **2** to deal (in) □ **traffic lights** lights of changing colours for controlling traffic at road junctions or street crossings

**traffic** *verb* ↦ **traffics, trafficking, trafficked**

**tragedy** *noun* (*pl* **tragedies**) **1** a very sad event **2** a play about unhappy events and with a sad ending □ **tragedian** *noun* **1** an actor who specializes in tragic roles **2** a person who writes tragedies □ **tragic** *adj* of tragedy; very sad □ **tragically** *adv*: *he was tragically killed in an accident*

**trail** *verb* **1** to draw along, in or through: *trailing his foot through the water* **2** to hang down (from) or be dragged loosely behind **3** to hunt (animals) by following footprints *etc* **4** to walk wearily **5** of a plant: to grow over the ground or a wall □ *noun* **1** an animal's track **2** a pathway through a wild region **3** something left stretching behind: *a trail of dust* □ **trailer** *noun* **1** a vehicle pulled behind a car **2** a short film advertising a longer film to be shown at a later date

**train** *noun* **1** a railway engine with carriages or trucks **2** a part of a dress which trails behind the wearer **3** the attendants who follow an important person **4** a line (of thought, events *etc*) **5** a line of animals carrying people or baggage □ *verb* **1** to prepare yourself by practice or exercise for a sporting event, job *etc* **2** to educate **3** to exercise (animals or people) in preparation for a race *etc* **4** to tame and teach (an animal) **5** (with **on** or **at**) to aim, point (a gun, telescope *etc*) at **6** to make (a tree or plant) grow in a certain direction ▫ **trainee** *noun* someone who is being trained ▫ **trainer** *noun* someone who trains people or animals for a sport, circus *etc* ▫ **training** *noun* **1** preparation for a sport **2** experience or learning of the practical side of a job

**trait** *noun* a point that stands out in a person's character: *patience is one of his good traits*

**traitor** *noun* **1** someone who goes over to the enemy's side, or gives away secrets to the enemy **2** someone who betrays trust

**traitorous** *adj* like a traitor; treacherous

**trajectory** *noun* (*pl* **trajectories**) the curved path of something (*eg* a bullet) moving through the air or through space

**tram** *noun* a long car running on rails and driven by electric power for carrying passengers (*also called*: **tramcar**) ▫ **tramline** *noun* **1** a rail of tramway **2** (**tramlines**) *tennis* the parallel lines marked at the sides of the court ▫ **tramway** *noun* a system of tracks on which trams run

**trammel** *noun* something that hinders movement ▫ *verb* to hinder

**trammel** *verb* ⇔ **trammels, trammelling, trammelled**

**tramp** *verb* **1** to walk with heavy footsteps **2** to walk along, over *etc*: *tramping the streets in search of a job* ▫ *noun* **1** someone with no fixed home and no job, who lives by begging **2** a journey made on foot **3** the sound of marching feet **4** a small cargo-boat with no fixed route

**trample** *verb* **1** to tread under foot, stamp on **2** (*usually* with **on**) to treat roughly or unfeelingly **3** to tread heavily

**trampoline** *noun* a bed-like framework holding a sheet of elastic material for bouncing on, used by gymnasts *etc*

**trance** *noun* a sleep-like or half-conscious state

**tranquil** *adj* quiet, peaceful ▫ **tranquillity** *noun*: *she loved the tranquillity of the valley*

**tranquillize** *verb* to make calm ▫ **tranquillizer** *noun* a drug to calm the nerves or cause sleep

**trans-** *prefix* across, through: *transatlantic*
ⓘ From Latin *trans* meaning 'across' or 'beyond'

**transact** *verb* to do (a piece of business) ▫ **transaction** *noun* a piece of business, a deal

**transatlantic** *adj* **1** crossing the Atlantic Ocean: *transatlantic yacht race* **2** across or over the Atlantic: *transatlantic friends*

**transcend** *verb* **1** to be, or rise, above **2** to be, or do, better than

**transcribe** *verb* **1** to copy from one book into another or from one form of writing (*eg* shorthand) into another **2** to adapt (a piece of music) for a particular instrument

**transcript** *noun* a written copy ▫ **transcription** *noun* **1** the act of transcribing **2** a written copy

**transept** *noun* the part of a church which lies across the main part

**transfer** *verb* **1** to remove to another place **2** to hand over to another person ▫ *noun* **1** the act of transferring **2** a design or picture which can be transferred from one surface to another ▫ **transferable** *adj* able to be transferred ▫ **transference** *noun*

**transfer** *verb* ⇔ **transfers, transferring, transferred**

**transfigure** *verb* to change (greatly and for the better) the form or appearance of ▫ **transfiguration** *noun* a change in appearance, *esp* to something more beautiful, glorious, or exalted

**transfix** *verb* **1** to make unable to move or act (*eg* because of surprise):

*transfixed by the sight* **2** to pierce through (as with a sword)

**transform** *verb* to change in shape or appearance completely and often dramatically □ **transformation** *noun* □ **transformer** *noun* an apparatus for changing electrical energy from one voltage to another

**transfuse** *verb* **1** to pass (liquid) from one thing to another **2** to transfer (blood of one person) to the body of another □ **transfusion** *noun* (*in full* **blood transfusion**) the introduction of blood into a person's body by allowing it to drip through a needle inserted in a vein

**transgress** *verb* to break a rule, law *etc* □ **transgression** *noun* the act of breaking a rule, law *etc*; a sin

**transient** *adj* not lasting, passing □ **transience** *noun*

**transistor** *noun* **1** a small device, made up of a crystal enclosed in plastic or metal, which controls the flow of an electrical current **2** a portable radio set using these

**transit** *noun* **1** the carrying or movement of goods, passengers *etc* from place to place **2** the passing of a planet between the sun and the earth □ **transition** *noun* a change from one form, place, appearance *etc* to another □ **transitional** *adj* involving transition; temporary: *the country will pass through a transitional period between constitutions* □ **transitory** *adj* lasting only for a short time

**transitive** *adj*, *grammar* of a verb: having an object, *eg* the verb '*hit*' in 'he *hit* the ball'

**translate** *verb* to turn (something said or written) into another language □ **translation** *noun* **1** the act of translating **2** something translated □ **translator** *noun* someone who translates

**transliterate** *verb* to write (a word) in the letters of another alphabet

**translucent** *adj* allowing light to pass through, but not transparent □ **translucence** *noun* a translucent quality

**transmit** *verb* **1** to pass on (a message, news, heat) **2** to send out signals which are received as programmes □ **transmission** *noun* **1** the act of transmitting **2** a radio or television broadcast □ **transmitter** *noun* an instrument for transmitting (*esp* radio signals)

**transmit** ⇔ transmits, transmit*ting*, transmit*ted*

**transom** *noun* a beam across a window or the top of a door

**transparency** *noun* (*pl* **transparencies**) **1** the state of being transparent **2** a photograph printed on transparent material and viewed by shining light through it

**transparent** *adj* **1** able to be seen through **2** easily seen to be true or false: *a transparent excuse*

**transpire** *verb* **1** of a secret: to become known **2** to happen: *tell me what transpired* **3** to let out (moisture *etc*) through pores of the skin or through the surface of leaves

**transplant** *verb* **1** to lift and plant (a growing plant) in another place **2** to remove (skin) and graft it on another part of the same body **3** to remove (an organ) and graft it in another person or animal □ *noun* **1** the act of transplanting **2** a transplanted organ, plant *etc* □ **transplantation** *noun* the transfer of an organ or tissue from one person to another, or from one part of the body to another

**transport** *verb* **1** to carry from one place to another **2** to overcome with strong feeling: *transported with delight* **3** *historical* to send (a prisoner) to a prison in a different country □ *noun* **1** the act of transporting **2** any means of carrying persons or goods: *rail transport* **3** strong feeling:

*transports of joy* □ **transportation** *noun* **1** the act of transporting **2** means of transport **3** *historical* punishment of prisoners by sending them to a prison in a different country

**transpose** *verb* **1** to cause (two things) to change places **2** to change (a piece of music) from one key to another □ **transposition** *noun*

**transverse** *adj* lying, placed *etc* across: *transverse beams in the roof*

**transvestite** *noun* someone who likes to wear clothes intended for the opposite sex

**trap** *noun* **1** a device for catching animals *etc* **2** a plan or trick for taking someone by surprise **3** a bend in a pipe which is kept full of water, for preventing the escape of air or gas **4** a carriage with two wheels □ *verb* to catch in a trap, or in such a way that escape is not possible □ **trapdoor** *noun* a door in a floor or ceiling □ **trapper** *noun* someone who makes a living by catching animals for their skins and fur

**trap** *verb* ⇨ traps, trapp*ing*, trapp*ed*

**trapeze** *noun* a swing used in performing gymnastic exercises or feats

**trapezium** *noun* a figure with four sides, two of which are parallel

**trappings** *noun pl* **1** clothes or ornaments suitable for a particular person or occasion **2** ornaments put on horses

**trash** *noun* something of little worth, rubbish □ **trashy** *adj* worthless

**trauma** *noun* **1** injury to the body **2** a very violent or distressing experience which has a lasting effect **3** a condition (of a person) caused in this way □ **traumatic** *adj* very upsetting, unpleasant or frightening: *moving to a new house can be traumatic*

**travail** *noun, old* hard work

**travel** *verb* **1** to go on a journey **2** to move **3** to go along, across **4** to visit foreign countries □ *noun* the act of travelling □ **traveller** *noun* **1** someone who travels **2** a travelling representative of a business firm who tries to obtain orders for his firm's products

**travel** *verb* ⇨ travels, travell*ing*, travell*ed*

**traverse** *verb* to go across, pass through □ *noun* **1** something that crosses or lies across **2** a path across a rock face *etc* **3** a zigzag track of a ship

**travesty** *noun* (*pl* **travesties**) a poor or ridiculous imitation: *a travesty of justice*

**trawl** *verb* to fish by dragging a trawl along the bottom of the sea □ *noun* a wide-mouthed, bag-shaped net □ **trawler** *noun* a boat used for trawling

**tray** *noun* a flat piece of wood, metal *etc* with a low edge, for carrying dishes

**treachery** *noun* (*pl* **treacheries**) the act of betraying those who have trusted you □ **treacherous** *adj* **1** likely to betray **2** dangerous: *treacherous road conditions* □ **treacherously** *adv*

**treacle** *noun* a thick, dark syrup produced from sugar when it is being refined

**tread** *verb* **1** to walk on or along **2** (with **on**) to put your foot on **3** to crush, trample under foot □ *noun* **1** a step **2** a way of walking **3** the part of a tyre which touches the ground □ **treadle** *noun* part of a machine which is worked by the foot □ **treadmill** *noun* **1** *historical* a mill turned by the weight of people who were made to walk on steps fixed round a big wheel **2** any tiring, routine work □ **tread on someone's toes** to offend or upset them □ **tread water** to keep yourself afloat in an upright position by moving your arms and legs

**tread** verb ⇔ treads, treading, trodden, trod

**treason** noun disloyalty to your own country or its government, eg by giving away its secrets to an enemy □ **treasonable** adj consisting of, or involving, treason

**treasure** noun 1 a store of money, gold etc 2 anything of great value or highly prized □ verb 1 to value greatly 2 to keep carefully because of its personal value: she treasures the mirror her mother left her □ **treasurer** noun someone who has charge of the money of a club □ **treasure-trove** noun treasure or money found hidden, the owner of which is unknown □ **Treasury** or **treasury** noun (pl **treasuries**) the part of a government which has charge of the country's money

**treat** verb 1 to deal with, handle, act towards: I was treated very well in prison 2 to try to cure (someone) of a disease 3 to try to cure (a disease) 4 to write or speak about 5 to buy (someone) a meal, drink etc 6 to try to arrange (a peace treaty etc) with □ noun something special (eg an outing) that gives much pleasure: they went to the theatre as a treat □ **treatment** noun 1 the act of treating (eg a disease) 2 remedy, medicine: a new treatment for cancer 3 the way in which someone or something is dealt with: rough treatment

**treatise** noun a long, detailed essay etc on some subject

**treaty** noun (pl **treaties**) an agreement made between countries

**treble** adj 1 threefold, three times normal: wood of treble thickness 2 high in pitch: treble note □ verb to become three times as great □ noun 1 the highest part in singing 2 a child who sings the treble part of a song

**tree** noun 1 the largest kind of plant with a thick, firm wooden stem and branches 2 anything like a tree in shape

**trefoil** noun a three-part leaf or decoration

**trek** noun 1 a long or wearisome journey 2 old a journey by wagon □ verb 1 to make a long hard journey 2 old to make a journey by wagon

**trek** verb ⇔ treks, trekking, trekked

**trellis** noun (pl **trellises**) a network of strips for holding up growing plants

**tremble** verb 1 to shake with cold, fear, weakness 2 to feel fear (for another person's safety etc) □ noun 1 the act of trembling 2 a fit of trembling

**tremendous** adj 1 very great or strong 2 informal very good, excellent □ **tremendously** adv, informal very

**tremor** noun a shaking or quivering

**tremulous** adj 1 shaking 2 showing fear: a tremulous voice

**trench** noun (pl **trenches**) a long narrow ditch dug in the ground (eg by soldiers as a protection against enemy fire) □ verb to dig a trench in □ **trenchcoat** noun a kind of waterproof overcoat with a belt

**trenchant** adj 1 going deep, hurting: a trenchant remark 2 of a policy etc: effective, vigorous

**trend** noun a general direction: the trend of events □ **trendy** adj, informal fashionable

**trepidation** noun fear, nervousness

**trespass** verb 1 to go illegally on private land etc 2 (with **on**) to demand too much of: trespassing on my time 3 to sin □ noun (pl **trespasses**) the act of trespassing □ **trespasser** noun

**tress** noun (pl **tresses**) 1 a lock of hair 2 (**tresses**) hair, esp long

**trestle** noun a wooden support with legs, used for holding up a table, platform *etc*

**tri-** *prefix* three: *triangle/ tricycle*
ⓘ From Latin *tres* and Greek *treis*,
both meaning 'three'

**trial** *noun* **1** the act of testing or
trying (*eg* something new) **2** a test
**3** the judging (of a prisoner) in a
court of law **4** suffering □ **on trial
1** being tried (*esp* in a court of law)
**2** for the purpose of trying out:
*goods sent on trial* **3** being tested:
*I'm still on trial with the company*
□ **trial and error** the trying of
various methods or choices until the
right one is found

**triangle** *noun* **1** a figure with three
sides and three angles: △ **2** a
triangular metal musical
instrument, played by striking with
a small rod □ **triangular** *adj* having
the shape of a triangle

**triathlon** *noun* a sporting contest
consisting of three events, often
swimming, running and cycling

**tribe** *noun* **1** a people who are all
descended from the same ancestor
**2** a group of families, *esp* of a
wandering people ruled by a chief
□ **tribal** *adj* belonging to or done by
a tribe or tribes: *tribal warfare*
□ **tribesman, tribeswoman** *noun* a
person who belongs to a particular
tribe

**tribulation** *noun* great hardship or
sorrow

**tribunal** *noun* **1** a group of people
appointed to give judgement, *esp* on
an appeal **2** a court of justice

**tribune** *noun*, *historical* a high
official elected by the people in
ancient Rome

**tributary** *noun* (*pl* **tributaries**) **1** a
stream that flows into a river or
other stream **2** someone who gives
money as a tribute

**tribute** *noun* **1** an expression, in word
or deed, of praise, thanks *etc*: *a
warm tribute to his courage* **2** money
paid regularly by one nation or ruler

to another in return for protection
or peace

**trice** *noun*: **in a trice** in a very short
time

**triceps** *noun* a muscle at the back of
the arm that straightens the elbow

**trick** *noun* **1** a cunning or skilful
action to puzzle, amuse *etc* **2** in card
games, the cards picked up by the
winner when each player has played
a card □ *adj* meant to deceive: *trick
photography* □ *verb* to cheat by
some quick or cunning action
□ **trickery** *noun* cheating □ **trickster**
*noun* someone who deceives by
tricks □ **tricky** *adj* not easy to do

**trickle** *verb* **1** to flow in small
amounts **2** to arrive or leave slowly
and gradually: *replies are trickling
in* □ *noun* a slow, gradual flow

**tricolour** or *US* **tricolor** *noun* the flag
of France, consisting of three
upright stripes of red, white and
blue

**tricycle** *noun* a three-wheeled bicycle

**trident** *noun* a three-pronged spear

**tried** *past form of* **try**

**triennial** *adj* **1** lasting for three years
**2** happening every third year

**tries** *see* **try**

**trifle** *noun* **1** anything of little value
**2** a small amount **3** a pudding of
whipped cream, sponge-cake, wine
*etc* □ *verb* **1** (with **with**) to act
towards them without sufficient
respect: *in no mood to be trifled with*
**2** to amuse yourself in an idle way
(with): *he trifled with her affections*
**3** to behave in a light, thoughtless
manner

**trifling** *adj* very small in value or
amount

**trigger** *noun* a small lever on a gun
which, when pulled with the finger,
causes the bullet to be fired □ *verb*
(often with **off**) to start, be the cause
of, an important event, chain of
events *etc*

**trigonometry** *noun* the branch of mathematics which has to do chiefly with the relationship between the sides and angles of triangles □ **trigonometric** or **trigonometrical** *adj*

**trilby** *noun* a man's hat with an indented crown and narrow brim

So called because a hat of this shape was worn by an actress in the original stage version of George du Maurier's novel, *Trilby* (1894)

**trill** *verb* to sing, play or utter in a quivering or bird-like way □ *noun* a trilled sound; in music, a rapid repeating of two notes several times

**trillion** 1 a million million millions 2 (originally *US*) a million millions

**trilogy** (*pl* **trilogies**) a group of three related plays, novels *etc* by the same author, meant to be seen or read as a whole

**trim** *verb* 1 to clip the edges or ends of: *trim the hedge* 2 to arrange (sails, cargo) so that a boat is ready for sailing 3 to decorate (*eg* a hat) □ *noun* 1 the act of trimming 2 dress: *hunting trim* □ *adj* tidy, in good order, neat □ **in good trim** 1 in good order 2 fit

**trim** *verb* ⋄ **trims, trimming, trimmed**

**trimming** *noun* 1 a decoration added to a dress, cake *etc* 2 a piece of cloth, hair *etc* cut off while trimming

**Trinity** *noun* in Christianity, the union of Father, Son and Holy Ghost in one God

**trinket** *noun* a small ornament (*esp* one of little value)

**trio** *noun* (*pl* **trios**) 1 three performers 2 three people or things

**trip** *verb* 1 (often with *up*) to stumble, fall over 2 to move with short, light steps 3 (with *up*) to make a mistake □ *noun* 1 a journey for pleasure or business 2 a light short step 3 (**trips**) *slang* the drug LSD □ **tripper** *noun* someone who

goes on a short pleasure trip

**trip** *verb* ⋄ **trips, tripping, tripped**

**tripartite** *adj* 1 in or having three parts 2 of an agreement: between three countries

**tripe** *noun* 1 part of the stomach of the cow or sheep used as food 2 *informal* rubbish, nonsense

**triple** *adj* 1 made up of three 2 three times as large (as something else) □ *verb* to make or become three times as large

**triplet** *noun* 1 one of three children or animals born of the same mother at one time 2 three rhyming lines in a poem 3 *music* a group of three notes played in the time of two

**triplicate** *noun*: **in triplicate** in three copies

**tripod** *noun* a three-legged stand (*esp* for a camera)

**trisect** *verb* to cut into three □ **trisection** *noun* trisecting, dividing into three parts

**trite** *adj* of a remark: used so often that it has little force or meaning

**triumph** *noun* 1 a great success or victory 2 celebration after a success: *ride in triumph through the streets* □ *verb* 1 to win a victory 2 to rejoice openly because of a victory □ **triumphal** *adj* used in celebrating a triumph □ **triumphant** *adj* victorious; showing joy because of, or celebrating, triumph □ **triumphantly** *adv*

**trivet** *noun* a metal tripod for resting a teapot or kettle on

**trivia** *noun pl* unimportant matters or details

**trivial** *adj* of very little importance □ **triviality** *noun* (*pl* **trivialities**) 1 something unimportant 2 trivialness □ **trivialness** *noun* the state of being trivial

**trod** and **trodden** *see* **tread**

**troglodyte** *noun* a cave-dweller

**troll** *noun* a mythological creature,

giant or dwarf, who lives in a cave

**trolley** *noun* (*pl* **trolleys**) **1** a small cart (*eg* as used by porters at railway stations) **2** a supermarket basket on wheels **3** a hospital bed on wheels for transporting patients **4** a table on wheels, used for serving tea *etc* □ **trolley-bus** *noun* a bus which gets its power from overhead wires

**trombone** *noun* a brass wind instrument with a sliding tube which changes the notes

**troop** *noun* **1** a collection of people or animals **2** (**troops**) soldiers **3** a unit in cavalry *etc* □ *verb* **1** to gather in numbers **2** to go in a group: *they all trooped out* □ **trooper** *noun* a horse-soldier □ **troop the colours** to carry a regiment's flag past the lined-up soldiers of the regiment

**trophy** *noun* (*pl* **trophies**) **1** something taken from an enemy and kept in memory of the victory **2** a prize such as a silver cup won in a sports competition *etc*

**tropic** *noun* **1** either of two imaginary circles running round the earth at about 23 degrees north (**Tropic of Cancer**) or south (**Tropic of Capricorn**) of the equator **2** (**tropics**) the hot regions near or between these circles □ *adj* of the tropics □ **tropical** *adj* **1** of the tropics **2** growing in hot countries: *tropical fruit* **3** very hot

**trot** *verb* **1** of a horse: to run with short, high steps **2** of a person: to run slowly with short steps **3** to make (a horse) trot □ *noun* the pace of a horse or person when trotting □ **trotters** *noun pl* the feet of pigs or sheep, *esp* when used as food

**trot** *verb* ↔ trots, trotting, trotted

**troubadour** *noun*, *historical* a medieval travelling singer-musician, *esp* in France

**trouble** *verb* **1** to cause worry or sorrow to **2** to cause inconvenience to **3** to make an effort, bother (to): *I*

*didn't trouble to ring him* □ *noun* **1** worry, uneasiness **2** difficulty; disturbance **3** something which causes worry, difficulty *etc* **4** a disease **5** care and effort put into doing something □ **troubleshooter** *noun* someone whose job is to solve difficulties (*eg* in a firm's business activities) □ **troublesome** *adj* causing difficulty or inconvenience

**trough** *noun* **1** a long, open container for holding animals' food and water **2** an area of low atmospheric pressure **3** a dip between two sea waves

**trounce** *verb* **1** to punish or beat severely **2** to defeat heavily

**troupe** (*say* troop) *noun* a company of actors, dancers *etc*

**trousers** *noun pl* an outer garment for the lower part of the body which covers each leg separately □ **trouser** *adj* of a pair of trousers: *trouser leg*

**trousseau** *noun* (*pl* **trousseaux** or **trousseaus** - *say both* **troos**-ohz) a bride's outfit for her wedding

**trout** *noun* a freshwater or sea (**sea-trout**) fish, used as food

**trowel** *noun* **1** a small spade used in gardening **2** a similar tool with a flat blade, used for spreading mortar

**troy weight** a system of weights for weighing gold, gems *etc*

**truant** *noun* someone who stays away from school *etc* without permission □ **truancy** *noun* □ **play truant** to stay away from school, work *etc* without permission

**truce** *noun* a rest from fighting or quarrelling agreed to by both sides

**truck** *noun* **1** a wagon for carrying goods on a railway **2** a strong lorry for carrying heavy loads □ **trucker** *noun*, *US* a lorry driver □ **have no truck with** to refuse to have dealings with

**truculent** *adj* fierce and threatening, aggressive □ **truculence** *noun*

**trudge** *verb* to walk with heavy steps, as if tired

**true** *adj* **1** of a story *etc*: telling of something which really happened **2** correct, not invented or wrong: *it's true that the earth is round* **3** accurate **4** faithful: *a true friend* **5** real, properly so called: *the spider is not a true insect* **6** rightful: *the true heir* **7** in the correct or intended position □ **truism** *noun* a statement which is so clearly true that it is not worth making □ **truly** *adj* **1** really: *Is that truly what he said?* **2** genuinely; honestly: *I'm truly sorry* **3** completely, utterly: *a truly classless society*

**truffle** *noun* a round fungus found underground and much valued as a flavouring for food

**trump** *noun* **1** a suit having a higher value than cards of other suits **2** a card of this suit □ *verb* to play a card which is a trump □ **trump card 1** a card which is a trump **2** something kept in reserve as a means of winning an argument *etc* □ **trump up** to make up, invent □ **turn up trumps** to play your part well when things are difficult

**trumpery** *noun* (*pl* **trumperies**) something showy but worthless

**trumpet** *noun* **1** a brass musical instrument with a clear, high-pitched tone **2** the cry of an elephant □ *verb* **1** to announce (*eg* news) so that all may hear **2** to blow a trumpet **3** of elephants: to make a long, loud cry

**truncated** *adj* **1** cut off at the top or end **2** shortened: *a truncated version*

**truncheon** *noun* a short heavy staff or baton such as that used by police officers

**trundle** *verb* to wheel or roll along

**trunk** *noun* **1** the main stem of a tree **2** the body (not counting the head, arms or legs) of a person or animal **3** the long nose of an elephant **4** a large box or chest for clothes *etc* **5** *US* the luggage compartment of a car **6** (**trunks**) short pants worn by boys and men for swimming □ **trunkcall** *noun* the former name for a **national call** □ **trunk road** a main road

**truss** *noun* (*pl* **trusses**) **1** a bundle (*eg* of hay, straw) **2** a system of beams to support a bridge **3** a kind of supporting bandage □ *verb* **1** to bind, tie tightly (up) **2** (often with **up**) to prepare (a bird ready for cooking) by tying up the legs and wings

**trust** *noun* **1** belief in the power, truth or goodness of a thing or person **2** something (*eg* a task or an item of value) handed over to someone in the belief that they will do it, guard it *etc* **3** charge, keeping: *the child was put in my trust* **4** arrangement by which something (*eg* money) is given to someone for use in a particular way **5** a number of business firms working closely together □ *verb* **1** to have faith or confidence (in) **2** to give (someone something) in the belief that they will use it well *etc*: *I can't trust your sister with my tennis racket* **3** to feel confident (that): *I trust that you can find your way here* □ **trustee** *noun* someone who keeps something in trust for another □ **trustful** or **trusting** *adj* ready to trust, not suspicious □ **trustworthy** *adj* able to be trusted or depended on □ **trusty** *adj* able to be trusted or depended on □ **take on trust** to believe without checking or testing

**truth** *noun* **1** the state of being true **2** a true statement **3** the facts □ **truthful** *adj* **1** telling the truth, not lying **2** of a statement: true □ **truthfully** *adv*

**try** *verb* **1** to attempt, make an effort (to do something) **2** to test by using: *try this new soap* **3** to test severely, strain: *you're trying my patience*

**4** to attempt to use, open *etc*: *I tried the door but it was locked* **5** to judge (a prisoner) in a court of law □ *noun* (*pl* **tries**) **1** an effort, an attempt **2** one of the ways of scoring in Rugby football □ **trying** *adj* hard to bear; testing □ **try on** to put on (clothing) to see if it fits *etc* □ **try out** to test by using

**try** *verb* ⟿ tries, trying, tried

■ (verb, meaning 1) attempt, endeavour, venture, undertake, seek, strive; (verb, meaning 2) test, sample; (verb, meaning 5) hear, judge

**tsar** or **tzar** or **czar** *noun, historical* the emperor of pre-revolutionary Russia

**tsarina** or **tzarina** or **czarina** *noun, historical* **1** the wife of a tsar **2** an empress of Russia

**tsetse** (*say* tset-si) *noun* or **tsetse fly** an African biting fly which spreads dangerous diseases

**T-shirt** *another spelling of* **tee-shirt**

**tub** *noun* **1** a round wooden container used for washing *etc*; a bath **2** a round container for ice-cream *etc*

**tuba** *noun* a large brass musical instrument giving a low note

**tubby** *adj* fat and round

**tube** *noun* **1** a hollow, cylinder-shaped object through which liquid may pass **2** an organ of this kind in humans, animals *etc* **3** a container from which something may be squeezed **4** an underground railway system **5** a cathode ray tube □ **tubing** *noun* a length or lengths of tube □ **tubular** *adj* shaped like a tube

**tuber** *noun* a swelling on the underground stem of a plant (*eg* a potato)

**tuberculosis** *noun* an infectious disease affecting the lungs

**TUC** *abbrev* Trades Union Congress

**tuck** *noun* **1** a fold stitched in a piece of cloth **2** *informal* sweets, cakes *etc* □ *verb* **1** to gather (cloth) together into a fold **2** to fold or push (into or under a place) **3** (with **in** or **up**) to push bedclothes closely round (someone in bed) □ **tuck shop** a shop in a school where sweets, cakes *etc* are sold □ **tuck in** *informal* to eat with enjoyment or greedily

**Tuesday** *noun* the third day of the week

**tuft** *noun* a bunch or clump of grass, hair *etc*

**tug** *verb* **1** to pull hard **2** to pull along □ *noun* **1** a strong pull **2** a tugboat □ **tugboat** *noun* a small but powerful ship used for towing larger ones □ **tug-of-war** *noun* a contest in which two teams, holding the ends of a strong rope, pull against each other

**tug** *verb* ⟿ tugs, tugging, tugged

**tuition** *noun* **1** teaching **2** private coaching or teaching

**tulip** *noun* a type of flower with cup-shaped flowers grown from a bulb

Based on a Persian word for 'turban', because of the similarity in shape

**tulle** *noun* a kind of cloth made of thin silk or rayon net

**tumble** *verb* **1** to fall or come down suddenly and violently **2** to roll, toss (about) **3** to do acrobatic tricks **4** to throw into disorder □ *noun* **1** a fall **2** a confused state □ **tumbledown** *adj* falling to pieces □ **tumbler** *noun* **1** a large drinking glass **2** an acrobat □ **tumble to something** to understand it suddenly

**tumbrel** or **tumbril** *noun, historical* a two-wheeled cart of the kind used to take victims to the guillotine during the French Revolution

**tummy** *noun* (*pl* **tummies**), *informal* the stomach

**tumour** *noun* an abnormal growth on or in the body

**tumult** *noun* **1** a great noise made by a crowd **2** excitement, agitation

□ **tumultuous** *adj* with great noise or confusion: *a tumultuous welcome*

**tun** *noun* a large cask, *esp* for wine

**tuna** *noun* (*pl* **tuna** or **tunas**) a large sea fish, used as food (*also called*: **tunny**)

**tundra** *noun* a level treeless plain in Arctic regions

**tune** *noun* **1** notes put together to form a melody **2** the music of a song □ *verb* **1** to put (a musical instrument) in tune **2** to adjust a radio set to a particular station **3** (sometimes with **up**) to improve the working of an engine □ **tuneful** *adj* having a pleasant or recognizable tune □ **tunefully** *adv* □ **tuning fork** a steel fork which, when struck, gives a note of a certain pitch □ **change your tune** to change your opinions, attitudes *etc* □ **in tune 1** of a musical instrument: having each note adjusted to agree with the others or with the notes of other instruments **2** of a voice: agreeing with the notes of other voices or instruments **3** in agreement (with) □ **to the tune of** to the sum of

**tungsten** *noun* an element, a grey metal

**tunic** *noun* **1** a soldier's or police officer's jacket **2** *historical* a loose garment reaching to the knees, worn in ancient Greece and Rome **3** a similar modern garment: *gym tunic*

**tunnel** *noun* **1** an underground passage (*eg* for a railway train) □ *verb* **1** to make a tunnel **2** of an animal: to burrow

**tunnel** *verb* ⇝ tunnels, tunnel*ling*, tunnel*led*

**tunny** *same as* **tuna**

**turban** *noun* **1** a long piece of cloth wound round the head, worn by Muslims **2** a kind of hat resembling this

**turbid** *adj* of liquid: muddy, clouded

**turbine** *noun* an engine with curved blades, turned by the action of water, steam, hot air *etc*

**turbo-** *prefix* using a turbine engine ⓘ From Latin *turbo* meaning 'a spinning-top'

**turbot** *noun* a type of large flat sea fish, used as food

**turbulent** *adj* **1** disturbed, in a restless state **2** likely to cause a disturbance or riot □ **turbulence** *noun* irregular movement of air currents, *esp* when affecting the flight of aircraft

**tureen** *noun* a large dish for holding soup at table

**turf** *noun* **1** grass and the soil below it **2** (with **the**) the world of horse-racing □ *verb* to cover with turf □ **turf out** *informal* to throw out

**turgid** *adj* **1** swollen **2** of language: sounding grand but meaning little, pompous

**turkey** *noun* (*pl* **turkeys**) a large farmyard bird, used as food

**Turkish bath** a type of hot air or steam bath in which someone is made to sweat heavily, is massaged and then slowly cooled

**turmoil** *noun* a state of wild, confused movement or disorder

**turn** *verb* **1** to go round: *wheels turning* **2** to face or go in the opposite direction: *turned and walked away* **3** to change direction: *the road turns sharply to the left* **4** to direct (*eg* attention) **5** (**turn on**) to move, swing *etc*: *the door turns on its hinges* **6** of milk: to go sour **7** to become: *his hair turned white* **8** of leaves: to change colour **9** to shape in a lathe **10** to pass (the age of): *she must have turned 40* □ *noun* **1** the act of turning **2** a point where someone may change direction, *eg* a road junction: *take the first turn on the left* **3** a bend (*eg* in a road) **4** a spell of duty: *your turn to wash the dishes* **5** an act (*eg* in a circus) **6** a short stroll: *a turn along the beach* **7** a fit of dizziness, shock *etc* **8** requirement: *this will serve our turn* □ **turncoat** *noun* someone who betrays their party, principles *etc* □ **turning** *noun* **1** the act of turning **2** a point where a road *etc* joins another **3** the act of shaping in a lathe □ **turning-point** a crucial point of change □ **turnover** *noun* **1** rate of change or replacement (*eg* of workers in a firm *etc*) **2** the total amount of sales made by a firm during a certain time □ **turnpike** *noun* **1** *historical* a gate across a road which opened when the user paid a toll **2** *US* a road on which a toll is paid □ **turnstile** *noun* a gate which turns, allowing only one person to pass at a time □ **turntable** *noun* **1** a revolving platform for turning a railway engine round **2** the revolving part of a record-player on which the record rests □ **by turns** or **in turn** one after another in a regular order □ **do someone a good** (or **bad**) **turn** to act helpfully (or unhelpfully) towards someone □ **to a turn** exactly, perfectly: *cooked to a turn* □ **turn against** to become hostile to □ **turn down 1** to say no to, refuse (*eg* an offer, a request) **2** to reduce, lessen (heat, volume of sound *etc*) □ **turn in 1** to go to bed **2** to hand over to those in authority □ **turn off 1** to stop the flow of (a tap) **2** to switch off the power for (a television *etc*) □ **turn on 1** to set running (*eg* water from a tap) **2** to switch on power for (a television *etc*) **3** to depend (on) **4** to become angry with (someone) unexpectedly **5** *slang* to arouse sexually □ **turn out 1** to make to leave, drive out **2** to make, produce **3** to empty: *turn out your pockets* **4** of a crowd: to come out, gather for a special purpose **5** to switch off (a light) **6** to prove (to be): *he turned out to be right* □ **turn to 1** to set to work **2** to go to for

help *etc* □ **turn up 1** to appear, arrive **2** to be found **3** to increase (*eg* heat, volume of sound *etc*) □ **turn someone's head** to fill them with pride or conceit

**turnip** *noun* a plant with a large round root used as a vegetable

**turpentine** *noun* an oil from certain trees used for mixing paints, cleaning paint brushes *etc*

**turpitude** *noun* wickedness

**turquoise** *noun* a greenish-blue precious stone

Literally 'Turkish stone', because first found in Turkestan

**turret** *noun* **1** a small tower on a castle or other building **2** a structure for supporting guns on a warship □ **turreted** *adj* having turrets

**turtle** *noun* a kind of large tortoise which lives in water □ **turtledove** *noun* a type of dove noted for its sweet, soft song □ **turn turtle** of a boat *etc*: to turn upside down, capsize

**tusk** *noun* a large tooth (one of a pair) sticking out from the mouth of certain animals (*eg* an elephant, a walrus)

**tussle** *noun* a struggle □ *verb* to struggle, compete

**tussock** *noun* a tuft of grass

**tutor** *noun* **1** a teacher of students in a university *etc* **2** a teacher employed privately to teach individual pupils □ *verb* to teach □ **tutorial** *adj* of a tutor □ *noun* a meeting for study or discussion between tutor and students

**tutu** *noun* a ballet dancer's short, stiff, spreading skirt

**tuxedo** *noun* (*pl* **tuxedos** or **tuxedoes**) *US* a dinner-jacket

**TV** *abbrev* television

**twaddle** *noun, informal* nonsense

**twain** *noun, old* two □ **in twain** *old* in two, apart

**twang** noun 1 a tone of voice in which the words seem to come through the nose 2 a sound like that of a tightly-stretched string being plucked □ verb to make such a sound

**tweak** verb to pull with a sudden jerk, twitch □ noun a sudden jerk or pull

**tweed** noun 1 a woollen cloth with a rough surface 2 (**tweeds**) clothes made of this cloth □ adj made of tweed

**tweezers** noun pl small pincers for pulling out hairs, holding small things etc

**twelve** noun the number 12 □ adj 12 in number □ **twelfth** adj the last of a series of twelve □ noun one of twelve equal parts

**twenty** noun the number 20 □ adj 20 in number □ **twentieth** adj the last of a series of twenty □ noun one of twenty equal parts

**twice** adv two times

**twiddle** verb to play with, twirl idly □ **twiddle your thumbs** 1 to turn your thumbs around one another 2 to have nothing to do

**twig** noun a small branch of a tree

**twilight** noun 1 the faint light between sunset and night, or before sunrise 2 the time just before or after the peak of something: the twilight of the dictatorship

**twill** noun a kind of strong cloth with a ridged appearance

**twin** noun 1 one of two children or animals born of the same mother at the same birth 2 one of two things exactly the same □ adj 1 born at the same birth 2 very like another 3 made up of two parts or things which are alike

**twine** noun a strong kind of string made of twisted threads □ verb 1 to wind or twist together 2 to wind (about or around something)

**twinge** noun a sudden, sharp pain

**twinkle** verb 1 of a star etc: to shine with light which seems to vary in brightness 2 of eyes: to shine with amusement etc □ **twinkling** noun: **in a twinkling** in an instant

**twirl** verb 1 to turn or spin round quickly and lightly 2 to turn round and round with the fingers □ noun a spin round and round

**twist** verb 1 to wind (threads) together 2 to wind round or about something 3 to make (eg a rope) into a coil 4 to bend out of shape 5 to bend or wrench painfully (eg your ankle) 6 to make (eg facts) appear to have a meaning which is really false □ noun 1 the act of twisting 2 a painful wrench 3 something twisted: a twist of tissue paper □ **twister** noun, informal a dishonest and unreliable person

**twitch** verb 1 to pull with a sudden light jerk 2 to jerk slightly and suddenly: a muscle in his face twitched □ noun 1 a sudden jerk 2 a muscle spasm

**twitter** noun 1 high, rapidly repeated sounds, as are made by small birds 2 slight nervous excitement □ verb 1 of a bird: to make a series of high quivering notes 2 of a person: to talk continuously

**two** noun the number 2 □ adj 2 in number □ **two-faced** adj deceitful, insincere □ **twofold** adj double □ **two-time** verb to have a love affair with two people at the same time

**tycoon** noun a business man of great wealth and power

Based on a Japanese title for a warlord

**tympani** another spelling of **timpani**

**type** noun 1 kind 2 an example which has all the usual characteristics of its kind 3 a small metal block with a raised letter or sign, used for printing 4 a set of these 5 printed lettering □ verb 1 to print with a typewriter 2 to use a typewriter 3 to identify or classify as a particular type ▫ **typecast** *verb* to give (an actor) parts very similar in character ▫ **typescript** *noun* a typed script for a play *etc* ▫ **typewriter** *noun* a machine with keys which, when struck, print letters on a sheet of paper ▫ **typist** *noun* someone who works with a typewriter and does other secretarial or clerical tasks

**typhoid** *noun* an infectious disease caused by germs in infected food or drinking water

**typhoon** *noun* a violent storm of wind and rain in Eastern seas

**typhus** *noun* a dangerous fever carried by lice

**typical** *adj* having or showing the usual characteristics: *a typical Irishman/ typical of her to be late* ▫ **typically** *adv*

**typify** *verb* to be a good example of: *typifying the English abroad*

**typify** ⊳ typifies, typifying, typified

**typography** *noun* the use of type for printing ▫ **typographical** *adj* relating to or involving printing or typography

**tyranny** *noun* (*pl* **tyrannies**) the rule of a tyrant ▫ **tyrannical** or **tyrannous** *adj* like a tyrant, cruel ▫ **tyrannize** *verb* to act as a tyrant; rule over harshly

**tyrant** *noun* a ruler who governs cruelly and unjustly

**tyre** or *US* **tire** *noun* a thick rubber cover round a motor or cycle wheel

**tyro** another spelling of **tiro**

**tzar, tzarina** another spelling of **tsar, tsarina**

# Uu

**ubiquitous** (*say* yoo-**bik**-wit-*u*s) *adj* **1** being everywhere at once **2** found everywhere ▫ **ubiquity** *noun* existence everywhere

**udder** *noun* a bag-like part of a cow, goat *etc* with teats which supply milk

**UFO** (*say* yoo-ef-**oh** or **yoo**-foh) *abbrev* unidentified flying object

**ugly** *adj* **1** unpleasant to look at or hear: *ugly sound* **2** threatening, dangerous: *gave me an ugly look* ▫ **ugliness** *noun* ▫ **ugly duckling** an unattractive or disliked person who later turns into a beauty, success *etc*

**UHF** *abbrev* ultra high frequency

**UHT** *abbrev* **1** ultra-heat treated **2** ultra high temperature

**ukelele** (*say* yook-*e*-**lei**-li) *noun* a small, stringed musical instrument played like a banjo

**ulcer** *noun* an open sore on the inside or the outside of the body

▫ **ulcerated** *adj* having an ulcer or ulcers ▫ **ulcerous** *adj* affected with ulcers

**ulterior** *adj* beyond what is admitted or seen: *ulterior motive*

**ultimate** *adj* last, final ▫ **ultimately** *adv* finally, in the end

**ultimatum** *noun* a final demand sent with a threat to break off discussion, declare war *etc* if it is not met

**ultra-** *prefix* **1** very: *ultra-careful* **2** beyond: *ultramicroscopic* ▫ **ultramarine** *adj* of a deep blue colour ▫ **ultrasonic** *adj* beyond the range of human hearing ▫ **ultraviolet** *adj* having rays of slightly shorter wavelength than visible light

⊚ From Latin *ultra* meaning 'beyond'

**umber** *noun* a mineral substance used to produce a brown paint

**umbilical** adj of the navel □ **umbilical cord** a tube connecting an unborn mammal to its mother through the placenta

**umbrage** noun a feeling of offence or hurt: *took umbrage at my suggestion*

**umbrella** noun an object made up of a folding covered framework on a stick which protects against rain

Literally 'little shadow' and originally used to refer to a sunshade

**umlaut** (say oom-lowt) noun a character (¨) placed over a letter to modify its pronunciation

**umpire** noun 1 a sports official who sees that a game is played according to the rules 2 a judge asked to settle a dispute □ verb to act as an umpire

**umpteen** adj many, lots

Originally *umpty*, a signaller's slang term for a dash in Morse code

**UN** abbrev United Nations

**un-** prefix 1 not: *unequal* 2 (with verbs) used to show the reversal of an action: *unfasten*

**unabashed** adj shameless, blatant

**unable** adj lacking enough strength, power, skill *etc*

**unaccountable** adj not able to be explained □ **unaccountably** adverb: *she was feeling unaccountably depressed*

**unaccustomed** adj not used (to)

**unadulterated** adj pure, not mixed with anything else

**unanimous** (say yoo-**nan**-im-us) adj 1 all of the same opinion: *we were unanimous* 2 agreed to by all: *a unanimous decision* □ **unanimously** adj: *he was elected unanimously* □ **unanimity** (say yoo-na-**nim**-it-i) noun

**unapproachable** adj unfriendly and stiff in manner

**unarmed** adj not armed

**unassuming** adj modest

**unattached** adj 1 not attached

**2** single, not married or having a partner

**unaware** adj not knowing, ignorant (of): *unaware of the danger* □ **unawares** adverb 1 without warning 2 unintentionally

**unbalanced** adj mad; lacking balance: *unbalanced view*

**unbearable** adj too painful or bad to be endured

**unbending** adj severe

**unbounded** adj not limited, very great: *unbounded enthusiasm*

**unbridled** adj not kept under control: *unbridled fury*

**unburden** verb: **unburden yourself** to tell your secrets or problems to someone else

**uncalled** adj: **uncalled for** quite unnecessary: *your remarks were uncalled for*

**uncanny** adj strange, mysterious □ **uncannily** adverb

**uncared** adj: **uncared for** not looked after properly

**unceremonious** adj informal, off-hand

**uncertain** adj 1 not certain, doubtful 2 not definitely known 3 of weather: changeable

**uncharted** adj 1 not shown on a map or chart 2 little known

**uncle** noun 1 the brother of your father or mother 2 the husband of your father's or mother's sister

**unclean** adj dirty, impure

**uncoil** verb to unwind

**uncomfortable** adj not comfortable

**uncommon** adj not common, strange □ **uncommonly** adj very: *uncommonly talented*

**uncompromising** adj not willing to give in or make concessions to others

**unconditional** adj with no conditions attached; absolute

**unconscious** adj 1 senseless,

stunned (*eg* by an accident) **2** not aware (of) **3** not recognized by the person concerned: *unconscious prejudice against women* □ *noun* the deepest level of the mind

**uncouth** *adj* **1** clumsy, awkward **2** rude

**uncover** *verb* **1** to remove a cover from **2** to disclose

**unction** *noun* anointing; anointment □ **unctuous** *adj* oily, ingratiating

**undaunted** *adj* fearless; not discouraged

**undecided** *adj* not yet decided

**undeniable** *adj* not able to be denied, clearly true

**under** *prep* **1** directly below or beneath **2** less than: *costing under £5* **3** within the authority or command of: *under General Montgomery* **4** going through, suffering: *under attack* **5** having, using: *under a false name* **6** in accordance with: *under our agreement* □ *adverb* in or to a lower position, condition *etc* □ **go under 1** to sink beneath the surface of water **2** to go bankrupt, go out of business □ **under age** younger than the legal or required age □ **under way** in motion, started

**under-** *prefix* **1** below, beneath: *underfoot* **2** lower in position or rank: *under-secretary* **3** too little: *underpay*

**underachieve** *verb* to achieve less than your potential

**underarm** *adverb* of bowling *etc*: with the arm kept below the shoulder

**undercarriage** *noun* the wheels of an aeroplane and their supports

**underclothes** *noun pl* clothes worn next to the skin under other clothes

**undercover** *adj* acting or done in secret: *an undercover agent* (ie a spy)

**undercurrent** *noun* **1** a flow or movement under the surface **2** a

half-hidden feeling or tendency: *an undercurrent of despair in her voice*

**undercut** *verb* to sell at a lower price than someone else

**underdeveloped** *adj* **1** not fully grown **2** of a country: lacking modern agricultural and industrial systems, and with a low standard of living

**underdog** *noun* the weaker side, or the loser in any conflict or fight

**underdone** *adj* of food: not quite cooked

**underestimate** *verb* to estimate at less than the real worth, value *etc*

**underfoot** *adj* under the feet

**undergo** *verb* **1** to suffer, endure **2** to receive (*eg* as medical treatment)

**undergo** ⇔ undergoes, undergoing, underwent, undergone

**undergraduate** *noun* a university student who has not yet passed final examinations

**underground** *adj* **1** below the surface of the ground **2** secret, covert □ *noun* a railway which runs in a tunnel beneath the surface of the ground

**undergrowth** *noun* shrubs or low plants growing amongst trees

**underhand** *adj* sly, deceitful

**underlie** *verb* to be the hidden cause or source of □ **underlying** *adj*

**underline** *verb* **1** to draw a line under **2** to stress the importance of, emphasize

**underling** *noun* someone of lower rank

**undermine** *verb* to do damage to, weaken gradually (health, authority *etc*)

**underneath** *adj & prep* in a lower position (than), beneath: *look underneath the table/ wearing a jacket underneath his coat*

**undernourished** *adj* not well nourished

**underpants** noun pl underwear covering the buttocks and upper legs

**underpass** noun a road passing under another one

**underpay** verb to pay too little

**underpin** verb to support from beneath, prop up

**underprivileged** adj not having normal living standards or rights

**underrate** verb to think too little of, underestimate

**undersell** verb **1** to sell for less than the true value **2** to sell for less than someone else

**undersigned** noun: **the undersigned** the people whose names are written at the end of a letter or statement

**undersized** adj below the usual or required size

**underskirt** noun a thin skirt worn under another skirt

**understand** verb **1** to see the meaning of **2** to appreciate the reasons for: *I don't understand your behaviour* **3** to have a thorough knowledge of: *do you understand economics?* **4** to have the impression that: *I understood that you weren't coming* **5** to take for granted as part of an agreement □ **understandable** adj **1** reasonable, natural or normal: *he reacted with understandable fury* **2** able to be understood: *his speech was barely understandable*

**understand** ↔ understand**s**, understand**ing**, **understood**

■ (meaning 1) grasp, comprehend, discern, perceive; (meaning 2) fathom; (meaning 4) believe, gather, conclude

**understanding** noun **1** the ability to see the full meaning of something **2** an agreement **3** condition: *on the understanding that we both pay half* **4** appreciation of other people's feelings, difficulties *etc* □ adj able to understand other people's feelings, sympathetic

**understate** verb to represent something as being less important or smaller than it really is □ **understatement** noun a statement which does not give the whole truth, making less of certain details than is actually the case

**understudy** noun (pl **understudies**) an actor who learns the part of another actor and is able to take their place if necessary

**undertake** verb **1** to promise (to do something) **2** to take upon yourself (a task, duty *etc*): *I undertook responsibility for the food* □ **undertaker** noun someone whose job is to organize funerals □ **undertaking** noun **1** something which is being attempted or done **2** a promise **3** the business of an undertaker

**under-the-counter** adj hidden from customers' sight; illegal

**undertone** noun **1** a soft voice **2** a partly hidden meaning, feeling *etc*: *an undertone of discontent*

**undertow** noun a current below the surface of the water which moves in a direction opposite to the surface movement

**undervalue** verb to value (something) below its real worth

**underwater** adj under the surface of the water

**underwear** noun underclothes

**underweight** adj under the usual or required weight

**underwent** past form of **undergo**

**underworld** noun **1** the criminal world or level of society **2** the place where spirits go after death

**underwrite** verb **1** to accept for insurance **2** to accept responsibility or liability for □ **underwriter** noun someone who insures ships

**undesirable** adj not wanted

**undeveloped** *adj* not developed

**undivided** *adj* not split, complete, total: *undivided attention*

**undo** *verb* **1** to unfasten (a coat, parcel *etc*) **2** to wipe out the effect of, reverse: *undoing all the good I did* **3** *old* to ruin, dishonour (*esp* a reputation): *alas, I am undone* □ **undoing** *noun* ruin, dishonour

**undo** ➾ undo**es**, undo**ing**, undo**ne**, und**id**

**undoubted** *adj* not to be doubted □ **undoubtedly** *adj* without doubt, certainly

**undreamt-of** *adj* more *etc* than could have been imagined

**undress** *verb* to take your clothes off

**undue** *adj* too much, more than is necessary: *undue expense* □ **unduly** *adverb* excessively; unreasonably: *unduly worried*

**undulate** *verb* **1** to move as waves do **2** to have a rolling, wavelike appearance □ **undulating** *adj* □ **undulation** *noun*

**undying** *adj* unending, never fading: *undying love*

**unearth** *verb* to bring or dig out from the earth, or from a place of hiding □ **unearthly** *adj* **1** strange, as if not of this world **2** *informal* absurd, *esp* absurdly early: *at this unearthly hour*

**uneasy** *adj* anxious, worried □ **uneasiness** *noun*

**unemployed** *adj* **1** without a job **2** not in use □ **unemployment** *noun* **1** the state of being unemployed **2** the total number of unemployed people in a country □ **the unemployed** unemployed people as a group

**unenviable** *adj* not arousing envy: *unenviable task*

**unequal** *adj* **1** not equal; unfair: *unequal distribution* **2** lacking enough strength or skill: *unequal to the job* □ **unequalled** *adj* without an

equal, unique

**unequivocal** (*say* un-i-**kwiv**-*o*k-al) *adj* clear, not ambiguous: *unequivocal orders*

**unerring** *adj* always right, never making a mistake: *unerring judgement*

**uneven** *adj* **1** not smooth or level **2** not all of the same quality *etc*: *this work is very uneven*

**unexceptionable** *adj* not causing objections or criticism

From the sense of 'exception' found in the phrase 'to take exception to something' (= to object to it)

➾ Do not confuse:
   **unexceptionable** and
   **unexceptional**

**unexceptional** *adj* not exceptional, ordinary

From the sense of 'exception' meaning 'something unlike the rest'

**unexpected** *adj* not expected, sudden

**unfailing** *adj* never failing, never likely to fail: *unfailing accuracy*

**unfair** *adj* not just

**unfaithful** *adj* **1** not true to your marriage vows **2** failing to keep promises

**unfasten** *verb* to loosen, undo (*eg* a buttoned coat)

**unfathomable** *adj* not understandable, not clear

**unfeeling** *adj* harsh, hard-hearted

**unfettered** *adj* not restrained

**unfit** *adj* **1** not suitable **2** not good enough, or not in a suitable state (to, for): *unfit for drinking/ unfit to travel* **3** physically under par

**unfold** *verb* **1** to spread out **2** to give details of (a story, plan) **3** of details of a plot *etc*: to become known

**unforgettable** *adj* unlikely to ever be forgotten; memorable

**unfortunate** *adj* **1** unlucky **2** regrettable: *unfortunate turn of phrase*

**unfounded** *adj* not based on fact; untrue

**unfurl** *verb* to unfold (*eg* a flag)

**ungainly** *adj* clumsy, awkward

**ungracious** *adj* rude, not polite

**ungrateful** *adj* not showing thanks for kindness

**unguarded** *adj* **1** without protection **2** thoughtless, careless: *unguarded remark*

**unguent** (*say* ung-gwent) *noun* ointment

**unhappy** *adj* **1** miserable, sad **2** unfortunate □ **unhappily** *adj*

**unhealthy** *adj* **1** not well, ill **2** harmful to health: *unhealthy climate* **3** showing signs of not being well: *unhealthy complexion*

**unheard-of** *adj* very unusual, unprecedented

**unhinged** *adj* mad, crazy

**unholy** *adj* **1** evil **2** outrageous

**uni-** *prefix* one, a single: *unilateral/ unit*
  ⓘ From Latin *unus* meaning 'one'

**unicorn** *noun* a mythological animal like a horse, but with one straight horn on its forehead

**uniform** *adj* the same in all parts or times, never varying □ *noun* the form of clothes worn by people in the armed forces, children at a certain school *etc* □ **uniformity** *noun* sameness: *the uniformity of modern architecture*

**unify** *verb* to combine into one □ **unification** *noun*

**unify** ⇨ unifi*es*, unifi*ying*, unifi*ed*

**unilateral** *adj* **1** one-sided **2** involving one person or group out of several □ **unilateralism** *noun* the abandoning of nuclear weapons by one country, without waiting for others to do likewise

**uninhibited** *adj* not inhibited, unrestrained

**uninitiated** *adj* not knowing, ignorant

**uninterested** *adj* not interested

❧ Do not confuse with: **disinterested**. It is generally a negative thing to be **uninterested** (= bored). It is generally a positive thing to be **disinterested** (= fair), especially if you are trying to make an unbiased decision.

**uninterrupted** *adj* **1** continuing without a break **2** of a view: not blocked by anything

**union** *noun* **1** the act of joining together **2** partnership; marriage **3** countries or states joined together **4** a trade union □ **unionist** *noun* **1** a member of a trade union **2** someone who supports the union of the United Kingdom □ **Union Jack** the flag of the United Kingdom

**unique** *adj* without a like or equal: *a unique sense of timing*

❧ Do not confuse with: **rare**. You can talk about something being **rare**, quite **rare**, very **rare** *etc*. It would be incorrect, however, to describe something as 'very **unique**', since things either are or are not **unique** - there are no levels of this quality.

**unisex** *adj* suitable for either men or women

**unison** *noun* **1** exact sameness of musical pitch **2** agreement, accord □ **in unison** all together

**unit** *noun* **1** a single thing, person or group, *esp* when considered as part of a larger whole: *army unit/ storage unit* **2** a fixed amount or length used as a standard by which others are measured (*eg* metres, litres, centimetres *etc*) **3** the number one □ **unitary** *adj* **1** forming a unit, not divided **2** using or based on units □ **unity** *noun* **1** complete agreement **2** the state of being one or a whole **3** the number one

**unite** *verb* **1** to join together; becom

one **2** to act together □ **united** *adj*

**universe** *noun* all known things, including the earth and planets □ **universal** *adj* **1** relating to the universe **2** relating to, or coming from, all people: *universal criticism* □ **universally** *adverb* (sense 2): *universally acclaimed*

**university** *noun* (*pl* **universities**) a college which teaches a wide range of subjects to a high level, and which awards degrees to students who pass its examinations

**unkempt** *adj* untidy

**unkind** *adj* not kind; harsh, cruel

**unleaded** *adj* of petrol: not containing lead compounds

**unleash** *verb* **1** to set free (a dog *etc*) **2** to let loose (*eg* anger)

**unleavened** (*say* un-lev-end) *adj* of bread: not made to rise with yeast

**unless** *conj* if not, except in a case where: *unless he's here soon, I'm going* (*ie* if he's not here soon)

**unlike** *adj* different, not similar □ *prep* **1** different from **2** not characteristic of: *it was unlike her not to phone*

**unlikely** *adj* **1** not probable: *it's unlikely that it will rain today* **2** probably not true: *an unlikely tale*

**unload** *verb* **1** to take the load from **2** to remove the charge from a gun

**unlucky** *adj* **1** not lucky or fortunate **2** unsuccessful □ **unluckily** *adverb*

**unmanly** *adj* weak, cowardly

**unmask** *verb* **1** to take a covering off **2** to show the true character of **3** to bring to light (a plot *etc*)

**unmentionable** *adj* not fit to be spoken of, scandalous, indecent

**unmistakable** *adj* very clear; impossible to confuse with any other: *unmistakable handwriting*

**unmitigated** *adj* complete, absolute: *unmitigated disaster*

**unmoved** *adj* not affected, unsympathetic: *unmoved by my pleas*

**unnatural** *adj* not natural, perverted

**unnecessary** *adj* not necessary; avoidable

**unnerve** *verb* to disconcert, perturb

**UNO** *abbrev* United Nations Organization

**unobtrusive** *adj* not obvious or conspicuous; modest

**unpack** *verb* to open (a piece of luggage) and remove the contents

**unpalatable** *adj* **1** not pleasing to the taste **2** not pleasant to have to face up to: *unpalatable facts*

**unparalleled** *adj* not having an equal, unprecedented: *unparalleled success*

**unpick** *verb* to take out sewing stitches from

**unpleasant** *adj* not pleasant, nasty

▪ disagreeable, objectionable, repulsive

**unprecedented** *adj* never having happened before

**unprepossessing** *adj* not attractive

**unprincipled** *adj* without (moral) principles

**unprintable** *adj* not suitable to be printed; obscene

**unquestionable** *adj* undoubted, certain

**unravel** *verb* **1** to unwind, take the knots out of **2** to solve (a problem or mystery)

**unravel** ⟵ unravel**s**, unravel**ling**, unravel**led**

**unreal** *adj* **1** not real, imaginary **2** *informal* amazing, incredible

**unremitting** *adj* never stopping, unending: *unremitting rain*

**unrequited** *adj* of love: not given in return, one-sided

**unrest** *noun* a state of trouble or discontent, *esp* among a group of people

**unrivalled** *adj* without an equal

**unruly** adj 1 badly behaved 2 not obeying laws or rules □ **unruliness** noun

**unsavoury** adj very unpleasant, causing a feeling of disgust

**unscathed** adj not harmed

**unscrew** verb to loosen (something screwed in)

**unscrupulous** adj having no scruples or principles

**unseat** verb 1 to remove from a political seat 2 to throw from the saddle (of a horse)

**unseemly** adj unsuitable, improper: unseemly haste

**unseen** adj not seen □ **sight unseen** (bought etc) without having been seen, at the buyer's risk

**unsettle** verb to disturb, upset □ **unsettled** adj 1 disturbed 2 of weather: changeable 3 of a bill: unpaid □ **unsettling** adj disturbing, upsetting

**unsightly** adj ugly

**unsociable** adj not willing to mix with other people

**unsolicited** adj not requested: unsolicited advice

**unsophisticated** adj 1 simple, uncomplicated 2 naive, inexperienced

**unsound** adj 1 incorrect, unfounded 2 not sane

**unspeakable** adj too bad to describe in words: unspeakable rudeness

**unstinting** adj unrestrained, generous

**unstoppable** adj not able to be stopped

**unsung** adj not celebrated, neglected: an unsung Scots poet

**unsuspecting** adj not aware of coming danger

**unswerving** adj solid, unwavering

**untenable** adj unjustifiable: the government's position is untenable

**unthinkable** adj 1 very unlikely 2 too bad to be thought of

**untidy** adj not neat or well-organized

**untie** verb 1 to release from bonds 2 to loosen (a knot)

**until** prep up to the time of: can you wait until Tuesday? □ conj up to the time that: keep walking until you come to the corner

**untimely** adj 1 happening too soon: untimely arrival 2 not suitable to the occasion: untimely remark

**unto** prep, old to

**untold** adj 1 not yet told: the untold story 2 too great to be counted or measured: untold riches

**untoward** adj 1 unlucky, unfortunate 2 inconvenient

**untrue** adj 1 not true, false 2 unfaithful

**untruth** noun a lie □ **untruthful** adj lying or dishonest

**unusual** adj 1 not usual 2 rare, remarkable □ **unusually** adverb to an unusual degree: unusually cold for the time of year

■ uncommon, exceptional, anomalous

**unvarnished** adj 1 not varnished 2 plain, straightforward: the unvarnished truth

**unveil** verb 1 to remove a veil from 2 to remove a cover from (a memorial etc) 3 to bring to light, disclose

**unwaged** adj unemployed

**unwarranted** adj uncalled-for, unnecessary

**unwell** adj not in good health

**unwieldy** adj not easily moved or handled □ **unwieldiness** noun

**unwind** verb 1 to wind off from a ball or reel 2 to relax

**unwitting** adj 1 unintended: unwitting insult 2 unaware □ **unwittingly** adverb: I unwittingly caused a lot of trouble

**unwonted** adj unaccustomed, not

usual: *unwonted cheerfulness*

**unworthy** *adj* **1** not worthy **2** low, worthless, despicable **3** (with *of*) not deserving: *unworthy of attention* **4** below someone's usual standard, out of character: *that remark is unworthy of you*

**up** *adverb* **1** towards or in a higher or more northerly position: *walking up the hill/ they live up in the Highlands* **2** completely, so as to finish: *drink up your tea* **3** to a larger size: *blow up a balloon* **4** as far as: *he came up to me and shook hands* **5** towards a bigger city *etc*, not necessarily one further north: *going up to London from Manchester* □ *prep* **1** towards or in the higher part of: *climbed up the ladder* **2** along: *walking up the road* □ *adj* **1** ascending, going up: *the up escalator* **2** ahead in score: *2 goals up* **3** better off, richer: *50 up on the deal* **4** risen: *the sun is up* **5** of a given length of time: ended: *your time is up* **6** *informal* wrong: *what's up with her today?* □ **up-and-coming** *adj* likely to succeed □ **on the up and up** progressing steadily, getting better all the time □ **up and about 1** awake **2** out of bed after an illness □ **ups and downs** times of good and bad luck □ **up front 1** at the front **2** of money: paid in advance **3** candidly, openly □ **up to 1** until: *up to the present* **2** capable of: *are you up to the job?* **3** dependent on, falling as a duty to: *it's up to you to decide* □ **up to 1** *doing: up to his tricks again* □ **up to scratch** of the required standard □ **up to speed** fully competent at a new job *etc*

**up** ↔ *upper, upmost* or *uppermost*

**upbeat** *adj, informal* cheerful, optimistic

**upbraid** *verb* to scold

**upbringing** *noun* the rearing of, or the training given to, a child

**update** *verb* to bring up to date □ *noun* **1** the act of updating **2** new information: *an update on*

*yesterday's report*

**upend** *verb* to turn upside down

**upfront** or **up-front** *adj* **1** candid, frank **2** foremost

**upgrade** *verb* **1** to raise to a more important position **2** to improve the quality of □ *noun, computing* a newer version of a software program

**upheaval** *noun* a violent disturbance or change

**upheld** *past form of* **uphold**

**uphill** *adj* **1** going upwards **2** difficult: *uphill struggle* □ *adv* upwards

**uphold** *verb* **1** to defend, give support to **2** to maintain, keep going (*eg* a tradition)

**uphold** ↔ *upholds, upholding, upheld*

**upholster** *verb* to fit (furniture) with springs, stuffing, covers *etc* □ **upholstery** *noun* **1** covers, cushions *etc* **2** the skill of upholstering

**upkeep** *noun* **1** the act of keeping (*eg* a house or car) in a good state of repair **2** the cost of this

**upland** *noun* **1** high ground **2** (**uplands**) a hilly or mountainous region

**uplift** *verb* to raise the spirits of, cheer up

**up-market** *adj* of high quality or price, luxury

**upon** *prep* **1** on the top of: *upon the table* **2** at or after the time of: *upon completion of the task*

**upper** *adj* higher, further up □ *noun* **1** the part of a shoe *etc* above the sole **2** *slang* the drug amphetamine □ **upper-case** *adj* of a letter: capital, *eg A* not *a* (*contrasted with:* **lower-case**) □ **upper-class** *adj* belonging to the highest social class, aristocratic □ **upper hand** advantage; dominance, control □ **uppermost** *adj* highest, furthest up

**upright** adj **1** standing up, vertical **2** honest, moral □ noun an upright post, piano etc

**uprising** noun a revolt against a government etc

**uproar** noun a noisy disturbance □ **uproarious** adj very noisy

**uproot** verb **1** to tear up by the roots **2** to leave your home and go to live in another place

**upset** verb (say up-set) **1** to make unhappy, angry, worried etc **2** to overturn **3** to disturb, put out of order **4** to ruin (plans etc) □ adj (say up-set) distressed, unhappy etc, ill □ noun (say up-set) **1** distress, unhappiness, worry etc **2** something that causes distress

upset verb ⇨ upsets, upsetting, upset

▪ (verb, meaning 1) distress, trouble, worry, agitate, discompose, disconcert; (verb, meaning 2) tip, spill; (verb, meanings 3 and 4) topple, overthrow, destabilize; (adj) dismayed, troubled, disconcerted, shaken

**upshot** (say up-shot) noun a result or end of a matter: what was the upshot of all this?

**upside-down** adj & adv **1** with the top part underneath **2** in confusion

**upstage** adv away from the footlights on a theatre stage □ adj, informal haughty, proud □ verb to divert attention from (someone) to yourself

**upstairs** adv in or to the upper storey of a house etc □ noun the upper storey or storeys of a house □ adj in the upper storey or storeys: upstairs bedroom

**upstanding** adj **1** honest, respectable **2** strong and healthy **3** old standing up

**upstart** (say up-staht) noun someone who has risen quickly from a low to a high position in society, work etc

**upstream** adv higher up a river or stream, towards the source

**upsurge** (say up-serj) noun a rising, a swelling up

**uptake** (say up-teik) noun: **quick on the uptake** quick to understand

**uptight** adj nervous, tense

**up-to-date** adj **1** modern, in touch with recent ideas etc **2** belonging to the present time **3** containing all recent facts etc: an up-to-date account □ **up to date 1** to the present time **2** containing recent facts etc **3** aware of recent developments

**upturn** noun a positive change, an improvement

**upward** adj moving up, ascending □ **upwards** adv from lower to higher, up □ **upwardly-mobile** adj moving to a higher social status □ **upwards of** more than

**uranium** (say yoo-**rei**-ni-um) noun a radioactive metal

**urban** adj relating to a town or city (contrasted with: **rural**) □ **urbanization** noun the process of urbanizing □ **urbanize** verb to make urban

**urbane** adj polite in a smooth way □ **urbanity** noun **1** smoothness of manner **2** (pl **urbanities**) urbane actions

**urchin** noun a dirty, ragged child

Originally meaning 'hedgehog', the prickly sense of which survives in sea urchin

**urge** verb **1** to drive (on) **2** to try to persuade: urging me to go home **3** to advise, recommend: urge caution □ noun a strong desire or impulse

**urgent** adj **1** requiring immediate attention **2** asking for immediate action □ **urgently** adv: medical supplies are needed urgently □ **urgency** noun

**urine** noun the waste liquid passed out of the body of animals and humans from the bladder □ **urinary** *adj* of or relating to urine or the passing of urine □ **urinate** *verb* to pass urine from the bladder

**urn** *noun* **1** a vase for the ashes of the dead **2** a metal drum with a tap, used for heating water for tea or coffee

**US** or **USA** *abbrev* United States of America

**us** *pron* used by a speaker or writer in referring to themselves together with other people (as the object in a sentence): *when would you like us to come?*

**usage** *noun* **1** the act or manner of using **2** the established way of using a word *etc* **3** custom, habit **4** treatment: *rough usage*

**use** *verb* **1** to put to some purpose: *use a knife to open it* **2** to bring into action: *use your common sense* **3** (often with **up**) to spend, exhaust (*eg* patience, energy) **4** to treat: *he used his wife cruelly* □ *noun* **1** the act of using **2** value or suitability for a purpose: *no use to anybody* **3** the fact of being used: *it's in use at the moment* **4** custom □ **no use** useless □ **used to 1** accustomed to **2** was or were in the habit of (doing something): *we used to go there every year*
  ⊙ From Latin *uti* meaning 'to use', and *usus* meaning 'a using'.
  ─────────────────────────
  ◧ (verb, meanings 1 and 2) utilize, employ, exploit (verb, meaning 3) consume, expend

**used** *adj* **1** employed, put to a purpose **2** not new: *used cars*

**useful** *adj* serving a purpose; helpful □ **usefully** *adv*

**useless** *adj* having no use or effect

**user** *noun* someone who uses anything (*esp* a computer) □ **user-friendly** *adj* easily understood, easy to use

**usher, usherette** *noun* someone who

shows people to their seats in a theatre *etc* □ *verb* **usher someone in** or **out** to lead or convey them into or out of a room, building *etc*

**USSR** *abbrev*, *historical* Union of Soviet Socialist Republics

**usual** *adj* **1** done or happening most often: *usual method* **2** customary: *with his usual cheerfulness* **3** ordinary □ *noun* a customary event, order *etc* □ **usually** *adv* on most occasions

**usurp** (*say* yoo-**zerp**) *verb* to take possession of (*eg* a throne) by force □ **usurper** *noun*

**usury** (*say* **yooz**-yu-ri) *noun* the lending of money with an excessively high rate of interest □ **usurer** *noun* a money-lender who demands an excessively high rate of interest

**utensil** *noun* an instrument or container used in the home (*eg* a ladle, knife, pan *etc*)

**uterus** *noun* (*pl* **uteri** - *say* **yoo**-te-rai) the womb

**utilitarian** *noun* concerned with usefulness, rather than beauty, pleasure *etc*

**utility** *noun* (*pl* **utilities**) **1** usefulness **2** a public service supplying water, gas *etc*

**utilize** *verb* to make use of □ **utilization** *noun*: *careful utilization of resources*

**utmost** *adj* **1** the greatest possible: *utmost care* **2** furthest □ **do your utmost** to make the greatest possible effort

**utopia** (*say* yoo-**toh**-pi-*a*) *noun* a perfect place, a paradise □ **utopian** *adj* unrealistically ideal

Literally 'no place', coined by Thomas More for his fictional book *Utopia* (1516)

**utter**[1] *verb* to produce with the voice (words, a scream *etc*) □ **utterance** *noun* something said

**utter²** *adj* complete, total: *utter darkness* □ **utterly** *adv* completely, absolutely □ **uttermost** *adj* most complete, utmost

**U-turn** *noun* a complete change in direction, policy *etc*

**UVA** *abbrev* ultraviolet radiation

## Vv

**v** *abbrev* versus

**vacancy** *noun* (*pl* **vacancies**) 1 a job that has not been filled 2 a room not already booked in a hotel *etc*

**vacant** *adj* 1 empty, not occupied 2 of an expression: showing no interest or intelligence □ **vacantly** *adv*

**vacate** *verb* to leave empty, cease to occupy

**vacation** *noun* 1 the act of vacating 2 a holiday

**vaccine** *noun* a substance made from the germs that cause a disease, given to people and animals to try to prevent them catching that disease □ **vaccinate** *verb* to give a vaccine to, *eg* by injection into the skin □ **vaccination** *noun*

**vacillate** *verb* to move from one opinion to another; waver □ **vacillation** *noun*

**vacuous** *adj* 1 empty 2 empty-headed, stupid □ **vacuously** *adv*

**vacuum** *noun* a space from which all, or almost all, the air has been removed □ **vacuum cleaner** a machine which cleans carpets *etc* by sucking up dust □ **vacuum flask** a container with double walls enclosing a vacuum, for keeping liquids hot or cold

**vagabond** *noun* 1 someone with no permanent home; a wanderer 2 a rascal, a rogue

**vagaries** *noun pl* strange, unexpected behaviour: *vagaries of human nature*

**vagina** *noun* the passage connecting a woman's genitals to her womb

**vagrant** *adj* unsettled, wandering □ *noun* a wanderer or tramp, with no settled home □ **vagrancy** *noun*

**vague** *adj* 1 not clear; not definite 2 not practical or efficient; forgetful □ **vaguely** *adv*

**vain** *adj* 1 conceited, self-important 2 useless: *vain attempt* 3 empty, meaningless: *vain promises* □ **in vain** without success □ **vainly** *adv*

**valance** *noun* a decorative frill round the edge of a bed

**vale** *noun*, *formal* a valley

**valediction** *noun*, *formal* a farewell □ **valedictory** *adj*

**valentine** *noun* 1 a greetings card sent on St Valentine's Day, 14 February 2 a sweetheart, a lover

**valet** (*say* **val**-et or **val**-ei) *noun* a manservant □ *verb* 1 to work as a valet 2 (*say* **val**-et) to clean out (a car) as a service

**valetudinarian** (*say* val-i-tyood-i-**neir**-ri-an) *noun* someone who is over-anxious about their health

**valiant** *adj* brave □ **valiantly** *adv*

**valid** *adj* 1 sound, acceptable 2 legally in force: *valid passport* □ **validity** *noun*

**valley** *noun* (*pl* **valleys**) low land between hills, often with a river flowing through it

**valour** *noun* courage, bravery □ **valorous** *adj*

**valuable** *adj* of great value □ **valuables** *noun pl* articles of worth

**value** *noun* 1 worth; price 2 purchasing power (of a coin *etc*) 3 importance 4 usefulness 5 *algebr* a number or quantity put as equal to an expression: *the value of x is 8* □ *verb* **1** to put a price on **2** to think highly of □ **valuation** *noun* **1** the act of valuing **2** an estimated price or value □ **valueless** *adj* □ **valuer** *noun* someone trained to estimate the value of property □ **value-added tax** a government tax raised on the selling-price of an article, or charged on certain services

**valve** *noun* **1** a device allowing air, steam or liquid to flow in one direction only **2** a small flap controlling the flow of blood in the body **3** an electronic component found in older television sets, radios *etc*

**vamp** *noun* the upper part of a boot or shoe □ *verb* **1** to patch **2** to play improvised music

**vampire** *noun* a dead person supposed to rise at night and suck the blood of sleeping people

**van**[1] *noun* a covered or closed-in vehicle or wagon for carrying goods by road or rail

**van**[2] *noun*, *short for* **vanguard**

**vandal** *noun* someone who pointlessly destroys or damages public buildings *etc* □ **vandalism** *noun* □ **vandalize** *verb*

**vane** *noun* **1** a weathercock **2** the blade of a windmill, propeller *etc*

**vanguard** *noun* **1** the leading group in a movement *etc* **2** the part of an army going in front of the main body

**vanilla** *noun* a sweet-scented flavouring obtained from the pods of a type of orchid

**vanish** *verb* **1** to go out of sight **2** to fade away to nothing

**vanity** *noun* (*pl* **vanities**) **1** conceit **2** worthlessness **3** something vain and worthless

**vanquish** *verb* to defeat

**vantage point** a position giving an advantage or a clear view

**vapid** *adj* dull, uninteresting

**vaporize** *verb* to change into vapour □ **vaporizer** *noun* a device which sprays liquid very finely

**vapour** *noun* **1** the air-like or gas-like state of a substance that is usually liquid or solid: *water vapour* **2** mist or smoke in the air

**variable** *adj* changeable; that may be varied □ *noun* something that varies *eg* in value

**variance** *noun* a state of differing or disagreement □ **at variance** in disagreement or conflict □ **variant** *noun* a different form or version □ *adj* in a different form

**variation** *noun* **1** a varying, a change **2** the extent of a difference or change: *variations in temperature* **3** *music* a repetition, in a slightly different form, of a main theme

**varicose vein** a swollen or enlarged vein, usually on the leg

**variegated** *adj* marked with different colours; multicoloured

**variety** *noun* (*pl* **varieties**) **1** the quality of being of many kinds, or of being different **2** a mixed collection: *a variety of books* **3** a sort, a type: *a variety of potato* **4** mixed theatrical entertainment including songs, comedy, *etc*

**various** *adj* **1** of different kinds: *various shades of green* **2** several: *various attempts* □ **variously** *adv*

▣ different, diverse, many, several, heterogeneous

**varnish** *noun* a sticky liquid which gives a glossy surface to paper, wood *etc* □ *verb* **1** to cover with varnish **2** to cover up (faults *etc*)

**vary** *verb* **1** to make, be, or become different **2** to make changes in (a routine *etc*) **3** to differ, disagree

**vary** ⇨ **varies**, **varying**, **varied**

**vase** *noun* (*say* vahz *or US* veiz) *noun* a jar of pottery, glass *etc* used as an ornament or for holding cut flowers

**Vaseline** noun, trademark a type of ointment made from petroleum

**vassal** noun historical a tenant who held land from an overlord in return for certain services

**vast** adj of very great size or amount □ **vastly** adv □ **vastness** noun

**VAT** abbrev value-added tax

**vat** noun a large tub or tank, used eg for fermenting liquors and dyeing

**vaudeville** noun theatrical entertainment of dances and songs, usually comic

**vault** noun 1 an arched roof 2 an underground room, a cellar □ verb to leap, supporting your weight on your hands, or on a pole

**vaunt** verb to boast

**VCR** abbrev video cassette recorder

**VDU** abbrev visual display unit

**veal** noun the flesh of a calf, used as food

**veer** verb 1 to change direction or course 2 to change mood, opinions, etc

**vegan** (say vee-gan) noun a vegetarian who uses no animal products

**vegetable** noun a plant, esp one grown for food □ adj 1 of plants 2 made from or consisting of plants

**vegetarian** noun someone who eats no meat, only vegetable or dairy foods □ adj consisting of, or eating, only vegetable or dairy foods

**vegetate** verb 1 to grow as a plant does 2 to lead a dull, aimless life □ **vegetation** noun 1 plants in general 2 the plants growing in a particular area

**vehement** adj emphatic and forceful in expressing opinions etc □ **vehemence** noun □ **vehemently** adv

**vehicle** noun 1 a means of transport used on land, esp one with wheels 2 a means of conveying information, eg television or newspapers

**veil** noun 1 a piece of cloth or netting worn to shade or hide the face 2 something that hides or covers up □ verb 1 to cover with a veil 2 to hide □ **take the veil** to become a nun

**vein** noun 1 one of the tubes which carry the blood back to the heart 2 a small rib of a leaf 3 a thin layer of mineral in a rock 4 a streak in wood, stone etc 5 a mood or personal characteristic: a vein of cheerfulness

**veldt** (say velt) noun, South African open grass-country, with few or no trees

**vellum** noun 1 a fine parchment used for bookbinding, made from the skins of calves, kids or lambs 2 paper made in imitation of this

**velocity** noun rate or speed of movement

**velour** (say ve-loor) noun a fabric with a soft, velvet-like surface

**velvet** noun a fabric made from silk etc, with a thick, soft surface □ adj 1 made of velvet 2 soft or smooth as velvet; silky □ **velvety** adj

**venal** (say vee-nal) adj 1 willing to be bribed 2 done for a bribe; unworthy ⊚ From Latin venalis meaning 'for sale'

⬥ Do not confuse with: **venial**. **Venal** is related to the verb 'vend', since they both contain the concept of selling (from Latin venum). **Venial** comes from the Latin venia (= forgiveness) and means 'forgivable'.

**vend** verb to sell □ **vendor** noun □ **vending machine** a machine with sweets etc for sale, operated by putting coins in a slot ⊚ From Latin vendere meaning 'to sell'

**vendetta** noun a bitter, long-lasting quarrel or feud

**veneer** verb 1 to cover a piece of wood with another thin piece of finer quality **2** to give a good appearance to what is really bad □ *noun* **1** a thin surface layer of fine wood **2** a false outward show hiding some bad quality: *a veneer of good manners*

**venerable** *adj* worthy of respect because of age or wisdom

**venerate** *verb* to respect or honour greatly □ **veneration** *noun*

**venereal disease** (*say* vi-**neer**-ri-al) a disease contracted through sexual intercourse

**Venetian blind** a window blind formed of thin movable strips of metal or plastic hung on tapes

**vengeance** *noun* punishment given, harm done in return for wrong or injury, revenge □ **with a vengeance** with unexpected force or enthusiasm

**vengeful** *adj* seeking revenge □ **vengefully** *adv*

**venial** (*say* vee-ni-al) *adj* of a sin: not very bad, pardonable (*compare with:* **cardinal**)
ⓘ From Latin *venialis* meaning 'pardonable'

🔦 Do not confuse with: **venal**. **Venial** comes from the Latin *venia* (= forgiveness). **Venal** literally means 'willing to be bought' and is related to the verb 'vend', since they both contain the concept of selling (from the Latin *venum*).

**venison** *noun* the flesh of a deer, used as food

**venom** *noun* **1** poison **2** hatred, spite □ **venomous** *adj* □ **venomously** *adv*

**vent** *noun* **1** a small opening **2** a hole to allow air or smoke to pass through **3** an outlet **4** a slit at the bottom of the back of a coat *etc* □ *verb* to express (strong emotion) in some way □ **give vent to** to express, let out

**ventilate** *verb* **1** to allow fresh air to pass □ **through** (a room *etc*) **2** to

talk about, discuss □ **ventilation** *noun* □ **ventilator** *noun* a grating or other device for allowing in fresh air

**ventriloquist** *noun* someone who can speak without appearing to move their lips and can project their voice on to a puppet *etc* □ **ventriloquism** *noun*

Literally 'stomach speaker' and originally meaning someone possessed by a talking evil spirit

**venture** *noun* an undertaking which involves some risk: *business venture* □ *verb* **1** to risk, dare **2** to do or say something at the risk of causing annoyance: *may I venture to suggest* □ **venturesome** *adj*

**venue** *noun* the scene of an event, *eg* a sports contest or conference

**veracious** *adj* truthful □ **veracity** *noun*
ⓘ From Latin *verax* meaning 'truthful'

🔦 Do not confuse with: **voracious**

**veranda** or **verandah** *noun* a kind of terrace with a roof supported by pillars, extending along the side of a house

**verb** *noun* the word that tells what someone or something does in a sentence, *eg* 'I *sing*' / 'he *had* no idea'

**verbal** *adj* **1** of words **2** spoken, not written: *verbal agreement* **3** of verbs

**verbatim** *adj* in the exact words, word for word: *a verbatim account*

**verbose** *adj* using more words than necessary □ **verbosity** *noun*

**verdant** *adj* green with grass or leaves

**verdict** *noun* **1** the judge's decision at the end of a trial **2** someone's personal opinion on a matter

**verdigris** *noun* the greenish rust of copper, brass or bronze

**verdure** *noun* green vegetation

**verge** *noun* **1** the grassy border along the edge of a road *etc* **2** edge, brink □ **verge on** to be close to: *verging on the absurd*

**verger** *noun* a church caretaker, or church official

**verify** *verb* to prove, show to be true, confirm □ **verifiable** *adj* □ **verification** *noun*

verify ⇔ verifies, verifying, verified

**verily** *adj, old* truly, really

**verisimilitude** *noun* realism, closeness to real life

**veritable** *adj* **1** true **2** real, genuine

**verity** *noun* truth

**vermicelli** *noun* a type of food like spaghetti but in much thinner pieces

**vermilion** *noun* a bright red colour

**vermin** *noun pl* animals or insects that are considered pests, *eg* rats, mice, fleas *etc* □ **verminous** *adj*

**vernacular** *noun* the ordinary spoken language of a country or district □ *adj* in the vernacular

**vernal** *adj* of the season of spring

**verruca** *noun* a wart, *esp* on the foot

**versatile** *adj* **1** able to turn easily from one subject or task to another **2** useful in many different ways □ **versatility** *noun*

**verse** *noun* **1** a number of lines of poetry forming a planned unit **2** poetry as opposed to prose **3** a short division of a chapter of the Bible □ **versed in** skilled or experienced in

**version** *noun* **1** an account from one point of view **2** a form: *another version of the same tune* **3** a translation

**versus** *prep* against (*short form*: **v**)

**vertebra** *noun* (*pl* **vertebrae**) one of the bones of the spine

**vertebrate** *noun* an animal with a backbone

**vertex** *noun* (*pl* **vertices**) the top or summit; the point of a cone, pyramid or angle

**vertical** *adj* **1** standing upright

**2** straight up and down □ **vertically** *adv*

⊠ horizontal

**vertigo** *noun* giddiness, dizziness

**verve** *noun* lively spirit, enthusiasm

**very** *adv* **1** to a great extent or degree: *seem very happy* **2** exactly: *the very same* □ *adj* **1** same, identical: *the very people who claimed to support him voted against him* **2** ideal, exactly what is wanted: *the very man for the job* **3** actual: in *the very act of stealing* **4** mere: *the very thought of blood*

⊠ (adv, meaning 1) extremely, most, greatly, highly, deeply, truly, remarkably, excessively, exceedingly, acutely, particularly, absolutely, noticeably, unusually

**vespers** *noun pl* a church service in the evening

**vessel** *noun* **1** a ship **2** a container for liquid **3** a tube carrying fluids in the body: *blood vessels*

**vest** *noun* **1** an undergarment for the top half of the body **2** *US* a waistcoat

**vestibule** *noun* an entrance hall; a lobby

**vestige** *noun* a trace, an indication of something's existence □ **vestigial** *adj*

**vestment** *noun* a ceremonial garment, worn *eg* by a religious officer during a service

**vestry** *noun* (*pl* **vestries**) a room in a church in which vestments are kept

**vet¹** *noun, informal* a veterinary surgeon

**vet²** *verb* to examine, check

vet ⇔ vets, vetting, vetted

**vetch** *noun* a plant of the pea family

**veteran** *adj* old, experienced □ *noun* **1** someone who has given long service **2** an old soldier **3** *US* anyone who has served in the armed forces

**veterinary** *adj* relating to the treatment of animal diseases □ **veterinary surgeon** a doctor who treats animals

**veto** (*say* vee-toh) *noun* (*pl* **vetoes**) **1** the power to forbid or block (a proposal) **2** an act of forbidding or blocking □ *verb* to forbid, block

**veto** *verb* ⇔ vetos, vetoing, vetoed

Latin for 'I forbid', a phrase originally used by people's tribunes in the Roman Senate when objecting to proposals

**vex** *verb* to annoy; cause trouble to □ **vexation** *noun* □ **vexatious** *adj*

**VHF** *abbrev* very high frequency

**via** *prep* by way of: *travelling to Paris via London*

**viable** *adj* able to be managed, practicable: *viable proposition*

**viaduct** *noun* a long bridge taking a railway or road over a river *etc*

**viands** *noun pl*, *old* food

**vibrant** *adj* full of energy; lively, sparkling

**vibrate** *verb* **1** to shake, tremble **2** to swing to and fro rapidly **3** of sound: to resound, ring □ **vibration** *noun*

**vicar** *noun* an Anglican member of the clergy who is in charge of a parish □ **vicarage** *noun* the house of a vicar

**vicarious** *adj* **1** in place or on behalf of another person **2** not experienced personally but imagined through the experience of others: *vicarious thrill*

**vice** *noun* **1** a bad habit, a serious fault **2** wickedness, immorality **3** a tool with two jaws for gripping objects firmly

**vice-** *prefix* second in rank to: *vice-chancellor/ vice-president* ⊙ From Latin *vicis* meaning 'a turn'

**vice versa** *adv* the other way round: *I needed his help and vice versa (ie he needed mine)*

**vicinity** *noun* **1** nearness

**2** neighbourhood

**vicious** *adj* wicked; spiteful □ **viciously** *adv* □ **vicious circle** a bad situation whose results cause it to get worse

If you have trouble spelling the '-sh-' sound in **vicious**, remember the single 'c' in the related word 'vice'.

**vicissitude** (*say* vi-**sis**-it-yood) *noun* **1** change from one state to another **2** (**vicissitudes**) changes of luck, ups and downs

**victim** *noun* **1** someone who is killed, harmed, etc, intentionally or by accident **2** an animal for sacrifice □ **victimize** *verb*

**victory** *noun* (*pl* **victories**) success in any battle, struggle or contest □ **victor** *noun* a winner of a contest *etc* □ **victorious** *adj* successful in a battle or other contest

**victuals** (*say* **vit**-alz) *noun pl*, *old* food

**video** *adj* **1** relating to the recording and broadcasting of TV pictures and sound **2** relating to recording by video □ *noun* (*pl* **videos**) **1** a videocassette recorder **2** a recording on videotape **3** *US* television □ *verb* to make a recording by video □ **videocassette** *noun* a cassette containing videotape □ **videocassette recorder** a tape recorder using videocassettes for recording and playing back TV programmes □ **videotape** *noun* magnetic tape for carrying pictures and sound

**video** *verb* ⇔ videos, videoing, videoed

**vie** *verb*: **vie with** to compete with, try to outdo

**vie** ⇔ vies, vying, vied

**view** *noun* **1** a range or field of sight: *a good view* **2** a scene **3** an opinion □ *verb* **1** to look at **2** to watch (television) **3** to consider □ **viewpoint** *noun* **1** a place from which a scene is viewed **2** a personal opinion (also **point of view**) □ **in**

**view 1** in sight **2** in your mind as an aim □ **in view of** taking into consideration □ **on view** on show; ready for inspecting □ **with a view to** with the purpose or intention of

**vigil** *noun* a time of watching or of keeping awake at night, often before a religious festival

**vigilant** *adj* watchful, alert □ **vigilance** *noun*

**vigilante** (*say* vij-i-**lan**-tei) *noun* a private citizen who assumes the task of keeping order in a community

**vigorous** *adj* strong, healthy; forceful □ **vigorously** *adv*

**vigour** *noun* strength of body or mind; energy

**Viking** *noun, historical* a Norse invader of Western Europe

**vile** *adj* **1** very bad **2** disgusting, revolting □ **vilely** *adv*

**vilify** *verb* to say bad things about vilify ⇨ vilifies, vilifying, vilified

**villa** *noun* a house in the country *etc* used for holidays

**village** *noun* a collection of houses, not big enough to be called a town □ **villager** *noun*

**villain** *noun* a scoundrel, a rascal □ **villainous** *adj* □ **villainy** *noun*

**villein** *noun, historical* a serf

**vindicate** *verb* **1** to clear from blame **2** to justify

**vindictive** *adj* revengeful; spiteful

**vine** *noun* **1** a climbing plant that produces grapes (also **grapevine**) **2** any climbing or trailing plant

**vinegar** *noun* a sour-tasting liquid made from wine, beer *etc*, used for seasoning or pickling

**vineyard** (*say* **vin**-yad) *noun* an area planted with grapevines

**vintage** *noun* **1** the gathering of ripe grapes **2** the grapes gathered **3** wine of a particular year, *esp* when of very high quality **4** time of origin or manufacture □ *adj* **1** of a vintage

**2** of wine: of a particular year **3** very characteristic of an author, style *etc*: *vintage Monty Python* □ **vintage car** a car made between 1919 and 1930

**viola** (*say* vi-**oh**-la) *noun* **1** a stringed instrument like a large violin **2** a member of the family of plants which include violets and pansies

**violate** *verb* **1** to break (a law, a treaty *etc*) **2** to harm sexually, *esp* rape **3** to treat with disrespect **4** to disturb, interrupt □ **violation** *noun* □ **violator** *noun*

**violent** *adj* **1** acting with great force: *violent storm* **2** caused or characterized by violence: *a violent film* **3** uncontrollable: *violent temper* □ **violence** *noun* □ **violently** *adv*

---

◼ (meaning 1) intense, devastating, tumultuous; (meaning 2) brutal, bloodthirsty; (meaning 3) impetuous, intemperate, fiery

---

**violet** *noun* a kind of small bluish-purple flower

**violin** *noun* a musical instrument with four strings, held under the chin and played with a bow □ **violinist** *noun*

**violoncello** *see* **cello**

**VIP** *abbrev* very important person

**viper** *noun* **1** an adder **2** a vicious or treacherous person

**virago** *noun* (*pl* **viragos**) a noisy, bad-tempered woman

**virgin** *noun* someone who has never had sexual intercourse □ **virginal** *adj* □ **the Virgin Mary** the mother of Christ

**virginals** *noun* an early type of musical instrument, with a keyboard

**virile** *adj* manly; strong, vigorous □ **virility** *noun*

**virtual** *adj* in effect, though not in strict fact □ **virtually** *adv* almost, nearly □ **virtual reality** a computer-created environment that the person operating the computer is able to be a part of

**virtue** noun **1** goodness of character and behaviour **2** a good quality, eg honesty, generosity etc **3** a good point □ **by virtue of** because of

**virtuosity** noun brilliance of technique

**virtuoso** noun (pl **virtuosos**) a highly skilled artist, esp a musician

**virtuous** adj good, just, honest □ **virtuously** adv

**virulent** adj **1** full of poison **2** bitter, spiteful **3** of a disease: dangerous □ **virulence** noun

**virus** noun (pl **viruses**) a germ that is smaller than any bacteria, and causes diseases such as mumps, chickenpox etc □ **viral** adj

**visa** noun a permit given by the authorities of a country to allow someone to stay for a time in that country

**visage** (say **viz**-ij) noun, old the face

**viscera** (say **vis**-e-ra) noun pl the inner parts of the body

**viscount** (say **vai**-kownt) noun a title of nobility next below an earl □ **viscountess** (say **vai**-kownt-es) noun a title of nobility next below a countess

**viscous** (say **vis**-kus) adj of a liquid: sticky, not flowing easily □ **viscosity** noun

**visible** adj able to be seen □ **visibility** noun **1** the clearness with which objects may be seen **2** the extent or range of vision as affected by fog, rain etc □ **visibly** adv

**vision** noun **1** the act or power of seeing **2** something seen in the imagination **3** a strange, supernatural sight **4** the ability to foresee likely future events □ **visionary** adj seen in imagination only, not real □ noun (pl **visionaries**) someone who dreams up imaginative plans

**visit** verb **1** to go to see; call on **2** to stay with as a guest □ noun **1** a call at a person's house or at a place of interest etc **2** a short stay □ **visitation** noun **1** a visit of an important official **2** a great misfortune, seen as a punishment from God □ **visitor** noun

■ (verb) see

**visor** (say **vai**-zor) noun **1** a part of a helmet covering the face **2** a movable shade on a car's windscreen **3** a peak on a cap for shading the eyes

**vista** noun a view, esp one seen through a long, narrow opening

**visual** adj relating to, or received through, sight: visual aids □ **visual display unit** a device like a television set, on which data from a computer's memory can be displayed

**visualize** verb to form a clear picture of in the mind □ **visualization** noun

**vital** adj **1** of the greatest importance: vital information **2** necessary to life **3** of life **4** vigorous, energetic: a vital personality □ **vitality** noun life; liveliness; strength; ability to go on living □ **vitalize** verb to give life or vigour to □ **vitally** adv essentially; urgently

**vitamin** noun one of a group of substances necessary for health, occurring in different natural foods

**vitiate** (say **vish**-i-eit) verb to spoil, damage

**vitreous** adj of or like glass

**vitriol** noun sulphuric acid □ **vitriolic** adj biting, scathing

**vituperation** noun abusive criticism or language

**vivacious** adj lively, sprightly □ **vivaciously** adv □ **vivacity** noun

**vivid** adj **1** life-like **2** brilliant, striking □ **vividly** adv

**vivisection** noun the carrying out of

experiments on living animals

**vixen** *noun* 1 a female fox 2 an ill-tempered woman

**vizier** *noun, historical* a minister of state in some Eastern countries

**vocabulary** *noun* (*pl* **vocabularies**) 1 the range of words used by an individual or group 2 the words of a particular language 3 a list of words in alphabetical order, with their meanings

**vocal** *adj* 1 of the voice 2 expressing your opinions loudly and fully □ **vocalist** *noun* a singer

**vocation** *noun* 1 an occupation or profession to which someone feels called to dedicate themselves 2 a strong inclination or desire to follow a particular course of action or work

**vociferous** *adj* loud in speech, noisy

**vodka** *noun* an alcoholic spirit made from grain or potatoes

**vogue** *noun* the fashion of the moment; popularity □ **in vogue** in fashion

**voice** *noun* 1 the sound produced from the mouth in speech or song 2 ability to sing 3 an opinion □ *verb* to express (an opinion *etc*)

**void** *adj* 1 empty, vacant 2 not valid □ *noun* an empty space

**volatile** *adj* 1 of a liquid: quickly turning into vapour 2 of a person: changeable in mood or behaviour, fickle

**volcano** *noun* (*pl* **volcanoes**) a mountain with an opening through which molten rock, ashes *etc* are periodically thrown up from inside the earth □ **volcanic** *adj*

Named after *Vulcan*, the Roman god of fire

**vole** *noun* any of a group of small rodents, including the water rat

**volition** *noun* an act of will or choice: *he did it of his own volition*

**volley** *noun* (*pl* **volleys**) 1 a number

of shots fired or missiles thrown at the same time 2 an outburst of abuse or criticism 3 *tennis* a return of a ball before it reaches the ground □ *verb* 1 to shoot or throw in a volley 2 to return (a ball) before it reaches the ground

**volt** *noun* the unit used in measuring the force of electricity □ **voltage** *noun* electrical force measured in volts

**voluble** *adj* speaking with a great flow of words □ **volubility** *noun*

**volume** *noun* 1 a book, often one of a series 2 the amount of space taken up by anything 3 amount: *volume of trade* 4 loudness or fullness of sound □ **voluminous** *adj*

**voluntary** *adj* 1 done or acting by choice, not under compulsion 2 working without payment □ *noun* (*pl* **voluntaries**) a piece of organ music of the organist's choice played at a church service

**volunteer** *noun* someone who offers to do something of their own accord, often for no payment □ *verb* 1 to act as a volunteer 2 to give (information, an opinion *etc*) unasked

**voluptuous** *adj* full of, or too fond of, the pleasures of life

**vomit** *verb* to throw up the contents of the stomach through the mouth □ *noun* the matter thrown up by vomiting

**voracious** *adj* very greedy, difficult to satisfy: *voracious appetite* □ **voracity** *noun*
Ⓔ From Latin *vorax* meaning 'devouring'

❀ Do not confuse with: **veracious**

**vortex** *noun* (*pl* **vortices** or **vortexes**) 1 a whirlpool 2 a whirlwind

**vote** *verb* 1 to give your support to (a particular candidate, a proposal *etc*) in a ballot or show of hands 2 to decide by voting □ *noun* 1 an expression of opinion or support by roting **2** the right to vote ▫ **voter** *noun*

**ouch** *verb*: (with **for**) to say that you re sure of or can guarantee: *I can ouch for his courage*

**oucher** *noun* a paper which can be xchanged for money or goods

**ouchsafe** *verb* to give or grant (a eply, privilege *etc*)

**ow** *noun* a solemn promise or eclaration, *esp* one made to God ▫ *verb* **1** to make a vow **2** to hreaten (revenge *etc*)

**owel** *noun* **1** a sound made by the oice that does not require the use of he tongue, teeth or lips **2** the letters *a, e, i, o, u* (or various combinations of them), and sometimes *y*, which represent those sounds

**voyage** *noun* a journey, usually by sea ▫ *verb* to make a journey

**vulgar** *adj* **1** coarse, ill-mannered **2** indecent **3** of the common people ▫ **vulgarity** *noun* ▫ **vulgarly** *adv* ▫ **vulgar fraction** a fraction not written as a decimal, *eg* $\frac{1}{3}$, $\frac{4}{5}$

**vulnerable** *adj* **1** exposed to, or in danger of, attack **2** liable to be hurt physically or emotionally ▫ **vulnerability** *noun*

**vulture** *noun* a large bird that feeds mainly on the flesh of dead animals

---

## Ww

**ad** *noun* **1** a lump of loose material eg wool, cloth, paper) pressed ogether **2** a bunch of banknotes ▫ **wadding** *noun* soft material (eg otton wool) used for packing or adding

**addle** *verb* to walk with short, nsteady steps, moving from side to ide as a duck does ▫ *noun* the act of vaddling

**ade** *verb* **1** to walk through deep vater or mud **2** to get through with ifficulty: *still wading through this ook* ▫ **wader** *noun*

**afer** *noun* **1** a very thin, light type of iscuit, as that eaten with ice-cream a very thin slice of anything

**affle** *noun* **1** *US* a light, crisp cake nade from batter, cooked in a **vaffle-iron 2** pointless, long-drawn-out talk ▫ *verb* to talk long nd meaninglessly

**aft** *verb* to carry or drift lightly hrough the air or over water

**ag** *verb* to move from side to side or p and down ▫ *noun* **1** an act of vagging **2** someone who is always oking

**wag** *verb* ▫ **wags, wagging, wagged**

**wage** *verb* to carry on (a war *etc*) ▫ *noun* (often **wages**) payment for work

**wager** *noun* a bet ▫ *verb* to bet

**waggle** *verb* to move from side to side in an unsteady manner ▫ *noun* an unsteady movement from side to side

**wagon** or **waggon** *noun* **1** a four-wheeled vehicle for carrying loads **2** an open railway carriage for goods **3** *US* a trolley for carrying food

**wagtail** *noun* a small black and white bird with a long tail which it wags up and down

**waif** *noun* an uncared-for or homeless child or animal ▫ **waifs and strays** homeless children or animals

**wail** *verb* to cry or moan in sorrow ▫ *noun* a sorrowful cry

**wain** *noun, old* a wagon

**wainscot** *noun* a skirting-board

**waist** *noun* the narrow part of the body, between ribs and hips

**waistcoat** *noun* a short, sleeveless jacket, often worn under an outer jacket

**wait** *verb* **1** to put off or delay action **2** (with *for*) to remain in expectation or readiness for: *waiting for the bus to come* **3** to be employed as a waiter or waitress □ *noun* **1** a delay **2** (*waits*) singers of Christmas carols □ **waiting list** a list of people waiting for something in order of priority □ **waiting room** a room in which to wait at a railway station, clinic *etc* □ **wait on 1** to serve (someone) at table **2** to act as a servant to

■ (verb, meaning 1) delay, linger

**waiter, waitress** *noun* someone whose job it is to serve people at table in a restaurant

**waive** *verb* to give up (a claim or right) □ **waiver** *noun* **1** the act of waiving **2** a document indicating this

Ⓘ From Old French *guesver* meaning 'to abandon'

◭ Do not confuse with: **wave**

**wake¹** *verb* (often with *up*) to stop sleeping □ *noun* **1** a night of watching beside a dead body **2** a feast or holiday □ **wakeful** *adj* not sleeping, unable to sleep □ **waken** *verb* to wake, arouse or be aroused □ **waking** *adj*

**wake** *verb* ⇔ wakes, waking, woke or waked, woken

**wake²** *noun* a streak of foamy water left in the track of a ship □ **in the wake of** immediately behind or after

**walk** *verb* **1** to move along on foot **2** to travel along (streets *etc*) on foot □ *noun* **1** an act of walking **2** a manner of walking **3** a distance to be walked over **4** a place for walking: *a covered walk* □ **walkie-talkie** *noun* a portable radio set for sending and receiving messages □ **walking stick** a stick used for

support when walking □ **Walkman** *noun*, *trademark* a personal stereo □ **walk-over** *noun* an easy victory □ **walk of life** someone's rank or occupation

■ step, stride, pace, proceed, advance, march, plod, tramp, traipse, trek, trudge, saunter, amble, stroll, tread, hike, promenade, move

**wall** *noun* **1** a structure built of ston brick *etc* used to separate or enclos **2** the side of a building □ *verb* (wit *in, off etc*) to enclose or separate with a wall □ **wallflower** *noun* **1** a sweet-smelling spring flower **2** someone who is continually without a partner at a dance *etc* □ **wallpaper** *noun* paper used in house decorating for covering wal □ *verb* to cover with wallpaper □ **o the wall** unusual, eccentric

**wallaby** (*pl* **wallabies**) a small kind of kangaroo

**wallet** *noun* a small folding case for holding bank-notes, credit cards *e*

**wallop** *verb*, *informal* to beat, hit □ *noun*

**wallow** *verb* to roll about with enjoyment in water, mud *etc*

**walnut** *noun* **1** a tree whose wood is used for making furniture **2** the nu it produces

**walrus** *noun* (*pl* **walruses**) a large se animal, like a seal, with two long tusks

**waltz** *noun* (*pl* **waltzes**) **1** a ballroo dance for couples with a circling movement **2** music for this dance, with three beats to each bar □ *verb* to dance a waltz

**wan** (*say* won) *adj* pale and sickly looking

**wand** *noun* a long slender rod used k a conjuror, magician *etc*

**wander** *verb* **1** to roam about with no definite purpose; roam **2** to go astray **3** to be mentally confused because of illness *etc* □ **wanderer** *noun*

**wanderlust** *noun* a keen desire for travel

**wane** *verb* **1** to become smaller (*contrasted with:* **wax**) **2** to lose power, importance *etc* □ **on the wane** becoming less

**wangle** *verb* to get or achieve through craftiness, skilful planning *etc*

**want** *verb* **1** to wish for **2** to need, lack □ *noun* **1** poverty **2** scarcity, lack □ **wanted** *adj* looked for, *esp* by the police □ **wanting** *adj* **1** absent, missing; without **2** not good enough **3** feeble-minded **4** (with **in**) lacking: *wanting in good taste*
ⓔ From Old Norse *vant* meaning 'lacking', and *vanta* meaning 'to lack'

◼ (verb, meaning 1) desire, crave, covet, yearn for; (verb, meaning 2) require

**wanton** *adj* thoughtless, pointless, without motive: *wanton cruelty*

**war** *noun* an armed struggle, *esp* between nations □ *verb* (with **against**) to fight in a war, make war against □ **warfare** *noun* the carrying on of war □ **warhead** *noun* the part of a missile containing the explosive □ **warlike** *adj* fond of war **2** threatening war □ **warship** *noun* a ship armed with guns *etc* □ **on the warpath** in a fighting or angry mood

**warble** *verb* ⟿ wars, warring, warred

**warble** *verb* to sing like a bird, trill □ **warbler** *noun* a type of song-bird

**ward** *verb*: (with **off**) to keep off, defend yourself against (a blow *etc*) □ *noun* **1** a hospital room containing a number of beds **2** one of the parts into which a town is divided for voting **3** someone who is in the care of a guardian □ **warden** *noun* someone who guards a game reserve **2** someone in charge of a

hostel or college □ **warder** *noun* a prison guard

**wardrobe** *noun* **1** a cupboard for clothes **2** someone's personal supply of clothes

**warehouse** *noun* a building where goods are stored

**wares** *noun pl* goods for sale
ⓔ From Old English *waru*

**warm** *adj* **1** fairly hot **2** of clothes: keeping the wearer warm **3** of a person: friendly, loving □ *verb* to make or become warm □ **warmth** *noun* □ **warm-blooded** *adj* having a blood temperature higher than that of the surrounding atmosphere □ **warm-hearted** *adj* kind, generous

**warn** *verb* **1** to tell (someone) beforehand about possible danger, misfortune *etc* **2** to give cautionary advice to: *I warned him not to be late* □ **warning** *noun* a remark, notice *etc* that warns

**warp** *verb* **1** to become twisted out of shape **2** to distort, make unsound: *his previous experiences had warped his judgement* □ *noun* the threads stretched lengthwise on a loom, which are crossed by the weft

**warrant** *noun* a certificate granting someone a right or authority □ *verb* to justify, be a good enough reason for: *the crime does not warrant such punishment* □ **I warrant you** or **I'll warrant** you may be sure, I assure you

**warren** *noun* **1** a collection of rabbit burrows **2** a building with many rooms and passages; a maze

**warrior** *noun* a great fighter

**wart** *noun* a small hard growth on the skin

**wary** *adj* cautious, on guard □ **warily** *adv*

**was** *past form of* **be**

**wash** *verb* **1** to clean with water, soap *etc* **2** to cover yourself with water *etc* **3** of water: to flow over or against **4** to sweep (away, along *etc*) by force of water □ *noun* (*pl* **washes**) **1** a washing **2** a streak of foamy water left behind by a moving boat **3** a liquid with which anything is washed **4** a thin coat of paint *etc* □ **washer** *noun* **1** someone or something that washes **2** a flat ring of metal, rubber *etc* for keeping joints tight □ **washing** *noun* **1** the act of cleaning by water **2** clothes to be washed □ **washing machine** an electric machine for washing clothes □ **washing-up** *noun* dishes to be washed □ **wash your hands of** to have nothing further to do with □ **wash up** to wash the dishes

**wasp** *noun* a stinging, winged insect, with a slender, yellow and black striped body

**wassail** *verb, old* to have a convivial drinking session

**waste** *adj* **1** thrown away, rejected as useless: *waste paper* **2** of land: uncultivated, barren and desolate □ *verb* **1** to spend (money, time, energy) extravagantly, without result or profit **2** to decay or wear away gradually □ *noun* **1** extravagant use, squandering **2** rubbish, waste material **3** uncultivated land **4** an expanse of water, snow *etc* □ **wastage** *noun* **1** an amount wasted **2** loss through decay or squandering □ **wasteful** *adj* causing waste, extravagant □ **wastepaper** basket a basket for paper rubbish □ **wastepipe** *noun* a pipe for carrying away dirty water or semi-liquid waste □ **waster** or **wastrel** *noun* an idle, good-for-nothing person

**watch** *verb* **1** to look at, observe closely **2** (often with **over**) to look after, mind **3** *old* to keep awake □ *noun* (*pl* **watches**) **1** the act of keeping guard **2** someone who keeps, or those who keep, guard **3** a sailor's period of duty on deck **4** a small clock worn on the wrist or kept in a pocket □ **watchful** *adj*

alert, cautious □ **watchfully** *adv* □ **watchdog** *noun* **1** a dog which guards a building **2** an organization which monitors business practices *etc* □ **watchman** *noun* a man who guards a building *etc* at night □ **watchword** *noun* a motto, a slogan

---

■ (verb, meaning 1) observe, view, regard, mark; (verb, meaning 2) guard, superintend, supervise

---

**water** *noun* **1** a clear, tasteless liquid which falls as rain **2** a collection of this liquid in a lake, river *etc* **3** urine □ *verb* **1** to supply with water **2** to dilute or mix with water **3** of the mouth: to fill with saliva **4** of the eyes: to fill with tears □ **watery** *adj* **1** full of water **2** too liquid, textureless □ **water butt** a large barrel for rain water □ **water-closet** *noun* a toilet, a lavatory (*short form* WC) □ **water-colour** *noun* **1** a paint which is mixed with water, not oil **2** a painting done with this paint □ **watercress** *noun* a plant which grows beside streams, with hot-tasting leaves which are eaten in salads □ **waterfall** *noun* a place where a river falls from a height, often over a ledge of rock □ **waterlily** *noun* a plant which grows in ponds *etc*, with flat floating leaves and large flowers □ **waterlogged** *adj* **1** filled with water **2** soaked with water □ **watermark** *noun* a faint design on writing paper showing the maker's name, crest *etc* □ **watermelon** *noun* a large melon with red juicy flesh and a thick, green rind □ **water polo** a ball-game played in a pool between teams of swimmers □ **waterproof** *adj* not allowing water to pass through □ *noun* an overcoat made of waterproof material □ **watershed** *noun* a ridge separating the valleys of two rivers □ **water-skiing** *noun* the sport of being towed very fast on skis behind

a motorboat □ **watertight** adj so closely fitted that water cannot leak through □ **waterway** noun a channel along which ships can sail □ **waterworks** noun pl **1** a place which purifies and stores a town's water supply **2** euphemistic the urinary system **3** informal tears
ⓔ From Old English wæter

**watt** noun a unit of electric power □ **wattage** noun electric power measured in watts

**wattle** noun **1** interwoven twigs and branches used for fences etc **2** an Australian acacia tree **3** a fleshy part hanging from the neck of a turkey

**wave** noun **1** a moving ridge on the surface of the water **2** a ridge or curve of hair **3** a vibration travelling through the air carrying light, sound etc **4** a hand gesture for attracting attention, or saying hello or goodbye **5** a rush of an emotion (eg despair, enthusiasm etc) □ verb **1** to make a wave with the hand **2** to move to and fro, flutter: flags waving in the wind **3** to curl, curve □ **wavy** adj □ **wavelength** noun the distance from one point on a wave or vibration to the next similar point
ⓔ From Old English wafian meaning 'to wave'

**🖎 Do not confuse with: waive**

**waver** verb **1** to be unsteady, wobble **2** to be uncertain or undecided
ⓔ From Old Norse vafra meaning 'to flicker'

**wax** **1** the sticky, fatty substance of which bees make their cells **2** a fatty substance in the ear **3** a quickly hardening substance used for sealing letters etc □ adj made of wax □ verb **1** to rub with wax **2** to grow, increase (contrasted with: **wane**) □ **waxy** adj □ **waxen** adj □ **waxworks** noun pl a museum displaying wax models of famous people

**way** noun **1** an opening, a passage: the way out **2** road, path **3** room to go forward or pass: block the way **4** direction: he went that way **5** route: do you know the way? **6** distance: a long way **7** condition: in a bad way **8** means, method: there must be a way to do this **9** manner: in a clumsy way **10** someone's own wishes or choice: he always gets his own way □ **by the way** incidentally, in passing □ **by way of 1** travelling through **2** as if, with the purpose of: by way of a favour □ **in the way** blocking progress □ **make your way** to go
ⓔ From Old English weg

**wayfarer** noun, old a traveller on foot

**waylay** verb to wait for and stop (someone)

**wayside** noun the edge of a road or path □ adj located by the side of a road

**wayward** adj wilful, following your own way

**WC** abbrev water-closet

**we** pron used by a speaker or writer in mentioning themselves together with other people (as the subject of a verb): we are having a party this weekend

**weak** adj **1** not strong, feeble **2** lacking determination, easily persuaded **3** easily overcome: weak opposition □ **weakly** adj **1** in a weak way **2** lacking strength, sickly □ **weakness** noun **1** lack of strength **2** a fault; a special fondness (for): a weakness for chocolate □ **weaken** verb □ **weakling** noun a person or animal that is lacking in strength

**weal** noun a raised mark on the skin caused by a blow from a whip

**wealth** noun **1** riches **2** a large quantity: wealth of information □ **wealthy** adj rich

**wean** (say ween) verb **1** to make (a child or young animal) used to food other than the mother's milk

**2** (with **from** or **off**) to make (someone) gradually give up (a bad habit *etc*)

**weapon** *noun* **1** an instrument used for fighting, *eg* a sword, gun *etc* **2** any means of attack

**wear** *verb* **1** to be dressed in, have on the body **2** to arrange in a particular way: *she wears her hair long* **3** to have (a beard, moustache) on the face **4** to damage or weaken by use, rubbing *etc* **5** to be damaged in this way **6** to last: *wear well* □ *noun* **1** use by wearing: *for my own wear* **2** damage by use **3** ability to last **4** clothes *etc*: *school wear* □ **wearable** *adj* □ **wearer** *noun* □ **wear and tear** damage by ordinary use □ **wear off** to pass away gradually □ **wear on** to become later: *the afternoon wore on* □ **wear out** **1** to make or become unfit for further use **2** to exhaust

**wear** *verb* ⇨ wear*s*, wear*ing*, wore, worn

**weary** *adj* **1** tired, having used up your strength or patience **2** tiring, boring □ *verb* to make or become tired, bored or impatient □ **wearing** *adj* □ **wearisome** *adj* □ **weary of** tired of, bored with

**weary** ⇨ wear*ies*, wear*ying*, wear*ied*

**weasel** *noun* a small wild animal with a long and slender body, that lives on mice, birds *etc*

**weather** *noun* the state of the atmosphere, *eg* heat, coldness, cloudiness *etc* □ *verb* **1** to dry or wear away through exposure to the air **2** to come safely through (a storm, difficulty *etc*) □ **weathercock** or **weathervane** *noun* a flat piece of metal that swings in the wind to show its direction

**weave** *verb* **1** to pass threads over and under each other on a loom *etc* to form cloth **2** to plait cane *etc* for basket-making **3** to put together (a story, plan *etc*) **4** to move in and out between objects, or move from side to side: *weaving through the traffic* □ **weaver** *noun*

**weave** ⇨ weave*s*, weav*ing*, wove, woven

**web** *noun* **1** the net made by a spider, a cobweb **2** the skin between the toes of ducks, swans, frogs *etc* **3** something woven □ **webbed** *adj* of feet: having the toes joined by a web □ **web-footed** having wedded feet

**wed** *verb* to marry □ **wedding** *noun* **1** marriage **2** a marriage ceremony □ **wedlock** *noun* the state of being married

**wed** ⇨ wed*s*, wed*ding*, wed*ded*

**we'd** *short for* **1** we would; we should **2** we had

**wedge** *noun* **1** a piece of wood, metal *etc* thick at one end with a thin edge at the other, used in splitting wood, forcing two surfaces apart *etc* **2** anything shaped like a wedge □ *verb* **1** to fix or become fixed with a wedge **2** to push or squeeze (in): *wedged in amongst the crowd*

**Wednesday** *noun* the fourth day of the week

**wee** *adj, Scottish* small, tiny

**weed** *noun* **1** a useless, troublesome plant **2** a weak, worthless person **3** (**weeds**) a widow's mourning clothes □ *verb* to clear (a garden *etc*) of weeds

**weedy** *adj* **1** full of weeds **2** like a weed **3** thin and puny, unmanly

**week** *noun* **1** the space of seven days from Sunday to Saturday **2** the working days of the week, not Saturday and Sunday □ **weekly** *adj* happening, or done, once a week □ *adv* once a week □ *noun* (*pl* **weeklies**) a newspaper, magazine *etc* coming out once a week □ **weekday** *noun* any day except Saturday and Sunday □ **weekend** *noun* Saturday and Sunday
ⓒ From Old English *wice*

**weep** verb **1** to shed tears **2** to ooze, drip: *a weeping wound*

**weep ◁ weeps, weeping, wept**

**weeping willow** a willow tree with drooping branches

**weevil** noun a small beetle that destroys grain, flour *etc*

**weft** noun the threads on a loom which cross the warp

**weigh** verb **1** to find out how heavy (something) is by putting it on a scale *etc* **2** to have a certain heaviness: *weighing 10 kilogrammes* **3** to raise (a ship's anchor) **4** of burdens *etc*: to press down, be heavy or troublesome **5** to consider (a matter, a point) carefully **6** to consider (something) important □ **weigh in** to test your weight before a boxing match □ **weigh out** to measure out a quantity by weighing it on a scale

**weight** noun **1** the amount that anything weighs **2** a piece of metal weighing a certain amount: *a 100 gramme weight* **3** a load **4** importance □ verb to make heavy by adding or attaching a weight □ **weightless** adj **1** weighing nothing or almost nothing **2** not affected by gravity, so able to float about □ **weightlessness** noun absence of the pull of gravity □ **weighty** adj **1** heavy **2** important

**weir** noun a dam across a stream

**weird** adj **1** mysterious, supernatural **2** odd, strange

**welcome** verb **1** to receive with warmth or pleasure **2** to accept gladly: *I welcome the challenge* □ noun a welcoming, a warm reception □ adj received with pleasure □ **welcome to** permitted to do or take □ **you're welcome!** used in reply to an expression of thanks

**weld** verb **1** to join (pieces of metal) by pressure, with or without heating **2** to join closely □ noun a joint made by welding

**welfare** noun comfort, good health □ **welfare state** a country with a health service, insurance against unemployment, pensions for those who cannot work *etc*

**well** noun **1** a spring of water **2** a shaft in the earth to extract water, oil *etc* **3** an enclosed space round which a staircase winds □ verb (often with **up**) to rise up and gush: *tears welled up in her eyes* □ adj in good health □ adv **1** in a good and correct manner: *write well* **2** thoroughly: *well beaten* **3** successfully: *do well* **4** conveniently: *it fits in well with my plans* □ exclam expressing surprise, or used in explaining, narrating *etc* □ **well-advised** adj wise □ **well-behaved** adj with good manners □ **well-being** noun welfare; contentment □ **well-disposed** adj (with **to**) inclined to favour □ **well-informed** adj having or showing knowledge □ **well-known** adj **1** familiar **2** celebrated, famous □ **well-meaning** adj having good intentions □ **well-meant** adj rightly, kindly intended □ **well-off** adj rich □ **well-read** adj having read many good books □ **well-to-do** adj rich □ **well-wisher** noun someone who wishes someone success □ **as well as** in addition to □ **it is as well** or **it is just as well** it is a good thing, it is lucky

**well adv ◁ better, best**

**we'll** short for we will; we shall

**wellingtons** noun pl high rubber boots covering the lower part of the legs

**welt** noun **1** a firm edging or band, *eg* on the wrist or waist of a garment **2** a weal

**welter** verb to roll about, wallow □ noun **1** great disorder or confusion **2** a muddled mass, a jumble: *a welter of information*

**wench** noun (*pl* **wenches**) *old* a young woman, a girl

**wend** verb: **wend your way** to make your way slowly

**went** past form of **go**

**wept** past form of **weep**

**were** past form of **be**

**we're** short for we are

**werewolf** noun a mythical creature which changes periodically from a human into a wolf

**west** noun one of the four chief directions, that in which the sun sets □ adj in the west □ adv to or towards the west □ **westerly** adj **1** lying or moving towards the west **2** of wind: from the west □ **western** adj relating to, or in, the west □ noun a film or story about life among the early settlers in the western United States □ **westward** adj & adv towards the west □ **westwards** adv towards the west

**wet** adj **1** soaked or covered with water or other liquid **2** rainy: a wet day □ noun **1** water **2** rain □ verb to make wet □ **wet suit** a suit that allows water to pass through but retains body heat

**wet** verb ⇔ wets, wetting, wet or wetted

**whack** noun a loud, violent slap or blow □ verb to slap or hit violently

**whale** noun a very large mammal living in the sea □ **whaler** noun a ship engaged in catching whales

**wharf** noun (pl **wharfs** or **wharves**) a landing stage for loading and unloading ships

**what** adj & pron used to indicate something about which a question is being asked: what are you doing? □ adj any that: give me what money you have □ conj anything that: I'll take what you can give me □ adj, adv & pron used for emphasis in exclamations: what rubbish! □ **whatever** adj & pron **1** anything (that): show me whatever you have **2** no matter what: whatever happens

□ **whatsoever** adj at all: nothing whatsoever to do with me □ **what about?** used in asking whether the listener would like something: what about a glass of milk? □ **what if?** what will or would happen if: what if he comes back? □ **what with** because of: what with doing no exercise and being overweight, he had a heart attack

**wheat** noun a grain from which the flour used for making bread etc is made □ **wheaten** adj **1** made of wheat **2** wholemeal

**wheedle** verb to beg or coax, often by flattery

**wheel** noun **1** a circular frame or disc turning on an axle, used for transporting things **2** a steering-wheel of a car etc □ verb **1** to move or push on wheels **2** to turn like a wheel or in a wide curve **3** to turn round suddenly: wheeled round in surprise □ **wheelbarrow** noun a handcart with one wheel in front, two handles and legs behind □ **wheelchair** noun a chair on wheels for an invalid

**wheeze** verb to breathe with difficulty, making a whistling or croaking sound □ noun **1** the sound of difficult breathing **2** informal a joke

**whelk** noun a type of small shellfish, used as food

**whelp** noun **1** old a young lion **2** a puppy □ verb of a lion, dog etc: to give birth to young

**when** adv at what time: when did you arrive? □ adv & conj the time at which: I fell when I was coming in □ relative pron at which: at the time when I saw him □ conj seeing that, since: why walk when you have a car? □ **whenever** adv & conj **1** at any given time: come whenever you're ready **2** at every time: I go whenever I get the chance

**whence** adv, old from what place: whence did you come? □ conj to the place from which: *he's gone back whence he came*

**where** *adv & conj* to or in what place: *where are you going?/ I wonder where we are* □ *relative pron & conj* (in the place) in which, (to the place) to which: *go where he tells you to go* □ **whereabouts** *adv & conj* near or in what place: *whereabouts is it?* □ *noun* the place where someone or something is: *I don't know her whereabouts* □ **whereas** *conj* **1** when in fact: *they thought I was lying, whereas I was telling the truth* **2** but, on the other hand: *he's tall, whereas I'm short* □ **whereupon** *adv & conj* at or after which time, event *etc* □ **wherever** *adv* to what place: *wherever did you go?* □ *conj* to any place: *wherever you may go*

**whet** *verb* **1** to sharpen (a knife *etc*) by rubbing **2** to make (desire, appetite *etc*) keener □ **whetstone** *noun* a stone on which to sharpen blades

**whet** ← whet*s*, whet*ting*, whet*ted*

**whether** *conj* **1** either if: *whether you come or not* **2** if: *I don't know whether it's possible*

**which** *adj & pron* **1** used to refer to a particular person or thing from a group: *which colour do you like best?* **2** the one that: *show me which dress you would like* □ *relative pron* referring to the person or thing just named: *I bought the chair which you are sitting on* □ **whichever** *adj & pron* any (one), no matter which: *I saw trees whichever way I turned* □ **which is which** which is one and which is the other: *they are twins and I can't tell which is which*

**whiff** *noun* a sudden puff or scent: *whiff of perfume*

**while** or **whilst** *conj* **1** during the time that: *while I'm at the office* **2** although: *while I sympathize, I can't really help* □ **while** *noun* a space of time □ *verb* (with **away**) to pass (time) without boredom: *he*

whiled away the time by reading

**whim** *noun* a sudden thought or desire □ **whimsical** *adj* **1** full of whims, fanciful **2** humorous

**whimper** *verb* to cry with a low, whining voice □ *noun* a low, whining cry

**whine** *verb* **1** to make a high-pitched, complaining cry **2** to complain unnecessarily □ *noun* an unnecessary complaint

**whinge** *verb* to whine, complain peevishly □ *noun* a peevish complaint □ **whingeing** or **whinging** *adj*

**whinge** *verb* ← whinge*s*, whinge*ing* or whing*ing*, whinge*d*

**whinny** *verb* of a horse: to neigh □ *noun* (*pl* **whinnies**) a neighing sound

**whinny** *verb* ← whinn*ies*, whinn*ying*, whinn*ied*

**whip** *noun* **1** a lash with a handle, for punishing, urging on animals *etc* **2** a member of parliament who sees that the members of their own party attend to give their vote when needed □ *verb* **1** to hit or drive with a lash **2** to beat (eggs, cream *etc*) into a froth **3** to snatch (away, off, out, up *etc*): *whipped out a revolver* **4** to move fast, like a whip □ **whipping** *noun* a beating with a whip

**whip** *verb* ← whip*s*, whip*ping*, whip*ped*

**whippet** *noun* a breed of racing dog, like a small greyhound

**whir** or **whirr** *noun* a sound of fast, continuous whirling □ *verb* to move or whirl with a buzzing noise

**whir** *verb* ← whir*s*, whirr*ing*, whirr*ed*

**whirl** *verb* **1** to turn round quickly **2** to carry (off, away *etc*) quickly □ *noun* **1** a fast circling movement **2** great excitement, confusion □ **whirlpool** *noun* a place in a river or sea where the current moves in a circle □ **whirlwind** *noun* a violent current of wind with a whirling motion

**whisk** *verb* **1** to move quickly and lightly, sweep: *their car whisked past* **2** to beat or whip (a mixture) □ *noun* **1** a quick sweeping movement **2** a kitchen utensil for beating eggs or mixtures **3** a small bunch of twigs *etc* used as a brush

**whisker** *noun* **1** a long bristle on the upper lip of a cat *etc* **2** (**whiskers**) hair on the sides of a man's face, sideburns

**whisky** or *Irish* & *US* **whiskey** *noun* (*pl* **whiskies** or **whiskeys**) an alcoholic spirit made from grain

Based on Scottish Gaelic *uisge beatha*, meaning 'water of life'

**whisper** *verb* **1** to speak very softly, using the breath only, not the voice **2** to make a soft, rustling sound □ *noun* a soft sound made with the breath

**whist** *noun* a type of card game for four players

**whistle** *verb* **1** to make a high-pitched sound by forcing breath through the lips or teeth **2** to make such a sound with an instrument **3** to move with such a sound, like a bullet □ *noun* **1** the sound made by whistling **2** any instrument for whistling

**whit** *noun* a tiny bit: *not a whit better*

**white** *adj* **1** of the colour of pure snow **2** pale or light-coloured: *white wine* **3** of a pale-coloured complexion □ *noun* **1** something white **2** someone with a pale-coloured complexion **3** the part of an egg surrounding the yolk □ **whiteness** *noun* □ **white elephant** something useless and costly or troublesome to maintain □ **white-hot** *adj* having reached a degree of heat at which metals glow with a white light (hotter than **red-hot**) □ **whiten** *verb* to make or become white or whiter □ **whitewash** *noun* a

mixture of ground chalk and water, or lime and water, for whitening walls *etc* □ *verb* **1** to put whitewash on **2** to cover up the faults of, give a good appearance to

**whitebait** *noun* the young of herring or sprats

**whither** *adv* & *conj*, *old* to what place

**whiting** *noun* a small type of fish related to the cod

**Whitsun** *noun* the week beginning with the seventh Sunday after Easter

**whittle** *verb* **1** to pare or cut (wood *etc*) with a knife **2** (with **away** or **down**) to make gradually less: *whittled away his savings*

**whiz¹** or **whizz** *verb* **1** to move with a hissing sound, like an arrow **2** to move very fast

whiz ↔ whizzes, whizzing, whizzed

**whiz²** *noun* or **whizz kid** someone who achieves rapid success while relatively young

**who** *pron* used to refer to someone or some people unknown or unnamed (only as the subject of a verb): *who is that woman in the green hat?* □ *relative pron* referring to the person or people just named: *do you know who those people are?* □ **whoever** *pron* any person or people

**whole** *adj* **1** complete **2** all, with nothing or no one missing **3** not broken **4** in good health □ *noun* the entire thing □ **wholly** *adv* □ **wholefood** *noun* unprocessed food produced without the aid of artificial fertilizers □ **wholehearted** *adj* enthusiastic, generous □ **wholemeal** *noun* flour made from the entire wheat grain □ **wholesale** *noun* the sale of goods in large quantities to a shop from which they can be bought in small quantities by ordinary buyers (*compare with*: retail) *adj* **1** buying or selling in large quantities **2** on a

large scale: *wholesale killing*
□ **wholesaler** *noun* a person who buys goods on a large scale and sells them in smaller quantities to shopkeepers for sale to the public
□ **wholesome** *adj* giving health, healthy □ **on the whole** when everything is taken into account

**who'll** *short for* who will; who shall

**whom** *pron* **1** used to refer to someone or some people unknown or unnamed (only as the object of a sentence): *to whom am I speaking?* **2** which person: *do you know to whom I gave it?* □ *relative pron* referring to the person or people just named: *the person whom I liked best*

**whoop** *noun* a loud cry, rising in pitch □ *verb* to give a whoop
□ **whooping-cough** *noun* an infectious disease in which violent bouts of coughing are followed by a whoop as the breath is drawn in

**whose** *adj & pron* belonging to whom?: *whose handwriting is this?*
□ *relative pron* of whom: *the man whose wife I know*

**why** *adv & pron* for which reason?: *why did you not stay?* □ **the whys and wherefores** all the reasons, details

**wick** *noun* the twisted threads in a candle or lamp which draw up the oil or grease to the flame

**wicked** *adj* **1** evil, sinful **2** mischievous, spiteful □ **wickedly** *adv*

**wicker** *adj* of a chair: made of woven willow twigs

**wicket** *noun* **1** a small gate or door, *esp* in or beside a larger one **2** *cricket* the set of three stumps, or one of these, at which the ball is bowled **3** the ground between the bowler and the batsman

**wide** *adj* **1** broad, not narrow **2** stretching far: *a wide grin* **3** general, big: *a wide selection*

**4** measuring a certain amount from side to side: *5 centimetres wide* □ *adv* **1** off the target: *the shots went wide* **2** (often with **apart**) far apart: *hold your arms wide* □ **widely** *adv* **1** over a wide area; among many: *widely believed* **2** far apart □ **wide-awake** *adj* fully awake; alert □ **wide-eyed** *adj* with eyes wide open in surprise *etc* □ **widen** *verb* □ **wideness** *noun* a wide state or quality □ **wide-open** *adj* opened to the full extent
□ **widespread** *adj* spread over a large area or among many people
□ **wide of the mark** off the target, inaccurate

**widow** *noun* a woman whose husband is dead □ **widower** *noun* a man whose wife is dead

**width** *noun* **1** measurement across, from side to side **2** large extent

**wield** *verb* **1** to swing or handle (a cricket bat, sword *etc*) **2** to use (power, authority *etc*)

**wife** *noun* (*pl* **wives**) **1** a married woman **2** the woman to whom a man is married

**wig** *noun* an artificial covering of hair for the head

**wiggle** *verb* to move from side to side with jerky or twisting movements □ *noun* a jerky movement from side to side □ **wiggly** *adj*

**wigwam** *noun*, *historical* a conical tent of skins made by some Native Americans

**wild** *adj* **1** of an animal: not tamed **2** of a plant: not cultivated in a garden **3** uncivilized **4** unruly, uncontrolled **5** of weather: stormy **6** frantic, mad: *wild with anxiety* **7** of a guess *etc*: rash, inaccurate
□ *noun* (usually **wilds**) an uncultivated or uncivilized region
□ **wildlife** *noun* wild animals, birds *etc* in their natural habitats

**wilderness** *noun* a wild, uncultivated or desolate region

**wile** *noun* a crafty trick

**wilful** *adj* fond of having one's own way; intentional

**will** *noun* 1 the power to choose or decide 2 desire: *against my will* 3 determination: *the will to win* 4 feeling towards someone: *a sign of goodwill* 5 a written statement about what is to be done with your property after your death □ *verb* 1 to influence someone by exercising your will: *he willed her to win* 2 to hand down (property *etc*) by will 3 (*past form* **would**) also used to form future tenses of other verbs when the subject is **he, she, it, you** or **they**: *you will see me there* 4 *informal* often used for the same purpose when the subject is **I** or **we**: *I will tell you later* 5 used for emphasis, or to express a promise, when the subject is **I** or **we**: *I will do it if possible* (*see also* **shall**, **would**) □ **at will** as or when you choose □ **with a will** eagerly

**will** *verb* ⇨ wills, willing, willed

ⓘ Noun, and verb meanings 1 and 2: come from Old English *willa* meaning 'will' or 'determination'; verb meanings 3, 4 and 5: come from Old English *wyllan* meaning 'to wish' or 'to be willing'.

**willing** *adj* ready to do what is asked; eager

■ disposed, compliant, agreeable, amenable

**will-o'-the-wisp** *noun* a pale light sometimes seen by night over marshy places

**willow** *noun* 1 a tree with long slender branches 2 its wood, used in cricket bats

**willynilly** *adv* 1 whether you wish or not 2 notwithstanding other people's feelings

From the phrase *will I, nill I*, meaning 'whether I want or don't want'

**wilt** *verb* 1 of a flower or plant: to droop 2 to lose strength

**wily** *adj* cunning

**wimp** *noun*, *informal* an ineffectual person

**win** *verb* 1 to gain by luck or in a contest 2 to gain (the love of someone *etc*) by effort 3 to come first in a contest 4 (often with **over**) to gain the support or friendship of □ *noun* an act of winning; a victory □ **winning** *adj* 1 victorious, successful 2 charming, attractive: *winning smile* □ **winnings** *noun pl* money *etc* that has been won

**win** *verb* ⇨ wins, winning, won

■ (verb, meanings 1 and 2) acquire, attain, procure, secure; (verb, meaning 3) prevail, triumph

**wince** *verb* to shrink or start back in pain *etc*, flinch

**winch** *noun* (*pl* **winches**) 1 a handle or crank for turning a wheel 2 a machine for lifting things, worked by winding a rope round a revolving cylinder □ **winch up** to lift up with a winch

**wind**[1] *noun* 1 a current of air 2 breath 3 air carrying a scent 4 air or gas in the stomach 5 the wind instruments in an orchestra □ *verb* to put out of breath □ **windy** *adj* 1 of weather: with a strong wind blowing 2 of a place: exposed to strong winds □ **winder** *noun* a key *etc* for winding a clock □ **winding** *adj* curving, twisting □ **windfall** *noun* 1 a fruit blown from a tree 2 an unexpected gain, *eg* a sum of money □ **wind instrument** a musical instrument sounded by the breath □ **windmill** *noun* a mill driven by sails which are moved by the wind, used for pumping water, grinding grain *etc* □ **windpipe** *noun* the tube leading from the mouth to the lungs □ **windscreen** or *US* **windshield** *noun* a pane of glass in front of the driver of a car *etc* □ **windsurfer** *noun* a board with a sail for riding the waves

□ **windsurfing** *noun* the sport of riding the waves on a sailboard or windsurfer □ **windswept** *adj* exposed to strong winds and showing the effects of it: *windswept hair* □ **windward** *adj & adv* in the direction from which the wind blows □ **get the wind up** *informal* to become afraid □ **get wind of** *informal* to hear about in an indirect way

**wind²** *verb* **1** to turn, twist or coil **2** (sometimes with **up**) to screw up the spring of (a watch, clockwork toy *etc*) **3** to wrap closely □ **wind up** **1** to bring or come to an end: *wind up a meeting* **2** *informal* to annoy, tease □ **wind your way** to make your way circuitously

**wind** *verb* ⬦ *winds, winding, wound*

**windlass** *noun* a machine for lifting up or hauling a winch

**window** *noun* an opening in a wall, protected by glass, which lets in light and air

**wine** *noun* **1** an alcoholic drink made from the fermented juice of grapes or other fruit **2** a rich dark red colour

**wing** *noun* **1** one of the arm-like limbs of a bird, bat or insect by means of which it flies **2** one of the two projections on the sides of an aeroplane **3** a part of a house built out to the side **4** the side of a stage, where actors wait to enter **5** *football etc* a player positioned at the edge of the field **6** a section of a political party: *the left wing* □ *verb* **1** to wound (a bird) in the wing **2** to soar □ **winged** *adj* **1** having wings **2** swift □ **on the wing** flying, in motion □ **under someone's wing** under the protection or care of someone

**wink** *verb* **1** to open and close an eye quickly **2** to give a hint by winking **3** of lights *etc*: to flicker, twinkle □ *noun* **1** an act of winking **2** a hint given by winking □ **forty winks** a

short sleep

**winkle** *noun* a small edible shellfish (*also called*: **periwinkle**) □ **winkle out** to force out gradually

**winnow** *verb* to separate the chaff from the grain by wind

**winsome** *adj* charming

**winter** *noun* the cold season of the year □ *adj* of or suitable for winter □ *verb* **1** to pass the winter **2** to keep, feed (sheep *etc*) during the winter □ **wintry** *adj* **1** cold, frosty **2** cheerless, unfriendly: *a wintry look*

**wipe** *verb* **1** to clean or dry by rubbing **2** (with **away**, **out**, **off** or **up**) to clear it away □ *noun* the act of cleaning by rubbing □ **wiper** *noun* one of a pair of moving parts which wipe the windscreen of a car □ **wipe something out** to totally destroy it

**wire** *noun* **1** a thread-like length of metal **2** the metal thread used in communication by telephone *etc* **3** *informal* a telegram □ *adj* made of wire □ *verb* **1** to bind or fasten with wire **2** *informal* to send a telegram **3** to supply (a building *etc*) with wires for carrying an electric current □ **wiry** *adj* **1** made of wire **2** of a person: thin but strong □ **wireless** *adj* of communication: by radio waves □ *noun, old* a radio set

**wisdom** *noun* the quality of being wise □ **wisdom teeth** four large back teeth which appear after childhood

**wise** *adj* **1** very knowledgeable **2** judging rightly; sensible

**wish** *verb* **1** to feel or express a desire **2** (often with **for**) to long for, desire: *she wished for peace and quiet* **3** to hope for on behalf of (someone): *wish someone luck* □ *noun* (*pl* **wishes**) **1** desire, longing **2** a thing desired or wanted **3** an expression of desire: *make a wish* **4** (**wishes**) expression of hope for another's happiness, good fortune *etc*: *good* *wishes* □ **wishful** *adj* wishing, eager □ **wishful thinking** basing your belief on (false) hopes rather than known facts □ **wishbone** *noun* a forked bone in the breast of fowls □ **wish someone well** to feel goodwill towards them

**wishywashy** *adj* **1** of liquid: thin and weak **2** feeble, not energetic or lively **3** lacking colour

**wisp** *noun* a small tuft or strand □ **wispy** *adj*

**wistful** *adj* thoughtful and rather sad □ **wistfully** *adv*

**wit** *noun* **1** (often **wits**) intelligence, common sense **2** the ability to express ideas neatly and funnily **3** someone who can do this □ **at your wits' end** unable to solve your difficulties, desperate □ **keep your wits about you** to keep alert □ **to wit** namely, that is to say

**witch** *noun* (*pl* **witches**) **1** a woman with magic power obtained through evil spirits **2** an ugly old woman □ **witchcraft** *noun* magic performed by a witch □ **witch doctor** someone believed to have magical powers to cure illnesses *etc*

**with** *prep* **1** in the company of **2** by means of: *cut it with a knife* **3** in the same direction as: *drifting with the current* **4** against: *fighting with his brother* **5** on the same side as **6** having: *a man with a limp* **7** in the keeping of: *leave the keys with me*

**withdraw** *verb* **1** to go back or away **2** to take away, remove: *withdraw cash/ withdraw troops* **3** to take back (an insult *etc*) □ **withdrawal** *noun* □ **withdrawn** *adj* **1** of a place: lonely, isolated **2** of a person: unwilling to communicate with others, unsociable

**withdraw** ⋄ withdraw*s*, withdraw*ing*, withdrew, withdrawn

**wither** *verb* **1** to fade, dry up or decay **2** to make to feel very unimportant or embarrassed: *she*

*withered him with a look* □ **withering** *adj* **1** drying up, dying **2** of a remark *etc*: scornful, sarcastic

**withers** *noun pl* the ridge between the shoulder bones of a horse

**withhold** *verb* to keep back, refuse to give

**withhold** ⋄ withhold*s*, withhold*ing*, withheld

**within** *prep* inside the limits of: *keep within the law* □ *adv* on the inside

**without** *prep* **1** in the absence of: *we went without you* **2** not having: *without a penny* **3** outside the limits of: *without the terms of the agreement* □ *adv*, *old* **1** on the outside **2** out-of-doors

**withstand** *verb* to oppose or resist successfully

**witness** *noun* (*pl* **witnesses**) **1** someone who sees or has direct knowledge of a thing **2** someone who gives evidence in a law court **3** proof, evidence □ *verb* **1** to see, be present at **2** to sign your name to confirm the authenticity of (someone else's signature) **3** to give or be evidence □ **bear witness** to give or be evidence of: *bear witness to his character*

**witticism** *noun* a witty remark

**wittingly** *adv* knowingly

**witty** *adj* clever and amusing

**wizard** *noun* a man believed to have the power of magic □ **wizardry** *noun*

**wizened** *adj* dried up, shrivelled: *a wizened old man*

**woad** *noun* **1** a blue dye **2** the plant from which it is obtained

**wobble** *verb* to rock unsteadily from side to side □ *noun* an unsteady rocking □ **wobbly** *adj*

**woe** *noun* **1** grief, misery **2** a cause of sorrow, a trouble □ **woeful** *adj* sorrowful; pitiful □ **woefully** *adv* □ **woebegone** *adj* dismal, sad-looking

**wok** *noun* an Asian cooking-pan

shaped like a large bowl

**wolf** noun (pl **wolves**) a wild animal like a dog that hunts in packs □ verb to eat greedily □ **cry wolf** to give a false alarm □ **keep the wolf from the door** to keep away hunger or want

**woman** noun (pl **women**) 1 an adult human female 2 human females in general 3 a domestic help □ **womanly** adj □ **womanhood** noun the state of being a woman
Ⓔ From Old English wif meaning 'a woman', and man meaning 'man' or 'human being'

**womb** noun the part of a female mammal's body in which the young develop and stay till birth

**wombat** noun a small, beaver-like Australian animal, with a pouch

**women** pl of **woman**

**won** past form of **win**

**wonder** noun 1 the feeling produced by something unexpected or extraordinary; surprise, awe 2 something strange, amazing or miraculous □ verb 1 to be curious or in doubt: I wonder what will happen 2 to feel surprise or amazement (at, that) □ **wonderful** adj 1 arousing wonder; strange, marvellous 2 excellent □ **wonderment** noun, old amazement □ **wondrous** adj, old wonderful

**wont** (say wohnt) adj, old accustomed (to do something) □ noun habit: as is his wont

**won't** short for will not

**woo** verb 1 to try to win the love of (someone) 2 to try to gain (eg success) □ **wooer** noun

**woo** ⇌ woos, wooing, wooed

**wood** noun 1 a group of growing trees 2 the hard part of a tree, esp when cut for use □ **wooded** adj covered with trees □ **woody** adj 1 like wood 2 wooded □ **woodcut** noun 1 a picture engraved on wood 2 a print made from this engraving

□ **woodcutter** noun someone who fells trees, cuts up wood etc □ **wooden** adj 1 made of wood 2 dull, stiff, not lively: a wooden speech □ **woodenly** adv □ **woodland** noun land covered with trees □ **woodlouse** noun (pl **woodlice**) a small beetle-like creature with a jointed shell, found under stones etc □ **woodpecker** noun a bird that pecks holes in the bark of trees with its beak, in search of insects □ **woodwind** noun wind instruments, made of wood or metal, eg the flute or clarinet □ **woodwork** noun 1 the making of wooden articles 2 the wooden parts of a house, room etc □ **woodworm** noun the larva of a beetle that bores holes in wood and destroys it

**wool** noun 1 the soft hair of sheep and other animals 2 yarn or cloth made of wool □ **woollen** adj made of wool □ noun a knitted garment made of wool □ **woolly** adj 1 made of, or like, wool 2 vague, hazy: a woolly argument □ noun (pl **woollies**) a knitted woollen garment

**word** noun 1 a written or spoken sign representing a thing or an idea 2 (**words**) talk, remarks: kind words 3 news: word of his death 4 a promise: break your word □ verb to choose words for: he worded his refusal carefully □ **wordy** adj using too many words □ **wording** noun choice or arrangement of words □ **have words** informal to quarrel □ **in a word** in short, to sum up □ **take someone at their word** to treat what they say as true □ **take someone's word for something** to trust that what they say is true □ **word for word** in the exact words

**wore** past form of **wear**

**work** noun 1 a physical or mental effort to achieve or make something 2 a job, employment: out of work 3 a task: I've got work to do

4 anything made or done
5 something produced by art, *eg* a book, musical composition, painting *etc* 6 manner of working, workmanship: *poor work* 7 (**works**) a factory 8 (**works**) the mechanism (*eg* of a watch) 9 (**works**) deeds: *good works* □ *verb* 1 to be engaged in physical or mental work 2 to be employed 3 to run or operate smoothly and efficiently 4 of a plan *etc*: to be successful 5 to get into a position slowly and gradually: *the screw worked loose* 6 to organize, manage, control □ **workable** *adj* able to be done, practical □ **worker** *noun* someone who works at a job □ **working** *adj* operating properly, not broken □ **working class** the social class including manual workers □ **working day** or **working hours** the hours each day that someone spends at work, on duty *etc* □ **workman** *noun* someone who works with their hands □ **workmanlike** *adj* done with skill □ **workmanship** *noun* 1 the skill of a workman 2 manner of making something □ **workshop** *noun* a room or building where manufacturing, craftwork *etc* is done □ **work out** 1 to solve 2 to discover as a result of deep thought 3 of a situation: to turn out all right in the end □ **work up** to arouse, excite: *working himself up into a fury* ⊕ From Old English *weorc*

---

■ (verb, meaning 1) toil, drudge; (verb, meaning 3) function

---

**world** *noun* 1 the earth and all things on it 2 the people of the world 3 any planet or star 4 the universe 5 a state of existence: *the next world* 6 a particular area of life or activity: *the world of fashion* 7 a great deal: *a world of good* □ **worldly** *adj* concerned with material things such as money, possessions *etc*, not the soul or spirit □ **worldwide** *adj* extending throughout the world

□ *adv* throughout the world
⊕ From Old English *world/ weorold* meaning 'age or life of man'

**worm** *noun* 1 a small creeping animal without a backbone, often living in soil 2 *informal* a low, contemptible person 3 something spiral-shaped, *eg* the thread of a screw 4 (**worms**) the condition of having threadworms *etc* in the intestines 5 *computing* a kind of virus □ *verb* 1 to move gradually and stealthily (in or into) 2 (**worm out**) to draw out (information) bit by bit

**wormwood** *noun* a plant with a bitter taste

**worn** *adj* 1 damaged by use 2 tired, worn-out □ **worn-out** *adj* tired, exhausted

---

■ anxious, apprehensive, overwrought, distraught

---

**worry** *verb* 1 of a dog: to shake or tear (something) with its teeth 2 to annoy 3 to make troubled and anxious 4 to be troubled and anxious □ *noun* (*pl* **worries**) 1 uneasiness, anxiety 2 a cause of unease or anxiety □ **worried** *adj*

**worry** ⇔ worri*es*, worry*ing*, worri*ed*

---

■ (verb, meaning 3) agitate

---

**worse** *adj* 1 bad or evil to a greater degree 2 more ill □ *adv* badly to a greater degree, more severely: *it's snowing worse than ever* □ **worsen** *verb* □ **worse off** in a worse position, less wealthy *etc*

**worship** *noun* 1 a religious ceremony or service 2 deep reverence, adoration 3 a title used in addressing a mayor, provost *etc* □ *verb* 1 to pay honour to (a god) 2 to adore or admire deeply □ **worshipful** *adj* 1 full of reverence 2 worthy of honour

**worship** ⇔ worship*s*, worship*ping*, worship*ped*

**worst** adj bad or evil to the greatest degree □ adv badly to the greatest degree □ verb to beat, defeat □ **at worst** under the least favourable circumstances □ **if the worst comes to the worst** if the worst possible circumstances occur

**worst** verb ↪ worsts, worst*ing*, worst*ed*

**worsted** (*say* woors-tid) noun **1** a type of fine woollen yarn **2** a strong cloth made of this

**worth** noun **1** value; price **2** importance **3** excellence of character *etc* □ adj **1** equal in value to **2** deserving of: *worth considering* □ **worthless** adj of no merit or value □ **worthwhile** adj deserving time and effort □ **worthy** adj **1** (often with **of**) deserving, suitable **2** of good character □ noun (*pl* **worthies**) a highly respected person: *local worthy* □ **worth your while** worth the trouble spent

**would** verb **1** the form of the verb **will** used to express a condition: *he would go if he could* **2** used for emphasis: *I tell you I would do it if possible* **3** old expressing a wish: *I would that he were gone* □ **would-be** adj trying to be or pretending to be: *would-be actor*

ⓔ From Old English *wolde* which is the past tense of *wyllan* meaning 'to wish'

**wound** noun **1** a cut or injury caused by a weapon, in an accident *etc* **2** a hurt to someone's feelings □ verb **1** to make a cut or injury in **2** to hurt the feelings of □ **wounded** adj

**wraith** (*say* reith) noun an apparition of a living person, often as a warning of death

**wrangle** (*say* **rang**-gl) verb to quarrel noisily □ noun a noisy quarrel

**wrap** (*say* rap) verb **1** to fold or roll round **2** (with **up**) to cover by folding or winding something round □ noun a cloak or shawl □ **wrapper** noun a loose paper cover, *eg* round a book or sweet

**wrap** verb ↪ wraps, wrapp*ing*, wrapp*ed*

**wrath** (*say* roth or rawth or rath) noun violent anger □ **wrathful** adj

**wreak** (*say* reek) verb to cause: *wreak havoc*

**wreath** (*say* reeth) noun **1** a ring of flowers or leaves **2** a curling wisp of smoke, mist *etc*

**wreathe** (*say* reedh) verb to encircle

**wreck** (*say* rek) noun **1** destruction, *esp* of a ship by the sea **2** the remains of anything destroyed, *esp* a ship **3** someone whose health or nerves are in bad condition □ verb to destroy □ **wreckage** (*say* rek-ij) noun the remains of something wrecked

**wren** (*say* ren) noun a very small type of bird

**wrench** (*say* rench) verb **1** to pull with a violent, often twisting, motion **2** to sprain (your ankle *etc*) □ noun (*pl* **wrenches**) **1** a violent twist **2** a tool for gripping and turning nuts, bolts *etc* **3** sadness caused by parting from someone or something

**wrest** (*say* rest) verb, *formal* to twist or take by force

**wrestle** (*say* **re**-sl) verb **1** to fight with someone, trying to bring them to the ground **2** (with **with**) to think deeply about (a problem *etc*) □ **wrestler** noun **wrestling** noun the sport in which two people fight to throw each other to the ground

**wretch** (*say* rech) noun (*pl* **wretches**) **1** a miserable, pitiable person: *a poor wretch* **2** a worthless or contemptible person

**wretched** (*say* **rech**-id) adj **1** very miserable **2** worthless, very bad □ **wretchedly** adv

**wriggle** (*say* **ri**-gl) verb **1** to twist to and fro **2** to move by doing this, as a worm does **3** to escape (out of a difficulty *etc*)

**wring** (*say* ring) *verb* **1** to twist or squeeze (*esp* water out of wet clothes) **2** to clasp and unclasp (your hands) in grief, anxiety *etc* **3** to cause pain to: *the story wrung everybody's heart* **4** to force out (*eg* a promise) □ **wringer** (*say* **ring**-er) *noun* a machine for forcing water from wet clothes

**wring** ⤙ wring*s*, wring*ing*, wrung

**wrinkle** (*say* **ring**-kl) *noun* a small crease or fold on the skin or other surface □ *verb* to make or become wrinkled □ **wrinkly** *adj*

**wrist** (*say* rist) *noun* the joint by which the hand is joined to the arm

**writ** (*say* rit) *noun* a formal document giving an order (*esp* to appear in a law court

**write** (*say* rait) *verb* **1** to form letters with a pen, pencil *etc* **2** to put into writing: *write your name* **3** to compose (a letter, a book *etc*) **4** to send a letter (to) **5** *computing* to copy (a data file) □ **writer** *noun* □ **writing** *noun* □ **write down** to record in writing □ **write off** to regard as lost for ever □ **write up** to make a written record of

**write** ⤙ write*s*, writ*ing*, wrote, writt*en*

**writhe** (*say* raidh) *verb* to twist or roll about, *eg* in pain

**wrong** (*say* rong) *adj* **1** not correct **2** not right or just **3** evil **4** not what is intended: *take the wrong turning* **5** unsuitable: *the wrong weather for camping* **6** mistaken: *you are wrong if you think that* □ *noun* **1** whatever is not right or just **2** an injury done to another □ *verb* to do wrong to, harm □ **wrongly** *adv* □ **wrongdoer** *noun* someone who does wrong □ **wrongdoing** *noun* immoral or illegal behaviour or actions □ **wrongful** *adj* not lawful or just □ **go wrong 1** to fail to work properly **2** to make a mistake or mistakes □ **in the wrong** guilty of injustice or error

---

□ (adj, meaning 1) fallacious; (adj, meaning 2) reprehensible; (adj, meanings 2 and 3) iniquitous; (adj, meaning 5) unseemly, indecorous, incongruous, inapt; (adj, meaning 6) erroneous

---

**wrote** *past form of* **write**

**wrought** (*say* rawt) *adj, old* made, manufactured □ *verb, old, past form* of **work** □ **wrought iron** iron hammered, rather than cast, into shape

**wrung** *past form of* **wring**

**wry** (*say* rai) *adj* **1** slightly mocking or bitter: *wry remark* **2** twisted or turned to one side □ **wryly** *adv*

---

## Xx

**xenophobia** (*say* zen-*o*-**foh**-bi-*a*) *noun* hatred of foreigners or strangers

**Xerox** (*say* **zeer**-roks) *noun, trademark* **1** a photographic process used for copying documents **2** a copy made in this way □ *verb* (**xerox**) to copy by Xerox

**Xmas** *noun, informal* Christmas

**X-rays** *noun pl* rays that can pass through material impenetrable by light, and produce a photographic image of the object through which they have passed □ **X-ray** *noun* a shadow picture produced by X-rays on photographic film □ *verb* to take a photographic image of with X-rays

**XTC** *noun, slang* the drug Ecstasy

**xylophone** *noun* a musical instrument consisting of a series of graded wooden bars which are struck with hammers

# Yy

**yacht** *noun* a sailing or motor-driven boat for racing, cruising *etc* □
**yachtsman, yachtswoman** *noun* a man or woman who sails a yacht

**yak** *noun* a Tibetan long-haired ox

**yam** *noun* a tropical root vegetable, similar to a potato

**Yank** or **Yankee** *noun, Brit informal* an American

**yank** *verb, informal* to tug or pull with a violent jerk □ *noun* a violent tug

**yap** *verb* to bark sharply
**yap** ⇔ ya**ps**, ya**pping**, ya**pped**

**yard** *noun* **1** a measure of length (0.9144 of a metre, or 3 feet) **2** a long beam on a mast for spreading sails **3** an enclosed space used for a particular purpose: *shipbuilding yard* **4** *US* a garden □ **yardstick** *noun* **1** a standard for measurement **2** a yard-long measuring stick

**yarn** *noun* **1** wool, cotton *etc* spun into thread **2** one of several threads forming a rope **3** a long, often improbable, story

**yarrow** *noun* a strong-smelling plant with flat clusters of white flowers

**yashmak** *noun* a veil covering the lower half of the face, worn by Islamic women

**yawl** *noun* a small rowing boat or fishing boat

**yawn** *verb* **1** to take a deep breath unintentionally with an open mouth, because of boredom or sleepiness **2** of a hole: to be wide open, gape □ *noun* an open-mouthed deep breath

**ye** *pron, old* you

**yea** (*say* yei) *interjection, old* yes

**year** *noun* **1** the time taken by the earth to go once round the sun, about 365 days **2** the period 1 January to 31 December **3** a period of twelve months starting at any point **4** (**years**) age: *wise for her years* □ **yearly** *adj* □ **yearling** *noun* a year-old animal
ⓔ From Old English *gear*

**yearn** *verb* **1** to long (for, to do something *etc*) **2** to feel pity or tenderness (for) □ **yearning** *noun* an eager longing

**yeast** *noun* a substance which causes fermentation, used to make bread dough rise and in brewing

**yell** *verb* to give a loud, shrill cry; scream □ *noun* a loud, shrill cry

**yellow** *noun* the colour of gold, egg-yolks *etc* □ *adj* of this colour □ *verb* to become yellow, due to ageing

**yelp** *verb* to give a sharp bark or cry □ *noun* a sharp bark or cry

**yen**¹ *noun* the standard unit of Japanese currency

**yen**² *noun, informal* a strong desire, longing

**yeoman** (*say* yoh-man) *noun, historical* a farmer with his own land □ **yeomanry** *noun* □ **Yeomen of the Guard** the company acting as bodyguard to the British king or queen on certain occasions

**yes** *interjection* expressing agreement or consent □ *noun* **1** an expression of agreement or consent **2** a vote in favour

**yesterday** *noun* **1** the day before today **2** the past □ *adv*

**yet** *adv* **1** by now, by this time: *have you seen that film yet?* **2** still, before the matter is finished: *we may win yet* □ *conj* but, nevertheless: *I am defeated, yet I shall not surrender* □ **yet another** and another one still □ **yet more** still more

**Yeti** noun, another name for the **Abominable Snowman**

**yew** noun **1** a tree with dark green leaves and red berries **2** its wood

**yield** verb **1** to give in, surrender **2** to give way to pressure or persuasion **3** to produce (a crop, results etc) □ noun an amount produced; a crop □ **yielding** adj

**yob** or **yobbo** (pl **yobboes** or **yobbos**) noun a lout, a hooligan

**yodel** verb to sing in a style involving frequent changes between an ordinary and a very high-pitched voice

**yodel** ⇨ yodels, yodelling, yodelled

**yoga** noun a Hindu system of philosophy and meditation, often involving special physical exercises

**yoghurt** or **yogurt** noun a semi-liquid food product made from fermented milk

**yoke** noun **1** a wooden frame joining oxen when pulling a plough or cart **2** a pair of oxen or horses **3** something that joins together **4** a frame placed across the shoulders for carrying pails etc **5** slavery, domination **6** a part of a garment fitting over the neck and shoulders **7** a part of a skirt fitting closely over the hips □ verb **1** to put a yoke on **2** to join together

**yokel** noun, derogatory an unsophisticated country person; a rustic

**yolk** noun the yellow part of an egg

**Yom Kippur** noun the Day of Atonement, a Jewish fast day

**yonder** adv, old in that place (at a distance but within sight) □ adj that (object) over there: by yonder tree

**yore** noun: **of yore** old formerly, in times past

**you** pron the person(s) spoken or written to, used as the sing or pl subject or object of a verb: what did you say?

**you'd** abbrev **1** you would; you should **2** you had

**you'll** abbrev you will; you shall

**young** adj **1** in early life **2** in the early part of mental or physical growth □ noun **1** the offspring of animals **2** (the young) young people □ **youngster** noun a young person ⊚ From Old English geong

**your** adj belonging to you: it's your life

**you're** short for you are

**yours** pron belonging to you: is this pen yours? □ **Yours**, **Yours faithfully**, **Yours sincerely** or **Yours truly** expressions used before a signature at the end of a letter

**yourself** pron (pl **yourselves**) **1** used reflexively: don't trouble yourself **2** used for emphasis: you yourself can't go

**youth** noun **1** the state of being young **2** the early part of life **3** a young person **4** young people in general □ **youthful** adj **1** young **2** fresh and vigorous □ **youth hostel** a hostel where hikers etc may spend the night

**you've** abbrev you have

**yo-yo** noun, trademark a toy consisting of a reel which spins up and down on a string

**Yule** or **Yuletide** noun, old Christmas

**yuppie** or **yuppy** noun (pl **yuppies**) a young well-paid urban professional

# Zz

**zany** *adj, informal* crazy, madcap

**zap** *verb* 1 to strike, shoot *etc* suddenly 2 to move rapidly; zip
**zap** ⇨ zaps, zapping, zapped

**zeal** *noun* 1 enthusiasm 2 keenness, determination □ **zealous** (*say* zel-us) *adj* □ **zealously** *adv*

**zealot** (*say* zel-ot) *noun* a fanatical enthusiast

**zebra** *noun* a striped African animal of the horse family □ **zebra crossing** a pedestrian street crossing, painted in black and white stripes

**zenith** *noun* 1 the point of the heavens exactly overhead 2 the highest point, the peak

**zephyr** (*say* zef-er) *noun, formal* a soft, gentle breeze

**zero** *noun* 1 nothing or the sign for it (0) 2 the point (marked 0) from which a scale (*eg* on a thermometer) begins □ **zero hour** the exact time fixed for some action

**zest** *noun* 1 relish, keen enjoyment 2 orange or lemon peel *etc* □ **zestful** *adj* □ **zestfully** *adv*

**zigzag** *adj* having sharp bends or angles □ *verb* move in a zigzag direction
**zigzag** ⇨ zigzags, zigzagging, zigzagged

**zinc** *noun* a bluish-white metal

**zip** *noun* 1 a fastening device for clothes, bags *etc*, consisting of two rows of metal or nylon teeth which interlock when a sliding tab is pulled between them 2 a whizzing sound, *eg* made by a fast-flying object 3 *informal* energy, vigour □ *verb* 1 to fasten with a zip 2 to whiz, fly past at speed
**zip** *verb* ⇨ zips, zipping, zipped

**zither** *noun* a flat, stringed musical instrument, played with the fingers

**zodiac** *noun* an imaginary strip in space, divided into twelve equal parts □ **signs of the zodiac** the divisions of the zodiac used in astrology, each named after a group of stars

**zombie** *noun* 1 a corpse reanimated by witchcraft 2 a very slow or stupid person

**zone** *noun* 1 any of the five main bands into which the earth's surface is divided according to temperature: *temperate zone* 2 a section of a country, town *etc* marked off for a particular purpose: *no-parking zone* □ *verb* to divide into zones

**zoo** *noun* a place where wild animals are kept and shown to the public

**zoo-** *prefix* of or relating to animals ⊚ From Greek *zoion* meaning 'animal'

**zoology** *noun* the science of animal life □ **zoological** *adj* □ **zoologist** *noun*

**zoom** *verb* 1 to move with a loud, low buzzing noise 2 to make such a noise 3 of an aircraft: to climb sharply at high speed for a short time 4 of prices: to increase sharply 5 to use a zoom lens on a camera □ **zoom lens** *photography* a lens which makes a distant object appear gradually nearer without the camera being moved

*Notes*

*Notes*